DICTIONARY OF

American History

Third Edition

EDITORIAL BOARD

DICTIONARY OF
American History

Third Edition

Stanley I. Kutler, *Editor in Chief*

Volume 4
Girl Scouts to Kwanzaa

New York • Detroit • San Diego • San Francisco • Cleveland • New Haven, Conn. • Waterville, Maine • London • Munich

Dictionary of American History, Third Edition

Stanley I. Kutler, *Editor*

For more information, contact
Charles Scribner's Sons
An imprint of the Gale Group
300 Park Avenue South
New York, NY 10010

LIBRARY OF CONGRESS CATALOGING-IN-PUBLICATION DATA

Dictionary of American history / Stanley I. Kutler.—3rd ed.
p. cm.
Includes bibliographical references and index.
ISBN 0-684-80533-2 (set : alk. paper)
1. United States—History—Dictionaries. I. Kutler, Stanley I.
E174 .D52 2003
973'.03—dc21

Printed in United States of America
10 9 8 7 6 5 4 3 2 1

CONTENTS

DICTIONARY OF
American History

Third Edition

G

(Continued)

GIRL SCOUTS OF THE UNITED STATES OF AMERICA. Juliette Gordon Low founded the Girl Scouts of the United States of America with eighteen members on 12 March 1912 in Savannah, Georgia. The British general Sir Robert Baden-Powell, founder of the Boy Scouts, and his sister Agnes Baden-Powell, founder of the Girl Guides, inspired Low. In 1915, when the organization was incorporated in the United States, there were fifteen thousand members. At first, it was closely modeled on the Girl Guides, but it soon became more distinctive under Low's leadership.

The purpose of the organization as Low conceived it was to encourage self-development, citizenship, and love of the out-of-doors in girls and young women. Low's marital experience led her to emphasize the ability to be self-supporting, in part because when her husband died, he left his estate to his mistress, forcing Low to sue in court to get her fair share of the inheritance. The organization also reflected the period in which she was living. During the Progressive Era, women were expanding their roles outside the domestic sphere by joining women's clubs and organizations. Though the Girl Scouts encouraged enlightened housekeeping and child care, they also emphasized independence, physical fitness, and careers for women.

Girl Scout activities reflected historical changes. During World War I scouts aided the war effort by volunteering in hospitals, growing gardens, and selling war bonds. In 1917 the first troop of physically disabled girls came together in New York City; in the 1920s the first African American troops were organized. By 1929 there were 200,000 Girl Scouts, and in 1930 a troop of Native American girls was organized. During the Depression, Girl Scouts collected food and clothing for distribution to the needy. The fund-raising effort for which the Girl Scouts has been most well known was launched in 1936 when the first Girl Scout cookies were sold.

Girl Scouts collected lard and scrap metal during World War II as their membership soared to one million by 1944. In 1958 the Girl Scouts purchased a headquarters in New York City that was still its home at the end of the century. In the 1960s Girl Scouts backed the civil rights movement and established desegregated troops. When the women's movement echoed many of the Girl Scout themes of career preparation and independence in the 1970s, it was only natural that they would reinforce one another. Betty Friedan, author of *The Feminine Mystique* (1963), became a member of the national board. In the 1980s scouts began to address contemporary problems such as teen suicide and child abuse. Seeking to reach their goal of nontraditional careers for women, the Girl Scouts in 1996 entered an agreement with the American Society of Mechanical Engineers to encourage young women's achievement in math and science. With regard to policy on gay membership, Connie Matsui, national president of the Girl Scouts, confirmed in 2001 that the organization did not discriminate on the basis of sexual orientation. In 2001 membership was 2.7 million Girl Scouts and 915,000 adults.

Throughout its existence, the Girl Scouts has been a progressive force in American society. The organization has led in movements toward racial, social, and sexual equality. It has trained many of the nation's women leaders. Two-thirds of women serving in Congress in 1999 were former scouts. The Girl Scout message of independence, citizenship, self-sufficiency, physical fitness, and love of the outdoors has been influential in many American women's lives.

BIBLIOGRAPHY

Girl Scouts of America. *75 Years of Girl Scouting*. New York: Girl Scouts of America, 1986.

Perry, Elizabeth Israels. "The Very Best Influence: Josephine Holloway and Girl Scouting in Nashville's African American Community." *Tennessee Historical Quarterly* 52 (1993): 73–85.

Revzin, Rebekah E. "American Girlhood in the Early Twentieth Century: The Ideology of Girl Scout Literature, 1913–1930." *Library Quarterly* 68 (1998): 261–275.

Strickland, Charles. "Juliette Low, the Girl Scouts, and the Role of American Women." In *Woman's Being, Woman's Place: Female Identity and Vocation in American History*. Edited by Mary Kelly. Boston: G. K. Hall, 1979.

Bonnie L. Ford

See also **Boy Scouts of America; Junior Leagues International, Association of.**

Henry arose with an unearthly fire burning in his eye. He commenced somewhat calmly—but the smothered excitement began more and more to play upon his features and thrill in the tones of his voice. The tendons of his neck stood out white and rigid like whipcords. His voice rose louder and louder until the walls of the building and all within them seemed to shake and rock in its tremendous vibrations. Finally his pale face and glaring eyes became terrible to look upon. Men leaned forward in their seats with their heads strained forward, their faces pale and their eyes glaring like the speaker's. His last exclamation—"Give me liberty or give me death"—was like the shout of a leader which turns back the rout of battle!

SOURCE: Report of Henry's speech by a witness, "an old Baptist clergyman," reprinted in *Patrick Henry: Life, Correspondence, and Speeches,* vol. 1, pp. 267–268.

"GIVE ME LIBERTY OR GIVE ME DEATH!" concluded Patrick Henry's rousing speech delivered to the Virginia Convention on 23 May 1775. In the days leading up to Henry's speech, the colonies' breach with Britain had become critical. To many Virginians, war seemed imminent. However, false rumors of the British ministry's willingness to back away from unpopular policies such as the Coercive Acts had spread, causing some to consider reconciliation again. The immediate occasion of the speech was the convention's proposed positive response to the Jamaica assembly's 1774 petition to the king, which asserted colonial rights but also emphasized the colony's loyalty and its desire for harmonious relations with Britain. Henry retorted that Britain would never reconcile with the colonies on terms that would ensure colonial rights and insisted war was the only realistic option. Rather than have the convention place false hope in compromise, Henry offered a resolution to prepare the colony's defenses for the inevitable clash with Britain. He rose to defend his motion and enjoyed one of his finest moments as an orator, giving a speech that was long and clearly remembered by those in attendance. In concluding, Henry asked, "Is life so dear or peace so sweet as to be purchased at the price of chains and slavery?" His answer: "Forbid it, Almighty God! I know not what course others may take, but as for me, give me liberty or give me death!" The speech rallied the convention's spirit of resistance, the resolution passed, and Virginia took a major step toward independence.

BIBLIOGRAPHY

Henry, William Wirt. *Patrick Henry: Life, Correspondence, and Speeches.* 3 vols. New York: Scribners, 1891.

Mayer, Henry. *A Son of Thunder: Patrick Henry and the American Republic.* New York: Franklin Watts, 1986.

McCants, David A. *Patrick Henry, the Orator.* New York: Greenwood Press, 1990.

Meade, Robert Douthat. *Patrick Henry.* 2 vols. Philadelphia: Lippincott, 1957–1969.

Aaron J. Palmer

See also **Coercive Acts; Colonial Policy, British; Revolution, American: Political History; Virginia; Virginia Resolves.**

GLAIZE, THE. An old buffalo wallow on the Maumee River at the mouth of the Auglaize River (at what later became Defiance, Ohio, fifty miles southwest of Toledo), the Glaize emerged as a multicultural settlement during the late eighteenth century. Although the area was a hunting ground for the Ottawas and other native groups, it did not become a place of permanent residence until the period of the American Revolution, when French and English traders established a fort and trading post, around which were founded at least seven Indian villages inhabited primarily by Shawnees, Delawares, and Miamis. The combined population of these towns at its peak in 1792 was about two thousand persons. In that year, the Glaize became headquarters for a multitribal confederacy that, armed and fed by British trading agents, resisted American expansion in the Northwest Territory.

As the area's economic and diplomatic center, the Glaize became a natural target for the American forces as they pushed forward in 1794. Troops under General Anthony Wayne scattered the population and razed most of the community's permanent buildings in August of that year and the American general established his headquarters nearby. Final defeat of the Northwest Confederacy occurred at the Battle of Fallen Timbers on 20 August 1794. Subsequently, the Glaize ceased to be a vital community. Prominent individuals associated with the Glaize include Blue Jacket, Little Turtle, Big Cat, James and Simon Girty, John Kinzie, George Ironside, and Billy Caldwell.

BIBLIOGRAPHY

Tanner, Helen Hornbeck. "The Glaize in 1792: A Composite Indian Community." *Ethnohistory* 25 (1978): 15–39.

Michael Sherfy

See also **Fallen Timbers, Battle of; Greenville Treaty.**

GLASS CEILING, a discriminatory barrier to the advancement of women into the upper echelons of business, the professions, and government. After discrimination by sex in employment was outlawed by the CIVIL RIGHTS ACT OF 1964, it was understood that women would not be seen in top jobs in substantial numbers until many had achieved the necessary experience at intermediate levels. However, the paucity of women in the highest positions decades later suggested that they faced persisting barriers—hence the perception of a "glass ceiling." Even in the absence of an impenetrable barrier at some particular level, fewer promotional opportunities for women than for men at each of many levels produced a scarcity of women at and near the top.

BIBLIOGRAPHY

Davidson, Marilyn J., and Cary L. Cooper. *Shattering the Glass Ceiling: The Woman Manager.* London: Paul Chapman, 1992.

Morrison, Ann M., Randall P. White, Ellen Van Velsor, and the Center for Creative Leadership. *Breaking the Glass Ceiling: Can Women Reach the Top of America's Largest Corporations?* Reading, Mass.: Addison-Wesley, 1992.

Barbara R. Bergmann

See also **Discrimination: Sex; Women in Public Life, Business, and Professions.**

GLASSMAKING. American glassmaking at the beginning of the twenty-first century is a vast industry supplying global markets. Flat glass, used for fenestration, the automotive industry, and television and computer screens, accounts for the bulk of production; American glass works provide immense amounts of glass for international building projects. Though basic techniques of the modern flat glass industry have been in place since the mid-twentieth century, continual improvements are made in manufacturing, especially in developing new combinations of layering and coating glass for specific purposes.

Early American Glassmaking

An early attempt at glassmaking took place in Jamestown, Virginia, in 1608. Production was probably limited to blowing crude bottles and glass beads used as barter with Native Americans. Other glass works came and went in Massachusetts, New York, and Pennsylvania until 1780, when a glass factory was established in Glassboro, New Jersey. This glass works passed through many ownerships until 1919, when Owens Bottle Company bought and modernized it with automatic production.

Two names stand out in early American glassware. The first is Henry William Stiegel (called "Baron" Stiegel). Stiegel became, through marriage, the owner of an iron furnace, and went on to own a second iron furnace and three glass manufacturing houses. Between 1763 and 1774, Stiegel's factory in Manheim, Pennsylvania, produced superior decorated and colored flint glassware (also called lead glass), a heavy, brilliant glass that is used also to make paste jewelry. Stiegel's success inspired other glassmakers, and glassmaking spread to Pittsburgh and the Ohio River Valley. These new glass works not only supplied window and bottle glass to the newly settled country, but also created table glassware with discernible Midwestern designs. The second important name in early American glassware is John Frederick Amelung, who established the New Bremen Glassmanufactory in Frederick County, Maryland, in 1784. Using free-blown, mold-blown, cut, and particularly impressive engraved methods, Amelung produced items that were as advanced as high-quality European glassware.

Glassmaking. In this 1908 photograph by Lewis W. Hine, taken at the Seneca Glass Works in Morgantown, W.Va., a glassblower prepares a piece while the mold boys watch and get ready to detach the mold from the hot glass. © CORBIS

New Glassmaking Techniques

In the first quarter of the nineteenth century, glassmakers in America began to use two significant techniques. Factories in New York, New England, and Pennsylvania adopted a technique called "blown three-mold": usually three molds were needed for each piece, and the glassmaker would blow glass into incised metal molds to produce imitation cut glass. In Pittsburgh, at the New England Glass Company in Boston, and at the Boston and Sandwich Glass Company in Sandwich, Massachusetts, glass was at first pressed into a mold by hand, but after 1825 mechanical means were used. This innovation boosted small family businesses into a flourishing industry that spread across the country and abroad. Fancy-looking, inexpensive glassware became readily available as techniques improved. Using coal instead of wood for melting furnaces gave higher, more consistent temperatures. Natural gas, discovered in western Pennsylvania in 1859, proved to be even more controllable and cheaper than either coal or wood. American glassware companies, benefiting from increasing numbers of skilled European immigrants, produced distinctive articles in varying shapes, colors, and effects.

Sheet glass in the eighteenth and nineteenth centuries was made by blowing glass, using one of two methods. The Boston Crown Glass Company used the crown method from 1793 to about 1827: glass was blown, rotated to form a large plate, then cut and formed into rectangular sheets. The cylinder method required a large (six foot by two foot) cylinder to be blown, then opened to form a flat sheet. This became the more popular method because it created larger panes.

Twentieth-Century Innovations

By the twentieth century, flat glass was produced mechanically by drawing glass upward with a metal rod or bait and onto a metal roller. The glass was then passed over a flattening table to be cut into large sheets and commercially sized panes.

Wherever flat glass had to be free from distortion—in mirrors, auto glass, and shop-front windows—plate glass was formed by rolling, then was polished and buffed to a high sheen on both sides to an even thickness. Mirrors were made by backing glass with mercury and tin, later by using silver nitrate. Plate glass with a high proportion of lead was used as safety glass to protect medical personnel from radiation. A three-layer safety glass was developed in 1956 for use in atomic-energy plants.

Sheet glass is sometimes made with wire mesh fed into the molten glass to prevent shattering. Double-glazing and insulating glass that performs like a thermos is commonly used for windows as an energy-saving device. Glass rolled or pressed with figured designs give textured effects, commonly used in bathroom windows. Frosted glass is plate glass etched with hydrofluoric acid to produce a matte effect, sometimes called obscure glass. Sandblasting gives a similar effect but makes a weaker pane and is harder to clean. Safety glass for automobile windows is made by laminating a sheet of plastic—originally celluloid, but later a clear, non-yellowing polyvinyl chloride (PVC) type of plastic—between two sheets of plate glass to prevent windows from shattering when struck. Bullet-resistant glass uses several layers of glass and plastic.

Another innovation, glass brick, became a popular architectural device in the mid-twentieth century as it let natural light into such areas as hallways. Pyrex, in use by 1920, is one of several trademarked names for the heat-resistant glass-cooking utensils made by adding boric oxide to silica and alkali. Stovetop vessels were introduced in 1936. Borosilicate glass is resistant not only to high heat, but also to corrosive materials.

Glass fiber (also called fiber glass or spun glass) was used in ancient Egypt to decorate glass vessels. Glass fiber is produced by modern methods to make fine filaments, which can be combined to form single strands and woven into fireproof textiles for translucent undercurtains. Glass wool is made by forming filaments into mats that are used for heat insulation, electrical insulation, and air filters, and to reinforce plastics on aircraft parts, boats, buildings, and cars.

By the end of the twentieth century, with growing interest in environmental concerns, recycled glass had been used for various products from soda bottles to road building.

Fine Glassware and Art Glass

Probably the most recognized (and imitated) American art glassmaker was Louis Comfort Tiffany. In the last two decades of the nineteenth century, Tiffany used iridescent effects and fantastic colorings in his free-blown and manipulated wares.

In the twentieth century, the name Steuben became associated with high-quality blown glassware. The Steuben factory was acquired by Corning Glass Works during World War I to help meet wartime need for technical glass. A chemical formula was developed that could make glass as pure rock crystal. In 1933, Steuben Glass assembled a design, production, and marketing team that produced fine modern American glassware inspired by colonial designs. Inexpensive American glassware from the twentieth century includes milk glass usually used in kitchens, and, from the Great Depression of the 1930s, Carnival or Depression glass that was a popular giveaway to draw the public to gas stations and fairgrounds. This fine glassware had become a nostalgic collectable by the late twentieth century.

Much of the American art or studio glass production was centered just north of Seattle at the beginning of the twenty-first century. Renowned glass artist Dale Chihuly helped found the Pilchuck Glass School in that area in 1971.

BIBLIOGRAPHY

Glass Association of North America. Home page at http://www.glasswebsite.com.

Lee, Ruth Webb. *The Sandwich Glass Handbook.* Rutland, Vt.: Tuttle, 1985.

McKearin, George S., and Helen McKearin. *American Glass: The Fine Art of Glassmaking in America.* New York: Crown, 1941.

———. *Two Hundred Years of American Blown Glass.* Garden City, N.Y.: Doubleday, 1950.

Morse, Joseph Laffan, ed. *The Universal Standard Encyclopedia,* Volume 2. New York: Unicorn, 1954.

Chippy Irvine

GLASS-STEAGALL ACT, an emergency banking measure passed by Congress in 1932. Its first two provisions permitted particular member banks to use collateral normally ineligible for rediscount to borrow from Federal Reserve banks at one percent above the rate on normally eligible paper. The act authorized the Federal Reserve

Board to permit Federal Reserve banks to use U.S. government obligations, gold, and eligible paper to secure Federal Reserve notes. This act stabilized the banking system only temporarily.

The following year, Congress passed the Glass-Steagall Act of 1933, also called the Banking Act of 1933, which created the Federal Deposit Insurance Corporation and separated investment and commercial banking. Congress repealed the Glass-Steagall Act of 1933 in 1999, with the passing of the Financial Services Modernization Act of 1999 (Gramm-Leach-Bliley Act), thus removing the regulations barring mergers among banking, securities, and insurance businesses.

BIBLIOGRAPHY

McElvaine, Robert S. *The Great Depression: America 1929–1941.* New York: Times Books, 1984; 1993.

Frederick A. Bradford
Cynthia R. Poe

See also **Banking; Exchanges; Federal Reserve System.**

GLEBES were lands set aside for the clergy by American colonists, consistent with English tradition. The proprietors of townships in the New England colonies, in drawing lots for their land, reserved a share for a minister for his support. The presence of a minister, they reasoned, would induce people to migrate to the new community. The minister's allotment could be substantial—as much as four lots of 100 acres each, one for his farm and three that he could sell or rent. Whereas New England glebes generally passed into private ownership in the first generation of the community's development, in the South, notably in Virginia, glebes ranging from 100 to 250 acres were intended as permanent farms for the support of the ministers of the established church and could be rented but not sold. Members of churches other than the established church resented having to contribute to the purchase of glebes, however. Those opposed to the institution in Virginia, spurred by a wave of evangelical revivals in the area, succeeded in 1802 in securing the adoption of the Sequestration Act, which provided for the sale of glebes by the overseers of the poor for the benefit of the indigent. Not geared to reliance on the voluntary contributions of members as were other churches, the Episcopal Church was weakened by the new law. In other southern states the glebes remained in the hands of the church and were sometimes worked by ministers whose incomes were small or by tenants.

BIBLIOGRAPHY

Hall, David D. *The Faithful Shepherd: A History of the New England Ministry in the Seventeenth Century.* Chapel Hill: University of North Carolina Press, 1972.

Paul W. Gates/A. R.

See also **Church of England in the Colonies; Church and State, Separation of; Great Awakening; Land Policy.**

GLIDERS. The military glider, unique to World War II, became obsolete after the war as aviation developed, especially with the production of successful HELICOPTERS.

The Germans conducted the first glider mission in 1940. Recognizing the possibilities, the British and Americans implemented their own glider programs designed to discharge, in a small area, large numbers of fully armed troops ready for immediate combat, thus eliminating the costly time required to assemble paratroopers. Gliders also made it possible to deliver vehicles and weapons too heavy for parachutes.

The Germans made the most imaginative use of gliders to land troops silently on top of the Belgian Fort Eben-Emael in May 1940. Within ten minutes they blinded that great fortress, virtually putting it out of action. In May 1941 the only large-scale employment of gliders by the Luftwaffe played a significant role in Operation Merkur, the successful airborne assault on Crete. A daring, small-scale glider mission liberated Benito Mussolini from imprisonment at Gran Sasso in the Abruzzi Mountains in Italy in 1943. Elsewhere, minor glider missions substituted when transport aircraft operations were not feasible.

Allied forces used gliders on a larger scale. The first operation, in 1943, a British-American assault on Sicily, provided valuable experience despite being inept and costly. Use of gliders on D day in Normandy was largely successful but indecisive. The largest Allied glider mission, part of Operation Market-Garden in September 1944, employed 2,596 gliders to secure a bridgehead across the Rhine River at Arnhem, Netherlands, but had limited success. Operation Varsity, the last glider operation of the war, near Wesel, Germany, on 23 March 1945, employed 1,348 gliders and was considered a tremendous success.

BIBLIOGRAPHY

Craven, Wesley F., and James Lea Cate, eds. *The Army Air Forces in World War II.* Chicago: University of Chicago Press, 1950–1958.

U.S. Air Force. *USAF Historical Studies*, Air Force Historical Research Agency, nos. 1, 97, and 167.

John A. McQuillen Jr./C. W.

See also **D Day; World War II, Air War against Germany.**

GLOBAL WARMING. Gases created through human industrial and agricultural practices (primarily carbon dioxide from burning fossil fuels and wood, as well as methane, nitrous oxide, and chlorofluorocarbons) increase the heat-reflecting potential of the atmosphere, thereby raising the planet's average temperature.

Early Scientific Work

Since the late nineteenth century, atmospheric scientists in the United States and overseas have known that significant changes in the chemical composition of atmospheric gases might cause climate change on a global scale. In 1824, the French scientist Jean-Baptiste Fourier described how the earth's atmosphere functioned like the glass of a greenhouse, trapping heat and maintaining the stable climate that sustained life. By the 1890s, some scientists, including the Swedish chemist Svante Arrhenius and the American geologist Thomas Chamberlain, had discerned that carbon dioxide had played a central role historically in regulating global temperatures.

In 1896, Arrhenius provided the first quantitative analysis of how changes in atmospheric carbon dioxide could alter surface temperatures and ultimately lead to climatic change on a scale comparable with the ice ages. In 1899, Chamberlain similarly linked glacial periods to changes in atmospheric carbon dioxide and posited that water vapor might provide crucial positive feedback to changes in carbon dioxide. In the first decade of the twentieth century, Arrhenius further noted that industrial combustion of coal and other fossil fuels could introduce enough carbon dioxide into the atmosphere to change the temperature of the planet over the course of a few centuries. However, he predicted that warming would be delayed because the oceans would absorb most of the carbon dioxide. Arrhenius further posited various societal benefits from this planetary warming.

Developing Scientific Consensus

Over the course of the twentieth century, scientists confirmed these early predictions as they probed further into the functioning of the earth's atmospheric system. Early in the century, dozens of scientists around the world contributed to an internationally burgeoning understanding of atmospheric science. By the century's close, thousands of scientists collaborated to refine global models of climate change and regional analyses of how rising temperatures might alter weather patterns, ecosystem dynamics, agriculture, oceans and ice cover, and human health and disease.

While no one scientific breakthrough revolutionized climate change science or popular understanding of the phenomenon, several key events stand out to chart developing scientific understanding of global warming. In 1938, Guy S. Callendar provided an early calculation of warming due to human-introduced carbon dioxide and contended that this warming was evident already in the temperature record. Obscured by the onset of World War II and by a short-term cooling trend that began in the 1940s, Callendar's analysis received short shrift. Interest in global warming increased in the 1950s with new techniques for studying climate, including analysis of ancient pollens, ocean shells, and new computer models. Using computer models, in 1956, Gilbert N. Plass attracted greater attention to the carbon dioxide theory of climate change. The following year, Roger Revelle and Hans Suess showed that oceanic absorption of atmospheric carbon dioxide would not be sufficient to delay global warming. They stressed the magnitude of the phenomenon:

> Human beings are now carrying out a large scale geophysical experiment of a kind that could not have happened in the past nor be reproduced in the future. Within a few centuries we are returning to the atmosphere and oceans the concentrated organic carbon stored in sedimentary rocks over hundreds of millions of years. (Cristianson, *Greenhouse*, pp. 155–156)

At the same time, Charles Keeling began to measure the precise year-by-year rise in atmospheric carbon dioxide from the Mauna Loa Observatory in Hawaii. In 1965, the President's Scientific Advisory Committee issued the first U.S. government report that summarized recent climate research and outlined potential future changes resulting from increased atmospheric carbon dioxide, including the melting of the Antarctic ice cap, the rise of sea level, and the warming of oceans.

By the late 1970s, atmospheric scientists had grown increasingly confident that the buildup of carbon dioxide, methane, chlorofluorocarbons, and related gases in the atmosphere would have a significant, lasting impact on global climate. Several jointly written government reports issued during President Jimmy Carter's administration presented early consensus estimates of global climate change. These estimates would prove consistent with more sophisticated models refined in the two decades following. A 1979 National Research Council report by Jule G. Charney, *Carbon Dioxide and Climate: A Scientific Assessment*, declared that "we now have incontrovertible evidence that the atmosphere is indeed changing and that we ourselves contribute to that change. Atmospheric concentrations of carbon dioxide are steadily increasing, and these changes are linked with man's use of fossil fuels and exploitation of the land" (p. vii). The Charney report estimated a doubling of atmospheric carbon dioxide concentrations would probably result in a roughly 3-degree Celsius rise in temperature, plus or minus 1.5 degrees.

Global Warming Politics

As climate science grew more conclusive, global warming became an increasingly challenging political problem. In January 1981, in the closing days of the Carter administration, the Council on Environmental Quality (CEQ) published *Global Energy Futures and the Carbon Dioxide Problem.* The CEQ report described climate change as the "ultimate environmental dilemma," which required collective judgments to be made, either by decision or default, "largely on the basis of scientific models that have severe limitations and that few can understand." The report reviewed available climate models and predicted that carbon dioxide–related global warming "should be observable now or sometime within the next two decades"

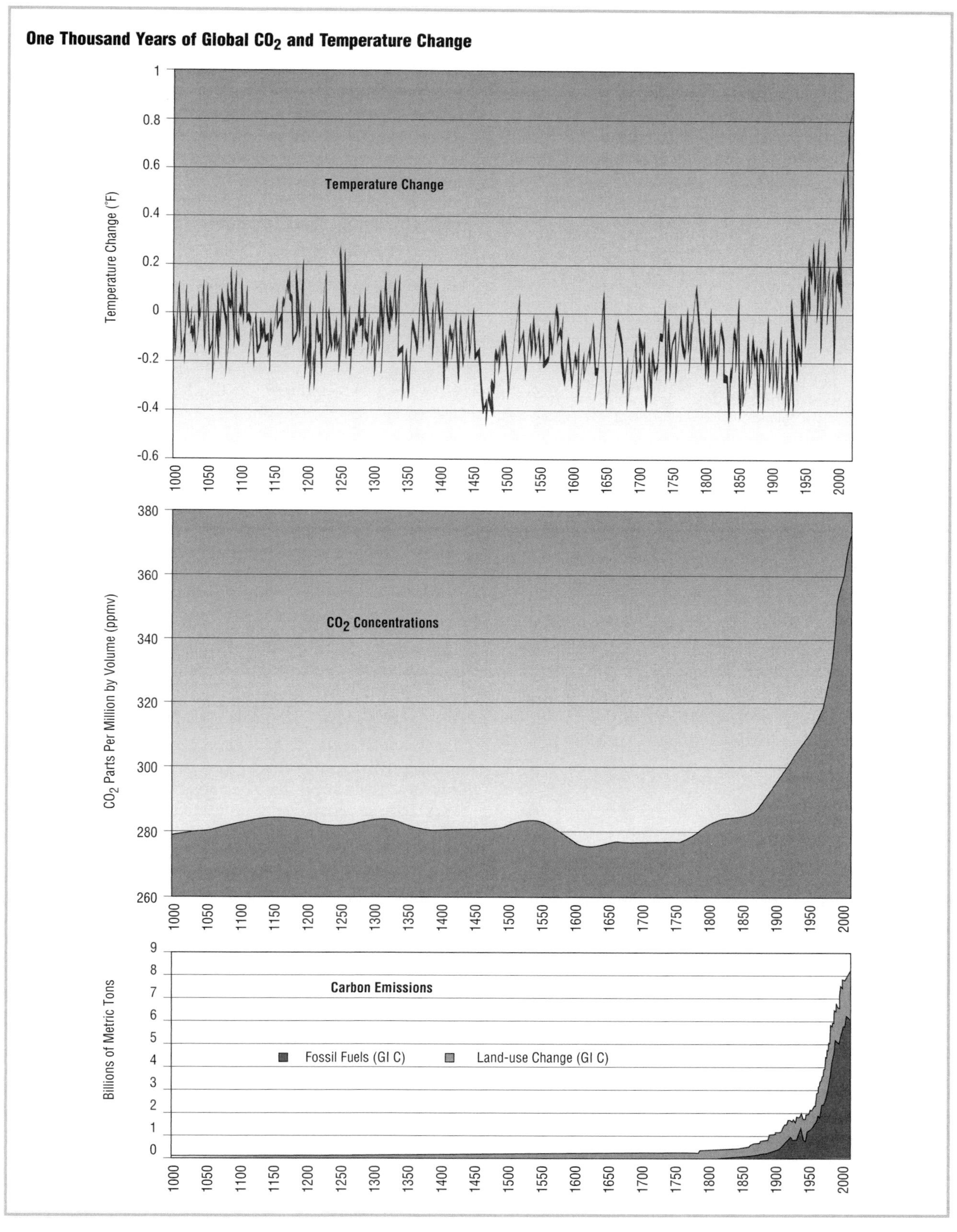
One Thousand Years of Global CO_2 and Temperature Change
Temperature Change
Temperature Change (°F)
1
0.8
0.6
0.4
0.2
0
-0.2
-0.4
-0.6
1000
1050
1100
1150
1200
1250
1300
1350
1400
1450
1500
1550
1600
1650
1700
1750
1800
1850
1900
1950
2000
CO_2 Concentrations
CO_2 Parts Per Million by Volume (ppmv)
380
360
340
320
300
280
260
Carbon Emissions
Billions of Metric Tons
9
8
7
6
5
4
3
2
1
0
Fossil Fuels (GI C)
Land-use Change (GI C)

(p. v). With atmospheric carbon dioxide increasing rapidly, the CEQ report noted that the world was already "performing a great planetary experiment" (p. 52).

By the early 1980s, the scientific models of global warming had established the basic contours of this atmospheric phenomenon. Federal environmental agencies and scientific advisory boards had urged action to curb carbon dioxide emissions dramatically, yet little state, federal, or international policymaking ensued. Decades-old federal and state subsidies for fossil fuel production and consumption remained firmly in place. The federal government lessened its active public support for energy efficiency initiatives and alternative energy development. Falling oil and natural gas prices throughout the decade further undermined political support for a national energy policy that would address the problem of global warming.

A complicated intersection of climate science and policy further hindered effective lawmaking. Scientists urged political action, but spoke in a measured language that emphasized probability and uncertainty. Many scientists resisted entering the political arena, and expressed skepticism about their colleagues who did. This skepticism came to a head in reaction to the government scientist James Hansen's efforts to focus national attention on global warming during the drought-filled summer of 1988. As more than 400,000 acres of Yellowstone National Park burned in a raging fire, Hansen testified to Congress that he was 99 percent certain that the earth was getting warmer because of the greenhouse effect. While the testimony brought significant new political attention in the United States to the global warming problem, many of Hansen's scientific colleagues were dismayed by his definitive assertions. Meanwhile, a small number of skeptical scientists who emphasized the uncertainty of global warming and the need to delay policy initiatives fueled opposition to political action.

In 1988, delegates from nearly fifty nations met in Toronto and Geneva to address the climate change problem. The delegates formed the Intergovernmental Panel on Climate Change (IPCC), consisting of more than two thousand scientists from around the world, to assess systematically global warming science and policy options. The IPCC issued its first report in 1990, followed by second and third assessments in 1995 and 2001. Each IPCC report provided increasingly precise predictions of future warming and the regional impacts of climate change. Meanwhile, books like Bill McKibben's *The End of Nature* (1989) and Senator Albert Gore Jr.'s *Earth in the Balance* (1992) focused popular attention in the United States on global warming.

Yet these developments did not prompt U.S. government action. With its major industries highly dependent on fossil fuel consumption, the United States instead helped block steps to combat climate change at several international conferences in the late 1980s and 1990s. At the United Nations Conference on Environment and Development in Rio de Janeiro in 1992, U.S. negotiators successfully thwarted a treaty with mandatory limits on greenhouse gas emissions. As a result, the Rio conference adopted only voluntary limits. In 1993, the new administration of Bill Clinton and Albert Gore Jr. committed itself to returning United States emissions to 1990 levels by the year 2000. The administration also attempted to adjust incentives for energy consumption in its 1993 energy tax bill. Defeated on the tax bill and cowed when Republicans gained control of Congress in 1994, however, the Clinton administration backed away from significant new energy and climate initiatives.

At the highly charged 1997 United Nations Conference on Climate Change in Kyoto, Japan, more than 160 countries approved a protocol that would reduce emissions of carbon dioxide, methane, nitrous oxide, and three chlorofluorocarbon substitutes. In the United States, powerful industry opponents to the Kyoto Protocol, represented by the Global Climate Coalition (an industry association including Exxon, Mobil, Shell Oil, Ford, and General Motors, as well as other automobile, mining, steel, and chemical companies), denounced the protocol's "unrealistic targets and timetables" and argued instead for voluntary action and further research. Along with other opponents, the coalition spent millions of dollars on television ads criticizing the agreement, focusing on possible emissions exemptions for developing nations. Although the Clinton administration signed the Kyoto Protocol, strong Senate opposition to the agreement prevented ratification. In 2001, President George W. Bush withdrew his executive support for the protocol.

Growing Signals of Global Warming

By the end of the 1990s, climate science had grown increasingly precise and achieved virtual worldwide scientific consensus on climate change. The 2001 report of the Intergovernmental Panel on Climate Change concluded that global average surface temperature had increased by 0.6 degrees Celsius during the twentieth century, largely due to greenhouse gas emissions. Carbon dioxide concentrations in the atmosphere had increased by approximately 30 percent since the late nineteenth century, rising from 280 parts per million (ppm) by volume to 367 ppm in 1998.

By 2001, signs of global warming were increasingly widespread. With glaciers around the world melting, average sea levels rising, and average precipitation increasing, the 1990s registered as the hottest decade on record in the past thousand years. Regional models predicted widespread shifting of ecosystems in the United States, with alpine ecosystems expected largely to disappear in the lower forty-eight states while savannas or grasslands replace desert ecosystems in the Southwest. The IPCC 2001 report estimated an increase of between 1.4 and 5.8 degrees Celsius by 2100, a projected increase in global temperature very likely "without precedent during at least the last 10,000 years."

BIBLIOGRAPHY

Christianson, Gale E. *Greenhouse: The 200-Year Story of Global Warming.* New York: Walker, 1999.

Council on Environmental Quality. *Global Energy Futures and the Carbon Dioxide Problem.* Washington, D.C.: Government Printing Office, 1981.

Handel, Mark David, and James S. Risbey. *An Annotated Bibliography on Greenhouse Effect Change.* Cambridge, Mass.: Massachusetts Institute of Technology, Center for Global Change Science, 1992.

Intergovernmental Panel on Climate Change. *Climate Change 2001: Impacts, Adaptations, and Vulnerability.* Edited by James J. McCarthy et al. Cambridge, U.K.: Cambridge University Press, 2001.

———. *Climate Change 2001: Mitigation.* Edited by Bert Metz et al. Cambridge, U.K.: Cambridge University Press, 2001.

———. *Climate Change 2001: The Scientific Basis.* Edited by J. T. Houghton et al. Cambridge, U.K.: Cambridge University Press, 2001.

McKibben, Bill. *The End of Nature.* 10th anniv. ed. New York: Anchor, 1999.

National Research Council. *Carbon Dioxide and Climate: A Scientific Assessment.* Washington, D.C.: National Academy of Sciences, 1979.

Paul Sabin

See also **Climate; Conservation.**

"GO WEST, YOUNG MAN, GO WEST" was an expression first used by John Babsone Lane Soule in the *Terre Haute Express* in 1851. It appealed to Horace Greeley, who rephrased it slightly in an editorial in the *New York Tribune* on 13 July 1865: "Go West, young man, and grow up with the country." When the phrase gained popularity, Greeley printed Soule's article to show the source of his inspiration. The phrase captured the imaginations of clerks, mechanics, and soldiers returning from the Civil War, many of whom moved west to take up a homestead.

BIBLIOGRAPHY

Cross, Coy F. *Go West, Young Man!: Horace Greeley's Vision for America.* Albuquerque: University of New Mexico Press, 1995.

J. W. Ellison/c. w.

See also **Homestead Movement; West, American; Westward Migration.**

GODEY'S LADY'S BOOK. In 1830 in Philadelphia, Louis Godey first published *Godey's Lady's Book* as the *Lady's Book.* In 1837 Godey bought the *Ladies Magazine* of Boston and made its editor, Sarah Josepha Hale, the literary editor of his periodical. Despite her publicly active role as an author, Hale's writings preached the message of separate-gendered spheres. This combination of Godey and Hale gave the magazine its high standing. During the forty years of their association, *Godey's* became one of the most famous and influential periodicals in America. In matters of fashions, etiquette, home economics, and standards of propriety, *Godey's* was the supreme arbiter. As did all similar magazines of the time, *Godey's* included fashion plates featuring clothing designs from Paris, then the sole fashion center. *Godey's* also served as the model for later home magazines. Shortly before the Civil War, it enjoyed a monthly circulation of 150,000 copies. The growing American middle class found this publication most useful. Following the sale of Godey's interests and Hale's retirement in 1877, the magazine moved to New York, where it finally expired in 1892. In later years *Godey's* faced competition from other periodicals, such as *Ladies' Home Journal,* which still publishes today.

BIBLIOGRAPHY

Okker, Patricia. *Our Sister Editors: Sarah J. Hale and the Tradition of Nineteenth-Century American Women Editors.* Athens: University of Georgia Press, 1995.

Tebbel, John William. *The Magazine in America, 1741–1990.* New York: Oxford University Press, 1991.

Tonkovich, Nicole. *Domesticity with a Difference: The Nonfiction of Catharine Beecher, Sarah J. Hale, Fanny Fern, and Margaret Fuller.* Jackson: University Press of Mississippi, 1997.

E. H. O'Neill/A. E.

See also **Clothing and Fashion; Literature: Popular Literature; Magazines, Women's.**

GOLD ACT. During the Civil War the federal government issued paper money called greenbacks to help fund the war effort. In 1864 the depreciation of greenbacks was measured by the premium on gold, and speculators were blamed for the fluctuations in the premiums. Congress responded by passing the Gold Act in June 1864. The act made it unlawful to buy or sell gold for future delivery or to buy or sell foreign exchange to be delivered after ten days. The result was such an aggravation in the fluctuation of the price of gold that the act was repealed on 2 July 1864.

BIBLIOGRAPHY

Friedman, Milton. *Money Mischief: Episodes in Monetary History.* New York: Harcourt Brace Jovanovich, 1992.

Hammond, Bray. *Sovereignty and an Empty Purse: Banks and Politics in the Civil War.* Princeton, N.J.: Princeton University Press, 1970.

James D. Magee/A. G.

See also **Exchange, Bills of; Gold Exchange; Gold Standard; National Bank Notes.**

GOLD BUGS. Borrowed from the title of the Edgar Allan Poe story "The Gold Bug" (1843), this label by the

1870s referred to those who favored basing the U.S. monetary system on gold to the exclusion of silver. As the struggle over monetary issues intensified, generating heated rhetoric and wonderful cartoons, the term became more derogatory. After 1893, it was applied especially to gold supporters within the Democratic Party. That shrinking group, predominantly urban businesspeople and professionals, supported President Grover Cleveland's repeal of the SHERMAN SILVER PURCHASE ACT, and in 1896 they bolted the party to create and support the National Democratic ticket of John Palmer.

BIBLIOGRAPHY

Friedman, Milton, and Anna Jacobson Schwartz. *A Monetary History of the United States, 1867–1960.* Princeton, N.J.: Princeton University Press, 1963.

Philip R. VanderMeer

See also **Gold Standard.**

GOLD CLAUSE CASES, *Norman v. Baltimore and Ohio Railroad Company,* 294 U.S. 240 (1935); *Nortz v. United States,* 294 U.S. 317 (1935); and *Perry v. United States,* 294 U.S. 330 (1935). In order to prevent a potentially disastrous run on U.S. gold reserves during the Great Depression, Congress enacted legislation canceling the government's obligation to repay certain of its debts in gold. When the new law was challenged as unconstitutional under the Constitution's contracts clause, the U.S. Supreme Court upheld it by a 5 to 4 vote. By doing so, the Court reaffirmed Congress's plenary authority over monetary policy and prevented further harm to the national economy.

BIBLIOGRAPHY

Hall, Kermit L., ed. *The Oxford Companion to the Supreme Court of the United States.* New York: Oxford University Press, 1992.

Katherine M. Jones

GOLD DEMOCRATS. Repudiating the free-silver platform of the Democratic presidential candidate, William Jennings Bryan, Gold Democrats organized the National Democratic Party in September 1896. They nominated Senator John M. Palmer of Illinois for president on a conservative, gold platform, thus providing an anti-Bryan ticket for those Democrats who could not stomach voting for Republican candidates. Nevertheless, many Gold Democrats either voted for Republican William McKinley or avoided voting, with the result that Palmer polled only 134,635 votes. Gold Democrats did not nominate candidates in 1900, because some drifted back to the Democratic Party and others turned to the Republican Party.

BIBLIOGRAPHY

Glad, Paul W. *McKinley, Bryan, and the People.* Philadelphia: Lippincott, 1964.

Jones, Stanley L. *The Presidential Election of 1896.* Madison: University of Wisconsin Press, 1964.

*Jeannette P. Nichols/*A. G.

See also **Free Silver; Gold Standard; Silver Democrats.**

GOLD EXCHANGE was organized in New York City in 1862. Wall Street brokers had bought and sold gold in exchange for greenbacks since the first of that year, but early makeshift arrangements proved inadequate. Upon establishing the exchange, the founding brokers provided that any respectable citizen could become a member by paying $100 a year to defray expenses, and 450 men joined. At first, gold was actually delivered, but after 1863, traders exchanged Treasury Department certificates of deposit. When business increased significantly, sales and purchases were cleared daily through the Gold Exchange Bank. The gold exchange was a commercial necessity and served a useful purpose until the United States resumed gold redemption at the beginning of 1879.

BIBLIOGRAPHY

Shapiro, Eli, Ezra Solomon, and William L. White. *Money and Banking.* New York: Holt, Rinehart and Winston, 1968.

*Frederick A. Bradford/*C. W.

See also **Gold Standard; Greenbacks; Treasury, Department of the.**

GOLD MINES AND MINING. Gold mining in the United States began in the foothills of the Appalachian Mountains in North Carolina following the chance discovery of a nugget of free gold in 1799. Limited but continuous activity there and in Georgia after the opening of gold deposits in 1828–1829 resulted in the production of an estimated $24.5 million in gold in the years before 1848. This record was completely and dramatically eclipsed in the goldfields of CALIFORNIA after the discovery of gold at Coloma by James Wilson Marshall in January 1848. The gold flakes that Marshall found in the run at John Sutter's mill were not the first gold found in California; Mexicans had worked placer deposits near Los Angeles since 1842. But the Coloma strike touched off a mass migration to the goldfields of the newly acquired territory. The first decade of California mining, 1848–1858, saw some $550 million in gold extracted.

The early California mines were placer deposits of free, or pure, gold mixed with sand and gravel. The mining pan became the basic tool of the placer miner. He recovered the gold by agitating water and debris in the pan; the gold, being heavier than the sand or gravel, settled to the bottom of the pan. Refinements such as the rocker, sluice, tom, dredge, and hydraulic nozzle are all

Golden Rule Mine. The entrance to a mine in Tuolumne County, Calif., east of San Francisco. NATIONAL ARCHIVES AND RECORDS ADMINISTRATION

devices employing the same principle as the pan—that of washing the gold-bearing debris with water. The only chemical process used was mercury-gold amalgamation. Mercury and gold have a natural affinity for each other and, when brought into contact, form an amalgam. Separated from other debris, the amalgam can be heated, driving the mercury off as a vapor, leaving a residue of free gold.

In time, as the easily worked California placer deposits began to be exhausted, interest turned to lode mining, the mining of free gold in streaks or veins embedded in quartz or rock. Lode mining called for relatively complicated and expensive methods of crushing the ore, and early tools such as the Spanish *arrastre* were soon replaced by steam-powered stamp mills. Washing and amalgamation followed the pulverizing of the ore to recover the gold. The Empire and the North Star mines at Grass Valley were California's most successful lode mines.

The California gold mining initiated a continuing series of gold strikes in the trans-Mississippi West, and the experiences of California miners proved valuable lessons in the new camps. Mining laws and mining methods, with many ingredients borrowed from Spanish mining via Mexico, were exported from California to the new fields. In 1859 the Comstock lode in NEVADA, with its rich gold and silver ores, gave rise to the boomtown of Virginia City. The year before, small placer deposits had been found near Cherry Creek in what was to become Colorado, touching off the Pike's Peak rush in the spring of 1859. In the following decade camps were opened in Idaho and Montana, and the Black Hills region of South Dakota experienced the same pattern in the years after 1875. The Alaska fields were first mined in the 1880s, with later and richer discoveries in 1898 near Cape Nome and in 1902–1903 in the Fairbanks region. Goldfield and Tonopah provided Nevada with a second rush in 1903–1905.

Most of the gold discovered was free gold, and mechanical methods of separation were sufficient for recovery. Even so, as mines were extended farther and deeper, more extensive methods were required to extract the ore. Fortunately, through borrowings from abroad and on-site innovations, technology kept pace with need. The Comstock operations in Nevada in 1865–1875 were especially noted for application and adaptation of new techniques. The compressed-air drill and the diamond-studded rotary drill were borrowed from France; the new explosives nitroglycerine and dynamite, used for blasting, were introduced from Sweden; and A. S. Hallidie of San Francisco perfected the flat, woven-wire cable used in hoists.

Where gold is found in combination with other elements, the problems of extraction are more complex. Advances in metallurgical chemistry were necessary before such ores could be profitably worked. One of the first successful chemical processes for separation of refractory ores was the cyanide process, perfected in 1887. This process involved the placing of finely crushed gold ores in a solution of potassium cyanide, where the gold cyanide that formed could be removed either with zinc or by electrolysis. This process and others such as chlorination and oil-flotation were available when the Cripple Creek fields of Colorado were opened in 1891. The nation's richest mining district developed from the telluride ores of Cripple Creek; the two biggest producers, the Portland and the Independence mines, accounted for more than $100 million in gold in the years after 1891. The new chemical processes also made possible the reworking of older mines to recover gold from low-grade ores and the development of new areas in which low-grade ores existed, such as the San Juan region of Colorado, with its Camp Bird, Liberty-Bell, and Smuggler-Union mines.

Mine production reached its highest levels in the decade 1905–1915, when an annual average of 4,513,480 fine ounces of gold was produced in the United States. After World War I gold mining decreased markedly. High-grade ores had been exhausted, and the costs of extraction and refining had increased. After 1920 the Homestake mine at Lead made South Dakota the leading gold-producing state. In 1970 three states (South Dakota, Nevada, and Utah) mined 84 percent of the 1,743,000 fine ounces of gold produced in the United States.

BIBLIOGRAPHY

Gudde, Erwin Gustav. *California Gold Camps: A Geographical and Historical Dictionary of Camps, Towns, and Localities Where Gold Was Found and Mined, Wayside Stations and Trading Centers.* Berkeley: University of California Press, 1975.

James, Ronald Michael. *The Roar and the Silence: A History of Virginia City and the Comstock Lode.* Reno: University of Nevada Press, 1998.

Paul, Rodman Wilson. *The California Gold Discovery: Sources, Documents, Accounts, and Memoirs Relating to the Discovery of Gold at Sutter's Mill.* Georgetown, Calif.: Talisman Press, 1966.

Carl Ubbelohde / A. G.

Gold Miners. The dream was of easy riches; the reality, hard work with rewards for only a few.
GRANGER COLLECTION, NEW YORK

See also **Forty-Niners; Merchant Adventurers; Mining Towns;** *and vol. 9:* **The Vigilantes of Montana.**

GOLD PURCHASE PLAN, formulated by President Franklin D. Roosevelt's financial adviser, George F. Warren, and sometimes referred to as the Warren Plan, was put into operation in October 1933 and ended in January 1934. Under this plan the RECONSTRUCTION FINANCE CORPORATION was authorized to buy gold newly mined in the United States and, if necessary, on the world markets at prices to be determined from time to time after consultation with the president and the secretary of the treasury. The theory of the Gold Purchase Plan, apparently, was to bring about an increase in the domestic commodity price level by raising the price of gold. In this respect it was a failure.

BIBLIOGRAPHY

Friedman, Milton, and Anna Jacobson Schwartz. *A Monetary History of the United States, 1867–1960.* Princeton, N.J.: Princeton University Press, 1963.

Leuchtenburg, William E. *Franklin D. Roosevelt and the New Deal, 1932–1940.* New York: Harper & Row, 1963.

Frederick A. Bradford / A. G.

See also **Banking: Banking Crisis of 1933; Federal Reserve System; Gold Exchange; Gold Standard; Hard Money.**

GOLD RESERVE ACT. In response to the GREAT DEPRESSION, and at the request of President Franklin D. Roosevelt, Congress passed the Gold Reserve Act on 30 January 1934; the measure nationalized all gold by ordering the Federal Reserve banks to turn over their supply to the U.S. Treasury. In return the banks received gold certificates to be used as reserves against deposits and Federal Reserve notes. The act also authorized the president to devalue the gold dollar so that it would have no more than 60 percent of its existing weight. Under this authority the president, on 31 January 1934, fixed the value of the gold dollar at 59.06 cents.

BIBLIOGRAPHY

Friedman, Milton, and Anna Jacobson Schwartz. *A Monetary History of the United States, 1867–1960.* Princeton, N.J.: Princeton University Press, 1963.

Erik McKinley Eriksson / A. G.

See also **Banking: Banking Crisis of 1933; Federal Reserve System; Gold Exchange; Gold Standard; Hard Money.**

GOLD RUSH, CALIFORNIA. When James Marshall looked into the American River and saw gold alongside John Sutter's sawmill on 24 January 1848, he unintentionally initiated a set of events that dramatically transformed both California and the United States. Al-

San Francisco Bay, c. 1851. A steady procession of ships transformed San Francisco almost overnight from village to city, ethnically diverse and initially lawless, until tamed by vigilante justice. THE GAMMA LIAISON NETWORK

though Marshall and Sutter attempted to prevent news of their discovery from spreading, within a few months word had reached San Francisco. A visitor in June found the city nearly abandoned because of "gold fever." By September eastern newspapers offered their readers breathless reports of the incredible riches ready for the taking.

The term "rush" is appropriate. By 1850, California's American- and European-born population had increased tenfold, with San Francisco alone growing from a sleepy village of 1,000 to a bustling city of 35,000. Ships that docked in San Francisco Bay at the height of the fever risked losing their entire crews to the goldfields. The state's non-Indian population increased from about 14,000 before the discovery to nearly 250,000 in 1852 even though an average of 30,000 prospectors returned home each year. Although 80 percent of the "forty-niners" were from the United States and all states were represented, this migration also was a global event, drawing gold seekers from California Indian bands, East Asia, Chile, Mexico, and western Europe. For the United States it was the largest mass migration to date, flooding the previously lightly traveled trails to the West Coast as more than 1 percent of the nation's population moved to California in just a few years.

The apparent availability of wealth drew so many so fast. In a time when farm workers could expect to earn a dollar for a long day's work and skilled craftspeople earned perhaps half again as much, it was not uncommon for early arrivals to the goldfields to make $16 a day. The chance for such prosperity struck many Americans as not merely a potential individual windfall but as a fulfillment of their rapidly expanding country's promise of economic democracy. Just nine days after Marshall's discovery, California, ceded in the Treaty of Guadalupe-Hidalgo by a defeated and occupied Mexico, formally became a part of the United States. It seemed that average Americans, whatever their previous backgrounds or origins, were reaping nature's bounty.

The hordes of newcomers made gold rush California a society distinct from the migrants' various homelands. The diversity of nationalities, the sharp fluctuations in economic prospects, and the overwhelming preponderance of men all kept social life in the goldfields unsettled. At the time gold rush California was for many a sharp contrast to the sobriety and respectability of middle-class America. "But they were rough," wrote Mark Twain of the forty-niners in *Roughing It.* "They fairly reveled in gold, whiskey, fights, fandagos, and were unspeakably happy."

It was for good reason that mining camps and towns instantly acquired reputations for wildness. Probably half of the women in early mining camps were prostitutes. Alcohol, isolation, and struggles over access to gold made for high rates of homicide and other violence. Gender roles were less predictable and more flexible than in the homes of most migrants. The small percentage of women meant that men had to perform traditionally feminine domestic tasks or pay others, often women entrepreneurs, good money to do so, and this may have given married women more power and options. But the quick end of

Roughing It. Miners often paid deluxe prices for meager accommodations. © CORBIS

easy riches and the arrival of significant numbers of white women in the 1850s signaled the end of gold rush society. Newly arrived middle-class women saw themselves as "taming" California, curtailing gambling, drinking, prostitution, and much of the openness in gender roles that had characterized the region.

While the promise of easy riches drew many migrants, the reality was often not what they had hoped. Miners worked long hours in remote places, generally living in ramshackle accommodations and paying exorbitant prices for food, shelter, and clothing. The gold deposits accessible to hand digging quickly played out, and all that remained were buried veins that could be exploited only by well-capitalized ventures employing hydraulic equipment and other expensive machinery. Most miners who remained were no longer independent prospectors but rather the employees of large mining companies. Indeed, most of the gold rush fortunes were not made by extracting the nearly $300 million in gold dug in six years but rather by marketing supplies to the miners. The German immigrant Levi Strauss, for example, sold so many work pants to gold diggers that his name became the generic term for jeans (Levis).

For others the gold rush was an outright disaster. The numbers, diseases, and violence of newcomers overwhelmed most of the state's Native American peoples, initiating a demographic collapse that brought them to the edge of extinction. White discrimination, embodied most clearly in heavy taxes on foreign miners, kept most Chinese, Latin American, and African American prospectors out of the choice diggings. Even the rush's originators failed to profit. Marshall and Sutter were soon overtaken by the course of events and were ruined. Their sawmill was idled by the flight of able-bodied men to the diggings, and squatters occupied much of Sutter's expansive lands, killing most of his livestock and destroying his crops. Both men died in poverty and anonymity.

But what destroyed Sutter and Marshall created American California, with important consequences for the nation as a whole. The gold rush made the Golden State the most populous and prosperous western territory even as it removed tens of thousands of men from their families and communities for years. Connecting the West Coast to the rest of the country added to the impetus to build the transcontinental railways, to defeat the last independent Indian nations on the Great Plains, and to settle the interior West. Finally, the wealth it produced, even greater and more easily acquired in legend, made thousands flock to later discoveries of gold in Nevada, Colorado, and Alaska.

BIBLIOGRAPHY

Holliday, J. S. *The World Rushed In: The California Gold Rush Experience.* New York: Simon and Schuster, 1981.

Johnson, Susan Lee. *Roaring Camp: The Social World of the California Gold Rush.* New York: Norton, 2000.

Roberts, Brian. *American Alchemy: The California Gold Rush and Middle-Class Culture.* Chapel Hill: University of North Carolina Press, 2000.

Rohrbough, Malcolm J. *Days of Gold: The California Gold Rush and the American Nation.* Berkeley: University of California Press, 1997.

Benjamin H. Johnson

See also **California; Forty-Niners;** *and vol. 9:* **Constitution of the Committee of Vigilantes of San Francisco.**

GOLD STANDARD. The gold standard is a monetary system in which gold is the standard or in which the unit of value—be it the dollar, the pound, franc, or some other unit in which prices and wages are customarily expressed and debts are usually contracted—consists of the value of a fixed quantity of gold in a free gold market.

U.S. experience with the gold standard began in the 1870s. From 1792 until the Civil War, the United States, with a few lapses during brief periods of suspended specie payments, was on a bimetallic standard. This broke down in the early days of the Civil War, and from 30 December 1861 to 2 January 1879, the country was on a depreciated paper money standard. The currency act of 1873 dropped the silver dollar from the list of legal coinage but continued the free and unlimited coinage of gold and declared the gold dollar to be the unit of value. There was a free market in the United States for gold, and gold could be exported and imported without restriction. Nonetheless, for six more years the United States continued on a de facto greenback standard. In accordance with the provisions of the RESUMPTION ACT of 1875, paper dollars became officially redeemable in gold on 2 January 1879.

Under the gold standard as it then operated, the unit of value was the gold dollar, which contained 23.22 grains of pure gold. Under free coinage, therefore, anyone could take pure gold bullion in any quantity to an American mint and have it minted into gold coins, receiving $20.67

(less certain petty charges for assaying and refining) for each ounce.

The Gold Standard Act of 1900 made legally definitive a gold-standard system that had existed de facto since 1879. This act declared that the gold dollar "shall be the standard unit of value, and all forms of money issued or coined by the United States shall be maintained at a parity of value with this standard." That meant that the value of every dollar of paper money and of silver, nickel, and copper coins and of every dollar payable by bank check was equal to the value of a gold dollar—namely, equal to the value of 23.22 grains of pure gold coined into money. Thenceforth global trends would contribute to domestic cycles of inflation and deflation. If the supply of gold thrown on the world's markets relative to the demand increased, gold depreciated and commodity prices increased in the United States and in all other gold-standard countries. If the world's demand for gold increased more rapidly than the supply of gold, gold appreciated and commodity prices in all gold-standard countries declined.

Until the Great Depression there was general agreement among economists that neither deflation nor inflation is desirable and that a stable unit of value is best. Since then, some economists have held that stable prices can be achieved only at the expense of some unemployment and that a mild inflation is preferable to such unemployment. While gold as a monetary standard during the half-century 1879–1933 was far from stable in value, it was more stable than silver, the only competing monetary metal, and its historical record was much better than that of paper money. Furthermore, its principal instability was usually felt during great wars or shortly thereafter, and at such times all other monetary standards were highly unstable.

During the late nineteenth century, the major nations of the world moved toward the more dependable gold coin standard; between 1873 and 1912 some forty nations used it. World War I swept all of them off it whether they were in the war or not. At the Genoa Conference in 1922, the major nations resolved to return to the gold standard as soon as possible (a few had already). Most major nations did so within a few years; more than forty had done so by 1931.

But not many could afford a gold coin standard. Instead, they used the gold bullion standard (the smallest "coin" was a gold ingot worth about eight thousand dollars) or the even more economical gold exchange standard, first invented in the 1870s for use in colonial dependencies. In the latter case the country would not redeem in its own gold coin or bullion but only in drafts on the central bank of some country on the gold coin or gold bullion standard with which its treasury "banked." As operated in the 1920s, this parasitic gold standard, preferentially dependent on the central banks of Great Britain, France, and the United States, allowed credit expansion on the same reserves by two countries.

It was a hazardous system, for if the principal nation's central bank was in trouble, so were all the depositor nations. In 1931 the gold standards of Austria, Germany, and Great Britain successively collapsed, the last dragging down several nations on the gold exchange standard with it. This was the beginning of the end of the gold standard in modern times. Many of the British, notably economist J. M. Keynes, alleged that both the decline in Great Britain's foreign trade and its labor difficulties in the late 1920s had been caused by the inflexibility of the gold standard, although it had served the nation well for the previous two centuries. Others argued that Britain's problems were traceable to its refusal to devalue the depreciated pound after the war or to obsolescence in major industries. In any event, Britain showed no strong desire to return to the gold standard.

Meanwhile, in the United States the gold coin standard continued in full operation from 1879 until March 1933 except for a brief departure during the World War I embargo on gold exports. At first the panic of 1929, which ushered in the long and severe depression of the 1930s, seemed not to threaten the gold standard. Britain's departure from the gold standard in 1931 shocked Americans, and in the 1932 presidential campaign, the Democratic candidate, Franklin D. Roosevelt, was known to be influenced by those who wanted the United States to follow Britain's example. A growing number of bank failures in late 1932 severely shook public confidence in the economy, but it was not until February 1933 that a frightened public began to hoard gold. On 6 March 1933, soon after he took office, President Roosevelt declared a nationwide bank moratorium for four days to stop heavy withdrawals and forbade banks to pay out gold or to export it. On 5 April the president ordered all gold coins and gold certificates in hoards of more than a hundred dollars turned in for other money. The government took in $300 million of gold coin and $470 million of gold certificates by 10 May.

Suspension of specie payments was still regarded as temporary; dollar exchange was only a trifle below par. But the president had been listening to the advice of inflationists, and it is likely that the antihoarding order was part of a carefully laid plan. Suddenly, on 20 April, he imposed a permanent embargo on gold exports, justifying the step with the specious argument that there was not enough gold to pay all the holders of currency and of public and private debts in the gold these obligations promised. There never had been, nor was there expected to be. Dollar exchange rates fell sharply. By the Thomas Amendment to the Agricultural Adjustment Act of 12 May 1933, Congress gave Roosevelt power to reduce the gold content of the dollar as much as 50 percent. A joint resolution of Congress on 5 June abrogated the gold clauses to be found in many public and private obligations that required the debtor to repay the creditor in gold dollars of the same weight and fineness as those borrowed. In four cases the SUPREME COURT later upheld this abrogation.

During the autumn of 1933, the Treasury bid up the price of gold under the Gold Purchase Plan and finally set it at $35 an ounce under the Gold Reserve Act of 30 January 1934. Most of the resulting profit was subsequently used as a stabilization fund and for the retirement of national bank notes. The United States was now back on a gold standard (the free gold market was in London). But the standard was of a completely new kind, and it came to be called a "qualified gold-bullion standard." It was at best a weak gold standard, having only external, not internal, convertibility. Foreign central banks and treasuries might demand and acquire gold coin or bullion when the exchange rate was at the gold export point, but no person might obtain gold for his money, coin, or bank deposits. After France left gold as a standard in 1936, the qualified gold-bullion standard was the only gold standard left in a world of managed currencies.

Although better than none at all, the new standard was not very satisfactory. The thirty-five-dollar-an-ounce price greatly overvalued gold, stimulating gold mining all over the world and causing gold to pour into the United States. The "golden avalanche" aroused considerable criticism and created many problems. It gave banks excess reserves and placed their lending policies beyond the control of the FEDERAL RESERVE SYSTEM. At the same time citizens were not permitted to draw out gold to show their distrust of the new system or for any other reason. As for its stated intent to raise the price of gold and end the Depression, the arrangement did neither. Wholesale prices rose only 13 percent between 1933 and 1937, and it took the inflation of WORLD WAR II to push them up to the hoped-for 69 percent. Except for a brief recovery in 1937, the Depression lasted throughout the decade of the 1930s.

The appearance of Keynes's *General Theory of Employment, Interest and Money* in 1936 and his influence on the policies of the Roosevelt administration caused a revolution in economic thinking. The new economics deplored oversaving and the evils of deflation and made controlling the business cycle to achieve full employment the major goal of public policy. It advocated a more managed economy. In contrast, the classical economists had stressed capital accumulation as a key to prosperity, deplored the evils of inflation, and relied on the forces of competition to provide a self-adjusting, relatively unmanaged economy. The need to do something about the Great Depression, World War II, the KOREAN WAR, and the COLD WAR all served to strengthen the hands of those who wanted a strong central government and disliked the trammels of a domestically convertible gold-coin standard. The rising generation of economists and politicians held such a view. After 1940 the Republican platform ceased to advocate a return to domestic convertibility in gold. Labor leaders, formerly defenders of a stable dollar when wages clearly lagged behind prices, began to feel that a little inflation helped them. Some economists and politicians frankly urged an annual depreciation of the dollar by 2, 3, or 5 percent, allegedly to prevent depressions and to promote economic growth; at a depreciation rate of 5 percent a year, the dollar would lose half its buying power in thirteen years (as in 1939–1952), and at a rate of 2 percent a year, in thirty-four years. Such attitudes reflected a shift in economic priorities because capital seemed more plentiful than before and thus required less encouragement and protection.

There remained, however, a substantial segment of society that feared creeping inflation and advocated a return to the domestically convertible gold-coin standard. Scarcely a year passed without the introduction in Congress of at least one such gold-standard bill. These bills rarely emerged from committee, although in 1954 the Senate held extensive hearings on the Bridges-Reece bill, which was killed by administration opposition.

After World War II a new international institution complemented the gold standard of the United States. The International Monetary Fund (IMF)—agreed to at a United Nations monetary and financial conference held at Bretton Woods, New Hampshire, from 1 July to 22 July 1944 by delegates from forty-four nations—went into effect in 1947. Each member nation was assigned a quota of gold and of its own currency to pay to the IMF and might, over a period of years, borrow up to double its quota from the IMF. The purpose of the IMF was to provide stability among national currencies, all valued in gold, and at the same time to give devastated or debt-ridden nations the credit to reorganize their economies. Depending on the policy a nation adopted, losing reserves could produce either a chronic inflation or deflation, unemployment, and stagnation. Admittedly, under the IMF a nation might devalue its currency more easily than before. But a greater hazard lay in the fact that many nations kept part of their central bank reserves in dollars, which, being redeemable in gold, were regarded as being as good as gold.

For about a decade dollars were much sought after. But as almost annual U.S. deficits produced a growing supply of dollars and increasing short-term liabilities in foreign banks, general concern mounted. Some of these dollars were the reserve base on which foreign nations expanded their own credit. The world had again, but on a grander scale, the equivalent of the parasitic gold-exchange standard it had had in the 1920s. Foreign central bankers repeatedly told U.S. Treasury officials that the dollar's being a reserve currency imposed a heavy responsibility on the United States; they complained that by running deficits and increasing its money supply, the United States was enlarging its reserves and, in effect, "exporting" U.S. inflation. But Asian wars, foreign aid, welfare, and space programs produced deficits and rising prices year after year. At the same time, American industries invested heavily in Common Market nations to get behind their tariff walls and, in doing so, transmitted more dollars to those nations.

Possessing more dollars than they wanted and preferring gold, some nations—France in particular—demanded gold for dollars. American gold reserves fell from $23 billion in December 1947 to $18 billion in 1960, and anxiety grew. When gold buying on the London gold market pushed the price of gold to forty dollars an ounce in October 1960, the leading central banks took steps to allay the anxiety, quietly feeding enough of their own gold into the London market to lower the price to the normal thirty-five dollars and keep it there. When Germany and the Netherlands upvalued their currencies on 4 and 6 March 1961, respectively, their actions had somewhat the same relaxing effect for the United States as a devaluation of the dollar would have had. On 20 July 1962 President John Kennedy forbade Americans even to own gold coins abroad after 1 January 1963. But federal deficits continued, short-term liabilities abroad reaching $28.8 billion by 31 December 1964, and gold reserves were falling to $15.5 billion.

Repeatedly the Treasury took steps to discourage foreign creditors from exercising their right to demand gold for dollars. The banks felt it wise to cooperate with the Americans in saving the dollar, everyone's reserve currency. By late 1967, American gold reserves were less than $12 billion. In October 1969 Germany upvalued the mark again, and American gold reserves were officially reported at $10.4 billion. The patience of foreign creditors was wearing thin. During the first half of 1971, U.S. short-term liabilities abroad shot up from $41 billion to $53 billion, and the demand for gold rose. On 15 August 1971 President Richard M. Nixon announced that the U.S. Treasury would no longer redeem dollars in gold for any foreign treasury or central bank. This action took the nation off the gold standard beyond any lingering doubt and shattered the dollar as a reliable reserve currency. At a gathering of financial leaders of ten industrial nations at the Smithsonian Institution in Washington, D.C., on 17 to 18 December 1971, the dollar was devalued by 7.89 percent in the conversion of foreign currencies to dollars, with some exceptions. In 1972 gold hit seventy dollars an ounce on London's free market for gold, and the United States had its worst mercantile trade deficit in history.

In early 1973 another run on the dollar began. The Treasury announced a 10 percent devaluation of the dollar on 12 February, calling it "a means toward easing the world crisis" and alleging that trade concessions to the United States and greater freedom of capital movements would follow. The new official price of gold was set at $42.22, but on the London market gold soon reached $95 and went to $128.50 in Paris in mid-May. A third devaluation seemed possible but was avoided, at least outwardly. The nine Common Market nations all "floated" their currencies, and Germany and Japan announced they would no longer support the dollar. By midsummer the dollar had drifted another 9 percent downward in value. The U.S. Treasury refused to discuss any plans for a return to gold convertibility. Nevertheless the United States and all other nations held on to their gold reserves. Several European nations, notably France and Germany, were willing to return to a gold basis.

In the 1970s opponents of the gold standard insisted that the monetary gold in the world was insufficient to serve both as a reserve and as a basis for settling large balances between nations, given the rapid expansion of world trade. Supporters of the gold standard distrusted inconvertible paper money because of a strong tendency by governments, when unrestrained by the necessity to redeem paper money in gold on demand, to increase the money supply too fast and thus to cause a rise in price levels. Whereas opponents of the gold standard alleged there was insufficient monetary gold to carry on international trade—they spoke of there being insufficient "liquidity"—supporters stressed that national reserves did not have to be large for this purpose, since nations settled only their net balances in gold and not continually in the same direction.

A period of severe inflation followed the Nixon administration's decision to abandon the gold standard. Nevertheless, despite the economic turmoil of the 1970s, the United States did not return to the gold standard, choosing instead to allow the international currency markets to determine its value. In 1976 the International Monetary Fund established a permanent system of floating exchange rates, a development that made the gold standard obsolete and one that allowed the free market to determine the value of various international currencies. Consequently, as inflation weakened the American dollar, the German Mark and Japanese Yen emerged as major rivals to the dollar in international currency markets.

In the 1990s the American dollar stabilized, and, by the end of the decade, it had regained a commanding position in international currency markets. The robust global economic growth of the 1980s and 1990s appeared to vindicate further the decision to vacate the gold standard. In 2002 the European Union introduced into circulation the Euro, a single currency that replaced the national currencies of nearly a dozen European nations, including major economic powers such as Germany, France, and Italy. The Euro quickly emerged as a highly popular currency in international bond markets, second only to the dollar. Although the long-term direction of international currency markets remains unclear, it seems certain that neither the United States nor Europe will ever return to the gold standard.

BIBLIOGRAPHY

Chandler, Lester Vernon. *American Monetary Policy, 1928–1941.* New York: Harper & Row, 1971.

De Cecco, Marcello. *The International Gold Standard: Money and Empire.* New York: St. Martin's Press, 1984.

Eichengreen, Barry J. *Golden Fetters: The Gold Standard and the Great Depression, 1919–1939.* New York: Oxford University Press, 1992.

Golden Gate Bridge. A view of the renowned San Francisco bridge in 1936, the year before its completion as one of the longest suspension bridges in the world. © CORBIS-BETTMANN

Gallarotti, Giulio M. *The Anatomy of an International Monetary Regime: The Classical Gold Standard, 1880–1914.* New York: Oxford University Press, 1995.

Kemmerer, Edwin Walter. *Gold and the Gold Standard: The Story of Gold Money, Past, Present and Future.* New York: McGraw-Hill, 1944.

Mehrling, Perry G. *The Money Interest and the Public Interest: American Monetary Thought, 1920–1970.* Cambridge, Mass.: Harvard University Press, 1997.

Ritter, Gretchen. *Goldbugs and Greenbacks: The Antimonopoly Tradition and the Politics of Finance, 1865–1896.* New York: Cambridge University Press, 1997.

Schwartz, Anna, and Michael D. Bordo, eds. *A Retrospective on the Classical Gold Standard, 1821–1931.* National Bureau of Economic Research. Chicago: University of Chicago Press, 1984.

Donald L. Kemmerer / A. R.

See also **Banking: Banking Crisis of 1933; Bimetallism; Debt, Public; Free Silver; Gold Bugs; Gold Purchase Plan; Gold Reserve Act; Great Depression; Inflation; International Monetary Fund; Keynesianism; Money; Specie Payments, Suspension and Resumption of; Treasury, Department of the.**

GOLDEN GATE BRIDGE, erected across the entrance of the harbor at San Francisco, California, at a cost of approximately $35 million, by the Golden Gate Bridge and Highway District, created by the California legislature (1923, 1928). The bridge links San Francisco peninsula with counties along the Redwood Highway to the north. The central span is 4,200 feet long, supported by towers that rise 746 feet from the water's surface; and the total length, including approaching viaducts, is one-and-three-quarter miles. The bridge has six lanes for motor traffic and sidewalks for pedestrians. Construction began 5 January 1933, and the bridge was opened to traffic 28 May 1937.

BIBLIOGRAPHY

Petroski, Henry. *Engineers of Dreams: Great Bridge Builders and the Spanning of America.* New York: Knopf, 1995.

Van der Zee, John. *The Gate: The True Story of the Design and Construction of the Golden Gate Bridge.* New York: Simon and Schuster, 1986.

P. Orman Ray / A. R.

See also **Bridges; California; New Deal; Reconstruction Finance Corporation; Roads; San Francisco.**

GOLDEN HIND, originally named the *Pelican,* the first English vessel to circumnavigate the globe, sailed from Plymouth, England, on 13 December 1577. It was rechristened the *Golden Hind* by its commander, Sir Francis Drake, in Magellan Strait. Sailing up the South American coast, it plundered Spanish treasure ships and reached the vicinity of present-day San Francisco on 15 June 1579. The *Golden Hind* sailed home around the Cape of Good Hope, reaching Plymouth on 26 September 1580.

BIBLIOGRAPHY

Roche, T. W. E. *The Golden Hind.* London [Serial]; New York: Praeger, 1973.

Louis H. Bolander/A. R.

See also **California; Explorations and Expeditions: British.**

Golf Legends. Early American superstars (*right to left*) Gene Sarazen, Walter Hagen, and Bobby Jones (standing with Johnny Parnell at far left) pose at the Woodland Country Club in Newton, Mass., on 5 September 1928. AP/Wide World Photos

GOLF originated in England and Scotland, and though American colonists played, the game quickly disappeared from the United States after the Revolutionary War. It came back in the 1880s, when the founders of the first country clubs discovered that golf suited their needs better than the traditional pastimes of horsing and hunting. Until the 1970s, private courses outnumbered municipal and daily-fee courses open to the public. The link between golf and the country club largely determined how the game developed, who played it, and how it has been perceived.

Elites developed country clubs in the late-nineteenth century to restore social order in the face of rapid immigration, industrialization, and urbanization. Country club members found golf especially appealing because it promised to revive the health of upper-class Victorians, some of whom believed they were suffering from a collective attack of nerves called neurasthenia. By the 1920s, country clubs had become appealing to the middle class. Modest clubs marked class, religious, and social distinctions as surely as wealthy white Protestant clubs did, but they also introduced golf to a wider audience. In 1916, there were fewer than 1,000 courses; by 1930, there were almost 6,000.

Golf also provided some of the earliest opportunities for women in sport. Though some clubs discriminate against women even today (by restricting weekend play to men, for example, or requiring wives or daughters to join in the names of husbands or fathers), many allowed women to play from the beginning. Men considered golf appropriate for the feminine constitution and temperament. It required more finesse than brute strength, and golfers competed against themselves and the course, not each other. Given the chance to play, however, women established themselves on their own terms. Olympic champion Babe Didrikson Zaharias pursued golf later in her career because she believed it would soften her unpopular androgynous image, but she immediately became famous for her powerful drives.

In 1894, representatives of the leading clubs created golf's first governing body, the United States Golf Association (USGA), to promote the increasingly popular game, set rules, and sponsor tournaments. In 1916, a group of professionals, fed up with USGA policies that clearly favored amateurs, formed the Professional Golfers Association (PGA). The Ladies Professional Golfers Association was constituted in 1950.

American golfers lagged behind Europeans until 1913, when Francis Ouimet shocked the golf world by defeating England's best at the U.S. Open. Ouimet, who learned the game as a caddie, was the first of many working-class kids who taught themselves golf by carrying equipment at private clubs that would never accept them as members. The list also includes Walter Hagen, Gene Sarazen, Ben Hogan, and Byron Nelson. Hagen and Bobby Jones, an aristocratic amateur, dominated the game in the 1920s and became America's first golf superstars. Hagen won eleven "majors" in his career: two U.S. Opens, four British Opens, and five PGA Championships. Jones, who in the 1930s founded the fourth major, the Masters, took three British Opens and four U.S. Opens, plus five U.S. amateur titles. Together they established golf as a spectator sport.

During the Depression and World War II, golf's reputation suffered. Americans were feeling sober, and nothing seemed to symbolize the frivolous leisure class better than rich men in knickers chasing a ball around the manicured lawn of a private club. In the 1950s, the civil rights movement focused attention on the game's racism and on the segregation of most country clubs. As private organizations, the clubs were not required to integrate, and most did not. Many cities transferred public courses to private owners to keep them white. The golf establishment did not confront its race problem until 1990, when civil rights groups threatened to picket the PGA Championship, scheduled for the all-white Shoal Creek Country Club. Shoal Creek quickly admitted a black member, and the PGA promised to hold subsequent tournaments only at integrated courses. The same year, the U.S. Open champion Tom Watson resigned from his club because it refused a Jewish member. The desire for PGA events has encouraged most clubs to open their admission policies, but actual progress remains slow.

Nevertheless, golf has enjoyed years of fantastic growth. In the 1960s, Arnold Palmer, whose loyal fans are known as "Arnie's Army," and Jack Nicklaus, the "Golden Bear," helped make televised golf a success. At the beginning of the twenty-first century the game thrives internationally, with celebrated players from all over the world and Ryder Cup competition between national teams. In 2002, Tiger Woods led the surge in the sport's popularity. As the game's most dominant player and first African American star, he introduced golf to a much wider demographic. With about 10,000 municipal or daily-fee courses and only half that many private courses, golf has become more accessible than ever.

BIBLIOGRAPHY

Cayleff, Susan E. *Babe: The Life and Legend of Babe Didrikson Zaharias.* Urbana: University of Illinois Press, 1995.

Chambers, Marcia. *The Unplayable Lie: The Untold Story of Women and Discrimination in American Golf.* New York: Pocket Books, 1995.

Lowe, Stephen R. *Sir Walter and Mr. Jones: Walter Hagen, Bobby Jones, and the Rise of American Golf.* Chelsea, Mich.: Sleeping Bear Press, 2000.

Moss, Richard J. *Golf and the American Country Club.* Urbana: University of Illinois Press, 2001.

Jeremy Derfner

See also **Recreation; Sports; Victorianism.**

Gone With the Wind. A reissue poster for the 1939 blockbuster, showing Clark Gable (as Rhett Butler) and Vivien Leigh (as Scarlett O'Hara). THE KOBAL COLLECTION

GONE WITH THE WIND. Both the novel (1936) and the motion picture (1939) are significant icons of the 1930s, revealing a great deal about the decade of the Great Depression. The novel won the Pulitzer Prize in 1936. *Gone With the Wind* depicts important intellectual and cultural developments. First, the "Lost Cause" concept—the romantic tragedy of the Confederacy's defeat in the CIVIL WAR—was popular with the public and academic community in the South. The notion that Yankee capitalism had defeated the South's genteel plantation life naturally led to the second equally popular idea—the "Needless War" doctrine. According to this theory, abolitionists, with their fixation on slavery, had caused the conflict between the states. These sentiments, alone and in combination, contributed to the myth that the South was a gracious but doomed alternative to heartless modern America. Slavery and the role of African Americans in the Civil War were ignored in the popular culture and by many historians. Despite protests from the African American press, black entertainers were assigned their traditional roles as either villains or clowns, though actress Hattie McDaniel did win an Academy Award for her role in the film. The hardships of the Great Depression and the coming of World War II, which prompted a bitter struggle between isolationists and internationalists, added to the distant charm of the Old South as portrayed in *Gone With the Wind.*

The novel by Margaret Mitchell was an instant success. Published by Macmillan in 1936, the 1,057-page tome was a hymn to the Lost Cause, despite the author's intent to combine an F. Scott Fitzgerald approach with historical recreation. The book sold more than fifty thousand copies in a single day, was a bestseller for two years, and, by 1965, had sold more than 12 million authorized copies.

Mitchell was born in Atlanta in 1900 to an established Georgia family. She grew up with tales of the Lost Cause and a romantic ideal of the Civil War. Well-educated and witty, she wrote for newspapers and magazines. She married twice but had no children. A delightful storyteller, she was a gracious presence on the Atlanta social scene. With the novel's great success, Mitchell was thereafter known as the author of *Gone With the Wind.* She never wrote another novel and directed that upon her death most of her literary manuscripts be destroyed. Mitchell died in 1949 after she was struck by a speeding automobile.

Selznick International Pictures bought the screen rights to *Gone With the Wind* for $50,000. The classic motion picture features a moving musical score and talented cast, including Vivien Leigh, Clark Gable, Olivia De Havilland, and Leslie Howard. The movie had a spectacular debut in Atlanta in 1939 and continued to be a leading money producer long after its release. Filled with assumptions of the Lost Cause and the Needless War doctrine, the movie does not ignore the sexual tension between the heroine and the hero. The movie has a minor but clear feminist subtext.

Historical interpretations come and go but, undoubtedly, *Gone With the Wind* endures as a monument to the Lost Cause. It is also a product of the 1930s, when many Americans sought an escape from the twin horrors of economic depression and the impending European war. Though not great literature, the story endures as a vital example of how some Americans prefer to think about the Civil War.

BIBLIOGRAPHY

Harwell, Richard. *Gone With the Wind, as Book and Film.* Columbia: University of South Carolina Press, 1983. Good collection of contemporary reviews and essays.

Pressly, Thomas. *Americans Interpret Their Civil War.* Princeton, N.J.: Princeton University Press, 1954. A brilliant analysis of how historical interpretations interact with other aspects of the culture.

Pyron, Darden Asbury, ed. *Recasting "Gone With the Wind" in American Culture.* Miami: University Presses of Florida, 1983. A far-ranging analysis of how the novel and movie fit into American culture.

Pyron, Darden Asbury. *Southern Daughter, The Life of Margaret Mitchell.* New York: Oxford University Press, 1991. A solid biographical study.

Donald K. Pickens

See also **Film; Literature: Popular Literature.**

GONZÁLEZ, ELIÁN, CASE. On Thanksgiving Day 1999, two men fishing off the coast of Fort Lauderdale, Florida, spotted a small boy floating in the ocean, supported by an inner tube. The boy was taken to a hospital, where he recovered. His mother and a dozen others had drowned in an attempt to escape Cuba and reach the United States. Elián's relatives in Miami—the closest being a great-uncle—sought to keep the boy with them. They did this in the face of Cuban demands that he be returned, and despite the likelihood that the U.S. family court system would try to reunite him with his father, Juan Miguel—even though the father was a Fidel Castro loyalist. Hundreds of sympathizers kept vigil at the relative's small house in Little Havana, forming prayer circles, and damning Attorney General Janet Reno for maintaining that the family courts should rule on the case.

At first, opinion among Cuban Americans was mixed. José Basulto, a Bay of Pigs veteran and leader of the prominent anti-Castro Brothers to the Rescue, initially said he thought the boy should be reunited with his father. Some younger Cuban Americans—self-described as Generation Ñ—argued that the issue should be settled in family court. Once Castro began using the case as a pretext for a series of anti-American tirades, however, the lines were drawn: the community's economically and politically powerful militant right wing used support for Elián's right to remain in Miami as a litmus test, and most Cuban Americans either publicly backed the "Keep Elián" position or kept silent.

Anonymous donors gave Elián's relatives a car, trips to Disneyland, and a lavish assortment of toys and clothes for the bewildered boy. He was sent to a private school, one of a chain owned by a hard-line anti-Castroite, but when reporters and photographers hounded his every move, he had to be taken from school and kept at his great-uncle's home. The intense media presence in Miami encouraged demonstrations staged by community leaders, who beseeched the crowds to defend Elián at all costs. On one occasion, a large group of demonstrators attacked a radio talk show host from Portland, Oregon, for wearing a T-shirt that read, "Send the Boy Home."

On Holy Saturday, 22 April 2000, Attorney General Reno ordered in a special team of agents from the Immigration and Naturalization Service, who stormed the house around 5:00 A.M. Most were dressed in military uniforms and carried weapons. Despite negative publicity created by a journalist's photograph of the terrorized boy facing an angry, armed soldier, outside of Miami most Americans strongly supported reuniting the boy with his father, who had come to the United States to wait out the judicial process. Even after Elián was seized, media coverage, especially in Miami, continued its feeding frenzy, although the hundreds of photographers and reporters camped day and night across the street from Elián's house began to dwindle away. When Elián and his father, stepmother, and stepbrother returned to Cuba after being turned over by the FBI, Castro made the boy into a hero and had hundreds of thousands of Cuban schoolchildren rally in mass support of the little boy. He then settled the family in the quiet city of Cárdenas.

BIBLIOGRAPHY

Domínguez, Jorge. "Your Friend, Fidel." *Harvard Magazine* 102, no. 6 (July–August 2000): 35–39.

Levine, Robert M. *Secret Missions to Cuba: Fidel Castro, Bernardo Benes, and Cuban Miami.* New York: St. Martin's and Palgrave, 2001.

Robert M. Levine

See also **Cuba, Relations with; Cuban Americans.**

GOOD NEIGHBOR POLICY. The Good Neighbor Policy grew out of the experience of the administrations of Presidents Calvin Coolidge (1923–1929) and Herbert Hoover (1929–1933), but it was formally promulgated by President Franklin D. Roosevelt (1933–1945). In his 1933 inaugural address, Roosevelt asserted, "In the field of world policy I would dedicate this nation to the policy of the good neighbor—the neighbor who resolutely respects himself and, because he does so, respects the rights of others." The Good Neighbor Policy centered on nonintervention and noninterference. It also came to be associated with trade reciprocity. By the time Roosevelt was elected to the presidency, there was growing Latin American opposition to U.S. military intervention and some searching criticism of U.S. policy in the United States itself.

The Good Neighbor Policy flowed in significant measure from the calculation that U.S. goals in the Caribbean and Central America, in particular, could be better served by strengthening diplomatic and commercial relations instead of engaging in the gunboat diplomacy and military intervention of the late nineteenth and early twentieth centuries. For example, the experience of Henry L. Stimson, Coolidge's special representative to Nicaragua in 1927, and other officials involved in U.S.-Nicaraguan relations in the late 1920s and early 1930s played an important role in the reorientation of U.S. policy in the region after 1933. U.S. marines had operated in Nicaragua from 1912 to 1925, helping to establish and train the Nicaraguan National Guard. Following a brief withdrawal, the United States sent marines back to Nicaragua in 1926 after renewed fighting between political factions there. Washington reacted in particular against the Mexican government's support for the political faction opposed to the pro-U.S. grouping. The second military intervention brought criticism from some politicians in the United States who thought that it undermined Washington's status and power in the eyes of Latin Americans and actually encouraged opposition to the United States in Latin America.

As the 1930s progressed, the Good Neighbor Policy was elaborated via a range of public treaties and private directives in the context of rising U.S. political and economic influence in the region. Despite the stated anti-interventionism of the Good Neighbor Policy, the United States operated within a structure of Pan-American cooperation that was often more interventionist than before. U.S. intervention in the 1930s, however, was carried out by ambassadors, foreign service officers, and economic and military advisers backed up by economic assistance and private capital, instead of by the marines and gunboats of the past. For example, Roosevelt established the Export-Import Bank in 1934 to loan money to U.S. exporters in order to facilitate overseas sales; by the end of the 1930s, it was funding projects throughout Latin America. The United States also negotiated reciprocal trade treaties with a number of Latin American republics that often had important political implications. The countries of Central America, for example, increased their imports from the United States in this period, becoming more dependent on U.S. agricultural products in particular, in exchange for political recognition and support. By the end of the 1930s, Washington had also set up new structures linking the U.S. military with its Latin American counterparts.

The Good Neighbor Policy was, and often still is, viewed as successful for a variety of reasons, including the fact that it strengthened hemispheric relations in the lead up to, and during, World War II. However, Roosevelt's Good Neighbor Policy also gave direct and indirect support to dictatorships in the region. For example, Roosevelt and his successors provided sustained support for the authoritarian regimes of Anastasio Somoza (1936–1956) in Nicaragua, Rafael Trujillo (1930–1961) in the Dominican Republic, and Fulgencio Batista (1934–1958) in Cuba. This was a major contradiction of the Good Neighbor Policy, and it became more pronounced with the onset of the Cold War after 1945. The formal violation of Roosevelt's pledge of nonintervention, which was understood to mean the actual landing of U.S. soldiers, did not occur until troops were sent into the Dominican Republic in April 1965, where they remained as an occupation force until July 1966. However, in the context of the Cold War, the United States had already instigated or carried out a number of covert interventions in the 1950s and early 1960s. The most well known are probably the Central Intelligence Agency–orchestrated overthrow of the democratically elected government of Guatemala in 1954 and the unsuccessful invasion of Cuba at the Bay of Pigs in 1961, both of which involved the training and equipping of exiles and the provision of logistical or air support by the United States.

BIBLIOGRAPHY

Gellman, Irwin F. *Roosevelt and Batista: Good Neighbor Diplomacy in Cuba, 1933–1945.* Albuquerque: University of New Mexico Press, 1973.

———. *Good Neighbor Diplomacy: United States Policies in Latin America, 1933–1945.* Baltimore: Johns Hopkins University Press, 1979.

Green, David. *The Containment of Latin America: A History of the Myths and Realities of the Good Neighbor Policy.* Chicago: Quadrangle Books, 1971.

Roorda, Eric Paul. *The Dictator Next Door: The Good Neighbor Policy and the Trujillo Regime in the Dominican Republic, 1930–1945.* Durham, N.C.: Duke University Press, 1998.

Wood, Bryce. *The Making of the Good Neighbor Policy.* New York: Columbia University Press, 1961.

———. *The Dismantling of the Good Neighbor Policy.* Austin: University of Texas Press, 1985.

Mark T. Berger

See also **Caribbean Policy; Cuba, Relations with; Dominican Republic; Guatemala, Relations with; Latin America, Relations with; Nicaragua, Relations with.**

GOTHIC LINE. In June 1944, when the Germans gave up Rome to the Allies, Adolf Hitler ordered his troops in Italy to retreat north and make a defensive stand in the Apennines near the Po River valley. The Gothic Line, as it came to be called, was a belt of fortifications ten miles deep and about two hundred miles long, in naturally strong defensive terrain, across Italy from Carrara to Pesaro. Impressed laborers from occupied countries began construction in mid-1943, and work to strengthen the positions continued even after German combat troops occupied the line in mid-1944. By August, 2,400 machine-gun posts, 500 gun and mortar positions, 120,000 meters of barbed wire, several Panther tank-gun turrets embedded in steel and concrete bases, and many miles of antitank ditches had been incorporated into the line.

After entering Rome on 4 June, the American and British armies drove north. Two months later they were near Pisa, Arezzo, and Ancona and on the Gothic Line approaches. On 25 August the Allies attacked. Against stiff resistance, the British captured Rimini on 21 September, and the Americans took the Futa and Giogo passes on the road to Bologna. Winter weather forced the Allies to halt their offensive operations until April 1945, when they broke the Gothic Line. American troops entered the Po River valley and took Bologna on 21 April. Unable to stop the Allied advances, the German commander, Gen. Heinrich von Vietinghoff, agreed to an unconditional surrender on 29 April, thereby bringing to an end the bitterly fought Italian campaign of World War II.

BIBLIOGRAPHY

Clark, Mark Wayne. *Calculated Risk.* New York: Harper, 1950.

MacDonald, Charles Brown, and Sidney T. Mathews. *Three Battles.* Washington, D.C.: Center of Military History, U.S. Army, 1993.

Orgill, Douglas. *The Gothic Line: The Autumn Campaign in Italy, 1944.* London: Heinemann, 1967.

Martin Blumenson/A. R.

See also **Anzio; Gustav Line; Monte Cassino; Salerno; World War II.**

GOVERNMENT OWNERSHIP. According to American economic and political ideology, government is supposed to keep its distance from the private sector, and on the whole it does. The government owns much less in the United States than in Europe, where many countries have taken over airlines, mines, and telecommunications systems. Nevertheless, the United States has never been a perfect haven for private interests. Each of the 90,000 American governments (federal, state, county, city, water district, etc.) owns something, be it land, buildings, resources, or a business. The government can own entities that it runs as regular departments (such as local sanitation departments), or it can own what are known as public enterprises or government corporations, which are created and wholly or partly owned by the government but are run essentially as businesses (for example, the New Jersey Turnpike Authority).

Government ownership is as old as the United States. The post office has existed since the nation's founding, and the first Bank of the United States (1791) was partially funded by the federal government. On the local level, Philadelphia built one of the first public waterworks in the country in 1799. In the early nineteenth century, governments chartered many corporations to build "internal improvements." For example, New York created the Erie Canal Commission in 1816 to pay for and manage the state's canal system.

In the first half of the nineteenth century, government also came to own a considerable amount of land as it purchased (Louisiana) or conquered (California) territory. Congress and the president typically gave away federal land or sold it cheaply. The Homestead Act (1862) offered 160 acres to any person willing to live on and work the land for five years. By the 1870s, however, the fledgling conservation movement had inspired governments to limit the private acquisition of public land. In 1872 Yellowstone became the first national park, and forest preserves were set aside starting in 1891. Despite the psychic importance of property ownership in the United States, the federal government still owns about a third of all land (much of it in the West), though private businesses and individuals are permitted to use much of it for various purposes, including recreation, grazing, and mineral extraction.

In the late nineteenth century, cities (and counties) started creating public companies to deliver important services such as education, water, fire protection, sanitation, electricity, and mass transit, all of which had once been private. The transition was piecemeal. New York, for example, offered public water and sewers in the 1830s and 1840s, took over street cleaning in 1881, and bought out two private subway companies in 1940, but it never owned utilities. Since the 1980s, a movement to reprivatize government-owned services has borne fruit with the rise of charter schools and private prisons.

Government corporations, which are created by government but run as businesses, took off during the New

Deal. The pioneering Tennessee Valley Authority (1933), which still provides electric power, forced energy companies to lower costs. In the late 1990s, there were more than 6,000 government corporations in existence, including the Federal National Mortgage Association (Fannie Mae), Amtrak, the Legal Services Corporation, the Empire State Development Corporation, and the United States Postal Service (converted from government department to corporation in 1971). These public enterprises compete with private lenders, transit companies (such as Greyhound), lawyers, real estate developers, and shipping companies (for example, United Parcel Service, FedEx).

BIBLIOGRAPHY

Hibbard, Benjamin H. *A History of Public Land Policies.* Madison: University of Wisconsin Press, 1965.

Mitchell, Jerry. *The American Experiment with Government Corporations.* Armonk, N.Y.: M. E. Sharpe, 1999.

Jeremy Derfner

See also **Privatization.**

GOVERNMENT PUBLICATIONS. The various divisions of the federal government produce a vast collection of documents on an enormous range of subjects. In addition to common publications such as the federal budget and presidential papers, government departments write reports about everything from beekeeping and naval history to crime trends and national health disasters. Many of these documents are available to the public either directly through the Government Printing Office (GPO) or in one of more than 1,000 federal depository libraries across the country. In 2001 GPO distributed tens of millions of copies of about 15,000 different government publications. Nevertheless, most Americans underuse these documents because they tend to be hard to find. Libraries give them a separate classification system and shelve them in their own section, and very few bookstores sell them.

The U.S. Constitution mandates the printing of a single government publication, the journals of House and Senate proceedings. Congress's printing needs increased quickly, but it continued to hire private printers on a contract basis for the first half of the nineteenth century. Private firms tended to produce sloppy work and to overcharge for it, and Congress was rarely satisfied with its makeshift printing arrangements. In 1795, for example, Congress hired a printer to produce a multivolume set of federal statutes, but he finished less than half of it. Twenty years later, another printer was hired and failed to do the same job, which was not completed until 1845, when the contract finally went to a Boston firm. Congressional business could be stalled for days while members waited for crucial documents.

Congress experimented with various solutions to its printing problem. The first proposal for a formal government body in charge of printing appeared in 1819, but both houses hired full-time private printers instead. The poor service persisted, however, and Congress restored competitive bidding on a per-job basis in 1846 and created a Joint Committee on Printing to oversee the process. But even after a superintendent of public printing was appointed in 1852, service failed to improve. In 1860, after two investigations, Congress finally created the Government Printing Office, which bought a large plant and hired a staff of 350.

At first, GPO's major responsibility was to the members of Congress, who needed the quick and accurate turnaround of key documents to conduct their business. The office's mission changed radically, however, with the passage of the Printing Act of 1895. GPO would continue to address the government's printing needs, but it would also be responsible for disseminating information to the public. Congress appointed a superintendent of public documents, who was responsible for compiling detailed indexes, selling documents, and sending them to libraries. GPO's structure and objectives have remained largely the same since then. Its formal mission is to "inform the Nation," and the superintendent still administers the distribution of publications and puts together a comprehensive list of available documents, the *Monthly Catalogue of United States Government Publications.*

Well before GPO adopted its public service function, however, the government had been interested in making sure documents were available to people. The Federal Depository Library System was created in 1813, when Congress required the secretary of state to send a copy of the House and Senate journals to every university, college, and historical society in every state. But as the government generated more material, such a comprehensive provision proved unworkable. In 1859, senators and representatives selected a limited number of libraries from their states and districts to participate in the system, and by 1922 the libraries were asked to request the specific classes of publications in which they were most interested. In 2001 there were about 1,300 federal depository libraries.

Government documents are also available to the public through GPO's *Monthly Catalogue*, through GPO's extensive Web site (GPO Access), and at eighteen GPO bookstores in big cities throughout the country. GPO Access was established in 1994 by an act of Congress, and by 2001 it included 225,000 free government publications, and visitors were downloading an average of 30 million per month. GPO also pioneered the use of microfilm and CD-ROM to cope with a deluge of paper, but it still produces more than 100,000 tons of paper documents a year.

Though the modern GPO belongs to the legislative branch of government, it runs mostly like a business. It employs a unionized staff of about 3,000, and the president appoints its chief executive officer, known officially as the public printer. The office gets two appropriations, one for congressional printing and another for legally required distributions. Otherwise, it pays for itself. About 130 federal government departments hire GPO for their printing needs, including passports and census and tax forms. In 2001, GPO revenue exceeded $700 million.

Government documents are striking in their volume and variety. In 2001, GPO divided its publications into 131 categories, including wildlife (116 titles), arms control (127), aging (39), earth science (160), Civil War (192), radiation (48), music (221), and voting and elections (245). Since 1873, GPO has printed the *Congressional Record*, which contains the verbatim transcript of all business conducted on the floors of both houses. Every morning, it sends out 9,000 copies of the previous day's debates. In 1935 the office started printing the *Federal Register*, which collects a tangle of executive rules and regulations. Other notable publications include: U.S. Supreme Court decisions, various censuses, the *Congressional Directory*, numerous annual reports, government periodicals, and the *Statistical Abstract of the United States*. In the late 1990s, GPO's two most important documents were the *Starr Report* and several rulings in the Microsoft antitrust case.

BIBLIOGRAPHY

Kling, Robert E. *The Government Printing Office*. New York: Praeger, 1970.

Relyea, Harold. *Title 44, United States Code—Public Printing and Documents: A Brief Historical Overview*. Washington, D.C.: Library of Congress, Congressional Research Service, 1979.

Schmeckebier, Laurence Frederick, and Roy B. Eastin. *Government Publications and Their Use*. Washington, D.C.: Brookings Institution, 1969.

Smith, Culver H. *The Press, Politics, and Patronage: The American Government's Use of Newspapers, 1789–1875*. Athens: University of Georgia Press, 1977.

Jeremy Derfner

See also **Census, U.S. Bureau of the; Libraries.**

GOVERNMENT REGULATION OF BUSINESS.

GOVERNMENT REGULATION OF BUSINESS. Since colonial times, government has regulated business. The need for more responsive and effective business regulation was at least part of the reason for the fight for independence and the establishment of the federal government. As the U.S. economy became more industrialized and the United States grew to be a world power in the nineteenth century, the federal government passed business laws that favored social reforms over the interests of big business. In the twentieth century, government involvement continued to expand until the 1970s, when both business and the public began to call for less regulation. At the beginning of the twenty-first century, the ruinous effects that utility deregulation had on California's economy and the corporate accounting scandals that came to light in late 2001 raised the possibility of a new era of federal intervention into business practices.

Business Regulation and the Birth of a New Nation

In 1649 the British Parliament passed the NAVIGATION ACTS to regulate trade with and within the North American colonies. During the first one hundred years these trade laws were in effect, the British did little to enforce them. Colonial Americans north of Maryland profited from a thriving trade with other colonies in North America and the West Indies. The British, who exported cotton from the southern colonies, dominated commerce in that region.

By 1764, however, England had incurred significant war debts, and the British Parliament decided to finance this debt by enforcing the long neglected Navigation Acts, which tipped the balance of trade in England's favor. In that same year, the Currency Act banned the American colonies from printing their own paper money, which they had been doing since 1690. As a result, the colonies were forced to pay debt in gold and silver. Reserves of these precious metals were quickly drained, and a depression ensued. Economic conditions were worsened by a series of new taxes that further serviced England's war debts. In 1765 the STAMP ACT taxed most legal and printed documents, as well as dice and playing cards. The TOWNSHEND ACTS of 1767 levied duties on glass, pigment for paint, paper, and tea.

For nearly a century, the American colonists had been able to develop and regulate their economic system. Suddenly the British Parliament began to impose a series of regulations that the colonists had no part in formulating. The regulations themselves, the lack of legislative participation, and the manner in which these rules were enforced in the colonies sparked resentment that flamed to open hostility as the British responded to colonial protests with ever-stricter regulations and methods of enforcement. The northern trading centers, which had enjoyed the greatest degree of independence, were hardest hit by England's new policies, and Boston soon became the center of opposition to British rule. By 1771 the trade deficit with Britain grew to £2.86 million. In response to the economic hardship these regulations created and the authoritarian manner in which the rules were enforced, the Revolutionary War broke out in 1775 at Lexington and Concord, Massachusetts.

During the colonial period, provincial legislatures capped wage and commodity prices, and master craftsmen had to secure municipal licenses. After the Revolutionary War, the new state governments continued most local regulation and, in addition, imposed tariff duties. The central government that was created under the ARTICLES OF CONFEDERATION from 1781 to 1789 lacked certain basic powers to regulate commerce between the states and to enforce contractual obligations. These flaws were among the factors that led to the current form of federal government created by the U.S. Constitution, which vested the U.S. Congress with authority to regulate interstate commerce. The adoption of the Constitution ended state tariff regulation and imposed a moderate federal system of protection, with discriminatory tonnage taxes favoring American ships and subsidies for New England's fisheries.

From State Regulation to Federal Regulation

Aside from wars and its fluctuating tariff policies, the federal government at the beginning of the nineteenth century was chiefly important to business in guaranteeing a uniform national currency and security for contracts, making gifts of land, and offering the protection of the due process of law. During this century, states actively began to promote business. Incorporation by special act was relatively easy, and starting with New York State in 1811, manufacturing was encouraged by "general" incorporation laws requiring only the payment of a small fee. State courts soon gave corporations the benefit of limited liability. Pennsylvania in particular bought stock in scores of manufacturing and transportation enterprises. Many of the states went into banking and canal construction. Subsequently, RAILROADS received much state and local assistance and often had directors representing the public interest.

In 1824 the Supreme Court strengthened the federal government's power to regulate interstate commerce with its decision in *GIBBONS V. OGDEN*, which involved the authority to license shipping. Steamboat operator Thomas Gibbons had secured only a federal license to run his business in New York State waters, which were controlled by a monopoly created through a state licensing system. A member of this monopoly, Aaron Ogden tried to shut down Gibbons's business by suing him for failing to have the proper New York State licenses. The Court ruled in favor of Gibbons and declared that commerce involved not only buying and selling but also transportation and navigation. By giving Congress the sole authority to regulate interstate transportation, this decision cleared the way for the United States to create a national transportation system that has continued to benefit business.

By 1860 only a few transportation and banking enterprises remained in state hands. As the railroads enabled Americans to travel more easily from state to state, new state regulations were enacted to protect the interests of local businesses. Stricter licensing laws kept out-of-state doctors, lawyers, and even barbers from competing with local practitioners. Laws governing the quality of major export products protected the reputation of a city or state. Regulation of railroad rates was attempted to benefit local shippers, but here the states ran into trouble with the commerce power of Congress.

In 1866 the Fourteenth Amendment secured citizens against the deprivation of property or equal protection of the law without due process. By the 1880s the amendment was being interpreted by the Supreme Court to mean that property included the return on such intangible assets as stocks or bonds and that due process meant judicial review of the substance of law. This interpretation rendered the state regulation of national business completely ineffective and further encouraged federal action to correct problems in interstate commerce. This power permitted a long series of railroad regulatory acts, starting in 1887, that were generally advantageous to shippers. In the twentieth century, these acts would leave the railroads in a weak position in competition against the automobile and airplane.

Antitrust Law

The 1880s saw the advent of the trust, which enabled a handful of businesses to gain nearly complete control over many commodity-based industries. The founder of the Standard Oil Company, John D. Rockefeller, was the first to achieve monopoly-like domination over an industry. He had gained this power under his company's so-called Trust Agreement. In 1882 the public learned of this agreement, and the term "trust" entered the American vocabulary as a word signifying MONOPOLY. At one point Standard Oil controlled more than 90 percent of the nation's petroleum refining. The huge profits that Standard Oil earned under its Trust Agreement drew the attention of other investors, and by 1887 there existed the Cotton Oil Trust, the Linseed Oil Trust, and the Distiller and Cattle Feeders Trust, which was also known as "The Whisky Trust." The way TRUSTS concentrated wealth and economic power in the hands of a few business tycoons so alarmed the American public that Congress passed the SHERMAN ANTITRUST ACT in 1890.

Despite this legislation, almost fifty other trusts were formed by 1897. The Supreme Court dealt a serious blow to the federal government's ability to enforce the Sherman Act with its 1895 decision in *UNITED STATES V. E. C. KNIGHT COMPANY*, also known as the "The Sugar Trust Case." The Court took the position that refining sugar was an activity confined to a specific locale and that the federal government therefore could not use its power to regulate interstate commerce as a means to break up the trust. The Court ruled against the federal government although E. C. Knight controlled nearly 98 percent of the sugar refining industry and was able to set the retail price of sugar throughout the entire country.

Efforts to curb trusts languished until Theodore Roosevelt was elected to the presidency in 1904 on a TRUST-BUSTING platform. By that time 185 trusts had been formed; their creation had been aided by an 1889 New Jersey law that allowed companies chartered in that state to hold the stock of other companies. Similar legislation was enacted in several other states including Delaware and Maine, and trusts took the form of holding companies. One such HOLDING COMPANY was the Northern Securities Company, which monopolized railroad transportation from the Great Lakes to the Pacific Coast. Roosevelt successfully invoked the Sherman Act to break the monopoly, which was dissolved by order of the Supreme Court in 1904. When the Court ordered the dissolution of the Standard Oil and American Tobacco trusts in 1911, it ruled that these trusts placed "unreasonable restraint" on trade. This implied that the Court would tolerate "reasonable restraints," and monopolistic-like business entities continued to grow. Congress passed further antitrust legislation with the Clayton Act in 1914, which outlawed unfair methods of competition. The act created the FEDERAL TRADE COMMISSION to enforce this legislation. Business eventually responded to this type of regulation by creating CONGLOMERATES that diversify holdings instead of concentrating them in a single sector of industry.

Regulation and Deregulation in the Twentieth Century

At the turn of the nineteenth century, the public's dismay at business practices fostered further federal regulation. In 1906 writer and social activist Upton Sinclair published *THE JUNGLE*, a novel that exposed the unsanitary practices of the meatpacking industry. The public furor created by this book motivated the federal government to pass the Pure Food and Drug Act (1906), which Congress continued to strengthen throughout the first half of the twentieth century.

Social activists also promoted the cause of CHILD LABOR reform, which was embraced by the Congress and presidents. The first child labor laws were passed during the administration of President Woodrow Wilson (1913–1921), but they were struck down by the Supreme Court. Similar laws passed in 1919 and 1935 were also ruled unconstitutional by the Court, which held that Congress had overstepped its authority by directly placing controls on state and local commerce. An amendment to the Constitution protecting children against abusive labor practices was passed by Congress in 1924 but failed to gain state ratification. The 1938 FAIR LABOR STANDARDS ACT, which regulated child labor and afforded other worker protections, finally stood up to constitutional scrutiny by the Court in 1941.

President Franklin D. Roosevelt's NEW DEAL legislation, enacted in an effort to revive the U.S. economy suffering from the stock market crash of 1929 and the ensuing GREAT DEPRESSION of the 1930s, effectively made the federal government the nation's chief regulator of business and the economy. Roosevelt's legislation reformed the banking system and securities industries, which had practically collapsed during the decade. He tried to jump-start the economy through massive government employment programs, many of which served to improve the country's business infrastructure. The massive military expenditures needed to fight World War II, however, were what provided the economic stimulus needed to end the depression. Apart from building and maintaining a national highway system, military spending continues to be the federal government's greatest direct involvement with the business community.

As the twentieth century wore on, regulation by federal or state act with subsequent judicial interpretation was largely replaced by control through administrative orders of commissions. Between 1887 and 1940 the federal government created a score of commissions and boards governing aspects of business and labor, and from about 1900 on, the states followed suit. The most important of the national agencies came to be the Federal Trade Commission, which had broad regulatory powers over corporate practices. On the whole this change in regulatory enforcement pleased business. Commissions came to be staffed by members of the enterprises they regulated, who understood the problems involved. Appearance before a commission was quicker, cheaper, and generally more satisfactory than the slow and costly processes of legal proceedings in state or federal court.

The federal government had been continually expanding its role in regulating business since the Sherman Act. After ninety years of almost uninterrupted growth, the 1970s proved to be a transitional period for federal regulation. The start of the decade saw the creation of three new federal regulatory bodies: the Occupational Safety and Health Administration (OSHA), the ENVIRONMENTAL PROTECTION AGENCY (EPA), and the Consumer Protection Agency. From 1971 to 1974 the government directly intervened into the private sector with a series of wage and price controls designed to curb inflation that had been plaguing the U.S economy since 1965. However, inflation, combined with social programs and business regulations often criticized as excessive, and the huge federal budget deficits incurred to finance these programs and regulations resulted in political pressure that ended the expansion of federal business regulation. By the end of the decade, several regulatory agencies, including the INTERSTATE COMMERCE COMMISSION and the CIVIL AERONAUTICS BOARD, had been abolished, and the airline, telecommunications, railroad, trucking, and television and radio broadcasting industries had been deregulated.

The 1980s and 1990s saw further DEREGULATION. Consumers as well as business have benefited from this trend, but there have been notable failures. Deregulation of the savings and loan industry led to a series of bank failures in the late 1980s that cost the federal government more than $1 trillion. In 2001, deregulation of California's power industry created electricity shortages, raised wholesale and retail prices, and forced two of that states largest utility companies to declare bankruptcy. The energy trading company, Enron, along with other energy brokers, which were all created because of deregulation, has been accused of conspiring to manipulate California's power supply and creating the state's energy crisis.

In December 2001 Enron became the center of another scandal when its bankruptcy, the largest to date in the nation's history, revealed that the company had used deceptive accounting practices to inflate its earning reports and stock price. This was the first in a series of corporate bankruptcies to involve fraudulent bookkeeping that shook an already weak stock market in 2002. To restore investor confidence, the federal government exercised its regulatory authority to promote greater scrutiny of the securities, accounting, and power utility industries.

The accounting scandals of the early twenty-first century recall the business scandals of the late 1800s and early 1900s when antagonism between business and government regulators became ingrained. Despite this antipathy, the two sides have, in fact, benefited from each other. Government regulations ensuring the enforceability of contracts and property rights are such basics that business in the United States could not function properly without them. Likewise, without the economic growth created by private business, the U.S. government could not sustain itself. Although the current system of federal and state regulations may sometimes be self-contradictory, and, in addition, confusing to the business community, it is a relatively loose one, leaving the United States as one of the nations whose business welfare depends most on the decisions of private entrepreneurs.

BIBLIOGRAPHY

Laffont, Jean-Jacques, and Jean Tirole. *Competition in Telecommunications.* Cambridge, Mass.: MIT Press, 2000.

Lai, Loi Lei, ed. *Power System Restructuring and Deregulation.* New York: Wiley, 2001.

Macey, Jonathan R., Geoffrey P. Miller, and Richard Scott Carnell. *Banking Law and Regulation.* 3d ed. Gaithersburg, Md.: Aspen Publishers, 2000.

Peritz, Rudolph J. R. *Competition Policy in America, 1888–1992: History, Rhetoric, Law.* New York: Oxford University Press, 1996.

Singer, Jonathan W., and Keneth E. Montague, eds. *Broken Trusts: The Texas Attorney General Versus the Oil Industry, 1889–1909.* Vol. 12, *Oil and Business History Series.* College Station: Texas A&M University Press, 2002.

Viscusi, W. Kip, John M.Vernon, and Joseph E. Harrington Jr. *Economics of Regulation and Antitrust,* 3d ed. Cambridge, Mass.: MIT Press, 2000.

John Wyzalek

See also **Constitution of the United States; Enron Scandal; Interstate Commerce Laws; Interstate Highway System; Pure Food and Drug Movement;** *and vol. 9:* **Women in Industry (Brandeis Brief).**

GOVERNORS. The term "governors" describes the chief executives of the American colonies and, later, of the states of the Union. The governor's role has evolved over the course of American history, but on the whole it has been relatively weak as governors lost power struggles at turns to state legislatures, other executive officials, and the federal government. Since about 1970, however, as the considerable legal restraints on their authority have been loosened, governors have steadily gained power and importance.

The Colonial Era

In the early seventeenth century, when the colonies were still owned by private charter companies, governors served primarily as corporate managers and were vested with only vague political authority. But as the Crown began to assert greater control over its possessions in America, governors were given an expanded role as the king's colonial proxies. By the middle of the eighteenth century only Connecticut and Rhode Island survived as charter colonies and they elected chief executives annually. The rest of the English territories were proprietary colonies or royal provinces, with governors who were either approved or appointed directly by the king.

On paper, proprietary and royal governors enjoyed broad powers over all the functions of colonial government. They were given the authority to appoint judges and other officials, veto legislation, and adjourn the assembly. Their political dominance, however, was greater in theory than in practice. Governors served at the pleasure of the king, who often tried to make day-to-day decisions about colonial administration. Moreover, colonial assemblies (like the English Parliament) were given the power of the purse, and they could wring significant concessions from uncooperative governors by withholding money and even refusing to pay their salaries. Governors grew increasingly vulnerable as the Revolution approached. As representatives of the Crown, they had to enforce the succession of unpopular laws, such as the Stamp and Coercive Acts, that would lead to war. In the mid-1770s, the colonists removed royal and proprietary governors from office and paved the way for the creation of independent state governments.

The Early Republic

The first state constitutions provided for strong legislatures and weak governors. The framers' recent experience with the Crown and its colonial representatives had convinced them that executive power led inevitably to despotism, whereas legislative power was impervious to tyranny because it was republican—that is, accountable to the people. Though rules differed in each state, in general governors were appointed to brief terms by a legislature that they could no longer summon or dissolve. Governors lacked veto power and could make decisions only with the advice and consent of an executive council chosen by the legislature. By and large, the first state constitutions envisioned governors who merely administered the laws passed by the assembly.

These early state governments, however, were so ineffectual and chaotic that the new Republic was forced to reconsider the rejection of executive power. Philadelphia's Constitutional Convention of 1787 created a presidential office with more independence and authority over national government than any governor had over state government (then or later). Gradually, the individual states tried to approximate the federal model, adopting new constitutions that vested executives with greater authority. For example, Illinois's first constitution, passed in 1818, provided for a popularly elected governor with four-year terms and significant appointment powers. New York's 1821 constitution granted the gubernatorial veto.

Nevertheless, the office of governor remained comparatively powerless, and the persistent weakness of American governors can be traced to the precedent set in the early Republic.

The Jacksonian Era

In the 1830s and 1840s, a new political philosophy held that all white men, not just elite landowners, were the proper guardians of American democracy. In this view, voters mattered more than legislators, and the already aging model that gave assemblies authority over governors fell completely out of favor. Most states, reflecting the new importance placed on voters, wrote new constitutions that sought to free governors from legislative authority and make them directly accountable to the people.

In general, the new constitutions gave governors veto power and made the office an elected rather than appointed one. Both reforms validated governors' claims of authority. With a powerful weapon to use against the legislature and a popular mandate, the governors had gained political independence.

A third reform, however, significantly reduced governors' control over their own executive branch. In the spirit of popular democracy and suffrage for all white men, most states adopted some form of what became known as the long ballot, whereby voters selected a large number of state officers. For example, New York's 1846 constitution called for the election of not only the governor but also a lieutenant governor, secretary of state, treasurer, comptroller, attorney general, three canal commissioners, three prison inspectors, and a state engineer.

These elected executive officials claimed their own popular mandates, articulated their own political visions, worked to achieve their own objectives, and often belonged to their own party factions. Governors had little hope of putting together an efficient administration with a clear chain of command or a single set of goals. The problem only worsened as state governments grew more complex with the passage of time and the accretion of responsibilities. Progressive-Era administrations demonstrated a special fondness for proliferating bureaucracy. Illinois, for example, supported just twenty state agencies in 1850, but by 1925 that number had increased to more than 170. Governors found it nearly impossible to administer such sprawling organizations.

The Progressive Era

Government grew so rapidly during the Progressive Era (about 1890 to 1920, though historians continue to debate the dates) because Americans' faith in the power of government was exploding. Industrial society seemed to be spinning out of control, and Progressives turned to government to fix a host of problems from alcoholism and corruption to child labor and corporate monopoly. Despite the often-crippling hodgepodge of agencies, then, state executives were empowered to take aggressive action on a range of issues, and governors temporarily escaped their narrow spheres of influence.

Woodrow Wilson began his political career serving as governor of New Jersey from 1910 to 1912, and he pushed through several good-government measures. Hiram Johnson, California's governor from 1910 to 1917, passed the Public Utilities Act, giving an independent state commission the power to regulate the powerful Southern Pacific Railroad. Robert La Follette served as Wisconsin's governor from 1900 to 1906; he became the most renowned Progressive governor, and his state was regarded as a model for the rest of the nation. Wilson, Johnson, and La Follette achieved power earlier governors could only have imagined, and the reputation of state government in general improved. Future presidents Theodore Roosevelt, Woodrow Wilson, Calvin Coolidge, and Franklin D. Roosevelt all gained prominence as governors during the first third of the twentieth century.

The Great Depression and States' Rights

When the Great Depression hit, however, the brief moment of gubernatorial power ended. States did not have the resources to cope with the huge demand for government services, and governors who still lacked coherent authority could not respond adequately to the crisis. During the New Deal, Washington, D.C., became firmly entrenched as the center of American government, and the foreign policy crises of World War II and the Cold War kept all eyes on national affairs. Governors again sunk into relative powerlessness and obscurity, and for thirty years after World War II no governor was elected president.

In the 1950s and 1960s, governors generally made news only in their embarrassing capacity as spokespeople for segregation and states' rights in the South. Southern senators and representatives urged their constituents to defy the Supreme Court's *Brown v. Board of Education* decision that outlawed segregation in public education, but it fell to governors to implement the legal and political strategy of "massive resistance." Governors such as Orval Faubus of Arkansas, Ross Barnett of Mississippi, and George Wallace of Alabama symbolized southern racism and provincialism. But the governors' empty rhetoric of states' rights also forced the federal government to display its supremacy to the humiliation of the states.

In 1957, when Faubus refused to enforce a federal court order desegregating Central High School in Little Rock, President Dwight Eisenhower called in the army and troops remained on campus for the entire school year. Similarly, Wallace famously stood in a doorway at the University of Alabama to prevent the enrollment of black students, but he was forced to relent when federal marshals arrived.

The Modern Governor

In the 1960s, states finally addressed their collective governor crisis by reorganizing and consolidating executive administration. Between 1965 and 1975, forty states underwent at least a partial reorganization. Many states were unable to get rid of the long ballot that remains a favorite target of reformers, but they eliminated most of the other checks on their governors. States have consolidated and rationalized their labyrinthine bureaucracies, collapsing hundreds of agencies into dozens and placing them under accountable department heads. They have given governors the authority to make annual budgets, and almost all states have extended the term of office to four years and allow governors to serve at least two consecutive terms. Many experts argue that these changes have attracted more talented candidates and produced the innovative administrations that now serve as models for national government.

From 1976 until the end of the twentieth century, every president except George H. W. Bush had been a former governor. Bill Clinton and George W. Bush modeled their presidencies closely on their experiences as governors. It may still be too soon to conclude that American governors have finally emerged from ineffectiveness, but without question they are more powerful than ever before.

BIBLIOGRAPHY

Black, Earl. *Southern Governors and Civil Rights: Racial Segregation as a Campaign Issue in the Second Reconstruction.* Cambridge, Mass.: Harvard University Press, 1976.

Kallenbach, Joseph E. *The American Chief Executive: The Presidency and the Governorship.* New York: Harper and Row, 1966.

Lipson, Leslie. *The American Governor: From Figurehead to Leader.* Chicago: University of Chicago, 1939.

Osborne, David. *Laboratories of Democracy: A New Breed of Governor Creates Models for National Growth.* Boston: Harvard Business School Press, 1988.

Ransone, Coleman Bernard. *The American Governorship.* Westport, Conn.: Greenwood Press, 1982.

Sabato, Larry. *Goodbye to Good-Time Charlie: The American Governor Transformed, 1950–1975.* Lexington, Mass.: Lexington Books, 1978.

Sanford, Terry. *Storm over the States.* New York: McGraw-Hill, 1967.

Jeremy Derfner

See also **State Constitutions.**

GRAFFITI. From the Italian *graffito* (scribbling), the practice of drawing symbols, images, or words on private or public surfaces without permission. Ancient Romans wrote graffiti, as have many of the world's cultures. The modern graffiti movement, associated with the hip-hop culture of break dancing and rap music, started primarily among black and Latino teenagers in Philadelphia and New York in the late 1960s. In 1971, the *New York Times* ran a story about "Taki 183," a messenger who had been writing his "tag," or stylized signature, all over New York, and graffiti took off. "Taggers" and "burners," who painted elaborate "pieces," short for masterpieces, usually wrote on subway cars, which had the advantage of moving their writing across the city.

Graffiti elicited strong opinions. To graffiti writers, it was a thriving subculture. To many intellectuals, it was a new and vital art form. To city officials, however, graffiti was illegal vandalism. New York established an antigraffiti task force and an undercover graffiti police unit and spent many millions of dollars on experimental solvents and train yard security improvements. By the mid-1980s, New York had cut down on graffiti, but by then the art form had spread across the United States and to Europe. A new kind of "gang graffiti" that marks territory and sends messages to rival gangs became common in Los Angeles in the late 1980s.

BIBLIOGRAPHY

Abel, Ernest L., and Barbara E. Buckley. *The Handwriting on the Wall: Toward Sociology and Psychology of Graffiti.* Westport, Conn.: Greenwood Press, 1977.

Phillips, Susan A. *Wallbangin': Graffiti and Gangs in L.A.* Chicago: University of Chicago Press, 1999.

Powers, Stephen. *The Art of Getting Over: Graffiti at the Millennium.* New York: St. Martin's Press, 1999.

Jeremy Derfner

See also **Art: Self-Taught Artists.**

GRAIN FUTURES ACT. The Grain Futures Act, passed on 21 September 1922, reestablished government control over commodity exchanges, which had been nullified by invalidation of the act of 24 August 1921 (*Hill v. Wallace*, 259 U.S. 44 [1922]). Omitting tax provisions, Congress reenacted similar regulations, based solely on the power to regulate interstate commerce, which were upheld by the SUPREME COURT in an assertion of the "stream-of-commerce" doctrine (*Chicago Board of Trade v. Olsen*, 262 U.S. 1 [1923]). The Grain Futures Administration assisted the secretary of agriculture in enforcement of the provision that all trading in grain futures must be at grain exchanges designated as contract markets submitting daily reports. The Commodity Exchange Act of 15 June 1936 further expanded federal control over other agricultural products by eliminating the exemptions for owners and growers of grain and their associations. This act was superseded in 1974 by the Commodity Futures Trading Commission Act.

BIBLIOGRAPHY

Fite, Gilbert Courtland. *George N. Peek and the Fight for Farm Parity.* Norman: University of Oklahoma Press, 1954.

Saloutos, Theodore, and John D. Hicks. *Agricultural Discontent in the Middle West, 1900–1939.* Madison: University of Wisconsin Press, 1951.

George C. Robinson / T. M.

See also **Agriculture; Commerce Clause; Exchanges.**

GRAMM-RUDMAN-HOLLINGS ACT (1985), officially the Balanced Budget and Emergency Deficit Control Act, was championed by Republican U.S. Senators Philip Gramm of Texas and Warren Rudman of New Hampshire, and Democratic U.S. Senator Ernest Hollings of South Carolina. Passage of this bipartisan legislation was spurred by concern over large and growing federal deficits during the 1980s and the inability of Congress and the administration to raise taxes or cut spending sufficiently to resolve the problem. The act specified a schedule of gradually declining deficit targets leading to a balanced budget in 1991. It also specified that if the administration and Congress were unable to reach agreement on a budget deficit that came within $10 billion of the targets specified in the bill, automatic and across-the-board spending reductions would be implemented in all programs except SOCIAL SECURITY, interest payments on the national debt, and certain low-income entitlements.

In the years following passage of the bill, Congress revised the deficit reduction schedule and the target year for balancing the federal budget. The most significant revision occurred in 1990, when Congress, faced with a deficit of $110 billion, enacted the Budget Enforcement Act, which cut the deficit substantially, made the deficit targets more flexible, and extended the target date for balancing the budget until 1995. The Omnibus Budget Reconciliation Act of 1993 established new limits on discretionary government spending for fiscal years 1996 through 1998.

In 1998 the budget deficit was eliminated and the federal government ran a surplus for the first time in more than a quarter of a century. Despite the balanced budgets of the late 1990s, federal deficits remain a major issue in American politics, particularly in light of the impending retirement of the baby-boom generation in the early twenty-first century.

BIBLIOGRAPHY

Congressional Budget Office. *The Economic and Budget Outlook: Fiscal Years 1995–1999.* Washington, D.C.: Government Printing Office, 1994.

Hahm, Sung Deuk, et al. "The Influence of Gramm-Rudman-Hollings Act on Federal Budgetary Outcomes, 1986–1989." *Journal of Policy Analysis and Management* 11 (1992): 207–234.

Masters, Nicholas A. *The Congressional Budget Process.* Washington, D.C.: U.S. Government Printing Office, 1993.

Michael H. Spiro / A. G.

See also **Budget, Federal; Congress, United States; Debt, Public; Demography and Demographic Trends.**

GRAND ARMY OF THE REPUBLIC (GAR), founded in 1866 for veterans of all ranks of the Union Army, became the first mass organization of American veterans to exercise significant political influence. Although theoretically a non-partisan organization, it functioned, in fact, as if it were an adjunct of the Republican Party whose leaders urged veterans to "vote as you shot." Important national commanders included Senator John A. Logan (1826–1886) and Wisconsin governor Lucius Fairchild (1831–1896), both former generals who became highly partisan Republican politicians. The latter called upon God to "palsy" President Grover Cleveland for ordering some captured Confederate standards returned to the appropriate southern states.

Relatively slow to grow in the immediate postwar years, membership spurted during the 1880s, rising from 87,718 members in 1881 to a peak of 409,489 in 1890, after which an inevitable decline set in. At its final encampment, in 1949, only six members attended. The last member died in 1956.

The GAR's political influence was demonstrated by its successful advocacy before Congress of ever more generous pensions. Initially, it stressed benefits it provided for members. In many ways it resembled the proliferating fraternal benefit organizations, with which it competed for members. But by the later 1870s, its stress shifted to gaining governmental benefits for its members. At the time of the GAR's first major victory in Washington—the passage of the so-called Arrears Act of 1879—the cost of veterans benefits was about ten cents of every federal dollar; by 1893, such costs had risen to forty-three cents of every dollar. Civil War pensions were then restricted to benefits for "disabled" veterans and widows of veterans. In 1904, however, Theodore Roosevelt's commissioner of pensions issued an order declaring that old age is, ipso facto, a disability, so that, at age sixty-two, veterans were deemed 50 percent disabled, at age sixty-five, 75 percent disabled, and at age seventy disability was total. Any veteran who reached that age was entitled to twelve dollars a month, a significant amount for most Americans at a time when the average annual wage was $490. By the eve of American entry into World War I, the top pension had risen to thirty dollars a month and a veteran's widow was entitled to twenty-five dollars a month.

Most Southerners, many Democrats, and mugwumps of every variety had long condemned the GAR and its pension lobby. Carl Schurz, for example, a Union veteran himself, wrote articles about "The Pension Scandal," while Charles Francis Adams insisted that "every dead-beat, and malingerer, every bummer, bounty-jumper, and suspected deserter" sought a pension.

During World War I, largely in reaction to their memories of GAR-inspired pension abuse, two Southern-born Democrats, Woodrow Wilson and his son-in-law William Gibbs McAdoo, tried to take the pension issue out of postwar politics with a prototypical Progressive measure. It provided military personnel with family allotments and the opportunity to purchase special cut-rate "war risk insurance," which Congress approved overwhelmingly. This did not, of course, prevent postwar veteran-related legislation from becoming a political issue until well into the Great Depression.

BIBLIOGRAPHY

Daniels, Roger. *The Bonus March: An Episode of the Great Depression.* Westport, Conn.: Greenwood, 1971. Chapter 1, "Something for the Boys," surveys veterans benefits through World War I.

Davies, Wallace E. *Patriotism on Parade: The Story of Veterans' and Hereditary Organizations in America, 1783–1900.* Cambridge, Mass.: Harvard University Press, 1955. Relates the GAR to its predecessors.

Dearing, Mary R. *Veterans in Politics: The Story of the GAR.* Baton Rouge: Louisiana State University Press, 1952. Reprint, Westport, Conn.: Greenwood Press, 1974. A history that focuses on the GAR's lobbying role.

McConnell, Stuart C. *Glorious Contentment: The Grand Army of the Republic, 1865–1900.* Chapel Hill: North Carolina University Press, 1992. A modern history, stressing the social history of the GAR.

Skocpol, Theda. "America's First Social Security System: The Expansion of Benefits for Civil War Veterans." *Political Science Quarterly* 108 (1993): 85–116. An imaginative interpretation.

Roger Daniels

See also **Pensions, Military and Naval; Veterans' Organizations.**

GRAND BANKS. Several parts of the continental shelf off the eastern coast of North America lie under less than six hundred feet of water. Covering over fifty thousand square miles, Newfoundland's Grand Banks is the most extensive of these areas. Here, conditions favor the growth of phytoplankton, minute organisms which are the first link in a food chain that includes a small fish known as capelin, northern cod, and humans. In the spring, the cod pursue the capelin when they move close to the coast to spawn. It is here, inshore, that people have been fishing for cod for the longest time. Whether aboriginal Newfoundlanders, who first arrived five thousand years ago, fished for cod is unclear. According to a 1529 account, the Beothuks did not do so. Possibly on the basis of information dating from the earlier Viking voyages to Newfoundland and points beyond around A.D. 1000, English and Portuguese vessels seem to have happened upon these fishing grounds even before the official discoverer of Newfoundland, John Cabot, noted their fabulous abundance in 1497. Soon, fishers and merchants from the European Atlantic kingdoms had developed a seasonal inshore fishery producing for southern European markets. In this "dry" fishery, crews split, salted, and dried the cod on shore over the summer before returning to Europe. Beginning around 1550, the French pioneered the "wet" or "green" fishery on the Banks proper, heavily salting the cod on board and returning home directly. By the 1570s, hundreds of vessels and thousands of men were active in the two fisheries.

In the seventeenth century, some of the French and English who now dominated the fishery began wintering in Newfoundland. French residents were forced to leave the island in the eighteenth century, although the French migrant fishery continued in northern Newfoundland. By 1815, English-speaking Newfoundlanders had largely replaced English migrant fishers inshore. Offshore, schooners based in New England and Newfoundland had begun to make inroads on the Europeans vessels' share of the catch. By the later nineteenth century, the Europeans were generally French, and Brazil had joined Europe and the Caribbean as a major market. Pressure on the resource would increase over the long term. But it was no doubt twentieth-century technology, especially the voracious factory-freezer ship introduced in the 1950s, that put it at risk. Europeans, some of them from as far away as Russia, returned in force to the Banks and even inshore in the post–World War II period, catching unprecedented quantities of an already dwindling fish stock. Catches of cod peaked in the late 1960s. Experts continue to weigh the long-term effects of climatic change on cod populations, but they now agree that overfishing was the primary factor in the decline of the inshore and Banks fisheries. International fisheries organizations and even the Canadian government, which imposed a two-hundred-mile management zone covering most of the Grand Banks in 1977, were slow to act decisively to conserve the resource. By 1992, the stock was so depleted that Canada was forced to close its Grand Banks fishery, putting thousands out of work. Reopened in the late 1990s, the cod fishery operates in the early twenty-first century on a severely reduced scale. Recovery, if it happens at all, will take decades. Meanwhile, in 1997, a consortium of companies began tapping another of the Banks' riches, the vast Hibernia oil field, discovered in 1979.

BIBLIOGRAPHY

Gentilcore, R. Louis, ed. *Historical Atlas of Canada.* Vol. 2, *The Land Transformed, 1800–1891.* Toronto: University of Toronto Press, 1993.

Harris, Michael. *Lament for an Ocean: The Collapse of the Atlantic Cod Fishery.* Toronto: McClelland and Stewart, 1998.

Historical Atlas of Canada. Vol.1, *From the Beginning to 1800.* Vol. 2, *The Land Transformed, 1800–1891.* Vol. 3, *Addressing the Twentieth Century, 1891–1961.* Toronto: University of Toronto Press, 1987, 1990, 1993.

Marshall, Ingeborg. *A History and Ethnography of the Beothuk.* Montreal: McGill-Queen's University Press, 1996.

Vickers, Daniel. *Farmers and Fishermen. Two Centuries of Work in Essex County, Massachusetts, 1630–1850.* Chapel Hill: University of North Carolina Press, 1994.

Wright, Miriam. *A Fishery for Modern Times: The State and the Industrialization of the Newfoundland Fishery, 1934–1968.* Oxford: Oxford University Press, 2001.

Thomas Wien

See also **Cod Fisheries.**

GRAND CANYON, a gorge of the Colorado River, from four to eighteen miles wide and in places more than

Grand Canyon. A view of the Colorado River and a portion of the spectacular canyon walls.
NATIONAL ARCHIVES AND RECORDS ADMINISTRATION

a mile deep, winding some 280 miles from Marble Canyon, near the Arizona-Utah line, to Grand Wash Cliffs in northern Mohave County of ARIZONA.

The first written description of the canyon is Pedro de Castañeda's account of a small group of Spanish explorers who found it after hearing stories of a large canyon during a visit to the Hopis in 1540. The canyon was little known until Lt. Joseph C. Ives and Dr. J. S. Newberry visited its lower end in April 1858 and brought back the first geological description of the region. Maj. John Wesley Powell made the first journey down the Colorado River through the canyon with nine men, 24 May–30 August 1869. Congress created Grand Canyon National Park, 673,575 acres, on 26 February 1919, and two years later the completion of a railroad from Williams, Arizona, facilitated tourist travel to the canyon. In 1932, an additional 198,280 acres encompassing Toroweap Point of the canyon was set aside as the Grand Canyon National Monument. In 1966, the SIERRA CLUB successfully spearheaded a drive to prevent the erection of a dam at the lower end of the canyon.

BIBLIOGRAPHY

Morehouse, Barbara J. *A Place Called Grand Canyon: Contested Geographies.* Tucson: University of Arizona Press, 1996.

Pyne, Stephen J. *How the Canyon Became Grand: A Short History.* New York: Viking, 1998.

Rufus Kay Wyllys / C. W.

See also **Colorado River Explorations; Explorations and Expeditions: Spanish; National Park System; Tourism.**

GRAND CENTRAL TERMINAL, at Forty-second Street and Park Avenue in New York City, stands as a magnificent Beaux Arts monument to America's railroad age. At the heart of the terminal, the Grand Concourse—New York City's secular cathedral—serves as the crossroads for

Grand Central Terminal. Sunbeams shining through high lunette windows illuminate parts of the vast Grand Concourse. © HULTON-DEUTSCH COLLECTION /CORBIS

midtown Manhattan. The terminal and two-story underground train yard, stretching from Forty-second to Fifty-sixth Streets between Madison and Lexington Avenues, replaced the first Grand Central constructed in 1871 by Commodore Cornelius Vanderbilt and his New York Central and Harlem Railroads.

In 1901, William J. Wilgus, the New York Central's chief engineer, proposed a multifaceted plan of stunning complexity for a new facility. The railroad planned to build a new terminal building and a two-story underground train yard and to electrify operations in Manhattan, the Bronx, and Westchester Counties. To pay for the enormous cost, Wilgus proposed developing the air rights over the two-story underground train yard by creating luxury hotels, commercial office space, and apartments.

Excavation removed three million cubic feet of rock and dirt. Construction of the underground train yard consumed thirty thousand tons of steel, three times more than needed for the Eiffel Tower. Electrification proceeded in parallel with the construction. Whitney Warren and the partnership of Charles Reed and Alan Stem of Minneapolis designed the complex. Warren, trained at the École des Beaux-Arts in Paris, drew the plans for the monumental terminal building on Forty-second Street to serve as a magnificent gateway to New York.

Hailed at its opening in 1913 as the "greatest railway terminal in the world," the new Grand Central transformed the area around Forty-second Street into a harmonious blend of hotels, office buildings, and apartments, many connected directly by underground passageways to the terminal. Park Avenue, north of Grand Central, became New York City's grand boulevard, lined with luxury apartments and hotels built over the underground train yard.

Despite Grand Central's success, the New York Central and all of the nation's railroads soon entered a period of rapid decline. Grand Central suffered as the railroad struggled for decades to remain solvent. As decline continued after World War II, the railroad in 1954 announced plans to destroy the terminal and replace the Grand Concourse with a tall office building. New Yorkers rallied to save Grand Central and New York City passed its landmarks preservation law designating the building a landmark. A bitter court battle ensued until the U.S. Supreme Court in 1978 upheld Grand Central's landmark status.

Deterioration continued during the long court battle until the newly formed Metro-North Railroad assumed operation of the terminal. Restoration plans were formulated and financing secured to restore Grand Central. On 1 October 1998, after the restoration was completed, a rededication drew dignitaries and ordinary New Yorkers to celebrate the rebirth of one of the city's glories: Grand Central Terminal, the crossroads of New York City.

Kurt C. Schlichting

See also **New York City; Railroads.**

GRAND OLE OPRY began in Nashville, Tennessee, in November 1925 as weekly radio broadcasts playing old time, or hillbilly (later called country and western), music from the fifth floor of the National Life and Accident Insurance Company building. Founded by George Dewey Hay, known on air as "the Solemn Ol' Judge," who had helped organize a similar program in Chicago, the program was originally called the *WSM* ("We Shield Millions") *Barn Dance* and became the enduring *Grand Ole Opry* in 1928. The show thrived during the radio era of the 1920s and grew with the emerging recording industry and the advent of television. The popularity and expanded exposure of *Opry* performers gave birth to live tours and *Opry* films. Many bluegrass and country and western performers were launched or promoted by the *Opry*, including Hank Williams Sr., the Carter Family, Ernest Tubb, Bill Monroe, Lester Flatt and Earl Scruggs, Patsy Cline, Loretta Lynn, Dolly Parton, and the comedienne Minnie Pearl. One of the most enduring *Opry* careers was that of Roy Acuff, who was with the *Opry* from the 1930s until his death in 1992. In 1943, the *Opry*, after moving to successively larger venues, became a live stage show at the Ryman Theater Auditorium in Nashville. It remained there until 1974, when it moved to the 4,400-seat Grand Ole Opry House at Opryland Amusement Park, an entertainment center on the outskirts of Nashville.

BIBLIOGRAPHY

Dawidoff, Nicholas. *In the Country of Country: A Journey to the Roots of American Music.* New York: Vintage Books, 1997.

Malone, Bill C. *Country Music U.S.A.* Austin: University of Texas Press, 1985

Deirdre Sheets

See also **Music: Bluegrass; Music: Country and Western.**

GRAND PORTAGE received its name from voyageurs, who found the nine miles between Lake Superior and the Pigeon River the longest portage in their regular canoe route from Montreal to the Rocky Mountains. About 1780 the name came to mean the British North West Company post at the lake end of the portage. At the height of its prosperity, about 1795, Grand Portage had a stockade, sixteen buildings, a pier, a canoe yard, a garden, domestic animals, and schooner connection with Sault Ste. Marie. In 1804 the transfer of activities from Grand Portage to Fort William, Ontario, occurred in accordance with JAY'S TREATY of 1794, thus ending Grand Portage's heyday.

BIBLIOGRAPHY

Lass, William E. *Minnesota: A History.* New York: Norton, 1998.

Grace Lee Nute/A. E.

See also **North West Company; Voyageurs.**

GRAND PRAIRIE, a geographical division of north TEXAS extending about 200 miles south from the Red River, two to three counties in width. The Grand Prairie, in combination with the Black Prairie, formed the Cretaceous Prairies of Texas. Deep, clay subsoil covered most of the Grand Prairie, and, along with the dense root structure of prairie grasses, posed a formidable challenge to early settlers interested in farming. The Grand Prairie's period of settlement and county organization was 1846–1858. Its luxuriant grass made it the first important cattle-grazing region of Texas, and the quality of its soil and nearness to timber made it an early prairie farming area.

BIBLIOGRAPHY

Connor, Seymour V. *Texas: A History.* New York: Crowell, 1971.

Greer, J. K. *Grand Prairie.* Dallas, Tex.: Tardy, 1935.

L. W. Newton/F. H.

See also **Agriculture; Cattle; Prairie.**

GRANDFATHER CLAUSE, a legal provision exempting someone from a new qualification or regulation. More specifically, through seven southern state constitutional amendments passed from 1895 to 1910, grandfather clauses exempted men who had the right to vote on 1 January 1867 or, in some states, those who had fought in American wars and their descendants, from literacy or property tests for voting. Proponents contended that poor, illiterate whites would still be able to vote, while African Americans, who could not vote in the South in 1866, would again be disfranchised. Grandfather clauses were temporary and were declared unconstitutional under the Fifteenth Amendment by the U.S. Supreme Court in *Guinn and Beal v. United States* (1915).

BIBLIOGRAPHY

Kousser, J. Morgan. *The Shaping of Southern Politics: Suffrage Restriction and the Establishment of the One-Party South, 1880–1910.* New Haven, Conn.: Yale University Press, 1974.

J. Morgan Kousser

See also **Disfranchisement.**

GRANGER CASES. In the face of increasing activism calling for the regulation of railway rates by the Grangers (members of the National Grange of the Order of Patrons of Husbandry) and other groups, several Midwestern states asserted regulatory authority over the railroad industry, enacting what were known as the Granger Laws. Illinois's 1870 constitution called for the state legislature to "prevent unjust discrimination and extortion" in freight and passenger rates, and Illinois, along with Wisconsin, Iowa, and Minnesota moved to regulate railroads and warehouses within their borders. Most of the state laws were poorly drawn and were eventually appealed as the railroads created uniform rates by raising them to the maximum allowed by law.

Illinois's regulations were the strongest and became the subject of *Munn v. Illinois* (1877), the most important of the eight Granger Cases. Fourteen Chicago warehouses, including that of the Munn Brothers, stored the grain produced by seven states. In *Munn v. Illinois,* the Court was asked to determine whether the state could regulate a private industry that served a public function. In a 5 to 4 decision, the Court sided with Illinois and established the Public Interest Doctrine, declaring that states could properly regulate private entities that served a public function. Chief Justice Morrison R. Waite, writing for the Court, declared that when "one devotes his property to a use in which the public has an interest, he, in effect, grants to the public an interest in that use, and must submit to be controlled by the public for the public good." Nationwide, other states followed suit, and the movement eventually gave rise to federal regulatory entities such as the Interstate Commerce Commission.

BIBLIOGRAPHY

Cashman, Sean Dennis. *America in the Gilded Age: From the Death of Lincoln to the Rise of Theodore Roosevelt.* New York: New York University Press, 1993.

Ely, James W., Jr. *The Chief Justiceship of Melville W. Fuller, 1888–1910.* Columbia: University of South Carolina Press, 1995.

R. Volney Riser

See also **Interstate Commerce Commission; Public Interest Law.**

GRANGER MOVEMENT. The Granger movement grew out of a farmers' lodge, the Patrons of Husbandry, founded in 1867 by Oliver Hudson Kelley. While employed by the Department of Agriculture, Kelley made a tour of the South and was struck by the enslavement of southern farmers to outworn methods of agriculture. He believed the situation could best be remedied by an organization that would bring farmers together in groups for the study and discussion of their problems. Accordingly, with the help of a few interested friends, he devised a secret ritualistic order, equally open to women and to men, and became its first organizer. Each local unit, or Grange, was admonished to select among its officers a "lecturer," whose duty should be to provide some educational diversion, such as a lecture or a paper, for every meeting.

In 1868 Kelley started west for his home in Minnesota and began recruiting among his former neighbors. His organization won adherents, less for its social and educational advantages than for the opportunity it presented for farmers to unite against railroads and elevators and to institute cooperative methods of buying and selling. By the end of 1869 there were thirty-seven active Granges in Minnesota. A year later, the order expanded into nine states. During the panic of 1873 there were Granges in every state of the Union but four. Membership claims reached a maximum during the mid-1870s of about 800,000, with the total number of Granges estimated at about 20,000. The center of Granger activity remained during the entire period in the grain-growing region of the upper Mississippi Valley.

The grievances that drove the northwestern farmers into these organizations grew out of their almost complete dependence on outside markets for the disposal of their produce and on corporation-owned elevators and railroads for its handling. The high prices that accompanied the Civil War in the United States and the Bismarckian wars in Europe enabled the farmers, during those wars, to pay the high charges the corporations exacted. After these conflicts, when prices began to drop, the grain growers found themselves in acute distress. In 1869 they paid at the rate of 52.5 cents a bushel to send grain from the Mississippi River to the Atlantic seaboard and nearly half as much to send it from an Iowa or Minnesota farm to Chicago. Elevators, often owned by the railroads, charged high prices for their services, weighed and graded grain without supervision, and used their influence with the railroads to ensure that cars were not available to farmers who sought to evade elevator service.

Rumblings of farmer revolt began in the late 1860s, and in 1869 the legislature of Illinois passed an act that required the railroads to charge only "just, reasonable, and uniform rates." The act, however, provided no adequate means of enforcement, and nothing came of it. The next year, Illinois adopted a new constitution in which the legislature was authorized to make laws to correct railway abuses and extortions. Acting on this authority, the legislature of 1871 set maximum freight and passenger rates and established a board of railroad and warehouse commissioners to enforce them. These laws the railroads flatly refused to obey, a position in which they were sustained by the state supreme court. In late 1873, however, a more carefully drawn law ran the gauntlet of a revised supreme court, for in the meantime at a judicial election the angered farmers had replaced one of the offending judges with a judge more Granger-minded.

By that time, the Grange had become far more political than educational in nature and, ably assisted by a host of unaffiliated farmers' clubs, was in the thick of the fight for state regulation of railroads and elevators. At Granger lodge meetings and picnics, farmers exhorted one another to nominate and elect to office only those who shared their views. In case corporation control over the Republican and Democratic Parties could not be overthrown, they planned to form independent, reform, or antimonopoly parties through which to carry on the fight. So many farmers made Independence Day 1873 an occasion for airing these views that the celebration was long remembered as the Farmers' Fourth of July. On that day, many rural audiences listened with approval to the reading of a "Farmers' Declaration of Independence," which recited farmers' grievances and asserted their determination to use the power of the state to free themselves from the tyranny of monopoly. Victories at the polls led to the passage of a series of so-called Granger laws for the regulation of railroads and warehouses, not only in Illinois but also in several other northwestern states. These measures were not always well drawn, and for the most part they were soon repealed or drastically modified. Nevertheless, the U.S. Supreme Court, in *Munn v. Illinois* and a number of other cases, all decided in 1877, sustained the Granger contention that businesses of a public nature could, in accordance with the federal Constitution, be subjected to state regulation—a precedent of far-reaching consequence.

Equally important as the political activities of the various Granges were their business ventures. Granges founded numerous cooperative elevators, creameries, and general stores, although most of these establishments failed to survive the ruthless competition of private business. The Granges tried many other experiments also, such as buying through purchasing agents or through dealers who quoted special prices to Grangers, patronizing mail-order houses, and manufacturing farm machinery. The last-mentioned undertaking, ill conceived and overdone, resulted in serious financial reverses and had much to do with the sudden decline in Granger popularity that, beginning about 1876, brought the movement to an untimely end.

Despite its short span of life, the Granger movement had taught farmers many things. They had learned that their political power, when they chose to use it, was great. They found that business cooperatives, although hazardous, might limit the toll paid to middlemen and that such social and educational activities as the Grange had fostered could greatly brighten rural life. The Patrons of Husbandry as a lodge survived the Granger movement, won new eastern adherents to replace the western deserters, and in the twentieth century even recovered some of its influence in politics.

BIBLIOGRAPHY

Buck, Solon J. *The Agrarian Crusade.* New Haven: Yale University Press, 1920.

———. *The Granger Movement.* Lincoln: University of Nebraska Press, 1963.

Cartensen, Vernon R., ed. *Farmer Discontent, 1865–1900.* New York: Wiley, 1974.

Marti, Donald B. *Women of the Grange.* New York: Greenwood Press, 1991.

Nordin, Dennis S. *Rich Harvest: A History of the Grange, 1867–1900.* Jackson: University Press of Mississippi, 1974.

Woods, Thomas A. *Knights of the Plow: Oliver H. Kelley and the Origins of the Grange in Republican Ideology.* Ames: Iowa State University Press, 1991.

John D. Hicks / H. S.

See also **Agrarianism; Farmers Institutes; *Munn v. Illinois;* Patrons of Husbandry; Populism.**

GRANTS-IN-AID. A general term for money given to state or local governments by Congress. In many cases, grants are earmarked for specific purposes (these are called categorical grants). The federal government uses grants-in-aid to induce states and cities to fund programs they show little interest in or cannot afford. The first grants (1862) were land grants to states for public universities. During the New Deal, impoverished cities received federal money for a variety of initiatives (public housing and unemployment insurance, for example). Since World War II, the practice has grown increasingly common. In the late-1990s, Congress appropriated more than $200 billion annually (about 15 percent of federal spending) for grants-in-aid.

BIBLIOGRAPHY

Brown, Lawrence D., James W. Fossett, and Kenneth T. Palmer. *The Changing Politics of Federal Grants.* Washington, D.C.: Brookings Institution, 1984.

Jeremy Derfner

GRASSHOPPERS regularly destroyed crops from the start of American AGRICULTURE to the early 1950s. These insects fall roughly into migratory and nonmigratory groups. Although migratory grasshoppers (locusts) generally did the most damage, every species caused problems in some part of America. Locusts usually attacked sparsely settled regions, while nonmigratory species typically struck more settled regions. Especially serious attacks occurred in New England in 1743, 1749, 1754, and 1756 and recurred into the nineteenth century, especially in Vermont and Maine. California missions suffered heavily several times in the 1820s, as did farms in Missouri and Minnesota. Grasshoppers appeared in the GREAT BASIN and on the GREAT PLAINS in 1855 and at odd intervals thereafter. The great grasshopper plagues of the Plains occurred in 1874–1876. The need for research to prevent attacks factored significantly into the 1863 creation of the Division of Entomology (renamed the Bureau of Entomology in 1904) in the U.S. Department of Agriculture.

The hopperdozer, a device for catching and killing insects, made its first recorded appearance in 1878, but it may have been used as early as 1858. It consisted of a shallow pan on skids with a large screen behind the pan, which farmers pulled across fields. Grasshoppers jumped up, hit the screen, and fell into a pan filled with kerosene or poison. Farmers used hopperdozers well into the twentieth century. Control by bran and molasses mixed with arsenic remained the chief means of effective control until the discovery of the hydrocarbon insecticides, such as chlordane, in the mid-1940s.

In the twentieth century the worst grasshopper attacks occurred in 1931, 1934, 1936, and 1939. The worst of these was the 1936 invasion, which destroyed crops and forage on a grand scale throughout the Midwest and South and especially on the Great Plains. The menace of grasshoppers declined during World War II, and thereafter the use of new insecticides has kept grasshoppers in check.

BIBLIOGRAPHY

Schlebecker, J. T. "Grasshoppers in American Agricultural History." *Agricultural History* 27 (1953): 85–93.

Sorensen, W. Conner. *Brethren of the Net: American Entomology, 1840–1880.* Tuscaloosa: University of Alabama Press, 1995.

John T. Schlebecker / C. W.

See also **Agriculture, Department of; Insecticides and Herbicides.**

GRAY PANTHERS. In 1970, Maggie Kuhn organized a group of recently retired friends to discuss the challenges facing retirees, including loss of income, uncertain social roles, and lack of networking opportunities, but also a newfound independence, such as speaking out against the Vietnam War. After a New York talk show producer nicknamed them the "Gray Panthers," Kuhn's group struck a nerve with other retirees, who wanted to join. The Gray Panthers used the media to gain a national forum for issues ranging from race relations to health-care reform. As membership grew, the group organized local networks and in 1985 opened a public policy office in Washington, D.C.

BIBLIOGRAPHY

Kuhn, Maggie. *No Stone Unturned: The Life and Times of Maggie Kuhn.* New York: Ballantine, 1991.

Bob Batchelor

See also **Old Age; Retirement.**

GREAT AWAKENING. Some historians denominate essentially all revivalistic activity in Britain's North American colonies between 1740 and 1790 as the "Great Awakening," but the term more properly refers only to those revivals associated with the itinerant Anglican preacher George Whitefield that occurred between 1739 and 1745. Evangelicals in Britain as well as America attended to Whitefield's perambulations on both sides of the Atlantic, giving the Awakening an international dimension; indeed, American events made up just one portion of a trans-European movement among eighteenth-century Protestants to exalt spiritual experience as faith's hallmark as opposed to adherence to systematized creeds and catechisms.

The Awakening elaborated upon strains of revivalism that had been developing piecemeal within Reformed Protestant traditions. As far back as the 1680s, Solomon Stoddard had hosted "refreshings" within the Congregational church in Northampton, Massachusetts, elevating parishioners' religious and moral commitment by heightening their fear of hell while emphasizing that salvation could be obtained only through conversion (the New Birth)—the Holy Spirit's infusion of grace into the soul. His grandson, Jonathan Edwards, anatomized the process, detailing how, with God's help, a minister heading a settled congregation—the New England norm—might inspire multiple conversions relatively quickly. During the 1720s, Theodorus Frelinghuysen initiated a similar interest in "heart-religion" among New Jersey's Dutch Reformed churches. His example animated Gilbert Tennent, a Pennsylvania Presbyterian whose father, William, similarly advocated the importance of conversion at his Neshaminy seminary. The Tennents' preaching warmed Presbyterian settlers from Scotland and Ulster who were accustomed to holding Sacramental Seasons—four-day devotions climaxed by highly affective celebrations of the Lord's Supper. Reformed churches had thus independently discovered various means of inducing collective conversions through heightened religious excitement before Whitefield commenced his second American tour in 1739. Whitefield's unique contribution was to foment religious excitement in all of these traditions simultaneously, make them each fully cognizant of the others, exaggerate the behavioral manifestations of the New Birth, and demonstrate the degree to which highly effusive appeals to large audiences could stimulate conversion and recruit the unchurched.

George Whitefield. The English evangelist. Nominally an Anglican priest but in practice a Reformed Protestant who led the Calvinistic Methodist Church for a time, he spread the revivalism called the Great Awakening throughout the American colonies and England between 1739 and 1745. GETTY IMAGES

Whitefield appropriated secular culture in order to challenge it. Condemning the stage for diverting playgoers from God, he dramatized both the Word and himself theatrically. Critical of the "Consumption Revolution" brought about by both middle-class arrogations of aristocratic taste and burgeoning industrial production because it lured people into luxuriousness, he took advantage of the emerging transatlantic press, itself a market phenomenon, to advertise the Gospel while commodifying himself. An apostle for spontaneously seizing grace, he calculated his evangelical campaigns carefully, pioneering the use of advance men to announce his movements and the printed word—his own journals and others' press reports—to trumpet his progress. In less than two years, he visited every province from Georgia to New Hampshire, attracting the largest crowds anyone in those colonies had ever witnessed. His ordination notwithstanding, Whitefield preferred Reformed Protestant predestinarianism to the Church of England's Arminianism, but in the pulpit he downplayed dogma and minimized the importance of denominational affiliation to stress the necessity of being born again. He wanted "just Christians," he said, and anyone willing to take Christ by faith would qualify. Capable, remarked contemporary actor David Garrick, of moving audiences to paroxysms simply by pronouncing "Mesopotamia," Whitefield excited thousands to manifest their conversion by shrieking, groaning, laughing, or singing. Preaching often to people who, unlike New Englanders, belonged either to churches that did not emphasize conversion or to no church at all, he characterized the New Birth as a decision for Christ that any believer could make in defiance or in the absence of clerical authority, an act manifested by a brief, highly charged (even convulsive) experience that conferred salvation but did not, as for Puritans, also energize the believer to reform society morally. This shift toward a normative understanding of conversion as occurring outside a settled ecclesiastical order identifies an emergent "evangelical" conception of the New Birth as essentially an individualized experience.

Whitefield did not fare well in the South, where he angered Anglicans by chastising them for ignoring conversion and slaveowners for keeping Christ from their slaves (though he never condemned slavery itself). He enjoyed greater influence among northern Congregationalists, Presbyterians, Lutherans, and German Reformed, all churches with conversionist traditions. Anglicans, Quakers, and German sectarians, all non-Reformed Protestants, paid him little heed, as of course did the smattering of Roman Catholics. Increasingly, however, Whitefield in particular and revivalism in general came under fire for promoting discord rather than godliness. In his wake, churches were disrupted by itinerant preachers inveighing against unconverted ministers and by "New Lights" censoring congregants deemed unregenerate. Under such strains the Presbyterians schismed from 1741 to 1758, and the Congregational Standing Order lost one-third of its churches, many of which ultimately became Baptist. Whitefield suffered a tepid reception when he returned to America in 1744, and by the next year, the colonists had turned their attention to saving their skins from the French rather than their souls from the Devil.

The Great Awakening created a new definition of a "revival of religion" as a specific event manifesting God's gracious dispensation toward a church, town, or people. It elevated the rate of conversion, but a drop in succeeding years suggests that it accelerated the pace of church membership only temporarily, by lowering the age at which people already likely to convert claimed Christ rather than by attracting a substantial number of outsiders to the churches. Discovery that church-formation continued briskly before and after the 1740s intimates that the Awakening did not have such a prominent impact on Christianizing the American people as had been supposed. The Awakening did mark an important attempt to proselytize Amerindians and Africans, though the numbers baptized were quite small, but it had no discernible effect on the American Revolution, none of whose ideology, politics, or organization of protest can be traced directly to revivalism. Most important, the Awakening did demonstrate the revival's power to recruit large numbers of church members during a short period of time. The Whitefieldian model—more effective for spurring conversion and cohering churches among the trans-Appalachian West's dispersed, unorganized populations than its Edwardsean counterpart—would become the engine driving the evangelization of nineteenth-century America.

BIBLIOGRAPHY

Crawford, Michael J. *Seasons of Grace: Colonial New England's Revival Tradition in Its British Context.* New York: Oxford University Press, 1991.

Lambert, Frank. *Inventing the "Great Awakening."* Princeton, N.J.: Princeton University Press, 1999.

Schmidt, Leigh Eric. *Holy Fairs: Scottish Communions and American Revivals in the Early Modern Period.* Princeton, N.J.: Princeton University Press, 1989.

Ward, W. R. *The Protestant Evangelical Awakening.* Cambridge, Mass.: Cambridge University Press, 1992.

Charles L. Cohen

See also **Evangelicalism and Revivalism.**

GREAT BASIN. On his first expedition to the 189,000-square-mile region that he named the Great Basin, 1843–1844, John Charles Frémont explored the rim of that area, which lies between the Wasatch Mountains on the east and the Sierra Nevada on the west, including most of Nevada and the western third of Utah. Frémont was in search of the mythical Buenaventura River.

The second expedition, 1845–1846, was organized for the purpose of exploring the Great Basin more fully. Frémont and his party set out south and west of the Great Salt Lake and crossed the Great Salt Desert into central Nevada. There he divided his party. Edward Kern went southwest, while Frémont and his group went northwest to California. The expeditions collected scientific data, made sketches of the scenery, and noted unusual physical features. Frémont named many rivers, lakes, springs, mountains, passes, and deserts in the Great Basin, generally after the members of his expeditions.

The early emigrant trails and cutoffs across the Great Basin branched off the Oregon Trail at South Pass, Wyoming. The Salt Lake–Los Angeles road turned southwest at Salt Lake, continued to the Virgin River, and extended southwest over the Old Spanish Trail. At the Virgin River, William's short route, or light-hand road, turned west across Nevada to Death Valley. Another important offshoot, the Humboldt Trail, crossed the Forty-Mile desert to the Carson River and from there followed mountain passes into California. The Great Basin was threaded with ramifications of these trails and cutoffs and was heavily traveled by early emigrants.

BIBLIOGRAPHY

Coy, Owen Cochran. *The Great Trek.* Los Angeles: Powell Publishing, 1931.

Faragher, John Mack. *Women and Men on the Overland Trail.* New Haven, Conn.: Yale University Press, 1979.

Unruh, John D. *The Plains Across: The Overland Emigrants and the Trans-Mississippi West, 1840–60.* Urbana: University of Illinois Press, 1979.

Effie Mona Mack / A. R.

See also **Frémont Explorations; Gold Rush, California.**

GREAT BOOKS PROGRAMS. In 1919, Columbia professor John Erskine began teaching a radical course on literature's "great books," discarding the weightiness of scholarship to allow students to engage in critical conversation about the texts. In 1931 his former student Mortimer Adler, with President Robert M. Hutchins of the University of Chicago, began a similar course. Combating trends toward academic specialization, they sought to provide core humanistic training and a democratic foundation for society. Widely implemented by universities, programs based on the "Great Books" remain a key part of core curricula. Hutchins and Adler created a program for adults in 1947 with the establishment of the Great Books Foundation. Based on cooperative learning, or "shared inquiry," the program motivates participants to think critically about the texts, spurred by curiosity rather than the proddings of an instructor. Great Books discussion groups were especially popular with the middle class through the 1950s–1970s, but interest tapered off in the 1980s. The foundation started its Junior Program in 1962, expanding it to the classroom in 1992 to integrate reading, writing, and discussion. The foundation's goals include enlarging the Great Books canon to include non-Western works and rejuvenating interest in discussion groups. Hutchins and Adler's legacy continued through their editions of the *Encyclopaedia Britannica*'s *Great Books of the Western World*, used extensively in seminar courses and discussion groups.

BIBLIOGRAPHY

Adler, Mortimer J. *Reforming Education: The Opening of the American Mind.* New York: Macmillan, 1988.

Ashmore, Harry S. *Unseasonable Truths: The Life of Robert Maynard Hutchins.* Boston: Little, Brown, 1989.

"The Great Conversation Continues: The Great Books Foundation 1947–1997." Chicago: Great Books Foundation, 1997.

Meaghan M. Dwyer

GREAT BRITAIN, RELATIONS WITH. The United Kingdom and the United States have shared a faith in commercial and geographic expansion and in rights guaranteed by written laws, commonalities of religion and language, and a belief that each was a chosen people destined to rule whole continents. Commercial competition and conflicting aspirations for the Western Hemisphere made the two frequent rivals throughout the nineteenth century. It took opposition to common adversaries through two world wars and the Cold War to develop the special relationship with which they entered the twenty-first century.

In 1776, 90 percent of white colonists traced their roots to Protestant immigrants from Britain. After the French and Indian War (1754–1763), however, London damaged these bonds by limiting westward expansion and through heavy taxation. Armed with predictions that their population would double in every generation, revolutionaries such as Benjamin Franklin preached that demography held the key to independence and to eventual continental dominance.

More than 30 percent of Americans remained loyal to the British Crown throughout the Revolution (1775–1783), and rebel leaders justified their revolt as a defense of rights guaranteed to free Britons. Theirs was not a fratricidal attempt to sever ties with the British people, Thomas Jefferson wrote in the Declaration of Independence, it was instead a war waged solely against Britain's tyrannical King George III. This intermingling of loyalties and war aims has led many historians to consider the conflict more a transatlantic British civil war than a traditional revolution.

America's 1778 accord with France, Britain's traditional enemy, marked the diplomatic turning point of the war. French money and naval power enabled George Washington's continental armies to win a decisive victory at Yorktown in 1781. London soon sued for peace, and American diplomats agreed to terms on 30 November 1782, breaking their promise to France that they would not sign a separate accord. Franklin and his fellow diplomats believed their country needed British trade to prosper and an accessible frontier to grow, and the 1783 Peace of Paris promised both. It gave Americans access to valuable Newfoundland fishing grounds and a western boundary of the Mississippi River in exchange for guarantees protecting loyalists and British debts. With peace in hand, a bitter Parliament moved immediately to contain future Yankee expansion, by refusing to relinquish forts on the American side of the Canadian border, and by closing the lucrative West Indies to American traders.

Peace only reinforced the new country's position as Britain's economic vassal, as Americans purchased three times what they sold to Britain in 1783 alone. A postwar depression brought on in part by Parliament's punitive measures invigorated investment in domestic manufacturing and spurred the search for alternative markets, however, while also aiding proponents of a federal government powerful enough to regulate foreign trade. By 1795, the percentage of American imports originating in Britain had declined from nearly 90 percent to a more manageable 35 percent (where it remained until the 1850s), accounting for nearly 20 percent of Britain's overall trade. Across the Atlantic, the embarrassing defeat in North America prompted Parliament to implement naval and financial reforms, and helped reorient London's imperial aspirations toward India and Asia, changes that enabled Britain's eventual triumph over Napoleonic France. The defeat at Yorktown, therefore, paradoxically sewed the seeds of victory at Waterloo, just as British economic efforts to weaken and divide its former colonies after 1783 helped spawn the more cohesive federal constitution.

Relations with the New Nation

Dependence on Atlantic trade soon brought Europe's troubles to America. The 1789 French Revolution sparked a series of bloody wars that ravaged Europe for a generation. Many Americans initially saw opportunity in the Old World's woes, but dreams of political isolation vanished as French and British raiders preyed on American vessels. Britain seized 250 American ships in 1793 alone, risking war and disrupting the tariff fees considered vital to Treasury Secretary Alexander Hamilton's national financial program. President George Washington dispatched Chief Justice John Jay to London in search of a peaceful solution, but Britain refused to cease badgering American ships or to halt the hated impressment of American crews into the Royal Navy. Jay did win trade concessions in India and procured another British pledge to relinquish its Canadian strongholds. His work was harshly criticized at home for his failure to secure neutral shipping rights, but JAY'S TREATY solidified American claims to the Ohio Valley and opened commercial routes so lucrative that American vessels carried 70 percent of India's trade by 1801.

The Napoleonic Wars drew America deeper into the European conflict, and French and American ships waged an undeclared war by 1799. British warships temporarily convoyed Yankee vessels filled with grain for British soldiers fighting in Spain, but this Anglo-American rapprochement was short-lived. Britain embargoed European ports controlled by Napoleon in 1807, in counter to France's 1806 embargo on British trade. Trapped between two European juggernauts, the United States could do little to protect its vessels against a British fleet that possessed three ships for every American cannon. President Thomas Jefferson responded with an embargo of his own on European trade in 1807, but when sanctions failed and British naval impressment continued to rise, a sharply divided Congress declared war in 1812.

The WAR OF 1812 solved little, but, although British marines burned Washington, D.C., the United States proved its permanence. Britain could not conquer it, nor would Americans forsake their claims to Maine and the Northwest. Freed from the fear of European invasion after hostilities ended with the 1814 Treaty of Ghent, the United States could finally turn its attention fully toward development and expansion. By 1820, more people lived in states formed after 1789 than had lived in the entire country in 1776. The focus of Anglo-American relations moved west as well. Settlers from both countries poured into new territories as distant as Oregon, aided by boundary settlements such as the 1817 Rush-Bagot Pact, which demilitarized the Great Lakes and the United States–Canadian border in the East, and the Anglo-American Convention of 1818 that established the forty-ninth parallel as the border to the Rocky Mountains in the West. These were mutually advantageous pacts: stability allowed Britain to save money and troops for more daunting imperial trouble spots, while Americans believed their demographic advantages ensured eventual dominance over any accessible land.

British officials hoped to counter Washington's territorial gains with growing commercial power throughout the Western Hemisphere. In 1823, Britain's foreign minister, George Canning, offered President James Monroe a joint declaration forbidding further European colonization in the New World in exchange for a promise that neither country would annex more Latin American territory. Monroe refused. He longed for Texas and Cuba, and realized that London would prevent further French, Spanish, or Russian expansion into potential British markets no matter what America promised. Monroe therefore unilaterally declared the New World off limits, a policy later called the MONROE DOCTRINE.

Anglo-American expansion into Oregon Territory, a landmass larger than France, Germany, and Hungary combined, brought the two countries close to war in the 1840s. London could not stem the tide of American settlers, and American hawks urged President James Polk to claim the entire region, Canadian areas included, but he blinked first when London mobilized its fleet for war. The ensuing 1846 Oregon Treaty peacefully extended the Canadian-American border along the forty-ninth parallel to the Pacific, providing the United States with the Columbia River and Puget Sound, while Britain retained Vancouver Island. Growing British and American interests in Latin America prompted the 1850 CLAYTON-BULWER TREATY, whereby each nation promised equal access to any future isthmian canal. When coupled with the Monroe Doctrine, this accord highlights each nation's willingness to work together rather than see a third power gain influence in the New World.

The American Civil War and the Path to Partnership

America's bloody Civil War (1861–1865) nearly extinguished the trend toward Anglo-American cooperation. Britain had banned slavery in 1833, and pervasive abolitionism made Britons overwhelmingly supportive of the Union cause. Yet Confederate statesmen presumed Britain's ravenous appetite for cotton (more than 80 percent of which came from the South) would bring London to their aid. They were terribly mistaken. London's recognition of the Confederacy as a warring belligerent infuriated the North, however, and British officials vigorously protested the Union's seizure of two Southern diplomats from the British ship *Trent* in 1862. President Abraham Lincoln's release of the men defused the crisis, though not before Britain had dispatched troops to protect Canada.

Following the war, friendly diplomacy ruled Anglo-American relations for thirty years. Diplomatic lethargy did nothing to halt growing Anglo-American ties, including the fashionable trend of intermarriages between America's nouveau riche and the upper crust of British society that produced the prime ministers Winston Churchill and Harold Macmillan, among others. Anglo-American culture fused during this period as at no time since the Revolution. Nathaniel Hawthorne and Ralph Waldo Emerson were read as frequently as Henry Wadsworth Longfellow and John Greenleaf Whittier in both countries, and actors from London and New York plied their trade equally in each. It was not until 1896 that a crisis threatened these amiable relations, when Washington flexed its growing might in Latin America by demanding arbitration for a boundary dispute between British Guinea and Venezuela. London eventually conceded to Washington's demands, a symbolic concession that America had become the hemisphere's dominant power.

The Venezuela crisis marked the last instance Britain and America threatened each other with war. In all, arbitration diffused 126 Anglo-American disputes before 1900, and the twentieth century began with talk of "Anglo-Saxonism" and of shared Anglo-American strategic interests. In 1898, Secretary of State John Hay termed friendly Anglo-American relations the "one indispensable feature of our foreign policy." British leaders wholly agreed with Hay's assessment, ceding control of the Western Hemisphere to the United States in the 1900s (after gaining access to America's future isthmian canal through the 1901 HAY-PAUNCEFOTE TREATIES) by removing their last troops from Canada and the West Indies in 1906. Britain's support of Hay's 1899 call for an "open door" in China for foreign investment symbolized London's growing willingness to follow Washington's international lead, and British and American troops fought side-by-side to suppress China's 1901 Boxer Rebellion.

Allies of a Kind

Europe plunged once more into war in 1914, and President Woodrow Wilson declared his country neutral, "in thought as well as in action." Most Americans, however, sided with the Allied cause. Germany threatened American interests in Latin America and the Pacific, and whereas the Allied blockade of the Central Powers (mildly) hindered American trade, Germany's submarine (U-boat) assaults on transatlantic shipping risked American lives and livelihoods. When Berlin began unrestricted submarine warfare in 1917, the United States entered the conflict.

Anglo-American financial ties made American intervention inevitable. Britain engaged $3.5 billion in American loans to finance the war, and American exports to the Allies doubled in every year of the conflict, reaching $4 billion by 1917. The Central Powers received less than one-tenth that amount. These fruits of America's industrial might, and the service of more than one million American infantrymen in France (where some 50,000 lost their lives) helped secure the Allied victory, while the conflict transformed the United States from a net debtor to a net creditor. America's share of world trade rose from 12.5 percent in 1914 to 25 percent in 1920, while Britain's share tumbled from 15.4 percent to 11.8 percent. This financial reversal highlights the war's most significant affect on Anglo-American relations, as the United States finally became unquestionably the stronger power.

Victory revealed Anglo-American divisions and the limits of American power. Wilson rejected the imperialist war aims of Britain and France, and called America their wartime "associate" rather than their ally. He considered the devastating war an opportunity to reform Europe's devious diplomatic style in favor of a more democratic international system, though he was not above using America's newfound financial might to get his way. Armed with Fourteen Points with which to remake the world, Wilson's idealism ran headlong into European pragmatists, chief among them Britain's prime minister, Lloyd George. His constituents demanded spoils for their victory, George said. They had suffered three million dead and wounded, while in America "not a shack" had been destroyed. He rejected Wilson's demands for a lenient German peace settlement and for decolonization, leaving the British Empire intact and the president without a treaty acceptable to his Senate.

Despite isolationist claims to the contrary, Americans in the 1920s engaged the world as never before. New York replaced London as the world's financial center and the globe's leading investor, and the number of American visitors to Europe leaped from 15,000 in 1912 to 251,000 in 1929. These newcomers were not always welcomed, especially after Washington refused to cancel London's war debt. British critics considered their spilled blood to be payment enough, and they railed against the commercial "invasion" from across the Atlantic. They complained that 95 percent of movies shown on British screens in 1925 came from Hollywood, and rebuffed visiting Yankee executives preaching "efficiency" and "standardization" as replacements for traditional production techniques. "Americanization" itself became a profane word in many British circles, though America's commercial and cultural influence seemed omnipresent.

These economic tensions did not preclude Anglo-American cooperation, and the two nations led the charge for naval disarmament throughout the 1920s. Yet, hamstrung by the Great Depression and by America's failure to join the League of Nations, the two countries refused to coordinate in punishing Japan's invasion of Manchuria in 1931, or to enforce German compliance with postwar treaties. By the mid-1930s, London and Washington had each erected restrictive trade barriers in self-defeating efforts to combat the global economic contagion. Convinced that trade had pulled their country into Europe's past wars, Congress passed a series of Neutrality Acts limiting future American financial ties to warring nations.

Americans could therefore only watch as Europe moved once more toward war.

The Special Relationship

Unlike Wilson a generation before, President Franklin Roosevelt rejected strict neutrality when war broke out in 1939. He considered Britain to be America's best defense against Germany, and he circumvented the Neutrality Acts by authorizing "cash and carry" sales, whereby London paid up front for goods and transported them on British ships. Roosevelt went even further a year later, directing the transfer of fifty aging destroyers to the Royal Navy in exchange for British bases. Such aid proved insufficient. "The moment approaches when we shall no longer be able to pay," Prime Minister Winston Churchill secretly cabled Roosevelt in 1940, who responded with the LEND-LEASE program, which ultimately provided nearly $21 billion in wartime aid.

The two countries were de facto allies long before the United States entered the war. They had coordinated military policy since 1938, especially for protection against a new generation of U-boats, and they shared war aims published as the ATLANTIC CHARTER four months before the Pearl Harbor attack. They promised victory would bring worldwide self-determination, freedom of the seas, freedom from want and fear, and unfettered access to global resources, each of these attacks against fascism but also against colonialism. A sworn imperialist, Churchill's need for American aid forced him to accept Washington's leadership in defining these goals, and this pattern of American dominance continued throughout the war. An American, Dwight D. Eisenhower, commanded Allied troops in Europe, while Washington controlled the war in the Pacific and the eventual occupation of Japan. Britain left the war in financial ruin; America left the war as the world's most powerful state.

Special Relationship. Prime Minister Margaret Thatcher *(left)* and President Ronald Reagan, close conservative allies in the 1980s, pose with their respective spouses, Dennis Thatcher and Nancy Reagan, at the White House. © UPI/CORBIS-BETTMANN

American diplomats again hoped to remake the world in their image. They began with Britain, and demanded that London open its empire to American goods as the price of postwar aid. Just as in 1918, Washington proved uninterested in absolving British war debts as payment for wartime sacrifices, and Britain reluctantly negotiated a further $3.5 billion in much-needed American reconstruction aid in 1945. Three years later, their funds exhausted, British diplomats led the way in seeking MARSHALL PLAN aid for Europe as a whole. In atomic weapons, too, Britain gave way, this time to an American monopoly, despite their collaborative wartime effort to split the atom, and despite American assurances that atomic energy would be a collaborative affair at war's end.

The Cold War gave London and Washington little recourse but to work together against global communism, and indeed the story of their Cold War relationship is one of long-term mutual dependence trumping short-term disagreements. They jointly broke the Soviet Union's blockade of Berlin in 1948–1949; they led the United Nations effort in the Korean War (1950–1953); and they helped charter the North Atlantic Treaty Organization (NATO), designed to thwart Soviet advances in Europe. Although publicly allied at nearly every turn, America's dominance and seemingly excessive anticommunism rankled British policymakers. Successive Whitehall governments strove to decrease their economic dependence on Washington by developing their own atomic bomb in the 1950s; by diminishing their reliance on American aid; by refusing to support American anticommunist trade restrictions, particularly Washington's complete embargo of communist China; and by pursuing a European solution to the troubled Middle East. This last effort ended in failure, after Gamal Nasser's 1956 nationalization of the Suez Canal imperiled Europe's access to Middle Eastern oil. London moved to retake the canal by force, but it never coordinated these moves with Washington, where furious policymakers criticized Britain's old-fashioned imperialism, which mocked America's anticolonial rhetoric. President Eisenhower's brief refusal to support the faltering pound ended Britain's involvement in the debacle, proving once more London's dependence on the United States.

America's Cold War plans equally relied on British political and strategic support. Britain's economy ranked third largest in the world (behind the United States and the USSR), and only Washington contributed more to the free world's defense. President John F. Kennedy consulted with Prime Minister Harold Macmillan every night of the Cuban missile crisis in 1962, for example, and successive British leaders took seriously their responsibility to temper American power with London's long global experience. In truth, each power needed the other. Their mutual interests in expanding democracy and trade overshadowed their divergent anticommunist approaches, even when British support for the Vietnam War never matched American expectations.

Britons gained a measure of cultural revenge for Hollywood and Coca-Cola in the early 1960s, when an unceasing stream of rock-and-roll bands (the British invasion) flooded American airwaves, beginning with the Beatles in 1964. The pound was never as strong as this musical influence, however, and American policymakers repeatedly propped up the faltering currency throughout the 1960s and 1970s. The two nations extended the breadth of their diplomatic relationship when London supported President Jimmy Carter's innovative emphasis on human rights diplomacy in the late 1970s. Prime Minister Margaret Thatcher and President Ronald Reagan, two like-minded conservatives, reinvigorated the special relationship in the 1980s: Reagan supported Thatcher's decision to defend the Falkland Islands from Argentina in 1982, and the prime minister's 1984 advice to trust the Soviet Union's Mikhail Gorbachev helped move the United States toward a new détente. The end of the Cold War did little to change this perception. British and American forces led the Allied effort in the 1991 Gulf War, and jointly struck Iraq's military throughout the ensuing decade. Indeed, the two countries moved seemingly in unison from the conservatism of Reagan-Thatcher to the new liberalism of Bill Clinton and Tony Blair, arguably the closest pair of Anglo-American leaders ever, their personal alliance symbolic of two nations whose financial and cultural development was, in the end, separated only by distance rather than ideology. Indeed, as final proof of Anglo-American intimacy, when terrorists destroyed the World Trade Center towers in September 2001, Britain lost more citizens than any other foreign nation.

BIBLIOGRAPHY

Allen, H. C. *Great Britain and the United States: A History of Anglo-American Relations, 1783–1952.* New York: St. Martin's, 1955.

Collier, Basil. *The Lion and the Eagle: British and Anglo-American Strategy, 1900–1950.* New York: Putnam, 1972.

Dobson, Alan P. *The Politics of the Anglo-American Economic Special Relationship, 1940–1987.* New York: St. Martin's, 1988.

Dunning, William A. *The British Empire and the United States: A Review of Their Relations during the Century of Peace following the Treaty of Ghent.* New York: Scribners, 1914.

Kunz, Diane B. *The Economic Crisis of the Suez Crisis.* Chapel Hill: University of North Carolina Press, 1991.

Ovendale, Ritchie. *Anglo-American Relations in the Twentieth Century.* New York: St. Martin's, 1998.

Jeffrey A. Engel

See also **British Debts; Colonial Policy, British; Ghent, Treaty of; Neutrality; Revolution, American; World War I War Debts;** *and vol. 9:* **Address to President Lincoln by the Working-Men of Manchester, England; Madison's War Message.**

GREAT DEPRESSION, the longest, deepest, and most pervasive depression in American history, lasted from 1929 to 1939. Its effects were felt in virtually all corners of the world, and it is one of the great economic calamities in history.

In previous depressions, such as those of the 1870s and 1890s, real per capita gross domestic product (GDP)—the sum of all goods and services produced, weighted by market prices and adjusted for inflation—had returned to its original level within five years. In the Great Depression, real per capita GDP was still below its 1929 level a decade later.

Economic activity began to decline in the summer of 1929, and by 1933 real GDP fell more than 25 percent, erasing all of the economic growth of the previous quarter century. Industrial production was especially hard hit, falling some 50 percent. By comparison, industrial production had fallen 7 percent in the 1870s and 13 percent in the 1890s.

From the depths of depression in 1933, the economy recovered until 1937. This expansion was followed by a brief but severe recession, and then another period of economic growth. It was not until the 1940s that previous levels of output were surpassed. This led some to wonder how long the depression would have continued without the advent of World War II.

In the absence of government statistics, scholars have had to estimate unemployment rates for the 1930s. The sharp drop in GDP and the anecdotal evidence of millions of people standing in soup lines or wandering the land as hoboes suggest that these rates were unusually high. It is widely accepted that the unemployment rate peaked above 25 percent in 1933 and remained above 14 percent into the 1940s. Yet these figures may underestimate the true hardship of the times: those who became too discouraged to seek work would not have been counted as unemployed. Likewise, those who moved from the cities to the countryside in order to feed their families would not have been counted. Even those who had jobs tended to see their hours of work fall: the average work week, 47 to 49 hours in the 1920s, fell to 41.7 hours in 1934 and stayed between 42 and 45 until 1942.

The banking system witnessed a number of "panics" during which depositors rushed to take their money out of banks rumored to be in trouble. Many banks failed under this pressure, while others were forced to merge: the number of banks in the United States fell 35 percent between 1929 and 1933.

While the Great Depression affected some sectors of the economy more than others, and thus some regions of the country more than others, all sectors and regions experienced a serious decline in output and a sharp rise in unemployment. The hardship of unemployment, though concentrated in the working class, affected millions in the middle class as well. Farmers suffered too, as the average price of their output fell by half (whereas the aggregate price level fell by only a third).

The Great Depression followed almost a decade of spectacular economic growth. Between 1921 and 1929, output per worker grew about 5.9 percent per year, roughly double the average in the twentieth century. Unemployment and inflation were both very low throughout this period as well. One troublesome characteristic of the 1920s, however, was that income distribution became significantly less equal. Also, a boom in housing construction, associated in part with an automobile-induced rush to the suburbs, collapsed in the late 1920s. And automakers themselves worried throughout the late 1920s that they had saturated their market fighting for market share; auto sales began to slide in the spring of 1929.

Technological advances in production processes (notably electrification, the assembly line, and continuous processing of homogenous goods such as chemicals) were largely responsible for the advances in productivity in the 1920s. These advances induced the vast bulk of firms to invest in new plants and equipment In the early 1920s, there were also innovative new products, such as radio, but the decade after 1925 was the worst in the twentieth century for new product innovation.

Hard Times. A couple of men call San Francisco's Howard Street home. As Dorothea Lange's photograph indicates, the Great Depression still had not run its course as of February 1937. LIBRARY OF CONGRESS

Causes of the Great Depression

In 1929 the standard economic theory suggested that a calamity such as the Great Depression could not happen: the economy possessed equilibrating mechanisms that would quickly move it toward full employment. For example, high levels of unemployment should put downward pressure on wages, thereby encouraging firms to increase employment. Before the Great Depression, most economists urged governments to concentrate on maintaining a balanced budget. Since tax receipts inevitably fell during a downturn, governments often increased tax rates and reduced spending. By taking money out of the economy, such policies tended to accelerate the downturn, though the effect was likely small.

As the depression continued, many economists advised the federal government to increase spending, in order to provide employment. Economists also searched for theoretical justifications for such policies. Some thought the depression was caused by overproduction: consumers did not wish to consume all that was produced. These analysts often attributed overproduction to the increased disparity in income that developed in the 1920s, for the poor spend a greater percentage of their income than do the rich. Others worried about a drop in the number of profitable investment opportunities. Often, these arguments were couched in apocalyptic terms: the Great Depression was thought to be the final crisis of capitalism, a crisis that required major institutional restructuring. Others, notably Joseph Schumpeter, pointed the finger at technology and suggested that the Great Depression reflected the failure of entrepreneurs to bring forth new products. He felt the depression was only temporary and a recovery would eventually occur.

The stock market crash of 1929 and the bank panics of the early 1930s were dramatic events. Many commentators emphasized the effect these had in decreasing the spending power of those who lost money. Some went further and blamed the Federal Reserve System for allowing the money supply, and thus average prices, to decline.

John Maynard Keynes in 1936 put forward a theory arguing that the amount individuals desired to save might exceed the amount they wanted to invest. In such an event, they would necessarily consume less than was produced (since, if we ignore foreign trade, total income must be either consumed or saved, while total output is the sum of consumption goods and investment goods). Keynes was skeptical of the strength of equilibrating mechanisms and shocked many economists who clung to a faith in the ability of the market system to govern itself. Yet within a decade the profession had largely embraced his approach,

PERSONAL EFFECTS OF THE DEPRESSION

The study of the human cost of unemployment reveals that a new class of poor and dependents is rapidly rising among the ranks of young sturdy ambitious laborers, artisans, mechanics, and professionals, who until recently maintained a relatively high standard of living and were the stable self-respecting citizens and taxpayers of the state. Unemployment and loss of income have ravaged numerous homes. It has broken the spirit of their members, undermined their health, robbed them of self-respect, and destroyed their efficiency and employability. Many households have been dissolved, little children parcelled out to friends, relatives, or charitable homes; husbands and wives, parents and children separated, temporarily or permanently. . . . Men young and old have taken to the road. Day after day the country over they stand in the breadlines for food. . . . The law must step in and brand as criminals those who have neither desire nor inclination to violate accepted standards of society. . . . Physical privation undermines body and heart. . . . Idleness destroys not only purchasing power, lowering the standards of living, but also destroys efficiency and finally breaks the spirit.

SOURCE: From the 1932 Report of the California Unemployment Commission.

in large part because it allowed them to analyze deficient consumption and investment demand without reference to a crisis of capitalism. Moreover, Keynes argued that, because a portion of income was used for taxes and output included government services, governments might be able to correct a situation of deficient demand by spending more than they tax.

In the early postwar period, Keynesian theory dominated economic thinking. Economists advised governments to spend more than they taxed during recessions and tax more than spend during expansions. Although governments were not always diligent in following this prescription, the limited severity of early postwar business cycles was seen as a vindication of Keynesian theory. Yet little attention was paid to the question of how well it could explain the Great Depression.

In 1963, Milton Friedman and Anna Schwartz proposed a different view of the depression. They argued that, contrary to Keynesian theory, the deflationary actions of the Federal Reserve were primarily at fault. In the ensuing decades, Keynesians and "monetarists" argued for the supremacy of their favored theory. The result was a recognition that both explanations had limitations. Keynesians struggled to comprehend why either consumption or investment demand would have fallen so precipitously as to trigger the depression (though saturation in the housing and automobile markets, among others, may have been important). Monetarists struggled to explain how smallish decreases in the money supply could trigger such a massive downturn, especially since the price level fell as fast as the supply of money, and thus real (inflation-adjusted) aggregate demand need not have fallen.

In the 1980s and 1990s, some economists argued that the actions of the Federal Reserve had caused banks to decrease their willingness to loan money, leading to a severe decrease in consumption and, especially, investment. Others argued that the Federal Reserve and central banks in other countries were constrained by the gold standard, under which the value of a particular currency is fixed to the price of gold.

Some economists today speak of a consensus that holds the Federal Reserve, the gold standard, or both, largely responsible for the Great Depression. Others suggest that a combination of several theoretical approaches is needed to understand this calamity.

Most economists have analyzed the depression from a macroeconomic perspective. This perspective, spawned by the depression and by Keynes's theories, focuses on the interaction of aggregate economic variables, including consumption, investment, and the money supply. Only fairly recently have some macroeconomists begun to consider how other factors, such as technological innovation, would influence the level of economic activity.

Beginning initially in the 1930s, however, some students of the Great Depression have examined the unusually high level of process innovation in the 1920s and the lack of product innovation in the decade after 1925. The introduction of new production processes requires investment but may well cause firms to let some of their workforce go; by reducing prices, new processes may also reduce the amount consumers spend. The introduction of new products almost always requires investment and more employees; they also often increase the propensity of individuals to consume. The time path of technological innovation may thus explain much of the observed movements in consumption, investment, and employment during the interwar period. There may also be important interactions with the monetary variables discussed above: in particular, firms are especially dependent on bank finance in the early stages of developing a new product.

Effects of the Great Depression

The psychological, cultural, and political repercussions of the Great Depression were felt around the world, but it had a significantly different impact in different countries. In particular, it is widely agreed that the rise of the Nazi Party in Germany was associated with the economic turmoil of the 1930s. No similar threat emerged in the United States. While President Franklin Roosevelt did introduce a variety of new programs, he was initially elected on a traditional platform that pledged to balance the budget. Why did the depression cause less political change in the United States than elsewhere? A much longer experience with democracy may have been important. In addition, a faith in the "American dream," whereby anyone who worked hard could succeed, was apparently retained and limited the agitation for political change.

Effects on individuals. Much of the unemployment experience of the depression can be accounted for by workers who moved in and out of periods of employment and unemployment that lasted for weeks or months. These individuals suffered financially, to be sure, but they were generally able to save, borrow, or beg enough to avoid the severest hardships. Their intermittent periods of employment helped to stave off a psychological sense of failure. Yet there were also numerous workers who were unemployed for years at a time. Among this group were those with the least skills or the poorest attitudes. Others found that having been unemployed for a long period of time made them less attractive to employers. Long-term unemployment appears to have been concentrated among people in their late teens and early twenties and those older than fifty-five. For many that came of age during the depression, World War II would provide their first experience of full-time employment.

With unemployment rates exceeding 25 percent, it was obvious that most of the unemployed were not responsible for their plight. Yet the ideal that success came to those who worked hard remained in place, and thus those who were unemployed generally felt a severe sense of failure. The incidence of mental health problems rose, as did problems of family violence. For both psychological and economic reasons, decisions to marry and to have children were delayed. Although the United States provided more relief to the unemployed than many other countries (including Canada), coverage was still spotty. In particular, recent immigrants to the United States were often denied relief. Severe malnutrition afflicted many, and the palpable fear of it, many more.

Effects by gender and race. Federal, state, and local governments, as well as many private firms, introduced explicit policies in the 1930s to favor men over women for jobs. Married women were often the first to be laid off. At a time of widespread unemployment, it was felt that jobs should be allocated only to male "breadwinners." Nevertheless, unemployment rates among women were lower than for men during the 1930s, in large part because the labor market was highly segmented by gender, and the service sector jobs in which women predominated were less affected by the depression. The female labor force participation rate—the proportion of women seeking or possessing paid work—had been rising for decades; the 1930s saw only a slight increase; thus, the depression acted to slow this societal change (which would greatly accelerate during World War II, and then again in the postwar period).

Breadline. Out-of-work men wait to receive food—in this instance, cabbage and potatoes—from a federal relief agency in Cleveland, Ohio, 1933. ASSOCIATED PRESS/WORLD WIDE PHOTOS

Many surveys found unemployment rates among blacks to be 30 to 50 percent higher than among whites. Discrimination was undoubtedly one factor: examples abound of black workers being laid off to make room for white workers. Yet another important factor was the preponderance of black workers in industries (such as automobiles) that experienced the greatest reductions in employment. And the migration of blacks to northern industrial centers during the 1920s may have left them especially prone to seniority-based layoffs.

Cultural effects. One might expect the Great Depression to have induced great skepticism about the economic system and the cultural attitudes favoring hard work and consumption associated with it. As noted, the ideal of hard work was reinforced during the depression, and those who lived through it would place great value in work after the war. Those who experienced the depression were disposed to thrift, but they were also driven to value their consumption opportunities. Recall that through the 1930s it was commonly thought that one cause of the depression was that people did not wish to consume enough: an obvious response was to value consumption more.

The New Deal. The nonmilitary spending of the federal government accounted for 1.5 percent of GDP in 1929

Soup Kitchen. Eleanor Roosevelt, wife of the president-elect, helps feed unemployed women at the Grand Central Restaurant in New York, 1932. ASSOCIATED PRESS/WORLD WIDE PHOTOS

but 7.5 percent in 1939. Not only did the government take on new responsibilities, providing temporary relief and temporary public works employment, but it established an ongoing federal presence in social security (both pensions and unemployment insurance), welfare, financial regulation and deposit insurance, and a host of other areas. The size of the federal government would grow even more in the postwar period. Whether the size of government today is larger than it would have been without the depression is an open question. Some scholars argue for a "ratchet effect," whereby government expenditures increase during crises, but do not return to the original level thereafter. Others argue that the increase in government brought on by the depression would have eventually happened anyhow.

In the case of unemployment insurance, at least, the United States might today have a more extensive system if not for the depression. Both Congress and the Supreme Court were more oriented toward states' rights in the 1930s than in the early postwar period. The social security system thus gave substantial influence to states. Some have argued that this has encouraged a "race to the bottom," whereby states try to attract employers with lower unemployment insurance levies. The United States spends only a fraction of what countries such as Canada spend per capita on unemployment insurance.

Some economists have suggested that public works programs exacerbated the unemployment experience of the depression. They argue that many of those on relief would have otherwise worked elsewhere. However, there were more workers seeking employment than there were job openings; thus, even if those on relief did find work elsewhere, they would likely be taking the jobs of other people.

The introduction of securities regulation in the 1930s has arguably done much to improve the efficiency, fairness, and thus stability of American stock markets. Enhanced bank supervision, and especially the introduction of deposit insurance from 1934, ended the scourge of bank panics: most depositors no longer had an incentive to rush to their bank at the first rumor of trouble. But deposit insurance was not an unmixed blessing; in the wake of the failure of hundreds of small savings and loan institutions decades later, many noted that deposit insurance allowed banks to engage in overly risky activities without being penalized by depositors. The Roosevelt administration also attempted to stem the decline in wages and prices by establishing "industry codes," whereby firms and unions in an industry agreed to maintain set prices and wages. Firms seized the opportunity to collude and agreed in many cases to restrict output in order to inflate prices; this particular element of the New Deal likely served to slow the recovery. Similar attempts to enhance agricultural prices were more successful, at least in the goal of raising farm incomes (but thus increased the cost of food to others).

International Effects

It was long argued that the Great Depression began in the United States and spread to the rest of the world. Many countries, including Canada and Germany, experienced similar levels of economic hardship. In the case of Europe, it was recognized that World War I and the treaties ending it (which required large reparation payments from those countries that started and lost the war) had created weaknesses in the European economy, especially in its financial system. Thus, despite the fact that trade and capital flows were much smaller than today, the American downturn could trigger downturns throughout Europe. As economists have come to emphasize the role the international gold standard played in, at least, exacerbating the depression, the argument that the depression started in the United States has become less central.

With respect to the rest of the world, there can be little doubt that the downturn in economic activity in North America and Europe had a serious impact. Many Third World countries were heavily dependent on exports and suffered economic contractions as these markets dried up. At the same time, they were hit by a decrease in foreign investment flows, especially from the United States, which was a reflection of the monetary contraction in the United States. Many Third World countries, especially in Latin America, responded by introducing high tariffs and striving to become self-sufficient. This may have helped them recover from the depression, but probably served to seriously slow economic growth in the postwar period.

Developed countries also introduced high tariffs during the 1930s. In the United States, the major one was the Smoot-Hawley Tariff of 1930, which arguably encouraged other countries to retaliate with tariffs of their own. Governments hoped that the money previously spent on imports would be spent locally and enhance employment. In return, however, countries lost access to foreign markets, and therefore employment in export-oriented sectors. The likely effect of the increase in tariffs was to decrease incomes around the world by reducing the efficiency of the global economy; the effect the tariffs had on employment is less clear.

BIBLIOGRAPHY

Barnard, Rita. *The Great Depression and the Culture of Abundance: Kenneth Fearing, Nathanael West, and Mass Culture in the 1930s.* New York: Cambridge University Press, 1995. Explores the impact of the depression on cultural attitudes and literature.

Bernanke, Ben S. *Essays on the Great Depression.* Princeton, N.J.: Princeton University Press, 2000. Emphasizes bank panics and the gold standard.

Bernstein, Michael A. *The Great Depression: Delayed Recovery and Economic Change in America, 1929–1939.* New York: Cambridge University Press, 1987. Argues for the interaction of technological and monetary forces and explores the experience of several industries.

Bordo, Michael D., Claudia Goldin, and Eugene N. White, eds. *The Defining Moment: The Great Depression and the American Economy in the Twentieth Century.* Chicago: University of Chicago Press, 1998. Evaluates the impact of a range of New Deal policies and international agreements.

Friedman, Milton, and Anna J. Schwartz. *A Monetary History of the United States, 1867–1960.* Princeton, N.J.: Princeton University Press, 1963.

Hall, Thomas E., and J. David Ferguson. *The Great Depression: An International Disaster of Perverse Economic Policies.* Ann Arbor: University of Michigan Press, 1998.

Keynes, John M. *The General Theory Of Employment, Interest, and Money.* New York: St. Martin's Press, 1964. Original edition published in 1936.

Margo, Robert A. "Employment and Unemployment in the 1930s." *Journal of Economic Perspectives* 7, no. 2 (spring 1993): 41–59.

Rosenbloom, Joshua, and William Sundstrom. "The Sources of Regional Variation in the Severity of the Great Depression: Evidence from U.S. Manufacturing 1919–1937." *Journal of Economic History* 59 (1999): 714–747.

Rosenof, Theodore. *Economics in the Long Run: New Deal Theorists and Their Legacies, 1933–1993.* Chapel Hill: University of North Carolina Press, 1997. Looks at how Keynes, Schumpeter, and others influenced later economic analysis.

Rothermund, Dietmar. *The Global Impact of the Great Depression, 1929–1939.* London: Routledge, 1996. Extensive treatment of the Third World.

Schumpeter, Joseph A. *Business Cycles: A Theoretical, Historical, and Statistical Analysis of the Capitalist Process.* New York: McGraw-Hill, 1939.

Szostak, Rick. *Technological Innovation and the Great Depression.* Boulder, Colo.: Westview Press, 1995. Explores the causes and effects of the unusual course that technological innovation took between the wars.

Temin, Peter. *Did Monetary Forces Cause the Great Depression?* New York: Norton, 1976. Classic early defense of Keynesian explanation.

———. *Lessons from the Great Depression.* Cambridge, Mass.: MIT Press, 1989. Emphasizes the role of the gold standard.

Rick Szostak

See also **Agricultural Price Support; Banking: Bank Failures, Banking Crisis of 1933; Business Cycles; Keynesianism; New Deal;** *and vol. 9:* **Advice to the Unemployed in the Great Depression, June 11, 1932.**

GREAT GATSBY, THE, a novel by F. Scott Fitzgerald that, over the several decades after its publication in 1925, came to be regarded as one of the most elegant, efficient, and profound pieces of fiction ever written in the United States. *The Great Gatsby* is a concentrated meditation on "the American dream," understood as the faith that anyone, even of the most humble origins, can attain wealth and social standing in the United States through talent and individual initiative. Fitzgerald explores the compelling appeal of this dream, and the circumstances that render it as deceptive as it is enduring.

Fitzgerald's protagonist is a young man from North Dakota, James Gatz, who changes his name to Jay Gatsby and manufactures a persona "out of his own Platonic self-conception." While in his soldier's uniform just prior to service in World War I, Gatsby falls in love with Daisy, a beautiful, rich young woman whose voice has "the sound of money." After the war, Gatsby pursues Daisy, even though she has by then married a gruff and tasteless man of her own class. Gatsby buys a huge, garish mansion on Long Island near Daisy's home and tries to impress her and her social set with lavish parties financed, as some of his guests rightly suspect, by the illegal sale of alcoholic beverages. But Daisy rejects Gatsby's suit, as her feelings and behavior are controlled by the conventions of her class in ways that the innocent "American dreamer" does not understand. In the end, it is inherited wealth and social standing that determine much more of one's destiny than is determined by talent and individual initiative, readers of *The Great Gatsby* are led to conclude.

Much of the power of *The Great Gatsby* derives from Fitzgerald's having provided readers with an opportunity to simultaneously see through the pretender's illusions and identify deeply with his aspirations and even love him for having made the effort. Gatsby himself "turned out all right in the end," Fitzgerald's narrator insists. The problem was "the foul dust that floated in the wake of Gatsby's dreams," meaning the particulars of American history, the class structure, and all the webs of social circumstance in which an individual's capacities for hope are embedded. The generic human impulses that drive us to better ourselves often impel us to foolish pursuits, and to ignore the conditions under which our striving actually takes place—but those impulses themselves are to be treasured.

BIBLIOGRAPHY

Sklar, Robert. *F. Scott Fitzgerald: The Last Laocoön.* New York: Oxford University Press, 1967.

David A. Hollinger

See also **Jazz Age.**

GREAT LAKES. The Great Lakes, also called the Inland Seas, consist of five connecting freshwater lakes in east central North America that straddle the international border between Canada and the United States. Collectively they constitute the world's largest body of freshwater, with a surface area of 94,000 square miles (244,000 sq. km) and 5,500 cubic miles (23,000 cu. km) of water. The lakes contain approximately 18 percent of the world's supply of freshwater, with only the polar ice caps having more. From west to east, the lakes are Superior (the largest and deepest of the lakes), Michigan, Huron, Erie (the shallowest), and Ontario (the smallest); they collectively extend about 850 miles (1370 km) west to east and 700 miles (1125 km) from north to south. The Great Lakes form the western portion of the greater St. Lawrence hydrographic system, extending from Minnesota to the Atlantic Ocean.

Lake Superior connects to Huron through Sault Sainte Marie (St. Marys River), and Lake Michigan joins Huron via the Straits of Mackinac. A major inlet north of Lake Huron is Georgian Bay, which lies entirely within Canada. Waters from the three upper Great Lakes (Superior, Michigan, and Huron) flow through the St. Clair River, Lake St. Claire, and the Detroit River into Lake Erie, which in turn is connected to Lake Ontario through the Niagara River and Niagara Falls. The five lakes then drain northeastward into the Atlantic Ocean through the St. Lawrence River. The Great Lakes' drainage basin covers 295,200 square miles (764,570 sq. km) and includes portions of eight states (Minnesota, Wisconsin, Michigan, Illinois, Indiana, Ohio, Pennsylvania, and New York) and the Canadian province of Ontario, which extends along the north shore of four of the lakes. Lake Michigan lies entirely within the boundaries of the United States; the international boundary bisects the other four lakes.

Geologically, the Great Lakes system began to develop three million years ago, during the Precambrian Era, a time of volcanic activity and geological stress that formed major mountain systems that later eroded. Most of central North America was covered by marine seas during the Paleozoic Era, and major continental glaciers advanced over the Great Lakes region beginning about one million years ago. As a result of a series of glacial formations and retreats, glacial deposits and large volumes of meltwater created a basin larger than the present-day Great Lakes. The most recent Great Lakes basin formed between 32,000 and 10,000 years ago; lake levels stabilized about 2,400 years ago. Five biotic provinces are defined on the basis of floral and faunal characteristics, and include Hudsonian to the extreme north, Canadian (Georgian Bay, Lake Nipissing, and the Ottawa River), Carolinian-Canadian Transition (present-day Wisconsin, Michigan, and southern Ontario), Illinoisan (southern Lake Michigan basin), and Carolinian (Ohio, Pennsylvania, and western New York).

Paleo-Indian hunters and gatherers occupied the Great Lakes basin before 9500 B.C.E. and were followed by semisedentary Early Archaic peoples who exploited a wider variety of large and small fauna and diverse flora. More populous and technologically advanced Late Archaic peoples formed small sedentary communities beginning in 3,000 B.C.E. The Archaic-Woodland Transition (1500–100 B.C.E.) was characterized by large sedentary villages, plant domestication, the development of pottery, and cultural adaptations to diverse econiches. The Middle Woodland period (c. 200 B.C.E.–500 C.E.) saw the development of Hopewell culture in Ohio and adjacent states, characterized by circular and serpentine earthworks, enormous artificial mounds, elaborate burial practices, and long-distance trade systems for exotic goods used in burials, such as marine shells from Florida and obsidian from Wyoming. Other areas of the Great Lakes continued an Early Woodland pattern.

The subsequent Late Woodland period (500–1600 C.E.) saw the incursions of peoples and ideas from the Mississippi Valley; an emphasis on the cultivation of maize, beans, squash, and sunflowers; larger populations and settlements; and territorial conflicts between tribes. At European contact a number of major tribes were established in the Great Lakes basin, among them the Ojibwe, Menominee, Winnebago, Miami, Potawatomi, Fox, Sauk, Kickapoo, and Mascouten tribes in the upper Great Lakes region, and the Erie, Iroquois (Seneca, Oneida, Cayuga, Onondaga, and Mohawk), and Wenro south of lakes Erie and Ontario, with the Ottawa, Petun, Huron, and Neutral tribes north of those lakes. Miamis, Mascoutens, Mesquakies, and Shawnees occupied the area around Lake Michigan.

The French explorer Jacques Cartier, seeking a northwest passage to the Orient, located the St. Lawrence River during the years of 1534 and 1535. Samuel de Champlain visited lakes Ontario and Huron in 1610, initiating a period of French exploration characterized by missionaries, fur traders, and territorial conflicts between the emerging New France and British colonies along the Atlantic seaboard. The Ottawa River provided a route for Jesuit missionaries and French trappers and traders, who soon visited the upper lakes. Jean Nicolet reached the shores of

TABLE 1

Great Lakes: Physical Features and Population

	Superior	Michigan	Huron	Erie	Ontario	Combined
Elevation[a] (feet)	600	577	577	569	243	
Length (miles)	350	307	206	241	193	
Breadth (miles)	160	118	183	57	53	
Average Depth[a] (feet)	483	279	195	62	283	
Maximum Depth[a] (feet)	1,332	925	750	210	802	
Volume[a] (cu mi)	2,900	1,180	850	116	393	5,439
Water Area (sq mi)	31,700	22,300	23,000	9,910	7,340	94,250
Land Drainage Area[b] (sq mi)	49,300	45,600	51,700	30,140	24,720	201,460
Total Area (sq mi)	81,000	67,900	74,700	40,050	32,060	295,710
Shoreline Length[c] (miles)	2,726	1,638	3,827	871	712	10,210[d]
Retention Time (years)	191	99	22	2.6	6	
Outlet	St. Marys River	Straits of Mackinac	St. Clair River	Niagara River/ Welland Canal	St. Lawrence River	
Population U.S. (1990)	425,548	10,057,026	1,502,687	10,017,530	2,704,284	24,707,075
Canada (1991)	181,573		1,191,467	1,664,639	5,446,611	8,484,290
Totals	607,121	10,057,026	2,694,154	11,682,169	8,150,895	33,191,365

a. Measured at Low Water datum.
b. Land drainage area for Lake Huron includes St. Marys River; for Lake Erie includes the St. Clair-Detroit system; for Lake Ontario includes the Niagara River.
c. Including islands.
d. These totals are greater than the sum of the shoreline length for the lakes because they include the connecting channels (excluding the St. Lawrence River).

SOURCE: Government of Canada and United States Environmental Protection Agency (1995), 4.

Lake Michigan in 1634, and Isaac Jogues and Charles Raymbault ventured to Sault Sainte Marie seven years later. By 1672 the Jesuits had compiled and published an accurate map of Lake Superior. The Iroquois Wars (1641–1701) and a period of French incursion, settlement, and fortifications (1720–1761) followed. By 1673 Louis Jolliet and Jacques Marquette had begun explorations of the upper Mississippi River, followed by Robert Cavelier, Sieur de La Salle, and his expedition (1678–1684). By 1683 a highly accurate map of all the Great Lakes, based on these and other expeditions and journeys, was compiled by Father Louis Hennepin.

Drawn by the fur trade and seeking new lands, English traders from Albany began to explore the upper Great Lakes in the 1690s. To counter this, in 1701 Antoine de la Mothe Cadillac established Fort Pontchartrain du Détroit, which commanded the narrow river between Lake Erie and Lake Huron. It became the focus of French control of the upper lakes and denied access to English traders and exploration. The conflict between the English and French for the control of North America, which centered on the Great Lakes, involved a series of wars and minor conflicts that covered a period of seventy-five years and included participation by Native Americans on both sides. The FRENCH AND INDIAN WAR culminated with the surrender of French Canada to the British in 1760. Pontiac's War (1763–1764) heralded a transitional period with American exploration, migrations, and settlement of the region along the southern shores of the Great Lakes. Notably the Definitive Treaty of Peace signed between Britain and the United States in 1783, ending the Revolutionary War, included an article that called for control of the lakes to be shared between British Canada and the American colonies.

The WAR OF 1812 (1812–1815), between the Americans and the British, also involved Native Americans on both sides in the region of Detroit and the Niagara Frontier. Many of the engagements were fought on and adjoining the Great Lakes. A major naval engagement, the battle of Lake Erie (10 September 1813), was won by the Americans and helped to ensure the sovereignty of the United States through the Treaty of Ghent (1814) and the Rush-Bagot Agreement (1817), which established limitations on naval forces on the Great Lakes.

The promise of agricultural land was a major attraction for immigrants; hence agrarian settlements and fisheries developed on both the American and the Canadian sides of the border during the 1800s. City building, nation building, and industrialization were hallmarks of the nineteenth century as dairying, fruit and vegetable cultivation, logging, and forest exploitation gave way to iron and steel production, papermaking, and chemical manufacture in the twentieth century. The forests around the Great Lakes provided hardwoods and pine, while the Lake Superior region yielded high-quality iron ore and copper. Major agricultural products included corn, wheat, soybeans, grapes, pork, and beef cattle. The industry of the region was, and remains, highly diversified, but significant quantities of iron ore, coal, minerals, grain, and manufactured products are transported throughout the Great Lakes and shipped overseas. Notable transportation improvements included the construction of the Erie Canal, from Albany to Buffalo, New York (completed in 1825); the Canadian Lachine Canal, bypassing rapids in the St. Lawrence River; and the Welland Canal (1829), joining lakes Erie and Ontario. The latter two were surpassed in 1959 by the completion of the St. Lawrence Seaway.

Commercial fishing began about 1820 and peaked between 1889 and 1899 but native fish diminished and have been replaced by introduced species. Sport fishing, water recreation, and cultural tourism have become economically significant in spite of a deterioration in water quality and habitat that accompanied urbanization and industrialization. Pollution, pathogens, eutrophication, toxic contaminants, diminished oxygen levels, the introduction of exotic flora and fauna (such as zebra mussels), and a recent drop in lake water levels are of major concern to inhabitants of the Great Lakes basin.

Perhaps surprisingly, a number of upper Great Lakes cities were founded earlier than many of the settlements situated along the shores of the lower lakes. In the main lakes the early settlements were fur trading posts, such as Green Bay in modern Wisconsin at the mouth of the Fox River, established in 1634 and with a population of more than 103,000 by 2000. Other posts were established at Chicago in 1673; at Thunder Bay, Ontario, in 1678; and at Duluth, Minnesota, in 1692. In the lower lakes Hamilton, Ontario, was established in 1669 and by 2000 was an industrial center with 320,000 inhabitants; Buffalo, New York, a former Seneca Indian village settled by Europeans in 1679, was by 2000 an industrial city with more than 300,000 inhabitants. Detroit, settled in 1701, has become a center of automotive production and has a population exceeding 1,045,000 in 2000. Established in 1720, Toronto, now the capital of the province of Ontario and a financial and commercial center, had a 2000 census of 640,000. Because explorers, missionaries, and travelers could bypass Lake Erie by venturing from Lake Ontario and the Ontario River to the upper lakes, settlements along Lake Erie were founded late in the region's history. These include Erie, Pennsylvania, in 1753 (in 2000 an industrial and agricultural community of 105,000); Cleveland, Ohio, in 1786 (a major center of heavy industry with a population exceeding 506,000 in 2000); London, Ontario, in 1792 (by 2000 an industrial and agricultural center with more than 303,000 persons); and Toledo, Ohio, in 1794 (another industrial community, with 323,000 persons in 2000). Rochester, New York, now a center for imaging science, was founded on the Genessee River, which flows into Lake Ontario, in 1789; Milwaukee, Wisconsin, situated at the mouth of the river of the same name, was founded in 1800 and was a major center of the brewing industry. In 2000 Rochester had a population of 217,000, and Milwaukee's census exceeded 617,000. Chicago grew from a trading post to become a leading rail and lake transport hub, as well as an industrial and commercial center with a population of 2,840,000 in 2000.

BIBLIOGRAPHY

Ashworth, William. *Great Lakes Journey: A New Look at America's Fresh-water Coast.* Detroit: Wayne State University Press, 2000.

Bogue, Margaret B. *Around the Shores of Lake Superior: A Guide to Historic Sites.* Madison: University of Wisconsin Press, 1979.

———. *Fishing the Great Lakes: An Environmental History, 1783–1933.* Madison: University of Wisconsin Press, 2000.

Burns, Noel M. *Erie: The LakeThat Survived.* Totowa, N.J.: Rowman & Allanheld, 1985.

Cantor, George. *The Great Lakes Guidebook,* 3 vols. Ann Arbor: University of Michigan Press, 1978–1980.

———. *The Great Lakes Guidebook: Lake Huron and Eastern Lake Michigan.* Ann Arbor: University of Michigan Press, 1985.

———. *The Great Lakes Guidebook: Lakes Ontario and Erie.* Ann Arbor: University of Michigan Press, 1985.

Gentilcore, R. Louis, ed. *Historical Atlas of Canada, vol. 2: The Land Transformed, 1800–1891.* Toronto: University of Toronto Press, 1990.

Government of Canada and United States Environmental Protection Agency. Great Lakes Factsheet No. 1. In *The Great Lakes: An Environmental Atlas and Resource Book,* 3d ed., 1995. Available from http://www.epa.gov/glnpo/atlas/fact1txt.html.

Harris, R. Cole, ed. *Historical Atlas of Canada, vol. 1: From the Beginning to 1800.* Toronto: University of Toronto Press, 1987.

Hatcher, Harlan H. *The Great Lakes.* London and New York: Oxford University Press, 1944.

———. *Lake Erie.* Indianapolis and New York: Bobbs-Merrill, 1945. Reprinted Westport, Conn: Greenwood, 1971.

Hatcher, Harlan H., and Erich A. Walter. *Pictorial History of the Great Lakes.* New York: Crown, 1963.

Hough, Jack L. *Geology of the Great Lakes.*Urbana: University of Illinois Press, 1958.

Karpinski, Louis C. *Maps of Famous Cartographers Depicting North America: An Historical Atlas of the Great Lakes and Michigan,* 2d ed. Amsterdam: Meridian, 1977. First published 1880.

Kerr, Donald, ed. *Historical Atlas of Canada, vol. 3: Addressing the Twentieth Century, 1891–1961.* Toronto: University of Toronto Press, 1993.

Kuchenberg, Tom. *Reflections in a Tarnished Mirror: The Use and Abuse of the Great Lakes.* Sturgeon Bay, Wis.: Golden Glow, 1978.

Landon, Fred. *Lake Huron.* New York: Russell & Russell, 1972. First published 1944.

Ludwigson, John O. *Two Nations, One Lake: Science in Support of Great Lakes Management.* Ottawa: Canadian National Committee for International Hydrological Decade, 1974.

Mason, Ronald J. *Great Lakes Archaeology.* New York: Academic Press, 1981.

McGucken, William. *Lake Erie Rehabilitated: Controlling Cultural Eutrophication, 1960s–1990s.* Akron, Ohio: University of Akron Press, 2000.

Office of the Great Lakes. *Great Lakes Trends: Into the New Millennium.* Lansing: Michigan Department of Environmental Quality, 2000.

Pound, Arthur. *Lake Ontario.* Port Washington, N.Y.: Kennikat Press, 1970.

Skaggs, David C. *A Signal Victory: The Lake Erie Campaign. 1812–1813.* Annapolis, Md.: Naval Institute Press. 1997.

St. John, John R. *A True Description of the Lake Superior Country.* Grand Rapids, Mich.: Black Letter-Press, 1976.

Tanner, Helen H., ed. *Atlas of Great Lakes Indian History.* Norman: University of Oklahoma Press for The Newberry Library, 1987.

Thompson, Mark L. *Graveyard of the Lakes.* Detroit: Wayne State University Press, 2000.

Thwaites, Reuben Gold. *The Jesuit Relations and Allied Documents.* 73 vols. Cleveland: Burrows Brothers, 1896–1901.

Charles C. Kolb

See also **Expeditions and Explorations: French; Michigan, Upper Peninsula of; Tribes.**

GREAT LAKES NAVAL CAMPAIGNS OF 1812. After the fall of New France in 1760, the British navy ruled the Great Lakes. Its undisputed authority of the northern waters proved valuable during PONTIAC'S WAR (1763–1764) and the American Revolution (1775–1783). Following the advent of American authority on the lakes (1796), both governments supported armed vessels as necessary to maintain their authority.

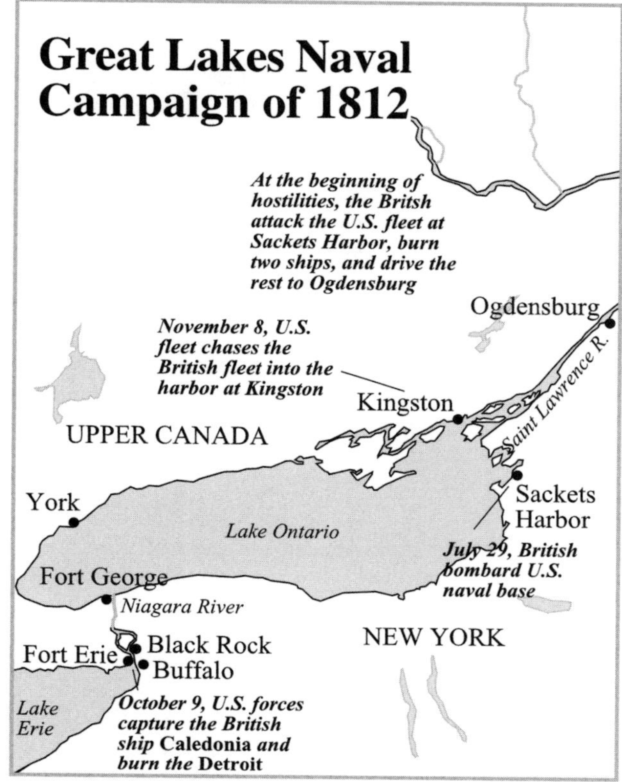

A potent challenge to British naval supremacy came during the War of 1812. After losing two schooners to the British at Sackets Harbor in the early months of the War of 1812, the Americans realized the need to establish adequate naval protection on the northern waters. When Commodore Isaac Chauncey arrived at Sackets Harbor on 6 October 1812 to assume command of American naval operations, he ordered Lt. Jesse D. Elliott to purchase vessels for a new fleet. On 8 October two British ships cast anchor across the Niagara off Fort Erie. Seeing an opportunity, Elliott's force boarded the ships early the following morning; the *Caledonia* was captured, and the *Detroit* grounded and was burned.

One month later, Chauncey's reconstructed squadron of ten vessels left Sackets Harbor to intercept the British fleet returning southward from Fort George. The flagship *Royal George* was pursued into Kingston harbor, at the eastern end of Lake Ontario, but there, with the aid of the shore batteries, it drove off the American fleet. On 11 October the British schooner *Simcoe* was destroyed, and before the campaign closed, three merchant ships were captured by the Americans. In September 1813 Commodore Oliver Hazard Perry's American fleet won the Battle of Lake Erie, thus securing American control of Lake Erie and making an invasion into Canada possible.

With the return of peace, both nations faced the necessity of building new fleets on the lakes to safeguard their respective interests. This prospect was averted through an agreement initiated by President James Monroe in 1815 and made formal two years later with the Great Lakes Disarmament Agreement.

BIBLIOGRAPHY

Coles, Henry L. *The War of 1812.* Chicago: University of Chicago Press, 1965.

Morison, Samuel Eliot. *"Old Bruin": Commodore Matthew C. Perry, 1794–1858.* Boston: Little, Brown, 1967.

Pratt, Fletcher. *Preble's Boys: Commodore Preble and the Birth of American Sea Power.* New York: Sloane, 1950.

Robert W. Bingham/A. R.

See also **Canadian-American Waterways; Great Lakes; Lake Erie, Battle of; Navy, United States; Niagara Campaigns; Ships of the Line; War of 1812.**

GREAT LAKES STEAMSHIPS date from 1816, when the first such ship, the Canadian *Frontenac*, entered service, followed by the American *Walk-in-the-Water* in 1818. During most of the nineteenth century, sailing ships continued to haul most of the bulk cargoes (iron ore, coal, stone), whereas steamships took over most of the package freight and passenger business. Most of the wooden vessels on the Lakes served a dual role as package freight and passenger carriers.

To avoid paying track usage fees to competing railroads, many East Coast railroad companies used these boats as connector lines between where their rail lines ended along Lakes Ontario and Erie and debarkation points at Milwaukee, Chicago, and other western Lakes ports, where they either had arrangements with subsidiary lines or business partnerships with other carriers. These early vessels were first side-wheel-powered like river vessels (including the *Frontenac* and the *Walk-in-the-Water*), but by the 1850s, John Ericsson's invention of a submerged propeller became increasingly popular. Passenger quarters were located along the upper decks, and cargo was carried below the main deck, with large gangway doors in the sides to facilitate ease of movement. Fire remained an ever-present danger, as were storms, which frequently occurred with little warning on the Lakes.

As the lumber regions of Michigan, Wisconsin, and Minnesota became active in the 1870s, a new type of vessel was used to haul this type of awkward cargo. At the same time, this design also served in the iron ore, the stone, and the coal trade and quickly became the dominant vessel arrangement for these routes. The first of these vessels, the *R. J. Hackett* (1869), conceived of by Cleveland ship owner E. M. Peck, placed the navigating cabins at the bow and the engines and crew's quarters at the back of the hull, leaving a long, open deck broken by hatches to provide access to the vessel's holds. The high bow and stern cabins protected lumber cargos stored on deck from the wind and waves, and provided ready access to the holds for other bulk cargos. While the *R. J. Hackett* and many other vessels of this type were still built of wood, iron and steel would follow in time.

A landmark use of iron occurred in 1843 with the construction of the gunboat USS *Michigan*, a vessel that served until the 1920s. The *Michigan* skirted the limits of the Rush-Bagot Treaty (1817), which declared the GREAT LAKES a nonmilitary zone. The iron *Onoko* (1882) and the steel *Spokane* (1886) served on the Lakes for over thirty years, far exceeding the average life of wooden vessels. By the twentieth century, iron was replaced with cheaper and stronger steel vessels, which continued to grow in size from the 1880s to the present day.

By 1927 the number of vessels had grown to 765 and their gross registered tonnage to 2,887,427 tons, according to a report of the Lake Carriers' Association. The members of this group included major U.S. flag carriers. Together with its Canadian counterpart, the Dominion Marine Association, it formed an important lobbying group. The number of vessels cited above includes those in the bulk, package, and automobile trade of the United States and Canada, but excludes passenger steamers and railroad car ferries. About thirty passenger lines operated on the upper Great Lakes, although after the 1920s their number dropped precipitously, and passenger traffic ended by the late 1960s. Bulk cargoes consisted primarily of iron ore, coal, limestone, and wheat. Vessels reached a length in excess of 600 feet with a carrying capacity of 10,000 tons. Package freight carriers lost their ties to railroads through a court case in 1916 and had to survive on their own.

The standard bulk carrier was a long, narrow, and deep vessel with machinery in the stern, navigating bridge forward, and crew quarters both forward and aft. Cargo was handled through large hatches extending nearly the full width of the deck. Though the vessels were almost identical in profile to the *R. J. Hackett*, a number of innovations had taken place to provide either an alternative or to improve the basic design. One alternative, called a whaleback, was created by a Scottish immigrant, Alexander McDougall, in 1888. The design featured a rounded upper deck, flat sides, and a bottom that tapered to points or "snouts" at the ends. McDougall envisioned a vessel sitting low in the water that waves would simply wash over, limiting the resistance offered by a conventional hull. Fewer than fifty of these vessels were built, as they proved economically unsuccessful, and only one remains, the *Meteor*, as a museum in Superior, Wisconsin.

The disastrous storm of November 1913 that sank over a dozen vessels and cost 250 sailors' lives prompted other changes, such as improved lifeboats, stronger one-piece hatch covers (pioneered by McDougall's whalebacks), and the slow adoption of radio communication. Continued sinkings, highly sensationalized, indicated the glacial nature of change in the vessel industry.

The heyday of the Great Lakes steamship took place between 1890 and 1929 as hundreds of new vessels steamed out of shipyards, most to serve in the rapidly expanding iron ore routes for lower Lake steel mills. The steel industry grew into a vertically integrated business with owners controlling mines, vessels, and mills during the 1890s. Fierce competition eventually resulted in the formation of the United States Steel Corporation, the largest steel producer, in 1901. From that point on, independent vessel owners declined for the next several decades as major steel companies built their own fleets and consolidated their hold on the shipment of ore. World War I and the boom of the 1920s stimulated the growth of the industry and made many owners feel that continual expansion was possible. The Great Depression erased that vision and nearly two-thirds of the ore-carrying fleet became inactive along with the passenger vessels and package freight carriers throughout the 1930s.

The demand for vessels to serve in the Atlantic brought an end to package freight carriers, which were already losing business to the speedier and year-round operations of railroads and trucks. Bulk freighters were more successful, although they were affected by the decline in the output of Mesabi Range high-grade iron ore and the opening of the Saint Lawrence Seaway in 1959. Before its opening, Great Lakes steamships remained confined to the lakes above Lake Erie since vessels built especially for the iron ore and coal trades were too large to pass through the Welland Canal at Niagara Falls. The projected earnings of the Seaway never fully materialized, and with the growth of container shipping and cargo airlines, the Seaway will continue to experience declining revenues.

High construction and labor costs, intensified railroad competition, and the midwinter icing conditions made owners prefer to convert to diesel fuel and install automatic boiler controls and bow thrusters for older vessels rather than place new building orders. That changed with a new vessel, the *Stewart J. Cort,* put into operation in 1972, which was the forerunner of the 1,000-foot, self-loading vessels of capacity 58,000 gross tons, three times that of the older bulk carriers, but operated by crews of the same size. This shipbuilding spurt was triggered by the Merchant Marine Act of 1970, which extended ocean-going tax and subsidy benefits to lakers, demand for which subsequently increased for transporting low-sulfur Rocky Mountain coal for Midwest utilities and iron to meet a projected shortage of steel.

The collapse of the American steel industry in the early 1980s shattered these hopes for the ship owners and put many venerable companies out of business. Consolidation and dismantling of many vessels, even those of recent vintage, reduced the U.S. and Canadian fleets to fewer than one hundred vessels, with only half to two-thirds of those operating in any given year. The drive for economy prompted a new innovation with integrated tug and barge units operating instead of traditional ships and their large crews. Self-unloading vessels have also become the rule on the Great Lakes since they offer the flexibility of delivery to suitable locations. Great Lakes steamships have operated for nearly two hundred years, but their future has never been more uncertain.

BIBLIOGRAPHY

LesStrang, Jacques. *Cargo Carriers of the Great Lakes.* New York: Crown, 1982.

———. *Great Lakes/St. Lawrence System.* Boyne City, Mich.: Harbor House, 1985.

Matthew L. Daley

See also **Canadian-American Waterways; Shipbuilding; Trade, Domestic; Transportation and Travel.**

GREAT LAW OF PENNSYLVANIA was enacted 7 December 1682 by an assembly of freeholders called at Upland (Chester) by William Penn shortly after his arrival in Pennsylvania. It expanded upon a body of laws that Penn had submitted, known as the Laws Agreed upon in England (also known as Penn's Frame of Government). The Great Law established liberty of conscience, extended manhood suffrage, and limited the death penalty to relatively few offenses. Through these statutes, which remained the basis of law in colonial Pennsylvania, Penn attempted to legislate a perfectly moral state.

BIBLIOGRAPHY

Geiter, Mary K. *William Penn.* New York: Longman, 2000.

Lockridge, Kenneth A. *Settlement and Unsettlement in Early America.* Cambridge: Cambridge University Press, 1981.

Robert Fortenbaugh / s. b.

See also **Colonial Settlements; Religious Liberty; Suffrage: Colonial Suffrage.**

GREAT MEADOWS, ten miles east of present-day Uniontown, Pennsylvania, was the site of the first battle in the French and Indian War. On 2 April 1754 a force of Virginians under Col. Joshua Fry, with Maj. George Washington second in command, embarked from Alexandria to engage the French at Fort Duquesne, Pennsylvania. Washington's first experience as a military commander occurred at dawn on 27 May, when he launched a successful surprise attack on a small French force north of Great Meadows. By June Fry had died and Washington was in command. Bunkered at Fort Necessity near Great Meadows, Washington's force was attacked on 3 July by about five hundred French and four hundred Indians. His provisions almost gone, Washington capitulated. After a prisoner exchange, the English force marched with its wounded back to Virginia.

BIBLIOGRAPHY

Cleland, Hugh. *George Washington in the Ohio Valley.* Pittsburgh: University of Pittsburgh Press, 1955.

Washington, George. *Washington and the West.* New York: The Century, 1905.

Solon J. Buck / a. r.

See also **Braddock's Expedition; Colonial Wars; Duquesne, Fort; French and Indian War; French Frontier Forts.**

GREAT MIGRATION. In March 1630, the *Arbella* set sail from Southampton, England, for America, thus beginning an unprecedented exodus of English men, women, and children to North America that lasted for ten years. Of the eighty thousand who left England between 1630 and 1640, approximately twenty thousand sailed to New England. The other emigrants sailed to the Chesapeake Bay region, the West Indies, and other areas.

Most but not all of the Great Migration immigrants to New England were Puritans from the eastern and southern counties of England who wanted to escape a situation they considered intolerable. King Charles I (reigned 1625–1649) dissolved Parliament and insisted on ruling England without interference. Archbishop William Laud, a staunch Anglican, began to purge the Church of England of Puritan members. Finally, a depression in the cloth industry caused economic stress in the counties where the Puritans lived. Hoping to flee this persecution and economic depression, the Puritans joined the ranks of those attempting to organize companies and obtain charters to establish colonies in the New World. The most successful of these companies, the Massachusetts Bay Company, received its charter from Charles I on 4 March 1629.

Although the Massachusetts Bay Company was organized as a joint-stock company, it had a dual purpose from the beginning. Some investors were interested in earning profits through trade, while others hoped to establish a colony that would provide a refuge for persecuted Puritans. Unlike the separatist Pilgrims who preceded them to the New World, the Puritans were nonseparating Congregationalists who hoped to reform the Church of England. Like the Pilgrims, however, they immigrated in family groups rather than as individuals. With the signing of the Cambridge Agreement in August 1629, twelve Puritan members of the Massachusetts Bay Company, led by the future governor of Massachusetts, John Winthrop, shifted the focus of the colony away from trade and in so doing secured a safe haven for Puritans in Massachusetts.

Less than a year after the signing of the Cambridge Agreement, Winthrop and approximately one hundred people set sail in the *Arbella.* The ship reached Salem, Massachusetts, in June 1630 and was soon joined by several more ships in the Winthrop fleet. The Puritans originally settled in Salem but relocated to Charlestown before finally founding a capital in Boston in October 1630. By the end of 1630, seventeen ships carrying close to two thousand passengers had arrived in Massachusetts. The Great Migration came to an abrupt halt in 1640, but by then almost two hundred ships carrying approximately twenty thousand people had left England for Massachusetts.

BIBLIOGRAPHY

Fischer, David Hackett. *Albion's Seed: Four British Folkways in America.* New York: Oxford University Press, 1989.

Pomfret, John E., with Floyd M. Shumway. *Founding the American Colonies, 1583–1660.* New York: Harper and Row, 1970.

Jennifer L. Bertolet

See also **Cambridge Agreement; Colonial Settlements; Massachusetts Bay Colony; Puritans and Puritanism.**

GREAT PLAINS, a geographically and environmentally defined region covering parts of ten states: Montana, North Dakota, South Dakota, Nebraska, Wyoming, Kansas, Colorado, Oklahoma, Texas, and New Mexico. Running between Canada and Mexico, the region stretches from the 98th meridian (altitude 2,000 feet) to the Rocky Mountains (altitude 7,000 feet). This eastward-sloping, treeless, semi-arid, shortgrass plateau's annual rainfall is between thirteen and twenty inches, and the region's continental climate creates an environment of extremes: excessive heat and cold, and violent weather patterns. Along with deep, rich soils, its other valuable resource is the Ogallala Aquifer, a large, nonrenewable water source underlying much of the region. The region's culture, its boom and bust economy, and its importance to American history cannot be understood apart from its environment.

Great Plains Farmstead. This 1942 photograph by John Vachon of a stretch of Dewey County, S.D., captures the region's often bleak, challenging, and endless vistas. LIBRARY OF CONGRESS

Evidence suggests that the first human occupation of the Plains occurred at the end of the last ice age (around 10000 B.C., when the Clovis and then Folsom peoples inhabited the region). Between 5000 and 2000 B.C., a long drought made the region uninhabitable. Around 1000 A.D. the drought receded and the Eastern Woodland culture entered the central Plains to farm stream bottoms. The climate shifted again and many of its inhabitants withdrew, as others took their place.

The first documented European visit to the Plains was made in 1540 by the Spanish explorer Francisco Vasquez de Coronado. One hundred and fifty years later, the French investigated trading opportunities with Plains tribes in the region. American interest in the Plains was cemented with its purchase from France in 1803. In the twenty years after the Louisiana Purchase, three government expeditions led to the common perception of this region as the Great American Desert. Trails were blazed through the Plains from the 1830s, taking settlers to California and Oregon, and, by the late 1870s, the military had forced many Indian nations such as the Arapahos, Cheyennes, and Apaches onto reservations.

Euro-American settlement began at the close of the Civil War. Peace, the sense of manifest destiny, technological developments, and an unusually generous period of rainfall between 1878 and 1887 made the Plains appear especially inviting. Relying on free access to land and water, cattle ranching boomed in the 1870s and 1880s, but later declined as a result of the increasing number of small farmers and the harsh winter of 1886–1887. Boom times came in the mid-1910s, as Plains farmers increased production to supply World War I. An economic bust followed due to overproduction, and this, combined with the prolonged drought of the 1930s and poor agricultural practices, led to the region's most terrible ecological and social catastrophe, the Dust Bowl.

Post–World War II farmers sought to minimize weather unpredictability by mechanizing irrigation in order to utilize the Ogallala Aquifer. From 1940 to 1980, production tripled even as crop prices declined. By 1990, 40 percent of America's beef was fattened and slaughtered within a 250-mile radius of Garden City, Kansas. The decline in the aquifer, combined with low commodity prices, led to a depressed regional economy, and a decreasing and aging population at the turn of the twenty-first century. Unlike many other American regions, the Great Plains resists the traditional story of progress: its environment sets the context for repetitive boom-and-bust economic cycles.

BIBLIOGRAPHY

Opie, John. *Ogallala: Water for a Dry Land: A Historical Study in the Possibilities for American Sustainable Agriculture.* Lincoln: University of Nebraska Press, 1993.

Webb, Walter Prescott. *The Great Plains.* Lincoln: University of Nebraska Press, 1981. Reprint of the original 1931 edition.

West, Elliott. *The Contested Plains: Indians, Goldseekers, and the Rush to Colorado.* Lawrence: University of Kansas Press, 1998.

Amanda Rees

See also **Archaeology and Prehistory of North America; Dust Bowl;** *and vol. 9:* **Across the Plains to California in 1852; Living in the Dust Bowl, 1934.**

GREAT SALT LAKE in northwestern Utah is relatively shallow (about 35 feet), and its size (about 2,000 square miles) and salinity fluctuate widely with precipitation patterns. The fur trader James Bridger visited the lake in December 1824, becoming the first documented non-Native to do so, though another fur trapper, Etienne Provost, may have visited two months earlier. Native peoples had lived in the area for at least 10,000 years. Shoshone and Ute Indian territories overlapped on the eastern shore. John C. Frémont explored the lake in 1843, followed by Howard Stansbury in 1849–1850. Salt, magnesium, and chlorine are extracted commercially. The lake is an important stopover for migratory birds.

Great Salt Lake. A 1972 view of the east shore of this vast, shallow lake in Utah. LIBRARY OF CONGRESS

BIBLIOGRAPHY

Madsen, Brigham D., ed. *Exploring the Great Salt Lake: The Stansbury Expedition of 1849–1850.* Salt Lake City: University of Utah Press, 1989.

Morgan, Dale L. *The Great Salt Lake.* Lincoln: University of Nebraska, 1986. Original edition was published in 1947.

Stum, Marlin. *Visions of Antelope Island and Great Salt Lake.* Logan: Utah State University Press, 1999.

Steven M. Fountain

See also **Utah;** *and vol. 9:* **An Expedition to the Valley of the Great Salt Lake of Utah.**

GREAT SMOKY MOUNTAINS, part of the Appalachian Mountains that run along the North Carolina–Tennessee boundary, are about fifty miles long with sixteen peaks above six thousand feet. Originally known as the Iron Mountains, they were inhabited by Cherokee Indians until about 1789. Little about the Smokies was recorded until Samuel B. Buckley, Thomas L. Clingman, and Arnold Henry Guyot explored them in the 1850s. Guyot published the first comprehensive scientific study of the whole region. The mountains are so called because of a blue haze that looks like rising smoke, characteristic of the region. The Great Smoky Mountains became a national park in 1934.

BIBLIOGRAPHY

Brown, Margaret Lynn. *The Wild East: A Biography of the Great Smoky Mountains.* Gainesville: University Press of Florida, 2000.

Frome, Michael. *Strangers in High Places: The Story of the Great Smoky Mountains.* Garden City, N.Y.: Doubleday, 1966; Knoxville: University of Tennessee Press, 1980, 1993.

Pierce, Daniel S. *The Great Smokies: From Natural Habitat to National Park.* Knoxville: University of Tennessee Press, 2000.

Hugh T. Lefler/H. S.

See also **Appalachia.**

GREAT SOCIETY, the program of liberal reform put forward by President Lyndon Johnson in his 1964 commencement address at the University of Michigan that proposed expanding the size and scope of the federal

Architect of the Great Society. President Lyndon Johnson and the first lady, Lady Bird Johnson, take part in a State Department "Salute to Congress," 7 October 1965. Library of Congress

government to diminish racial and economic inequality and improve the nation's quality of life. Johnson sponsored legislation that strengthened African American voting rights and banned discrimination in housing and public service provision. The War on Poverty, a collection of community empowerment and job programs, directed resources toward the inner cities and the Medicare and Medicaid programs provided health insurance to the poor and elderly, respectively. While many Great Society programs were subsequently abandoned, in the early 2000s, Democrats continued to defend the social insurance and civil rights changes Johnson enacted.

BIBLIOGRAPHY

Andrews, John A. *Lyndon Johnson and the Great Society.* Chicago: Ivan R. Dee, 1998.

Richard M. Flanagan

GREAT TRAIN ROBBERY, THE, a motion picture released by the Edison Manufacturing Company in 1903, was written, directed, and photographed by Edwin S. Porter. Based on a Butch Cassidy robbery, its cast included Gilbert M. "Bronco Billy" Anderson, who became one of the first stars of western films. This twelve-minute silent movie, one of cinema's earliest narrative films, used fourteen shots to tell the story of a robbery and the ensuing chase. The film features several innovations, including a panning shot, but the true cinematic breakthrough involves Porter's use of cuts, in which he avoided dissolves and fades, to create a continuous narrative that shows events happening simultaneously but in different places. Other filmmakers were using similar techniques at the time, but the incredible commercial success of *The Great Train Robbery* has given it a special historical and cinematic significance. Arguably the first western film, it was definitely the first influential one and the forefather of the genre. This tale also greatly influenced early crime and chase films. Its famous ending, in which a bandit fires a pistol at the camera, provided contemporary audiences with a thrill. Permanent movie theaters, then called nickelodeons, began to spread after this film, when investors saw the financial potential of movies.

The Great Train Robbery. Two outlaws coerce the engineer in a scene from this historically significant, and very influential, 1903 short film. © corbis-Bettmann

BIBLIOGRAPHY

Cook, David A. *A History of Narrative Film.* 3d ed. New York: Norton, 1996.

Musser, Charles. *Before the Nickelodeon: Edwin S. Porter and the Edison Manufacturing Company.* Berkeley: University of California Press, 1991.

Justin Cober

See also **Film.**

GREAT VALLEY is a term applied to the region in California between the Sierra Nevada and the Coast Ranges, drained by the Sacramento and San Joaquin rivers. Jedediah Smith first explored and trapped in the valleys in 1822, but, on his second attempt in 1827, the California authorities ordered him to leave. The Hudson's Bay Company then sent trappers in for ten years (1829–1838), by the Willamette Valley from Fort Vancouver, and reaped a rich harvest. The valleys, now known usually as the Central Valley, are the agricultural heartland of California.

BIBLIOGRAPHY

Howard, Thomas Frederick. *Sierra Crossing: First Roads to California.* Berkeley: University of California Press, 1998.

Phillips, George Harwood. *Indians and Intruders in Central California, 1769–1849.* Norman: University of Oklahoma Press, 1993.

Carl L. Cannon / S. B.

See also **California; Fur Trade and Trapping; Hudson's Bay Company; West, American; Westward Migration.**

GREECE, RELATIONS WITH. The primary factors in Greek-American relations are American philhellenism, Greek emigration to the United States, and U.S. foreign aid to Greece.

During the Greek War of Independence (1821–1832), the United States supported Greece, with heartfelt speeches on its behalf delivered in the American Senate. Over time, though, Greece came to view American support with ambivalence, as the line between support and intervention blurred. In the nineteenth century, Greece's foreign policy was based on the "Great Idea," a never-realized expansionist program that called for the Greek conquest of Asia Minor. The United States, along with the Great Powers, opposed it, lest its success lead to a disastrous shift in the region's power balance.

In 1924 the United States passed the Johnson-Reed Act, limiting the immigration of southern Europeans. Greece, sunk into economic depression by the worldwide postwar slump and a dramatically burgeoning population (between 1907 and 1928 the Greek population went from about 2.6 million to 6.2 million), could no longer find relief in emigration, as it had in past times of economic difficulty. Historically, Greece has relied heavily on the income sent home by its Greek-American émigré population. Such receipts plunged in the interwar period.

During World War II and the Greek Civil War (1946–1949), U.S.-Greek relations intensified as Greece became a critical pawn in the emerging Cold War. Allied with the United States during World War II, Greece's resistance to German occupation turned to civil strife when the two main groups of the resistance—one communist and the other royalist—turned against each other.

The United States proclaimed the TRUMAN DOCTRINE in 1947, funneling huge amounts of financial and military aid into Greece. Greece was consequently allied with the United States during the Korean conflict and throughout the Cold War. Between 1946 and 1996, the United States provided Greece with more than $11.1 billion in economic and security assistance. Direct aid programs ceased by 1962; military assistance continued. In 1995, for example, Greece was the fourth-largest recipient of U.S. security assistance, receiving loans totaling $255.15 million.

In 1953 Greece and the United States signed a defense cooperation agreement and established American military installations on Greek territory. The Mutual Defense Cooperation Agreement provides for U.S. military assistance to Greece and the operation of a major U.S. military facility in Crete.

Toward the end of the twentieth century, links between the two countries became more economic and cultural than diplomatic. The United States is the single largest foreign investor in Greece, with investments of at least $900 million in 1994; more than one million Americans are of Greek origin. Diplomatic and economic ties underwent some restructuring with Greece's integration into the European Community at the end of the twentieth century.

BIBLIOGRAPHY

Allison, Graham T., and Kalypso Nicolaidis, eds. *The Greek Paradox: Promise vs. Performance.* Cambridge, Mass.: MIT Press, 1997.

Gallant, Thomas W. *Modern Greece.* New York: Arnold, 2001.

K. E. Fleming

See also **Truman Doctrine.**

GREELY'S ARCTIC EXPEDITION. The Greely Expedition, marketed to the public as the first attempt by the United States to begin a new era of scientific research in the Arctic, was instead largely another expedition in the tradition of romantic polar exploration and tragedy. Its intent was first to act as a search party for the lost naval expedition aboard the *Jeannette*, and second to establish a scientific station on Lady Franklin Bay as part of the U.S. contribution to the first International Polar Year (IPY), a systematic simultaneous study of the Arctic environment slated for 1882–1883. But the ulterior motives of the expedition, decided long before it was folded into the IPY, were to beat the record set by the English for farthest north, and to attempt the North Pole itself.

Except for two Eskimo hunters, no one in the twenty-five-man party had previous Arctic experience. But Lieutenant Adolphus W. Greely had wisely planned his provisions for his stay in the Arctic; the tragedy of the expedition came not from their stay, but their means of egress. In the summer of 1881, Greely and his men landed on the far northern shores of Ellesmere Island on Lady Franklin Bay. Here they established Fort Conger; but scarcely before the ship that dropped them off left the harbor, there were significant tensions in the party. The friction was in part the result of personality conflicts and jealousies, but also because Greely had alienated his men.

From October 1881 through February 1882, the men passed the time carrying out their scientific duties; for example, they made meteorological, magnetic, tidal, and pendulum observations. In April 1882, a smaller party reached the farthest north. Greely himself surveyed Grinnell Land, in the middle of Ellesmere Island. In August 1882, they waited for a supply ship that never arrived; it was caught in the ice two hundred miles south. Another relief ship had splintered in the ice pack. They spent another winter; the summer of 1883 passed, again without a relief ship. Although game was plenty at Fort Conger and supplies would have lasted another winter, Greely followed orders and left by boat in the beginning of August 1883. But Greely did not know that the relief ships, in their haste to find them, did not adequately provision the caches toward which they retreated.

On their southward journey, the party became trapped on a free-drifting ice floe at the mercy of the winds, currents, and tides. After thirty-two days, the floe began to break up, and finally they reached the shores of Ellesmere, near Cape Sabine. The only remaining rations would last a mere fifty days; with rations cut, the starving crew began the slow suffering from frostbite, scurvy, and infections, and men died throughout the winter and spring.

The next rescue was planned amid public debate on the folly of polar exploration; Congress had difficulty passing the appropriations bill. But a relief party left in late April, and by late June they reached the seven survivors, although one died shortly thereafter. The highly publicized dramas of the Greely Expedition overshadowed much of its scientific achievement, and that of the International Polar Year itself.

BIBLIOGRAPHY

Barr, William. "Geographical Aspects of the First International Polar Year, 1882–1883." *Annals of the Association of American Geographers* 73, no. 4 (1983): 463–484.

Greely, A. W. *Three Years of Arctic Service: An Account of the Lady Franklin Bay Expedition of 1881–84, and the Attainment of the Farthest North.* New York: Scribners, 1886.

Vogel, Hal, Steve Shapiro, and Daniel Zimmerman. "The Rise and Set of Arctic Moon." *Polar Record* 27, no. 160 (1991): 43–46.

Annette Watson

See also **Polar Exploration.**

GREEN BAY is a city in Wisconsin at the mouth of the Fox River on Green Bay inlet, separated from Lake Michigan by the Door Peninsula. Originally called La Baye and La Baye des Puans by the French explorers who came there in the 1630s, the settlement was renamed Green Bay in 1839 after it was merged with a trading post. It is the oldest settlement in the state. The area served as a French trading post and fort during conflicts with the British and had permanent settlers only sporadically until 1745, when the trading post there became permanent. Situated at the end of the Fox River system of portages to the Mississippi River, the settlement was particularly attractive to settlers after the opening of the Erie Canal in 1825. The settlers platted a village in 1829 and incorporated Green Bay as a city in 1854. It served as a major port for lumbering from about 1850 and, from 1890, as a processing site for dairy, agricultural goods, and paper products. The city has a total land area of 43.9 square miles. Its population rose from 87,899 in 1980 to 96,466 in 1990 and 102,313 in 2000. Green Bay, like many other northern cities, has continued to experience growth despite its location in the Rust Belt.

The Receiver. An appropriate statue in Green Bay, Wisc., home of the Green Bay Packers football team. GREEN BAY AREA VISITOR & CONVENTION BUREAU

BIBLIOGRAPHY

Martin, Deborah B. *History of Brown County, Wisconsin, Past and Present.* 2 vols. Chicago: S. J. Clarke, 1913.

Thompson, William Fletcher, ed. *The History of Wisconsin.* 3 vols. Madison: State Historical Society of Wisconsin, 1973–1985.

Matthew L. Daley

See also **Wisconsin.**

GREEN BERETS. *See* **Special Forces.**

GREEN CARD. Alien registration receipt cards, colloquially called "green cards," are issued to aliens who qualify as lawful permanent residents as proof of their status. The 2002 version of the card was actually light pink in color. Cards issued before 1976, however, were green. All older versions of the green card expired in 1996. The I-551 cards expire after ten years and need to be renewed before expiration. Permanent resident children must apply for a new card when they reach their fourteenth birthday. Expiration of the card does not affect an individual's status as a lawful permanent resident, but an expired card cannot be used to establish employment eligibility or as a visa for travel.

The current card is machine readable and contains the alien's photograph, fingerprints, and signature as well as optical patterns to frustrate counterfeiting. If a resident's card is lost, mutilated, or destroyed, a replacement card may be issued. If the permanent resident is naturalized, permanently leaves the country, is deported, or dies, the card must be surrendered.

To qualify for permanent resident status and receive a card, an alien must fit into one of several categories. The Immigration and Nationality Act (INA), as amended, established a set of preferred immigrant categories, each limited by a numerical quota. An alien may be sponsored by certain family members in the United States. An employment-based status is granted to workers with extraordinary ability, people with advanced degrees, people whose labor is needed in the United States, religious workers, foreign employees of the government, and entrepreneurs who create employment opportunities for Americans. The so-called diversity category includes immigrants from underrepresented countries. Refugees and people granted asylum may also apply for permanent residence after one year.

The card serves as a permit for employment in the United States and a visa. Permanent residents may use the card to return to the United States after a temporary absence not exceeding one year. If more than a year passes before the resident returns to the United States, the card is no longer valid as a reentry permit. If the permanent resident has been abroad for more than one year but less than two, he or she must obtain a reentry permit from the INS. If the resident is absent from the United States for longer than two years, he or she must obtain a special immigrant visa from a U.S. consulate, usually after establishing that he or she has not abandoned his or her permanent resident status.

The potential use of the card to reenter the United States should not be confused with the maintenance of lawful permanent residence status. To maintain lawful permanent resident status while abroad, an alien must demonstrate the intent to remain in the United States as a permanent resident. The INS generally examines the length of and purpose for the resident's absence; whether or not the resident continues to file U.S. tax returns, maintains a U.S. address, bank account, and driver's license; the location of the resident's close family members; and the location and nature of the resident's employment.

For the holder of a green card to be eligible for naturalization, he or she generally must reside in the United States continuously for five years following establishment of permanent residence. The required period is reduced to three years if the resident is the spouse of a U.S. citizen. If the resident is absent from the country for more than six months but for less than a year, the continuity of residence is broken unless the resident can supply a reasonable explanation for the absence. An absence of one year or more destroys the continuity of residence unless the resident takes appropriate steps prior to the expiration of a year.

BIBLIOGRAPHY

Aleinikoff, Thomas Alexander, David A. Martin, and Hiroshi Motomura. *Immigration: Process and Policy.* 4th ed. St. Paul, Minn.: West Group, 1998.

Gordon, Charles, Stanley Mailman, and Stephen Yale-Loehr. *Immigration Law and Procedure.* New York: Matthew Bender, 1988; supplemented through 2002.

Legomsky, Stephen H. *Immigration and Refugee Law and Policy.* Westbury, N.Y.: Foundation Press, 1997.

Daniel Kanstroom

See also **Immigration.**

GREEN MOUNTAIN BOYS. Beginning in 1749, the New Hampshire governor Benning Wentworth issued numerous patents to land in the Green Mountains, counting on a vague border with New York to at least temporarily make the claims profitable. Settlers, moving in orderly, family-centered groups, took advantage of the new patents and moved into the area, establishing towns that were, although varied in religion and ethnic background, far from a wild frontier. In 1770, New Yorkers attempted to use a 1764 royal decision that the land belonged to them to move in Dutch settlers on new patents. Reacting to this incursion, Ethan Allen, a recent immigrant, formed the Green Mountain Boys, a group of men determined to protect their families' lands, who used intimidation, violence, and harassment to drive off the hated "Yorkers." Allen and his men successfully evaded the authorities, even posting a mock reward for their enemies in retaliation for bounties posted on their heads.

When the American Revolution began, Allen volunteered the Green Mountain Boys for service, transforming them into soldiers, not just outlaws. Using their knowledge of the area and Fort Ticonderoga's weaknesses, Allen and Henry Knox seized the fort and its cannon, which eventually forced the British out of Boston. When Allen volunteered for the ill-fated Montreal expedition, the rest of the men stayed behind under Colonel Seth Warner and fought at the Battle of Bennington. Ira Allen, Ethan Allen's brother, led the Green Mountain Boys to declare an independent Vermont in 1777, fighting off claims by both New Hampshire and New York while politically maneuvering for support within the Continental Congress. Although Ethan Allan died in 1789, his family and his Green Mountain Boys survived to see Vermont become a state in 1791.

BIBLIOGRAPHY

Bellesiles, Michael A. *Revolutionary Outlaws.* Charlottesville: University Press of Virginia, 1993.

Hoyt, Edwin P. *The Damndest Yankees.* Brattleboro, Vt.: Stephen Green Press, 1976.

Margaret D. Sankey

See also **Bennington, Battle of; New Hampshire; Ticonderoga, Capture of; Vermont.**

GREENBACK MOVEMENT. To meet the enormous demands of the Civil War, the federal government in 1863 began issuing large quantities (as much as from $300 to $400 million in circulation between 1862 and 1879) of "greenbacks," notes not redeemable for gold. At the close of the war, fiscal conservatives expected a return to the gold standard and a constriction in the monetary supply. However, the increased cash available was attractive, not as a wartime expediency but as a monetary policy, to a growing group of Greenbackers. Frequently westerners and southerners, they were alienated by the limited supply of specie-backed notes available through the eastern-dominated national banking system, and felt that the conservative policies of the system limited their ability to expand entrepreneurial activity, particularly in the newly settled West. Many Greenbackers sprang from the Jacksonian tradition of agrarian and antimonopolistic politics, and far from being the yokels and bumpkins that their political rivals depicted, they campaigned for an imaginative and dynamic new system of fiscal management in the United States.

As early as 1868, Greenbackers saw a political proposal from Ohio Democrat George Pendleton ("The Pendleton Plan"), which suggested that greenbacks be continued, tied to an incontrovertible bond scheme. The bonds proposed would widen the supply of cash, and because the amount of money could be expanded or contracted by the number of bonds sold, make the country's money supply respond to the demands of the population. Although this plan was not adopted, the bond plan remained a priority for Greenbackers until the return to the gold standard in 1879. Greenbackers were a disparate and organizationally dispersed group, which was both advantageous and a drawback for the Greenback Party, which emerged as a political entity by the early 1870s. Positively, the party could draw on the organizational resources of various groups, such as the Grange, for meeting space and financial support. Negatively, as a third party, it lacked the patronage and machinery required to compete with the Republicans and Democrats, especially as many supporters of greenbacks were often concerned with other issues—like Reconstruction in the southern states, women's rights, and labor problems—and divided by them as well. Some candidates, like Daniel Russell of North Carolina, ran for Congress on both the Greenback and Republican ticket, but others—caught between the two major parties—were successful at only the state level. (The party's candidates were particularly successful in Illinois, where they enjoyed tremendous agrarian support.)

During the 1870s, the debate over greenbacks remained a clash between the conservative "goldbugs," as Greenbackers derisively called their opponents, and the Greenbackers, who defined themselves as antimonopolist, entrepreneurial, democratic, and—with these values—representing the best of America. Their detractors accused them of being the least desirable of citizens: shiftless debtors who saw in easy money a way to quick riches. The debate officially ended when, with Republican organizations in the Midwest winning over voters and Greenbackers unable to push for a national policy, the gold standard was returned in 1879. Many followers of the movement, however, continued their political activities under the banner of the Populist Party.

BIBLIOGRAPHY

Ritter, Gretchen. *Goldbugs and Greenbacks: The Antimonopoly Tradition and the Politics of Finance in America.* Cambridge, U.K.: Cambridge University Press, 1997.

Unger, Irwin. *The Greenback Era: A Social and Political History of American Finance, 1865–1879.* Princeton, N.J.: Princeton University Press, 1964.

Margaret D. Sankey

See also **Gold Bugs; Granger Movement; Farmers' Alliance; Inflation.**

GREENBACKS, the popular name for the U.S. notes issued during the Civil War as legal tender for all debts except tariff duties and interest on the public debt. They served as the standard of value in ordinary commercial transactions after their issue in 1862. The $450 million in greenbacks that was authorized was later permanently reduced to $346,681,016. Although heavily depreciated during the Civil War, greenbacks were much favored by rural proponents of inflationary monetary policies, who rallied for their continuance in the late 1860s and 1870s. Organized as the Greenback Party, the proponents succeeded in postponing the resumption of specie payments until the Resumption Act of 1875, which by 1879 had returned the greenback to a value on par with metallic currency.

BIBLIOGRAPHY

Ritter, Gretchen. *Goldbugs and Greenbacks.* Cambridge: Cambridge University Press, 1997.

Unger, Irwin. *The Greenback Era.* Princeton, N.J.: Princeton University Press, 1964.

Elmer Ellis/A. R.

See also **Currency and Coinage; Resumption Act; Specie Payments, Suspension and Resumption of.**

Innovative Community. In this 1946 photograph by Gretchen Van Tassel, children play on a pedestrian path alongside row houses and open space in Greenbelt, Md. LIBRARY OF CONGRESS

GREENBELT COMMUNITIES. Among the numerous public works projects undertaken by the New Deal during the 1930s, one of the most innovative was the three "greenbelt" towns: Greenbelt, Maryland, outside Washington, D.C.; Greenhills, Ohio, north of Cincinnati; and Greendale, Wisconsin, near Milwaukee. The towns took their names from the wide belt of open land surrounding each, separating them from adjacent suburban developments and reinforcing their sense of local cohesion. The New Deal's Resettlement Administration constructed the towns between 1935 and 1938, giving jobs to twenty-five thousand unemployed workers. Exemplifying the most advanced planning ideas, Greenbelt, the largest of the three towns, received the most public attention. Its 885 dwellings were carefully arranged on super blocks with generous amounts of open space. The town center contained a municipal building, retail stores, a movie theater, a gas station, a swimming pool, and a public school that also served as a community center. Pedestrian paths wound through each neighborhood, passed safely under major roads, and linked all the dwellings to the town center. Greenhills (676 dwellings) and Greendale (572 dwellings) followed the same general plan as Greenbelt but on more modest scales.

The greenbelt communities received widespread praise for their innovative designs, but because influential private real estate interests strongly opposed such development, no others were built. Following World War II, Congress ordered the U.S. Housing Administration to sell the towns. Many residents of Greenhills and Greendale purchased their dwellings. The greenbelt lands, nearly all of which lay outside the village boundaries, were bought by real estate developers, who covered them with more expensive houses. In Greenbelt, where far more unoccupied land lay within the town boundaries, residents formed a housing cooperative and purchased the original town and a large section of the surrounding territory. Frustrated by attempts to manage and develop the unoccupied land, the cooperative decided to sell it to private developers, who covered the property with housing units and commercial centers. By the year 2000 Greenbelt contained 10,180 houses and 21,456 residents. Greendale had 6,011 houses and 14,405 residents, and Greenhills had 1,639 houses and 4,103 residents. In spite of their inability to control the postwar development of the lands surrounding their towns, the "greenbelters" continued to exhibit the strong sense of community spirit that characterized their actions during the New Deal era and passed this spirit on to many of the new residents.

BIBLIOGRAPHY

Alanen, Arnold R., and Joseph A. Eden. *Main Street Ready-Made: The New Deal Community of Greendale, Wisconsin.* Madison: State Historical Society of Wisconsin, 1987.

Arnold, Joseph L. *The New Deal in the Suburbs: A History of the Greenbelt Town Program, 1935–1954.* Columbus: Ohio State University Press, 1971.

Knepper, Cathy D. *Greenbelt, Maryland: A Living Legacy of the New Deal.* Baltimore: Johns Hopkins University Press, 2001.

Miller, Zane L. *Suburb: Neighborhood and Community in Forest Park, Ohio, 1935–1976.* Knoxville: University of Tennessee Press, 1981.

Williamson, Mary Lou, ed. *Greenbelt: History of a New Town, 1937–1987.* Norfolk, Va.: Donning Publishers, 1987.

Joseph L. Arnold

See also **Resettlement Administration.**

GREENFIELD VILLAGE. *See* **Henry Ford Museum and Greenfield Village.**

GREENVILLE TREATY of 3 August 1795 resulted directly from General "Mad" Anthony Wayne's victory over a confederation of Native warriors at Fallen Timbers (near modern Toledo, Ohio) in 1794. Over 1,100 Indians attended Wayne's council, which began in earnest in mid-July. Wayne read the Indians copies of the Treaty of Paris (1783) and the new Jay's Treaty (1794) to drive home the point that Britain had abandoned the Ohio Country, and the United States was now sovereign in the region. Jay's Treaty, in which Britain promised to evacuate its forts in American territory, proved crucial to Wayne's case. This agreement (this was probably the first the Indians had heard of it) convinced most of the confederacy's chiefs and warriors that the British material aid necessary for continued resistance would cease, and that they should therefore make peace with the Americans and cede the Ohio Country to the young nation.

Many of the Indian leaders present accepted the American terms. Chief Little Turtle of the Miamis delivered a rebuttal speech denying former British claims to Ohio. He proposed a compromise, in which the new boundary would extend no farther north than Fort Recovery (in present-day Mercer County, Ohio). Wayne insisted on his original proposal, however. He made extensive use of liquor, presents, spies, and bribes to further the American agenda, and on 3 August, representatives from all the tribes present marked the treaty. Little Turtle held out until 12 August, but then relented in a private council with Wayne.

The treaty allotted annuities (yearly payments) of $1,000 in trade goods (minus the cost of shipping) each to the Wyandots, Delawares, Shawnees, Miamis, Ottawas, Chippewas, and Potawatomis. A $500 annuity (minus shipping) went to the Kickapoos, Weas, Eel Rivers, Piankashaws, and Kaskaskias. Ideally, the annuities went to the chiefs who had signed the treaty and were then distributed to their people, though this was not always the case in practice. The Kickapoos disdained what they saw as an inconsequential annuity, and declined even to collect it for several years. The United States received all of modern-day Ohio, minus the northwest quadrant. Wayne further reserved 150,000 acres on the Ohio River opposite Louisville, Kentucky, for the veterans of George Rogers Clark's Vincennes campaign. The treaty also reserved numerous small plots of land for the United States and the old French holdings, which became the subject of later dispute.

The Greenville Treaty established a general peace between Americans and Indians in the Old Northwest that held until 1811. It inexpensively opened most of Ohio to rapid American settlement, and proved that Indian lands could be purchased, rather than merely taken. The treaty also, through the annuity system, increased Indian dependence on manufactured goods and established some chiefs, like Little Turtle, as prominent leaders. American officials would later force these tribes into land cession treaties by threatening to withhold their Greenville annuities. While it seemed Wayne had negotiated with the confederation, in reality he met with disgruntled, feuding villagers who could not even agree on the distribution of their annuities. A great many of the chiefs who attended the treaty died soon after from disease, further compromising Indian leadership in the Old Northwest. Wayne's use of bribery, spies, and threats of force helped him play one tribe against another to secure the treaty. His aide-de-camp, William Henry Harrison, utilized all these tactics when he became governor of Indiana Territory in 1800.

BIBLIOGRAPHY

Kappler, Charles J., ed. *Indian Treaties 1778–1883.* New York: Interland, 1972.

Sword, Wiley. *President Washington's Indian War: The Struggle for the Old Northwest, 1790–1795.* Norman: University of Oklahoma Press, 1985.

White, Richard. *The Middle Ground: Indians, Empires, and Republics in the Great Lakes Region, 1650–1815.* New York: Cambridge University Press, 1991.

Robert M. Owens

See also **Fallen Timbers, Battle of; Indian Land Cessions; Indian Policy, U.S.: 1775–1830; Indian Treaties; Jay's Treaty.**

GREENWICH VILLAGE. Called Sapokanikan by the original native inhabitants who used the area mostly for fishing, Greenwich Village is one of the most vibrant and diverse neighborhoods in Lower Manhattan. During the 1630s, Dutch settlers called this area Noortwyck and used it for farms. It remained sparsely populated until the English conquered it in 1664. By 1713 it had evolved into a small village renamed Grin'wich. Because of its proximity to the commercial activities centered near the Hudson River, it began to take on a more commercial orientation after the American Revolution. A series of epidemics between 1803 and 1822 increased the area's population when residents from more crowded parts of the city fled north. By 1840 the area had been transformed from a small farming hamlet to a thriving business and residential center. Land developers bought up and divided the remaining farmland, and the marshy tracts were filled in.

Greenwich Village. Outside Cafe Bizarre on West Third Street, 1959. © BETTMANN/CORBIS

Fashionable Greek Revival–style townhouses sprang up around Washington Square Park.

During the nineteenth century the Village was transformed not only by its affluent residents but also by the many educational and cultural institutions that flourished there. New York University was founded in 1836 and private galleries, art clubs, and learned societies abounded. The neighborhood began another transformation by the end of the nineteenth century when German, Irish, and Italian immigrants flooded into the area to work in the manufacturing concerns based in the southeastern part of the neighborhood. As these immigrants moved in, many single-family residences were subdivided into smaller units or demolished and replaced by tenements. By World War I, a range of political and cultural radicals and bohemians had moved in, and the neighborhood began to take on the character that has marked it since as a home to and focal point for diverse social, cultural, educational, and countercultural movements.

In the 1950s, the Village provided a forum for the beat generation and produced such literary luminaries as Jack Kerouac and Allen Ginsberg. The 1960s through the early 1970s marked the arrival of an openly gay community, hippies, antiwar activists, and an assortment of countercultural and underground movements. In 1969, police and gay residents met in a violent confrontation known as the Stonewall Rebellion. The next year members of a radical terrorist group, the Weathermen, blew themselves up while building a bomb in a Greenwich Village townhouse. In the 1980s, the Village became a center for the mobilization against the AIDS epidemic. At the start of the twenty-first century, the Village is a major tourist mecca and continues to be one of the most dynamic and diverse neighborhoods in New York City.

BIBLIOGRAPHY

Burrows, Edwin G., and Mike Wallace. *Gotham: A History of New York City to 1898.* New York: Oxford University Press, 1999.

Gold, Joyce. *From Trout Stream to Bohemia: A Walking Guide to Greenwich Village History.* New York: Old Warren Road Press, 1988.

Miller, Terry. *Greenwich Village and How It Got That Way.* New York: Crown, 1990.

Faren R. Siminoff

See also **New York City.**

GRENADA INVASION. The United Kingdom ruled the Caribbean island of Grenada from 1763 until independence in 1974. The country's first prime minister, Sir Eric Gairy, ruled until 1979, when a coup led by Maurice Bishop overthrew his government. By late summer 1983, Bishop's New Jewel Movement had split into two factions. On 19 October the more left-wing element, under Deputy Prime Minister Bernard Coard and General Hudson Austin, which favored closer ties to communist states, arrested and subsequently executed Bishop and some of his ministers. Two days later, the Organization of Eastern Caribbean States (OECS) met and voted to intervene militarily to restore order. Lacking adequate forces, the OECS appealed to nonmember states Jamaica, Barbados, and the United States. A 23 October meeting of British and U.S. diplomats with Grenadian officials proved unproductive.

Amid growing concern in Washington for the safety of U.S. nationals in Grenada, President Ronald Reagan authorized the commitment of U.S. forces. On 25 October a combined force of six thousand troops from the United States and one thousand troops from Jamaica, Barbados, and the OECS landed on Grenada in a military action named Operation Urgent Fury. By 28 October the troops had secured the island. The operation was a military success, although not free from error. U.S. public opinion narrowly supported the INTERVENTION, but the United Nations Security Council and later the General Assembly voted to deplore the action as a flagrant violation of international law. Depending on one's viewpoint, Operation Urgent Fury either destroyed a democratic regime or ended a growing threat to regional and U.S. security interests.

BIBLIOGRAPHY

Hopf, Ted. *Peripheral Visions: Deterrence Theory and American Foreign Policy in the Third World, 1965–1990.* Ann Arbor: University of Michigan Press, 1994.

Payne, Anthony, Paul Sutton, and Tony Thorndike. *Grenada: Revolution and Invasion.* New York: St. Martin's Press, 1984.

Weber, Cynthia. *Simulating Sovereignty: Intervention, the State, and Symbolic Exchange.* Cambridge: Cambridge University Press, 1995.

Richard W. Turk/A. E.

See also **Caribbean Policy; Latin America, Relations with.**

GRIFFON, first sailing vessel on the upper Great Lakes, was built in 1679 by Robert Cavelier, Sieur de La Salle, above Niagara Falls to transport men and supplies between Niagara and his projected Illinois colony. In August of that year, the *Griffon* carried La Salle, accompanied by Father Louis Hennepin, to Green Bay, from which the ship was sent back to Niagara laden with furs for La Salle's creditors. Vessel and crew disappeared on the voyage, and their fate remains a mystery. Frequent reports of the discovery of its remains have been published, but all have lacked substantial foundation; the numerous pictures of the *Griffon* are likewise fictional.

BIBLIOGRAPHY

MacLean, Harrison J. *The Fate of the Griffon.* Toronto: Griffin House, 1974.

M. M. Quaife/A. R.

See also **Explorations and Expeditions: French; La Salle Explorations; Mackinac, Straits of, and Mackinac Island.**

GRIGGS V. DUKE POWER COMPANY, 401 U.S. 424 (1971). Prior to the passage of Title VII of the Civil Rights Act of 1964, which prohibited employment discrimination, employers throughout the South and elsewhere in the United States used racial classifications to intentionally discriminate against African Americans in hiring decisions. The 8-0 Supreme Court decision in *Griggs* established new definitions of employment discrimination, influencing wide-ranging areas of public policy. The issue was whether the new law prohibited Duke Power Company from requiring a high school education and the passing of a standardized general intelligence test as conditions of employment when the standards were not significantly related to job performance. Blacks were disqualified by the standards at a substantially higher rate than white applicants, and the jobs at issue had previously been filled only by whites as part of a long-standing practice of discrimination. The district court had decided that the company's examination program was not intentionally discriminatory.

The Supreme Court reversed the decision, holding that the law prohibited not only overt discrimination but also practices ostensibly "neutral" but discriminatory in operation, such as screening tests, that result in a disparate (unfavorable) impact on blacks. This "disparate impact" precedent established the right to sue under Title VII regardless of discriminatory intent and placed the burden of proof on the employer to show that the conduct was based on "business necessity." The Court shifted the burden of proof back to the plaintiff in *Price Waterhouse v. Hopkins* (1989) and *Ward's Cove Packing Co., Inc., v. Atonio* (1989), but the Civil Rights Act of 1991 reinstated the *Griggs* theory. Thus, *Griggs* helped sustain affirmative action programs in the employment field.

BIBLIOGRAPHY

Gray, C. Boyden. "Disparate Impact: History and Consequences." *Louisiana Law Review* 54 (July 1994).

Halpern, Stephen C. *On the Limits of the Law: The Ironic Legacy of Title VI of the 1964 Civil Rights Act.* Baltimore: Johns Hopkins University Press, 1995.

Nieman, Donald G. *Promises to Keep: African-Americans and the Constitutional Order, 1776 to the Present.* New York: Oxford University Press, 1991.

Tony Freyer/A. R.

See also **Affirmative Action; Civil Rights Movement; *Ward's Cove Packing Co., Inc., v. Atonio.***

GRISTMILLS. From colonial times and into the first half of the nineteenth century, gristmills flourished in America by meeting an important local need in agricultural communities: grinding the farmers' grain and levying a toll, usually in kind, for the service. In some especially productive localities, mills grew large and millers operated as merchants, buying and exporting the area's surplus grain. Beginning in the mid-nineteenth century, however, the opening of the great grain-producing areas of the West, railroad construction, steam power, and the growth and concentration of industry eventually drove most of the small local mills out of business. Relics of the once decentralized American milling industry can still be found along the streams of many of the older states. The massive grinding stones of gristmills were once much sought after as ornaments for courtyards or gardens.

BIBLIOGRAPHY

Lockwood, J. F. *Flour Milling.* Liverpool, N.Y.: Northern Publishing Company, 1945.

Storck, John. *Flour for Men's Bread.* Minneapolis: University of Minnesota Press, 1952.

W. A. Robinson/C. W.

See also **Agriculture; Cereal Grains; Corn; Elevators, Grain; Wheat.**

GRISWOLD V. CONNECTICUT, 381 U.S. 479 (1965). When the state Planned Parenthood League opened a clinic in New Haven, Connecticut, in 1961, two staff members were arrested and fined under a rarely used law for giving advice and a prescription for a contraceptive to a married couple. The law, a legacy of Anthony

Comstock's anti-vice campaign of the late nineteenth century, had been interpreted to ban the use of contraceptives and the opening of public clinics, which meant that women could not attain access to reliable contraception unless they could afford private physicians.

The Supreme Court decision in *Griswold v. Connecticut* reversed the Connecticut law by extending constitutional protection to the individual's right to Privacy. However, the Supreme Court was uncertain about the source of this right. The plurality opinion, written by Justice William O. Douglas, argued that several provisions of the Bill of Rights combine to create "penumbras"—that is, rights not explicitly set forth but nonetheless guaranteed by implication—and thus protected "zones of privacy." A married couple's choice about parenthood lay within that zone. Two dissenters from the right of privacy, Hugo Black and Potter Stewart, accused the majority of writing their personal opinions into constitutional doctrine and violating the principle of judicial self-restraint. It was a curious decision: No one publicly opposed the legalization of birth control, but many legal scholars agreed with the dissenters' accusations. Eight years later, *Roe v. Wade* (1973) revealed the explosive potential of *Griswold* and other privacy decisions as precedents by ruling that the right of privacy included a limited right to elective abortion.

BIBLIOGRAPHY

Baer, Judith A. *Women in American Law: The Struggle toward Equality from the New Deal to the Present.* New York: Holmes and Meier, 1996.

Ball, Howard, and Phillip Cooper. *Of Power and Right: Hugo Black, William O. Douglas, and America's Constitutional Revolution.* New York: Oxford University Press, 1992.

*Judith A. Baer/*A. R.

See also **Birth Control Movement; *Roe v. Wade.***

GROSJEAN V. AMERICAN PRESS COMPANY,

297 U.S. 233 (1936). To stifle criticism from his political enemies, U.S. senator Huey Long of Louisiana persuaded the legislature of his state to place a 2 percent license tax on the sale of advertising in newspapers with a weekly circulation of more than twenty thousand (which covered most of the state's opposition newspapers). Nine Louisiana newspaper publishers challenged the law in court. In *Grosjean v. American Press Company*, Justice George Sutherland wrote for a unanimous U.S. Supreme Court, holding the Louisiana law unconstitutional under the due process clause of the U.S. Constitution because it abridged the freedom of the press.

BIBLIOGRAPHY

Hair, William Ivy. *The Kingfish and His Realm: The Life and Times of Huey P. Long.* Baton Rouge: Louisiana State University, 1991.

R. Blake Brown

See also **Due Process of Law; First Amendment.**

GROUP LIBEL LAWS.

Otherwise known as hate speech laws or codes, group libel laws penalize speech or other communication that attacks or defames a particular group on the basis of its race, ethnicity, gender, sexual orientation, religion, or other such characteristic. These laws are typically based on the belief that group libel, particularly against groups that suffer from social prejudice and discrimination, cements the groups' subordinated status, helps create a social climate that encourages violence against the group, and causes the targeted group to curtail its own speech.

These statutes and codes, when enacted by governmental bodies or public institutions such as public universities, raise serious First Amendment issues. Since the speech is categorized and penalized because of its content, the statutes must overcome the general constitutional presumption against content-based restrictions on speech. Nevertheless, in *Beauharnais v. Illinois* (1952), the U.S. Supreme Court narrowly upheld the constitutionality of a state statute criminalizing the libel of a group of citizens. The Court said that, like "fighting words" (words that would cause the average addressee to fight), libel against individuals or groups was not within a constitutionally protected category of speech.

While *Beauharnais* has never been expressly overruled, a number of cases have so weakened its rationale that its holding would not likely survive if tested. Indeed, in *R.A.V. v. City of St. Paul* (1992), the Court struck down a local ordinance that made it a crime to place on public or private property a symbol or object likely to arouse "anger, alarm, or resentment . . . on the basis of race, color, creed, religion, or gender." The defendant had been charged under the ordinance after burning a cross in the yard of an African American family. Even though the "speech" at issue fell into the analytical category of "fighting words," which the Court had previously maintained was of low constitutional value, the Court held that the ordinance was viewpoint based and thus on its face unconstitutional. *R.A.V.* thus suggests that group libel laws and hate speech codes will fail constitutional attack, absent some special context that would allow the speech restriction to satisfy strict scrutiny.

BIBLIOGRAPHY

Freedman, Monroe H., and Eric M. Freedman, eds. *Group Defamation and Freedom of Speech.* Westport, Conn.: Greenwood Press, 1995.

Matsuda, Mari. "Public Response to Racist Speech: Considering the Victim's Story." *Michigan Law Review* 87 (1989): 2357–2381.

Sunstein, Cass R. *Democracy and the Problem of Free Speech.* New York: Free Press, 1993.

Kent Greenfield

See also **Hate Crimes; Libel.**

GUADALCANAL CAMPAIGN. To check the Japanese advance and open the way for a strategic offensive against Rabaul, the Allies planned to seize bases in the southern Solomon Islands. On 7 August 1942 Maj. Gen. Alexander A. Vandegrift's First Marine Division landed on Guadalcanal and nearby Tulagi, scattering small Japanese forces on both islands. The Japanese reaction was swift. First, Japanese aircraft struck at the beachhead. Then, in a surprise night attack against Allied naval forces early on 9 August (the Battle of Savo Island), seven Japanese cruisers and a destroyer sank three American cruisers, an Australian cruiser, and an American destroyer. Rear Adm. Richmond K. Turner and Adm. Frank J. Fletcher were forced to withdraw ships from the area, leaving the marines alone to defend the Guadalcanal airfield. Undaunted by the loss of the aircraft carrier *Ryuto* at the battle of the Eastern Solomons (August 23–25), the Japanese landed thousands of troops on the island in nightly destroyer runs ("Tokyo Express"). In mid-September, the Japanese, now about a division strong, attacked the marine positions (the Battle of Bloody Ridge), only to be repulsed with heavy losses.

For the next month, heavy air and sea battles took place in the Guadalcanal area. While further Japanese reinforcement efforts were frustrated in a series of naval actions, the marines were soon replaced by more than fifty thousand army troops under Maj. Gen. Alexander Patch. The Japanese, short on supplies and weakened by disease, fell back before heavy American attacks. In early February 1943, the thirteen thousand Japanese survivors were evacuated in night operations, leaving Guadalcanal in American hands.

BIBLIOGRAPHY

Frank, Richard B. *Guadalcanal.* New York: Random House, 1990.

Griffith, Samuel B., II. *The Battle for Guadalcanal.* New York: Lippincott, 1963.

Hammel, Eric M. *Guadalcanal, Decision at Sea: The Naval Battle of Guadalcanal, November 13–15, 1942.* New York: Crown, 1988.

Stanley L. Falk/A. R.

See also **Aircraft Carriers and Naval Aircraft; Bismarck Sea, Battle of; Bougainville; Marine Corps, United States; Rabaul Campaign; World War II; World War II, Navy in.**

GUADALUPE HIDALGO, TREATY OF. On 2 February 1848, a senior State Department clerk, Nicholas P. Trist, signed a treaty at the town of Guadalupe Hidalgo (just outside of Mexico City) ending the war with Mexico. The previous fall, Gen. Winfield Scott had completed his advance from Vera Cruz along Mexico's Gulf coast, through the mountains and into the capital, Mexico City.

In April 1847, President James K. Polk had sent Trist, a loyal Democrat, to spy on Scott, a Whig whom Polk feared might oppose him in the election of 1848. After Scott gained the capital, Polk's appetite for Mexican territory seemingly increased, and he considered demanding all of Mexico. In early October 1847, Polk ordered Trist recalled. When Trist learned in November of the recall, he stalled, informed Mexican authorities he had to leave, and got Mexican leaders on 24 January 1848 to agree to earlier U.S. land demands. Trist signed the Treaty of Guadalupe Hidalgo nine days later and sent it to the president. Thus, he negotiated and signed a treaty on behalf of the United States after he had been dismissed from his position.

The treaty called for Mexico to cede more than half its original territory, including the present-day states of California, Arizona, Nevada and Utah and parts of New Mexico, Colorado, and Wyoming. It also made adjustments to the Mexico-Texas border (the Rio Grande became the boundary instead of the Rio Nueces). In all, Mexico ceded more than 500,000 square miles. In return, the United States paid Mexico some $15 million, most of which went to Americans with claims against the Mexican government.

The gain of land from this treaty caused problems in the U.S. Senate because of the deepening debate over the expansion of slavery. Subsequent problems in establishing the U.S.-Mexican border in southern Arizona and New Mexico would be resolved with the Gadsden Purchase in 1853, establishing what is the current boundary.

BIBLIOGRAPHY

Bauer, Karl Jack. *The Mexican War, 1846–1848.* New York: Macmillan, 1974.

Drexler, Robert W. *Guilty of Making Peace: A Biography of Nicholas P. Trist.* Lanham, Md.: University Press of America, 1991.

Eisenhower, John S.D. *So Far from God: The U.S. War with Mexico, 1846–1848.* Norman: University of Oklahoma Press, 2000.

Francaviglia, Richard, and Douglas W. Richmond, eds. *Dueling Eagles: Reinterpreting the U.S.-Mexican War, 1846–1848.* Fort Worth: Texas Christian University Press, 2000.

Charles M. Dobbs

See also **Compromise of 1850; Gadsden Purchase; Mexican-American War; Wilmot Proviso.**

GUAM, the westernmost territory of the United States, was captured by American forces in June 1898 during the Spanish-American War, and ceded to the United States by the Treaty of Paris, signed 10 December 1898. Ferdinand Magellan is credited with discovery of the island in 1521. The island, which is about thirty miles long and four to ten miles wide, is the southernmost of the Mariana Islands. It was then inhabited by natives who had migrated from Asia, probably the Malay Archipelago, about 3,500 years earlier. Following its cession in 1898, Guam was administered by naval officers, pursuant to executive orders of the president. On 1 August 1950, its administration was transferred to the Department of the Interior under the Organic Act. Until 1970, under this act, the chief executive of Guam was a governor appointed by the president, but a 1968 amendment provided for popular election thereafter. A unicameral legislature (one legislative chamber) of twenty-one members is the lawmaking authority. A court with the jurisdiction of a federal district court and local jurisdiction has been established, its decisions subject to appeal to the U.S. Court of Appeals. The people of Guam have been citizens of the United States since 1950.

During World War II, Guam was occupied by Japanese forces from December 1941 to 21 July 1944 when it was recaptured by United States Marines. It has since played a key role in U.S. Pacific defenses. In 2000, its population of approximately 150,000 was largely employed in military-related pursuits, but tourism continues to provide a lively and increasing source of economic activity. Major exports include petroleum products, construction materials, and fish, and Guam's largest trading partners are the mainland United States and Japan. English and Chamorro are the principal languages on the island, and more than 98 percent of the population is Roman Catholic.

BIBLIOGRAPHY

Carano, Paul, and Pedro C. Sanchez. *A Complete History of Guam.* Rutland, Vt.: Tuttle, 1964.

Rogers, Robert F. *Destiny's Landfall: A History of Guam.* Honolulu: University of Hawaii Press, 1995.

Ruth G. Van Cleve / A. G.

See also **Japan, Relations with; Spanish-American War, Navy in; Territorial Governments; Territories of the United States.**

GUANO, nitrate-rich bat dung that is an excellent fertilizer, was first imported into the United States in 1824 by John S. Skinner, a proponent of progressive agriculture and the editor of the first U.S. farm journal, *American Farmer.* The agricultural press, picking up on progressive farming techniques that made use of various fertilizers (composed of bones, seaweed, rock phosphate, night soil, or various manures) to boost production, began to focus attention on the value of guano as an almost magical fertilizer. Its advocates urged farmers to try it, regaling them with fabulous stories of its productive power, but its use was insignificant until the 1840s and never spread far beyond the relatively small, if influential, group of progressive farmers. Its high price, owing in part to a Peruvian monopoly of the principal source, led to declining use after 1854.

BIBLIOGRAPHY

Mathew, W. M. *The House of Gibbs and the Peruvian Guano Monopoly.* London: Royal Historical Society, 1981.

Skaggs, Jimmy. *The Great Guano Rush.* New York: St. Martin's Press, 1994.

Fred Cole / C. W.

See also **Agriculture; Fertilizers.**

GUANTÁNAMO BAY, U.S. naval base, naval air station, and U.S. Marine Corps base near the eastern end of the south coast of Cuba. This 36,000-acre compound fell under American control under the terms of the Platt Amendment of 1901, by which the United States obtained the right to intervene in Cuba and to buy or lease territory for naval stations. A new treaty in 1934 eliminated the right of intervention but reasserted prior stipulations in regard to Guantánamo Bay. The Cuban Communist government of Fidel Castro later denied the validity of the treaties, but the United States retained the base. The site has an excellent deep-water land-locked harbor.

BIBLIOGRAPHY

Fitzgibbon, Russell H. *Cuba and the United States, 1900–1935.* Menasha, Wis.: George Banta Publishing, 1935; New York: Russell and Russell, 1964.

Paterson, Thomas G. *Contesting Castro: The United States and the Triumph of the Cuban Revolution.* New York: Oxford University Press, 1994.

Charles B. MacDonald / A. R.

See also **Caribbean Policy; Cuba, Relations with; Treaties with Foreign Nations.**

GUATEMALA, RELATIONS WITH. Guatemala, the most populated Central American country, has historically been the most economically powerful nation in the region, though that power rested with a select elite and U.S. business interests. United States policy in Central America has consisted of defending and promoting American trade and security. In Guatemala, the United States enjoyed considerable influence through informal interests that until 1954 made military intervention unnecessary. The United States held sway over the economy through its dominance in trade and commerce, made possible by authoritarian and dictatorial regimes. The U.S. United Fruit Company (UFCO) was the single largest landowner. Through its banana monopoly, UFCO controlled the railroad, harbors, and steamships vital to national commerce. To the detriment of most Guatemalans, the company prospered by accommodating dictators who kept exploited laborers under control and satisfied the United States' desire for order and stability.

In 1944, a middle-class, student-supported revolution put an abrupt end to dictator Jorge Ubico. This brought about a period of reforms and democratization, including the 1944 elections, the freest the country had seen, and, in 1952, far-reaching land reforms. The banana company vigorously objected to the expropriation of its unused lands. Predictably, UFCO and the U.S. government claimed communists, not maldistribution of national resources, were causing Guatemalan social and political problems. In 1954, the United States organized, funded, and directed a coup to topple the constitutionally elected Jacobo Arbenz Guzman government. The United States wanted to discourage nationalists from challenging American interests, especially in its own "backyard." Although the United States justified its covert intervention on Cold War grounds, close ties between UFCO and the administration of President Dwight Eisenhower provided additional incentive.

The military's return to power lasted more than thirty years and was supported by U.S. funding, which exceeded that of any other Central American country between 1954 and 1970. John F. Kennedy's Alliance for Progress attempted to force Guatemalan reform, but U.S. plans favored big business, caused a growing disparity between rich and poor, and perpetuated Guatemalan dependence. Despite U.S. aid and failed attempts at reform, worsening social conditions and political repression fostered growing rebellion. Beginning in the late 1960s, the U.S.-trained Guatemalan military brutally and often indiscriminately repressed the political opposition, the death toll reaching more than fifty thousand by 1976. Attempting to promote human rights, President Jimmy Carter's administration ceased military aid, but Guatemalan military leaders found other suppliers in western Europe and Israel. The Ronald Reagan administration revived the Cold War and was willing to forgive the abuses of authoritarianism, but Congress blocked arms shipments until a civilian headed the Guatemalan government. In 1985, the Guatemalan military selected its civilian figurehead. Congress resumed military aid and increased economic assistance, but after thirty years of warfare, the rebels still operated throughout most of the country.

BIBLIOGRAPHY

Dosal, Paul J. *Doing Business with the Dictators: A Political History of United Fruit in Guatemala, 1899–1944.* Wilmington, Del.: SR Books, 1993.

Gleijeses, Piero. *Shattered Hope: The Guatemalan Revolution and the United States, 1944–1954.* Princeton, N.J.: Princeton University Press, 1991.

Immerman, Richard H. *The CIA in Guatemala: The Foreign Policy of Intervention.* Austin: University of Texas Press, 1982.

LaFeber, Walter. *Inevitable Revolutions: The United States in Central America.* 2d ed. New York: Norton, 1993.

Leonard, Thomas M. *Central America and the United States: The Search for Stability.* Athens: University of Georgia Press, 1991.

Dominic A. Cerri

See also **Alliance For Progress; Cold War;** *and vol. 9:* **Maya in Exile: Guatemalans in Florida.**

GUERRILLA WARFARE. "Guerrillas" is a term originally applied to quasi-military and irregular groups of Spanish partisans who fought against Napoleon in the Peninsular War (1808–1814), but the type of warfare implied by the term is found everywhere in history, from the most ancient times to the present. The spectrum of guerrilla activity runs from conventional military operations by organized groups to uncoordinated, spontaneous, individual acts of sabotage, subversion, or terrorism carried out against an enemy. Guerrillas normally operate outside of constituted authority.

American guerrilla warfare during colonial times, the Revolution, and the War of 1812 was based to a large degree on knowledge of the Indian tactics of hit-and-run raids, ambush, and cover and concealment. During the Revolutionary War, for example, Francis Marion, the "Swamp Fox" of the southern campaign, used these techniques against the more traditionally organized British forces. In the war with Mexico (1846–1848), enemy guerrillas caused the U.S. army much trouble. The 1850s saw the rise of partisan bands on both sides of the border-state issue, who carried on guerrilla activity that was more often banditry than support for a cause. This activity continued through the Civil War, enlarged by deserters on both sides who raided for profit. Many of these groups—the James and Younger gangs were the most notorious—continued their brigandage well after the war ended.

Until 1917, American troops engaged in guerrilla and partisan activities while fighting Indians in the West and while aiding those fighting for independence in Cuba. They also fought Boxers in China, insurrectionists in the Philippines, and bandits on the Mexican border. Not until World War II were Americans again involved in guerrilla warfare. In the Philippines especially, many American soldiers and civilians, finding themselves cut off, fought with Filipino guerrillas against the Japanese. In all theaters, troops furnished assistance to partisans fighting their homeland's invaders. Most often, the Office of Strategic Services carried out this aid.

In the Korean War, Americans participated in a number of activities either directed at the enemy's guerrilla campaign in the south or in support of South Korean guerrilla operations in the north. In the Vietnam War, commanders directed a major part of the pacification effort at eliminating communist guerrilla activities in the countryside. Small numbers of insurgents effectively tied down major elements of both U.S. and South Vietnamese military forces in every province and district in the country. The ability of the insurgents to blend into the populace and the terror tactics used to ensure their security made their dislodgment and elimination extremely difficult.

BIBLIOGRAPHY

Appleman, Roy E. *South to the Naktong, North to the Yalu; June–November 1950.* Washington, D.C.: Office of the Chief of Military History, Department of the Army, 1961.

Morton, Louis. *Decision to Withdraw to Bataan.* Washington, D.C.: Center of Military History, U.S. Army, 1990. Originally published in Greenfield, Kent R., ed., *Command Decisions,* Center of Military History, U.S. Army, 1960.

Zook, David H., and Robin Higham. *A Short History of Warfare.* New York: Twayne, 1966.

John E. Jessup Jr. / C. W.

See also **Booby Traps; Special Forces; Terrorism; Vietnam War.**

GUFFEY COAL ACTS. Sponsored by the United Mine Workers of America and guided through Congress by Pennsylvania's Senator Joseph Guffey in August 1935, the Bituminous Coal Conservation Act formed an integral part of the Franklin D. Roosevelt administration's effort to create federal regulatory power under the National Industrial Recovery Act. Intended to stabilize an historically chaotic industry, the act sought to establish price controls and production quotas; afford protection to labor; retire marginal coal lands; and, generally, treat the bituminous coal industry, a major source of the nation's heat and fuel, as a public utility. Before portions of the act became operative, the U.S. Supreme Court, by a 5 to 4 decision in the case of *Carter v. Carter Coal Company* (1936), declared sections of the 1935 act unconstitutional.

Recast and amended in light of New Deal political victories and fresh judicial possibilities, it was redesignated the Guffey Coal Act of 1937 and easily passed through Congress. The new act retained key provisions of the original 1935 act, such as federal price-fixing and using taxes to compel compliance with its provisions. Administration of the act, embodying the most complex and comprehensive administrative power ever granted a regulatory agency in peacetime, was vested in the National Bituminous Coal Commission. Although Congress subsequently extended the act through 1943, it was largely unsuccessful. Unfortunate compromises, multiple standards, and the baffling complexities and rivalries of the bituminous coal industry, led Congress to allow the Guffey Act to expire in 1943.

BIBLIOGRAPHY

Brand, Donald Robert. *Corporatism and the Rule of Law: A Study of the National Recovery Administration.* Ithaca, N.Y.: Cornell University Press, 1988.

C. K. Yearley / C. W.

See also ***Carter v. Carter Coal Company*; Codes of Fair Competition; National Recovery Administration.**

GUGGENHEIM MUSEUM. The Solomon R. Guggenheim Museum, located on the Upper East Side of Manhattan in New York City, is an international showplace for twentieth-century art, that is committed to the exhibition of nonobjective art and a movement "from the materialistic to the spiritual . . . from objectivity to non-objectivity." The Guggenheim's holdings began with the private collection of the American mining magnate Solomon R. Guggenheim (1861–1949). He began actively collecting art in 1928, after a visit to Wassily Kandinsky's studio in Dessau, Germany. Inspired by Kandinsky's active, abstract style, Guggenheim spent much of the second half of his life building a robust collection of European and American conceptual and abstract art in collaboration with the German avant-garde artist Hilla Rebay. Guggenheim amassed paintings, sculptures, and collages by many of the twentieth century's most radical artists, such as Kandinsky, Marc Chagall, René Magritte, Willem de Kooning, Jackson Pollock, Alberto Giacometti, Pablo Picasso, and Constantin Brancusi. These holdings, in combination with important later acquisitions, such as the Thannhauser Collection of Impressionist and post-Impressionist art, serve as the core of the contemporary Guggenheim Museum's collection.

At the Guggenheim collection's first exhibition space, a former automobile showroom on East Fifty-fourth Street in New York City, called the Museum of Non-Objective Painting, Rebay oversaw exhibitions of revolutionary new forms of art developed by artists like Kandinsky, Paul Klee, and Piet Mondrian. In 1943, Guggenheim commissioned Frank Lloyd Wright to design and build a permanent home for the collection. Wright conceived of his spiral design as a space where the visitor could view art "truthfully." He believed that the building would force visitors to rethink their ideas about architecture in much the same way that nonobjective art forced viewers to reconsider the definition of painting and sculpture. The planned building immediately became the locus of considerable controversy. After significant financial, political, and intellectual struggles, the museum opened in 1959, four months after Wright's death. It remains one of the world's most profound architectural expressions.

In addition to the Guggenheim New York, Guggenheim museums include the Venice-based Peggy Guggenheim Collection, a rich collection of objects ranging in style from cubism to surrealism to abstract expressionism accumulated by Solomon's niece. The Deutsche Guggenheim Berlin opened in 1997. The Frank O. Gehry–designed Guggenheim Bilbao, Spain, which also opened in 1997, is an undulating titanium-clad structure that further stretches the definition of the modern museum. Special exhibitions as well as multimedia and high-technology art are shown at the Guggenheim Las Vegas, designed by Rem Koolhaas. Also in Las Vegas is the Guggenheim Hermitage Museum, a collaboration with the State Hermitage Museum in St. Petersburg, Russia.

Guggenheim Museum. Frank Lloyd Wright displays a model of his dramatic design for the art museum's second home, 1945; it was finally completed and opened to the public fourteen years later. AP/WIDE WORLD PHOTOS

BIBLIOGRAPHY

Art of Tomorrow: Fifth Catalogue of the Solomon R. Guggenheim Collection of Non-Objective Paintings. New York: Solomon R. Guggenheim Foundation, 1939.

Davis, John H. *The Guggenheims: An American Epic.* New York: Morrow, 1978.

Krens, Thomas. "The Genesis of a Museum." In *Art of the Century: The Guggenheim Museum and Its Collection.* New York: Solomon R. Guggenheim Foundation, 1993.

Stern, Robert A. M., Thomas Mellins, and David Fishman. *New York 1960: Architecture and Urbanism between the Second World War and the Bicentennial.* New York: Monacelli Press, 1995.

Joshua Perelman

See also **Architecture; Art: Painting; Museums.**

GUILFORD COURTHOUSE, BATTLE OF (15 March 1781). Pursued closely by General Charles Cornwallis, General Nathanael Greene retreated northward through North Carolina into Virginia, collecting recruits as he went, then turned south again. At Guilford Courthouse, North Carolina, Greene arranged his 4,404 men—3,000 were militia—for battle. On the afternoon of 15 March 1781, Cornwallis, with 2,213 veterans, attacked. In the ensuing battle, Greene lost 79 men, and 184 were wounded, while nearly 1,000 militia dispersed to their homes. Cornwallis lost 93 men, 413 were wounded, and 26 were missing—nearly one-fourth of his force. The British held the field, but the battle was a strategic victory for the Americans. Cornwallis soon withdrew to Wilmington, North Carolina, abandoning all the Carolinas save for two or three coastal towns.

BIBLIOGRAPHY

Middlekauff, Robert. *The Glorious Cause: The American Revolution, 1763–1789.* New York: Oxford University Press, 1982.

Rankin, Hugh F. *The North Carolina Continentals.* Chapel Hill: University of North Carolina Press, 1971.

Thayer, Theodore. *Nathanael Greene: Strategist of the American Revolution.* New York: Twayne, 1960.

Nelson Vance Russell / A. R.

See also **Revolution, American: Military History; Southern Campaigns.**

GUINN AND BEAL V. UNITED STATES, 238 U.S. 347 (1915), grew out of the attempt by the State of Oklahoma to include in its constitution, on a permanent basis, the grandfather-clause principle, a legal device that had been used by white southern legislators since the 1890s to prevent black Americans from voting. The Supreme Court decided that the provision represented a clear violation of the purpose and intent, if not the express provisions, of the Fifteenth Amendment.

BIBLIOGRAPHY

Elliott, Ward E. Y. *The Rise of Guardian Democracy.* Cambridge, Mass.: Harvard University Press, 1974.

Nieman, Donald G. *Promises to Keep: African-Americans and the Constitutional Order, 1776 to the Present.* New York: Oxford University Press, 1991.

W. Brooke Graves / A. R.

See also **Disfranchisement; Grandfather Clause; Suffrage: African American Suffrage.**

GULF OF SIDRA SHOOTDOWN (19 August 1981). As part of a response to Libya's support of international terrorism, two U.S. Navy F-14 Tomcat fighter planes deliberately flew over the Gulf of Sidra, claimed by Libya as its own territory. When two Libyan warplanes fired a missile at the U.S. planes, the Tomcats shot down both Libyan planes. President Ronald Reagan celebrated by pantomiming a gunslinger shooting from both hips and reasserting that the gulf was international waters. Libya's support for international terrorism continued nonetheless, leading to further incidents in the Gulf of Sidra and eventually the U.S. bombing of Tripoli and Benghazi in April 1985.

BIBLIOGRAPHY

Davis, Brian L. *Qadaffi, Terrorism, and the Origins of the U.S. Attack on Libya.* New York: Praeger, 1990.

El Warfally, Mahmoud. *Imagery and Ideology in U.S. Policy toward Libya, 1969–1982.* Pittsburgh: University of Pittsburgh Press, 1988.

Simons, Geoff. *Libya: The Struggle for Survival.* New York: Macmillan, 1993.

J. Garry Clifford / T. D.

See also **Arab Nations, Relations with; Pan Am Flight 103; Terrorism.**

GULF STREAM. A powerful, warm, surface current in the North Atlantic Ocean, east of North America, the Gulf Stream is one of the strongest known currents. It originates in the Gulf of Mexico as the Florida Current, with an approximate temperature of 80 degrees Fahrenheit, a breadth of no more than fifty miles and a depth of a mile or more. It passes through the Straits of Florida and up along the eastern coast of the United States to the Grand Banks of Newfoundland, Canada, driven northward by southwest winds.

As the Gulf Stream reaches Cape Hatteras, North Carolina, the cold Labrador Current that flows from the north separates it from the coast. At this confluence, the warm Gulf Stream waters combine with the cold winds accompanying the Labrador Current, forming one of the densest concentrations of fog in the world. Because of this immense heat transfer, atmospheric storms tend to intensify in this region. Also at this location, the Gulf Stream is split into two currents: the Canary Currents, which are diverted southeast and carry cooler waters to the Iberian Peninsula and northwestern Africa; and the North Atlantic Drift, which flows northwest toward western Europe, providing temperate waters to the western coastal areas of Europe. The water temperature decreases with the northward flow and the breadth of the current spans several hundred miles at its widest. The average speed of the Gulf Stream is four miles per hour, slowing to one mile per hour as the current widens to the north. The Gulf Stream transports as much as 3.99 billion cubic feet of water per second, an amount greater than that carried by all of the world's rivers combined. The current's core, or jet, follows the contours of the continental rise.

The Spanish explorer Juan Ponce de León was the first to describe the Gulf Stream in 1513 as he searched for the fountain of youth in what is now Florida. The Gulf Stream played a major role in the settling of southeastern regions of the United States. North America's oldest city, St. Augustine, sits on the coast of eastern Florida where the Gulf Stream flows. It was founded during the Spanish period, fifty years or so after De León's trek. When the United States acquired Florida, land speculators quickly moved in and formed large plantations. Tourism in the region escalated soon after, and continued to thrive in the early 2000s, especially along Florida's Treasure Coast. The Gulf Stream was also popularized in art, as evidenced in Winslow Homer's 1899 painting *The Gulf Stream.*

Another major contribution of the Gulf Stream is its warming effect on the climates of adjacent land areas that it passes, especially in northern latitudes, where the coastal weather is quite temperate, even in winter. The Gulf Stream is known as a western-boundary current, a current that is located on the western side of every ocean basin. It is part of a clockwise-rotating system of currents in the North Atlantic. The Gulf Stream is the most extensively studied ocean current in the world, but many questions about it remain unanswered.

BIBLIOGRAPHY

Groves, Donald G., and Lee M. Hunt. *The Ocean World Encyclopedia.* New York: McGraw-Hill, 1980.

Mary Anne Hansen

See also **Climate; Grand Banks; Oceanography.**

GULF WAR OF 1991. *See* **Persian Gulf War.**

GUN CONTROL laws impose restrictions, limitations, or prohibitions on the ownership and use of firearms.

Colonial Era

The first American gun control laws were mandates that families own firearms, that they carry firearms on certain occasions (such as when going to church), and that they train with firearms periodically. These laws sometimes overlapped with militia laws, which required most able-bodied males to participate collectively in the military defense of their communities, using firearms supplied by themselves. However, the state gun control laws tended to go further, requiring gun ownership of people who were not part of the militia (for example, female heads of household).

In England gun control laws had frequently been imposed to disarm religious dissidents or the lower classes, especially during the restoration of the Stuart kings from 1660 to 1688. Colonial America had no analogous laws, although the Massachusetts Bay Colony in the 1630s did disarm the supporters of the religious dissident Anne Hutchinson, whose antinomian heresy favored a less rigid interpretation of the Bible.

Unlike religion, race has been a long-standing concern of American gun control laws. In 1640 Virginia's first recorded legislation about blacks barred them from owning guns. Fear of slave revolts led other southern colonies to enact similar laws. Southern militias enforced the laws preventing blacks from bearing arms, although this was far from the only function of the militia. Many colonial governments attempted to forbid trading firearms with Indians, but these laws were frequently evaded. Similar state and territorial laws in the nineteenth century also had little success.

Nineteenth Century

In antebellum nineteenth-century America, there were very few gun control laws of any kind that applied to white people. The major exception was a restriction on carrying concealed weapons, which was especially common in the South and which may have been an effort to suppress dueling.

An 1822 Kentucky decision, *Bliss v. Commonwealth,* interpreted the state constitution to declare a concealed handgun ban unconstitutional. Most courts, however, ruled that concealed handguns were an exception to the general right to bear arms under the Second Amendment and its many state constitutional analogues.

In 1846 with its *Nunn v. State* decision, the Georgia Supreme Court ruled that a ban on the sale of most handguns violated the Second Amendment of the Constitution. During the nineteenth century, several states enacted special restrictions on edged weapons that were considered suitable only for criminal use (especially bowie knives and dirks). State courts often but not always upheld these laws against constitutional challenges. Usually courts interpreted the state constitution to parallel the federal Second Amendment, and ruled that both state and federal constitutions protected an individual's right to bear arms—primarily the type of arms useful for "civilized warfare," such as rifles, shotguns, muskets, handguns, and swords, but not billy clubs or bowie knives. A minority of courts went further, and extended protection to arms that were useful for personal protection, even if not useful for militia-type service.

In the 1857 *Dred Scott v. Sandford* case, U.S. Supreme Court chief justice Roger B. Taney defended his holding that free blacks could not be citizens, for if blacks were citizens, they would have the right to "the full liberty of speech in public and private upon all subjects upon which its [a state's] own citizens might speak; to hold public meetings upon political affairs, and to keep and carry arms wherever they went." As with most other laws regarding free blacks, state-based restrictions on gun ownership by free blacks grew more severe in the decades leading up to the Civil War. In the early republic North Carolina had enrolled free blacks in its militia, but such a policy had become unthinkable by the 1850s.

Immediately after the Civil War several southern states enacted "black codes," which were designed to keep former slaves in de facto slavery and submission. To provide practical protection for defensive gun ownership by the freedmen, the Republican Congress passed the Freedmen's Bureau Acts (1866 and 1868) and the Civil Rights Act of 1871, and sent the Fourteenth Amendment to the states for ratification. Many southern states, however, reacted by passing gun control laws that were facially neutral, but designed to disarm only blacks. For example, Tennessee in 1871 banned all handguns except the "Army and Navy" models. Former confederate soldiers already owned their high-quality service pistols. Freedmen were precluded from obtaining the inexpensive pistols that were beginning to proliferate in the American market. Other southern states enacted licensing and registration laws. Class violence was the main motive for gun control in the North. For example, an 1879 Illinois law forbade mass armed parades, a measure targeted at fraternal labor organizations. In *Presser v. Illinois* (1886), the U.S. Supreme Court ruled that such parade bans did not violate the Second Amendment.

Twentieth Century

Concerns about anarchists, immigrants, and labor unrest became a powerful basis for gun control in the early twentieth century. South Carolina banned handgun sales and carrying in 1902, allowing only sales to and carrying by sheriffs and their special deputies (company "goons"). The ban was repealed in the 1960s. In 1911 Timothy Sullivan, a state senator from New York, authored the state's Sullivan Law, making a license a requirement for owning handguns and a separate, difficult-to-obtain license a requirement for carrying handguns. The law was sparked by concerns about gun crimes being perpetrated by immigrants, especially Italians and Jews. The Sullivan Law has usually been enforced with great stringency by the New York City Police Department, making it nearly impossible for New Yorkers to obtain a permit to own a handgun.

Oregon (1913) and Hawaii (1934) enacted handgun controls because of labor unrest tied to immigrant radicals. In 1934 California enacted a one-day waiting period (later expanded to fifteen days) for handgun purchases because of concerns about communism, as exemplified by San Francisco's "Red Raids." Many states enacted restrictions or prohibitions on gun possession by aliens.

Racial tension remained an important motive for gun control. Although blacks had been disarmed by the police and did not fight back against white mobs in the East St. Louis riot of 1917, the Missouri legislature still enacted a law requiring a police permit to obtain a handgun. In Michigan handgun permit laws were enacted after Dr. Ossian Sweet, a black man, shot and killed a person in a mob that was attacking his house because he had just moved into an all-white neighborhood. The Detroit police stood nearby, refusing to restrain the angry crowd. Defended by the civil rights attorney Clarence Darrow, Sweet was acquitted in a sensational 1925 trial.

Nationwide alcohol prohibition and the resulting gangster violence led to demands for additional gun control. The first federal law, banning the mail-order delivery of handguns, was enacted in this period. A number of states enacted licensing laws for the carrying of concealed weapons. Based on the model Uniform Pistol and Revolver Act, the laws were usually supported by gun rights advocates as a successful tactic to defuse calls for handgun prohibition. Federally, the National Firearms Act of 1934 imposed a $200 tax and a registration requirement on the ownership of machine guns, short-barreled shotguns, and other weapons thought to be favored by gangsters. A 1938 federal law required firearms dealers to possess federal licenses.

Gun confiscation laws in fascist and communist countries were widely reviled in the United States, and almost no gun control laws were enacted in the 1940s and 1950s. In 1941 Congress amended the Property Requisition Act (allowing the president to seize material needed for war) with specific language to protect the Second Amendment and to prevent the confiscation of personal firearms.

President John F. Kennedy's assassination in 1963 did not immediately lead to more gun control laws, but the urban riots of 1965–1968, sharply rising violent crime rates, and the 1968 assassinations of Martin Luther King Jr. and Robert Kennedy spurred a massive wave of gun controls. Illinois and New Jersey enacted statewide gun licensing; California, aiming at the Black Panthers, restricted the unconcealed carrying of firearms. New York City required the registration of long guns; and many

> [T]his is one of the fundamental principles, upon which rests the great fabric of civil liberty, reared by the fathers of the Revolution and of the country. And the Constitution of the United States, in declaring that the right of the people to keep and bear arms, should not be infringed, only reiterated a truth announced a century before, in the act of 1689, 'to extend and secure the rights and liberties of English subjects'—Whether living 3,000 or 300 miles from the royal palace. . . .
>
> If a well-regulated militia is *necessary* to the *security* of the State of Georgia and of the United States, is it competent for the General Assembly to take away this security, by disarming the people? What advantage would it be to tie up the hands of the national legislature, if it were in the power of the *States* to destroy this bulwark of defence? In solemnly affirming that a well-regulated militia is necessary to the *security* of a *free State,* and that, in order to train properly that militia, the unlimited right of the *people* to *keep* and *bear* arms shall not be impaired, are not the sovereign people of the State committed by this pledge to preserve this right inviolate . . .
>
> The right of the whole people, old and young, men, women and boys, and not militia only, to keep and bear *arms* of every description, and not *such* merely as are used by the *militia,* shall not be *infringed,* curtailed, or broken in upon, in the smallest degree; and all this for the important end to be attained: the rearing up and qualifying a well-regulated militia, so vitally necessary to the security of a free State. Our opinion is, that any law, State or Federal, is repugnant to the Constitution, and void, which contravenes this *right,* originally belonging to our forefathers, trampled under foot by Charles I. and his two wicked sons and successors, re-established by the revolution of 1688, conveyed to this land of liberty by the colonists, and finally incorporated conspicuously in our own *Magna Charta!* And Lexington, Concord, Camden, River Raisin, Sandusky, and the laurel-crowned field of New Orleans plead eloquently for this interpretation! And the acquisition of Texas may be considered the full fruits of this great constitutional right.
>
> —*Excerpt from* Nunn v. State, *1846*

other states and localities enacted laws, especially restrictions on gun carrying.

The federal Gun Control Act (GCA) of 1968 greatly tightened restrictions on firearms dealers, and created a federal list of "prohibited persons" (including convicted felons, persons dishonorably discharged from the military, and drug users) who were barred by federal law from possessing firearms. Concerns about abusive enforcement of the GCA led Congress in 1986 to pass the Firearms Owners' Protection Act, which invoked the Second, Fourth, and Fifth Amendments and restricted search and seizure powers of the federal Bureau of Alcohol, Tobacco and Firearms. The 1986 law also eased the 1968 restrictions on interstate sales of long guns and ammunition.

During this time the first enduring national gun control groups were founded. After a series of name changes, the groups became known as the Brady Campaign and the Coalition to Stop Gun Violence. Several other national groups were formed in the 1980s and 1990s, as well as many state or local affiliates of the national groups. Some celebrities became public advocates for gun control, including the comedian Rosie O'Donnell.

The two terms of the Clinton administration saw an explosion of gun control activity, with the enactment in 1993 of the Brady Act (imposing a waiting period that sunset in 1998) and the requirement that gun sellers use the "National Instant Check System" (a Federal Bureau of Investigations database of convicted felons) before selling guns to a customer at retail. The manufacture of so-called "assault weapons" (guns with a military appearance) was banned in 1994, as was the manufacture of magazines holding more than ten rounds. About a half dozen states have some kind of "assault weapon" law. The administration imposed many other restrictions, especially on gun dealers. According to President Bill Clinton, an antigun control backlash delivered the U.S. House and Senate to the Republicans in the 1994 elections and cost Al Gore the presidency in the 2000 election.

By the early twenty-first century almost all states adopted some kind of "preemption" law to limit or abolish local-level gun controls, thus reserving gun control legislation exclusively to the state legislature; preemption laws became especially popular after handguns were banned by the city of Washington, D.C., and by two Chicago suburbs, Morton Grove and Oak Park.

In 1988 Florida started a trend which by 2002 had led 33 states to adopt "shall issue" laws, requiring authorities to issue concealed handgun carry permits to all adult applicants who pass background checks and (in most states) a safety training class. During the early and mid-1990s when concern about youth violence was especially intense, many states enacted restrictions on juvenile gun (especially handgun) possession.

Over the years, about two dozen court cases have found a local, state, or federal gun control law to violate the Second Amendment or the right to bear arms clause that is contained in forty-four state constitutions. Most gun control laws, however, have withstood legal challenge.

BIBLIOGRAPHY

Carter, Gregg. *The Gun Control Movement.* New York: Twayne, 1997.

Cottrol, Robert, ed. *Gun Control and the Constitution.* New York: Garland, 1993.

Cramer, Clayton. *For the Defense of Themselves and the State: The Original Intent and the Judicial Interpretation of the Right to Keep and Bear Arms.* Westport, Conn.: Praeger, 1994.

Halbrook, Stephen P. *Freedmen, The Fourteenth Amendment, and the Right to Bear Arms, 1866–1876.* Westport, Conn.: Praeger, 1988.

Kopel, David B. *The Samurai, the Mountie, and the Cowboy: Should America Adopt the Gun Controls of Other Democracies?.* Buffalo, N.Y.: Prometheus, 1992.

Young, David, ed. *The Origin of the Second Amendment.* Ontonagon, Mich.: Golden Oak, 1995.

David B. Kopel

See also **Brady Bill.**

GUNBOAT DIPLOMACY can be defined in a general way as any aggressive diplomatic activity carried out with the implicit or explicit use of military (usually naval) power. However, the term is most often associated with the activities of the Great Powers in the second half of the nineteenth century and the early twentieth century. In this period, the construction of steel-hulled vessels of relatively shallow draught (gunboats) that were heavily armed provided new opportunities for the projection of power on the part of rival imperial powers. In the case of the United States, gunboat diplomacy is probably most closely associated with Washington's diplomatic and military interventions in the Caribbean during the early decades of the twentieth century.

With the promulgation of the Roosevelt Corollary to the Monroe Doctrine in 1904 by President Theodore Roosevelt, the use of naval power as an instrument of U.S. foreign policy in the Caribbean and Latin America was explicitly foregrounded. Roosevelt, who had fought in the Spanish-American War (1898), wanted to make the United States the dominant power in the circum-Caribbean and across the Pacific. The U.S. Navy grew in size by ten battleships and four cruisers during Roosevelt's presidency. Under his stewardship the United States played a key role in Panama's break with Colombia and the building of the Panama Canal. He also presided over direct naval intervention in the Dominican Republic. Between 1905 and 1907, gunboat diplomacy ensured U.S. financial supervision and control in that nation while avoiding, at least initially, both the costs and the enmity that went with the establishment of a formal colony. The use of gunboat diplomacy, including the deployment of marines, in support of direct U.S. control over government finances was also central to Washington's involvement in Nicaragua between 1916 and 1933. Meanwhile, the United States intervened in Haiti in 1915, ostensibly out of concern that Germany was planning to establish submarine bases there; U.S. Marines remained in Haiti until 1934.

The high period of gunboat diplomacy can be said to have ended in 1933 with the adoption of the Good Neighbor Policy by President Franklin D. Roosevelt (1933–1945). In the years prior to and immediately after World War II, the United States generally sought to exert its influence in Latin America and other parts of the world without resorting to the explicit use of military force that had characterized gunboat diplomacy.

With the onset of the Cold War, however, Washington turned increasingly to overt and covert forms of naval and military intervention in the Caribbean, Latin America, and beyond. Although Cold War conflict was governed by new imperatives, a number of Washington's post-1945 interventions are still regarded by some observers as updated forms of gunboat diplomacy.

BIBLIOGRAPHY

Cable, James. *Gunboat Diplomacy, 1919–1991: Political Applications of Limited Naval Force.* 3d ed. New York: St. Martin's Press, 1994.

Challener, Richard D. *Admirals, Generals, and American Foreign Policy, 1898–1914.* Princeton, N.J.: Princeton University Press, 1973.

Healy, David. *Drive to Hegemony: The United States in the Caribbean, 1898–1917.* Madison: University of Wisconsin Press, 1988.

Langley, Lester D. *The Banana Wars: United States Intervention in the Caribbean, 1898–1934.* Rev. ed. Lexington: University Press of Kentucky, 1985.

Mark T. Berger

See also **Caribbean Policy; Dominican Republic; Good Neighbor Policy; Haiti, Relations with; Latin America, Relations with; Nicaragua, Relations with.**

GUNBOATS, in the simplest sense, are tiny men-of-war that are extremely overgunned in proportion to size. Their influence dates to the 1776 Battle of Valcour Island on Lake Champlain when Benedict Arnold, with fifteen green-timber boats with cannon, halted a British invasion from Canada. (The *Philadelphia*, one of eleven gunboats sunk during the battle, was raised and restored in 1935 and is exhibited in the Smithsonian Institution. Search teams subsequently found the remaining sunken gunboats, the last being discovered in 1997.)

The gunboats sent to Tripoli during the first Barbary War typically carried twenty to twenty-three men and two twenty-four- or thirty-two-pound cannons in a hull seventy feet long. The boats were effective only along a coast, since, for them to be stable on the open sea, their crews had to stow the cannons below deck. To President Thomas Jefferson, anxious to avoid entanglement in the Napoleonic Wars, such a limitation seemed a virtue.

Congress authorized further commissions, and 176 gunboats were at hand for the War of 1812. The gunboats were almost entirely worthless. Since the token two dozen U.S. blue-water frigates and sloops were highly effective at sea, the U.S. Navy learned an important lesson—do not overinvest in any single type of man-of-war.

In the Civil War, improvised gunboats were found on embattled rivers everywhere. Often, their heavy guns inhibited Confederate movement or prevented such Union disasters as those at Shiloh and Malvern Hill. In the decades before the Spanish-American War, European neocolonialism introduced "gunboat diplomacy," calling for larger, hybrid craft that could safely cross oceans, assume a year-round anchorage on a foreign strand, and possess sufficient shallow draft to go up a river. The 1892 U.S.S. *Castine*, for example, on which Chester W. Nimitz (who became U.S. commander of the Pacific Fleet in World War II) served as a lieutenant, was 204 feet overall, weighed 1,177 tons, and had eight four-inch rifles, making it a far stronger man-of-war than the famous destroyer type then emerging. Of the score of American gunboats before World War II, the half-dozen-strong Chinese Yangtze River patrol was immortalized in the novel *Sand Pebbles* by Richard McKenna. In real life, the *Panay* was sunk without provocation on 12 December 1937 by Japanese bombers. The others in the Far East were destroyed early in World War II.

The inshore fighting of World War II led to the building of forty-one small gunboats (patrol gunboat, or PG) and twenty-three still smaller motor gunboats (patrol gunboat motor, or PGM), with the emphasis on a multiplicity of automatic weapons and on rocket launchers for shore bombardment. The Soviet Union became particularly interested in such vessels, and, by 1972, had at least 200 gunboats.

The U.S. Navy had no interest in modernizing gunboats until the Vietnam War spawned a variety of tiny types used in swarms, either to police the shoreline or to penetrate the riverways. The heaviest types revived the name of "monitor." Since the Vietnam War, the U.S. Navy has developed heavily armed and computerized hydrofoil gunboats capable of exceeding seventy knots and fitted for nighttime amphibious operations.

BIBLIOGRAPHY

Friedman, Norman. *U.S. Small Combatants, Including PT-Boats, Subchasers, and the Brown-Water Navy: An Illustrated Design History.* Annapolis, Md.: Naval Institute Press, 1987.

Lundeberg, Philip K. *The Gunboat Philadelphia and the Defense of Lake Champlain in 1776.* Basin Harbor, Vt.: Lake Champlain Maritime Museum, 1995.

Tucker, Spencer. *The Jeffersonian Gunboat Navy*. Columbia: University of South Carolina Press, 1993.

R. W. Daly / A. R.

See also **Barbary Wars; Navy, United States; *Panay* Incident; Warships; World War II, Navy in.**

GUNPOWDER. *See* **Explosives.**

GUSTAV LINE, a belt of German fortifications in southern Italy during World War II. Hoping to halt the Allied invasion of Italy south of Rome, in November 1943 Field Marshal Albert Kesselring ordered the formation of three defensive belts forty miles deep. The Barbara Line and the Bernhard Line were forward positions designed to gain time to build the final and strongest Gustav Line. Allied troops called all three the Winter Line. Running from Minturno, through Cassino, across the Apennines, and behind the Sangro River to the Adriatic, it blocked the approaches to Rome through Avezzano in the east and through the Liri Valley in the west.

The Germans rooted the Gustav Line in the high ground of Sant' Ambrogio, Monte Cassino, and other peaks that gave them perfect observation over the valleys of the Rapido and Garigliano rivers. Veteran troops had concrete bunkers, machine-gun emplacements, barbed wire, mines, mortars, and artillery to employ against attackers.

Trying to enter the Liri Valley and advance to Anzio, the U.S. Fifth Army attacked the Gustav Line in mid-January 1944. British units crossed the Garigliano but were unable to break the defenses, while American attempts to cross the Rapido and to surmount Monte Cassino failed. After air bombardments destroyed the abbey on Monte Cassino, attacks by New Zealand troops on 15 February and 15 March also failed.

On 11 May, General Alphonse Juin's French Expeditionary Corps broke the Gustav Line, enabling Polish troops to take Monte Cassino, British and Canadian forces to move up the Liri Valley, and American units to advance up the coast to Anzio. Having fought magnificent defensive battles in the Gustav Line, Kesselring withdrew, abandoned Rome, and moved into new defensive positions along the Gothic Line in the northern Apennines.

BIBLIOGRAPHY

Blumenson, Martin. *Bloody River: The Real Tragedy of the Rapido*. Boston: Houghton Mifflin, 1970, 1998.

D'Este, Carlo. *Anzio and the Battle for Rome*. New York: HarperCollins, 1991.

Fisher, Ernest F., Jr. *Cassino to the Alps*. Washington, D.C.: United States Government Printing Office, 1977, 1993.

Martin Blumenson / A. R.

See also **Anzio; Gothic Line; Monte Cassino; Salerno.**

GYPSIES is the general term as well as a self-designation for a number of distinct ethnic groups that differ from one another socially, politically, and economically. Each group maintains social distance from each other and from non-Gypsies. A source of fascination and suspicion, itinerant Gypsies were subject to expulsion by authorities. Between 1859 and 1931, twelve states passed laws, subsequently repealed, to tax or regulate "roving bands of nomads, commonly known as gypsies."

The Romnichels emigrated from England as families primarily from 1850 to 1910. Some purchased land and created settlements or "Gypsy corners"; land ownership provided an assured camping place, loan collateral, or supplementary income. Romnichel immigrants were cutlers, basket makers, and rat catchers, but with the increased use of horses in agriculture and urban transportation, this group's primary occupation became horse trading. They traded horses while traveling and shipped animals by rail to urban sales stables. When the horse trade declined following World War I, they resorted to previously secondary occupations, such as manufacturing rustic furniture, basketry, fortune-telling, driveway paving, and septic tank cleaning.

Although their religious preferences were conventionally Protestant, many formed fundamentalist Christian congregations. Kindreds, identified by surnames, are associated with distinctive cultural and psychological traits that are important in social evaluations based on an ideology distinguishing ritually clean from unclean behavior.

Rom families emigrated from Serbia and the Russian empire during the late nineteenth and early twentieth centuries in groups as large as two hundred persons. Although Rom occupations included horse trading, fortune-telling, and repairing industrial equipment, coppersmithing, the wipe tinning of copper kettles, was a specialty. When new technologies replaced copper vessels and horses, Roma developed urban fortune-telling businesses, using vacant stores for both houses and businesses and contracting with amusement parks and carnivals. Local ordinances and Rom territoriality based on the fortune-telling business dictated population density. Driveway sealing and paving, trade in scrap metal or used vehicles, and auto body repair also became common occupations. During the Great Depression, spurred by the Rom leader Steve Kaslov and Eleanor Roosevelt, the Works Progress Administration (WPA) and social service agencies in New York City established short-lived adult education classes and a coppersmith workshop for this group.

Rom kinship is strongly patrilineal, and household organization is patrilocal. Conflicts are resolved by juridical systems that impose fines or the threat of banishment. Their ideology separates pure from impure, good luck from bad, male from female, and Gypsy from non-Gypsy. Marriages are arranged by families and include a bride price, or couples elope. Roma generally are Roman Catholic or Eastern Orthodox, and their communal rituals echo Serbian Orthodox practices. However, some Roma founded Pentecostal Christian churches that preached against earlier practices.

Ludars immigrated to the United States between 1880 and 1910 from Bosnia and speak a Romanian dialect. Animal exhibitors, they arrived with trained bears and monkeys. Initially, they worked in horse trading and industrial wage labor. The Great Depression forced some to take WPA-sponsored road construction work, while the WPA circus employed a Ludar showman and his performing bear. Subsequent occupations included carnival concessions, manufacturing outdoor furniture, driveway paving, and seasonal agricultural work.

From 1908 to 1939, Ludars established permanent camps on leased land, particularly in the Bronx and Queens, New York; Stickney Township near Chicago; and Delaware County, Pennsylvania, from which they made seasonal journeys or commuted to tell fortunes from house to house. Ludar religion is traditionally Eastern Orthodox, and marriages, arranged by parents with a bride price, are performed by a justice of the peace or in Orthodox or Catholic churches.

Slovak Gypsies, historically sedentary, immigrated to the United States during the late nineteenth and early twentieth centuries primarily from Saros County in eastern Slovakia. Speaking a dialect of Romani, the men arrived singly or in small groups, and their wives and children followed later. Defined by musical performances, some settled in New York City, where they played in saloons, hotels, and theaters. Others, including the WPA Gypsy orchestras, established settlements in western Pennsylvania; Youngstown and Cleveland, Ohio; Detroit; and Chicago, where they played for ethnic and general audiences and performed industrial labor. Most remained Roman Catholics.

BIBLIOGRAPHY

Gropper, Rena C. *Gypsies in the City: Culture Patterns and Survival.* Princeton, N.J: Darwin Press, 1975.

Lockwood, William G., and Sheila Salo. *Gypsies and Travelers in North America: An Annotated Bibliography.* Cheverly, Md.: Gypsy Lore Society, 1994.

Salo, Matt T. "Gypsy Ethnicity: Implications of Native Categories and Interaction for Ethnic Classification." *Ethnicity* 6, no. 1 (1979): 73–96.

Salo, Matt T., and Sheila Salo. "Gypsy Immigration to the United States." In *Papers from the Sixth and Seventh Annual Meetings, Gypsy Lore Society, North American Chapter.* Edited by Joanne Grumet. New York: Gypsy Lore Society, 1986.

———. "Romnichel Economic and Social Organization in Urban New England, 1850–1930." *Urban Anthropology* 11, no. 3–4 (1982): 273–313.

Sutherland, Anne. *Gypsies: The Hidden Americans.* Prospect Heights, Ill.: Waveland Press, 1986.

Matt T. Salo
Sheila Salo

See also **Ethnohistory; Immigration.**

HABEAS CORPUS, WRIT OF, is a legal procedure by which a court inquires into the lawfulness of a person's confinement. It takes the form of an order from a court or judge requiring the custodian to produce the prisoner in court for a judicial investigation into the validity of the detention. In the words of Chief Justice John Marshall, "The writ of habeas corpus is a high prerogative writ, known to the common law, the great object of which is the liberation of those who may be imprisoned without sufficient cause. It is in the nature of a writ of error, to examine the legality of the commitment" (*Ex Parte Watkins*, 1830).

Habeas corpus is celebrated as "the great writ of liberty," and has a special resonance in Anglo-American legal history, because the availability of the procedure means that if an individual is found to have been imprisoned illegally the court can release him or her, thus enforcing the rule of law and frustrating governmental oppression. "Its root principle is that in a civilized society, government must always be accountable to the judiciary for a man's imprisonment: if the imprisonment cannot be shown to conform with the fundamental requirements of law, the individual is entitled to his immediate release" (*Fay v. Noia*, 1963).

The use of the writ against the Crown can be traced to the fifteenth century, with the judges drawing their authority both from the common law and from statutes. The most significant English legislation was the Habeas Corpus Act of 1679, which was widely copied throughout the American colonies and remained influential well into the nineteenth century. All states today retain the procedure in one form or another. Reflecting the importance attached to the writ, the U.S. Constitution (Article 1, section 9, clause 2) forbade its suspension "unless when in Cases of Rebellion or Invasion the public Safety may require it," and the Judiciary Act of 1789 authorized the federal courts to issue it. Pursuant to this authority, the early Supreme Court ordered the release of prisoners taken during the Whiskey Rebellion (*United States v. Hamilton*, 1795) of an individual detained in the District of Columbia for no better reason than that "he was an evil doer and disturber of the peace" (*Ex Parte Burford*, 1806), and of two of Aaron Burr's alleged coconspirators who had been arrested by the army (*Ex Parte Bollman*, 1807).

While there have been limited suspensions of the writ on several occasions, the most widespread occurred during the Civil War under orders from President Abraham Lincoln, for which he subsequently received congressional authority. In 1867, the Reconstruction Congress passed a statute explicitly authorizing the federal courts to adjudicate petitions filed by state prisoners asserting that they were being held "in custody in violation of the Constitution or law or treaties of the United States." The current federal habeas corpus statutes (28 *U.S. Code*, sections 2241, 2254) are direct descendants of the 1867 act.

Like other Reconstruction legislation, the act was narrowly construed by the Supreme Court during the last decades of the nineteenth century. This attitude underwent a change in the first quarter of the twentieth century, as exemplified by *Moore v. Dempsey* (1923), in which the Supreme Court held that the writ should issue to investigate allegations by black petitioners that their state convictions for murder in the wake of a massive race riot in Phillips County, Arkansas, had been procured by egregious government misconduct, including physical torture.

While the Supreme Court broadened its recognition of substantive constitutional rights against the states during the second half of the twentieth century, the occasions for the use of the writ of habeas corpus in federal court by state prisoners increased, especially in criminal cases. As a result, there were a number of unsuccessful efforts through the 1940s and 1950s to amend the federal statute so as to limit the writ's availability. Such proposals reappeared frequently during the 1970s and 1980s. In 1996, following the bombing of a federal building in Oklahoma City, Congress passed the Anti-Terrorism and Effective Death Penalty Act. This act rewrote the procedural rules governing the writ in an effort to speed up judicial proceedings, particularly in capital cases. Interpretations of the statute by the Supreme Court during the first five years of its effectiveness reflected the view that these changes were not, however, intended to work any fundamental changes in the scope of the rights that prisoners could vindicate through the writ. For example, in the case of *Immigration and Naturalization Service v. St. Cyr* (2001), the Court ruled that the act did not repeal habeas jurisdiction over immigrants confined pending deportation.

BIBLIOGRAPHY

Freedman, Eric M. *Habeas Corpus: Rethinking the Great Writ of Liberty.* New York: New York University Press, 2001.

Liebman, James S., and Randy Hertz. *Federal Habeas Corpus Practice and Procedure.* 4th ed. Charlottesville, Va.: Lexis Law Publishing, 2002.

Eric M. Freedman

See also **Constitution of the United States.**

HAGUE PEACE CONFERENCES (1899, 1907), which met at the Hague in the Netherlands, reflected a contemporary peace movement, alarm over the growing alliance system and arms race, early agitation for some type of world organization, and desires to codify international law. The first conference was prompted by Tsar Nicholas II of Russia, who in a rescript issued on 24 April 1898 sought "the progressive development of the present armaments" and "the most effective means of insuring to all peoples the benefits of a real and durable peace."

Delegates from twenty-six states, including the United States and Mexico from the Western Hemisphere, assembled for the first conference from 18 May to 29 July 1899. The U.S. delegation was headed by Andrew D. White, the U.S. minister to Russia and former president of Cornell University. The conference reached modest agreement on rules of land and maritime warfare. The agreements outlawed three innovations in weapons (asphyxiating gases, expanding or "dumdum" bullets, and projectiles or explosives from balloons), but the conferees failed to make headway on limiting arms. On 29 July every participating nation agreed to the Convention for the Pacific Settlement of International Disputes, which advanced the concept of resolving differences through mediation by a third party, international commissions, or the international tribunal at the Hague. It was stipulated, however, that the arbitration was not compulsory and did not extend to questions involving national honor or integrity. The U.S. delegation insisted on a reservation concerning disputes involving application of the Monroe Doctrine. To facilitate arbitration, the delegates created the Permanent Court of Arbitration, essentially a list of judges from which powers could select a panel if the need arose.

The second conference met from 15 June to 18 October 1907. In 1904, fifteen representatives of the Interparliamentary Union, an association of legislators from various nations, had met in St. Louis, Missouri. Under the leadership of Representative Richard Barthold (Republican from Missouri), the legislators agreed to work toward a second conference. In his 1904 annual message, President Theodore Roosevelt proposed the meeting but graciously allowed the tsar to take credit. Forty-four governments sent delegates, this time including nineteen from the Americas. Joseph H. Choate, a former ambassador to Great Britain, headed the U.S. delegation. Armament discussions again failed, but conventions developed on laws of war, naval warfare, and neutrality, plus one renouncing the right to use force to collect debts. The 1907 convention renewed the declaration prohibiting the charge of projectiles from balloons but did not reaffirm the declarations concerning gas and bullets. A revised Convention for the Pacific Settlement of International Disputes included a provision for an International Court of Prize, which served as a court of appeal in case neutral ships were captured in wartime. Delegates could not agree on how to create a court of arbitral justice, something strongly supported by the United States, but the relevant commission unanimously adopted a resolution supporting "the principle of obligatory arbitration." The conference adopted a revised version of the Drago Doctrine, formulated on 29 December 1902 by Louis M. Drago, the foreign minister of Argentina. That doctrine specified that European powers must not use armed force to collect national debts owed by American nations to foreign creditors.

Peace workers anticipated a third conference in 1915, because the delegates in 1907 had believed periodic meetings were the best way to handle international problems. Although World War I ended that hope, suggestions for another assembly appeared well into the 1930s. The assumptions implicit in such thinking, plus the precedents of 1899 and 1907 in the form of conventions, declarations, and stated desires, contributed substantially to later and more fully developed international institutions, including the League of Nations, the United Nations, and international courts of justice.

BIBLIOGRAPHY

Davis, Calvin D. *The United States and the First Hague Peace Conference.* Ithaca, N.Y.: Cornell University Press, 1962.

———. *The United States and the Second Hague Peace Conference: American Diplomacy and International Organization, 1899–1914.* Durham, N.C.: Duke University Press, 1975.

Kuehl, Warren F. *Seeking World Order: The United States and International Organization to 1920.* Nashville, Tenn.: Vanderbilt University Press, 1969.

Justus D. Doenecke
Warren F. Kuehl

See also **International Court of Justice; International Law; Peace Conferences.**

HAGUE V. COMMITTEE ON INDUSTRIAL ORGANIZATION, 307 U.S. 496 (1939). Decided by the U.S. Supreme Court in 1939 on a five to two vote, *Hague v. Committee on Industrial Organization* enjoined Frank ("Boss") Hague, mayor of Jersey City, and other city officials from enforcing local ordinances to harass labor organizers. The case marked a victory for the new industrial union organization, known as the CIO; it also marked the first time that the Supreme Court invoked the First Amendment to protect labor organizing. The case is significant as the source of the "public forum" doctrine, as the Supreme Court repudiated its own older doctrine that government ownership of the land on which streets and parks are situated gave officials the same right as private landlords to refuse access to those public spaces.

BIBLIOGRAPHY

Kaplan, Benjamin. "The Great Civil Rights Case of *Hague v. CIO*: Notes of a Survivor." 25 *Suffolk University Law Review* 25 (1991): 913.

William E. Forbath

See also **American Federation of Labor-Congress of Industrial Organizations; Trade Unions.**

HAIRSTYLES throughout U.S. history have reflected political, social, and cultural trends as well as personal taste in grooming.

The Puritans, who were among the first European settlers in the United States, cut their hair in a way that expressed their staunch Christian beliefs and antimonarchist politics. In their native England, Puritan men were known as "Roundheads" because they cut their hair short in contrast to their monarchist enemies, the Cavaliers, who sported the courtly style of long, flowing locks. As the Puritans secured their base of power in seventeenth-century colonial Massachusetts, they passed such laws as the one in 1634 that banned long hair if it was "uncomely" or harmed "the common good."

As the colonies grew and were settled by other Europeans, the Puritan hair ethic was replaced by a hair aesthetic that to date is unique in American history. Early eighteenth-century hairstyles, rooted in European royal fashions, were distinctive for their extravagant use of wigs, hair extensions, curling, crimping, and powdering for both men and women. The 1700s was the only period in U.S. history when it was socially acceptable for men to wear long hair and wigs. Even military men styled their hair long, tied back into a pigtail, and powdered it white or gray. In the decades just prior to the Revolution, American women of the upper class mirrored the high hairstyles of their European counterparts and used cushions, pads, wigs, and wires to have their hairstyles reach new heights. Patriotic fervor felled these towers of hair, which had become synonymous with the English royalty, and women's hairstyles became more modest. By the end of the eighteenth century, men were also opting for simpler hairstyles and were abandoning their wigs, powder, and pigtails.

A Line of Curls. Women show off hairstyles featuring curls and ringlets at a convention of hairdressers in Hartford, Conn. AP/ Wide World Photos

In the nineteenth century, more elaborate hairstyles gradually returned for women. Chignons, curls, and braids all had their moment of style, and women often used wigs or hair extensions to achieve their coifs. Between 1859 and 1860, $1 million worth of hair was imported into the United States for wig making. By the end of the century, women's hair reached another high note when hair extensions were commonly used for a top-knotted style that later became known as "the Gibson girl."

In the early 1800s, two hairstyle controversies involved men. The first occurred in 1803 when Lieutenant Colonel Thomas Butler was court-martialed for favoring the longer style of the previous century and thereby disobeying General James Wilkinson's 1801 decree that military men's hair be cropped. The second occurred in 1830, when James Palmer, who wore a beard, moved to Fitchburg, Massachusetts. Since the colonial era, beards were uncommon on men, and Palmer's beard so outraged the townspeople of Fitchburg that he was physically assaulted, refused communion in church, and eventually jailed.

Palmer was, evidently, slightly ahead of his time in the United States. At about the same time as his arrest in Massachusetts, European Romantic writers were growing beards as a sign of the Romantic movement's revolutionary character and its deep tie to nature. The American Romantic poet Walt Whitman, like his European counterparts, wore a full beard. By mid-century, however, beards became such commonplace fashion that in 1853 the War Department officially issued regulations about how military men could wear beards. Civil War general Ambrose Burnside popularized the style of side-whiskers that became known by the corrupted version of his last name, sideburns. As the 1800s drew to a close, so did the fashion of facial hairstyles for men.

During the twentieth century, hairstyles were often used as symbols of social revolution. At the beginning of the century, women began to experience unprecedented social freedom. In the 1920s newly liberated women demonstrated the cut with past social restrictions by having their hair cut into bobs. Later in the twentieth century, long hair was a symbol of the 1960s' peace and counterculture movements. The Black Liberation Movement also expressed its revolutionary "Black Is Beautiful" stance with the full and natural hairstyle known as the Afro, which was popular in the late 1960s and early 1970s. In prior decades, fashionable black hair was "conked," or chemically treated to straighten its natural tight curl. In the 1980s and onward, black Americans expressed a renewed pride in their ancestry by wearing braided styles traditional to African countries.

Throughout the twentieth century, hairstyles were generally less formal and easier to maintain than they had been in previous centuries. The 1950s' and 1960s' bouffant and beehive styles, which required quantities of hair spray, hair extensions, and padding, were notable exceptions and recalled the high hairstyles of the eighteenth and nineteenth centuries. In general, as the formalities and conventions of American society have relaxed over time so have Americans' hairstyles, which in the early twenty-first century have mainly required a cut and combing to be fashionable.

BIBLIOGRAPHY

Corson, Richard. *Fashions in Hair: The First Five Thousand Years.* New York: Hastings House, 1965.

Simon, Diane. *Hair: Public, Political, Extremely Personal.* New York: St. Martin's Press, 2000.

John Wyzalek

See also **Clothing and Fashion.**

HAITI, RELATIONS WITH. Relations between the United States and Haiti, the two oldest republics in the Western Hemisphere, have often been troubled. For most of the nineteenth and early twentieth centuries, race played a key role in the contact between the two nations. During the last several decades, other issues—immigration, security, and narcotics trafficking—have dominated their relationship.

In 1804, following years of rebellion against their French masters, Haitians were able to declare the independence of their island nation (which also encompassed the present-day nation of the Dominican Republic until 1844). Despite profitable trade relations with Haiti, the United States did not recognize the new republic. Southern congressmen, and their slave-owning constituents, were appalled at the thought of the "negro republic" and the dangerous message it might send to the millions of enslaved African Americans in the United States. It was not until 1862, during the Civil War, that the United States extended formal diplomatic recognition to Haiti. Still reflecting the intense racism in America, however, the Department of State appointed mostly African Americans—including Frederick Douglass—to head the U.S. diplomatic mission in Haiti in the post–Civil War period.

In the years following the Civil War, the American focus on Haiti began to sharpen as the United States pursued aggressive commercial and territorial overseas expansion. American industry, which needed both markets and sources for raw materials, saw Haiti as a relatively untapped resource. United States officials and businessmen worked assiduously to secure the Haitian market, and by the turn of the century, the United States ranked second only to France in trade with the Caribbean nation. The United States also developed a keen strategic interest in Haiti, for the American navy was clamoring for a Caribbean port to serve as a coaling station and base from which to protect America's lines of trade in the region. Môle St.-Nicolas, the finest port in Haiti, fit the bill nicely. Throughout the late nineteenth century, the United States attempted to secure a lease on the port, but Haiti refused.

During the early 1900s, U.S. concern with Haiti intensified. Part of the concern revolved around the increasing German economic presence in Haiti that threatened in some instances to displace American interests. Both the French and German governments were not above using diplomatic pressure and threats of intervention to induce Haiti to pay its debts or offer concessions. In 1910, the United States attempted to blunt the Europeans' penetration of Haiti by convincing the Haitian government to accept a major loan and offer American businesses profitable economic concessions. In 1915, Haitian political instability exploded into violence and the nation's president was seized and murdered by an angry crowd. In response, President Woodrow Wilson ordered U.S. marines into the nation to restore order and protect American interests. Thus began an American occupation of Haiti that lasted until 1934. During those years, American control of the Haitian economy became complete, despite occasional revolts by Haitian peasants.

By the late 1920s and early 1930s, with the Great Depression in full swing, the costly, and sometimes bloody, occupation of Haiti became extremely unpopular with the American people. President Franklin Roosevelt, as part of his Good Neighbor policy, promised to end the American military presence. With the withdrawal of U.S. forces in 1934, the Haitian military—armed and trained by the United States during the occupation—filled the political void. The key figure who emerged from the political uncertainty in Haiti following the U.S. withdrawal was François "Papa Doc" Duvalier, who used the military to gain election to the presidency in 1957. Duvalier soon proved himself to be a completely corrupt and brutal dictator, who used his secret police force (the Tonton Macoutes) to intimidate and murder his opposition. He managed, however, to maintain good relations with the United States because of his professed tough stance against communism. In 1971, the old dictator passed away and was immediately replaced by his teenage son, Jean-Claude.

Beginning in the 1980s, U.S.-Haitian relations began to deteriorate rapidly. A new emphasis on human rights by President Jimmy Carter was part of the reason, and the American government began to hammer away at the blatant human rights abuses in Haiti. However, other factors were also involved. Drug trafficking became a widespread problem in Haiti, and U.S. officials chided the Haitian government for its ineffective measures to stem the flow of narcotics into America. Hundreds, and then thousands, of Haitian "boat people," attempting to flee the brutal political repression and poverty of their homeland, flooded into the United States. Most were immediately returned to Haiti, resulting in a cry of racism from Haitian American groups who compared the cold shoulder turned to Haitian immigrants to the warm welcome enjoyed by Cuban refugees. These and other issues increased American concerns about the security of Haiti and fears of radical forces taking control from the Duvalier regime.

Haitian Refugees. One of the many boatloads of Haitians who fled their country and tried—not always successfully—to reach the United States during the three years before the U.S. military and other forces restored the deposed president Jean-Bertrand Aristide to power in 1994. AP/Wide World Photos

In 1986, Duvalier fled Haiti amidst growing political instability and frequent riots. His departure did little to improve the lot of the average Haitian or to soothe American concerns for the future of the nation. What followed was a confusing procession of juntas, provisional governments, and postponed, cancelled, or rigged elections, all under the savagely brutal hand of the Haitian military. Under intense diplomatic and economic pressure from the United States, Haitian elections were held in December 1990, resulting in the selection of Jean-Bertrand Aristide as the new president. Within a year, however, Aristide was forced from office by the military. The United States responded with economic sanctions and threats of intervention if Aristide was not restored to power. As chaos and violence engulfed Haiti, the United States, with support from the United Nations and the Organization of American States, organized and led a multinational force into Haiti in September 1994. Aristide was restored to power. He was succeeded by Réné Preval, who was elected in 1996.

Most of the multinational force was withdrawn from Haiti, leaving a United Nations peacekeeping force of six thousand. The goal of the UN force was to maintain order, train a new Haitian police force, and oversee future elections. The United States pumped millions of dollars of economic assistance into Haiti during the late 1990s. While many of the worst examples of political corruption and brutality began to come to an end following the U.S.-led intervention, the situation in Haiti remained tense and uncertain. Despite American and international economic assistance, the Haitian economy continued to perform badly, and Haiti remained one of the poorest nations in the world. As of 2002, illegal immigration from Haiti remained a source of friction with the United States, as did the issue of drug trafficking. It seemed unlikely that any of these problems would disappear in the years to come.

BIBLIOGRAPHY

Logan, Rayford W. *The Diplomatic Relations of the United States and Haiti, 1776–1891.* Chapel Hill: University of North Carolina Press, 1941.

Plummer, Brenda Gayle. *Haiti and the United States: The Psychological Moment.* Athens: University of Georgia Press, 1992.

Renda, Mary A. *Taking Haiti: Military Occupation and the Culture of U.S. Imperialism, 1915–1940.* Chapel Hill: University of North Carolina Press, 2001.

Schmidt, Hans. *The United States Occupation of Haiti, 1915–1934.* New Brunswick, N.J.: Rutgers University Press, 1971.

Michael L. Krenn

See also **Caribbean Policy; Intervention.**

HAKLUYT'S *VOYAGES*, the short title of a collection of original records of English voyages overseas before 1600. The full title is *The Principall Navigations, Voiages, and Discoveries of the English Nation* (published, folio, 1589; expanded to three volumes, 1598–1600). The editor was Richard Hakluyt, clergyman, geographer, and promoter and historiographer of the English expansion. The materials he collected after 1600 were in part included in the more ambitious, but much less careful or complete, work of Samuel Purchas, *Purchas his Pilgrimes* (1625, four volumes, folio).

Hakluyt's American section, volume 3 of the *Voyages* and part 2 of Purchas, is an admirable body of source materials for the early history of the English in the New World, the first such collection published for any European nation. For virtually every voyage of importance, Hakluyt procured a full narrative by a participant and added many official documents and private letters. He thus preserved the original and often unique records of the voyages of Jacques Cartier, Sir John Hawkins, Sir Francis Drake, Sir Martin Frobisher, John Davys, Thomas Cavendish, Sir Walter Raleigh (to Guiana), and (in *Purchas*) Henry Hudson and William Baffin. He also preserved the records of the colonial projects of French Florida, Adrian Gilbert's Newfoundland, and Raleigh's Virginia.

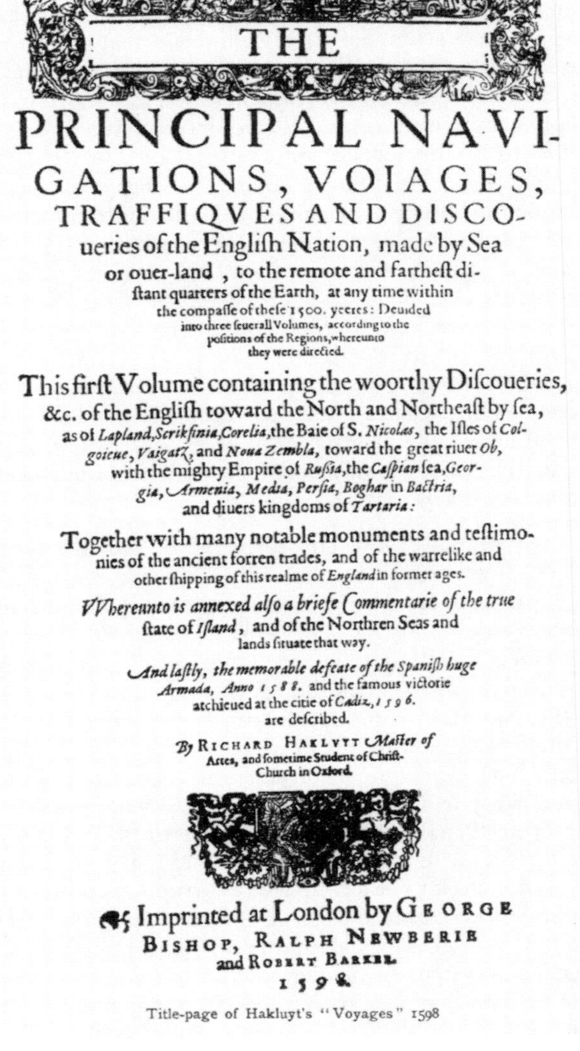

THE

PRINCIPAL NAVIGATIONS, VOIAGES, TRAFFIQVES AND DISCOueries of the Englifh Nation, made by Sea or ouer-land, to the remote and fartheft diftant quarters of the Earth, at any time within the compaffe of thefe 1500. yeeres: Deuided into three feuerall Volumes, according to the pofitions of the Regions, whereunto they were directed.

This firft Volume containing the woorthy Difcoueries, &c. of the Englifh toward the North and Northeaft by fea, as of *Lapland, Scrikfinia, Corelia*, the Baie of S. *Nicolas*, the Ifles of *Colgoicue, Vaigatz*, and *Noua Zembla*, toward the great riuer *Ob*, with the mighty Empire of *Rufsia*, the *Cafpian* fea, *Georgia, Armenia, Media, Perfia, Boghar* in *Bactria*, and diuers kingdoms of *Tartaria*:

Together with many notable monuments and teftimonies of the ancient forren trades, and of the warrelike and other fhipping of this realme of *England* in former ages.

VVhereunto is annexed alfo a briefe Commentarie of the true ftate of *Ifland*, and of the Northren Seas and lands fituate that way.

And laftly, the memorable defeate of the Spanifh huge Armada, Anno 1588. and the famous victorie atchieued at the citie of *Cadiz*, 1596. are defcribed.

By RICHARD HAKLVYT *Mafter of* Artes, and fometime Student of Chrift-Church in Oxford.

Imprinted at London by GEORGE BISHOP, RALPH NEWBERIE and ROBERT BARKER. 1598.

Title-page of Hakluyt's "Voyages" 1598

Hakluyt's *Voyages*. The 1598 title page of Richard Hakluyt's rich collection of material on the earliest English voyages to the New World. NORTH WIND PICTURE ARCHIVES

BIBLIOGRAPHY

Parks, G. B. *Richard Hakluyt and the English Voyages.* New York: Ungar, 1961.

George B. Parks/A. R.

See also **Explorations and Expeditions: British.**

***HALF MOON*,** the ship the Dutch East India Company provided for the voyage of exploration made by Henry Hudson in 1609, in the course of which the HUDSON RIVER was discovered. A vessel of eighty tons, it was a flat-bottomed two-master. Called by the Dutch a *vlieboot*, a term derived from the island of Vlieland, it has been translated into English, without reference to its derivations, as "flyboat." Later employed in the East India trade, the *Half Moon* was wrecked in 1615 on the shore of the island of Mauritius, then owned by the Dutch.

BIBLIOGRAPHY

Syme, Ronald. *Henry Hudson.* New York: Marshall Cavendish, 1991.

A. C. Flick/A. R.

See also **Albany; Explorations and Expeditions: British; New York State.**

HALF-BREEDS. *See* **Indian Intermarriage.**

HALFWAY COVENANT. As the second generation of Puritans began to move away from their parents' exceedingly strict definition of sainthood, church elders were faced with a serious problem. If, as they reached adulthood, children of the founders of MASSACHUSETTS and CONNECTICUT gave no acceptable proof of that spiritual experience called regeneration, should they be granted full church membership? In June 1657, an intercolonial ministerial conference at Boston attempted to answer through the Halfway Covenant, whereby membership was granted to the children whose parents had experienced regeneration but, pending regeneration of their own, participation in the Lord's Supper and voting in the church were withheld. Although a Massachusetts synod proclaimed it for all Massachusetts churches (1662), controversy continued for more than a century.

BIBLIOGRAPHY

Foster, Stephen. *The Long Argument: English Puritanism and the Shaping of New England Culture, 1570–1700.* Chapel Hill: University of North Carolina Press, 1991.

Rutman, Darrett B. *Winthrop's Boston: A Portrait of a Puritan Town, 1630–1649.* Chapel Hill: University of North Carolina Press, 1965.

Raymond P. Stearns/A. R.

See also **Congregationalism; Meetinghouse; "New England Way"; Puritans and Puritanism; Religion and Religious Affiliation; Religious Thought and Writings.**

HAMBURG RIOT (8 July 1876), the pivotal clash in the struggle between the RADICAL REPUBLICANS and the Democrats for the control of SOUTH CAROLINA. Several hundred armed white men gathered in Hamburg to force the disarming of a black militia company accused of obstructing the streets. In the melee that followed, one white man and seven black men were killed. Daniel H. Chamberlain, the Republican governor, called the affair a massacre engineered for political purposes. His remarks alienated the governor's white supporters and assured victory for the enemies of compromise in the state Democratic convention the following August.

BIBLIOGRAPHY

Holt, Thomas C. *Black over White: Negro Political Leadership in South Carolina During Reconstruction.* Urbana: University of Illinois Press, 1977.

Zuczek, Richard. *State of Rebellion: Reconstruction in South Carolina.* Columbia: University of South Carolina Press, 1996.

Francis B. Simkins/A. R.

See also **Reconstruction; Red Shirts; Riots.**

HAMILTON'S ECONOMIC POLICIES. In 1789, Congress created the Department of the Treasury, including the cabinet post of secretary of the Treasury, and required the secretary to report directly to Congress. President George Washington appointed Alexander Hamilton as the first secretary of the Treasury.

During 1790 and 1791, Hamilton embarked on an ambitious plan of economic nationalism. He intended the plan to solve the economic problems that had plagued the United States since the American Revolution and to provide the means to defend the new republic. Beginning in January 1790 with the "Report on the Public Credit," he advanced his plan in a series of reports to Congress. His plan contained seven central elements.

Foreign Debts

The first element called for paying off in full the loans that foreign governments had made to the Continental Congress during the Revolution. In 1790 the principal on these loans amounted to roughly $10 million. The United States owed two-thirds of these debts to France, one-third to the Netherlands, and a small amount to Spain. In addition, unpaid interest of about $1.6 million had accrued. Hamilton proposed that the federal government pay the interest out of tax revenues and borrow, over a fifteen-year period, enough capital to repay the principal of the loans. No one in Congress or the administration challenged Hamilton's arguments that the United States had a legal and moral obligation to pay off these debts, and that it had to do so in order to establish the credit of the United States, and its citizens, in European financial markets.

Domestic Debts

The second element was more controversial. This was Hamilton's proposal for repaying the debts that the Continental Congress and the Confederation government had incurred by borrowing domestically—that is, from individuals and American state governments. These debts, amounting to about $42.4 million, had resulted from the selling of bonds to supporters of the Revolution and the issuing of various notes to pay soldiers and farmers and merchants who had supplied the revolutionary armies. This proposal consisted of two parts.

Alexander Hamilton. The first secretary of the Treasury.
LIBRARY OF CONGRESS

First, Hamilton recommended "redemption" of the debt at full value. By "redemption," he meant offering to trade the complicated morass of notes and bonds of varying durations and interest rates for new, long-term federal bonds. These new securities would pay fixed, attractive rates of interest. Second, Hamilton recommended that the federal government maintain this new debt as a permanent feature of the fiscal landscape. To demonstrate the commitment of the federal government to maintaining the value of this permanent debt, Hamilton proposed creating a "sinking fund," based on the method used by the British government to manage its debt. The Treasury would establish this fund within a national bank (which Hamilton promised to propose soon) and supply it with surplus revenues of the post office and the proceeds of a new European loan. A management committee consisting of the secretary of the Treasury, the vice president of the United States, the speaker of the House, the chief justice, and the attorney general would then use this fund to purchase public securities if they circulated below their par value. In so doing, the committee would maintain a floor under the price of these securities.

Hamilton believed that the two parts of the plan would work together. The plan would create a class of wealthy citizens who, because they were long-term creditors of the new national government, would be loyal to it and take an active interest in its affairs. As a consequence, the central government would be strong and able to finance wars or fund major national projects. In addition, the permanent debt, because its owners could readily convert it into money or other assets, would provide capital to meet the needs of an expanding economy.

Members of Congress generally agreed with Hamilton that the new federal government had a legal obligation to pay the domestic debts that the Confederation government had incurred. Article VI of the Constitution provides that "All Debts contracted . . . before the Adoption of this Constitution, shall be as valid against the United States under this Constitution, as under the Confederation." But many in Congress, including James Madison, argued that the federal government ought to negotiate down the domestic debts and take into account the interests of those who had first owned the securities. Critics pointed out that the inflation of the war years and the depressed conditions of the 1780s had forced many of the original owners, including revolutionary war soldiers, to sell them at substantial losses. The speculators, including wealthy American merchants, Dutch investors, and even British investors, who had bought these deeply discounted notes, stood to reap huge windfall gains under Hamilton's redemption program. The critics wanted Hamilton to scale back the redemption of debts held by speculators and provide some compensation to the original owners of the domestic debt. Madison proposed offering speculators only "the highest price which has prevailed in the market" and distributing the savings to the original owners.

Hamilton, however, believed that the federal government would be unable to determine who had been the original owners of federal securities. Moreover, he was convinced that the best way of demonstrating the trustworthiness of the federal government was to pay back the debts at something close to their full value. This demonstration was necessary, Hamilton was certain, in order for the federal government to borrow in the future without having to pay excessive rates of interest. Hamilton was persuasive, and nearly half of the members of the House of Representatives owned the domestic debt that Hamilton sought to redeem. In February 1790, the House voted down Madison's plan.

Debts of the States

The third element of Hamilton's policies was the proposal that the federal government take over the $25 million in debt that the state governments had accumulated during the Revolution. With this "assumption" program, Hamilton sought to strengthen further the nation's financial reputation, to bolster the nation's stock of capital, and to enhance the financial power of the federal government.

All of the states had debts from the war, but their efforts to pay off the debts had varied greatly. Massachusetts and South Carolina had been sluggish in paying off their war debts and had much to gain from assumption. Four southern states—Georgia, North Carolina, Virginia, and Maryland—had been aggressive in paying off their debts. For them, assumption threatened to be costly, requiring them to subsidize the plan through new federal taxes.

Secretary of State Thomas Jefferson was worried about the cost of assumption, and about Hamilton's political intentions. To Jefferson, assumption threatened the Republic by dangerously centralizing financial power. Madison agreed with Jefferson, and in April 1790 they were able to defeat assumption in its first test within the House of Representatives. By July, however, Madison and Jefferson had softened their opposition. For one thing, Hamilton had lowered the assumption program to $21.5 million and agreed to adjust the accounts so that Virginia's net payments to the federal government would be zero. For another, he agreed to support moving the nation's capital from New York to a site in Virginia on the banks of the Potomac River after a ten-year interlude in Philadelphia. Madison and Jefferson hoped the move would stimulate economic development of their state, weaken the kind of ties that Hamilton sought to promote between the federal government and the financial elites of New York and Philadelphia, and bring the government more under the influence of Virginia's leaders. In addition, Madison and Jefferson became worried that if the fledgling government failed to pass a funding bill the divergence of sectional interests might break up the new union. They allowed southern votes to shift to support for Hamilton's plan for assumption of the state debts, and in July it won congressional endorsement in what historians later called the Compromise of 1790.

Taxation

The fourth central element of Hamilton's financial program was taxation. On 4 July 1789, even before Congress had created the Treasury, President Washington signed into law a tariff act designed to raise revenues for the new government. The act established a complex set of duties on imports, rebates for re-exported goods, and special favors for imports carried in American vessels. The act yielded more than $1 million per year, but this was far less than the $3 million that Hamilton estimated would be required each year for interest payments to the holders of federal debt. Therefore, in January 1790 in the "Report on the Public Credit," Hamilton recommended an increase in tariffs and the introduction of internal taxation in the form of an excise tax on distilled spirits. However, he stopped short of proposing direct taxes—by which he, and the Constitution, meant poll taxes and property taxes. He worried that these taxes would create a popular backlash, and he wanted to encourage state cooperation with his financial program by leaving direct taxation as the exclusive province of state and local governments.

In August 1790, Congress passed four separate acts that adopted, with only minor changes, Hamilton's proposals for paying off foreign debts, redeeming domestic debts, assuming state debts, and increasing tariffs. At the same time, Congress asked Hamilton to submit a formal proposal for establishing the tax on distilled spirits. In December 1790, Hamilton advanced a formal proposal for the tax and, in March 1791, with little debate, Congress adopted it in the Excise Act of 1791.

The Bank of the United States

In December 1790, Hamilton also proposed the fifth element in his financial plan: the federal chartering and funding of a powerful institution—a national bank, which would be called the Bank of the United States and modeled to some extent on the Bank of England. The bank was to be a commercial bank, which was a rare institution in America. State governments had chartered only four of them. Like these four, the Bank of the United States would accept deposits, issue bank notes (as loans or as evidence of deposits), discount commercial paper, and loan short-term funds to the government. But Hamilton wanted more. The Bank of the United States, in Hamilton's view, would be very different from the other commercial banks. One difference would be its sheer size. Hamilton proposed capitalization for the bank that would make it five times the size of all the other commercial banks combined. This meant that the bank could expand significantly the size of the nation's money supply and thus enhance economic activity.

In contrast to the other banks, the Bank of the United States would conduct business on a national scale and thus be able to expedite the movement of federal funds around the nation. In an era of slow communication, this ability promised to enhance the efficiency and power of both the federal government and the nation's capital markets. Another difference, the participation of the federal government as a partner in the bank's ownership, would enable the government to share in the returns from the bank's operations and thus enhance federal revenues. A final difference, the requirement that investors in the bank use long-term obligations of the federal government to purchase bank stock, would support the price of government bonds. Hamilton meant for these differences, taken as a package, to reinforce other elements in his economic program.

In February 1791, Congress passed a bill that adopted most of Hamilton's specific ideas for the new bank. Congress provided for a twenty-year charter, a pledge that the government would not charter another bank during that period, a capitalization of $10 million, 20 percent ownership by the federal government, a requirement that 75 percent of the stock subscribed by private parties be purchased with United States securities, and a provision for locating the headquarters of the bank in Philadelphia.

During the congressional debates over the bank, Madison and other Virginians became concerned that locating the bank in Philadelphia for twenty years might interfere with moving to the permanent capital in ten years. They demanded that Congress reduce the term of the charter to ten years, but Pennsylvania supporters of the bank blocked the reduction. Madison then claimed that Congress had no power to charter the bank, or any corporation. In so doing, he advanced a "narrow" interpretation of the powers of Congress under the Constitution. While Congress rejected Madison's claim, President Washington took his argument seriously. In addition, Washington worried about jeopardizing the move of the capital to the Potomac site, which was near his home of Mount Vernon. However, Hamilton made a powerful case to Washington that the Constitution implied the power to create corporations and this "broad" interpretation swayed the president, who signed the bill creating the Bank of the United States.

The Mint

In January 1791, while the Bank of the United States was still under debate, Hamilton submitted the "Report on the Establishment of a Mint." The creation of a mint, the sixth element of his economic program, followed the call of the Constitution for a national coinage. Hamilton's goal was to create a system of coinage that would be uniform across the United States and provide monetary stability. Uniformity and stability would promote commerce, enhance the credit worthiness of the United States, and protect the value of tax revenues. Hamilton personally preferred gold coinage but he recognized the political reality that many members of Congress worried about the shortage of gold and the potential deflationary impact of a gold standard. Hamilton proposed, instead, a bimetallic standard based on the minting of both gold and silver coins. Both gold and silver coins would be legal tender, and the mint would buy gold or silver at an official ratio of fifteen ounces of silver to one ounce of gold. The most common coin in circulation was the Spanish silver dollar, and it had provided the unit with which the new nation valued its debts. To ease the transition, Hamilton recommended adopting the dollar as the basic unit for the coinage of the new republic, and keeping the silver content of the new dollar close to that of the Spanish one. In addition, to facilitate small transactions, he recommended an elaborate fractional coinage. Congress adopted almost all of Hamilton's proposals in the Coinage Act of 1792.

Promotion of Manufacturing

In January 1791 the House of Representatives asked Hamilton to prepare a plan for the seventh element of his program: "the encouragement and promotion of such manufactories as will tend to render the United States independent of other nations for essentials, particularly for military supplies" (*Journal of the House of Representatives of the United States*, 15 January 1791, quoted in Jacob E. Cooke, ed., *The Reports of Alexander Hamilton*, p. 115). In December of that year, Hamilton responded with the last of his reports, the "Report on Manufactures." Hamilton went beyond the charge to consider preparations for war; he recommended an ambitious, national program of industrial advancement. Hamilton made a case that, complementing America's vast agricultural sector, manufacturing, and especially the introduction of machine production, would contribute to "The Produce and Revenue of the Society" (Alexander Hamilton, "Report on Manufactures," quoted in Cooke, ed., *The Reports of Alexander Hamilton*, p. 127). He concluded that the development of modern manufacturing in America would be difficult because of "fear of want of success in untried enterprises" (Hamilton, "Report on Manufactures," p. 140) and competition from European manufacturers, who had reaped the benefits of the mercantilist policies of European governments.

To overcome these obstacles, the federal government should, Hamilton argued, adopt a broad range of policies that would encourage Americans to spend their money and their energy on the advancement of technological change in industry. The policies included, in addition to the public finance measures that Hamilton had already championed successfully, tariffs crafted to protect new industries; exemptions from tariffs for raw materials important to industrial development; prohibitions on the exporting of raw materials needed by American industry; promotion of inventions; award of premiums and bonuses for "the prosecution and introduction of useful discoveries" by a federal board; inspection of manufactured goods to protect consumers and enhance the reputation abroad of American manufacturing; and improvement of transportation facilities.

In response, in March 1792, Congress passed most of the tariff program Hamilton had proposed: increases in tariffs on manufactured goods, including the iron and steel of Pennsylvania, and reductions in tariffs on raw materials. However, Congress rejected the rest of Hamilton's policy for manufactures. Jefferson and Madison hated the prospect of an industrial revolution and believed that Hamilton had already gained excessive power and might even be plotting to replace the Republic with a monarchy. (Their suspicion was incorrect.) In addition, prominent merchants feared that Hamilton's industrial program would disturb their profitable trade with Great Britain.

The Aftermath

Some of Hamilton's economic policies, especially the creation of the Bank of the United States and excise taxation, stimulated the development of organized opposition to the Washington administration and led to the formation of what became the Republican Party of Thomas Jefferson and James Madison. Particularly troublesome to Hamilton was the Whiskey Rebellion in 1794, in which thousands of farmers in western Pennsylvania challenged the legitimacy of the excise tax on distilled spirits. They waved banners denouncing tyranny and embracing "liberty, equality, and fraternity," the ideals of the French Revolution. With Hamilton's enthusiastic support, President Washington mobilized 15,000 troops to suppress the rebellion.

Hamilton's economic policies may have undermined the future of the Federalist Party, but they established a fiscally strong federal government, just as Hamilton had planned. In 1793, under Hamilton's tax regime, the federal government collected enough revenue to pay off interest on the public debt ($2.8 million in 1793), fund the army and navy (over $1 million in 1792), and still balance the federal budget. By 1795 the regular payment of interest enabled the Treasury to float new loans in the Netherlands and pay off its debts to Spain and France. Meanwhile, Hamilton redeemed the domestic debts, including the debts of state government, and the new securities circulated at close to par value. Vigorous capital markets, in turn, contributed to a dramatic economic expansion that began in the early 1790s and continued for a decade. Finally, Hamilton's economic policies established a model of a central government that worked creatively, positively, and effectively to unleash the nation's economic energies. For the next two centuries, Hamilton's model would influence the development of the federal government as an integral part of American capitalism.

BIBLIOGRAPHY

Brown, Roger H. *Redeeming the Republic: Federalists, Taxation, and the Origins of the Constitution.* Baltimore: Johns Hopkins University Press, 1993. Emphasizes the role of fiscal concerns in the movement for the Constitution.

Bruchey, Stuart. *Enterprise: The Dynamic Economy of Free People.* Cambridge, Mass.: Harvard University Press, 1990. Contains an incisive assessment of Hamilton's program.

Cooke, Jacob E., ed. *The Reports of Alexander Hamilton.* New York: Harper and Row, 1964.

Elkins, Stanley, and Eric McKitrick. *The Age of Federalism: The Early American Republic, 1788–1800.* Oxford and New York: Oxford University Press, 1993. Best book on the rise and fall of the Federalists.

Ellis, Joseph J. *Founding Brothers: The Revolutionary Generation.* New York: Knopf, 2001. Contains insightful essay on the Compromise of 1790.

Ferguson, E. James. *The Power of the Purse: A History of American Public Finance, 1776–1790.* Chapel Hill: University of North Carolina Press, 1961. Best history of the financing of the American Revolution.

McDonald, Forrest. *Alexander Hamilton: A Biography.* New York: Norton, 1979. Intertwines Hamilton's ideas with the development of his political career.

Mitchell, Broadus. *Alexander Hamilton: The National Adventure, 1788–1804.* New York: Macmillan, 1962. Contains lucid and detailed discussion of Hamilton's program.

W. Elliot Brownlee

See also **Bank of the United States; Compromise of 1790; Currency and Coinage; Mint, Federal; Revolution, American: Financial Aspects; Sinking Fund, National.**

HAMPTON ROADS CONFERENCE. In February 1865, Confederate Vice President Alexander Stephens, representing the Richmond government, met with President Abraham Lincoln and Secretary of State William Seward on the *River Queen* in Hampton Roads, Virginia, to discuss terms of peace. Lincoln offered peace on the basis of (1) reunion, (2) emancipation, and (3) the disbanding of Confederate troops, with a personal promise of sympathetic treatment. The Confederate representatives were not empowered to accept any terms except independence, and the conference adjourned without further agreement. In April, Richmond fell to the Union army, and, by May, the final Confederate armies in the field had surrendered.

BIBLIOGRAPHY

McPherson, James M. *Battle Cry of Freedom: The Civil War Era.* New York: Oxford University Press, 1988.

Thomas, Emory M. *The Confederate Nation: 1861–1865.* New York: Harper and Row, 1979.

James Elliott Walmsley / A. G.

See also **Civil War; Confederate States of America; Emancipation Proclamation; Peace Movement of 1864; Unconditional Surrender.**

HANDICAPPED, EDUCATION OF THE.
See **Disabled, Education of the.**

HANGING, a method of execution brought over from England by the early settlers of America. Other severe practices of inflicting death, while not extensive, were occasionally resorted to during the colonial period. With the adoption of the U.S. Constitution, which prohibited "cruel and unusual punishment," these other methods were abandoned. Hanging remained the sole legal means of effecting CAPITAL PUNISHMENT until the innovations of electrocution, gas, and lethal injection.

Notwithstanding the provision in the Constitution, hanging, as it was conducted, was cruel. Not only was it the occasion of festivities, during which a body was often left suspended for an entire day, but also it lacked the slightest essentials of science. The condemned man or woman was frequently flung from a ladder, or placed on a cart that was wheeled out from under the body; instead of sustaining a quick, painless death, the victim suffered the agonies of slow strangulation.

The historical significance of hanging stemmed, in part, from its public display. Hangings in antebellum America were local community events in which residents were taught important societal lessons, including the perils of a life of crime and the power of the authorities. Hangings, however, were not always sanctioned by the state. Lynch mobs enforced extralegal and barbarous death sentences of hanging and mutilation on thousands of African Americans, primarily in the South.

Opponents of the death penalty and critics of public executions joined forces in the mid-nineteenth century. For the latter group, the efforts were a success, as many northern states began relegating hangings to jails. As late as 1965, however, six states still used hanging for capital punishment. However, merely removing executions from the witnessing gaze of large crowds was not the goal for antideath penalty advocates, and they continued to fight for abolition altogether. They won a victory in Michigan in 1846, when that state became the first in the nation to outlaw execution as a method of punishment; Rhode Island and Wisconsin followed with similar laws in the 1850s.

Rather than abolishing the death penalty, many states changed the method of execution. New York became the first state to construct an electric chair, which, in 1888, replaced the gallows. State hangings continued into the 1930s. The last public hanging occurred in Covington, Kentucky, in 1936.

In the early twenty-first century, public outcry against the death penalty began to rise. Among the movement's participants are opponents in the two states that still allow hanging as a method of execution: Montana and Washington. (Washington hanged two inmates in the 1990s. Delaware used hanging as a means of execution in 1996 though the state outlawed the method for those people sentenced after 1986.)

BIBLIOGRAPHY

Banner, Stuart. *The Death Penalty: An American History*. Cambridge, Mass.: Harvard University Press, 2002.

Bedau, Hugo. *The Death Penalty in America: An Anthology*. Garden City, N.Y.: Anchor Books, 1967.

Marquart, James W., Sheldon Edland-Olson, and Jonathan R. Sorensen. *The Rope, the Chair, and the Needle: Capital Punishment in Texas, 1923–1994*. Austin: University of Texas Press, 1994.

Sellin, Johan Thorsten, ed. *Capital Punishment*. New York: Harper and Row, 1967.

Lewis E. Lawes
Caroline Waldron Merithew

HANSSEN ESPIONAGE CASE. In July 2001, Federal Bureau of Investigation agent Robert Hanssen pleaded guilty in federal court to fifteen charges of spying for the Soviets and the Russians. His action resolved the most serious case of spying in the history of the FBI and the worst in the United States since the former Central Intelligence Agency officer Aldrich H. Ames received life in prison in 1994. Hanssen, a Chicago native, spent much of his twenty-five-year FBI career in counterintelligence, where he had access to highly sensitive cases and documents. Beginning in 1979 and continuing off and on until his arrest in 2001, the self-taught computer expert hacked into ultra-secret government databases to obtain his information, which he passed on to his handlers via dead drops near his suburban Washington, D.C., home. The material—some six thousand pages of highly classified documents and more than twenty-five computer disks—included information on nine double agents (two of whom were later executed) and details about several top-secret communications programs and U.S. nuclear war preparations. For his efforts, Hanssen received $1.4 million in cash and diamonds, which he apparently used to finance the education of his six children. A former stripper said that Hanssen, a devout Roman Catholic, gave her cash, expensive gifts, and a trip to Hong Kong. Hanssen's motivation for spying remains murky, although in a 1999 letter to his handlers he claimed to have made his decision as early as age fourteen. His arrest in February 2001 and the severity of his crimes sparked an intense debate within the federal government over whether or not Hanssen should be executed. Instead of asking for the death penalty, however, federal prosecutors opted for extensive debriefings to determine the extent of his espionage. On 10 May 2002, after the debriefings, Hanssen was sentenced to life in prison without parole.

BIBLIOGRAPHY

Havill, Adrian. *The Spy Who Stayed Out in the Cold: The Secret Life of FBI Double Agent Robert Hanssen*. New York: St. Martin's Press, 2001.

Richelson, Jeffrey T. *A Century of Spies: Intelligence in the Twentieth Century*. New York: Oxford University Press, 1995.

Vise, David A. *The Bureau and the Mole: The Unmasking of Robert Philip Hanssen, the Most Dangerous Double Agent in FBI History*. New York: Atlantic Monthly Press, 2002.

Mary Jo Binker

See also **Spies.**

HANTAVIRUS refers both to a family of biological viruses that can be transmitted from animals to humans and to hantavirus pulmonary syndrome—the highly fatal infection caused by the viruses. Most often transmitted by exposure to the droppings of rodents, especially deer mice, infected individuals experience fever, nausea, vomiting, muscle and head aches, and, if left untreated, respiratory distress that can result in death. Other hantaviruses produce kidney disease.

As of 2003, an effective treatment for hantavirus was not yet available. Although long recognized in other countries, the disease was fairly rare in the United States, and the likelihood of infection was low. The first outbreak in the United States occurred in May 1993 in the Four Corners area of Arizona, Colorado, New Mexico, and Utah, and by April 2001, 283 cases of the disease had been reported in thirty-one states.

BIBLIOGRAPHY

Hjelle, B., S. Jenison, G. Mertz, et al. "Emergence of Hantaviral Disease in the Southwestern United States." *Western Journal of Medicine* 161, no. 5 (1994): 467–473.

Schmaljohn, C. S., and S. T. Nichol, eds. *Hantaviruses.* Berlin and New York: Springer Verlag, 2001.

D. George Joseph

See also **Epidemics and Public Health.**

HARD MONEY is specie, that is, gold and silver coin. During much of the eighteenth century, the Revolution, and the Confederation, many Americans suffered from the inflation of paper MONEY. The Constitution says that "No State shall . . . make any Thing but gold and silver Coin a Tender in Payment of Debts" (Article I, Section 10), which put the United States on a hard money basis. Since then, debtor classes and some business groups have repeatedly tried, often with success, to modify the intent of these words.

Those who favored hard money have at different times fought different opponents. In the 1830s the fight was against banks, particularly the second BANK OF THE UNITED STATES, which President Andrew Jackson and Senator Thomas Hart Benton of Missouri alleged defrauded the people and mixed in politics. Jackson's followers, including President Martin Van Buren, set up the INDEPENDENT TREASURY SYSTEM in 1840–1841, but the Whigs abolished it. President James K. Polk founded a more enduring system in 1846. Van Buren's and Polk's systems put the treasury on a hard money basis, although some modifications soon had to be made.

For Secretary of the Treasury Salmon P. Chase (1861–1864), also a hard money proponent, it was a bitter pill to have to ask Congress for three issues of legal tender notes (GREENBACKS) to carry on the CIVIL WAR. Later, as chief justice, Chase said that making paper money legal tender was unconstitutional (*Hepburn v. Griswold* [1870]).

In the later 1860s and 1870s hard money advocates demanded a return to the gold standard, which was finally achieved on 2 January 1879; an 1873 law had already eliminated silver as part of the monetary base. The hard money advocates opposed any expansion of government paper money, in contrast with the views of the Greenback Party. But they did not oppose national bank notes if these were redeemable in specie.

When the United States abandoned the GOLD STANDARD in the spring of 1933, American citizens lost the right to demand redemption of paper money or bank deposits in gold coin, and they did not regain it with the limited return to a gold standard in January 1934. The era of hard money had ended. On 15 August 1971, the United States took the final step in establishing an irredeemable paper money standard.

BIBLIOGRAPHY

Friedman, Milton, and Anna Jacobson Schwartz. *A Monetary History of the United States, 1867–1960.* Princeton, N.J.: Princeton University Press, 1963.

McFaul, John M. *The Politics of Jacksonian Finance.* Ithaca, N.Y.: Cornell University Press, 1972.

Timberlake, Richard H. *Monetary Policy in the United States: An Intellectual and Institutional History.* Chicago: University of Chicago Press, 1993.

Donald L. Kemmerer / A. R.

See also **Currency and Coinage; Inflation; Mint, Federal; Specie Circular; Specie Payments, Suspension and Resumption of; Treasury, Department of the.**

HARDWARE TRADE refers to hardware stores that sell a number of basic hardware lines such as tools, builders' hardware, paint, glass, housewares and household appliances, cutlery, and roofing materials, no one of which accounts for more than half the sales of the establishments. These products are sold to individual family consumers, farmers, large and small builders, industrial plants that use many such items as components in their own products, and other enterprises. Only a few of these products, such as some hand tools and building fixtures, have strong brand identification. They originate in a variety of manufacturing sources. They tend to be heavy, and dealers must maintain substantial inventories that turn over slowly. All these factors complicate the distribution system.

During the colonial and revolutionary periods, American settlers used hardware they had brought with them, along with goods imported from abroad and a small amount manufactured in this country. Businesses were not sharply differentiated. Producers often sold small quantities direct to consumers and to distributors. Large, prosperous iron merchants in New York and other major coastal importing centers sold to all types of customers, including country general stores.

During the early nineteenth century, firms began to take on more specialized roles. Manufacturers sold directly to industrial users and to wholesalers. The wholesalers in turn concentrated more on selling to retail stores, including general stores, and to some types of industrial users. Generally they expected the retailers to travel to the wholesale centers, often during specially designated market weeks, to purchase their supplies for the selling season. As population density increased and transportation facilities improved, suppliers began sending out traveling financial agents to help collect bills and, eventually, traveling salesmen to collect orders. In 1830, Scovill Manufacturing Company of Connecticut, a manufacturer of brass fittings and buttons, became one of the first hardware companies to employ traveling salesmen.

Competition increased sharply for local hardware stores and wholesalers with the growth of mail-order houses and large downtown department stores in the later decades of the century. Retailer attempts to organize boycotts and obtain punitive tax legislation on these new forms of distribution were unsuccessful in hindering their growth. During the 1920s and 1930s, the opening of urban retail department stores by mail-order companies such as Sears Roebuck and Montgomery Ward provided additional competition for the independent hardware stores. After World War II, yet more competition emerged in the form of discount department stores such as Kmart and Wal-Mart, then by the growth of home building supply stores such as Home Depot and Lowe's, which sold lumber as well as hardware items in warehouse-like "big box" stores.

In the 1920s and 1930s many of the independent hardware retailers formed cooperative chains in which independently owned stores engaged in joint wholesaling and purchasing activities, shared advertising campaigns, and other commercial activities. Prominent among these ventures were Cotter and Company and American Wholesale Supply, both of which eventually merged into the TrueStar organization. Retail census figures for 1997 show 15,748 establishments with sales of $13.6 billion.

BIBLIOGRAPHY

Barger, Harrold. *Distribution's Place in the American Economy Since 1869.* Princeton, N.J.: Princeton University Press, 1955.

Cory, Jim. "Mom & Pop in the '90s." *Hardware Age* (October 1990): 58–67.

Marber, Allen. "Eighteenth Century Iron Merchants, A Modern Marketer." In *Marketing in Three Eras.* Edited by Terence Nevett and Stanley C. Hollander. East Lansing: Michigan State University Department of Marketing, 1987.

Stanley C. Hollander

See also **Iron and Steel Industry; Retailing Industry; Stores, General; Traveling Salesmen.**

HARLEM. The New York City neighborhood—bounded by the Harlem River to the northeast and Washington Heights to the north, and by 110th Street to the south and Morningside Heights to the southwest—that eventually became the biggest and one of the most important black communities in the United States. Harlem began as a farming village in Dutch New Amsterdam. It remained an agricultural community until after the Civil War, when rapid population growth pushed New Yorkers uptown. By 1880, elevated trains ran as far north as 129th Street, and the neighborhood attracted tens of thousands of upper-class whites, with poorer Italians and Jews settling to the east and south.

Real estate speculators turned quick profits in booming Harlem, but in 1905, the market collapsed and blacks flooded into the overdeveloped neighborhood. Black New Yorkers desperately needed a place to go at the beginning of the twentieth century. The black population was growing even faster than the rest of the city, and increasing racial violence made most neighborhoods unsafe. During the 1920s, roughly 120,000 blacks, most new arrivals from the Caribbean and the South, migrated to Harlem, and an equal number of whites moved out. At the same time, Puerto Rican immigrants established "El Barrio" in East Harlem, known today as Spanish Harlem.

At first, Harlem represented great promise for blacks. Unlike most northern ghettos, it featured beautiful new buildings on wide streets. In the 1920s, the Harlem Renaissance brought together a talented group of artists, writers, and musicians that included Aaron Douglas, Romare Bearden, Zora Neale Hurston, Langston Hughes, and Duke Ellington. Harlem also established itself at the center of black political culture in the United States. The National Association for the Advancement of Colored People and the National Urban League, as well as Marcus Garvey's nationalist Universal Negro Improvement Association (see Black Nationalism) and the labor leader A. Philip Randolph's Brotherhood of Sleeping Car Porters maintained headquarters there. Later, Malcolm X worked primarily out of Harlem, and the community elected two of the most prominent African Americans in congressional history, Adam Clayton Powell Jr. (1944–1970) and Charles Rangel (1970–).

By the eve of the Great Depression, the huge influx of people had overwhelmed both the housing market and the job market; the latter made even tighter by racist hiring practices. Gradually, Harlem became a slum. The depression hit hard, and unemployment approached 50 percent. Despite a number of ill-conceived urban renewal efforts, Harlem has struggled with unemployment, poverty, health crises, and crime since World War II. The sweeping economic prosperity of the 1990s renewed interest in Harlem and sections of the neighborhood were rebuilt, but its core remains very poor.

BIBLIOGRAPHY

Greenberg, Cheryl Lynn. *Or Does It Explode?: Black Harlem in the Great Depression.* New York: Oxford University Press, 1991.

Hamilton, Charles V. *Adam Clayton Powell, Jr.: The Political Biography of an American Dilemma.* New York: Atheneum, 1991.

Markowitz, Gerald E., and David Rosner. *Children, Race, and Power: Kenneth and Mamie Clark's Northside Center.* Charlottesville: University Press of Virginia, 1996.

Osofsky, Gilbert. *Harlem: The Making of a Ghetto: Negro New York, 1890–1930.* New York: Harper and Row, 1968.

Jeremy Derfner

See also **African Americans; New York City; Puerto Ricans in the United States.**

HARLEM, BATTLE OF (16 September 1776). After the Battle of Long Island, George Washington withdrew his demoralized troops to Manhattan Island and established a line from the mouth of the Harlem River across the island to Harlem (now Morningside) Heights. On the morning of 16 September 1776, about one thousand British appeared on the Harlem Plains. Washington ordered a company of Connecticut Rangers and three Virginia companies to strike at the enemy's rear. Although the leaders of both companies were killed, reinforcements sent down from the heights drove the British back. This small victory greatly heartened the American troops, and Washington held his position for another month.

BIBLIOGRAPHY

Bliven, Bruce, Jr. *Battle for Manhattan.* New York: Holt, 1956.

Alvin F. Harlow / A. R.

See also **Harlem; White Plains, Battle of.**

HARLEM RENAISSANCE. Known also by the names Black Renaissance or New Negro Movement, the Harlem Renaissance represented a cultural movement among African Americans roughly between the end of World War I (1918) and the beginning of the Great Depression (1929). The names given to this movement reveal its essential features. Certainly the words "black" and "Negro" mean that this movement centered on African Americans, and the term "renaissance" indicates that something new was born or, more accurately, that a cultural spirit was reawakened in African American cultural life. Although most historians remember the Harlem Renaissance as a literary movement, in fact, African Americans during the 1920s also made great strides in musical and visual arts, as well as science. Finally, the focus on HARLEM—an old Dutch-built neighborhood of New York City—indicates that this "renaissance" was something of an urban phenomenon. In fact, the exciting developments in African American cultural life of the 1920s were not limited to Harlem, but also had roots in other urban communities where black Americans migrated in great numbers: East St. Louis, Illinois; Chicago's south side; and Washington, D.C.

The artists of the Harlem Renaissance forwarded two goals. Like the journalists and other "crusaders" of the Progressive era, black authors tried to point out the injustices of racism in American life. Second, newspaper editors, activists, authors, and other artists began to promote a more unified and positive culture among African Americans. Early efforts to publicize a more unified consciousness among African Americans included two publications in 1919: Robert Kerlin's collection of editorial material in *Voice of the Negro* and Emmett Scott's *Letters from Negro Migrants.* On the political front, leaders such as Marcus Garvey began to put forth plans for black economic self-sufficiency, political separatism, and the creation of a cross-national African consciousness.

Several important developments during the World War I era gave rise to the Harlem Renaissance. First, black southerners since the turn of the century had been moving in large numbers to the North's industrial cities. As a result, southern blacks who had been denied their political rights and had resorted to sharecropping as a means of livelihood came into contact with northern African Americans who were more often the descendants of free blacks and, therefore, had better access to education and employment. Additionally, black Americans moving to the cities had much to complain about. World War I, the so-called war to make the world safe for democracy, had been a bitter experience for most African Americans. The U.S. Army was rigidly segregated, race riots broke out in many American cities during or immediately after the war, and the North was residentially and economically segregated like the South, despite the absence of JIM CROW LAWS.

Zora Neale Hurston. The author of *Their Eyes Were Watching God* (1937), other fiction, and collections of African American folklore. AP/WIDE WORLD PHOTOS

Not all of the forces driving the Harlem Renaissance were negative, however. An influential anthropologist of the time, Zora Neale Hurston, observed that many white American artists began to employ aspects of African American culture in their works; she called these people "Negrotarians." Significant among these were Frank Tannenbaum, author of *Darker Phases of the South* (1924), and Paul Green, whose 1926 production of *In Abraham's Bosom* with a mostly black cast won the Pulitzer Prize.

Literature

The literary works of the Harlem Renaissance were products of their writers' racial consciousness but also dem-

Nella Larsen. A nurse and a writer, best known for her first novel, *Quicksand* (1928). THE BEINECKE RARE BOOK AND MANUSCRIPT LIBRARY

onstrated a profundity and beauty that placed many of these writers among the great literary figures of the century. An important originator of the movement, James Weldon Johnson, gave impetus to other black writers in 1922 by publishing the work of contemporary black poets in a volume entitled *The Book of American Negro Poetry.* Writing throughout the 1920s, Johnson published his reflections on the decade of black artistic creation in his autobiographical *Black Manhattan* (1930). Johnson was joined by another early and influential writer, Jamaican-born Claude McKay. McKay gained notoriety with awareness-raising poems such as "The Lynching." McKay, like fellow Caribbean native Marcus Garvey, displayed the defiance and anger felt by black Americans in the wake of World War I.

The most influential African American poet of the 1920s would prove to be the eloquent Langston Hughes, called the Poet Laureate of the Harlem Renaissance. Early Hughes's poetry such as "The Negro Speaks of Rivers" and "Mother to Son" reflected his roots in African American culture; these poems were published in *The Weary Blues* (1926). Later Hughes's work—four poems on the infamous (mis)trial of nine black men accused of rape in Alabama—revealed his heightened political consciousness and were published as *Scottsboro Limited* (1932). In the waning years of the Harlem Renaissance, Hughes turned to satirical short stories on black life with a collection entitled *The Ways of White Folks* (1934).

Perhaps one of the best fiction writers of the Harlem Renaissance was Jessie Redmon Fauset. Well educated at Ivy League schools, Fauset represented the "talented tenth" of African Americans that W. E. B. Du Bois hoped would excel to the point of proving blacks' value to American society. Fittingly, Fauset represented blacks in her novels as mainstream Americans, choosing to weave race issues within her wider interest in cultural problems such as social status and economic well-being. Her most important works included *There Is Confusion* (1924), *Plum Bun* (1928), and *Comedy: American Style* (1933). Other writers—E. Franklin Frazier and Alain Locke, for example—hoped to advance the position of African Americans through scholarship by exposing the problems facing black Americans to induce change, as progressive journalists and novelists had done with health and safety issues before.

Music

Black Americans during the 1920s excelled in fields other than literature. We often remember JAZZ as the product of black migration to New Orleans, but the other cities that black artists called home—New York, Chicago, St. Louis, for example—witnessed the development of jazz music as well. Important jazz pianists such as the unofficial "mayor" of Harlem, Fats Waller, and Art Tatum played music at house parties and other gatherings in Manhattan, making music an integral part of the black experience in the urban North. African American bandleaders—Duke Ellington, Count Basie, and Fletcher Henderson—and vaudeville blues singers—Gertrude "Ma" Rainey and Bessie Smith—performed for black and white audiences, thereby influencing popular music in general.

Like Jessie Fauset, composer William Grant Still brought to the Harlem Renaissance a background in American higher education. Trained at the Oberlin Conservatory of Music, Still used traditional African American musical idioms to create European-style symphonic music. He was the first black composer to have a symphony played by a major orchestra, the first to conduct a major orchestra, and the first to have an opera produced by a major opera company. In 1931, Still legitimized Afro-inspired aesthetics in Western musical forms in premiering a tribute to the Harlem Renaissance aptly entitled the *Afro-American Symphony*.

Visual Art

In the world of visual art, the leading graphic artist, and illustrator for many of James Weldon Johnson's works, was Aaron Douglas. In northern cities, black artists such as Douglas wanted to capture their people's movement, energy, and soul as jazz musicians had. One of the most successful artists to do this was Archibald J. Motley Jr. Using vibrant color and flowing shapes, Motley reflected in his work the fast-paced urban life he observed in Chicago.

Countee Cullen. The prolific poet and one of the most prominent figures of the Harlem Renaissance. AP/Wide World Photos

The Harlem Renaissance as a movement represented a rebirth of African American culture in the United States. As a product of black urban migration and black Americans' disappointment with racism in the United States, the renaissance was aimed at revitalizing black culture with pride. In political life, literature, music, visual art, and other cultural areas, African Americans in the 1920s put forth their individual and collective sense of dignity in the face of an American culture that often considered them second-class citizens.

BIBLIOGRAPHY

Franklin, John Hope, and Alfred A. Moss Jr. *From Slavery to Freedom: A History of African Americans.* 8th ed. Boston: McGraw-Hill, 2000. See chapter eighteen, 400–417. Classic, and still excellent, account of the Harlem Renaissance, balancing narrative with interpretation of primary evidence.

Huggins, Nathan Irvin. *Harlem Renaissance.* New York: Oxford University Press, 1971. Standard monograph on the movement.

———, ed. *Voices from the Harlem Renaissance.* New York: Oxford University Press, 1976. Vast collection of primary documents from the period.

Kellner, Bruce, ed. *The Harlem Renaissance: A Historical Dictionary for the Era.* Westport, Conn.: Greenwood Press, 1984. A useful reference tool on people, places, and a variety of other subjects pertaining to the movement.

Kramer, Victor. *The Harlem Renaissance Re-Examined.* New York: AMS, 1987. A large volume of scholarly essays on a wide range of topics within the movement.

Perry, Margaret. *The Harlem Renaissance: An Annotated Bibliography and Commentary.* New York: Garland Publishing, Inc., 1982. A wonderful research tool on nineteen influential period authors, complete with citations of published works.

Singh, Amritjit. *The Novels of the Harlem Renaissance: Twelve Black Writers, 1923–1933.* University Park: The Pennsylvania State University Press, 1976. Literary study of wide cross-section of black authors.

Waldron, Edward E. *Walter White and the Harlem Renaissance.* Port Washington, N.Y.: Kennikat Press, 1978. A monograph on the influential civic leader's role during the period.

R. A. Lawson

HARPERS FERRY, CAPTURE OF. On 9 September 1862, in Frederick, Maryland, General Robert E. Lee issued his famous "lost order." To clear the enemy from his rear, Lee directed General Thomas J. ("Stonewall") Jackson to capture the garrison at Harpers Ferry, Virginia (now West Virginia), and then hurry northward to rejoin the main army. The combined forces would then move through Hagerstown into Pennsylvania. But the "lost order" had come into the Union general George B. McClellan's possession. The defenders of Harpers Ferry put up unexpected resistance against Jackson's siege on September 14 and did not surrender until the following day. Jackson rejoined Lee at Sharpsburg twenty-four hours late, a delay that nearly led to disaster at the Battle of Antietam.

BIBLIOGRAPHY

Gallagher, Gary W., ed. *The Antietam Campaign.* Chapel Hill: University of North Carolina Press, 1999.

Teetor, Paul R. *A Matter of Hours: Treason at Harper's Ferry.* Rutherford, N.J.: Fairleigh Dickinson University Press, 1982.

Thomas Robson Hay / A. R.

See also **Antietam, Battle of; Maryland, Invasion of.**

HARPERS FERRY RAID. The Harpers Ferry raid from 16 to 18 October 1859 was led by the abolitionist John Brown. Brown captured the U.S. arsenal at Harpers Ferry, Virginia (subsequently West Virginia), at the confluence of the Potomac and Shenandoah Rivers. With the weapons seized there, he intended to arm the great number of slaves he thought would join him. But the plot was a failure, and Brown and most of his followers were either killed outright or captured and later executed. Nevertheless, the raid, and the myth of John Brown it created, accelerated the sectional divide over slavery and indirectly helped achieve Brown's agenda.

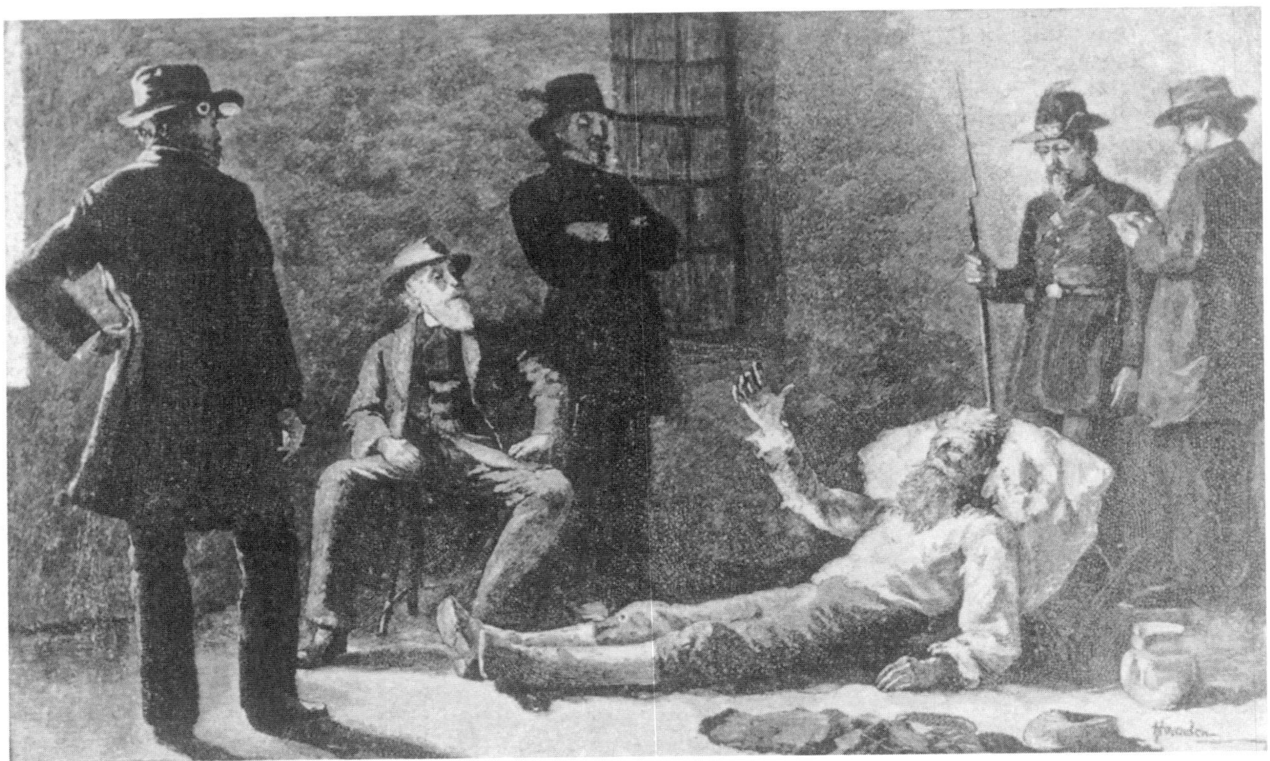

John Brown. The wounded abolitionist lies down among his captors after his failed attempt to seize the federal arsenal at Harpers Ferry, Va., and provoke a mass insurrection by slaves; his raid was a contributing factor leading to the Civil War, and many Northerners came to regard him as a beloved martyr.

Background

John Brown was born in Connecticut in 1800. He was a deceitful businessman, a defendant in litigation in twenty-one separate cases. However, he was able to inspire loyalty among low and influential men alike. He had become an ardent sympathizer of the slaves by the 1830s. In 1855 he moved with five of his sons to Kansas, where the slavery issue was bitterly contested. On 24 May 1856, Brown led a party on a raid of Pottawatomie Creek, a frontier community near Lawrence. In what has become known as the Pottawatomie Massacre, Brown and his followers killed five proslavery men. The massacre exacerbated national tensions over slavery by suggesting that antislavery forces were willing to commit violence. It also suggested that Brown saw himself as an agent of God. Murky evidence about Pottawatomie allowed Brown to avoid arrest. From 1856 to 1859 he traveled between Kansas and New England, organizing antislavery raiding parties. In early 1858 he began seeking support for the Harpers Ferry raid.

The Plot

By 1858 Brown had cultivated support among leading northern antislavery and literary figures. That year he approached his contacts with a plan to take an armed force into Virginia to rally the slaves, and resist by force any effort to prevent their being freed. Evidently Brown viewed Virginia, a slave state, as ready for black revolt. Brown consulted with Frederick Douglass, Gerrit Smith, George Stearns, Franklin Sanborn, Thomas Wentworth Higginson, Theodore Parker, and Samuel Gridley Howe. Several tried to dissuade Brown, but all except Douglass ended up agreeing to provide him with the money necessary to launch the Harpers Ferry raid. They became known as the Secret Six.

John Brown's intentions at Harpers Ferry are mysterious. After his capture he asserted that freeing slaves was his only object, not killing slaveholders. On the other hand, on 8 May 1858 in Ontario, Canada, he shared with several dozen Negroes and white men a "provisional constitution" that provided for confiscating all the personal and real property of slave owners and for maintaining a government throughout a large area. Since Brown did not expect to have more than a hundred men in his striking force, the large army necessary for this operation would have to be composed of liberated slaves. Moreover, Brown's little band already had plenty of guns at its disposal. Therefore, the only thing to be gained by attacking the federal arsenal at Harpers Ferry was weapons, presumably to arm thousands of slaves. We can conclude that Brown did not intend to kill people in the Harpers Ferry raid unless they got in his way. But he also intended to encourage a great many slaves to defend their freedom and to give them the means to do so.

Brown planned to strike at Harpers Ferry in the summer of 1858, but his plans were interrupted by Hugh Forbes, an English soldier of fortune he had hired to train troops. Disenchanted by Brown's reneging on his wages, Forbes publicized the plot by describing it to U.S. senators Henry Wilson and William Seward. Wilson chastised the Secret Six, warning them that Brown's scheme would compromise the antislavery cause. The Secret Six told Brown that he must go back to Kansas, which he did in June 1858. In December he led a raid into Missouri, where his band killed a slaveholder and liberated eleven slaves whom they carried (in midwinter) all the way to Ontario. This was Brown's most successful operation ever. It could have capped his antislavery career and gained him a solid footnote in Civil War history books. But Brown saw his destiny in Virginia.

The Raid

In the summer of 1859, Brown went to Maryland and rented a farm five miles from Harpers Ferry. There he waited, mostly in vain, for additional men and money. By mid-October 1859 he had twenty-two followers and probably recognized that his force never would be any stronger. On the night of 16 October, he and his band marched toward the Potomac with a wagonload of arms, cut the telegraph wires, crossed and captured the bridge, and moved into Harpers Ferry. Brown quickly seized the armory and its rifle works. He then sent out a detail to capture two local slaveholders along with their slaves. This mission was accomplished. Meanwhile, Brown's men had stopped a Baltimore and Ohio train, inadvertently killing the African American baggage master, but then allowed the train to go on its way. On the morning of 17 October, Brown took a number of the armory's employees hostage as they came in for work. Otherwise he remained in the engine works of the arsenal, perhaps waiting, in his mind, for the slaves to rise. By mid-morning, Maryland and Virginia militia were on their way to Harpers Ferry, and the president of the Baltimore and Ohio railroad reported to Washington that some sort of insurrection was in progress. By the afternoon of the 17th, the militia had gained control of the bridges, driving off or killing Brown's outposts. By 10 P.M., Lieutenant Colonel Robert E. Lee, U.S. Cavalry, with his aide Lieutenant J. E. B. Stuart, had arrived to take charge.

Lee followed military protocol for the situation. He offered the Virginia militia a chance to capture the engine works (which they declined), gave the insurrectionists a chance to surrender, and was careful to avoid shooting Brown's prisoners. On 18 October, Lee sent Stuart to negotiate with the leader of the raid. A veteran of Kansas, Stuart was astonished to recognize Brown. Once Brown refused to surrender, Stuart waved in a dozen marines who charged with bayonets. It was all over in moments, without a shot fired. One marine and two of Brown's men were killed. Brown himself was wounded but was saved from death because his assailant, in command of the assault team, had only a dress sword. Altogether, Brown's force had killed four civilians and wounded nine. Of his own men, ten were dead or dying, five had escaped the previous day, and seven were captured.

Brown's scheme—leading an army of twenty-two men against a federal arsenal and the entire state of Virginia—was amazingly amateurish. He left behind at his Maryland farm many letters that revealed his plans and exposed all of his confederates. He seized Harpers Ferry without taking food for his soldiers' next meal. Most bizarrely, Brown tried to lead a slave insurrection without notifying the slaves. As an abolitionist, he took it as an article of faith that slaves were seething with discontent and only awaited a signal to throw off their chains. But the Harpers Ferry raid was so poorly planned and executed that slaves, even had they been as restive as Brown assumed, could not participate.

The Consequences

In the six weeks that followed the raid, Republican and Democratic leaders denounced Brown's act. But he had shown a courage that won him grudging admiration in the South and legendary status in the North. Brown recognized that the manner of his death might be a great service to the antislavery cause. After a one-week trial, during which he lay wounded on a pallet, he was convicted of murder, treason, and insurrection. When he received his death sentence, he uttered words that became oratory of legend:

> Had I interfered in behalf of the rich, the powerful, the intelligent, the so-called great . . . every man in this court would have deemed it an act worthy of reward rather than punishment. . . . Now, if it is deemed necessary that I should . . . mingle my blood . . . with the blood of millions in this slave country whose rights are disregarded by wicked, cruel, and unjust enactments, I say, let it be done.

When Brown was hung at nearby Charles Town, on 2 December 1859, church bells tolled in many northern towns, cannons fired salutes, and prayer meetings adopted memorial resolutions. The execution dramatically deepened moral hostility to slavery. Such expressions of grief turned southern enchantment with Brown into panic. Southerners identified Brown with the abolitionists, the abolitionists with Republicans, and Republicans with the whole North. Abraham Lincoln's election in 1860 fed rumors that the Republicans were letting loose dozens of John Browns on the South. Radical southern newspapers claimed Harpers Ferry showed that the South could have no peace as a part of the Union. John Brown's raid moved southern sentiments from mediation toward revolution.

Once the Civil War erupted, the ghost of John Brown inspired the Northern armies through the popular song "John Brown's Body." Its best-known version spoke of John Brown's body moldering in the grave, of his departure to become a soldier in the army of the Lord, and of hanging the Confederate president, Jefferson Davis, on a sour apple tree. In November 1861, Julia Ward Howe, the wife of Secret Six member Samuel Gridley Howe, visited an army camp and heard the song. She awoke in the middle of the night with a creative urge to write down the words of "The Battle Hymn of the Republic." Upon publication, this version of the John Brown song became exalted. The words of the "Battle Hymn" have come down through the years as the noblest expression of what the North was fighting for in the Civil War.

BIBLIOGRAPHY

Oates, Stephen B. *To Purge This Land with Blood: A Biography of John Brown.* New York: Harper and Row, 1970. The best overall work among many.

Rossbach, Jeffery. *Ambivalent Conspirators: John Brown, the Secret Six, and a Theory of Slave Violence.* Philadelphia: University of Pennsylvania Press, 1982. Evaluates Brown's and his supporters' assumptions about the slaves' responsiveness.

United States National Park Service. *John Brown's Raid.* Washington, D.C.: Office of Publications, National Park Service, 1974. Good visual representation of key locations at Harpers Ferry at the time of the raid.

Timothy M. Roberts

See also **Antislavery; "Battle Hymn of the Republic".**

HARRIS V. McRAE, 448 U.S. 297 (1980), a case in which the Supreme Court upheld by a 5 to 4 vote the power of Congress to exclude elective abortions from coverage under the Medicaid program. The Hyde Amendment, named after Representative Henry Hyde and passed in several versions since 1976, barred the use of federal funds for abortions except when the mother's life was in danger or when the pregnancy resulted from rape or incest (the latter clause was later repealed). Although a Republican, Hyde received enough bipartisan support for the bill to be enacted by a Democratic Congress and president.

Cora McRae was one of several pregnant Medicaid recipients who brought suit, alleging that the Hyde Amendment violated the due process clause of the Fifth Amendment and the religion clauses of the First Amendment. At the time, the plaintiffs had reason for optimism because the Supreme Court had held that the government must subsidize other rights, such as the right to counsel, for the indigent. In addition, Congress had established the Medicaid program in 1965 under Title XIX of the Social Security Act specifically to give federal aid to states choosing to reimburse the indigent for medical treatments they could not afford. McRae contended that Title XIX obligated states receiving Medicaid funds to fund medically necessary abortions despite the Hyde Amendment's provisions. Indeed the federal district court granted McRae injunctive relief, ruling (491 F. Supp. 630) that although the Hyde Amendment amended (rather than violated) Title XIX, it nevertheless did violate both the Fifth and First Amendments.

In 1977, however, the Supreme Court upheld state laws similar to the Hyde Amendment, suggesting that abortion would not be treated like other rights. *Harris v. McRae* applied the same reasoning to the national government, reversing and remanding the district court ruling while holding the Hyde Amendment constitutional. "Although government may not place obstacles in the path of a woman's exercise of her freedom of choice," wrote Justice Potter Stewart, "it need not remove those of its own creation. Indigency falls in the latter category." The dissenters, especially Thurgood Marshall, argued that the decision ignored "another world 'out there' " in which poor women could not get abortions without assistance from Medicaid. The Hyde Amendment foreshadowed a number of attacks on abortion rights after 1989, both in individual state legislatures and, in 1995, in a federal ban on abortions in military hospitals and for those covered by federal health plans. The Hyde Amendment was still in effect in the early 2000s, although states retained the right to subsidize abortions with their own funds.

BIBLIOGRAPHY

Baer, Judith A. *Women in American Law.* New York: Holmes and Meier, 1991.

Bingham, Marjorie. *Women and the Constitution.* St. Paul, Minn.: The Upper Midwest Women's History Center, 1990.

Hoff-Wilson, Joan. *Law, Gender, and Injustice.* New York: New York University Press, 1991.

Judith A. Baer / A. R.

See also **Abortion; Medicare and Medicaid; Pro-Choice Movement; Pro-Life Movement; Women's Health.**

HARRISBURG CONVENTION. After the Tariff of 1824 proved unsatisfactory to the woolen interests and following the defeat of the Woolens Bill of 1827, the friends of protection called a convention at Harrisburg, Pennsylvania, to agree on a new bill. Protectionist advocates held meetings throughout the northern states and sent 100 delegates from thirteen states to the convention at Harrisburg, from 30 July to 3 August 1827. The convention produced a memorandum to Congress that set forth the special needs of the woolens manufacturers and the general value of protection. Because the tariff bill of 1828 was drafted and passed for political ends, the demands of the memorandum were ignored.

BIBLIOGRAPHY

Stanwood, Edward. *American Tariff Controversies in the Nineteenth Century.* New York: Russell and Russell, 1967.

Robert Fortenbaugh / C. W.

See also **Tariff; Textiles; Wool Growing and Manufacture.**

HARTFORD CONVENTION. From 15 December 1814 to 5 January 1815, a convention of delegates from throughout New England met at Hartford, Connecticut, to plan regional opposition to the Republican Party's federal policies. Its members hoped to bring an end to a string of defeats for the Federalist Party in general and for New England Federalists in particular. In addition, they sought to gain increased governmental support for a New England destabilized by the ongoing War of 1812.

The convention numbered twenty-six delegates. They were sent by the legislatures of Connecticut, Rhode Island, and Massachusetts, and by county caucuses in Vermont and New Hampshire. Some radical Massachusetts Federalists had lobbied for such an event since at least 1808, but more moderate men controlled the convention. British military successes in northern New England had prevented a fuller deputation from the newer New England states.

The agrarian, expansionist, anti-British cast of the Republican Virginia Dynasty's policies inured to the detriment of the New England states. Those states' economies relied heavily on foreign trade and an expanding manufacturing sector, and their self-conception was strongly shaped by the Puritan experiments at Plymouth and Massachusetts Bay. Unlike Virginia, New England stood in federal politics for hostility to the French Revolution, for foreign trade, and for a stand-pat position on westward expansion.

Following President Thomas Jefferson's 1803 Louisiana Purchase, New Englanders began to fear that a huge new swath of territory would be settled by southerners and fall under permanent Republican control. What might have been a Republican interregnum now appeared to be only the onset of New England's permanent reduction to minority status in the Union. The Jeffersonian embargo on foreign trade in 1807, keystone of Jefferson's second presidential term, did great damage to New England's economy. What made it worse was that the Republicans in Congress, who less than a decade before had complained of the Alien and Sedition Acts' arbitrariness, gave the president extremely broad enforcement powers.

New England opposed the War of 1812, and this opposition went so deep that Massachusetts Governor Caleb Strong refused to deploy his state's militia to defend the District of Maine against invasion. Part of the Hartford Convention's purpose, however, was to urge the federal administration to defend New England more vigorously, and in response to Strong's actions, Madison deployed volunteers to counter potential insurrection in Massachusetts. Nonetheless, one Hartford Convention delegate, former Secretary of State Timothy Pickering, expected Union forces to be defeated by the British in Louisiana regardless of what the convention might decide.

The convention met in secret, which aroused great hopes and anxieties, depending on the observer. In the end, it merely called for a second convention in June in case the war had not ended and proposed a set of amendments to the federal Constitution. It also lent its prestige to the notion of interposition, formerly associated primarily with the Republican Party.

On Christmas Eve 1814, in the midst of the convention, the Treaty of Ghent was concluded, and on 8 January 1815, Andrew Jackson's forces won their famous victory at New Orleans. Amidst the paroxysms of patriotism, the Hartford Convention's participants found themselves branded "traitors" and suspected of wanting to break apart the Union, something none of its members had considered in 1814. The Federalist Party, which had played a pivotal role in founding the Republic, was permanently wrecked by the Hartford Convention. By decade's end, it virtually had ceased to exist.

BIBLIOGRAPHY

Banner, James M., Jr. *To the Hartford Convention: The Federalists and the Origins of Party Politics in Massachusetts, 1789–1815.* New York: Knopf, 1970.

Ben-Atar, Doron, and Barbara B. Oberg, eds. *Federalists Reconsidered.* Charlottesville: University Press of Virginia, 1998.

Dwight, Theodore. *History of the Hartford Convention: With a Review of the Policy of the United States Government, Which Led to the War of 1812.* New York: N. and J. White; Boston: Russell, Odiorne, 1833.

Ketcham, Ralph. *James Madison: A Biography.* New York: Macmillan, 1971.

Rutland, Robert A. *The Presidency of James Madison.* Lawrence: University Press of Kansas, 1990.

K. R. Constantine Gutzman

See also **Federalist Party; Republicans, Jeffersonian; War of 1812.**

HARTFORD WITS. Originally the Connecticut Wits, this group formed in the late eighteenth century as a literary society at Yale College and then assumed a new name, the Hartford Wits. Their writings satirized an outmoded curriculum and, more significantly, society and the politics of the mid-1780s. Their dissatisfaction with the Articles of Confederation appeared in the *The Anarchiad* (1786–1787), written by David Humphreys, Joel Barlow, John Trumbull, and Lemuel Hopkins. In satirizing democratic society, this mock-epic promoted the federal union delineated by the 1787 Federal Convention at Philadelphia. After the ratification of the Constitution, most of the Wits, including Timothy Dwight, became Federalist spokesmen for order and stability. Barlow, however, became a radical Republican. From a common origin, the Wits ultimately took up positions across the early Republic's ideological spectrum.

BIBLIOGRAPHY

Elliott, Emory. *Revolutionary Writers: Literature and Authority in the New Republic, 1725–1810.* New York: Oxford University Press, 1982.

Howard, Leon. *The Connecticut Wits.* Chicago: The University of Chicago Press, 1943.

John Saillant

See also **Articles of Confederation; Federalist Party; Yale University.**

HARVARD UNIVERSITY. Puritans so dreaded an uneducated ministry that in 1636, only six years after the founding of Massachusetts Bay, the colony's General Court voted money "towards a schoale or colledge." Named after the Reverend John Harvard, a private benefactor, Harvard College opened in 1638 in a house inside a cattle yard donated by the town of Cambridge, and in 1642, it graduated the first class of nine men. In 1650, the legislature granted an official charter providing for governance by a small, self-perpetuating corporation and a larger board of overseers to be chosen by the magistrates; half were to be ministers.

The Seventeenth and Eighteenth Centuries

The college's charge was "the education of youth in all manner of good literature Artes and sciences." This meant four years of grammar, rhetoric, logic, ethics, natural science, metaphysics, arithmetic, geometry, astronomy, and history as well as Latin, Greek, and (for interpreting the Old Testament) Hebrew. Prospective ministers, the majority of Harvard's graduates for several generations, studied theology for an additional three years. But the established Congregational Church seldom interfered in either curriculum or training.

Following the English (rather than the European) model, students lived in dormitory rooms and ate meals with tutors at "commons." The tutors, ill-paid and often no older than the students, answered to the president of the college, who also taught. Henry Dunster was a formidable early president (1640–1654), as was Increase Mather (1685–1701), a famous Boston divine. Order was a chronic problem. Harvard students, many of whose families paid their tuition with farm produce, consumed much "beef, bread, and beer" and fathers frequently had to pay for broken windows. During a somnolent eighteenth century, posted student social rankings were a chief preoccupation.

Major Changes and Enhanced Independence

Under the presidencies of John T. Kirkland (1810–1828) and especially Josiah Quincy (1829–1845), Harvard—now with a medical college (1782) and law school (1817)—erected new buildings, established permanent professorships, and increased its enrollments. Fewer boys came from the New England hinterlands, and more from Boston's economic and cultural elite, grown rich from commerce, finance, and manufacturing. Scions of the plantation South arrived. By the time of the Civil War, faculty were better paid, even affluent, mixing easily with Boston society. Ministers were increasingly rare and serious researchers and men of letters more common, as in, for example, the fields of criticism (James Russell Lowell), chemistry (Josiah Cooke), geology (Louis Agassiz), and economics (Francis Bowen). President James Walker (1853–1860) remarked, "Now a professor is as much a layman as a lawyer or a physician is." Instruction itself grew more secular; only 10 percent of antebellum Harvard graduates became ministers, a startlingly low figure for nineteenth-century America.

At midcentury, Harvard—still state chartered and partially state funded—faced two challenges: one from religious conservatives opposed to the university's religious liberalism, and another from political liberals opposed to its exclusiveness and its hostility to abolitionism. In response, the institution moved to insulate itself from political interference by severing its relation to the state government, forgoing funds but jettisoning politically appointed overseers. The corporation and president dealt with a lesser challenge—this from faculty demanding greater control—by firmly grasping (as a professor put it) "the money, the keys, and the power."

The Regimes of Charles W. Eliot and A. Lawrence Lowell

Charles W. Eliot's presidency (1869–1909) witnessed further change. Student numbers rose to fifteen hundred. Students from the defeated South largely disappeared, to be replaced by representatives of the new economic power centers, New York City in particular. Raised in privilege, students led "gilded" lives at Harvard, immersed in clubs, sports, and society and earning "gentlemen's Cs." Private gifts, from wealthy alumni and others, increased dramatically. President Eliot, trained in chemistry, introduced an elective system that relaxed the traditional college curriculum. But the most profound innovation came when Eliot laid the foundations of the graduate school in 1872. The stress on advanced instruction and research produced unrivaled departments of history (Henry Adams, Edward Channing), philosophy (Josiah Royce, William James), fine arts (Charles Eliot Norton), and English (George Lyman Kittredge), among many others. Eliot strengthened the law and medical schools and established a professional school of business administration. By the end of Eliot's term, Harvard, with its illustrious alumni, lavish patronage, national reach, and distinguished faculty, was the premier institution of higher education in the country, a position it has largely maintained.

President A. Lawrence Lowell (1909–1933), a political scientist, established new professional schools (public health, engineering) but elsewhere modified Eliot's legacy. Focusing anew on undergraduates, Lowell introduced major fields, the tutorial system, and the house plan, which lodged the three upper classes with tutors in residential units, partly as a way to undermine the influence of the Harvard clubs. Lowell's defense of the right of students and faculty to dissent—to oppose U.S. entry into World War I or be prolabor—led to tension with the corporation but enhanced Harvard's reputation for academic integrity. Lowell tolerated new ethnic groups, making Harvard perhaps the most tolerant of American universities. Yet he also helped impose a quota on the admission of Jewish students, fearing that they would crowd out Protestant applicants and develop "inappropriate ethnic consciousness."

Research Science, Student Radicalism, and an Enlarged Endowment

The presidencies of the chemist James B. Conant (1933–1953) and the classicist Nathan Pusey (1953–1971) marked a deemphasis on undergraduates and a dramatic shift in resources toward research science at the expense of the traditional liberal arts. Harvard became a chief recipient of federal research grants during World War II and the Cold War, which triggered the appointment of top researchers in key scientific and engineering fields and the construction of substantial new facilities for them. As of 1967, Harvard had trained 16 percent of Nobel Prize winners, more than any other university. By 1971, total enrollments were 40,000 and the operating budget was $200 million.

The struggle to maintain high academic standards while addressing radical activist demands and the needs of a suffering Cambridge consumed much of the administration of President Derek Bok (1971–1991), a lawyer who expanded Harvard's global presence and applicant pool. His successor, Neil Rudenstine (1991–2001), concentrated on increasing the university's endowment, which rose from $1.3 billion in the early 1970s to over $15 billion by the end of the century. This made Harvard the wealthiest university in the United States by a substantial margin, which prompted criticism of its high yearly tuition ($35,000) and low pay rates for janitorial and other staff. Lawrence Summers, an economist and former secretary of the Treasury, was appointed Harvard's twenty-seventh president in 2001.

BIBLIOGRAPHY

Hawkins, Hugh. *Between Harvard and America: The Educational Leadership of Charles W. Eliot.* New York: Oxford University Press, 1972.

Hershberg, James. *James B. Conant: Harvard to Hiroshima and the Making of the Nuclear Age.* New York: Knopf, 1993.

Morison, Samuel Eliot. *Three Centuries of Harvard, 1636–1936.* Cambridge, Mass.: Harvard University Press, 1936.

Story, Ronald. *The Forging of an Aristocracy: Harvard and the Boston Upper Class, 1900–1970.* Middletown, Conn.: Wesleyan University Press, 1980.

Yeomans, Henry A. *Abbott Lawrence Lowell, 1856–1943.* Cambridge, Mass.: Harvard University Press, 1948.

Ronald Story

See also **Education, Higher: Colleges and Universities, Denominational Colleges, Women's Colleges; Ivy League; Law Schools; Medical Education; Science Education.**

HAT MANUFACTURE, COLONIAL RESTRICTION ON. Colonial manufactures, stimulated by the abundance of furs in New England and New York, made and exported hats to neighboring colonies, the West Indies, and southern Europe through the early eighteenth century. But in 1732, the influential Company of Felt-Makers in London persuaded Parliament to forbid colonial exportation of hats, require a seven years' apprenticeship, exclude blacks, and limit each manufacturer to two apprentices. New York exported hats labeled "British" from 1733 to 1735 and John Adams stated that Massachusetts hatmakers disregarded the law, but the industry's rapid growth after independence in 1783 suggests that the law had an inhibiting effect during the colonial period.

BIBLIOGRAPHY

Kammen, Michael G. *Empire and Interest: The American Colonies and the Politics of Mercantilism.* Philadelphia: Lippincott, 1970.

McCusker, John J., and Kenneth Morgan, eds. *The Early Modern Atlantic Economy.* New York: Cambridge University Press, 2000.

Lawrence A. Harper / B. P.

See also **Beaver Hats; Colonial Commerce; Colonial Policy, British; Fur Trade and Trapping; Mercantilism; Navigation Acts.**

HATCH ACT (1939), as amended, regulates partisan political activities by U.S. civil servants. The Democratic senator Carl Hatch of New Mexico, protesting the political involvement of federal employees in primaries and general elections, sponsored the bill that became the Hatch Act in order to ban federal employees from participating actively in political campaigns or from using their positions to coerce voters.

The Pendleton Act of 1883 and several executive orders limited partisan political activity by career civil servants. But the number of federal government workers ballooned from 14,000 in 1883 to 560,000 in 1926, so that by the 1930s, conservative Democrats and Republicans feared that these restrictions were insufficient, and that civil servants might shape elections of presidents, senators, and representatives. Also, they believed that the administration of Democratic president Franklin Roosevelt was using relief monies to influence elections. New Deal liberals seeking renomination or attempting to unseat conservative Democrats in Kentucky, Tennessee, and Pennsylvania were accused of diverting Works Progress Administration funds to enhance their prospects at the polls. In January 1939, the Senate Campaign Expenditures Committee upheld those accusations.

Hatch complained that the Democratic National Committee was obtaining gifts from persons working for—and corporations having contracts with—the federal government, and that several relatives of rival New Mexico Democratic senator Dennis Chavez had coerced WPA officials. In January 1939, Hatch introduced legislation to neutralize the federal civil service. While permitting federal employees to vote, his measure prohibited the assessment or solicitation of funds from WPA employees or the removal of any personnel because of refusal to change political affiliation. Section 9 prevented federal officials and workers from using their position to interfere in presidential or congressional elections. Non-policymaking federal officials could not be removed for partisan reasons. Enforcement was left to department heads, with a one-thousand-dollar fine or one-year term of imprisonment for violators.

In April 1939 the Senate adopted his measure with little fanfare, but the House Judiciary Committee infuriated Hatch by deleting section 9. The full House, however, restored much of it in July. President Roosevelt, who privately harbored reservations about section 9, reluctantly signed the bill into law on 2 August. The Hatch Act magnified the influence of local bosses, rural legislators, and labor unions. The original measure, therefore, was broadened in 1940 to include 250,000 state employees paid wholly or partially from federal funds and to require the nonpayment and removal of violators. A 1950 amendment reduced the penalty to ninety days suspension without pay.

Hatch Act supporters considered a politically neutral civil service the best way to achieve an impartial government and protect federal workers from coercion or threats by superiors. They regarded a government employee's attempts to influence the votes of others as inconsistent with the spirit of the Constitution and wanted to limit the growing influence of government employee unions.

In *United Public Workers v. Mitchell* (1947), the U.S. Supreme Court by a 4–3 vote upheld the constitutionality of the Hatch Act, stating that public employment was a privilege subject to reasonable conditions. The Commission on Political Activity of Government Personnel in 1966 recommended relaxing restrictions and penalties. A 1972 U.S. district court ruled that the Hatch Act was vague, overly broad, and contrary to the First Amendment, but the U.S. Supreme Court in June 1973 again upheld it.

Critics claimed that the Hatch Act denied millions of federal employees the First Amendment rights of freedom of speech and association and discouraged political participation among people who otherwise would be vigorous political activists. Democratic President Bill Clinton encouraged Congress to overhaul the Hatch Act, and. the Federal Employees Political Activities Act of 1993 permitted most federal civil servants to run for public office in nonpartisan elections, contribute money to political organizations, and campaign for or against candidates in partisan elections. Federal officials, however, were still barred from engaging in political activity while on duty, soliciting contributions from the general public, or running as candidates for office in partisan elections.

BIBLIOGRAPHY

Eccles, James R. *The Hatch Act and the American Bureaucracy.* New York: Vantage Press, 1981.

Ponessa, Jeanne. "The Hatch Act Rewrite." *Congressional Quarterly Weekly Report* (13 November 1993), 3146–3147.

Porter, David L. "Senator Carl Hatch and the Hatch Act of 1939." *New Mexico Historical Review* 47 (April 1973): 151–164.

———. *Congress and the Waning of the New Deal.* Port Washington, N.Y.: Kennikat Press, 1980.

David L. Porter

See also **Campaign Financing and Resources; Civil Service.**

HATE CRIMES. Hate crimes are crimes committed because of the victim's race, gender, national origin, religion, sexual orientation, or other protected status. The federal government, most states, and many localities have enacted laws or regulations to define such acts as separate crimes in themselves or to augment penalties for existing crimes when motivated by hatred or bias. Because definitions vary across jurisdictions, acts as disparate as lynching, assault while calling the victim derogatory names, cross burning, or making intimidating threats on the basis of the victim's race or other protected status might be considered hate crimes. Whatever the definition, statistics show that incidences of hate crime were on the rise in the late twentieth century.

On the federal level there is no hate crime law per se, though legislative efforts to enact such a law came close to succeeding in the late 1990s. Prior to 1994, federal prosecutors combating hate crimes depended primarily on civil rights statutes, including those protecting voting activities, fair housing, and the enjoyment of public accommodations. In 1994 Congress added to federal authority to prosecute hate crimes by providing sentence enhancements for any existing federal offense if the defendant selected the victim "because of the actual or perceived race, color, religion, national origin, ethnicity, gender, disability, or sexual orientation" of the victim. Also in 1994, Congress passed the Violence against Women Act, which provided a civil cause of action for gender-motivated violence. The Supreme Court, however, voted 5 to 4 in *United States v. Morrison* (2000) to strike down the relevant provisions as being outside Congress's legislative authority under the commerce clause and the Fourteenth Amendment.

During the last two decades of the twentieth century, nearly every state enacted a hate crime law of some kind. Most of these statutes took the form of sentence enhancements for existing crimes. Others defined new substantive criminal offenses or created new private causes of action.

Hate crime statutes raise a number of serious policy and legal questions. Some critics believe that hate crime statutes pose serious First Amendment difficulties by distinguishing among criminals based on their beliefs. Other critics charge that the statutes are unconstitutionally vague or send the inappropriate message that crimes committed for reasons other than bias are not as serious. Supporters of hate crime statutes assert that the constitutional concerns can be surmounted and that the statutes are necessary to make clear society's strong belief that bias-motivated crimes are particularly detrimental to the social fabric.

Some of the constitutional issues raised by hate crime statutes were the focus of two Supreme Court cases in the early 1990s. In *R.A.V. v. City of St. Paul* (1992), the Court struck down a local ordinance that outlawed placing on public or private property a symbol or object likely to arouse "anger, alarm, or resentment . . . on the basis of race, color, creed, religion, or gender." The defendant had been charged under the ordinance after burning a cross in the yard of an African American family. Even though the "speech" at issue fell into the analytical category of "fighting words," which the Court had previously maintained was of low constitutional value, the Court held that the ordinance was viewpoint based and thus facially unconstitutional.

In *Wisconsin v. Mitchell* (1993), the Court upheld, against a First Amendment challenge, a state statute that increased a defendant's punishment for battery because he selected his victim on the basis of the victim's race. In a unanimous opinion the Court rejected the defendant's argument, adopted by the lower court, that the penalty enhancement represented punishment for bigoted thought. The state could legitimately punish criminal conduct motivated by bias more than the same criminal conduct without such motivation because of the greater harm likely to flow from the former. After *R.A.V.* and *Mitchell*, hate crimes statutes in the form of penalty enhancements became the preferred form at both the federal and the state levels.

BIBLIOGRAPHY

Jacobs, James B., and Kimberly Potter. *Hate Crimes.* New York: Oxford University Press, 1998.

"Symposium: Federal Bias Crime Law." *Boston University Law Review* 80 (2000): 1185–1449.

Wang, Lu-in. *Hate Crimes Law.* St. Paul: West, 1993. Comprehensive reference source on federal and state hate crime law.

Kent Greenfield

See also **Crime; Discrimination; Group Libel Laws.**

HAWAII. When Captain James Cook arrived in the Hawaiian Islands in the 1770s, he found a people living in the most isolated location on earth who had developed a highly sophisticated agriculture based mainly on the cultivation of *kalo* (taro), some of which was grown in impressive irrigation systems. The subsistence economy was based on agriculture and the harvest of products from the sea. Items moved between farmers and fishermen through reciprocal gift exchanges that were not driven by values or timetables. Absent any metals, pottery clay, or textile fibers, the people developed a highly advanced culture based on the materials provided by the islands.

Politically, the people were ruled by regional *mo'i* (kings) of whom there might be several on one island. Religiously and legally the society was regulated by a religion based on a *kapu* (tabu) system that consisted of prohibitions, restrictions, and directions, all of which depended for their enforcement on the authority and punitive powers of the *kahuna* (priests). Under this system, women were prohibited from eating certain foods or dining with men and were restricted in other ways. The daily life of Hawaiians was also regulated by the *konohiki* (landlords), under whom they lived in a semifeudal status.

The *maka'ainana* (commoners) were subject to arbitrary exactions from the *ali'i* (chiefs) in whose presence they were required to prostrate themselves, and were also subject to a formal tax annually during the *makahiki* season, which occurred late in every year and brought concentrations of people from the surrounding area. The burden of taxation was lightened through its accompaniment by a festival that included sports and games. It was during the *makahiki* festival that Captain Cook sailed into Kealakekua Bay, where he later met his unfortunate end, and the presence of the unusually large number of people may have caused him to exaggerate the population of the islands.

Early Merchant Trade

Despite their "discovery" by Cook, the islands at first seemed to offer nothing of economic benefit to the West, and their location away from established trade routes discouraged follow-up voyages. John Ledyard, an American who accompanied Cook, was struck, however, by the potential profits to be gained by trading the furs of the Pacific Northwest for the products of China at Canton. Ledyard's efforts to interest American businessmen in such a venture were met with skepticism until his stories were confirmed by the publication of the journals of the expedition, whereupon both English and American merchant ships set out to exploit the trade.

It was the fur trade between the Pacific Northwest and Canton that made the Hawaiian Islands a desirable way station and a convenient stopover between trading seasons. Thus began the rapid transformation of the islands and their people. Reciprocal gift exchanges quickly gave way to barter, then to trade and the beginnings of a commercial agriculture that focused on growing the products sought by the Westerners, many of them newly introduced to the islands. The reliance on stone and other indigenous products for tools and weapons was now supplemented by the use of metals. Western firearms were also introduced. These were used, with the help of Western advisers, by Kamehameha, a *mo'i* of the island of Hawaii, to unify all of the islands under his control as king of Hawaii.

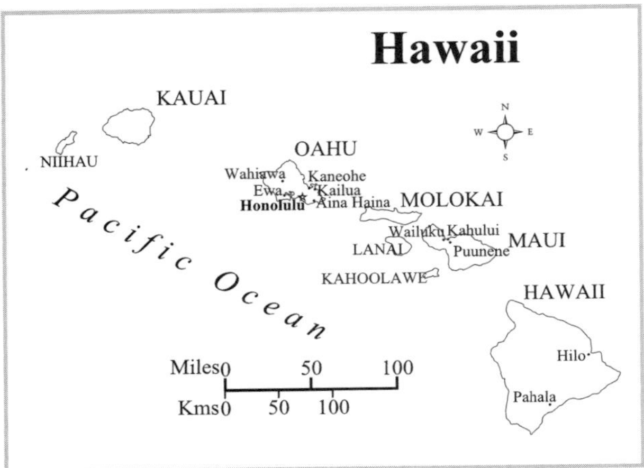

The discovery of sandalwood in the islands, and its marketability in Canton, gave Hawaii an economic value it had not previously possessed and brought Western (mainly American) merchants to Honolulu to deal in this precious commodity, especially after Kamehameha's death in 1819 ended his monopoly over the trade. The *ali'i* scrambled to exploit the sandalwood forests for access to the goods of the West that the fragrant wood provided, incurring debts with foreign merchants to be paid later in deliveries of sandalwood. The beginnings of a monetary economy began to intrude into the traditional subsistence way of life even in the most remote areas.

Forced Westernization and the Rise of the Sugar Industry

After Kamehameha's death, the traditional *kapu* system was thrown out by his successor, Liholiho, under the influence of Kamehameha's widow, Kaahumanu, whom he had appointed as *kuhina nui* (regent, prime minister) to advise the new king. The overthrow set the Hawaiian people adrift in a particularly chaotic time. In 1820, two events occurred that would further contribute to the transformation of the islands and to the stresses on the Hawaiian people: the arrival of the first Puritan missionaries from New England and the introduction of the first whaling ships to Hawaii's harbors. Their arrival accelerated the revolution in Hawaiian life that had been inaugurated by Cook's arrival, the main features of which would be: (1) the transition from a society in which wealth, power, and status were based on land to one in which they were increasingly measured in money; (2) the increasing control of that monetary economy—and the wealth and power and status associated with it—by Westerners rather than by the Hawaiian *ali'i;* (3) the transition from a rural, largely subsistence lifestyle to an urban, consumerist one, with the accompanying rise of individualism at the expense of the traditional communalism; (4) the replacement of the traditional religion and its related social controls by a religion ill-suited to the Hawaiians in the form of Calvinist Christianity; (5) the destructive effects of the Calvinist missionaries in their efforts to replace all traditional culture with the Calvinists' own version of acceptable diversions, laws, and institutions; (6) the introduction of Western laws, practices, and institutions that were easily understood by the Westerners, but which increasingly placed the Hawaiians at a disadvantage in coping with these alien devices; (7) the blurring of class distinctions between commoners and chiefs that resulted in the loss of power and influence by the traditional leadership of the Hawaiian people, creating a vacuum increasingly filled by the missionaries and other Westerners; and (8) the integration of Hawaii into the global economy, with the accompanying globalization of Hawaiian culture and daily life.

By the 1890s, commercialism, urbanization, and individualism had replaced subsistence agriculture and rural communalism as the key features of life in the islands, while large sugar plantations marketing their products in foreign lands had largely supplanted the *kuleana* (small fields) of Hawaiian farmers. The Hawaiian religion had been replaced by Christianity, and the *kapu* system by Puritan law codes, while the traditional prerogatives of the *ali'i* and of the *mo'i* had been usurped by a new white "*ali'i*" ruling in the name of a Republic of Hawaii within which the franchise of Hawaiians had been so sharply restricted that they were a minority of voters.

While there were many milestones in the march toward this fate, a major one certainly was passage by the kingdom's legislature of the alien land law in 1850, which made it possible for foreigners for the first time to own land in fee simple. Before this act, the economic penetration by foreign interests had been limited largely to commerce. Once the security of land ownership was provided, however, foreign interests, mainly American, were willing to undertake the investment in productive ventures like sugar plantations and mills. As declining demand for whale oil and whalebone caused whaling to die out in the 1860s and 1870s, the growing, processing, and exportation of sugar rose in importance. The ratification by the United States in 1875 of a reciprocity treaty with the Kingdom of Hawaii enormously accelerated the growth of the sugar industry. The effect, however, was to make the kingdom almost totally dependent on sugar for its prosperity, and the sugar industry, in turn, almost totally dependent on the American market. Like the tentacles of an octopus, the sugar plantations reached out everywhere for lands on which to grow the valuable crop.

Another effect of the reciprocity act was to accelerate the importation of laborers (mainly Chinese and Japanese) to work on the plantations, since there were not enough Hawaiians to do the work. The Hawaiian population, estimated at between 300,000 and 500,000 at the time of Cook's arrival, had shrunk by the end of the 1870s to fewer than 60,000, while between 1876 and 1890 the sugar planters imported 55,000 Chinese and Japanese laborers. In 1876, the Hawaiians, despite their reduced numbers, still accounted for 90 percent of the population of the islands. By 1890, they were not even a majority in their own land.

Annexation

The combination of the reciprocity act and the "bayonet constitution" forced by the white oligarchy on King Kalakaua in 1887 solidified the position and prosperity of that oligarchy in Hawaii. The reciprocity act permitted the shipment of sugar to the American market duty-free, thus putting it on the same basis as domestically produced sugar and at an advantage in competition with other foreign sugar. The 1887 constitution assured these planters and businessmen of control over the government of the kingdom, thus making them secure in their extensive investments in the islands. In the early 1890s, however, both profits and power were undermined by two events, one in Washington and one in Honolulu.

The first was the passage into law of the McKinley Tariff in 1890, which deprived Hawaiian sugar of all the advantages it had received by granting duty-free status to all foreign sugar while providing a bounty to domestic sugar producers. The second was the death of King Kalakaua and the succession of Liliuokalani as queen, who came to the throne determined to recover for the crown the powers it had lost in the 1887 constitution.

In January 1893, a combination of circumstances centering on the queen's proposal to promulgate a new constitution on her own initiative touched off a virtually bloodless coup. At a critical moment, U.S. forces were moved ashore from the USS *Boston*, then in Honolulu harbor, at the instigation of the U.S. minister to Hawaii, John L. Stevens. A provisional government was established under Sanford B. Dole and a mission was dispatched to Washington, D.C., to negotiate a treaty for annexation of the islands by the United States.

The timing was unfortunate, for a Republican sympathetic to annexation, Benjamin Harrison, was about to turn over the White House to an unsympathetic Democrat, Grover Cleveland. The treaty negotiated with the Harrison administration was stalled in the Senate until Cleveland's inauguration, whereupon Cleveland launched an investigation that seemed to reveal the culpability of the preceding administration in the overthrow. Denied the support of the White House, the annexation treaty drew dust in the Senate until the election of Republican William McKinley in 1896 and the Spanish-American War brought the renewed enthusiasm for expansion that made possible Hawaii's annexation by joint resolution of Congress. On 12 August 1898 the flag of the United States was raised over Iolani Palace in Honolulu.

Once under the U.S. Constitution, the sugar planters might have been more secure in their profits, but their political power was eroded by the guarantee of franchise to all Hawaiian adult males, which made up the majority of eligible voters. In the first territorial election, the Hawaiians' own Home Rule Party elected a majority of the legislature and also the territory's delegate to Congress. Placed on the defensive, the planters negotiated an agreement with Prince Jonah Kalanianaole Kuhio, an heir to the throne of the defunct monarchy, to run on the Republican ticket for delegate to Congress, thereby attracting enough Hawaiian voters to the Republican side to give the planter-controlled Republicans effective political domination until World War II.

During the next forty years, however, conditions were created for the political transformation of Hawaii by the arrival of tens of thousands of new immigrants, mainly now from the Philippines; by the coming to voting age of the sons and daughters of these and earlier immigrants; and by the rise of a labor movement in Hawaii. The Great Depression and New Deal of the 1930s did not impact Hawaii as much as they did the mainland United States, but they did exert an influence. Hawaii received a share of the public-works and work-relief spending that improved its infrastructure just in time for the needs of World War II. These programs were administered by federal officials from the mainland that breathed new life into the Hawaii Democratic Party. Legislation like the National Industrial Recovery Act and the National Labor Relations Act gave enormous stimulus to the unionization of Hawaii's workers. At the same time, the tendency on the part of some in the Franklin D. Roosevelt administration to deal with Hawaii as an "insular possession" like the Philippines and Puerto Rico, rather than as a territory of the United States, as in the case of the Jones-Costigan Sugar Act, convinced many that only statehood could provide the security that Hawaii's economy required.

World War II and Postwar Political Change

Within twenty-four hours of the Japanese attack on Pearl Harbor on 7 December 1941, life in the islands changed, as the territory came under a rigorous martial law that worked closely with the white oligarchy (generally referred to as the Big Five, which consisted of Alexander and Baldwin, American Factors, C. Brewer and Company, Castle and Cooke, and Theo H. Davies and Company). On the surface it appeared to be only a brief interruption of normal conditions and that the 1930s status quo would return after the war. But numerous new factors were introduced during the war years that accelerated the changes already under way in the 1930s. For one, the war brought many new workers from the mainland who brought their union loyalties and an antipathy to the big businesses that ruled Hawaii and the political party that represented them. Many of these workers stayed after the war ended, as did many servicemen who had been exposed to the islands for the first time. Another factor was that many of Hawaii's minorities went off to fight in the war, most notably the Americans of Japanese ancestry (AJAs) who made up the famed 100th Infantry Battalion, and 442d Regimental Combat Team. Taking advantage of their veterans' benefits after the war, many would go on to receive college degrees and even postgraduate and professional degrees and would commit themselves to bringing reforms to Hawaii.

By 1954, a Democratic Party that had been reinvigorated by the leadership of former policeman John A. Burns, working with AJAs like Daniel K. Inouye and others, was able to capture control of both houses of the territorial legislature. (By 2002, the Democrats were still in control of both houses.) The loss of the Big Five's political control was soon followed by the weakening of their economic control as well. As Hawaii's delegate to Congress, Burns worked tirelessly in behalf of statehood for the islands. He was finally successful in 1959, when Congress approved a statehood bill. On 17 June of that year the voters of Hawaii ratified statehood by a margin of 17–1, and on 21 August, President Dwight D. Eisenhower signed the bill admitting Hawaii as the fiftieth state in the Union.

Hawaii since Statehood

In a special 1959 election, the last appointed governor of the territory, Republican William Quinn, became the first elected governor of the state, when he staged a surprising victory over John Burns. But in 1962, Burns defeated Quinn, ushering in an unbroken succession of Democratic governors for the remainder of the twentieth century. Meanwhile, the Democratic Party's strategy changed from that of a working-class party to one racially oriented, based on appeals to the descendants of Hawaii's immigrant plantation laborers of whatever class.

Statehood did not save Hawaii's sugar industry. The combination of rising costs and foreign competition brought the demise of the industry by the end of the twentieth century. Left at least temporarily without a viable industry, the state of Hawaii was forced to rely almost entirely on tourism for its prosperity, with tourists sought from all over the world, particularly Asia. Tourism, however, was dependent on economic conditions in the source countries. Frequent economic crises on the U.S. mainland and in Asia during these decades revealed how fragile Hawaii's economic base had become when they triggered severe recessions in the islands that continued into the twenty-first century.

Meanwhile, traditional Hawaiian culture, so long dormant that its very survival was being questioned, staged a renaissance in the 1970s, inspired in large part by developments on the U.S. mainland including the civil rights and ethnic studies movements of the 1960s. The Hawaiian renaissance encompassed both cultural and political elements, with a resurgence of interest in both traditional and more recent Hawaiian culture and language, together with the beginnings of Hawaiian political activism in opposition to development on Oahu and the U.S. Navy bombing of the island of Kahoolawe. Two laws passed during the Lyndon Johnson presidency contributed to both aspects of the renaissance. The creation of the National Foundation on the Arts and Humanities in 1965 provided money to encourage the growth and understanding of arts and humanities. With government patronage available, Hawaiians and others interested in traditional Hawaiian culture were stimulated to undertake creative activities, pursue traditional arts and crafts, and learn and disseminate information about the culture. The Model Cities program inaugurated by the federal government in 1966 encouraged grassroots political activism and provided broader opportunities for the participation and leadership of Hawaiians.

The influence of the Hawaiian renaissance profoundly affected the state's constitutional convention in 1978, particularly the "Hawaiian package" of amendments that the new constitution included. The new constitution recognized the Hawaiian language as one of the official languages of the state (just eleven years after its use was still prohibited), confirmed the Hawaiians in various traditional rights, and established the Office of Hawaiian Affairs to represent the interests of native Hawaiians. Four years later, the leader of the Hawaiian forces within the convention, John Waihee, was elected lieutenant governor of the state, and in 1986, he was elected to the first of two terms as governor.

The twentieth century ended with many Hawaiians seeking the culmination of the renaissance in some degree of sovereignty, and many others continuing the resurgent interest in Hawaiian culture and language amid new opportunities available in the state's schools and colleges. It also ended with signs of a possible resurgence of the Republican Party as an apparent result of decades that Hawaii had spent in the economic doldrums.

BIBLIOGRAPHY

Daws, Gavan. *A Shoal of Time: A History of the Hawaiian Islands.* New York: Macmillan, 1968.

Fuchs, Lawrence H. *Hawaii Pono: A Social History.* New York: Harcourt, Brace, and World, 1961. Reprint, San Diego: Harcourt, Brace, and Jovanovich, 1983.

Kuykendall, Ralph S. *The Hawaiian Kingdom.* 3 vols. Honolulu: University of Hawaii, 1938–1967.

Gary Dean Best

See also **Honolulu; Sugar Industry.**

HAY–BUNAU-VARILLA TREATY was signed on 18 November 1903 by Secretary of State John M. Hay and Philippe Bunau-Varilla, a French canal investor who had helped organize the Panamanian revolt against Colombia and acted as the new ruling junta's envoy to Washington. The treaty provided that the United States guarantee the independence of Panama, while receiving in perpetuity a ten-mile-wide strip of territory for the construction of a canal. The United States was made fully sovereign over this zone and retained the right to intervene elsewhere in Panama as necessary to keep order. In return, the United States agreed to pay Panama $10 million and an annuity of $250,000 from canal revenues. The U.S. Senate ratified the treaty on 23 February 1904. Because of U.S. support for Panamanian secession, relations with Colombia remained fragile until Washington paid that country $25 million in restitution, or "canalimony," under the Thomson-Urrutia Treaty of 1921.

BIBLIOGRAPHY

LaFeber, Walter. *The Panama Canal: the Crisis in Historical Perspective.* Updated ed. New York: Oxford University Press, 1989.

Major, John. *Prize Possession: The United States and the Panama Canal, 1903–1979.* Cambridge, U.K., and New York: Cambridge University Press, 1993.

Schoonover, Thomas D. *The United States in Central America, 1860–1911: Episodes of Social Imperialism and Imperial Rivalry in the World System.* Durham, N.C.: Duke University Press, 1991.

Max Paul Friedman

See also **Panama Canal.**

HAYBURN'S CASE, 2 Dallas 409 (1792), refers to one of the earliest assertions of the independence of the American judiciary, and one of the first instances of federal judicial review. A 1791 federal statute granting pensions to Revolutionary War veterans mandated that the U.S. circuit courts determine whether petitioners qualified. The act gave the secretary of war the power to deny pensions if he believed the courts to be in error. Circuit judges protested that the act, in giving an executive official power to overrule a judicial determination, violated the Constitution's principle of separation of powers. The appeal lodged before the Supreme Court of circuit judges' refusal to act was rendered moot when a new statutory pension plan did not involve judges.

BIBLIOGRAPHY

Casto, William R. *The Supreme Court in the Early Republic: The Chief Justiceships of John Jay and Oliver Ellsworth.* Columbia: University of South Carolina Press, 1995.

Stephen B. Presser

See also **Judicial Review.**

HAY-HERRÁN TREATY was signed by Secretary of State John M. Hay and Dr. Tomás Herrán, the Colombian minister, on 22 January 1903. It allowed the French-controlled New Panama Canal Company to sell its option on a canal route through Panama to the United States. In addition, Colombia would give the United States a 100-year lease on a ten-kilometer-wide strip of land across Panama for construction of a canal. The United States agreed to pay Colombia $10 million and an annuity of $250,000 starting nine years after ratification of the treaty. The U.S. Senate approved the treaty in March 1903. In August of that year, however, the Colombian Senate rejected the treaty. The primary arguments against the treaty centered on the question of money and issues of Colombian sovereignty. President Theodore Roosevelt was furious at the Colombian action, and in November 1903 a revolution broke out in Panama that resulted in its independence from Colombia. Shortly thereafter, the United States signed an agreement with Panama giving America the right to construct a canal through that country.

BIBLIOGRAPHY

Lael, Richard L. *Arrogant Diplomacy: U.S. Policy Toward Colombia, 1903–1922.* Wilmington, Del.: Scholarly Resources, 1987.

Miner, Dwight C. *The Right for the Panama Route: The Story of the Spooner Act and the Hay-Herrán Treaty.* New York: Columbia University Press, 1940.

Michael L. Krenn

See also **Panama Canal.**

HAYMARKET RIOT. In April and early May 1886, the idea of a national strike for the eight-hour day gained momentum among the labor activists of CHICAGO. On 3 May police fired on strikers at the McCormick Harvesting Machine Company, killing four. August Spies, editor of the semianarchist *Arbeiter-Zeitung,* issued circulars demanding revenge and announcing a mass meeting the next evening at the Haymarket Square. About 1,300 people attended the meeting, although many dispersed when it began to rain. Amid general anticipation of violence, large police reserves were concentrated nearby. Mayor Carter H. Harrison attended the meeting, but he soon left, judging the speeches innocuous. Contravening Harrison's advice, 180 police advanced on the meeting and ordered the crowd to disperse. At this point, a bomb, thrown by an unknown hand, fell among the police, leaving seven dead and seventy injured.

Popular fears of a general anarchist plot made an impartial investigation impossible; eight alleged anarchists were convicted on a conspiracy charge, and four were hanged. The eight-hour movement collapsed beneath the stigma of radicalism. Governor John P. Altgeld pardoned the three surviving prisoners in 1893, declaring that the trial had been a farce—an opinion severely condemned by the conservative press but highly praised by organized labor.

BIBLIOGRAPHY

Avrich, Paul. *The Haymarket Tragedy.* Princeton, N.J.: Princeton University Press, 1984.

Nelson, Bruce C. *Beyond the Martyrs: A Social History of Chicago's Anarchists, 1870–1900.* New Brunswick, N.J.: Rutgers University Press, 1988.

Harvey Wish / A. R.

See also **Anarchists; Chicago; Labor; Strikes; Wages and Salaries; Work; and picture (overleaf).**

Haymarket Riot. An engraving published in *Harper's Weekly* on 15 May 1886 depicts the chaos touched off by the fatal explosion, during a mass meeting at the Chicago square on 4 May. LIBRARY OF CONGRESS

HAY-PAUNCEFOTE TREATIES. The first Hay-Pauncefote Treaty, signed 5 February 1900 by Secretary of State John Hay and Sir Julian Pauncefote, the British ambassador, modified the CLAYTON-BULWER TREATY of 1850, which provided for a joint protectorate by England and the United States of any trans-isthmian canal. It permitted the construction and maintenance of a canal under the sole auspices of the United States. The U.S. Senate amended the treaty to have it supersede the Clayton-Bulwer Treaty and to give the United States the right to fortify the canal. Great Britain declined to accept the Senate amendments, and the second Hay-Pauncefote Treaty was negotiated, signed on 18 November 1901. Article I declared that it should supersede the Clayton-Bulwer Treaty. Article II provided that a canal might be constructed under the auspices of the United Sates and that it would have all the rights incident to such construction as well as the right to regulate and manage the canal. Article III stipulated that the canal should be free and open to the vessels of all nations "on terms of entire equality" and that the charges of traffic should be "just and equitable." The United States was virtually accorded the sole power to assure the neutrality of trans-isthmian transit. Fortification of the canal was not mentioned, but during the negotiations the British foreign secretary admitted that the United States would have the right to fortify. This treaty made feasible the construction of a canal through Central America by the United States and enabled it to consider the Nicaragua route as an alternative to the Panama route. On 16 December the Senate overwhelmingly ratified the second treaty. Acquiescence of the British reflected their preoccupation with growing German power in Europe, acknowledgment of Washington's predominance in Central America, and the rise of the United States to great power status.

BIBLIOGRAPHY

LaFeber, Walter. *The Panama Canal: The Crisis in Historical Perspective.* Updated ed. New York: Oxford University Press, 1989.

Major, John. *Prize Possession: The United States and the Panama Canal, 1903–1979.* Cambridge, U.K., and New York: Cambridge University Press, 1993.

Schoonover, Thomas D. *The United States in Central America, 1860–1911: Episodes of Social Imperialism and Imperial Rivalry in the World System.* Durham, N.C.: Duke University Press, 1991.

Max Paul Friedman
William Spence Robertson

See also **Panama Canal.**

HAYS, FORT (1867), one of a system of military posts established in KANSAS to support the government's campaign against Plains Indians. Gen. Philip H. Sheridan for a time made his headquarters at Fort Hays, as did Gen. George A. Custer in 1867–1869. Hays City, a railroad town nearby, looms large in western mythology. There, in 1869, frontier marshal James Butler ("Wild Bill")

Hickok maintained order with his revolvers. The following year, he killed three soldiers in an altercation and fled to escape execution by Sheridan. As late as 1874, residents fought a street battle with black soldiers from the fort, in which six of the latter were killed.

BIBLIOGRAPHY

Oliva, Leo E. *Fort Hays, Frontier Army Post, 1865–1889.* Topeka: Kansas State Historical Society, 1980.

Paul I. Wellman / A. R.

See also **Army Posts; Cow Towns; Military Service and Minorities: African Americans.**

HAYWOOD-MOYER-PETTIBONE CASE, one of the great criminal cases involving organized labor in the United States. Developing in 1905 after Harry Orchard planted a bomb that killed former Idaho Gov. Frank Steunenberg, the case involved the principal officers of the old WESTERN FEDERATION OF MINERS. The assassin turned state's evidence and accused the three union leaders, Charles H. Moyer, president; William ("Big Bill") Haywood, secretary-treasurer; and George A. Pettibone, formerly prominent in the union but at that time retired. Using questionable methods, these men were extradited from Colorado to Idaho. A jury of farmers and ranchers acquitted Haywood, the first to be tried. Pettibone, too, was acquitted, and Moyer was released without trial.

BIBLIOGRAPHY

Grant, Luke. "Idaho Murder Trial," *Outlook*, vol. 85, and "The Haywood Trial: A Review," *Outlook*, vol. 86.

Hayes, Arthur G. *Trial by Prejudice.* New York: Covici, Friede, 1933.

Gordon S. Watkins / C. W.

See also **Coeur d'Alene Riots; Extradition.**

HAZARDOUS WASTE is a by-product, usually of manufacturing, medical and scientific research, and consumer detritus (disintegrating materials), that is dangerous to human health and wildlife. The substances defined as hazardous received their initial analysis in the industrial hygiene movement between 1900 and 1930, which focused on substances in the workplace. The movement's concern with hazardous industrial substances seldom extended beyond the factory walls. Although public health authorities in the late nineteenth century considered industrial pollution a major problem, the focus shifted after the acceptance of the germ theory of disease. Public health officers and sanitary engineers focused on bacterial wastes as the primary threat to human health. When they considered industrial wastes, they concentrated on their nonpathogenic effects. It was only after World War II that professionals began to pay greater attention to health and the environment.

Hazardous Waste Site. Signs warn visitors away from Times Beach, Mo., a town so badly contaminated by dioxin in the oil sprayed on streets to control dust, that the federal government spent $30 million to move the town's 2,000 residents elsewhere in 1983, demolish all the buildings, and burn the soil before creating the 500-acre Route 66 State Park there. GREENPEACE PHOTO

The first federal legislation regarding hazardous waste was the 1970 Solid Waste Disposal Act. Section 212 required that the Environmental Protection Agency (EPA) investigate the storage and disposal of hazardous wastes. The resulting 1974 report to Congress on the disposal of hazardous wastes led to the passage in 1976 of the Resource Conservation and Recovery Act (RCRA), which defined hazardous wastes that can cause illness or pose a hazard to health and to the environment when improperly stored, transported, or managed. In 1980, the EPA announced regulations implementing cradle-to-grave controls for handling hazardous wastes.

RCRA did not touch on the dangers of wastes buried in industrial and municipal landfills. For decades, industries had disposed of hazardous materials in landfills. Land disposal of wastes increased in the post-World War II period, as states put limits on water disposal. These older sites, in many cases abandoned or closed, posed a threat to groundwater supplies. The case of LOVE CANAL, a chemical waste dump formed by the Hooker Chemical and Plastics Corporation in Niagara Falls, New York, and from which toxic chemical wastes migrated to endanger neighboring residential areas, focused public and governmental attention on the problem in the late 1970s.

Congress responded to the perceived danger of these sites in 1980 by approving the Comprehensive Environmental Response, Compensation, and Liability Act (CERCLA), or SUPERFUND, which provided $1.6 billion for the cleanup of toxic wastes. Under CERCLA, the EPA established procedures of site-specific risk assessments to determine whether the hazardous wastes were a threat to human health. The Superfund Amendments and Reauthorization Act in 1986 increased the fund to $9.6 billion. The Superfund Act and its amendments sought to cover the costs of cleanup by requiring retrospective liability.

That is, it made those people and companies responsible for creating hazardous waste sites liable for the costs of cleanup. The amendments also required that firms that imported, processed, or produced more than 50,000 pounds per year of any of the EPA's listed chemicals and compounds, register them in the EPA's annual Toxics Release Inventory. The slow pace of cleanups, however, as well as cumbersome procedures, convinced many experts that Superfund was not only underfunded but imposed unreasonable standards of cleanliness, given future site uses.

One of Superfund's main tools was a trust fund that contained money contributed by corporations that were taxed to help pay for cleanup operations at Superfund sites. In 1995, that legislation expired. In the following years, Democratic President Bill Clinton annually attempted to renew the legislation, but the Republican-controlled legislature consistently blocked his efforts. Once Republican President George W. Bush came into office, the White House ceased to agitate for renewal. Many critics see the Superfund program as fundamentally flawed because it spends too much money in court battles to determine who is responsible for cleaning up hazardous sites. Furthermore, they argue that taxing the chemical and petrochemical industries to clean up sites that they did not pollute is unfair. In 2001, $860 million was available for Superfund cleanup, but that amount was projected to fall to $28 million by 2003.

BIBLIOGRAPHY

Anderson, Terry L., ed. *Political Environmentalism: Going Behind the Green Curtain.* Stanford, CA: Hoover Institution Press, 2000.

Barnett, Harold C. *Toxic Debts and the Superfund Dilemma.* Chapel Hill: University of North Carolina Press, 1994.

Hird, John A. *Superfund: The Political Economy of Environmental Risk.* Baltimore: Johns Hopkins University Press, 1994.

Mazur, Allan. *A Hazardous Inquiry: The Rashomon Effect at Love Canal.* Cambridge, Mass: Harvard University Press, 1998.

Switzer, Jacqueline Vaughn. *Environmental Politics: Domestic and Global Dimensions.* New York: St. Martin's Press, 1994; 1998.

Joel A. Tarr / A. E.

See also **Energy, Department of; Energy Industry; Environmental Business; Environmental Protection Agency; Times Beach; Waste Disposal; Water Pollution.**

HEAD START, an antipoverty preschool program initiated in 1965 under the Economic Opportunity Act, was designed to serve the needs of children from low-income families. It was based on the philosophy that early intervention, coupled with compensatory education, would enable children from impoverished backgrounds to adjust to school and community. Originally a summer program, it expanded to full-year sessions comparable to a regular school year after educators and psychologists determined that the short program was not sufficient to obtain meaningful results. Most classes operate five days a week, with sessions of half and full days. In the 1970s the target population was broadened to include children with handicaps and children whose first language is not English. Established during the Democratic presidency of Lyndon B. Johnson, Head Start has received bipartisan government support, and, in 1991, it received its largest allocation ever—nearly $2 billion—with passage of the Head Start Expansion and Quality Improvement Act to ensure availability of Head Start to every eligible four-year-old.

Supported by the U.S. Department of Education, Head Start offers a child development program to improve health, social and emotional adjustment, intellect, and self-esteem. Although a federal agency oversees Head Start, the program is administered through local organizations, mostly community action agencies, which submit proposals for funding. In 1995 grantees ran approximately 24,000 classes. Each program site must meet several requirements, including the provision of educational activities, health care, and meals and snacks as part of an overall nutrition program. Classes resemble a nursery school, with activities modified to meet the needs of individuals and the group. Families receive instruction in areas such as nutrition and the use of community services and resources. Parents are encouraged to participate as members of advisory boards and as volunteers and staff members. A family-needs assessment and annual home visiting are mandated. Because the program concentrates on meeting the needs of each child, it necessitates a high adult-student ratio, the ideal being one adult (including volunteers) to every five children. As of 1994, every class was required to have at least one teacher with a child development associate degree (CDA) or other early childhood degree or credential. The CDA degree is one of many offshoots of Head Start, developed out of the program's need for an affordable body of well-trained caregivers. Some programs are attempting to recruit teachers with bachelor's degrees, but low salaries are a deterrent. Several states supplement federal allocations to narrow the gap between Head Start and public school salaries.

Head Start has produced mixed results. Difficulty in carrying out studies has led to an appraisal of specific program elements. During the program's early days, researchers found improvement in IQ scores, but follow-up studies in New York City public elementary schools revealed that six months after leaving Head Start, participants scored no higher on achievement tests than non-participants with similar socioeconomic backgrounds. A widely publicized 1969 study by the Westinghouse Learning Corporation concluded that full-year Head Start programs barely affected achievement and that summer programs yielded negative effects. Analysis of these data several years later, corrected for sample selection bias, found positive effects. Most analysts agree that Head Start produces immediate benefits for children—improved health, higher scores on academic tests, and increased self-esteem. Many parents receive training and become directly involved in their children's education. Long-term results are less dramatic and clear-cut. Data from a 1987 study of 3,500 Philadelphia Head Start children showed no lasting effect on achievement scores, but the children were more likely to attend school regularly in the age-appropriate grade. Studies confirm that Head Start graduates fare better than their counterparts on such measures as repeating a grade and placement in special education classes. Edward Zigler, a psychologist and proponent of Head Start, contends that, although the program can be viewed as highly successful, particularly if evaluations consider family changes, it cannot compensate for deficits attributable to a wide range of community problems. Despite its growth, Head Start serves fewer than half of all eligible students. In 2002 it served about 915,000 children.

Home Start is an evolving program that works with parents and children directly in their homes and provides a combination of home and center activity. Behind this approach is the premise that intervention with parents, the first and primary educators of children, can produce positive effects on their families. Home Start is considered particularly effective with children in rural areas where resources and transportation are scarce.

In 2002 President George W. Bush announced his intention to strengthen and improve Head Start and other early childhood development programs, but he failed to include funding for such improvements in his 2003 budget. Children's advocates argued that without increasing child-care funding and funding to other early childhood programs, no progress would be made.

BIBLIOGRAPHY

Ellsworth, Jeanne, and Lynda J. Ames, eds. *Critical Perspectives on Project Head Start: Revisioning the Hope and Challenge.* Albany: State University of New York Press, 1998.

Lacy, Gary L. *Head Start Social Services: How African American Mothers Use and Perceive It.* New York: Garland, 1999.

Mills, Kay. *Something Better for My Children: The History and People of Head Start.* New York: Dutton, 1998.

Peters, Barbara J. *The Head Start Mother: Low-income Mothers' Empowerment Through Participation.* New York: Garland, 1998.

Zigler, Edward, and Susan Muenchow. *Head Start: The Inside Story of America's Most Successful Educational Experiment.* New York: Basic Books, 1992.

Myrna W. Merron/D. B.

See also **Child Care; Childhood; Education; Education, Cooperative; Education, Experimental; Family; Maternal and Child Health Care; Poverty; War on Poverty.**

HEALTH AND HUMAN SERVICES, DEPARTMENT OF. The U.S. Department of Health and Human Services (HHS) officially opened on 4 May 1980 after the Department of Education Organization Act of 1979 removed the education components from the Department of Health, Education, and Welfare. As the federal government's chief organization for the provision of health care and social welfare services, in fiscal year 2002, HHS operated through eleven divisions, employed 65,000 people, and had a budget of $460 billion. Its major responsibilities included administering Temporary Assistance to Needy Families, a state-federal welfare program that succeeded the Aid to Families with Dependent Children program, and the MEDICARE AND MEDICAID health-care programs that reached about one in every four Americans.

The Federal Security Agency

The origins of the department go back to 1937, when the President's Committee on Administrative Management recommended that President Franklin D. Roosevelt be allowed to submit reorganization plans to Congress that would have the effect of law if Congress failed to act in sixty days. Although Congress refused to grant the president the power to create cabinet-level departments in this manner, it did allow him to start subcabinet agencies. Hence, in April 1939, Roosevelt sent Congress a reorganization plan that included the creation of the Federal Security Agency (FSA). The agency brought together the federal government's health, education, and welfare programs. In particular, it included the previously independent Social Security Board, which ran the nation's major social insurance and welfare programs; the public works programs of the New Deal; the Office of Education from the Department of the Interior; and the Public Health Service from the Department of the Treasury.

President Harry Truman tried and failed to elevate the FSA into a cabinet-level department of welfare. Congress decided not to enact the president's proposal in part because of fears that the FSA administrator, Oscar Ewing, would use the new department as a vehicle to promote the cause of national health insurance. In the meantime, the configuration of the department changed as the FOOD AND DRUG ADMINISTRATION was added from the Department of Agriculture in 1940 and the CHILDREN'S BUREAU was added from the Department of Labor in 1946.

The Department of Health, Education, and Welfare

Although President Dwight Eisenhower was no supporter of national health insurance, he nonetheless submitted plans for the Department of Health, Education, and Welfare (HEW) in March 1953 and presided over the creation of the department in April. The name for the new department reflected in part the preferences of the Republican senator Robert Taft of Ohio, who strongly opposed starting a department of welfare and believed that an alternative, a department of human resources, sounded too totalitarian. Oveta Culp Hobby, the former commander of the Women's Air Corps and the publisher of the *Houston Post*, became the first secretary of health, education, and welfare. Her successors have included Marion Folsom (1955–1958), Arthur Flemming (1958–1961),

John Gardner (1965–1968), and Elliot Richardson (1970–1973).

The most celebrated events during the life of HEW included the licensing of the Salk polio vaccine in 1955, the expansion of the social security program to include disability protection in 1956, the passage of major new welfare legislation to reorient Aid to Dependent Children (renamed Aid to Families with Dependent Children) from income maintenance to rehabilitation in 1962, the beginning of significant federal responsibility for funding the nation's public schools after enactment of the Elementary and Secondary Education Act of 1965, and the passage of Medicare and Medicaid in 1965. This last event created a major new federal presence in the area of health care finance and made the federal government the single largest health insurer in the country. Within HEW, it led in 1977 to the creation of the Health Care Financing Administration (HCFA), an important new operating agency that would hire more than four thousand employees by 1993. Along with the commissioner of social security, the director of the NATIONAL INSTITUTES OF HEALTH, the surgeon general, and the administrator of the Food and Drug Administration, the HCFA administrator became a prominent official within the department.

During the era of HEW, the SOCIAL SECURITY program expanded to reach more people and pay more generous benefits to the elderly, people with disabilities, the families of the elderly and the disabled, and the survivors of workers who died before reaching retirement age. As one indication of its growth, the program collected $3.9 billion from the nation's workers in 1953 and $103 billion in 1980. Congress passed major social security legislation in 1954, 1956, 1958, 1965, 1968, 1969, 1971, and 1972, each time making the program more generous. During this same period, the federal government spent a growing amount of money to fund medical research. The budget of the National Institutes of Health, for example, grew at an annual rate of 30 percent during the 1950s and 1960s.

President Jimmy Carter supplied the impetus for breaking up HEW and starting the Department of Health and Human Services (HHS). Pressure to create a department of education came from the National Education Association, which had 1.8 million members and had endorsed Carter in 1976. Joseph A. Califano, Carter's choice as HEW secretary, tried to talk the president out of recommending the education department, arguing that it would only increase interest-group pressure on the president and that none of the groups that had studied government reorganization had recommended a federal department of education. Califano lost the internal argument within the Carter administration in part because of the enthusiasm of the Democratic senator Abraham Ribicoff of Connecticut, a former HEW secretary who had found the department to be unmanageable. Congress then agreed to create the Department of Education.

Health and Human Services in Operation

On 4 May 1980, Patricia Roberts Harris's job changed from secretary of HEW to secretary of HHS. She presided over a department with 140,000 employees and a budget of $226 billion. The structure of HHS in 1980 was the same as the structure of HEW in 1979, with only the Education Division and the vocational rehabilitation program missing. The four major operating agencies of HHS were the Office of Human Development Services, the Public Health Service, HCFA, and the Social Security Administration (SSA). Through February 2002, six people followed Harris in the job, including Otis R. Bowen, Louis Sullivan, and Tommy Thompson. During the 1980s, the major events at HHS concerned health care finance. President Ronald Reagan chose Richard Schweiker, a former U.S. senator, as his secretary of HHS. Schweiker worked on changing the way in which the federal government reimbursed hospitals under Medicare from retrospective, or payment after the fact based on costs, to prospective, or payment in advance determined by the diagnosis of the person being treated. Margaret Heckler, a former U.S. representative, took over on 9 March 1983 and implemented the reforms that Schweiker had put in place. She also coped with the political controversy surrounding the removal of thousands of people from the disability rolls maintained by HHS. The disability controversy related to a larger political dialogue over whether the Reagan administration had been fair in the cuts it had made in many social welfare programs as part of the Omnibus Budget Reconciliation Act of 1981.

During the 1990s, HHS lost one of its major operating agencies when the SSA became an independent entity on 31 March 1995. The Democratic Senator Daniel Moynihan of New York was a major sponsor of this legislation. The departure of SSA left the Public Health Service—with such major subdivisions as the National Institutes of Health, the Food and Drug Administration, and the CENTERS FOR DISEASE CONTROL AND PREVENTION—as the largest operating division of the department.

President William Clinton made health insurance and welfare reform his two priorities in the HHS realm. Despite a major publicity campaign and the active support of Donna Shalala, a former university president who served as his HHS secretary, the president failed in 1993 to get his health insurance proposals through Congress. He fared better with his initiative to end welfare as an open-ended entitlement and to substitute a program that left more discretion to the states than previously and made a job, rather than an income maintenance grant, the central objective of the welfare program.

Although presidents tried to highlight different issues at different times, the fact remained that HHS was the agency of the government responsible for federal policy in a bewildering number of areas, from curing and caring for those affected by acquired immune deficiency syndrome and leading public health campaigns to discourage people from smoking, to preserving the health insurance rights of people with disabilities, assessing the risk of cancer from additives to the nation's food supply, and assuring the long-range solvency of the Medicare program.

BIBLIOGRAPHY

Altmeyer, Arthur J. *The Formative Years of Social Security.* Madison: University of Wisconsin Press, 1966.

Califano, Joseph A., Jr. *Governing America: An Insider's Report from the White House and the Cabinet.* New York: Simon and Schuster, 1981.

Miles, Rufus E. *The Department of Health, Education, and Welfare.* New York: Praeger, 1974.

Strickland, Stephen P. *Politics, Science, and Dread Disease: A Short History of United States Medical Research Policy.* Cambridge, Mass.: Harvard University Press, 1972.

Sundquist, James L. *Politics and Policy: The Eisenhower, Kennedy, and Johnson Years.* Washington, D.C.: Brookings Institution, 1968.

Edward D. Berkowitz

See also **Education, Department of; Epidemics and Public Health; Health Care; New Deal; Welfare System.**

HEALTH CARE. The term "health care system" refers to a country's system of delivering services for the prevention and treatment of disease and for the promotion of physical and mental well-being. Of particular interest to a health care system is how medical care is organized, financed, and delivered. The organization of care refers to such issues as who gives care (for example, primary care physicians, specialist physicians, nurses, and alternative practitioners) and whether they are practicing as individuals, in small groups, in large groups, or in massive corporate organizations. The financing of care involves who pays for medical services (for example, self-pay, private insurance, Medicare, or Medicaid) and how much money is spent on medical care. The delivery of care refers to how and where medical services are provided (for example, in hospitals, doctors' offices, or various types of outpatient clinics; and in rural, urban, or suburban locations).

Health care systems, like medical knowledge and medical practice, are not fixed but are continually evolving. In part, health care systems reflect the changing scientific and technologic nature of medical practice. For instance, the rise of modern surgery in the late nineteenth and early twentieth centuries helped create the modern hospital in the United States and helped lead to the concentration of so many medical and surgical services in hospital settings. However, the rise of "minimally invasive" surgery a century later contributed to the movement of many surgical procedures out of hospitals and into doctors' offices and other outpatient locations. A country's health care system also reflects in part the culture and values of that society. Thus, physicians in the United States, Canada, France, Germany, and Great Britain follow similar medical practices, but the health care systems of these nations vary considerably, reflecting the different cultural values and mores of those societies.

Traditional Medical Practice in America

For the first century of the republic, almost all physicians engaged in "general practice"—the provision of medical and surgical care for all diseases and for all patients, regardless of sex and age. Typically, doctors engaged in "solo practice," whereby they practiced by themselves without partners. Doctors' offices were typically at their homes or farms. Reflecting the rural makeup of the country, most physicians resided in rural settings. House calls were common. Payment was on the "fee-for-service" basis. Doctors would give patients a bill, and patients would pay out of pocket.

Medicine at this time was not an easy way for an individual to earn a living. Many physicians could not be kept busy practicing medicine, and it was common for doctors to have a second business like a farm, general store, or pharmacy. Physician income, on average, was not high, and doctors often received payment in kind—a chicken or box of fruit rather than money. Doctors also experienced vigorous competition for patients from a variety of alternative or lay healers like Thomsonians, homeopaths, and faith healers.

In the last quarter of the nineteenth century and first quarter of the twentieth century, fueled by the revolution in medical science (particularly the rise of bacteriology and modern surgery), the technologic capacity and cultural authority of physicians in the United States began to escalate. Competition for patients from alternative healers diminished, and most Americans thought of consulting a doctor if they needed medical services. The location of care moved to doctors' offices for routine illnesses and to hospitals for surgery, childbirth, and major medical problems. Indeed, the hospital came to be considered the "doctor's workshop." In 1875, there were 661 hospitals in the United States containing in aggregate about 30,000 beds. By 1930, the number of acute care hospitals had increased to around 7,000, and together they contained about one million beds. Since most hospitals were concentrated in cities and large towns, where larger concentrations of patients could be found, doctors were increasingly found in larger metropolises. In the 1920s, the U.S. population was still 50 percent rural, but already 80 percent of physicians resided in cities or large towns.

Before World War II (1939–1945), about 75 to 80 percent of doctors continued to engage in general practice. However, specialty medicine was already becoming prominent. Residency programs in the clinical specialties had been created, and by 1940 formal certifying boards in the major clinical specialties had been established. Decade by decade, fueled by the growing results of scientific research and the resultant transformation of medical practice—antibiotics, hormones, vitamins, antiseizure medica-

Table 1

Specialization in Medicine

American Board of Ophthalmology	1916
American Board of Pediatrics	1933
American Board of Radiology	1934
American Board of Psychiatry and Neurology	1934
American Board of Orthopedic Surgery	1934
American Board of Colon and Rectal Surgery	1934
American Board of Urology	1935
American Board of Pathology	1936
American Board of Internal Medicine	1936
American Board of Anesthesiology	1937
American Board of Plastic Surgery	1937
American Board of Surgery	1937
American Board of Neurological Surgery	1940

tions, safer childbirth, and many effective new drugs and operations—the cultural authority of doctors continued to grow. By 1940, competition to "regular medicine" from alternative healers had markedly slackened, and the average U.S. physician earned 2½ times the income of the average worker. (Some medical specialists earned much more.) Most physicians continued in solo, fee-for-service practice, and health care was not yet considered a fundamental right. As one manifestation of this phenomenon, a "two-tiered" system of health care officially existed—private rooms in hospitals for paying patients, and large wards for indigent patients where as many as thirty or forty "charity" patients would be housed together in one wide open room. In many hospitals and clinics, particularly in the South, hospital wards were segregated by race.

The Transformation of Health Care, 1945–1985

The four decades following World War II witnessed even more extraordinary advances in the ability of medical care to prevent and relieve suffering. Powerful diagnostic tools were developed, such as automated chemistry analyzers, radioimmunoassays, computerized tomography, and nuclear magnetic resonance imaging. New vaccines, most notably the polio vaccine, were developed. Equally impressive therapeutic procedures came into use, such as newer and more powerful antibiotics, antihypertensive drugs, corticosteroids, immunosuppressants, kidney dialysis machines, mechanical ventilators, hip replacements, open-heart surgery, and a variety of organ transplantations. In 1900, average life expectancy in the United States was forty-seven years, and the major causes of death each year were various infections. By midcentury, chronic diseases such as cancer, stroke, and heart attacks had replaced infections as the major causes of death, and by the end of the century life expectancy in the United States had increased about 30 years from that of 1900. Most Americans now faced the problem of helping their parents or grandparents cope with Alzheimer's disease or cancer rather than that of standing by helplessly watching their children suffocate to death from diphtheria.

These exceptional scientific accomplishments, together with the development of the civil rights movement after World War II, resulted in profound changes in the country's health care delivery system. Before the war, most American physicians were still general practitioners; by 1960, 85 to 90 percent of medical graduates were choosing careers in specialty or subspecialty medicine. Fewer and fewer doctors were engaged in solo practice; instead, physicians increasingly began to practice in groups with other physicians. The egalitarian spirit of post–World War II society resulted in the new view that health care was a fundamental right of all citizens, not merely a privilege. This change in attitude was financed by the rise of "third-party payers" that brought more and more Americans into the health care system. In the 1940s, 1950s, and 1960s, private medical insurance companies like Blue Cross/Blue Shield began providing health care insurance to millions of middle-class citizens. In 1965, the enactment of the landmark Medicare (a federal program for individuals over 65) and Medicaid (joint federal and state programs for the poor) legislation extended health care coverage to millions of additional Americans. Medicare and Medicaid also brought to an end the era of segregation at U.S. hospitals, for institutions with segregated wards were ineligible to receive federal payments. Third-party payers of this era continued to reimburse physicians and hospitals on a fee-for-service basis. For providers of medical care, this meant unprecedented financial prosperity and minimal interference by payers in medical decision-making.

Despite these accomplishments, however, the health care system was under increasing stress. Tens of millions of Americans still did not have access to health care. (When President Bill Clinton assumed office in 1993, the number of uninsured Americans was estimated at 40 million. When he left office in 2001, that number had climbed to around 48 million.) Many patients and health policy experts complained of the fragmentation of services that resulted from increasing specialization; others argued that there was an overemphasis on disease treatment and a relative neglect of disease prevention and health promotion. The increasingly complicated U.S. health care system became inundated with paperwork and "red tape," which was estimated to be two to four times as much as in other Western industrialized nations. And the scientific and technological advances of medicine created a host of unprecedented ethical issues: the meaning of life and death; when and how to turn off an artificial life-support device; how to preserve patient autonomy and to obtain proper informed consent for clinical care or research trials.

To most observers, however, the most critical problem of the health care system was soaring costs. In the fifteen years following the passage of Medicare and Medicaid, expenditures on health care in dollars increased

TABLE 2

U.S. Health Care Costs

	Dollars	Percentage of GDP
1950	$12.7 billion	4.5 percent
1965	$40 billion (est.)	6 percent
1980	$230 billion	9 percent
2000	$1.2 trillion	14 percent

nearly sixfold, and health care costs rose from 6 percent to 9 percent of the country's gross domestic product (GDP). Lee Iacocca, while president of Chrysler in the late 1970s, stunned many Americans by pointing out that U.S. automobile companies were spending more per car on health premiums for workers than for the steel that went into the automobiles. Public opinion polls of the early 1980s revealed that 60 percent of the population worried about health care costs, compared with only 10 percent who worried about the quality of care. Millions of Americans became unwillingly tied to their employers, unable to switch to a better job because of the loss of health care benefits if they did so. Employers found their competitiveness in the global market to be compromised, for they were competing with foreign companies that paid far less for employee health insurance than they did. In the era of the soaring federal budget deficits of the Reagan administration, these problems seemed even more insurmountable.

The Managed Care Era, 1985–Present

In the mid-1980s, soaring medical care costs, coupled with the inability of federal regulations and the medical profession on its own to achieve any meaningful cost control, led to the business-imposed approach of "managed care." "Managed care" is a generic term that refers to a large variety of reimbursement plans in which third-party payers attempt to control costs by limiting the utilization of medical services, in contrast to the "hands off" style of traditional fee-for-service payment. Examples of such cost-savings strategies include the requirement that physicians prescribe drugs only on a plan's approved formulary, mandated preauthorizations before hospitalization or surgery, severe restrictions on the length of time a patient may remain in the hospital, and the requirement that patients be allowed to see specialists only if referred by a "gatekeeper." Ironically, the first health maintenance organization, Kaiser Permanente, had been organized in the 1930s to achieve better coordination and continuity of care and to emphasize preventive medical services. Any cost savings that were achieved were considered a secondary benefit. By the 1980s, however, the attempt to control costs had become the dominant force underlying the managed care movement.

Unquestionably, the managed care movement has brought much good. It has forced the medical profession for the first time to think seriously about costs; it has encouraged greater attention to patients as consumers (for example, better parking and more palatable hospital food); and it has stimulated the use of modern information technologies and business practices in the U.S. health care system. In addition, the managed care movement has encouraged physicians to move many treatments and procedures from hospitals to less costly ambulatory settings, when that can be done safely.

However, there have been serious drawbacks to managed care that in the view of many observers have outweighed its accomplishments. Managed care has not kept its promise of controlling health care costs, and in the early years of President George Walker Bush's administration, the country once again faced double-digit health care inflation. In the view of many, the emphasis on cost containment has come at the erosion of the quality of care, and the dollar-dominated medical marketplace has been highly injurious to medical education, medical schools, and teaching hospitals. Managed care has also resulted in a serious loss of trust in doctors and the health care system—creating a widespread fear that doctors might be acting as "double agents," allegedly serving patients but in fact refusing them needed tests and procedures in order to save money for the employing organization or insurance company. As a result, the twenty-first century has opened with a significant public backlash against managed care and a vociferous "patients' rights movement."

Ironically, many of the perceived abuses of managed care have less to do with the principles of managed care than with the presence of the profit motive in investor-owned managed care organizations. Nonprofit managed care organizations, such as Kaiser Permanente, retain about 5 percent of the health premiums they receive for administrative and capital expenses and use the remaining 95 percent to provide health care for enrollees. For-profit managed care companies, in contrast, seek to minimize what they call the "medical loss"—the portion of the health care premium that is actually used for health care. Instead of spending 95 percent of their premiums on health care (a "medical loss" of 95 percent), they spend only 80, 70, or even 60 percent of the premiums on health services, retaining the rest for the financial benefit of executives and investors. Some astute observers of the U.S. health care system consider the for-profit motive in the delivery of medical services—rather than managed care per se—the more serious problem. However, since 90 percent of managed care organizations are investor-owned companies, the for-profit problem is highly significant.

Future Challenges

The U.S. health care system has three primary goals: the provision of high-quality care, ready access to the system, and affordable costs. The practical problem in health care policy is that the pursuit of any two of these goals aggravates the third. Thus, a more accessible system of high-quality care will tend to lead to higher costs, while a low-cost system available to everyone is likely to be achieved at the price of diminishing quality.

Certain causes of health care inflation are desirable and inevitable: an aging population and the development of new drugs and technologies. However, other causes of soaring health care costs are clearly less defensible. These include the high administrative costs of the U.S. health care system, a litigious culture that results in the high price of "defensive medicine," a profligate American practice style in which many doctors often perform unnecessary tests and procedures, the inflationary consequences of having a "third party" pay the bill (thereby removing incentives from both doctors and patients to conserve dollars), and the existence of for-profit managed care organizations and hospital chains that each year divert billions of dollars of health care premiums away from medical care and into private wealth. Clearly, there is much room to operate a more efficient, responsible health care delivery system in the United States at a more affordable price.

Yet the wiser and more efficient use of resources is only one challenge to our country's health care system. In the twenty-first century, the country will still face the problem of limited resources and seemingly limitless demand. At some point hard decisions will have to be made about what services will and will not be paid for. Any efforts at cost containment must continue to be appropriately balanced with efforts to maintain high quality and patient advocacy in medical care. Better access to the system must also be provided. Medical insurance alone will not solve the health problems of a poor urban community where there are no hospitals, doctors, clinics, or pharmacies. Lastly, the American public must be wise and courageous enough to maintain realistic expectations of medicine. This can be done by recognizing the broad determinants of health like good education and meaningful employment opportunities, avoiding the "medicalization" of social ills like crime and drug addiction, and recognizing that individuals must assume responsibility for their own health by choosing a healthy lifestyle. Only when all these issues are satisfactorily taken into account will the United States have a health care delivery system that matches the promise of what medical science and practice have to offer.

BIBLIOGRAPHY

Fox, Daniel M. *Health Policies, Health Politics: The British and American Experience, 1911–1965.* Princeton, N.J.: Princeton University Press, 1986.

Fuchs, Victor R. *The Health Economy.* Cambridge, Mass.: Harvard University Press, 1986.

Gray, Bradford H. *The Profit Motive and Patient Care: The Changing Accountability of Doctors and Hospitals.* Cambridge, Mass.: Harvard University Press, 1991.

Hiatt, Howard H. *America's Health in the Balance: Choice or Chance?* New York: Harper and Row, 1987.

Ludmerer, Kenneth M. *Time to Heal: American Medical Education from the Turn of the Century to the Era of Managed Care.* New York: Oxford University Press, 1999.

Lundberg, George D. *Severed Trust: Why American Medicine Hasn't Been Fixed.* New York: Basic Books, 2000.

Mechanic, David. *Painful Choices: Research and Essays on Health Care.* New Brunswick, N.J.: Rutgers University Press, 1989.

Rodwin, Marc A. *Medicine, Money, and Morals: Physicians' Conflicts of Interest.* New York: Oxford University Press, 1993.

Rosen, George. *The Structure of American Medical Practice, 1875–1941.* Edited by Charles E. Rosenberg. Philadelphia: University of Pennsylvania Press, 1983.

Rosenberg, Charles E. *The Care of Strangers: The Rise of America's Hospital System.* New York: Basic Books, 1987.

Starr, Paul. *The Social Transformation of American Medicine: The Rise of a Sovereign Profession and the Making of a Vast Industry.* New York: Basic Books, 1982.

Stevens, Rosemary. *In Sickness and in Wealth: America's Hospitals in the Twentieth Century.* New York: Basic Books, 1989.

Kenneth M. Ludmerer

See also **Health and Human Services, Department of; Medicare and Medicaid.**

HEALTH FOOD INDUSTRY. The health food industry, a $4-billion-dollar-a-year business in the early 1990s, was founded on the fact that American consumers increasingly regarded health as a primary concern when buying food. The average food bill per individual at that time was more than four thousand dollars per year, of which almost half was spent on food away from home. As people became more concerned about healthful food in the 1980s and 1990s, consumption of organic foods increased. Because they are cultivated without synthetic additives, fertilizers, or pesticides—some of which are proven carcinogens that often leach into public water supplies—organic foods are better for consumers because many pesticides are systemic, meaning that the food absorbs so that they cannot be washed off. Organic coffee began gaining popularity as an alternative to conventional coffee sprayed with synthetic chemicals. From the late 1970s, increasing numbers of U.S. consumers turned to bottled water as an alternative to alcohol and chlorinated tap water as part of a health regimen.

Beside natural foods, food supplements such as vitamins and herbal products made up a large part of the health food industry. These supplements constituted a form of alternative medicine for people disenchanted with over-the-counter drugs and concerned about side effects of pharmaceuticals. Despite Food and Drug Administration regulations prohibiting the manufacturers of food supplements from making specific medical claims, sales of herbal supplements rose 70 percent to $22.7 million in supermarkets alone during 1993.

The health food industry bonanza was largely based on the connection made by the scientific community between disease and fatty foods, and on the fact that the average consumer in the United States ate more than sixty-five pounds of fat each year. Many manufacturers began to make processed foods with low-fat and low-calorie ingredients and claimed that these products were more healthful and more nutritious than the more standard options. In the 1980s and early 1990s, the food industry reduced fat content in meat, cheese, dips, dressings, and desserts. A number of firms promoted vegetarian burgers. Mail-order businesses for natural foods thrived. Some firms produced natural and organic meats by raising drug-free animals; others produced meat alternatives based on soy and wheat protein. Alternative restaurants came in four types: vegetarian, vegan, health food, and organic. Foods such as venison, buffalo, odorless garlic, and quinoa became popular in these restaurants. McDonald's Corporation experimented in the 1990s with a healthful burger, the McLean, developed by replacing fat with an algae product called carrageenan, a gum-like substance used to bind ingredients. A fat substitute, Simplesse, was developed in the form of frozen ice cream with half the calories of regular ice cream. Another 1990s trend in fast, healthful food was called sous-vide food, consisting of food items sealed in vacuum-packed bags, in which they could remain fresh for weeks and were prepared by boiling water. The use of irradiation to kill harmful bacteria in foods was being reexamined as a result of fatalities from tainted hamburgers.

BIBLIOGRAPHY

Belasco, Warren J. *Appetite for Change: How the Counterculture Took the Food Industry, 1966–1988.* Ithaca, N.Y.: Cornell University Press, 1993.

Grad, Lauri Burrows. "New Foods for the '90s." *Redbook* (May 1992): 136–138.

Sims, Laura S. *The Politics of Fat: Food and Nutrition Policy in America.* Armonk, N.Y.: M. E. Sharpe, 1998.

John J. Byrne/c. w.

See also **Fertilizers; Food, Fast; Food and Drug Administration; Hydroponics; Organic Farming; Vegetarianism.**

HEALTH INSURANCE. Most Americans believe medical care should be available to every citizen. Yet the United States is the only wealthy democracy that does not insure millions of its citizens, and Americans pay higher health care costs than patients in any other country. From 1970 to 1996 the percentage of Americans without medical insurance climbed from 10.9 to 15.6. At the turn of the twenty-first century over 40 million Americans lacked any type of coverage and roughly the same number were underinsured against serious illnesses.

A poorly designed health care system explains why so many either lack coverage or must worry about losing insurance if they lose or change jobs. In the United States, health insurance is closely linked to employment. Government-sponsored programs cover only certain groups—veterans and military servicemembers, the elderly and the poor, and Native Americans. Most Americans enroll in a plan offered by their employer. Coverage therefore depends on both government policies and the ability of private employers to offer job-related benefits.

In the early twentieth century, most Americans lacked health insurance. In 1915, the American Association for Labor Legislation (AALL) urged state lawmakers to provide coverage for low-income families. Fifteen states were considering legislation before opponents of government-sponsored insurance attacked the proposals as "un-American" forms of "socialism." Although critics defeated the AALL legislation, Congress established a national hospital system for veterans in 1921.

In the 1930s the depression put medical care beyond the reach of many middle-class Americans. The influential American Medical Association (AMA) nevertheless opposed both private and public insurance plans, and AMA opposition forced President Roosevelt to exclude health care provisions from his Social Security Act. Over AMA objections, cash-strapped hospitals nevertheless began implementing new prepayment schemes. At Baylor University, a plan devised by Dr. Justin Ford Kimball offered hospitalization benefits in exchange for monthly prepayments. By 1940, fifty-six "Blue Cross" programs were offering hospital benefits to 6 million subscribers. In 1943 the AMA itself established Associated Medical Care Plans, the model for "Blue Shield," to maintain some control over the reimbursements paid to doctors.

After World War II, President Truman called on a Republican-controlled Congress to enact universal health coverage. When Congress did not act, Truman won the 1948 election, and the Democrats won back Congress. Truman renewed his campaign for universal coverage, but the AMA spent millions to thwart him. Weak support among voters and political divisions among Democrats contributed to the plan's defeat. So, too, did the relative availability of private insurance after the war. Many employers now offered benefits to attract scarce workers, and tax policies encouraged them by exempting revenues used to pay employee premiums. Moreover, after labor unions won the right to bargain for health insurance, many union members gained employer-financed coverage.

In the 1950s many elderly, unemployed, and chronically ill Americans remained uninsured. When Democrats swept Congress and the presidency in 1964, Lyndon Johnson made government-sponsored health insurance for the elderly a top priority. In 1965 Congress amended the Social Security Act to create Medicare and Medicaid, providing health coverage for the elderly and the poor. Under Medicare, age and social security status determined eligibility; under Medicaid, income determined eligibility, and benefits varied by state.

Since the 1960s, health care costs have consumed an ever larger percentage of the gross national product, and the problem of cost containment has dominated health care discourse. President Nixon elevated health maintenance organizations, or HMOs, to the top of his health care agenda. In 1973 Congress passed the Health Maintenance Organization Act, which financed the creation of HMOs (prepaid group practices that integrate financing and delivery of services) and required employers to offer HMO plans. Since then, the number of Americans insured by HMOs has skyrocketed.

In 1960 fewer than 50 percent of Americans had health insurance; at the beginning of the twenty-first century roughly 85 percent were covered by private insurance, Medicare, or Medicaid. In 1992, 38.9 million Americans still lacked health insurance. Upon his election, President Clinton kept a campaign promise by introducing a plan to reform health care financing, control costs, and extend coverage to the uninsured. Clinton's "Health Security" plan featured universal coverage, employer mandates, and complex regulatory mechanisms.

Health insurance companies and other interest groups spent millions of dollars to defeat the Clinton initiative. Republican Party strategists feared that Democrats would earn the confidence of middle-class voters if Health Security became law. Antigovernment conservatives used moral suasion and grassroots mobilization to undermine the Clinton plan. Opponents successfully portrayed Health Security as a choice-limiting takeover of the health care system by liberals and bureaucrats. The Clinton plan would have guaranteed every American a choice, however, of at least three different plans, including a fee-for-service option. From 1992 to 1997 enrollment in HMOs and other health plans that limit one's choice of doctors soared by 60 percent. By the beginning of the twenty-first century, over half of all insured American workers were enrolled in employer-sponsored HMOs.

BIBLIOGRAPHY

Bok, Derek. *The Trouble with Government.* Cambridge, Mass.: Harvard University Press, 2001.

Gamble, Vanessa Northington. "Health Care Delivery." In *Encyclopedia of the United States in the Twentieth Century.* Edited by Stanley I. Kutler et al. Vol. 2. New York: Scribners, 1996.

Skocpol, Theda. *Boomerang: Health Care Reform and the Turn Against Government.* New York: Norton, 1997.

Justin Suran

See also **Health Care; Health Maintenance Organizations; Insurance; Medicare and Medicaid.**

HEALTH MAINTENANCE ORGANIZATIONS

(HMOs), combining both provision of service and insurance functions in the health industry, have organizational antecedents in the late nineteenth century with doctors who provided medical care to members of fraternal organizations in return for a fixed periodic fee per member. By the early 1920s, Washington and Oregon hosted dozens of clinics that offered prepaid medical care, often to employees of specific firms through the employers. These built on models developed in the region's lumber mills. In the Midwest, a few doctors financed hospitals in the 1920s by selling shares in return for guaranteed access to the facilities.

In the early 1930s, the successful industrialist Henry Kaiser responded positively to the physician Sidney Garfield's suggestion that the doctor treat Kaiser's construction firm employees in return for a modest fee per employee. This practice spread to other Kaiser facilities. The construction boom of World War II expanded Kaiser's firms and also his demand for labor; his health plan took on the general outline of a modern health maintenance organization with its own medical and hospital sites and paid physicians providing group practice care to the insured employees. At the end of the war, the plan opened membership to the general public. This Kaiser Foundation Health Plan owned medical facilities, clinics, and hospitals, and employed doctors to provide medical care in return for a fixed fee. In contrast with a health maintenance organization, formal health insurance allows the insured to select the provider and then pays the provider a fee for service. Blue Cross, established at Baylor University in 1933, was among the first to offer health insurance. Blue Cross provided insurance for physicians' services; Blue Shield, to cover hospital costs, began a few years later.

Although the precursors of the modern HMO existed well before World War II, the number of persons covered by the organizations was relatively small. This reflected the relatively low demand, and cost, of medical care. Physicians primarily diagnosed and provided palliative care; patients either recovered or they didn't. After the war, successes in developing anesthesia and antibiotics began to revolutionize medical care for ordinary citizens. Surgery became more tolerable and more successful. The intense competition for labor during the war led firms, kept by wage and price controls from raising wages, to offer health insurance to attract and keep workers. The government deemed this fringe benefit nontaxable. As this form of compensation spread during the war and continued afterward, it provided the financial wherewithal to expand demand for the amazing services that new medical technology could provide.

In explaining why competitive markets likely would fail to provide an efficient level of medical services, economists in the mid-1960s pointed to these demand-increasing features combined with the information asymmetry between sellers (physicians) and buyers (patients). Under this argument, relatively ill-informed patients depend upon well-informed doctors as their agents to provide appropriate care. Because patients increasingly carried health insurance, often through their employers, they did not have incentives to question the physicians' advice. Doctors hence could create demand for their own services. Third-party payments led to moral hazard, with neither seller nor buyer motivated to monitor costs. Adverse selection, as those consumers most likely to need insurance opted for more generous programs, joined moral hazard as factors inflating demand. Rapid changes in medical technology focused on doing more, not on containing costs. The expansion in 1965 of federal government programs to provide access to medical care for the poor (Medicaid) and the elderly (Medicare) further expanded demand.

The term "health maintenance organization" originated in the 1970s and is credited to Paul Ellwood, a policy adviser to the federal government on medical care. The term became institutionalized with the HMO Act of 1973, as the federal government struggled to control rapidly expanding medical costs. Other political and economic problems in the 1970s superseded concern for medical care costs, but by 1980, these costs accounted for 8.8 percent of gross domestic product (GDP) and were rising rapidly. In response, both private firms that paid for employees' health insurance premiums and governments that were financing care for the poor and the elderly sought mechanisms to control costs. Managed care organizations looked attractive. Managed care attempts to manage the cost and quality of medical care directly, in contrast to the passive role played by insurers under a fee-for-service arrangement. Managed care runs a full gamut of options, from managed indemnity to preferred provider organization (PPO) to point-of-service (POS) arrangements to a full health maintenance organization. Thus, the HMO is a subset of managed care.

Increasingly, however, medical plans offer a continuum of plans including an HMO, PPO, and POS. HMOs and closely related organizations do share the characteristic of providing medical care for a prepaid periodic fee. Care comes from either medical employees of the HMO or from medical practitioners with whom the HMO contracts. In some cases, the medical practitioners own the organization. Typically, customers access the medical community through an oversight doctor, the primary care physician (PCP). The PCP guides the patient via referrals if necessary to specialists in the organization or on a list approved by the organization.

As medical costs in 1993 hit 13.4 percent of GDP and industry analysts predicted a rise to 20 percent of GDP within a decade, interest in health maintenance organizations continued to grow. The loosely affiliated state and regional Blue Cross–Blue Shield organizations had been shifting since 1960 from fee-for-service insurance organizations to health maintenance organizations. HMO membership increased from roughly three million in the late 1940s to about six million in the mid-1970s. By the early 1990s, the plans enrolled about thirty-seven million people. In 2000, HMO membership was slightly greater than eighty million, down a little from 1999's almost eighty-one million. The slight decline represents an exodus of HMOs from the Medicare market in response to limits on federal government payments. Medical expenditures as a percentage of GDP dropped slightly between 1993 and 1998. Despite hopes for stabilization, costs began to rise in 2000, accounting for 13.2 percent of GDP. As the U.S. population ages, pressure mounts for more extensive insurance coverage of prescription drugs, and other payment and provision models remain even more unpopular, continued evolution of health maintenance organizations seems likely.

BIBLIOGRAPHY

Arrow, Kenneth. "Uncertainty and the Welfare Economics of Medical Care." *American Economic Review* 53 (1963): 941–973.

Birenbaum, Arnold. *Managed Care: Made in America.* Westport, Conn.: Praeger, 1997.

Cutler, David. "A Guide to Health Care Reform." *Journal of Economic Perspectives* 8 (1994): 13–29.

Dranove, David. *The Economic Evolution of American Health Care: From Marcus Welby to Managed Care.* Princeton, N.J.: Princeton University Press, 2000.

Miller, Irwin. *American Health Care Blues: Blue Cross, HMOs, and Pragmatic Reform since 1960.* New Brunswick, N.J.: Transaction, 1996.

Robbins, Dennis A. *Managed Care on Trial: Recapturing Trust, Integrity, and Accountability in Healthcare.* New York: McGraw-Hill, 1998.

Wong, Kenman L. *Medicine and the Marketplace: The Moral Dimensions of Managed Care.* Notre Dame, Ind.: University of Notre Dame Press, 1998.

Ann Harper Fender

See also **Health Care; Health Insurance; Medicare and Medicaid.**

HEART DISEASE. *See* **Cardiovascular Disease.**

HEART IMPLANTS. Because of the high rate of congestive heart failure, physicians in the United States sought to solve the problem through cardiac transplants. In 1964, James Hardy attempted the first such operation, inserting a chimpanzee's heart into a terminally ill patient who died three hours after the surgery. After Christiaan Barnard of South Africa made the first successful human cardiac transplant in 1967, university hospitals in the United States began using Barnard's method. Among the most successful were Norman Shumway and his team at Stanford University—they developed a combined heart and lung transplant in 1980. Meanwhile, Denton Cooley, in 1969, implanted the first completely artificial heart in a human, and in the early 1980s, Willem Kolff and Robert Jarvik produced artificial hearts to keep patients alive until donor hearts became available.

By the late 1980s, cardiac implants had become the established treatment for terminal heart disease. With immunosuppression therapies and the curtailment of infectious diseases, cardiologists overcame most implant rejections and greatly prolonged survival rates of transplant patients—80–90 percent after one year, and 70–80 percent after five years by the early 1990s. A Kentucky man successfully received the first fully self-contained artificial heart on 3 July 2001, marking a new era in heart implantation.

Medical ethicists have raised questions about priority lists for receiving heart transplants. Some physicians believe in assigning priority to primary transplant candidates because repeat transplant patients have poorer survival chances than first-time candidates. While 2,299 patients received heart transplants in 1993 in the United States, more than 3,000 remained on the waiting list at the end of that year.

BIBLIOGRAPHY

Fye, Bruce W. *American Contributions to Cardiovascular Medicine and Surgery.* Bethesda, Md.: National Library of Medicine, 1986.

Ubel, Peter A., et al. "Rationing Failure: The Ethical Lessons of the Retransplantation of Scarce Vital Organs," *Journal of the American Medical Association* 270, no. 20 (November 1993): 2469–2474.

Ruth Roy Harris / c. w.

See also **Bioethics; Cardiovascular Disease; Medicine and Surgery; Transplants and Organ Donation.**

HEATING. House warming continued to depend on the primitive fireplace, often without a chimney, through the seventeenth century. In the mid-eighteenth century, the first steps were taken in developing a science of heat as the thermometer came into use and the effect of absorption and release of heat on evaporation and freezing (latent heat) was observed. By the end of the century, scientists were measuring the heat generated by combustion and other chemical and physical processes. Stoves were being designed on these new scientific principles, especially in France.

In 1744 Benjamin Franklin issued a pamphlet describing his famous "Pennsylvania fireplace." Stoves were already in use in America, especially by German immigrants, but they were not "scientific"—Franklin's stove was, thanks principally to information previously published in Europe. Invented in 1739 or 1740, Franklin's fireplace, while set into the existing house fireplace, projected into the room to achieve the maximum possible heat radiation. The smoke followed a circuitous route in reaching the chimney so as to extract the maximum possible heat from it.

In Europe ancient architectural traditions inhibited the introduction of stoves, which were usually as unaesthetic as they were utilitarian. In America, Franklin's fireplace was not particularly popular either, but it ushered in a fever of invention of what came to be called Franklin stoves, Rittenhouse stoves, or Rumford stoves—the second being a more efficient version of the first, and the third, a by-product of the multifarious activities of Benjamin Thompson, an American Tory living in Europe (where he was known as Count Rumford). Rumford's activities ranged from the study of the science of heat to the organization of public soup kitchens that incorporated elaborate cooking stoves. Most complicated of the new stoves, perhaps, were those designed by Charles Willson Peale and his son Raphael to heat Independence Hall, where Peale had his museum. Through the above inventions the stove gradually became independent of the fireplace, which it replaced as the household hearth. Stove plates—that is, the sides and backs of stoves—became the largest single product of the American iron industry.

Heating. A woman dressed in Puritan garb does her spinning close to the hearth to stay warm in this photograph from c. 1906. LIBRARY OF CONGRESS

Central heating, the warming of entire buildings, had been known in ancient times to both the Romans and the Chinese, both of whom made hollow heating ducts in the floors and walls of houses. The American architect B. H. Latrobe made such an installation in the U.S. Capitol building in 1806. But more common was the kind of central heating introduced by Daniel Pettibone in 1808 in the Pennsylvania Hospital in Philadelphia. It was a stove in which the smokepipe was enclosed within a larger pipe through which hot air circulated to five upper-story rooms. In either case the principle of convection was used: hot air expands on heating, causing it to be lighter and to rise, thus inducing a vacuum that cold air rushes in to fill (and to be heated). A general circulation and mixing of the air results.

Heating by passing hot water through pipes had been used in European horticultural greenhouses in the eighteenth century, and this method was subsequently used to heat buildings as they became too large to be heated efficiently by stoves. The U.S. Capitol, which seems to have seen experimentation with all types of heating, was adapted in 1857–1867 to hot-water heat. At the same time, many factories came to be heated by the "waste" heat from the steam engines with which they were powered, and piped steam became an alternative to hot water. Both systems were installed in the skyscrapers—far too large to be heated by stoves or by the natural convection of hot air—that began to appear in Chicago in the 1880s.

The heating properties of natural gas were known as early as the nineteenth century, but transporting the gas proved a technical barrier until after World War II when advances in metallurgy and welding allowed the construction of thousands of miles of pipe by the close of the 1960s.

The 1973 oil crisis caused many families to investigate alternative heating strategies for their homes. Some turned to natural gas and new solar technology, while most individuals began investigating how to seal door and window leaks that increased heating bills. The trend formed the foundation of the first U.S. Department of Energy weatherizing assistance program, which continued to operate through the close of the twentieth century.

BIBLIOGRAPHY

Beattie, Donald, ed. *History and Overview of Solar Heat Technologies.* Cambridge, Mass.: MIT Press, 1997.

Clark, John G. *Energy and the Federal Government: Fossil Fuel Policies, 1900–1946.* Urbana: University of Illinois Press, 1987.

Goodwin, Crauford, ed. *Energy Policy in Perspective: Today's Problems, Yesterday's Solutions.* Washington, D.C.: Brookings Institution, 1981.

Vietor, Richard H. K. *Energy Policy in America Since 1945: A Study of Business-Government Relations.* New York: Cambridge University Press, 1984.

Wright, Lawrence. *Home Fires Burning: The History of Domestic Heating and Cooking.* London: Routledge & K. Paul, 1964.

Robert P. Multhauf / A. R.; F. B.

See also **Air Conditioning; Energy, Renewable; Energy Industry; Franklin Stove; Kerosine Oil; Oil Crises; Petroleum Industry.**

HELENA MINING CAMP. In September 1864 John Cowan and Robert Stanley, after spending the summer in unsuccessful prospecting, discovered gold at Last Chance Gulch, Prickly Pear Valley, thus opening the Helena Mining Camp, the most productive in Montana. Gold seekers from Bannack, Alder Gulch, and elsewhere hurried to the new diggings, which soon adopted the name Helena; the district became known as Rattlesnake. Red Mountain, Ten Mile, and Unionville also produced large quantities of gold. On Silver Creek, Thomas Cruse developed the Drum Lummon mine, which he sold in 1882 for $1.5 million. As prospectors exhausted the placer mines, quartz mining developed, and silver and lead became important.

BIBLIOGRAPHY

Malone, Michael P. *Montana: A History of Two Centuries.* Seattle: University of Washington Press, 1991.

Smith, Duane A. *Rocky Mountain West: Colorado, Wyoming, and Montana, 1859–1915.* Albuquerque: University of New Mexico Press, 1992.

Paul C. Phillips / A. E.

See also **Gold Mines and Mining; Lead Industry; Mining Towns; Montana; Prospectors; Silver Prospecting and Mining.**

HELICOPTERS. Few inventions have changed transportation and military aviation as rapidly and dramatically as the helicopter. The quest for powered flight assumed two forms—horizontal takeoff and vertical takeoff—and helicopters and their cousins autogiros, emerged as solutions to the problem of vertical flight. Researchers who pursued vertical flight options sought to capitalize on the increased battlefield surveillance and reconnaissance potential that such craft could provide. Additionally, helicopters promised to offer an inexpensive method of maintaining liaison between central command centers and subordinate units. Experiments with autogiro and helicopter designs occurred throughout Europe, Russia, and the United States from the early 1900s through the interwar years. In 1939, Igor Sikorsky successfully tested his VS 300, the first helicopter with a main rotor that provided lift and a tail rotor that provided directional stability. Sikorsky's solution to the problems of simultaneously lifting and controlling the aircraft launched the helicopter industry in the United States.

Although U.S. forces gained some experience with helicopters late in World War II, the first substantial use of the vertical-takeoff craft came in the Korean War. Between 1950 and 1953, helicopters proved their worth in casualty evacuation, search and rescue, troop insertion, cargo transport, and reconnaissance. In 1950, General Douglas MacArthur requested an increase in the number of helicopters for use as organic aircraft within division, corps, and army headquarters units. U.S. Marine Corps units also used helicopters as organic airlift and combat support assets to bolster tactical combat effectiveness. Perhaps the greatest contribution helicopters made to the war effort in Korea came in the form of aeromedical evacuation. Countless numbers of wounded soldiers owed their survival to dedicated helicopter crews who carried them to field hospitals for emergency medical care. By the end of the Korean War, the U.S. military was committed to developing the helicopter's potential for nearly every conceivable mission.

After the war, helicopter designers concentrated on developing powerful craft that could carry greater payloads over longer distances. Certain industries—oil exploration, for example—came to depend on the economical transportation ability inherent in helicopter technology. The military concentrated on making helicopters an integral

Helicopter. Rangers exit a U.S. Marine helicopter to attack Vietcong positions around Da Nang, South Vietnam, on 30 April 1965, near the start of American escalation in the Vietnam War. NATIONAL ARCHIVES AND RECORDS ADMINISTRATION

maneuver element of land warfare. The French use of helicopters to patrol and pacify large territories in the Algerian War foreshadowed the U.S. Army's airmobile concepts that came to typify the Vietnam War between 1964 and 1973. Moreover, U.S. army doctrine contained an implicit comparison between lightly armed, mobile guerrilla forces and the mobility that conventional forces obtained using heliborne troops. With this in mind, the army created air cavalry divisions with an assortment of assault, attack, heavy and medium transport, command and control, search and rescue, and medical evacuation helicopters.

The vision of helicopters as organic aviation assets in nearly every army echelon characterized U.S. involvement in the Vietnam War. Army leaders attempted to use helicopters to achieve "vertical envelopments" of Vietcong and North Vietnamese regular forces. According to this concept, ground reconnaissance missions would locate and fix enemy forces until air cavalry units arrived to launch the main American assault. The strategy first emerged in the dramatic Battle of the Ia Drang Valley in 1965, involving the First Cavalry Division (Airmobile) in which U.S. forces engaged and defeated two North Vietnamese army regiments in South Vietnam's central highlands.

Heroic search and rescue crews penetrated heavily defended Vietcong and North Vietnamese positions throughout the war to pluck downed aircrews and wounded soldiers from certain imprisonment or death. Fittingly, the last images of U.S. involvement in Vietnam included helicopters evacuating embassy personnel and refugees from the roof of the U.S. embassy in Saigon (now Ho Chi Minh City) as the South Vietnamese government collapsed in March 1975. In the post-Vietnam era, the U.S. military continued to develop robust helicopter forces. The U.S. Navy in the twenty-first century continued to rely on a wide range of helicopters to support fleet operations in such roles as antisubmarine warfare, troop insertion, countermine operations, search and rescue, and cargo movement. U.S. Air Force special operations units relied on the high-tech Sikorsky MH-53 J/M aircraft, and the U.S. Army developed the Boeing AH Apache Longbow to dominate the combined arms battlefield.

Civilian use of helicopters exploded after the Vietnam War. The same characteristics—speed, mobility, and vertical takeoff and landing—that made helicopters attractive to military forces also appealed to police, emergency services, and firefighting institutions. Law enforcement helicopters from federal to local levels assisted ground units in surveillance and pursuit operations. Emergency service helicopters supported myriad tasks that produced dramatic lifesaving results. Helicopters enhanced firefighting efforts whether in large-scale wildfires or in combating hazardous industrial fires.

BIBLIOGRAPHY

Allen, Matthew. *Military Helicopter Doctrines of the Major Powers, 1945–1992.* Westport, Conn.: Greenwood Press, 1993.

Boyne, Walter J., and Donald S. Lopez, eds. *Vertical Flight: The Age of the Helicopter.* Washington, D.C.: Smithsonian Institution Press, 1984.

Fay, John. *The Helicopter: History, Piloting, and How It Flies.* 4th ed. New York: Hippocrene, 1987.

Francis, Devon F. *The Story of the Helicopter.* New York: Coward-McCann, 1946.

Futrell, Robert Frank. *The United States Air Force in Korea, 1950–1953.* Rev. ed. Washington, D.C.: Office of Air Force History, 1983.

Momyer, William W. *Airpower in Three Wars: World War II, Korea, Vietnam.* Washington, D.C.: Department of the Air Force, 1978.

Anthony Christopher Cain

See also **Air Cavalry; Air Power, Strategic.**

"HELL ON WHEELS," a term applied to the temporary rails-end towns, or construction camps, of the Union Pacific Railroad. Construction westward along the 42d parallel began in 1865, laying a record-setting average of over a mile of track a day using only picks, shovels, and mules. The term reflected the rough work camps of the all-male, largely Irish laborers, who fought, drank, and caused general hell along the rail as they progressed westward over the prairie and through the mountains.

BIBLIOGRAPHY

Bain, David Haward. *Empire Express: Building the First Transcontinental Railroad.* New York: Viking, 1999.

Williams, John Hoyt. *A Great & Shining Road: The Epic Story of the Transcontinental Railroad.* New York: Times Books, 1988.

Dan E. Clark / H. S.

See also **Railroads; Transcontinental Railroad, Building of.**

HELL'S ANGELS. A motorcycle club founded by Arvid Olsen and a group of World War II veterans in San Bernardino, California. Attempting to duplicate the sense of excitement and brotherhood they felt in the military (they had "Hell's Angels" painted on their fighter planes), the group turned to motorcycles and donned the leather jackets, boots, helmets, and goggles that they wore during the war.

The group gained notoriety on 4 July 1947, when it attended an American Motorcycle Association rally in Hollister, California. A riot broke out, and the Hell's Angels ransacked the town, leading to the state police being called in to restore order.

Stanley Kramer immortalized the Hollister incident in *The Wild One* (1954), starring Marlon Brando and Lee Marvin. The movie made the Hell's Angels famous around the world and turned the motorcycle into a symbol of social deviance. Hunter S. Thompson's 1967 book, *Hell's Angels: A Strange and Terrible Saga*, perpetuated the group's outlaw mystique. Hired as bodyguards for a Rolling Stones concert in 1969, they killed a man who pulled a gun, thus symbolizing the violence of the 1960s.

A 1997 court affidavit claimed the motorcycle gang had 1,800 members worldwide, with international headquarters in Oakland, California. A decentralized organization that constantly battles the federal government, branches of Hell's Angels have faced criminal charges from drug trafficking to racketeering.

BIBLIOGRAPHY

Barger, Ralph "Sonny." *Hell's Angel: The Life and Times of Sonny Barger and the Hell's Angels Motorcycle Club.* New York: Morrow, 2000.

Thompson, Hunter S. *Hell's Angels: A Strange and Terrible Saga.* New York: Ballantine Books, 1967.

Bob Batchelor

HELPERITES. *See* ***Impending Crisis of the South.***

HELSINKI ACCORDS. As part of the emerging East-West détente, in November 1972 talks opened in Helsinki to prepare for a Conference on Security and Cooperation in Europe. Between 3 July 1973 and 1 August 1975, representatives of thirty-five states, including the United States, Canada, the Soviet Union, the Vatican, and all of the European states except Albania, discussed the future of Europe.

On 1 August 1975 leaders from the participating nations signed the Helsinki Final Act. It included three "baskets." Basket I contained a "Declaration on Principles Guiding Relations between Participating States." It legitimated the present borders within Europe, outlawed the use of force, prohibited intervention in the internal affairs of any state, and required respect for human rights and the self-determination of peoples.

Basket II addressed "Cooperation in the Field of Economics, of Science and Technology, and of the Environment." It sought to encourage increased East-West trade, scientific collaboration, and industrial management, and recognized the interdependence of societies across Europe.

Basket III dealt with "Cooperation in Humanitarian and other Fields." It provided a basis for increased person-to-person contacts between Eastern and Western Europe, encouraged the freer movement of peoples and ideas, and promised to facilitate the reunification of families long separated by Cold War conflict.

Critics were quick to point out that these agreements lacked enforcement mechanisms. Moreover, they gave the communist governments in the Soviet Union and Eastern Europe legitimate standing as equals with the democratic regimes in the West. The Helsinki Accords, however, also legitimized human rights in the most repressive parts of Eastern Europe and the Soviet Union. Dissidents, like the founders of "Charter 77" in Czechoslovakia, used the language of the Helsinki Accords to justify their criticisms of communist governments. Many of the dissidents inspired by the Helsinki Accords led the anticommunist revolutions of 1989. In addition, many of the "new thinkers" in the Soviet Union who attained power after 1985—including Mikhail Gorbachev—explained that they hoped to build a more humane European civilization, as outlined in the Helsinki Accords. Seeking stability, Soviet leaders signed the Final Act in 1975; in so doing they unleashed domestic forces they could not control.

BIBLIOGRAPHY

English, Robert. *Russia and the Idea of the West: Gorbachev, Intellectuals, and the End of the Cold War.* New York: Columbia University Press, 2000.

Garthoff, Raymond L. *Détente and Confrontation: American-Soviet Relations from Nixon to Reagan.* Washington, D.C.: The Brookings Institution, 1994.

Maresca, John J. *To Helsinki: The Conference on Security and Co-operation in Europe, 1973–1975.* Durham, N.C.: Duke University Press, 1985.

Jeremi Suri

See also **Cold War.**

HEMP. Although England sought hemp from its American colonies to rig its sailing ships, and although the British government and colonial legislatures tried to encourage its production by bounties, it never became an important export crop. But the virgin clearings and moderate climate of America did invite its small-scale cultivation. Many colonial homesteads had hemp patches—hemp and tow cloth were familiar household manufactures, and local cordage supplied colonial shipyards.

After the American Revolution, when settlers began developing the rich Ohio Valley bottomlands, hemp became a staple crop in Kentucky. Lexington erected mills for manufacturing it, and Southwesterners used hemp cordage and bale cloth to pack their cotton crops. Output peaked around 1860 at about 74,000 tons, of which Kentucky produced 40,000 tons and Missouri 20,000 tons. Thereafter, the advent of the steamship, the substitution of steel for hemp cordage, and the introduction of artificial fibers lessened demand. American production of hemp for fiber ceased shortly after World War II.

With some twenty-five thousand uses, industrial hemp has undergone a revival in many countries such as France and Canada. The United States, however, continues to ban commercial hemp production because of fears by the Drug Enforcement Agency that the plant, which belongs to the same species as marijuana, would be put to illicit use. Agricultural advocacy groups have protested the DEA policy, pointing out that the THC content of hemp is so low that it would be useless as a drug and that the prohibition places American farmers at competitive disadvantage, depriving them of the income from a highly useful and potentially lucrative crop.

BIBLIOGRAPHY

Hopkins, James F. *A History of the Hemp Industry in Kentucky.* Lexington: University of Kentucky Press, 1951.

Nader, Ralph. "Farm Aid: The DEA Should Get Out of Regulating Hemp Agriculture." *San Francisco Bay Guardian,* April 3, 2000. Available at http://www.sfbg.com/nader/95.html.

Victor S. Clark / c. w.

See also **Bounties, Commercial; Narcotics Trade and Legislation; Shipping, Ocean.**

HENNEPIN, LOUIS, NARRATIVES OF. The Hennepin narratives consist of the three known narratives of exploration written by Father Louis Hennepin, a Franciscan friar born in Belgium around 1640. He migrated to Canada, then known as New France, in 1675. Here he engaged in missionary activities among the Native Americans located along the Lower St. Lawrence River near Kingston, Ontario. Late in 1678 he accompanied Robert Cavelier, Sieur de La Salle, on his expedition to the mouth of the Mississippi River. Hennepin wrote an account of this expedition, *Description of Louisiana: Newly Discovered to the Southwest of New France by Order of the King* (1683). When the party reached the mouth of the Illinois River, Hennepin and two Frenchmen left de La Salle to explore the Upper Mississippi in 1680.

On 11 or 12 April 1680 Hennepin and his two companions were taken prisoner by the Dakotas, who resided in what is now Minnesota. They traveled to a major Dakota village near Mille Lacs, in central Minnesota. The Dakotas took them bison hunting in the western prairies and provided Hennepin with a view of their daily lives and customs. The trio was eventually rescued by a Frenchman, Daniel Greysolon, Sieur du Luth.

Description of Louisiana, his first narrative, was a best-seller by the standards of the day, and encouraged a dramatic increase of interest in the Upper Mississippi region. It was translated into Italian, Dutch, and German almost immediately. His narrative recounted the adventures of the trip and described the geography, flora, and fauna of the Upper Mississippi. To appeal to readers he tended to stress the more sensational aspects of Dakota life. He was the first European to see Lake Pepin, and he described and named St. Anthony Falls in what later became Minneapolis, Minnesota. It is widely believed to be a fairly truthful account of the expedition, although there are remarkable similarities between his account and the official account of de la Salle's trip written by Claude Bernou.

Hennepin went on to write at least two other narratives. *New Discovery of a Very Large Country* was published in 1698. In this narrative he claimed for himself the exploration of the Lower Mississippi and the discovery of the mouth of the great river, discoveries usually attributed to de la Salle and Louis Jolliet. His third narrative, *The New Voyage,* was also published in 1698 and was a compilation of his and others' earlier works.

BIBLIOGRAPHY

Hennepin, Louis. *Father Louis Hennepin's Description of Louisiana: Newly Discovered to the Southwest of New France by Order of the King.* Translated by Marion Cross. Minneapolis: University of Minnesota Press, 1938.

Polly Fry

See also **Explorations and Expeditions: French; La Salle Explorations.**

HENRY, FORT (now Wheeling, W. Va.), originally Fort Fincastle, was built in June 1774 by Col. William Crawford from plans drawn by George Rogers Clark. In 1776 it was renamed Fort Henry in honor of Patrick Henry, governor of Virginia. On 10 September 1782, Fort Henry was attacked by Indians and British in one of the final battles of the American Revolution.

At the outbreak of the Civil War, the fort fell into Confederate hands. On 6 February 1862, seventeen thousand Union troops under General Ulysses S. Grant, supported by gunboats under Commodore Andrew Foote, moved by water against Fort Henry on the Tennessee River. Confederate General Lloyd Tilghman safely evacuated most of his small garrison and surrendered after a brief fight.

BIBLIOGRAPHY

Cooling, B. Franklin. *Forts Henry and Donelson—The Key to the Confederate Heartland.* Knoxville: University of Tennessee Press, 1987.

Selby, John E. *The Revolution in Virginia, 1775–1783.* Williamsburg, Va.: Colonial Williamsburg Foundation, 1988.

Charles H. Ambler / A. R.

See also **Donelson, Fort, Capture of; Revolution, American: Military History; Shiloh, Battle of.**

HENRY FORD MUSEUM AND GREENFIELD VILLAGE. An indoor-outdoor museum of American history in Dearborn, Michigan, the Henry Ford Museum and Greenfield Village was founded by Henry Ford in 1929 as the Edison Institute. The twelve-acre Henry Ford Museum focuses on American innovation. Greenfield Village consists of eighty-one public acres of historic homes and buildings.

While other wealthy Americans were collecting fine art, by 1912 Henry Ford was assembling a collection of objects produced and used by ordinary Americans, including spinning wheels and steam engines. Ford believed that these objects told the real history of America, a history that was not reflected in textbooks. Ford's agents also began collecting buildings of both ordinary and great Americans, such as the homes of the Wright brothers and Noah Webster. The public, learning of Ford's interest in everyday things, began shipping objects to Dearborn as well. The centerpiece of Greenfield Village was Thomas Edison's reconstructed Menlo Park, New Jersey, laboratory. Ford, who idolized Edison, named the museum in his honor and dedicated it on 21 October 1929, the fiftieth anniversary of Edison's invention of the electric light. The international publicity arising from the 1929 event generated more interest in Ford's historical venture, although regular visiting hours for the public did not begin until 1933. Following Ford's interest in "learning by doing," students at the Edison Institute School studied in the buildings and learned from the collections. More than 270 students were attending kindergarten through college by the late 1930s.

After Ford's death in 1947, the pace of collecting slowed and the staff struggled to fund the operation. In 1966, the institution was reorganized as an independently supported educational organization. The school system closed in 1969. The museum's highest attendance was over 1.7 million in 1976, sparked by the celebration of the American bicentennial. In the 1980s, the museum began a process of institutional self-evaluation, wrote its first mission statement, and developed a rigorous collections program. At the beginning of the twenty-first century, the mission focuses on developing educational experiences centered on themes of American ingenuity, resourcefulness, and innovation.

Anniversary and Birth. Thomas Edison, seated with *(left to right)* his associate Francis Jehl, President Herbert Hoover, and Henry Ford, joins in celebrations marking the fiftieth anniversary of Edison's electric light and the birth of the Edison Institute, the core of what would become Greenfield Village. © SCHENECTADY MUSEUM; HALL OF ELECTRICAL HISTORY FOUNDATION/CORBIS

In 2000, Henry Ford Museum and Greenfield Village was Michigan's leading cultural attraction with 1.6 million visitors. In 1997, the museum opened the Henry Ford Academy, a public charter high school, serving four hundred students from Wayne County, with classes held in the museum and the village. Recent additions to the complex included an operating railroad roundhouse in Greenfield Village, Buckminster Fuller's futuristic Dymaxion House, and a 400-seat IMAX Theatre in the Henry Ford Museum. The Benson Ford Research Center opened in 2002.

BIBLIOGRAPHY

An American Invention: The Story of Henry Ford Museum and Greenfield Village. Dearborn, Mich.: Henry Ford Museum and Greenfield Village, 1999.

Barnard, Eunice Fuller. "Ford Builds a Unique Museum." *New York Times Magazine* (5 April 1931).

Upward, Geoffrey C. *A Home for Our Heritage: The Building and Growth of Greenfield Village and Henry Ford Museum, 1929–1979.* Dearborn, Mich.: Henry Ford Museum Press, 1979.

Wamsley, James S. *American Ingenuity: Henry Ford Museum and Greenfield Village.* New York: Abrams, 1985.

Judith E. Endelman

See also **Science Museums.**

HEPBURN ACT. Congress passed the Hepburn Act to clarify and increase the authority of the Interstate

Commerce Commission over railroads and certain other types of carriers. It authorized the commission to determine and prescribe just and reasonable maximum rates, establish through routes, and prescribe and enforce uniform systems of accounts. The law also strengthened the Elkins Act of 1903, dealing with personal discrimination; forbade railroads from transporting, except for their own use, many commodities in which they were financially interested; restricted the granting of free passes; and increased the number of commissioners from five to seven. The commission's orders were made binding without court action, thus requiring carriers to assume the burden of initiating litigation that tested the validity of the orders.

BIBLIOGRAPHY

Cooper, John Milton, Jr. *Pivotal Decades: The United States, 1900–1920.* New York: Norton, 1990.

Eisner, Marc Allen. *Regulatory Politics in Transition.* 2d ed. Interpreting American Politics Series. Baltimore: Johns Hopkins University Press, 2000. The original edition was published in 1993.

Kolko, Gabriel. *Railroads and Regulation, 1877–1916.* Princeton, N.J.: Princeton University Press, 1965.

Hobart S. Perry/C. P.

See also **Elkins Act; Interstate Commerce Commission; Railroad Rate Law.**

HERMITAGE, the estate of Andrew Jackson, near Nashville, Tenn., bought by Jackson in 1795. He moved to it in 1804, selling all but 6,000 acres of the original 28,000-acre tract. The log cabin that served as Jackson's home was replaced by a brick house in 1819; when this burned in 1834, the present Hermitage building, in a Greek Revival style, was erected on the old site. After Jackson's death the Hermitage was occupied by Andrew Jackson Jr., until 1888, although it had been bought by Tennessee in 1856 to be preserved as a shrine.

BIBLIOGRAPHY

Horn, Stanley F. *The Hermitage, Home of Old Hickory.* Richmond, Va.: Garrett and Massie, 1938.

Perry, Lewis. *Boats Against the Current: American Culture Between Revolution and Modernity, 1820–1860.* New York: Oxford University Press, 1993.

R. S. Cotterill/A. R.

See also **Architecture; Jacksonian Democracy; Old Hickory.**

HERPETOLOGY. Contributions to the study of American reptiles prior to 1800 were made primarily by European travelers. Notable among the earliest contributors were the Englishman Mark Catesby and the Philadelphian William Bartram, who traveled throughout the southeastern United States making natural history observations on many organisms, including the alligator. Some American reptiles were described by Carolus Linnaeus in his *Systema Naturae* (1758).

In the late 1700s and early 1800s, a number of foreign naturalists and European scientists worked on American reptiles that had been sent to them, thereby adding to the

Hermitage. An early view of the grounds of Andrew Jackson's estate near Nashville, Tenn. © CORBIS

knowledge of existing forms. Additions to the growing list of American reptiles were also made by John Eaton LeConte of the U.S. Army; Thomas Say, who traveled with the Stephen H. Long expedition to the Rocky Mountains (1820); and Richard Harlan, a practicing physician. Harlan attempted to draw together the body of information on American reptiles with his *Genera of North American Reptiles and a Synopsis of the Species* (1826–27) and *American Herpetology* (1827), but these contributions only partly alleviated some of the confusion regarding taxonomic matters that had developed by that time.

John Edwards Holbrook, a Charleston, S.C., physician, produced the first major contribution to U.S. knowledge of American reptiles. Holbrook's *North American Herpetology* (1836, 1842) was a milestone in herpetology. The success and influence of his work probably related to its completeness for the time and to the superb color lithographs drawn from living examples by talented artists. His work caught the attention of European scientists and brought a measure of recognition to the rise of science in America.

In the period immediately after the appearance of Holbrook's *North American Herpetology*, a number of expeditions sponsored by the U.S. government were organized to explore the American West. Notable among these were Charles Wilkes's expedition to the Pacific Northwest, Howard Stansbury's expedition to the Great Salt Lake, George M. Wheeler's explorations west of the 100th meridian, Maj. William H. Emory's Mexican boundary survey, Capt. Randolph B. Marcy's exploration of the Red River, Capt. Lorenzo Sitgreaves's expedition down the Zuni and Colorado rivers, and the Pacific Railroad surveys. Spencer Fullerton Baird brought back large collections of reptiles to museums, in particular the U.S. National Museum, which he helped establish in 1857. The reptiles collected by the U.S. exploring teams were studied by a number of scientists, including Baird. By 1880 most of the expeditions to the West had been completed and the results published, providing a first glimpse of the diversity and extent of the American reptile fauna.

Several herpetofaunal surveys were published by eastern states, including those by David Humphreys Storer for Massachusetts (1839) and James E. DeKay for New York (1842–1844). Louis Agassiz of the Museum of Comparative Zoology at Harvard added much to the knowledge of the embryology of the turtle in his *Contributions to the Natural History of the United States of America* (1857).

From the 1880s to the early 1900s a number of individuals made important contributions to the study of American reptiles. Samuel Garman of the Museum of Comparative Zoology compiled from scattered reports of various U.S. expeditions an important treatise on American snakes, *North American Reptilia, Part I, Ophidia* (1883). This work remained of considerable value to scientists until outdated by the appearance of *The Crocodilians, Lizards, and Snakes of North America* (1900) by Edward Drinker Cope. Leonhard Hess Stejneger of the U.S. National Museum introduced the careful designation of type specimens and type localities into the description of new species, produced an important treatise entitled *The Poisonous Snakes of North America* (1895), and later wrote with Thomas Barbour five editions of *A Check List of North American Amphibians and Reptiles* (1917). These checklists provided a concise synopsis of the known species of reptiles and amphibians and reference for other workers. In *The Reptiles of Western North America* (1922), John Van Denburgh of the California Academy of Sciences described new species of western reptiles and provided information on geographic distributions.

Since the 1920s, scientific investigations, centered in American universities, have been made on every conceivable aspect of the biology of reptiles. Some of the more important contributors have been Frank N. Blanchard, who was a pioneer in field studies of reptiles and developed marking techniques; and Henry Fitch, who subsequently produced some of the most complete field studies of reptiles to date. Clifford H. Pope and Archie Carr greatly expanded the knowledge of North American turtles; Carr later made pioneering contributions on sea turtles and their conservation. Alfred S. Romer contributed to the work on fossil reptiles; his *Osteology of the Reptiles* (1956) was still the standard reference for that field of research twenty years later. Laurence M. Klauber made many contributions on western reptiles and introduced refined statistical techniques. His book *Rattlesnakes* (1956) remained the most complete herpetological monograph produced by the mid-1970s. Detailed lizard population studies were published by W. Frank Blair, in *The Rusty Lizard* (1960).

During the 20th century several scientists produced semipopular works that served to generate wide interest in reptiles. Raymond Lee Ditmars probably did more to stimulate interest in the study of reptiles than any other individual. He routinely lectured to a wide variety of audiences and published many books, but his *Reptile Book*, first appearing in 1907, was one of the most stimulating to young naturalists. Karl P. Schmidt produced the *Field Book of Snakes* (1941) in coauthorship with D. Dwight Davis. Roger Conant wrote the first of the newest type of field guides, *A Field Guide to Reptiles and Amphibians* (1958), that contained range maps, color illustrations, and synoptic information about the organisms. Robert C. Stebbins further improved the field guide format with his *Field Guide to Western Reptiles and Amphibians* (1966). In addition to field guides, herpetofaunal surveys have been written for most of the states and have stimulated interest. Some of the better state surveys are those by Paul Anderson, *The Reptiles of Missouri* (1965), and Philip W. Smith, *The Amphibians and Reptiles of Illinois* (1961).

Few American reptiles have attracted more scientific and popular attention than the rattlesnake, a venomous snake of the pit viper family. The rattlesnake emerged as a central revolutionary icon and appeared frequently in patriotic propaganda; a flag featuring a coiled rattlesnake on a yellow background, with the caption "Don't Tread on Me," was presented to the Continental Congress by Col. Christopher Gadsden of South Carolina and unofficially adopted by Capt. Esek Hopkins as a commodore's flag. The rattlesnake holds an important place in American folklore: for example, the legendary virtue of rattlesnake oil for rheumatism; the cleverness of the roadrunner—which really does kill rattlesnakes—in corralling a sleeping rattler with cactus joints and then making him bite himself to death; or the thousands of authentic stories told around camp fires every summer. A few people die from rattlesnake bites annually, but the spread of land developments is steadily diminishing the snake population.

Three major societies sponsor periodicals to handle the great increase in the number of scholarly contributions within the field of herpetology: *Copeia* (1913–) is published by the American Society of Ichthyologists and Herpetologists, *Herpetologica* (1936–) is published by the Herpetologists' League, and the *Journal of Herpetology* (1968–) is published by the Society for the Study of Amphibians and Reptiles.

BIBLIOGRAPHY

Adler, Kraig, ed. *Contributions to the History of Herpetology*. Oxford, Ohio: S.S.A.R., 1989.

Gillespie, Angus K., and Jay Mechling, eds. *American Wildlife in Symbol and Story*. Knoxville: University of Tennessee Press, 1987.

Kessel, E. L. *A Century of Progress in the Natural Sciences, 1853–1953*. San Francisco: 1955.

J. Frank Dobie
Richard D. Worthington/A. R.

See also **Museums; Science Museums; Science Education.**

HESSIANS. *See* German Mercenaries.

HIDDEN PERSUADERS, THE,

was the first of a series of best-selling books by Vance Packard, a social critic and former journalist. Published in 1957, the book attacked the advertising industry for using controversial new psychological techniques to influence consumers. Packard's critique sold more than a million copies, a remarkable accomplishment for a nonfiction work of the time, and its three-word title soon became an established part of the nation's vocabulary. The centerpiece of Packard's attack was a consumer analytical technique called motivation research, which had been developed from psychoanalytic theory. Advertisers used the technique, according to Packard, to probe the psyches of American consumers in an effort to identify their unconscious desires. He claimed that the results of these investigations were used to manipulate consumers to buy the products and services being promoted by the advertisers' corporate clients.

Not surprisingly, the advertising industry contested Packard's charges. It claimed that motivation research had played a positive role in advertising by helping it identify the complex motives underlying consumer behavior. Moreover, industry spokespersons argued that Packard had overstated the power of motivation research, a circumstance they contended had resulted from his naive acceptance of advertisers' enthusiastic accounts of their successes with the psychological technique. Despite these industry responses, *The Hidden Persuaders* hit a responsive chord with many members of the American public in the 1950s who evidently found compelling Packard's Orwellian portrait of the advertising industry as Big Brother, secretly but powerfully exploiting the postwar prosperity of American consumers.

Monroe Friedman

See also **Advertising.**

HIDE AND TALLOW TRADE.

In California under the Spanish regime, missions and ranchers depended chiefly on the sale of hides and tallow for a livelihood. In 1822 William A. Gale, a former fur trader, interested Bryant, Sturgis and Company of Boston in the products from the region's large cattle herds, and Boston ships took over the trade. The discovery of gold in California threatened to destroy the trade until the coming of the railroad induced a gradual revival.

In the region east of California and west of the Mississippi River, the cattle trade boomed after the Civil War, although few cattle were killed for hides alone. Buffalo hide had long been an important article of commerce, and with the coming of the railroad, buffalo were slaughtered in huge numbers. Both whites and Indians became hide hunters, and from Texas to Canada the plains were strewn with carcasses, until by the mid-1880s the vast herds had been extinguished.

BIBLIOGRAPHY

Bancroft, Hubert Howe. *History of California*. 7 vols. San Francisco: The History Company, 1884–1890. Reprint, Santa Barbara, Calif.: W. Hebberd, 1963–1970.

Isenberg, Andrew C. *The Destruction of the Bison: An Environmental History, 1750–1920*. Studies in Environmental History Series. New York: Cambridge University Press, 2000.

Frank Edward Ross/C. W.

See also **Buffalo (Bison); Fur Trade and Trapping.**

HIGHER CRITICISM

is a term applied to a type of biblical studies that emerged in mostly German academic circles in the late eighteenth century, blossomed in English-speaking academies during the nineteenth, and faded out in the early twentieth. Early modern biblical studies were customarily divided into two branches.

"Lower" or textual criticism addressed critical issues surrounding the Bible's extant manuscripts, canon, and variant readings. The other genre was called "higher" criticism, which, as Benjamin Jowett of Oxford University once said, sought to investigate and interpret biblical documents like any other document of antiquity. Higher critics were interested not only in the Bible's primal literary sources but also in the operative and undisclosed assumptions of biblical writers themselves.

Inevitably, the same intellectual energies that fueled the burgeoning historical studies in nineteenth-century Germany and England were applied to the biblical studies as well. By the mid-nineteenth century the term "higher criticism" was employed to describe the application of the historical-critical method derived from other historical disciplines to the Bible and its many authors. These newer biblical studies were also influenced by prevailing Enlightenment presuppositions, especially those espoused by Kant and Hegel. For these reasons, higher criticism came to be viewed as a radical departure from earlier biblical studies in the precritical eras. In established Catholic, Protestant, and Jewish religious communities, the term came to be associated with the desacralizing of the Bible. Scholars in academic circles, however, employed the newer critical methods while trying to free biblical studies from the heavy hand of theological conviction.

By the 1830s American Protestant scholars in Cambridge, Andover, and Princeton were well aware of the German higher critics. Each of these three academic centers responded differently, however, to the higher critics' writings. At Harvard, Joseph Buckminster and Andrews Norton heeded a donor's generosity and promoted "a critical knowledge of the Holy Scriptures." At Andover Seminary, Moses Stuart and Edward Robinson cautiously endorsed liberal scholarship from Germany. At Princeton Theological Seminary, a young Charles Hodge returned from studies in Germany and mounted a countermovement to higher criticism through his journal, *The Biblical Repertory and Princeton Review*. Other religious communities, such as Protestant theologians in the South, conservative Jewish scholars, and traditional Roman Catholic academics, usually responded to the higher critics with suspicion and distaste.

By the late nineteenth century, increasing numbers of English-speaking scholars viewed the newer critical methods as promising, responsible, and liberating. William Rainey Harper of the University of Chicago, Charles A. Briggs of Union Theological Seminary, Charles Bacon of Yale, and William Robertson Smith in Scotland incorporated the higher critics' revisionism into their writings about biblical hermeneutics. In sharp and deepening opposition, conservative Roman Catholic, Protestant, and Jewish scholars wrote feverishly to counter the growing consensus of higher critics. At stake were contentious issues such as Julius Wellhausen's hypothesis of multiple authorship of the Pentateuch, David F. Strauss's analysis of the role of myth in the narratives about Jesus, and F. C. Bauer's recasting of historical background of the Pauline epistles.

By the end of the nineteenth century two responses to higher criticism seemed inescapable: in academic circles there was no returning to the precritical methods of biblical hermeneutics; in ecclesial circles, however, there was deepening reluctance to trust the "assured results" of higher critics' scholarship. Both of these positions came to poignant focus when the Presbyterian professor Charles A. Briggs of Union Theological Seminary was tried for heresy for his more modernist views about the Bible in 1892–1893. By the opening decade of the twentieth century the term "higher criticism" was deemed too simplistic and amorphous. By then biblical scholars from divergent religious traditions and university doctoral studies were eager to broker the hermeneutical insights adapted from a wider and more secular scholarship in the fields of history, literary criticism, modern philosophy, and science.

BIBLIOGRAPHY

Brown, Jerry W. *The Rise of Biblical Criticism in America, 1800–1870.* Middletown: University of Connecticut Press, 1969.

Coggins, R. J., and J. L. Houlden, eds. *A Dictionary of Biblical Interpretation.* London: SCM Press, 1990.

Fogarty, Gerald P. *American Catholic Biblical Scholarship.* San Francisco: Harper and Row, 1989.

Hayes, John H., gen. ed. *Dictionary of Biblical Interpretation.* 2 vols. Nashville, Tenn.: Abingdon Press, 1999.

Sarna, Jonathan, and N. H. Sarna. "Jewish Biblical Scholarship and Translations in the United States." In *The Bible and Bibles in America.* Edited by Ernest S. Frerichs. Atlanta: Scholars Press, 1988.

John W. Stewart

See also **Bible.**

HIGHER LAW is that purported body of legal principles, partaking of the divine, that is eternally and universally valid in human society. As the Roman orator Cicero explained it, it is "right reason in agreement with nature . . . [it is] one eternal and unchangeable law . . . valid for all nations and all times, and [there is] . . . one master and ruler, that is, God, [who is] the author of this law, its promulgator, and its enforcing judge." Christian legal theorists, such as St. Augustine and St. Thomas Aquinas, gave similar descriptions of this all-encompassing system. Under the rubric of "natural law," the jurist Sir William Blackstone recognized it as a part of the English common law in his famous *Commentaries* (1765–1769), which profoundly influenced American common law, and its expositors such as Joseph Story and James Kent. The nature of the American legal system, and whether it admits of higher law, or whether it simply consists of the temporal pronouncements of the American people and their legislatures, has been a much-mooted question throughout American history. In the late eighteenth century, higher-law notions were used to explain the presence of natural rights in America, and higher-law principles were said, by the abolitionists, to justify resistance to the provisions of the U.S. Constitution that permitted slavery. Higher-law notions fell into disrepute following their use in the late nineteenth and early twentieth centuries, particularly through the doctrines of freedom of contract, to frustrate state and federal regulation of the economy. In the late twentieth century, pursuant to the doctrines of legal realism, which became ascendant in American legal education beginning in the 1960s, American constitutional and private law has generally been understood only to be the product of American legislators and judges. Still, when, in 1974, President Gerald Ford pardoned the disgraced former President Richard Nixon, he claimed that he did so on the basis of a "higher law" than the Constitution, and when the Supreme Court, under Chief Justice Earl Warren, rendered a series of decisions dramatically enhancing individual rights, the Court's critics and supporters recognized that the Court was turning to higher-law notions of fairness and justice to support its rulings. The higher-law notion of inalienable rights granted by a Creator was acknowledged in the Declaration of Independence, and in the late twentieth century, several scholars sought to demonstrate that the Constitution itself was created to secure those rights.

BIBLIOGRAPHY

Corwin, Edward S. *The "Higher Law" Background of American Constitutional Law.* Ithaca, N.Y.: Cornell University, 1955.

Gerber, Scott Douglas. *To Secure These Rights: The Declaration of Independence and Constitutional Interpretation.* New York: New York University Press, 1995.

Sandoz, Ellis. *A Government of Laws: Political Theory, Religion, and the American Founding.* Baton Rouge: Louisiana State University, 1989.

Stephen B. Presser

See also **Common Law.**

HIGHWAY BEAUTIFICATION ACT. In his 1965 State of the Union Address, President Lyndon Johnson called for the creation of a Great Society—an ambitious legislative agenda to improve the quality of American life. Inspired by his wife, Lady Bird Johnson, President Johnson made highway beautification one of the signature themes of the Great Society and introduced legislation in Congress to preserve scenic beauty by removing and regulating billboards along America's highways. During congressional deliberations, the administration received support from urban planners, garden clubs, and a fledgling environmental movement. An alliance of advertisers, business owners, sign operators, and landowners, however, substantially weakened the proposal. Dissatisfied, President Johnson nevertheless signed the Highway Beautification Act into law on 22 October 1965, promising that it would be the first of many steps toward a more beautiful America.

One of the nation's first modern environmental laws, the act prohibited the construction of new billboards on scenic and rural federal-aid highways and required the removal of illegal billboards erected without proper permits. Billboards not meeting established standards were to be removed. To carry out these provisions, the act offered federal funding and financial incentives to the states. Despite limited amendments in 1975 and again in 1991 to strengthen the act, the act has so far failed to meet expectations. As one marker, by the turn of the millennium there were an estimated 450,000 billboards on federal-aid highways, compared to 330,000 billboards in 1965.

The act has failed for several reasons. First, exceptions built into the act itself limited its effectiveness. Second, by mandating that sign rights be compensated rather than amortized, Congress increased the cost of billboard removal beyond expectations. Eventually, federal funds for the program simply evaporated from the budget. Finally, the act imposed financial penalties for state actions that did not conform to the act's framework. In the end, the act failed because of loopholes, insufficient federal funding, and because the act hobbled state initiatives.

BIBLIOGRAPHY

Albert, Craig J. "Your Ad Goes Here: How the Highway Beautification Act of 1965 Thwarts Highway Beautification." *University of Kansas Law Review* 48 (2000): 463.

Floyd, Charles F., and Peter J. Shedd. *Highway Beautification: The Environmental Movement's Greatest Failure.* Boulder, Colo.: Westview Press, 1979.

Shannon C. Petersen

See also **Conservation; Great Society.**

HIGHWAYS. *See* **Interstate Highway System; Roads; Transportation and Travel.**

HIJACKING, AIRPLANE. Often known as skyjacking, airplane hijacking is a form of air piracy usually perpetrated against commercial aviation. It can range from acts of individuals motivated by personal reasons—such as escaping the political, social, or economic conditions of their homeland—to violent acts of political extortion committed by highly organized terrorist groups or criminal organizations. A distinction is usually drawn between hijacking, involving an unauthorized person or group of people seizing control of an aircraft, and other acts of airplane-related terrorism such as bombing. The ability of airplanes to traverse oceans and national borders, along with the public's marked increase in reliance on air travel, has led many terrorist organizations to choose airplane hijacking as a means for publicity or extortion. This has confronted governments with a truly global security problem as authorities struggle to keep pace with the ingenuity and brazenness of terrorist groups.

By the turn of the twenty-first century, over one thousand hijackings of commercial airplanes had been reported worldwide. The first reported act of airplane hijacking was committed on 21 February 1931 in Peru. The first reported hijacking of a U.S. airplane occurred on 1 May 1961, when a hijacker forced a domestic flight to detour to Cuba. Hijackings were relatively rare, however, until the period between 1967 and 1972, when they reached epidemic proportions, peaking in an eleven-day period in early September 1970, when six hijackings were reported worldwide among the eighty for the year. Although hijacking during this period was chiefly identified first with Cuba and then the Middle East, U.S. domestic aviation was not immune. One notable incident occurred on 24 November 1971, when a mysterious figure known as "D. B. Cooper" parachuted out of a plane after having extorted $200,000 from the airline. Despite a massive manhunt he was never found, although would-be emulators proved decidedly less successful.

In response to the rash of hijackings, new security measures were implemented by the U.S. Federal Aviation Administration (FAA), the airlines, and various government law enforcement agencies. These included searches of passengers and their luggage prior to boarding and a "sky marshals" program involving armed law enforcement officers aboard some flights. In 1973 metal detection and X-ray devices became mandatory at all airports. Although the new security measures led to longer check-in times and some passenger inconvenience, they also led to a dramatic reduction in the number of U.S. hijackings.

By the 1990s, however, death tolls worldwide were rising. The hijacking of a domestic Chinese flight on 2 October 1990 resulted in 132 deaths. On 23 November 1996, a hijacked Ethiopian flight resulted in 123 deaths. But by far the worst case of airplane hijacking occurred on 11 September 2001. It was the first hijacking in the United States in a decade and the first one with fatalities since 1987. In a coordinated attack, four U.S. domestic flights were hijacked and, without warning or demands, two planes were deliberately crashed into the two World Trade Center towers in New York City and another into the Pentagon in Washington, D.C. The fourth plane crashed in rural Pennsylvania. The 266 passengers and crew in the planes died instantly, nearly 200 people at the Pentagon were killed, and some 3,000 people in the World Trade Center towers perished when the buildings collapsed.

BIBLIOGRAPHY

Arey, James A. *The Sky Pirates.* New York: Scribners, 1972.

Criminal Acts against Civil Aviation. Washington, D.C.: U.S. Department of Transportation, Federal Aviation Administration, Office of Civil Aviation Security, 1986–.

David G. Coleman

See also **Terrorism.**

Hindu Temple. The white towers of this brown brick temple, seen during construction in St. Louis in 1998, are covered with deeply carved figures and situated over shrines to the primary Hindu deities. © G. John Renard

HINDUISM. Americans learned about Hinduism in the late eighteenth century from European scholars and from missionaries and traders returning from India. Henry David Thoreau and Ralph Waldo Emerson incorporated Hindu themes in their transcendental philosophy in the 1830s and 1840s. The first Indian to successfully promote Hinduism in America was Swami Vivekananda, who represented Hinduism at the World's Parliament of Religions in Chicago's 1893 Columbian Exposition. He went on to establish Vedanta Societies in major American cities, teaching a variety of Hinduism that emphasizes social reform, religious tolerance, and the unity of self (*atman*) and Absolute (*Brahman*). Swami Paramahansa Yogananda's Self-Realization Fellowship, established in 1935 to teach kriya yoga, soon surpassed Vedanta in popularity. In the 1960s, transcendental meditation and the International Society of Krishna Consciousness, or Hare Krishna Society, gathered large numbers of followers among Americans seeking spiritual alternatives to mainstream religion, and the civil rights movement drew inspiration from Indian nationalist Mohandas K. Gandhi's interpretation of the Hindu tradition of *ahimsa* (nonviolence).

After the passage of less restrictive immigration laws in 1965, a large influx of Asian Indian immigrants brought a new plurality of Hindu practices to the United States. They contributed the first major, Indian-style Hindu temples, built to accommodate immigrant Hindus, to the American landscape. In 2000, there were approximately one million Hindus in the United States.

BIBLIOGRAPHY

Jackson, Carl T. *The Oriental Religions and American Thought: Nineteenth-Century Explorations.* Westport, Conn.: Greenwood Press, 1981.

———. *Vedanta for the West: The Ramakrishna Movement in the United States.* Bloomington: Indiana University Press, 1994.

Tweed, Thomas A., and Stephen Prothero, eds. *Asian Religions in America: A Documentary History.* New York: Oxford University Press, 1999.

Susan Haskell

See also **Asian Religions and Sects.**

HIPPIES. On 5 September 1965, in an article in the *San Francisco Examiner* about the new "Bohemian" scene developing in the Haight-Ashbury district, Michael Fallon labeled its members "hippies." The label stuck and was thereafter applied to any young person who experimented with drugs, exhibited an unconventional appearance, enjoyed new forms of "acid" music and art, expressed disdain for mainstream values and institutions, investigated exotic religions, or espoused a philosophy that combined the beats' existentialism with a colorful, expressive joie de vivre all their own. Although initially treated as a harmless curiosity by the media, Ronald Reagan, then governor of California, spoke for many Americans when he defined a hippie as someone who "dresses like Tarzan, has hair like Jane, and smells like Cheetah."

BIBLIOGRAPHY

Lee, Martin A., and Bruce Shlain. *Acid Dreams: The Complete Social History of LSD: The CIA, the Sixties, and Beyond.* New York: Grove Weidenfeld, 1992.

Perry, Charles. *The Haight-Ashbury: A History.* New York: Vintage Books, 1985.

Wolfe, Tom. *The Electric Kool-Aid Acid Test.* New York: Farrar, Straus and Giroux, 1968.

Rick Dodgson

Hippies. "Flower children" play with the world in Golden Gate Park, San Francisco, to celebrate the start of the Summer of Love, 1967. AP/WIDE WORLD PHOTOS

See also **Antiwar Movements; Counterculture; Youth Movements.**

HISPANIC AMERICANS. According to the 2000 Census, Hispanic Americans make up 12.5 percent of the total population of the United States and are now the nation's largest ethnic minority group, surpassing African Americans by a margin of 0.2 percent.

The nation's 20.5 million Hispanics of Mexican heritage (often called Chicanos) constitute 66 percent of the Hispanic American population and make up about 7.3 percent of the total U.S. population. At nearly 3.5 million, Puerto Ricans living in the United States are the second largest Hispanic American group; Cuban Americans are third largest, with a population of just over 1.24 million. Hispanics in the United States also come from all the countries of Central and South America including El Salvador, Nicaragua, Ecuador, Columbia, Brazil, Uruguay, Venezuela, and the Dominican Republic. Each Hispanic subgroup has its own culture, language, customs and way of life.

From the Los Angeles barrios populated mostly by Chicanos to Cubans in South Florida, Puerto Ricans in New York City to Brazilians in Boston, Hispanic peoples and cultures have become part of American cities and towns.

Spanish Exploration and Conquest

The Spanish presence in the United States dates back to the early days of European exploration of the Americas. In 1513, Spanish explorer Juan Ponce de Leon discovered a sunny spit of North America's southeastern coast that he dubbed "La Florida" (Land of Flowers). In 1565, the Spanish finally began settling Florida with the founding of St. Augustine. In the 1540s, Francisco Vásquez de Coronado's expeditionary force traversed what is now America's Southwest; in 1610, Santa Fe, New Mexico, was established as the Spanish provincial capital. Spain's oppression of the native peoples resulted in the bloody PUEBLO REVOLT of 1680. A decade later, when the Spanish returned, they were more careful in their treatment of the indigenous peoples; the centuries-old blend of Native American and Spanish culture remains deeply rooted in that area.

The Spanish claim on "Alta California" was firmly established in 1769 when Father Junipero Sera, a Roman Catholic priest, founded San Diego de Alcalá, the first of California's twenty-one Spanish missions. For some sixty-five years, until the end of Spanish rule in the region, the powerful, well-financed missions infused the region with Catholicism and Spanish culture. After Mexico gained independence from Spain in 1821, it allowed the indigenous peoples who had worked the mission lands to settle them as ranches.

United States Expansion

Mexico's territorial disputes with the aggressively expansionist United States resulted in the MEXICAN-AMERICAN WAR, which began in 1846 and ended in 1848 with the signing of the Treaty of Guadalupe Hidalgo. The terms of this treaty had Mexico ceding 55 percent of its territory to the United States. Mexican residents of the ceded lands—which encompassed modern-day Texas, Arizona, California, and New Mexico and portions of Colorado, Utah and Nevada—became U.S. citizens.

The brief SPANISH-AMERICAN WAR of 1898 further expanded the U.S. sphere of influence into formerly Spanish territories. As Spain relinquished its faltering grip on Cuba and PUERTO RICO (both of which had been battling for independence for years), as well as Guam and the Philippines, the United States stepped in as a new colonial administrator.

In July 1898, the United States invaded Puerto Rico as a prelude to the anticipated hand-off by Spain already being brokered by negotiators. The island, which had been colonized by the Spanish after its discovery by Columbus in 1493, had been on the verge of instituting its own long-anticipated independence from Spain. The arrival of the American military, which controlled the island until a civilian government was established in 1900, effectively transferred Puerto Rico from one colonial steward to another.

Puerto Rico

In 1917, the JONES ACT granted residents of Puerto Rico U.S. citizenship. Puerto Ricans were allowed to elect their own governor in 1948; in 1952, Puerto Rico adopted a constitution and became a commonwealth. Spanish was recognized as Puerto Rico's official language after fifty years of English-speaking rule. Puerto Ricans, however, lack some privileges of true citizenship: those who live in Puerto Rico cannot vote in U.S. presidential elections (though they participate in party nominating conventions) and have only "shadow" (non-voting) representation in Congress. They also pay no U.S. income taxes.

Puerto Rican Americans have long walked a tightrope of loyalties made taut by the tension of pride in their dual cultures and frustration over America's continued rule of their homeland. The Puerto Rican Nationalist Party, founded in 1936, has been and continues to be an active and sometimes violent voice for independence; more moderate activists have sought statehood for Puerto Rico.

In 1950, a crackdown on Nationalist protestors in Puerto Rico left more than thirty dead,and the violence soon spread to Washington, D.C. On 1 November 1950, a pair of armed Puerto Rican Nationalists stormed Blair House, where President Harry S. Truman and his family were living during White House renovations. The president was unharmed, but a Secret Service agent was killed and several others were wounded. In 1954, four Puerto Rican Nationalists opened fire on the floor of the House of Representatives, wounding five congressmen. Political strife and revolution often preceded Hispanic migrations to the United States in the twentieth century—those events, themselves, were often influenced by U.S. military involvement in Central or South America.

Hispanic Immigrants and Political Muscle

Revolutions in Mexico, Cuba, Nicaragua and the Dominican Republic, and civil wars in Guatemala and El Salvador during the twentieth century were among the many violent upheavals that led millions of people to seek sanctuary in the United States. With these immigrants came the same rich, yet dividing languages and cultures, ethnicity and social strata that had marked their former lives. Thus, the different groups found it difficult to stand together under such broad labels as "Hispanics" or "Latino." Facing increased anti-immigration sentiments and movements such as the "English First" effort to make English the "official" language of the United States, Hispanics, especially recent immigrants, are often torn between devotion to the culture of their homelands and the need for political and social clout in American life—most easily gained by joining forces with others who share similar, though far from identical, backgrounds and experiences.

The Washington, D.C.–based National Council of La Raza (NCLR), founded in 1968, is on the leading edge of advocacy for Hispanic rights. Through lobbying and public education, leadership development and community support, the NCLR is actively building the political and societal muscle of America's largest growing minority group.

BIBLIOGRAPHY

Acuna, Rudolfo. *Occupied America: A History of Chicanos.* 4th ed. New York: Longman, 2000.

Bonilla, Frank, et al., eds. *Borderless Borders: U.S. Latinos, Latin Americans, and the Paradox of Interdependence.* Philadelphia: Temple University Press, 1998.

Clayton, Lawrence A., ed. *The Hispanic Experience in North America.* Columbus: Ohio State University Press, 1992.

Cruz, José E. *Identity and Power: Puerto Rican Politics and the Challenge of Ethnicity.* Philadelphia: Temple University Press, 1998.

Gonzalez, Juan. *Harvest of Empire: A History of Latinos in America.* New York: Viking, 2000.

Horner, Louise L., ed. *Hispanic Americans, 2002: A Statistical Sourcebook.* Palo Alto, Calif.: Information Publications, 2002.

Noble, Judith, and Jaime Lacasa. *The Hispanic Way.* Lincolnwood, Ill.: Passport Books, 1991.

Rodriguez, Clara E. *Changing Race: Latinos, the Census and the History of Ethnicity in the United States.* New York: New York University Press, 2000.

Suro, Roberto. *Strangers Among Us: Latino Lives in a Changing America.* New York: Knopf, 1998.

Laura A. Bergheim

See also **Cuba, Relations with; Cuban Americans; Guadalupe Hidalgo, Treaty of; Latin America, Relations with;**

Puerto Ricans in the United States; *and vol. 9:* **Chicano Nationalism: The Key to Unity for La Raza; Pachucos in the Making.**

HISS CASE. The Hiss case, which spanned the years from 1948 through 1950, helped pave the way for McCarthyism and, in particular, the Cold War search for communists thought to have infiltrated the State Department during the administrations of Franklin D. Roosevelt and Harry S. Truman. The principals included Alger Hiss, a former State Department official; Whittaker Chambers, a self-confessed former Soviet agent; and Richard Nixon, a freshman congressman and member of the House Committee on Un-American Activities (HUAC).

The Hiss case broke during the HUAC hearings in the summer of 1948 when Chambers accused Hiss of membership, some ten years earlier, in a communist cell with a mission to influence New Deal policies and programs. When Chambers repeated the charge on the *Meet the Press* radio program without benefit of congressional immunity, Hiss sued for libel. Chambers then expanded his charge, accusing Hiss of passing State Department documents for transmittal to the Soviet Union. As proof, he produced microfilm and other documents (some of which were allegedly typed on a Woodstock typewriter once owned by the Hiss family). Some of these documents were hidden in, among other places, a hollowed-out pumpkin on Chambers's Maryland farm.

With Nixon and HUAC doggedly pursuing Hiss through a detailed comparison of his statements under oath compared to those of Chambers, the case quickly moved into federal courts. As the statute of limitations had run out on any possible espionage charge, Hiss was tried twice on two counts of perjury—having denied under oath the passing of documents and that he had seen Chambers after 1 January 1937. The first trial ended in a hung jury. On 21 January 1950, the second trial ended in conviction. Less than a month later, in a Lincoln's Day speech in Wheeling, West Virginia, Senator Joseph R. McCarthy claimed to have a list of 205 additional communists (he later reduced the number to fifty-seven) who had also infiltrated the State Department.

Hiss served nearly four years of a five-year sentence and steadfastly maintained his innocence until his death on 15 November 1996. To some partisans, the case symbolized a generation on trial, as Hiss appeared to be the prototypical New Dealer. A former clerk for Supreme Court justice Felix Frankfurter, he worked in the Agricultural Adjustment Administration before joining the State Department. He accompanied President Roosevelt to the World War II summit at Yalta, and served as secretary general of the United Nations founding conference. He then moved on to the Carnegie Endowment for International Peace. When Senator McCarthy spoke of "twenty years of treason," his reference was to the Democratic Party, in particular to officials in the Roosevelt-Truman administration who seemed to cherish the popular front world that had produced men like Hiss.

Alger Hiss. The former State Department official, accused of espionage, swears to tell the truth; people remain divided over whether he did, though many consider that Soviet archival material made available to some researchers after the breakup of the Soviet Union proves his guilt. AP/Wide World Photos

The Hiss case has continued to stir controversy. The Nixon White House tapes revealed the president's obsession with the case as Watergate spun out of control. Then, after amendments in 1974 to the Freedom of Information Act of 1966, Hiss received some forty thousand pages of FBI, CIA, Justice Department, and State Department documents pertaining to his civil service career and subsequent prosecution. These documents, particularly the FBI files, led Hiss to file a petition in federal court for a writ of *coram nobis.* His request that the perjury verdict be overturned because of prosecutorial misconduct was denied on 15 July 1982 by Judge Richard Owen (who had been appointed by President Nixon). Hiss carried his appeals forward to the United States Supreme Court, which on 11 October declined to hear his suit. A few months later, on 26 March 1984, President Ronald Reagan posthumously awarded Chambers a presidential Freedom Medal.

In the 1990s, the Hiss case was kept alive by the National Security Agency's release of decoded Soviet messages transmitted to and from Moscow during World War II (the Venona cables); document searches by Dmitri Antonovich Volkogonov, Russian president Boris Yeltsin's military adviser and overseer of Soviet intelligence archives; and the release, after fifty-one years, of grand jury transcripts, including the testimony of Hiss, Chambers, and Nixon.

BIBLIOGRAPHY

Chambers, Whittaker. *Witness*. Chicago: Regnery Gateway, 1984.

Hiss, Alger. *Recollections of a Life*. New York: Holt, 1988.

Theoharis, Athan. *Beyond the Hiss Case: The FBI, Congress, and the Cold War*. Philadelphia: Temple University Press, 1982.

Tiger, Edith, ed. *In re Alger Hiss: Petition for a Writ of Error Coram Nobis*. 2 vols. New York: Hill and Wang, 1979, 1980.

Weinstein, Allen. *Perjury: The Hiss-Chambers Case*. New York: Knopf, 1978.

Kenneth O'Reilly

See also **Cold War; House Committee on Un-American Activities; McCarthyism.**

HISTORIOGRAPHY, AMERICAN. Historiography refers to the history of historical writing. It also encompasses the philosophy, scope, and methods employed in historical work.

The Colonial Period

American historical writing has a long, if sporadic, history until the middle of the nineteenth century. Initial works of history in the seventeenth century were often composed by men who had participated in the events described. Typical of this genre was John Smith's *The Generall Historie of Virginia, New England and the Summer Isles* (1624). Captain Smith described his years in the Jamestown wilderness, the starvation endured by the settlers, and his "rescue" by the Indian princess Pocahontas. Smith's vivid descriptions and personality coexisted with his desire to settle scores and to fabricate material.

In the colonies to the north, a group of capable chroniclers described the early history of settlements in New England. Between 1630 and 1650, William Bradford wrote his *History of Plimoth Plantation*, although the work was not published in full until 1856, with a definitive edition appearing in 1912. Bradford, who began his journey to the New World from Holland and who served as governor of Plymouth Colony, covered the controversies of the early years of the colony: the natural disasters and near starvation of the settlers until the kindly intervention of local Indian tribes. John Winthrop's journal, covering the Massachusetts Bay Colony for the period 1630–1639, chronicled religious disputes with Anne Hutchinson and Roger Williams, the growth of a theodicy, and the daily life of the community.

A handful of other significant works of history appeared in the seventeenth century, most notably Edward Johnson's *The Wonder-Working Providence of Sion's Savior in New England* (1654); Increase Mather's *A Brief History of the War with the Indians* (1676), his account of King Philip's War; and Cotton Mather's *Magnalia Christi Americana* (1702). The method employed in most of these histories combined documents with occasional reflections on them. The narrative holding them together was a descriptive thread designed to capture the trials and tribulations of colonial settlement. Among the Puritan historians especially, a philosophy of history animated each line of the text. In their work as settlers and historians, these men announced that they were following God's divine plan, founding, as Winthrop famously stated, "A City Upon a Hill." Their work was intended to help lay the foundation for that endeavor.

Revolutionary War Era

In the years leading up to the American Revolution, loyalist historians condemned the colonial movement toward independence from Great Britain. George Chalmers, William Smith, and Thomas Hutchinson, most famously, in *History of the Colony and Province of Massachusetts Bay* (1764), offered interventions, through history, into the politics of the era. They failed, however, to stem the tide of revolutionary fervor and their influence in America was minimal.

The revolutionary period and its immediate aftermath was dominated by attempts to move away from local histories toward national ones. David Ramsay's *The History of the American Revolution* (1789) was notable for its strident nationalism and Federalist perspective, as well as for its tendency toward plagiarism. Despite the patriarchy that marked American society in this era, two women contributed importantly to the historiography. Both of them were wealthy and well connected. Hannah Adams's *A Summary History of New England* (1799) demonstrated an Enlightenment view on religious affairs, condemning the intolerance of her Puritan forefathers. Mercy Otis Warren's *History of the Rise, Progress, and Termination of the American Revolution* (1805) was a work that rendered moral and political reflections upon the leading actors of the Revolution. Fiercely democratic and idealist, Warren used her study to speculate on human nature, on the passions and reason. Warren followed her ancestors in positing that human action was part of a providential plan. Thus she combined aspects of Calvinist and Enlightenment thought within her history of the figures of the Revolution.

Romantic History

American historical writing blossomed in the 1830s during the period of the American literary renaissance associated with Ralph Waldo Emerson, Henry David Thoreau, and Walt Whitman. Writers turned to the American continent to record the romance of America and the unfolding of a new type of individual, the American democrat. Although their politics differed somewhat, both George Bancroft and Francis Parkman were Romantic historians with a vision of American progress. Trained in

Germany and conversant with transcendental strains of philosophy, Bancroft's ten-volume *History of the United States* (1834–1874) was a paean to the development of freedom and equality. American nationalism, exemplified by the populist revolution in American democracy associated with Andrew Jackson, of which Bancroft was an adherent, is written on every page of his history. Parkman's historical writing was a literary event of the highest order. He rendered judgments like an Olympian deity. His major theme, captured most famously in the volume *Montcalm and Wolfe: The French and Indian War* (1884), depicted the American wilderness as an arena where the French empire, associated with the decay of absolutism, was inevitably pushed aside by a British empire on the cutting edge of colonial American liberty and democracy. For Parkman, history was a tale of heroic figures locked in struggle. But great white men were invariably caught up in forces and circumstances not of their own choosing. Parkman, in particular, was quite conversant with the frontier, and he was attentive to nature as a force in history. His histories, however, slighted the importance of Native Americans, except in their role as savage combatants in larger colonial contests. The work of Bancroft and Parkman, for all of its self-conscious literary concerns, was built upon diligent research and concern with getting the facts right, although sometimes the quest for narrative power and political meaning got in the way.

History as a Science

The Romantic school of historians was soon to become a minor element in American historical writing. In the post–Civil War years, American society began a search for institutional authority and expertise. In field after field, professional scholarship, dedicated to the ideals of liberal capitalism, progress, and objectivity, came to the fore. In 1884, the American Historical Association was founded, an organization devoted to the advancement of historical research in America. Initially, the organization was populated with both professional and gentleman scholars. Indeed, at the time of the founding of the association, there were fewer than two dozen full-time teachers of history in America's colleges. By the turn of the century, with the explosion of higher education in America, historical study had become a central part of the curriculum. With this development came graduate programs, such as the one at Johns Hopkins University, where seminars trained scholars in the latest in European historical research, dedicated to the collection of sources, the careful scrutiny of documents, and employment of the scientific method.

By the 1880s, practicing historians in America, be they university trained or not, were attracted to the idea of a scientific history. Historians were practicing their craft, after all, under the long and imposing shadow cast by Darwinian and other evolutionary theories. The very notion of evolution, of development from a simple to a complex organism, had predated Darwin and was part of the legacy of Romanticism. Historians, in any case, were determined to demonstrate that history, rather than being cyclical or hodgepodge, had an interior logic, no less so than biology. For some historians, history could be reduced to a set of scientific rules. John Fiske, in his popular works of history influenced by the evolutionary views of the French thinker Auguste Comte and the English philosopher Herbert Spencer, attempted to chart American development as a necessary process, one exemplifying laissez-faire economics and individualism. His *The Discovery of America* (1892) was an archaeological and ethnographic analysis of the development of a continent, with the ascendancy of the white settlers assured by the logic of scientific evolutionary forces. Science, as law and method, was the operating belief among diverse historians. All celebrated John William Draper and Andrew Dickson White's view of history as the triumph of science over superstition. Herbert Baxter Adams at Johns Hopkins University was convinced that history was a natural science and the seminar was a laboratory for the application of scientific methods to the study of history. Adams and his followers maintained that history was rightly the study of political institutions, their development over time from a germ (with origins in Germany) to the democratic communities of Puritan New England.

No historian grappled more with the philosophical implications of scientific history than Henry Adams. Adams began as a reasonably conventional historian, focusing his energies on the period of American history between the presidential administrations of his grandfather, John Adams, and his father, John Quincy Adams. With an eye for detail, historical research, and literary craftsmanship, Adams's nine-volume *History of the United States During the Administrations of Thomas Jefferson and James Madison* (1889–1891) was an exhaustive work of professional history. In articles addressed to the profession and, most famously, in his autobiography, Adams's relation to science soured. Unlike many of his colleagues who viewed evolution and history as progressive and optimistic, Adams's science mirrored his growing pessimism in the face of social change and dislocation in the 1890s. Science revealed chaos as much as order, devolution more than progress. Adams's philosophy of science seemingly led historians into an intellectual and philosophical cul-de-sac.

The Progressive Historians

At the moment when Adams's philosophy of history indicated a downward spiral, a new generation of historians committed to social change and professionalism came to the fore. With Adams, they were well aware of the clash of interests that had defined American history, and they too rejected the genteel tradition in America that celebrated America as the apotheosis of liberty and freedom. In their vision of history as present politics, historians such as Frederick Jackson Turner, Vernon L. Parrington, and James Harvey Robinson revolutionized the study of history. These Progressive Era historians, often inspired by the political reformism of their age and the scope of the developing social sciences, attempted to capture the forces that had created, and that continued to inform, the economic and political reality of America. Their historical assumptions were akin to those of the muckrakers in politics: exposure of the reality hidden from view would open up the possibility of reform. Knowledge was possibility and power.

The Progressive historians were professionally trained and joined only loosely in their political allegiances. But they were all dedicated to using history to understand the dynamics of American society. Turner began the revolution in historical thought with his important address, "The Significance of the Frontier in American History" (1893). In a relatively short piece, Turner proclaimed that understanding the frontier and sectional nature of America explained American democracy, individualism, and self-sufficiency. He rejected any reliance on the evolution of British or Germanic traditions (the germ theory) in America, focusing instead on how the American character was shaped by the savage challenge of the frontier. His large theories were sketched deftly and presumptively. Turner's essay ended in tantalizing fashion: the four-hundred-year history of the American pioneer being molded by the frontier environment was over: what was to happen next?

The clash between the pioneer and frontier that defined Turner's histories was less prominent in the work of other Progressive Era historians. Parrington and Charles A. Beard, for instance, viewed the American past as a series of conflicts between various interest groups. Working from this perspective, they overturned pietistic visions about the motives of the founders and the openness of American society. Beard's most important work, *An Economic Interpretation of the Constitution of the United States* (1913), argued that economic interests rather than abstract ideals underwrote the Constitution. And the subtext of such an argument was apparent: economic interests were continuing to define American politics in the twentieth century. Building upon the Populist and Progressive critique of the monied interests, Parrington presented in his *Main Currents in American Thought* (1927) a Jeffersonian, liberal critique of aristocratic power and capitalist concentration of wealth. His was a political reading of American literature, in the American grain.

The native-born radicalism of Beard and Parrington was particularly appealing in its methodology. Beard and Parrington presented many examples of class and interest conflict in America but without the apparatus of Marxian terminology. With the exception of work by W. E. B. Du Bois on Reconstruction and by Herbert Aptheker on slave revolts, little historical writing in America until the 1960s was explicitly Marxist in methodology. Yet the clash of interests and classes was present in some of the best historical writing from the 1940s. The liberal activist historian Arthur M. Schlesinger Jr., for instance, in *The Age of Jackson* (1945), forthrightly presented the Jacksonian revolution in terms of its conflict of interests, while also undermining earlier interpretations that simplified the sectional dynamics of the revolution. Moreover, Schlesinger's Jacksonian thrust represented an intervention into contemporary politics, a stirring defense of Franklin D. Roosevelt and the New Deal.

Consensus History

Focus on the clash of interests with hints of class conflict in historical writing diminished in the years after World War II. With the conflict of ideologies between the United States and the Soviet Union, in the midst of sustained economic growth, and under the dark cloud of McCarthyism and conformity, historians came to emphasize the factors that held Americans of all classes and nationalities together. Consensus history was a wide tent, holding within it works as diverse and influential as Richard Hofstadter's *The American Political Tradition* (1948), Daniel J. Boorstin's *The Genius of American Politics* (1953), David Potter's *People of Plenty* (1954), and Louis Hartz's *The Liberal Tradition in America* (1955). These works were of a piece in their observation that the history of America was marked by a lack of ideological conflict. Hofstadter, for all of his emphasis on consensus, was too much of an ironist to rest content in the recognition that the pull of American politics was toward the middle. Hartz demonstrated how America's lack of a feudal past forced it to be a nation of Lockean individualism. He found this problematic in many ways. Boorstin and Potter were less ironic in their depictions of consensus. For Potter, abundance of land and material goods, as well as opportunity, beneficently shaped the American character. Boorstin, the most conservative of the consensus historians, celebrated the lack of ideological thinking in America. He concentrated on the "genius" of an American polity rooted in opportunity and historical circumstance; Americans did things rather than relying on abstract and inherited thought. Boorstin's view supported both American consensus and exceptionalism.

History and the Social Sciences

The postwar period and the early 1960s were marked by historical writing that was deeply influenced by the social sciences, especially psychology and sociology. This was hardly new, since in the 1910s, James Harvey Robinson had called upon historians to employ social science in their writings. But in the 1960s, the turn to social science–influenced history exploded. This new interest may have been an attempt by historians to add the cachet of social scientific rigor to their analyses. In the best cases, it gave historians new ways of conceptualizing historical data; in the worst cases, it reduced historical complexity to formulae. Hofstadter's deeply influential *The Age of Reform* (1955) employed the concept of "status anxiety" to explain the motivations and rhetoric behind the Populist and Progressive movements. This sometimes led Hofstadter to play down the importance of real grievances in favor of psychological explanations of displacement, nostalgia, and conspiracy as the motivating factors in history. The work of Erik Erikson and other psychologists marked a significant turn in history. Erikson paved the way with his groundbreaking work of psychohistory, *Young Man Luther* (1958), where he demonstrated how Martin Luther's religious protest and intensity were rooted in his childhood experiences. Soon historians followed suit with interpretations that seemed less beholden to historical causation than to psychological reduction. David Donald's biographical examination of the abolitionist Charles Sumner seemed to care more for Sumner's psychological quirks than for his devotion to a great cause.

Perhaps Stanley M. Elkins's *Slavery: A Problem in American Institutional and Intellectual Life* (1959) was the most daring, and problematic, application of psychological and sociological concepts to a historical problem. Elkins maintained that slaves had acted in a docile, lazy, and nonrebellious manner. But he revised traditional racist historical interpretations of the slave personality by Ulrich B. Phillips and William A. Dunning by rejecting such attributes as inherent to any racial group. Instead, using concepts such as "significant other" and work done by psychologists of the concentration camp experience, as well as comparative historical analysis of slave institutions, Elkins contended that the Sambo personality was the result of a psychological breaking of the individual, akin to that which occurred in concentration camps. Yet, as later historians demonstrated, despite all of the social science paraphernalia that informed Elkins's work, he missed much of the complexity of slavery and the disjuncture between the concentration and the slave camp experiences.

Interpretations of Slavery

Elkins stepped into an arena of American historiography that had been transformed by Kenneth M. Stampp's *The Peculiar Institution* (1956). Borrowing from anthropology, Stampp demonstrated respect for the sophistication of African cultures, and he recorded the injustice and inhumanity of slavery at the moment when the modern civil rights movement was in motion. Moreover, Stampp was clear in his liberal conviction that African Americans were not different from individuals of other races. Of course, Stampp was not the first historian to condemn slavery. Important work by African American historians such as W. E. B. Du Bois had examined the plight of blacks in America with great depth. But their work had been largely ignored by the profession. With the rise of the civil rights movement, and in the wake of the controversy of Elkins's interpretation, the institution and personality of the slave and the role of the African American in American life became central to historical investigation. Important works by John W. Blassingame, George Rawick, and Lawrence Levine redefined and expanded the study of slavery. This was in marked contrast to the earlier excision of blacks from serious historical analysis.

The most sophisticated work of analysis, building upon Marxian and Hegelian foundations, was by Eugene Genovese. In *Roll, Jordan, Roll* (1974), Genovese argued that the slave system was based upon negotiations between master and slave. The paternalistic ideology of the slaveholders allowed the slaves some room in which to take control of their lives. The unwritten contract between slave and slaveholder, as defined by Genovese, permitted slaves to retain their humanity and the slaveholders to be viewed as antagonistic to the capitalist model of production. While influential, Genovese's analysis came under attack, especially as a new generation of historians of the slave experience began to focus on the complexity of slavery in different regions, the imposition of work rules upon slaves, the prevalence of slave resistance and running away, and on the distinctions in the slave experience on account of gender and position within the plantation hierarchy.

The Radical Reinterpretation of America

By the 1960s, the days of consensus history had been shattered, replaced by a new skepticism and widening of the subject matter of history. A new generation of radical historians would build upon the work of Howard Zinn, Staughton Lynd, Gabriel Kolko, and, most importantly, William Appleman Williams. Williams's *The Tragedy of American Diplomacy* (1959) and *The Contours of American History* (1961) echoed themes that had appeared in Beard's history. Williams argued that American diplomacy, while not evil in intent, was often misdirected and distanced from its presumed ideals. Williams wrote radical history in an American idiom. He would have a wide audience with an emerging generation of radical historians in the 1960s that confronted an America distanced from its ideals of freedom and equality. The war in Vietnam, the prevalence of American racism, and economic inequality fed into the radical critique of America. This critique began to turn upside down all areas of historical inquiry. Earlier visions of the Progressives as reformists were replaced by interpretations of the era as corporate capitalist. If initial accounts of the dropping of the atomic bomb at the end of World War II had been supportive of the act, analyses of New Left historians pictured the use of the bomb less as a military necessity than as the first strike in the Cold War against the Soviet Union. If early accounts of the Cold War had invariably blamed the Soviet Union, the history of the New Left attempted to demonstrate, at the least, that the United States' imperial goals played a significant role in the onset of conflict. If earlier histories of labor had focused on the hierarchy of unions, New Left historians celebrated history from the bottom up.

History from the Bottom Up

The desire to move away from elitist history, to get to the experiences of the common person and to undermine historical myths, informed much of the social history of the 1960s and 1970s. Labor history became an important field of study. Influenced by the stirring call of the British historian E. P. Thompson in *The Making of the English Working Class* (1963) to study the class consciousness of workers as it developed, American historians such as Herbert Gutman and David Montgomery contributed important work. Armed with sophisticated methods of quantitative analysis and the turn to census records, historians sought to test whether America was an upwardly mobile nation, as myth would have it. In works such as Stephan Thernstrom's *Poverty and Progress* (1964), a new generation of urban historians argued that upward mobility was less common than imagined, that Americans were constantly on the move, and that economic success was often uncertain for most Americans.

The New Left had a revolutionary impact on the scope of historical analysis and on the politics of the profession. If some of their analyses have since been found to be problematic, especially in terms of Soviet intentions, the movement opened the profession to new fields of analysis, shattered many prevailing assumptions, and demonstrated that historical analysis has relevance to contemporary problems.

Women's and Gender History

In the 1970s, another major gap in the historical record began to be bridged. Although Mary Ritter Beard and Eleanor Flexner had done important earlier work on the history of women in America, the study of women in American history by the 1970s emerged as a major revolution in historiography. Gerda Lerner led the way toward women's history as a central element to the study of history. This was the initial phase in women's history—to put women back into the picture of history. The second phase of women's history, as outlined by Joan Wallach Scott, was to apply gender analysis to the past. Now the history of labor unions, politics, and the family came under critical scrutiny to establish how women's identities were forged. Despite the impositions of a patriarchal society, as Carroll Smith-Rosenberg noted, women were able to build networks of mutual support and encouragement. As gender analysis came into the profession, many traditional interpretations of major movements in American history were revised. Thanks to the work of Theda Skocpol, Nancy Cott, Ellen Carol DuBois, and Kathryn Kish Sklar, twentieth-century liberalism came to be seen as an outgrowth of a maternalist consciousness, connected with the important work of women in social reform.

A More Inclusive History and the Problem of Synthesis

A new willingness to challenge assumptions and to be more inclusive came to define historical practice. In the field of Western historiography, thanks to the work of Patricia Nelson Limerick, Donald Worster, Richard White, and Quintard Taylor, which built on an older, outsider tradition exemplified by the popular historian Bernard De Voto, triumphalist interpretations of the settlement of the West were rejected. Now the history of the West was comprehended in terms of the displacement of the Native American, the battle over land and water rights, and the inclusion of women, African Americans, and Mexicans as major players in the history of Western development.

By the 1980s, the profession of history had been transformed in a host of ways, not only by dint of the expansive subject matter that now fell under the purview of history, but also in terms of the implications of historical analysis for American society. Gone was the ideal of consensus; in its place was a vision of American history rent by class, racial, and gender division. For some conservative historians, this shift represented the triumph of a radical agenda, the undermining of traditional values, and an assault upon foundational assumptions. But other historians, many with liberal politics, began to worry that something had been lost, as well as gained, in the new historical focus and the flowering of specialized studies. Thomas Bender, in an influential article, noted that with the fragmentation of historical analysis the ideal of a synthetic history had fallen by the wayside. Social history seemed disconnected from analyses of power and politics. Historians appeared unwilling to offer generalizations that could transcend the academic specialties that historians had so carefully cultivated. Gone was the possibility of a common core of knowledge for historians. Few articles in the leading historical journals could speak across disciplinary lines or offer a new vision of an American public culture. But the call for synthesis fell on deaf ears, in part because of the diversity of the historical profession and the fear of an imposed and artificial order on the new data of history. Most importantly, concerns shifted in the wake of a linguistic challenge to history in the 1980s that provoked a new set of issues and concerns for historical practice.

Postmodern Challenges

The greatest challenge to historiography came from a theoretical questioning of the foundations of historical practice and method. Certainly historians such as Charles Beard and Carl Becker had already questioned the ideal of objectivity. They were well aware that present interests influenced the subject matter to be studied and the interpretations to be applied to the past. A broader methodological attack appeared in Peter Novick's *That Noble Dream* (1988). Epistemological issues dealing with the theory and philosophy of historical study had traditionally been ceded to philosophers, and they rarely intruded upon the consciousness of practicing historians. Instead, historians, borrowing models from the social sciences, upheld the need to be fair to the sources and to strive for objectivity. Postmodernist theories, especially in the hands of Hayden White and others, began to challenge the practice and patience of historians. Historians were forced to confront the argument that history is a narrative endeavor, that all social reality is understood through language, and that our comprehension of the facts is not a knowledge of something but a representation of something. This understanding of the linguistic nature of social reality, in its best moments, forced historians to become more reflective about their own assumptions, about how their work constituted a narrative. It also led some historians, such as Simon Schama, James Goodman, and

John Demos, to attempt to tell a story from multiple perspectives and to diminish the lines between historical fact and fiction. In its worst moments, the postmodern turn seemed to strip historians of any special relationship to truth claims and perhaps to turn history into an exercise in futility.

For many historians, the solution to the challenge of postmodernism was to split the differences. Historians could no longer practice history without attention to language and representation, nor could they claim that the contextualization of data was an unproblematic endeavor. But in the view of Thomas Haskell, David A. Hollinger, and others, the new historical consciousness was pragmatic, open to a plurality of methods, and based upon the willingness of historians to recognize that context was plural, rather than singular. The truth claims of historians, in the pragmatic mode, were open to debate with the presumption that certain contexts could be demonstrated to be compelling for particular and discernible reasons.

The challenge and opportunity of diversity and postmodernism and the need for larger synthesis led, by the end of the twentieth century, to new areas of study premised on an emphasis on the interrelatedness of groups. Gender and queer theory are predicated upon the belief that identity is constructed and relational. The work of George Chauncey and Leila Rupp established new connections between outsiders and dominant society. Ann Douglas's study of the Harlem Renaissance demonstrated how interracial relations ("mongrelization," in her terminology) brought together white pragmatist theorists and African American thinkers and artists. In the new field of whiteness studies, as pioneered by David Roediger, Eric Lott, Noel Ignatieff, George Lipsitz, and Matthew Frye Jacobson, historians have demonstrated how racial categories were constructed and how they shifted over time, thus allowing certain excluded groups to later be subsumed under the designation "white." "Whiteness" is no longer a term of neutrality but a concept laden with power and privilege. These works have placed the dynamic between different groups in American society at the center of historical analysis. But grand syntheses or compilations of historical data have not been driven from the field of history. In the initial volumes of the *Oxford History of the United States*, begun in 1982, the historians James McPherson, James T. Patterson, and David M. Kennedy have attempted to bring together political and diplomatic with social and cultural history.

The profession of history, and historiography, changes with the times. In the age of the Internet, the scope of the profession expands. Hypertext computer programs may render problematic traditional historical emphasis on linear development. The coming of the computer book and Web publishing may allow monographic historical studies with small readerships to become financially feasible and easily accessible. The precise future of historical research may be impossible to predict, but the challenges of the Internet, popular film histories by Ken Burns, and the need to balance diversity with synthesis will have to be met.

BIBLIOGRAPHY

Appleby, Joyce, Lynn Hunt, and Margaret Jacobs. *Telling the Truth about History*. New York: Norton, 1994.

Bender, Thomas. "Wholes and Parts: The Need for Synthesis in American History." *Journal of American History* 73 (June 1986): 120–136.

Cotkin, George. "'Hyping the Text': Hypertext, Postmodernism, and the Historian." *American Studies* 37 (Fall 1996): 103–116.

Diggins, John Patrick. "Consciousness and Ideology in American History: The Burden of Daniel J. Boorstin." *American Historical Review* 76 (February 1971): 99–118.

Harlan, David. *The Degradation of American History*. Chicago: University of Chicago Press, 1997.

Haskell, Thomas L. *Objectivity Is Not Neutrality: Explanatory Schemes in History*. Baltimore: Johns Hopkins University Press, 1998.

Higham, John, with Leonard Krieger and Felix Gilbert. *History: The Development of Historical Studies in the United States*. Englewood Cliffs, N.J.: Prentice-Hall, 1965.

Hofstadter, Richard. *The Progressive Historians: Turner, Beard, Parrington*. New York: Knopf, 1968.

Hollinger, David A. *In the American Province: Studies in the History and Historiography of Ideas*. Bloomington: Indiana University Press, 1985.

Holt, W. Stull. *Historical Scholarship in the United States and Other Essays*. Seattle: University of Washington Press, 1967.

Jameson, J. Franklin. *The History of Historical Writing in America*. 1891. Reprint, New York: Antiquarian Press, 1961.

Kraus, Michael, and David D. Joyce. *The Writing of American History*. Norman: University of Oklahoma Press, 1985.

Loewenberg, Bert James. *American History in American Thought: Christopher Columbus to Henry Adams*. New York: Simon and Schuster, 1972.

Novick, Peter. *That Noble Dream: The "Objectivity Question" and the American Historical Profession*. Cambridge, U.K.: Cambridge University Press, 1988.

Ross, Dorothy. "Historical Consciousness in Nineteenth-Century America." *American Historical Review* 89 (October 1984): 909–928.

Scott, Joan Wallach. *Gender and the Politics of History*. New York: Columbia University Press, 1988.

Singal, Daniel Joseph. "Beyond Consensus: Richard Hofstadter and American Historiography." *American Historical Review* 89 (October 1984): 976–1004.

Smith, William Raymond. *History as Argument: Three Patriotic Historians of the American Revolution*. The Hague: Mouton, 1966.

Van Tassel, David D. *Recording America's Past: An Interpretation of the Development of Historical Studies in America, 1607–1884*. Chicago: University of Chicago Press, 1960.

White, Hayden. *Metahistory: The Historical Imagination in Nineteenth-Century Europe*. Baltimore: Johns Hopkins University Press, 1975.

Wish, Harvey. *The American Historian: A Social-Intellectual History of the Writing of the American Past.* New York: Oxford University Press, 1960.

George B. Cotkin

See also **Ethnohistory; Progressive Movement; Romanticism; Sociology; Women's Studies.**

HIV. *See* **Acquired Immune Deficiency Syndrome.**

HO-CHUNK. *See* **Winnebago/Ho-Chunk.**

Hockey. Youngsters play hockey at a park in New Ulm, Minn., 1975. National Archives and Records Administration

HOCKEY in the United States originated during the summer of 1894. American and Canadian college students participating in a tennis tournament in Niagara Falls, Canada, learned that during the winter months they played different versions of the same game. The Canadians played hockey, the Americans a game they called "ice polo." Boasting of their prowess, the students challenged each other to a competition. In a series of matches staged that next winter in Montreal, Ottawa, Toronto, and Kingston, the Canadians won all the hockey games and managed to tie two of the ice polo contests. Within a few years American colleges and amateur clubs along the Eastern Seaboard had forsaken ice polo for hockey.

At approximately the same time, Minnesotans learned about hockey from their neighbors in Manitoba; players from the upper peninsula of Michigan also challenged Canadians in hockey games. The debut of the Western Pennsylvania and Interscholastic Hockey leagues brought hockey also to Pittsburgh and its environs. By the turn of the twentieth century, hockey had become popular in three separate regions of the United States.

Early Leagues

In 1904, a northern Michigan dentist named J. L. Gibson found enough eager investors from mining companies to form the first professional hockey league. Although the International Professional Hockey League (IPHL) enjoyed some success, it survived only three seasons, disappearing in 1907.

Two years later, in 1909, mining entrepreneur Michael John O'Brien and his son Ambrose joined forces with P. J. Doran, owner of the Montreal Wanderers whose team had been excluded from the Canadian Hockey Association (CHA), to organize the National Hockey Association (NHA), the immediate predecessor of the National Hockey League (NHL). When the NHA began play on 5 January 1910, it had five teams based in three small Ontario towns, Colbalt, Haileybury, and Renfrew, and two teams in Montreal, the Wanderers and an all French-Canadian squad known as Les Canadiens.

So popular did the NHA become that it competed effectively against the CHA. When representatives of the rival leagues met to discuss a merger, NHA officials agreed to take only two clubs from the CHA, the Ottawa Senators and the Montreal Shamrocks, causing the collapse of the CHA. The now seven-team NHA became the top professional hockey league in North America.

Because they could not afford to neglect the family business in British Columbia to play hockey in eastern Canada, Frank and Lester Patrick left the NHA and founded the Pacific Coast Hockey Association (PCHA) in 1911. The PCHA carried out innovations in the rules and style of play that have been incorporated into the modern game, such as tabulating assists (the NHA did the same in 1913), permitting goaltenders to sprawl to make saves (the NHA required them to remain standing), and adding blue lines to divide the ice into zones (the NHA left the ice surface unmarked). PCHA rules also permitted the players to pass the puck forward while in the neutral zone, whereas the NHA permitted only backward passing and required skaters to carry the puck (that is, to push the puck along the ice with their sticks) toward the opponent's goal. In 1913 the NHA and the PCHA agreed to play an annual five-game series to determine the championship of professional hockey and claim the coveted Stanley Cup, named for Lord Frederick Arthur Stanley, the governor-general of Canada.

The Advent of the National Hockey League

During the World War I the NHA teams lost players to military service, attendance declined, and owners reduced salaries. With so many players in the armed forces, the NHA board of directors voted to dismantle their partnership and, in November 1917, reorganized as the National Hockey League. The National Hockey League inaugurated play on 19 December 1917 as a four-team circuit, with the Canadiens and Wanderers based in Montreal, the Senators in Ottawa, and the Arenas in Toronto. (Quebec had received the rights to a franchise, but the owners did not put a team on the ice in 1917). After a fire on 2 January 1918 reduced the Westmount Arena to ashes and left the Wanderers homeless, the team withdrew from the league, having played only four games.

Survival of the fittest was the law for both franchises and players during the early years of the National Hockey League. The teams struggled to fill their arenas and to make profits. The players endured a vicious brand of hockey in which fists and sticks took their toll. They also accepted extraordinarily low salaries, even by the standards of the day. Harry Cameron, the highest paid player on the Stanley Cup champion Toronto Arenas in 1918, earned a paltry $900 per year. The Montreal Canadiens and the Ottawa Senators dominated the NHL from 1917 until 1926. Between them, they represented the league in six of the first nine Stanley Cup series played against teams from the Pacific Coast Hockey Association or the Western Canada Hockey League.

Growth and Contraction

In 1924 the NHL expanded into the United States when the Boston Bruins entered the league. Before the 1925–1926 season, the New York Americans and the Pittsburgh Pirates came in, and Canadians feared that the Americans were about to steal their national game.

Between 1926 and 1942 the NHL grew from a tiny circuit of Canadian teams into the major North American professional hockey league. The growth of the NHL was not lost on the owners of teams in the Pacific Coast Hockey Association and the Western Canada Hockey League. In 1926 the Patrick brothers concluded they could no longer compete with the NHL and so dissolved their league, selling many of the players' contracts to NHL teams.

With the onset of the Great Depression in 1929, teams from smaller markets, such as the Ottawa Senators and the Pittsburgh Pirates, struggled to compete and eventually suspended operations. In 1941, after moving to Brooklyn, the New York Americans also withdrew from the NHL. The six surviving NHL teams were the Boston Bruins, the Chicago Black Hawks, the Detroit Red Wings, the Montreal Canadiens, the New York Rangers, and the Toronto Maple Leafs. Many regard the twenty-five year period between 1942 and 1967 as the "Golden Age of Hockey." Yet competition among the "Original Six" was uneven. The Bruins, Black Hawks, and Rangers struggled; the Maple Leafs, Red Wings, and Canadiens dominated.

The stability that had characterized the National Hockey League between 1942 and 1967 gave way to the tumult of the years 1968 through 1979. The prospect of substantial profits and the threat of a new professional hockey league combined to induce NHL owners to add six new teams: the Los Angeles Kings, the Minnesota North Stars, the Philadelphia Flyers, the Pittsburgh Penguins, the Oakland Seals, and the St. Louis Blues. In 1970 the NHL expanded to fourteen teams, adding the Buffalo Sabers and the Vancouver Canucks, and split into two divisions, with the Original Six clubs playing in the East and the expansion teams in the West. Predictably, the Original Six teams dominated the NHL immediately after expansion. The Montreal Canadiens won Stanley Cups in 1971 and 1973, and then enjoyed a sting of four consecutive championships between 1975–1976 and 1978–1979.

The World Hockey Association, 1972–1979

The invention of Gary Davidson and Dennis Murphy, who had also organized the American Basketball Association, the World Hockey Association (WHA) began play in 1972 and for seven years competed with the NHL. With franchises in Chicago, Cleveland, Edmonton, Houston, Los Angeles, Minnesota, New England (later Hartford, Connecticut), New York, Ottawa, Philadelphia, Quebec, and Winnipeg, the league gained immediate credibility when such established NHL stars as Gordie Howe, Bobby Hull, Frank Mahovlich, and Jacques Plante signed with association teams. Along with the NHL players who vaulted to the new league, the WHA advertised a host of young talent, including Mike Gartner, Mark Howe, Mark Messier, and Wayne Gretzky, each of whom later made his mark in the NHL.

The WHA operated on a slender budget before going out of existence in 1979, with four franchises, the Edmonton Oilers, Quebec Nordiques, Hartford Whalers, and Winnipeg Jets, joining the NHL. During its existence, however, the league offered an exciting brand of hockey, only slightly inferior to the quality of play in the NHL, and the inter-league competition for players succeeded in raising the average salaries in both leagues. The principal response of the NHL to the WHA was additional expansion, planting franchises in Atlanta (later Calgary) and Long Island in 1972, and in Kansas City (later Colorado and New Jersey) and Washington in 1974. Such preemptive strikes forestalled the establishment of WHA teams in those markets.

The Europeans Arrive

The American Olympic hockey squad excited new interest in the sport with the celebrated "Miracle on Ice" in 1980, while the New York Islanders and the Edmonton Oilers ruled the NHL throughout the decade. More important, the demographic composition of the NHL began to change. The percentage of Canadian players declined from 82.1 percent in 1980 to 75.5 percent by 1989, while the number of U.S. and European players rose.

The Russians arrived in force during the late 1980s and early 1990s, especially after the disintegration of the Eastern Bloc in 1989 and the collapse of Soviet Union in 1991. By 1998, 22.5 percent of NHL players came from outside Canada and the United States. Swedes, Finns, Czechs, Slovaks, Latvians, Russians, and a smattering of Germans composed the international roster of the NHL. The influx of Americans, Europeans, and Russians resonated with fans. NHL attendance grew throughout the decade. In 1979 average attendance was 12,747 per game. Ten years later, it had climbed to 14,908.

Problems and Prospects

Fundamental changes also took place off the ice during the 1980s and 1990s, especially in the reorganization of the National Hockey League Players Association (NHLPA). By the end of the 1980s, many players feared that Alan Eagleson, the executive director of the NHLPA since its inception in 1967, had grown too close to management to represent the players effectively. Eagleson survived two attempts to oust him in 1989. Only after his resignation in 1991, however, did players learn that he had embezzled from the pension fund and committed fraud in the process of arranging international hockey tournaments. Convicted of these charges in January 1998, Eagleson was fined and imprisoned, becoming the first Honored Member to have his plaque removed from the Hockey Hall of Fame.

On 1 January 1992, lawyer and agent Bob Goodenow assumed control of the NHLPA. In April 1992, after only four months in office, Goodenow called the first players' strike in league history. The strike cost NHL president John Ziegler his job, and the NHL Board of Governors elected Gary Bettman, the former senior vice president of the National Basketball Association, as the first commissioner.

Even before Bettman assumed control of the NHL, team owners determined to increase its exposure. That aspiration was, in part, the rationale for expanding the league again during the 1990s. Two new franchises, the Tampa Bay Lightning and a second version of the Ottawa Senators, began play in 1992, and the Board of Governors also awarded franchises to Anaheim and Florida.

Despite its growing popularity, the NHL suffered through a series of crises during the 1990s, including franchise relocations, the financial and legal problems of various NHL owners, and a damaging lockout in 1994–1995 that shortened the regular season to 48 games. The lockout temporarily halted the momentum that Bettman had kindled, but during the late 1990s the league still managed to expand into new markets and attract new fans. The Nashville Predators began play in 1998; Atlanta also received an expansion franchise, the Thrashers, in 1999. For the 2000–2001 season, Minneapolis-St. Paul, which had lost its team when the North Stars moved to Dallas in 1993, got the Minnesota Wild, while the Blue Jackets began play in Columbus, Ohio. Although continuing to prosper, at the beginning of the twenty-first century, the NHL was threatened by the financial instability of small-market Canadian teams, dramatically escalating player salaries, and the prospect of another protracted labor dispute.

BIBLIOGRAPHY

Bernstein, Ross. *Frozen Memories: Celebrating a Century of Minnesota Hockey.* Minneapolis: Nordin Press, 1999.

Diamond, Dan, et al. *The NHL Official Guide and Record Book.* New York: Total Sports Publishing, 2000.

Diamond, Dan, et al., eds. *Total Hockey: The Official Encyclopedia of the National Hockey League,* 2d ed. Kansas City, Mo.: Andrew McMeel, 2000.

Falla, Jack, et al. *Quest for the Cup: A History of the Stanley Cup Finals, 1893–2001.* Berkeley, Calif: Thunder Bay, 2001.

McFarlane, Brian. *The History of Hockey.* Champaign, Ill.: Sports Publishing, 1997.

McKinley, Michael. *Etched in Ice: A Tribute to Hockey's Defining Moments.* Vancouver, B.C.: Greystone, 2002.

———. *Putting a Roof on Winter: Hockey's Rise from Sport to Spectacle.* Toronto: Douglas and McIntyre, 2000.

Mark G. Malvasi

See also **Recreation; Sports.**

HOGS are not indigenous to the Western Hemisphere. In 1493 Christopher Columbus first introduced them to the Caribbean island of Hispaniola. Some forty-six years later, they arrived in what is now the continental United States with Hernando de Soto's expedition. It is likely that de Soto's expedition left behind some of the hogs, either deliberately or accidentally.

The first important importation of hogs into the thirteen original colonies accompanied the establishment of Jamestown in 1607. Their introduction in the Massachusetts Bay area by the English and in the Delaware River region of Pennsylvania and New Jersey by the English, Germans, and Swedes soon followed. Thus, by the end of the seventeenth century, hogs were well established in the Middle Atlantic and New England colonies.

American breeds of hogs emerged from these early sources, but more significant development of breeds took place after the extensive importations from western Europe during the first half of the nineteenth century. The eight leading breeds are the Chester White, Duroc, Hampshire, Poland China, Spotted, Berkshire, Yorkshire, and American Landrace. Purebred hogs, while relatively small in number compared to the total commercial production in the United States, serve as an important seedstock source for commercial nonpurebred herds.

Marked changes in the type and conformation of hogs raised in the United States have occurred since the 1930s as a result of changes in consumer preference and a decline in the use of lard. Breeders have developed a meat-type hog: a lean, meaty animal providing an increased yield of preferred lean cuts and a reduced yield of fat. Improved breeding and selection programs have been applied to all breeds of hogs with advances in nutritional knowledge that permit the maximum expression of the animal's potential for lean tissue development.

Marketing patterns continue to change. During the early 1800s, herds were driven to cities on the eastern seaboard. Later, with population shifts and the development of transportation systems, packing centers arose in Cincinnati and Chicago. The latter eventually became the center of the industry. After World War II, as other stockyards located throughout the Midwest became increasingly important, that of Chicago declined; hogs were no longer marketed in Chicago after 1970.

The production of hogs continues as one of the major U.S. agricultural enterprises. Iowa, which was home to fifteen million hogs in 2001, easily leads the nation in pork production. North Carolina is in second place with 9.5 million hogs. Especially in North Carolina, however, an increasing number of American hogs are raised not on family farms but rather on large-scale factory operations. Promoters of the practice claim that it improves efficiency and brings jobs to economically depressed areas. Critics, by contrast, dispute that factory hog farms are more efficient and also worry about the environmental, economic, and health implications of this style of production. Most frequently, they argue that factory farms have yet to discover a suitable way to deal with hog waste, which can pollute groundwater and smell unbearably strong.

BIBLIOGRAPHY

Hallam, Arne, ed. *Size, Structure, and the Changing Face of American Agriculture.* Boulder, Col.: Westview Press, 1993.

Horwitz, Richard P. *Hog Ties: Pigs, Manure, and Mortality in American Culture.* New York: St. Martin's Press, 1998.

Tansey, Geoff, and Joyce D'Silva, eds. *The Meat Business: Devouring a Hungry Planet.* New York: St. Martin's Press, 1999.

Thu, Kendall M., and E. Paul Durrenberger, eds. *Pigs, Profits, and Rural Communities.* Albany: State University of New York Press, 1998.

R. J. Davey/A. E.

See also **Agriculture; Livestock Industry; Meatpacking.**

HOHOKAM is the name given by archaeologists to a prehistoric culture centered along the Salt, Gila, Verde, and Santa Cruz Rivers in the low, hot Sonoran desert of southern Arizona between approximately 300 B.C. and A.D. 1450. The name Hohokam means "those who have gone" in the language of the O'odham, the contemporary Native American inhabitants of southern Arizona. The Hohokam cultural sequence initially was defined at the site of Snaketown in the lower Gila Valley southeast of Phoenix, by the early twentieth century archaeologists Harold Gladwin and Emil Haury. Since the 1980s, knowledge of the Hohokams has greatly expanded as a result of cultural resource management archaeology projects conducted in the Phoenix and Tucson basins. Hohokam chronology is subdivided into four periods: Pioneer (A.D. 300–775), Colonial (A.D. 775–975), Sedentary (A.D. 975–1150), and Classic (A.D. 1150–1350). The Red Mountain phase predates the Pioneer period, and the El Polvoron phase post-dates the Classic period.

By the beginning of the first millennium A.D., prehistoric hunters and gatherers in southern Arizona had begun to experiment with agriculture and to settle in small villages along the major river systems. The Hohokam culture emerged from this substrate. During the Preclassic (Pioneer, Colonial, and Sedentary phases), the Hohokams lived in semi-subterranean pit house villages. Houses were clustered together around courtyards with associated work areas, trash mounds, and cemeteries. Public architecture included ball courts and mounds capped with caliche. The Hohokams grew maize, squash, cotton, beans, agave, and tobacco. They built extensive networks of irrigation canals along the Salt and Gila Rivers. They produced buff, brown, and red-painted pottery using the paddle-and-anvil technique. Frogs, lizards, birds, and other animals were commonly depicted on pottery as well as in shell and stone. Exotic artifacts of the Hohokams include: groundstone palettes, bowls, and figurines; baked-clay figurines; carved and acid-etched Pacific marine shell jewelry; iron pyrite mirrors; and turquoise mosaics. The Hohokams cremated their dead and sometimes placed the remains inside ceramic vessels. The Preclassic reached its zenith during the Sedentary phase, when Hohokam culture extended from northern Mexico in the south to Flagstaff, Arizona, in the north. Mexican influences are seen in the presence of ball courts, copper bells made using the lost-wax casting technique, macaws, and cotton textiles.

Changes in settlement patterns, architecture, ceramics, burial practices, and trade relations occurred during the Classic period. Ball courts were no longer constructed. Aboveground adobe houses were grouped into walled compounds surrounding rectangular, earthen platform mounds. Platform mounds were built at regular intervals along river and irrigation canal systems, suggesting these sites were administrative centers allocating water and coordinating canal labor. Polychrome pottery appeared, and inhumation burial replaced cremation. Shell and other exotic trade continued, but on a smaller scale than during the Preclassic. Social and climatic factors led to a decline and partial abandonment of the area after A.D. 1400. During the Postclassic El Polvoron phase, people lived in dispersed "ranch"-style villages of shallow pit houses. Large-scale irrigation systems were abandoned, and farming was replaced by a mixed subsistence strategy.

BIBLIOGRAPHY

Gumerman, George J., ed. *Exploring the Hohokam: Prehistoric Desert Peoples of the American Southwest.* Albuquerque: University of New Mexico Press, 1991.

Haury, Emil W. *The Hohokam, Desert Farmers and Craftsmen: Excavations at Snaketown 1964–1965.* Tucson: University of Arizona Press, 1976.

Reid, Jefferson, and Stephanie Whittlesey. *The Archaeology of Ancient Arizona.* Tucson: University of Arizona Press, 1997.

Ruth M. Van Dyke

See also **Ancestral Pueblo (Anasazi).**

HOLDING COMPANY. A holding company is characterized by its ownership of securities (generally common stock) of other companies for the purpose of influencing the management of those subsidiary companies, rather than for investment or other purposes.

Some holding companies, often called "pure" holding companies, confine their operations to owning and managing other firms, whereas other holding companies are themselves operating companies. This distinction was formerly of greater significance than it is now, because—until the passage of the first limiting legislation in the 1930s—pure holding companies that controlled operating companies in several regulated industries, including banking and public utilities, were free of state and federal regulations imposed on operating companies. Through acquisition of separate firms, holding companies could enter activities and geographical areas barred to regulated operating companies. Many loopholes in regulations governing these industries were closed by the Public Utility Holding Company Act of 1935 and the Bank Holding Company Act of 1956.

The holding company emerged as a common form of business organization around 1900, some decades after its first use in railroads (1853) and communications (1832). The earliest holding companies had charters granted by special acts of state legislature that explicitly permitted them to control stock of other corporations; the courts in most states usually ruled that this power had to be granted by explicit legislative enactment. However, a few early general incorporation acts did provide for charters granting such powers. Nevertheless, the widespread use of holding companies followed, especially upon liberalization of general incorporation acts by New Jersey and several other states starting in 1889. This development suggests that the wide use of charters in New Jersey and, later, in Delaware stemmed from other factors, including favorable tax treatment and the financial, technological, and marketing demands and opportunities of large-scale business.

The holding company, depending upon circumstances, offers financial, administrative, and legal advantages over other forms of business organization. It usually has better access to securities markets than do the member operating companies individually, making it easier to secure the capital necessary to conduct large-scale operations. It permits a combination of firms with control of a smaller portion of voting stock than is necessary for a merger of those firms. (One objection to the holding company, however, is the sometimes meager protection it provides to the rights of minority stockholders.) It affords a convenient method of centralizing control of the policies of different businesses while leaving control of their operations decentralized. Pyramiding—the use of a number of holding companies placed on top of each other—especially when combined with a heavy reliance on borrowed funds at each level, permits business organizers to acquire control of a large volume of assets with relatively little investment. Separate incorporation of properties located in different states or engaged in different activities often simplifies the holding company's accounting, taxation, and legal problems and may free the holding company of legal restrictions to which it might otherwise be subject.

As business organizers moved to exploit these advantages toward the turn of the twentieth century, the holding company device became the dominant form of large-scale business organization. Long used in the railroad industry, it was extended there, notably with formation of the Northern Securities Company in 1901. The formation, also in 1901, of United States Steel—then called the "world's greatest corporation"—signaled the adoption of holding company organizations in mining and manufacturing. Somewhat later, extensive holding-company systems were formed in banking and finance and in public utilities. Many of the latter were noted for their extensive pyramiding and their combination of diverse, widely scattered holdings.

Under attack from the beginning, holding companies have remained controversial and the subject of continuing demands for public control. Those formed around the turn of the twentieth century were enveloped from birth in the antitrust agitation of the period. The public utility holding companies of the 1920s were likewise attacked as monopolistic. The attack on them, which gained intensity and focus with the failure of a number of the systems in the early 1930s, led to the passage in 1935 of the Public Utility Holding Company Act. Corporations controlling two or more banks were brought under federal control in 1956. Attention in the 1960s and early 1970s shifted to the conglomerate (the highly diversified holding company), and to the financial congeneric (the bank-centered one-bank holding company, which limited its operations to banking and other closely related financial services). Both were subjected to a measure of federal control in the early 1970s: the Justice Department initiated a number of antitrust suits to block some acquisitions of the former, and Congress, in 1970, amended the Bank Holding Company Act of 1956 to circumscribe activities of the latter.

In the late twentieth century, federal regulators continued to scrutinize anticompetitive or monopolistic acquisitions, especially in the media and telecommunications industry. In the year 2000 alone, the government blocked a potential merger between American Telephone and Telegraph (AT&T) and the media giant Time Warner, and another proposed merger between long-distance telephone providers WorldCom and Sprint.

BIBLIOGRAPHY

Berle, Adolf A., Jr., and Gardiner C. Means. *Modern Corporation and Private Property.* New Brunswick, N.J.: Transaction Publishers, 1991.

Chandler, Alfred D., Jr. *The Visible Hand: The Managerial Revolution in American Business.* Cambridge, Mass.: Harvard University Press, 1977.

Means, Gardiner C. *The Corporate Revolution in America: Economic Reality versus Economic Theory.* New York: Crowell-Collier Press, 1962.

Wm. Paul Smith / T. G.

See also **Antitrust Laws; AT&T Divestiture; Conglomerates; Corporations; Leveraged Buyouts; Mergers and Acquisitions; Monopoly; Restraint of Trade; Trusts.**

HOLIDAYS AND FESTIVALS. Referring most broadly to periods of time free from work, the word "holiday" is derived from the word "holyday," and refers generally to special days of celebration and commemoration. These can be based on religion, politics, or regional, ethnic, or racial affiliation, and may or may not be officially recognized. For instance, neither Halloween (31 October) nor Valentine's Day (14 February) are official holidays in the sense that businesses and government agencies close down or that the government acknowledges them as special. However, both are widely celebrated in the United States. Other holidays receive government recognition at the local level (such as Evacuation Day, 17 March, in Suffolk County, Massachusetts), the state level (such as Juneteenth, 19 June, in Texas), or the national level (for example, Independence Day, 4 July).

Some holidays, such as Halloween and Valentine's Day, have been celebrated in Europe and America for centuries and a number of them are related to pre-Christian celebrations. Among those on the American calendar having ancient origins is Valentine's Day. Moreover, many distinctly American holidays were heavily influenced by preexisting festivals. The American Thanksgiving, for instance, commemorates a feast at Plymouth Colony in 1621 that was most likely inspired by British harvest home traditions. Other holidays, however, are created in America as social circumstances demand. Examples are Martin Luther King Jr.'s birthday and the African American holiday of Kwanzaa.

Holidays and Controversy

Holidays are frequently contested. The holiday for Martin Luther King Jr.'s birthday, for instance, was resisted by President Ronald Reagan and the officials of several states. Likewise, while Kwanzaa is regarded by its participants as reinforcing a sense of community, it is seen as divisive by those not participating.

Kwanzaa is celebrated from 26 December through 1 January. It was invented in the mid-1960s by Dr. Maulana Kerenga. Believing that African Americans were alienated from the Eurocentrism and the commercialism of Christmas, he adapted some African symbols and harvest traditions to construct a festival for African Americans. It is intended not to supplant, but to complement Christmas. Many families celebrate both. Kwanzaa is not a religious holiday; rather, it speaks to ethnic and racial identity and tradition within the United States. In this sense Kwanzaa involves the cultural dynamics of identity politics, reflects the growing awareness of pluralism in the United States, and helps create that sense of pluralism as well. Invented to express ethnic and racial identity, the celebration is sometimes a site of racial debate and exclusion.

Similar dynamics can be seen in the increasingly national celebration of Cinco de Mayo, a Mexican celebration of a military victory. In the United States it has become something of a pan-Latino holiday. Some regard it as a conflation of a great variety of national and regional Latin American cultures and therefore as doing an injustice to their real differences. Similarly, traditional occasions such as the Day of the Dead (Día de los Muertos) are growing in popularity in the United States. A manifestation of a culturally diverse population, it can also be seen as a standardization, since the Day of the Dead traditions presented in schools, museums, and cultural centers are largely based on phenomena found mostly in central and southern Mexico.

The adaptation of traditional celebrations in the United States indicates that they serve different purposes under different circumstances, and that meanings change with personal, social, and cultural contexts. Still, even the major, long-standing holidays such as Independence Day, Thanksgiving, and Christmas are sites of identity politics and contestation. For instance, in the eighteenth and nineteenth centuries African Americans, free and slave, held countercelebrations near the Fourth of July as an ironic commentary on the celebration of freedom in a land of slaves. Subsequently, Native Americans declared Thanksgiving a National Day of Mourning.

Cyclical and Noncyclical Observances in Early America

Throughout history, peoples around the world have marked important occasions, significant times of year, and important points in the life cycle with rituals, festivals, and celebrations. For example, European colonists found elaborate ceremonial systems in place among Native Americans. They reflected the hunting, pastoral, and agricultural economies of the tribes. The American Thanksgiving is often thought to be modeled entirely on the British Harvest Home festival, but the Native peoples who taught the colonists how to grow food also influenced the 1621 celebratory meal with their own harvest celebration traditions. Their foods remain staples of the symbolic meal eaten every Thanksgiving.

Although harvest celebrations were allowed in early America, thanksgivings were actually days of fasting and prayer in recognition of nonrecurring events both in Puritan New England and elsewhere. President George Washington declared 26 November 1789 as a national thanksgiving holiday to thank God for victory in the War of Independence as much as to commemorate the Puritans of 1621. The holiday was not regularized as the fourth Thursday of every November until 1863.

Christmas

The Puritans of Massachusetts believed that holidays were not biblically justified, and therefore did not observe them or allow others to do so. Christmas, for example, was banned in Massachusetts from 1659 to 1681. It was in the middle colonies, where Anglicanism held sway, that Christmas developed. At first a rowdy occasion, Christmas was in the seventeenth and early eighteenth centuries a carnivalesque celebration. During the nineteenth century, however, Christmas changed into a more demure and domestic family holiday. The Christmas tree tradition was borrowed from Germany. Santa Claus derived from European traditions of St. Nicholas, the British Father Christmas, and other mid-winter gift bearers. But the American Santa Claus also owes much to American authors such as Washington Irving, who described him in *Knickerbocker Tales* (1809); Clement Moore, who is said by some to have written "A Visit from St. Nicholas"; and cartoonist Thomas Nast.

Independence Day

Independence Day was celebrated from the day on which the Declaration of Independence was adopted and read before the population of the colonies: 4 July 1776. Before independence and as late as 1800, British customary holidays such as Guy Fawkes Day were observed in New England, as were official commemorations in honor of the monarchy. The Fourth of July continued the bonfire and fireworks customs of those celebrations. Soon, it became an occasion for lengthy oratory, picnics, sports, and a reading of the Declaration.

African American Celebrations

African Americans celebrated these holidays by putting their own historically and culturally derived spin on them. Africans in bondage, for instance, were usually allowed Christmas or New Year's as a holiday. From all accounts, the celebrations were very much African in nature, with masquerading and musical performances. Such festivals were found throughout the African diaspora. Similarly, a Dutch Easter celebration in New York State known as Pinkster became an occasion for an African American celebration in the African-derived style. For African Americans as well as whites, the Fourth of July entailed speech making, feasting, and sports, but might be celebrated on a different day, perhaps in implicit protest. In addition, emancipation celebrations were held. The first of August recognized the abolition of slavery in Haiti in 1837. Since the Civil War, emancipation celebrations have been held at different times around the country. In Texas, 19 June, known as Juneteenth, is a legal holiday.

Other Holidays

The Civil War begat Memorial Day. The period between the Civil War and World War I gave rise to many other holidays, including Flag Day and Labor Day. Along with these official holidays, the United States hosts a wide variety of festivals that reflect its multiculturalism. Some ethnic celebrations, such as St. Patrick's Day, have become nationally celebrated; some, such as the Mexican Cinco de Mayo, are growing in popularity.

BIBLIOGRAPHY

Cressy, David. *Bonfires and Bells: National Memory and the Protestant Calendar in Elizabethan and Stuart England.* Berkeley: University of California Press, 1989.

Litwicki, Ellen M. *America's Public Holidays, 1865–1920.* Washington, D.C.: Smithsonian Institute Press, 2000.

Santino, Jack. *All around the Year: Holidays and Celebrations in American Life.* Urbana: University of Illinois Press, 1994.

———. *New Old-Fashioned Ways: Holidays and Popular Culture.* Knoxville: University of Tennessee Press, 1996.

Jack Santino

See also **Christmas; Flag Day; Independence Day; Kwanzaa; Labor Day; Memorial Day; Thanksgiving Day.**

HOLLYWOOD. An area of the city of Los Angeles famous primarily for its association with the film industry,

Hollywood. The movie star Eddie Murphy puts his footprints in cement on the Walk of Fame. AP/WIDE WORLD PHOTOS

Hollywood was originally a small independent agricultural community. It merged with Los Angeles in 1910 in order to obtain an adequate water supply. At approximately the same time, the film industry began to locate in the region, seeking to take advantage of natural sunlight that allowed year-round filming and a diverse southern California landscape that provided cheap scenery. In 1914, the director Cecil B. DeMille decided to locate his studio in Hollywood permanently, and other companies followed. By the 1920s, Hollywood had beaten out rivals such as Culver City and Burbank as the place most associated with the film industry, although in fact movie lots were scattered throughout the Los Angeles area. The growing power and romance of film made Hollywood a cultural icon and a major tourist attraction. In the 1950s and 1960s, Hollywood also began to attract television studios and record companies. While still home to many entertainment-related companies and remaining a popular destination for starstruck visitors, the area's actual role in film production began to lag in the 1970s. Soaring production and living costs in Los Angeles led many companies to seek opportunities elsewhere, and Hollywood itself struggled with problems associated with urban blight.

BIBLIOGRAPHY

Friedrich, Otto. *City of Nets: A Portrait of Hollywood in the 1940s.* New York: Harper and Row, 1986.

Starr, Kevin. *Inventing the Dream: California through the Progressive Era.* New York: Oxford University Press, 1985.

Torrence, Bruce T. *Hollywood: The First 100 Years.* Hollywood, Calif.: Hollywood Chamber of Commerce, 1979.

Daniel J. Johnson

See also **Film; Los Angeles.**

HOLMES V. WALTON, a case decided by the Supreme Court of New Jersey in 1780. It is cited as one of the precedents for the doctrine of judicial review. The court declared unconstitutional a statute that provided in certain classes of cases that a jury might consist of six men. The legislature subsequently repealed the voided portion of the act. Thus, the right of the courts to pass upon the constitutionality of legislation was not denied, but the legislature claimed the final power to define the functions of each department of government.

BIBLIOGRAPHY

Hall, Kermit L. *The Supreme Court and Judicial Review in American History.* Bicentennial Essays on the Constitution. Washington, D.C.: American Historical Association, 1985.

William S. Carpenter/A. R.

See also **Hayburn's Case; Judicial Review; Jury Trial.**

HOLOCAUST MUSEUM. The dedication of the United States Holocaust Memorial Museum in Washington, D.C., on 22 April 1993 brought to fruition a process begun on 1 May 1978, when President Jimmy Carter announced the formation of the President's Commission on the Holocaust, chaired by the Holocaust survivor and eventual Nobel laureate Elie Wiesel. Motivations for the project were complex: it was a political response to the administration's tension with American Jews, and it was a cultural response to the increasing power of Holocaust memory among both American Jews and the wider culture.

Holocaust Museum. The entrance in 1993, the year the museum opened. AP/Wide World Photos

The commission envisioned a living memorial that would include memorial, museum, and educational space, and it proposed a civic ritual, the "Days of Remembrance" ceremonies, which would become an annual part of the nation's ritual calendar. Early struggles hinted at the enduringly volatile nature of the project. The commission and the Carter administration argued bitterly about the proper balance between Jewish and non-Jewish Holocaust victims in an attempt to construct an official definition of the Holocaust and in the selection of members for a body designed to implement its recommendations: the United States Holocaust Memorial Council, which first met on 28 May 1980, also chaired by Elie Wiesel.

Those tasked with the creation of the museum had to address issues about the location and representation of the Holocaust in a national American museum. Should this be an "official" American memory? Why? If so, where should the memory be located? In New York, home to the largest Jewish community outside of Israel, or in the nation's capital, on space adjacent to the national Mall, suggesting the Holocaust memory should be enshrined as a central American memory? Should the building be a neutral container, or should the architecture itself be expressive of the event?

After visiting Holocaust sites in Europe, the New York architect James Ingo Freed created an evocative building that removed visitors from American space, through what some called an "atrium from hell," windows that never allow a full view of the Mall, and elevators that transport visitors into the cold and dark exhibition space.

The creators of the museum also struggled with issues of Holocaust representation. What is the proper relationship between Jews and "other" victim groups in a museum exhibition? Do photographs taken by Nazis victimize the dead yet again? Is women's hair—shorn from victims before gassing—an appropriate artifact with which to tell the story?

Supported in part by federal funds, the museum has become an influential model of an activist memorial environment, seeking to awaken civic sensibilities through the telling of a cautionary tale. The Oklahoma City National Memorial was consciously modeled after the United States Holocaust Memorial Museum.

BIBLIOGRAPHY

Linenthal, Edward T. *Preserving Memory: The Struggle to Create America's Holocaust Museum.* New York: Viking, 1995. Reprint, New York: Columbia University Press, 2001.

Novick, Peter. *The Holocaust in American Life.* Boston and New York: Houghton Mifflin, 1999.

Weinberg, Jeshajahu, and Rina Elieli, *The Holocaust Museum in Washington.* New York: Rizzoli, 1995.

Young, James E. *At Memory's Edge: After-Images of the Holocaust in Contemporary Art and Architecture.* New Haven, Conn.: Yale University Press, 2000.

———. *The Texture of Memory: Holocaust Memorials and Meaning.* New Haven, Conn.: Yale University Press, 1993.

Edward T. Linenthal

See also **Genocide; Jews; Museums.**

HOLY CROSS, PRIESTS OF, are members of the religious congregation of the same name (in Latin, *Congregatio a Sancta Cruce*). The congregation was formed in 1837 by Basil Anthony Moreau near Le Mans, France, to assist in local parishes, hospitals, and educational institutions and to work in foreign missions. In 1841 Edward Sorin, C.S.C., introduced the congregation into the United States and the following year founded the University of Notre Dame near South Bend, Ind. The Priests of Holy Cross teach and assist at King's College in Wilkes-Barre, Pa.; Stonehill College in North Easton, Mass.; and the University of Portland in Portland, Oreg.; and from 1865 to 1970 they published the popular weekly magazine *The Ave Maria.* They serve as parish priests in several dioceses throughout the United States and assist as missionaries in Asia, Africa, and South America. There were approximately 1,100 priests in the Congregation of Holy Cross in 1974, more than half of whom are members of the three provinces of the United States. By 2000, there were approximately 1,700 members of the Congregation of Holy Cross, made up of roughly 900 priests and 800 brothers.

BIBLIOGRAPHY

Armstrong, Philip, C.S.C. *A More Perfect Legacy: A Portrait of Brother Ephrem O'Dwyer, C.S.C., 1888–1978.* Notre Dame, Ind.: University of Notre Dame Press, 1995.

Sorin, Edward. *Chronicles of Notre Dame du Lac.* Notre Dame, Ind.: University of Notre Dame Press, 1992.

Thomas E. Blantz, C.S.C. / A. R.

See also **Catholicism; Missions, Foreign.**

HOLY EXPERIMENT. "Holy Experiment" was William Penn's term for the ideal government he established for Pennsylvania in 1681, when he obtained the charter for that colony from King Charles II of England. Penn believed that the charter was a gift from God, "that an example may be set up to the nations: there may be room there, though not here, for such an holy experiment." This "experiment," Penn believed, would be a success only if the colony was settled with people of virtue, whose spirituality would shape Pennsylvania society, law, and politics. A member of the Religious Society of Friends, or Quakers as they were derisively called, Penn shared with his coreligionists a belief that, by virtue of their direct knowledge of and communion with God's divine authority, their precepts of religious liberty, political freedom, and pacifism were bound to take root in the new colony.

The first law the assembly passed guaranteed religious liberty and toleration for all who "shall confess and acknowledge one Almighty God to be the Creator, Upholder and Ruler of the world." The spiritual, legal, and political commitment to religious toleration loomed large to those Friends who had been persecuted in England. Economic, political, and religious divisions, however, undermined the colony's spiritual foundations within a few years of its establishment. An ineffective council, designated by Penn to be the executive branch of government in his absence, could do little to uphold the experiment's ideals. Most historians agree that between Penn's departure for England in 1684 and his return to the colony in 1699, the political ideals inherent in the Holy Experiment largely failed.

BIBLIOGRAPHY

Bronner, Edwin B. *William Penn's Holy Experiment: The Founding of Pennsylvania, 1681–1701.* New York: Temple University Press, 1962.

Illick, Joseph E. *Colonial Pennsylvania: A History.* New York: Scribners, 1976.

Leslie J. Lindenauer

See also **Pennsylvania; Quakers.**

HOME OWNERS' LOAN CORPORATION. For middle-class America the Home Owners' Loan Corporation, founded in 1933, was a crucial New Deal benefit. Americans had always held to an ideal of individualism that included a home of one's own; but in the years leading up to the New Deal, only four out of every ten Americans managed to attain that status. A key reason for the majority's failure was the restrictive mortgage system. Usually, borrowers were required to make down payments averaging around 35 percent for loans lasting only five to ten years at interest of up to 8 percent. At the end of that brief loan period, mortgage holders had to hope they could refinance or else come up with the remaining cost of the property. The minority of home buyers who could manage such terms assumed the additional risk of dealing with local institutions that did not offer loan mortgage insurance and were often dangerously underfunded, especially in areas outside the main cities.

This shaky system was unable to withstand the shock of the 1929 economic collapse. The number of mortgages issued nationwide dropped from 5,778 in 1928 to a mere 864 in 1933, and many banks went under, dragging homeowners down with them. Faced with this dire situation, the New Deal had a basic choice. It could follow the urging of the Federal Reserve Board chairman, Marriner Eccles, echoing the most influential economist of the age, John Maynard Keynes, that money should be pumped into the lagging building trades in order to gain both work for the unemployed and badly needed public housing. Or it could follow the lead of Herbert Hoover, who in 1932 had created the Federal Home Loan Bank to provide federal funding for lenders in the private housing market. Franklin Roosevelt, when he succeeded Hoover as president, inclined toward the latter course, but with government oversight and a focus on hard-pressed homeowners, rather than on the institutions controlling their mortgages.

In June 1933, the Home Owners' Loan Act, following the president's lead, sailed through Congress. The law authorized $200 million to set up the Home Owners' Loan Corporation (HOLC) with authority to issue $2 billion in tax-exempt bonds. The money raised would enable the HOLC to rescue imperiled mortgages by offering financing up to 80 percent of assessed value, to a maximum of $14,000. There followed a rush to file applications in 1934 by those holding 40 percent of all mortgaged properties, of which half with lowest risk were accepted. As intended, the main beneficiaries were homeowners at the lower end of the middle class with incomes in the $50 to $150 monthly range, persons who in the private market would have lost their homes.

The HOLC permanently changed the prevailing mortgage system. It offered money at 5 percent, provided insurance for its loans through the Federal Housing Authority and the Federal Savings and Loan Insurance Corporation, and allowed up to twenty-five years for repayment. To reach far-flung clients the HOLC dispersed into regional centers. Every loan situation was handled individually, including personal visits to prevent default. Given wide discretion to act, agents improved the chances clients would meet their obligations by helping them find work, collect insurance claims and pensions, attract tenants for rental space, qualify for public assistance, and even locate foster children to take in for a fee. The success of this sympathetic outreach was best demonstrated by the fact that the foreclosure rate for HOLC's risky mortgages was no greater than that for much safer mortgages accepted by banks and insurance companies.

HOLC policies favored single-family homes outside the central cities, thus setting in motion the rapid growth of suburbs after World War II. The suburban ideal of privately financed housing also inclined toward segregation on the grounds that racially homogeneous areas were most stable and thus posed the lowest credit risk. That bias, shared by private sector bankers and realtors, excluded most minorities from much consideration. The HOLC Loan Experience Card specified race and immigrant status as a consideration, and the records of the agency showed that from 1933 to 1936, the period it was authorized to issue loans, 44 percent of its help went to areas designated "native white," 42 percent to "native white and foreign," and 1 percent to Negro. Typifying the plight of the cities, the half of Detroit where blacks lived was excluded outright, as was a third of Chicago.

Despite its shortcomings, New Deal innovation helped account for home ownership rising from 40 percent of the population in the prosperous 1920s to almost 70 percent by the mid-1990s, with vast new tracts outside the cities of the Northeast and in new, sprawling urban areas in the South and Southwest setting the most conspicuous example. The historian David Kennedy did not exaggerate in claiming that the HOLC and the housing legislation it set in motion "revolutionized the way Americans lived."

BIBLIOGRAPHY

Gelfand, Mark I. *A Nation of Cities: The Federal Government and Urban America, 1933–1965.* New York: Oxford University Press, 1975.

Harriss, C. Lowell. *History and Policies of the Home Owners' Loan Corporation.* New York: National Bureau of Economic Research, 1951.

Jackson, Kenneth T. *Crabgrass Frontier: The Suburbanization of the United States.* New York: Oxford University Press, 1985.

Alan Lawson

See also **Building and Loan Associations; New Deal.**

HOME RULE is the principle or practice of self-government by localities. The U.S. Constitution makes no mention of local jurisdictions, so a state legislature must grant a city or county a charter, or the right to draft its own charter, to create a structure and powers for local government. Into the nineteenth century most American towns and counties functioned in the English tradition of local self-government on most matters, often by establishing municipal corporations empowered to provide public services and regulate local economic matters. As urban populations expanded with immigration and industrial development, many municipal governments found their ability to deliver services such as fire and police protection overwhelming and the process of awarding city contracts (especially in public utilities) increasingly corrupt. State legislatures, many still dominated by rural and agricultural interests, were often unresponsive, and boss-run political machines entered the void in many big cities. Reformers calling for "good government" promoted home rule as one remedy, theorizing that government closest to the people would hold public officials accountable and eliminate corrupt and inefficient politics from the businesslike formation of effective policy. The Missouri Constitution of 1875 included the first state provision of the right of municipalities to draft their own charters, and many states followed suit throughout the Progressive Era. A version of this "home rule movement" for counties gained some momentum in the mid-twentieth century, but only 129 of more than 3,000 counties ever adopted any kind of charter.

The specific character of home rule varies by state. As of 2000, forty-six states allowed some form of home rule for municipalities (the exceptions being Alabama, Hawaii, Nevada, and New Hampshire) and thirty-seven for counties. Thirty-seven states provide for structural home rule, permitting communities to incorporate and create local governments, while thirty-one allow functional home rule, in which city or county governments may exercise power in such areas as public works, social services, and economic development.

Advocates of the expansion of home rule claim that local control makes government more responsive, allows for flexible and innovative approaches to local problems, and relieves state legislatures of parochial issues. Detractors emphasize, however, that few issues are strictly local in nature, especially as the populations of central cities decline and metropolitan areas become more important. Enhanced local autonomy may hinder cooperation among neighboring localities and exacerbate tensions over policies involving overlapping state-local jurisdictions, especially in the areas of taxation and public spending.

The nation's capital is a special case of the home rule question, as the governance of Washington, D.C., sometimes involves conflicts between local and national interests. An elected city council and/or mayor governed Washington for much of the nineteenth century, until Congress took direct control of legislation for the District for a century starting in 1874. The limited home rule charter governing the District since 1974 allows an elected mayor and council to make laws for local affairs but reserves veto powers to Congress, even though citizens of Washington have no voting representative in the national legislature. A constitutional amendment to grant full home rule for the District failed in 1978, reflecting the stalled aspirations of home rule advocates nationwide.

BIBLIOGRAPHY

Harris, Charles Wesley. *Congress and the Governance of the Nation's Capital: The Conflict of Federal and Local Interests.* Washington, D.C.: Georgetown University Press, 1995.

Krane, Dale, Platon N. Rigos, and Melvin B. Hill Jr. *Home Rule in America: A Fifty-State Handbook.* Washington, D.C.: CQ Press, 2001.

Jeffrey T. Coster

See also **Charters, Municipal; Local Government.**

HOME SCHOOLING, the practice of educating one's own children, saw dramatic growth over the last two decades of the twentieth century. Home schoolers numbered about 15,000 in the 1970s; by 1999 850,000 children were learning at home. Long the normative practice on the American frontier, parent-directed EDUCATION was almost entirely eclipsed with the accomplishment of universal compulsory schooling in the early twentieth century. But in the wake of the "anti-Establishment" cultural ferment of the 1960s and 1970s, home schooling re-emerged, championed by advocates across a wide ideological spectrum.

The contemporary home school movement has a dual history. One branch began in the left-liberal alternative school movement of the 1960s, a cause that sought to democratize teacher-student relationships and give students greater discretion in directing their own educations. John Holt, long an advocate of alternative schooling, began to promote home education (which he called "unschooling") in the 1970s. Before his death in 1985, Holt nurtured a national grassroots network of home school converts. Another branch grew out of the conservative Protestant day school movement, specifically through the work of Raymond and Dorothy Moore, whose several books and national speaking tours advocating home education reached a ready audience of religious families already skeptical of public schools.

One of the first tasks of the fledgling movement was to secure the legality of the practice. Spurred by a small but well-organized home school lobby, judicial and legislative activity throughout the 1980s rendered home education legal throughout the United States by the end of the decade. The process of legalization was facilitated by the distinctive jurisdictional structure of American education. Because authority over schooling is largely in the hands of state and local governments in the United States, activists were able to wage localized battles and win victories in piecemeal fashion.

By the beginning of the twenty-first century, home education was not only legal but also broadly accepted in the United States. Home schooling was made easier by favorable laws, an elaborate network of support and advocacy groups at the local and national levels, and a vital sector of small businesses that supplied curriculum materials of all kinds to a growing home school market.

While the home school movement is a nominally international one, with at least a few adherents in most nations of the industrialized world, it is a distinctively American invention. The basic ideas that animate home education—that each learner is unique, that government schools are not doing their job well, and that educational professionals are unnecessary for sound instruction—are in keeping with the individualism and skepticism of formal authority that have characterized the national culture throughout its history.

BIBLIOGRAPHY

Bielick, Stacey, Kathryn Chandler, and Stephen Broughman. *Homeschooling in the United States: 1999* (NCES 2001-033). U.S. Department of Education. Washington, D.C.: National Center for Education Statistics, 2001. The first nationally representative survey of the U.S. home school population.

Moore, Raymond, and Dorothy Moore. *Home Grown Kids.* Waco, Tex: Word Books, 1981. A popular defense of home education.

Stevens, Mitchell L. *Kingdom of Children: Culture and Controversy in the Homeschooling Movement.* Princeton, N.J.: Princeton University Press, 2001. A sociological account of the rise of home education in the United States.

Mitchell Stevens

HOME SHOPPING NETWORKS, or electronic retailing, began in the 1980s in the form of television hucksters selling cubic zirconia jewelry and various knickknacks. Then came lengthy "infomercials," costly television advertisements, often with celebrity hosts, that gave the impression of regular programming. By the 1990s the increase in the number of two-income families with little time for leisure; new concerns about poor service and rising crime rates at shopping malls; and the desire for quality merchandise at bargain prices had boosted interest in home shopping. These changing demographics and consumer attitudes gave televised home shopping a new prestige, and the industry earned $3 billion a year and reached more than 100 million homes.

The two largest services in the mid-1990s were QVC Network and Home Shopping Network, Inc. The popularity of home shopping was evidenced by Joan Rivers's *Can We Shop* show; Softbank on Hand, a CD-ROM with more than a hundred commercial programs for software shoppers; and the purchase by Home Shopping Network of the Internet Shopping Network to establish home shopping via computer. Some shopping channels use high-pressure tactics, such as horn blowing and whistle blasting to get viewers' attention, while others use more low-key marketing approaches. Large retail companies, such as Macy's and Spiegel, began their own cable channels, which combined programming and entertainment with selling. These retailers expressed great interest in interactive television shopping, in which the home consumer can call up any product at will, view it from various sides, obtain detailed information about the product, order by punching in a credit card number, and have it delivered within twenty-four hours. The next stage in interactive television may be "virtual shopping," in which the viewer will be able to "try on" a garment by creating a computerized self-image on the screen, realistic to skin tone, color of hair and eyes, and body measurements.

By the end of the twentieth century, television home shopping channels continued to generate a brisk trade for retailers. However, corporate mergers between retail, media, and Internet companies had all but ensured that future innovations in home shopping would be oriented around the "information appliance," the much anticipated marriage of television and the Internet. Moreover, in the heated race to gain footholds in electronic commerce, the traditional television-based home shopping networks did not always fare well. In May 1999, investors in the profitless online portal Lycos rejected a proposal to merge with Barry Diller's Home Shopping Network, even though the latter made a profit.

BIBLIOGRAPHY

Evans, David S., and Richard Schmalensee. *Paying with Plastic: The Digital Revolution in Buying and Borrowing.* Cambridge, Mass.: MIT Press, 1999.

Kare-Silver, Michael de. *E-Shock, the Electronic Shopping Revolution: Strategies for Retailers and Manufacturers.* New York: AMACOM, 1999.

Wice, Nathaniel. "Lycos Shareholders Scare Off Suitor."*Time Digital* (May 10, 1999).

John J. Byrne/A. R.

See also **Electronic Commerce; Internet; Mail-Order Houses; Television: Programming and Influence.**

HOMEOPATHY, a system of medicine developed by the German physician Samuel Hahnemann in the 1790s, was introduced in the United States in the 1820s by Hahnemann's colleagues and students. One of these, Constantine Hering, founded the world's first homeopathic medical school in Allentown, Pennsylvania, in 1835. With Hering and his students in the vanguard, American homeopathy became the world leader in the field for the rest of the nineteenth century. After falling into relative obscurity after the 1910s, homeopathy has enjoyed a significant revival among consumers and medical professionals since the 1970s.

Homeopathy is based on an ancient medical principle, the law of similars, from the observation that a substance that causes a particular set of symptoms in a healthy person can cure those symptoms when they arise in the process of an illness. Homeopathic medicines are investigated in provings, standardized trials in healthy human subjects; information from accidental overdoses and poisonings and from verified clinical cures is also included in the profile of a medicine's sphere of action. A second fundamental principle is the minimum dose: homeopaths have found that the most effective medicinal dose is the smallest one capable of causing a curative response. Homeopathic medicines are manufactured by potentization, a process of serial dilution and agitation that produces microdoses of the natural substances from which the medicines are derived. A final principle is holism and individualization: the medicine is selected on the basis of the total symptom picture of the particular case.

Professionalizing early through the establishment of schools and hospitals, homeopaths formed the first national medical organization in North America, the American Institute of Homeopathy, in 1844. Throughout the rest of the nineteenth century, homeopathic medical schools in Philadelphia, New York, Cleveland, Chicago, and cities as far west as San Francisco produced a steady stream of practitioners, with a high of almost 500 graduates in 1897; on average, 12 percent of graduates were women. Resistance from orthodox physicians continued throughout the century in the form of professional ostracism, although by 1902 it was estimated that 15,000 licensed American physicians included homeopathy in their practices.

Homeopathy's success in the nineteenth century can be attributed to several factors. Its efficacy in epidemics of cholera, yellow fever, and influenza as well as in the treatment of chronic and intractable diseases was striking and converted many physicians; its adaptability for home care attracted mothers, who carried it into their communities; and its perceived affinities with Swedenborgianism, a mystical Christian philosophy, made it popular among the intellectual and social elite. Many prominent figures used homeopathy, including Elizabeth Cady Stanton, James Garfield, and the family of William and Henry James.

Historians have argued that ideas derived from homeopathy influenced the direction of conventional medicine in the second half of the nineteenth century, with the concept of the minimum dose encouraging the turn away from the drastic treatments of conventional medicine and the law of similars leading, in a creative misreading, to the development of vaccination. The assimilation of certain aspects of homeopathy by orthodox physicians is one factor cited for its decline, others being controversy among homeopaths about therapeutic techniques, the growing acceptance of empiricist laboratory science and especially bacteriology as medical authority, and the economic dominance of the orthodox medical-pharmaceutical industry. The 1910 Flexner Report on American medical education may have hastened the closing of some homeopathic colleges. It seems clear that the homeopathic medical schools, employing orthodox practitioners among their faculty, produced a hybrid profession that could not maintain a separate identity in the face of an increasingly powerful orthodox medical system.

Homeopathy's eclipse during the twentieth century is measured by a steep decline in its number of practitioners and by the homeopathic colleges' closing or conversion to conventional training. Still, professional organizations provided education for practitioners and consumers, and a handful of physicians kept the discipline alive. In the 1970s, disenchantment with the conventional medical system led consumers and practitioners to explore homeopathy among other forms of alternative and complementary medicine. Since then the shift from crisis intervention to preventive medicine, the concern over increasingly prevalent chronic disease, the search for cost-effective treatments, and the rejection of materialist philosophies in health care have fueled homeopathy's swift growth in popularity.

Developments since the 1980s include the establishment of postgraduate and comprehensive training programs throughout the United States; the 1991 founding of the Council for Homeopathic Certification, a profession-wide board that sets standards and conducts testing of practitioners; and the steady growth of membership in the National Center for Homeopathy, an educational organization for consumers and professionals. An increase in the amount of legal action against practitioners has paralleled the rebirth of the profession, as some licensing boards consider homeopathy to be outside their licensees' scope of practice. However, leading medical journals have published articles on clinical and scientific research in homeopathy; the number of medical schools offering some exposure to homeopathy is increasing; and many states have moved to license naturopathic physicians, making homeopathy more widely available. Its cost effectiveness has attracted some insurance companies' attention, but homeopathy's ultimate position in relation to the conventional medical system remains to be seen.

BIBLIOGRAPHY

Coulter, Harris. *Divided Legacy: A History of the Schism in Medical Thought.* 4 vols. Berkeley: North Atlantic Books, 1973, 1975, 1977, 1994. See especially vols. 3 and 4 for treatment of homeopathy in the United States.

Rogers, Naomi. *An Alternative Path: The Making and Remaking of Hahnemann Medical College and Hospital of Philadelphia.* New Brunswick, N.J.: Rutgers University Press, 1998.

Winston, Julian. *The Faces of Homeopathy: An Illustrated History of the First 200 Years.* Tawa, N.Z.: Great Auk Publishing, 1999.

Ann Jerome Croce

See also **Medicine, Alternative; Swedenborgian Churches.**

HOMESTEAD MOVEMENT. It is difficult to fix a starting date for the movement that culminated in 1862 with the passage of the Homestead Act. The notion of free land had been ingrained in the thoughts and minds of settlers moving westward since colonial days, but until the West became politically powerful, the demand passed unheeded. The revenue motive was basic in determining the public land policy of the new nation, and more than three-quarters of a century elapsed between the passage of the Land Ordinance of 1785 and the passage of the Homestead Act.

Nevertheless, since its establishment, Congress had received petitions requesting that free land be given to settlers. In 1797, the settlers of the Ohio River area submitted such a petition, and two years later the residents of the Mississippi Territory followed suit. In 1812, Representative Jeremiah Morrow of Ohio presented a request from the True American Society, arguing that every American was entitled to a piece of free land. A few years later, in 1825, Senator Thomas Hart Benton of Missouri proposed a law that would give free land to settlers. By the 1830s and 1840s, the movement for free land had gained support from the president, organized labor, and the newly formed National Reform Party. In 1832, President Andrew Jackson weighed in on the issue when he stated, "The public lands should cease as soon as practicable to be a source of revenue." Thus, the basic doctrines of homestead legislation steadily attracted adherents.

In 1846, Felix G. McConnell of Alabama and Andrew Johnson of Tennessee introduced homestead bills in Congress. The latter was an ardent supporter of the homestead movement until final passage of the bill in 1862. A general bill for free land had come to a vote in Congress in 1852, but it was defeated in the Senate. At the same time, Horace Greeley, publisher of the *New York Tribune*, presented his views on the matter, stating that the public land system should "be so modified that every person needing Land may take possession of any quarter-section not previously located, and that none other than a person needing land shall be allowed to acquire it at all."

The homestead movement became a central political issue in 1848, when the Free Soil Party voiced its support for free land for settlers "in consideration of the expenses they incur in making settlements in the wilderness . . . and of the public benefits resulting therefrom." Four years later, the party supported the ideal even more vigorously but on different grounds. In 1852 it asserted that "all men have a natural right to a portion of the soil; and that, as the use of the soil is indispensable to life, the right of all men to the soil is as sacred as their right to life itself." Therefore, the party contended, "the public lands of the United States belong to the people, and should not be sold to individuals nor granted to corporations, but should be held as a sacred trust for the benefit of the people, and should be granted in limited quantities, free of cost, to landless settlers." These two platforms contained the primary arguments used by advocates of free land, namely, reward for public service and natural right.

Although the homestead movement had numerous supporters, it also faced strong opposition, as evidenced by the failure of a bill to pass before 1862. Many southerners opposed homestead legislation because they feared it would result in the peopling of the territories by antislavery settlers. On the other hand, many easterners disapproved of the movement because they feared its success would adversely affect the eastern economy. They contended westward migration would increase, thereby lowering land values in the East and depriving the federal government of an important revenue source. The Know-Nothing Party and other anti-alien groups opposed the movement because it would give free land to foreign immigrants.

In 1860, the homestead movement experienced both a setback and a small victory. In that year, Congress passed a bill that would have sold land for 25 cents an acre, but President James Buchanan vetoed the bill, arguing that it was unconstitutional. At the same time, however, the new Republican Party demanded that Congress pass a homestead bill. A Republican victory and southern secession enabled the party to carry out its program. On 20 May 1862, President Abraham Lincoln signed the Homestead Act, and the goal sought by generations of westerners since the inception of the public land policy was finally achieved.

The Homestead Act allowed "any person who is the head of a family, or who has arrived at the age of twenty-one years, and is a citizen of the United States, or who shall have filed his declaration of intention to become such" the right to claim 160 acres of land, a quarter-section, for free. The claimant need only pay a small filing fee and live on and improve the land for five years. If he so chose, the homesteader could buy the land for $1.25 an acre after six months. Originally, settlers could only homestead on surveyed land, but in 1880, Congress extended the act to include the unsurveyed public domain.

Although approximately 274 million acres were claimed and 400,000 farms were established under the Homestead Act, the law never came close to meeting the expectations of its supporters. The lands of the West were too arid to support traditional farming techniques, and a farm of 160 acres was simply too small. Congress attempted to address the problems with a series of acts passed between 1873 and 1916. The Timber Culture Act (1873) granted 160 acres to the head of a family who agreed to plant and maintain forty acres of trees for ten years. The Desert Land Act (1877) encouraged irrigation of arid lands by granting 640 acres at $1.25 an acre to anyone who agreed to irrigate the land within three years of filing. In 1909, the Enlarged Homestead Act expanded the original act to 320 acres instead of 160. The Stock-Raising Homestead Act (1916) authorized homestead entries of 640 acres on grazing lands. Congress even applied the homestead principle to Indian lands with the passage of the Dawes General Allotment Act in 1877. These acts, however, also failed to achieve the desired results.

BIBLIOGRAPHY

Fite, Gilbert C. *The Farmers' Frontier, 1865–1900.* New York: Holt, Rinehart, 1966.

Hibbard, Benjamin Horace. *A History of the Public Land Policies.* Madison: University of Wisconsin Press, 1965.

Shannon, Fred A. *The Farmer's Last Frontier: Agriculture, 1860–1897.* New York: Farrar and Rinehart, 1945.

White, Richard. *"It's Your Misfortune and None of My Own:" A History of the American West.* Norman: University of Oklahoma Press, 1991.

Jennifer L. Bertolet
Dan E. Clark

See also **Free Soil Party; Land Acts; Land Policy; Timber Culture Act; Westward Migration.**

HOMESTEAD STRIKE, at the Carnegie Steel Company plant at Homestead, Pennsylvania, in 1892, was one of the most violent labor struggles in U.S. history. The company, owned by Andrew Carnegie and managed by Henry Clay Frick, was determined to break the Amalgamated Association of Iron, Steel, and Tin Workers union, which represented 750 of Homestead's 3,800 laborers. Frick closed the mill and locked the workers out on 1 July, after they rejected his proposed 22 percent wage cut. While Carnegie remained at his castle in Scotland, Frick hired three hundred Pinkerton Detective Agency guards to battle the workers. A gunfight erupted when the Pinkertons attempted to land at the Monongahela River docks, and altogether at least sixteen people were killed and more than sixty wounded. The fighting ended on 12 July, when Pennsylvania National Guard troops arrived. The lockout continued for almost five months, while steel production continued at Carnegie's other plants. The Amalgamated Association was ultimately driven from Homestead, forcing the remaining desperate workers to return to their jobs. In the following decade, the average workday rose from eight to twelve hours, and wages dropped an average of 25 percent. By 1903 all other steel plants in the country had defeated the union as well.

BIBLIOGRAPHY

Demarest, David P., and Fannia Weingartner, eds. *"The River Ran Red": Homestead 1892.* Pittsburgh: University of Pittsburgh Press, 1992.

Krause, Paul. *The Battle for Homestead, 1880–1892: Politics, Culture, and Steel.* Pittsburgh: University of Pittsburgh Press, 1992.

John Cashman

See also **Steel Strikes.**

HOMESTEADERS AND THE CATTLE INDUSTRY. Beginning in the late 1860s, cattle grazing on the open range of the western plains from Texas to Montana became the major industry. During the years following the Civil War, a vast stream of cattle poured north out of Texas to COW TOWNS in Kansas and Nebraska. From these towns, fat, mature animals went to market while young steers and breeding animals traveled farther north or west to stock new ranges.

Most of the cattle driven north each year grazed on ranges in the public domain throughout western Kansas, Nebraska, Dakota, Montana, Wyoming, and other western states and territories. Ranchers held them there for growth and fattening. The unwritten law of the range known as "cow custom" determined the boundaries of each rancher's pasturelands. Usually, the ranch's headquarters lay near the center of the range, and along the ranch's borders were cow camps from which riders looked after the cattle and kept them within the limits of their own range. Despite their efforts, some would stray across the line onto the pasturelands of neighboring ranchers, which made it necessary to hold roundups each spring and autumn. At the spring roundup, COWBOYS branded calves. At the fall roundup, grazers separated their fat, mature animals from the remainder and sent them to market for slaughter.

Cowboys drove cattle over the state lands of western Texas and northward from Texas over the great Indian reservations of Indian Territory, as well as those farther north, and over the public domain of the central and northern plains. All of this huge region constituted the so-called cow country. Settlers taking up homesteads steadily advanced westward along its eastern border, but for a time, ranchers could replace the erstwhile grazing area lost to farmers by opening large tracts of hitherto unwatered lands for use as pasturage with the construction of dams across ravines and the drilling of deep wells from which windmills pumped water.

The first shipments of dressed beef to Europe, especially Great Britain, began in 1875. Shipments steadily increased until Europe imported more than 50 million pounds in 1878 and more than 100 million pounds in 1881. The enormous influx of American beef so alarmed the cattle raisers of northern Britain that a parliamentary commission came to the United States to visit the range area and report on conditions. Its report, publicized in 1884, told of great profits to be made in ranching, which encouraged British investors to send huge sums of capital to the United States for investment in ranching enterprises. Many Britons came to the cow country to give their personal attention to ranching. By 1884 British investors had placed more than $30 million of capital into ranching on the Great Plains. Among the large British enterprises were the Prairie Land and Cattle Company, the Matador, and the Espuela Land and Cattle Company.

An enthusiasm for grazing cattle on the open range amounting almost to a craze had also swept over the United States before 1885. Prominent lawyers, U.S. senators, bankers, and other businessmen throughout the eastern United States formed cattle companies to take advantage of the opportunities offered for ranching on the great open ranges to the west. The destruction of the buffalo herds made it necessary to feed the many large tribes of western Indians, and this resulted in the awarding of valuable beef contracts for that purpose with the privilege of pasturing herds upon the various reservations.

The invention of BARBED WIRE and the rapid extension of its use after 1875 brought about the enclosure of considerable tracts of pastureland. Congress enacted laws that forbade the fencing of lands of the public domain, and orders of the Indian Bureau prohibited the enclosure of lands on Indian reservations. While the United States government and its various agencies could not strictly enforce such laws and orders, they were not without effect.

Perhaps the year 1885 marks the peak of the open-range cattle industry. By that time, most of the range was fully stocked and much of it overstocked. During the summer of 1886, ranchers drove large herds north from Texas and spread them over the ranges in the most reckless fashion possible. Then came the terrible winter of 1886–87 in which hundreds of thousands of cattle died of cold and starvation. Spring came to find nearly every rancher on the central and northern plains facing ruin. The open-range cattle industry never recovered from the results of that tragic winter.

Moreover, homesteaders, contemptuously called nesters by ranchers, rapidly were settling the range area, including large Indian reservations. Ranchers largely had kept homesteaders to the east between 1867 and 1885, but on 25 February 1885, Congress passed a law that prohibited interference with settlers. On 7 August 1885, President Grover Cleveland followed it with an enforcement proclamation. Beginning in the spring of 1886, settlers, who streamed west in covered wagons on a 1,000-mile front, occupied the public domain on the plains. In many regions, sheep were replacing cattle anyway. The struggle between ranchers and farmers continued in some isolated parts of the mountain states until the early twentieth century, but in most areas, the end of the open-range cattle period arrived by 1890.

BIBLIOGRAPHY

Evans, Simon M., Sarah Carter, and Bill Yeo, ed. *Cowboys, Ranchers, and the Cattle Business: Cross-border Perspectives on Ranching History.* Calgary: University of Calgary Press, 2000.

Jordan, Terry G. *Trails to Texas: Southern Roots of Western Cattle Ranching.* Lincoln: University of Nebraska Press, 1981.

Massey, Sara R., ed. *Black Cowboys of Texas.* College Station: Texas A & M University Press, 2000.

Patterson, Paul E. *Great Plains Cattle Empire: Thatcher Brothers and Associates, 1875–1945.* Lubbock: Texas Tech University Press, 2000.

Remley, David A. *Bell Ranch: Cattle Ranching in the Southwest, 1824–1947.* Albuquerque: University of New Mexico Press, 1993.

Bliss Isely / A. E.

See also **Agriculture; Cattle; Cattle Brands; Cattle Drives; Chisholm Trail; Livestock Industry; Meatpacking; Rodeos; Trail Drivers.**

HOMEWORK. Schoolwork assigned to be done outside of the school hours. The history of homework in the United States is a varied one, both in substance and in perceived value. Over the years, its presentation has changed markedly, and its popularity has waxed and waned.

In the early 1800s, in an agrarian society, the school year was short and homework was of little significance. There was little time for it, because children living on farms had a multitude of chores. In the late 1800s, as a result of the industrial revolution, families moved to the cities and became more urbanized. At this time, educational philosophers perceived the mind as a passive, blank slate upon which learning would be imprinted. The formal learning of the time, in large part, consisted of a classroom experience that entailed much memorization, drill, and recitation. Homework, which was structured similarly, was deemed an important reinforcement of what was learned. Many people, however, believed that homework could cause physical, emotional, or mental illness, since it kept children from fresh air and physical exercise.

In the early 1900s, educator Edward Bok was instrumental in addressing and supporting concerns about the value of homework. In his writings he suggested that no homework should be assigned to those students less than 15 years of age and only one hour per night to those students 15 and older. The Progressive Education Movement had begun to ask questions about the structure of teaching. Supporters of this movement viewed learning as an active process of problem solving, far different from the passive learning philosophy of the past. This change in perception caused memorizing and reciting to lose its place as the primary approach to education. In 1930, the Society of the Abolition of Homework was established. This group stressed its concerns about the health risks that members felt homework presented, including eyestrain, lack of sleep, limited development in certain areas due to lack of free play, and even physical deformities.

In response to Russia's launching of the space satellite *Sputnik* in 1957, the pendulum swung again. A fifty-year trend toward less homework came to a halt. As the United States became committed to compete with the Russians, a cry came out for more and better education in both math and science. The vast majority of educators and parents called for more homework. The National Defense Education Act supported this effort and, in turn, the value of homework. By the 1960s, homework was seen as a major factor in scholastic achievement, although in 1966 the National Education Association (NEA) did suggest some limits in amount. The NEA suggested no homework for the early elementary school child; no more than one hour a day, four days a week, for upper elementary and junior high school students; and approximately one and one-half hours a night for senior high school students.

In the 1980s, policymakers continued to encourage educators to increase the amount of homework given. In 1983 the government's document, *A Nation at Risk*, declared that much of what ailed the U.S. economy could be attributed to the inadequacies of the schools and stressed the need for more homework and a longer school day. Even though researcher Harris Cooper reported in 1989 that his extensive studies indicated the amount of homework done in the elementary grades has little or no effect on later academic achievement, homework's value at all levels was continually supported by the vast majority of educators. Comparisons to the educational approaches, school hours, and the amount of homework assigned by other countries became prevalent. Although ongoing research is inconclusive, studies have indicated that students in other countries (whether they are assigned more homework than U.S. students or not) still outperform U.S. students on tests in math and science. This would bring into question the value of increasing homework for students in U.S. schools.

The debate continues. At the beginning of the twenty-first century, new questions and concerns about homework and approaches to homework have evolved. Among them: "Is a more intensified approach to education, including a great deal of homework, necessary for us as a nation to compete in a global marketplace?" and "Is it fair and healthy for the schools to impose more work on families who are generally overworked and who already have their free time overtaxed?"

Studies done at Carnegie-Mellon University show that real competence is the result of extensive practice. An additional finding from the 1999 National Assessment for Educational Progress concludes that 17-year-olds who typically spend more that two hours a day doing homework have higher average reading scores than those who spend less than an hour per day or no time at all on homework.

Experts perceive that homework is a good way to review, reinforce, and practice what has been taught. Homework is also considered to be a good way to assimilate new information related to what has been studied. In addition, homework is judged as an avenue that allows teachers to assess students' understanding of what has been presented. It is also seen as a method of preparation for the next day's work and a valuable way to study for tests. In addition, it is purported to teach direction following, organizational skills, time management, and research skills, as well as supporting the communication between parents and the school. Some feel that homework builds character.

Negative arguments include that homework suppresses creativity and chokes the desire to learn. Many also observe that it creates unnecessary anxiety for the child and the family and can have a negative impact on the family as a whole. Others feel that assigning homework is unfair without support available to children whose families have little time or little knowledge about the technology taught and the approaches to teaching that are considered valuable today.

At the beginning of the twenty-first century, homework was given in greater quantities than in the past, in part due to the increased difficulty in getting into top colleges and the more challenging job market that faced graduates. The resources available to students who wished support with their homework also grew. Homework hotlines were available, as were special homework tutors and tutorial programs offered in learning centers. In addition, numerous Internet nodes offered homework support, and many schools had afterschool programs where time was set aside for children to work on their homework under supervision.

BIBLIOGRAPHY

Cooper, Harris M. *The Battle over Homework.* Thousand Oaks, Calif.: Corwin Press, 1994.

Kralovec, Etta, and John Buell. *The End of Homework.* Boston. Beacon Press. 2000.

National Center for Educational Statistics. *The Condition of Education 2001.* Washington, D.C.: Department of Education, 2001.

Dawn Duquès

See also **Education.**

HOMOSEXUALITY. *See* **Sexual Orientation.**

HONKY-TONK GIRLS were women with no particular skill who entertained cowboys in saloons, later called honky-tonks, during the 1800s in the state of Texas. They would sing and dance and drink alongside any cowboy they met in the saloon. They were carefree, happy people who made the cowboys feel important for the evening.

The spirit of the honky-tonk has evolved into modern-day country music. The songs of country singer Loretta Lynn, whose first big hit in 1960 was titled, "Honky Tonk Girl," are classic examples of honky-tonk music. Most honky-tonk music contains stories about religion, family, and hard luck. Its roots are with the common people, similar to the roughhouse cowboy.

BIBLIOGRAPHY

Honky-Tonk Music, Microsoft Encarta Encyclopedia, 2002.

Rice, James, "Texas Honky Tonk Music," 1985, available from http://www.ssqq.com/information.

Donna W. Reamy

HONOLULU. Honolulu, the capital of the state of Hawaii, is on the southeast coast of the island of Oahu. Its name means "sheltered harbor." This "crossroads of the Pacific" between the Americas and Asia is an export-import site for goods and people.

As a consequence of high-rise construction, Honolulu is America's most crowded city. According to the 2000 Census, about 80 percent (876,156) of Hawaii's residents live in Honolulu's 60 square miles. This is about 1,460 persons per square mile, compared to 79.6 persons per square mile in the United States overall. This ranks Honolulu among the fifty largest U.S. cities, and counties and fifty-first largest Standard Metropolitan Statistical Area.

More than 21 percent of Honolulu's residents are foreign born. (Only Los Angeles and New York City have higher percentages.) English is a second language for more than 26 percent. Twenty-one percent are white and 10 percent are Hispanic, African American, or Native American. More than 65 percent are Asian. The largest Asian immigrant populations are Filipino, Japanese, Korean, Chinese, and Vietnamese.

Diversity is not new. Tahitians arrived in pre-recorded history, mixing with already-present islanders. The British discovered the bay settlement in 1794. Honolulu became a world hub for traders, whalers, and fishermen. Western missionaries followed in the 1820s; Chinese and Filipino plantation laborers came in the 1830s. By 1884, Honolulu's Chinatown had five thousand inhabitants and Chinese owned 60 percent of wholesale and retail establishments and 85 percent of restaurants. Military occupations—Russian (1816), British (1843), and French (1849)—added variety. From 1845, Honolulu was home to Hawaii's monarchy. American investors moved in after the treaty of reciprocity between Hawaii and the United States in 1875.

Incorporated as a city in 1907, Honolulu is the state's commercial and industrial hub and the headquarters for county, state, and regional federal government institutions. Its economy is tied to Asian and American markets. Military installations, including Pearl Harbor naval base, are important strategically and economically; Japan considered Pearl Harbor important enough to bomb in 1941. Honolulu International Airport is among the busiest U.S. airports. Tourism contributes to skyscraper hotels, shopping centers, and retail businesses. Honolulu harbor bustles with luxury cruise liners, freighters, and intra-island barges. Extensive docks and warehouses serve pineapple canneries, sugar refineries, garment manufacturers, dairy enterprises, and aluminum, cement, oil, and steel industries.

Educational institutions—the University of Hawaii, Chaminade University, and Hawaii Pacific University—contribute to research and development industries in astronomy, biomedicine, geophysics, oceanography, and satellite communications. World-class cultural institutions include Bishop Museum, a premier resource for Pacific culture studies; the Honolulu Academy of Arts, among the world's most beautiful museums; and the Iolani Palace, the only royal palace in the United States.

A temperate climate of from seventy-two to seventy-eight degrees year-round supports agriculture and outdoor recreation. But like most cities in the early twenty-first century, Honolulu faces environmental and social issues such as urban sprawl, water quality, and open space preservation.

BIBLIOGRAPHY

Beechert, Edward D. *Honolulu: Crossroads of the Pacific.* Columbia: University of South Carolina Press, 1991.

Stone, Scott C. S. *Honolulu: Heart of Hawaii.* Tulsa, Okla.: Continental Heritage Press, 1983.

Ellen Sue Blakey

See also **Asian Americans; Hawaii; Pearl Harbor.**

HOOD'S TENNESSEE CAMPAIGN

HOOD'S TENNESSEE CAMPAIGN (October–December 1864). After the evacuation of Atlanta, Confederate president Jefferson Davis visited General J. B. Hood's army and proposed a move northward to cut General William Tecumseh Sherman's communications to Chattanooga, with the possibility of moving on through Tennessee and Kentucky to "the banks of the Ohio."

In an effort to lure Sherman west, Hood marched in early October to Tuscumbia on the Tennessee River. He waited there for three weeks anticipating Sherman's pursuit. Instead, Sherman, forewarned by a speech from Davis, sent the Army of the Ohio under General J. M. Schofield to reinforce Colonel George H. Thomas's force at Nashville. On 15 November, Sherman began his ruinous raid to the sea.

Hood ignored Sherman and pushed into Tennessee to scatter the Union forces gathering at Nashville. On 29 November, he failed to cut off Schofield's retreating army near Spring Hill; the next day, Hood was repulsed with heavy losses at the Battle of Franklin. Schofield hurriedly retreated into Nashville. Hood followed, but delayed for two weeks, awaiting Thomas's move. On 15 and 16 December, Thomas attacked with precision, crushed the left of Hood's line, and forced the Confederate army to withdraw to shorter lines. For the first time, a veteran Confederate army was driven in disorder from the field of battle. Thomas's cavalry pursued vigorously but was unable to disperse Hood's army, which crossed the Tennessee River and turned westward to Corinth, Mississippi. Hood soon relinquished his command to General Richard Taylor. The war in the West was over.

BIBLIOGRAPHY

Ash, Stephen V. *Middle Tennessee Society Transformed, 1860–1870: War and Peace in the Upper South.* Baton Rouge: Louisiana State University Press, 1988.

Groom, Winston. *Shrouds of Glory: From Atlanta to Nashville: The Last Great Campaign of the Civil War.* New York: Atlantic Monthly Press, 1995.

Hay, Thomas R. *Hood's Tennessee Campaign.* New York: Neale, 1929.

Thomas Robson Hay/A. R.

See also **Nashville, Battle of; Sherman's March to the Sea; Tennessee, Army of.**

Hoosac Tunnel. The west portal, North Adams, Mass., as seen in a photograph taken c. 1900. LIBRARY OF CONGRESS

HOOSAC TUNNEL, opened in 1876 after 22 years of construction that claimed nearly 200 lives, extends 4.73 miles through the Hoosac Mountains of Massachusetts, a southern extension of the Green Mountains. It was started in 1855 by the Troy and Greenfield Railroad as part of a plan to divert western trade to Boston. The state aided the railroad but was forced to take over the tunnel when the railroad failed in 1863. In 1887 the tunnel was turned over to the Fitchburg Railroad, which became a part of the Boston and Maine. Compressed air drills were first used in the United States in 1866 in the construction of this tunnel.

BIBLIOGRAPHY

Carman, Bernard R. *Hoot Toot & Whistle: The Story of the Hoosac Tunnel & Wilmington Railroad.* Brattleboro, Vt.: Greene Press, 1963.

Cleveland, F. A., and F. W. Powell. *Railroad Promotion and Capitalization.* New York: Longmans, Green & Co., 1981.

James D. Magee/A. R.

See also **Allegheny Mountains, Routes Across; Railroads; Tunnels.**

HOOVER COMMISSIONS. In the mid-1900s, two commissions on organization of the executive branch of government were set up by unanimous votes of the two chambers of the U.S. Congress. Appointed by President Harry S. Truman, former president Herbert Hoover served as chairman of the first commission, which functioned from 1947 to 1949 to deal with the growth of government during World War II. Under President Dwight D. Eisenhower, Hoover chaired the second commission (1953–1955), dealing with government growth during the Korean War. Both commissions sought to reduce expenditures to the lowest amount consistent with essential services and to end duplication and overlapping of government services and activities. The commissions were nonpartisan. Of the personnel for each, four were named by the president, four by the vice president, and four by the Speaker of the House.

The first commission created twenty-four task forces of experts to study as many phases of government; the second created nineteen. Task forces reported to the commission, which, after studies by their staffs and members, reported their findings to Congress. The first commission made 273 recommendations; the second, 314. Of these, about half could be carried out by administrative action; the rest required legislation. More than 70 percent of the recommendations were put into effect.

Hoover estimated that the first commission brought a total savings of $7 billion and the second more than $3 billion yearly. Among reforms resulting from the commissions' studies were passage of the Military Unification Act of 1949; creation of the General Services Agency; formation of the Department of Health, Education, and Welfare; cost accounting and modernized budgeting; reduction of government competition with private business; development of a federal career service; coordination of federal research; and a general reduction of red tape.

BIBLIOGRAPHY

Best, Gary Dean. *Herbert Hoover: The Postpresidential Years, 1933–1964.* Stanford, Calif.: Hoover Institution Press, 1983.

Smith, Richard Norton. *An Uncommon Man: The Triumph of Herbert Hoover.* New York: Simon and Schuster, 1984.

Neil MacNeil/A. G.

See also **Bureaucracy.**

HOOVER DAM. Located in the Black Canyon on the Colorado River, Hoover Dam lies about thirty miles southeast of Las Vegas, Nevada. The federal government built it for flood control, navigation, irrigation, water storage, and power generation. Farmers in the region experienced disastrous Colorado River floods before the dam was constructed.

Herbert Hoover first proposed a dam for the Colorado River when he became secretary of commerce in 1921. At the time his plan involved a dam in Boulder Canyon. After he became president, Hoover proposed an "upper" and a "lower" basin, a compromise that made a dam possible by dividing the water among the states af-

Hoover Dam. An aerial view of the impressive engineering feat, which impounds the vast reservoir called Lake Mead. © CHARLES E. ROTKIN/CORBIS

fected by the river and its tributaries. Arizona, California, Colorado, Nevada, New Mexico, Utah, and Wyoming entered the Colorado River Compact in 1922, and in 1928 Congress authorized the construction of Boulder Dam, which later became the Hoover Dam.

During the Great Depression the government contractor, Six Companies, six formerly independent companies that had merged to get the job, constructed the dam, the highest concrete arch dam in the United States. Lake Mead, the reservoir the dam impounds, is one of the largest human-made lakes in the world, with an area of 247 square miles. The dam itself is 726.4 feet from the foundation rock on the roadway to the crest, with towers and ornaments extending another 40 feet above the crest. It weighs more than 6.6 million tons. With 17 turbines, the power facility has a nameplate capacity of 2.074 million kilowatts.

Of the thousands of people who worked on the dam between 1930 and 1936, ninety-six workers died from accidents directly relating to the building of the dam and dozens more from related ailments. Before the dam could even be started, Boulder City had to be built to house the workers, and miles of highways and railroads from the dam site to Boulder City and from there to Las Vegas had to be constructed. In the first step of building the dam, men attached to ropes were hoisted over the edge of the canyon, where they scraped loose rock from the canyon walls by hand. Four tunnels diverted the flow of the river, and a ton of dynamite was required to dig fourteen feet. The dam itself was made up of columns filled slowly with concrete. To cool the chemical heat released by the concrete, ice water ran through the equivalent of 582 miles of one-inch diameter pipes embedded in the concrete. After the columns were filled and cooled, grout was poured between them to make the structure monolithic.

The Hoover Dam was seen as a triumph of humans over nature. It was the first human-made structure to exceed the masonry mass of the Great Pyramid of Giza. By the twenty-first century the dam was regarded ambivalently, sustaining environmentalists' criticism that it in fact damaged or destroyed an ecosystem.

BIBLIOGRAPHY

Carothers, Steven W., and Bryan T. Brown. *The Colorado River through Grand Canyon: Natural History and Human Change.* Tucson: University of Arizona Press, 1991.

Dunar, Andrew J., and Dennis McBride. *Building Hoover Dam: An Oral History of the Great Depression.* New York: Twayne, 1993.

Stevens, Joseph E. *Hoover Dam: An American Adventure.* Norman: University of Oklahoma Press, 1988.

Ruth Kaplan

See also **Conservation; Hydroelectric Power.**

HOPEDALE COMMUNITY. *See* **Utopian Communities.**

HOPEWELL is the name given to a distinctive, widely shared cultural expression flourishing between A.D. 1 and 400 among locally rooted societies from the Kansas City area to upstate New York, and from southern Ontario and northern Wisconsin to peninsular Florida. Hopewell has no single point of origin, being drawn from diverse cultural traditions. Single autonomous small villages dominated cultural and political life. However, these interconnected prehistoric cultures have a common identity based upon their distinctive artifacts and the equally distinctive style with which these artifacts were decorated. Much of this artwork has been found in graves and graveside areas in and under burial mounds, and unmounded structures connected with burial rites. The singular decorative style developed in the Lower Mississippi Valley centuries earlier. During the Hopewellian Period, the Marksville cultural tradition of the Lower Valley exerted particularly strong influences upon the Havana Tradition of the Illinois Valley and adjoining Midwest. A hallmark of this period was far-flung trade in ritually important materials such as obsidian from western Oregon, silver from Ontario, native copper from the Kewennaw peninsula of Michigan, shark teeth, alligator teeth, and marine shells from the Gulf Coast of Florida, and sheets of mica from the Appalachians of North Carolina.

Hopewell. An aerial view of the Great Serpent Mound in southern Ohio (now in a state park): about 1,330 feet long, 20 feet wide, and an average of 3 feet high. LIBRARY OF CONGRESS

Religion was dominated by shamanic practices that included tobacco smoking. Stone smoking pipes and other carvings evince a strong affinity to the animal world, particularly in the depictions of monstrous human and animal combinations. These artifacts mark the earliest archaeologically documented use of domesticated tobacco.

Hopewell's distinctive technological accomplishments include various objects of cold hammered native copper such as prestigious ornaments (breastplates, skullcap headdresses, mica cutouts, and copper beads and bracelets), ritual equipment (pan pipes), and utilitarian pieces (ax and adze heads, and awls). Spool-shaped ornaments hammered from copper and secured in the earlobes required intricate fabrication and represent the apogee of Hopewellian technical expertise. Other distinctive artifacts included clay figurines, meteoric iron nodules, and atlatl weights.

Hopewell also produced some of the most noteworthy earthen architecture of the Eastern Woodlands. The most distinctive stamp to earthen constructions in this era are the geometric embankments that enclose communal ritual areas. The famous octagon embankment at Newark, Ohio, measures a maximum of 1,720 feet across. Large squares and circles often conjoined in complex but geometrically regular configurations testify to the knowledge of a simple but sophisticated mathematics that was applied to a complicated symbolism. Most mounds were dome-shaped creations of circular or oval ground plans, and some attained enormous size. The earliest platform mounds make their appearance during this period. Notable examples of earthworks include Mound City (Ohio), Seip (Ohio), Fort Ancient (Ohio), Marksville (Louisiana), and Pinson (Tennessee).

Hopewell's agriculture was based upon domesticated plants native to the Eastern Woodlands including squash, sunflower, sumpweed and chenopodium. In this period, maize, the tropical grain that was to become so important a thousand years later, made its first appearance in small amounts.

BIBLIOGRAPHY

Brose, David S., and N'omi B. Greber, eds. *Hopewell Archaeology: The Chillicothe Conference.* Kent, Ohio: Kent State University Press, 1979.

Kennedy, Roger G. *Hidden Cities: The Discovery and Loss of Ancient North American Civilization.* New York: Free Press, 1994.

Pacheco, Paul J., ed. *A View from the Core: A Synthesis of Ohio Hopewell Archaeology.* Columbus: Ohio Archaeological Council, 1996.

Romain, William F. *Mysteries of the Hopewell: Astronomers, Geometers, and Magicians of the Eastern Woodlands.* Akron, Ohio: University of Akron Press, 2000.

James A. Brown

See also **Archaeology and Prehistory of North America; Indian Mounds.**

HOPI. The name Hopi is derived from the word *Hopituh*, which best translates as people who are mannered, civilized, and adhere to the Hopi way. The Hopi way is a marvelous and complex system of relationships, behavior, language, industry, philosophy, and thought. Hopis believe that humankind emerged into the present world from another place. The emergence story begins with a covenant made with Maasaw, a deity who first occupied this world. The story recounts the time when Hopis asked Maasaw for permission to live on this land. Maasaw responded, "It is up to you. All I have to offer you is my planting stick, a pouch of seeds, and a gourd of water. My life is simple but hard. If you commit to this way of life, you may live here with me." Maasaw laid several ears of corn before the different groups of people who emerged with the Hopis and asked the leaders of each group to choose one ear of corn apiece. The Hopi leader did not rush forward but waited until others made their selection. The only remaining ear was a short ear of blue corn. Maasaw said to the Hopi leader, "You did not rush forward, you have shown patience and humility, which is symbolized by this short ear of corn. Here, take this and become my people." The Hopis took the stubby ear of blue corn, which represented a long life but one full of challenges and hard work. They agreed to live according to Maasaw's instructions, which became a spiritual covenant that has guided Hopis since the earliest times to the present.

Hisatsinoms (Earliest People), the ancestors of present-day Hopis, built and occupied communities throughout the greater Southwest. Monumental architectural remains can be seen at locations such as Mesa Verde in Colorado, Chaco Canyon in New Mexico, and Wupatki in Arizona. These and other sites were settled by extended families or clans who, over time, migrated to the center of the Hopi world. Clans remain as the single most important unit of organization and identity for Hopis. Bear, Tobacco, Sand, Snake, Flute, Roadrunner, Sun, Snow, Corn, and Spider are examples of clan names. Each has its own history, specializations, and ways that it interacts with other clans. The last point is particularly important as one can only marry outside of one's clan. To do otherwise would be considered incest.

In the twenty-first century, the Hopis resided in twelve independent villages in northeastern Arizona. Oraibi, the oldest of the villages, is also considered the oldest continuously inhabited community in all of North Amer-

Hopi Pueblo. Amid typically harsh Hopi land in northeastern Arizona, 1920; the pueblo is Walpi, the oldest settlement (c. 1700) atop First Mesa. Library of Congress

Hopi Bride. A woman in traditional dress for a wedding; Hopis can marry only outside their own clan. LIBRARY OF CONGRESS

ica. The villages range in age from Oraibi, which is more than a thousand years old, to communities such as Polacca, which was settled in the early part of the last century. Most of the villages were established on mesas or escarpments that extend southward from a larger land formation known as Black Mesa. These village sites were strategically selected according to a plan that would help to protect residents and their way of life from marauding enemies and unwanted visitors.

In 1540, Spanish soldiers reached the Hopi area and defeated a group of Hopis who were defending an early village site. During the next 140 years, the Spanish attempted to colonize and missionize the Hopis. In 1680, indigenous populations over a wide geographical area staged a revolution against the Spanish government, and its military, missions, and civilians. For the Hopis, the Pueblo Revolt of 1680 was not only a revolution against a colonial government, it was a concerted effort to rid the area of forces that threatened Hopituh and their covenant with Maasaw. Colonial jurisdiction over the northern reaches of New Spain remained until 1821, when Mexico declared independence from Spain. Hopis lived under Mexican rule until 1848, the year that also marked the signing of a treaty between the United States and Mexico at the close of the Mexican War. In 1882, the Hopi Indian Reservation was established by executive order of President Chester A. Arthur. The reservation land base is nearly 3,000 square miles. The Hopi Tribal Council and Government was organized in 1935, and its constitution was approved by the secretary of the interior in 1936. Hopis are now federally recognized as "the Hopi Tribe."

In 2001, the Hopi Tribe's Enrollment Office reported a total population of 11,095. Between 75 and 80 percent of this population lived in the Hopi area. Others lived and worked in urban areas or were in college or military service. Hopi children attended community schools staffed by Hopi and non-Hopi educators and governed by local school boards. At about age eight, boys and girls begin their traditional Hopi religious education and training with the supervision of a close adult adviser.

Agriculture is central to Hopi culture. In fact, Hopi culture is often referred to as a "corn culture." With an annual precipitation of twelve inches or less, the Hopis have employed dry farming technology to sustain themselves and adjust to an arid land that can be harsh and unpredictable. Dry farming requires patience, humility, hard work, and most of all, a heart full of prayer. Harvest time is a joyful time and everyone partakes of the new crops.

The Hopis are among the most studied groups of people in Native North America. In 1980, there were well over 3,000 books and monographs published about Hopis. Since 1980, that number has probably increased exponentially. Recent scholarship has involved a number of Hopi scholars. The *Hopi Dictionary* published in 1998, for example, is a monumental work that includes more than

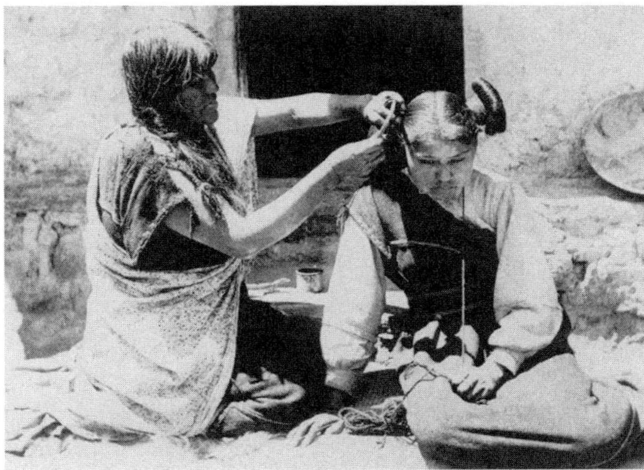

Hopi Hairstyles. A woman arranges the hair of a girl, c. 1909. LIBRARY OF CONGRESS

30,000 terms and was developed by Hopi and other language specialists. Hopis speak a Shoshonean language that is a branch of a larger language family known as Uto-Aztecan. *The Hopi Dictionary* is intended to help Hopi speakers to write and read the language. The Hopi Tribe publishes the newspaper *Hopi Tutuveni,* which uses both English and the Hopi syllabary. In 2001, the first Hopi public radio station went on the air. The station's call letters, KUYI, symbolically translate to water.

The Hopi artistic expressions in jewelry, pottery, painting, textiles, and basket making are well known to the art market and the world of collectors. Visitors are welcome to visit the Hopi Cultural Center on Second Mesa and may also arrange for guided tours of some of the villages. However, the Hopi people also desire to protect their rights to privacy and safeguard their religious knowledge and ceremonies. The Hopi Cultural Preservation Office is charged with the responsibility of representing Hopi interests both within and outside the Hopi reservation. This responsibility requires the involvement not only of the Hopi government, but also of the Hopi villages, clans, and religious societies, which must cooperate with each other as well. This is in keeping with the covenant between Maasaw and Hopituh.

BIBLIOGRAPHY

Hopi Dictionary Project. *Hopi Dictionary/Hopìikwa Lavàytutuveni: A Hopi-English Dictionary of the Third Mesa Dialect.* Tucson: University of Arizona Press, c. 1998.

James, Harry C. *Pages from Hopi History.* Tucson: University of Arizona Press, 1994.

Ortiz, Alfonso, ed. *Southwest.* Vol. 9 of *Handbook of North American Indians.* Edited by William C. Sturtevant. Washington, D.C.: Smithsonian Institution Press, 1979.

Secakuku, Alph H. *Following the Sun and Moon: Hopi Kachina Tradition.* Flagstaff, Ariz.: Northland Publishing, 1995.

Hartman H. Lomawaima
Stewart Koyiyumptewa

See also **Agriculture, American Indian; Indian Languages; Indian Oral Literature; Indian Religious Life; Pueblo Revolt.**

HORIZONTAL TARIFF BILL,

a federal tariff law, effective 1 May 1872, that cut protective duties by 10 percent. Another act admitted tea and coffee free. The bill was a compromise that allowed protectionists to prevent more drastic cuts in protective duties. The reduction was repealed in 1875 to meet an alleged need for more revenue.

BIBLIOGRAPHY

Goldstein, Judith. *Ideas, Interests, and American Trade Policy.* Ithaca, N.Y.: Cornell University Press, 1993.

James D. Magee / A. R.

See also **Tariff; Trade, Foreign.**

HORNBOOK,

the primer or first reading book used in colonial schools. Long used in England, colonists brought it with them to America. The hornbook was not really a book at all but simply a sheet of paper mounted on a board and covered with transparent horn. The board ended in a handle that a child held while reading. The handle was perforated so that it might be attached to the child's belt. Hornbooks contained the alphabet in capital and small letters, followed by combinations of vowels with consonants to form syllables, the Lord's Prayer, and Roman numerals.

BIBLIOGRAPHY

Beatty, Barbara. *Preschool Education in America: The Culture of Young Children from the Colonial Era to the Present.* New Haven, Conn.: Yale University Press, 1995.

Cohen, Sheldon S. *A History of Colonial Education, 1607–1776.* New York: Wiley, 1974.

Charles Garrett Vannest / S. B.

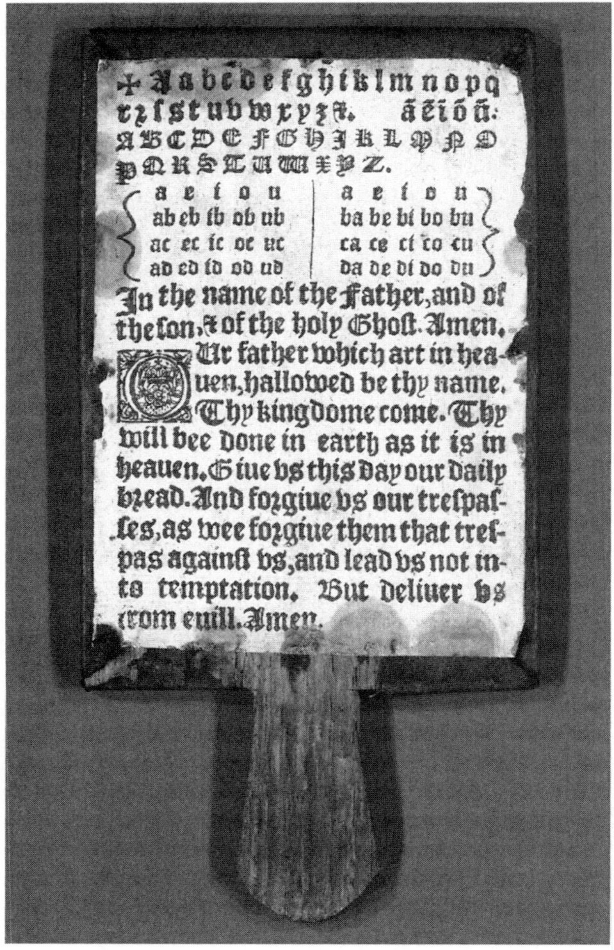

Hornbook. This early primer includes the alphabet and the Lord's Prayer. FOLGER SHAKESPEARE LIBRARY

See also **Colonial Society; Dame School; Education;** ***New England Primer.***

HORSE. The horse in America dates at least from the single-hoofed *Equus caballus* that emerged in Pleistocene times, about 1 million years ago. Ancestors of the modern horse began a westward migration from North America across the land bridge between the north coast of Alaska and that of Siberia. Some paleontologists suspect that the horse disappeared in America not more than, and possibly less than, 10,000 years ago.

The horse was reintroduced into the Western Hemisphere with the voyages of discovery by Christopher Columbus for Spain at the end of the fifteenth century. These Spanish steeds, derived from Moorish stock, first landed in the Caribbean in November 1493. The Spanish horses acclimated rapidly and within twenty years formed the chief supply for the Spanish mainland expeditions. Other European explorers brought horses to eastern and western parts of the New World in the sixteenth and seventeenth centuries. English colonists imported European horses. In the British colonies as a whole, horses were valued for riding, hunting, and racing.

The adoption of the horse by Native Americans, after the initial impact, increased rapidly and proved a major implement of change for the nomadic Plains tribes. By 1660, Indians had learned the value of horses and had begun to use them. During the next forty years the horse spread into the plains and mountains with great rapidity. In 1805 and 1806 Meriwether Lewis and William Clark noted the use of horses by Indians. With horses, the Kiowa ranged more than 1,000 miles in a summer. Some eastern forest tribes, once partially agricultural, moved out into the grassland with acquired horses and turned to hunting. The equestrian tribes were often at war with one another and raided white settlements to steal more horses.

Horses were crucial for transportation and inland migration prior to the development of the railroad. Extractive industries, manufacturers, and city distributive systems were all dependent on horsepower. The stagecoach was the first inland interregional utility, and the post rider opened communication with outlying settlements. Horses drew canal boats and railcars and served hunters, trappers, and miners. Cow horses carried cowboys on long cattle drives, herding livestock. The night horse was used to stand guard. Cavalry mounts and supply teams were adjuncts of military organizations and campaigning on every front. Approximately 1,500,000 horses and mules died during the Civil War (1861–1865).

The twentieth-century revolution worked by the internal combustion engine resulted in a displacement of horses for power and transportation. Tractor-drawn corn planters could plant an average of seventy acres of corn, compared to a horse-drawn average of only sixteen acres. From about 26 million farm horses and mules in the United States in 1920, the number declined to slightly more than 3 million horses and mules on farms in 1960.

American Breeds

American horse breeders carefully selected breeding stock and monitored pedigrees in an attempt to cultivate desired characteristics. Sometimes especially swift or capable horses were produced by chance. Superb horses were occasionally discovered and of unknown parentage. These animals were retained as studs or broodmares in the hopes that their talents or physical attributes would be transmitted to offspring. As a result, breeds unique to the United States were developed, especially in the twentieth century, to meet performance needs. Breed associations were formed to preserve genetic records and promote specific types of horses.

The American Quarter Horse is the first horse breed distinctive to the United States. Descended from a mixture of American breeds and imported bloodstock during the colonial period, Quarter Horses are exceptionally sturdy, muscular, versatile, and fast. They accompanied Americans from Atlantic colonies to the western frontier, where they were valued for their cow sense. Cattlemen, including those at the famous King Ranch in Kingsville, Texas, developed outstanding lines of Quarter Horses. One of the King Ranch Quarter Horses, Wimpy, was named grand champion stallion at the 1941 Fort Worth Exposition. The American Quarter Horse Association, founded in 1940, assigned Wimpy its first registration number, and he became a leading foundation sire. Quarter Horses fill many roles. The All-American Futurity at Ruidoso Downs, New Mexico, distributes a $2 million purse to Quarter Horses that sprint 440 yards. The American Quarter Horse Heritage Center and Museum at Amarillo, Texas, preserves this breed's history.

Justin Morgan's horse Figure, foaled in Massachusetts in 1793, founded a line notable not only for speed but also for light draft. Rhode Island developed one of the most distinctive and noted types of the period in the Narragansett pacer, a fast, easy-gaited saddle horse, but one not suited for driving or draft purposes. The stylishly moving American Saddlebred represents a mixture of Narragansett Pacer, Arabian, Standardbred, and Thoroughbred ancestors. Established in 1891, The American Saddle Horse Breeder's Association (later renamed American Saddlebred Horse Association) was the first American breed association, and Denmark was designated the main foundation sire.

Tennessee Walking Horses represent a conglomeration of breeds which produced a gaited horse that is renowned for its running walk. This breed is based on the line of foundation sire Allan F-1. The Racking Horse has a comfortable, natural four-beat gait which southern planters valued. Ozark settlers bred the Missouri Fox Trotter, which had a sliding gait that eased travel in hilly areas.

Most modern Appaloosas are related to the horses bred by the Nez Perce Indians. These spotted horses of-

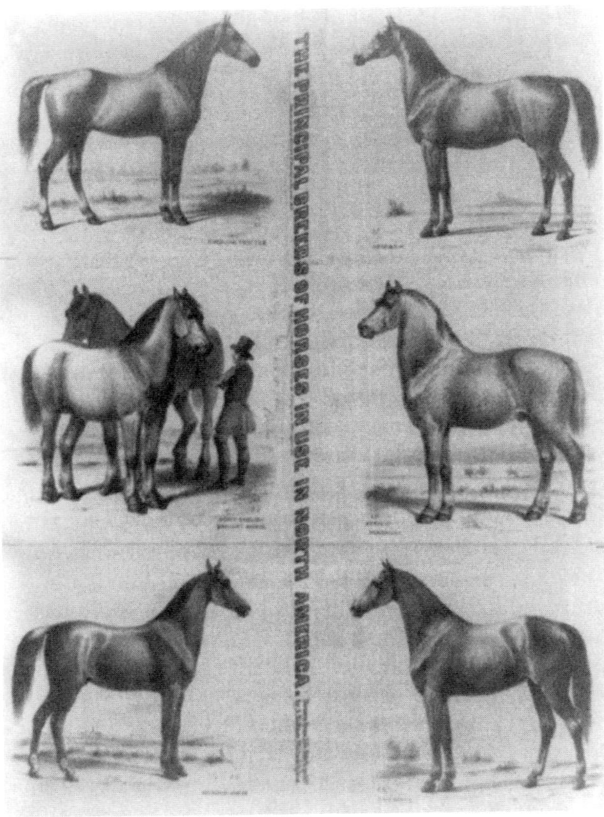

Horses. Augustus Kollner's lithograph, c. 1872, depicts what he identifies as the "principal breeds of horses in use in North America" *(clockwise from upper left):* American trotter, Arabian horse, Normandy horse, racehorse, Morgan horse, and heavy English draft horse. LIBRARY OF CONGRESS

ten also have Quarter Horse, Thoroughbred, and Arabian ancestry. Joker B. and Colida were two of the Appaloosa Horse Club's outstanding foundation stallions after that association was formed in 1938. The Pony of the Americas (POA) was created by crossing an Appaloosa mare and a Shetland pony stallion. The resulting foal, Black Hand, became the POA foundation sire, establishing a breed especially for children to ride and show.

The American Cream Draft Horse is the sole draft breed created in the United States. Representatives of this breed are descended from a pink-skinned, cream-colored Iowa mare named Old Granny. After mechanization resulted in the slaughter of many draft horses, the American Minor Breeds Conservancy cited the American Cream Draft Horse as an endangered breed.

Horse Culture

By the beginning of the twenty-first century, 6.9 million horses were living in the United States and were used by 1.9 million horse owners for recreational or commercial purposes. Approximately one-half of American horses are kept for their owners to enjoy and ride for pleasure. About one-third of horses are used primarily for shows and competitions. An estimated 725,000 horses race or are used as broodmares and studs on racehorse farms. Slightly more than one million horses fill working roles such as agricultural laborers and police mounts. Others are used as rodeo stock or for polo teams.

Although horses are found throughout the United States, Kentucky's Bluegrass region is specifically identified with equines. The center of American horse racing activity, Kentucky is home to major racing stables and tracks. The Kentucky Horse Park and the International Museum of the Horse were established at Lexington, Kentucky, in 1978 to educate people about horses and to host significant equine-related artistic, cultural, and sporting events. This thousand-acre site includes the Hall of Champions and the grave of the famous racehorse Man o' War. The museum is the world's largest equestrian museum and examines the history of human-horse interactions, providing online access to exhibits via the Internet. The daily Parade of Breeds highlights representatives of distinctive American horse breeds.

Pony, 4-H, and local riding clubs offer opportunities for equestrians to learn about horses. Riders barrel race at rodeos. Equestrians also compete at such prestigious events as the National Horse Show, held annually at Madison Square Garden in New York since 1883. Members of the United States Equestrian Team participate in international equestrian sporting events including the Olympics.

Legislation and Statistics

The American Society for the Prevention of Cruelty to Animals was organized in 1866 to protest horse abuse. During the late nineteenth century, George T. Angell established similar humane groups in Massachusetts to protect horses. Congress passed the Horse Protection Act (HPA) in 1970, then amended it in 1976 with further revisions in 1983 to provide legal measures to prevent abusive treatment of horses. Specifically, the HPA forbids people from soring horses. This procedure involves application of stimulants, such as chemical pastes or sharp chains, to make a horse step higher or perform more spectacularly than normal in order to win competitions or earn higher prices at sales. After receiving training and being licensed by a United States Department of Agriculture (USDA)–approved horse agency, a Designated Qualified Person (DQP) monitors horses at shows and auctions to inspect, detect, and bar any animals that have been sored.

The HPA declares that soring of horses for exhibitions or sales as well as the interstate transportation of sored animals to horse shows is prohibited. People convicted of soring horses are usually prevented from participating in future shows and sales for a specific time period, occasionally being disqualified for life, fined as much as $5,000, and sometimes sentenced to as much as a two-year prison term. State and local governments often prosecute people for committing acts that violate regional animal welfare legislation.

In 1996, the American Horse Council Foundation, created in 1969, commissioned a study to evaluate how the horse industry impacts the U.S. economy. The study determined that the American horse industry contributes annually $25.3 billion of goods and services to the national economy and pays taxes totaling $1.9 billion. The horse industry provides more income to the gross domestic product than such significant industries as furniture and tobacco manufacturing, motion picture production, and railroad transportation.

Throughout the United States, breeding, training, and boarding stables, horse show arenas, racetracks, and auction barns hire workers for various tasks, ranging from grooms and stable hands to jockeys and stable managers. At least 7.1 million people participate in some aspect of the horse industry. More Americans are employed by the horse industry than work in media broadcasting, railroad, or tobacco, coal, and petroleum manufacturing positions. Millions more are active as spectators at equine events.

BIBLIOGRAPHY

American Horse Council Home page at: http://www.horsecouncil.org/

American Quarter Horse Association. Home page at http://www.aqha.com.

Appaloosa Horse Club. Home page at http://www.appaloosa.com.

Kentucky Horse Park and the International Museum of the Horse. Home page at http://www.imh.org.

Tennessee Walking Horse Breeders' and Exhibitors' Association. Home page at http://www.twhbea.com.

Cypher, John. *Bob Kleberg and the King Ranch: A Worldwide Sea of Grass.* Austin: University of Texas Press, 1995.

Denhardt, Robert M. *The Quarter Running Horse: America's Oldest Breed.* Norman: University of Oklahoma Press, 1979.

Edwards, Elwyn Hartley. *The Encyclopedia of the Horse.* Photography by Bob Langrish and Kit Houghton. Foreword by Sharon Ralls Lemon. London and New York: Dorling Kindersley, 1994.

Gray, Bob. *Great Horses of the Past.* Houston: Cordovan Corp., 1967.

Hillenbrand, Laura. *Seabiscuit: An American Legend.* New York: Random House, 2001.

Horse Industry Directory. Washington, D.C.: Published annually by the American Horse Council in cooperation with American Horse Publications, 1976–.

Mellin, Jeanne. *The Complete Morgan Horse.* Lexington, Mass.: S. Greene Press, 1986.

Ward, Kathleen Rauschl. *The American Horse: From Conquistadors to the 21st Century.* Belleville, Mich.: Maple Yard Publications, 1991.

Zeh, Lucy. *Etched in Stone: Thoroughbred Memorials.* Lexington, Ky.: Blood-Horse, 2000.

Tom Fulton
Elizabeth D. Schafer

See also **Horse Racing and Showing; Indians and the Horse; Mule; Mustangs; Pony Express; Rodeos.**

HORSE MARINES is a term that refers to cavalrymen doing the work of marines or vice versa. The expression became associated with an episode in TEXAS in 1836, following the Battle of San Jacinto. As Maj. Isaac Burton's Texas Rangers made a reconnaissance along the coast to establish the extent and speed of the Mexican withdrawal, they sighted and captured three Mexican supply ships. Burton's detachment became known as the Horse Marines. In a broader sense the term designates, with humorous derision, almost any military or naval incongruity.

BIBLIOGRAPHY

Robinson, Charles M. *The Men Who Wear the Star: The Story of the Texas Rangers.* New York: Random House, 2000.

Winders, Richard Bruce. *Mr. Polk's Army: The American Military Experience in the Mexican War.* College Station: Texas A&M University Press, 1997.

Jim Dan Hill / H. R. S.

See also **Marine Corps, United States; Mexican-American War; San Jacinto, Battle of; Texas Rangers.**

HORSE RACING AND SHOWING. Both horse racing and horse showing antedate the history of the United States. The first settlers in the early colonies, particularly in Virginia, engaged in horse racing, one of the few accepted sports of the time. These races tended to be ad hoc affairs. Typically, they were run over the comparatively short distance of a quarter mile and took place—because of the lack of an established course—on whatever pathways through the forest were available or over the roads of settlements. Colonists began breeding horses that could sprint over the quarter mile distance in the late seventeenth century and early eighteenth century. Institutionalized racing began in New York shortly after it became a British colony, when Governor Richard Nicolls held horse races in the late 1660s at Hempstead on Long Island; the winners were awarded the first known sporting trophies in America. Thoroughbred racing following the British example was introduced by Governor Samuel Ogle of Maryland and first staged at Annapolis in 1745, fifteen years after the first thoroughbred stallion had been imported from England. Despite its attraction for local audiences, organized horse racing on a large scale did not begin before the end of the Civil War. Horses had been used extensively by both sides during the conflict, and after 1865 horse breeding in the South, particularly in the state of Virginia, was devastated. Kentucky took over as the leading state in horse breeding, and New York soon was unsurpassed in racing. Over the next thirty-five years until the turn of the century, horse racing, particularly thoroughbred racing, grew rapidly, with more than three hundred tracks operating across the nation.

Two main types of horse racing have evolved since the Civil War. The first employs jockeys, who ride either on a flat track—often an oval—for distances mostly between three-quarters of a mile and two miles or on the turf course used in the steeplechase, a race in which obstacles must be jumped. The other type is harness racing, in which a horse pulls a small two-wheeled carriage, or "sulky," with a driver over a one-mile course. Here, the horse is not permitted to gallop. Harness racing is governed by the United States Trotting Association, formed in 1938, and its notable races include the Hambletonian, the Kentucky Futurity, and the Little Brown Jug.

Horse racing became a year-round activity during the 1930s when winter racing was organized in Florida and California. The interwar period also saw the first introduction of technology into horse racing with the adoption in 1929 of the mechanical starting gate, which was followed in 1936 by the photo-finish camera. In 1942 the Thoroughbred Racing Associations of the United States was founded in Chicago. During the late 1960s, the first female jockeys were licensed. The heyday of thoroughbred racing came after World War II when track attendance increased from 26 million in 1946 to 53.3 million people in 1974; purses went up from $56 million to $5.2 billion during that period. By the start of the twenty-first century, the number of racetracks had declined to approximately 150, used both for races with jockeys and for harness races.

The number of foals registered each year increased dramatically after World War II, from almost 6,000 to more than 51,000 in 1986. Since 1986 that number has steadily declined to less than 37,000 in 1999. This decline is due no doubt to the fact that racehorses have become a considerable investment. The price for the most traded group of future racehorses, yearlings (about 9,000 horses), increased by more than 100 percent between 1991 and 2001. In 2001 the average cost of a yearling was $52,549, but prices can be well over $1 million—in 1981 the European champion Storm Bird was sold for $30 million. While only a handful of horses from each year's crop will ever win a race—and still fewer will ever generate considerable income—large purses have been won by star equine performers. Kelso earned $1,977,896 in eight seasons of racing (1959–1966), and Secretariat earned more than $1.3 million in only two seasons (1972–1973). Secretariat generated even more income from stud duty at a price of more than $6 million. In the 1970s three horses—Secretariat (1973), Seattle Slew (1977), and Affirmed (1978)—for the first time after a quarter of a century won the famous Triple Crown (the Kentucky Derby, Preakness, and Belmont Stakes). The 1985 American champion Alysheba generated total earnings of more than $6.6 million; Cigar—named Horse of the Year in both 1995 and 1996—earned $9,999,815.

Betting

Betting was a traditional ingredient of horse racing even in the early colonies. At many races, each owner of a horse put up a stake, and the total amount made up the winner's purse. Spectators participated in auction pools in which contestants were auctioned off, and the purchaser of the winner collected the pool minus a commission. After the Civil War, bookmakers took over and made betting a profitable business that soon attracted criminals who realized the opportunities for foul play. One form of foul play was the manipulation or doping of horses, which led to much public indignation. In 1894, to eliminate corruption, prominent track and stable owners formed the American Jockey Club, modeled on the English Jockey Club. The sport spread as the nation grew, despite being outlawed in a number of states because it was considered too close to gambling.

Bookmakers paid a flat fee to the racing association for the privilege of operation, and some of their fee money, plus some of the income from admissions, was used to supplement purses. A direct tie between purse money and volume of wagering, however, did not exist. Purses were modest and not sufficient to make winning a race more profitable than a betting coup at good odds. In 1908, however, the pari-mutuel system of wagering regained a foothold in the United States after having been tried and discarded during the nineteenth century. In this system, the odds are based on the relative amounts that have been bet on a horse, and the wagerer stakes his money on whether a particular horse will win the race, finish second, or come in third.

Betting transformed horse racing from a semi-private sport into a very large public entertainment business in which not only racing associations, owners, and jockeys but also state governments derived income directly proportional to the volume of wagering. Tracks now were able to offer larger purses, which attracted more horses and stimulated wagering. Although the number of races has declined since the late 1980s from almost 75,000 to a little over 55,000 in 2001, gross purses have increased from about 700 million to over one billion dollars in 2001. Handle (the total amount bet) in pari-mutuel wagering on U.S. thoroughbred racing increased by 55 percent between 1990 and 2001 from $9.385 billion to $14.550 billion. While horse racing is still a major spectator sport, ontrack betting has gone down during this period. Offtrack betting has increased to make up more than 85 percent of all bets in 2001. The relatively easily extracted pari-mutuel tax has become an important source of state revenue since the Great Depression of the 1930s, when states were desperately seeking revenue. The generated annual gross revenues exceeded more than $3.25 billion in 1998. States have not only allowed offtrack betting to make up for the decline in ontrack betting, they have also

Judge Roy Bean. The "law west of the Pecos," in western Texas, 1882–1902; here (*seated, facing right*) he tries an accused horse thief outside his saloon (named for the English actress Lillie Langtry, "the Jersey Lily," whom he knew only from illustrations). NATIONAL ARCHIVES AND RECORDS ADMINISTRATION

permitted ontrack betting on races taking place at other locations, which bettors monitor via simulcast satellite television transmissions. Some states also now allow account wagering that permits bettors to telephone their wagers from anywhere. The latest development is Internet betting.

Pari-mutuel wagering on horse racing is legal in forty-three U.S. states. These states have increasingly supplied subsidies to purses to make horse racing more attractive and to secure the flow of revenues. In New Jersey, for example, purses were boosted by a one-time $11.7 million subsidy from the state legislature in 2001. California has become the state with most races (5,107 in 2001, with gross purses of over $172 million), followed by West Virginia (4,379 races, with gross purses of around $66 million), Pennsylvania (3,992 races, with gross purses of around $50 million), and Florida (3,968 races, with gross purses of around $83 million). New York now ranks fourth in number of races (3,851) but second in gross purses ($145 million).

Horse Shows

Horse shows have developed alongside racing into a large number of different disciplines, including dressage, jumping, vaulting, and endurance. The first attempts to organize the sport were made in 1918, when the Association of American Horse Shows was formed on the eastern seaboard of the United States. By 1924 the Association had spread across the nation, enrolling sixty-seven shows. With seven recognized divisions, the Association incorporates the American Royal, Devon, and National horse shows as member competitions. In 2001 it adopted the name USA Equestrian. It recognizes twenty-six breeds and disciplines, and has over 80,000 individual members and more than 2,700 member competitions.

In 1999 there were 725,000 horses involved in racing, and almost 2 million in horse showing. Horse racing and showing remains an important industry and is the second most frequented spectator sport in the United States, surpassed only by baseball.

BIBLIOGRAPHY

Duke, Jacqueline, ed. *Thoroughbred Champions: Top 100 Racehorses of the 20th Century.* Lexington, Ky.: Blood-Horse, 1999.

Hickok, Ralph. *The Encyclopedia of North American Sports History.* New York: Facts on File, 1992.

Longrigg, Roger. *The History of Horse Racing.* London: Macmillan, 1972.

National Museum of Racing and Hall of Fame Online. Homepage at http://www.racingmuseum.org/.

Thalheimer, Richard, and Mukhtar M. Ali. "Intertrack Wagering and the Demand for Parimutuel Horse Racing." *Journal of Economics and Business* 47, no. 4 (October 1995): 369–383.

Michael Wala

See also **Horse.**

HORSE STEALING, often punishable as a crime against property, was significant throughout American history. Widely practiced by Ohio Valley Indians and banditti alike against eighteenth-century western settlers, it was difficult to trace and punish. Further west and southwest, populations were even more dependent on horses than the easterners. The culture of the Plains Indians was a horse culture; they raided horses from Mexico, from one another, and from settlers. Here, horse thieves were severely punished and, without benefit of trial by jury, were often hanged from the limbs of cottonwood trees. Following the Civil War, gangs of organized horse thieves operated out of Texas, using hideouts for stolen horses and selling them after driving them hundreds of miles from home.

BIBLIOGRAPHY

Dobie, J. Frank. *The Flavor of Texas.* Austin, Tex.: Jenkins, 1975.

Howard, Robert W. *Horse in America.* Chicago: Follett, 1965.

J. Frank Dobie / H. R. S.

See also **Fencing and Fencing Laws; Horse.**

HOSPITALS. Hospitals are institutions in which illnesses, injuries, and disabilities are diagnosed and treated. Deploying advanced medical technology, modern American hospitals are capable of providing medical services beyond those available in physicians' offices or outpatient facilities. In the United States, hospitals are operated either privately or by government entities. Some private hospitals operate for profit; others are operated by religious or secular charitable organizations on a nonprofit basis. Hospitals may function independently or participate in multihospital systems or networks.

The first American hospital was established in 1752. Subsequently, sustained growth in the quantity and quality of American hospitals has been fostered by technological and educational advances, government policies, and public and private HEALTH INSURANCE mechanisms that have generally shifted the burden of paying for hospital services away from the individual patient.

The development of American hospitals may be traced through five historical stages. In the formative stage (1750–1850), private charitable organizations established voluntary hospitals that treated patients free of charge while, at the same time, public almshouses (which also provided nonmedical social services to poor, mentally ill, dispossessed, and disabled individuals) were gradually transformed into public hospitals. Next, the era of specialization (1850–1890) gave rise to specialized hospitals (for example, children's hospitals) and nursing emerged as a trained profession. The subsequent era of surgery (1890–1930) was spurred by the introduction of anesthesia and aseptic practices, which facilitated rapid growth in surgical practice, and thereby expanded the role of for-profit hospitals. In the era of insurance and expansion (1930–1975), the emergence of hospital insurance, MEDICARE, AND MEDICAID changed the way hospital care was financed. These programs, along with expanded federal assistance for the construction of new community hospitals and Veterans Administration hospitals, financed a proliferation of new and expanded hospitals. Finally, in the era of cost containment (1975–2000), earlier trends toward expansion and deployment have been largely reversed and replaced by countervailing trends towards hospital consolidation, diversification, and integration.

1750–1850: The Formative Era

Traditionally, care for the sick was one of many social services that public almshouses provided to the poor and dispossessed. In the eighteenth century, certain public almshouses evolved into public hospitals by focusing on caring for the sick. In this manner, Philadelphia Almshouse became Philadelphia General Hospital, New York Almshouse became Bellevue Hospital, and Baltimore County Almshouse became part of Baltimore City Hospitals.

In 1752, the Pennsylvania Hospital became the first permanent general hospital specifically chartered to care for the sick. In 1791, New York Hospital followed; in 1821 came Massachusetts General Hospital. These voluntary hospitals did not generally charge fees, but instead were supported by charitable donations. Although most patients admitted for treatment in voluntary hospitals were poor, the admissions process was selective. Patients deemed contagious, immoral, or otherwise undesirable (alcoholics, for example) were transferred to almshouses. Such selectivity was designed to reduce the hospital's mortality rate and to improve its reputation. Despite these efforts towards respectability, however, people of means generally stayed away from hospitals.

1850–1890: The Era of Specialization

For several reasons, the ability of hospitals successfully to treat illness and injury substantially improved during the mid-nineteenth century. First, Florence Nightingale's success in promoting cleanliness and proper ventilation on hospital wards improved hospital mortality rates years before germ theory explained why. Second, NURSING schools were established during this period, graduating trained professional nurses who made indispensable contributions to hospital care. Third, in the 1870s, Johns Hopkins University adopted systematic clinical instruction and investigations. Consequently, hospitals became central to medical education and scientific training as well as treatment.

As hospitals became more successful at treating illness and injury, they gradually transformed from storehouses where the impoverished could convalesce (or die) into medical treatment centers of choice for individuals from across the social spectrum. As part of this transformation, specialty hospitals emerged. Some were developed to pull children, mentally ill, and disabled people out of almshouses and into institutions dedicated to serving their particular needs. In addition, specialized religious and ethnic hospitals were established by certain religious and immigrant groups. These hospitals arose in response to actual discrimination and also to satisfy certain unique needs of group members—last rites among Catholics and kosher meals among Jews, for example.

During this time, ward-style hospitals in which relatively poor patients were attended by the hospital's on-staff physicians remained the norm. Slowly, however, private rooms were added, attracting middle-class and wealthy patients who retained their choice of physician.

1890–1920: The Era of Surgery

The groundwork for the era of surgery was laid by two important mid-nineteenth-century developments. First, in 1846, Dr. William Morton introduced anesthesia at Massachusetts General Hospital. Then, in 1867, Dr. Joseph Lister demonstrated antiseptic surgery in London. These two demonstrations set the stage for the emergence of surgery, which would thrust hospitals into their central role in treating illness and injury.

Dr. Lister's method of performing antiseptic surgery was soon superseded by aseptic surgery, which involves creating a sterile surgical field rather than sterilizing at various points during a procedure. As aseptic surgery proliferated, surgical mortality rates plummeted. However, sterile surgical fields required a more complex environment than most home kitchens or doctors' offices could provide. Consequently, by 1900, almost all surgery was performed in hospitals. Pressure on hospital bed space caused by the increase in surgical admissions forced hospitals to admit sick patients only during the acute phase of their illness rather than for their entire treatment. With sicker patients in residence for shorter periods, the costs of providing hospital care predictably increased.

As mortality rates fell and positive results emerged, more people were willing to pay for surgery. Accordingly, patient fees gradually replaced charitable donations as hospitals' primary source of revenue. This shift generally enabled physicians to wrest control over hospital admissions away from hospital board members. However, not every physician was able to obtain hospital admitting privileges. In response, some physicians built their own hospitals or increased pressure on existing hospitals to open their facilities to all physicians.

1930s–1960s: The Era of Insurance and Expansion

Until 1929, private hospitals were financed exclusively by charitable contributions, patient fees, or both. In 1929, however, Baylor University Hospital successfully introduced prepaid hospital care when it offered fifteen-hundred schoolteachers the opportunity to purchase up to twenty-one days of hospital inpatient care per year (whether used or not) for six dollars per person. Other hospitals followed suit, some issuing joint offerings that allowed subscribers to preserve greater choice among hospitals and physicians.

The need for prepaid hospital care became more acute during the Great Depression, when private voluntary hospitals faced a crisis of declining occupancy and decreased charitable contributions while public hospitals swelled with nonpaying patients. To survive this crisis, in 1932 a number of private hospitals agreed to provide certain hospital services for a fixed payment regardless of the cost of delivering the services. These prepaid services plans, which functioned like hospitalization insurance, provided blanket coverage for a list of services rather than reimbursing the hospital for each service provided. The plans, known as Blue Cross Plans, remained under the control of the voluntary hospitals.

Blue Cross Plans charged standard rates without regard to a policyholder's income. Not surprisingly, the plans attracted mainly middle-class subscribers. Yet Blue Cross Plans proved viable, and kept the voluntary hospitals viable too. Indeed, the financial success of Blue Cross Plans induced commercial indemnity insurers to offer similar hospitalization coverage to groups and individuals. By the 1950s, more Americans obtained hospitalization coverage from commercial insurers than from Blue Cross. Even while Blue Cross plans and private hospitalization insurance proliferated, however, many poor and elderly Americans who were the most vulnerable to sickness and its costs remained uninsured.

Beginning in the late 1940s, public and private hospitals began to receive additional financial support from Congress. In 1946, the Hospital Survey and Construction Act (Hill-Burton Act) funded the construction of many new community hospitals nationwide. In 1965, Congress authorized the federal Medicare program, which pays for hospital and medical care for individuals aged sixty-five or older and those with long-term disabilities. Shortly thereafter, Medicare was supplemented by Medicaid, a joint federal-state program that provides medical and hospital insurance to low-income people under sixty-five and to those who have exhausted their Medicare benefits.

1975–2000: The Era of Cost Containment

The introduction from the 1930s through the 1960s of Blue Cross Plans, private health insurance, Medicare, and Medicaid all contributed to pushing consumer demand for medical and hospital care to unprecedented levels. As the overall demand for health services escalated, so did overall costs, which consumed 15 percent of the gross domestic product in 2001.

Insurers responded to escalating health care costs by creating new mechanisms, including managed care, to control costs and access to services. Some managed care plans employ utilization review, require pre-authorization of hospitalization, or negotiate for reduced fee payments to participating providers in exchange for patient volume. Alternatively, to discourage excess medical services, other managed care plans pay participating physicians a fixed monthly fee per patient, regardless of the services used. These new insurance mechanisms have reduced average hospital lengths of stay and occupancy levels. By moving health services from hospitals to outpatient settings wherever possible, managed care plans have diminished the role of hospitals in the American health care system.

Hospitals have responded to these changes by diversifying their activities, increasing on-site outpatient services or even providing outpatient services off-site. Hospitals also have affiliated with one another to create multihospital systems and networks, and have vertically integrated with physicians through a variety of organizational structures. These organizations were intended to offset the negotiating power of the insurers, but have met with only limited success, if that.

At the start of the twenty-first century, hospitals continue to play an unparalleled role in providing essential medical services, facilitating medical research, and training new physicians. However, whether hospitals will retain their central role in American medical care is open to question.

BIBLIOGRAPHY

Starr, Paul. *The Social Transformation of American Medicine*. New York: Basic Books, 1982.

Linda Dynan

HOSTAGE CRISES. While taking hostages has been widespread throughout history, a spate of international hostage crises involving Westerners in the 1970s and 1980s caused the practice to become chiefly identified with Middle East terrorist organizations. Taking hostages gave such organizations leverage over their state enemies in the form of direct extortion or publicity. For the United States, hostage crises have often posed severe national security and political threats. Since the early 1970s the public has become aware of a psychological phenomenon known as the Stockholm syndrome, in which some hostages come to display an emotional attachment toward their captors.

The 1970s saw several international hostage crises, including the terrorist group Black September's seizure of eleven Israeli athletes at the 1972 Olympic Games in Munich. All of the hostages and five of the eight terrorists died. In late February 1977 the Ugandan dictator Idi Amin initiated a somewhat unconventional hostage crisis when he banned all Americans in Uganda, numbering approximately two hundred, from leaving the country. The crisis was resolved peacefully within a few days. American involvement in the turmoil of the Middle East led to a wave of more conventional and more violent terror attacks in the late 1970s, including the Iran hostage crisis of 1979–1981, that continued through the mid-1980s.

On 4 November 1979 militant students loyal to the Muslim leader Ayatollah Ruhollah Khomeini, fearing a U.S. plot to restore to power the recently deposed shah, Reza Pahlavi, stormed the U.S. embassy in Teheran and took sixty-five Americans hostage. When Khomeini endorsed the action and provided Iranian government support, the stage was set for a prolonged international crisis. President James Earl Carter's administration attempted to free its diplomats by several methods, including an abortive rescue mission, all to no avail. The crisis lasted over a year and Carter paid a heavy political price for the failures in the 1980 election campaign, which he ultimately lost to Ronald Reagan. As a final humiliation for Carter, the hostages were finally released on 20 January 1981, only hours after Reagan was sworn in as president.

Reagan, however, had his own hostage problems with Shiite Iran as the Middle East situation deteriorated. Shortly after Israel invaded Lebanon in June 1982, extremist Shiite groups with ties to Iran, including one known as Hezbollah (Party of God), began to seize Western hostages and demand the release of Islamic activists from Israeli jails. By early 1985 Hezbollah had seized seven U.S. citizens. In response, the Reagan administration devised a complicated, secret, and constitutionally questionable process of ransoming the hostages with secret arms sales involving Israel and Nicaraguan rebels (contras). The plan was a net failure, and leaked news of the transactions sparked a serious political scandal and a highly publicized congressional investigation that ultimately tainted the second Reagan administration. The last of the U.S. hostages, the Associated Press journalist Terry Anderson, who was held hostage for over five years, was released in December 1991.

Another unconventional hostage situation arose during the Persian Gulf crisis of 1990 and 1991. The Iraqi dictator Saddam Hussein held approximately two thousand Westerners hostage as "human shields" against bombing raids by the U.S.–led coalition.

BIBLIOGRAPHY

Christopher, Warren, et al. *American Hostages in Iran: The Conduct of a Crisis*. New Haven, Conn.: Yale University Press, 1985.

Walsh, Lawrence E. *Firewall: The Iran-Contra Conspiracy and Cover-Up*. New York: Norton, 1997.

David G. Coleman

See also **Iran Hostage Crisis; Iran-Contra Affair; Persian Gulf War; Terrorism;** *and vol. 9:* **Interrogation of an Iran Hostage.**

HOTELS AND HOTEL INDUSTRY. The primary purpose of hotels is to provide travelers with shelter, food, refreshment, and similar services and goods, offering on a commercial basis things that are customarily furnished within households but unavailable to people on a journey away from home. Historically hotels have also taken on many other functions, serving as business exchanges, centers of sociability, places of public assembly and deliberation, decorative showcases, political headquarters, vacation spots, and permanent residences. The hotel as an institution, and hotels as an industry, transformed travel in America, hastened the settlement of the continent, and extended the influence of urban culture.

Hotels in the Early Republic

The first American hotels were built in the cities of the Atlantic coast in the 1790s, when elite urban merchants began to replace taverns with capacious and elegant establishments of their own creation. They hoped thereby to improve key elements of the national transportation infrastructure and increase the value of surrounding real estate, while at the same time erecting imposing public monuments that valorized their economic pursuits and promoted a commercial future for the still agrarian republic. Unlike earlier public accommodations, hotels were impressive structures, readily distinguishable as major public institutions due to their tremendous size, elaborate ornamentation, and sophisticated academic styles. They were often designed by important architects like James Hoban, Charles Bulfinch, and Benjamin Latrobe. Hotels also had a distinctive internal arrangement incorporating grand halls for the use of the public and featuring dozens of bedchambers, which for the first time offered private space to all guests. Building on such a massive scale was tremendously expensive, and hotels cost from eight to thirty times as much as had been spent on even the finest taverns. Early hotels quickly became important centers of politics, business, and sociability. The City Hotel in New York, for example, became the center of the Gotham elite's business pursuits and elegant society balls, and Washington's Union Public Hotel housed the U.S. Congress in 1814–1815 after the British army destroyed part of the Capitol. The first generation of hotel building continued into the first decade of the nineteenth century before being brought to a close by the financial failure of many of the first projects and the economic disruptions surrounding the War of 1812.

Nineteenth-Century Hotels

A second period of hotel construction began around 1820, driven by the American transportation revolution. Steam navigation and the coming of the canal age, especially the opening of the ERIE CANAL in 1825, extended the range of movement along the nation's internal waterways and greatly increased the volume of travel in America. Urban merchant-capitalists constructed a new generation of hotels as part of their mercantilist strategy to claim expanding economic hinterlands for their cities and states. The first of these hotels appeared in leading commercial centers along coastal trade routes, beginning with Baltimore's City Hotel (1826), Washington's National Hotel (1827), Philadelphia's United States Hotel (1828), and Boston's renowned Tremont House (1829). These were followed by similar establishments built at key points along the Ohio and Mississippi rivers, notably Cincinnati's Pearl Street House (1831), Louisville's Galt House (1834), and the St. Charles in New Orleans (1837). These and other second-generation American hotels were much larger and more numerous than their predecessors and established the rectilinear, city-block hotel as a set architectural form that would be repeated in locations all across the growing nation. This phase of hotel development was brought to a close by the prolonged depression that followed the panic of 1837.

The third generation of hotels was catalyzed by the rapid growth of the American railroad system in the decades after 1840, a development that freed long-distance travel from the limitations of the river system and reconfigured the nation's transportation network along an east-west axis. Hotels continued to multiply in the East and also proliferated along the advancing frontier of settlement, rising over the prairies and plains in the 1840s and 1850s and appearing in the mountain West in the 1860s and 1870s. The westward advance of hotel construction soon linked up with a counterpart that had originated with Anglo settlement of the Pacific coast and extended eastward. By the time of the centennial, America boasted both a transcontinental railroad and a continental hotel network. Hotelkeepers had meanwhile come to see their operations as constituting an integrated national system. In the 1840s, they embraced new theories and methods of hotel management based on closer supervision and regimentation of employees and regularized contact among managers. In the 1850s, hotel proprietors began to organize their first local trade associations, and in the 1870s they established specialized publications like *Hotel World* and the *National Hotel Gazette* that served the industry nationwide. Visitors from overseas constantly commented on the size, extent, and excellence of the nation's hotel system, revealing that as early as midcentury, the American hotel had surpassed the hostelries of Europe and become the leading international standard for public accommodation.

Hotel development also involved diversification of hotel types. Most early hotels had been large urban luxury establishments, but newer variants quickly emerged. Resort hotels, designed to accommodate the rising tide of tourists, were built in scenic rural landscapes far from the cities where the hotel form had been born. Commercial hotels, more simply furnished and less expensive than the luxury variant, served the growing ranks of traveling salesmen and other commercial workers set in motion by the burgeoning economy. Railroad hotels were built at regular intervals along track lines to provide passengers and crews with places to eat and rest in the decades before the introduction of sleeping cars. Residential hotels, dedicated to the housing needs of families increasingly unable to afford private houses in expensive urban real estate markets, served as the prototypes for apartment buildings. And a frontier hotel form, characterized by wood construction, whitewash, and tiered porches, was built in hundreds of new settlements where travelers and lumber were common but capital was scarce. These and other hotel types soon far outnumbered luxury hotels, though the latter variety received the most attention from journalists, authors, and printmakers, and therefore tended to stand for all hotels in the popular imagination.

Hotels were vital centers of local community life in American cities and towns. Their role as important public spaces was in part a continuation of traditional uses of taverns, one that was further amplified by hotels' conspicuous architecture, central location, and spacious and inviting interiors. Merchants and other businesspeople continued to use hotel space for offices, commercial exchanges, and accommodations, but the popular uses of hotels far transcended their economic function. Well-appointed hotel parlors and ballrooms were favored venues for card parties, cotillions, and other sociable events that involved seeing and being seen in refined public settings. By the same token, voluntary associations ranging from debating societies to ethnic brotherhoods and charitable organizations regularly hired hotel assembly rooms and dining halls for their meetings and banquets. Hotels also became major loci of political activity. Political parties and factions often set up their headquarters in hotels, where they held caucuses and made nominations. Hotels served as important public forums, a fact revealed by the large number of published images of political figures making speeches from hotel windows and balconies, hobnobbing in lobbies, and raising toasts in crowded halls. Indeed, such was the political importance of hotels that they were often attacked in periods of domestic strife. The Civil War era, for example, was marked by the burning or cannonading of numerous hotels by Southern sympathizers.

Hotels also extended their influence over distances because they functioned as a powerful system of cultural production and diffusion. Their role in accommodating travelers made hotels into a frontier between individual communities and the world beyond, with hotel guests acting as cultural emissaries who carried new ideas about aesthetics and technology along the routes of their journeys. Innovations in interior decorative luxury were among the ideas most commonly transmitted. Hotelkeepers spent heavily on refined furnishings as part of their efforts to attract guests, and in so doing transformed decor into a showcased capital good. Because a hotel could afford to spend far more on amenities than could a private family, its interiors constantly tempted guests to emulate a higher standard of living. Midwestern travelers who stayed at fine hotels in St. Louis or New York City, for example, were impressed with the elegance of their surroundings and sought to reproduce them back home in Illinois, Iowa, and Nebraska. Hotels similarly became showcases for household and communications technologies. Indoor plumbing, central heating, elevators, and gas and electric lighting first saw wide public use in hotels, as did the telegraph and the telephone. Authors from Stephen Crane to Bret Harte recognized the ways in which hotels were setting a new pace in American life, and in his classic *The American Scene* (1907), Henry James found himself "verily tempted to ask if the hotel-spirit may not just be the American spirit most seeking and most finding itself."

Hotels in the Age of Auto and Air Travel

The rise of the automobile in the early twentieth century reordered the nation's transportation regime and marked the beginning of a new hotel age that lasted for more than two decades. The nineteenth-century American hotel system had been predicated upon long-distance, point-to-point, steam-driven water and rail transportation, and the gradual transition to automobility wrought major changes in the hotel industry. In an effort to secure the patronage of drivers, existing hotels added parking facilities, and new establishments incorporated them into their building plans. Other developers created the motor hotel, or motel, a new hotel variant which, instead of being located in cities and other travel destinations, was typically sited on inexpensive land along the roads in between. The automobile also influenced the hotel industry in construction and management techniques, as Fordist mass production fostered a corresponding drive for standardization and scale in hotels. E. M. Statler was the foremost figure in this cause. In 1908, he opened the first chain of hotels dedicated to his belief that hospitality should be made as similar as possible in every location. Statler's success with a business model based on cost cutting and scientific management made him the leading hotelier of his time and an important influence upon twentieth-century hotel administration. By 1930, as the Great Depression was putting a definitive end to this period of hotel building, the Census Bureau counted more than 17,000 hotels in the United States.

The American hotel industry expanded at a previously unseen pace following World War II. The three-decade economic boom of the postwar years increased the incidence of commercial travel and sent incomes soaring, and the success of organized labor distributed wealth more evenly and made paid vacations a reality for millions of workers. Meanwhile, the creation of the interstate highway system and the emergence of safe and reliable passenger aircraft made travel easier and more broadly subscribed than ever before. Hotels emerged as an important terrain of struggle in the conflictual domestic politics of the era. When civil rights activists demanded an end to racial discrimination in public accommodations, the special legal status of hotel space became a crucial consideration in the litigation strategy of the National Association for the Advancement of Colored People (NAACP). It was no coincidence that the constitutionality of the Civil Rights Act of 1964 was definitively established by the Supreme Court's ruling in *Heart of Atlanta Motel v. United States*.

Hotels were similarly implicated in international politics. Americans ventured abroad in increasing numbers during the postwar years, and the nation's hotel industry expanded globally in order to accommodate them. In the context of Cold War geopolitics, American-owned hotels in foreign countries also served as exemplars of the benefits and vitality of capitalism. Conrad Hilton in particular spoke of his company's overseas properties, particularly those along the IRON CURTAIN, as valuable assets in the fight against communism. In a world simultaneously divided by politics and connected by transportation, hotels were important symbolic sites.

The American hotel industry benefited greatly from the uneven prosperity of the 1980s and 1990s and entered the twenty-first century as a large and fast-growing segment of the national economy. The hotels of the United States employed well over 1.4 million people and collected more than $100 billion per year in receipts. They formed a dense network of 53,000 properties comprising some 4 million guest rooms nationwide. Internationally, the industry operated more than 5,000 overseas hotels with over half a million rooms.

From its beginnings as an experimental cultural form, the American hotel became a ubiquitous presence on the national landscape and developed into an immense and vital national industry. The hotel system transformed the nature of travel, turning it from an arduous and uncertain undertaking of the few into a predictable and commonplace activity of the many. On the way, the hotel became instrument, ornament, symptom, and symbol of America's continental and international empire.

BIBLIOGRAPHY

Boorstin, Daniel. "Palaces of the Public." In *The Americans: The National Experience.* New York: Vintage, 1965.

Groth, Paul. *Living Downtown: The History of Residential Hotels in the United States.* Berkeley: University of California Press, 1994.

Harris, Neil. "Living with Lobbies." In *Cultural Excursions: Marketing Appetites and Cultural Tastes in Modern America.* Chicago: University of Chicago Press, 1990.

Raitz, Karl B., and John Paul Jones III. "The City Hotel as Landscape Artifact and Community Symbol." *Journal of Cultural Geography* 9 (1988): 17–36.

Sandoval-Strausz, A. K. "For the Accommodation of Strangers: The American Hotel, 1789–1908." Ph.D. diss., University of Chicago, 2002.

Wharton, Annabel Jane. *Building the Cold War: Hilton International Hotels and Modern Architecture.* Chicago: University of Chicago Press, 2001.

A. K. Sandoval-Strausz

See also **Resorts and Spas; Taverns and Saloons; Transportation and Travel.**

HOUMA. The Houmas (Ouma) are an American Indian tribe of the Muskogean language family first encountered in 1682 by René-Robert Cavalier de la Salle on the east bank of the Mississippi River, opposite from the mouth of the Red River. Their population in 1699 was estimated at about 700 individuals living in upwards of 150 cabins. They were closely related to the Choctaw, Chickasaw, and Chakchiuma tribes. Baton Rouge, the capital of Louisiana, was named for the red pole on the Mississippi that established the southern boundary of their hunting territory.

The Houmas remained steadfast allies of Louisiana throughout the French period (1699–1766), helping not only to feed New Orleans by selling goods in the public markets, but also as military allies; their villages constituted the first line of defense from the north for New Orleans and the settlements just upriver of the city (known as the German Coast). The French alliance cost the Houmas dearly: not only did they suffer from epidemics, but they had conflicts with neighboring and regional tribes, and were targets of slave raiders from South Carolina. They moved near New Orleans after 1706, although over the next decade or so they moved upriver into present-day Ascension Parish, near the head of Bayou Lafourche. As early as 1739, due to their continually dwindling numbers, the Houmas were reportedly combining with other local tribes.

There are few accounts of the Houmas during the Spanish period (1766–1803), and they virtually disappear from the historical record within a decade of the Louisiana Purchase of 1803. Some time later, they moved down Bayou Lafourche into present-day Lafourche and Terrebonne Parishes. By the early twentieth century, the anthropologist John Swanton had visited them and written a report for the Smithsonian's Bureau of American Ethnology that concluded that the historic Houmas were all but extinct as a people. He characterized the people who called themselves Houmas as a tri-racial isolate who identified themselves as Indian, but who were so intermarried with whites and blacks that they were racially little different from the Cajuns among whom they lived.

During the 1970s and 1980s the Houma organized themselves as the United Houma Nation, Incorporated, and sought federal recognition as an Indian tribe. Although they have been denied federal recognition, they were recognized by the state of Louisiana, and they continue to press their status as American Indians and to seek federal recognition. As of 2002, the tribal council claimed to represent over 20,000 tribal members.

BIBLIOGRAPHY

Bowman, Greg, and Janel Curry-Roper. *The Houma Indian People of Louisiana: A Story of Indian Survival.* Houma, La.: United Houma Nation, 1982.

Davis, Dave. "A Case of Identity: Ethnogenesis of the New Houma Indians." *Ethnohistory* 48 (2001): 473–494.

Swanton, John R. "The Indians of the Southeastern United States." *Bureau of American Ethnology Bulletin* 137. 1946; Reprint ed. Washington, D.C.: Smithsonian Institution, 1979.

Michael James Foret

HOUSE COMMITTEE ON UN-AMERICAN ACTIVITIES. The House Committee on Un-American Activities (HUAC) searched for communists and other suspected subversives for nearly forty years. Founded in 1938 as the House Special Committee to Investigate Un-American Activities and chaired by a conservative Texas Democrat, Martin Dies, HUAC became a standing committee of the House in 1945. In 1969 it announced a new focus, domestic terrorism, and received a new name, the House Internal Security Committee. Six years later, in the wake of Vietnam and Watergate, the full House abolished the committee.

Prior to HUAC's founding, congressional investigations of subversion were episodic. The most notable occurred in 1919, 1930, and 1934, and the sponsor of the committee's founding resolution, Samuel Dickstein, a New York Democrat, had been involved in several of those efforts. Where Dickstein was primarily concerned with native fascism and all other forms of anti-Semitism, however, the committee came to focus on ostensible left-wing subversion. Its basic charge was that communists and their sympathizers had infiltrated nearly all of the New Deal's alphabet agencies.

During the Cold War years, HUAC made its mark on two fronts. First, beginning in 1947, the committee held hearings on President Harry S. Truman's Federal Employee Loyalty Program. The most important of these investigations involved Edward Condon, director of the National Bureau of Standards, and Alger Hiss, a former State Department official. When Chairman J. Parnell Thomas, a New Jersey Republican, asked to see Condon's loyalty file, President Truman declined—citing both privacy and constitutional grounds, namely the separation of powers. That refusal not only allowed HUAC to charge the administration with covering up a sham of a loyalty program; it also broadened the debate. Could a sitting president refuse a congressional request for information? This debate over "executive privilege" would continue—and eventually involved a freshman congressman sitting on the committee, Richard M. Nixon.

Nixon was also the HUAC member who most determinedly pursued Alger Hiss. When Hiss was convicted of perjury in January 1950 for having denied under oath the passing of documents to a self-confessed Soviet agent, the committee's basic point about the adequacy of a loyalty program run by a Democratic president appeared, at least to its partisans, a proven fact.

The second front on which HUAC made its mark was investigating communist infiltration of the film industry. The initial hearings were orchestrated with the help of J. Edgar Hoover's FBI. The FBI identified both "unfriendly" witnesses who were not expected to answer the committee's questions during the televised hearings, and "friendly" witnesses who could be counted on to cooperate fully. Screen Actors Guild president Ronald Reagan, who actually had an FBI informant code designation, was among those in the latter category. Ultimately, these hearings resulted in a First Amendment challenge to the committee's authority by the so-called Hollywood Ten. The Supreme Court rejected that challenge.

Thereafter, HUAC played a substantial role in establishing and policing the Hollywood blacklists. Any actor, writer, director, or other film industry employee named as a communist would find himself or herself without work, and the only way off the blacklist was to appear as a friendly witness before the committee and "name names"—that is, inform on friends and acquaintances. A witness who received a committee subpoena could remain silent only by citing the Fifth Amendment's protection against self-incrimination. Citing free speech or any other constitutional protection would result, as the Hollywood Ten discovered, in both the blacklist and a federal prison sentence for contempt of Congress.

In the 1960s, the committee kept at communist infiltration while adding hearings on such new subjects as the Ku Klux Klan and Students for a Democratic Society. However, with the decline of McCarthyism and the gradual eroding of the Hollywood blacklist, HUAC's heyday had passed. There would be no more klieg lights and screaming newspaper headlines. The committee spent its last years toiling in relative obscurity.

BIBLIOGRAPHY

Goodman, Walter. *The Committee: The Extraordinary Career of the House Committee on Un-American Activities.* New York: Farrar, Straus and Giroux, 1968.

Navasky, Victor S. *Naming Names.* New York: Viking Press, 1980.

O'Reilly, Kenneth. *Hoover and the Un-Americans: The FBI, HUAC, and the Red Menace.* Philadelphia: Temple University Press, 1983.

Kenneth O'Reilly

See also **Anticommunism; Blacklisting; Cold War; Hiss Case;** *and vol. 9:* **The Testimony of Walter E. Disney before the House Committee on Un-American Activities 24 October 1947.**

HOUSE DIVIDED. When he accepted the Republican nomination to the U.S. Senate at Springfield, Ill., on 16 June 1858, Abraham Lincoln paraphrased a sentence from the Bible (Mark 3:25) in order to emphasize his belief that eventually slavery had to be extinguished: "A house divided against itself cannot stand." Lincoln continued, "I believe this government cannot endure permanently half slave and half free. I do not expect the Union to be dissolved—I do not expect the house to fall—but I do expect it will cease to be divided." Lincoln's opponent, Stephen A. Douglas, favored allowing the people of each state to determine whether to allow slavery within their midst.

BIBLIOGRAPHY

Foner, Eric. *Free Soil, Free Labor, Free Men: The Ideology of the Republican Party Before the Civil War.* New York: Oxford University Press, 1995 (orig. pub. 1970).

Johannsen, Robert W. *Lincoln, the South, and Slavery: The Political Dimension.* Baton Rouge: Louisiana State University Press, 1991.

Oates, Stephen B. *With Malice Toward None: The Life of Abraham Lincoln.* New York: Harper & Row, 1977.

Theodore M. Whitfield / C. P.

See also **Antislavery; Equality, Concept of; Irrepressible Conflict; Lincoln-Douglas Debates; Republican Party;** *and vol. 9:* **A House Divided.**

HOUSE MADE OF DAWN by N. Scott Momaday was published in 1968 and won the Pulitzer Prize for fiction in 1969, the only book by a Native American to receive this honor. It is widely regarded as his masterpiece. Momaday, who is of Kiowa and Cherokee-Anglo descent, was born in Lawton, Oklahoma, in 1934 and later lived on reservations in the southwest. A scholar as well as a writer, he received a bachelor's degree from the University of New Mexico and a Ph.D. from Stanford.

Taking its title from a Navajo ceremonial song, the book details the life of a young Indian man named Abel, who is caught between the traditional Navajo life and the more destructive, urban world of postwar America. The novel's structure is intricate and combines a modernist form with references to Native ceremonial practices to create a haunting and redemptive work. The book has earned Momaday comparisons to William Faulkner and James Joyce. *House Made of Dawn* is now considered one of the significant novels of the twentieth century and the impetus for the renaissance in American Indian literature.

BIBLIOGRAPHY

Schubnell, Matthias. *N. Scott Momaday: The Cultural and Literary Background.* Norman: University of Oklahoma Press, 1985.

Stephanie Gordon

See also **Literature: Native American Literature.**

HOUSE OF BURGESSES, the first popularly elected legislature in America. It first met as a one-house assembly in Virginia on 30 July 1619, with a governor, Sir George Yeardley, four members of the council, and two burgesses from each of the boroughs, to preserve the same rights as the residents of Britain for Virginia's freeholders, the white male property holders. The house determined the eligibility of its own members, passed local laws, carried out the provisions of the governor and the charter, and regulated taxes. It developed into a two-house legislature, with little English influence by the mid-seventeenth century. On 29 June 1776, the house declared Virginia's independence from Great Britain and wrote the state's first constitution.

BIBLIOGRAPHY

Griffith, Lucille Blanche. *The Virginia House of Burgesses, 1750–1774.* University: University of Alabama Press, 1970.

Morton, Richard Lee. *Colonial Virginia.* Chapel Hill: University of North Carolina Press, 1960.

Quitt, Martin H. *Virginia House of Burgesses, 1660–1706: The Social, Educational, and Economic Bases of Political Power.* New York: Garland, 1989.

Michelle M. Mormul

See also **Assemblies, Colonial; Chesapeake Colonies; Virginia.**

HOUSE OF REPRESENTATIVES. *See* **Congress, United States.**

HOUSE-GREY MEMORANDUM. In 1916, as U.S. relations with both Germany and Great Britain became more tense, President Woodrow Wilson sought to mediate an end to the conflict in Europe. The first effort was the House-Grey Memorandum negotiated by Wilson's trusted adviser, Colonel Edward M. House, and the British foreign secretary, Sir Edward Grey. The memorandum, issued on 22 February 1916, called for the United States to invite the warring powers to a peace conference, and if the Allied Powers accepted and the Central Powers rejected this invitation, the United States "would probably enter the war against Germany." Nothing came of this initial effort. Wilson toned down the guarantee of American physical force, while the belligerents still had hopes of victory.

BIBLIOGRAPHY

Williams, Joyce G. *Colonel House and Sir Edward Grey: A Study in Anglo-American Diplomacy.* Lanham, Md.: University Press of America, 1984.

Charles M. Dobbs

HOUSING

Native American and Colonial Housing

Native Americans built a wide variety of houses on the North American continent thousands of years before European colonization. Some were simple triangular tipis, engineered to resist the wind and keep out the cold but easily moveable; others were earthen, wood and covering, stone, or adobe houses. Often the shapes of these dwellings reflected the features of the land around them as their builders sought a safe accommodation with nature. Native Americans lived in single-family structures, extended-family structures, and multiunit structures. In the mid-sixteenth century Spaniards explored the Southwest, where they found Native Americans living in remarkable cliff dwellings and pueblos. The Europeans added their own

Aleut House. An early-twentieth-century Indian shelter in Alaska: a hole in the earth, covered by a framework of driftwood that is held up with whalebone. LIBRARY OF CONGRESS

concepts of housing to indigenous materials and methods of construction to create a distinctive style still common in the Southwest. European colonists arriving on the eastern seaboard in the seventeenth century built houses of masonry or wood that imitated Old World houses. The few remaining from the colonial period are readily identifiable as Dutch, French, or English. In forested New England, colonial houses were built of wood. In Virginia and Maryland the colonists built masonry houses, using the clay soil to make bricks and oyster shells to make mortar. The earliest colonial houses were simple one- or two-room, one-story buildings.

During the colonial period there emerged several types of American houses that incorporated distinctive environmental adaptations. New England houses were designed for difficult winters with sharply sloped roofs, low ceilings, small rooms, and small windows. The houses of the Southwest faced inward onto courtyards, had thick adobe walls, high ceilings, and small windows in outer facades. The houses of the Middle Atlantic states and the South were built with high ceilings, large windows, central halls, and long porches. Houses were placed on hills to capture breezes or sheltered to avoid harsh winds. Not until central heating and air conditioning did such adaptations to climate become less crucial.

Settlement of the West and the Urbanization of America

Nineteenth-century settlers beyond the Appalachians at first built modest houses that utilized the resources available to them. Those in woodland areas built log cabins. Faced with treeless prairies, the immigrants who settled the Great Plains in the second half of the nineteenth century built dugouts or sod houses and sometimes houses of stone. However, when the railroads brought cut lumber and other building supplies, wood-framed houses in styles popular on the east coast became typical in the interior portions of the country.

In 1860 four times as many people lived in rural as in urban areas, but by 1920 rural and urban populations were approaching parity. Industry transformed America between the Civil War and the early twentieth century from a rural agricultural nation to one in which cities were growing rapidly as people came to them from both foreign countries and rural areas. The Census of 1890 counted some 12.7 million families in the United States. That number was 11 percent more than the number of dwelling units, with an even worse housing ratio in the eastern industrialized cities. For example, in 1900 three-quarters of New York City's population lived in squalid, overcrowded tenements. In 1890 Jacob Riis published *How the Other Half Lives*, a shocking description of slum life among New York City immigrants.

On the other hand, the houses of the more prosperous were being equipped with electric lights, central heating, and indoor bathrooms by the 1880s. New forms of public transportation, primarily electric streetcars, made possible the development of housing away from city centers. A nationwide speculation boom in land acquisition and subdivision of building lots developed in the 1880s, and by the end of 1892, the housing market in the United States was oversupplied.

At the end of the nineteenth century, the new American industrialists began displaying their wealth by building showplace houses in cities and more rural settings. Newport, Rhode Island, was a favorite location for the fabulous summer homes of the wealthy. The elegance and luxury of this housing stood in sharp contrast to city tenements and the shacks of the poor in the South.

Frank Lloyd Wright and Suburbanization

Before World War I, a comprehensive movement of social and political reform known as progressivism took a stand against the ostentatious lifestyles of the wealthy and condemned the wretchedness of slum housing. Frank Lloyd Wright envisioned the ideal suburban house for the independent American family, a free-standing house on its own plot of ground. Wright proposed that American housing development be spread over the entire country with each family occupying one house on one acre of land. A vast network of roads could link it all together in a culture without cities. It is this pattern of sprawl, so sharply in contrast to the centralized settlements brought to the United States from Europe, that has come to prevail in the United States.

Wright's Prairie Houses incorporated a new form of interior design that featured large fireplaces in the center of the house and an open flowing floor plan. The symbolism of the houses was sanctuary for the American family, natural surroundings, escape from the crowded conditions of the city, and rejection of the artificiality of overwrought design. Wright's designs were part of a movement away from the formal Queen Anne houses so dominant in the second half of the nineteenth century and toward the simpler Craftsman or bungalow styles.

Prosperity, Depression, and World War II

Between 1923 and 1927 a period of economic prosperity brought with it one of the greatest housing booms in the history of the country. The new availability of automobiles stimulated construction of houses in the suburbs, where land was relatively cheap. More than seven million new dwelling units were started in the 1920s; annual housing peaked at 937,000 units in 1925, a figure that would be unsurpassed for the next twenty years. By 1932, housing production had fallen to 134,000 units and the industry, along with the rest of the economic and financial structure of the country, was spiraling downward. Property values fell by more than 25 percent from 1929 to 1932, eliminating homeowner equity and increasing mortgage debt from 36 percent of value in 1928 to 61 percent in 1932. As foreclosures increased, approximately one million people were forced into homelessness. The administration of President Franklin D. Roosevelt drew housing into the purview of the federal government during the 1930s by creating, along with several other programs, the Federal Housing Administration to provide federal insurance for home loans.

Apartment House. The upscale Beresford Apartments, completed in 1929 and located on Central Park West on the Upper West Side of Manhattan. © Lee Snider/corbis

The crisis of World War II produced the first mass production of prefabricated houses. Builders devised factory-built, standardized building components such as wall and ceiling panels, and utilized light metal framing with girders and trusses that allowed for greater spans. Poured concrete foundations became standard. Many technological advances were made with the help of leading universities such as the Massachusetts Institute of Technology. This cooperative effort established the basis for the hugely expanded postwar construction industry. The small, craft-oriented, homebuilding industry became more like the rest of American industry in general.

Postwar Prosperity, the Flight from the Cities, and Racial Discrimination

Americans came out of World War II with higher incomes to buy better houses. Housing starts in 1946, at 1,023,000, were higher than they had been in 1925, the previous record year, and they reached nearly 1.5 million in 1949. During this boom period the average cost of building a house rose from $4,625 in 1945 to $7,525 in 1949. Veterans Administration guaranteed loans were a major factor in helping to house the millions of servicemen returning from the war. The proportion of nonfarm home ownership rose from 41.1 percent in 1940 to 50.8 percent in 1945, the fastest increase of such magnitude to take place in the twentieth century. By 1956 the owner-occupied portion of nonfarm occupancy would be 59 percent, a huge increase from that of 1940.

The 1950 Census showed an improvement in the physical condition of the country's housing. Based on a standard of more than one person per room, overcrowding was reduced from 20 percent in 1940 to 15 percent in 1949. As the country continued its emergence from the depression and war years, those who could afford it largely fled the cities, leaving behind a poor minority population, a diminished commercial core, and growing slums. An American Public Health Association Report in 1948 recognized racial segregation and substandard housing in central cities as major problems. The Housing Act of 1949 favored "a decent home and a suitable living environment for every American family," but it was years before racial segregation in housing was addressed comprehensively. In 1962 President John F. Kennedy issued an executive order barring discrimination in the sale, lease, or occupancy of residential property owned or operated by the federal government. The Civil Rights Act of 1964 barred racial discrimination in any housing requiring federal funding assistance and the Fair Housing Act of 1968 established equal housing opportunity as official U.S. policy.

Expanding Suburbs, More Apartment Buildings

The new American middle class wanted the suburban houses that prosperity could make available to them in the postwar period. The ideal was a single-family house for the nuclear family on a large lot away from the deteriorating inner city. Builders acquired large tracts of land relatively inexpensively at the perimeters of towns and cities, secured government-insured advance financing, installed streets and other infrastructure, and mass produced standardized ranch-style housing. Production of mobile homes, which had been around since the 1930s when they were called trailers, began to expand rapidly in the 1960s as assembly-line techniques were improved.

The development of the elevator and steel frame construction had promoted intense multistory apartment building construction in the late nineteenth century in large cities where land was too expensive to justify single-family houses. Yet in 1960 only about 5 percent of housing units were in apartment buildings of ten or more units, except for New York City, Chicago, Los Angeles, Miami, and Washington, D.C. Apartment construction increased in the 1960s as a result of smaller households and higher per-household income. There was a surge of luxury apartment buildings with balconies, swimming pools, large lobbies, and tenant services such as guest screening, message and package reception, and security features. In addition to rental units, condominium and cooperative apartments, which had some of the features of home ownership, became popular.

Seeking the American Dream

Despite the energy crisis of the mid-1970s and decreasing family size, houses became larger as they were recognized as the best hedge against inflation and the most important source of wealth creation for families. Three bedrooms and two bathrooms became standard. Total housing starts, including shipments of mobile homes, reached an astonishing 21,482,000 in the 1970s. This production level was at the rate of approximately one new dwelling unit for every ten people in the country. The median price of new conventional single-family dwellings rose from $23,400 to $62,900 during the decade. Economist Alan Greenspan estimated in 1977 that the market value of the nation's entire stock of single-family, owner-occupied houses was increasing at an annual rate of $62.2 billion, almost all of which was being converted to cash through mortgages. This money was recirculating in the economy, bringing the United States out of the mid-1970s recession and spurring more housing production. Capital gains from housing outstripped by three to one the gains taken by private investors in the stock market at this time.

In the late 1970s builders began to create new types of housing clusters including duplexes, triplexes, and four-plexes. Large landscaped developments often included a mix of detached houses, apartment buildings, and townhouses around a central feature such as a golf course or other recreational facility. Eventually the more expensive of these developments would become socially segregated "gated" communities with access limited to residents and their guests.

By the 1980s the national homeownership rate was nearly 65 percent, with the highest rate among people from ages fifty-five to sixty-five. The incidence of new two-story houses increased, and all new houses had more bedrooms, bathrooms, and fireplaces. At the other end of the scale were the homeless whose numbers reached an estimated 500,000 to 750,000 during the 1980s.

By 1999 the average new house had two or more stories, three bedrooms, 2.5 bathrooms, central heating and air conditioning, a working fireplace, and a two-car garage. Its average size was 2,250 square feet, 50 percent larger than the average new house in 1970.

The number of housing units in the United States at the end of the twentieth century was nearly 116 million, with 91 percent of these occupied on a full-time basis. Approximately one-third of the remaining 9 percent were seasonal, recreational, or occasionally used dwellings, an indication of the housing prosperity of Americans. More than 66 percent of the units occupied on a full-time basis were occupied by their owners; in 1900 only 36.5 percent of dwelling units were owner occupied. The average household size at the end of the century was 2.6, a number that had been 4.8 in 1900 and 3.7 in 1940.

Housing is an essential component of the nation's economy and a prime indicator of national economic direction. Home ownership is usually the major form of investment for individuals and households, and a key to financial stability and upward social mobility. Home ownership has long been the American Dream, the goal toward which many strive.

BIBLIOGRAPHY

Doan, Mason C. *American Housing Production: 1880–2000, A Concise History.* Lanham, Md.: University Press of America, 1997.

Ford, Larry R. *Cities and Buildings, Skyscrapers, Skid Rows, and Suburbs.* Baltimore: Johns Hopkins University Press, 1994.

Kostof, Spiro. *America by Design.* New York: Oxford University Press, 1987.

Welfeld, Irving. *Where We Live: A Social History of America's Housing.* New York: Simon and Schuster, 1988.

Wright, Gwendolyn. *Building the American Dream: A Social History of Housing In America.* Cambridge, Mass.: MIT Press, 1983.

Judith Reynolds

See also **Apartment Houses; Architecture; Architecture, American Indian; Electrification, Household; Greenbelt Communities; Plumbing; Suburbanization; Tenements; Urbanization;** *and vol. 9:* **In the Slums, 1890.**

HOUSING AND URBAN DEVELOPMENT, DEPARTMENT OF. The Department of Housing and Urban Development (HUD) has a broad and complex mission, accomplished through a number of programs and in conjunction with such entities as Fannie Mae and Freddie Mac as well as the Federal Housing Authority. HUD coordinates and regulates housing loans under these entities, provides subsidies for public housing throughout the United States, assists in providing loans to health care facilities, and has numerous programs to assure the provision of adequate housing particularly in urban areas and to under-served populations in the United States. In addition, HUD is active in assuring the maintenance of the Fair Housing laws in federal programs, provides grants to various entities involved in providing housing, and continually adds programs in these areas.

When President Lyndon B. Johnson signed the legislation creating the Department of Housing and Urban Development on 9 September 1965, he envisioned that HUD would be responsible for federal participation in the thinking and planning of large urban areas and would provide a focal point for innovation and imagination related to the problems of America's growing cities. He also anticipated that HUD would strengthen the federal government's relationship with states and cities on urban issues. He hoped that the department would be able to encourage growth while retarding the decay of the expanding urban centers throughout the country. It was a vision that was originally introduced by President John F. Kennedy in his 1961 State of the Union address. In 1966, the statutory objectives of HUD were translated into the Model Cities and Metropolitan Development Act, and then in 1968 the Housing Act was passed, followed in 1970 by the Housing and Urban Development Act.

From Kennedy and Johnson's vision of the federal government's participation and cooperation in providing adequate housing and urban development that protects and promotes opportunities of diverse ethnic populations and the poorest families in the country, HUD made significant strides during its first three years. It made the Federal Housing Administration a key part of HUD's mission to develop low-income housing, initiated cross-communication between programs so that related issues could be addressed in a coordinated way, involved neighborhood groups in spearheading inner-city rehabilitation through the Model Cities program, and looked for innovative ways to fund private housing for lower-income families. Unfortunately HUD has failed to capitalize on its strong beginnings. Since the Johnson presidency, HUD has proven to be a department that has become the poor cousin within the cabinet—underfunded and racked with scandal, fraud, and abuse. Virtually all of the presidents since Johnson have disagreed with the fundamental aims and purposes for which HUD was established and have attempted to undermine both the power and prestige of the department. Even those who have supported HUD's goals have been unable to overcome its now long history of failure.

President Nixon's HUD secretary from 1969 to 1973, George Romney, actually placed a moratorium on all federal housing programs in 1973, and during Nixon's abbreviated second term, James T. Lynn, Romney's successor, oversaw HUD's decline to a second-tier position within the cabinet.

During the administrations of Gerald Ford and Jimmy Carter, HUD was not able to overcome this reputation. Ford's administration was caught up in post-Watergate caretaking, and Jimmy Carter's administration was quickly besieged by the Iran hostage crisis that came to define his presidency. Carter's post-presidency commitment to and activist role in the nonprofit organization Habitat for Humanity suggests that significant opportunities for strong presidential leadership on the issues of community renewal, fair housing, and innovative programs for financing low-income housing were missed during his administration.

In 1981, President Reagan appointed Samuel R. Pierce Jr., a New York attorney, to be the new secretary of HUD. Pierce's term—lasting the full eight years of the Reagan presidency, the longest of any HUD secretary since its inception—resulted in the appointment of an independent counsel to investigate corruption within the agency. This led ultimately to seventeen criminal convictions, including that of Pierce's former executive assistant. During the same time period, HUD's operating appropriations were cut from $24.9 billion in 1981 to $7.5 billion in 1989—with fraud and corruption taking an estimated $2 billion of the dramatically reduced funds over the eight-year period. (The criminal convictions netted $2 million in criminal fines but only returned some $10 million in squandered HUD monies.) While tainted by the gross mismanagement of the agency, Pierce himself was never charged with any of the corruption that characterized his term at HUD.

The gutting of HUD programs and the ensuing scandals made recovery for HUD in the 1990s problematic at a time when a national economic recession and the spiraling effects of inner-city decay, drugs, and gangs in public housing stretched limited resources and existing programs to the breaking point. Jack Kemp, secretary of HUD in George H. W. Bush's administration (1989–1992), had the difficult two-prong task of trying to respond to the independent counsel's investigation of the previous HUD administration while initiating a comprehensive audit and extensive reform of existing HUD programs and policies. At the same time, he was attempting to promote aggressive programs to assist those mired in the cycle of inner-city poverty and still remain true to his conservative beliefs that market-based policies provided the best long-term hope for the poor to pull themselves out of poverty. Kemp's program HOPE (Home-ownership and Opportunity for People Everywhere) was launched on 10 November 1989 and under its umbrella included programs such as enterprise zones and low-income housing tax credits for first-time home buyers. HOPE, along with a Senate initiative to generate new housing construction called HOME, were folded into the National Affordable Housing Act of 1990. Underfunding and lack of congressional support caused many of these programs to wither and die quietly on the legislative vine.

In 1993, Bill Clinton won the presidency, and with his down-home roots and populist support, particularly among African Americans, many had great hopes for a return to the Kennedy-era "Camelot" with a focus on the renewal of America's dilapidated and struggling cities where large populations of ethnic minorities were trapped. Clinton tapped Henry Cisneros, the former mayor of San Antonio, Texas, to be the secretary of HUD. However, scandal again enveloped the secretary's office when Cisneros became the target of an independent counsel's investigation for misuse of government funds. Ultimately Cisneros was indicted on charges that he had lied about the money he had spent supporting his former girlfriend and pleaded guilty to a misdemeanor.

Despite the scandal, the Clinton administration did focus attention on the massive drug problem that had turned many public housing projects into war zones. In his 23 January 1996 State of the Union address, Clinton announced what would become HUD's "one strike and you're out" policy, with zero tolerance for drug-related activities or violence for those living in public-assisted housing. While the program had detractors, and the zero tolerance policy led to some Orwellian results, Clinton's new HUD secretary, Andrew M. Cuomo, worked with Congress to implement the program along with tightening the reins of HUD to overcome the years of mismanagement.

The twelfth secretary of Housing and Urban Development, appointed by President George W. Bush, was the first Cuban American cabinet member in U.S. history. Mel Martinez arrived from Cuba in 1962 during an airlift of children. He began life in America in a foster home, not speaking a word of English. From these humble beginnings, he assumed leadership of HUD, charged with implementing policies and programs that address the needs of some 5.4 million families. Unfortunately, by 2002, housing and urban issues had once again taken a backseat to more pressing national and international concerns, and observers thought it unlikely that HUD would become a priority in the Bush administration.

BIBLIOGRAPHY

Kotlowitz, Adam. *There Are No Children Here: The Story of Two Boys Growing Up in America.* New York: Doubleday, 1991.

Nenno, Mary K. *Ending the Stalemate: Moving Housing and Urban Development into the Mainstream of America's Future.* Lanham, Md.: University Press of America, 1996.

Karenbeth Farmer
M. H. Hoeflich
Broadus Mitchell

See also **City Planning; Corruption, Political.**

HOUSTON. The city of Houston, Texas—fourth largest city in the United States, world petroleum and petrochemical capital, national corporate center, and major international port—has long been noted for its ag-

Houston Oil. This 1939 photograph by Russell Lee shows a refinery along the Houston Ship Channel. LIBRARY OF CONGRESS

gressive business leadership and impressive record of economic growth. Houston's phenomenal development ranks as one of the most astonishing examples of urban growth in United States history.

In 1836, only John and Augustus Allen, the visionary New Yorkers who founded the city on the coastal prairies of southeast Texas, fifty miles inland from Galveston Island, glimpsed Houston's potential. Hampered by its location on Buffalo Bayou, a scarcely navigable, sluggish little stream, Houston was overshadowed in importance by the seaport of Galveston. Southeast Texas itself was only a peripheral area of the Deep South whose long-dominant urban entrepôt was New Orleans.

Named after Sam Houston, hero of the fight for Texas independence, the city served briefly as capital of the Texas Republic (1837–1839), but its future did not lie in becoming a seat of government. Like other southern inland cities Houston specialized in rail development, serving as a railhead for Galveston and as a collection and shipment point for cotton and other agricultural goods produced in the region. Before the Civil War, Houston became a regional railroad center with five rail lines fanning out in all directions. Postbellum expansion linked the city to the national rail network in 1873.

After the Civil War, Houston businessmen determined to make Houston a major port city. Buffalo Bayou was difficult to navigate even for small boats, so Houston boosters began a drive to dredge a navigable channel toward the Gulf of Mexico. Charles Morgan, a Gulf Coast shipowner, headed the project, which resulted in the opening of a twelve-foot-deep waterway to Clinton. Houston entrepreneurs enlisted federal assistance to resume the ship channel project in 1881 until the waterway cut through Galveston Bay and Buffalo Bayou to a turning basin above Harrisburg in 1914. The Houston Ship Channel, subsequently widened and deepened, made Houston a major inland port.

Houston was spared the fate of Galveston, which was completely destroyed by a hurricane in 1900. With the elimination of its rival to the south, the path was clear for Houston to develop into the dominant urban center in southeast Texas. The cornerstone of the city's bid for regional dominance and national prominence was set with the advent of the Texas oil boom that followed the discovery of oil at nearby Spindletop in 1901. The oil boom led to the formation of three of the world's major oil companies: Texaco (originally the Texas Company), Gulf, and Exxon (originally Humble). Houston became the national capital of an integrated industry consisting of energy business headquarters, drilling operations, producing wells, pipelines, refineries, and port facilities. The Houston Ship Channel developed into a major world petrochemical industry corridor.

The city's extraordinary growth, interrupted by the Great Depression of the 1930s, resurged with the onset of World War II. As wartime industrial production expanded into the South, Houston shared in the largesse by acquiring numerous new defense plants and contracts in the petroleum, petrochemical, and shipbuilding industries. These new and expanded industries acted as a catalyst for postwar growth. Postwar Houston experienced rapid urban population and spatial growth. The city, having incorporated several surrounding suburbs in the late 1940s, surpassed New Orleans in population in 1950. The Bayou City was on its way to becoming a major national metropolis. By 1984, it had surpassed Philadelphia as the nation's fourth largest city behind New York City, Los Angeles, and Chicago.

Urban Houston. A panoramic view of the city's skyline, 1910. Library of Congress

In the 1960s, the emergence of the economic phenomenon known as the Sunbelt witnessed enhanced economic diversification and growth. Houston's private and public leaders could boast of many accomplishments. Securing the Manned Spaceflight Center (later the Johnson Space Center) in 1960 was a defining achievement of the period.

The oil boom of the 1970s brought even greater prosperity, but collapsing oil prices in the 1980s produced Houston's most severe economic downturn since the Great Depression. A return to former prosperity in the 1990s meant greater population, spatial and economic growth, and also created a movement toward greater economic diversification that included such fields as business services, medical research, health services, international banking, and tourism.

Houston was still the fourth most populous city in the United States in 2000. With 1,953,631 people, it is part of the Houston-Galveston-Brazoria Consolidated Metropolitan Statistical Area, the nation's tenth most populous CMSA, with 4,669,571 people in 2000.

The only major American city to eschew zoning as a planning tool, Houston is generally regarded as one of the best examples of a private enterprise city in a nation where the public sector receives its cues from business leadership. Nevertheless, it has managed to adapt well to new political trends. In 1981, the city's voters elected Houston's first woman mayor, Kathryn J. Whitmire; in 1997 they chose its first African American mayor, Lee P. Brown.

BIBLIOGRAPHY

Angel, William D., Jr. "To Make A City: Entrepreneurship on the Sunbelt Frontier." In *The Rise of the Sunbelt Cities*. Edited by David C. Perry and Alfred J. Watkins. Beverly Hills, Calif.: Sage Publications, 1977.

Johnston, Margurite. *Houston, The Unknown City, 1836–1946*. College Station: Texas A&M University Press, 1991.

Kaplan, Barry J. "Houston: The Golden Buckle of the Sunbelt." In *Sunbelt Cities, Politics and Growth Since World War II*. Edited by Richard M. Bernard and Bradley R. Rice. Austin: University of Texas Press, 1983.

McComb, David G. *Houston, The Bayou City*. Austin: University of Texas Press, 1969.

Parker, Robert E. and Joe R. Feagin. "Military Spending in Free Enterprise Cities: The Military-Industrial Complex in Houston and Las Vegas." In *The Pentagon and the Cities*. Edited by Andrew Kirby. London: Sage Publications, 1992.

Conrad L. Rein

See also **Petrochemical Industry; Petroleum Industry; Texas.**

HOW TO WIN FRIENDS AND INFLUENCE PEOPLE. Dale Carnegie (1888–1955) was a Missouri-born teacher, sprung from a struggling farm family. After a brief, unsuccessful acting career, he began to offer public-speaking classes in a New York YMCA in 1912. In 1936, his book *How to Win Friends and Influence People*, based on two and a half decades of teaching classes in speech and assertiveness, succeeded spectacularly and went on to sell 15 million copies. It was essentially a book of advice to salesmen and executives who wanted to manipulate their customers and employees. Its commonsense advice included the injunctions to gaze intently on your interlocutor, to use a dazzling smile, to remember his name, and praise him lavishly. Above all, said Carnegie, make the people you meet feel important and they in turn will respect and admire you. He added that the feeling must come from within—if it was insincere, it was worthless. The author had changed the spelling of his name (originally Carnagey) to match the name of industrialist-millionaire Andrew Carnegie, whom he idolized. He littered the text of his book with the older Carnegie's sayings, jostling them against quotations by John D. Rockefeller, Jesus, Lao-tzu, and Confucius.

Carnegie's success is attributable partly to the fact that his book appeared in the depths of the Great Depression and offered solace and hope to a generation of discouraged businessmen. It also contributed to the growing literature of industrial psychology and welfare capitalism, which emphasized the importance of good human relations in a smoothly operating commercial system. Ironically, it had little to say about making friends (hostile reviewers treated it as a manual on the cynical perfection of insincerity) but did describe methods for avoiding confrontation and strife. Carnegie himself disarmed critics by insisting, "I've never claimed to have a new idea. . . . I deal with the obvious."

BIBLIOGRAPHY

Kemp, Giles, and Edward Claflin. *Dale Carnegie: The Man Who Influenced Millions*. New York: St. Martin's, 1989.

Meyer, Donald. *The Positive Thinkers: Religion as Pop Psychology from Mary Baker Eddy to Oral Roberts*. New York: Pantheon, 1980.

Patrick N. Allitt

See also **Psychology; Self-Help Movement.**

HOWARD, FORT, built in 1816 on the site of the former French Fort La Baye and of the British Fort Edward Augustus, was the first American post at Green Bay, Wis., and was for many years the lone Americanizing force in a predominantly French settlement. Its garrison was called out in the Red Bird uprising (1827) and in the Black Hawk War (1832). The garrison was withdrawn in 1841; troops were again brought there at the close of the Mexican-American War, when Lt. Col. B. L. E. de Bonneville was the last commandant.

BIBLIOGRAPHY

Kellogg, Louise Phelps. "Old Fort Howard." *Wisconsin Magazine of History* 18 (1934).

Prucha, Francis P. *A Guide to the Military Posts of the United States, 1789–1895*. Madison: State Historical Society of Wisconsin, 1964.

Louise Phelps Kellogg / A. R.

See also **Army Posts; Fox-Wisconsin Waterway; Green Bay; Wisconsin.**

HUBBLE SPACE TELESCOPE. Although astronomer Lyman Spitzer first suggested the idea of a space-based telescope in 1946, it was not until 24 April 1990 that one was placed in orbit around the earth. Named after the pioneering astronomer Edwin P. Hubble, it promised to overcome distortions caused by the earth's atmosphere. The forty-three-foot-long telescope could look seven times farther into space than the most powerful terrestrial observatories.

Computer problems in 1982 thwarted the $2 billion telescope's initial launching. Rescheduled for October 1986, its launch was again delayed by the tragedy in January 1986 that killed the crew of the space shuttle *Challenger*. Four years later, the Hubble Space Telescope finally was lifted into space. Two months after the telescope was placed in orbit, scientists announced that its 94.5-inch primary mirror, polished to incredible smoothness, was flawed, resulting in blurred images. Ironically, the telescope was myopic. Investigation showed that engineers easily could have detected this problem prior to launch. Scientists had to delay or cancel experiments.

In December 1993 the crew of the space shuttle *Endeavour* fitted the telescope with corrective optics and

Hubble Space Telescope. The device has expanded the frontiers of the visible universe. © CORBIS

made other repairs. After this $629 million outer-space repair job, the telescope worked perfectly. It took detailed views of nebulae and star clusters. In October 1994 astronomers announced that data from the telescope showed that the universe was between eight billion and twelve billion years old, younger than earlier estimates by nearly half. Astronomers announced in January 1996 that the telescope was detecting hundreds of galaxies never before seen, which they speculated could be the most distant and oldest galaxies ever observed.

BIBLIOGRAPHY

Fischer, Daniel, and Hilmar Duerbeck. *The Hubble: A New Window to the Universe.* Translated by Helmut Jenkner and Douglas Duncan. New York: Copernicus, 1996.

Peterson, Carolyn Collins, and John C. Brandt. *Hubble Vision: Further Adventures with the Hubble Space Telescope.* 2d ed. New York: Cambridge University Press, 1998.

Brent Schondelmeyer / A. R.

See also ***Challenger*** **Disaster; Observatories, Astronomical; Space Program.**

HUCKLEBERRY FINN. Ernest Hemingway wrote that "all modern American literature comes from one book by Mark Twain called *Huckleberry Finn.* . . . All American writing comes from that. There was nothing before. There has been nothing as good since."

The Adventures of Huckleberry Finn was published in 1885, and in that year the public library in Concord, Massachusetts, became the first institution to ban the novel. Twain's use of the word "nigger" later led some schools and libraries to ban the book. *Huckleberry Finn* was first attacked during Twain's day because of what some described as its indecency; later, it would be attacked as racist. But by the end of the twentieth century, its status as one of the greatest of American novels was almost universally recognized.

Huck Finn, the protagonist and narrator of the novel, is around thirteen or fourteen years of age. He is being raised by Miss Watson and the Widow Douglas, both of whom blindly accept the hypocritical religious and moral nature of their society and try to help Huck understand its codes and customs. They represent an artificial life that Huck wishes to escape. Huck's attempt to help Jim, a runaway slave, reunite with his family makes it difficult for him to understand what is right and wrong. The book follows Huck's and Jim's adventures rafting down the Mississippi River, where Huck gradually rejects the values of the dominant society, especially its views on slavery.

BIBLIOGRAPHY

Blair, Walter. *Mark Twain and Huck Finn.* Berkeley: University of California Press, 1960.

Smith, Henry Nash. *Mark Twain: The Development of a Writer.* Cambridge, Mass.: Belknap Press, 1962.

James Varn

HUDSON RIVER. From its Adirondack origin in Lake Tear of the Clouds to its southern terminus in upper New York Bay, the Hudson River, 306 miles in length, drains an area of about 13,370 square miles. While its waters were long traveled and fished by Indians, the first European to see the Hudson was probably Giovanni da Verrazano, an Italian sailing for the French, who explored the area in 1524. Although other Europeans reached the Hudson during the sixteenth century, settlement occurred only after Henry Hudson's September 1609 voyage of exploration. Hudson, an Englishman in the employ of the Dutch East India Company, was seeking a northwest passage to the Far East. On his ship, the *Half Moon,* he sailed about 150 miles up the river that now bears his name.

After Hudson reported on the availability of furs along the river, Amsterdam fur traders established a Dutch trading post at Fort Nassau (near present-day Albany) in 1613. In 1623, the newly created West India Company took over the fort, renaming it Fort Orange, while the vast territory claimed by the Dutch was called New Netherland, with its principal settlement, New Amsterdam, at the southern tip of Manhattan Island. Much of the settlement of New Netherland was concentrated on the Hudson River, with a few large patroonships established along its banks. The river and the territory remained in Dutch hands until 1664, when Sir Richard

Hudson River. Steamboats like Robert Fulton's *Clermont*, launched in 1807, revolutionized transportation and accelerated New York State's economic growth. © UPI/CORBIS-BETTMANN

Nicolls led a force of Englishmen who seized the territory and renamed it New York.

The Hudson played a significant role during the American Revolution, with both the British and the Americans seeking to maintain control of the waterway. On 12 July 1776, Admiral Lord Richard Howe sent two British warships, the *Phoenix* and the *Rose*, thirty miles up the Hudson to Tarrytown. To prevent the British from moving further north, logs were used to float an iron chain across the river from the fort at West Point to Constitution Island.

New York's most dramatic growth followed the end of the Revolution, when the Six Nations of the Iroquois ceded most of their territory to the state, permitting settlers to move up the Hudson and then west. Growth was further accelerated with the 1807 invention of the steamboat. Steamboats sparked the state's economic development and eventually fostered a tourist industry by attracting wealthy city residents north to the Catskills and Adirondacks. Even more rapid economic growth followed the opening of the ERIE CANAL in 1825, as goods from Lake Erie ports were moved through New York State and then down the Hudson to shipping facilities in New York City. The completion of the Hudson River Railroad in 1851 further spurred trade and encouraged wealthy New Yorkers to build homes along the Hudson.

The beauty of the Hudson River valley sparked a revolution in American art with the development of the HUDSON RIVER SCHOOL of painters. By the early nineteenth century, artists such as Thomas Cole, Asher Durand, John Kensett, Thomas Doughty, Jasper Cropsey, George Inness, and John Casilear created American landscapes that celebrated the natural beauty of the area. The river and its mountains also served as a favored locale in the literary works of such American writers as Washington Irving and James Fenimore Cooper.

The river has paid a price for progress and development. By the twentieth century, the Hudson had become a polluted waterway. The river was the focal point for conservationists when, in 1962, Con Edison made a proposal to build a hydroelectric plant on the river at Storm King Mountain. Opposition to the plant prompted the U.S. Court of Appeals to insist that the planners consider the effects of the plant on the environment. In the ensuing battle, the pressure brought by environmental groups led Con Edison to drop the Storm King project in 1980. A later environmental battle concerned the dumping of over one million pounds of the carcinogenic substance polychlorinated biphenyl (PCB) in the Hudson by major corporations situated on its banks. In 2001, the Environmental Protection Agency ordered General Electric to begin a $500 million dredging operation of the Hudson River to remove the PCBs.

BIBLIOGRAPHY

Carmer, Carl. *The Hudson.* New York: Fordham University Press, 1992.

Dunwell, Frances F. *Hudson River Highlands.* New York: Columbia University Press, 1992.

Lossing, Benson J. *The Hudson.* Hensonville, N.Y.: Black Dome Press, 2000.

Mary Lou Lustig

See also **New York State.**

HUDSON RIVER SCHOOL, a group of nineteenth-century painters inspired by the American landscape. In the realm of the arts, nineteenth-century Americans were torn between a conviction that their country was possessed of unique virtues and a belief that they should copy European masters. In one respect, what painters could learn from the Old World fitted exactly the conditions of their new land. The European Romantic movement taught a reverence for nature at its wildest, and along with that an awe in the presence of power, darkness, and mystery, all of them evocable in scenes of natural grandeur. Americans possessed a landscape such as the Romantic imagination sought, presenting itself not in quiet and domesticated detail but in great spaces broken into by deep forests, wild waters, and violent storms.

Painters were discovering similar moods on the European continent, to be sure. But the peculiar mating of Romanticism, transmitted to the United States in the form of transcendentalism, with a wilderness that Americans saw as their unspoiled and inviting heritage awakened a distinctive artistic sensibility. In the second and third quarters of the nineteenth century, American nature was captured particularly by a group of painters known collectively as the Hudson River school. The designation "Hudson River school" was first applied dismissively late in the century, but has since become an honored name.

Kindred Spirits. This 1849 painting by Asher B. Durand is typical of the Hudson River school's transcendentalist reverence for nature. © Francis G. Mayer/Corbis

Early in the nineteenth century, much of the American concept of good painting took its definition from the American Academy of Fine Arts, which drew on formal European composition. The National Academy of Design, founded in 1825, was an instrument for the propagation of the Romantic venture. Practitioners traveled into remote regions to make sketches; much of their finished work took place in studios in New York City. Albert Bierstadt drew on western scenery, notably in his *Rocky Mountains, Landers Peak* (1863) and his *Lower Yellowstone Falls.* Frederic Edwin Church mined landscape in Ecuador, including an active volcano. Others included Thomas Doughty, Thomas Cole, George Inness, and Asher Brown Durand. Adherents to the new aesthetic had faith in the instruction given by nature on its own terms. Some of the Hudson River paintings do not depict an exact geographic scene but one heightened by the painter's imagination. However, they were generally of a mind with Henry David Thoreau, whose writings depict spiritual patterns in nature yet describe them in the most exquisitely precise detail of a veined leaf, a colony of ants, a rivulet of water tracing downhill. The result, or at least the effort of such an apprehension of nature, therefore brought together enterprises that coexist uneasily: an intellectual construct in Romanticism, scientific inquiry, and artistic execution.

In the mid-1830s, the British immigrant Cole carried out a more abstract and idealized work in his ambitious series *The Course of Empire*, an essay on canvas describing through stages the hope and folly of human endeavor. It goes from the violent landscape *Savage State* through *Pastoral or Arcadian* and *Consummation of Empire* to *Destruction to Desolation*, depicting ruined colonnades amid a reasserted nature. Such explicit instruction in the evils of overcivilization was the exception. More common were presentations of a nature of commanding force yet life-giving to humanity if it will accept it in itself. Durand's familiar *Kindred Spirits*, painted in 1849, puts the figures of Cole and William Cullen Bryant atop a crag looking over a rugged yet benign wilderness. Their communion with each other and their surroundings catches the transcendentalist perception of a oneness between mind and nature.

By the century's last quarter, artistic aims and techniques were changing. Part of the reason, doubtless, was a decline in Romanticism in its transcendentalist American form, which intellectuals had for a time adopted as virtually a reigning American ethos. A new aesthetic developed in France, the Barbizon school, was competing with the manner of the Hudson River painters. One artist, George Inness, bridged the shift. Artists continued to seek majesty and refreshment in nature; but they sought a freer and more personally experimental rendering of natural scenery.

BIBLIOGRAPHY

Cooper, James F. *Knights of the Brush: The Hudson River School and the Moral Landscape.* New York: Hudson Hills Press, 1999.

Howat, John K. *The Hudson River and Its Painters.* New York: Penguin Books, 1972.

Lassiter, Barbara Babcock. *American Wilderness: The Hudson River School of Painting.* Garden City, N.Y.: Doubleday, 1977.

David Burner

See also **Art: Painting.**

HUDSON'S BAY COMPANY. The Hudson's Bay Company resulted from the western explorations of Pierre Esprit Radisson and Médard Chouart, Sieur de Groseilliers, in the mid-seventeenth century. On trips into Wisconsin and Minnesota country, they learned from NATIVE AMERICANS of a great fur country northwest of Lake Superior that might be reached via Hudson Bay. This idea, linked with one of a probable northwest passage through Hudson Bay, led the Frenchmen to England in the middle 1660s. There they assembled a sort of syndicate of wealthy and influential men that grew into the Hudson's Bay Company, and received its charter on 2 May 1670, as the Governor and Company of Adventurers of England Trading into Hudson's Bay. Under that charter and supplemental charters the company still operates, making it one of the oldest commercial corporations.

Much of the company's effect on the United States sprang from a bitter struggle that raged between it and the North West Company. During the heyday of the fur trade, the company had posts in most parts of what is now Canada and a few forts on U.S. soil, mostly along the boundary line west from Grand Portage. Near the Red River of the North (now Manitoba), Thomas Douglas, fifth Lord Selkirk—one of the North West Company's largest stock owners—had established a colony on company lands in 1811. The Hudson's Bay Company and the North West Company resolved many of their differences by merging in 1821, but Selkirk died in the same year, leaving the company to administer his colony. Members of Selkirk's colony had contributed to the establishment of Fort Saint Anthony (now Fort Snelling) in 1819, and the misfortunes of the colonists continued to lead many of them to emigrate to Fort Snelling, making them some of Minnesota's earliest European settlers. Red River cart traffic with MINNESOTA settlements, proximity to U.S. soil, and the colonists' discontent with company rule led to annexation hopes and schemes on both the part of the colonists and the United States between 1849 and the final surrender of the company's territories in 1869.

Missionaries provided the second major effect of the Hudson's Bay Company. Operating under the aegis of the company, they not only attempted to convert Native American and mixed-race groups, they also played an important part in the company's expansion into OREGON country. Company men appeared in Oregon in 1821 to carry on the fur trade begun years earlier by the North West Company. Although a joint occupation agreement existed between the United States and Great Britain from 1818 to 1846, Dr. John McLoughlin, the company's chief factor, helped Oregon become American by welcoming American traders, explorers, missionaries, and settlers. The decline of the fur trade and the threat of war were the final factors that convinced Great Britain in 1846 to abandon its claims south of the forty-ninth parallel. The Hudson's Bay Company continues to operate today, albeit without its monopoly of trade, its territory, and administrative rights in the West that were granted under its first charter.

BIBLIOGRAPHY

MacKay, Douglas. *The Honourable Company: A History of the Hudson's Bay Company.* Indianapolis, Ind.: Bobbs-Merrill, 1936.

Newman, Peter C. *Company of Adventurers.* New York: Viking, 1985.

Rich, E. E., ed. *The History of the Hudson's Bay Company 1670–1870.* London: Hudson's Bay Record Society, 1958–1959.

Grace Lee Nute / F. B.

See also **Corporations; Fur Companies; Fur Trade and Trapping; North West Company.**

HUGUENOTS. The term "Huguenot," of unknown origin, was first applied to French Calvinists during the religious struggles of the sixteenth century. Henry IV granted religious toleration to his Protestant subjects by the Edict of Nantes (1598), but Louis XIV revoked it in 1685. During periods of persecution, approximately 300,000 French Protestants fled to Prussia, Switzerland, Holland, England, and the Dutch and English colonies. Fewer than 3,000 Huguenot refugees arrived in America before 1710. In America, the label Huguenot came to refer more broadly to French-speaking Calvinists, whether French, Swiss, or Walloon.

Attempted Huguenot settlements in Florida and South Carolina in 1562 and 1564 failed. In 1623, Huguenots, largely Walloons, settled New Amsterdam. Peter Minuit, the first director general of New Netherland, was a Walloon, and Jean Vigne, the first white child born on Manhattan Island, was French and probably Huguenot. Fort Orange (Albany), Kingston, and New Paltz in New York were Huguenot settlements. Some 200 or 300 Huguenot families came to Boston after Louis XIV's Dragonnades, which persecuted Protestants by billeting unruly soldiers in their homes.

After 1685, increasing numbers of Huguenots came to America, settling in Rhode Island, in Hartford and Milford in Connecticut, and in New Rochelle, New York. They mingled with other settlers in Delaware, Maryland, and Pennsylvania, where they were called Dutchmen and confused with German settlers. In Virginia, the first of the "French Protestant Refugees," as the name appears officially in Virginia records, was Nicholas Martiau. He arrived before 1620 and is the earliest known Virginia ancestor of George Washington. The shipload coming to

Manakintowne on 23 July 1700, and two more shiploads in the same year, made up the largest single settlement of Huguenots in America. King William Parish was set aside for them, but this group with its local church and pastor was absorbed into the Church of England. The parishioners soon intermarried with the English people of the colony.

Huguenots began coming to South Carolina in 1670, played a large part in the settlement of Charleston in 1680, and by 1687 had established four settlements largely or wholly French: Jamestown on the Santee River, the "Orange Quarter" on the Cooper River, Saint-John's in Berkeley County, and Charleston. In 1732, 360 French-Swiss Protestants settled Purysburg on the Savannah River, and in 1764 the last French colony was founded, New Bordeaux in Abbeville County.

Traditionally, historians have emphasized the rapid assimilation of the Huguenots into American society, linguistically, religiously, and economically. The most recent interpretations are more circumspect. While the Huguenots did indeed learn English, conform to Anglicanism, and contract exogamous marriages, such behavior may better be described as acculturation, in that Huguenot values influenced the evolution of the dominant Anglo-American culture. The process of assimilation may also have been more gradual than earlier historians believed. Huguenots transacted public business in English but continued to use French in private correspondence through most of the eighteenth century. Among merchant families, exogamous marriages served to maintain and expand their place within the Atlantic commercial network known as the Protestant International. Calvinist religious practices persisted despite conformity, giving a low-church tone to the Church of England.

The late nineteenth century witnessed a revival of Huguenot ethnicity as exemplified in the creation of Huguenot heritage societies and the adoption of a Huguenot flag (a Maltese cross and dove against a blue background). In Charleston at the end of the twentieth century, Huguenot descendants continued to take pride in their Huguenot church, the only one still in existence in America.

BIBLIOGRAPHY

Bosher, John F. "Huguenot Merchants and the Protestant International in the Seventeenth Century." *William and Mary Quarterly*, 3d ser., 52 (January 1995): 77–102.

Butler, Jon. *The Huguenots in America: A Refugee People in New World Society.* Cambridge, Mass.: Harvard University Press, 1983.

Van Ruymbeke, Bertrand. "The Huguenots of Proprietary South Carolina: Patterns of Migration and Settlement." In *Money, Trade and Power: The Evolution of South Carolina's Plantation System.* Edited by Jack P. Greene, Rosemary Brana-Shute, and Randy J. Sparks. Columbia: University of South Carolina Press, 2001.

Leslie Choquette
James Elliott Walmsley

See also **New Amsterdam; Walloons.**

HUMAN EXPERIMENTATION. *See* **Clinical Research.**

HUMAN GENOME PROJECT. The Human Genome Project (HGP) is an ambitious international effort to understand the hereditary instructions that make each human being unique. Its original goal was to locate the 100,000 or so human genes and read the entire genetic script—all three billion bits of information—by the year 2005, although technological advances moved up the expected completion date to 2003 and allowed the project to release a "working draft" of the human genome sequence in June 2000.

Launched in 1990, the project is supported in the United States by the National Institutes of Health and the Department of Energy. The HGP expects to identify the genes involved in both rare and common diseases, perhaps enabling early detection and treatment of disease and new approaches to prevention. In addition, gene discovery might predict someone's likelihood of getting a disease long before symptoms appear. In some cases, preventive actions can then be undertaken that may avert disease, as with familial breast cancer; or they can detect disease at its earliest stages, when treatment tends to be more successful. Errors in human genes cause an estimated three thousand to four thousand clearly hereditary diseases, including Huntington's disease, cystic fibrosis, sickle-cell anemia, neurofibromatosis, and Duchenne muscular dystrophy. Moreover, altered genes play a part in cancer, heart disease, diabetes, Alzheimer's disease, and many other common illnesses.

The HGP is designed to provide tools and techniques to enable scientists to find genes quickly. The first of these tools are maps of each chromosome. The ultimate goal is to decode, letter by letter, the exact sequence of all 3 billion nucleotide bases that make up the human genome—a daunting task that spurred researchers from many fields (biology, physics, engineering, and computer science, to name a few) to develop automated technologies to reduce the time and cost of sequencing. The ability to probe genes could be a double-edged sword, however. For some diseases, for example, ability to detect a nonfunctional gene has outpaced doctors' ability to do anything about the disease it causes. Huntington's disease is a case in point. Although a test for high-risk families has been available for years, only a handful of individuals have decided to be tested. The reason seems to be that, because there is no way to cure or prevent Huntington's disease, some would rather live with uncertainty than with the knowledge that they will be struck some time in midlife with a fatal disease. There is also the uncertainty of what might happen if a health insurance company or a potential employer learns that an individual is destined to develop Huntington's disease. Might that person be denied coverage or turned down for a job? Because of such concerns, the HGP has, since its inception, devoted about 5 percent of its $3 billion budget to inquiry aimed at anticipating and resolving the ethical, legal, and social issues likely to arise from its research. This marks one of the first times scientists are exploring the consequences of their research before crises arise.

Controversy enveloped the HGP in 1998 when Craig Venter's Celera Genomics, a private corporation, announced its attention to compete with the government-funded project and to beat it in the race to decode the human genome. Some observers doubted the value of the private effort, pointing to duplication of effort between Celera and the HGP. Others criticized Celera's goal of seeking patents on individual genes. Despite a joint 2000 statement by U.S. President Bill Clinton and British Prime Minister Tony Blair declaring that the basic information on the human genome should be considered public property, by June 2000 the U.S. Patent and Trademark Office had granted some two thousand gene patents and was considering twenty-five thousand more.

On 12 February 2001 HGP and Celera issued a joint statement stating that they had learned that humans have about thirty thousand genes—many fewer than scientists had anticipated—and that the final decoding might be possible within a few years.

BIBLIOGRAPHY

Clark, Carol. "On the Threshold of a Brave New World." CNN Interactive, 2001. Available at http://www.cnn.com.

Cooper, Necia G., ed. *The Human Genome Project: Deciphering the Blueprint of Heredity.* Mill Valley, Calif.: University Science Books, 1994.

Davis, Joel. *Mapping the Code: The Human Genome Project and the Choices of Modern Science.* New York: Wiley, 1990.

Lee, Thomas F. *The Human Genome Project: Cracking the Genetic Code of Life* New York: Plenum Press, 1991.

Leslie Fink / C. W.

See also **DNA; Energy, Department of; Genetics; Medical Research; National Institutes of Health.**

HUMAN RESOURCES. *See* **Industrial Relations.**

HUMAN RIGHTS. The concept of human rights has evolved over time, and various countries have emphasized different aspects of human rights principles and policy. Some nations have emphasized traditional civil and political rights (both individual and collective), whereas others—particularly communist and socialist regimes—have emphasized the concept of economic and social rights. Some governments have embraced both sets of principles.

In the United States, the concept of certain individual and collective rights—in particular, civil and political rights—as "natural" or "unalienable" can be traced back to colonial times, reflecting the influence of John Locke and other political theorists. This concept was clearly set forth in the Declaration of Independence and was codified in the Constitution and the Bill of Rights. The United States has long regarded international human rights standards as universal. It has rejected the arguments of nations such as China, which claim that such standards can be discounted as mere "Western" concepts and argue that human rights should be viewed through the prism of each nation's history and culture. Unlike many governments, the United States acknowledges that some human rights problems persist within its territory despite its generally good record and accepts that universal human rights standards involve study and criticism of such matters.

Initiatives since World War II

World War II (1939–1945) gave impetus to the modern development of basic principles of human rights and to the general acceptance of the idea that the human rights practices of individual countries toward their own citizens are legitimate matters of international concern. The 1945 United Nations Charter included a general commitment to respect for human rights, but it was the Universal Declaration of Human Rights (adopted by the UN General Assembly in 1948) that provided the basic statement of what have become widely accepted international human rights standards. The former first lady Eleanor Roosevelt played a key role in the formulation of the Universal Declaration.

Human rights principles, policy, and practices became an increased focus of popular and public attention in the United States during the last quarter of the twentieth century. Several influential nongovernmental organizations (NGOs) were formed during this period to monitor and report on human rights matters. For example, both Human Rights Watch and the Lawyers Committee for Human Rights were formed in 1978, and Physicians for Human Rights was formed in 1986. In addition, both the legislative and the executive branches of the U.S. government took significant steps during this period to make the promotion of human rights a government priority.

The new emphasis on human rights led to a congressional requirement for the annual submission by the Department of State of "a full and complete report" on the status of human rights practices around the world. The first of the Country Reports on Human Rights Practices was submitted in 1977 (covering 1976). It surveyed the situation in eighty-two countries in less than 300 pages. By 2000, 194 individual reports were included, covering virtually every country in the world, and the overall report was more than 5,000 pages. The Country Reports evolved and expanded over the years, covering many of the rights included in the Universal Declaration and multilateral accords to which the United States is a party, as well as some rights in internationally accepted covenants to which the United States is not a party. Over time, the Country Reports added coverage of specific problems that became matters of public concern. For example, in the 1990s, Congress mandated coverage of children, indigenous people, refugees, and worker rights, and the State Department itself expanded coverage of women's rights, people with disabilities, and religious, national, racial, and ethnic minorities. Problems noted in the Country Reports can lead to the denial of aid and trade preferences. The Country Reports were initially subject to criticism as biased in some cases by policy concerns, and for many years the Lawyers Committee for Human Rights published an annual critique. However, by the late 1990s, the Country Reports were widely acknowledged to be a comprehensive and credible account of global human rights practices, and the Lawyers Committee had ceased publishing its critique.

In 1976, Congress established within the State Department a coordinator for human rights and humanitarian affairs; in 1977, under the Carter administration, which established human rights as a foreign policy priority, this position was upgraded to assistant secretary. In 1994, the Bureau of Human Rights and Humanitarian Affairs was reorganized and renamed the Bureau of Democracy, Human Rights, and Labor, to reflect both a broader scope and a more focused approach to the interlocking issues of democracy, human rights, and worker rights.

Broadening Human Rights Concerns

American efforts to encourage respect for human rights increased significantly during the 1990s. The United States ratified the International Covenant on Civil and Political Rights (ICCPR) in 1992 (however, by the early twenty-first century it had not yet ratified the International Covenant on Economic, Social, and Cultural Rights, or a number of other key international conventions). While the Universal Declaration did not entail any legal obligations, the ICCPR bound nations to respect its provisions and report on their observance; the United States submitted its first report under the ICCPR in 1994.

Also in 1994, Congress created the position of senior adviser for women's rights in the State Department, and women's rights became a major focus of U.S. activity. In 1995, First Lady Hillary Clinton played a leading role in equating women's rights and human rights at the Fourth World Conference on Women in Beijing. In 2000, the focus on women's rights was reflected in the Victims of Trafficking and Violence Protection Act, which required a State Department report to Congress; the first report was submitted in 2001. Trafficking in persons—particularly women and children—is a significant transnational human rights problem, which became the focus of increased international attention in the late 1990s.

In the mid-1990s, growing public and congressional concern about religious persecution abroad led to calls for increased government action and reporting about such abuses. In 1996, Secretary of State Warren Christopher established the Advisory Committee on Religious Freedom Abroad to advise the secretary and the president on integrating the protection and promotion of religious freedom into U.S. foreign policy. In 1998, Congress passed the International Religious Freedom Act, which provided for an ambassador-at-large, a bipartisan U.S. Commission on International Religious Freedom, an annual State Department report, and possible sanctions against nations that restricted religious freedom.

During the 1990s, the United States placed increasing emphasis on encouraging democratization, promoting justice and accountability, and assisting the development of civil society. Through both direct assistance and the work of the National Endowment for Democracy, the United States promoted the development of key institutions and processes that provide the foundation for democratic governance, including support for free elections, free media, and free trade unions, training in the rule of law and the administration of justice, the empowerment of women, and the creation of NGOs and other institutions of civil society.

The United States also worked extensively with NGOs and international organizations to promote and protect human rights. The development of transnational human rights networks and a global human rights community, particularly after the 1993 World Conference on Human Rights in Vienna and the Beijing Women's Conference, facilitated international debate over issues of democratization and justice. The 1998 arrest of General Augusto Pinochet in London at the request of a Spanish judge who wanted to try Pinochet in Spain for torture and political killings during his seventeen-year rule in Chile marked a watershed development. Although the British government ultimately allowed Pinochet to return home, his sixteen-month detention was a precedent for the globalization of efforts to assure justice and accountability. His near extradition helped generate a worldwide movement to hold heads of state accountable for human rights abuses committed while they were in power.

The U.S. government has played an active role in multilateral forums such as the UN Human Rights Commission in Geneva, pressing for resolutions critical of human rights abuses in countries such as China and Cuba. The United States has supported the efforts of regional bodies such as the Organization of American States and the Organization for Security and Cooperation in Europe, and has worked to build multilateral coalitions for human rights sanctions, monitoring, and relief efforts.

The United States also has worked to build new institutions to advance the protection of human rights. It supported the creation of the office of the UN high commissioner for human rights in 1993. Abuses and atrocities in Europe and Africa in the 1990s, including genocide in Rwanda and "ethnic cleansing" in Bosnia, led to sustained efforts to further accountability and justice. In response to these crises, the United States played a key role in the establishment of the International Criminal Tribunals for the Former Yugoslavia and Rwanda. The United States also supported the establishment and efforts of national or international "truth commissions," where internal conflicts and the transition from authoritarian rule made them an essential part of the peace process. Such truth commissions can provide a forum for victims to detail atrocities committed and discredit the perpetrators, particularly if prosecution is impractical or impossible, as in South Africa.

However, at times, the United States has not fully supported some international institutions. Although in late 2000 it signed the treaty to establish an International Criminal Court, concern in Congress in particular that the court might be able to prosecute U.S. service personnel abroad has prevented ratification. In 2001, the U.S. government renounced the accord. Also in 2001, concern that some nations would seek to use the World Conference against Racism for political purposes led the United States to limit its participation.

The United States played a major role in developing the Convention against Torture, which it signed in 1992 and ratified in 1994. Subsequently, the executive branch established regulations to ensure that those who were likely to be tortured if returned to their country of origin could not be extradited or deported. The National Institute of Mental Health has provided significant funding for research into the problems of survivors of torture, and the Office of Refugee Resettlement in the Department of Health and Human Services has provided funding to organizations in major cities to identify torture survivors among refugee communities. The U.S. Agency for International Development has supported programs around the world to assist torture victims, and the United States has been the largest single donor to the UN Voluntary Fund on Torture. Since 1980, the United States has supported civil claims by torture victims. In 1992, the president and Congress worked together to enact the Torture Victims Protection Act and, in 1998, the Torture Victims Relief Act to support the efforts of torture victims who sought refuge in the United States to seek justice and compensation for their suffering.

The United States has focused increasingly on issues of worker rights and, particularly in the late 1990s, on problems such as forced labor (including forced child labor) and sweatshop labor. As part of its anti-sweatshop initiative, the U.S. government has awarded millions of dollars in grants to organizations that promote justice in the workplace. During the 1990s, the United States increasingly sought to promote corporate social responsibility in the global struggle for human rights. This concept entailed recognition that profits could not be considered apart from human costs, in terms of human rights, labor standards, and environmental issues, and that these factors should be integrated into business practices. The United States has worked closely with the International Labor Organization on worker rights problems around the world. The Department of State's Advisory Committee on Labor Diplomacy was established in 1999, as was the position of special representative for international labor affairs. In 2000, the United States played a leading role in the development and adoption of a business code of conduct aimed at preventing abuses by governments in developing nations where international corporations operate. A group of major energy and mining companies joined with human rights organizations in adopting this voluntary statement of principles.

At the start of the twenty-first century, the cause of democracy and respect for human rights continued to progress. In its 2000–2001 survey, Freedom in the World, Freedom House reported that there were 86 free countries, 58 partly free countries, and 48 countries rated not free (in which basic political rights and civil liberties were denied). This represented an improvement compared with the figures of 65, 50, and 50, respectively, in its 1990–1991 survey. Nonetheless, violations of basic human rights, severe persecution, and egregious abuses, still form a systematic pattern in much of the world.

BIBLIOGRAPHY

Andreopoulos, George J., and Richard Pierre Claude, eds. *Human Rights Education for the Twenty-First Century.* Philadelphia: University of Pennsylvania Press, 1997.

Brown, Peter G., and Douglas MacLean, eds. *Human Rights and U.S. Foreign Policy: Principles and Applications.* Lexington, Mass.: Lexington Books, 1979.

Claude, Richard Pierre, and Burns H. Weston, eds. *Human Rights in the World Community: Issues and Action.* 2d ed. Philadelphia: University of Pennsylvania Press, 1992.

Dunne, Tim, and Nicholas J. Wheeler, eds. *Human Rights in Global Politics.* Cambridge, U.K.: Cambridge University Press, 1999.

Hannum, Hurst, ed. *Guide to International Human Rights Practice.* 3d ed. Ardsley, N.Y.: Transnational, 1999.

Human Rights Watch World Report 2000. New York: Human Rights Watch, 1999.

Koh, Harold Hongju, and Ronald C. Slye, eds. *Deliberative Democracy and Human Rights.* New Haven, Conn.: Yale University Press, 1999.

Meron, Theodore, ed. *Human Rights in International Law: Legal and Policy Issues.* Oxford: Clarendon Press, 1984.

Marc J. Susser

See also **Bill of Rights in U.S. Constitution; United Nations;** *and vol. 9:* **Human Rights Not Founded on Sex, October 2, 1837.**

HUMPHREY'S EXECUTOR V. UNITED STATES, 295 U.S. 602 (1935), restricted the president's power to remove members of the so-called independent agencies. In October 1933, President Franklin D. Roosevelt removed Federal Trade Commissioner William E. Humphrey, not for neglect of duty or malfeasance, as stipulated in the Federal Trade Commission Act, but because of differences of opinion. Humphrey denied the validity of this action, and, in a suit that continued after Humphrey's death, the SUPREME COURT held unanimously that Congress intended to create the FEDERAL TRADE COMMISSION as an independent body and therefore meant to limit the president's removal power to the causes enumerated in the act, and that such limitations were not unconstitutional. Congress has authority, the Court declared, to require such a body to act independently of executive control and may forbid removal except for cause.

BIBLIOGRAPHY

Herring, E. Pendleton. *Public Administration and the Public Interest.* New York: Russell and Russell, 1967. The original edition was published in 1936.

Leuchtenburg, William E. "The Case of the Contentious Commissioner: Humphrey's Executor v. U.S." In *Freedom and Reform: Essays in Honor of Henry Steele Commager.* Edited by Harold M. Hyman and Leonard W. Levy. New York: Harper and Row, 1967.

Ransom E. Noble Jr.
Andrew C. Rieser / A. R.

See also **Federal Agencies; *Myers v. United States*; Removal, Executive Power of.**

HUNDRED. The hundred was a colonial administrative unit based on its English counterpart: an area occupied by one hundred families and served by local officials. In Virginia, the hundred began as a settlement of one hundred families but soon became a strictly territorial unit for judicial, military, and political purposes. In Maryland, hundreds were territorial units for elections, public levies, and preservation of the peace. In Virginia, Maryland, and Delaware, the establishment of larger administrative units such as boroughs and counties diminished the function of hundreds, although they remained important subdivisions and continued to exist in many places in the early 2000s.

BIBLIOGRAPHY

Carr, Lois Green, Philip D. Morgan, and Jean B. Russo, eds. *Colonial Chesapeake Society.* Chapel Hill: University of North Carolina Press, 1988.

Shelby Balik
Percy Scott Flippin

See also **Borough; Colonial Settlements.**

HUNKERS, the name applied to the conservative faction of New York's Democratic Party in the 1840s. The Hunkers favored spending state surpluses on canals, making internal improvements, and liberally chartering state banks. They supported James K. Polk for president, and they deprecated antislavery agitation. Patronage disputes promoted discord with the progressive element of the party, known as the Barnburners. The Barnburners withdrew from the state Democratic convention in 1847 and the national convention in 1848. A coalition formed in 1850 failed to elect Horatio Seymour governor. By 1853 the terms "Hards" and "Softs" were being used to replace the labels "Hunkers" and "Barnburners."

BIBLIOGRAPHY

Benson, Lee. *The Concept of Jacksonian Democracy: New York as a Test Case.* Princeton, N.J.: Princeton University Press, 1961.

Donovan, Herbert D. A. *The Barnburners: A Study of the Internal Movements in the Political History of New York State and of the Resulting Changes in Political Affiliation, 1830–1852.* New York: New York University Press, 1925.

Philip G. Auchampaugh / A. G.

See also **Barnburners.**

HUNTINGTON LIBRARY AND MUSEUM, a library of rare Anglo-American books and manuscripts; an art museum specializing in eighteenth-century English, American, and French paintings; and a botanical garden. The railway magnate Henry Edwards Huntington (1850–1927) and his second wife, Arabella Duval Huntington (1850–1924), created and developed the Huntington Library and Museum. Located in San Marino, California, the library and museum became both a visitor attraction and a research center.

Huntington's original collecting ideal, to document British and American history as expressed in art, literature, politics, and ecology, remained the objective of the institution after his death. Highlights of the collection include the Ellesmere manuscript of Chaucer's *Canterbury Tales* (c. 1410); a Gutenberg Bible (c. 1455); Thomas Gainsborough's *The Blue Boy* (c. 1770); the Hastings correspondence; eighteenth-century material relating to the British civil war, Oliver Cromwell, and colonial interests; as well as first editions and letters of Shakespeare, William Blake, Mary Shelley, and John Ruskin. Similarly the collection features American documents dating from the original colonies onward. Examples include papers relating to the signing of the Declaration of Independence and many of its signatories; Native American treaties and land grants; and papers, letters, and documents of such figures as Benjamin Franklin, Henry David Thoreau, Nathaniel Hawthorne, Ralph Waldo Emerson, Harriet Beecher Stowe, Mark Twain, and Henry James. The library also houses a collection of over 400,000 rare titles relating to women and women's history from 1455 onward.

Established by Huntington as a trust in 1919 and opened to the public in 1928, the library and museum are situated on the grounds of Henry and Arabella Huntington's former estate. The museum occupies the Huntingtons' beaux arts mansion, while the library resides in a separate building. Both were designed by the architect Myron Hunt.

Born in Oneonta, New York, Henry E. Huntington established his fortune as a railroad magnate and land

Hurons. Members of this now widely scattered Indian confederation pose in tribal costume on a reservation near Fredericton, New Brunswick, Canada. UNIVERSITY OF PENNSYLVANIA MUSEUM ARCHIVES

speculator in California. His career began as a manager for his uncle Collis Huntington, who shared ownership of the Central Pacific and Southern Pacific Railroads. After Collis Huntington's death in 1900, Henry Huntington expanded the family interests to include the municipal rail system in Los Angeles and property development along his lines. At the same time he cemented his control of Los Angeles's urban development by investing in water and power.

Although he began collecting books and manuscripts in 1903, Huntington emerged as a major book and manuscript collector after his retirement in 1911, when he purchased much of the Hoe collection of illuminated manuscripts and the E. Dwight Church Library of English literature and Americana for a reputed $1.3 million. The prizes of his early collecting were one of only two known 1603 editions of *Hamlet* and a large amount of material relating to the American Revolution, including hundreds of pamphlets and selections from George Washington's correspondences. After this purchase Huntington collected voraciously. A year later his library ranked as the third largest private library in the United States. Considered the premier American book collector by 1915, Huntington decided to create a permanent house for his collection on his San Marino ranch.

BIBLIOGRAPHY

Cannon, Carl L. *American Book Collectors and Collecting from Colonial Times to the Present.* New York: H. W. Wilson, 1941.

Dickinson, Donald C. *Henry E. Huntington's Library of Libraries.* San Marino, Calif.: Huntington Library, 1995.

Henry E. Huntington Library and Art Gallery. *The Huntington Art Collections: A Handbook.* San Marino, Calif.: Huntington Library, 1986.

Schad, Robert O. *Henry Edwards Huntington: The Founder and the Library.* San Marino, Calif.: Henry E. Huntington Library and Art Gallery, 1931.

Thorpe, James. *Henry Edwards Huntington: A Biography.* Berkeley: University of California Press, 1994.

Joshua Perelman

See also **Collecting; Libraries; Museums.**

HURON/WYANDOT. The Hurons were a confederation of four or five tribes, whose foundation originated in the fifteenth or sixteenth century. At the time of European contact, there were twenty thousand Hurons living close to the banks of Georgian Bay in the modern province of Ontario, Canada, in semi-sedentary farming communities, which relocated every fifteen to twenty years when the grounds were no longer productive and wood for heating fuel was exhausted.

This matrilineal and matrilocal society traces its origins back to a first woman, Aataentsic, who is at the core of the creation myth. Clan segments—the groupings of people related to the women lineage living in the same longhouse—were the basic social units. The political system was based on councils representing kinship networks at the village, tribe, and confederation levels. The Hurons played a central role in the commercial and diplomatic networks of their region.

Starting in 1634, misfortunes descended on the Hurons. Terrible epidemics followed by Iroquois attacks brought about the complete destruction of Huronia by 1650. Most of the survivors were reduced to captivity; a few hundred survivors took refuge close to the French settlement at Quebec. A similar number of traditionalist Hurons, together with the Tobacco Indians, formed the Wyandot community of the Great Lakes region, first at Michilimackinac and later in Detroit. Within this group, the Huron chief Kondiaronk played a decisive role in the conclusion of the 1701 Great Peace in Montreal, which ended the war with the Iroquois. In 1697, the Quebec-region Hurons settled in Lorette (now Wendake), Quebec, to become a prosperous community of approximately two thousand people. The American removal policy forced the Great Lakes Wyandots to settle in Oklahoma. Only a few hundred still live in that state, where they have no reservation territory. The remainder of the three thousand Wyandots of the United States are scattered throughout the country.

BIBLIOGRAPHY

Barbeau, Marius. *Huron and Wyandot Mythology.* Ottawa, Canada: Government Printing Bureau, 1915.

Heidenreich, Conrad. *Huronia: A History and Geography of the Huron Indians, 1600–1650.* Toronto: McClelland and Stewart, 1971.

Trigger, Bruce G. *The Children of Aataentsic. A History of the Huron People to 1660.* 2 vols. Montreal: McGill-Queen's University Press, 1976.

Denys Delâge

See also **Warfare, Indian.**

Hurricane Fran. An enhanced satellite photograph, taken from a television screen at the National Hurricane Center in Miami, shows the swirling vortex apparently headed for Charleston, S.C., in September 1996; in fact, the storm made landfall—and caused heavy damage—in North Carolina. AP/Wide World Photos

HURRICANES, intensely powerful storms that originate at sea in tropical waters. Hurricanes are characterized by circular wind patterns, in which violent winds spiral around the eye of the storm, and they can be hundreds of miles wide. Hurricanes travel great distances and most never reach land, but those that do often devastate coastal areas. The combination of high winds, torrential rains, and tidal surges can cause many deaths and massive property damage. By definition, a tropical storm becomes a hurricane when its sustained winds reach 74 miles per hour. Hurricane winds have reached 150 and even 200 miles per hour, but the most deadly aspect is the tidal surge. Sea levels can rise 15 or even 20 feet, with storm surges flooding low-lying areas and drowning many people.

Scientists use the term "tropical cyclone" to describe these violent storms. The word "hurricane" is derived from the languages of native peoples of the Caribbean, and refers to Western Hemisphere storms. Tropical cyclones also occur in the Eastern Hemisphere, developing in the Pacific Ocean, where they are called typhoons or cyclones. The term "tornado," however, describes a different phenomenon; tornadoes originate over land and are typically 700 yards in diameter.

Because warm water is their energy source, tropical cyclones are seasonal. Hurricane season in the Atlantic lasts from June through November. Most storms occur between August and October, and early September is the riskiest period for major storms. Hurricane season is a serious matter throughout the Caribbean and Central America, and nations from Cuba to Honduras have suffered terrible losses. The high-risk areas in the United States lie along the Gulf Coast from Texas to Florida, and the Atlantic coast from Florida to the Carolinas, but New England has also experienced deadly storms.

Hurricanes are classified by intensity: category 1 storms have sustained winds of 74–95 mph, while category 5 storms have winds over 155 mph and tidal surges over 18 feet. Scientists believe that two category 5 storms hit the modern United States, the most intense being the 1935 Florida Keys storm, when barometers dropped to 26.35 inches. This powerful hurricane was neither the deadliest nor the costliest in American history. There have been several storms of greater national significance. Of course, every town that experiences a hurricane is changed, and the storm becomes part of local history.

Most communities buried their dead, rebuilt their buildings, and moved forward. Certain hurricanes, however, rose beyond local significance and are considered national tragedies with relief efforts much like San Francisco's earthquake and Chicago's fire.

The Galveston storm ranks first among American hurricanes. The hurricane that struck Galveston, Texas, in September 1900 killed over 8,000 people, including 6,000 in the island city, and remains the deadliest natural disaster in U.S. history. The tidal surge rose rapidly, flooding much of the barrier island. Galveston's highest elevation was only 8.7 feet above sea level, and when the waves receded, a wall of wreckage and bodies remained. The nation rallied to Galveston's relief, and Galvestonians adopted the new city commission form of government to manage the recovery. Galveston constructed a massive sea wall and pumped in sand to raise the entire city's grade. In 1915, another category 4 hurricane hit Galveston, but the seawall held and the rebuilt city survived.

In one decade, three major hurricanes battered southern Florida, arriving in 1926, 1928, and 1935. The September 1926 storm directly hit Miami, as the eye of the storm passed over the young city. Scientists estimate that if this hurricane followed the same path today, it would cause an astounding $70 billion of property damage. The storm surge flooded Miami Beach and ravaged Moore Haven, an agricultural settlement on Lake Okeechobee. Well over 300 people drowned, and the response included stronger building codes for southern Florida. The 1928 storm struck near Palm Beach, but also did its deadliest work in Florida's low-lying interior. Lake Okeechobee rose 15 feet, devastating Belle Glade, a community of black migrant farm workers. This natural disaster was America's second deadliest, and estimates range from 1,800 to 2,500 dead. Relief came slowly, but eventually included a vast canal system and a huge rock levee to prevent Lake Okeechobee from overflowing. This federal flood control program dramatically altered the Everglades ecosystem. The third major hurricane in this era was the category 5 storm that hit the Florida Keys in 1935. Hundreds of war veterans were building highway bridges between these islands on a federal work relief program. Winds rose to 200 miles per hour and the tidal surge topped 18 feet. The train sent to evacuate the workers arrived too late, and over 400 people died, including 250 veterans. Many Americans were outraged that the veterans were left in harm's way, and pressure grew for better hurricane warnings.

There were other deadly storms between 1935 and 1960, including the unusual 1938 hurricane that killed 600 people in New England. Radar became a tool for tracking tropical storms in the 1950s, and hurricanes were given women's names starting in 1953. Few large hurricanes struck the United States in the 1960s, 1970s, and 1980s. But in 1989, a category 4 hurricane pounded the Carolinas. This storm was named Hugo (men's names were added in 1978) and it caused more property damage than any prior hurricane. But Hugo's record did not stand long. In August 1992, Hurricane Andrew's 16-foot storm surge hit southern Florida, setting a new record with property losses of $25–30 billion. Andrew battered Homestead, Florida City, and Miami's outskirts, killing nearly fifty people and seriously damaging over 100,000 homes. Hugo and Andrew exposed a new generation to the deadly threat of hurricanes.

While property damage has increased in recent hurricanes, fatalities have fallen due to earlier warnings by the National Hurricane Center, better evacuations, and safer buildings. However, many more Americans have moved to coastal locations, and areas like the Florida Keys are increasingly difficult to evacuate. Gulf and Atlantic coast communities remain at risk each hurricane season, and a direct hit on Miami, New Orleans, or Houston could be catastrophic. Tropical storms remain unpredictable, and there is no more deadly example of nature's power than the hurricane.

BIBLIOGRAPHY

Barnes, Jay. *Florida's Hurricane History.* Chapel Hill: University of North Carolina Press, 1998.

Bixel, Patricia Bellis, and Elizabeth Hayes Turner. *Galveston and the 1900 Storm: Catastrophe and Catalyst.* Austin: University of Texas Press, 2000.

Elsner, James B., and A. Birol Kara. *Hurricanes of the North Atlantic: Climate and Society.* New York: Oxford University Press, 1999.

Steinberg, Theodore. *Acts of God: The Unnatural History of Natural Disaster in America.* New York: Oxford University Press, 2000.

William C. Barnett

See also **Disasters; Galveston; Mexico, Gulf of; Miami; Tornadoes; Weather Service, National.**

HURTADO V. CALIFORNIA, 110 U.S. 516 (1884). The issue in this case was whether a conviction for murder without grand jury indictment was a violation of the due process clause of the Fourteenth Amendment. The State of California had provided a criminal procedure based merely on information or formal accusation by the prosecution. In 1884 the Supreme Court held that such conviction was not forbidden by the Constitution. In line with this principle, the Court in *Twining v. New Jersey* (1908) exempted the states from guaranteeing another Fifth Amendment civil liberty, freedom from compulsory self-incrimination.

BIBLIOGRAPHY

Kelly, Alfred H., Winfred A. Harbison, and Herman Belz. *The American Constitution: Its Origins and Development.* 7th ed. New York: Norton, 1991.

Leonard C. Helderman / A. R.

See also **Due Process of Law; Jury Trial.**

HUTCHINSON LETTERS, between Massachusetts Governor Thomas Hutchinson and officials in London—particularly Thomas Whately—discussing colonial unrest and urging abridgment of colonial liberties. For the rest of his life after the publication of these letters—which effectively destroyed his career—Hutchinson doggedly pursued the mystery of who had turned the letters over to colonial agent Benjamin Franklin, who in turn sent them to Massachusetts. Between 1768 and the end of 1771, Hutchinson wrote Whately at least thirteen letters, six of which were published in America in 1773. Although the letters were for the most part restrained and merely cautionary, and contained little that the public had not heard Hutchinson express before, their publication provided a catalyst for colonial protest.

BIBLIOGRAPHY

Bailyn, Bernard. *The Ordeal of Thomas Hutchinson.* Cambridge, Mass.: Harvard University Press, 1974.

Pencak, William. *America's Burke: The Mind of Thomas Hutchinson.* Washington, D.C.: University Press of America, 1982.

Leslie J. Lindenauer

See also **Colonial Policy, British.**

HYDROELECTRIC POWER. The capability to produce and deliver electricity for widespread consumption was one of the most important factors in the surge of American economic influence and wealth in the late nineteenth and early twentieth centuries. Hydroelectric power, among the first and simplest of the technologies that generated electricity, was initially developed using low dams of rock, timber, or granite block construction to collect water from rainfall and surface runoff into a reservoir. The water was funneled into a pipe (or penstock) and directed to a waterwheel (or turbine) where the force of the falling water on the turbine blades rotated the turbine and its main shaft. This shaft was connected to a generator, and the rotating generator produced electricity. One gallon (about 3.8 liters) of water falling 100 feet (about 30 meters) each second produced slightly more than 1,000 watts (or one kilowatt) of electricity, enough to power ten 100-watt light bulbs or a typical hairdryer.

There are now three types of hydroelectric installations: storage, run-of-river, and pumped-storage facilities. Storage facilities use a dam to capture water in a reservoir. This stored water is released from the reservoir through turbines at the rate required to meet changing electricity needs or other needs such as flood control, fish passage, irrigation, navigation, and recreation. Run-of-river facilities use only the natural flow of the river to operate the turbine. If the conditions are right, this type of project can be constructed without a dam or with a low diversion structure to direct water from the stream channel into a penstock. Pumped-storage facilities, an innovation of the 1950s, have specially designed turbines. These turbines have the ability to generate electricity the conventional way when water is delivered through penstocks to the turbines from a reservoir. They can also be reversed and used as pumps to lift water from the powerhouse back up into the reservoir where the water is stored for later use. During the daytime when electricity demand suddenly increases, the gates of the pumped-storage facility are opened and stored water is released from the reservoir to generate and quickly deliver electricity to meet the demand. At night when electricity demand is lowest and there is excess electricity available from coal or nuclear electricity generating facilities the turbines are reversed and pump water back into the reservoir. Operating in this manner, a pumped-storage facility improves the operating efficiency of all power plants within an electric system. Hydroelectric developments provide unique benefits not available with other electricity generating technologies. They do not contribute to air pollution, acid rain, or ozone depletion, and do not produce toxic wastes. As a part of normal operations many hydroelectric facilities also provide flood control, water supply for drinking and irrigation, and recreational opportunities such as fishing, swimming, water-skiing, picnicking, camping, rafting, boating, and sightseeing.

Origins of the Hydroelectric Industry 1880–1930

Hydroelectric power technology was slow to develop during the first ten years of the hydroelectric era (1880–1889) due to the limitations of direct current electricity technology. Some pioneering hydropower developments using direct current technology are described below.

The Grand Rapids Electric Light and Power Company in Michigan connected a dynamo to a waterwheel for the Wolverine Chair Factory in July 1880 and this installation powered 16 brush-arc lamps.

A dynamo was connected to a hydropower turbine at Niagara Falls in 1881 to power the arc lamps for the city streets.

The first hydropower facility in the western United States was completed in San Bernardino, California, in 1887.

By 1889 there were about 200 small electric generating facilities in the United States that used water for some or all of their electricity production.

The potential for increasing hydroelectric development was dramatically enhanced in 1889 when alternating current technology was introduced, enabling electricity to be conveyed economically over long distances.

The next 30 years of the modern era of hydroelectric development, 1890 to 1920, began with the construction of individual hydroelectric facilities by towns, cities, cooperatives, and private manufacturing companies for their own specific needs, and ended with the organization of the first utility system in the country. Cities and towns used hydroelectric facilities to provide electricity for trolley systems, streetlights, and individual customers. Co-

Opening of Boulder Dam. A view from an airplane of the result when President Franklin D. Roosevelt pressed a button on the other side of the country on 11 September 1936: millions of cubic feet of water per minute pouring into the Colorado River from outlets on both sides of the dam. © BETTMANN/CORBIS

operatives brought together groups of individuals and businesses to establish a customer pool that could finance and construct hydroelectric facilities for their own needs. Hundreds of small factories and paper mills in New England, the South, and throughout the Midwest constructed hydroelectric facilities for their own specific industrial use. Just prior to World War I, Southern Power Company purchased a large number of hydroelectric facilities from cites, towns, cooperatives, and factories, and consolidated them into the first regional utility power system in the United States. By 1920 hydroelectric facilities supplied 25 percent of the electricity used in the United States.

The hydroelectric industry matured between 1920 and 1930. During this period, electrical grid systems expanded, reaching more customers who were eager to receive and use electricity. Industrial production grew to satisfy the demand for consumer goods, requiring additional electricity. To meet the increasing demand, town and city electrical systems and regional utility systems grew in number and size throughout the more populated areas of the country. By 1930 hydroelectric facilities were delivering almost 30 percent of the nation's electricity needs.

The Hydroelectric Industry Prospers 1930–1980

The hydroelectric industry prospered from 1930 to 1980 for a number of reasons. Considerable federal funding was provided from 1930 through the 1960s for the construction of large federal dams and hydroelectric facilities. A major percentage of the massive increases in electricity required for wartime production during the 1940s was met by the construction of a sizable number of hydroelectric facilities; and to meet escalating electricity needs in response to the dramatic expansion of consumer demand and industrial production throughout the decades of the 1950s, 1960s, and 1970s, many new electric generating facilities, including hydroelectric developments, were constructed.

In the 1930s, major federal funding for new dam and hydroelectric facility development was allocated for three locations: the Tennessee River under authority of the TENNESSEE VALLEY AUTHORITY (TVA), the Colorado River under authority of the U.S. Bureau of Reclamation (Bureau), and the Columbia River under authority of the Bureau and the U.S. Army Corps of Engineers (COE). The TVA was established during the Great Depression in 1933 to develop multiple-use water resource projects in the Tennessee River system and spur economic development in Tennessee. It began construction in 1935 on a series of dams with hydroelectric facilities, which included almost 30 dams by the time the system was completed in 1956. Most of the TVA growth took place during World War II when the electrical demand necessary to develop the atomic bomb in the region surged by 600 percent between 1939 and 1945.

The Bureau, established in 1902 to promote the development of the western United States through the construction of federal irrigation dams, completed the world famous HOOVER DAM on the Colorado River in 1936. Hoover Dam, which opened three years ahead of schedule, was a public works project intended to relieve unemployment during the Great Depression and provide critical electricity to meet the growing needs of the City of Los Angeles, California. At the same time, the Bureau and COE undertook the development of the great dams on the Columbia River in the northwestern United States. Within six years of the initial operation of Hoover, the Bureau completed Grand Coulee Dam on the Columbia

Boulder Dam Power Unit, 1941. An atypical picture by the nature photographer Ansel Adams: one of a series showing electrical equipment and wires associated with Boulder Dam (renamed Hoover Dam in 1947). NATIONAL ARCHIVES AND RECORDS ADMINISTRATION

Shasta Dam. In Russell Lee's 1942 photograph, workers hose away dirt and rock during construction of the dam, which opened in 1945 on the Sacramento River in Northern California. LIBRARY OF CONGRESS

River, still the largest dam in the northwestern United States. During the mid-1940s, Grand Coulee supplied the electricity needed to produce planes and other war material to support U.S. victory in World War II. Bonneville Dam, completed in 1938 by the COE and also located on the Columbia River, was a public works project to help relieve regional unemployment during the Great Depression. Like Grand Couleee, Bonneville also supplied critical electricity in support of World War II production efforts. In 1940 hydroelectric plants supplied more than 35 percent of the nation's electricity.

Grand Coulee and Bonneville, along with the other large hydroelectric projects constructed in the northwest region from the 1940s through the 1960s, supplied between 80 and 90 percent of the electricity consumed in the states of Washington and Oregon by 1980. However, the portion of the nation's electricity supplied by hydroelectric facilities had declined to 12 percent. Federal support for constructing dams where a hydroelectric plant could be included was declining and initial steps were being taken to alter the primary mission of the Bureau and COE from developing new projects to operating and maintaining existing facilities.

Regulation of the Hydroelectric Industry 1899–1986

Hydroelectric power development has always been closely linked to political influences. Federal recognition of the necessity to control development on the nation's waterways began with the passage of the Rivers and Harbors Act in 1899, less than twenty years after the appearance of the first hydroelectric facility. The rapid expansion of interest in natural and water resources led to the creation of the Inland Waterways Commission in 1907. This Commission issued a report advocating a national policy to regulate development on streams or rivers crossing public lands. A White House Natural Resources Conference the following year proposed increased development of the nation's hydroelectric resources. As a result, the Federal Water Power Act (FWPA) was passed in 1920, establishing the Federal Power Commission (FPC) with the authority to issue licenses for non-federal hydroelectric development on public lands and waterways. Recognizing that the FWPA did not extend to all waterways, Congress enacted the Federal Power Act (FPA) in 1935 to amend the FWPA. The FPA extended the FPC's authority to all hydroelectric projects built by utilities engaged in interstate commerce. The FPA also required that the effects of a project on other natural resources be considered along with the electricity to be produced by the project.

From 1940 to 1980, twenty-two federal laws were passed that affect the hydroelectric licensing decisions of the FPC (renamed the Federal Energy Regulatory Commission [FERC] in 1977). Included among these laws are the Fish and Wildlife Coordination Act, Wilderness Act, National Historic Preservation Act, Wild and Scenic Rivers Act, National Environmental Policy Act, Endangered

Species Act, Federal Land Policy and Management Act, Soil and Water Resources Conservation Act, Public Utility Regulatory Policies Act, and Energy Security Act. The enactment of these laws coincided with increasing concerns that negative environmental consequences result from dam construction. These concerns included flooding large land areas, disrupting the ecology and the habitat of fish and wildlife, changing the temperature and oxygen balance of the river water, creating a barrier to the movement of fish upstream and downstream, and modifying river flows. By 1980 concerns that the salmon runs in the Columbia River system were in jeopardy prompted congress to pass the Pacific Northwest Power Planning and Conservation Act. This Act established the Northwest Power Planning Council, which is responsible for the protection and recovery of salmon runs in the Columbia River system. The implementation of many of these laws resulted in a more complex and expensive process to obtain a license for a hydroelectric facility.

The Hydroelectric Industry Stabilizes 1986–2000

The Electric Consumers Protection Act (ECPA) of 1986, which increased the focus on non-power issues in the hydroelectric licensing process, has contributed to an increase in development costs to the point where new hydroelectric facilities are often only marginally competitive with other conventional electric generating technologies. Since 1986, the time required to obtain a hydroelectric license has grown from two years to four years and the licensing cost has doubled for projects of all sizes. Even with more efficient technology, hydroelectric generation increased only slightly between 1986 and 2000. By 1986, the average size of all hydroelectric projects in the United States was about 35,500 kilowatts. After 1986, new projects completing the licensing and construction process average less than 5,000 kilowatts in size.

The recent availability of cheap natural gas and the minimal permitting requirements for gas-fired electricity generating plants has resulted in a dramatic increase in the construction of these plants. These gas-fired plants are meeting the increasing electricity demand more economically than other generating resources.

In today's climate of increased environmental awareness, the construction of new dams is often viewed more negatively than in the past. Therefore, the construction of a new dam for hydroelectric generation is rare. Only six hydroelectric projects were constructed between 1991 and 2000 with new dam or diversion structures and all of these structures are less than 30 feet (10 meters) in height. Hydroelectric facilities are installed at only about 2 percent of the nation's dams.

Present Geographical Distribution of the Industry

Almost 70 percent of all U.S. hydroelectric generation is produced in the western United States during an average water year. The northwestern states of Washington, Oregon, Montana, Wyoming, and Idaho generate about 50 percent of all hydroelectric output. The mountains are high and water is plentiful in this region, yielding optimal conditions for hydroelectric generation. Another 20 percent of the nation's hydroelectric output occurs in the southwestern states of Colorado, Utah, Nevada, California, Arizona, and New Mexico. While these states have terrain similar to those in the northwest, the climate is drier. The southeastern states of Virginia, North Carolina, Tennessee, South Carolina, Georgia, Alabama, Mississippi, and Florida contribute about 10 percent of U.S. hydroelectric production. This region includes large TVA and utility dams with hydroelectric plants. The State of New York produces over 8 percent of the nation's hydroelectricity. At a capacity of 2,500,000 kilowatts, the New York Power Authority's Robert Moses Niagara hydroelectric project is the primary contributor of this electricity. The remainder of the country produces 12 percent of U.S. hydroelectric generation.

The Financial Picture of the Hydroelectric Industry

The financial status of the hydroelectric industry is generally healthy due to long equipment life and low maintenance and operating costs. Hydroelectric facilities in the United States had total capital value in 2000 of about $159 billion based on average new facility costs compiled by DOE of $1,700 to $2,300 per kilowatt of capacity. The gross revenue for the industry in 2000 was about $18 billion based on U.S. electricity production of 269 billion kilowatt hours and DOE's $0.066/kilowatt hour estimate for the national average value of electricity. Using DOE's data, net profit for the industry in 2000 was calculated to be about $11 billion after deducting licensing and regulatory costs (about $500 million), capital costs (about $4.6 billion), and operation and maintenance costs (about $1.9 billion). In the mid-1990s, the hydroelectric industry directly employed nearly 48,000 people and their earnings totaled approximately $2.7 billion according to DOE. Another 58,000 people indirectly provided services and material needed to operate and maintain hydroelectric dams and generating facilities. Few businesses that are 125 years old are as efficient and as important to the U.S. economy as the hydroelectric industry.

Future Directions for the Hydroelectric Industry

The hydroelectric industry has been termed "mature" by some who charge that the technical and operational aspects of the industry have changed little in the past 60 years. Recent research initiatives counter this label by establishing new concepts for design and operation that show promise for the industry. A multi-year research project is presently testing new turbine designs and will recommend a final turbine blade configuration that will allow safe passage of more than 98 percent of the fish that are directed through the turbine. The DOE also recently identified more than 30 million kilowatts of untapped hydroelectric capacity that could be constructed with minimal environmental effects at existing dams that presently have no hydroelectric generating facilities, at existing hydro-

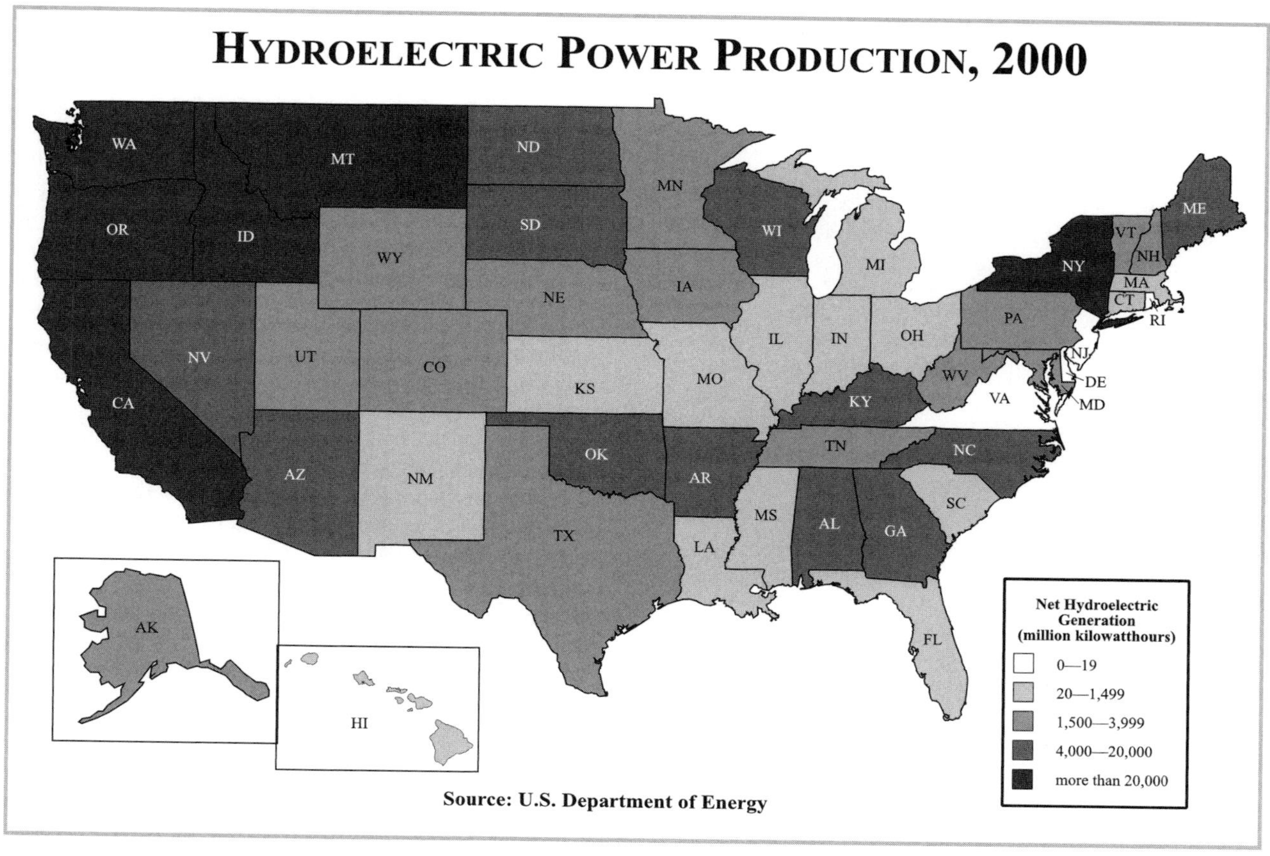

electric projects with unused potential, and even at a number of sites without dams. Follow-up studies will assess the economic issues associated with this untapped hydroelectric resource. In addition, studies to estimate the hydroelectric potential of undeveloped, small capacity, dispersed sites that could supply electricity to adjacent areas without connecting to a regional electric transmission distribution system are proceeding. Preliminary results from these efforts have improved the visibility of hydroelectric power and provide indications that the hydroelectric power industry will be vibrant and important to the country throughout the next century.

BIBLIOGRAPHY

Barnes, Marla. "Tracking the Pioneers of Hydroelectricity." *Hydro Review* 16 (1997): 46.

Federal Energy Regulatory Commission. *Hydroelectric Power Resources of the United States: Developed and Undeveloped.* Washington, 1 January 1992.

———. *Report on Hydroelectric Licensing Policies, Procedures, and Regulations: Comprehensive Review and Recommendations Pursuant to Section 603 of the Energy Act of 2000.* Washington, May 2001.

Foundation for Water and Energy Education. *Following Nature's Current: Hydroelectric Power in the Northwest.* Salem, Oregon, 1999.

Idaho National Engineering Laboratory and United States Department of Energy—Idaho Operations Office. *Hydroelectric Power Industry Economic Benefit Assessment.* DOE/ID-10565. Idaho Falls, November 1996.

———. *Hydropower Resources at Risk: The Status of Hydropower Regulation and Development 1997.* DOE/ID-10603. Idaho Falls, September 1997.

United States Department of Energy, Energy Information Administration. *Annual Energy Review 2000.* DOE/EIA-0384 (2000). Washington, August 2001.

United States Department of Energy—Idaho Operations Office. *Hydropower: Partnership with the Environment.* 01-GA50627. Idaho Falls, June 2001.

Richard T. Hunt

See also vol. 9: **Power.**

HYDROGEN BOMB, a type of nuclear weapon, also known as the "superbomb," that derives some of its energy from the fusion of the nuclei of light elements, typically isotopes of hydrogen. Physicists recognized the fusion or thermonuclear reaction as the source of the sun's energy as early as 1938. During World War II, scientists of the Manhattan Project saw the possibility of creating a thermonuclear weapon, but they decided to concentrate first on building a fission or atomic bomb because any fusion bomb would likely require a fission device to initiate its thermonuclear "burning."

Although by 1945 the United States had developed and used the atomic bomb, only modest theoretical research on fusion was done before the first Soviet atomic test of August 1949. Many of the scientists of the U.S. Atomic Energy Commission and its General Advisory Committee opposed development of the hydrogen bomb on both practical and moral grounds, but advocates within Congress, the military, and elsewhere argued that any restraint shown by the United States in the matter would not be reciprocated by a Soviet Union still ruled by Joseph Stalin. Following a theoretical design breakthrough in February 1951 by Stanislaw Ulam and Edward Teller, the United States conducted the world's first thermonuclear test in November 1952. The device exploded with a force equivalent to more than 10 million tons of TNT, approximately seven hundred times the power of the fission bomb at Hiroshima. Within hours of the blast, the resulting mushroom cloud had spread across one hundred miles of sky, its stem alone measuring thirty miles across. In August 1953 the Soviet Union detonated its first boosted fission weapon, a bomb that used thermonuclear fuel to increase in a limited way its explosive yield, and in November 1955 the Soviet Union tested its first "true" thermonuclear weapon. By the 1960s, largely due to the hydrogen bomb, both superpowers had acquired the ability to obliterate as much of the other as they wished in a matter of hours. The world had entered the era of "mutual assured destruction."

BIBLIOGRAPHY

Federation of American Scientists. "The High Energy Weapons Archive: A Guide to Nuclear Weapons." Available at http://nuketesting.enviroweb.org/hew/.

Hewlett, Richard G., and Francis Duncan. *A History of the United States Atomic Energy Commission*. Volume 2: *Atomic Shield, 1947–1952*. Washington, D.C.: U.S. Atomic Energy Commission, 1972. Comprehensive official history.

Rhodes, Richard. *Dark Sun: The Making of the Hydrogen Bomb*. New York: Simon and Schuster, 1995.

Richard G. Hewlett
David Rezelman

See also **Arms Race and Disarmament; Nuclear Weapons.**

HYDROPONICS, a method of growing plants in nutrient solutions, without soil. Under normal conditions, soil captures and stores nitrogen, potassium, and other mineral nutrients, which plant roots absorb gradually. Hydroponics, in contrast, immerses roots directly in liquid nutrient solutions. Plants are either suspended above water with their roots submerged, or they are placed in sand or in sterile growing mediums and regularly flooded with liquid nutrients. Proponents say this minimizes nutrient loss and allows more precise control over the nutrients the plants receive.

The principles of hydroponic gardening have been used since ancient times. They were brought to popular attention in the United States in 1937 by Dr. W. F. Gericke, who introduced the word "hydroponic" (from the Greek words for "water" and "work") and publicly displayed immense tomato plants cultivated by this method. Hydroponics became a brief fad. Although popular interest subsided, hydroponic methods continued to be developed and studied. In World War II, soldiers on Pacific islands grew their vegetables hydroponically, and in the 1960s large commercial hydroponic greenhouses and multiacre hydroponic farms were established in many locations around the United States.

In the early 2000s hydroponic systems ranged from small home setups to large enterprises. Advocates saw hydroponics as a way to increase the world's food supply and as a form of cultivation suitable for the confines of spacecraft. However, most people viewed hydroponics as a supplement to traditional growing methods rather than as a replacement. It is not suitable for all plants, must be done carefully, and can require large amounts of water.

BIBLIOGRAPHY

Nicholls, Richard. *Beginning Hydroponics: Soilless Gardening*. Philadelphia: Running Press, 1990.

Resh, Howard M. *Hydroponic Food Production: A Definitive Guidebook of Soilless Food-Growing Methods*. 5th ed. Santa Barbara, Calif.: Woodbridge Press, 1995.

John Townes / c. w.

See also **Agriculture; Gardening; Organic Farming.**

HYGIENE. Before the eighteenth century, physicians and priests were the principal students of health science in Europe and the New World. For centuries, the study of medicine had been divided into theory and practice. Theory included physiology, etiology, and semiotics, whereas practice included hygiene and therapeutics. Traditionally educated physicians understood and employed hygienic practices as well as therapeutic ones.

Priests, often viewing disease as punishment for sin, assumed major roles as health educators during the early Middle Ages, and they dispensed moral advice hand in hand with medical advice. Accordingly it was a clergyman, Thomas Thatcher, a pastor at Weymouth, Massachusetts, who prepared the first medical tract in the North American colonies during the third quarter of the seventeenth century.

In the eighteenth century, as superstition declined and social roles were secularized, teachers and government authorities assumed responsibilities as health educators. Simon-André Tissot, a Swiss physician, wrote his *Advice to the People in General with Their Health* (1761), declaring that owners of estates and schoolteachers should be instructed in matters of health and disease and should be expected to teach the uneducated. Sustaining this emphasis, Bernard Faust, a German physician, issued his *Catechism of Health* in 1794. Four years later, with the enthusiastic recommendation of Benjamin Rush in Philadelphia, an English edition of Faust's book was published in New York.

Faust had lived in a political system that championed effective health care. Officials in the absolutist states of western Europe believed that an enlightened government should protect the health of its people. Several of these governments established systems of medical police that regulated the personal lives of their citizens from the cradle to the grave with a plethora of laws and administrative agencies. Most nineteenth-century political leaders in the United States rejected the rigid paternalism of these systems. Nevertheless, with the lobbying of interested physicians, health legislation did appear in numerous states before the Civil War.

Thomas Cooper (1759–1839), trained as a lawyer and physician, saw a need for regulation of such nuisances as gambling, swearing, public drunkenness, filth and sewerage, vagrants and beggars, "careless and desperate drivers" of stagecoaches, and the firing of guns in the streets. Two outstanding New York City physicians, David Hosack and John Griscom, encouraged politicians to adopt legislation relating to epidemic diseases, constructing houses, locating cemeteries, and protecting sources of water. By 1832, most of the larger American cities had created boards of health that enacted various kinds of regulations, and twenty states had adopted licensure regulations for practitioners.

However, in caring for patients, American practitioners as a profession did not honor traditional attention to hygienic practices. Only a few individual physicians, beginning with Benjamin Rush, evinced a special interest in hygiene. These physicians acknowledged new British works on health and translated some key European treatises. Elisha Bartlett (1804–1855), John Bell (1796–1872), and Robley Dunglison (1798–1869) prepared original monographs on personal hygiene. An underlying theme, expressed succinctly by Bell, was the belief that "rules for the preservation of beauty" were the "same rules to be followed for the support of health," both physical and mental; these rules were also "in entire harmony" with those by which each individual was "required to maintain his ethical and religious relations with his fellow men." Like other physician-authors of the period, Bell discussed skin care, dress, exercise, diet, longevity, and certain aspects of public hygiene. Encouraged by such physicians, a democratization of health education occurred and some citizens, at Boston in 1837, founded the American Physiological Society in order to learn "that part of Human Physiology which teaches the influence of air, cleanliness, exercise, sleep, food, drink, medicine, etc., on human health and longevity." Although short-lived, this group reflected the growing concern among American citizens for an understanding of human physiology and appropriate hygienic practices.

By 1876, there was still no comprehensive American treatise on hygiene. The situation changed abruptly with the emergence of a preventive medicine based on the bacteriological discoveries begun by Louis Pasteur and continued by many others during the last quarter of the century. These discoveries offered a rational basis for many of the sanitary reforms that legislatures began to enact and provided justification for new kinds of specific hygienic practices, both personal and public. Although public health workers were primarily concerned with the control of contagious and epidemic diseases well into the first decades of the twentieth century, the National Committee for Mental Hygiene was organized in 1908. Eight years later (June 1916), the Johns Hopkins School of Hygiene and Public Health incorporated mental hygiene into its original prospectus. An emerging interest in occupational hygiene reinforced attention to mental hygiene.

Although a few doctors studied health problems associated with the work of miners, metalworkers, shoemakers, bakers, and numerous other craftsmen during the eighteenth and nineteenth centuries, it was not until the turn of the twentieth century that American physicians and other health professionals began to give significant attention to occupational hygiene and the prevention of diseases associated with particular occupations.

Between 1870 and 1930 bacteriological discoveries, statistical surveys of disease, health regulations of industrial workers, and other forms of health legislation led to a conceptualization of hygiene as a public concern rather than a strictly private matter. The first texts on hygiene and public health were written, and the Massachusetts Institute of Technology established the first school of public health in 1912. In medical schools, hygiene became part of the curriculum in public health or preventive medicine courses. Most authorities considered personal hygiene primarily a matter of infectious disease control.

A redefinition of health began to emerge in the mid-nineteenth century, reflected in the World Health Organization's view of health as a complete state of physical, mental, and social well-being. With the mushrooming demand for medical care among citizens who saw health care as a right rather than a privilege, the emergence of multiple new groups of professionals providing health care, and the surge of scientific knowledge about ways to prevent disease and maintain health, hygiene resumed its original position as an integral component of medical and liberal education.

BIBLIOGRAPHY

Bennett, James T. *From Pathology to Politics: Public Health in America.* New Brunswick, N.J.: Transaction Publishers, 2000.

Bullough, Bonnie. *Preventive Medicine in the United States, 1900–1990: Trends and Interpretations.* Canton, Mass.: Science History Publications, 1992.

Duffy, John. *The Sanitarians: A History of American Public Health.* Urbana: University of Illinois Press, 1990.

Rosen, George. *A History of Public Health.* Baltimore: Johns Hopkins University Press, 1993.

Chester R. Burns/C. W.

See also **Epidemics and Public Health; Health Care; Johns Hopkins University; Massachusetts Institute of Technology; Medicine, Occupational; Mental Illness.**

HYLTON V. UNITED STATES (1796). The question of whether a tax on carriages imposed by an act of Congress (5 June 1794) was a direct tax and therefore subject to the constitutional rule of apportionment to the states, was decided in the negative. Three justices—Samuel Chase, William Paterson, and James Iredell—sitting without their colleagues, decided unanimously that the tax was an excise or duty and not a direct tax. The case is chiefly important for the implied assumption that the Court had the authority to review the constitutionality of an act of Congress.

BIBLIOGRAPHY

Brown, Roger H. *Redeeming the Republic: Federalists, Taxation, and the Origins of the Constitution.* Baltimore: Johns Hopkins University Press, 1993.

Currie, David P. *The Constitution in Congress: The Federalist Period, 1789–1801.* Chicago: University of Chicago Press, 1997.

Phillips Bradley/A. R.

See also **Income Tax Cases; Judicial Review; Taxation.**

HYMNS AND HYMNODY. The separatist Mayflower Pilgrims brought to Plymouth a book titled *The Booke of Psalmes: Englished both in Prose and Metre* (1612), by Henry Ainsworth. The Massachusetts Bay Puritans brought with them a version of the 150 psalms by Thomas Sternhold and John Hopkins. Eventually perceived as too inaccurately translated, in 1636 the Puritans began creating a psalmbook more suited to their ideology. In 1640, *The Whole Book of Psalmes Faithfully Translated into English Metre*, eventually known as *The Bay Psalm Book*, became the first book printed in British America, and marked the beginnings of American psalmody. No tunes were included in the book until the ninth edition, printed in 1698, which had fourteen tunes.

Isaac Watts's *Hymns and Spiritual Songs* (1707) was reprinted in America in 1739, while his *The Psalms of David Imitated* (1719), with Watts's free translation of the psalms, was reprinted there in 1729. In 1712, the Reverend John Tufts published his *Introduction to the Art of Singing Psalm Tunes*, the first music instruction book printed in America. The second edition contained thirty-seven tunes and was bound with *The Bay Psalm Book*. The Reverend Thomas Prince, pastor of the Old South Church of Boston, significantly revised it; he included fifty hymns, all but eight attributed to Isaac Watts. American hymns before 1720 in the New England Protestant churches were primarily psalms sung in either common meter (composed of stanzas alternating eight and six syllables per line), short meter (two lines of six syllables each, followed by one line of seven syllables and one line of six syllables), or long meter (each line with eight syllables), employing the same few tunes repeatedly. A technique known as lining out, in which a leader would read a line and the congregation would then sing it, was developed in England in the 1600s for a mostly illiterate people who lacked psalmbooks. It evolved in America, assisted by educated New England ministers who had studied music. A controversy developed among colonial churches involving "regular" singing of the psalms as written and the lining out method of singing, eventually giving rise to singing schools. The American singing school movement, begun in New England around 1720, arose from schools organized by local ministers. They later turned into social events held in taverns and private homes. American folk hymns derived from secular folk songs set to sacred texts by rural singing school teachers. John Wyeth's *Repository of Sacred Music, Part Second* (1813) is the earliest singing school tunebook to contain a significant number of folk hymns. Folk hymns from the oral tradition were published in numerous shape-note tunebooks. These employed diamonds, squares, ovals, and triangles to represent different notes. Two such systems of notation were published, one by William Smith and William Little in 1798 (*The Easy Instructor*) and one by Andrew Law in 1803 (*The Musical Primer*). Smith and Little's book, which used staff lines, was the more popular. This system of reading and singing became quite popular, especially in the antebellum South, at least partially because of the publication of John Wyeth's *Wyeth's Repository of Sacred Music* (1810). Shape-note singing endures as Sacred Harp singing.

The text of many hymns was considered too severe for American children and so compilations of Sunday School songs became quite popular around 1860. They emphasized the joys of heaven, the love of Christ for the person singing, and the satisfaction gained in living the Christian life.

Camp meeting songs, or spirituals, were a type of folk hymn associated with camp frontier meetings of the early and middle 1800s. They drew a broad mix of people from a vast area, including slaves, whose music was an important ingredient in the mix. The songs often employed the text of such well-known hymn writers as Isaac Watts and Charles Wesley, and were characterized by free rhythms, a chorus, simple harmonic progressions, and the use of minor keys.

By the 1880s, Sunday School songs had given way to the gospel song. The American gospel song developed within the framework of the evangelicalism emerging from the urban north, and was characterized by simplicity, an emphasis on personal experience, the absence of adoration and worship, and an admonition to turn away from sin and sorrow. Gospel songs had fewer stanzas than camp meeting songs, and were always sung in a major key. Frances Jane Crosby was a prolific gospel hymnist, producing more than nine-thousand texts. During the latter half of the twentieth century, gospel hymnody became more popular along with the rise in fundamentalism and Pentecostalism.

Early in the twentieth century, a revival of hymn writing occurred in the United States. Some of the greatest hymns in the English language were written after 1965 during the period known as the New English Renaissance. In 1922, the Hymn Society of America was founded and it continues to encourage the composition of new works. At the turn of the twenty-first century, churches have debated traditional versus contemporary styles of worship, a debate encompassing the types of music used in worship services.

BIBLIOGRAPHY

Bealle, John. *Public Worship, Private Faith: Sacred Harp and American Folksong.* Athens: University of Georgia Press, 1997.

Ninde, Edward S. *The Story of the American Hymn.* New York: Abingdon Press, 1921.

Christine E. Hoffman

See also ***Bay Psalm Book;*** **Camp Meetings; Music: African American, Gospel.**

I

I LOVE LUCY, a television program that aired weekly on the CBS network from 1951 to 1957. This half-hour situation comedy was among the most popular shows in television history, ranking first in the Nielsen ratings for four of its six seasons. Reruns have continued to air since the late 1950s, making this one of the best known of American television series. The program was created and produced by Jess Oppenheimer, who also wrote for the show with Madelyn Pugh Davis and Bob Carroll Jr.

Desi Arnaz starred as Cuban American bandleader Ricky Ricardo, who worked in a New York City nightclub. Lucille Ball, Arnaz's wife on the show and off, played Lucy Ricardo, his childlike and mischievous wife. Vivian Vance and William Frawley portrayed Ethel and Fred Mertz, the Ricardos' neighbors, landlords, and best friends. Lucille Ball emerged as a master of physical comedy; her slapstick routines were well suited to the small television screen.

I Love Lucy. Lucille Ball and Desi Arnaz in a scene from their comedy series, one of the most popular, influential, and enduring in the history of television. THE KOBAL COLLECTION

The extraordinary popularity of *I Love Lucy* had a dramatic impact on American television. It was shot on film in Los Angeles at a time when most TV shows were broadcast live from New York City. Before long, however, and partially as a result of *Lucy*'s success, most prime-time television production moved from New York City to Hollywood and from a live, theatrical aesthetic to a filmed, Hollywood style. Because *I Love Lucy* was on film, it could be sold perpetually in reruns. Within a few years, most of the TV industry had moved its productions to film.

BIBLIOGRAPHY

Oppenheimer, Jess. *Laughs, Luck—and Lucy: How I Came to Create the Most Popular Sitcom of All Time.* Syracuse, N.Y.: Syracuse University Press, 1996.

Robert Thompson

See also **Television: Programming and Influence.**

ICE SKATING, a sport brought to North America from Europe in the 1740s, takes three basic forms. Figure skating, solo or in pairs, includes jumps and spins with varying degrees of difficulty, combined with movement and dance. Speed skating (and short-track speed skating) is racing on ice. Ice hockey is a team sport played on ice. In the mid-nineteenth century, skates were made of steel with straps and clamps to fasten them to shoes. Later in the century, the blade with the permanently attached shoe was developed by the American ballet dancer and vanguard figure skater Jackson Haines, who also introduced the elements of dance and music into the previously rigid form of figure skating.

British soldiers stationed in Canada introduced a game called "shinty," which combined field hockey with ice skates. The game was originally played with a ball, but in the 1860s a puck was introduced. Regulations and associations quickly developed to govern the popular and reck-

Ice Skating. In this 1875 print, recreational skaters move together in New York's Central Park. © BETTMANN/CORBIS

less sport, and in 1892 the Canadian governor general, Frederick Arthur, Lord Stanley of Preston, donated a cup to be given to the top Canadian team after an annual playoff. The Stanley Cup is still the object the National Hockey League (NHL) competes for in its championship games. Professional women's hockey debuted in the late 1990s.

The first recorded speed-skating race in England was in the Fens during 1814. World championships for speed skating (men only) began in the 1890s. In 1892, the world governing body of both speed and figure skating—The International Skating Union (ISU)—was founded. Six years later, the first ISU-sanctioned event was held. In 1914, pioneer figure skater George H. Browne organized the first International Figure Skating Championships of America under the sponsorship of the ISU of America. In 1921, the United States Figure Skating Association (USFSA) was formed to govern the sport and promote its national growth.

As an Olympic sport, figure skating (considered an indoor sport) debuted in the 1908 Olympic Summer Games in London, with competitions held for men, women, and pairs. It became a winter sport at the first-ever 1924 Winter Games in Chamonix, France. Originally, figure skating was executed in a stiff, formal style. Compulsory movements consisted of curves and turns, in or against the direction of movement, and executed to form several circle forms in a row. Although music, more fluid movements, pirouettes, spins, and ever-increasing athleticism were continually added to the performance roster, compulsory figures remained a part of Olympic competition until 1991. Ice hockey was included in the summer Olympics in 1920 and in the inaugural winter games of 1924, where men's speed skating was also an event. Women's speed-skating championships were first held in 1936 and included in the Olympics in 1960. Ice dancing, a figure-skating discipline, became an Olympic event in 1976 and short-track speed skating in 1992.

American skaters have won more Olympic medals to date—forty by 2002—than competitors from any other country. The first American Olympic skating gold medal winner was Charles Jewtraw, who won the 500-meter speed-skating event in 1924. That same year, Beatrix Loughran took the silver medal for women's figure skating. The winning tradition continued through the turn of the twenty-first century, with Tara Lipinski winning the gold in 1998, and Sarah Hughes winning the gold in 2002. During the last decades of the twentieth centuries, many Olympic medallists such as Dorothy Hamill, Peggy Fleming, and Scott Hamilton enjoyed lasting popularity, and figure skating competitions became highly watched events.

BIBLIOGRAPHY

Brennan, Christine. *Edge of Glory: The Inside Story of the Quest for Figure Skating's Olympic Gold Medals.* New York: Penguin, 1999.

Smith, Beverley. *Figure Skating: A Celebration.* New York: St. Martin's Press, 1994.

United States Figure Skating Association. *The Official Book of Figure Skating.* Introduction by Peggy Fleming. New York: Simon and Schuster, 1998.

Deirdre Sheets

See also **Olympic Games, American Participation in.**

ICELAND, U.S. FORCES IN. After the invasion of Norway and Denmark in April 1940, Great Britain realized that Germany might take over Iceland. Therefore, on 10 May 1940 the British occupied the island without the consent of the Icelandic government. The Icelanders hoped, instead, to entrust their protection to a nonbelligerent and asked the United States to place the island under its jurisdiction. The U.S. government, deciding that national security required the survival of Britain and that this could be maintained only by a secure convoy line across the Atlantic, agreed to station troops in Iceland.

The first American troops arrived on 7 July 1941. American forces increased prodigiously after the United States declared war on Germany in December 1941. By mid-1943 the military force peaked at approximately 40,000 troops and seventy-five fighter-interceptor planes. After mid-1943, as the war turned against Germany, the United States gradually reduced its Icelandic garrison. By September 1944 the troops numbered 8,500; by the end of the war, a mere 1,000. This remaining force left in April 1947, after the United States turned over the American air base at Keflavik to Iceland in return for postwar landing rights for U.S. military aircraft.

American forces returned in February 1951, when the North Atlantic Treaty Organization, of which Iceland had become a member, sought to bolster its defenses in Europe. The number of American troops stabilized during the 1970s at approximately 1,000, serving as personnel for antisubmarine defenses, a fighter squadron, and a radar base. The almost continuous presence of U.S. forces in Iceland after World War II helped connect the previously isolated island nation with the rest of the world.

BIBLIOGRAPHY

Bittner, Donald F. *The Lion and the White Falcon: Britain and Iceland in the World War II Era.* Hamden, Conn.: Archon Books, 1983.

Neuchterlein, Donald E. *Iceland, Reluctant Ally.* Ithaca, N.Y.: Cornell University Press, 1961.

John J. Hunt / E. M.

See also **North Atlantic Treaty Organization.**

IDAHO. Few states are as dramatically differentiated, both geographically and culturally, as Idaho. According to the 2000 census, just 1,293,953 people inhabited its 82,751 square miles, or 15.6 people per square mile. Idaho stretches 479 miles from north to south. It has eighty mountain ranges, and at 5,000 feet above sea level, is the fifth highest state in the Union. Forests cover 41 percent of the state and 82 percent of land in the north, and the state receives 100 million acre-feet of water annually in the form of rain and snow, to supply 16,000 miles of rivers and streams. The most important tributary is the Snake River, which flows for 1,000 miles before draining into the Columbia. Culturally, the state is divided between the Mormon southeast, the new high-tech industries of Boise and the southwest, and the north, formerly devoted to mining and lumbering, and now working to develop tourist attractions.

Indians and Trappers

Native American settlement in Idaho was split between the Shoshones of the Great Basin in the south, who had access to the resources of the Snake and Boise Rivers with their fish and game, and the Nez Perce and Coeur d'Alene tribes in the north. The arrival of the Lewis and Clark Expedition in 1805 preceded the entry of trappers and traders into the region. In 1810, Fort Henry was erected as the first American habitation. A trade war was pursued between the Hudson's Bay Company and independent American trappers, which lasted into the 1840s. Fort Hall and Fort Boise were established as part of this competition, but ultimately came to be staging posts on the Oregon Trail. The rise of Oregon "fever" in the 1840s led 53,000 settlers to take the trail in the next two decades.

Miners and Mormons

Idaho Territory had no formal settlements until the incorporation of Franklin in 1860. In the north, however, there were a set of mining camps, which were illegally established on the Nez Perce Indian reservation to service the diggings at Orofino Creek and Pierce City. The gold rush proved alluring to depression-hit farmers, and the territory produced $3 million of gold dust by 1861. Such communities were unstable and had a large proportion of saloons and theaters. Mormon pioneers made their first permanent settlement in Idaho in the 1860s as part of Brigham Young's plans for colonization. Theirs was a much harder existence but a more stable community life, centered on family and religion, with homesteads clustered around a ward meetinghouse and supported by cooperative organizations.

State Formation

In 1853, Washington Territory was separated from Oregon and the future Idaho Territory was divided between them. Six years later, Oregon became a state and southern Idaho was added to Washington Territory. Idaho Territory was created in 1863, with only 32,342 residents. Congress removed portions of the future territories of Montana and

Wyoming in 1868, but Idaho was still too sprawling to be well administered. The north fought to be annexed by Washington Territory in the 1880s, but President Grover Cleveland vetoed a bill to separate it. The territorial legislature propitiated the north by locating the state university at Moscow. In 1889, Idaho held a special convention and drafted a constitution that Congress approved, and a year later it became a state.

Developing the Land

There was little active government in Idaho during the Civil War, and many Confederate sympathizers and migrants from the border states settled in the region. In 1864, the legislature moved the capital to Boise, a site with much fertile land and a mild climate. Boise became a trade and transportation hub and two-thirds of Idaho farms were located in the Boise area by 1870. Cattle raising became common in the 1860s, and farming succeeded mining as the principal occupation in the 1870s, although it was as dependent as mining on outside financing. With irrigation, the Snake River valley became capable of development, and in the northern region of the Palouse, wheat growing was developed on a grand scale.

Silver Mining and Lumber Production

Lead and silver strikes at Wood River (1880) and the Coeur d'Alene (1883-1884) produced a new source of wealth for Idaho. The town of Hailey near Wood River had Idaho's first electric lighting and first telephone service. Initial placer methods were succeeded by hard-rock mining financed by outside investors, most notably the Sunshine Mine in the Coeur d'Alene, with the largest recorded silver production in the world. Eastern and Californian demand for timber spurred the creation of the Clearwater Timber Company by Frederick Weyerhaeuser in 1900, and by 1903, most private timberland was in the hands of the big timber companies. In 1904, production had reached 350 million board feet and by 1925, 1,100 million board feet.

Building a Transport Network

Mining, lumbering, and wheat growing companies required an effective railroad network to transport their products. In 1882, Pocatello, in the southeast, became a major railroad center, with a complex of railroad shops that was more unionized and ethnically diverse than other parts of the state, and far less Mormon than most towns in the east. The expansion of the network continued into the twentieth century, and by 1918, there were 2,841 miles of track in Idaho. Railroad stations were a matter of community pride and stimulated town growth, even though they also created dependency on the railroad timetable.

Immigration and Anti-Mormonism

The changes of the 1880s brought newcomers to Idaho. These included the Basques, who were known to work as shepherds but often worked in mining and dam construction; they developed their own hotels and boardinghouse culture. The 1880s also saw the rise of anti-Mormonism, because of the perception of the Latter-day Saints as outsiders who tended to vote as a bloc for the Democratic Party. Under the leadership of Fred Dubois, a campaign was waged against the Mormon practice of polygamy, and the legislature passed a measure in 1882 that barred Latter-day Saints from voting, holding office, or serving on a jury, although most of these restrictions were abandoned in 1893.

The Politics of the 1890s

During the 1890s, miners' support for silver monetization made Populism a political force in Idaho. Organized labor grew rapidly, and in 1907, there were forty-five unions with 2,240 members. In the Coeur d'Alene in 1892 and 1899, there were violent attacks on mine property. In 1899, Governor Frank Steunenberg declared martial law and many miners were imprisoned. In 1905, Harry Orchard planted a bomb at Steunenberg's home that killed the governor. The subsequent kidnap and prosecution of miners' leader William Haywood in 1906 set the stage in the following year for one of the more colorful trials of the century, with Senator William Borah as the prosecutor and the radical lawyer Clarence Darrow for the defense.

Idaho in the Progressive Era

Violent protest was not, however, the only means of bringing about reform. During the 1890s, Boise's Columbian Club created the first traveling library in the West. In 1900, there were about fifteen reform clubs in Idaho that pushed for progressive legislation. Although the Republican Party was strong in the state, Idaho saw the introduction of the direct primary, initiative, referendum, recall, and workers' compensation, as well as prohibition. Equally important was the irrigation of the Snake River plain, with the assistance of the federal Reclamation Bureau. By 1915, over 19 million acres (about 35 percent of state) had been formed into twenty-two national forests. Such assistance, however, created a problem of dependence on federal resources and technological expertise. The rise of irrigated land led to the "selling" of Idaho in the East by communities and railroads. Tourism was also pushed through such instruments as *National Geographic.*

Idaho in the 1920s

During World War I, Idaho contributed 20,000 men to the armed forces; produced food, minerals, and timber for aircraft; and purchased many war bonds and savings stamps. The state also fought the syndicalist Industrial Workers of the World, who were campaigning in the mining towns and lumbering camps for an eight-hour day and higher wages. Governor Moses Alexander asked for federal troops to quell unrest in the towns of Wallace and Lewiston, and the state legislature passed a criminal syndicalism law. The agricultural depression of 1921 prompted some out-migration and twenty-seven banks failed in the 1920s. Nevertheless, Idaho completed a basic network of highways and electric railroads for a number of communities, including Boise. Motorization spurred the creation of all-weather roads and then larger schools, and caused the demise of many remote villages. A north-south highway was completed by 1920, making possible direct communication between the two halves of the state. During the 1920s, Idaho experienced a farm revolt that led to the creation of the Progressive Party, which elected candidates in 1922 and controlled three county governments. But the Republican Party remained dominant.

The Great Depression

Of the Pacific Northwest states, Idaho suffered most during the Great Depression. Farm prices fell 44 percent between 1929 and 1930; the Snake River plain experienced severe drought and declining production through the early 1930s; and average income fell 49.3 percent between 1929 and 1932. The Democrat C. Ben Ross was elected governor in 1930 and Idaho voted strongly for the Democrats in 1932. The state was fifth in the nation in New Deal per capita spending, with programs for construction, electricity in the countryside, and agricultural relief. The development of hydroelectric power by the federal government was a serious political issue in the Pacific Northwest, but Idaho proved less keen on the idea of public power than Washington and Oregon, and the legislature rejected public utility districts in 1937.

World War II and the Transformation of Idaho

During World War II, 60,000 Idahoans—11 percent of the state's population—served in the armed forces. Air bases were established at Boise and Pocatello, while the largest inland naval base was located at Sandpoint, training 293,381 sailors. After the war, the Strategic Air Command maintained Mountain Home Air Force Base for refueling, while on the Snake River, the federal government built the National Reactor Testing Station with fifty-two reactors, which produced the first electricity from nuclear power in 1951.

Postwar Reconstruction

After 1945, Idaho saw the rise of manufacturing and of firms like Morrison-Knudsen, a construction company that had worked on Hoover Dam, Albertson's grocery and drugs, one of the largest retail outlets in the United States, and the J. R. Simplot Company, with interests in food processing, fertilizers, and ranching. Other employers included Boise Cascade, one of the nation's largest producers of plywood; Micron Technology, a semiconductor company founded in 1978; and Hewlett Packard. The federal Idaho National Engineering Laboratory employed 10,000 people in the early 1990s or 5 percent of the state's jobs. Boise emerged as a major northwestern city, experienced suburban growth, and retained its small-town ambiance. It was the only city in the central Northwest with more than 100,000 residents. Big growth in the 1970s was followed by a recession in the early 1980s, especially in mining and timber. Resource-based communities turned to tourism for salvation and a large in-migration took place, mostly from California, during the late 1980s and early 1990s. During the 1990s, the state's population grew 28.5 percent.

Politics in the Late Twentieth Century

Despite holding the governorship from 1971 to 1994 and producing influential figures like Senator Frank Church, the Democratic Party became increasingly irrelevant in Idaho. The Republicans held the majority of seats in the state legislature from 1961 to the beginning of the twenty-first century. During the 1980s, union power declined, and Idaho's first right-to-work law was enacted. Idahoans voted for Republican Bob Dole over Democrat Bill Clinton by a margin of 18 percent in 1996 and for Republican George W. Bush over Democrat Al Gore by a margin of 39 percent in 2000.

BIBLIOGRAPHY

Arrington, Leonard J. *History of Idaho.* 2 vols. Moscow: University of Idaho Press, 1994.

Ashby, LeRoy. *The Spearless Leader: Senator Borah and the Progressive Movement in the 1920s.* Urbana: University of Illinois Press, 1972.

Ewert, Sara E. Dant. "Evolution of an Environmentalist: Senator Frank Church and the Hells Canyon Controversy." *Montana: The Magazine of Western History* 51, no. 1 (Spring 2001): 36–51.

Fahey, John. *The Inland Empire: Unfolding Years, 1879–1929.* Seattle: University of Washington Press, 1986.

Malone, Michael P. *C. Ben Ross and the New Deal in Idaho.* Seattle: University of Washington Press, 1970.

May, Dean L. *Three Frontiers: Family, Land, and Society in the American West, 1850–1900.* New York: Cambridge University Press, 1994.

Schwantes, Carlos A. *In Mountain Shadows: A History of Idaho.* Lincoln: University of Nebraska Press, 1991.

Wells, Merle W. *Gold Camps and Silver Cities: Nineteenth Century Mining in Central and Southern Idaho.* Moscow: Idaho Department of Lands, Bureau of Mines and Geology, 1983.

Jeremy Bonner

See also **Coeur d'Alene Riots; Oregon Trail; Silver Prospecting and Mining; Tribes: Northwestern.**

ILLINOIS. The fertile plains of Illinois have served as a center for commerce and transportation since prehistoric times. Located in the center of the North American continent, Illinois has boundaries that are largely defined by three great rivers—the Mississippi, Ohio, and Wabash—and by the southern shore of Lake Michigan. A Paleo-Indian culture existed in Illinois at least as early as 8000 B.C.E. About 1000 C.E. a great Woodland (or Mississippian) Indian culture established its capital at Cahokia, near present-day East St. Louis. Here at least twenty thousand inhabitants built huge earthen mounds, fortified their city with an elaborate log stockade, conducted trade with peoples on the Atlantic and Gulf coasts, and dominated the economic and political life of the Mississippi River valley. Cahokia had been abandoned for two hundred years or more when the first Europeans arrived. In 1673 Jacques Marquette, a French Jesuit priest, and Louis Jolliet (Joliet) explored the Fox and Illinois rivers by canoe and met with peaceful Illini and Kaskaskia Indians. With their Indian guides the two French explorers reached the Mississippi River. Jolliet observed that a canal dug at the strategic portage where the Chicago River disappeared into the sandy marshes along the shore of Lake Michigan would link the Great Lakes to the Mississippi River and the Gulf of Mexico. On a return voyage in 1675, Marquette established his first mission, the Church of the Immaculate Conception, on the north bank of the Illinois River. By 1680 the location of Marquette's mission was occupied by the Grand Village of the Kaskaskia (or Grand Village of the Illinois) and had grown to nearly seven thousand residents under the leadership of the French adventurer Robert Cavelier, Sieur de La Salle, who also built Fort Crevecoeur, near the present site of Peoria, and Fort St. Louis, at Starved Rock near La Salle, in 1680 and 1682, respectively.

For nearly a century French priests and soldiers slowly established outposts along the rivers of the Illinois country, including the Holy Family mission at Cahokia (near the ancient mound city) in 1699 and Kaskaskia, on the banks of the Mississippi, in 1703. Fort de Chartres developed from a rude wooden stockade to a formidable stone fortress between 1720 and 1753, and was intended to serve as the headquarters of an anticipated French colonial empire stretching across most of the central part of North America. Unable to transplant great numbers of settlers, the French colonial administration monitored trade with the Indians and governed with only a modest military presence. Overextended and outnumbered by the expansion of British colonization into the Ohio River valley, the French ultimately lost a war for empire in North America. In 1763, following the French and Indian War, the British gained control of all French lands in North America under the terms of the Treaty of Paris and, after delays caused by Pontiac's War, the British military peacefully took possession of the great Fort de Chartres. With the arrival of the British, many of the French abandoned Illinois and relocated across the Mississippi in the area around St. Louis, Missouri. In 1774 the British Parliament, anxious to assure their French subjects in the Mississippi valley that they would be well and effectively governed, passed the Quebec Act, placing all of the area that would become the Old Northwest, including Illinois, under the control of British authorities in Canada. This action nullified claims to this area by colonies such as Virginia, and was viewed as one of the "Intolerable Acts" by the Americans on the eve of the Revolutionary War.

During the American Revolution, George Rogers Clark led a Virginia militia unit across southern Illinois on foot to attack a surprised British garrison at Kaskaskia on 4 July 1778. Clark claimed all of Illinois for his native state. Virginia relinquished its claim on 1 March 1784, and Illinois (along with Ohio, Indiana, Michigan, Wisconsin, and all of Minnesota east of the Mississippi River) became part of the Northwest Territory governed under the Ordinances of 1785 and 1787. Conflicts between Indians and land-hungry white settlers defined the territorial period, and in 1811 the ineffective territorial governor, Ninian Edwards, sadly informed native chiefs: "My Children, I have found it almost impossible to prevent white people from rushing to your towns, to destroy your corn, burn your property, take your women and children prisoners, and murder your warriors." Still, Indian resistance led by Tecumseh's federation slowed white settlement, and the massacre of the garrison at Fort Dearborn (CHICAGO) in 1812 spread terror throughout the frontier.

Following the War of 1812, Indian resistance to white settlement was largely eliminated, and settlers streamed into southern Illinois, via the Ohio River, from Kentucky, Virginia, Tennessee, and the Carolinas. Meanwhile, pioneers from New England and the Middle Atlantic states arrived in northern Illinois, often through the Great Lakes. The distinct political and cultural differences still evident in Illinois can be traced to this early settlement pattern. On 3 December 1818 the Illinois Territory became the nation's twenty-first state, with a northern boundary set at 42°30′ to provide a generous shoreline on Lake Michigan and land for fourteen northern counties. At the time of its admission to the Union, Illinois probably had only about thirty-five thousand white inhabitants and several thousand slaves, most of them scattered on hardscrabble farms along crude trails in the southernmost part of the state between Shawneetown, on the Ohio River, and Kaskaskia. Much of the land along the Mississippi, known as the "American Bottom," was swampy, prone to flooding, and notorious for its disease-carrying mosquitoes. With the exception of the lead mining district around Galena in the state's northwest corner, the population in the first decades of statehood remained in the southernmost parts of the state. This rough, hilly region was called "Little Egypt" by the early pioneers, because they felt the land between the Mississippi and Ohio rivers resembled the Nile River delta; as a result of this perceived resemblance, residents in this region named one of their most important towns Cairo. State government was housed at Kaskasia in a small, rented cabin that eventually was carried away by flood waters, and the state's first governor, the semiliterate Shadrach Bond, favored the introduction of slavery as a means of providing a much-needed workforce. By 1820 Illinois had fifty-five thousand inhabitants and the capital was moved to Vandalia, the terminus of the new National Road (today U.S. Route 40).

During its formative years the state government grappled with myriad problems resulting from the state's rapid and diverse development. An effort to amend the state's constitution to allow slavery was defeated in an 1824 referendum by a vote of 6,640 to 4,972. However, sympathy for slavery remained strong in southern Illinois, which bordered on the slave states of Kentucky and Missouri. In 1837 Elijah Lovejoy, an abolitionist newspaper publisher, was murdered in Alton and his press destroyed. In 1832, following the brief but bloody Black Hawk War, the Sauk and Fox Indians were forced to relinquish all claims to lands in Illinois. The Illinois governor proved powerless in his feeble attempts to quell anti-Mormon sentiment in western Illinois; in 1844 a vigilante-militia in Carthage murdered the charismatic leader of the Church of Jesus Christ of Latter-Day Saints (Mormons),

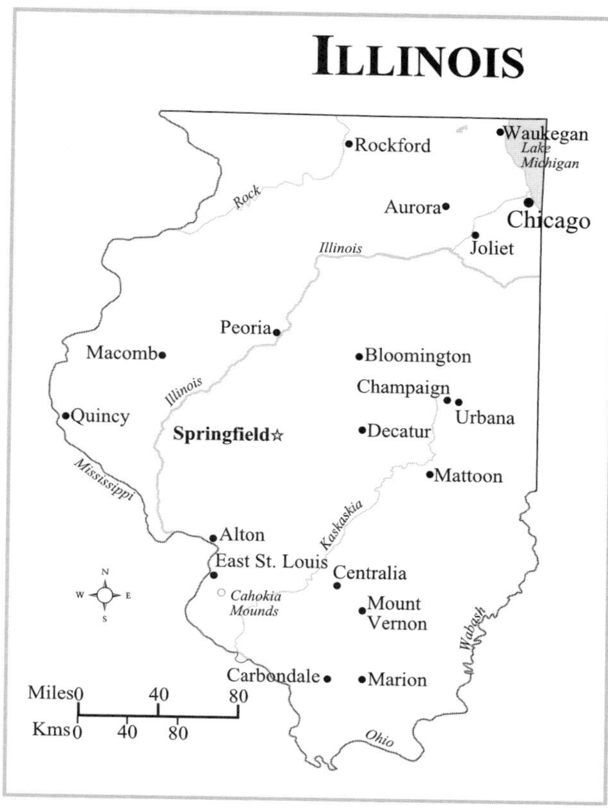

Joseph Smith, and his brother, Hyrum. Several thousand of Smith's followers, under the leadership of Brigham Young, soon abandoned their settlement at Nauvoo and began their journey to Utah. In 1837 the legislature once again moved the capital, this time to Springfield—in the very center of the state and closer to the most fertile and rapidly developing regions. The first decades of statehood witnessed an extraordinary growth in the state's population; it reached nearly half a million people by 1840, almost a tenfold increase since statehood just two decades earlier. Key to this amazing growth, as settlers filled the rich prairie lands of central and northern Illinois, was an excellent transportation system. Steamboats navigated the Mississippi, Ohio, Wabash, and Illinois rivers, facilitating the movement of settlers and goods. The legislature approved "an Act to establish and maintain a general system of internal improvements" in 1837, and this led to the construction of the one-hundred-mile Illinois and Michigan Canal. Opened in 1848, it linked the rising metropolis of Chicago with the Illinois River at La Salle, from which river traffic could proceed from Lake Michigan to the Mississippi River and ultimately the Gulf of Mexico. The canal was not commercially successful because it soon faced competition from railroads. Chartered in 1851, the Illinois Central Railroad (for which Abraham Lincoln served as an attorney) used federal and state subsidies, along with \$25 million of private capital, to construct more than seven hundred miles of track connecting Chicago with Cairo and Galena to form a Y across the fertile prairie. By the mid-1850s Illinois had the nation's most modern network of railroads and Chicago had become the Midwest's railroad center.

In 1860, the year an Illinois Republican, Abraham Lincoln, was elected president, following his loss to Stephen A. Douglas in the nationally significant election for the U.S. Senate just two years earlier, the state's population had swelled to 1,715,000; over a quarter of a million of them served in the Civil War, and thirty-four thousand died fighting for the Union. Although pro-slavery, Confederate sympathizers (COPPERHEADS) in Illinois organized themselves as the Sons of Liberty or Knights of the Golden Circle and opposed the Union cause, sometimes with violence, there was otherwise little opposition to the war in the state. Meanwhile, Chicago prospered as the Union's central warehouse for military operations in the West.

Between the Civil War and the turn of the century, farmers transformed vast stretches of prairie grassland into neat, square fields of corn and other grains, and pasture for cattle and hogs. However, farm foreclosures caused by high taxes, overproduction, low prices, and exploitation by railroads led to unrest in rural areas. Meanwhile, in Chicago and other industrial centers, and in coal mining towns, expansion brought overcrowding, poor working conditions, and a new flood of immigrant labor. When the major political parties ignored their plight, farmers responded by supporting third-party movements, such as the Grangers and the Populist party. In a victory for rural agitators, the landmark U.S. Supreme Court ruling *Munn v. Illinois* (1877) established the principle that state legislatures could regulate railroads. Workers sought to join unions, and violent labor clashes and strikes occurred throughout the state. In 1873 a rail strike virtually shut down the state, as did another strike in 1877. At the Haymarket Riot in 1886, a bomb killed seven Chicago policemen and led to the execution of four alleged anarchists the following year. The Pullman strike of 1894 ended with President Grover Cleveland ordering federal troops into Chicago to restore order. Illinois advanced as an agricultural and industrial giant, becoming the nation's third most populace state in 1890, with Chicago (devastated by fire in 1871 but quickly rebuilt) emerging as the nation's "Second City." The state was the national leader in wheat and corn production and second in livestock; it was also a leader in the mining of bituminous (soft) coal. At the same time that steel, farm equipment, and industrial machinery manufacturing grew in the northern cities of Joliet, Rock Island-Moline, Peoria, and Rockford, Chicago, with its port and railroad facilities, steel mills, manufacturing plants, Union Stockyards, and MEATPACKING businesses served as the hub of commerce in the north central United States. By the early twentieth century the Illinois poet Carl Sandberg could rightly proclaim Chicago the "Hog Butcher of the World" and the "City of Big Shoulders."

Political power in Illinois has traditionally rested in county courthouses and city halls, where local party organizations choose candidates, make key decisions on issues, and dole out favors and patronage. The Democrats and Republicans have generally shared power on a fairly equal basis throughout the state's history. In pre-Civil War Illinois the slavery issue gave Democrats an edge over Whigs and, later, Republicans. However, between the Civil War and the Great Depression, Republicans maintained the upper hand, largely due to the party's strength in the prosperous and rapidly growing northern and central regions of the state, and to its successful efforts to defeat reapportionment of the state legislature. Viewing with alarm the rise of Chicago with its huge and largely ethnic population (mainly Irish and eastern European), "downstate" Republican politicians successfully fought off all reapportionment schemes that would have appropriately recognized Chicago's rapidly growing population, which was 12 percent of the state's total in 1870, 35 percent in 1900, and 44 percent in 1930. Illinois's outmoded constitution of 1848 was replaced in 1870 by a poorly crafted document that neglected to provide home rule for cities, left the office of governor relatively weak, and set up an unorthodox system of cumulative voting that allowed voters to cast a ballot for one, two, or three candidates for the state House of Representatives, thus assuring at least one Republican or Democrat from every district.

Political rivalries in Illinois have traditionally been bitter and complex. Despite the efforts of reform-minded leaders such as Democratic governor John Peter Altgeld (1893–1897) and of a number of Progressives during the early twentieth century, political reform came slowly, and corruption and party patronage have characterized the state's political history. When congressional districts were redrawn, following the 1940 census, Chicago still had less than its correct share of districts. The courts had to force the state legislature's reapportionment in the 1960s; and when no agreement could be hammered out by 1964, all 177 members of the Illinois General Assembly were elected at large. A new state constitution in 1970 finally provided home rule to municipalities, established more equitable tax policies, and strengthened the governor and the state supreme court; but the unorthodox system of cumulative voting was not abandoned until 1981. Political patronage remained a scandal throughout most of the twentieth century in both Chicago and Springfield; and a U.S. Supreme Court decision in 1990 (*Rutan v. Republican Party of Illinois*) only altered rather than eliminated the practice. Illinois has more than thirty-six thousand elected officials, and some observers believe politics is so pervasive because so many political units comprise the complex fabric of Illinois government. There are 102 counties in Illinois, 1,300 cities and villages, 1,400 townships, and over 2,500 special governmental districts responsible for such diverse matters as libraries, airports, community colleges, water and sanitation, parks, and mosquito abatement. Illinois also has 960 elected school boards.

Throughout the twentieth century Illinois occupied a place among the nation's agricultural, commercial, and industrial leaders. It was home to such corporate giants as Sears, Montgomery Ward, International Harvester, Kraft Foods, Archer Daniels Midland, John Deere, and Caterpillar Tractor. The Great Depression hit Illinois even harder than other states, and in the early 1930s the state received more federal relief money than New York and Pennsylvania combined. Governor Henry Horner (1933–1941) used a suspension of the property tax to aid farmers and persuaded the legislature to enact taxes on gasoline and liquor (legal after the repeal of Prohibition) to fund relief efforts, but the economy did not fully recover until the nation began building up for war in 1940. Following World War II, Illinois enjoyed several decades of prosperity and growth. The completion of the St. Lawrence Seaway in 1959 transformed Chicago into an international port by linking the Great Lakes to the Atlantic, and by 1970 Chicago's O'Hare Airport was the nation's busiest. Illinois led the nation in corn and soybean production in 1971. The nation's first commercial nuclear power plant was built near Morris, Illinois, in the late 1940s, and Illinois, with its internationally renowned universities—the University of Chicago, Northwestern University, and the Chicago campus of the University of Illinois—provided an ideal location for research centers such as AT&T's Bell Laboratories, DeKalb Genetics, the Fermi National Accelerator Laboratory, and the Argonne National Laboratory.

In 1970 the state had a population of more than 11 million, a 10 percent increase over 1960. Illinois retained the twenty-four seats that it had held in the U.S. House of Representatives since the redistricting following the 1910 census. (It would lose four of these seats by the end of the century.) More than half the state's population lived in the Chicago metropolitan area. Although Chicago was then the nation's second most populous city, only two other cities in Illinois, Peoria and Rockford, had populations exceeding one hundred thousand. The completion of the Sears Tower in Chicago in 1974 (then the world's tallest building) called attention to Illinois as an economic powerhouse. However, in the late 1970s Illinois, like other Midwestern states in the nation's "Rust Belt," appeared to be in economic decline. Manufacturing plants relocated abroad in search of cheap, nonunionized labor, and farm prices declined due to overproduction (although the number of farms dwindled from 255,700 in the late nineteenth century to 80,000 in the late twentieth century). Illinois's coal production, once second only to Pennsylvania, dropped to sixth nationally by 1991, and production was only 30 percent of that of the nation's leader, Wyoming. Illinois lost manufacturing jobs, and its unemployment climbed from 7.1 percent in 1978 to a staggering 8.6 percent in 1986.

However, by the early 1990s Illinois had recovered, and a new economic base featuring banking, research, and new technologies emerged. The lands west and north of Chicago became the "silicon prairie," the fastest-growing high-technology corridor in the nation. Foreign capital poured into Chicago's revitalized banks. The accounting firm of Arthur Andersen provided financial services to corporate giants throughout the world, and though Chicago no longer housed stockyards, slaughterhouses, or giant grain elevators, the Chicago Board of Trade employed thirty-three thousand people and helped set prices for agricultural commodities throughout the world.

Because of its central location and extensive economic infrastructure, Illinois will likely continue to serve as a vital center of trade, transportation, and commerce in North America. With its large and ethnically diverse population, the "Prairie State" continues to be viewed as a political bellwether and a microcosm of the nation. Those wanting to gauge the mood of folks in the heartland continue to ask, "Will it play in Peoria?"

By 2000 Illinois's population had grown to 12,419,293, an expansion of 8.64 percent over 1990, but an increase that lagged the national growth rate of 13.1 percent. The state's Hispanic population grew by nearly 70 percent in the 1990s and comprised 12.3 percent of the population in 2000; African Americans comprised 15.1 percent of the total. All the population growth occurred in the northern part of the state. In 2000, 17.5 percent of the state's children lived in poverty despite Illinois's renewed prosperity. Political power in Illinois, still balanced between Republicans and Democrats, was located in three district geographic segments: Chicago, "downstate," and the "collar counties," comprised of sprawling suburbs and expanding cities surrounding the great metropolis. From 1977 and into the opening years of the twenty-first century, the Republicans held the governor's office, including during the four terms (1977–1991) of James "Big Jim" Thompson, a popular moderate Republican who managed to forge compromises with a legislature usually controlled by Democrats. His Republican successors, lacking his charisma, found dealing with the Democrats problematic, and because of declining state revenues in 2000, the funding of education and basic government services remained a chronically contentious issue.

Although the Illinois legislature failed to ratify the Equal Rights Amendment in 1982, thereby killing all chances of its becoming part of the U.S. Constitution, women in Illinois made significant gains in attaining state office. While the 1971–1972 General Assembly had only four female members, legislatures in the 1990s had more than forty. Reflecting the state's ethnic diversity, minority representation in the state legislature increased, from five African Americans in 1950 to more than twenty in the 1990s. In 1978 Roland Burris became the first African American to win statewide office when he was elected comptroller (he was subsequently elected attorney general); and in 1992 Carol Moseley Braun became the first black woman elected to the U.S. Senate by any state. At the beginning of the twenty-first century, Hispanics held seats in both the Illinois Senate and the House.

BIBLIOGRAPHY

Bridges, Roger D., and Rodney O. Davis. *Illinois: Its History and Legacy.* St. Louis, Mo.: River City, 1984.

Davis, G. Cullom. "Illinois: Crossroads and Cross Section." In *Heartland: Comparative Histories of Midwestern States.* Edited by James H. Madison. Bloomington: Indiana University Press, 1988.

Howard, Robert P. *Illinois: A History of the Prairie State.* Grand Rapids, Mich.: Eerdman's, 1972.

Nardulli, Peter F., ed. *Diversity, Conflict, and State Politics: Regionalism in Illinois.* Urbana: University of Illinois Press, 1989.

Michael J. Devine

ILLINOIS (INDIANS). The Illinois Indian tribe (they identified themselves as *inoca,* perhaps meaning "men"; the French later called them Illinois, and they are commonly referred to today as Illini) moved from Michigan to Illinois and Wisconsin by the 1630s. Illinois traders first contacted the French in 1666 at Chequamegon Bay, Lake Superior. The Illinois and Miami, speaking central Algonquian dialects, separated shortly before Jacques Marquette and Louis Jolliet arrived in the Illinois country in 1673. With more than 13,000 members by the mid-1650s, the tribe divided into a dozen subtribes. Dramatic population losses resulted from war, disease, Christianity, monogamy, alcoholism, and emigration. Illinois vulnerability was a consequence of dependency on their close allies, the French. As their numbers deteriorated, they combined into fewer subtribes (Cahokia, Kaskaskia, Michigamea, Moingwena, Peoria, and Tamaroa) and withdrew to the southwest, collecting along the east bank of the Mississippi south of the Illinois River. By 1736 the Illinois numbered just 2,500, and 80 in 1800; the last full-blood and his relatives left the state in 1833.

The Illinois constituted a tribe, not a confederacy, and maintained a tribal chief; the subtribes, however, often operated independently. Influential leaders included Rouensa, Chicago, and Ducoigne. Each man could marry several women, and would locate his families near his father. The tribe reckoned descent through the male line, and individuals became members of a clan and a moiety (division). The male role required prowess as hunter and warrior; and women tended to their dwellings, children, gathering, and agriculture. Men enjoyed a power and status advantage over women, but women employed considerable influence in their own realm.

In early spring the Illinois traditionally gathered in large semipermanent villages to plant crops and engage in communal buffalo hunting. Spring also saw them launch small war parties against such enemies as the Fox, Sauk, and Sioux. In the fall, they divided into small hunting villages of 200 or 300 cabins. Most Peorias moved west of the Mississippi River after 1765; eventually a few Kaskaskias joined them. Today, the Peorias, descendents of the Illinois and the Miamis, live in Peoria, Oklahoma.

BIBLIOGRAPHY

Blasingham, Emily J. "The Depopulation of the Illinois Indians." *Ethnohistory* 3 (1956): 193–224, 361–412. A most reliable examination of the depopulation of the Illinois tribe.

Illinois. The tribe was given its current name by the French, whom the Indians first encountered in 1666. LIBRARY OF CONGRESS

Callender, Charles. "Illinois." In *Handbook of North American Indians.* Edited by William C. Sturtevant et al. Vol. 15: *Northeast,* edited by Bruce G. Trigger. Washington, D.C.: Smithsonian Institution, 1978. A useful and authoritative account by an anthropologist.

Zitomersky, Joseph. *French Americans—Native Americans in Eighteenth-Century French Colonial Louisiana: The Population Geography of the Illinois Indians, 1670s–1760s.* Lund, Sweden: Lund University Press, 1994.

Raymond E. Hauser

ILLINOIS AND MICHIGAN CANAL. On 4 July 1836 the State of Illinois began construction of the Illinois and Michigan Canal to connect Lake Michigan and the Mississippi River. But the panic of 1837 soon forced Illinois to abandon work. Under the leadership of Governor Thomas Ford, however, Illinois devised new methods of financing and resumed construction. On 23 April 1848 the first boat passed through the canal.

The Illinois and Michigan Canal was profitable from its opening, and despite the growth of railroads, tolls exceeded its operation expenses until 1879. Traffic dwindled in the twentieth century, but sections of the canal stayed open until 1930. Of all North American artificial waterways, only the Erie Canal outranked it in importance.

BIBLIOGRAPHY

Ranney, Edward. *Prairie Passage: The Illinois and Michigan Canal Corridor.* Urbana: University of Illinois Press, 1998.

Redd, Jim. *The Illinois and Michigan Canal: A Contemporary Perspective in Essays and Photographs.* Carbondale: Southern Illinois University Press, 1993.

Paul M. Angle / A. E.

See also **Canals; Erie Canal; Lakes-to-Gulf Deep Waterway.**

ILLINOIS FUR BRIGADE, one of several trading expeditions sent out annually, between about 1816 and 1827, by the American Fur Company from its headquarters at Mackinac, at the confluence of Lakes Michigan and Huron, in Michigan Territory. The brigade, usually numbering ten or twelve bateaux loaded with trade goods, made its way down Lake Michigan and through the Chicago portage and Des Plaines River to the Illinois River. There it divided into small parties that spent the winter bartering with the Indians for furs. In the spring the brigade reassembled and returned by water to Mackinac. In 1828 the American Fur Company sold its Illinois interests to Gurdon S. Hubbard, the brigade's commander.

BIBLIOGRAPHY

Lavender, David. *The Fist in the Wilderness.* Garden City, N.Y.: Doubleday, 1964.

Stevens, Wayne Edson. *The Northwest Fur Trade: 1763–1800.* University of Illinois Studies in the Social Sciences, vol. 14, no. 3. Urbana: University of Illinois, 1928.

Paul M. Angle / T. D.

See also **American Fur Company; Fur Trade and Trapping; Indian Trade and Traders.**

IMMEDIATISM. The drive to end slavery at once, known as immediatism, had its origins in British abolitionists' frustration in the 1820s with Parliament's gradual approach to abolishing slavery in the West Indian colonies. The American abolitionist William Lloyd Garrison adopted the concept when he founded the antislavery newspaper the *Liberator* in 1831 and helped to establish the American Anti-Slavery Society in 1833. Using as a model the conversion experience of the Second Great Awakening, Garrisonian abolitionists wished to convert Americans to a belief that slaveholding was a sin. A sinner, once aware of his or her sin, should cease sinning immediately. Supporters of immediatism rejected moderate approaches to ending slavery such as colonization or political reform and demanded total emancipation and equal rights for black Americans. Most Americans did not support immediatism because it threatened too many economic and racial interests and because it seemed rash. Garrison believed that the U.S. Constitution was a proslavery document. Some of his supporters even called for a secession of free states from the Union. Once immediatism proved ineffectual, Garrison's argument that political action would compromise abolitionist principles was rejected by some abolitionists, who by the late 1830s were entering the political arena.

BIBLIOGRAPHY

Kraditor, Aileen S. *Means and Ends in American Abolitionism: Garrison and His Critics on Strategy and Tactics, 1834–1850.* New York: Pantheon Books, 1969.

Mayer, Henry. *All On Fire: William Lloyd Garrison and the Abolition of Slavery.* New York: St. Martin's Press, 1998. The best biography of Garrison and his philosophy of immediatism.

Stewart, James B. *Holy Warriors: The Abolitionists and American Slavery.* New York: Hill and Wang, 1976.

Timothy M. Roberts

See also **Antislavery.**

IMMIGRATION. Except for some 2.5 million Native Americans and Alaska natives, the 281 million persons recorded in the 2000 census are immigrants and their descendants. Some 70 million immigrants have come to what is now the United States, beginning with the Spanish settlers in Florida and New Mexico in the late sixteenth century. The United States only began counting immigrants in 1819, so the numbers before that time are problematic.

TABLE 1

Immigration by Centuries

16th–18th century	1,000,000
19th century	19,000,000
20th century	47,000,000
Total (legal or legalized)	67,000,000
Illegal Immigration (at least)	3,000,000
Total	70,000,000

Table 1 shows a reasonable estimate of total immigration, legal and illegal, by centuries; as it shows, more than two-thirds of all the immigrants who have come arrived in the twentieth century.

For a long time it seemed appropriate to many historians of immigration to focus on the so-called "century of immigration" that ran from 1815, the end of the Napoleonic Wars, to 1924, the date of the most restrictive immigration law in U.S. history. However, the large movements that occurred after World War II make such an emphasis inappropriate.

Beginning of the Twenty-First Century

Approximately 24 million immigrants—36 percent of all who have ever come—had arrived since 1960, leading many to fear that immigrants were swamping the nation. In fact, even in the immigrant-rich decade after 1990, the rate of immigration—computed by dividing the yearly number of immigrants by the total population—was well below peak level. In both the decade after 1850 and the one after 1900, the rate was over 10; for the first eight years after 1990, the rate was only 3.6. Such baseless fears about immigration—called "nativism" since the mid-nineteenth century—have often been present in America.

The Seventeenth and Eighteenth Centuries

Most of the million immigrants who arrived in the nearly two and a half centuries between the Spanish founding of St. Augustine, Florida, in 1565 and 1800 came during the years of peace between the 1680s and the 1770s. Between the outbreak of the American Revolution and Napoleon's final defeat in 1815 there was little nonmilitary immigration, although perhaps eighty thousand American Loyalists emigrated during and after the Revolution, mostly to Canada and Britain.

Since the largest single component of colonial immigration was English, and since Great Britain was the final European winner in the imperial wars of the era, the English language, English law, and English religious practices became norms to which later immigrants would be expected to conform. To be sure, the New World environment as well as distance and time worked cultural transformations, as did the influence of both aboriginal peoples and non-English immigrants. But the English were what John Higham has called the "charter group" and set norms for others to meet. About 48 percent of the total nonaboriginal population at the first census in 1790 has been estimated to be of English origin.

English: Virginia and the South. Permanent English settlement began at Jamestown, Virginia, in 1607 and, although there were non-English in most settlements, English immigrants predominated in every seventeenth-century colony except New York. The Virginia colony was for two decades a demographic disaster in which more than half of the immigrants died within a year or so. The immigrant population there and in other southern colonies was heavily male, so natural increase—the excess of births over deaths—did not begin much before the beginning of the eighteenth century, if then.

Why then did English immigrants continue to come? Most were probably ignorant of the true conditions and for many there was no choice. A majority of those English who migrated to the American South in the seventeenth and early eighteenth centuries were indentured servants. The dependence on tobacco growing in Virginia created almost insatiable demands for labor, which were eventually filled by enslaved African immigrants, but for decades, most indentured laborers were English and other Britons. Later in the eighteenth century about fifty thousand persons, overwhelmingly male, were "transported" from English prisons to British colonies.

But others came voluntarily, attracted by the availability of land and the possibility of wealth—what students of migration call a "pull factor," and/or repelled by wretched economic conditions and poor future prospects in England—a so-called push factor.

Maryland, where settlement conditions were less harsh than in Virginia, was founded as a refuge for English Catholics. Much of the gentry was Catholic, but they were soon outnumbered by Protestant lower orders. South Carolina had settlement patterns similar to those in Virginia, but, because of Charleston, the one city of any size in a southern colony, it had more non-British immigrants, including French Huguenots and a few Jews, among its elite population.

English: Massachusetts and New England. Most of the early migration to Massachusetts, beginning with the Pilgrims in 1620, was family migration, much of it religiously motivated. Most of the leading figures and a considerable number of the lesser lights were Protestant dissenters from the Church of England. For significant numbers of the "lesser sort," economic motives predominated. The largest increment of immigrants to New England, perhaps twenty-five thousand persons, came during the "great migration" of the two decades before 1641. Unlike the colonies on the Chesapeake, which were immigrant colonies until the beginning of the eighteenth century, persons born in the New World were a majority of the New England settlers within a few decades of set-

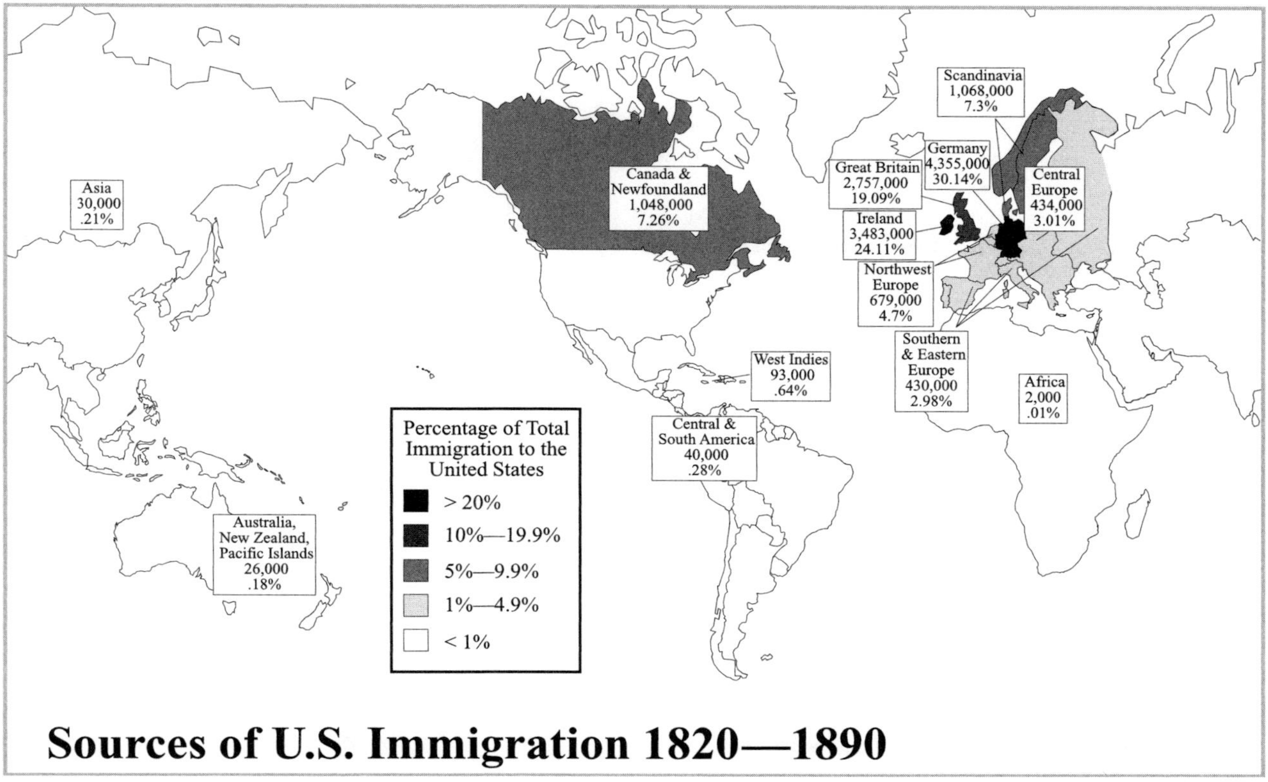

Sources of U.S. Immigration 1820—1890

tlement. New England was less affected by non-British immigration than any other section.

Africans. Africans and their descendents have never been more statistically prominent in American society than in the colonial period. The best estimate is that, at the first federal census in 1790, Africans and their descendents were about 20 percent of the population. The earliest Africans in British North America—brought to Jamestown in 1619—were first treated as indentured servants. By about 1700 in all parts of the American colonies, most Africans were enslaved. Philip Curtin's conservative 1969 estimate judged that almost 430,000 Africans were brought to what is now the United States, about 4.5 percent of all those brought to the New World by the African slave trade. Africans made up more than a third of all immigrants to the United States before 1810. Perhaps fifty thousand more were brought after the United States outlawed further imports of foreign slaves in 1808; those fifty thousand were the first illegal immigrants and the only ones before 1882. Africans and African Americans were found in every colony and state: in 1790 more than 90 percent of the 750,000 Negroes enumerated in the census lived in the South, a percentage that remained fairly constant until well after the World War II era.

Until well into the twentieth century, scholars believed that African immigrants were stripped of their culture and brought nothing but their labor to the United States. It is now clear that African contributions to early American culture were considerable, consisting largely of agricultural and craft techniques.

Other Europeans. The largest groups of non-English Europeans in the new United States were Irish, 7.6 percent; German, 6.9 percent; and Dutch, 2.5 percent; but they were distributed quite differently. The Irish, almost all of whom were Protestants, were dispersed widely throughout the colonies and had little impact as a group although a number of individuals were quite influential. The Germans, whose immigration in significant numbers began only in 1683, were heavily concentrated in Pennsylvania, where they constituted a third of the population. Many came as indentured servants, often called "redemptioners" because other relatives who had either come as free immigrants or had gained their freedom, would frequently purchase their remaining time. Their presence—and their politics—inspired some of the earliest American nativism. In 1751 Benjamin Franklin complained, "Why should Pennsylvania, founded by the English, become a colony of *Aliens*, who will shortly be so numerous as to Germanize us instead of our Anglifying them, and will never adopt our language or customs. . . ."

Franklin's fears, of course, were groundless. Although the English and Germans each constituted about a third of Pennsylvania's population, most of the rest were Britons—Irish, Scots, and Welsh. The only ethnic political power exercised by a non-English group was in New York, where the Dutch had been in charge until the bloodless

English conquest of 1660. Even though they were less than a sixth of the state's 1790 population, the Dutch, because of their status and wealth, continued to exercise significant political power. Although all of the American port cities, even Boston, contained considerable ethnic diversity in the colonial period, only New York was truly polyglot. Swedes had settled on the Delaware while a number of French Huguenots settled throughout the colonies: other French, the Acadians, were expelled by the British in 1755 from Nova Scotia and scattered throughout the colonies. Many wound up in Louisiana, which became an American territory after 1803.

The Nineteenth Century

The 19 million immigrants who came during the nineteenth century arrived at a generally accelerating pace, as table 2 indicates.

The Civil War in the first half of the 1860s and the economic slump during much of the 1890s account for the two decades in which the numbers decreased. But mere numbers do not properly indicate the impact of immigration: it is important to understand the rate or incidence of immigration. For example, in 1854 some 425,000 immigrants came, making it by far the heaviest single antebellum year for the arrival of immigrants. As there were about 26 million persons in the United States that year, the new immigrants amounted to, as such numbers are usually cited, 16 per 1,000 of the nation's people. Table 3 shows the rate of immigration per thousand averaged for each decade from the 1820s to the 1890s. Thus, the increase in actual numbers of immigrants from the 1860s to the 1870s was, in terms of incidence, a slight decrease. Beginning in 1850 each decennial census has recorded place of birth for every person enumerated, making it possible to calculate the percentage of foreign born in the population as indicated in table 4. The amazing consistency of the percentage of foreign-born persons shows clearly that, despite the fluctuations in other data, foreigners had a stable incidence in American life for a seventy-year period.

TABLE 2

Immigration to the United States, 1801–1900

Period	Number
1801–1820	Fewer than 100,000*
1821–1830	151,824
1831–1840	599,125
1841–1850	1,713,251
1851–1860	2,598,214
1861–1870	2,314,824
1871–1880	2,812,891
1881–1890	5,246,613
1891–1900	3,687,564
Total	c. 19,200,000

*No statistics were collected prior to 1819. The data are taken from official sources.

TABLE 3

Rate of Immigration per 1,000, 1821–1900

Period	Rate
1821–1830	1.2
1831–1840	3.9
1841–1850	8.4
1851–1860	9.3
1861–1870	6.4
1871–1880	6.2
1881–1890	9.2
1891–1900	5.3

TABLE 4

Foreign Born as a Percentage of Total Population, 1850–1920

Year	Percentage
1850	9.7
1860	13.2
1870	14.0
1880	13.3
1890	14.7
1900	13.6
1910	14.7
1920	13.2

From the 1830s through the 1860s a majority of immigrants were from just two ethnic groups—Irish and German. There were some 2.3 million of each, and in the 1850s and 1860s they were more than 70 percent of all immigrants. Their profiles, however, were quite different.

Irish. For the Irish, one terrible event, the potato famine of the second half of the 1840s, has dominated the memory of emigration, but there was substantial Irish immigration both before and after the famine. The root causes of Irish migration were mass poverty, underdevelopment, and a burgeoning population. Irish population almost doubled in the half-century after 1791 so that on the eve of the famine there were 8.1 million persons in Ireland. In the 1830s over 200,000 Irish had immigrated to the United States, and large numbers went to Canada and across the Irish Sea to England. Those Irish and their predecessors came largely as single men, and Irish labor was vital to much of the American "internal improvements" of the era. Some three thousand Irishmen had done most of the digging for the Erie Canal before1820 and several thousand dug the New Canal in New Orleans in the 1830s.

The great famine that began in 1845 had as its proximate cause an infestation of the fungus *Phytophthora infestans.* This blight was well known in Ireland: it had occurred at least twenty times in the previous 125 years and did not cause alarm at first. But in 1846 it struck more completely than ever before or since and triggered the last peacetime famine in western European history. Its impact was exacerbated by the disdain and ineptitude of the British government and Irish landlords as well as by the poverty and ignorance of the people. Disease, the constant companion of famine, took its toll. That and massive emigration in the next ten years reduced the population of Ireland by some 2.5 million people—nearly one person in three.

The migration of the famine years and beyond was largely family migration. Relatively few Irish settled in rural America, and the vast majority became residents of east coast cities between Boston and Baltimore, although there were large groups of Irish in such western cities as Cincinnati, Chicago, and San Francisco. They often filled the worst neighborhoods, such as the infamous Five Points in New York City. But they also began to fill the new urban occupations and came, in many cities, to dominate public services, particularly police and fire departments, and such new urban occupations as horse car drivers. And in city after city, they played a larger role in politics than their mere numerical incidence would indicate. Most became traditionally associated with the Democratic Party.

Before the end of the century, young, unmarried women became the majority of Irish emigrants. This reflected, in part, demographic and cultural changes greatly influenced by the famine and endemic poverty. Ireland had the oldest average age at marriage and the greatest percentage of persons who never married of any nation in western Europe. The Irish emigrants of these years were overwhelmingly Catholic and they soon came to dominate the Roman Catholic Church in America. For the Irish, and to a lesser degree for other Catholic immigrants, the immigrant church became what its historian, Jay P. Dolan, termed a fortress helping to protect its faithful from a largely hostile Protestant world.

Anti-Catholic hostility was nowhere stronger than among the Protestant Irish already in America. Most American Protestant Irish began, in the 1830s and 1840s, to call themselves Scotch Irish, a term never used in Ireland or anywhere else. They formed the backbone of the most militant anti-Catholic movements in the United States, including the so-called Know-Nothing movement of the 1840s and 1850s and the American Protective Association of the 1880s and 1890s.

Germans. The major push factor in nineteenth-century German immigration was the modernization of the German economy, which dislocated millions of Germans, a minority of whom chose emigration as a response. The Germans were the most numerous of nineteenth-century immigrants. They settled heavily in eastern cities from New York to Baltimore and in the midwestern area known as the German triangle, whose corners were Cincinnati, St. Louis, and Milwaukee. While most came in at eastern ports, a large number of those who settled in the "triangle" came to southern ports carried by ships in the cotton trade and made their way north by river boat and then railroad. Those in the cities worked largely at artisanal and mechanical pursuits, while one industry—the production of lager beer—was dominated by German producers and, for a time, consumers. Large numbers of German immigrants settled in rural areas, and some German American groups have shown very high levels of persistence in agriculture over several generations.

Although seventeenth- and eighteenth-century German migration was almost all Protestant, and although Protestants have probably been a majority of German immigrants in every decade except the 1930s, very sizable numbers of those since 1800 have been Catholics, and a significant minority of them have been Jewish. Among the German Protestants the majority have always been Lutherans, even during the colonial period, when a considerable number were Mennonites of various persuasions.

One of the most impressive aspects of German immigration was the vast cultural apparatus German Americans created: newspapers, magazines, theaters, musical organizations, and schools proliferated throughout the nineteenth and into the twentieth century. Some of these institutions, particularly the German *kindergartens*, had great influence on the national culture. The Germans were largely Republican in politics. On one of the great cultural issues of the era—Prohibition—most took the wet rather than the dry side.

Scandinavians. Almost 1.5 million Swedes, Norwegians, and Danes came to America in the nineteenth century, and perhaps 750,000 followed in the twentieth. Predominantly agricultural, Scandinavians were driven to migrate by expanding populations and a shortage of arable land. No European country sent a greater proportion of its population to America than Norway. Most Scandinavians settled initially in the upper Midwest and the Great Plains, with a large later migration, some of it second generation, to the Pacific Northwest. They were overwhelmingly Protestant: the major exception was some 25,000 Scandinavian converts to Mormonism whose passage to Utah was aided by a church immigration fund. The Scandinavian groups founded a relatively large number of colleges for the training of ministers of religion, the first ethnic groups to do so in any significant degree since the colonial era. In politics they were even more predominantly Republican than the Germans, with a heavy tilt toward the dry side of the Prohibition issue.

Era of Industrial Expansion, 1870s–1920

Prior to the Civil War, most immigrants settled in rural and small town America, although the incidence of immigrants in cities was higher than that of native-born Americans. In the latter decades of the nineteenth century, as the industrial sector of the American economy became more dynamic, the cities, and the jobs that they held, attracted more and more immigrants. At the same time, the spread of railroad networks in Europe and the development of shipping lines for whom immigrants were

"Huddled Masses . . . Breathe Free." After a view of the welcoming Statue of Liberty, new immigrants arrive at Ellis Island in New York Harbor, the primary gateway to America in the early twentieth century. LIBRARY OF CONGRESS

the major purpose rather than a sideline meant that more, and more ethnically varied, immigrants were able to cross the Atlantic. Although immigrants left from almost every port city in Europe, the lion's share left through Hamburg, Bremen, and Liverpool in the north and Genoa, Naples, and Trieste in the south. Conditions in the steerage sections in which most immigrants came were frightful, particularly on the vessels from southern ports, but at least in the age of steam the voyages were measured in days rather than weeks.

Contrary to the impression often given, immigrants from southern and eastern Europe did not begin to outnumber those from western Europe until the 1890s. Even in the first two decades of the twentieth century immigrants from western Europe were some two-fifths of all immigrants. Poles, Italians, and eastern European Jews were the dominant European immigrant groups from the 1890s, although every European nationality was represented. These later immigrants are often described as "new immigrants," a euphemism for "undesirable." The United States Immigration Commission, for example, in its 1911 report that was a stimulus for immigration restriction, described such immigrants as having "no intention of permanently changing their residence, their only purpose in coming to America being to temporarily take advantage of the greater wages paid for industrial labor in this country."

The charge of sojourning had been raised first against two non-European groups: the 250,000 Chinese who had begun to immigrate to California and the West Coast about the time of the gold rush of 1849, and the perhaps 500,000 French Canadians who poured into New England mill towns in the post–Civil War decades. While most Chinese immigrants were barred by the Chinese Exclusion Act of 1882, French Canadian immigrants remained unrestricted. The antisojourner argument ignored both the positive economic contributions that each group made and the fact that many Chinese and perhaps most French Canadian immigrants made permanent homes in the United States. The 1920 census identified some 850,000 first- and second-generation French Canadians, and some 60,000 Chinese.

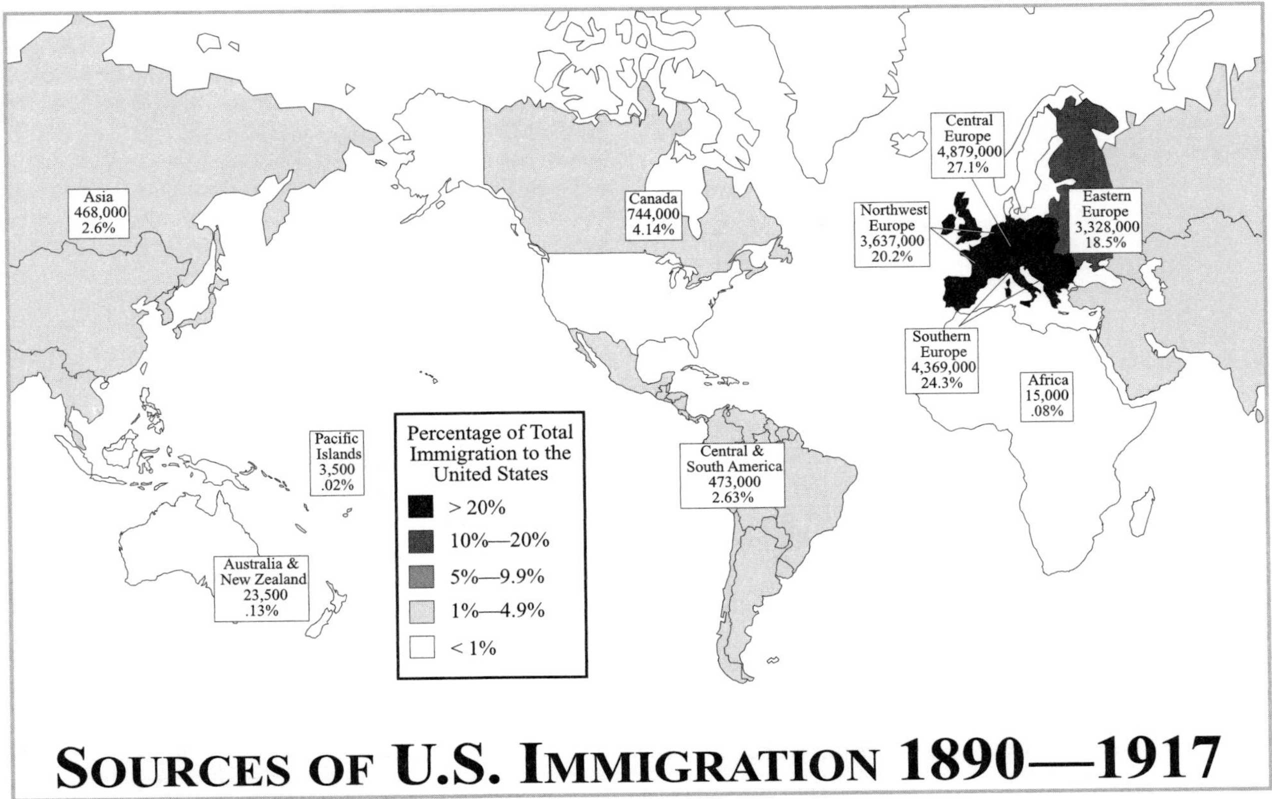

SOURCES OF U.S. IMMIGRATION 1890—1917

Many of the European immigrants of the industrial era did come as sojourners, and some came more than once. In one early-twentieth-century survey at Ellis Island, every tenth Italian reported having been in the United States before. Like their predecessors they were primarily motivated by economic opportunity; what set them off from most of their predecessors was that most found industrial rather than agricultural employment.

Poles are difficult to enumerate because immigration data reflect nationality rather than ethnicity and most Poles had German, Russian, or Austrian nationality. The best approximation of their number comes from the 1910 census, which showed nearly 950,000 foreign-born persons who said that their mother tongue was Polish. Poles settled largely in the industrial region around the Great Lakes, and were concentrated in cities between Buffalo and Milwaukee. Polish immigrants were chiefly employed in factory work, often in the dirtiest and most difficult jobs.

Between 1890 and 1920 more than four million Italians were recorded as entering the United States. No other group had come to the United States in such numbers in a comparable period of time. Their prime region of settlement was near the eastern seaboard between Boston and Philadelphia, with goodly settlements in Chicago and northern California. Unlike the Poles, Italians were concentrated in outdoor employment in road construction, railroad maintenance, and in the less-skilled aspects of the building trades. A significant number of young, mostly unmarried Italian and Italian American women were employed in the garment trades.

Like the Poles, eastern European Jews are difficult to track in the immigration data. Again in the 1910 census more than a million persons reported Yiddish or Hebrew as a mother tongue. (German Jewish immigrants would have reported German.) More than 850,000 of them were of Russian nationality, many of whom came from what is now Poland and the Baltic states; almost 125,000 came from some part of the Austrian Empire, and some 40,000 from Romania. Most had suffered some degree of persecution in Europe, and of all the immigrant groups in the industrial era, Jews were the least likely to sojourn. Almost all came intending to stay and did so. One scholar has calculated the remigration rate for European immigrants to the United States of various ethnicities in this era and found that fewer than 5 percent of Jews returned, as opposed to about a third of Poles and some 45 percent of Italians. Similarly, although there was a male majority for every European group of immigrants except the Irish, males were only about 55 percent of the Jews, while nearly two-thirds of the Poles and almost three-quarters of the Italians were male. For some of the other ethnic groups in this era both rates were even higher. Serb immigrants, for example, were calculated to have been 90 percent male and remigrated at a rate of almost 88 percent.

TABLE 5

Annual Immigration and Emigration, 1905–1914*

Year	Immigrants	Emigrants**	Net Migration
1905	1,026,499		
1906	1,100,735		
1907	1,285,349		
1908	782,870	395,073	387,797
1909	751,785	225,802	525,983
1910	1,041,570	202,436	839,134
1911	878,587	295,666	582,291
1912	838,172	333,262	504,910
1913	1,197,892	308,190	889,702
1914	1,218,480	303,338	915,142
Total	10,121,939		

*Fiscal year ending 30 June
**Emigrants not recorded before 1908

The ten years before the outbreak of World War I saw the highest number of legal immigrants entering the United States than in any ten-year period before or since. These figures added fuel to the raging restrictionist fires. But, as the data in table 5 show, return migration was also heavy; the incidence of foreign born in the population remained remarkably constant, as was shown in table 4.

The outbreak of World War I in 1914 transformed American migration patterns, both internal and external. The surge of Allied war orders beginning in the spring of 1915 plus the requirements of American "preparedness" and, after April 1917, war needs, increased the demands for workers in northern factories. The drastic drop in the numbers of European immigrants—from a million a year just before the war to an average of only about 100,000 annually between 30 June 1914 and 30 June 1919—helped to stimulate the so-called "Great Migration" of African Americans from the South to northern cities. This migration involved perhaps 500,000 persons between 1916 and 1918 and probably another million before the onset of the Great Depression of the 1930s.

1920s to 2000

In the 1920s, despite President Warren G. Harding's call for "normalcy," immigration was not allowed to return to the essentially laissez faire pattern that had prevailed for everyone except Asians throughout U.S. history. The Quota Acts of 1921 and 1924 put numerical caps on European immigration while stopping Asian immigration except for Filipinos, who, as American nationals, could not be excluded. (Asia, as defined by Congress, did not include Russian-Soviet Asia, or nations from Persia-Iran east.) The onset of the Great Depression plus administrative regulations designed chiefly to stop otherwise unrestricted Mexican immigration, reduced immigration significantly, and World War II reduced it even further as table 6 demonstrates.

The steady reduction in the number of immigrants and the accompanying decline in foreign born from 13.2 percent in 1920 to 6.9 percent in 1950 mask three important wartime developments that helped to reshape the patterns of American immigration in the second half of the twentieth century. These were the beginning of the refugee crisis, repeal of the Chinese exclusion acts, and the increase of the Mexican presence in the American labor force.

The anti-Semitic policies of Nazi Germany that began in 1933 precipitated the refugee crisis, which was neither fully understood nor dealt with adequately by the nations of the West. Vice President Walter Mondale's 1979 judgment that the western democracies "failed the test of civilization" is a good capsule summary. Many have blamed this aspect of the Holocaust on the 1924 immigration act. But while many of the supporters of that act had anti-Semitic motives, the quota system it set up, while stacked against immigrants from southern and eastern Europe, provided a relatively generous quota for Germany. Between 1933 and 1940, fewer than half of the 211,895 German quota spaces were filled. At the beginning of the Nazi era, few German Jews were ready to leave their native land; however, during much of the 1930s, willful obstruction by many American consular officials frustrated the attempts of German Jews to gain admission to the United States, often with fatal consequences.

The administration of Franklin D. Roosevelt, which innovated in so many areas of American life, was conservative on this issue: there was no New Deal for immigration. Critics have correctly pointed to the undemocratically recruited foreign service as largely culpable in denying asylum to many, but the president himself, out of political caution, on several occasions refused to act. The failure to support legislation to admit Jewish children and the refusal to allow refugee passengers on the ill-fated German liner *St. Louis* to land even though the ship was in American waters are clear examples of Roosevelt's misfeasance.

On the other hand, once war came the president exercised his vaunted administrative ingenuity to assist refugees. The most significant example of this was his instruction to Labor Secretary Frances Perkins to allow refugees who were in the United States on six-month visitor visas to "roll-over" such visas indefinitely every six months, making them, for all intents and purposes, resident aliens. Later arrangements were made with Canada to allow many such persons to make pro forma exits from the United States and return immediately on immigrant visas. And, in 1944, as awareness of the dimensions of the Holocaust grew, Roosevelt created the War Refugee Board by executive order. Its function was to save Jews and other refugees in Europe, but its mandate did not include bringing them to the United States. In June 1944 Roosevelt invented a way to get refugees into the country: something he called "parole power." He used it only once, in what historians have called a "token shipment" of nearly

TABLE 6

Immigration and Emigration, 1921–1945

Period	Immigration	Average	Emigration	Average	Net Immigration	Average
1921–1924	2,344,599	586,150	604,699	151,168	1,739,930	439,982
1925–1930	1,762,610	293,768	440,377	73,396	1,322,233	220,372
1931–1940	528,431	52,843	459,738	45,974	68,693	6,869
1941–1945	170,949	34,190	42,696	8,540	128,253	25,650

1,000 persons, almost all of them Jews who were kept in a camp at Oswego, New York, in the charge of the War Relocation Authority, whose major function was to warehouse Japanese Americans. Although the "parolees" were supposed to go back to Europe after the war, only one did. Roosevelt's successors used parole power to bring in hundreds of thousands of refugees, very few of them Jews, until the Refugee Act of 1980 regularized such admissions. Between 1946 and 2000 more than 3.5 million persons were admitted to the United States as refugees of one kind or another and many persons who were in fact refugees entered in other categories.

The repeal of the Chinese Exclusion Act in 1943, which also made alien Chinese eligible for naturalization, presaged a retreat from the blatant racism that had characterized American immigration policies. Similar legislation was passed regarding "natives of India" and Filipinos in 1946, and in 1952 the otherwise reactionary McCarran-Walter Act ended all ethnic bars to immigration and made naturalization color blind. Between 1943 and 2000, perhaps 8 million Asians, most of them from the formerly "barred zone," legally immigrated to the United States.

A third wartime initiative with long-term consequences for immigration was the so-called bracero program, which brought some 200,000 "temporary" Mexican workers to the United States, about half of whom worked in California. The program was restarted in 1951 during the Korean War and continued until 1964. In 1959 alone, 450,000 braceros were brought to the United States. None of these were counted as immigrants; many stayed or returned, contributing to the illegal immigrant phenomenon that loomed large in later immigration and even larger in rhetoric about it. The cumulative effect of the bracero program plus legal and illegal immigration was to make Mexico the largest single national contributor, by far, to immigration to the United States in the second half of the twentieth century. Since 1940 some 5 million Mexicans have either legally immigrated to the United States or been legalized later.

Tables 7 and 8 summarize the 26 million legal or legalized immigrants who entered the United States in the second half of the twentieth century. As table 8 demonstrates, not only did the total number of immigrants increase with each decade, but European immigration,

TABLE 7

Immigration and Foreign Born, 1951–2000

Years	Immigration (millions)	Foreign Born* (millions)	Percentage of Foreign Born
1951–1960	2.5	9.7	5.4%
1961–1970	3.3	9.6	4.7%**
1971–1980	4.5	14.1	6.2%
1981–1990	7.3	19.8	8.0%
1991–2000	8.4	29.3	10.4%

*In last year of period, i.e., 1960, 1970, etc.
**lowest figure ever recorded; no data before 1850

TABLE 8

Sources of Immigration to the United States, 1951–1998 (in millions)

Years	Europe	Asia	Americas	Africa	Other	Total
1951–1960	1.32	0.15	1.00	.01	.01	2.5
1961–1970	1.12	0.42	1.72	.03	.03	3.3
1971–1980	0.80	1.59	1.98	.08	.04	4.5
1981–1990	0.76	2.74	3.62	.18	.05	7.3
1991–1998	1.30	2.63	4.10	.31	.07	8.4
Total	5.30	7.53	12.42	.61	.20	26.0

which had always dominated American immigration, accounted for only one immigrant in five during the second half of the century.

Prior to the 1930s, almost all of the immigrants had come in at or near the bottom of the socioeconomic ladder, and this remained true for a majority of immigrants during the rest of the twentieth century. But, beginning with some of the distinguished refugees who fled from Hitler's Europe, a growing minority of immigrants came with educational credentials that surpassed those of most American natives. The so-called brain drain intensified during the latter decades of the century, as engineers and computer scientists were attracted to the various Silicon Valleys of America. At the other end of the spectrum, even larger numbers of immigrants came not to build America but to serve it. The service sector and agriculture, not the

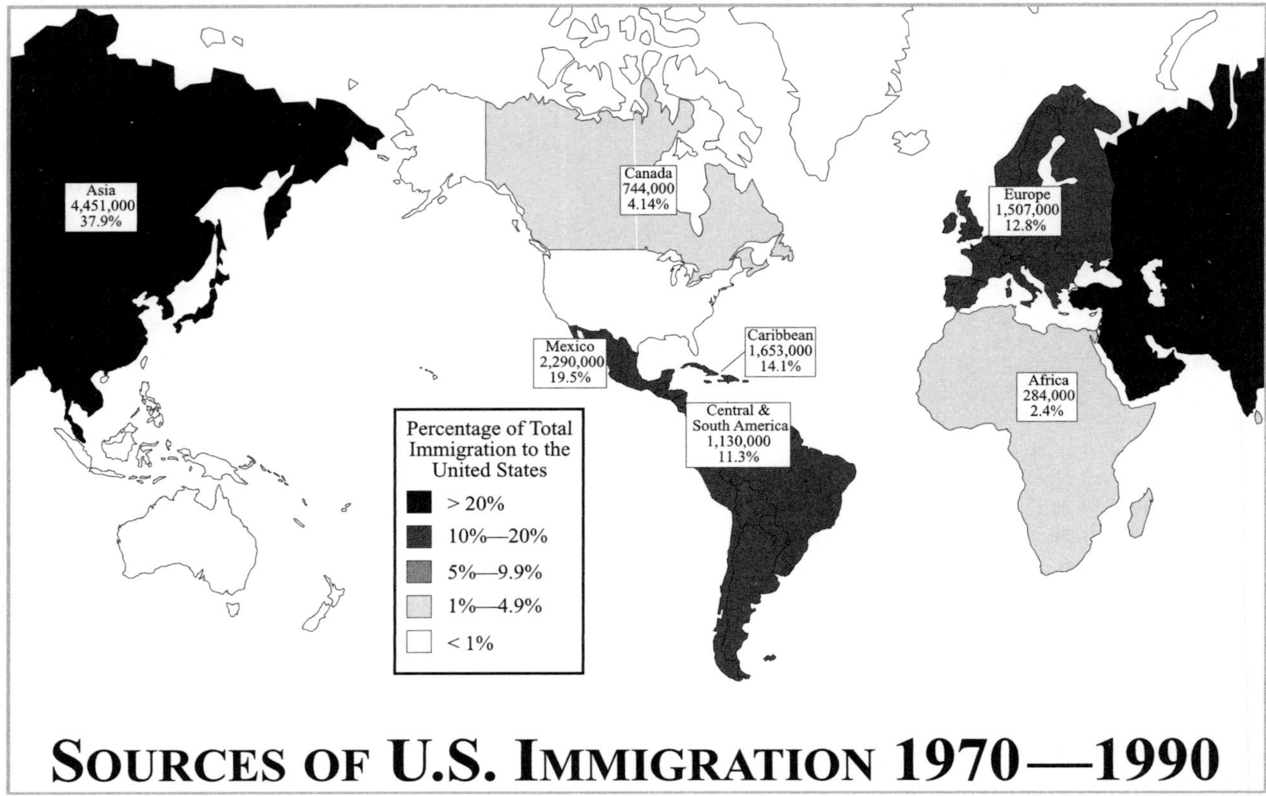

SOURCES OF U.S. IMMIGRATION 1970—1990

shrinking manufacturing sector, were the major employers of immigrant labor, legal and illegal. California farms, Arkansas chicken processors, fast food shops, and hotels and motels everywhere were among the largest employers.

Immigration policy since World War II. The shifts in American immigration policy that made the renewal of large-scale immigration possible are often attributed solely to the IMMIGRATION ACT OF 1965. As the foregoing suggests, this is a serious error. Between the 1943 repeal of the Chinese Exclusion Act and century's end, twenty-eight new substantive public laws revamped immigration and naturalization. Only a handful of the most significant can be noted here. Beginning with the hotly contested Displaced Persons Acts of 1948 and 1950—which brought some 400,000 European refugees, mostly gentiles, to the United States—a series of acts made taking refugees a part of the American consensus. By the end of the Eisenhower administration, the Fair Share Refugee Act symbolized the changed perception of American responsibility. Particularly noteworthy was the Carter administration's Refugee Act of 1980, which for the first time put the right to claim asylum into American law.

Two general statutes, the 1952 McCarran-Walter Act and the 1965 Immigration Act, transformed American immigration policy. While the most obvious innovation of the 1952 act was the ending of statutory racism in naturalization and immigration, it also eliminated overt gender bias in immigration. It seemed to continue the quota system much as it was enacted in 1924 but, because of other changes in the law, quota immigrants were only a minor fraction of legal immigration. Although the Japanese quota between 1953 and 1960 was only 185 a year—one-sixth of one percent of the Japanese population in the continental United States in 1920—a total of 46,250 Japanese legally immigrated in those seven years, almost all of them nonquota immigrants who were family members of U.S. citizens. European refugees, most of whom came from nations—or former nations—with tiny quotas were accounted for by "mortgaging quotas," mortgages that were never paid. When the quota system was abolished in 1965 the Latvian annual quota of 286, to give an extreme example, had been mortgaged to the year 2274.

The 1965 act ended national quotas and substituted putative hemispheric caps that seemed to limit immigration to less than half a million a year. At the same time, it so expanded family-based immigration and other nonquota immigration that the gross number of immigrants continued to rise steadily. By the late 1970s there was increasing concern in the media and in Congress about illegal immigration. After years of acrimonious debate, Congress passed a compromise measure, the Immigration Reform and Control Act of 1986 (IRCA). "Immigration Reform" had become a code phrase for reducing immigration. IRCA was widely hailed as a way to "fix" what was commonly called a "broken" immigration system, but the proposed fix exacerbated many of the problems that it was supposed to cure. The centerpiece of the bill was an "amnesty" supposed to legalize perhaps 3.1 million persons who had been illegally present in the United States since 1982. But congress set aside 350,000 "amnesty places" for "special agricultural workers" who need only have done 90 days of agricultural labor and lived in the United States since 1 May 1985. Subsequent Congresses increased the share for these agricultural workers significantly. Of the 2.68 million persons actually legalized under IRCA by the end of 1998 almost 1.25 million, some 47 percent, were "special agricultural workers" of one kind or another.

In the final analysis the amnesty provisions of IRCA not only increased significantly the number of legal immigrants in the United States, but also created a well-publicized precedent for future liberalizations, which would be impossible for Congress to resist. The legalization did not contribute to the number of immigrants present, but each person legalized could become, in time, a naturalized American citizen, some of whose relatives would be eligible for privileged admission status. A growing awareness of the failure of IRCA to achieve its goals—plus the conservative mood epitomized by the so-called Gingrich revolution resulting from the Republican sweep of the 1994 congressional elections—produced a spate of measures passed by Congress and signed by President Clinton. These measures "got tough" with legal immigrants by denying them all kinds of benefits—usually described as "welfare." Also, a number of statutes were designed to bolster the border patrol and, as the phrase went, "regain control of our borders." These measures had only transitory effects on stemming immigration, whether legal or illegal, but did, many authorities believe, discourage many persons illegally working in the United States from going back to Mexico, for fear of being unable to return.

At the same time, California voters overwhelmingly adopted the patently unconstitutional Proposition 187, which made illegal aliens ineligible for public social services including public school education, and required all state officials to report anyone suspected of being an illegal alien to the INS. Not surprisingly, the passage of Proposition 187—whose enforcement was immediately blocked by the courts—and a growing perception that much of the national legislation was unfair, produced some unintended consequences. Hispanic citizens mobilized to register and vote in increasing numbers, both the Republican Congress and the Democratic Clinton administration modified some of the anti-immigrant legislation and after California Democrats swept the 1998 elections the anti-immigrant consensus, which had seemed so strong just four years previously, disappeared. The 2000 presidential campaign saw both parties actively courting Hispanic voters. The early months of the administration of George W. Bush continued the positive attitude toward immigration that he had evinced as governor of Texas between 1995 and 2000—his White House Web site was available in Spanish—and a second, major amnesty program seemed all but inevitable. However, the terrorist destruction of New York City's World Trade Center on 11 September 2001 and the economic recession that had begun six months earlier put at least a temporary damper on such plans. Most students of American immigration expected that the same forces that had created the post–Great Depression boom in immigration—an expanding economy and an aging population—would, in the long run, create conditions in which large-scale immigration would continue.

BIBLIOGRAPHY

Berlin, Ira. *Many Thousands Gone: The First Two Centuries of Slavery in North America.* Cambridge, Mass.: Harvard University Press, 1998. An account of the varieties of the slave experience.

Bukowczyk, John J. *And My Children Did Not Know Me.* Bloomington: Indiana University Press, 1987. A brief history of Polish immigration.

Butler, Jon. *Becoming America: The Revolution before 1776.* Cambridge, Mass.: Harvard University Press, 2000. A striking analysis of the acculturation process.

Curtin, Philip D. *The African Slave Trade: A Census.* Madison: University of Wisconsin Press, 1969. A pioneering survey.

Daniels, Roger. *Coming to America: Immigration and Ethnicity in American Life.* 2d ed. New York: Harper Collins, 2002. An analytic narrative text.

Daniels, Roger, and Otis Graham. *Debating American Immigration, 1882–Present.* Lanham, Md.: Rowman and Littlefield, 2001. Dual approaches to twentieth-century immigration.

Diner, Hasia R. *Erin's Daughters in America: Irish Immigrant Women in the Nineteenth Century.* Baltimore: Johns Hopkins University Press, 1975. A gendered analysis.

Dolan, Jay P. *The Immigrant Church: New York's Irish and German Catholics, 1815–1865.* Baltimore: Johns Hopkins University Press, 1975. An analysis of the civic functions of the Roman Catholic Church.

Garcia, Maria Cristina. *Havana USA: Cuban Exiles and Cuban Americans in South Florida, 1959–1994.* Berkeley: University of California Press, 1996. A discriminating account of the Cuban American community.

Goodfriend, Joyce. *Before the Melting Pot: Society and Culture in Colonial New York City, 1664–1730.* Princeton, N.J.: Princeton University Press, 1992. An analysis of the most polyglot American colony.

Higham, John. *Strangers in the Land: Patterns of American Nativism, 1860–1925.* 2d ed. New Brunswick, N.J.: Rutgers University Press, 1988. The classic account of American Nativism.

Kitano, Harry H. L., and Roger Daniels. *Asian Americans: Emerging Minorities.* 3d ed. Upper Saddle River, N.J.: Prentice Hall, 2001. A survey of most Asian American ethnic groups.

Miller, Kerby A. *Emigrants and Exiles: Ireland and the Irish Exodus to North America.* New York: Oxford University Press, 1985. The standard account.

Morgan, Edmund S. *The Puritan Dilemma: The Story of John Winthrop.* Edited by Oscar Handlin. Boston: Little, Brown, 1958. An accessible biography of a seventeenth-century immigrant leader.

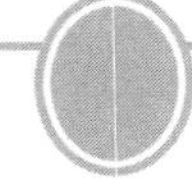

Preference Systems, 1952 and 1965 Immigration Acts

Immigration and Nationality Act, 1952

1. Highly skilled immigrants whose services are urgently needed in the United States and the spouses and children of such immigrants: 50%.
2. Parents of U.S. citizens over age twenty-one and unmarried adult children of U.S. citizens: 30%.
3. Spouses and unmarried children of permanent resident aliens: 20%.
4. Brothers, sisters, and married children of U.S. citizens and accompanying spouses and children: 50% of numbers not required for 1 through 3.
5. Nonpreference: applicants not entitled to any of the above: 50% of the numbers not required for 1 through 3 plus any not required for 4.

Immigration Act of 1965

Exempt from preference requirements and numerical caps: spouses, unmarried minor children, and parents of U.S. citizens.

1. Unmarried adult children of U.S. citizens: 20%.
2. Spouses and unmarried adult children of permanent resident aliens: 20%.
3. Members of the professions and scientists and artists of exceptional ability: 10% (requires certification from U.S. Department of Labor).
4. Married children of U.S. citizens: 10%.
5. Brothers and sisters of U.S. citizens over age twenty-one: 24%.
6. Skilled and unskilled workers in occupations for which labor is in short supply in the U.S.: 10% (requires certification from U.S. Department of Labor).
7. Refugees from communist or communist-dominated countries or from the Middle East: 6%.
8. Nonpreference: applicants not entitled to any of the above. (Since there have been more preference applicants than can be accommodated, this category has never been used. Congress eventually adopted the so-called lottery provision to provide for such persons.)

Reimers, David M. *Still the Golden Door: The Third World Comes to America.* 2d ed. New York: Columbia University Press, 1992. The standard account of the structural change in American immigration in the post–World War II decades.

Sanchez, George J. *Becoming Mexican American: Ethnicity, Culture, and Identity in Chicano Los Angeles, 1900–1945.* New York: Oxford University Press, 1993. The formative years of this community.

Wokeck, Marianne S. *Trade in Strangers: The Beginnings of Mass Migration to North America.* University Park: Pennsylvania State University Press, 1999. An account of the transportation of German immigrants before the American Revolution.

Yung, Judy. *Unbound Feet: A Social History of Chinese Women in San Francisco.* Berkeley: University of California Press, 1995. A gendered analysis.

Roger Daniels

See also **Chinese Exclusion Act; McCarran-Walter Act; Proposition 187; Refugee Act of 1980; Refugees;** *and vol. 9:* **Maya in Exile: Guatemalans in Florida.**

IMMIGRATION ACT OF 1965. Although technically just a group of amendments to the existing Immigration and Nationality Act, the Immigration Act of 1965, also known as the Hart-Celler Act, in actuality fundamentally reshaped American IMMIGRATION for the remainder of the twentieth century and beyond. It abolished the national origins system set up in the Immigration Act of 1924 and modified by the Immigration Act of 1952. While seeming to maintain the principle of numerical restriction, it so increased the categories of persons who could enter "without numerical limitation" as to make its putative numerical caps—170,000 annually for the Eastern Hemisphere with a maximum of 20,000 per nation plus 120,000 annually for the Western Hemisphere with no national limitations—virtually meaningless within a few years. Its expansion and modification of the existing preference systems is shown in the Sidebar. Although little noticed at the time and virtually ignored in most general histories of the period, it can be seen as one of three major legislative accomplishments of 1965, the high-water mark of late-twentieth-century liberalism, along with the Voting Rights Act and the establishment of the Medicare and Medicaid system.

The final passage of the 1965 act was somewhat anticlimactic. The struggle to scrap the 1924 national origins formula had been going on in earnest since the end of World War II. Liberal immigration policy goals were established by President Harry S. Truman's Commission on Immigration and Naturalization in its 1953 report, *Whom We Shall Welcome.* That report was highly critical of the 1952 McCarran-Walter Act, which was passed over Truman's veto. The reforms it urged and all attempts at systemic change were frustrated in Congress, although a number of statutes and executive branch actions added groups of immigrants, largely refugees, to the admissible mix.

The personnel changes in Congress accompanying President Lyndon Johnson's sweeping 1964 victory and the gradual diminution of religious, ethnic, and even racial prejudices in the nation at large made immigration reform an idea whose time had come. To be sure, a few restrictionist die-hards, such as Senator Sam Ervin (Democrat from North Carolina), tried to maintain the status quo. Ervin insisted that the McCarran-Walter Act was not discriminatory but was instead "like a mirror reflecting the United States, allowing the admission of immigrants according to a national and uniform mathematical formula recognizing the obvious and natural fact that those immigrants can best be assimilated into our society who have relatives, friends, or others of similar background already here." What Ervin never admitted was that the "mirror" was badly distorted, like those at amusement parks, and reflected not the population of the 1960s but that recorded in the 1920 census. But most in Congress simply acquiesced. The final passage of the bill in the Senate was by voice vote, while in the House it was approved overwhelmingly, 326 to 69.

Many scholars have characterized the 1965 act as a prime example of "unintended consequences," and it is clear that even its most influential advocate, President Johnson, seems not to have understood what its effects would be. In the signing ceremony staged on Liberty Island in New York Harbor, Johnson remarked: "This bill that we sign today is not a revolutionary bill. It does not affect the lives of millions. It will not reshape the structure of our daily lives, or really add importantly to our wealth or our power." The president was not indulging in uncharacteristic understatement. He and his advisers saw the 1965 act as redressing injuries done in 1924 and 1952, what he called the wrong done to those "from southern and eastern Europe."

In practice the law has worked quite differently from the ways in which any of its sponsors expected. Looking backward and expecting the future to resemble the past, they ignored the evidence of data available to them. As Table 1 shows, growing numbers of Latin Americans and Asians had been coming to the United States since World War II, and once such persons had permanent resident status, a whole cohort of relatives became eligible to enter the country as second preference immigrants. And as soon as these immigrants became U.S. citizens, as unprecedented numbers of them did in the minimum five-year waiting period, more persons became eligible as first, fourth, and fifth preference immigrants, while others could enter exempt from numerical preference. After the 1965 act went into effect, this kind of chain migration, in which related immigrants follow one another as links in a chain, accounted for a preponderance of all nonrefugee migration.

Perhaps the most misleading aspect of the law involves the presumed twenty thousand cap on entries from any one nation. That cap, which never affected Western Hemisphere nations, applies only to those entering from the Eastern Hemisphere who are subject to "numerical limitation." In 1985, for example, forty-eight thousand Filipinos and thirty-five thousand Koreans entered legally, to list only the two largest national groups from the Eastern Hemisphere entering in that year. The twenty thousand cap has been chimerical.

If scholars ignored or downplayed the 1965 law for a long time, by the 1980s, when immigration had become a major issue in American public life, many of the discussions, whether in blame or praise, overstated its influence. For example, a 1989 Rand study reported: "After a lull lasting more than 40 years, immigration to the United States began to increase considerably in the late 1960s after the passage of the 1965 Act." The two great changes that took place in American immigration in the second half of the twentieth century—the steady increase in the number of immigrants and the steady reduction of the once dominant share taken by European immigrants—were clearly in evidence before the enactment of the new law in October 1965, as Table 1 shows.

One can only speculate whether or not, had Congress understood what the results of its actions would be, the 1965 act would have been passed in anything like the form that it finally assumed. Most of the few scholars who have addressed this question have answered it in the negative.

TABLE 1

Legal Immigration to the United States by Decade and Region, 1941–2000 (in millions)

Decade	Number	% European	% Asian	% New World	% Other
1941–1950	1.0	60.0%	3.6%	34.3%	2.1%
1951–1960	2.5	52.7%	6.1%	39.7%	1.5%
1961–1970	3.3	33.8%	12.9%	51.7%	1.6%
1971–1980	4.5	17.8%	35.3%	44.1%	2.8%
1981–1990	7.3	10.4%	37.3%	49.3%	3.0%
1991–2000	c. 9.6	15.9%	31.3%	48.8%	4.0%

BIBLIOGRAPHY

Barkan, Elliott R. "Whom Shall We Integrate? A Comparative Analysis of the Immigration and Naturalization Trends of Asians before and after the 1965 Immigration Act (1951–1978)." *Journal of American Ethnic History* 1, no. 3 (Fall 1983): 29–57. Documents naturalization as a factor in chain migration.

Bean, Frank D., Georges Vernez, and Charles B. Keely. *Opening and Closing the Doors: Evaluating Immigration Reform and Control.* Santa Monica, Calif.: Rand, 1989. A social science study.

Gillon, Steven M. *"That's Not What We Meant to Do": Reform and Its Unintended Consequences in Twentieth-Century America.* New York: Norton, 2000. Chapter 4 deals with the 1965 Immigration Act.

Kennedy, Edward M. "The Immigration Act of 1965." *Annals* 367 (September 1966): 137–149. A contemporary account by a leading advocate of immigration reform.

Reimers, David M. *Still the Golden Door: The Third World Comes to America.* 2d ed. New York: Columbia University Press, 1992. The best account of post–World War II immigration.

Roger Daniels

See also **Immigration Restriction.**

IMMIGRATION RESTRICTION. Although slaves are not usually considered immigrants, the first formal inhibition of immigration by the United States was the prohibition of the foreign slave trade in 1808, which still allowed slave "visitors" brought by foreign masters. Similarly, an 1862 law prohibited American participation in the coolie trade. But free immigration was unimpeded until 1875. U.S. policy was to welcome immigrants, who were needed to help fill up what Americans saw as a largely empty and expanding country. No one put this better than President John Tyler in his annual message of 1841: "We hold out to the people of other countries an invitation to come and settle among us as members of our rapidly growing family."

But even as Tyler spoke, anti-immigration forces had begun to mobilize. Legislation taxing or otherwise impeding immigration enacted by some seaboard states was disallowed when the U.S. Supreme Court ruled in the Passenger Cases of 1849 that immigration was "foreign commerce" and could only be regulated by Congress. In the mid-1850s, the Know-Nothing Party, a mass Protestant anti-immigrant movement, elected eight governors, more than a hundred congressmen, mayors in Boston and Philadelphia, and a host of other officials but failed to get its program of severe immigration restriction and harsher laws against foreign-born Americans through Congress.

The first restriction of free immigrants was the Page Act of 1875, generated by concern about Chinese immigrants in the West. The law, which had little effect but considerable symbolic importance, excluded criminals and prostitutes, placed further restrictions against the "cooly trade," and prohibited the entry of any "oriental persons" without their consent, but entrusted the enforcement to the collectors at the various ports. The congressional debates show that many wanted Chinese immigration either limited or stopped completely. Four years later, Congress passed a bill barring any vessel that carried more than fifteen Chinese passengers, but President Rutherford B. Hayes vetoed it. His message showed that he, too, favored limiting Chinese immigration but was inhibited by a clause in the 1869 Burlingame Treaty with China that granted mutual rights of immigration. Hayes promised to renegotiate the treaty. A new treaty, effective in 1881, gave the United States the right to "regulate, limit, or suspend" the immigration of Chinese "laborers." Congress then passed a bill suspending the immigration of "Chinese laborers" for twenty years, which President Chester A. Arthur vetoed. He stated that he would approve a "shorter experiment." Congress responded with a bill suspending the immigration of Chinese laborers, "skilled and unskilled," for ten years, which Arthur signed in May 1882.

This misnamed Chinese Exclusion Act—it did not exclude Chinese merchants and their families—would, with fourteen subsequent statutes, bar most Chinese from immigrating to the United States until all fifteen laws were repealed in 1943. It represented a kind of legislative Rubicon and began an era of immigration restriction that continues to the present. That era can be divided into two parts. The first, stretching from 1882 until 1943, was one of increasing restriction, based largely on race and ethnicity, but also encompassing ideology, economics, and morality. Since 1943 immigration restriction has been lessened. It is important to note that statutes involving only Chinese were, in both 1882 and 1943, the hinges on which the golden door of American immigration both narrowed and widened.

General Immigration Restrictions

In August 1882, the first general immigration law set up a system whereby the federal government paid states to supervise incoming immigrants, levied a head tax—initially fifty cents—on each incoming alien passenger to finance the cost of supervision, and added an economic restriction by barring persons "likely to become a public charge." This LPC clause, originally interpreted as barring persons who, because of age or infirmity, could not support themselves, was later interpreted to bar the poor. A spate of subsequent laws over the next twenty-five years barred successively contract laborers (1885 and 1887); "idiots," "insane persons," those with a "loathsome or contagious disease," persons convicted of a variety of nonpolitical crimes, and "polygamists" (1891); and "anarchists or persons who believe in or advocate the overthrow by force and violence the Government of the United States" (1903). Then, on the eve of American entry into World War I, Congress enacted the Immigration Act of 5 February 1917 over President Woodrow Wilson's veto. It codified all previous exclusion provisions, imposed a much-debated literacy test that required the ability to read a passage in any recognized language, including Hebrew and Yiddish, expanded the grounds for mental health exclusion, and created a "barred zone" that was intended to keep out all Asians originating in nations east of Iran except for Japanese. However, the courts soon made an exception for Filipinos, who, it was ruled, were not "aliens" but "nationals" and thus could not be excluded from entry even though they, along with other Asians, were ineligible for citizenship. Japanese laborers, but not other Japanese, had been previously excluded by the Gentlemen's Agreement of 1907–1908 and thus were not included in the barred zone, which mentioned no nations but was expressed in degrees of latitude and longitude.

During these years organized opposition to immigration grew, but, except for the short-lived AMERICAN PROTECTIVE ASSOCIATION, an anti-Catholic group that flourished in the 1890s, it consisted of pressure groups devoted to propaganda and lobbying rather than mass political organizations. The most significant of these was the Immigration Restriction League founded by Harvard graduates in 1894, which was the chief proponent of the literacy test. These forces were greatly strengthened by the general xenophobia of the World War I and postwar eras.

The lame duck session of Congress in 1921 overwhelmingly passed the first bill to impose numerical limits on immigration, but Wilson killed it with a pocket veto. This Quota Law was reenacted as a temporary measure in the first weeks of Warren G. Harding's administration. It kept all of the existing restrictions, placed an annual cap or quota on immigration of about 350,000—3 percent of the number of foreign-born in the 1910 census—meted out largely to the nations of northern and western Europe, based on the presumed number of American residents born there. However, this and all subsequent bills limiting total immigration contained categories of persons designated as "not subject to numerical limitation." In the 1921 act, the chief of these were persons from the Western Hemisphere, to which were added, in its more permanent 1924 successor, alien wives—but not husbands—of U.S. citizens and their children under eighteen.

The Immigration Act of 1924 based its quota allocation not on 3 percent of the newly available 1920 census numbers, which showed a significant increase in the foreign-born from southern and eastern Europe—mostly Italians, Poles, and eastern European Jews—but on 2 percent of the 1890 census, when the incidence of such persons had been much smaller. This resulted in an initial annual quota of 164,667. Other provisions of the 1924 law included a bar on the immigration of "aliens ineligible to citizenship," which unilaterally abrogated the Gentlemen's Agreement by ending Japanese immigration, and the establishment of a "consular control system" that required visas of European immigrants. It also established a national-origins quota system, which went into effect on 1 July 1929. That system required a group of specialists, mostly academics, to determine the national origins of the American people and find out what percent of the entire American population in 1920 came from each eligible country. The experts, under the auspices of the American Council of Learned Societies, were instructed to exclude from their calculations immigrants and their descendants from the New World and Asia, as well as the descendents of "slave immigrants" and "American aborigines." The result ensured that quota immigration was not only "white" but largely British: the United Kingdom's allocation went from 34,007 to 65,721, almost 44 percent of the new quota, and most other national quotas were substantially reduced. This system, with increasingly significant modifications over time, remained the general basis for the allocation of quota visas until 1965, but by that time, quota spaces were a minority of annual admissions.

Relaxing Restrictions

The repeal of Chinese exclusion in 1943 was followed by similar exceptions for Filipinos and "natives of India" in 1946. The otherwise reactionary MCCARRAN-WALTER ACT of 1952 ended all ethnic and racial bars to immigration and naturalization and stopped overt gender discrimination as well. That act continued the national-origins system, but, beginning with the Displaced Persons Acts of 1948 and 1950, which admitted more than 400,000 European refugees outside of the quota system, a series of special legislative and executive actions for refugee admissions weakened its restrictive effect.

The passage of the Immigration Act of 1965, although technically a group of amendments to the 1952 act, greatly revamped and liberalized immigration law. It did away with national quotas by substituting numerical hemispheric caps (ending the Western Hemisphere's advantage) and expanded the annual number of visas and increased the percentage of visas reserved for family members of American residents. Spouses and minor children continued to be eligible without numerical limitation. Under its regime, total legal immigration increased steadily throughout the rest of the twentieth century. By 2000, for the first time in decades, the percentage of foreign-born in the population had reached 10 percent but still trailed the 13 to 14 percent levels that had prevailed between 1860 and 1920.

BIBLIOGRAPHY

Anbinder, Tyler Gregory. *Nativism and Slavery: The Northern Know Nothings and the Politics of the 1850s.* New York: Oxford University Press, 1992. The best account of mid-nineteenth-century nativism.

Anderson, David L. *Imperialism and Idealism: American Diplomats in China, 1861–1898.* Bloomington: Indiana University Press, 1985. Good for the diplomatic side of Chinese exclusion.

Daniels, Roger. *Coming to America: A History of Immigration and Ethnicity in American Life.* 2d ed. New York: HarperCollins, 2002. Contains summaries of policy and policy debates.

Higham, John. *Strangers in the Land: Patterns of American Nativism, 1860–1925.* 2d ed. New Brunswick, N.J.: Rutgers University Press, 1992. The classic account of nativism in its major phase.

Reimers, David M. *Unwelcome Strangers: American Identity and the Turn against Immigration.* New York: Columbia University Press, 1998. Best account of late-twentieth-century nativism.

Sandmeyer, Elmer Clarence. *The Anti-Chinese Movement in California.* 2d ed. Urbana: University of Illinois Press, 1991.

Solomon, Barbara Miller. *Ancestors and Immigrants.* Cambridge, Mass.: Harvard University Press, 1956. Definitive for the Immigration Restriction League.

Roger Daniels

See also **Immigration; Nativism;** *and vol. 9:* **Gentlemen's Agreement; Proclamation on Immigration Quotas.**

IMPEACHMENT. Article II, section 4, of the U.S. Constitution provides that "the President, Vice President and all civil Officers of the United States, shall be removed from Office on Impeachment for, and Conviction of, Treason, Bribery, or other high Crimes and Misdemeanors." Article I, section 2, gives the House of Representatives the "sole Power of Impeachment," and once impeachment articles are brought by the House, according to Article I, section 3, "The Senate shall have the sole Power to try all Impeachments. When sitting for that Purpose, they shall be on Oath or Affirmation. When the President of the United States is tried, the Chief Justice shall preside: And no Person shall be convicted without the Concurrence of two-thirds of the Members present." The penalties for impeachment are also carefully spelled out by the Constitution in Article I, section 3: "Judgment in Cases of Impeachment shall not extend further than to removal from Office, and disqualification to hold and enjoy any Office of honor, Trust or Profit under the United States: but the Party convicted shall nevertheless be liable and subject to Indictment, Trial, Judgment and Punishment, according to Law." While the president of the United States has general power to grant pardons and reprieves, this power, according to Article II, section 2, is expressly denied him "in Cases of Impeachment." The only other mention of impeachment in the Constitution is in Article III, section 2, which states, "The Trial of all Crimes, except in Cases of Impeachment, shall be by Jury."

Much mystery surrounds the proper grounds for impeachment and the precise nature of the proceedings. Impeachment as practiced in England carried with it criminal penalties and could result in the death of the offender. For the United States, however, it is merely a means of removing someone from office, though the conduct that gives rise to impeachment can also serve as a basis for a criminal prosecution. While the framers debated impeachment relatively little, it does appear clear that the language included in the Constitution represented a compromise between those who thought officeholders ought to be removable by the people's representatives for any "maladministration" and those who believed the president and the judges simply could not function if they were subject to removal from office at the discretion of the legislature. Thus, they limited impeachable offenses to "Treason, Bribery, or other high Crimes and Misdemeanors." Treason and bribery are clear enough, but the phrase "other high Crimes and Misdemeanors" is not. While the statement in Article III about trials by jury seems to link impeachments with crimes, several English impeachments that were models for the framers did not. And the word "misdemeanors" at the time of the writing of the Constitution meant only "misdeeds" rather than carrying the connotation of minor crimes, as it did later.

Relatively few federal officials have been impeached and tried, although the House has initiated impeachment proceedings against three presidents and one justice of the U.S. Supreme Court. The lower court judges who have been impeached have generally been convicted in their Senate trials, and all of them, with the exception of the first judge impeached, John Pickering, who was a habitual drunkard and probably was insane, were guilty of criminal conduct. Following impeachment, most of these judges went to prison or faded into obscurity, although one was subsequently elected as a member of the House of Representatives.

Associate Justice Samuel Chase

After Pickering's removal in 1803, the House began impeachment proceedings against Associate Justice Samuel Chase. Chase had been a strong partisan of John Adams in the election of 1800, and when Thomas Jefferson won that election, Chase found it difficult to hide his displeasure. He seemed sympathetic to the prosecution of Jeffersonian editors for seditious libel during the election campaign and afterward he railed against the administration during a grand jury charge in 1803. The House of Representatives voted articles against him in 1804 and his trial before the Senate in 1805 was a major social, political, and cultural event. Chase had committed no crimes, and his impeachment seems to have been brought both because of his harsh criticism of the Jeffersonians and because his jurisprudential notions on the roles of judge and jury differed from theirs. In the end many Jeffersonians became convinced Chase's removal would compromise the independence of the judiciary and the Senate could not find the required two-thirds vote for his conviction. Chase's acquittal established the principle that judges should not be removed for political reasons and his impeachment suggested the similar notion that judges should seek to remain above politics.

President Andrew Johnson

Andrew Johnson assumed the presidency following the assassination of Abraham Lincoln in 1865. The nation had just ended the Civil War and Congress and the new president were embroiled in disputes over how to accomplish the reconstruction of the Union. Many congressional Republicans suspected that Johnson harbored southern sympathies, so to restrict his ability to control the course of events Congress passed, over Johnson's veto, the Tenure of Office Act (1867), a statute restricting the president from removing any cabinet members until the Senate had confirmed their successors. The constitutionality of this statute was dubious, as the power to hire and fire subordinate executive officials would seem to be a presidential prerogative, but some, even at the time of the framing, believed that such removal could not take place without the concurrence of the same Senate that confirmed such appointments. Accordingly, when Johnson challenged Congress by dismissing his secretary of war, Edwin Stanton, whose sympathies were with Congress rather than with the president, the House brought articles of impeachment against Johnson. Johnson, too, was acquitted, but by only one vote. His impeachment was certainly the product of unusual circumstances, but it did seem to imply that ignoring congressional sentiment or abuse of office might constitute "high Crimes and Misdemeanors." Congress had even taken care to specify in the Tenure of Office Act that failure to follow the act would be a "high misdemeanor."

President Richard M. Nixon

The next case involving a presidential impeachment came more than a century later, and was also concerned with abuse of office, although the articles contemplated involved the commission of crimes as well. This was the proposed impeachment of President Richard M. Nixon and was the final chapter in a political crisis known as Watergate. The Watergate was an apartment complex in Washington, D.C., that housed the offices of the Democratic National Committee. During the presidential campaign of 1972, operatives eventually linked to persons working in Nixon' s White House broke into the offices, seeking materials that have never been revealed. The White House sought to cover up its involvement in the debacle, at one point even misleading the Federal Bureau of Investigation (FBI) by claiming that important Central Intelligence Agency (CIA) matters would be compromised if the federal investigatory agency probed too deeply into the White House's operatives. After the Supreme Court forced the White House to turn over taped evidence of meetings Nixon attended that involved plans to misuse the FBI and CIA for political damage control, the president's position became untenable. The Senate held hearings that exposed all sorts of official misconduct, and trials of the Watergate burglars revealed the connections with the White House. The House Judiciary Committee completed its hearings on impeachment articles and recommended impeachment to the full House. Nixon's political support deteriorated even among members of his own party, and in August 1974, before the full House could vote, he became the first president to resign his office. Doing so, he avoided becoming the first elected president to be impeached.

President William Jefferson Clinton

That dubious distinction went to William Jefferson Clinton in December 1998. The Nixon impeachment and the Chase impeachment were the models most often turned to in the proceedings against Clinton, although the genesis of his impeachment was different from theirs. During Clinton's campaign for the presidency in 1992 and his entire tenure in office, he was accused of financial chicanery and extramarital dalliances. His political opponents also charged that he and his wife misused White House facilities and staff positions for the benefit of themselves and their personal and political associates. Pursuant to the then-active Independent Counsel Law, a special prosecutor, the former federal judge Kenneth Starr, was appointed to investigate. The Independent Counsel Law required that Starr submit to Congress any evidence he found of impeachable offenses.

After an investigation that cost more than $50 million, Starr found no clear evidence of any wrongdoing with regard to financial manipulations or misuse of the White House. Nevertheless, Starr referred to Congress evidence he had discovered in connection with a private lawsuit brought against Clinton alleging sexual misconduct. The evidence demonstrated the president lied under oath in a deposition, sought to get others to file false affidavits, sought to conceal evidence, lied to a grand jury investigating these events, and sought through other means to "obstruct justice" in the case. To the end Clinton denied any wrongdoing, but the evidence of his perjury and obstruction of justice was clear and strong enough for the civil trial court judge to fine him for contempt. Clinton lost his license to practice law in Arkansas for five years.

A majority of the House of Representatives, following some exceptionally stormy hearings before the House Judiciary Committee, in December 1998 voted articles of impeachment against the president for his perjury and obstruction of justice. Virtually all of the House Republicans voted for the measure, and as they controlled the chamber and only a majority is required for impeachment, they prevailed. No witnesses appeared before the Senate, a first in impeachment trial proceedings, and the House managers were severely restricted in the evidence they were allowed to present. The Senate voted on 12 February 1999. Not one Senate Democrat voted to remove the president, though many criticized his misconduct. Fifty Republicans voted to convict on one of the charges and forty-five voted to convict on the other, numbers far short of the two-thirds majority, so Clinton served his remaining two years in office.

The great constitutional question in the Clinton proceedings was whether or not the president's conduct in a private lawsuit was proper grounds for impeachment and removal from office. If Clinton was guilty of the misconduct with which he was charged, and few reasonable observers doubted that he was guilty of the commission of many felonies, his detractors said this was intolerable in the only federal official who takes a constitutional oath to take care that the laws are faithfully executed. Further, the Republicans maintained that this evidence of bad character was sufficient to prove Clinton should not continue as president. Clinton's Democratic defenders argued that, even if he had done the things alleged, these were essentially private matters, that such personal peccadilloes were not disqualifications for public office. It was true that earlier impeachment cases seemed to involve grave matters of state or abuse of office and that Clinton's misdeeds seemed different in kind. Nevertheless, some scholars supporting the impeachment pointed out that the framers considered personal virtue important and wrote that impeachment was a tool to ensure that only "fit characters" served the nation. Clinton's acquittal and the political maelstrom his impeachment unleashed likely means that impeachment will be reserved in the near future for cases of clearly official misconduct. But it is also likely that the "character" issue will remain an important one in elective politics.

BIBLIOGRAPHY

Berger, Raoul. *Impeachment: The Constitutional Problems.* Cambridge, Mass.: Harvard University Press, 1973.

Gerhardt, Michael J. *The Federal Impeachment Process: A Constitutional and Historical Analysis.* 2d ed. Chicago: University of Chicago Press, 2000.

Hoffer, Peter Charles, and N. E. H. Hull. *Impeachment in America, 1635–1805.* New Haven, Conn.: Yale University Press, 1984.

Kutler, Stanley I. *The Wars of Watergate: The Last Crisis of Richard Nixon.* New York: Knopf, 1990.

Presser, Stephen B. "Would George Washington Have Wanted Bill Clinton Impeached?" *George Washington University Law Review* 67 (1999): 666–681.

Whittington, Keith E. *Constitutional Construction: Divided Powers and Constitutional Meaning.* Cambridge, Mass.: Harvard University Press, 1999.

Stephen B. Presser

See also **Constitution of the United States; Impeachment Trial of Andrew Johnson; Impeachment Trial of Bill Clinton; Impeachment Trial of Samuel Chase;** *and vol. 9:* **Constitutional Faith.**

IMPEACHMENT TRIAL OF ANDREW JOHNSON. President Andrew Johnson had been elected vice president on the Union Party ticket and succeeded Abraham Lincoln upon his assassination in 1865, and his impeachment in 1868 grew out of the struggle over Reconstruction after the Civil War. Johnson insisted that, as commander in chief of the armed forces, he had final authority over Reconstruction. Congress insisted that Reconstruction required legislative action. This conflict over who had final authority was exacerbated by differences over the terms of Reconstruction. The president insisted upon a speedy restoration of the southern states with generous amnesty and pardons for former Confederates and no provision for protecting the rights of African Americans beyond their emancipation. As part of this policy, he suspended the operation of some of Congress's wartime laws, convinced they were inappropriate in a time of peace. Without congressional authority, he reestablished state governments in the South and insisted that Congress must recognize their rights in the Union. Most Republicans demanded more radical political, social, and economic change in the South to foreclose future challenges to the Union and to protect the rights of southern Unionists and African Americans. They denied that the president alone could enact a Reconstruction policy. After more than a year of conflict, Congress finally passed a Reconstruction Act to begin the process anew under military control.

In the course of this struggle, Johnson used every resource at his command to carry his policy and defeat that of Congress. He vetoed every piece of congressional Reconstruction legislation. He sustained former Confederates in political struggles with southern Unionists and African Americans, fostering a climate that led to several race riots. He bitterly assailed the policies of Congress, and even appeared to question its legitimacy, calling it a "rump Congress," because it refused to seat congressmen-elect from the states he had reestablished. He urged white southerners to refuse to cooperate with congressional Reconstruction legislation. He sustained officials of southern governments, which the Reconstruction Act had left in place provisionally, in conflicts with the military officers the law had put in charge. In the course of this struggle, Johnson began removing Republican government officials and replacing them with men who would support him, as was customary in those days. In response, Congress passed the Tenure of Office Act over his veto.

The terms of this measure would prove crucial to the impeachment. It provided that no government officer could be removed until the Senate confirmed his replacement. However, the law created an exception to its general rule. It provided that the term of members of the cabinet would end one month after the end of the term of the president who appointed them. Before that time, the president had to secure the approval of the Senate to remove them.

In late summer of 1867, Johnson stepped up his campaign to defeat the operation of the Reconstruction Act. To gain complete control of the army, in August 1867 he suspended Secretary of War Edwin M. Stanton, who had the confidence of Republicans, and named General Ulysses S. Grant secretary of war ad interim. In doing so, he followed the procedure of the Tenure of Office Act, which allowed the president to suspend officials when the Senate was adjourned, subject to ratification of the decision when it reconvened. Over Grant's protests, Johnson then replaced officers who carried out the Reconstruction Act with too much enthusiasm with those who opposed the measure. Johnson's aggressive course forced Congress to amend its Reconstruction laws several times, and by the winter of 1867–1868, it seemed that Johnson might succeed in preventing their successful execution.

Fearing his power of obstruction, the Radical Republicans had urged Johnson's removal as early as 7 January 1867, when the Ohio representative James M. Ashley moved an impeachment resolution. It was referred to the House Committee on the Judiciary, which began to investigate charges that Johnson had used his presidential powers corruptly. After months of investigation, the committee divided over whether the president's actions constituted impeachable offenses. A narrow majority recommended impeachment to the House on 25 November 1867, over the objections of a minority, led by the committee chairman, James F. Wilson, who argued that impeachment lay only for an indictable violation of a specific law. Despite Johnson's aggressive course, on 7 December a majority of Republicans joined Democrats to defeat the resolution.

Emboldened by his victory, Johnson redoubled his efforts to disrupt the Reconstruction process, removing two more military commanders who enforced the law vigorously with more conservative replacements. However, he was frustrated when the Senate refused to agree to Stanton's removal and Grant returned the office of the secretary of war to him. Johnson was determined to force the issue, and on 21 February 1867 ordered Stanton's removal in apparent violation of the Tenure of Office Act; Stanton refused to give his office up to Johnson's temporary replacement. Faced now with what appeared to be a clear violation of law, on 24 February, the House passed an impeachment resolution without a dissenting Republican vote. On 2 March, it voted nine articles of impeachment and chose a committee to manage the impeachment before the Senate; it added two more articles the next day.

The Trial

Nearly all the articles of impeachment centered in one way or another on the removal of Stanton. Some impeached him for attempting to remove Stanton in violation of the Tenure of Office Act, others the attempt to name an ad interim replacement without first securing Senate confirmation as both the Constitution and the act required, and others repeated the same charges as part of a conspiracy to violate the Constitution and the act. The tenth article charged Johnson with attempting to stir hatred and contempt of Congress with the intent of setting aside its authority. The eleventh article restated all the charges in the general context of the struggle over Reconstruction. This was the only article that clearly placed Johnson's attempt to remove Stanton in the context of a general abuse of power rather than relying primarily on the violation of a specific statute.

The managers of impeachment were John A. Bingham and James F. Wilson, who had led the opposition to impeachment the previous December, and George S. Boutwell, Benjamin F. Butler, Thaddeus Stevens, Thomas Williams, and John A. Logan, with Bingham as chairman. President Johnson's lawyers included the former Supreme Court justice Benjamin R. Curtis; William M. Evarts, future attorney general, secretary of state, and U.S. senator from New York; the former attorney general Henry Stanbery; William S. Groesbeck of Ohio; and the Tennessee judge Thomas A. R. Nelson.

Despite the efforts of the managers and Radical Republicans in the Senate to speed the proceedings, the trial did not begin in earnest until 23 March. As the Constitution requires, the chief justice of the Supreme Court, Salmon P. Chase, presided. Supported by Democratic and conservative Republican senators, Chase stressed the legal aspects of the proceedings, over the objections of more

HARPER'S WEEKLY.
A JOURNAL OF CIVILIZATION

Vol. XII.—No. 587.] NEW YORK, SATURDAY, MARCH 28, 1868.

Impeachment Summons. President Andrew Johnson *(right)*, attended by Colonel William G. Moore, his private secretary, is handed the summons by George T. Brown, sergeant at arms of the Senate, to answer charges at his impeachment trial; it began on 30 March 1868, two days after this engraving by Theodore R. Davis appeared in *Harper's Weekly*. LIBRARY OF CONGRESS

Radical Republicans, who urged that the proceeding was essentially political. This stress on legalities aided the president's lawyers, enabling them to demand that all aspects of the charges be proven just as in an ordinary trial. By abstracting the charges from the political context, the president's counsel made them appear trivial and partisan. The managers' efforts to remind senators of the political context looked like appeals to partisanship that were out of place in a legal forum.

The Senate also rebuffed the managers' urgent requests to speed up the trial. As weeks of testimony and argument wore on, the sense of crisis receded, further helping the president's counsel to separate the articles from the bitter political and constitutional struggle of which they were a part. Johnson helped his cause by ending his interference in the South and proposing an acceptable replacement for Stanton as secretary of war. Public support for the impeachment began to wane.

The president's lawyers made somewhat inconsistent arguments, some of which could be persuasive only if one ignored the context in which he had tried to gain control of the army. They argued that the president had removed Stanton merely to create a court case in which he could challenge the constitutionality of the Tenure of Office Act. Even if the Tenure of Office Act was constitutional, which they denied, the president could not be removed merely for attempting to raise a court case on the question. On the other hand, Johnson's lawyers argued that the Tenure of Office Act did not cover Stanton because his term had ended one month after the death of Lincoln, the president who had appointed him. Even if Johnson had been wrong in this understanding, he could not be removed for a mere mistake. Johnson's lawyers never explained how the president could have intended to challenge the constitutionality of the Tenure of Office Act by removing an officer he did not believe was covered by it.

The impeachment managers argued that the president's intent to violate the law was clear and that the Senate had already decided it was constitutional by passing it. They argued that Stanton was protected from removal by the law, either because he was still serving the term to which Lincoln had appointed him, or if he were not, because he must then fall into the general category of government officers who could not be removed without Senate consent. Johnson's intent when he violated the act was irrelevant as long as he knowingly violated the law, the managers insisted. They also argued that the Constitution barred the appointment of a government officer without the confirmation of the Senate. The law permitted temporary appointments, such as Johnson had made when he attempted to remove Stanton, only when a position became vacant due to a death, illness, or resignation.

By May, as the trial wound to its conclusion, it was clear that Johnson might escape conviction. A number of Republican senators had joined Democrats to support the president's position on procedural issues and acceptance of testimony. Republican congressmen and constituents pressed wavering colleagues to vote to convict. To maximize the chances for conviction, the Senate voted first on the eleventh article, which had emerged as the strongest. On 16 May, senators divided 35 to 19 in favor of conviction, one vote short of the necessary two-thirds. The majority then forced an adjournment of ten days, during which the seven Republicans who had refused to convict came under renewed pressure. However, when the Senate resumed voting on 26 May, they reached the same result on the second and third articles. Knowing that there was even less support for conviction on the other articles, the Senate adjourned the entire proceeding.

Nearly all the Republicans who voted against conviction did so because they did not believe Stanton was within the terms of the Tenure of Office Act. It is also clear that they were worried about the effect of a conviction upon the future stability of the presidency as well as distrustful of Senator Benjamin F. Wade, who as Senate president pro tem would succeed Johnson as president. Although there were calls for retribution against the dissenters, no action was taken. Nonetheless, many of them later joined dissident Republican movements that challenged the party leadership.

BIBLIOGRAPHY

Benedict, Michael Les. *The Impeachment and Trial of Andrew Johnson.* New York: Norton, 1973.

Rehnquist, William H. *Grand Inquests: The Historic Impeachments of Justice Samuel Chase and President Andrew Johnson.* New York: Morrow, 1992.

Trefousse, Hans L. *The Impeachment of a President: Andrew Johnson, the Blacks, and Reconstruction.* New York: Fordham University Press, 1999.

Michael L. Benedict

See also **Impeachment; Reconstruction.**

IMPEACHMENT TRIAL OF BILL CLINTON.

On 19 December 1998 the Republican-controlled House of Representatives brought two articles of impeachment against President Bill Clinton, charging him with perjury and obstruction of justice. Both charges stemmed from Clinton's efforts to conceal the nature of his relationship with Monica Lewinsky, with whom he had had intermittent sexual encounters from November 1995 to April 1996 when she was a White House employee. On 12 February 1999 the Senate voted to acquit the president on both charges, capping a fourteen-month saga that dominated the news and brought partisan fighting in Washington to a fevered pitch.

The Road to Impeachment

The drama began with two would-be scandals that, apart from their implications for the Lewinsky matter, effectively came to naught. The first, which arose during the 1992 presidential campaign, involved alleged improprieties surrounding Clinton's 1978 investment in an Arkansas real estate deal known as Whitewater. After Clinton assumed the presidency in 1993, Congress held hearings on the matter, and under mounting pressure the president agreed on 12 January 1994 to appoint an Independent Counsel to investigate. In June 1994 the Counsel, Republican Robert Fiske, issued two reports exculpating Clinton. One month later, however, the Republican judge overseeing the Counsel's office replaced Fiske with the Kirkland and Ellis attorney Kenneth W. Starr, a former judge and staunch Clinton opponent who had served as solicitor general under President George H. W. Bush.

Concurrently, in December 1993 the conservative magazine *The American Spectator* reported claims by Arkansas state troopers that Clinton had conducted extramarital affairs while governor of Arkansas. The article attracted widespread attention among Washington journalists. On 6 May 1994, one woman cited in the article, Paula Jones, filed a sexual harassment lawsuit against the president, alleging he had made a lurid pass at her. Clinton fought the suit, but the Supreme Court ruled 9-0 on 27 May 1997 that it could proceed. Supported by conservative organizations and secretly assisted by Republican lawyers including Robert Bork and Theodore Olson, Jones's legal team gathered information about Clinton's sex life. They hoped to bolster Jones's claims with evidence of other harassment incidents.

Starting in October 1997, Linda Tripp, a Defense Department employee and friend of Monica Lewinsky, began secretly tape-recording her conversations with Lewinsky, which included discussions of Lewinsky's affair with Clinton two years earlier. Tripp, who disliked the president, hoped to expose the affair. In October, Tripp began sharing her information with a reporter for *Newsweek* magazine. In November she shared it with Jones's lawyers, who subpoenaed Lewinsky to testify. Lewinsky visited Clinton in December 1997 and discussed her testimony. On 7 January 1998 she signed an affidavit saying she had not had a "sexual relationship" with Clinton.

Meanwhile, Starr had broadened his Whitewater inquiry to probe a host of issues, including Clinton's sex life. Through back-channel contacts with Jones's lawyers, Starr learned of the Lewinsky affair. On 12 January 1998, Tripp gave Starr her tapes of Lewinsky disclosing the affair and suggesting that Clinton had encouraged her to deny it. Four days later Starr secured permission from Attorney General Janet Reno and a three-judge panel to investigate the affair.

On 17 January, Clinton, unaware of these developments, testified in the Jones case. Carefully parsing his language, he sought to avoid admitting to any extramarital sexual activity while also truthfully describing his behavior. His evasive answers, however, revealed the futility of his task. When asked, for example, if he had ever been alone with Lewinsky, he said, "I don't recall. It seems to me she brought things to me once or twice on the weekends." Such comments (and similar ones in Clinton's later testimony) became the bone of contention in the impeachment case. Clinton's critics would assert that they constituted perjury and required his ouster. The president would maintain that, although often ambiguous, they were literally truthful. Other supporters of the president would argue that, whatever their technical veracity, such statements were designed to conceal a private affair and did not warrant the removal of a president for just the second time in history.

By the time of Clinton's testimony, *Newsweek* was preparing to run its story, but at Starr's request, it agreed to wait. On 18 January the Drudge Report, an Internet gossip site, reported that *Newsweek* had held its story—thus publicly disclosing for the first time the news of Clinton and Lewinsky's affair. Mainstream news outlets began investigating the matter. On 21 January several news organizations reported the allegations, along with the fact that Starr was probing whether Clinton had committed or suborned perjury in the Jones suit.

Suddenly, newspapers and television networks sensed—and created—a scandal that riveted much of the nation for weeks and dominated the news for more than a year. Editors ordered their reporters to leave Havana, where they were covering the Pope's historic visit to Cuba, for Washington. Some commentators predicted Clinton would resign or be impeached imminently.

On 26 January, Clinton spoke at the White House, insisting, "I did not have sexual relations with that woman, Miss Lewinsky." Some observers accurately guessed that Clinton might be craftily denying that he and Lewinsky had had intercourse (which they had not) without disowning other intimate activities. Others jumped to the conclusion that he was lying. A few believed no extraordinary relationship had existed at all.

After a brief dip, Clinton's popularity quickly rebounded. By February his approval rating hovered at about 70 percent, where it remained throughout the year, despite intense criticism. For roughly the next six months, as Starr called witnesses before a grand jury, a stalemate ensued. Because Starr would not grant Lewinsky immunity from prosecution, she refused to testify. The inquiry stalled.

Starr's case suffered a blow on 1 April 1998, when U.S. District Court Judge Susan Webber Wright dismissed Jones's sexual harassment suit. The dismissal raised the prospect that Clinton's testimony in the Jones case, even if false, might be "immaterial" and technically not perjurious. Starr also drew fire for leaking grand jury testimony to sympathetic reporters in order to mobilize public pressure against the president.

In June, Lewinsky hired new lawyers, and on 27 July she "flipped." She met with Starr's staff for the first time and presented the details of her relationship with Clinton. Starr granted her immunity. Lewinsky also turned over a dress that was stained with semen, the DNA from which proved that Clinton and Lewinsky had been intimate. The next day, Clinton, whom Starr had subpoenaed to come before the grand jury, agreed to appear.

On 17 August, Clinton testified by closed-circuit television from the White House. He admitted his affair with Lewinsky while insisting he had not lied in his Jones testimony. He continued to use evasive language, for which he would later be impeached. That night, he delivered a televised address in which he apologized for a relationship with Lewinsky that he described as "not appropriate" and "wrong."

Most Americans said they were satisfied with the speech, wanted Clinton to stay in office, and hoped the investigation would be dropped. Many commentators in the media, however, joined the president's political foes in attacking his response as inadequate. In the following weeks, Clinton offered numerous additional apologies,

Grounds for Impeachment? A still from the videotape of President Bill Clinton's grand jury testimony, 17 August 1998. AP/WIDE WORLD PHOTOS

at one point labeling his relationship with Lewinsky "indefensible."

On 9 September, Starr submitted a 445-page report to Congress amid massive media attention. Starr charged Clinton with eleven impeachable offenses including perjury, obstruction of justice, and witness tampering. Two days later, the House of Representatives voted to make the Starr report available to the public. Publishers rushed their own editions into bookstores, and the report was posted on the Internet. The report drew comment mainly for its explicit sexual detail.

Impeachment and Acquittal

Despite continuing public support for the president, the House of Representatives, in which Republicans held a twenty-one-seat majority, voted on 8 October to begin impeachment hearings. First, the Judiciary Committee would have to decide whether to recommend impeaching Clinton; then the House would have to vote to impeach; and then the Senate would vote on whether to convict Clinton and remove him from office.

On 3 November, Election Day, the Republicans lost five seats in the House after running an advertising blitz attacking the president's integrity. Few anticipated the setback, which revealed public discontent with the impeachment drive. On 6 November, House Speaker Newt Gingrich resigned, stating that he was taking responsibility for the defeats, although it later emerged that Gingrich had been sexually involved with a staffer, whom he subsequently married. In the meantime, Paula Jones appealed the dismissal of her suit against Clinton, and the president, wanting to avoid further pitfalls, agreed on 13 November to pay her $850,000 if she would drop her demand for an apology. She did.

Impeachment hearings began 19 November with Starr as the main witness. Clinton participated by submitting written answers to eighty-one questions from the House Judiciary Committee. Throughout the next three months, a variety of elder statesmen and party leaders on both sides tried to negotiate a compromise under which Clinton would be censured and the impeachment charges dismissed, but these efforts repeatedly failed.

On 12 and 13 December the House Judiciary Committee, voting along party lines, approved four articles of impeachment. Two charged Clinton with perjury, a third with obstruction of justice, and a fourth with abuse of power. The House of Representatives heard arguments from both camps and planned to vote on impeachment on 16 December. But that day American and British forces attacked Iraq, hoping to thwart its development of weapons of mass destruction. Some Clinton critics, including Senate Majority Leader Trent Lott, accused the president of trying to divert attention from the impeachment vote, which was postponed until 18 December. Then, on the morning of 19 December, Representative Bob Livingston of Louisiana, whom Republicans planned to elect as Speaker, admitted that he too had committed adultery and was resigning from Congress. (House Judiciary chairman Henry Hyde and Georgia congressman Bob Barr faced similar exposures during the impeachment saga.)

That afternoon, the House approved two articles of impeachment. The first, charging Clinton with perjury in his 17 August grand-jury testimony, passed 228-206. Another, charging obstruction of justice, passed 221-212. The two other articles, charging perjury in the Jones case and abuse of power, failed by votes of 229-205 and 285-148, respectively.

After the votes, Congress adjourned, leaving the Senate trial for the next session. Despite ongoing but futile efforts to broker a censure compromise, the outcome was a foregone conclusion. Although the Republicans had a 55-45 majority, a two-thirds majority was needed to convict, and all but a few Democratic Senators had indicated they would not support the president's ouster.

Proceedings began on 7 January 1999. They followed the model of the 1868 impeachment trial of President Andrew Johnson. Supreme Court Chief Justice William Rehnquist presided as senators heard several days of testimony, first from the House Judiciary Committee Republicans who had voted for impeachment and then from Clinton's lawyers. A motion to dismiss the trial failed on 27 January, with one Democrat joining the Republicans in opposition. Then, three witnesses, including Lewinsky, gave additional testimony. The Senate hearings concluded on 9 February through 11 February with several days of debate among the Senators themselves.

On 12 February, the Senate voted. On Article One, charging perjury, ten Republicans joined all forty-five Democrats in voting to acquit Clinton. On Article Two, the Democrats were joined by five Republicans, again voting to acquit.

Afterward, commentators debated the significance of the ordeal. Some viewed it as a partisan power struggle, or an effort to oust a president who inspired deep hate among his foes. Others viewed it as a debate about the country's sexual mores, with Clinton's opponents fighting for a return to Victorian norms that punished aberrant behaviors and his supporters defending a new, more tolerant morality. The debate also revealed a gulf between the public, most of which wished to see Clinton stay in office, and elite journalists and politicians in Washington, who demanded Clinton's resignation. In the short run, the impeachment, although a stain on Clinton's record, probably harmed the Republicans more than the Democrats. Clinton remained enormously popular the whole time, while the Republicans saw their public standing drop. Some argued that the most lasting effect of the affair was to divert Clinton and the Congress from other concerns, keeping them from accomplishing more in his second term.

BIBLIOGRAPHY

Baker, Peter. *The Breach: Inside the Impeachment and Trial of William Jefferson Clinton.* New York: Scribner, 2000.

Toobin, Jeffrey. *A Vast Conspiracy: The Real Story of the Sex Scandal That Nearly Brought Down a President.* New York: Touchstone Books, 1999.

David Greenberg

See also **Impeachment; Impeachment Trial of Andrew Johnson; Political Scandals; Scandals;** *and vol. 9:* **Rose Garden Statement.**

IMPEACHMENT TRIAL OF SAMUEL CHASE.

On 2 May 1803, U.S. Supreme Court Justice Samuel Chase delivered a charge to a Baltimore grand jury in which he blasted Congress and the Jefferson administration for repealing the Judiciary Act of 1801 and thus unseating federal circuit court judges. He also lashed out at the Maryland legislature for eliminating property qualifications for the franchise and for interfering with the operation of Maryland's courts. Chase railed that America was risking a descent into "mobocracy," which he called "the worst form of all governments." Earlier, in the election year of 1800, he had earned the enmity of the Jeffersonians for his judicial conduct during seditious libel prosecutions of newspaper editors and others who were critical of the incumbent president, John Adams, and sympathetic to his challenger, Jefferson. Chase's active campaigning for Adams similarly secured their ire.

Thus, in 1804, the House of Representatives, with the tacit blessing of Jefferson, brought articles of impeachment against Chase, and he was tried before the Senate in 1805. There were eight articles, but the most important involved the 1803 grand jury charge and the allegedly partisan nature of Chase's conduct of the 1800 trial of James Thompson Callender, who had written a book critical of Adams, and of the trial for treason of John Fries, also in 1800.

The Senate prosecution of Chase was conducted by Representative John Randolph, a firebrand proponent of states' rights from Virginia. At the trial, Randolph presented an emotional but disorganized harangue against Chase. Chase was defended by the finest lawyers the Federalists could assemble, who emphasized that he was not accused of any crimes, but rather was impeached merely because he took legal positions not in accordance with the jurisprudential theories advanced by Jeffersonians. In particular, in the Callender and Fries trials Chase had sought to exclude evidence or arguments that he thought irrelevant and which might mislead the jury. Randolph argued that the juries should have been allowed to determine the law and the facts with a maximum of discretion, but Chase believed the jury had a more narrow role, to apply the law as given to it by the judge to the facts as found from the most reliable evidence. Chase's rulings were in keeping with what was to become American orthodoxy and Randolph's notions were no longer in the mainstream.

Chase's philippic before the Baltimore grand jury was more political than judicial, but the requisite two-thirds majority could not be found in the Senate even for conviction on that conduct. Persuaded that the prosecution of Chase represented an inappropriate attack on the independence of the judiciary, some Jeffersonian Republicans joined all the Federalist members of the Senate in voting to acquit, and thus Chase prevailed. The conventional wisdom regarding the outcome of Chase's impeachment—the only such proceeding ever brought against a U.S. Supreme Court justice—is that it showed that a judge could not be removed simply for taking politically unpopular positions. Less often observed is that the Chase impeachment caused the Supreme Court to shy away from overt displays of politics, and to a great extent, that it caused the federal judges to give up their role as "Republican schoolmasters" to the American public.

BIBLIOGRAPHY

Presser, Stephen B. *The Original Misunderstanding: The English, the Americans, and the Dialectic of Federalist Jurisprudence.* Durham, N.C.: Carolina Academic Press, 1991.

Whittington, Keith E. *Constitutional Construction: Divided Powers and Constitutional Meaning.* Cambridge, Mass: Harvard University Press, 1999.

Stephen B. Presser

See also **Impeachment; Supreme Court.**

IMPENDING CRISIS OF THE SOUTH, by Hinton Rowan Helper, was one of the most sensational books ever published in the United States. Appearing in the spring of 1857 as the nation was sliding toward civil war, the book became the centerpiece of an intense debate on the floor of the U.S. Congress. Helper, an obscure yeoman farmer from North Carolina, claimed that slavery was an economic disaster for the South and an insurmountable barrier to the economic advancement of the region's slaveless farmers. There was nothing new about this argument. Political economists had long claimed that slavery inhibited economic development and undermined small farmers, craftsmen, and manufacturers. Much of *The Impending Crisis* was a tedious recitation of dull statistics designed to prove this familiar argument. But Helper also added a shockingly inflammatory threat: If the southern planters did not voluntarily dismantle the slave system, he warned, the small farmers would launch a sustained class war across the South. Helper even hinted at a slave rebellion, although he himself had racist proclivities and little or no sympathy for the plight of the slaves. Coming at such a sensitive moment in national politics, it was no wonder southern leaders denounced Helper's northern supporters with such vehemence.

BIBLIOGRAPHY

Helper, Hinton Rowan. *The Impending Crisis of the South; How to Meet It.* Edited with an introduction by George M. Fredrickson. Cambridge, Mass.: Belknap Press, 1968.

James Oakes

See also **Slavery;** *and vol. 9:* **The Impending Crisis of the South: How to Meet It.**

IMPERIALISM. Americans have long thought of themselves as an "anti-imperial" people. The nation was, after all, founded in revolt against the British Empire. In the twentieth century, the rhetoric of national "self-determination" pervaded American discussions of foreign affairs. From Thomas Jefferson to Woodrow Wilson, the United States defined itself in opposition to the imperialism of other empires.

Imperialism, in this American usage, refers to the domination of another society against the expressed will of its people. Imperialism can be both formal and informal. In the case of formal empire—as in the British rule over the thirteen American colonies during the eighteenth century—a powerful foreign state manages the day-to-day political, social, and economic affairs in another land. Informal empire, in contrast, refers to a more indirect arrangement, whereby a foreign state works through local intermediaries to manage a distant society. In early nineteenth-century India, for example, British authorities negotiated favorable trade arrangements with native monarchs rather than bear the heavy costs of direct imperial control.

Close attention to these two kinds of imperialism has led many scholars to conclude that, despite popular assumptions, imperialism as a general term applies to American history. In particular, the years after the Civil War show abundant evidence of Americans expanding their economic, political, military, and cultural control over foreign societies. The post-1865 period is distinguished from previous decades, when the young Republic was both struggling for its survival and expanding over contiguous territory that it rapidly incorporated into the constitutional structures of the United States. Imperialism implies something different from continental expansion. It refers to the permanent subordination of distant societies, rather than their reorganization as states of equal standing in a single nation. America extended its federalist structure of governance across the North American continent before the Civil War. After that watershed, a powerful United States established areas of domination in distant lands, whose people were not allowed equal representation in governance. By the dawn of the twentieth century, the United States had a large informal empire and a smaller but still significant formal empire as well.

From the Civil War to the Twentieth Century

William Henry Seward, secretary of state during and immediately after the Civil War, recognized that the United States needed an overseas empire for its future peace and prosperity. The wounds of the bloody North-South conflict would heal, he believed, only with the promise of overseas benefits for all sections of the country. Informal U.S. expansion into foreign markets—especially in Asia and the Caribbean—provided farmers and industrialists with access to consumers and resources. At a time when the U.S. economy had begun to employ factory manufacturing, mechanized agriculture, and railroad transportation, large overseas outlets became necessary for prosperity. Americans were dependent on assured access to international markets, Seward believed, and this required expansion across the Atlantic and Pacific Oceans.

Seward began by building a "highway" to Asia. This included annexation of the Brooks Islands in 1867 (renamed the Midway Islands in 1903). The secretary of state also negotiated a treaty guaranteeing American businesses access to the island kingdom of Hawaii. The U.S. Senate eventually approved this treaty in 1875. Seward expected that the Brooks Islands and Hawaii would serve as important stepping-stones for American influence in the lucrative markets of China and Japan.

When the United States encountered resistance to its post–Civil War expansion in Asia, the government employed diplomatic and military pressures. In 1866, after the Japanese government closed itself to foreign trade, the United States joined other imperial powers—the British, the French, and the Dutch—in forcing Western access to the island nation over the objections of native interests. Seward dispatched a warship, the U.S.S. *Wyoming*, to join in naval exercises off the Japanese coast.

In China, the largest and most promising market, Seward used diplomacy instead of explicit force. According to the BURLINGAME TREATY, signed in September 1868, the Chinese government gave the United States trading access to designated coastal areas, with the additional right to build railroads and telegraphs facilitating penetration of the hinterland. In return, the United States allowed thousands of Chinese laborers to migrate across the Pacific. This arrangement helped to relieve China's overpopulation difficulties, and it provided American companies—particularly on the West Coast—with a large pool of low-wage workers. The U.S. government worked with the Chinese emperor to guarantee a market for the export of American products and the import of cheap labor.

Seward's imperialism set the stage for succeeding secretaries of state, but his policies inspired strong domestic resistance. By the time he left office in 1869, Seward had built an American overseas empire that included formal possessions, including the Brooks Islands and Alaska (1867), as well as larger informal areas of influence, which included Hawaii, Japan, and, most important of all, China. Many Americans expressed discomfort with this evidence of imperialism, including Republican Senator Charles Sumner and Horace Greeley, editor of the *New York Tribune.* Seward's other ambitious plans—including acquisition of the Danish West Indies (the U.S. Virgin Islands) and the construction of an isthmian canal connecting the Atlantic and Pacific Oceans through a sliver of Colombia—died at the hands of anti-imperialists on the floor of the U.S. Senate.

Despite these setbacks, Seward and his successors recognized the overriding imperialist trend in American foreign policy at the time. In addition to the economic advantages derived from overseas expansion, a series of internal social and cultural pressures pushed the United States to become more involved in managing distant societies. Religious belief—in particular a desire to spread Christian "civilization"—had motivated Western settlement across the North American continent during the period of manifest destiny, before the Civil War. Now these same urges inspired overseas proselytism. Ministers like Josiah Strong of the Home Missionary Society called upon thousands of their followers to establish churches and schools throughout China and other foreign countries. Christian missionaries would not only save less privileged souls, they would also display the profound righteousness of American society. As was the case with Britain and many other imperial powers in the nineteenth century, the United States defined its national identity by asserting superiority over—and a duty to convert—"Oriental" heathens.

American imperialism, in this sense, was part of a much larger international competition. Britain, France, and Russia—and by the last decades of the nineteenth century, Germany and Japan—were all competing for influence in Asia, Africa, and other "open" spaces for expansion. American leaders felt they had to adopt imperialistic policies of their own. Otherwise, the United States risked permanent exclusion from future opportunities abroad. Secretary of State John Hay's Open Door Notes of 1899 and 1900 codified this argument, proclaiming that the United States would assert its presence in China and other countries to make sure that other imperialist powers did not close off American access. As a self-conscious great power with a civilizing mission and a growing dependence on foreign markets, the United States needed its own empire—preferably informal. The historian Frederick Jackson Turner's influential 1893 essay, "The Significance of the Frontier in American History," captured this sense that the proving ground for American society was no longer on the North American continent, but now overseas.

One could not build an empire—even an informal one—without an adequate military. After an initial decade of demobilization after the Civil War, the United States embarked upon a period of extensive naval construction in the late nineteenth century. Alfred Thayer Mahan, president of the newly created Naval War College, outlined a new military doctrine for American imperialism in his widely read lectures, *The Influence of Sea Power upon History, 1660–1783.* First published in 1890, Mahan's text mined the history of the Roman and British empires to show that a large trading state could ensure its wealth and security by asserting dominance of the sea. A large battleship navy, in control of important strategic waterways and coaling stations across the globe, would guarantee the flow of commerce. It would also allow for the United States to influence foreign societies, transporting concentrated forces across great distances.

Largely as a consequence of Mahan's influence, the U.S. naval fleet grew consistently between 1890 and 1914. More ships created new opportunities for force projection. New overseas naval interests, in turn, justified ever larger estimates of strategic necessities. By 1898, the U.S. Navy had become both an advocate and a tool of American imperialism.

The United States used its growing naval power to force the declining Spanish empire out of Cuba and the Philippines. In both areas, America became the new imperial power. In 1901, the United States—now in formal control of Cuba—forced the native government of the island to include in its constitution a series of stipulations known as the PLATT AMENDMENT (named for Senator Orville Platt, a Republican from Connecticut). These included assurances of American political and economic domination. The U.S. Navy acquired possession of a major facility on the island, Guantánamo Naval Base. Washington also asserted the future right to intervene militarily in Cuba if U.S. interests were jeopardized. After granting the island nominal independence in 1902, the United States did indeed send an "army of pacification" to the island in 1906 for the purpose of repressing anti-American groups. The United States practiced a combination of informal and formal imperialism in Cuba.

In the case of the Philippines, the United States initially went to war with Spain in 1898 for the purpose of acquiring an informal naval coaling station. Native resistance to U.S. interests and a growing recognition in Washington that the archipelago would serve as an ideal point of embarkation for trade with the Chinese mainland led President William McKinley to declare the Philippines a permanent U.S. colony on 21 December 1898. America fought a bloody forty-one-month war to secure possession of the entire archipelago. During this PHILIPPINE INSURRECTION, the United States created an occupation army that waged total war on local resistance. Forty-two hundred Americans died in battle for possession of this colony. As many as twenty thousand Filipino insurgents also died. As never before, the United States had established direct control over a foreign society—seven thousand miles from North America—through brute force. At the dawn of the twentieth century, the evidence of American imperialism was unmistakable.

Liberal Imperialism

During the first half of the twentieth century, the United States was both an advocate of democracy and a practitioner of imperialism. The two are not necessarily contradictory. Presidents Theodore Roosevelt and Woodrow Wilson both believed they had an obligation to spread American ideas and interests across the globe. As a new world power, the United States had an apparent opportunity to remake the international system in a way that would eliminate the old ravages of war and corrupt alliances. Roosevelt and Wilson sought to replace militaristic aristocracies with governments that promised economic development and, eventually, democracy. International change of this variety would, they assumed, best serve America's long-term interests.

In the short run, however, the "new diplomacy" of Roosevelt and Wilson required more extensive American imperialism. When societies refused to follow the alleged tide of "modern" economic development and democracy symbolized by the United States, Washington felt an urge to intervene. On a number of occasions, U.S. leaders went so far as to force societies to be "free" on American terms. This was the rationale behind a series of early twentieth-century U.S. interventions in the Western Hemisphere that included, among others, Cuba, the Dominican Republic, Nicaragua, and Mexico. In each case, the United States asserted strategic and economic interests, and a long-term commitment to the betterment of the society under Washington's control. When U.S. military forces left their foreign areas of occupation, the threat of their redeployment served to intimidate those who wished to challenge U.S. influence.

In Europe and Asia, the United States pursued a consistent policy of informal imperialism during the first decades of the twentieth century. Contrary to the image of American diplomatic isolation before and after World War I, U.S. businesses worked with Washington's explicit—though often "unofficial"—support to build new overseas markets during this period. Investment firms like J. P. Morgan and Company lent large sums to countries such as Great Britain and France, forcing them to allow more American influence in the daily workings of their economies. Industrial concerns like Standard Oil, Singer Sewing Company, and International Harvester became more active in controlling natural resources overseas and marketing their products to foreign consumers. Perhaps most significant of all, intellectual and charitable groups like the Carnegie Council and the Rockefeller Foundation began to advise leaders in Europe, Asia, and Latin America on how they could make their societies and economies look more like that of the United States. Their seemingly "objective" counsels encouraged private property concentration, natural resource extraction, and increased trade—all factors that served to increase the influence of American firms.

The worldwide economic depression of the 1930s and the rise of fascism restricted much of the international commerce and communication that had flourished in the first decades of the century. These conditions, however, only heightened the pressures for informal American imperialism. Fearful that economic and political forces—especially in Germany—were moving against trade, economic development, and democracy, the U.S. government continued to encourage the activities of American companies and advisory groups abroad.

The administration of Franklin D. Roosevelt, in particular, sponsored the overseas marketing of Hollywood-produced films. Movies helped to proselytize the individual freedoms and personal prosperity that Americans believed were essential for a peaceful, liberal world. Hollywood helped nurture foreign consumers who would soon want to purchase the American-made automobiles and other products glorified on the silver screen. Most significant of all, policymakers like Roosevelt believed that movie exports would help inspire positive views of the United States in foreign societies. The president even thought this might work with Soviet leader Joseph Stalin—an avid consumer of American movies. Roosevelt hoped that Hollywood depictions of Soviet-American friendship would help solidify the two nations in their fight against Nazi fascism.

World War II and the Cold War

U.S. participation in World War II formalized America's liberal imperialism of the prior decades. As part of the Atlantic Charter—negotiated when Roosevelt and British Prime Minister Winston Churchill met in secret between 9 and 12 August 1941—the United States proclaimed that the war against fascism would end with a "permanent system of general security" that would embrace national self-determination, free trade, and disarmament. Citizens of foreign countries would benefit from "improved labor standards, economic advancement, and social security" when they restructured their societies to look like the

United States. The Atlantic Charter laid out an agenda for total war against the large standing armies, state-run economies, and dictatorial governments that characterized fascist regimes. This is what one scholar calls the "American way of war." Between 1941 and 1945, the United States deployed unprecedented military force—including two atomic bombs—to annihilate its most direct challengers in Asia and Europe. American commitments to free trade, economic development, and democracy required the unconditional surrender of Japanese, German, and Italian fascists. U.S. leaders and citizens not only asserted that their nation was the necessary "arsenal of democracy," they also proclaimed that they would remake the world after the horrors of war and genocide. The defeat of fascism would christen the "American Century," when the United States would play the unabashed role of liberal imperialist, planting the seeds of American-style economic growth and democracy across the globe.

The United States undertook this task with extraordinary resolve as soon as World War II came to a close in 1945. In the western half of Germany and the European continent, American policymakers rebuilt war-devastated societies. The Economic Recovery Program of 1947 (also known as the MARSHALL PLAN, after Secretary of State George Marshall) provided a staggering $13 billion of U.S. aid to feed starving people, reorganize industry, and jump-start economic production. Instead of the reparations and loans that weighed down European economies after World War I, the United States used the Marshall Plan to foster postwar stability, prosperity, and integration in Europe. With their economies organized along liberal capitalist lines, the west European countries developed favorable markets for American exports only a few years after the end of World War II.

In Japan and the western half of Germany, America's liberal imperialism was formal and incredibly successful. In both societies, U.S. officials helped to write new constitutions. The Japanese national charter of 1946 prohibited militarism and state control over the economy. It gave Japanese women the right to vote for the first time, promoted noncommunist labor unions, encouraged free public expression, and created new opportunities for American-style schooling. The new German "Basic Law," promulgated in 1949, similarly outlawed fascism and ensured individual rights, personal property ownership, and free elections. In both societies, the United States worked with a series of local politicians to uproot authoritarian traditions and impose liberal democracy. American officials sought to prevent future war, improve the lives of foreign citizens, and ensure U.S. strategic and economic interests. These goals were not incompatible; in fact, they reflected a formalization of American assumptions dating back to 1865.

The Soviet Union objected to America's liberal imperialism for obvious reasons. Joseph Stalin and his successors recognized that U.S. expansion in Europe and Asia prohibited the spread of communist ideals. Instead of the worker rights and economic equality championed by the Soviet Union—in words, if not in practice—American influence privileged personal liberties and individual wealth accumulation. The conflict between America's liberal democratic vision and the Soviet Union's communist alternative created an environment of competing imperialisms, which contemporaries called the "Cold War."

Throughout the 1950s and 1960s, Soviet criticisms of U.S. imperialism gained some popular support in Asian, African, and Latin American societies struggling for independence against inherited European and American domination. This was most evident in Indochina. Despite its anticolonial inclinations, U.S. leaders supported French colonialism in this region of Southeast Asia after World War II. In the eyes of U.S. policymakers, national independence for Vietnamese, Laotian, and Cambodian citizens threatened to undermine the stability and security of the region. Nationalist governments would allegedly threaten trade and economic development. Most significantly, American leaders feared that newly independent governments would fall under the influence of Soviet and, after 1949, Chinese communism. Liberal imperialism appeared necessary to contain communist expansion and prepare "underdeveloped" societies for eventual independence.

When Vietnamese nationalists—aided, as Washington predicted, by China and the Soviet Union—forced the French out of Indochina in 1954, the United States took over as a formal imperialist in the region. By the end of 1965, U.S. soldiers were fighting an extensive ground, sea, and air war against Vietnamese nationalists. Before the last U.S. troops withdrew from the region in 1975, hundreds of thousands—perhaps millions—of peasants had died or suffered dislocation as a consequence of American military activities. In addition, 58,193 U.S. soldiers perished in this war.

The Vietnam War illustrated the extended brutality of American imperialism during the Cold War. Longstanding economic and political impulses had combined with militant anticommunism to devastate much of Southeast Asia. Observers in countries around the world—including the United States—condemned American foreign policy for undermining the liberal purposes that it claimed to serve. The global revolt witnessed in 1968 on city streets across the United States, Europe, Asia, and Latin America was an international reaction against American imperialism.

After Vietnam and to the Twenty-First Century

American foreign policy was never the same after the Vietnam War. Aware of the resistance that the formal elements of American imperialism had inspired, policymakers returned to more informal mechanisms for asserting influence abroad. Economic globalization and human rights advocacy took center stage, along with continued anticommunism. The promise of American-style prosperity and individual rights—championed by politicians, businesspeople, and Hollywood writers—triumphed over the gray authoritarianism of communist regimes. By 1991, societies across the globe rushed to attract American investment and aid. Citizens sought out American cultural exports—including McDonald's, Coca-Cola, and Michael Jordan.

America's informal imperialism in the late twentieth century was remarkably effective. It did, however, inspire serious resistance. Instead of adopting communist slogans, as they had in the 1950s and 1960s, opponents of U.S. influence after 1991 turned largely to religion. Fundamentalisms of many varieties—Christian, Jewish, and Islamic—arose to challenge the decadence and hypocrisy of American liberal democracy. They condemned the United States for undermining traditional sources of authority and morality in foreign societies. They recognized that the free trade, economic development, and popular elections advocated by the United States would destroy many local hierarchies.

International terrorism—symbolized most frighteningly by the 11 September 2001 attacks on the World Trade Center and the Pentagon—emerged, in part, as a reaction to a long history of formal and informal American imperialism. This observation does not, in any way, justify the abhorrent terrorist activities. American imperialism has produced both positive and negative outcomes, as the contrast between post–World War II Japan and Vietnam makes clear. Nonetheless, the extraordinary overseas influence of the United States, dating back to 1865, has inspired violent resistance. Americans probably will not abandon their liberal imperialist assumptions in the twenty-first century, but they will surely develop new strategies for isolating and defeating foreign challengers.

BIBLIOGRAPHY

Cooper, John Milton, Jr. *The Warrior and the Priest: Woodrow Wilson and Theodore Roosevelt.* Cambridge, Mass: Harvard University Press, 1985. A superb comparative study that analyzes the politics and foreign policy of early twentieth-century America.

Gaddis, John Lewis. *Strategies of Containment: A Critical Appraisal of Postwar American National Security Policy.* New York: Oxford University Press, 1982. The best analysis of the sources and implications of America's anticommunist containment policy during the Cold War.

Gardner, Lloyd C. *Pay Any Price: Lyndon Johnson and the Wars for Vietnam.* Chicago: Elephant Paperbacks, 1997. A provocative analysis of how American liberal imperialism contributed to the Vietnam War.

Hahn, Peter L., and Mary Ann Heiss, eds. *Empire and Revolution: The United States and the Third World since 1945.* Columbus: Ohio State University Press, 2001. A useful survey of American imperialism in the "third world" during the Cold War.

Hogan, Michael J. *The Marshall Plan: America, Britain, and the Reconstruction of Western Europe, 1947–1952.* New York: Cambridge University Press, 1987. A penetrating account of how the Marshall Plan reconstructed Western Europe on America's model.

Hunt, Michael H. *Ideology and U.S. Foreign Policy.* New Haven, Conn.: Yale University Press, 1987. A stimulating account of how ideas about liberty, race, and revolution shaped American imperialism.

Iriye, Akira, ed. *The Cambridge History of American Foreign Relations: The Globalizing of America, 1913–1945.* New York: Cambridge University Press, 1993. A compelling discussion of Americanization in the first half of the twentieth century.

Knock, Thomas J. *To End All Wars: Woodrow Wilson and the Quest for a New World Order.* Princeton, N.J.: Princeton University Press, 1995. An excellent account of Wilson's liberal approach to foreign policy.

LaFeber, Walter. *The New Empire: An Interpretation of American Expansion, 1860–1898.* Ithaca, N.Y.: Cornell University Press, 1998. A classic history of American imperialism between the Civil War and the War of 1898.

Leffler, Melvyn P. *A Preponderance of Power: National Security, the Truman Administration, and the Cold War.* Stanford, Calif.: Stanford University Press, 1992. A rich account of how American values and fears of Soviet power drove foreign policy in the early Cold War.

McCormick, Thomas J. *China Market: America's Quest for Informal Empire, 1893–1901.* Chicago: Ivan Dee, 1990. A provocative account of American imperialism in Asia at the end of the nineteenth century.

Ninkovich, Frank. *The Wilsonian Century: U.S. Foreign Policy since 1900.* Chicago: University of Chicago Press, 1999. A compelling account of Wilson's influence on American imperialism in the twentieth century.

Rosenberg, Emily S. *Spreading the American Dream: American Economic and Cultural Expansion, 1890–1945.* New York: Hill and Wang, 1982. A thoughtful account of America's cultural and economic imperialism between the two world wars.

Smith, Tony. *America's Mission: The United States and the Worldwide Struggle for Democracy in the Twentieth Century.* Princeton, N.J.: Princeton University Press, 1994. A provocative analysis of American liberal imperialism.

Weigley, Russell F. *The American Way of War: A History of United States Military Strategy and Policy.* Bloomington: Indiana University Press, 1977. A compelling analysis of America's imperialistic approach to war.

Williams, William Appleman. *The Tragedy of American Diplomacy.* New York: Norton, 1988. Originally published in 1959 and one of the most important works on the history of American foreign relations—a penetrating discussion of economics, ideas, and imperialism.

Jeremi Suri

See also **Anti-Imperialists; China, Relations with; Cuba, Relations with; Hawaii; Intervention; Japan, Relations with; Philippines; Spanish-American War; Vietnam War;** *and vol. 9:* **Anti-Imperialist League Platform.**

IMPLIED POWERS. At the end of Section 8 of Article I of the U.S. Constitution, which enumerates the powers of Congress, the following clause appears: "The Congress shall have Power . . . to make all Laws which shall be necessary and proper for carrying into Execution the foregoing Powers, and all other Powers vested by this Constitution in the Government of the United States, or in any Department or Officer thereof." This clause is the source of the doctrine of implied powers.

During President George Washington's administration, the fight between the Federalists and the Antifederalists took not only a political but also a constitutional turn. Federalists favored broad construction of the Constitution so as to maximize the powers of the new central government, while Antifederalists sought to minimize those powers. Both groups seized upon the idea of implied powers. Alexander Hamilton argued that the necessary-and-proper clause means that Congress is not strictly limited to the enumerated "foregoing powers" but also has any powers that can be reasonably implied therefrom. Thomas Jefferson argued, on the contrary, that Congress had the authority to enact only those laws both necessary and proper for the implementation of one of the enumerated powers. Ultimately, the Hamiltonian theory won out, because it made better sense in an evolving world.

Hamilton and Jefferson were arguing over the constitutionality of the law creating the first Bank of the United States. Several years later, the Supreme Court, under John Marshall's leadership, resolved the dispute by adopting Hamilton's view in a case involving the second Bank of the United States, the case of *McCulloch v. Maryland* (1819). In ruling that Maryland could not tax the second bank, Marshall had at the same time to hold that Congress had the authority to charter the bank in the first place. He did so by adopting Hamilton's arguments. Included among the powers explicitly granted to Congress in the Constitution were the power to lay and collect taxes, borrow money, regulate commerce, declare and conduct war, and raise and support armies and navies. The Chief Justice said that it was in the best interests of the nation that Congress should be entrusted with the means to carry out these delegated powers and that the bank was a convenient, useful, and appropriate instrument for doing so. Concluding with a rhetorical flourish, Marshall wrote: "Let the end be legitimate, let it be within the scope of the constitution, and all means which are not prohibited, but consist with the letter and the spirit of the constitution, are constitutional."

Paradoxically, the Jeffersonian argument, if victorious, would have required greater judicial discretion, and thus greater judicial power than Marshall's view. It would have required courts to decide a means–ends question: Had Congress chosen a means that was necessary to the end in view and therefore a permissible means? Or had Congress chosen a means that was merely desirable or conducive to the end and therefore not permissible? As Daniel Webster argued in the *McCulloch* case, it would ill become a court to decide whether the bank corporation was the only possible means by which the currency power could be exercised; much more easily and modestly, it could decide whether there was a fair connection between the means and the ends.

Marshall's view arose out of his conviction that the Constitution was created for "an undefined and expanding future," the exigencies of which could not be foreseen by its framers; if such a document was to endure, the flexibility allowed by its own generality of wording and a liberal use of the implied powers doctrine by the Court would be necessary. In loosely construing the word "necessary" to mean "reasonable" or "convenient," Marshall succeeded in giving the Constitution the elasticity that has been perhaps its most remarkable characteristic and that, in the opinion of many scholars, accounts for its longevity. Together with the misnamed "doctrine of national supremacy" (national acts are supreme over state acts if both are otherwise constitutional) enunciated by Marshall in the same case, the doctrine of implied powers has enabled the Supreme Court to uphold the vast expansion of federal law and federal power necessary to meet the changing problems with which the nation has been confronted in the twentieth century. It has been a tool by which courts have upheld federal regulation under the commerce clause, laws enacted to carry out treaties, the federal government's exercise of the power of eminent domain, and the designation of treasury notes as legal tender—to give but a few examples.

There have been times, particularly between 1890 and 1937, when the courts have refused to approve federal legislation that they saw as an infringement on the powers of the states. These rulings generally applied the idea that the Tenth Amendment, in reserving unstated powers to the states, acts as a limitation on the scope of the implied powers of Congress. Thus, the Supreme Court twice struck down anti-child-labor laws, one framed under the commerce clause and the second under the tax clause. But during the half-century after the Court's liberalization in 1937 there were few, if any, such decisions.

Politically, there has always been a tendency toward adoption of the Jeffersonian view by the factions favoring states' rights, whereas those groups that lean toward nationalism tend toward loose construction. Since the issue of states' rights has proved to be an enduring one in American political life, the Jeffersonian argument has never quite been put to rest. It was revived during the 1950s by southerners opposed to federal intervention in race relations and during the 1960s by conservatives opposed to the Supreme Court's liberal decisions, especially those involving congressional use of the commerce and tax powers, during the tenure of Chief Justice Earl Warren. It wasn't until the 1990s, however, that there emerged a majority on the Supreme Court willing to circumscribe the scope of Congressional authority to enact legislation. In 1992, in the first of several cases striking down Congressional enactments, the Court held that the "take title" provision of the Low-Level Radioactive Waste Policy Act of 1985 exceeded the scope of Congress's enumerated powers (*New York v. United States*). The jury is still out on whether this and subsequent decisions (especially *United States v. Lopez*, 1995) mark a return to the jurisprudence of the early twentieth century or whether the Justices are simply demanding of Congress express and better documentation of the links between the authorized ends and the "necessary and proper" means Congress uses to attain them.

BIBLIOGRAPHY

Barnett, Randy E. "Necessary and Proper." *U.C.L.A. Law Review* 44, no. 3 (February 1997): 745.

Campbell, A. I. L." 'It is a *constitution* we are expounding': Chief Justice Marshall and the 'necessary and proper' clause." *Journal of Legal History* 12, no. 3 (December 1991): 190–245.

Engdahl, David E. "The Necessary and Proper Clause as an Intrinsic Restraint on Federal Lawmaking Power." *Harvard Journal of Law and Public Policy* 22, no. 1 (Fall 1998): 107–122.

Newmyer, R. Kent. *The Supreme Court Under Marshall and Taney.* New York: Thomas Y. Crowell Co., 1968.

Schwartz, Bernard. *A Commentary on the Constitution of the United States: The Powers of Government* Vol 1. *Federal and State Powers.* New York: Macmillan, 1963.

———. *A History of the Supreme Court.* New York: Oxford University Press, 1993.

Tugwell, Rexford G. *The Compromising of the Constitution (Early Departures).* Notre Dame, Ind.: University of Notre Dame Press, 1976.

VanAlstyne, William. "Implied Powers." *Society* 24, no. 1 (1986): 56–60.

White, G. Edward. *History of the Supreme Court of the United States.* Vols 3–4. *The Marshall Court and Cultural Change, 1815–1835.* New York: Macmillan, 1988.

Loren P. Beth / C. P.

See also **Education; Federal Government; General Welfare Clause; Hamilton's Economic Policies; Investigating Committees; Judicial Review; *McCulloch v. Maryland.***

IMPRESSMENT, CONFEDERATE. From the early part of the Civil War, the Confederate War Department practiced impressment, seizing supplies from producers and appropriating slaves for work on fortifications. In March 1863 it received congressional approval for impressment, but lack of official sanction had not prevented the practice before that time. Confederate policy ordered agents to impress only surplus supplies and slaves and to offer fair prices to the owners. Nevertheless, criticism of the administration of the law and the law itself increased with the growing suffering. By the winter of 1864–1865, the Confederacy had abandoned the system.

BIBLIOGRAPHY

Grimsley, Mark, and Brooks D. Simpson, ed. *The Collapse of the Confederacy.* Key Issues of the Civil War Era Series. Lincoln: University of Nebraska Press, 2001.

Henry T. Shanks / A. E.

See also **Army, Confederate; Civil War; Confederate States of America.**

IMPRESSMENT OF SEAMEN was one of the chief causes of bad relations between Great Britain and the United States during the early years of the Republic. Recruits for the Royal Navy were forcibly mustered in the eighteenth century by the press gang. While neutral vessels appear to have been so victimized prior to 1790, the problem became acute between that date and 1815. Under cover of the belligerent right of search, British boarding parties removed from the decks of foreign neutrals any seamen "deemed" British. The practice was steadfastly regarded in England as indispensable to sea power in the war with France. Although American seamen were the occasional victims of the press gang in England, and persons alleged to be British subjects were sometimes removed from American ships in British ports, the real issue concerned the impressment of seamen on the high seas. The American merchant marine, prospering and expanding under wartime conditions, offered unexcelled opportunities to British seamen. It is estimated that between 1790 and 1815 about twenty thousand—including deserters from the Royal Navy—signed up on American ships. Great Britain's traditional doctrine of inalienable allegiance conflicted with revolutionary America's doctrine of the right to change allegiance.

The British left the matter of determining nationality to the discretion of the press gang and boarding officers. Use of the English language appears to have been the main test applied. Of the ten thousand persons estimated to have been impressed from American ships, only one-tenth proved to be British subjects. The British returned native-born American seamen to the United States, without indemnity, if their citizenship could be established. But the British authorities took little responsibility in determining citizenship, and each separate case had to be handled by the American government. In the meantime, the impressed person had to remain in service and go wherever he was commanded.

As early as 1796 the United States issued certificates of citizenship to its mariners in an effort to protect them, but these "protections" were soon abused. The certificates were easily lost or were sold to British subjects. An American sailor could buy a certificate from a notary public for one dollar and sell it to a Briton for ten. The British consequently refused to honor the certificates. American protest against impressment dates from 1787. In 1792 President Thomas Jefferson tried to proceed on the simple rule that "the vessel being American shall be evidence that the seamen on board of her are such." Great Britain refused any concessions whatsoever to the principle. Three times the United States tried to negotiate a treaty in which each party would deny itself the right to impress persons from the other's ships, and it offered various concessions. Although linked with other issues of neutral trade, impressment came to assume first place in American diplomacy. The climax occurred in 1807 when four men were removed from the American frigate *Chesapeake*. In 1812 Congress alleged impressment to be the principal cause of the declaration of war against Great Britain, but in view of the ambitions of the American war hawks, this allegation can be discounted.

BIBLIOGRAPHY

Black, Jeremy, and Philip Woodfine, eds. *The British Navy and the Use of Naval Power in the Eighteenth Century*. Leicester, England: Leicester University Press, 1988.

Buel, Richard, Jr. *In Irons: Britain's Naval Supremacy and the American Revolutionary Economy*. New Haven, Conn.: Yale University Press, 1998.

Perkins, Bradford. *Prologue to War: England and the United States, 1805–1812*. Berkeley: University of California Press, 1961.

Zimmerman, James Fulton. *Impressment of American Seamen*. Studies in History, Economics, and Public Law, no. 262. Port Washington, N.Y.: Kennikat Press, 1966. The original edition was published in 1925.

Honor Sachs
Richard W. Van Alstyne

See also ***Chesapeake-Leopard*** **Incident; War of 1812.**

Eugene V. Debs. The labor leader and frequent Socialist candidate for president. LIBRARY OF CONGRESS

IN GOD WE TRUST is the motto that has appeared on most issues of U.S. coins since about 1864. Its use on coins stems from the rise of religious sentiment during the CIVIL WAR, which led many devout persons to urge that God be recognized on American coins. Accordingly, Secretary of the Treasury Salmon P. Chase asked the director of the mint at Philadelphia to have prepared a suitable device expressing this national recognition. Several other mottos were suggested—among them, "God Our Trust" and "God and Our Country." The use of "In God We Trust" is not required by law.

BIBLIOGRAPHY

Schwartz, Theodore. *A History of United States Coinage*. San Diego, Calif.: A. S. Barnes, 1980.

Thomas L. Harris / A. R.

See also **Evangelicalism and Revivalism; Treasury, Department of the.**

IN RE DEBS, 158 U.S. 564 (1895). Influenced by his attorney general, Richard Olney, and convinced that the Pullman strike of June–July 1894 was interfering with interstate commerce and the delivery of mails, President Grover Cleveland ordered troops into Chicago. Although the SHERMAN ANTITRUST ACT had proved of little value in controlling monopoly and Olney himself considered it useless, he asked and secured from the U.S. court in Chicago an injunction based on this act and on the law prohibiting obstruction of the mails. Described as the "omnibus injunction" because of its wide sweep, it forbade Eugene V. Debs, president of the AMERICAN RAILWAY UNION, and other officers "from in any way or manner interfering with, hindering, obstructing or stopping" the business of the railroads entering Chicago. Arrested for alleged violation of the injunction on 10 July, Debs and other leaders were found guilty, 14 December, of contempt and sentenced to jail, the sentences varying from three to six months (*United States* v. *Debs*, 64 Federal Reporter 724). Carried to the Supreme Court on a writ of habeas corpus, the sentence was upheld, on 27 May 1895, on the government's constitutional authority over interstate commerce and the mails. While the circuit court had based the injunction specifically on the Sherman Act, Justice David J. Brewer of the Supreme Court rested its decision on "broader grounds." Injunctions had traditionally been used to protect individuals in civil or criminal matters; with the Debs injunction, the Court dramatically expanded its reach into the preservation of national sovereignty and social order.

BIBLIOGRAPHY

Cooper, Jerry M. *The Army and Civil Disorder: Federal Military Intervention in Labor Disputes, 1877–1900.* Westport, Conn.: Greenwood Press, 1980.

Eggert, Gerald C. *Railroad Labor Disputes.* Ann Arbor: University of Michigan Press, 1967.

———. *Steelmasters and Labor Reform, 1886–1923.* Pittsburgh, Pa.: University of Pittsburgh Press, 1981.

H. U. Faulkner
Eric J. Marser

See also **Habeas Corpus, Writ of; Injunctions, Labor; Pullman Strike; Railroads; Strikes.**

IN RE GAULT, 387 U.S. 1 (1967), addressed the question of whether the criminal justice provisions of the Bill of Rights applied to minors. Chief Justice Earl Warren predicted this decision would become the Magna Carta for juveniles. The case involved Gerald Gault, a fifteen-year-old probationer, who had been arrested for making an obscene telephone call. Gault was held by the police while he was interrogated for several days, and, following the sort of informal proceeding then typical in juvenile courts, was sentenced to a state school until he turned twenty-one.

Justice Abe Fortas viewed Gault's case as a vehicle for reforming what he regarded as a failed juvenile justice system. The way to improve a system that simply bred criminals, Fortas believed, was to insist that juveniles be given many of the same rights that the Constitution guaranteed to adults. His *Gault* opinion declared that the Due Process Clause of the Fourteenth Amendment required giving juveniles written notice of the charges against them, allowing them to confront their accusers, and informing them that they had a privilege against self-incrimination and a right to be represented by an attorney (an appointed one if they were indigent). The effect of *Gault* was to affirm that children have constitutional rights, although their rights are somewhat more limited than the rights of adults.

BIBLIOGRAPHY

Kalman, Laura. *Abe Fortas: A Biography.* New Haven, Conn.: Yale University Press, 1990.

Walker, Nancy E., Catherine M. Brooks, and Lawrence S. Wrightsman. *Children's Rights in the United States: In Search of a National Policy.* Thousand Oaks, Calif.: Sage, 1999

Michal R. Belknap

See also **Due Process of Law; Juvenile Courts.**

IN RE NEAGLE, 135 U.S. 1 (1890), a case in which the U.S. Supreme Court asserted federal supremacy over state law. President Benjamin Harrison had directed David Neagle, a deputy U.S. marshal, to protect Justice Stephen J. Field of the Supreme Court against a death threat. Neagle shot and killed would-be assassin David S. Terry as Terry made a murderous assault on Field in California. Arrested by state authorities and charged with murder, Neagle was brought before the federal circuit court on a writ of habeas corpus and released on the ground that he was being held in custody for "an act done in pursuance of a law of the United States." His release was upheld by the Supreme Court.

BIBLIOGRAPHY

Kens, Paul. *Justice Stephen Field: Shaping Liberty from the Gold Rush to the Gilded Age.* Lawrence: University Press of Kansas, 1997.

P. Orman Ray/A. R.

See also **Assassinations and Political Violence, Other; Civil Service; Gilded Age; Supreme Court.**

INAUGURATION, PRESIDENTIAL. The presidential inauguration is the term used to designate the ceremony in which the duly elected president of the United States assumes the power and prerogatives of that office. According to the CONSTITUTION OF THE UNITED STATES, only one thing is required for the inauguration of a president: Article II, Section 1, provides that "before he enter on the Execution of his Office, he shall take the following Oath or Affirmation:—'I do solemnly swear (or affirm) that I will faithfully execute the Office of President of the United States, and will to the best of my Ability, preserve, protect and defend the Constitution of the United States.'"

Tradition has expanded the ceremony of taking the oath into a day-long festival attended by throngs of citizens and political partisans of the president. The ceremony begins with the taking of the oath of office by the president on a platform at the east front of the CAPITOL AT WASHINGTON, D.C. The oath is usually administered by the chief justice of the SUPREME COURT. The president then delivers his inaugural address, which adumbrates the themes of the new administration. The ceremony is witnessed by hundreds of dignitaries and thousands of spectators, while additional millions watch it on television. The afternoon is devoted to a parade from the Capitol, down Pennsylvania Avenue to the White House, led by the president and the first lady. In the evening the celebration concludes with several inaugural balls attended by the new president and his official party.

The official date for the inauguration was first set as 4 March by the Twelfth Amendment of the Constitution, passed in 1804. The date was changed in 1933 when the Twentieth Amendment set 20 January as the end of the presidential term, to shorten the period between the election of a new president and his inauguration.

George Washington took his oath of office on the balcony of Federal Hall in New York City on 30 April 1789 because the new government was not sufficiently organized for an earlier inauguration. He then delivered

Inaugural Address. After taking the oath of office, President John F. Kennedy delivers his memorable "Ask not . . ." speech on 20 January 1961. GETTY IMAGES

an inaugural address to both houses of Congress in the Senate chamber. President Andrew Jackson was the first to take the oath on a platform at the east front of the Capitol. The inaugural parade grew out of the escort of honor given to the incoming president as he went up to the Capitol to take the oath of office. The first organized procession from the Capitol back to the White House after the ceremony took place at the inauguration of President William Henry Harrison in 1841. The earliest inaugural ball took place in 1809, after the inauguration of President James Madison.

When the vice president takes the oath of office at the death of a president, all ceremonial formalities are dispensed with. The oath is administered as soon as possible by a justice or civil authority, and the ceremony consists simply of taking the oath in the words prescribed in the Constitution.

BIBLIOGRAPHY

Boller, Paul F., Jr. *Presidential Inaugurations.* New York: Harcourt, 2001.

Margaret Klapthor / A. G.

See also **Connecticut Compromise; Corrupt Bargain; Electoral College; Lame-Duck Amendment; Majority Rule; Midnight Judges; Republic.**

INCOME TAX. *See* **Taxation.**

INCOME TAX CASES. Confronted with a sharp conflict of social and political forces, in 1895 the Supreme Court chose to vitiate a hundred years of precedent and void the federal income tax of 1894 (*Pollock v. Farmers' Loan and Trust Company*, 157 U.S. 429; *Rehearing*, 158 U.S. 601). Not until 1913, after adoption of the Sixteenth Amendment, could a federal income tax again be levied.

The 1894 tax of 2 percent on incomes over $4,000 was designed by southern and western congressmen to rectify the federal government's regressive revenue system (the tariff and excise taxes) and commence the taxation of large incomes. Conservative opponents of the tax, alarmed by the rise of populism and labor unrest, saw the tax as the first step in a majoritarian attack on the upper classes.

Constitutionally, the tax seemed secure. The Court, relying on the precedent in *Hylton v. United States* (1796), had unanimously upheld the Civil War income tax in 1891 (*Springer v. United States*, 102 U.S. 586), declaring that an income tax was not a "direct tax" within the meaning of the Constitution and thus did not require apportionment among the states according to population. The Court had strongly intimated in *Hylton* that the only direct taxes were poll taxes and taxes on land.

Prominent counsel opposing the 1894 tax appealed to the Supreme Court to overthrow the *Hylton* and *Springer* precedents. Defenders of the tax, including Attorney General Richard Olney, warned the Court not to interfere in a divisive political issue. On 8 April the Court delivered a partial decision, holding by six to two (one justice was ill) that the tax on income from real property was a direct tax and had to be apportioned. Since a tax on land was direct, said Chief Justice Melville W. Fuller for the Court, so was a tax on the income from land. On other important issues the Court was announced as divided, four to four.

A rehearing was held, with the ailing justice sitting, and on 20 May the entire tax was found unconstitutional, five to four. Personal property was not constitutionally different from real property, the chief justice argued, and taxation of income from either was direct.

Public and professional criticism was intense, and the Democratic Party platform of 1896 hinted at Court packing to gain a reversal. From the perspective of the judicial role in the 1890s, the *Pollock* decisions, together with other leading cases of the period—such as the *E. C. Knight* case and the *Debs* injunction case—marked the triumph of a conservative judicial revolution, with far-reaching consequences.

BIBLIOGRAPHY

Ely, James W. *The Chief Justiceship of Melville W. Fuller, 1888–1910.* Chief Justiceships of the United States Supreme Court Series. Columbia: University of South Carolina Press, 1995.

Lasser, William. *The Limits of Judicial Power: The Supreme Court in American Politics.* Chapel Hill: University of North Carolina Press, 1988.

Arnold M. Paul
Andrew C. Rieser

See also **Hylton v. U.S.; In Re Debs; Pollock v. Farmers' Loan and Trust Company; Populism; Springer v. United States.**

INDEMNITIES, a diplomatic term for a nation's payments to compensate foreign citizens for injuries to their persons or properties. Such payments were more commonly described late in the twentieth century in terms of settlement of international claims. Indemnities differ from reparations, which have often denoted postwar nation-to-nation payments with punitive (and compensatory) functions.

Significant historical examples of indemnities paid to the United States have come in the context of damage to American merchant shipping. France paid millions of dollars in the 1830s for Napoleonic era spoliations—seizures of neutral American ships and cargos during the European wars of 1803 to 1815. British shipyards built Confederate commerce raiders during the Civil War, and Britain paid the United States more than $8 million under the 1871 Treaty of Washington for the resulting Union shipping losses. Also notable were Germany's payments after World War I for American civilians killed and ships sunk by its submarines. Expropriations have also occasioned indemnities, such as Albania's 1995 payment of $2 million for its then-communist government's seizure of American properties after World War II.

The United States has also made indemnities, sometimes for American mob violence to foreign citizens, such as the payments after three Italians were lynched in an 1891 New Orleans riot. Many twentieth-century indemnities have come after military accidents, such as a $2 million payment in 1955 for fallout poisoning on a Japanese fishing trawler after a United States hydrogen bomb test. More recently, surviving family members were paid when the USS *Vincennes* mistakenly shot down an Iranian airliner in 1988.

Indemnities often involve competing considerations for the paying nation. Governments may be slow for legal reasons to admit fault but quick for diplomatic reasons to demonstrate concern. These tensions are frequently resolved by characterization of payments as ex gratia humanitarian gestures and not admissions of liability. So, for example, Israel made an ex gratia payment after its accidental 1967 attack on the USS *Liberty.* The United States' payment in the Japanese trawler incident was also ex gratia.

The injured person's nation may also face thorny political issues attendant to indemnities. Notably, the president of the United States can agree to extinguish claims when it is in the national interest. This happened in 1981, when the American embassy hostages in Iran were released only after President Jimmy Carter waived their individual claims against the Iranian government. Subsequent recompense by the U.S. government in such cases is never certain. The Tehran embassy hostages were compensated by act of Congress in 1986. Conversely, claimants' heirs and insurers were still petitioning Congress for redress in 1915 with respect to certain spoliation claims against France that President John Adams had waived in 1800.

BIBLIOGRAPHY

Bemis, Samuel Flagg. *A Diplomatic History of the United States.* 5th ed. New York: Holt, Rinehart and Winston, 1965. Dated but comprehensive and valuable general source on indemnities through the mid-twentieth century.

Henkin, Louis. *Foreign Affairs and the United States Constitution.* 2d ed. Oxford: Clarendon Press, 1996. Useful discussion of constitutional issues involved in the historical context of the French spoliation claims settled in 1800.

Maier, Harold G. "Ex Gratia Payments and the Iranian Airline Tragedy." *American Journal of International Law* 83 (April 1989): 325–332. Useful legal and historical discussion of ex gratia payments.

Charles F. Bethel

See also ***Alabama*** **Claims; Iran Hostage Crisis.**

INDENTURED SERVANTS in colonial America were, for the most part, adult white persons who were

Indentured Servants. Female convicts transported from England arrive at Jamestown, Va., in this nineteenth-century colored engraving. THE GRANGER COLLECTION, LTD.

bound to labor for a period of years. There were three well-known classes: the free-willers, or redemptioners; those who were enticed to leave their home country out of poverty or who were kidnapped for political or religious reasons; and convicts. The first class represented those who chose to bind themselves to labor for a definite time to pay for their passage to America. The best known of these were Germans, but many English and Scottish men and women came in the same way. The second class, those who came to escape poverty or were forcibly brought to the colonies, was large because of the scarcity of labor in America. Their services were profitably sold to plantation owners or farmers, who indentured them for a period of years. The third class, convicts, were sentenced to deportation and on arrival in America were indentured unless they had personal funds to maintain themselves. Seven years was a common term of such service. The West Indies and Maryland appear to have received the largest number of immigrants of the third class.

Indentured servants made up a large portion of the population of the Chesapeake region, especially during the seventeenth century, when they accounted for 80 to 90 percent of European immigrants. The middle colonies of Pennsylvania, Delaware, and New Jersey also relied heavily on indentured servants, and in the eighteenth century more lived there than in any other region.

Most of the colonies regulated the terms of indentured service, but the treatment of individual servants differed widely. Some were mistreated; others lived as members of a family. It was commonly required that they be provided with clothing, a gun, and a small tract of land upon which to establish themselves after their service ended. These requirements applied especially to those who were unwilling servants. There was no permanent stigma attached to indentured servitude, and the families of such persons merged readily with the total population. Children born to parents serving their indenture were free. Terms of an indenture were enforceable in the courts, and runaway servants could be compelled to return to their masters and complete their service, with additional periods added for the time they had been absent.

When the prospects for upward mobility dimmed, as they did in the late-seventeenth-century Chesapeake region, indentured servants proved willing and ready to participate in violent rebellions and to demand wealthier colonists' property. The threat posed by great numbers of angry indentured servants might have been one of the reasons this type of servitude diminished over the course of the eighteenth century, with many farmers and plantation owners coming to rely instead on the labor of enslaved Africans.

Although indentured service of the colonial genre ceased after the American Revolution, similar kinds of contract labor were widespread in the United States during periods of labor shortage until the passage of the Contract Labor Law of 1885.

BIBLIOGRAPHY

Galenson, David W. *White Servitude in Colonial America: An Economic Analysis.* New York: Cambridge University Press, 1981.

Morgan, Edmund S. *American Slavery, American Freedom: The Ordeal of Colonial Virginia.* New York: Norton, 1975.

Salinger, Sharon. *"To Serve Well and Faithfully": Labor and Indentured Servants in Pennsylvania, 1682–1800.* New York: Cambridge University Press, 1987.

O. M. Dickerson / T. D.

See also **Apprenticeship; New Smyrna Colony; Slavery;** *and vol. 9:* **The History and Present State of Virginia; Indentured White Slaves in the Colonies.**

INDEPENDENCE. On 2 July 1776, the Continental Congress voted to sever all connections with the British Empire. Two days later, the delegates debated, revised, and finally approved the Declaration of Independence drafted by Thomas Jefferson. These actions were the climax to a decade of controversy that began when Parliament attempted to impose taxes on the American colonists with the Revenue Act of 1764 and the Stamp Act of 1765. Americans opposed these measures for various reasons, including a general aversion to taxation in any form. But the basic dispute was a constitutional one. Could Parliament enact legislation binding the American colonies "in all cases whatsoever," as its Declaratory Act of 1766 asserted? Americans argued that they could only be governed by their own legislative assemblies, not a distant Parliament to which they sent no members. But if the colonies were exempt from its jurisdiction, how could they remain part of the larger empire within which Parliament was the supreme source of law?

From an early point, observers in both countries worried that the dispute might end with the colonies seeking independence. Imperial officials had long fretted over the autonomy that the colonies enjoyed and the loose control the empire exerted. The British victory in the Seven Years' War (1756–1763) exacerbated those fears by removing the threat to colonial expansion posed by French control of Canada. Americans felt deep attachment to Britain and to the prosperity and security they enjoyed within the empire. Yet colonial legislatures repeatedly quarreled with royal governors and other imperial officials.

There is, however, little evidence that Americans actively sought independence. Through 1774, the colonists affirmed that their goal was the restoration of the rights they had previously enjoyed. Under the prevailing imperial policy of "salutary neglect," British authority rested lightly on Americans. Laws regulating daily life were enacted by the colonists' own assemblies. Within the empire, Americans accepted the framework for commerce laid down by successive navigation acts that Parliament had adopted beginning in 1651. Although they often violated specific regulations, the navigation system worked to the mutual advantage of both Britain and its colonies.

The Stamp Act and Townshend Acts

The adoption of the Stamp Act threw these understandings into crisis. Americans first objected that they were not bound by the acts of a legislature in which they were unrepresented. The British government responded that Americans were "virtually represented" in Parliament. When that claim proved unavailing, it further argued that Parliament was the sovereign source of law within the larger polity of which the colonies were indisputably a part. Because sovereignty was regarded as an absolute, unitary power, American arguments about representation would have to yield to the ultimate authority of Parliament.

In 1767, Parliament enacted the Townshend duties, exploiting a distinction some colonists had made between "internal" taxes like the Stamp Act and "external" duties on imported goods. Prompted by John Dickinson's influential *Letters from a Pennsylvania Farmer* (1767–1768), Americans replied that duties clearly levied as taxes were constitutionally unacceptable. A few writers suggested that the colonies were completely independent of Parliament, but still bound to the British Empire through their historic link to the crown.

This debate largely subsided after Parliament repealed the Townshend duties in March 1770, leaving only a duty on tea as a symbolic statement of its authority. In most colonies, politics reverted to normal and the harmony of the empire seemed restored.

The Tea Tax, the Coercive Acts, and the Continental Congress

In Massachusetts, however, a fresh controversy erupted between the royal governor, Thomas Hutchinson, and his detractors, led by Samuel Adams of Boston, after it was learned that Hutchinson and the provincial judges were to receive royal salaries, rendering them politically independent of the legislature. The debate ultimately led to a full-blown discussion of the constitutional rights of Americans and the constitutional powers of Parliament. It also disposed Hutchinson to enforce the new Tea Act that Parliament enacted in 1773. Rather than allow the dutied tea to land, as Hutchinson insisted it must, the Boston radicals dumped it into the town harbor. In response, Parliament enacted the Coercive Acts of 1774, closing the port of Boston, altering the provincial charter granted by the crown, and providing legal protection for British officials accused of crimes against Americans.

In town and county meetings, the American population mobilized to protest these measures, which demonstrated what allowing Parliament to legislate "in all cases whatsoever" could mean. Deputies from every colony but Georgia gathered in a Continental Congress at Philadelphia in September, and agreed to a program of opposition combining a commercial boycott of Britain with a demand that Parliament repeal its offensive legislation. In response to the British military occupation of Boston, Congress instructed the people of Massachusetts to take only defensive measures, but when the delegates adjourned in October, they understood that hostilities might erupt before they reconvened in May.

Armed Conflict and the Failure of Reconciliation

When war broke out at Lexington and Concord in Massachusetts during April 1775, a second Congress reviewed the American position but did not flinch, organizing the Continental Army that it named George Washington to command. Congress sent a new petition seeking redress to the crown, but the latter did not modify the positions it had taken in 1774. For its part, the government of Lord North, firmly backed by King George III, was committed to a policy of repression, believing that a decisive show of force would convince the Americans to retreat. New parliamentary acts declared the colonies in a state of rebellion and subjected their commerce to seizure.

Prospects for reconciliation dwindled with every passing month and independence became increasingly a matter of timing. Many Americans still resisted taking the final step of renouncing allegiance to the king. Even in Congress, moderates desperately hoped that Britain would send commissioners authorized to conduct serious negotiations. But the publication in January 1776 of Thomas Paine's electrifying pamphlet *Common Sense* made independence a legitimate subject of debate. In the spring, local meetings started to endorse the idea, as did the provincial convention of Virginia in May. Reports that Britain had begun contracting for Hessian mercenaries confirmed that the government was uninterested in negotiations.

In mid-May, Congress adopted a resolution authorizing the provincial conventions to establish new legal governments, resting on popular consent, to replace the old colonial governments that drew their authority from the crown. Three weeks later, it appointed committees to draft articles of confederation, a plan for foreign treaties, and a declaration of independence. A handful of delegates, led by John Dickinson, urged greater patience, but when the decisive vote came, Congress and the bulk of the politically active population supported the break with Britain. Seven years passed before their desires were secured.

BIBLIOGRAPHY

Bailyn, Bernard. *The Ideological Origins of the American Revolution.* Enlarged ed. Cambridge, Mass.: Harvard University Press, 1992. Immensely influential.

Christie, Ian R., and Benjamin W. Labaree. *Empire or Independence, 1760–1776: A British-American Dialogue on the Coming of the American Revolution.* New York: Norton, 1976. Balanced and shrewd assessment from both sides of the Atlantic.

Maier, Pauline. *American Scripture: Making the Declaration of Independence.* New York: Knopf, 1997. Provocative study of the decision and the document.

Rakove, Jack N. *The Beginnings of National Politics: An Interpretive History of the Continental Congress.* New York: Knopf, 1979.

Jack Rakove

See also **Committees of Correspondence; *Common Sense;* Continental Congress; Declaration of Independence; Revolution, American: Political and Military History.**

INDEPENDENCE, MO., city located in western Missouri, the seat of Jackson County, and part of the greater Kansas City metropolitan area. Founded in 1827 as a provisioning and starting point for the Santa Fe, California, and Oregon trails, the area had originally served as a trading post beginning in 1808 with Fort Osage. The city gained its name from its original settlers' admiration of President Andrew Jackson, who built his reputation as a people's president. The city also serves as the world

First Family of Independence, Mo. Former president Harry S. Truman and his wife, Bess, stand outside their home.

Fourth of July in Centre Square. A painting by John Lewis Krimmel, c. 1810–1812, part of a series he created over several years to show the changing celebrations in front of Independence Hall in Philadelphia. THE PENNSYLVANIA ACADEMY OF FINE ARTS

headquarters for the Reorganized Church of Jesus Christ of Latter-day Saints, a denomination of the older church that settled in the area prior to moving to the Utah Territory. During the Civil War, Union forces remained in control of the city and Confederate forces never threatened the area. During the latter part of the nineteenth century, the city served as a political adjunct to nearby Kansas City and produced the future President Harry S. Truman. He would remember the town as a bustling place without the troubles of Kansas City, providing the best of small-town life. After service as senator and president, Truman retired to his home in Independence and established his presidential library, one of the finest such institutions. The city has sustained its population during a time of urban renewal and has maintained its identity despite its suburban location.

The city continues as a manufacturing and food-processing center located along important highways centered on Kansas City. It continued to expand throughout the twentieth century, reaching an area of 77.8 square miles by 2001 and a population of 113,288, according to the 2000 census—up from 112,301 in 1990, but significantly higher than the 1980 figure of 111,806. The city is also situated in the sprawling Kansas City metropolitan region of nearly 1.8 million that covers eleven counties in Missouri and Kansas.

BIBLIOGRAPHY

Foerster, Bernd. *Independence, Missouri.* Indpendence, Mo.; Independence Press, 1978.

Matthew L. Daley

INDEPENDENCE DAY. The adoption of the Declaration of Independence on 4 July 1776 has caused that day to be taken as the birth date of the United States of America. Strangely, the commemoration of the Fourth of July received its first big impetus and had the pattern set for its celebration before the event even came to pass. On 3 July, John Adams wrote to his wife:

> The second day of July, 1776, . . . I am apt to believe . . . will be celebrated by succeeding generations as the great anniversary Festival. It ought to be commemorated, as the day of deliverance, by solemn acts of devotion to God Almighty. It ought to be solemnized with pomp and parade, with shows, games, sports, guns, bells, bonfires, and illuminations, from one end of this continent to the other, from this time forward forevermore.

Adams was thinking of the resolution of independence adopted on 2 July as the pivotal event, but the DECLARATION OF INDEPENDENCE soon completely obscured the resolution.

Independence Hall. The birthplace of the United States. HULTON ARCHIVE

The first anniversary does not appear to have been commemorated throughout the thirteen states, but there were elaborate celebrations in the principal cities, and parades, the firing of guns, the ringing of bells, decorations, illuminations, fireworks, and the drinking of toasts constituted the chief features in every instance. The practice of commemorating the Glorious Fourth soon spread widely, particularly after the adoption of the Constitution. As the years went by, some of the early features of the celebration declined or disappeared entirely, such as the thirteen guns and thirteen (or thirteen times thirteen) toasts. Meanwhile, sports and games, which at first were only a minor part of the festivities, became the greatest attraction. In country regions, the Fourth of July became a day for picnics, with exhibitions of skill in such contests as potato races, watermelon eating, and catching the greased pig, without much thought of the Declaration of Independence. Since 1777, fireworks, great and small, have held a prominent place. In the early 1900s, serious efforts were made to promote safety in Fourth of July celebrations, and in ensuing years the personal possession of fireworks has been outlawed in many states.

BIBLIOGRAPHY

Bodnar, John, ed. *Bonds of Affection: Americans Define Their Patriotism.* Princeton, N.J.: Princeton University Press, 1996.

Ellis, Joseph J. *Founding Brothers: The Revolutionary Generation.* New York: Knopf, 2000.

Maier, Pauline. *American Scripture: Making the Declaration of Independence.* New York: Knopf, 1998.

Edmund C. Burnett/A. G.

INDEPENDENCE HALL, a red-brick structure, near the center of Philadelphia, where the Declaration of Independence, Articles of Confederation, and Constitution were signed. Built between 1732 and 1757 for speaker Andrew Hamilton to serve as provincial Pennsylvania's state house, it became the meeting place of the Continental Congress during the American Revolution and retains many relics from that era. Adjoining Congress Hall, where the House and Senate met during the 1790s, and Old City Hall, where the Supreme Court deliberated, Independence Hall completes the grouping of historically important buildings on Independence Square.

Independence National Historical Park, established by the Eightieth Congress (1948) to preserve historical properties associated with the American Revolution, is a landscaped area of four city blocks and outlying sites that encompass Independence Square, Carpenters' Hall (meeting place of the First Continental Congress), the site of

Benjamin Franklin's home, the reconstructed Graff House (where Thomas Jefferson wrote the Declaration of Independence), City Tavern (center of revolutionary-war activities), restored period residences, and early banks. The park also holds the Liberty Bell, Franklin's desk, a portrait gallery, gardens, and libraries. A product of extensive documentary research and archaeology by the federal government, the restoration of Independence Hall and other buildings in the park set standards for other historic preservation and stimulated rejuvenation of old Philadelphia.

BIBLIOGRAPHY

Eberlein, Harold D., and Cortlandt V. D. Hubbard. *Diary of Independence Hall.* Philadelphia: J. B. Lippincott, 1948.

Hosmer, Charles B. *Presence of the Past: A History of the Preservation Movement in the United States Before Williamsburg.* New York: Putnam, 1965.

Kammen, Michael. *Mystic Chords of Memory: The Transformation of Tradition in American Culture.* New York: Knopf, 1991.

John D. R. Platt/A. R.

See also **Continental Congress; Declaration of Independence; Independence; Liberty Bell; Preservation Movement; Revolution, American: Political History.**

INDEPENDENCE ROCK is a giant granite outcropping, polished smooth by wind, rising only 136 feet above the surrounding terrain but measuring more than a mile in circumference. Located on the north bank of Wyoming's Sweetwater River, the rock was a landmark on the Oregon Trail. Migrants heading for CALIFORNIA and the PACIFIC NORTHWEST stopped here for fresh water and trail information, and many families carved their names into the granite to commemorate their passing. The rock was approximately two-fifths of the way from the trail's origin near Independence, Minnesota, to its terminus in Oregon's Willamette River Valley.

BIBLIOGRAPHY

Ellison, R. S. "Independence Rock and the Oregon Trail." *Midwest Review* (1927).

Lavender, David S. *Westward Vision: The Story of the Oregon Trail.* New York: McGraw-Hill, 1963.

Robert S. Thomas/W. P.

See also **Covered Wagon; Migrations, Internal; Oregon Trail; Wagon Trains; Westward Migration; Wyoming.**

INDEPENDENT COUNSEL LAW. *See* **Special Prosecutors.**

INDEPENDENT TREASURY SYSTEM, an alternative to a central bank. Critics of the first and second banks of the United States were legion. Jeffersonians and Jacksonians criticized their monopoly as sole financial agents of the U.S. Treasury and feared their significant financial power. President Andrew Jackson had little use for banks, and many citizens disliked the political influence usually required to obtain state bank charters.

By late 1837 the nation had twice experienced living under a central bank, had seen it liquidated, and then had endured a panic and a depression. The Democrats blamed it all on banks and wanted the Treasury to operate independently; the Whigs wanted a third central bank. In June 1840 Congress established an Independent Treasury System, but the first act of the Whig administration of President William Henry Harrison in March 1841 was to repeal the bill. After Harrison died in April, President John Tyler vetoed all attempts to set up a third central bank.

One of the major planks in Democratic candidate James K. Polk's platform in 1844 was to re-create the Independent Treasury System. Congress reestablished the system in August 1846 to trade only in gold and silver coin. The system tended to drain money out of commercial channels into government vaults, however, which damaged the economy. Because the system operated badly, the government made increasing use of banks, which promptly loaned money left in their hands. In 1914 the FEDERAL RESERVE SYSTEM (established 23 December 1913), a central bank, went into operation. The Independent Treasury System ended in 1921.

BIBLIOGRAPHY

Friedman, Jean E. *The Revolt of the Conservative Democrats: An Essay on American Political Culture and Political Development, 1837–1844.* Studies in American History and Culture, no. 9. Ann Arbor, Mich.: UMI Research Press, 1979.

Myers, Margaret G. *A Financial History of the United States.* New York: Columbia University Press, 1970.

Donald L. Kemmerer/C. W.

See also **Bank of the United States; Jacksonian Democracy; Jeffersonian Democracy.**

INDIA AND PAKISTAN, RELATIONS WITH. By the end of World War II, upwards of 250,000 U.S. soldiers had spent time in British India. However, both during and immediately after the war, the United States focused its military, diplomatic, and economic efforts on Europe and Pacific Asia far more than on south Asia. Britain itself left the Indian subcontinent on 15 August 1947, in part because of geopolitical and diplomatic considerations linked to the emerging Cold War centered on rivalry between the United States and the Soviet Union. Britain was already committed militarily in the Mediterranean and the Middle East, and the U.S. government had been arguing that rapidly turning India over to noncommunist Indians would prevent it from "falling" to the communists at a later date. Independence resulted in the partition of British India along communal lines and the transfer of power to the new nation-states of India and Pakistan. The violence and mass migration that resulted left between 200,000 and 500,000 people dead and turned another 12 million into refugees.

The issue that had been at the center of the violence was the fact that the new border between India and Pakistan ran right through the Punjab; however, the main bone of contention between the new nations would prove to be Kashmir, one of the many princely states that had continued to operate within the wider ambit of British rule up to 1947. With independence, the princely states were expected to accede to either India or Pakistan. In Kashmir (with a Hindu ruling elite and a majority Muslim population), the maharaja resisted joining either Pakistan or India. Then, in the context of a Pakistani-supported rebellion, the maharaja turned to the new Indian government for assistance, in exchange for "temporary" accession to India that would be followed at some point by a plebiscite on the future of Kashmir. The plebiscite never took place, and Indian military intervention successfully secured Indian control over much of the mountainous region. Both India and Pakistan have continued to maintain a military presence in Kashmir and have engaged in sporadic fighting along the so-called "Line of Control" ever since.

The Cold War, 1947–1979

While encouraging the British to leave the subcontinent, the United States had taken a limited interest in the new nation-states of India and Pakistan that emerged in South Asia in 1947. Immediately after 1945, Washington's primary geopolitical concern had been with western and southern Europe and northeast Asia. However, the United States began to change its assessment of south Asia with the establishment of the Peoples' Republic of China in late 1949 and the start of the Korean War in 1950. By the beginning of the 1950s, some policymakers, politicians, and journalists were arguing that South Asia was of central importance to a range of key U.S. foreign policy goals. India, under the charismatic leadership of Jawaharlal Nehru, was increasingly viewed as a possible political and economic model for Asia and the Third World. By the 1950s, Nehru's international profile and his commitment to a combination of parliamentary democracy, economic planning, and socialist principles that drew on Soviet, western European, and Chinese experience had helped to focus considerable world attention on India as a laboratory for postcolonial development. For some observers in the United States by this time, India was regarded as an important prize: they foresaw political and ideological benefits for Washington should it form an alliance with the most influential nonaligned government in Asia. According to this vision, if the United States strengthened ties with Nehru's government, Washington could help ensure that India would serve as an anchor for, and model of, democratic capitalist development in the Third World—to counter the explicitly anticapitalist and state-socialist alternatives exemplified by China and the Soviet Union.

For other U.S. strategists, however, Pakistan was the most important nation-state in the region for military-strategic reasons: they emphasized its proximity to the Soviet Union and its position in relation to the Middle East. By 1954, an emphasis on the relative importance of Pakistan led to a mutual security agreement between the United States and the Pakistani government. This was complemented by Pakistan's participation in the Southeast Asia Treaty Organization, formed in 1954, and in the Baghdad Pact, which was set up in 1955 (it was renamed the Central Treaty Organization in 1959 and was also known as the Middle East Treaty Organization). The flow of U.S. military assistance was driven by regional geopolitical considerations, but the strengthened military establishment that emerged in Pakistan viewed India as its primary enemy.

In 1953, Nehru used the impending military alliance between the United States and Pakistan to justify the cancellation of the planned plebiscite in Kashmir and substantially increase Indian defense spending. In this period the government in New Delhi also deepened its economic and military links to Moscow, while seeking to maintain good relations with the Chinese government. In response to these changes, the U.S. approach to south Asia shifted away from Pakistan somewhat and toward an emphasis on India by the end of the 1950s. The United States was worried that the Soviet Union was gaining influence in Indian government circles, as a result of its generous trade and aid arrangements.

There was growing concern that if the Indian government failed to achieve its national development plans, the strength of the country's communist movement would increase—and that economic decline in India could also enhance the Chinese government's prestige in international affairs. In these circumstances, the administrations of President Dwight Eisenhower (1953–1960) and particularly that of President John F. Kennedy (1961–1963) increased U.S. economic aid to India, while also trying to encourage improvement in Indo-Pakistani relations. With the apparent political stability in Pakistan under the military rule of the general, later field marshal, Ayub Khan (1958–1969), India and Pakistan, with the help of the World Bank, reached an agreement in 1960 about sharing irrigation water in the Indus basin. However, the issue of Kashmir proved more intractable. Furthermore, when the border dispute between China and India broke into open warfare in 1962 and the Indian army was quickly defeated (despite U.S. assistance), the Pakistani leadership concluded that it also had the military capability to defeat the Indian army. In 1965, by which time Nehru (who had died in May 1964) had been replaced as prime minister by Lal Bahadur Shastri (1964–1966), Ayub Khan instigated a war with India. The main arena of combat was Kashmir, where, despite expectations on the Pakistani side, the Indian army acquitted itself well. In September 1965, the government of Pakistan agreed to United Nations calls for a cease-fire. Subsequent negotiations (mediated by the Soviet Union) failed to change the position of either side on the issue of Kashmir.

Following the outbreak of war between India and Pakistan in 1965, Washington suspended all military and economic aid to both sides. Even food aid under PL480—a government program that supported commercial exports to third world countries—was disbursed via a "short tether" policy that involved shipping only enough food to last a couple of months. After 1965, the administration of President Lyndon Johnson (1963–1968) sought to limit U.S. aid and direct involvement in south Asia relative to the earlier period. Meanwhile, the political situation in Pakistan grew increasingly unstable by the end of the 1960s. In particular, relations between West and East Pakistan (separated by thousands of miles of Indian territory) deteriorated and the government of General Yahya Khan (1969–1971) launched a major wave of repression in East Pakistan. These events led to the Third Indo-Pakistani war in 1971. The Indian prime minister, Indira Gandhi (1966–1977, 1980–1984), sent the Indian army to the assistance of East Pakistan and facilitated its break with West Pakistan to form the new nation-state of Bangladesh. This was followed by a summit meeting between Mrs. Gandhi and the new president of Pakistan, Zulfikar Ali Bhutto (1971–1977). They agreed to resolve differences between their two countries peacefully in the future and affirmed respect for the existing cease-fire line in Kashmir. Following this, relations between India and Pakistan improved during the 1970s.

The New Cold War, 1979–1989

The Soviet invasion of Afghanistan in December 1979 had a major and immediate impact on U.S. relations with Pakistan and India. In 1978, U.S relations with Pakistan had worsened as a result of U.S. criticisms—most notably from President Jimmy Carter (1977–1981)—of human rights violations by the new military government of General Zia ul-Haq (1977–1988), which had overthrown the civilian government of Zulfikar Ali Bhutto (whom Zia executed). The relationship between the United States and Pakistan had also been undermined by Pakistan's attempts to develop nuclear weapons capability. In April 1979, in response to the Pakistani government's nuclear weapons initiative, the Carter administration suspended U.S. aid to Pakistan. However, once the Soviet Union entered Afghanistan, U.S. aid to Pakistan was restored and increased, and the Pakistani military, and military intelligence, played an important role (along with the Saudi Arabian and the Chinese governments) in supporting the loose coalition of resistance groups (Islamic Unity of Afghan Mujahideen) fighting the Soviet occupation. The dramatic turnaround in U.S.-Pakistani relations weakened the Carter administration's attempt to improve its relations with the Indian government. Under Prime Minister Morarji Desai (1977–1979), the Indian government sought to lessen its reliance on the Soviet Union. To this end, Desai and Carter signed the 1977 Delhi Declaration, which restated both governments' commitment to democracy and human rights. At the same time, Washington overrode restrictions on uranium sales to India as embodied in the U.S. Nonproliferation Act, which restricted the flow of nuclear materials to nation-states, such as India, if they did not agree to the system of safeguards outlined by the International Atomic Energy Agency.

These changes were insufficient to put U.S.-Indian relations on a more stable footing, once, after 1979, the United States resumed military and economic aid to Pakistan and began tilting toward China in the context of the war in Afghanistan. In 1980, Prime Minister Indira Gandhi, who had replaced Desai, moved to improve Indian relations with the Soviet Union. She announced a major arms deal, worth $1.6 billion, with the Soviet Union in May 1980. Then, in December, Leonid Brezhnev visited India and Mrs. Gandhi and the Soviet leader issued a public statement that condemned outside involvement in southwest Asia, a clear reference to U.S. involvement in the war in Afghanistan. Despite the strains on Indo-Pakistani relations that the 1979 Soviet invasion of Afghanistan created, Pakistan and India—along with Bangladesh, Nepal, Sri Lanka, Bhutan, and the Maldives—set up a cooperation committee in 1983 that provided a forum for regular ministerial-level meetings. However, in 1986, there were major confrontations between the Indian army and its Pakistani counterpart on the Siachin Glacier in Kashmir. This led to dramatic troop concentrations between December 1986 and February 1987. By 1988, there were some attempts to improve relations, but the secessionist uprising that got under way in Kashmir, with Pakistani support, during 1989 has ensured that Kashmir remains the key flash point of Indo-Pakistani relations and a source of concern in Washington.

The Post–Cold War Era, 1989–2001

The withdrawal of Soviet military forces from Afghanistan (between May 1988 and February 1989) and the end of the Cold War led to a significant geopolitical reorientation in south Asia. With the precipitous end of Soviet influence in the region, the United States turned its attention to two trends that were now seen to threaten regional stability. Both of these "new" threats were closely connected to Pakistan. In the 1990s, Washington became concerned about Islamic fundamentalism as Pakistan's foreign policy moved from an "anti-Soviet" to a "pro-Islamic" stance and the Pakistani government began to establish or improve relations with Afghanistan, Iran, and the former Soviet republics of central Asia. The United States also remained concerned about Pakistan's clandestine nuclear weapons program. In 1986, the U.S. Senate had passed a resolution calling on the State Department either to certify that Pakistan was not developing nuclear weapons or end the disbursement of U.S. military and economic aid. By 1990, U.S. aid to Pakistan had been terminated. This trend paralleled major improvements in U.S.-Indian relations. India's foreign policy was entering a new era following the demise of the Soviet Union. The government in New Delhi, concerned about Pakistan's nuclear capability, greeted the end of U.S. aid to Pakistan with approval. In the early 1990s, there was a push for naval and military cooperation between Washington and New Delhi. Meanwhile, the Indian government signaled a further break with state-directed economic development via the promulgation of a range of liberalizing initiatives after 1991 that also facilitated improved relations with the United States. However, a new era of cooperation between the United States and New Delhi did not really materialize. For example, in 1993, Indian repression and human rights violations in Kashmir were criticized by President Bill Clinton.

In the 1990s the conventional and nuclear arms race between Pakistan and India accelerated, while efforts to form some agreement between the two states regarding nuclear weapons were unsuccessful. India had first tested a nuclear device in 1974. Thereafter, New Delhi had resisted pressure that it sign the NUCLEAR NON-PROLIFERATION TREATY (NPT). The Indian government insisted it would only sign if all countries became signatories and if all major powers with nuclear weapons—including the United States—agreed to get rid of them. Pakistan also resisted demands that it sign the NPT, while the stakes were further raised when India made public in May 1998 that it had carried out five successful underground nuclear tests. These tests were aimed at countering the significant nuclear capability of China and the nuclear capacity that Pakistan had been working on for upwards of twenty years with the help of Beijing. Pakistan responded, despite U.S. efforts, by conducting two underground nuclear tests at the end of May 1998. Washington, with the support of Japan and a number of other nation-states, imposed sanctions on India and Pakistan in response. The Clinton administration subsequently reversed a number of the sanctions, allowing the International Monetary Fund to resume assistance to Pakistan when that country again appeared to be on the brink of a financial crisis. Nevertheless, until September 2001, many of the sanctions constraining the Pakistani military government of General Pervaiz Musharraf (who came to power in a coup in October 1999) remained in place. Then, within less than two weeks of the 11 September 2001 suicide bombing of the World Trade Center and the Pentagon, President George W. Bush lifted all U.S. sanctions on Pakistan and India. Pakistan, in particular, was central to Washington's new "war on terrorism," which was directed at Osama bin Laden and the Taliban regime in Afghanistan in the closing months of 2001.

BIBLIOGRAPHY

Jalal, Ayesha. *The State of Martial Rule: The Origins of Pakistan's Political Economy of Defence.* Cambridge, U.K.: Cambridge University Press, 1990.

McMahon, Robert J. *The Cold War on the Periphery: The United States, India, and Pakistan.* New York: Columbia University Press, 1994.

Perkovich, George. *India's Nuclear Bomb: The Impact on Global Proliferation.* Berkeley: University of California Press, 1999.

Rosen, George. *Western Economists and Eastern Societies: Agents of Change in South Asia, 1950–1970.* Baltimore: Johns Hopkins University Press, 1985.

Schofield, Victoria. *Kashmir in Conflict: India, Pakistan, and the Unfinished War.* London and New York: I. B. Tauris, 2000.

Tahir-Kheli, Shirin R. *India, Pakistan, and the United States: Breaking with the Past.* New York: Council on Foreign Relations Press, 1997.

Mark T. Berger

See also **Cold War; Southeast Asia Treaty Organizations.**

INDIAN AGENTS. The term "Indian agents" was not used officially until 1796, but the idea of assigning government "peace missionaries" to the Indian tribes began with Secretary of War Henry Knox in 1789. Knox hoped that agents would reduce friction between the tribes and the government by promoting "civilization" among the tribes and facilitating peaceful relations between the groups. U.S. treaties often stipulated that an agent would reside with a tribe. In 1793 the president gained the legal power to appoint agents, although initially Congress felt such positions would be temporary and did not renew the provision in the Trade and Intercourse Act of 1802 that authorized them. For the next thirty years there was no legal basis, except in treaties, for appointing Indian agents.

In the early nineteenth century, agents (who were legally forbidden from trading themselves) bore primary responsibility for supervising the government's Indian trading houses. During Thomas Jefferson's administration (1801–1809), trading houses worked to push Indians into dependence on manufactured goods. Trading houses, therefore, were forbidden from accepting any factory-produced items from Indians, who were restricted to trading hides and other raw materials. An agent would watch for violations in the trade and intercourse laws and report them to their superintendents (usually the governor of the territory), local military commanders, or the War Department. Finally, agents were charged with distributing annual payments, or annuities, to the chiefs, who would then redistribute them to their peoples. This system placed enormous reliance on the character of the individual agent.

While some agents were honest and efficient, mismanagement and corruption were frequent. Poor record keeping became standard, as agents often had little formal education, and government allocations lacked fine divisions between funds for private use and those for official business. Honesty and efficiency in the Indian agencies faced the dual challenges of a general public not especially concerned with Indians' welfare and an Indian Office preoccupied with keeping the peace.

In the years after the Civil War, periodic outbursts of public concern encouraged more efficient and humane administration of Indian policy at the agencies. Beginning in 1869, during President Ulysses S. Grant's administration, philanthropic Christian denominations gained control of many Indian agencies. These groups intended to improve the agencies, but overall they failed miserably. There were surprisingly few candidates for Indian agent who were both devout Christians and competent administrators. Even the most well-intentioned appointees proved largely inadequate to the task. By 1882 all the churches had withdrawn from the program.

Beginning in 1880, agents' duties included teaching Indians English as well as industrial and agricultural arts. Liquor was to be strictly prohibited. Setting Indians to "civilized" work became the priority, as idleness was seen as the worst enemy of Indian "progress." Despite these expectations, agents were often appointed for political reasons rather than for their qualifications.

In the interest of efficiency and fairness, reformers gradually managed to include agency personnel in the professional civil service. In 1896 President Grover Cleveland decreed that those seeking positions as agents, teachers, matrons, school superintendents, nurses, and physicians in the Indian Service would be required to pass competitive examinations before being appointed. While the new policy improved the quality of Indian agents, Indians themselves continued to hold only the most menial positions at the agencies. This pattern changed during the New Deal because a provision of the 1934 Indian Reorganization Act permitted Indians to gain appointment without taking the Civil Service exams. As a consequence of this shift, Indians began to be appointed agency superintendents (the title changed gradually after 1893). Among the first Native Americans to be named superintendents were Robert Yellowtail on the Crow reservation and Wade Crawford at the Klamath agency. By 1972 Native Americans held the majority of top-level executive positions in the Washington, D.C., office of the Bureau of Indian Affairs, as well as seven of the twelve area superintendent positions.

BIBLIOGRAPHY

Hoxie, Frederick E. *A Final Promise: The Campaign to Assimilate the Indians, 1880–1920.* Lincoln: University of Nebraska Press, 1984.

Jackson, Curtis E., and Marcia J. Galli. *A History of the Bureau of Indian Affairs and Its Activities among Indians.* San Francisco: R&E Research Associates, 1977.

Prucha, Francis Paul. *The Great Father: The United States Government and the American Indians.* Lincoln: University of Nebraska Press, 1984.

Schmeckebier, Laurence F. *The Office of Indian Affairs: Its History, Activities, and Organization.* Baltimore: Johns Hopkins University Press, 1927.

Robert M. Owens

See also **Bureau of Indian Affairs.**

INDIAN ART. *See* **Art, Indian.**

INDIAN BIBLE, ELIOT'S. Eliot's Indian Bible was a translation into Algonquian by John Eliot, a minister at Roxborough, Massachusetts. Eliot was one of a few ministers who had served as a missionary to American Indians in New England, and he had organized several "praying towns"—communities of converted Indians—in Massachusetts. Composed between 1650 and 1658, his was the first Bible printed by Protestants in the New World. In order to compose it, Eliot had not only to learn the language, in which effort he received help from many American Indians, but also to invent an orthography. Converted Indians on Martha's Vineyard used Eliot's Bible for more than a century.

BIBLIOGRAPHY

Cogley, Richard W. *John Eliot's Mission to the Indians before King Philip's War.* Cambridge, Mass.: Harvard University Press, 1999.

Morrison, Dane. *A Praying People: Massachusetts Acculturation and the Failure of the Puritan Mission, 1660–1690.* New York: P. Lang, 1995.

Perry Miller / S. B.

See also **King Philip's War; Martha's Vineyard; Massachusetts; Puritans and Puritanism.**

INDIAN BOARDING SCHOOLS. In 1769, Eleazar Wheelock established an Indian college in Hanover, New Hampshire, to convert the Natives to Christianity and civilization. While the founding of Dartmouth College predated the formation and growth of Indian boarding schools, the notion of "civilizing" the Indian was a robust construct that flourished for more than 150 years and became the cornerstone of federal policy on Indian education. The practice of removing Indian children from the "corrupt" influences of the Indian camp and placing them in boarding schools conducted by the federal government and various religious denominations became official policy after the Civil War and continued to varying degrees into the 1950s.

The number of Indian boarding schools grew rapidly after the Civil War in response to a new policy that emerged after President Ulysses S. Grant announced his new "peace policy," which placed the Bureau of Indian Affairs under the direction of various religious denominations who appointed agents, represented Indian interests, and established schools on the reservations. The federal government provided per capita payments and the land required to achieve the educational objectives of the Bureau of Indian Affairs and prepare a new generation of Indians for the realities of private land ownership and gradual assimilation into the dominant American culture. The ideas of cultural destruction, forced assimilation, and military regimen were popularized by Richard Henry

Pratt, who started the Carlisle Indian School in 1879, and became cornerstones of most Indian boarding schools in the United States. Regardless of affiliation, all Indian boarding schools sought to transform the Indian students by removing them from the reservation setting, teaching them industrial arts, converting them to European forms of Christianity, and inculcating in them a strong work ethic through the "outing system," which placed Indian students in work settings outside of the boarding school.

The curriculum at Indian boarding schools placed heavy emphasis on manual labor, industrial and domestic training, farming, English, and, depending on the sponsor, a large dose of religious indoctrination. The Bureau of Indian Affairs prohibited the use of Native languages, discouraged any manifestation of Indian culture, and limited contact between parents and students. Both government officials and church leaders favored boarding schools over day schools because the process of "civilizing" the students and converting them into sedentary farmers was easier when the influences of tribal life and indigenous culture were absent.

Between 1870 and 1930 the federal government and all of the major religious groups, especially Roman Catholics, established more than 150 on- and off-reservation boarding schools. Critics of the boarding schools and their curriculum argued that "the academic program provided at boarding schools precluded a successful transition to the white labor force and those who wished to return home discovered that the curriculum held no relevance to the reservation." The inadequate educational program and appalling conditions at Indian boarding schools were firmly documented in the Meriam Report (1928), which initiated a process of replacing boarding with day schools close to centers of Indian population.

The shuttering of boarding schools was accelerated when John Collier was appointed commissioner of Indian affairs in 1933. The passage of the Indian Reorganization Act in 1934 and Collier's commitment to fostering reforms in Indian policy significantly reduced the Indian boarding school population by the end of World War II. Community day schools, state-supported public schools, and nonresidential parochial schools were the dominant education institutions for Indian children by the mid-1950s.

BIBLIOGRAPHY

Adams, David Wallace. *Education for Extinction: American Indians and the Boarding School Experience, 1875–1928.* Lawrence: University Press of Kansas, 1995.

Ellis, Clyde. *To Change Them Forever: Indian Education at the Rainy Mountain Boarding School, 1893–1920.* Norman: University of Oklahoma Press, 1996.

James T. Carroll

See also **Dartmouth College; Education, Indian; Indian Policy, U.S., 1830–1900.**

INDIAN BRIGADE. The Indian Brigade consisted of three Union regiments composed largely of Cherokees, Creeks, and Seminoles. In 1862 Indians who were loyal to the Union fled to Kansas for safety and enlisted in two regiments. These Indians, together with some white troops, invaded the Indian Territory in the summer of 1862, where they were joined by a sufficient number of Indians formerly allied with the Confederacy to make up a third regiment. The brigade fought many minor engagements in northeastern Indian Territory.

BIBLIOGRAPHY

Abel, Annie Heloise. *The American Indian in the Civil War, 1862–1865.* Lincoln: University of Nebraska Press, 1992.

Hauptman, Laurence M. *Between Two Fires: American Indians in the Civil War.* New York: Free Press, 1995.

Edward Everett Dale / H. S.

See also **Cherokee; Creek; Indian Territory; Indians in the Civil War; Seminole.**

INDIAN CHILD WELFARE ACT (1978) brought national attention to the removal of American Indian children from their homes and subsequent placement in non-Indian homes. Prior to 1978, a disproportionate number (25 to 35 percent) of all American Indian children were taken from their homes by state social service agencies. Many of the children placed in non-Indian homes experienced loss of their cultural heritage and Indian identity.

The act regulates child custody cases involving American Indian children and shifts decision-making control from state agencies to tribal courts. Where abuse or neglect is substantiated and a child is taken into protective custody, the child is placed under the jurisdiction of the tribe and into the care of his or her extended family or of guardians who are American Indian. The provisions are designed to ensure that American Indian children are placed in homes that respect and understand American Indian cultural values. The act does not address the underlying causes of child abuse and neglect, such as poverty, alcoholism, or unemployment.

The law was challenged in the U.S. Supreme Court case *Mississippi Band of Choctaw Indians v. Holyfield* (1989). The Court upheld the tenets of the Indian Child Welfare Act in a landmark ruling by reaffirming the right of Indian tribes to retain exclusive jurisdiction in child custody cases.

The special emphasis placed on the role of tribal courts to decide child custody cases contributed to an expansion of tribal courts and social service agencies, and to unprecedented collaboration between tribes and non-Indian officials. Since passage of the act, fewer American Indian children are adopted into non-Indian homes. However, American Indian children continue to be separated from their families at a higher rate than non-Indian children. In many regions, there are not enough American

Indian foster families to take in needy children. Funding for the programs, staff, and facilities required to enforce the act continues to be limited.

BIBLIOGRAPHY

Jones, B. J. *The Indian Child Welfare Act Handbook: a Legal Guide to the Custody and Adoption of Native American Children.* Chicago: American Bar Association, 1995.

Josephy, Alvin M. Jr., Joane Nagel, and Troy Johnson, eds. *Red Power: the American Indians' Fight for Freedom.* 2d ed. Lincoln: University of Nebraska Press, 1999. The original edition was published in 1971.

Martha L. Chaatsmith

INDIAN CITIZENSHIP. Some early Indian treaties, such as that of 1830 with the Choctaw, provided for grants of citizenship to individual Indians. The Kickapoo Treaty of 1862 made citizenship dependent on acceptance of an allotment of land in severalty. Other treaties of the Civil War period, including that with the Potawatomi in 1861, required submission of evidence of fitness for citizenship and empowered an administrative body or official to determine whether the Indian applicant conformed to the standards called for in the treaties.

Following ratification of the Fourteenth Amendment in 1868, several Indian naturalization acts were passed by Congress. Most of them were similar to an 1870 law relating to the Winnebago of Minnesota. Section 10 of the Winnebago Act provided that an Indian might apply to the federal district court for citizenship, but had to prove to the satisfaction of the court that he was sufficiently intelligent and prudent to manage his own affairs, that he had adopted the habits of civilized life, and that he had supported himself and his family for the preceding five years.

The most important nineteenth-century legislation conferring citizenship on Indians was the Dawes General Allotment Act of 1887. The Dawes Act gave citizenship to Indians born within the United States who had received allotments, as well as to those who had voluntarily moved away from their tribes and adopted "the habits of civilized life." The following year, Congress extended citizenship to Indian women marrying persons who were already U.S. citizens.

Approximately two-thirds of the Indians of the United States had become citizens by 1924; in that year Congress passed a general Indian citizenship act, as a result of which all native-born Indians received full citizenship status. However, some states, citing the special relationship between the federal government and Native Americans, as well as a lack of state jurisdiction over them, denied Indians the right to vote until 1957.

Although in the past citizenship had been tied to the abandonment of tribal affiliation, by the early 2000s a Native American could be a U.S., state, and tribal citizen simultaneously. The United States retains the power to define who is and is not an Indian for purposes of determining who may be eligible for federal services, but the right of tribes to determine their own membership criteria has been upheld in court. Tribes use a variety of means to grant, deny, revoke, or qualify membership. Tribal citizenship is normally based on descent. Requirements vary from meeting a minimum degree of ancestry to tracing lineage to earlier tribal members.

BIBLIOGRAPHY

Cohen, Felix S. *Felix S. Cohen's Handbook of Federal Indian Law.* Charlottesville, Va.: Michie, 1982.

Frank Rzeczkowski

See also **Dawes General Allotment Act.**

INDIAN CIVIL RIGHTS ACT (1968), 25 U.S.C. Secs. 1301 et seq., was passed by Congress in an attempt to impose upon tribal governments certain restrictions and protections afforded by the U.S. Constitution. This represented a significant intrusion by the federal government into the internal affairs of tribes.

The U.S. Supreme Court had long made clear that although Indian tribes were subject to the dominant plenary power of Congress and the general provisions of the Constitution, tribes were nonetheless not bound by the guarantee of individual rights found in the Fifth Amendment. The most important decision affirming this principle is *Talton v. Mayes* (1896). Subsequent Supreme Court decisions affirmed the line of reasoning that tribes were not arms of the federal government when punishing tribal members for criminal acts and that Indian tribes were exempt from many of the constitutional protections governing the actions of state and federal governments. In the 1960s, Congress sponsored a series of hearings on the conduct of tribal governments and heard testimony regarding the abuses that some tribal members were enduring at the hands of sometimes corrupt, incompetent, or tyrannical tribal officials. The Indian Civil Rights Act (ICRA) was enacted in response to these revelations.

The most important provisions of ICRA were those that guaranteed (1) the right to free speech, press, and assembly; (2) protection from unreasonable search and seizure; (3) the right of a criminal defendant to a speedy trial, to be advised of the charges, and to confront any adverse witnesses; (4) the right to hire an attorney in a criminal case; (5) protection against self incrimination; (6) protection against cruel and unusual punishment, excessive bail, incarceration of more than one year and/or a fine in excess of $5,000 for any one offense; (7) protection from double jeopardy or ex post facto laws; (8) the right to a trial by a jury for offenses punishable by imprisonment; and (9) equal protection under the law, and due process. ICRA also stipulated that the writ of habeas corpus would be available in tribal court.

While ICRA included many familiar constitutional protections, it either ignored or modified others. The law did not impose the establishment clause, the guarantee of a republican form of government, the requirement of a separation of church and state, the right to a jury trial in civil cases, or the right of indigents to appointed counsel in criminal cases. Congress excluded these provisions because it recognized the unique political and cultural status of tribes.

The effects of the ICRA were substantial; by requiring tribes to meet certain standards, the law caused tribal judicial systems to mirror mainstream American courts and procedures. While the benefits to individual liberties were laudatory, the effect also homogenized tribal courts, and limited their sentencing powers.

In 1978, the Supreme Court dramatically limited the impact of ICRA in *Santa Clara Pueblo v. Martinez*. That case involved a request to prevent enforcement of a tribal ordinance denying tribal membership to children of female (but not male) members who marry outside the tribe. The petitioning mother claimed the ordinance discriminated against her child based upon sex and thus was a denial of equal protection and violated ICRA.

The Court held that tribal common-law sovereign immunity prevented a suit against the tribe. It concluded that Indian tribes are required to adhere to the substantial requirements of ICRA, but that in deference to tribal self-government, Congress did not intend for federal courts to oversee compliance with ICRA, except in habeas corpus proceedings or unusual circumstances. Since 1978 and *Martinez*, those persons who allege noncustodial violations of ICRA are limited to pursuing their claims in tribal forums. Generally federal courts play no enforcement role in any of the provisions of ICRA that don't involve the narrow review of the imposition of incarceration by tribal courts in criminal proceedings.

Proposals to amend the ICRA to provide for more effective enforcement by the federal courts have been made and remain controversial. However, any remedy must balance the rights of the individual tribal members with a respect for tribal sovereignty and self-government.

BIBLIOGRAPHY

Canby, William C., Jr. *American Indian Law in a Nutshell.* 3d ed. St. Paul, Minn.: West Group, 1998.

Johnson, Susan, Jeanne Kaufmann, John Dossett, and Sarah Hicks. *Government to Government: Understanding State and Tribal Governments.* Washington, D.C.: National Congress of American Indians/National Conference of State Legislatures, 2000.

O'Brien, Sharon. *American Indian Tribal Governments.* Norman: University of Oklahoma Press, 1989.

Sokolow, Gary A. *Native Americans and the Law: A Dictionary.* Santa Barbara, Calif.: ABC-CLIO, 2000.

John Low

See also **Indian Policy, U.S.: 1900–2000; Indian Political Life; Indian Tribal Courts.**

INDIAN CLAIMS COMMISSION. The U.S. Congress established the Indian Claims Commission (ICC) in August 1946 to adjudicate Native Americans' claims against the federal government for a century's worth of treaty violations, fraudulent land cessions, and financial mismanagement. Expected to last ten years, the three-member ICC operated until September 1978, when the U.S. Court of Claims reassumed jurisdiction over outstanding cases.

The impetus to create the ICC came from three main sources. Native Americans and white political leaders had been calling for a commission separate from the backlogged U.S. Court of Claims since 1910. Assimilationists intent on "terminating" federal guardianship of Native Americans hoped to eliminate a final legal and moral hurdle by "wiping the slate clean" of Indian demands for redress. Finally, federal officials wanted to address Native Americans' grievances as a reward for their contributions during World War II and to create a positive record of dealing fairly with America's minorities in the increasingly competitive atmosphere of the Cold War.

Nearly all of the 176 federally recognized Indian nations filed at least one claim before the ICC prior to the 1951 deadline. These filings produced 370 petitions combined by the court into 611 dockets. In most cases, Indian nations claimed the federal government had provided either inadequate or no compensation for land taken from them. Nearly a third of the petitions focused on the government's mismanagement of natural resources or trust funds. Ultimately, the ICC cleared 546 dockets and named

Indian Claims Commission. At the bill-signing ceremony creating the commission, on 13 August 1946, President Harry S. Truman turns to speak with *(left to right)* Senator Joseph O'Mahoney of Wyoming, Ute Indians Reginald Curry and Julius Murray, and Interior Department official Oscar Chapman. © Bettmann/corbis

342 awards totaling $818,172,606.64. These judgments ranged from several hundred dollars to $31.2 million.

Native Americans' experiences with the ICC were mixed. Many litigants resented the adversarial nature of its proceedings. Faced with the possibility of awarding billions of dollars, government lawyers battled to defeat the claims and refused to settle out of court. Both sides hired historians and anthropologists as "expert witnesses" to either prove or disprove aboriginal land title. Native Americans also objected to "gratuitous offsets," money the government deducted from awards for services rendered, and rightly complained that the awards did not include interest. In some cases, the government even stipulated how the awards could be spent before releasing funds to the successful plaintiffs. In addition, roughly $100 million went to attorney fees. Several nations did not believe justice could be found in monetary compensation. The Sioux and the Taos Pueblo rejected awards in the hopes of securing a return of their land.

Given the legal complexity, cultural conflicts, and political nature of the proceedings, it is not surprising that the ICC failed to satisfy every constituency. Nevertheless, in an important legacy of the claims process, besides the economic benefits, Native Americans gained valuable legal experience in asserting their sovereignty and in protecting their cultural identities, experience that continued to pay dividends into the twenty-first century.

BIBLIOGRAPHY

Churchill, Ward. "Charades, Anyone? The ICC in Context." *American Indian Culture and Research Journal* 24, no. 1 (winter 2000): 43–68.

Lieder, Michael, and Jake Page. *Wild Justice: The People of Geronimo vs. the United States.* New York: Random House, 1997.

Lurie, Nancy O. "The Indian Claims Commission." *Annals of the American Academy of Political and Social Science* 436 (1978): 97–110.

Rosenthal, H. D. *Their Day in Court: A History of the Indian Claims Commission.* New York: Garland, 1990.

Sutton, Imre, ed. *Irredeemable America: The Indians' Estate and Land Claims.* Albuquerque: University of New Mexico Press, 1985.

Wilkinson, Charles, et al. "The Indian Claims Commission." In *Indian Self-Rule: First-Hand Accounts of Indian White Relations from Roosevelt to Reagan.* Edited by Kenneth R. Philp. Logan: Utah State University Press, 1995.

Paul C. Rosier

See also **Indian Land Cessions; Indian Policy: U.S.: 1900–2000.**

INDIAN COUNTRY is a multifaceted term that historically has been used as a geographical designation, as a legal term, and as a cultural concept that encompasses the past, present, and future of American Indian people. It embodies the idea that there is "a place" for Indians. The existence of Indian Country, through the many evolutions of that term, represents an acknowledgment and agreement that Indian people will survive. It is a concession to the notion that the melting pot is not everyone's idea of the American dream, and that many Indian people desire to live in that place they call Indian Country.

The term "Indian Country," as a designated place and boundary line, appeared first in the PROCLAMATION OF 1763, the British edict that prohibited the survey, purchase, or settlement by colonists of lands west of the Appalachian Mountains. This Proclamation Line was meant to ensure that the Native tribes would be guaranteed sufficient territory so that trade and commerce, rather than war, would dominate Indian-white relations.

After its war of independence, the new United States saw the value of boundaries as a solution to ever-increasing conflict between Natives and non-Natives. Exercising its authority under concepts of international law and diplomacy, the United States quickly began negotiating with various tribes to secure treaties that established, among other things, borders between the United States and Indian Country. Many early treaties affirmed the underlying principle of the Proclamation Line, that the integrity and separateness of Indian territory would be maintained and preserved. For example, the 1795 Treaty of Greenville, signed by the United States and the tribes of the Great Lakes, demarcated which lands were available for settlement and which would remain the territory of the tribes.

The belief that America would include a place for its native inhabitants was also affirmed by the U.S. Congress in the trade and intercourse acts passed between 1790 and 1834, which governed white interaction with tribes in the newly reorganized Indian Country. As the non-Native population grew, the boundaries of what constituted Indian Country were continually changing and moving west, and by the time of passage of the Indian Removal Act in 1830, Congress had decided to eliminate any Indian Country east of the Mississippi River. By the end of the nineteenth century, Indian Country as a place had been fractioned off into the many Indian reservations dotting the United States, along with the area known before Oklahoma statehood as INDIAN TERRITORY. In 2002, American Indian reservations remain the most visible portions of Indian Country.

Congress's current definition of Indian Country dates from 1948. Essentially, it defines Indian Country as (a) all lands within the boundaries of an Indian reservation whether or not Indian owned; (b) all dependent Indian communities within the United States—that is, any land set aside by the federal government for the use, benefit, or occupancy of Indian people whether or not within the boundaries of a reservation; and (c) all "trust" and "restricted" allotments of lands for Indians whether or not these trust or restricted lands are within the boundaries of a reservation. This definition often determines whether jurisdiction in both criminal and civil lawsuits will be with the federal, state, or tribal courts. The definition also determines the applicability of many statutes meant to apply in some way specifically to Indian communities, such as the Indian Civil Rights Act (1968), the Indian Gaming Regulatory Act (1988), and the Native American Graves Protection and Repatriation Act (1990). Furthermore, in such civil matters as divorce, inheritance, taxation, child custody, and contract disputes, the question of whether the matter arose in Indian Country is important to the determination of rights and responsibilities when Indians are involved.

Reflecting the fact that the 2000 national census showed that well over half of the American Indians in the United States no longer lived on reservations, Indian Country has also come to stand for whatever area supports living, indigenous cultures. Whether at the American Indian Centers in cities such as Chicago, Minneapolis, Seattle, Los Angeles, and Oakland, at any of the more than one thousand powwows held each year throughout the United States, or at any place where Indian people gather in ceremonies or social events, Indian Country is wherever Indian spirit, pride, and community are found. It resides not only in law books and historical treatises but also in the earth of Indians' ancestors, in their homes, and in the hearts of Indian people everywhere.

BIBLIOGRAPHY

Deloria, Vine, Jr., and Clifford M. Lytle. *The Nations Within: The Past and Future of American Indian Sovereignty*. Rev. ed. Austin: University of Texas Press, 1998.

Oswalt, Wendell H. *This Land Was Theirs: A Study of Native Americans*. 7th ed. Boston: McGraw-Hill, 2002.

Pevar, Stephen L. *The Rights of Indians and Tribes: The Basic ACLU Guide to Indian and Tribal Rights*. 2d ed. Carbondale: Southern Illinois University Press, 1992.

Prucha, Francis Paul. *American Indian Treaties: The History of a Political Anomaly*. Berkeley: University of California Press, 1997.

John Low

See also **Indian Land Cessions; Indian Policy; Indian Removal; Indian Reservations; Indian Treaties.**

INDIAN DANCE. *See* **Dance, Indian.**

INDIAN ECONOMIC LIFE. In the two millennia before Columbus initiated continuous contact between Europe and the Americas, Indian economies were based on combinations of agriculture, fishing, hunting, and gathering. The horticultural practices of many gathering societies blurred the line between agriculture and gathering; Indians in many areas used fire and harvesting techniques to modify the productivity of the landscape for humans. As a result, berry patches, nut-bearing trees, basketry material, and forage for game animals were more prevalent than they would have been without human intervention. Indians of the Northeast woodlands practiced shifting agriculture as they rotated across the landscape, clearing the forest for fields of corn, beans, and squash around villages that moved every thirty to fifty years. Although they cultivated crops, they used the forest to restore soil productivity. In the desert Southwest, several large societies utilized irrigated agriculture; these societies went through cycles of growth and retreat as a result both of environmental and social changes.

Several areas developed sufficiently productive economies to support elite classes that controlled the economy and political system. In the Pacific Northwest, a title-holding class arose based on control and management of lucrative salmon runs. In the Mississippi Valley, an elite also developed, based in several large cities, of which Cahokia near present-day St. Louis is the most well known. At its height (in the thirteenth century), it had a population between 20,000 and 50,000.

These complicated local economies utilized long-distance trade for further enrichment; centers of trade were located throughout the continent—examples are on the Columbia River and the Dalles, at Cahokia on the Mississippi River, along the St. Lawrence River, and in the Southwest. The use of trade goods such as shell beads, stone tools, copper, flint products, and pottery has been confirmed in archaeological records; biodegradable goods were probably also traded, including hides, dried meat, canoes, cotton cloth, and baskets. Dried fish, oil, and human slaves were traded in the Pacific Northwest. Although markets and regional prices probably existed in the trading networks, actual exchange most likely invoked reciprocity rules that dominated in local economies.

Local economies were organized by many types of systems based on reciprocity and tied closely to the ecosystems in which the economies functioned. Leaders in most societies were expected to collect property and food that would be available for distribution to other members of the society, especially in times of need. Most well known of the reciprocity systems were the feasts used in the Pacific Northwest for distribution and governance, called "potlatches" by Europeans. The elite classes hosted feasts annually in order to celebrate family events (marriage, accession to titles) and simultaneously to generate recognition of property ownership and leadership authority. Fishing sites, small river drainages, and hunting grounds were held by "houses," groups of related kin who followed the directions of the men and women holding titles in the houses. Once the salmon harvesting and storing technology became linked to the house system two thousand years before contact, societies in the Pacific Northwest maintained their high population level and their way of life relatively unchanged until contact.

In the Northeast, Europeans after contact found that they had to enter into gift-giving relationships in order to conduct trade and make treaties with the indigenous people. The diplomatic and trade practices of the Iroquois Confederacy, for instance, linked gift exchange to peace making. Each town in the Confederacy had two sides ("moieties"), each of which shared food and other resources with the other. Women owned the agricultural land and organized horticultural production while men hunted.

Impact of Initial Contact with Europe

Because both the Old World and New World had developed different ways of managing their ecosystems, potential for productive trade and exchange of knowledge existed when European sailing vessels initiated contact. The New World had productive plants such as corn and potatoes, and valuable wildlife such as beaver and deer. The Old World had domesticated animals, metal tools, and wool cloth. Contact created huge changes in both worlds. Plants such as the potato participated in the agricultural revolution in northern Europe. The horse changed the Plains culture in North America.

Initial contact with Europeans led to the spread of diseases that decimated indigenous populations. The Atlantic Coast was depopulated all along its length. In the densely populated Southeast, for example, whole villages were abandoned. A consequence of this depopulation was that the first European settlers found land available for agriculture and found the tended countryside well stocked with berries and game.

During the seventeenth century, the remaining Indians and European settlers developed a lucrative trading system. Two of the main staples of the trade were furs in the north and deerskins in the south. The fur trade began late in the sixteenth century and lasted into the twentieth century. It was rooted in the demand for felt hats in Europe and was influenced by the competition for furs between the English and French (both with Indian intermediaries); by the establishment of large trading companies (among which the Hudson's Bay Company came to dominate); and by difficulties on the Indian side in defending the closed-access property systems that they were able to establish early in the trading system.

Throughout the postcontact period, Indians had difficulty excluding other Indians and non-Indian hunters from their lands; this inability to exclude others created "open access" to fish, beaver, deer, buffalo, berries, and other natural products useful to humans. An Indian community unable to exclude others from its common lands was unable to enforce conservation practices and the resources became depleted.

The problem of uncontrolled access to hunting grounds influenced the deerskin trade in the Southeast. In the eighteenth century, deerskins and furs were the fourth largest export from the British colonies, after tobacco, bread and flour, and rice. Trading in deerskins was profitable for middlemen and a significant source of tax revenue for colonial governments. With this large demand for the resource, controlling the hunting grounds was important, but proved to be difficult for Indians. The importance of hunting in generating income also increased the relative status of men compared to women, who tended crops.

Other changes also occurred as a result of contact with Europeans. Although Indians had domesticated many plants, they had not domesticated many animals. Animals introduced from Europe changed the options in hunting, gathering, and agriculture. The horse introduced dramatic changes on the Great Plains, inducing a move toward greater reliance on buffalo and less on agriculture. Sheep changed the use of the countryside among the Navajo, and cattle raising spread to California and the Southeast. Tobacco also became a cash crop in the region, allowing Indians to participate in the expanding system of commercial agriculture. By the nineteenth century, some southeastern Indians had even become slave owners.

Consequences of the Industrial Revolution

Although some believe trade itself degraded the Indians' power, in the colonial era both Indians and Europeans benefited from their exchanges. Indians participated significantly in both the fur and deerskin trades. After the industrial revolution began in England in the mid-eighteenth century, exchange between the continents did lead to faltering Indian economies. The resulting economic expansion in Europe and the Americas led to removal of native peoples from their lands. The open-access problems that had led to decimation of fish, beaver, and deer in much of the continent became a greater problem as the new capitalist economy expanded westward. Indians suffered because the sources of their livelihood were depleted and because the new governments of the United States and Canada did not recognize land ownership by the indigenous peoples.

After the War of 1812, the American economy began to grow rapidly and the non-Indian population began to flow westward. Fueled by the British demand for cotton, southern settlements spread first to the Mississippi, and then to Texas. Although the Cherokees had participated in the growth of the agricultural economy, and were strong competitors in the market, they were severely outnumbered and could not resist removal to Indian Territory.

Removal occurred in both the South and the North: by 1850 the United States east of the Mississippi River had very few resident Indians. The Iroquois of New York State mainly remained, and later joined the economy as laborers. Mohawks working in high-rise steel construction were well known. Other Indians on Cape Cod, Long Island, and in the rural areas of the South became wage laborers after having been displaced from their lands. This process of moving Indians to the margins of white society also occurred in California and the Great Basin.

Although many tribes had reservations in Nebraska and Kansas, in 1854 those states were opened for white settlement, and the Indians had to move to Indian Territory. In California, the explosion of white population following the discovery of gold in 1849 swept away a great many Indian communities and much of the Mexican hacienda system that had provided Native people with employment. Even as Indians in the Plains found that a reservation, once made, could be unmade, Indians in the Pacific Northwest were signing treaties that defined new reservations. Relying on salmon fishing and hunting, many of these tribes reserved their right to harvest fish and game outside of the reservations. These rights became compromised when open-access rules of harvest were also applied to those resources late in the nineteenth and early in the twentieth centuries. Salmon harvesting became industrialized as many salmon canneries were established on the Columbia River and in Puget Sound. On the reservations established from 1850 to 1890, Indians developed agriculture, as they were restricted from harvesting game outside of the reservations. For Indians in the Plains, open access to buffalo had led to the near-extinction of the species, and they had little choice but to find new sources of food.

The third main period of Indian economic history began with the division of reservations into individual landholdings, or allotments. This process accelerated following the passage of the Dawes General Allotment Act in 1887. Initially, the Indians' allotments were not to be sold, but by 1917 they were being sold in great numbers. On many reservations, lands not allotted were opened for non-Indian homesteading. On other reservations, the Bureau of Reclamation built irrigation projects, and on most of these reservations the best-irrigated land, often predominately Indian in ownership, quickly was purchased by non-Indians. Indians survived by working for wages or carrying out diminished subsistence activities, and through government support.

Early in the twentieth century, Indian ownership and control of resources fell to their historical low. Although the Indian Reorganization Act of 1934 ended land cessions, other policies accompanying the act allowed access to minerals and timber on Indian lands. After World War I, the few tribes that had built successful economies, based on timber and other resources, became the main targets for "termination" of their already diminished reservations. Some avoided termination, but many did not.

Revival in Late Twentieth Century

Fighting against termination began to create a resurgence of Indian political activity, which in turn lead to resurgence in economic activity. The 1960s brought both the end of the termination policy and the emergence of Indian activism, a process that was also encouraged by the civil rights movement. Throughout the 1970s, tribes began enterprises, and federal programs supported expanding reservation economies both with direct aid and indirectly through large housing programs. Under President Ronald Reagan in the 1980s, the supply of capital and resources from Washington to Indian Country shrank, but, simultaneously, some tribes were able to establish community-owned bingo and, later, casino gambling. This "gaming" economy became important for tribes located near large urban markets; such tribes became able to climb out of poverty. Other tribes, far from these markets, were not able to benefit from casino gambling. Many tribal enterprises—from farms to ranches to light industry and assembly plants—existed in other sectors at the end of the century. Private Indian enterprise was extensive; in 1997, the Census Bureau found almost 200,000 firms located throughout the country, with most in services (including entertainment and gaming), construction, and retail trade.

Although great change occurred in Indian economic life during the last five hundred years, Indian economies remained somewhat distinct from those of other minority groups in the United States. The 1997 Economic Censuses, for instance, were not able to collect data fully on Indians because the form of their enterprises did not conform to those of other people. No categories for "tribal corporations" or "subsistence hunters" were included, for example, and as a result, the census data was not complete. The persistence of these activities connected them to the precontact traditions of reciprocity in exchange and dependence on the continent's ecosystems.

BIBLIOGRAPHY

Barrington, Linda, ed. *The Other Side of the Frontier: Economic Explorations into Native American History.* Boulder, Colo.: Westview Press, 1999.

Boyd, Robert, ed. *Indians, Fire, and the Land in the Pacific Northwest.* Corvallis: Oregon State University Press, 1999.

Carlson, Leonard A. *Indians, Bureaucrats, and Land: The Dawes Act and the Decline of Indian Farming.* Westport, Conn.: Greenwood Press, 1981.

Littlefield, Alice, and Martha C. Knack, eds. *Native Americans and Wage Labor: Ethnohistorical Perspectives.* Norman: University of Oklahoma Press, 1996.

McDonnell, Janet A. *The Dispossession of the American Indian, 1887–1934.* Bloomington: Indiana University Press, 1991.

Moore, John H., ed. *The Political Economy of North American Indians.* Norman: University of Oklahoma Press, 1993.

Ray, Arthur J. *I Have Lived Here since the World Began: An Illustrated History of Canada's Native People.* Toronto: Lester and Key Porter, 1996.

Tanner, Helen Hornbeck, ed. *The Settling of North America: The Atlas of the Great Migrations into North America from the Ice Age to the Present.* New York: Macmillan, 1995.

U. S. Census Bureau. *American Indians and Alaska Natives: 1997 Economic Census, Survey of Minority-Owned Business Enterprise, EC97CS-6.* Washington: U. S. Government Printing Office, 2001.

Ronald L. Trosper

See also **Agriculture, American Indian; Buffalo; Dawes General Allotment Act; Fur Trade and Trapping; Indian Removal; Indian Reorganization Act; Indian Reservations; Indian Territory.**

INDIAN EDUCATION. *See* **Education, Indian.**

INDIAN INTERMARRIAGE. It is impossible to say when the first marriage between an American Indian and a non-Indian occurred. Perhaps it was a marriage with an American Indian ceremony. Surely it was between an American Indian woman and a man, probably a white man.

Over the centuries, Indian intermarriages increased. Colonists, fur traders, soldiers, and settlers, faced with a demographic imbalance of women of their own race, turned to Indian women as mates. More intermarriages occurred, however, in areas where the fur trade lasted longer, such as in parts of the Southeast and around the Great Lakes. Such unions were often frowned upon, eventually giving rise in some states to antimiscegenation laws forbidding marriages between whites and Indians or blacks. In response to the unions, the derogatory term "squaw man" was created, with the even more derogatory term "buck woman" created for white women married to Indian men.

As America sought to assimilate American Indians, intermarriages became more acceptable and frequent. In fact, one solution to the "Indian problem" was to dilute Indian blood (and Indian cultures) through intermarriage. In turn, tribes in propinquity to numbers of whites responded by bringing intermarried spouses into the tribe: the Cherokee constitution of 1839, for example, granted tribal membership to intermarried whites. In Canada, intermarriages produced a legally, racially, and culturally distinct people—the Métis. In the United States, unique, isolated groups developed, typically in the mid-Atlantic and southern states. Included here are the Brass Ankles, Cajuns and Creoles, Croatans, Guineas, Issues, Jackson Whites, Melungeons, Moors, Nanticokes, Red Bones, and Wesorts. The well-known LUMBEES could also be included in the list. In Oklahoma, mixed Indians and blacks were often designated as "red-black." In the Southwest and California, Spaniards and Mexicans—often racially mixed themselves—moved northward from Mexico and intermarried with native populations. In the missions that were established throughout the area, however, Indian women were forced into sexual relations without the formalities of marriage.

By the early twentieth century, intermarriages were becoming relatively common in some states. They produced more offspring than Indian–Indian unions, and U.S. policymakers realized that American Indians as a distinctive race might disappear through intermarriage and differential fertility. But as health conditions for "full bloods" improved, so did fertility rates. Eventually, the fertility of Indian–Indian marriages surpassed that of both Indian mixed marriages and the general U.S. population.

The American Indian population of the United States and Canada also reached its nadir of some 400,000 by the early twentieth century, down from more than 7 million around 1492. The American Indian population has increased since, more or less steadily, and in large part because of intermarriage. The 2000 U.S. Census enumerated some 2.5 million American Indians (plus more than 1.6 million reporting themselves as racially mixed); the 1996 Census of Canada enumerated some 800,000 Native Americans in Canada (554,000 American Indians, 41,000 Inuit [Eskimo], and 210,000 Métis). The total then becomes around 3.5 million (or around 5 million, if racially mixed Native Americans in the U.S. Census are included).

At the beginning of the twenty-first century, around two-thirds of all married American Indians in the United States were married to non-Indians, with intermarriage less prevalent in Canada. Rates varied by state and urbanization: they were higher in urban areas, lower on reservations or reserves; rates were higher in California and the Midwestern states, lower in Alaska and the Southwest and Northern Plains. If high intermarriage rates continue, at a future point American Indians may cease being a racial group and become an ethnic group with Indian ancestry and distinctive social and cultural characteristics.

BIBLIOGRAPHY

Price, Edward T. "A Geographic Analysis of White–Negro–Indian Racial Mixtures in Eastern United States." *Annals of the Association of American Geographers* 43 (1953): 138–155.

Sandefur, Gary D., and Trudy McKinnell. "American Indian Intermarriage." *Social Science Research* 15 (1986): 347–371.

Thornton, Russell. *American Indian Holocaust and Survival: A Population History Since 1492.* Norman: University of Oklahoma Press, 1987.

———. *The Cherokees: A Population History.* Lincoln: University of Nebraska Press, 1990.

Van Kirk, Sylvia. *Many Tender Ties: Women in Fur-Trade Society, 1670–1870.* Norman: University of Oklahoma Press, 1980.

Russell Thornton

See also **Creoles; Miscegenation.**

INDIAN LAND CESSIONS. In colonial America, France, with relatively few settlers, showed little interest in land acquisition and generally utilized Native negotiating forms—belts of wampum, Native-style councils, and formal alliances—to accomplish their diplomatic goals. Spain and England were more formally legalistic, and more interested in acquiring land. They preferred written agreements and adopted Native forms to "seal" their bargains. The great example of this practice was the Covenant Chain between Great Britain and the Iroquois. The European-style treaties negotiated by Spain and England proved advantageous in producing documents that could be enforced against European rivals and competing Indian tribes. During the eighteenth century, rapid European settlement and the improvement in European bargaining positions at treaty councils advanced the non-Indians' cause. Yet Indians still had the important option of playing one European nation against another in treaty negotiations, thereby avoiding trade or alliance monopolies.

With the rise of the United States after 1800, this key Indian negotiating tactic became more difficult to adopt.

Early Treaties

During the American Revolution, the United States negotiated a number of treaties with Indian nations, usually involving either alliance or armistice. Many of these early treaties reflected Native negotiating styles. But the treaty with the Delawares, 17 September 1778, proved a watershed. Utilizing legal language and enumerated articles, it set the pattern for most future treaties between the United States and Indians. It specified cession boundaries, annuity payments, and the roles of Indian agents and chiefs, and it was negotiated with an eye to European legal forms. This and subsequent U.S. treaties with Indians would be recognizable and enforceable.

In the years immediately after the Revolution, the rather weak United States had trouble controlling its western territory. Particularly troublesome to Indians was the assertion of settlers and government officials that the lands of the trans-Appalachian west, especially the Ohio Valley, belonged to the new nation by right of conquest from Britain. Britain had not consulted its unconquered Indian allies there before negotiating with the Americans, and these Native nations resisted American claims of hegemony. Indian military victories at Kekionga (modern Fort Wayne, Indiana) in 1790 and the upper Wabash (near modern Edgerton, Ohio) in 1791 forced American leaders to abandon the claim of conquest and instead to seek peaceful land purchases through treaties. Indian reluctance made it essential that the United States win a military victory to get the proud nations of the Old Northwest to negotiate. In 1794, the United States won the tactically small but strategically crucial victory at Fallen Timbers (near modern Toledo, Ohio). The victory, coupled with Britain's agreement (Jay's Treaty, finalized the following year) to evacuate its forts in the Great Lakes region, finally allowed the Americans to act. The result was the American triumph with the Greenville Treaty in 1795.

Negotiated in the summer of 1795 by General Anthony Wayne, the victor of Fallen Timbers, and hundreds of representatives from the Great Lakes–Ohio Valley tribes who had opposed him, Greenville set the precedent for subsequent U.S.-Indian treaties in the Old Northwest. The treaty required the cession of most of modern-day Ohio to the United States, in return for annual payments (or annuities) to the Indians. The treaty successfully inaugurated a general peace in the Old Northwest for the next fifteen years. It demonstrated that Indian lands would have to be purchased by the United States. Bribes and veiled threats of force, however, were prominent in Wayne's negotiations. The treaty also gave the United States a permanent method to use in later negotiations with these Indians, as annuities promised could always be withheld to obtain further concessions. Wayne's use of tough negotiating tactics and the ability to play one tribe's jealousies against another's did not go unnoticed. They became trademarks of his aide-de-camp at Greenville, William Henry Harrison, when Harrison became governor of Indiana Territory in 1800.

Indian Land Cessions. U.S. government officials meet with Indians in traditional dress from two tribes: the Sauk and Fox (forced out of Illinois in 1804, and again after the Black Hawk War of 1832, and eventually onto reservations in present-day Iowa, Kansas, and Oklahoma) and the Kansa (compelled in 1825 and 1846 to give up most of what is now Kansas, then moved entirely to Oklahoma in 1873).

As governor of Indiana (which initially held jurisdiction over present-day Illinois, Michigan, and Wisconsin) and commissioner plenipotentiary for Indian affairs north of the Ohio River between the Mississippi River and the Appalachian Mountains, Harrison had a significant impact on Indian relations. Patriotic, ruthless, and enthusiastic about land acquisition, Harrison proved willing and eager to carry out the policies of the new president, Thomas Jefferson. In general, Jefferson urged Harrison to buy Indian lands and to use treaty payments to give the Indians the necessary funds to become yeomen farmers. While benevolent in intent, the philosophy was also self-serving. Jefferson foresaw that Indians would become indebted to American traders, and that debt would make the chiefs more likely to sell lands to the United States. Over the next seven years, Harrison carried out this program with both zeal and skill.

In a flurry of treaty councils from 1803 to 1805, Harrison purchased millions of acres in what would become Indiana, Illinois, and Wisconsin. Invariably, the Indians involved received pennies per acre. By law, the government sold public lands in the Old Northwest at auction for at least a dollar per acre. Harrison utilized many tough negotiating techniques. He repeatedly threatened to withhold the Greenville annuities until chiefs agreed to meet with him to discuss land sales. He became a master of dividing and conquering his opponents—often inviting only some of the tribes who occupied a tract of land and securing an agreement with them. When these Indians, often desperate for additional annuities, agreed to a sale (often for lands they did not even occupy), Harrison could use them to put pressure on other tribes or chiefs who resisted. Whereas Indians formerly used the rivalries of European nations to their own advantage in treaty negotiations, by the nineteenth century the Americans could exploit the rivalries between different tribes. Harrison's councils and tactics established patterns for future U.S.-Indian treaties.

Removal

While confirming the boundary between Britain and the United States, the War of 1812 also did much to redefine and clarify U.S.-Indian relations east of the Mississippi. The Shawnee chief Tecumseh died facing Harrison's army during the invasion of Canada. General Andrew Jackson crushed the Red Stick Creeks, Tecumseh's numerous allies in the Southeast. With these twin blows, Indians in the eastern half of the United States ceased to be military threats and became obstacles to be removed. As commercial agriculture came to dominate the economies of the midwestern and southern states in the postwar era, Indians came to be defined as marginal figures in American life. President Jefferson's old dream of integrating Indians into American society vanished, and the racialized ideal of separating Indians and Americans took hold.

The removal period of the 1830s, most commonly associated with Andrew Jackson's presidency, offers the clearest example of the newly racialized concept of Indian relations and produced a new generation of land cessions. Most of the Five Civilized Tribes of the Southeast, the Cherokees, Choctaws, Chickasaws, Creeks, and Seminoles, had not opposed the United States during the War of 1812, and some had actively aided the United States against the Red Stick Creek faction. By the 1820s, the majority of them lived on small farms not unlike those of their white neighbors, and some had even adapted to plantation agriculture and owned slaves. The Cherokees, in particular, seemed "civilized," having drafted their own constitution and developed their own alphabet. The citizens of Georgia, however, remained determined to acquire Cherokee lands, and Jackson (president from 1829 to 1837) sympathized with Georgia. Further, he feared antagonizing other southern states in the midst of the budding nullification crisis with South Carolina, and supported the state's claims against the Cherokees. President Jackson approved the Removal Act of 1830, which authorized the chief executive to negotiate with all eastern tribes to secure their removal to lands west of the Mississippi. The Cherokees fought this act in court but they were unsuccessful.

By 1840, removal treaties (and subsequent forced relocations) had affected the Creeks, Choctaws, Chickasaws, and Seminoles in the Southeast, and the Miamis, Potawatomis, Kickapoos, and others in the Midwest. After the Cherokees' attempts at legal redress had failed, the other Civilized Tribes had little hope of resisting the pressure to cede their lands. The poorly organized, inadequately provisioned marches west, on which many Indians died of hunger, disease, and exposure, became known as the Trail of Tears. A faction of the Seminoles in Florida, under Chief Osceola, resisted removal by waging a guerrilla campaign and were never completely evicted from their lands.

Reservations

The removal era created the official view that Indians were backward peoples who could not coexist with whites. The government created the Bureau of Indian Affairs (BIA) in 1834 to deal with such people. Indians needed to be separated from the American population and confined to "colonies" where they could learn the arts of "civilization." Soon, colonies came to mean reservations. A further shift took place in 1849, when Indian affairs were transferred from the War Department to the Department of the Interior and inaugurated a new cycle of land cessions.

In the 1850s, the BIA held a firm commitment to the reservation policy. George Manypenny, who became the BIA's commissioner in 1853, argued that only by establishing permanent, fixed homes for Indians could they hope to adjust to American-style agriculture and the American doctrine of private property. Manypenny proposed a policy of allotment in severalty, in which reservations would be divided into individual plots of land that would be assigned to individual tribal members. Manypenny also sought to end the permanent cash annuity system, arguing that it was counter to the civilizing process. Instead, he proposed paying in animal stock, goods, or agricultural implements. These payments would diminish over time, forcing Indians to become self-sufficient. Manypenny personally negotiated nine treaties as commissioner; each implemented his plan with a different group and produced yet another round of land cessions, lending further weight to his influence on Indian policy.

The post–Civil War years saw a continuation of the policy of forcing tribes to cede large tracts of land in exchange for a clear title to a "reservation." In 1867, Congress authorized creation of the Indian Peace Commission, which attempted to implement this policy over a vast area of the West. Government officials hoped their efforts would secure a safe route for the new transcontinental railway as well as provide support for Indians as they adapted to new conditions. However, if Indians refused these measures, the commission would recommend force to suppress any resistance.

Initially, the Peace Commission gained some success through treaties at Medicine Lodge Creek, Kansas, and Fort Laramie, Wyoming, in 1867 and 1868. These treaties assigned reservations to several tribes and, in an admission of Indian military prowess, dismantled some American forts along the Bozeman Trail in Wyoming and Montana. The success of these treaties was matched by the 1868 treaty with the Navajos. Although the latter was

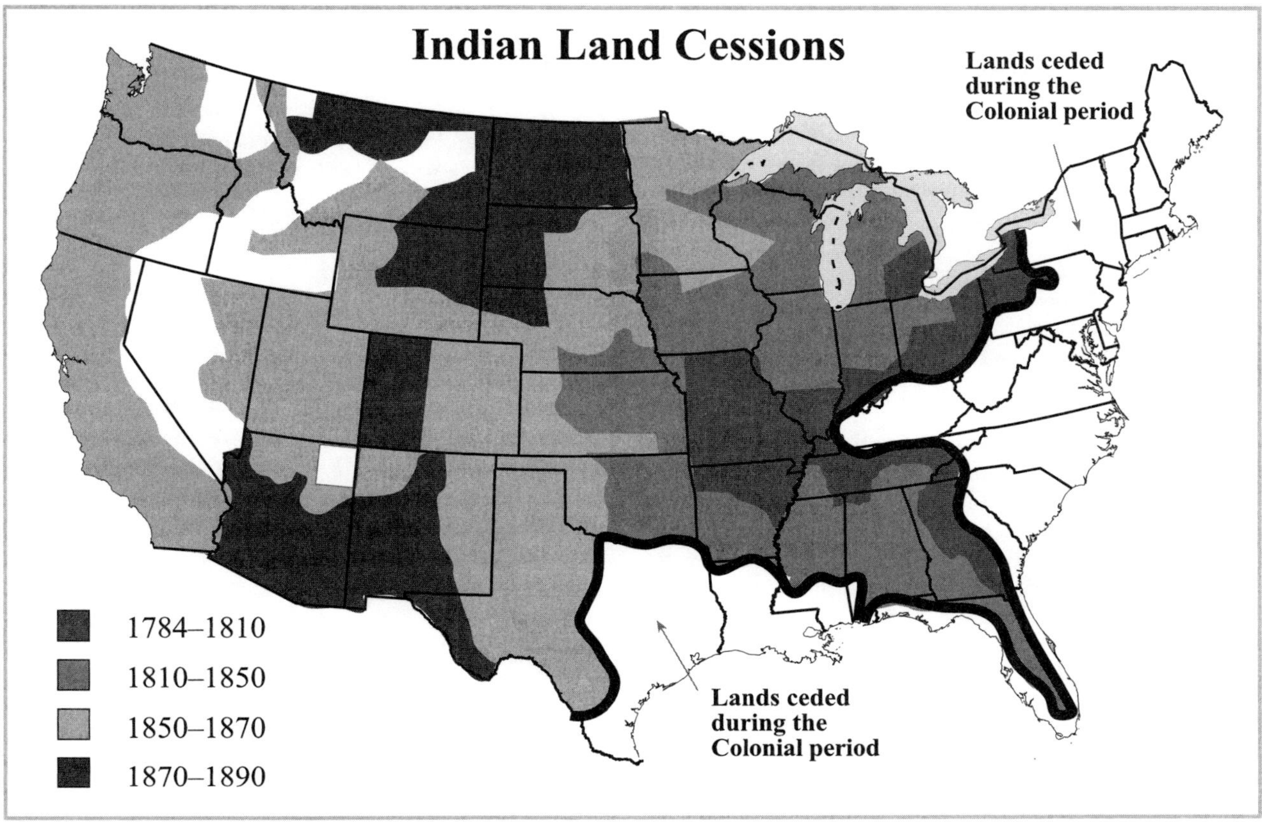

negotiated by the army, rather than the Peace Commission, it reflected the civilizing goals of peace, the creation of an Indian reservation, and annuity payments in goods and livestock rather than in cash.

By the 1870s, many reformers sought to do away with the treaty system, arguing that the balance of power between the United States and Indian tribes was now too skewed to allow for fair negotiations. In a rider to the Indian Appropriations Bill of 1871, the House of Representatives officially abandoned the practice of treating with Indian nations. Existing treaties, however, remained in effect. While 1871 marked the end of official "treaties," these were simply replaced by "agreements," or treaties by another name. The last major such document, the Great Sioux Agreement of 1889, split and reduced the Sioux reservations in North and South Dakota.

Allotment

In 1887, the Dawes General Allotment Act became law. Named for Senator Henry L. Dawes, chair of the Senate's Committee on Indian Affairs, the act authorized the president to allot each Indian head of household a section of land, usually 160 acres, and the new landholder would become a U.S. citizen. Once all Indian households were allotted their lands, the government could sell the surplus land to the public. Initially hailed by well-meaning reformers, the Dawes Act proved a disaster for Indians. Tribes were unable to slow the pace of allotment, and they had little influence on the price they were paid for their "surplus" lands. Following the Supreme Court's *Lone Wolf* decision in 1903, Congress could act unilaterally to seize these lands without compensation. In the allotment era, those who could not or would not become independent farmers suffered miserably. Revisions in the law allowing Indians to lease their lands helped briefly, but did nothing to encourage economic development among them. While Indians had held 155,632,312 acres of land in 1881, by 1900 they held just 77,865,373. Designed to make Indians independent, the Dawes Act instead cut them off from many traditional, communal means of support. The allotment system was largely dismantled in the 1930s under the leadership of President Franklin D. Roosevelt's commissioner of Indian affairs, John Collier.

Indian Land Claims

Since World War II, Indian tribes have successfully asserted their claims to land in several parts of the country. Many have been successful in reclaiming their collective rights, including those to land and the natural resources contained therein. The Indian Claims Commission Act of 1946 provided for a special tribunal to whom Indians might (within a five-year window) bring legal grievances against the U.S. government. The commission was not authorized to return lands to Indians, but $818 million was awarded to the tribes in compensation for past misdealing before the tribunal was dissolved in 1978.

Other tribes filed suits in U.S. courts. The Sioux tribe pursued claims to the Black Hills through the U.S. Court of Claims for decades. In 1980, the Supreme Court in *United States v. Sioux Nation of Indians* (1980) awarded them $100 million for these lands, but the Sioux rejected this offer. Other tribes pursued a congressional solution to their grievances. The Passamaquoddy and Penobscot tribes of Maine succeeded in winning $27 million (held in trust by the secretary of the Interior) following their legal challenge to an early nineteenth-century treaty. Alaskan Natives (supported by energy companies eager to gain access to oil) won nearly $1 billion and 45 million acres in the Alaska Native Claims Settlement Act (1971). Other cases remain unresolved. In *County of Oneida v. Oneida Indian Nation* (1985), the Supreme Court ruled 5–4 that Indians' right of occupancy to their lands was equal to whites' ownership in fee simple. Further, the Oneidas' sale of the land in question to the state of New York in 1795 was invalid because Indian land cessions were a question of federal jurisdiction. Subsequent negotiations with the state of New York over compensation for this illegal seizure remain unresolved.

BIBLIOGRAPHY

Deloria, Vine, Jr., and Raymond J. DeMallie, eds. *Documents of American Indian Diplomacy: Treaties, Agreements, and Conventions, 1775–1979.* Vol. 1. Norman: University of Oklahoma Press, 1999.

Esarey, Logan, ed. *The Messages and Letters of William Henry Harrison, 1800–1811.* Vol. 1. New York: Arno Press, 1975.

Goebel, Dorothy Burne. *William Henry Harrison: A Political Biography.* Indianapolis: Historical Bureau of the Indiana Library and Historical Department, 1926.

Horsman, Reginald. *Expansion and American Indian Policy, 1783–1812.* East Lansing: Michigan State University Press, 1967.

Hoxie, Frederick E. *A Final Promise: The Campaign to Assimilate the Indians, 1880–1920.* Lincoln: University of Nebraska Press, 1984.

Kappler, Charles J., ed. *Indian Treaties 1778–1883.* New York: Interland, 1972.

Philp, Kenneth R. *John Collier's Crusade for Indian Reform, 1920–1954.* Tucson: University of Arizona Press, 1977.

Prucha, Francis Paul. *The Great Father: The United States Government and the American Indians.* 2 vols. Lincoln: University of Nebraska Press, 1984.

Sugden, John. *Tecumseh: A Life.* New York: Henry Holt, 1997.

Sutton, Imre, ed. *Irredeemable America: The Indians' Estate and Land Claims.* Albuquerque: University of New Mexico Press, 1985.

Sword, Wiley. *President Washington's Indian War: The Struggle for the Old Northwest, 1790–1795.* Norman: University of Oklahoma Press, 1985.

Wilkinson, Charles F. *American Indians, Time, and the Law: Native Societies in a Modern Constitutional Democracy.* New Haven, Conn.: Yale University Press, 1987.

Robert M. Owens

See also **Alaska Native Claims Settlement Act; Cherokee Nation Cases; Dawes General Allotment Act; Greenville Treaty; Indian Claims Commission; Indian Policy, U.S.: 1775–1830, 1830–1900, 1900–2000; Indian Removal; Indian Reservations; Indian Treaties; *Lone Wolf v. Hitchcock;* Removal Act of 1830; Trail of Tears;** *and vol. 9:* **Fort Laramie Treaty of 1851; Life of Ma-ka-tai-me-she-kai-kiak, or Black Hawk.**

INDIAN LANGUAGES. Language is central to Indian identity. Although there are exceptions, in general, aboriginal group identity corresponded to the language that its members spoke. This tradition continues in that tribal designations often refer to language, even though in some cases few if any of its members may know the language.

At the time of the European contact, some 300 languages are estimated to have been in use among the indigenous habitants of the area north of Mexico and a surprisingly large number of these survive to the present day. In the 1990 U.S. census, 136 such languages were identified as household languages by respondents. Although census figures may involve overreporting and underreporting of both languages and their numbers of speakers, by adding in a conservative additional figure for languages found only in Canada, it can be asserted that perhaps half of the estimated number at the European contact are still in use.

Classification and History

The starting point for discussions of Indian languages is usually their relationships to one another or their classification. The primacy of this concern grows out of the tradition of historical and comparative linguistics, particularly with respect to many European languages in the Indo-European family. The success of the Indo-European tradition is based to some extent on the availability of data over time (as much as four thousand years) in some of the languages. Since no comparable record exists for Indian languages, however, their relationships and their classification have been more problematical.

Early students of Indian languages included Thomas Jefferson, who engaged in fieldwork and asked Meriwether Lewis and William Clark to bring back information on the languages of the tribes they encountered on the 1804–1806 expedition. Albert Gallatin, Jefferson's secretary of the Treasury, is also credited with later making the first serious attempt at a comprehensive classification. The definitive classification of Indian languages was produced by the Bureau of American Ethnology under the leadership of John Wesley Powell in 1891 and recognized fifty-eight distinct language families. Since then, generally accepted modifications of the Powell classification have been made that involve mergers of languages and groups with other groups and other rearrangements. However, the view of a large number (more than fifty, including isolates) of distinct language groups in North America has remained the orthodox one. There have, however, been attempts to reduce radically the number to as few as three stocks for the entire New World by postulating remote relations showing genetic unity among numbers of the Powellian families. This has led to considerable and sometimes acrimonious debate among experts. Substantial progress has been made in determining the internal relations within families and relating these to prehistoric and historic migrations. Advances have also been made in the reconstruction of earlier stages of the languages.

It is important to note that genetic classification of languages does not necessarily correspond to other classifications such as geographic or cultural. The geographic diversity of the Algonquian languages, which are spread over a huge part of the North American continent in several noncontiguous locations, including the high plains and both the east and west coasts, illustrates this well. Another kind of linguistic relationship among languages is illustrated by the Pueblo languages, which derive from three quite distinct families but show parallel patterns of expression and use because of the close geographic and cultural relations of their speakers. This kind of nongenetic relationship is called a linguistic area.

Writing

Although Indians recorded information using pictograms before contact with Europeans, they had no writing in the sense of a graphic system with which to directly represent language. The singular accomplishment of the Cherokee Sequoyah, who created a syllabary for his language in the early nineteenth century, is without parallel within the Indian world. Writing systems using the Latin alphabet and, in the case of Cree and Ojibwe, a geometric syllabary were developed initially by white missionaries and anthropologists, but Native speakers have taken responsibility for promulgating standardized orthographies. The strong tradition of orality has given many Indian languages as rigorous a set of conventions about usage as exists for formal, written English.

Language and Culture

Central to any discussion of Indian languages is the relationship between language and culture. Here, the focus has been the debate on the hypothesis associated with the linguist Edward Sapir and his student Benjamin Lee Whorf that language can determine ways in which its speakers view the world. Early evidence given by Whorf in support of the hypothesis has been rejected as untenable, but the debate continues to surface in scholarly discussions.

There can be no doubt, however, that Native culture is richly reflected in the Indian languages. Elaborate kinship systems found in these languages not only illustrate specific views of kinship, but also show the centrality of such relations to Indian life. Native systems of classification for the natural world are often subtle and complex.

American English has been greatly enriched by borrowing from Indian languages. Aside from the many place names, the two most commons types of borrowing are terms for native flora and fauna and for objects and concepts of the Native culture.

Prospects

At the start of the twenty-first century, all North American indigenous languages were classified as endangered. Navajo had by far the largest number of speakers, about 150,000, while most had fewer than 1,000, and many had only a very small number of elderly speakers. The most devastating influence was the pressure of the anglophone milieu in which Indians lived, under which only a small percentage of Indian children learned to speak their Native language at home. This led tribes to introduce ambitious programs of language maintenance and renewal as they took control of their education systems from preschool through graduate school.

BIBLIOGRAPHY

Campell, Lyle. *American Indian Languages: The Historical Linguistics of Native America.* Oxford: Oxford University Press, 1997.

Campbell, Lyle, and Marianne Mithun, eds. *The Languages of Native America.* Austin: University of Texas Press, 1979.

Ives, Goddard, ed. *The Handbook of North American Indians.* Vol. 17, *Languages.* Washington, D.C.: Smithsonian Institution Press, 1995.

Mithun, Marianne. *The Languages of Native North America.* Cambridge, U.K.: Cambridge University Press, 1999.

Silver, Shirley, and Wick R. Miller. *American Indian Languages: Cultural and Social Contexts.* Tucson: University of Arizona Press, 1997.

Gary Bevington

See also **Ethnology, Bureau of American; Education, Indian; Indian Oral Literature; Indian Oratory.**

INDIAN MEDICINE. *See* **Medicine, Indian.**

INDIAN MISSIONS represented an important form of contact between Indians and Europeans from the 1500s through the 1900s. No Native group escaped contact with Euro-American Christians seeking to restructure and transform Native beliefs and societies into Christian ones. Mission work provided the underpinnings of conquest for all three major European groups and the Americans: Spanish Catholics, French Catholics, English Puritans, and American Protestants. All saw the missions as a means to convert the Indians not only to Christianity but also to the missionaries' culture and society. Most apparently successful missions operated where Native culture had been decimated by disease and warfare. And through their writings, dictionaries, and other printed works, all missionaries ended up preserving cultural aspects of Native cultures.

The Rise and Decline of Missions: An Overview

The earliest missions to the Indians were Spanish and French Catholic and were staffed by the holy orders (Jesuit, Franciscan, and Augustinian). The monarchs of Spain sponsored their missions while those of France merely tolerated their own. By 1760, their missions had spread throughout the Spanish borderlands and New Spain. In the 1650s, John Eliot, an English Puritan, began PRAYING TOWNS in Massachusetts Bay. By 1717, small missions also became established in the southern colonies. Other efforts followed, including those of the American Board of Commissioners for Foreign Missions (Presbyterian-Congregationalist), the Missionary Society of the Methodist Episcopal Church, the Baptist Missionary Union, and other Protestant groups. The Presbyterian-Congregationalists ran the largest of the American missions, followed by the Methodists and then the Baptists. Protestant missionaries often remained blissfully unaware that many of the groups with whom they worked had already been exposed to Christianity through Catholic missions.

By the 1850s, the Protestant missionary societies had begun to ask the U.S. government to subsidize the mission system. It supplied money for teachers, equipment, and buildings. In return, it expected a pacified and cleared frontier. Because of their reliance on government money, some Protestant missionary societies and individual missionaries, like the Episcopal Bishop Henry Whipple of the Dakotas, became great advocates for the Indians to Congress. But groups like the INDIANS RIGHTS ASSOCIATION, founded in 1882, fought for what the missionaries wanted, not necessarily what the Indians wanted. Some missionary groups abandoned mission work to the Indians. Although the Presbyterians split over slavery, they maintained a steady mission presence. But as the Methodist and Baptist missionary societies split over missionary activity, both reduced the number of their missions.

The close relationship between the Protestant missionary societies and the federal government reached a pinnacle during the Peace Policy, which President Ulysses S. Grant established in 1869. It essentially turned the BUREAU OF INDIAN AFFAIRS over to Christian missionaries. Using the Society of Friends, or Quakers, as the leaders, Grant hoped that the policy would both reduce frontier problems and end missionary complaints against government policy. However, corruption continued and missionary groups fought over policy within the bureau. (Largely ignored, the Catholics formed their own Indian mission organization.) By 1876, the Peace Policy was dead and missions to the Indians were in decline.

From then until the early twentieth century, Indian missions were marginalized by the federal government so that they had to seek private funding. Their focus also shifted away from the Indians and toward groups outside of North America, as in Africa and India.

As Indians were forced onto reservations, both Protestant and Catholic missionary societies sought permanent inclusion within Native society through treaties giving the societies permanent land grants. However, as the government began to take over more of the functions previously filled by missionary societies, such as education, they lost influence both with the Native groups and the government.

The Southwest

Beyond the general history of mission work in the United States, regional differences existed. The Indians of the Southwest first experienced the mission system of the Spanish Catholics. Inspired by their expulsion of the Muslims from Spain in 1492, the Spanish sought to bring Catholicism to the newly discovered "heathen" of North America. They established missions throughout northern New Spain (West Texas, New Mexico, Arizona, and California). The Spanish Catholics structured their missions around agricultural work, spiritual work, and an aggressive transformation from Indian to Spanish culture. The Spanish missions suffered from a conflict of interest because their two sponsoring institutions, the church and the state, did not always agree about the fate of the Indians. The missions provided the Spanish with agricultural laborers and a way to secure the frontier. The Indians gained close contact with the Spanish, learning Spanish and Spanish ways. Although the PUEBLO REVOLT in 1680 disrupted New Mexican missions, those in southern California thrived. From the mid-1700s through the Mexican-American War (1846–1848), Catholic missionaries maintained a presence in California. After the war, American Protestants began to make incursions but had limited success converting the Indians.

The East

More competition for souls existed in the East. French Catholic and English Puritan missionaries invaded eastern North America with quite different approaches to the Natives and the mission system. The French Catholics lacked state sponsorship, while the Puritan state sponsored its missions. The French missionaries dealt with a vibrant mixed blood community of French trappers and Native women, both of whom often eschewed Catholicism. Without French military backing, Jesuits relied on the patience and support of the Indians they were trying to convert. The Jesuits tenaciously clung to their missions, in some cases for several hundred years, slowly achieving converts. While more tolerant of Native culture than the Protestants, the Jesuits emphasized the importance of the Madonna, given the importance of women in Native society.

The English Puritans worked with a Native population under attack by both the English and other Indian groups. Disease and warfare had decimated the Northeast tribes, leaving the remnants of some of the smaller tribes vulnerable to conversion. In 1650, John Eliot began establishing a system of praying towns. These replicas of English Puritan communities were intended to transform the Indians completely. Unfortunately, praying towns were also targets for English settlers when tensions erupted in the colonies. Angry English colonists attacked praying towns during many of the colonial conflicts, including King Philip's War in 1675 and 1676. Renewed epidemics and Indian efforts to migrate and build wider kin networks doomed these towns.

The Southeast, Northwest, and Great Plains

In the Southeast, Virginia and other southern colonies initially sought to convert the Indians. But when the Indians proved less than enthusiastic, the English abandoned the efforts. Overall, the English colonies offered some incentives for conversion. Converted and "civilized" Indians could own property and participate in trade and civic life. The so-called Five Civilized Tribes (Cherokee, Chickasaw, Creek, Choctaw, and Seminole) exploited these advantages by bringing in missionaries to help educate their people in the early nineteenth century. But Indian converts remained second-class citizens and vulnerable to changing political tides.

Indians along the Northwest Coast encountered Catholic missionaries through the French Canadian trading routes. While few converted, many adopted some of the concepts and language of Christianity, using French words to describe issues of sin and salvation. Protestants later took these words to mean that the Indians might once have been Christians. Beginning in the 1840s, American Protestants invaded in earnest. Marcus Whitman led a team of missionaries into Cayuse territory. With the tacit support of the federal government, he brought in white settlers. They, in turn, brought smallpox and tensions overland. In 1847, the Cayuse revolted against the missionaries, killing most of them, including Whitman, and attempting to eject the white settlers from their land. The Whitman Massacre galvanized the Protestant missionary movement to pacify the frontier by civilizing the Indian.

Later missionaries to the Northwest fought to outlaw large parts of Native culture, including the potlatch. Protestant missionaries, in particular, saw the potlatch as a waste of wage labor. With a growing number of Northwest Coast Indians working in salmon canneries and other industries after 1870, many missionaries hoped they would settle into Christian life. The potlatch defeated that purpose. American missionaries eventually convinced the U.S. government to outlaw the potlatch.

Unlike the other groups, the Great Plains peoples remained untouched by missionaries until well into the nineteenth century. The 1830s saw the invasion of Protestant missionaries, such as Stephen Return Riggs and Gideon Pond, into the Dakotas, Minnesota, and the Kansas-Nebraska Territory. They worked with both Plains Indian groups and those groups forced into the region by the federal government. Several of these missionaries became involved in policy, including Riggs of Minnesota and S. D. Hinman of the Dakotas. They acted as Indian agents and treaty negotiators, using their language skills to help settle the Indians on reservations, which the missionaries viewed as a necessary step toward Christianization.

BIBLIOGRAPHY

Beaver, R. Pierce. *Church, State, and the American Indians: Two and a Half Centuries of Partnership in Missions between Protestant Churches and the Government.* St. Louis, Mo.: Concordia, 1966.

Berkhofer, Robert. *Salvation and the Savage: An Analysis of Protestant Missions and American Indian Response, 1787–1862.* Lexington: University of Kentucky Press, 1965.

Devens, Carol. *Countering Colonization: Native American Women and Great Lakes Missions, 1630–1900.* Berkeley: University of California Press, 1992.

Higham, C. L. *Noble, Wretched, and Redeemable: Protestant Missionaries to the Indians in Canada and the United States, 1820–1900.* Albuquerque: University of New Mexico Press, 2000.

Kidwell, Clara Sue. *Choctaws and Missionaries in Mississippi, 1818–1918.* Norman: University of Oklahoma Press, 1995.

Vecsey, Christopher. *The Paths of Kateri's Kin.* Notre Dame, Ind.: University of Notre Dame Press, 1997.

Carol L. Higham

See also **Indian Policy, Colonial; Indian Policy, U.S.: 1775–1830, 1830–1900, 1900–2000; Indian Religious Life; Jesuits; Mission Indians of California;** *and vol. 9:* **A Dialogue between Piumbukhou and His Unconverted Relatives; Letter Describing Catholic Missions in California.**

INDIAN MOUNDS. Indian peoples built mounds made of earth in various shapes and sizes across eastern North America over several thousand years. These mounds were subjects of much speculation during the westward expansion of the United States, even though Thomas Jefferson had excavated one and deduced it to be the work of American Indians. Unfortunately, as the last eastern tribes were forced west of the Mississippi along the Trail of Tears, Jefferson's findings were forgotten, and the mounds were mistakenly thought to have been the work of a lost race of Mound Builders. That Mound Builder myth was finally laid to rest by the Smithsonian Institution's archaeologists in the 1890s, when Indian people were recognized to have built all of the mounds in the United States.

Archaeological discoveries in the twentieth and early twenty-first centuries reveal that many native groups built mounds down through the ages. Among the earliest were small burial mounds known from across the eastern United States during a period late in the fourth millennium B.C. called the "Middle Archaic." The Elizabeth Mounds site in Illinois has burials of men and women in a low mound dating to 4000 B.C., suggestive of large kin

Indian Burial Mound. This mound is in Marietta, Oh., a center of mound building dating back at least 2,000 years. LIBRARY OF CONGRESS

groups, sometimes called lineages or clans. Other Archaic mounds along the Green River in Tennessee and in coastal areas from the Carolinas to Louisiana date to the same time horizon. These mounds were often ring-shaped piles of mollusk shells. A similar series of mounds in northeastern Louisiana were made of earth. These include the impressive Watson Brake site mounds, ten mounds up to six meters high arranged around an elliptical "plaza" three hundred meters in length. By 1200 B.C., construction had begun at the unique "Late Archaic" mound site of POVERTY POINT in northeastern Louisiana. The main mound at that site may have been shaped in the form of a mythical bird of prey. This mound was twenty-one meters high and sat adjacent to a series of parallel loaf-shaped mounds and radiating isles or pathways arranged around a huge central space. The Poverty Point mounds suggest a level of sophistication in mound building not seen before this time.

Mound construction continued in places through the "Early Woodland" period (800–200 B.C.). In and around Ohio, ADENA mound-building groups produced centrally located but sparsely populated mound sites that usually included prominent conical burial mounds, some reaching heights of twenty meters. In the centuries that followed, during the period archaeologists call the "Middle Woodland" (200 B.C.–A.D. 300), mound building in the Midwest and Midsouth reached a new level of sophistication. Middle Woodland people sometimes built large flat-topped pyramids, huge earthen enclosures, and conical burial mounds. At the Pinson site in Tennessee, one four-sided flat-topped mound is eighteen meters high. It was probably a kind of stage that elevated a religious ritual or performance. In places like Newark, Ohio, earthen embankments were built in huge geometric shapes—circles, octagons, and squares covering up to twenty hectares of level ground. These enclosed spaces were probably sacred ritual areas. Processional avenues or "roads" led to and from these enclosed spaces. At other Middle Woodland sites across the Midwest and Midsouth, conical mounds were raised over the top of central tombs containing the bones of important people. The tombs beneath the burial mounds were sometimes crowded with the dead and their funerary objects. The funerary artifacts are often called HOPEWELL, named after a site in Ohio.

A lull in mound building, or a reduction in the scale of such construction, followed the Middle Woodland period in most places. However, in Georgia and northern Florida burial and platform mound construction continued during this "Late Woodland" period (A.D. 300–1000, with dates as late as European contact in some places). At sites named Kolomoki and McKeithen, archaeologists have found that prominent men and women directed mound building and mound-top use. In Ohio, the great Serpent Mound was built during this time, as were other effigy mounds—earthen mounds made in the shape of birds, snakes, and four-legged animals in Wisconsin and surrounding states. By A.D. 700 in Louisiana, Mississippi, and Arkansas, a new wave of mound building saw the construction of rectangular flat-topped mounds around large rectangular open plazas. These are so-called "Coles Creek" centers. In the Arkansas River valley, the site called Toltec has eighteen platform mounds and open plazas enclosed by a semicircular embankment of earth. However, like others of its type, Toltec was abandoned as a result of yet another new mound-building way of life that emerged in the Mississippi valley shortly after A.D. 1000. At that time, huge mounds were built at the site of CAHOKIA in southwestern Illinois. This huge construction effort marked the beginning of the "Mississippian" period, which lasted from A.D. 1000 up to European contact in parts of southeastern North America.

Cahokia appears to have been the only North American city-state ever to arise, a unique and extraordinarily large population center. Its largest central pyramid rose thirty meters above the surrounding floodplain of the mighty Mississippi. This central pyramid, called "Monks Mound," covered five hectares at its base, making it one of the largest monuments in the pre-Columbian New World (following pyramids at Teotihucan and Cholula in Mexico and Moche in Peru). Over a hundred more pyramidal mounds were clustered around Cahokia's many plazas, the largest of the plazas covering twenty hectares. These were, in turn, surrounded by neighborhoods of thatched-roof houses. Nearby were even more pyramidal mounds, most of which had four sides and flat tops. On their summits were built Mississippian temples, council houses, and the homes of important men and women. At Cahokia, and other Mississippian centers to the south, mound building was a regular, repetitive act that involved the entire community every year.

Numerous other Mississippian mounds are found at sites such as Moundville in Alabama, Shiloh in Tennessee, Etowah in Georgia, and Emerald or Winterville in Mississippi. Scores of such sites and their earthen platform mounds are testimony to a distinctive way of life that endured into historic times. Members of the Hernando de Soto expedition, in 1539–1543, and later European explorers and Euro-American pioneers observed that the mounds, the buildings on their summits, and even the chiefs and priests who lived on or took care of the mounds were sacred and highly revered. Mound building ceased shortly after European colonization and much was forgotten during the removal of Indian peoples from their homelands. Mounds remain as testimony to the rich and complex history of American Indians.

BIBLIOGRAPHY

Charles, Douglas K., Steven R. Leigh, and Jane E. Buikstra, eds. *The Archaic and Woodland Cemeteries at the Elizabeth Site in the Lower Illinois Valley.* Kampsville, Ill.: Kampsville Archeological Center, 1988.

Gibson, Jon L. *The Ancient Mounds of Poverty Point: Place of Rings.* Gainesville: University Press of Florida, 2001.

Lindauer, Owen, and John H. Blitz. "Higher Ground: The Archaeology of North American Platform Mounds." *Journal of Archaeological Research* 5 (1997): 169–207.

Pauketat, Timothy R. *Temples for Cahokia Lords: Preston Holder's 1955–1956 Excavations of Kunnemann Mound.* Ann Arbor: University of Michigan Press, 1993.

Russo, Michael. "A Brief Introduction to the Study of Archaic Mounds in the Southeast." *Southeastern Archaeology* 13 (1994): 89–93.

Squier, Ephraim, and Edwin H. Davis. *Ancient Monuments of the Mississippi Valley.* 1948. Reprint, edited by D. J. Meltzer. Washington, D.C.: Smithsonian Institution, 1998.

Timothy R. Pauketat

See also **Archaeology and Prehistory of North America.**

INDIAN MUSIC. *See* **Music: Indian.**

INDIAN ORAL LITERATURE nurtures and explores the connections native peoples see in the entire web of living and inert members. Rooted in both the land and the language, stories, in all their forms, relate people and species to their places of abode. These stories provide entertainment and education; they include informal accounts of personal events and nightly bedtime and just-so stories about how animals got their present colors, tails, behaviors, and such, as well as formally recited epics, which depict the creation of the world and other events, and take days or months to complete. In ancient times, the crippled and the blind earned food and lodging by telling stories and spreading news in camps and villages. Their repertoire included foibles, tales, fables, stories, and myths, as well as epics of great formal complexity. While the word "myth" connotes the imaginary in contemporary English, literary studies define it as a kind of cultural explanation, and native people accord it the weight of scientific proof and cosmic rationale.

Origin epics are the most distinctive. Throughout the Americas, there are seven major types of origin epics, including Earth Diver, who brought a speck of dirt from the ocean's floor to enable the world to be formed; Father Sky plus Mother Earth, who begat creation; Emergence from an underworld; Spider weaving the world; Tricksters democratizing private resources for future benefit to all succeeding beings; Twins vying to create useful or harmful consequences; and Dismemberment of a giant (like the Norse Ymir), whose body parts become pieces of the world—the skull becoming the dome of the sky, the bones turning into stones, the hair to vegetation, the blood becoming water, and the organs into species. None of these epics is entirely unique to the Americas; for example Earth Diver is circumpolar and Father Sky plus Mother Earth appears through the Pacific and ancient Japan. Even Ymir presents the story of Adam in reverse.

Text

Although the content of a story will vary with each telling, its grammar and literary style make its form distinct. Often a story has a title, a beginning ("Once upon a time"), and an ending ("The End," "Tied up"). The narrative will rely heavily on dialog between the characters, each of which has a distinct style of speech, like that of the modern cartoon characters Elmer Fudd and Daffy Duck. Some of the characters will have particles added on to their words when speaking. In languages like Navajo, where physical shape and internal consistency, such as "bulky," "roundish," "granular," "bundled," determine noun forms, humor is supplied by misapplying these shapes ("roundish" instead of human for a hunchback). Similarly, the difference between knowledge gained first-hand and that which is reported vicariously alerts listeners to lies and deceptions. Indeed, the very appearance of a trickster figure, such as Coyote or Hare, tells children that whatever the trickster does is likely to be very wrong. In this way moral, lessons were taught but not preached.

Other literary devices include the repetition of events, often four times the lengthening of vowels for emphasis (looong), the inversion of the norm (cross dressing), and the use of words in archaic or baby forms. Additionally, the level of the voice is raised or lowered, and whispers, lisps, and emphatic silences are used. Mythic events are adapted to fit the particular moment of telling.

Native speakers also develop a keen sense of chronology within their literature. Among the Iroquois of the Northeast, three epics explain the creation of the earth by Earth Grasper and the twins Sapling and Flint, the founding of the Iroquois League (1400s?), and then the Good Word of the prophet Handsome Lake about 1800. Among Tsimshians of the North Pacific, a dozen such epics layered through time not only outline the history of their world but also explain the founding of key dynastic houses. Because the earliest epics describe a newly glaciated world, these layerings extend over at least 10,000 years. Each serves to convey an array of names to be inherited, of resources to be claimed, of house sites to be occupied by season, and of art works (crests) to emblazon all of these connections.

Context

The context of a story—the particular season, or the presence of certain listeners—greatly influences how it is told, when it is told, and why it is told. For example, most epics should only be told in winter, when the land is quiet and the people relaxed. But if a child is visiting a place where an important event once happened, he or she may be told the story immediately, so a connection is made between the people, the place, and the event. Different families have distinct versions of the same event or epic. Often after one family has hosted a feast and told its version in public, other families will tell their versions in private, so the contrasts are made clear. Support for contested versions comes from "proofs" on the landscape; thus, the telling of an epic at such a place reinforces a family's claims. Among the Abenakis of the Northeast, human society began after a Frog disgorged all the earth's water. The water ran over the landscape in a treelike pattern, each branch ending in a lake inhabited by humans who gained a closeness with a particular species. At each telling, families agree on the dendritic flow of the water but strongly differ on the specific pond and particular species at the end, insisting that it must be their very own. Thus, a bear family will culminate its account with a pond inhabited by bears.

Texture

The way a narrator uses phrasing to create nuances of meaning and suspense can enhance or diminish the quality of each recitation. Age, gender, and pedigree also bear on a narrator's style. All Native American children are told stories and encouraged to repeat them. Those exhibiting keen memory and giving enjoyable performances are trained for public roles. Such artistry requires a broad range of knowledge. For example, when blind and thirsty Coyote goes in quest of a drink, he keeps running into trees. The audience will be able to discern the habitat from the type of tree that Coyote has run into, and will suspect he is near water when he falls into willows or is in the hills when he encounters pines.

Zuni storytellers add details consistent with their archaeological past to enrich their accounts and create an ideal mood. Hatchways, cotton dresses, and stone tools, while not always strictly accurate, enhance the literary quality of a story. Such complexity and nuance characterize superior performances and gain recognition for a narrator.

Scholarship

Most stories translate easily from native languages into English, Spanish, Russian, and other foreign languages, though native speakers say much of the emotional quality is lost in translation. Modern publications of Indian oral literature regard it as similar to Western drama, with long performances presented as lines, scenes, and acts. Stage directions provide data on the actions and voicings used, while shifts in the actual typography—such as capital letters for loud phrasings, italic letters for soft ones, and blank spaces for silences—suggest more than the actual wordings.

Academics concerned with folklore, anthropology, linguistics, and literature have developed a variety of explanations for Indian oral literature. Storytelling releases social pressures, especially those among family members. Epics help rationalize the cosmos, providing a basis for ritual and worship. The stories give intellectual consideration to the ironies, contradictions, and conflicts that exist in all species. While some explanations have been faddish (such as solar myths spreading from ancient Egypt), the ones noted above have endured, because they recognize the creative role that stories play.

Studies that emphasize a story's performance and context examine the phrasings, the audience, and the narrator. The look of the printed page also conveys much about how the dramatic manner interacts with the rules of the language itself.

Studies of the text emphasize the intellectual, cultural, and creative concepts embedded in each telling, such as the full and intimate knowledge of animal behavior and changes in the landscape over centuries, as well as the text's actual arrangement as "measured verse." Culturally important numbers, such as four, seven, and twelve, are used to organize lines and scenes into satisfying wholes, much the same way that basketry, weaving, and knitting use patterning by numbers to create texture and design. Such artistry also helps to identify the many examples of "fakelore" devised by Euro-Americans in the interest of "romantic" or "bloodthirsty" images of native peoples. Lovers leaps, star-crossed lovers, heartless battles to the death, forbidden sacred mountains, New Age mysteries, and a host of such Hollywood projections have nothing to do with traditional literatures.

Yet a basic interest in "motifs" continues. No story, myth, or epic stands alone. Certain themes are so common they have their own titles. Among these are Origin of Death, Bungling Host, Flood, Orpheus, Star Husband, Rolling Head, Dog Husband, Sun and Moon Incest, and Virgin Birth. They often appear in similar forms in the folklore of other cultures. These parallels speak to the overall human condition.

The role and importance of these tellings, whatever type or form, within the domain of literature can be summed up in the Native reminder that "our stories were our libraries."

BIBLIOGRAPHY

Miller, Jay. *Earthmaker: Tribal Stories from Native North America.* New York: Perigee, 1992.

Thompson, Stith. *Tales of the North American Indians.* Bloomington: Indiana University Press, 1966. Reprint of 1929 first edition.

Jay Miller

See also **Indian Languages; Indian Oratory; Literature: Native American Literature.**

INDIAN ORATORY. In most Indian societies, skill with the spoken word proved crucial to a leader's effectiveness. Obviously, this was in part because Native Americans are traditionally an oral people. Also, the stress on oratory reflected the general absence of coercive power among the North American tribes. A chief relied on persuasion, rather than force, to direct events. Great chiefs were by definition effective orators.

European orators, accustomed to written notes, were especially impressed with Indians' powers of memorization. Utilizing natural metaphors and sometimes lasting for hours, Indian speeches were well calculated to impress their target audiences. For non-Indian audiences, Indian oratory, even when translated, was often misunderstood. Great speeches of Indian leaders became merely monuments to what whites saw as Indian backwardness and another reason for the Indians' inevitable demise in the face of white settlement. "Logan's Lament," the speech of a Mingo chief who fought against the Virginians during Lord Dunmore's War in 1774, is one such "monument." In a speech that was probably doctored by Thomas Jefferson, Logan grieved over the unprovoked murder of his family and promised revenge. Logan also admitted that his people were doomed to extinction. Such romanticized speeches have often been used to essentialize Indians and excuse conquest.

BIBLIOGRAPHY

Vanderwerth, W. C. *Indian Oratory: Famous Speeches by Noted Indian Chieftains.* Norman: University of Oklahoma Press, 1971.

Wallace, Anthony F. C. *Jefferson and the Indians: The Tragic Fate of the First Americans.* Cambridge, Mass.: Harvard University Press, 1999.

Robert M. Owens

See also **Indian Oral Literature; Indian Political Life.**

INDIAN POLICY, COLONIAL. In the territories that ultimately became the United States, no single national Indian policy emerged during the colonial era. Four major European imperial powers, the Dutch, French, Spanish, and English, implemented separate Indian policies over an enormous expanse of time and territories. These policies were influenced by the nations' respective agendas, the resources at their disposal, and the particular circumstances each encountered in colonial America. Furthermore, while each of these imperial powers articulated some broad policy principles, many of the local colonial authorities were ultimately as instrumental in the formulation and implementation of policy as the home authorities. Certainly, the distance between the American colonies and their respective capitals made communications between these groups difficult and often required local colonial authorities to unilaterally implement policy. Despite the multiplicity of factors and agendas at work, however, some broad generalities regarding the policies of the four major imperial powers can be observed.

Dutch Policy

The Dutch settlements were designed to further what has been referred to as their "seaborne," global empire. The Dutch first began to explore the region that would become known as New Netherland when Henry Hudson's ship, the *Half Moon*, sailed up the Hudson River in 1609. By 1621, the Dutch West India Company was chartered, and in 1624, the Dutch settled on Manhattan Island naming their outpost New Amsterdam. Within a few years, Dutch settlements had extended into western Long Island as well as through the Hudson River Valley region as far north as Fort Orange (Albany). These settlements were established to further Dutch international trade. Early on, the Dutch realized that beaver pelts were a marketable commodity in Europe, and that in order to procure furs, it was essential to secure the cooperation of native communities. The Dutch Indian policy was, therefore, focused not on political domination but on linking these Native communities to the Dutch global trade network. Thus, until the British ousted them from the region in 1664, the Dutch shaped their relationship with their native neighbors in accord with the needs of the fur trade.

To secure the fur trade the Dutch attempted to form alliances by engaging in traditional native practices of reciprocity. Outwardly, they appeared to accomplish this, particularly with their principal northern trading partners, the Iroquois Confederacy, who were able to procure the choicest furs. This relationship was based on an agreement the Iroquois referred to as a "chain of iron." In return for furs, the Dutch supplied the Iroquois with European goods (most importantly firearms) and assistance in their rivalry with the Hurons, who resided in the Great Lakes region and were the allies of and fur suppliers to the French. The Dutch also supplied the Iroquois with wampum. Wampum, essential for the Native-European fur trade, were small, polished beads, made from two types of hard-shell clams, and only manufactured by the local, indigenous peoples living around the Long Island Sound. The Dutch also took steps to secure a steady supply of wampum from the Algonquian communities of southern New England, particularly the Narragansetts and the Pequots. In the 1630s, the Dutch attempted to implement an exclusive agreement with the Pequots for their trade. To further their economic goals the Dutch in

1633 even tried to plant a trading outpost, "New Hope," on the Connecticut River near present-day Hartford. This tactic was ultimately unsuccessful. Additionally, in an effort to stave off competing imperial claims, the Dutch explicitly recognized the natives as the original and legal owners of the soil and required all settlers to acquire native title through treaties or deeds.

However, the Dutch approach was not seamless and each settlement had a great deal of latitude to deal independently with their Indian neighbors. For example, large-scale violence between Dutch and Indians erupted in 1640 when Governor Willem Kieft attempted to subjugate indigenous communities near New Amsterdam. He demanded tribute from Long Island and Hudson Valley tribes. When they refused, he sent troops to enforce his demands. Unable to enforce his will on these tribes through military action he turned to the Mohawks to mediate a solution. Diplomacy failed, however, and hostilities resumed. As a result the Dutch States General recalled Kieft (who subsequently was lost at sea) and ordered an end to this type of coercive policy. Nevertheless, until the end of Dutch rule in 1664, hostilities between Dutch settlers and their native neighbors broke out sporadically, particularly where settler encroachments on native lands were most rampant.

French Policy

The fur trade sustained the French colonial empire in North America. At its most expansive, New France encompassed modern Ontario and Quebec and included the entire Great Lakes and Mississippi River drainage regions. Ostensibly, the French entered the race for New World lands to spread the Catholic religion to the Americas, but more realistically they hoped to replicate Spain's experience in Mexico.

Neither Jacques Cartier's expeditions (1534–1536) on the St. Lawrence River nor other sixteenth century expeditions found the desired riches. However, at the end of the sixteenth century a trading post was established at Tadoussac at the mouth of the Saguenay River and soon followed by posts at Quebec City and Montreal. New France relied upon the fur trade and therefore depended on the cooperation of a network of Algonquin and Huron allies. Similar to the Dutch, the French readily entered into traditional native forms of alliance building through exchanging "presents" of European goods, along with military and social obligations, for furs. In particular the French very quickly became enmeshed in their allies' ongoing conflict with the Iroquois Confederacy, fighting sporadically with this group until the Settlement of 1701. Ultimately this French form of alliance building with native peoples extended well into the Great Lakes region and down through the Ohio Valley.

The French were never able to attract large numbers of colonists to New France, and much of the European presence there consisted of fur traders known as *coureurs des bois* (runners of the woods) who often took native wives and adopted the trappings of native life. French Catholic missionaries were also present. The missions became particularly important because they were placed strategically so as to form a kind of human border between the English New England and New York colonies. One of the hallmarks of these missions, particularly those founded by the Jesuits, was that they tolerated the use of native languages and many of the indigenous peoples' traditional beliefs and lifestyles. Thus, what developed between the French and their native allies was a policy that combined political, military, social, and cultural reciprocity. Surprisingly, however, the French never formally recognized native title to their lands and did not enter into the types of deeds and treaties for land that characterized the Dutch and English policies.

Spanish Policy

Spanish imperial policy in colonial America was perhaps the most complicated and varied of any of the European powers. This was due to the vast geographic expanse of Spanish colonial holdings, which at their height covered territory in North America within the modern-day United States, as well as all of modern Mexico, most of Central and South America, and even much of the Caribbean Islands. This article looks only at Spanish Indian policy during the colonial era in what is today the United States. While the boundaries of colonial Spanish America were quite fluid, it most consistently comprised Florida, Texas, much of the southwest, and California, and is often referred to as the Spanish borderlands.

In general it can be said that Spanish policy was based on military force and depended on overt cultural coercion. The most commonly used "tools" of this policy were military conquest and the planting of presidios (military garrisons) to secure a region; Catholic missions designed to bring native communities within daily Spanish cultural and social control; and the settlement of pueblos (towns) and haciendas (plantations) to bring territory under the dominion of Spanish colonists. Along with such colonization went two uniquely colonial Spanish American institutions known as the encomienda and repartimento. The encomienda system involved the forced assignment of natives to work in mines and on plantations. Theoretically, in exchange for this labor the recipients were to pay taxes and provide their workers with instruction in the Catholic faith. The reality was usually far different. The most prevalent institution, however, in the Spanish borderlands was the repartimento, which mandated indigenous communities to supply a labor force to meet local colonial labor needs.

Typical of Spanish rule in the borderlands was the experience of the Pueblos in the Southwest, an agricultural people famous today for their apartment-like dwellings. In 1598, the Pueblos were invaded by a military expedition led by the Spanish conquistador, Juan de

Oñate. This led to the subsequent arrival of Franciscan missionaries, Spanish settlers, and the institutions of the encomienda and repartimento. In 1610, Santa Fe was built with forced Indian labor. The combination of a harsh tribute system and the attempt by Franciscan missionaries to suppress Pueblo cultural and religious practices caused great hardship for the Pueblo communities. It left the Pueblos stripped of their usual trading surplus and deprived them of the goods needed for traditional exchanges with their non-farming Apache and Navajo neighbors. The Pueblos' relative poverty led, in turn, to raids on towns by their former trading partners. Pueblo resistance to the Spanish system combined with droughts and epidemics led to the PUEBLO REVOLT of 1680. As a result, the Spanish were absent from the Rio Grande for a decade. Other areas of the Spanish borderlands experienced similar trials, but many of the indigenous groups in these areas were able to survive demographic losses and preserve their communities and identities.

English Policy

During the English colonial era, Indian policy was a complicated mix of colonial and imperial initiatives. Before 1755, local colonial authorities often took the lead in setting policy for each British colony. After 1755, this balance began to tip in favor of imperial-formulated policy. In that year, the British created two Indian departments in an attempt to regulate and control Indian policy and affairs. Unlike the French and Spanish, the English never focused on the conversion of native peoples to Christianity. Instead, despite some English missionary activity, the English were deeply influenced by the conviction that God had ordained America for the English.

The English made wide use of the treaty process. Very early in their dealings with native peoples, the English recognized title to the lands Indians historically possessed, and as with the Dutch, most individual colonies required some formal extinguishment of native title to perfect English title. By 1761 the British placed responsibility for such extinguishment with the British home government. The British Royal PROCLAMATION OF 1763 formalized this policy in the former French colonial domains. The ultimate English objective in their North American activities was to place ever-greater quantities of native lands under English possession and dominion.

The first permanent English settlement, Jamestown, Virginia (1607), pursued a policy of human and territorial conquest towards its native neighbors, the POWHATAN CONFEDERACY. This Confederacy consisted of some 15,000 Algonquian-speaking people living under the leadership of the werowance Powhatan. Relations between the two communities quickly deteriorated when the Jamestown settlers attempted to coerce their native neighbors to provision them with food and labor. From 1609 to 1610, the Powhatans nearly succeeded in starving the settlers out of existence. Only the timely arrival of reinforcements from England prevented the colony's demise. The two communities wavered between peace and war for almost fifteen years. However, by 1644, following a final and unsuccessful uprising, the Powhatans, ravaged by epidemics and warfare, finally submitted to the growing English settlement. From that time onward, the English settlers inhabiting the southern coastal regions pursued a policy of Indian removal, extermination, and enslavement. This policy was also replicated in large part in southern New England. In 1637, following their loss to the English settlers at the end of the PEQUOT WAR, the once-powerful Pequots were nearly annihilated and many of the survivors sold into slavery.

The Iroquois Confederacy's experience with the British, however, was somewhat different. In 1664 the English stepped into the shoes of the Dutch by virtue of their conquest of New Netherland. Almost immediately New York's colonial governor Sir Edmund Andros entered into an alliance with the Iroquois Confederacy called the "Covenant Chain." The Iroquois referred to this as a "chain of silver." The relationship between the English and Iroquois was an economic as well as a political one. By the mid-seventeenth century the Iroquois had become essential to the fur trade and their influence over other native groups extended as far west as the Ohio and even into the upper south. The Iroquois, particularly the Mohawks, assisted the English in suppressing many local native communities. They played this role in the New England conflict known as KING PHILIP'S WAR (1675–1676) and assisted the Virginia settlers in subduing the Susquehannocks after Bacon's Rebellion. They also served as a buffer between British America and New France, and despite minimal English military assistance engaged in intermittent warfare with New France until the Grand Settlement in 1701.

BIBLIOGRAPHY

Calloway, Colin G. *New Worlds for All: Indians, Europeans, and the Remaking of Early America.* Baltimore: Johns Hopkins University Press, 1997.

Cave, Alfred. *The Pequot War.* Amherst: University of Massachusetts Press, 1996.

Delage, Denys. *Bitter Feast: Amerindians and Europeans in Northeastern North America, 1600–1664.* Vancouver: University of British Columbia Press, 1993.

Richter, Daniel K. *The Ordeal of the Longhouse: The Peoples of the Iroquois League in the Era of European Colonization.* Chapel Hill: University of North Carolina Press, 1992.

Weber, David J. *The Spanish Frontier in North America.* New Haven, Conn.: Yale University Press, 1992.

White, Richard. *The Middle Ground: Indians, Empires and Republics in the Great Lakes Region, 1650–1815.* New York: Cambridge University Press, 1991.

Faren R. Siminoff

See also **Fur Trade and Trapping; Indian Land Cessions.**

INDIAN POLICY, U.S.

This entry includes 3 subentries:
1775–1830
1830–1900
1900–2000

1775–1830

U.S. Indian policy during the American Revolution was disorganized and largely unsuccessful. At the outbreak of the war, the Continental Congress hastily recruited Indian agents. Charged with securing alliances with Native peoples, these agents failed more often than they succeeded. They faced at least three difficulties. First, they had less experience with Native Americans than did the long-standing Indian agents of the British Empire. Second, although U.S. agents assured Indians that the rebellious colonies would continue to carry on the trade in deerskins and beaver pelts, the disruptions of the war made regular commerce almost impossible. Britain, by contrast, had the commercial power to deliver trade goods on a more regular basis. And third, many Indians associated the rebellious colonies with aggressive white colonists who lived along the frontier. Britain was willing to sacrifice these colonists in the interests of the broader empire (as it had done in the Proclamation of 1763), but for the colonies, visions of empire rested solely on neighboring Indian lands. Unable to secure broad alliances with Indian peoples, U.S. Indian policy during the Revolution remained haphazard, formed by local officials in response to local affairs.

Origins of the Civilization Policy, 1783–1800

At the conclusion of the American Revolution, the United States announced that it had conquered hostile Indian nations. In theory, all that remained was to settle treaties in which the defeated parties yielded to the demands of the victor. (The 1783 Treaty of Paris established peace between Britain and the United States and granted the new nation sovereignty over eastern North America, but made no mention of Native Americans.) The financial needs of the young Republic in part shaped this policy decision, for the United States hoped to use Indian lands to pay off the federal debt. Between 1784 and 1786, it signed a series of treaties with Ohio Indians that provided for massive, unremunerated land cessions. The treaties were disastrous for all involved. Indians protested vehemently against the cessions and made their point by attacking white colonists who moved aggressively onto their lands.

In light of these conflicts, Secretary of War Henry Knox reshaped U.S. Indian policy in 1786. Knox believed that the policy of conquest was both immoral and impractical. The United States had no right to take Indian lands without purchasing them, he said, and any attempt to seize lands would stain the reputation of the Republic. Moreover, the United States did not have the resources to fight Indian wars in the West. Knox instead developed a two-part plan. First, the United States would purchase Indian lands, which would be far less expensive than fighting for them. Second, the federal government would "civilize" Indians by instructing them in the economic and social practices of white Americans, thereby making them more willing to part with their vast hunting territories.

Subsequent treaties in both the South and the Old Northwest recognized Indian land title, but Knox's policy did not end hostilities. White colonists continued to stream onto Indian lands in Ohio Country, precipitating frequent and violent encounters. In 1790 and 1791, punitive expeditions undertaken by the United States ended in great victories for the Delawares, Shawnees, Miamis, and Algonquians in the Old Northwest. The defeat of Arthur St. Clair's forces in 1791 produced more American casualties than any other similar encounter in U.S. history (900 men killed or wounded). Nevertheless, in 1794, Anthony Wayne defeated the Indian alliance at the Battle of Fallen Timbers. The following year, the Treaty of Greenville opened all but the northwestern third of what later became Ohio to white colonization.

The Indian Policy of Thomas Jefferson, 1801–1824

Upon assuming office in 1801, Thomas Jefferson refined the plan of civilization. In what later became known as Jeffersonian Indian policy, the third president proposed to lead Indians from savagery to civilization by instructing men in agriculture and women in the domestic arts (household tasks such as spinning and weaving cloth). According to Jefferson, Indians—when versed in English, arithmetic, and Christianity—could eventually be incorporated into the Republic. His policy revealed an Enlightenment faith in progress and human reason; excepting Africans, he asserted, all humans had the innate ability to reason and to improve themselves. This apparently benevolent policy presumed the inferiority of indigenous cultures and predicted—in fact, encouraged—the disappearance of Native Americans as separate and distinct peoples.

Jeffersonian Indian policy ultimately failed. Its failure is best measured by the emergence of the Shawnee leader Tecumseh in the early nineteenth century. Drawing on a Native tradition of visionary revivalism, Tecumseh and his brother Tenskwatawa began urging Ohio Native Americans to return to their traditional ways. In 1810, Tecumseh traveled south to ask the Creeks and others to join him in a united attack against white colonists. Although most leaders rejected his plea, thousands of common Creeks and Seminoles, disillusioned with the plan of civilization, launched their own resistance to white authority. In the Old Northwest, Tecumseh's movement ended with the British and Indian defeat in the War of 1812. In the Southeast, it culminated in the Creek War of 1813 and 1814, in which U.S. troops put an end to radical resistance in the region.

Prelude to Removal

The Indian wars in the Old Northwest and the South, coupled with a rising demand by planters for southern cotton lands, led to more virulent attitudes toward Indians in the 1810s and 1820s. These attitudes would culminate in the 1830s with a formal government program to remove all Indians living east of the Mississippi River to territories in the West. Knox and Jefferson had insisted that the social and physical distinctions between Native peoples and whites were purely a product of environmental differences. They believed that, if raised in a patriarchal household in a democratic republic, clothed in European garb, and fed on a diet of domesticated beef, Indians would eventually look and behave like white Americans. By the 1820s, however, some Americans began asserting that there were immutable racial differences between Indians and whites. Since racial differences were immutable, these Americans argued, the plan of civilization was naïve at best and cruel and destructive at worst. Backed by the weight of science, they argued that removal would better serve Native peoples.

In fact, removal was first proposed by Jefferson in 1803, when he suggested that the Louisiana Purchase might provide eastern Indians with a new homeland. But it was not until the election of Andrew Jackson in 1828 that removal received the full support of the federal government. Jackson, a Tennessee frontiersman, a southerner, and an old Indian fighter, showed great consideration for the demands of his white compatriots and little sympathy for Native peoples. The combination did not bode well for Indians. In his first State of the Union address in 1829, Jackson outlined his plan to remove Native Americans to lands west of the Mississippi River. A year later, Jackson's removal policy became law. The law did not appear to condone coercion, but no matter; where Indians refused to relocate, federal troops drove them westward at gunpoint. By the end of the 1830s, tens of thousands of Indians had been forced off their eastern homelands.

BIBLIOGRAPHY

Calloway, Colin G. *The American Revolution in Indian Country: Crisis and Diversity in Native American Communities.* New York: Cambridge University Press, 1995.

Dowd, Gregory Evans. *A Spirited Resistance: The North American Indian Struggle for Unity, 1745–1815.* Baltimore: Johns Hopkins University Press, 1992.

Horsman, Reginald. *Expansion and American Indian Policy: 1783–1812.* East Lansing: Michigan State University Press, 1967.

McLoughlin, William G. *Cherokee Renascence in the New Republic.* Princeton, N.J.: Princeton University Press, 1986.

Prucha, Francis Paul. *American Indian Policy in the Formative Years: The Indian Trade and Intercourse Acts, 1780–1834.* Cambridge, Mass.: Harvard University Press, 1962.

Rogin, Paul. *Fathers and Children: Andrew Jackson and the Subjugation of the American Indian.* New York: Knopf, 1975.

Sheehan, Bernard W. *Seeds of Extinction: Jeffersonian Philanthropy and the American Indian.* Chapel Hill: University of North Carolina, 1973.

Wallace, Anthony F. C. *The Long, Bitter Trail: Andrew Jackson and the Indians.* New York: Hill and Wang, 1993.

———. *Jefferson and the Indians: The Tragic Fate of the First Americans.* Cambridge, Mass.: Belknap Press, 1999.

Claudio Saunt

See also **Creek War; Fallen Timbers, Battle of; Greenville Treaty; Indian Land Cessions; Indian Removal; Indians in the Revolution; Tippecanoe, Battle of.**

1830–1900

Between 1830 and 1900, Indians in the United States experienced dramatic change, such that by the turn of the century, most Indians were confined to impoverished reservations or on allotments carved out of those lands, where government officials exerted profound influence over many aspects of their lives. While policy in and of itself did not always produce this dramatic reversal in fortune, government initiatives consistently favored non-Indian interests and consistently undermined tribal ambitions.

Removal

Debates over Andrew Jackson's plan for Indian removal dominated policy discussions in 1830. Scarcely a novel idea, given generations of dispossession, Jackson's proposal broadened the pace and intensity of removal by relocating eastern Indians to western lands acquired via the Louisiana Purchase. Supported by settlers, as well as humanitarians who considered migration, the Indians' best hope for survival, the Indian Removal Act passed Congress in 1830 over the strong objections of critics who considered it a stain on the national honor.

But Indian removal proved quite complicated when applied to the Five Civilized Tribes (Cherokees, Creeks, Choctaws, Chickasaws, and Seminoles) of the Southeast, whose populations included "elite" classes of educated individuals who had embraced many aspects of Anglo-American culture. Shocked by Jackson's removal bill and Georgia's determination to extinguish by legislative fiat their recently founded republic, Cherokee leaders like John Ross lobbied Congress and appealed to the United States Supreme Court. This effort bore mixed results that proved highly significant for Indian peoples over the longer term, but were of little practical value to the Cherokees of the 1830s. In a pair of landmark decisions, *Cherokee Nation v. Georgia* (1831) and *Worcester v. Georgia* (1832), the Court ruled that Cherokees—and by extension all Indian nations—stood in a position of "domestic dependency" to the United States government. But while this constituted a reduced sovereignty, the Court also ruled that these same Indian nations lay outside the authority of individual states.

The *Worcester* decision declared Indian tribes an exclusively federal responsibility, and therefore should have protected the Cherokees, but Jackson refused to enforce the Court's will, and the resulting settler pressure moved tribes to sign removal agreements. Between 1831 and 1845, 45,000 of 60,000 eastern Indians endured painful relocation. Cherokees suffered famously, losing perhaps one-third of the 12,000 refugees who set out on the Trail of Tears. Forced to rebuild their lives and nations in the unfamiliar lands of Indian Territory, the Five Tribes later were forced to surrender lands as punishment for siding with the Confederacy. In 1898, the Curtis Act abolished their governments and subdivided their tribal domains.

Westward Expansion

Indian policy then turned westward, first focusing on securing overland corridors for white migrants, then developing into an effort to consolidate western peoples on large reservations. In California, the rush of miners seeking gold decimated indigenous populations, and some fell victim to a legislatively sanctioned bounty system that encouraged murder. In Oregon and Washington, sporadic violence and pressure from settler interests led to a comprehensive set of land surrender treaties negotiated by the territorial governor Isaac I. Stevens in the 1850s. While these treaties consolidated northwestern tribes on small parcels of land, they also recognized aboriginal fishing rights that proved decisive in twentieth-century fishing rights cases.

In the vast central region of the United States, settlers encountered significant populations of Plains peoples. At Fort Laramie, Wyoming, in 1851 an agreement designated, on paper, boundaries between major northern Plains tribes. Government negotiators concluded a similar agreement for the southern Plains at Fort Atkinson, Kansas, in 1853, but, as it turned out, neither agreement reduced intertribal conflict or minimized encounters with migrants. The more numerous and powerful Plains peoples, such as the Lakotas in the north, had little reason to participate in the extension of U.S. Indian policy over their homelands. Politically decentralized, with multiple and shifting leadership patterns, Plains societies also operated in ways not well suited to the expectations of treaty negotiators. Consequently, it remained an open question whether Native representatives held the authority either to make promises or to enforce treaty provisions, a problem exacerbated by faulty translations and less-than-candid treaty negotiators.

This combination of shifting power relations between tribes and the virtual certainty of misunderstandings between whites and Indians combined with the increasing pace of settlement to produce conditions ripe for conflict. When the Dakota conflict of 1862 and the horrific slaughter of Southern Arapahos and Southern Cheyennes at Sand Creek in 1864 presaged a new era of violent, and expensive, confrontation, policymakers attempted to reorient policy. At Medicine Lodge in 1867 and Fort Laramie in 1868, the distribution of gifts and promises led to Native endorsement of a plan that envisioned the consolidation of all western tribes on a few large reservations. The first components of what became known as the "peace policy," this effort also included placing the nomination and monitoring of Indian agents under the direction of religious denominations, the creation of the Board of Indian Commissioners to oversee the conduct of Indian policy, and, in 1871, the formal end of treaty making.

Inaugurated with great fanfare, the peace policy foundered almost immediately. Religious denominations proved no more effective in managing Indian agents than their civilian or military counterparts, corruption and mismanagement remained rampant, and, most significantly, the peace policy simply failed to keep the peace. In fact, the 1870s witnessed the last major surge of Indian-white violence, as Indians, predictably, rejected the government's demand that they surrender their way of life and relocate to reservations. They succumbed only after the destruction of bison herds and continued harassment at the hands of the military rendered independent life impossible.

Reservations and Allotment

Although intended as temporary "way stations" on the road toward assimilation, reservations were little more than grim prisons, where defeat, demoralization, and malnutrition produced a poverty of mind, body, and spirit. Self-styled "friends of the Indian" also found the results disappointing; concluding that tribalism was the Indian's problem and a strong dose of individuality its cure, they proposed another reorientation of Indian policy. Included was the creation of a system of off-reservation boarding schools modeled after Richard Henry Pratt's Carlisle Indian Industrial School (founded 1879). Designed around the motto "save the man, kill the Indian," off-reservation boarding schools isolated Indian children from their parents and subjected them to military discipline, all designed to strip them from their cultural moorings and render them more "assimilable." Thousands of Indian children passed through the boarding school system, and while many considered the experience tolerable, more found the isolation excruciating and the education more oriented toward producing manual laborers than leaders or professionals. Hundreds of children also perished at the schools.

Allotment, the other part of the 1880s assimilation program, involved subdividing reservation lands and assigning homesteads of 160, 80, or 40 acres to individuals or heads of families. Formalized in the 1887 Dawes General Allotment Act, allotment must rank among the most far-reaching, and damaging, of U.S. Indian policies. Designed to promote assimilation through values associated with private property holding, the Dawes Act proved more successful as a tool of dispossession. Granted U.S. citizenship upon the assignment to an allotment, Indian landholders remained subject to the authority of the Indian Office, which distributed assistance and enacted restrictions on religious practices and the most intimate details of life. Just as significantly, Indian landholders did not hold full title to their allotments. Designated the "trust period," and inserted into the Dawes Act to hamper the activities of swindlers, this measure prohibited Indians from selling allotments or entering into any contract touching upon the land for a period of twenty-five years.

Indians responded to the Dawes Act in a variety of ways. Some attempted to resist, but after the U.S. Supreme Court's decision in *Lone Wolf v. Hitchcock* (1903), it was clear that the federal government had the intention of imposing allotment, even if it violated the terms of treaties. Others attempted to live with allotment, and some succeeded in such a wide variety of ways as to demonstrate again Indian creativity and resilience. But as trust restrictions were weakened to permit leasing and sale of allotments, Indians increasingly lost control over their lands. By 1934 and the end of the allotment policy, the total Indian land base stood at about 52 million acres, down dramatically from the 150 million acres in 1880. Land loss translated to deepening poverty and social fragmentation. These twin results of allotment cleared the way for the Burke Act of 1906, which abolished the trust period for "competent" Indians, extended it indefinitely for those deemed "incompetent," and amounted to a pessimistic assessment of Indian capabilities. Now, "friends of the Indian" embraced the increasingly common conclusion that there would be a permanent Indian "underclass," at least as long as any distinctively "Indian" peoples survived.

BIBLIOGRAPHY

Adams, David Wallace. *Education for Extinction: American Indians and the Boarding School Experience, 1875–1928.* Lawrence: University Press of Kansas, 1995.

Deloria, Vine, Jr., and Clifford M. Lytle. *American Indians, American Justice.* Austin: University of Texas Press, 1983.

Harring, Sidney L. *Crow Dog's Case: American Indian Sovereignty, Tribal Law, and United States Law in the Nineteenth Century.* Cambridge, U.K.: Cambridge University Press, 1994.

Hoxie, Frederick E. *Parading Through History: The Making of the Crow Nation in America, 1805–1935.* Cambridge, U.K.: Cambridge University Press, 1995.

———. *The Final Promise: The Campaign to Assimilate the Indians, 1888–1920.* Lincoln: University of Nebraska Press, 2001.

McDonnell, Janet A. *The Dispossession of the American Indian, 1887–1934.* Bloomington: Indiana University Press, 1991.

Perdue, Theda, and Michael D. Green, eds. *The Cherokee Removal: A Brief History with Documents.* Boston: Bedford, 1995.

Prucha, Francis Paul. *The Great Father: The United States Government and the American Indians.* 2 vols. Lincoln: University of Nebraska Press, 1995.

Utley, Robert M. *The Indian Frontier of the American West, 1846–1890.* Albuquerque: University of New Mexico Press, 1984.

Brian C. Hosmer

See also **Cherokee Nation Cases; Indian Boarding Schools; Indian Land Cessions; Indian Reservations; Removal Act of 1830; Sand Creek Massacre; Trail of Tears; Wars with Indian Nations;** *and vol. 9:* **A Century of Dishonor; Fort Laramie Treaty of 1851.**

1900–2000

A complex mixture of forces shaped federal Indian policy in the twentieth century including the reform impulse among many humanitarians, regional economic pressures, Congress, federal agencies, missionaries, and Indian leaders. The relative weight of these forces varied throughout the decades.

The Allotment Policy

Federal Indian policy of the twentieth century cannot be understood without examining land allotment in the late nineteenth century. The basic feature of allotment was the assignment of tribal land to individual Indians. Although some 11,000 allotments were made prior to 1885, the Dawes General Allotment Act of 1887 guided the allotments afterward. The statute authorized the president to order the assignment of allotments to all enrolled Indians on reservations. Plots of 160 acres went to family heads; unmarried individuals eighteen or older and orphans received eighty acres; and those under eighteen were assigned forty acres. To guard against their sale, the law placed allotments under federal trust for twenty-five years, which meant the land could not be encumbered or sold. Allottees automatically gained U.S. citizenship.

The allotment policy was primary the work of eastern reformers who believed that education, Christian conversion, and allotment would end tribalism and traditional life, and Indians would quickly assimilate. Unfortunately, allotment caused huge land losses. In 1881, Indians held 155,632,312 acres of land, and by 1900, the figure had fallen to 77,865,373 acres. Despite these staggering losses, allotment and assimilation remained the centerpieces of Indian policy until 1933.

Early Twentieth Century

While the allotment-assimilation policy continued, several changes developed after 1900. The historian Frederick E. Hoxie, for example, has argued that Progressive reformers doubted Indians' ability to assimilate and relegated them to a menial social position. Other scholars have emphasized Progressives' policy goal of self-support after 1900, especially through irrigated farming and outside employment. Progressives also looked for a way to screen Indians to remove the more capable from government trust protections and services. This goal apparently shaped the Burke Act of 1906. The law amended the Dawes General Allotment Act by withholding citizenship from allottees until after the twenty-five-year trust period had expired. However, allottees before then could apply for "competency" and receive their citizenship and their allotments in fee simple. Most of those declared competent quickly sold their allotments at ruinous prices.

Western regional forces also began to assert more influence over Indian policy at the turn of the century. Western mining and agricultural interests resented the presence of nontaxable reservations in this undeveloped region and sought access to Indian resources. As more western territories became states, senators and representatives from the region dominated the Senate and House committees on Indian Affairs. Westerners also held many key positions in the Department of Interior and the BUREAU OF INDIAN AFFAIRS (BIA). Finally, federal agencies such as the Bureau of Reclamation and the Forest Service, which served powerful vested interests in the West, made sure that their constituents' needs were served. The weak BIA could seldom protect Indians against white pressures.

The policy of "forced patenting" during Commissioner Cato Sells's administration (1913–1921) epitomized Progressives' drive to "free" Indians from government control. Instead of Indians applying for competency, Sells and Secretary of the Interior Franklin K. Lane established "competency commissions" that toured reservations screening Indians and forcing those deemed competent to take fee simple titles to allotments. In 1917, Sells's "Declaration of Policy in the Administration of Indian Affairs" ended trust protection for all allottees under one-half Indian blood and boarding-school graduates. Forced patenting left thousands of Indians landless.

1920s Reform Agitation

After World War I the allotment-assimilation policy came under attack. John Collier, a young social worker, strongly opposed legislation that threatened Pueblo land titles in the Rio Grande Valley. Even though Congress approved a compromise measure in 1924, Collier took up other complaints, including Indians' poor oil revenues, lack of religious freedom on reservations, inferior education in Indian schools, and mismanagement of Indian finances. Unlike earlier reformers, Collier challenged the assimilation philosophy that had been central to Indian affairs for four decades. Collier's approach stressed cultural pluralism and encouraged Indians to retain their own traditions.

Collier's agitation produced a major investigation. In 1926–1927, the Institute for Government Research carried out an extensive survey of BIA field administration. The group's report, *The Problem of Indian Administration* (1928), blamed allotment and forced patenting for widespread poverty and condemned woeful education and health services. Major recommendations included upgrading BIA employees, increased funding, and adding a division of planning and administration to the BIA. Although the Herbert Hoover administration made several improvements, it never added the new division.

The Indian New Deal and World War II

The appointment of John Collier as Indian commissioner (1933–1945) caused marked changes in Indian policy. Early on, Collier demonstrated a more dynamic approach by arranging cooperative agreements with emergency programs such as the Civilian Conservation Corps and the Public Works Administration. These programs brought unprecedented expertise, funds, and employment opportunities to reservations. Collier's policy of cultural pluralism was reflected largely in the INDIAN REORGANIZATION ACT (1934). While several provisions of the original bill were lost in passage, what remained were procedures to create tribal governments and to charter business corporations. The act also halted allotment, established a revolving credit fund, and authorized money for scholarships and land acquisition.

Unfortunately, Collier's policies aroused intense criticism. Many traditional Indians resented mixed-bloods' domination of the tribal governments created under the Indian Reorganization Act. Other Indians believed Collier jeopardized past progress. White economic interests lashed the BIA when it blocked their use of reservation resources. This opposition and budget cuts kept the Collier administration on the defensive after 1938. The Indian New Deal softened the impact of the depression on Indians, but it was not a complete success.

World War II made Indian policy far less relevant than usual. Sensing this, Collier tried unsuccessfully to create an all-Indian army division in 1940. Two years later, he arranged with the War Relocation Authority to place Japanese Americans in camps on the Gila River and Colorado River reservations. The BIA also cooperated with the Selective Service in the registration and drafting of Indians. Despite such cooperation, the BIA was removed to Chicago in 1942, key personnel left the agency, budget cuts reduced services, and Collier remained on the defensive. The drift and stalemate of the BIA continued after Collier's resignation in 1945.

Termination

The appointment of Dillon S. Myer as Indian commissioner (1950–1953) ended the policy hiatus and initiated the termination policy. This policy involved ending BIA services by transferring them to other federal agencies or to states and the relocation of Indians to urban centers. In late 1951, Myer formed the Division of Program to gather data on reservations and to study ways to end BIA services. He soon ordered local agency employees to develop plans, with or without Indian cooperation, but the Republican victory in 1952 stalemated Myer's efforts.

Senator Arthur V. Watkins of Utah, chairman of the Senate Committee on Indian Affairs, became the architect of termination in 1953. House Concurrent Resolution 108, passed in August 1953, endorsed termination and ordered Department of the Interior officials to prepare termination legislation for individual tribes by 1 January 1954. Public Law 280 gave several states legal jurisdiction over reservations and permitted other states to extend jurisdiction unilaterally.

In February 1954, Senator Watkins and Representative E. Y. Berry of South Dakota started joint hearings on termination bills. Significant opposition arose during the proceedings. The National Congress of American Indians (NCAI) initially seemed unconcerned about the new policy but later strongly fought against termination. State officials during the hearings expressed reluctance about providing services to Indians unless compensated with federal funds. Other critics denounced the Indians' lack of preparation for termination. Over the next few years, Congress terminated eleven groups involving 13,263 Indians. Although this represented about 3 percent of enrolled Indians, termination caused tremendous hostility and anxiety.

Indian Commissioner Glenn L. Emmons (1953–1961) intensified the existing relocation program soon after his appointment. In 1956, he added job training to relocation. However, critics charged that relocation was a cruel attempt to force assimilation. Surprisingly, however, most Indians who left reservations did so on their own; only 25 percent of them relocated to cities because of the federal program.

Self-Determination

The inauguration of John F. Kennedy marked the start of self-determination, or allowing Indians greater voice in policy matters. Several events in 1961 signaled the new approach. Secretary of the Interior Stewart L. Udall quickly appointed a four-man study group to look at current Indian problems and suggest solutions. The panel's report on 7 October 1961 outlined three basic policy goals: economic self-sufficiency, greater Indian participation in American life, and equal citizenship. Also in 1961, the Commission on Rights, Liberties, and Responsibilities of American Indians filed a report that condemned termination as an ill-advised and hasty policy and demanded more government assistance to elevate Indians' standard of living. Finally, a meeting of 450 Indian leaders at the University of Chicago in June 1961 produced the Declaration of Indian Purpose, which advocated greater Indian control over policy making.

Kennedy's Indian commissioner, Philleo Nash (1961–1966), tried to end Indians' fears about termination. An anthropologist and experienced government administrator, Nash spent many months visiting Indian leaders and trying to restore confidence in the BIA. The Area Redevelopment Act of 1961 was a harbinger of future Indian affairs. It targeted areas of high unemployment and low income for loans and grants, and this included virtually all reservations. The funds that flowed to reservations through these antipoverty grants tended to break the BIA's monopoly on delivery of government services.

The trend of federal funding administered apart from the BIA increased during President Lyndon Johnson's War on Poverty. The Economic Opportunity Act of August 1964, for example, provided education and training benefits and allowed local initiatives. By mid-1968, sixty-three community action programs existed on 129 reservations. Indian policy had, in the meantime, become highly diffuse as more and more federal agencies offered services to reservations. President Johnson's executive order of 6 March 1968 established the National Council on Indian Opportunity to coordinate the many Indian programs. Chaired by Vice President Hubert Humphrey, the council was made up of five cabinet officers, the director of the Office of Economic Opportunity, and six Indian leaders. These developments strengthened tribal governments and taught local leaders how to lobby Congress and federal agencies.

During the 1968 campaign, Richard M. Nixon emphatically repudiated termination and promised Indian participation in major policy decisions. He repeated the same promises in his own special message to Congress in 1970. His contributions to self-determination included proposals that tribes be allowed to contract for services and that Indian school boards oversee education.

The Nixon administration policies took place during a highly charged period. The AMERICAN INDIAN MOVEMENT and other militant groups organized fish-ins, occupied Alcatraz, seized the BIA building, and occupied the village of Wounded Knee, South Dakota. Turmoil also erupted within the BIA as young Indian administrators clashed with conservative old hands. During major crises, White House staffers preempted BIA administrators, thereby undermining their authority.

The RED POWER movement reshaped policy but not in ways that met protestors' demands. Nixon officials responded to each crisis with face-saving settlements but made few concessions. The government frequently isolated militants by co-opting moderate groups such as the NCAI and the National Tribal Chairmen's Association. A good example of this strategy was authorizing the American Indian Policy Review Commission in 1975. This major investigation of Indian affairs consisted of eleven task forces made up almost entirely of Indians. The group's final report in May 1977 repeatedly advocated Indian sovereignty and the creation of an assistant secretary of interior for Indian affairs to help formulate policy. President Jimmy Carter established the new position later in the year. Congress also passed an unprecedented amount of legislation in the 1970s. Several laws dealt with Indian education, and others covered health care, civil rights, community colleges, child welfare, and religious freedom. Finally, Indians turned to the courts, where they won significant victories on such issues as hunting and fishing rights, tribal jurisdiction, gaming, and water rights. Case law, in effect, has often become policy since World War II.

BIBLIOGRAPHY

Fixico, Donald L. *The Invasion of Indian Country in the Twentieth Century: American Capitalism and Tribal Natural Resources.* Niwot: University Press of Colorado, 1998.

Hoxie, Frederick E. *A Final Promise: The Campaign to Assimilate the Indians, 1880–1920.* Lincoln: University of Nebraska Press, 1984.

Kvasnicka, Robert M., and Herman J. Viola, eds. *The Commissioners of Indian Affairs, 1824–1977.* Lincoln: University of Nebraska Press, 1979.

Olson, James S., and Raymond Wilson. *Native Americans in the Twentieth Century.* Provo, Utah: Brigham Young University Press, 1984.

Parman, Donald L. *Indians and the American West in the Twentieth Century*. Bloomington: Indiana University Press, 1994.

Prucha, Francis Paul. *The Great Father: The United States Government and the American Indians*. 2 vols. Lincoln: University of Nebraska Press, 1984.

Donald L. Parman

See also **Education, Indian; Indian Civil Rights Act; Indian Political Life; Indian Reservations; Indian Self-Determination and Education Assistance Act; Wounded Knee (1973);** *and vol. 9:* **Land of the Spotted Eagle.**

INDIAN POLITICAL LIFE. The evolution of the Native American societies, encountered by Europeans from the sixteenth century onward, occurred over many centuries. Indian societies were never static. Very likely, small hunter-gatherer bands of natives existed from the Lithic Period (13,000 years ago) onward, particularly in the Southwest, where hunting large game required group effort. Improvements in hunting technology, such as the bow and arrow, as well as better systems for the storing of food, such as baskets and pottery, led to more stability and more connectedness during the next stage of development, the Archaic. Early band development, at 6,000 to 7,000 years ago, likely placed considerable dependence upon a "Big Man," or male political leader. Siblings offered support in exchange for assistance. Age was also important. Elders always possessed a commodity that helped solidify leadership—they had knowledge of geography, other peoples, or even origin stories that helped give the band an identity.

Political organization in native North America took another shift when agriculture emerged in the American Southwest. When this process began approximately 2,000 years ago, native women (the principle farmers) likely increased their political power base. As corn, beans, and squash became common features of the Indian economy, communities became more sedentary. This shift also benefited women for it enabled them to maintain the activities of childrearing. Soon individuals were locating their family relations through the identity of their mothers, the keepers, and growers of the food supply. This practice produced matrilineal kinship systems.

Matrilineal Societies

As agriculture spread east to the Atlantic Coast, and north into the Rocky Mountains, matrilineal social development became the dominant form of native organization. Virtually every southeastern tribal society in existence at the time of European contact was matrilineal. And similar systems of order existed in the Virginia tidewater in Powhatan's confederacy, and northward into the lands of the Susquehanna and the Iroquois. Even in the Pacific Northwest, matrilineal systems predominated, as women formed the nucleus for food preparation and childcare in settled coastal towns. While after 1500, warfare and disease would break up some of these tribal traditions, 80 percent of Native Americans used matrilineal systems as a form of social organization. These matrilineal systems helped create the political control that Europeans first faced in the new continent.

Matrilineal societies generally were organized into clans, which included all the closely related people in a particular village. The clan leader was a matriarch, with various levels of influence existing depending upon age and capability of men and women who lived within her household or extended family. Clans often held particular affinity for some special animal, such as the beaver, the bear, or the deer. In order to prevent incest, a member of one clan could never marry the member of another. Indeed, to preserve the power and influence of a clan, the elders would often arrange marriages, and young women were not allowed to leave the compound so the elders could protect her. Within a matrilineal household, men owned nothing, had no control over food or clothing, and even faced stern taboos against speaking with their mothers-in-law. Men maintained separate organizations devoted to hunting or making war. As particular men grew in esteem within their respective clans, they were pushed forward to assume leadership roles. In some cases, actual elections brought the men to power. These local clan subchiefs, or headmen, resolved disputes by acting as intermediaries, a role suited for them because they owned little property. Often the subchiefs also joined in a council, in which every clan was represented. This band council determined any actions the village might take. Young men respected the decisions of the council because of their kinship connections to its members and because if they became disrespectful, they might never be given a wife or an opportunity to serve in a leadership capacity.

Occasionally, powerful clans would offer up both "peace" chiefs and "war" chiefs to speak for them. Rank in the council was decided by age, military prowess, and the power of an individual's clan. Such ranking was again often determined by clan mothers. Some evidence even suggests that clan chiefs could only serve at the bequest of the various clan mothers. Among some matrilineal societies, war could not be declared until the clan mothers agreed, and any decision regarding the relocation of the village was certainly considered only with the approval of the clan mothers.

Above the village, some matrilineal societies also created chieftainships, or larger political organizations that represented a number of villages. Oftentimes, a particularly strong and large village sat at the center of the chieftainship, being directed by a council that included representatives from various outlying towns. In some cases, supra-political elites came to control the chieftainships, with a particularly powerful political leader assuming command of the warriors. Powhatan was a good example of such a paramount chief. He was the political leader of some 10,000 Indians who lived along the Virginia coast when the English first arrived. His family was obviously very strong, as his brother followed him as chief at his death. Powhatan helped maintain his own political position by frequently selecting wives from among the young women of neighboring towns, taking some two-dozen in all. After they had given birth, the young women were sent back to their towns, where they lived an almost royal existence, being maintained by the chief. A similar political royalty emerged among the Natchez Indians of the central Mississippi River valley. Here, the "honored people," headed by the "Great Sun," or absolute ruler, sat at the top of the kin structure, followed by commoners and so-called slaves. This theocracy, while clearly an exception among matrilineal societies, still operated as a chieftainship, with a council that represented the various surrounding villages. The royalty that controlled the society derived its power from the clan mothers, as these women married commoners, who in turn produced children who became royalty. Male members of the royalty, who by contrast had to marry commoners, ended up having children who became commoners, thus preserving the female matrilineal line. The priesthood helped sanction the class structure and maintain the political authority of the honored people.

In the Southwest, religion played a key role in determining political leadership in Pueblo societies. While adopting a bilineal social structure (that is, tracing families through men and women), authority in Pueblo towns came directly from the various kin-ordered religious clans. Each town remained autonomous and, for direction, looked inward to its various ceremonies (many of which related to agriculture) and the clans that organized them. The Navajo Indians, to the north, while of Apachean origin, maintained more traditional matrilineal organization, as did most of the Northwest Coast Indians. When societies placed less emphasis upon farming, such as those in California or the Colombian Plateau, matrilineal systems generally gave way to patrilineal clan organization. Here, leadership emerged from the male members of the most successful clans. Councils, likewise, became assemblies of the most respected elders of the patrilineal clans.

The European Impact

Whether patrilineal or matrilineal, most indigenous societies in America at contact were intensely organized. Few were egalitarian, if the term is defined as one in which most members of the general society had a say in affairs. Young members of these societies, either male or female, had little political power. Given this political organization, one might expect that Europeans and American Indians could have established peaceful, mutually respectful relations. Unfortunately, much the opposite happened, for almost from the beginnings of contact, Europeans failed to understand the values and loyalties that held Indian societies together and failed to see the havoc that disease and war would have on traditional institutions.

The disruption of Native American political orders can be seen almost from the first entry of the earliest Europeans. In the Southwest, Spaniards used the sword and the Bible to reform Indian communities. Missionaries, supported by Spanish soldiers, invaded Indian towns, challenged native leaders, and forced a patriarchal system on the inhabitants. Indian men, who had traditionally acquired status from their religious roles, found their religion dismissed; most were forced to work in fields alongside their women. Disease quickly took its toll, as the number of Native American Pueblo communities declined from over one hundred in 1540 to a mere fourteen by 1800. Some Pueblo Indians fled and joined the roving Apache bands that had acquired horses. They returned to a more mobile existence that emphasized patrilocal social and political order. Apaches, in general, were making the transition from matrilineal organization—and some agriculture—to herding and raiding, occupations that supported patrilocal organization and strong male leadership.

The transition to patrilocal order, however, is best seen on the Great Plains, where the matrilineal societies of the Wichitas, Caddos, and Pawnees, which had dominated the region in 1540, saw their populations decline as others invaded their hunting grounds. Among the newcomers were Comanches, Arapahos, Cheyennes, and Lakotas, or Sioux people, who acquired horses after 1700 and built larger and larger populations. These new societies were all patrilocal and mobile.

Politically, women had little influence in these hunting camps and their men practiced polygamy, capturing women in raids on surrounding peoples. Such polygamy was virtually impossible in the traditional societies of the Wichitas, Caddos, or Pawnees, where the women owned the home and distributed food. Given the more flexible marriage system, Lakota populations would reach 50,000; Comanches would be nearly as populous by 1800. All of these societies were also much more warlike. Indeed, their men gained status and power from war.

Politically, the new Plains Indian societies placed considerable emphasis on training young men for raiding and war. The most important day in a young man's life was when elders offered to take him on a war party. His actions thereafter would determine his role in the society, some even opted to kill themselves if they failed as a warrior. Success in war led to invitations to join various male societies, these groups in turn having a profound impact on the political life of the community. For the Lakotas, the Fox Society and the Silent Eaters made decisions that the remainder of the band accepted. Most of these tribes had "soldiers' lodges," in one form or another, that directed the everyday happenings of the tribe, ordering its march from one locale to another. Soldiers had the absolute power to inflict corporal punishment when necessary.

Most of the Plains societies selected male chiefs to lead them. Band chiefs were often hereditary leaders who gave advice, listened to a council of elders, and issued proclamations based on the council's advice. Along with such civil authorities, Plains Indian societies also embraced various war chiefs, or men who were equipped both mentally and physically, to lead war parties. At times, war chiefs became all powerful. When they were successful, they could preempt the power of the tribal council. When they failed, the people usually abandoned them. The new Plains Indian societies, then, lacked the political order and traditions of the earlier, matrilineal-based societies.

As Europeans settled various portions of the Southwest and the East Coast, and then pushed into the interior, Native Americans often found it necessary to alter their political institutions. Acculturation, or the willing acceptance of change, led most southeastern tribes to adopt constitutional systems by the early 1800s. Increasingly, this led to more male-dominant political behavior, as matrilineal systems declined. By the 1830s and 1840s, the families of many Choctaws, Cherokees, and Creeks identified themselves by the name of the male patriarch, rather than the female. This meant men in tribal councils were given more political control, while women faced declining influence. After the removal policies of the Jackson Era were implemented, some southeastern societies even abandoned reinforcement of the reciprocal kinship relationships.

As the Plains Wars came to a halt after the American Civil War, Indians faced more forced political change. The federal government created the "reservation" as an institution designed to destroy all Indian custom and belief, including traditional political systems. Federal Indian agents replaced tribal law with federally funded and supported Indian judges and police. Tribal councils were largely ignored and agents used their massive control of food resources to reward younger men who traditionally would not have dared challenge traditional authority. Protestant and Catholic churches added to the dismantling of tribal political traditions by working to undermine Indian religion and promoting the nuclear rather than the extended Indian family. The federal government did the same after it passed the allotment law in 1887. By the early decades of the twentieth century, most vestiges of the older tribal political systems had disappeared in North America.

The Indian New Deal of 1934 allowed some return to tribal autonomy as it allowed tribes to reorganize their governments as corporations. Slowly by the 1960s and 1970s, tribes took back control of school and police systems. Yet, government strings, in the form of financial support, still remained and complete political "self-determination" had yet to materialize. When serious crime cannot be dealt with by the tribe, for example, the federal government still reserves the right to invade reservations and administer law and order; and health care systems are administered totally by the federal government.

BIBLIOGRAPHY

Anderson, Gary Clayton. *Kinsmen of Another Kind: Dakota-White Relations in the Upper Mississippi Valley, 1650–1862.* Lincoln: University of Nebraska Press, 1984.

———. *Sitting Bull and the Paradox of Lakota Nationhood.* New York: HarperCollins, 1996.

Faiman-Silva, Sandra. *Choctaws at the Crossroads: The Political Economy of Class and Culture in the Oklahoma Timber Region.* Lincoln: University of Nebraska Press, 1991.

Gutiérrez, Ramón A. *When Jesus Came, The Corn Mothers Went Away: Marriage, Sexuality, and Power in New Mexico, 1500–1846.* Palo Alto, Calif.: Stanford University Press, 1991.

Rountree, Helen C. *The Powhatan Indians of Virginia: Their Traditional Culture.* Norman: University of Oklahoma Press, 1989.

Van Kirk, Sylvia. *Many Tender Ties: Women in the Fur-Trade Society, 1670–1870.* Norman: University of Oklahoma Press, 1983.

Gary Clayton Anderson

See also **Agriculture, American Indian; Greenville Treaty; Indian Economic Life; Indian Social Life; Indians and the Horse; Powhatan Confederacy; Tribes; Warfare, Indian;** *and vol. 9:* **The Origin of the League of Five Nations; Land of the Spotted Eagle.**

INDIAN RELIGIOUS LIFE. One summer day in the early 1990s atop a grassy hillside on the Yankton Sioux reservation in South Dakota, an ad hoc crew of young men gathered to set up a large tent in preparation of a service of the NATIVE AMERICAN CHURCH. This service would involve the consumption of the church's sacrament, the flesh of peyote, a cactus that grows near the Texas-Mexico border. The tent poles, resting on the ground, were tree-size timbers. A man tied the tips of two of them together, and the men lifted the poles skyward. But the rope slipped and the poles slid apart. The process had to start all over. On the second attempt, the rope slipped and the poles misaligned another time. That's when one of the Yankton men said, "You know we have to do this four times." Everyone laughed. His joke played off of the fact that Yankton ceremonial protocol, to acknowledge the four cardinal directions and the spiritual powers associated with them, requires many ceremonial gestures and movements to be repeated four times. Tent construction, thankfully, does not. When their efforts succeeded the third time, that was it. The men began lifting other poles to rest within the V-shape formed where the first two raised poles crossed. Sheathing this skeleton with canvas, they enclosed a large space where dozens would later gather for worship.

A Navajo roadman had traveled to South Dakota to conduct the ceremony. He had spent an entire day sweeping, cleaning, and shaping the soil in accord with a very precise design, led an all-night service of prayer, song, and sacramental communion. For practitioners, peyote is a living, healing teacher who can help everyone, including individuals in dire need. Many stories relate how the spirit of peyote helped souls lost in the desert or drifting in despair, but the people gathered this particular evening radiated joy. They had a special reason to celebrate. The participants included many men and women who had just completed a SUN DANCE, an age-old Plains Indian religious practice. In a nearby ceremonial ground, the Sun Dancers had successfully endured four days of frequent dancing and constant fasting, concluding an entire year of dedicated prayer and preparation. Through the whole process, a Yankton medicine man had guided them. During the four days of the culminating ceremony, he had determined when they should start and stop dancing around the cottonwood tree, which had been specially selected and moved to the center of the circle. On his signal, the dancers lined up on a radius from that center and danced facing in one of the four cardinal directions. Then, again on his signal, they rotated one quarter of the way around the tree, lined up and danced to the next direction, and so on, until they had completed the fourfold circuit. They did this time and time again. Throughout the cycles, a community of relatives and friends, sitting in the brush arbor circling the dance ground, supported the dancers with good thoughts, prayers, gifts, and labor. Among other things, witnesses chopped wood to keep a fire going to heat rocks for a sweat lodge, a small domed tent where steam from water poured on the super-heated rocks cleansed the hearts and minds of the resting dancers.

After four days of dancing in the sun to the rhythmic voice of a large ceremonial drum, some of the dancers decided to make a final offering. Taking two razor cuts at a time to their shoulders or chests, they allowed a thin stick or bone skewer to be inserted through the fresh openings in their body. The dance leader then tied to the ends of the implanted stick a rope, pulled from the many attached to the top of the sacred tree. Toward the end of the dance, the now attached dancers approached the tree and rested their hands on it, then backed away until the ropes grew taut. They did this four times. The fourth time, they ran away from the tree and did not stop. The ropes grew taut, each dancer's skin stretched, and finally, with a popping sound, small divots of flesh tore away. These offerings recalled that of the primordial being, Inyan, one of the first superior gods, who allowed his blood to flow out to make all that is the living world. As the dancers emerged from the circle, they smiled and shook hands with everyone present. They had made a meaningful sacrifice for themselves, for relatives, for family members facing hard times, for the community, for their people.

Modern Challenges to Indian Religious Life

Not too long ago participants in these religious activities would have faced serious punishments. Indeed, during the latter decades of the nineteenth century and early decades of the twentieth, federal agents sought to eradicate the Sun Dance among Plains Indian nations and to ban the peyote religion wherever they encountered it. State officials especially targeted peyote worship, classifying the cactus as a narcotic on a level with cocaine or hashish, even though the evidence suggests peyote is not addictive. Government officials also sought to extinguish communal dances among PUEBLO Indians, potlatch ceremonies among northwestern tribes, world renewal ceremonies in northern California, fiestas in southern California, and other traditional practices. They assumed traditional ceremonies made Native men and women militant, pagan, and wasteful. They sought to replace these with Christianity.

During this period, the United States and Canada compelled Native children to attend boarding schools. In these institutions, teachers sought to force Indians to conform to white ways of acting, dressing, and believing. Facing these pressures from government authorities, all Native Americans developed ways to accommodate a hostile and powerful culture, without capitulating entirely or surrendering to despair. Some sought to continue their traditional practices, but in a way that did not attract attention. Some converted to Christianity and affiliated with established denominations. And many, including some Christians as well as some traditionalists, joined new Native-initiated religious movements.

New Religious Movements

During the late nineteenth century, Native Americans spread the peyote religion across Indian country, initially reaching Lipan APACHES, Tonkawas, KIOWAS, and COMANCHES in Oklahoma and later winning and healing the hearts of Anishinabe, MENOMINEE, Lakota (see SIOUX), NAVAJO, CREE, and other peoples. Because different peoples interpreted this tradition in different ways, there are various forms of peyote ceremonialism. Most incorporate Christian teaching and values. Indeed, on 10 October 1918, peyotists in Oklahoma organized the Native American Church, which they described as a good way to teach "the Christian religion and morality." This denomination and others defend practitioners of this religion, who continue to encounter discrimination and harassment.

During the 1880s, another new religious movement emerged in the Pacific Northwest. Known as the Indian Shaker religion, it continues to provide meaning to peoples in this area. It began near Olympia, Washington, with a Squaxin man named John Slocum and his wife, Mary Slocum. Employing Native American singing and words as well as Christian crucifixes, images of Jesus, and candles, Indian Shakers seek to heal the ill by shaking over them, brushing them with spirit power, and bell ringing. Shakers in the Indian Full Gospel Shaker Church use the Bible. In contrast, Shakers in the Indian Shaker Church, also known as the "1910 Church," do not. This schism epitomizes the complicated and sometimes vexed relationship between many Native peoples' religious life and Christian texts, symbols, and practices.

Still another new religious movement began in Mason Valley, Nevada, and gained devotees across the West. In 1889, a visionary Paiute healer named Wovoka revealed that Native Americans, by dancing a round dance and observing a peaceful moral code, could help generate a new earth full of life and free of loss and death. This message attracted Native visitors from near and far, and they took the new dance back to their peoples in the Great Basin, California, the Northwest, and the Great Plains.

Lakota Indians in South Dakota, sorely oppressed by the U.S. government, reinterpreted the religion as a way to bring back their ancestral ways and rid their land of white people. Although the PAIUTES called the religion Nänigükwa (Dance in a Circle), the Lakotas called it Wanagi Wacipi (Spirit Dance or GHOST DANCE). Authorities, fearing anything that countered their control, brought in soldiers, and on 29 December 1890 massacred approximately three hundred Minneconjou and Oglala men, women, and children at WOUNDED KNEE, South Dakota. CHEYENNE people developed yet another interpretation. They recognized Christian aspects in Wovoka's religion and referred to it as the "Dance to Christ." In a sense, participating in this movement provided some Native Americans with a fruitful way to appropriate elements of Christianity without converting to Christianity itself.

John Slocum and Wovoka were not the first Native prophets or visionaries to help people find new spiritual paths when ancestral ones were disrupted. All across the continent, an extraordinary range of fresh religious visions and new religious practices emerged to help Native American men and women respond to the challenges and opportunities associated with new peoples, technologies, plants, and animals as well as with colonialism, invasion, devastating new diseases, removal, forced assimilation, and missionization. Prophet-led revolts helped people from various tribes find common cause, but they also led to conflicts within Native nations and usually elicited brutal military responses and invasions by the armies of the United States. Witnessing these outcomes, many Native men and women gravitated toward less militant movements or made their peace with Christianity.

Even before the changes associated with contact and colonialism, there were religious innovators. During the fifteenth century in the Northeast, for example, a great leader called the Peacemaker taught thirteen laws that enabled Mohawks, Oneidas, Onondagas, Cayugas, and Senecas to live together in harmony and peace. United in a Great League of Peace and Power, they later brought the Tuscarora nation into their confederacy (1722) and called themselves the Haudenosaunee, "the people of the longhouse." Other Indians referred to them with an Algonquian word, Irinakoiw, and the French, borrowing this name, called them IROQUOIS. Today, the Iroquois remain an important presence in upstate New York, where they have recently won some important lawsuits related to unsettled land claims, established gaming operations, and launched strong language revitalization programs.

Renewing Religions and Identities

In the late twentieth and early twenty-first centuries, Native men and women were working to reclaim their rights and renew their traditions. In 1999, for example, young MAKAH men paddling a hand-carved canoe off the coast of Washington State pursued, harpooned, shot, landed, and butchered a gray whale. This act, which enraged some environmentalists, embodied the exercise of treaty rights guaranteed to a sovereign Native people. But it also symbolized the renewal of a profound relationship with the whale, a relationship vital in ancestral Makah tradition. Through whaling, the Makahs reclaimed an important part of their identity.

With great tenacity and imagination, with humor and legal argument, and with spirituality, contemporary Native Americans are strengthening their traditions. Yuchi men and women, like many speakers of endangered languages across the continent, are working to save their linguistic tradition. Zuni people have repatriated from museums statues of their war gods. Lakotas have reburied the ancestral remains of survivors of Wounded Knee and reclaimed from eastern museums clothing worn by its victims. Anishinabe people in Minnesota, Luiseño in California, and NEZ PERCE in Idaho have bought back tracts of land that hold spiritual and cultural significance to their peoples. Basket making and bird singing are regaining vigor in southern California, bringing Indians there into closer relationship with the land and giving new voice to ancestral stories of its creation. CHEROKEES are once again playing stickball in North Carolina.

Indian religious life has always enabled people to renew their worlds by providing the words, songs, acts, symbols, and values to deepen their participation in life and make things right again. But it is also the case that Native Americans have always sought to enrich their religious lives with fresh ideas, new visions, and original practices. As Indians reclaim their cultural patrimony, assert their treaty rights, regain some of their land bases, revitalize storytelling traditions, and preserve their languages, they are also renewing the wellsprings of their religious life. Everything is connected; the vitality of Indian religious life reflects the condition of Native lands, languages, and the communities. As the latter are renewed, so the former gains strength. Thanks to the creativity, vision, sacrifices, and persistence of modern Native American men and women, Indian religious life has a strong future. The summer will return. The drum will sound. A new Sun Dance will begin.

BIBLIOGRAPHY

Basso, Keith H. *Wisdom Sits in Places: Landscape and Language among the Western Apache.* Albuquerque: University of New Mexico Press, 1996.

Irwin, Lee. *The Dream Seekers: Native American Visionary Traditions of the Great Plains.* Norman: University of Oklahoma Press, 1994.

Kehoe, Alice Beck. *The Ghost Dance: Ethnohistory and Revitalization.* Fort Worth, Tex.: Holt, Rinehart, and Winston, 1989.

Martin, Joel W. *The Land Looks After Us: A History of Native American Religion.* Oxford, U.K., and New York: Oxford University Press, 2001.

Nelson, Richard K. *Make Prayers to the Raven: A Koyukon View of the Northern Forest.* Chicago: University of Chicago Press, 1983.

Stewart, Omer C. *Peyote Religion: A History.* Norman: University of Oklahoma Press, 1987.

Treat, James, ed. *Native and Christian: Indigenous Voices on Religious Identity in the United States and Canada.* New York: Routledge, 1996.

Vecsey, Christopher. *Imagine Ourselves Richly: Mythic Narratives of North American Indians.* New York: Crossroad, 1988.

Joel W. Martin

See also **Indian Bible, Eliot's; Nativist Movements (American Indian Revival Movements);** *and vol. 9:* **A Dialogue between Piumbukhou and His Unconverted Relatives; Land of the Spotted Eagle; A Letter from Wovoka.**

INDIAN REMOVAL. Indian removal, which involved transferring lands in the trans-Mississippi West to Native American groups who gave up their homelands east of the Mississippi, dominated U.S. government Indian policy between the War of 1812 and the middle of the nineteenth century. This practice, although not without detractors, had the support of several very important groups: speculators who coveted Indian lands, uneasy eastern settlers who feared Indian attacks, and missionary groups who felt that relocation would save the Indians from the degrading influences of their white neighbors.

Development of the Policy

The seeds of a removal program were sown in the series of negotiations with southeastern tribes that began with the first Treaty of Hopewell in 1785. Many citizens of the southeastern states, especially Georgia, believed that the federal government too often made concessions to powerful, well-organized tribes such as the Creeks and the Cherokees. In 1802, when Georgia was asked to cede the lands from which the states of Alabama and Mississippi would later be created, it did so only after extracting a promise from federal officials to "peaceably obtain, on reasonable terms," the Indian title to all land within Georgia's borders. In 1803, President Thomas Jefferson saw an opportunity to both appease Georgia and legitimize his controversial Louisiana Purchase by drafting a constitutional amendment authorizing Congress to exchange lands in the West for eastern lands occupied by Indians. While this amendment was never submitted for ratification, Congress enacted legislation the following year authorizing the president to administer such a removal and exchange policy provided that participating Indians continued their allegiance to the United States.

In ensuing years, several attempts were made to persuade the Cherokees and other major tribes to remove voluntarily to the West. While some groups favored escaping white harassment through resettlement, many more opposed the idea of leaving their ancestral homes. Their desire to stay was reinforced by the unhappy experiences of small groups of Cherokees, Delawares, Shawnees, and others who had accepted a land exchange and gone westward between 1785 and 1800. After the War of 1812 and the elimination of the British as a potential ally, Indian removal became a basic item in virtually all treaties with Native groups. In 1817 John C. Calhoun, a strong advocate of Indian removal, was named secretary of war by James Monroe. Calhoun joined forces with the war hero Andrew Jackson and Lewis Cass, governor of Michigan Territory, to urge formal adoption of a removal policy.

Several treaties, often of dubious legality, such as that signed by the Sauks at St. Louis in 1804, had called for westward removal at an indefinite time in the future. The formal adoption of a removal policy, however, picked up the pace considerably following the conclusion of peace with the British. The Delawares, for example, already having been pushed into Indiana, signed a removal treaty in 1818. The following year, several bands of Illinois Kickapoos agreed to resettle on Missouri lands formerly occupied by Osages. Cass pushed vigorously (and usually successfully) for treaties of cession and removal throughout the area between the Ohio and Mississippi Rivers. More famously, federal negotiators sought removal of all tribes in the Southeast. Treaties aimed at achieving this end were signed by the Choctaws in 1820 and by the Creeks in 1821.

Monroe withheld his full support of this removal policy until January 1825, when he delivered a special message to Congress describing forced resettlement in the West as the only means of solving "the Indian problem." Immediately thereafter, Calhoun issued a report calling for the resettlement of nearly 100,000 eastern Indians and recommended the appropriation of $95,000 for this purpose. Within a month after Calhoun's report was made public, the Creeks signed the Treaty of Indian Springs, agreeing to resettle on lands in the West by 1 September 1826, but many Creek leaders and some whites (including John Crowell, the Indian agent to the Cherokee) protested the manner in which the treaty had been negotiated. Crowell also recommended special federal protection for William McIntosh, the Creek leader who was the principal treaty signer. The requested protection was not forthcoming, however, and shortly thereafter McIntosh was assassinated by members of his own tribe. In 1826 the Creeks were successful in having the Treaty of Indian Springs set aside but, almost immediately, President John Quincy Adams negotiated the Treaty of Washington, which reimposed more or less the same terms on the Creeks.

The Removal Act

Andrew Jackson assumed the presidency in March 1829 and threw his political influence behind a national policy of Indian removal. He defended his stand by asserting that removal was the only course that could save Native Americans from extinction. The following year, after much debate, Congress passed the national Indian Removal Act, authorizing the president to set up districts within the Indian Territory for the reception of tribes agreeing to land exchanges. The act also provided for the payment of

indemnities to the Indians for assistance in accomplishing their resettlement, protection in their new settlements, and a continuance of the "superintendence and care" previously accorded them. Congress authorized $500,000 to carry out this act, and the pace of removal accelerated dramatically. Treaty negotiators set to work in the East and the West both to secure the permission of indigenous tribes in Indian Territory for eastern peoples to be resettled there and to convince eastern tribes to comply with removal. Under the supervision of General Winfield Scott and the federal army, the Cherokees began traveling their tragic Trail of Tears in 1838, three years after signing the controversial Treaty of New Echota. Although some groups, such as the Seminoles, resisted with force, most eastern tribes, including the so-called Civilized Tribes of the Southeast, had little choice but to accept what was offered them.

Treaties negotiated in the aftermath of the War of 1812 had already reduced the Native American population of the Old Northwest considerably, but Ohio, Indiana, and Illinois remained critical areas of activity for federal officials carrying out provisions of the Removal Act. With the Treaty of Wapaghkonnetta, signed in August 1831, the Shawnees gave up the last of their lands in Ohio in exchange for 100,000 acres in the Indian Territory. By the end of the following year, Ohio's Ottawas and Wyandots had also agreed to land exchanges, effectively eliminating that state's Native American population. In response to both the Indian Removal Act and the fear of Native reprisals inspired by the Black Hawk War of 1832, Indiana and Illinois were similarly cleared of Indians in the early 1830s. Most Sauks, Mesquakies, Winnebagoes, and Potawatomies were relocated to what is now Iowa. The Ojibways were confined to reservations in northern Michigan and Wisconsin. The Ottawas, Kaskaskias, Peorias, Miamis, and some New York Indians were assigned tracts along the Missouri border. The last treaty between the United States and the Indians of Illinois was made with the Kickapoos in February 1833, when that group agreed to relocate in Kansas. The Kickapoos suffered several subsequent removals (both voluntary and involuntary), and some of them ended up settling as far away as Mexico.

The westward journeys of these groups have been well documented and are infamous for their brutality. The best-known example is that of the Cherokees, who, during their removal from Georgia and North Carolina to the Indian Territory, lost nearly one-fourth of their number along the way. Those who reached their intended homes faced further difficulties. They quickly came into conflict with indigenous groups, and the lands set aside for them often became havens for criminals escaping prosecution. By 1850 the removal period was essentially over, but with the continued expansion of white settlement across the Mississippi, the Indian Territory was no longer a place where Native Americans could be isolated and left to their own devices. In the decades preceding the Civil War, the holdings of the relocated Indians were further reduced as new states were created out of the lands that had been "permanently" set aside for their use and occupancy.

By no means did all Native Americans east of the Mississippi move westward. Small pockets of Indian settlement remained in many eastern states. In some cases, those who remained behind were individual treaty signers and their families who had been given special grants of land within ceded areas. In others, especially in states along the eastern seaboard, certain groups were granted state-recognized reservations, some of which dated to the colonial period. In still other instances, they were persons who had chosen to disavow tribal ways and take up the "habits and arts of civilization" as practiced by the whites. Other individuals simply refused to leave and managed to remain hidden until the storm blew over, by which time their numbers were so insignificant that they were no longer viewed as threats by the whites around them.

Among the Indians escaping removal was a small band of several hundred fugitive Cherokees who fled to the mountains along the border between North Carolina and Tennessee, where they lived as refugees until 1842. In that year, in large part through the efforts of an influential trader named William H. Thomas, they received special permission to remain on lands set apart for their use in western North Carolina. These lands make up the Qualla Reservation, one of the largest reservations under federal supervision in the eastern United States.

By 1850, the federal government had concluded 245 separate Indian treaties. Through them, the United States had acquired more than 450 million acres of Indian land at a total estimated cost of $90 million.

BIBLIOGRAPHY

Green, Michael D. *The Politics of Indian Removal: Creek Government and Society in Crisis.* Lincoln: University of Nebraska Press, 1982.

Prucha, Francis Paul. *The Great Father: The United States Government and the American Indians.* 2 vols. Lincoln: University of Nebraska Press, 1984.

———. *American Indian Treaties: The History of a Political Anomaly.* Berkeley: University of California Press, 1994.

Wallace, Anthony F. C. *The Long, Bitter Trail: Andrew Jackson and the Indians.* New York: Hill and Wang, 1993.

Michael Sherfy

See also **Cherokee Nation Cases; Indian Land Cessions; Indian Territory; Removal Act of 1830; Trail of Tears;** *and vol. 9:* **A Century of Dishonor.**

INDIAN REORGANIZATION ACT. The Indian Reorganization Act (IRA) of 1934 represented a shift in U.S. Indian policy away from forced acculturation and assimilation. In 1928 the government-sponsored Meriam Report had documented problems of poverty, ill health, and despair on many reservations and recommended reforms in Bureau of Indian Affairs administration, including ending allotment and the phasing out of boarding schools. In 1933 the new administration of Franklin D. Roosevelt named John Collier, a former New York City social worker, to be commissioner of Indian affairs. Disillusioned with the materialistic and individualistic nature of industrial society, Collier proposed an Indian New Deal that would help preserve Native cultures and provide tribes with greater powers of self-government.

The IRA was the center of Collier's reform agenda. The act repudiated the Dawes General Allotment Act, barred further allotment, and set aside funds to consolidate and restore tribal landholdings. The IRA also provided for job training and vocational education and stipulated that Indians could gain employment in the BIA without recourse to civil service regulations. Finally, the act also allowed tribes to establish business councils with limited powers of home rule to enable them to develop reservation resources. A provision in Collier's original proposal to establish a special court of Indian affairs was rejected by Congress. Tribes were given the option of accepting or rejecting the IRA by referendum.

Despite Collier's rhetoric of self-determination, tribes felt pressured to accept the IRA just as they had felt pressed to accept previous government policies. Boilerplate BIA home rule charters showed little sensitivity to the diversity of Native life, and attempted to impose a one-size-fits-all solution to Indian problems. IRA referendums and majority rule tribal councils also ignored the consensus-driven traditions that persisted in many communities. The IRA attracted opposition from advocates of both assimilation and traditionalism, both inside and outside Indian communities. Ultimately, 174 tribes voted to accept the IRA and 78 tribes, including the Crow, Navajo, and Seneca, rejected it.

Despite its flaws and limitations, the IRA did represent a new recognition of Indian rights and culture. Although many of Collier's policies were altered in subsequent decades, both as a result of government-sponsored programs to terminate federal services to Indians and as a result of indigenous demands for greater sovereignty, the IRA and IRA-created governments remain influential in shaping U.S. Indian policy.

BIBLIOGRAPHY

Biolsi, Thomas. *Organizing the Lakota: The Political Economy of the New Deal on the Pine Ridge and Rosebud Reservations.* Tucson: University of Arizona Press, 1992.

Deloria, Vine, Jr., and Clifford M. Lytle. *The Nations Within: The Past and Future of American Indian Sovereignty.* New York: Pantheon, 1984.

Kelly, Lawrence C. *The Assault on Assimilation: John Collier and the Origins of Indian Policy Reform.* Albuquerque: University of New Mexico Press, 1983.

Taylor, Graham D. *The New Deal and American Indian Tribalism: The Administration of the Indian Reorganization Act, 1934–1945.* Lincoln: University of Nebraska Press, 1980.

Frank Rzeczkowski

See also **Bureau of Indian Affairs; Dawes General Allotment Act.**

INDIAN RESERVATIONS. Reservations have been a fundamental aspect of Native American existence for more than two centuries. For some, reservations are a living reminder of Euro-American colonialism and nation building exacted against indigenous people. Others insist that reservations today are the last remaining stronghold of sovereignty and cultural traditions, a reservoir that insures the perpetuation of Native American survival.

While the competing European colonial powers evolved political and legal mechanisms to deal with questions of Native American land title, the United States essentially followed the British model. The core principle was that Native American societies possessed a natural right to the soil as its original occupants. Thus, indigenous lands must be acquired by purchase, primarily negotiated through treaties and agreements. In addition to the treaties, the United States government used the concept of discovery, the rite of conquest, and military force to incorporate indigenous lands into the national fold.

In both the colonial period and the years that followed the American Revolution, reservations were an outgrowth of government land acquisition. Before the Revolution, various colonies created reservations that were subsequently recognized by legislatures as Indian reserves. The Second Continental Congress in 1775 established an Indian Department to deal with Indian affairs. After independence, the United States adopted a national policy of Indian administration by Constitutional mandate. The Constitution granted Congress plenary powers over Indian affairs in trade, treaties, warfare, welfare, and the right to take Indian lands for public purposes.

After 1778, Congress established federal Indian reservations by federal treaty or statute, conferring to the occupying tribe(s) recognized title over lands and the resources within their boundaries. Despite government promises of protection in exchange for land cessions, Secretary of War Henry Knox in 1789 lamented, "that all the Indian tribes once existing in those States, now the best cultivated and most populous, have become extinct . . . in a short period, the idea of an Indian on this side of the Mississippi will only be found in the page of the historian." Policymakers in the early republic believed that the attrition of Native Americans and the extinguishing of their reservations was an inevitable consequence of civilization's progress.

Indian Removal, 1816–1846

After the War of 1812, increasing conflicts between Native Americans and expanding Euro-American settlements demanded a solution. In 1830, Congress acted to create a policy of removal that would relocate Native Americans to "reserved lands" west of the Mississippi. President Andrew Jackson was the principal advocate of this policy, declaring in 1830 that "Humanity has often wept over the fate of the aborigines of this country, . . . but its progress has never for a moment been arrested, and one by one have many powerful tribes disappeared from the earth. . . . What good man would prefer a country covered with forests and ranges by a few thousand savages to our extensive republic . . . occupied by more than 12,000,000 happy people, and filled with all the blessings of liberty, civilization, and religion?"

Between 1828 and 1838, more than 80,000 Native Americans, particularly from the Southeast and the Old Northwest, were removed west of the Mississippi River. After relocation, the U.S. government acquired 15,355,767 acres of Indian lands for its citizens. Tribes suffered population losses when they were forced west and many tribal governments were weakened and disrupted as they attempted to create new governments on their western territories. The removal of Native American societies continued until 1877, although most relocations occurred before 1846.

Reservation Period, 1851–1880

While the removal created temporary space between "American civilization" and Indian Territory, that space quickly disappeared. As Euro-America pushed beyond the Mississippi river, policymakers had to devise new ways of alienating indigenous societies from their lands. To accomplish this task, on 3 March 1849 Congress created the Department of the Interior to manage public land, Indian land, and Indian affairs. The Indian Office moved quickly to address the "Indian problem." Under pressure from an expanding American population and American industry's demand for more natural resources, the new department took direct administrative responsibility for reservations. Beginning in 1851 and continuing for three decades, federal bureaucrats developed a series of policies for the final solution to the "Indian problem." Using treaties, coercion, and military force, the government actively consolidated Native American societies. Commissioner of Indian Affairs Luke Lea set forth the doctrine in 1851 by calling for the Indians' "concentration, their domestication, and their incorporation." Reservations came to be seen as instruments for the achievement of this goal. In a new flurry of treaty making, the United States acquired millions of acres of Indian land and assigned the tribes to reservations on a portion of their former territory.

In the years following the publication of the *Origin of Species* (1859), the desire to "domesticate" and "incorporate" Indians into American society was driven by the application of Darwinian evolutionary principles to the development of social life. Native Americans, like all non-Europeans, were believed to be intellectually, emotionally, and culturally inferior, but social evolution predicted that it might be possible to push Native Americans along the societal hierarchy toward civilization if they were forced to adopt Euro-American ways of life. For the remainder of the nineteenth century, this reasoning encouraged further acquisition of tribal land and the creation of additional reservations.

Although treaties were the primary mechanism for creating reservations, Congress suspended formal treaty making in 1871.Thereafter, federal reservations would be established by executive order, congressional act, or any legal combination recognized by the federal government. Before the turn of the century, 56 of 162 federal reservations were established by executive order. After 1919, however, only an act of Congress could establish reservations.

Forced Assimilation, 1880–1934

The rationale behind the twentieth-century reservation system was twofold: Native American resources could be further exploited with a minimum of cost and effort and, the controlled environment of the reservation would provide for a laboratory in social engineering. The reservation was conceived as a refuge for a declining race that could be elevated from their inferior status by assimilation. The Indian Office promoted these objectives by breaking up the "habits of savage life" by instilling "civilized" values through forced education, by insisting on agricultural labor, and by pushing the notion of private property and the development of monetary funds. To this end, the reservation was conceived as a controlled society where the habits of civilization could be molded under the direction of the Indian agent and agency personnel. From 1880 to 1934, ethnocide became an officially sanctioned policy.

The principal legal instrument for these new policies was the General Allotment Act, passed in 1887. After the

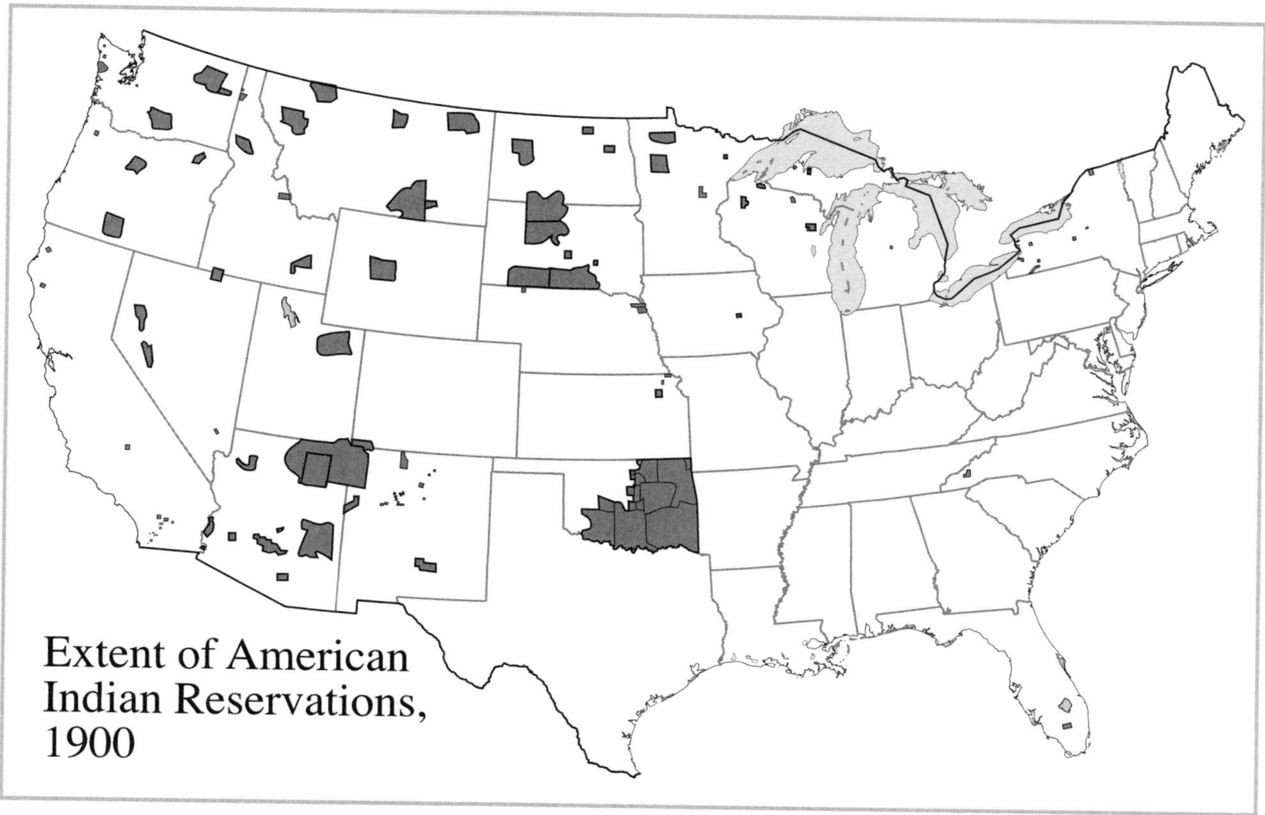

law's passage, more than one hundred reservations saw their lands fragmented into individual tracts of 160 acres or less. In 1906, the Burke Act granted local Indian Office officials the power to transfer land from trust status to fee patent status through application. The act expedited the transfer of Indian lands into Anglo hands. Over the next fifty years, the U.S. government was able to divest Native Americans of about 90 million acres. Indian lands decreased from 136 million acres in 1887 to about 48 million acres in 1934, when the act was finally repealed.

Despite oppressive government policies and actions, Native Americans were not passive victims of this new authoritarian reservation system. Native Americans continued to practice their cultural traditions and invent new ones. The Ghost Dance and the Native American Church stand as examples of Native American cultural persistence during this bleak period. In addition, the boarding school experience brought together young from various tribes who laid the seeds for the emergence of a pan-ethnic identity that cut across tribal lines. Some tribes also resisted government policies in court or before Congress.

Federal officials pressed their assimilationist agenda through the first decades of the twentieth century. The 1910 Omnibus Act, for example, though designed to solve heirship problems, authorized the Secretary of Interior to lease Indian lands, whether allotted or unallotted, and sell Indian resources. Between 1916 and 1920, Commissioner Cato Sells encouraged Indian Office personnel to force fee patent status of trust land of all competent Indians. By the 1920s, most tribes had lost the ability to control their resources and were in danger of losing valuable reservation resources.

As the federal government was dismantling Native American lands and societies, it also pressed them to volunteer for military service and to become U.S. citizens. After World War I, Indian veterans were granted U.S. citizenship under the Act of 1919. Five years later, all American Indians would be granted citizenship after the passage of the Indian Citizenship Act. Both pieces of legislation were intended to undermine Indian ties to their tribes.

Tribal Reorganization, 1928–1945

By the mid-1920s Native American leaders, sympathetic Indian rights organizations, and even some federal officials began to question the effectiveness of forced assimilation policies. In 1928, the Meriam Report, a nationwide study sponsored by the Indian Office, found that federal legislation injured American Indian progress. The report also noted that reservation life was plagued by endemic poverty, ill health, poor education, and social and economic dependency. The failures of allotment, forced assimilation, and deplorable living conditions on reservations outlined in the Meriam Report led to the passage of the 1934 Indian Reorganization Act. The legislation repealed the General Allotment Act, affirmed certain Native

Waiting for Rations. This 1890 photograph by George Trager shows Indians confined to the Pine Ridge Reservation, S.D., where they depended on meager U.S. government rations; starvation and resentment of white corruption led to the Sioux breakout that year, ending in the massacre at nearby Wounded Knee. NATIONAL ARCHIVES AND RECORDS ADMINISTRATION

American cultural traditions and practices, and authorized a political mechanism for strengthening self-government for federally recognized tribes. Two years later, the Oklahoma Indian Welfare Act of 1936 restored tribal governments (but did not reestablish reservations) to Oklahoma tribes. Alaskan Natives achieved similar reforms under the 1936 Alaskan Native Reorganization Act. One hundred and seventy-four tribes, bands, and communities incorporated themselves by this legal mechanism. While such legislative acts held the potential for economic and social development, the most important portion of the act suspended allotment and returned formerly ceded lands that remained in the public domain to trust status. Between 1935 and 1937, over 2 million acres of land reverted back to Indian holdings. Tribes also regained control of 7 million acres of leased grazing lands.

Termination, 1945–1961

Many policies strengthening Native American reservation societies were reversed following World War II. In addition to general hostility to all New Deal reforms, there was a growing belief among federal officials that the Bureau of Indian Affairs had outlived its purpose because it actually kept Indians from assimilating into American society.

To "get out of the Indian business," Congress passed the Indian Land Commission Claims Act of 1946, a measure designed to settle outstanding legal claims as a prelude to severing the government's ties to tribal nations. The desire to withdraw federal trusteeship for federally recognized tribes also led to a series of legislative acts that undermined reservation life. House Concurrent Resolution 108, adopted in 1953, declared Congress's intent to make the Indians subject to the same laws and entitled them to the same privileges and responsibilities as are applicable to other U.S. citizens. Soon thereafter Congress passed Public Law 83-280 transferring civil jurisdiction and criminal control of certain reservations to local state authorities. The next year, the Indian Health Service Branch was transferred from the Bureau of Indian Affairs to the U.S. Public Health Service. At the same time, the Bureau of Indian Affairs launched a relocation program to move Indians from reservations to target urban centers.

During the 1950s and 1960s, Congress acted to abolish (or "terminate") about 120 reservations. These included the Alabama-Coushatta of Texas, several California rancherias and reservation tribes, the Klamaths and the scattered tribes of Oregon, the Menominees of Wisconsin, and three Oklahoma tribes. For those terminated tribes the impact of the policy was devastating.

Although Congress did not officially reverse its termination policy until 1973, the program effectively ended in the early 1960s. Commissioner of Indian Affairs Phileo Nash, an anthropologist, introduced new programs to strengthen reservation political and economic development by building an economic infrastructure, promoting education, and on-the-job-training programs. By 1965, approximately fifty-six industrial plants were located on or near reservations.

Self-Determination, 1961 through the Early Twenty-first Century

From 1961 through the early 2000s, Native American political and legislative policies moved toward the general principle of self-determination on Indian reservations. Native American reaction against termination, combined with a growing sense of an indigenous pan-ethnic consciousness led to a reassertion of treaty rights among a number of tribes. Reservation-based tribes demanded greater authority over their affairs and urban Indians began to form organizations to bring attention to indigenous issues, including the need for strong reservation governments. The most successful urban protest group was the American Indian Movement, an organization that called for tribal sovereignty on reservations.

At the federal level, Lyndon B. Johnson's administration developed the War on Poverty to improve conditions in neglected areas of the country. Several tribes used these programs to take control of their own social welfare programs and to strengthen the administrative structure of their governments. The Bureau of Indian Affairs routinely opposed these efforts.

On the legislative front, congressional leaders grew increasingly sympathetic to tribal rights and reservation governments. The termination policy was officially renounced and several previously terminated tribes (most prominently the Menominees and Klamaths) were returned to tribal status. In 1975, Congress passed the Indian Self-Determination and Education Assistance Act, which established the principle that reservation governments could administer their own education and social service programs. While resisted by the Bureau of Indian Affairs, this new law opened the possibility that tribes could function as autonomous governments within the boundaries of their reservations.

Other pieces of legislation were passed to address social and cultural issues. In 1978, Congress passed the American Indian Religious Freedom Act with the intent to provide constitutional protection of indigenous religious freedom under the First Amendment. That same year, the Indian Child Welfare Act ended the practice of placing Indian children in non-Indian households and gave tribal courts a prominent role in adoption proceedings involving tribal members.

While reservation policies changed little in the 1980s, Congress approved two important pieces of legislation. The 1982 Indian Tribal Governmental Tax Status Act that permitted tribal governments to issue tax-exempt revenue bonds and the 1988 Indian Gaming Regulatory Act permitted gaming on reservations.

During the Clinton Administration the government-to-government relations between reservations and the United States was affirmed. President Clinton acknowledged that reservation communities were still plagued by poverty, poor health care, and unemployment, but he outlined a program for improvement that included greater tribal control over education, health care, and economic policy. Despite these declarations, throughout the 1990s, political attacks against Native American tribal sovereignty on reservations increased. Efforts were made to weaken the Indian Child Welfare Act and the Indian Gaming Regulatory Act. Amendments were made to the Clean Air Act to dissolve tribal authority over water policies on tribal lands. Funding for legal services and health care were cut. Proposals were made by states to tax gaming revenues.

It was discovered that billions of dollars held in trust by the federal government had been grossly misused and mismanaged. Many reservations and culturally sensitive sites off reservation were being targeted again for natural resource development. The federal government's relationship with tribes wavered between respect for tribal sovereignty and rights and attempts to extinguish tribal existence. The administration of George W. Bush was in the process of "downsizing" in order to meet balanced budget promises. Despite these attacks, reservation communities continued to persist into the twenty-first century.

The Reservation Situation in the Early Twenty-first Century

Census data since the 1960s reveals that the Native American population is growing at a tremendous rate. According to the 2000 census, there are 2,475,956 Native Americans in the United States, but only a portion of those individuals are citizens in one of the 510 federally recognized Native American tribes. Of that number, 437,079 American Indians, 182 Eskimos, and 97 Aleuts resided on 314 reservations and trust lands. About 50 percent of the 437,358 American Indians, Eskimos, and Aleuts reside on the ten largest reservations and trust lands.

A total of 56.2 million acres of land are held in trust by the United States for various tribes and individuals. About 82 percent of trust lands are owned by tribes, with 140 reservations entirely owned by tribes; approximately 17 percent are held by individuals; and less than one percent is held by the federal government. The largest reservation is the sixteen-million-acre Navajo reservation. It is home to about 269,202 Navajos. The Navajo reservation is unique in that since its establishment in 1868, it has progressively grown in size by executive orders and Congressional acts. In stark contrast, California rancherias and smaller reservations, primarily in California, Nevada, Oregon, and Washington, are less than 1,000 acres each.

The number of Native Americans living on reservations and trust lands vary substantially. According to the 2000 census, only ten reservations had a resident population of more than 7,000. These were the Navajo, Fort Apache, Gila River, Papago, Rosebud, San Carlos, Zuni Pueblo, Hopi, and Blackfeet reservations. Most had fewer than 1,000 residents. Since most reservation and trust lands are in the West, more than one-half of American

Indians reside in Oklahoma, California, Arizona, New Mexico, and Washington.

Indian reservations in the early 2000s, despite progress in health care and socio-economic development, remained a contradiction across the U.S. landscape. As reservation tribes struggled toward greater sovereignty and self-determination, they had to contend with numerous issues on a number of fronts. Many reservation communities struggled with a fragmented land base because of allotment, a growing hostility from non-Indian residents living on or near reservations, the need for greater economic self-sufficiency, and the task of building stronger cultural identities. Despite these challenges, many Native Americans continued to live on reservations. Reservations offered a strong sense of place and cultural identity. There is, across native North America, a new pride in tribal identity and a renaissance of traditions. Reservations have emerged as the focal point for the retention of unique cultural identities and for issues of sovereignty and self-determination, even for Indians who live in cities far from their tribal homelands. Across the Americas, indigenous people are recognizing that political struggle is essential to their basic right to exist as sovereign nations. Resistance and struggle are a part of daily existence for Native American people. A part of that resistance is not only surviving but also building a secure future for coming generations by enforcing basic human rights within a secure reservation land base. Reservations provide a geographical and political platform to expand their rights on a number of fronts.

BIBLIOGRAPHY

Berkhofer, Robert F., Jr. *The White Man's Indian: Images of the American Indian from Columbus to the Present.* New York: Knopf, 1978.

Bureau of the Census. *We the . . . First Americans.* Washington, D.C.: U.S. Department of Commerce, 1993.

Bureau of the Census. "American Indian Reservation Households Crowded in 1990." Washington, D.C.: U.S. Department of Commerce, 1995.

Champagne, Duane, ed. *Chronology of Native North American History: From Pre-Columbian Times to the Present.* Detroit: Gale Research, 1994.

Debo, Angie. *The Road to Disappearance: A History of the Creek Indians.* Norman: University of Oklahoma Press, 1941.

Dippie, Brian W. *The Vanishing American: White Attitudes and U.S. Indian Policy.* Middletown, Conn.: Wesleyan University Press, 1982.

Drinnon, Richard. *Facing West: The Metaphysics of Indian-Hating and Empire Building.* Minneapolis: University of Minnesota Press, 1980.

Foreman, Grant. *Indian Removal: The Emigration of the Five Civilized Tribes.* Norman: University of Oklahoma Press, 1953.

Green, Michael D. *The Politics of Indian Removal: Creek Government and Society in Crisis.* Lincoln: University of Nebraska Press, 1982.

Haller, John S., Jr. *Outcasts from Evolution: Scientific Attitudes of Racial Inferiority, 1859–1900.* Carbondale: Southern Illinois University Press, 1995.

Hoxie, Fredrick. *A Final Promise: The Campaign to Assimilate the Indians, 1880–1920.* Lincoln: University of Nebraska Press, 1984.

Jorgensen, Joseph B. "A Century of Political Economic Effects on American Indian Society, 1880–1980." *The Journal of Ethnic Studies* 6, no. 3 (1978): 1–74.

Marino, Cesare. "Reservations." In *Native America in the Twentieth Century.* Edited by Mary B. Davis. New York: Garland, 1994. 544–557.

Meredith, Howard. *A Short History of the Native Americans in the United States.* Malabar, Fla.: Kreiger, 2001.

Passel, Jeffery S., and Patricia A. Berman. "Quality of 1980 Census Data for American Indians." *Social Biology* 33, nos. 3–4 (1986): 163–182.

Pearce, Roy H. *Savagism and Civilization: A Study of the Indian and the American Mind.* Baltimore: John Hopkins University Press, 1965.

Rosenstiel, Annette. *Red and White: Indian Views of the White Man, 1492–1982.* New York: Universe Books, 1983.

Stuart, Paul. *The Indian Office: Growth and Development of an American Institution, 1865–1900.* Ann Arbor, Mich.: UMI Research Press, 1979.

Thornton, Russell. *American Indian Holocaust and Survival: A Population History since 1492.* Norman: University of Oklahoma Press, 1987.

Trigger, Bruce G. *A History of Archaeological Thought.* Cambridge, U.K.: Cambridge University Press, 1989.

Ubelaker, Douglas H. "Patterns of Demographic Change in the Americas." *Human Biology* 64, no. 3 (June 1992): 361–379.

U.S. Department of the Interior, Bureau of Indian Affairs. *American Indians Today: Answers to Your Questions.* Washington, D.C.: U.S. Department of the Interior, 1991.

Wissler, Clark. "The Rebirth of the 'Vanishing American.'" *Natural History* 34, no. 5 (1934): 415–430.

Gregory Campbell

See also **Bureau of Indian Affairs; Dawes General Allotment Act; Indian Policy, Colonial; Indian Policy, U.S; Indian Political Life; Indian Removal; Indian Reorganization Act; Indian Self-Determination and Education Assistance Act; Indian Territory; Removal Act of 1830; Westward Migration.**

INDIAN RIGHTS ASSOCIATION. In December 1882 Herbert Welsh, an artist and social reformer, and Henry Pancoast, a lawyer, founded the Indian Rights Association (IRA) in Philadelphia, Pennsylvania. The IRA, whose founding members were prominent businessmen and philanthropists, believed that American Indians' best hope for survival lay in a program of assimilation. This program involved education, conversion to Christianity, adoption of Anglo-Saxon legal institutions, private landholding, and the reduction of government rations.

The indefatigable efforts of Welsh and Charles Painter, the IRA's investigator and Washington lobbyist, made the IRA the most influential American Indian reform group of its time. The group monitored the implementation of legislation affecting American Indians, advocating legislation such as the **Dawes General Allotment Act** of 1887 and drafting legislation such as the Dawes Sioux Bill of 1884. Painter investigated complaints of abuse; Welsh used his connection with the editors of influential periodicals such as *Harper's Weekly* and the *New York Times*, as well as the IRA's own publications, to publicize Painter's findings.

After the turn of the century the IRA's activity diminished; Charles Painter had died in 1895 and Herbert Welsh was preoccupied with other reform activities. However, two former IRA officials, Francis Leupp and Charles Rhoads, became commissioners of Indian Affairs and pursued the IRA's policy of assimilation while in office.

The advent of John Collier as commissioner of Indian Affairs in 1933 ended the IRA's dominance over American Indian reform. The group's agenda has been modified during the twentieth century to include advocacy of global human rights. The IRA has continued its support of American Indian land rights, championing the Senecas in the Kinzua Dam controversy of the 1950s and 1960s, and helping the Pequot Indians to recover land in 1976. In the early twenty-first century its membership included prominent American Indians, and it supported American Indian education with financial assistance and public education.

BIBLIOGRAPHY

Erickson, Jackson T., ed. *Indian Rights Association Papers: A Guide to the Microfilm Edition, 1864–1973.* Glenrock, N.J.: Microfilming Corporation of America, 1975.

Hagan, William T. *The Indian Rights Association: The Herbert Welsh Years.* Tucson: University of Arizona Press, 1985.

Rebecca McNulty

See also **Bureau of Indian Affairs.**

INDIAN SELF-DETERMINATION AND EDUCATION ASSISTANCE ACT. Signed into law on 4 January 1975, this legislation completed a fifteen-year period of policy reform with regard to American Indian tribes. Passage of this law made self-determination, rather than termination, the focus of government action, reversing a thirty-year effort to sever treaty relationships with and obligations to Indian tribes. The disastrous consequences of termination, combined with aggressive Indian activism, had encouraged a reexamination of government policy. During the 1960s, the War on Poverty's Community Action programs, with their philosophy of "maximum feasible participation of the poor," also encouraged a change in direction. Significant too were President Lyndon B. Johnson's 1968 congressional message on Indian affairs entitled "The Forgotten American" and Richard M. Nixon's official repudiation of termination in 1970.

A policy of self-determination committed the federal government to encouraging "maximum Indian participation in the Government and education of the Indian people." The 1975 legislation contained two provisions. Title I, the Indian Self-Determination Act, established procedures by which tribes could negotiate contracts with the Bureau of Indian Affairs to administer their own education and social service programs. It also provided direct grants to help tribes develop plans to assume responsibility for federal programs. Title II, the Indian Education Assistance Act, attempted to increase parental input in Indian education by guaranteeing Indian parents' involvement on school boards.

Subsequent amendments to the Self-Determination Act adopted in the 1980s and 1990s launched self-governance. Under this program, tribes would receive bloc grants from the Indian Health Service and the Bureau of Indian Affairs to cover a number of programs. In 2000, about half of the bureau's total obligations to tribes took the form of self-determination contracts or bloc grants. Additionally, seventy-six tribes had contracted for health clinics, diabetes programs, mobile health units, alcohol and drug abuse clinics, and Community Health Representative programs through the Indian Health Service. As amended, the Indian Self-Determination and Education Assistance Act stands as one of the twentieth century's seminal pieces of federal Indian legislation.

BIBLIOGRAPHY

Castile, George Pierre. *To Show Heart: Native American Self-Determination and Federal Indian Policy, 1960–1975.* Tucson: University of Arizona Press, 1998.

Clarkin, Thomas. *Federal Indian Policy in the Kennedy and Johnson Administrations, 1961–1969.* Albuquerque: University of New Mexico Press, 2001.

Cobb, Daniel M. "Philosophy of an Indian War: Indian Community Action in the Johnson Administration's War on Indian Poverty, 1964–1968." *American Indian Culture and Research Journal* 22, no. 2 (1998): 71–102.

Philp, Kenneth R., ed. *Indian Self-Rule: First-Hand Accounts of Indian-White Relations from Roosevelt to Reagan.* Logan: Utah State University Press, 1995.

Daniel M. Cobb

See also **Education, Indian; Indian Policy, U.S., 1900–2000; Indian Political Life; Indian Reservations.**

INDIAN SIGN LANGUAGE. *See* **Sign Language, Indian.**

INDIAN SOCIAL LIFE. Although European contact affected Native people, adaptation and change have long characterized Indian communities. It can be difficult to differentiate recent changes from precontact trends already in process. In addition, new elements, such as the introduction of the horse by the Spanish, often altered lifestyles well before Native people came into direct contact with Euro-Americans. Across time and space, ongoing processes of indigenous adaptation and change complicate how we assess the transformations traditionally associated with the intrusion of Euro-Americans.

Northeastern Woodlands

The Northeast was a region of small, sedentary agricultural villages where women raised corn, squash, and beans. Summer wigwams were adjacent to seasonal food supplies and here families harvested berries and nuts, and hunted and fished. Village life was communal and emphasized generosity, loyalty, and bravery. The region was highly populated, so it suffered significantly from the first shock waves of epidemic disease associated with European encounter. Smallpox, chicken pox, measles, whooping cough, and typhus decimated coastal village populations by as much as 95 percent. Villages that persisted often did so as isolated settlements within a colonized English landscape.

The IROQUOIS were the region's most powerful confederacy, uniting the Cayugas, Mohawks, Oneidas, Onondagas, and Senecas. The Iroquois called themselves Haudensaunee, "people of the longhouse." They lived in elongated elm-bark structures, twenty-five feet wide and less than 100 feet long with some extending to 200 feet. Three to six families or hearths from the same maternal lineage lived in one dwelling. Marriage was a contract between two groups of kin, rather than a contract between individuals. Parents as well as elder relatives influenced the selection of marriage partners. However, the compatibility of the prospective couple remained important since newlyweds were incorporated into established longhouses. Noncompatible couples were permitted to divorce.

Cultural practices were altered by disease, warfare, and the continual incorporation of strangers. Among the matrilineal Seneca, the women of a longhouse might demand that the community go to war to replace a fallen male warrior. This cycle of retribution and replacement disrupted the eighteenth-century Iroquois, who were often a minority in their own villages while a majority were adoptees and slaves. The arrival of Jesuit missionaries further disrupted village life. Few Iroquois found Christianity an appealing alternative until Handsome Lake, a Seneca religious prophet, blended Christian practices with many of the traditional religious beliefs of the Seneca in the early nineteenth century. Handsome Lake's religious middle ground transformed gender and familial roles: men became agriculturalists, women became housewives, and the nuclear family displaced the familial networks of the longhouse. Longhouse churches have preserved the traditional feast calendar and traditional Iroquois behaviors have acquired the form of Christian commandments.

Southeastern Woodlands

During the precontact period large palisaded towns exerted political authority over this region. People lived in urban areas dominated by extensive ceremonial centers and large mound-like structures topped by temples and the houses of rulers and priests. Trade likely linked these towns to those of Mesoamerica.

Sometime between the eleventh and thirteenth centuries, political power became less centralized in southeastern towns and people dispersed into smaller communities. However, southeastern population centers remained larger and more complex in social organization than those of the Northeast. Towns housed interrelated families, linked through matrilineal descent. Each person was born into the mother's clan and the male relatives of one's mother often proved far more important than one's biological father. These hierarchically structured towns included chiefs whose power ranged from advisory to absolute. Ceremonial sites brought towns together for ritual feasts and housed competitive sports events, such as lacrosse. The importance of feasts and ceremonies speaks to the resiliency of indigenous tradition because they continued to bring people together. The Green Corn Ceremony, a four-day ceremony of Thanksgiving celebrated in early summer, has been followed for centuries. British defeat in the War of 1812 brought the first forced removals. Resettlement in Indian territory west of the Mississippi transformed most southeastern people into Oklahoma residents, but many communities retained their "town" focus and social structure.

Plains

Until the onset of the reservation period, plains life was inextricably linked to the buffalo hunt and to farming. Buffalo meat was dried, stored, and eaten during the winter months. Hides covered tipis, robes provided bedding, and sinew became thread. For Indians like the BLACKFEET, the buffalo was processed into one hundred different items of daily use. Another group of tribes farmed the bottom lands of the Missouri River and its tributaries. These plains farmers lived in large villages of "earth lodges," dirt-covered structures that could house as many as forty people.

Following the acquisition of horses in the eighteenth century, most Plains Indians became nomadic. Successful buffalo hunting required flexible living conditions. People resided in small groups known as tiospaye, which generally included extended families. Interrelated families camped together and joined other, more distantly related families to form bands.

Male work focused on hunting, warfare, and ceremonial life. The task of butchering was shared by men and women, but the drying and storing of meat, roots, and prairie fruits were women's work, as was the production of clothing, lodge covers, and robes. The woman generally owned the tipi. Over time, decimating epidemics and persistent raiding undermined the Plains Indians' farming villages and caused them to disappear as a significant part of the region's social life.

Kinship terminology tended to be generational, so the children of parents' siblings were referred to as brothers and sisters. Most Plains Indians practiced some system of avoidance and this usually affected affinal kin of the opposite sex. For instance, the Gros Ventre categorized relatives as those entitled to "respect" or those to whom avoidance was practiced. Interaction was often confined to siblings of the same sex and in-laws of the same generation.

The arrival of the horse introduced wealth differentials, but social divisions were lessened by community traditions of gift giving, which redistributed both food and horses. A prominent man with a large herd of horses usually had the largest tipi, which housed his wives and the young male relatives that lived with him. The other tipis clustered around him might include elderly women with their granddaughters or nieces whom they trained in women's tasks. Less prominent men lacking horses had smaller households. Authority on the plains was legitimated by participation in a ceremonial system based on one's relationship to the supernatural. Medicine power was essential to success—human figures seen in dreams or visions changed into animals, birds, insects, and snakes that bestowed power. Ceremonial practices differed among tribes but most practiced some form of the SUN DANCE. Leadership tended to be age based with respected elders acting as guides and teachers. Elders were also responsible for generating consensus and resolving conflict.

A series of nineteenth-century treaties relocated the various bands to reservations. There rules were established that forbade horse raids, scalp and war dances, and the Sun Dance. But, even after being settled on reservations the Plains tribes continued to view the generous distribution of property as a means to maintain authority and validate status.

Southwest

The Southwest is the longest area of continuous human habitation, outside of Mesoamerica. Local and community-based enclaves have long resisted assimilation, remained tenuously on their homelands, and have successfully maintained their lands, languages, and religions. Southwestern Indians maintain complex annual ceremonies that have been practiced for over 2,000 years.

The precontact fourteenth and fifteenth centuries were characterized by internal migration. Large population clusters broke up into smaller village enclaves. In the sixteenth century, the Spanish arrived and established the first colony on the Rio Grande in 1598; they were subsequently expelled during the PUEBLO REVOLT of 1680. Once the Spanish reestablished themselves they introduced a variety of technological changes that brought large domestic animals (such as horses and cattle), new crops (such as wheat), and metal tools and firearms into the region. Spanish reliance on a Christianized military intrusion dramatically changed the lifestyles, languages, and cultural beliefs of the people they colonized. Although many villages remained too remote for conquest, many people were captured by Spanish soldiers and forced to relocate to the Spanish missions. They became sedentary farmers and lived in nuclear families. Christianity challenged indigenous religions, but traditional beliefs were still followed, though often in secret. On the whole, the Spanish were far fewer in number and did not demand the vast land concessions that devastated indigenous homelands in the Northeast and Southeast. The peoples who lived in the Southwest experienced devastating changes in the last half of the nineteenth century when the U.S. military established hegemony over the region. It was then that Native communities faced resettlement on reservations. The Pueblos, whose homelands became their reservations, often fared the best while the nomadic hunters and traders, nations such as the APACHE and NAVAJO, faced deportation and mass starvation.

In the twentieth century, the U.S. government further attacked indigenous subsistence economies by substantially diminishing the land bases of many nations and forcing more intrusive policies of attendance at boarding schools. Although some ceremonies were criminalized, they were practiced in secret.

Farming has been and continues to be very important to the people of this region—corn, beans, cotton, and tobacco constitute the most important crops. Trade remains important in this region and people from various villages exchange food; minerals, such as turquoise; and native handicrafts, such as jewelry, baskets, and blankets.

Northwest Coast

The natural landscape has long structured the cultural life of the Northwest, providing raw materials for everything from food to clothing, housing, and transportation. Rich fish harvests, particularly salmon, and large red cedar forests shaped this region of hierarchically ranked communities, where status was inherited. Class divisions were rigid with rights and privileges as well as fishing and hunting areas determined by kinship. Marriage was an outgrowth of social organization. The lowest class of people were slaves, who were either purchased or captured. Unless freed, their status was permanent and hereditary. Marriage of a free person with a slave was considered disgraceful.

A rich ceremonial life, structured around the potlatch and elaborate gift giving, validated the status claims of the upper classes. From the Nootkans and Kwakiutl northward, the elite were ranked and from the Central Coast Salish southward, individual ranking was less developed. During the closing decades of the nineteenth century, disease became increasingly problematic, missionaries increased in number, and the government promoted assimilationalist policies. Wage labor and the construction of canneries on Indian lands proved particularly disruptive to long-established subsistence patterns. Initially, the Canadian and U.S. governments dismissed indigenous land rights. The skill and ability of Native people to seek legal redress in the courts reversed the descent into decline experienced by many communities.

Modern political organizations serve as governing bodies but the protocols followed by these groups follow traditional organizational structures. The Small Tribes Organization of Washington coordinates the land claim efforts and supports the fight for federal recognition. During the 1970s and 1980s, these tribes revived traditional dances and ceremonies, promoted traditional arts, created native language programs, and established tribal cultural centers. In many communities, carving has replaced fishing as the most prestigious occupation.

Despite repeated attempts to suppress the potlatch, it has persisted among Indians in the Northwest and even experienced a renascence in the 1960s when money was distributed, notable names bestowed, and dances incorporated into the ceremony. The Tlingit potlatch is perhaps the best known because they have used the ceremony to publicly commemorate important events.

Recent Trends

The kin-based communal nature of Indian life in most regions was undermined during the reservation period because the Bureau of Indian Affairs controlled all aspects of daily life. Households were weakened by a lack of economic opportunity for men. Male authority was also challenged by Christian missionaries who fostered movement toward the nuclear family, the English language, and the independence of children. The reservation period also fostered social interaction and while many traditional dances were banned, particularly war dances, dance forms were reinvented. Summer fairs have frequently taken the place of traditional activities, offering opportunities to visit friends and relatives on other reservations.

Collier's Indian New Deal was committed to rebuilding Indian communities, but it was the outbreak of World War II that represented a watershed in Native social life. Thousands of men enlisted in the army. Dance gatherings were used to send off and welcome home servicemen. These gatherings became the forerunners of the postwar powwow. The depression and then the army experience together led many young men to the cities to find work. The government also encouraged urban migration through a voluntary relocation program. At the same time, many who relocated to cities often returned to their reservations, when they retired. Tribal life was reinvigorated by new economic opportunities, particularly gaming, the revival of native religions, and a renewed emphasis on ritual activities. In addition, Indian organizations, like the National Congress of American Indians, coordinated intertribal efforts to return sacred lands. Together these changes produced unprecedented interaction, cultural innovation, and a sense of cultural revival across North America. These features continue to characterize American Indian social life in the twenty-first century.

BIBLIOGRAPHY

Anderson, Jeffrey D. *The Four Hills of Life: Northern Arapaho Knowledge and Life Movement.* Omaha: University of Nebraska Press, 2001.

Basso, Keith H. *Wisdom Sits in Places: Landscape among the Western Apache.* Albuquerque: University of New Mexico Press, 1996.

Bierwert, Crisca. *Brushed by Cedar, Living by the River: Coast Salish Figures of Power.* Tucson: University of Arizona Press, 1999.

Boyd, Robert. *The Coming of the Spirit of Pestilence: Introduced Infectious Diseases and Population Decline among Northwest Coast Indians, 1774–1874.* Vancouver: University of British Columbia Press, 1999.

Fowler, Loretta. *Arapaho Politics, 1851–1978: Symbols in Crisis of Authority.* Lincoln: University of Nebraska Press, 1982.

Harmon, Alexandra. *Indians in the Making: Ethnic Relations and Indian Identities around Puget Sound.* Berkeley: University of California Press, 1998.

Hoxie, Frederick E. *Parading through History: The Making of the Crow Nation in America, 1805–1935.* New York: Cambridge University Press, 1995.

Merrell, James H. *The Indians' New World: Catawbas and Their Neighbors from European Contact through the Era of Removal.* New York: W.W. Norton, 1989.

Saunt, Claudio. *A New Order of Things: Property, Power, and the Transformation of the Creek Indians, 1733–1816.* Cambridge, U.K.: University of Cambridge Press, 1999.

Wallace, Anthony F.C. *The Death and Rebirth of the Seneca.* New York: Vintage Books, 1972.

White, Richard. *The Middle Ground: Indians, Empires, and Republics in the Great Lakes Region, 1650–1815.* New York: University of Cambridge Press, 1991.

Susan Sleeper-Smith

See also **Agriculture, American Indian; Art, Indian; Indian Intermarriage; Indian Political Life; Indian Religious Life; Indian Reservations; Tribes;** *and vol. 9:* **Land of the Spotted Eagle.**

INDIAN TECHNOLOGY. Native Americans lived in harmony with their environments, but they also actively manipulated elements in those environments to meet their physical needs. Technology can be defined as the use of tools to increase the effects of human impact on the natural environment. The major tools used by Native Americans included fire for managing forest and grassland resources, various implements designed for hunting, agricultural implements, irrigation and other water management systems for agriculture, and astronomical tools.

Uses of Fire

The use of fire as a tool was widespread in the Americas. Although lightning-set fires were common, Indians set fires deliberately. On the East Coast of the United States, early historical accounts describe some forested areas as parklike—the forest floor was grassy with little underbrush. These conditions were maintained by natural and human-set fires. Fire promoted new growth of grass, which in turn provided an attractive habitat for deer. The lack of underbrush made it easier to hunt with bows and arrows. In what is now California, research has demonstrated that periodic burning of the chaparral increased the available browse for deer, leading to higher numbers and greater health of offspring. Burning also promoted long, straight branches of *Corylus* for basketry in California, and the soil around stands of wild sedge and ferns was cultivated to promote fine, straight roots. Basket making as a technology probably reached its highest point of sophistication in California.

Iroquoian agricultural communities in the Northeast Woodlands and Muskogeans in the Southeast used slash-and-burn techniques to clear and prepare their fields. Trees were girdled and left to die, and the dead trees were felled and burned, enriching and warming the soil for planting. On the Great Plains, fires were set to encourage the growth of new grasses and sometimes to drive game animals toward hunters or to surround them.

Hunting Technologies

The sinew-backed bow, arrow straighteners, and arrows and spears with stone points are all examples of Native technology. On the Northwest Coast and in the Arctic, sea animals were hunted with harpoons fitted with detachable heads that came loose from the shaft when they lodged in the animal. Makah whale hunters used long lines with sealskin floats attached to buoy the whale to prevent it from sounding and swamping their canoes. Throughout the Americas, weirs, nets, hooks, and spears were all used in fishing.

Development of Agriculture

Agriculture is a form of technology in that it involves direct human intervention in natural processes. Although the earliest domesticated plants were probably volunteers that favored the disturbed soil around human habitations, Native people could divert water to them, move them to more accessible locations, and ultimately collect and plant their seeds. Domestication creates a symbiotic relationship between plants and humans and changes the physical characteristics of seeds. They become larger, their coats become thinner, and they cling tightly to the plant so that they must be loosened and broadcast by humans. Hoes and planting sticks became part of the process of agriculture.

Although corn is generally considered the most important foodstuff domesticated by Native Americans, it originated in northern Mexico and made its way into the American Southwest by about 750 B.C. and into the Northeast by about A.D. 200–300. It followed far earlier domestication in the Northeast of sumpweed (c. 2000 B.C.), sunflowers (c. 1500 B.C.), and chenopodium (c. 1500 B.C.). The oily seeds of these plants supplemented the diets of hunter populations. Another important plant was the bottle gourd, which was used for containers rather than food. Scholars debate, however, whether the gourd was domesticated or simply gathered in the wild.

The traditional triad of foods raised by Native American populations—corn, beans, and squash—were introduced from Mesoamerica, and they gradually came to dominate the diets of Indian communities. They were generally planted in a form of intensive cropping. The corn plants provided support for climbing beans, while squash plants formed a ground cover that conserved moisture and kept soil temperatures moderate. Beans fixed nitrogen in the soil, necessary for healthy growth of the corn. Indian agriculturists took full advantage of the complementary nature of these three crops. The genetic variability of corn led to the development of specialized varieties. The Hopis in central Arizona developed a variety with a seed that produces a very long root and a very long shoot. The seed can be planted at a depth of about a foot, and the root grows down to reach ground moisture while the shoot pushes up through the soil. The Senecas in New York planted three different varieties that ripened at different times, had different uses, and represented three basic types of corn: dent, flour, and flint.

Irrigation Systems

A crucial aspect of technology in the arid Southwest was the control of water resources, both for agriculture and to meet the needs of daily life. The remains of extensive irrigation canals indicate that the Hohokams in the lower Arizona desert had a sophisticated water management system by about A.D. 800. The canals drew water along about 500 miles of the Salt River in the basin where Phoenix now sits. The canals represent a remarkable expenditure of energy. Some are as broad as 75 feet and nearly 100 miles long.

At Chaco Canyon in northeastern New Mexico, nine major Pueblo dwellings lined the banks of the lower Chaco River during a period beginning about A.D. 920. These and a number of smaller outlying pueblos housed nearly 10,000 people. The Pueblos thrived because of their ability to husband and control available water supplies. Pueblo Bonito, rising to a height of five stories in parts and containing about 800 rooms, is probably the best-known dwelling in this complex. Prior to A.D. 900, the Chaco River flooded seasonally, and crops were planted on the floodplain. Water also collected in natural basins along the rim of the canyon, and in heavy rains there was runoff from the rim down the sides of the canyon. By about 900, however, the river cut its way deeply into the canyon bottom and became so entrenched that it would not flood. Irrigation became necessary. Earthen dams were built to contain the streams' waters. Diversion walls and canals brought the water to the fields, and sluice gates controlled the flow. Diversion walls were built along the slopes of the main and side canyons to channel runoff water into canals. Bordered and gravel-mulched gardens preserved the soil moisture.

Between about A.D. 1020 and about 1120, perhaps 100,000 pine trees were cut for building and firewood in the Chaco Canyon area. Building largely ceased after 1120, however, and by about 1220 the pueblos were abandoned. The onset of drought in the San Juan River basin that lasted from 1130 to 1190 probably explains the abandonment. Even the sophisticated water control systems in Chaco Canyon could not deal with the severity and duration of the drought.

Archaeoastronomy and Technology

Time is a preoccupation in modern industrial societies, but Native people in North America also had a deep concern for the passage of time and the marking of important celestial events that coincided with changes in the seasons. Certain structures represent a sophisticated technology of telling time. At Fajada Butte near the pueblo ruins in Chaco Canyon, three slabs of stone leaning against a rock face on an outcropping of the butte cast patterns of light and shadow upon a spiral carved into a rock face. The spiral is bisected by a dagger of light just before noon on the day of the summer solstice. On the day of the winter solstice, two daggers of light brush the edges of the spiral. Although there is some debate about whether the slabs that create the shadows were deliberately placed there by human beings, the spiral is obviously a human artifact, and it demonstrates a sophisticated knowledge of celestial movements and a permanent marker of solstice events.

Although solstice observation is generally associated with agriculturists, there is evidence that it was also practiced by hunter peoples in North America. Medicine wheels in Saskatchewan indicate that the Blackfeet may have oriented their tepees on a north-south axis that allowed observation of eastern sunrise solstice sites. A medicine wheel at an elevation of about 7,500 feet in the Big Horn Mountains of Wyoming is a circle of stones with twenty-eight spokes radiating from a central cairn and six perimeter cairns. It provides sighting alignments for the summer and winter solstices and possibly for the helical rising of the bright stars Sirius, Vega, and Aldebaran.

Solstice alignment on a major scale appears in Mississippian mound sites in the southeastern and central United States. Computer analysis of twenty-eight mound sites in the lower Mississippi River valley revealed a regular pattern of orientation. The people who constructed these mounds around ceremonial plazas had all adopted a common distance measure of 155.8 feet, called the "Toltec Module" because it was first noted at a site in Arkansas that had a clear solstice orientation. It was also apparent that fully 75 percent of the Mississippian mound sites analyzed featured one or more solar alignments. Mound clusters generally had one clearly oriented for observation of winter solstice points, but summer solstice, equinoctial, and even some stellar sightings (most commonly Vega and Sirius) were also important. The alignment of mounds helped to alert a widespread population to the time for harvesting and planting their floodplain gardens.

Adaptation of New Technologies

The story of Peter Minuet buying Manhattan Island from the Indians for twenty-four dollars worth of beads and trinkets is deeply embedded in the American consciousness as an indicator of, at worst, the gullibility of American Indians or, at best, the lack of technological sophistication of Native people. The replacement of clay pots with copper kettles, deerskin clothing with woven cloth, and bows and arrows with guns is seen as the beginning of Indian cultural decline. These adaptations, however, represent more of an assimilation of new technologies into Indian worldviews than any Native belief that Europeans were culturally superior people.

European glass beads first used in trading were larger than the small seed beads used in contemporary beadwork. Clear beads resembled crystals that were used in divining while colored beads could resemble wampum, the white and purple cohoag shells that were ground into rounds, drilled, and strung. Wampum was not a trade item, and it was analogous to money only in that strings of wampum were given by killers to the families of their victims to assuage their guilt. Wampum strings were woven into belts, and the patterns carried meaning that was read into the belts by recitation of sacred texts. They were used to put into permanent form agreements between tribes, or between tribes and colonial governments and finally the United States government. The analogy of trade beads to wampum beads probably led the Canarsees, the tribe that Minuet encountered, to consider that they were striking an agreement with him rather than selling anything.

Copper kettles have a similar meaning. Thousands were acquired by Native people in exchange for furs and food, and because they were more durable than clay vessels, they were used as household items, but they are also found in burial sites. Much as some personal possessions were buried with the dead for use in another world, copper kettles were sometimes smashed flat or broken and placed over the head of the corpse in a manner similar to the use of clay pots.

Indians adopted guns primarily as weapons of war rather than for hunting. The bow and arrow were a more efficient hunting tool than the cumbersome muzzle-loading musket of European manufacture, and although more powerful, the musket was less accurate. Indians more quickly adopted the flintlock rifle, which was much faster to fire, over the musket. They also used guns in some ceremonies to produce a sound like thunder, which was considered a deity. Thus, technology and traditional belief systems were melded.

Although American Indians did not domesticate animals, use wheeled vehicles, or develop metallurgy (except for beaten copper ornaments), they were able to draw from their environments what they needed for survival, utilizing their human energy to cajole fire, water, plants, and animals into meeting their needs. They adapted European technologies (livestock, metal tools and weapons, glass beads) into their own cultures, using them for both utilitarian and spiritual purposes.

BIBLIOGRAPHY

Blackburn, Thomas C., and Kat Anderson, eds. *Before the Wilderness: Environmental Management by Native Californians.* Menlo Park, Calif.: Ballena Press, 1993.

Hurt, R. Douglas. *Indian Agriculture in America: Prehistory to the Present.* Lawrence: University Press of Kansas, 1987.

Larson, Lewis H. *Aboriginal Subsistence Technology on the Southeastern Coastal Plain during the Late Prehistoric Period.* Gainesville: University Presses of Florida, 1980.

Malone, Patrick M. *The Skulking Way of War: Technology and Tactics among the New England Indians.* Baltimore: Johns Hopkins University Press, 1993.

Miller, Christopher J., and George R. Hamell. "A New Perspective on Indian-White Contact: Cultural Symbols and Colonial Trade." *Journal of American History* 73, no. 2 (September 1986): 311–328.

Smith, Bruce D. *Rivers of Change: Essays on Early Agriculture in Eastern North America.* Washington, D.C.: Smithsonian Institution Press, 1992.

Stewart, Hilary. *Indian Fishing: Early Methods on the Northwest Coast.* Seattle: University of Washington Press, 1977.

Vivian, R. Gwinn. "Conservation and Diversion: Water-Control Systems in the Anasazi Southwest." In *Irrigation's Impact on Society.* Edited by Theodore E. Downing and McGuire Gibson. Tucson: University of Arizona Press, 1974.

Williamson, Ray A. *Living the Sky: The Cosmos of the American Indian.* Boston: Houghton Mifflin, 1984.

Clara Sue Kidwell

See also **Agriculture, American Indian; Corn; Indian Mounds; Irrigation; Wampum.**

INDIAN TERRITORY. Between 1820 and 1842, the Five Civilized Tribes were removed to Indian Territory, an area that encompassed most of current day Oklahoma. In 1866, the western portion of the territory was ceded to the United States for use as reservation land for other tribes. In 1889, a section of this western portion was opened to settlement and became Oklahoma Territory in 1890. An outcry for statehood soon emerged with settlers calling for the union of Oklahoma and Indian Territory. Cherokee Chief William Rogers and Choctaw Chief Green McCurtain opposed this union and led a constitutional convention to create a state of Sequoyah from the land known as Indian Territory. Congress ignored their proposal, and in 1907, Congress merged Indian and Oklahoma Territories into one state. With this action, Indian Territory disappeared.

BIBLIOGRAPHY

Burton, Jeffery. *Indian Territory and the United States, 1866–1906: Courts, Government, and the Movement for Oklahoma Statehood.* Norman: University of Oklahoma Press, 1995.

Veda Boyd Jones

See also **Indian Policy, U.S., 1830–1900; Sequoyah, Proposed State of;** *and vol. 9:* **Fort Laramie Treaty of 1851.**

INDIAN TRADE AND INTERCOURSE ACT. The Indian Trade and Intercourse Act was a set of measures enacted between 1790 and 1847 to improve relations with American Indians by granting the United States government sole authority to regulate interactions between Indians and non-Indians. The sale of Indian lands to individuals or states was forbidden. An 1834 renewal of the act also designated all U.S. lands west of the Mississippi River (except Louisiana, Missouri, and Arkansas Territory) as Indian Territory. Indian Territory gradually shrank and eventually vanished with the creation of Oklahoma in 1906. In spite of this reversal, the Penobscots and Passamaquoddies of Maine referred to the act in their 1972 suit for lands taken from them illegally in 1792. In 1980 they were awarded $81 million, which they used to expand reservation lands.

BIBLIOGRAPHY

Prucha, Francis Paul. *The Great Father: The United States Government and the American Indians.* Lincoln: University of Nebraska Press, 1995.

Paul W. Gates / J. H.

See also **Indian Policy, U.S., 1775–1830; Indian Territory; Passamaquoddy/Penobscot;** *and vol. 9:* **Fort Laramie Treaty of 1851.**

INDIAN TRADE AND TRADERS. The Indian trade of North America has traditionally been described as the web of economic relations between Europeans and their successors (Euro-Americans and Euro-Canadians) with Native Americans. Ever since Columbus's first landfall, Indians and whites have exchanged items of material and cultural significance as part of complex diplomatic and economic relationships entered into by two or more parties to secure exotic goods, establish and maintain political alliances, and ensure cohabitation of lands. By this same convention, the Indian trader has been portrayed as a Euro-American or Euro-Canadian male engaged in supplying Native Americans (male and female) with goods and services in exchange for Indian-made or -processed commodities such as furs, pelts, hides, and foodstuffs; geographic information; and, at times, Native political and social alliances. This individual, often portrayed as a backwoodsman or hunter-peddler, is historically associated directly with the beaver trade because of that animal's highly prized fur, used by Europeans in the manufacture of hats and coats by Europeans.

A more accurate view treats the Indian trade of North America as an ancient institution firmly established well before European contact and colonization. Linking both tribes and regions, this Indian trade involved individual traders as well as trader cultures that served as conduits between tribes separated by vast distances. Indian traders—female as well as male—met at Native American trading centers strategically located along major river systems or at hubs where several tribes seasonally passed en route to hunting, gathering, or fishing grounds. Examples include the ancient city of Cahokia in present-day Illinois, the Mandan-Hidatsa-Arikara villages (often called Middle Missouri Indian towns) in the present-day states of North Dakota and South Dakota, Zuni Pueblo in contemporary New Mexico, and passages or portages between important waterways such as Sault Sainte Marie and Niagara Falls in the Great Lakes region and the Dalles on the Columbia River. In addition to foodstuffs, fiberware and clayware, hides, and exotics ranging from obsidian and flint to seashells and pearls to precious gems and minerals passed hands in Indian lodges and at native trade fairs before A.D. 1500.

Early European-Indian Trade

After 1600, these same trails, watercourses, and meeting grounds became routes of European traffic and footprints for forts, factories, and towns placed at strategic points such as Albany, Augusta, Chicago, Detroit, Kodiak, Michilimackinac, Mobile, Natchitoches, Portland (Oregon), San Antonio, and St. Louis. Colonists introduced European mercantile ideas of inventories and profits based upon dynamics of supply and demand, often compromising Native systems, which operated on principles of barter exchange, gift-giving, and reciprocity. Whites who adhered to norms of Native trade did better than those who ignored or bypassed Indian protocol. The French succeeded best in the Indian trade business, becoming social as well as economic partners across North America. Up to the fall of New France in 1760 and beyond, French-Indian relations along the Saint Lawrence and Mississippi Rivers and in the Great Lakes region remained cordial, tied by kinship as well as economic partnerships.

Spanish, Dutch, English, Russian, and Swedish traders were less successful because of their more rigid expectations: they insisted that Indians conform to European trading standards. All colonists sought furs and hides, including deerskins, for a lucrative European and Cantonese fur market, making the occupation of the white or mixed-blood (métis or French-Indian and mestizo or Spanish-Indian) trader a common occupational type on all national and ethnic frontiers in North America. Each had government-licensed trading companies with wide powers to expand the respective nation's interests in addition to authority to trade, trap, hunt, and settle. Also, each country had independents, known in French parlance as *coureur de bois* (runners of the woods). From the Saint Lawrence to the Rio Grande and on to the Pacific Ocean, these "free" trappers and traders trekked and traded, earning reputations for adventure and exploration, and often compromising national interests for personal gain. Across every fur trade frontier, small concerns were absorbed by medium- and large-sized companies, whose workforces were under contract for specific terms of engagement and for set annual salaries.

Many major cities developed because of this nascent Indian trade. They include Albany and New York City (Dutch); Detroit, Mobile, Natchez, and Montreal (French); Charleston, Philadelphia, and Savannah (English); Pensacola, Santa Fe, and St. Louis (Spanish); Wilmington, Delaware (Swedish); and Kodiak, Alaska, and Fort Ross, California (Russian).

The Indian trade by itself did not result in total economic dependency of Native peoples on white suppliers of guns, blankets, kettles, knives, and other utilitarian items that made life more comfortable. Every tribe engaged in this European-supplied trade to a degree, some flourishing under the new formula of Indian-white trade, others suffering hardship and loss of economic position. Throughout the eighteenth century, most tribes of eastern and southeastern North America were locked into the Indian trade as way of life and expected French, British, and Spanish traders to protect their respective trade spheres from outside aggressors and internal rebellion.

Trade after the American Revolution

In the aftermath of the American Revolution, the Indian trade continued under different flags and more restrictive rules. Congress regulated Indian trade under a series of Trade and Intercourse Acts beginning in 1790, establishing government "factories" in the heart of Indian territories in 1796 with the intent of keeping settlers and alcohol out of Indian country. This segregationist approach was abandoned in 1822, allowing large and small companies to compete for Indian furs and favors in the western territories. In both Canada and the United States, independent traders and smaller firms were historically leveraged out of business by oligarchies such as the Montreal-based NORTH WEST COMPANY; the Philadelphia firm of BAYNTON, WHARTON, AND MORGAN; and Spanish, Indian, and English traders working for the British firm PANTON, LESLIE, AND COMPANY, based in Florida. Two near-monopolies—the London-based HUDSON'S BAY COMPANY (which absorbed the North West Company in 1821) and the New York-based AMERICAN FUR COMPANY (formed by John Jacob Astor in 1808) with its St. Louis-controlled Western Department (organized in 1822)—emerged in Canada and in the United States, respectively, up through the American Civil War.

As smaller, fur-bearing habitats were trapped out or settled, a new economic Indian trade prevailed from 1840 to 1890 on the western plains and prairies. This buffalo-hide trade supplied water- and steam-powered factories' demand for leather belts as well as military overcoats, rugs, and blankets. Once the buffalo were gone, economic dependency on reservations in Canada and the United

States gripped Indian communities, now reliant on annuities and the need to become herders and farmers.

Still, the Indian trade and the Indian trader, part of an international fur industry, continued in Alaska and in Canada's remote Yukon and Northwest Territories, where it remains important, as well as in the eastern Arctic. Across North America, Indians themselves have continued to function as Indian traders, many dealing in arts and crafts, others in horse breeding and trading; others in restoring buffalo, trading calves for other livestock and goods from one reserve to another; and still others in mitigating violations of treaties by swapping further litigation for restoration of tribal lands or monetary compensation.

BIBLIOGRAPHY

Chittenden, Hiram Martin. *The American Fur Trade of the Far West.* New York: Francis P. Harper, 1902.

Ewers, John C. *Plains Indian History and Culture.* Norman: University of Oklahoma Press, 1997.

Innis, Harold A. *The Fur Trade in Canada: An Introduction to Canadian Economic History.* New Haven, Conn.: Yale University Press, 1930.

Sturtevant, William C., gen. ed. *Handbook of North American Indians.* Vol. 4, *Indian-White Relations.* Edited by Wilcomb E. Washburn. Washington, D.C.: Smithsonian Institution, 1988.

William R. Swagerty

See also **Charleston Indian Trade; Fur Companies; Fur Trade and Trapping; Indian Economic Life; Missouri River Fur Trade; Mountain Men; Pacific Fur Company.**

INDIAN TRADING HOUSES were government-owned and operated stores that existed from 1795 to 1822 as part of the federal government's effort to regulate trade with Native Americans. During this period, twenty-eight trading posts were established, but only seven or eight were extant at any given time. The first stores were established at Coleraine, Georgia, and Tellico, Tennessee. The most important ones were located at Green Bay and Prairie du Chien, Wisconsin; Detroit and Mackinac, Michigan; Chicago, Illinois; Fort Wayne, Indiana; Chickasaw Bluffs, Mississippi; and Natchitoches, Louisiana.

The idea of winning the goodwill of the Indians by supplying them with goods from official stores originated in the colonial period. Massachusetts and South Carolina maintained such stores at different times; in 1753, Benjamin Franklin recommended that Pennsylvania establish a similar system. In 1775, the Continental Congress appointed a committee to devise a trading house system, also called a factory system. In 1793, President George Washington recommended the establishment of a series of trading posts at which Indians could secure goods at cost, and Congress established the first such posts with the Trading Houses Act in 1796. Congress intended the trading house system to strengthen military policy, promote peace on the frontier, protect the Indians against exploitation by private traders, and offset the British and Spanish influence over the Indians.

The trading houses sent in their orders for goods to the superintendent of Indian trade, whose office was in Philadelphia until 1808, when it was moved to Washington, D.C. The superintendent bought the goods on the open market or by bids and shipped them to the trading posts. The principal distributing points were Detroit, Saint Louis, and New Orleans. The post overseers, also known as factors, sold the goods to the Indians and received furs, skins, bear oil, beeswax, and other products in exchange. These products were shipped to the superintendent, who sold them at auction or in foreign markets.

Many difficulties arose under this system: freight rates were excessively high; delays were constant; the superintendent was limited to the domestic market in making his purchases and, as a result, frequently secured goods of inferior quality; skins and furs were often improperly treated, resulting in considerable losses; and the factors were forced to disobey instructions and sell on credit, thus losing money from uncollected accounts. The system did little to reduce foreign influence over Native Americans and was even less effective at preventing Indian exploitation by private traders.

The trading house system was never accepted as a permanent policy. Congress seldom assured its existence for longer than a two-year period. The superintendent and factors were thus unable to plan for the future. Private traders, Indian agents, and frontier merchants opposed the system; opponents circulated false stories and eventually secured its abolition. Sen. Thomas H. Benton of Missouri, inspired by the fur companies and his state's traders, led the fight that closed the system in 1822.

BIBLIOGRAPHY

Prucha, Francis P. *The Great Father: The United States Government and the American Indians.* Lincoln: University of Nebraska Press, 1984; 1986; 1995.

Wallace, Anthony F. C. *Jefferson and the Indians: The Tragic Fate of the First Americans.* Cambridge, Mass.: Belknap Press of Harvard University Press, 1999.

Edgar B. Wesley/J. H.

See also **Fur Trade and Trapping; Indians and Alcohol; Indian Policy, U.S. 1775–1830; Indian Trade and Traders.**

INDIAN TRAILS. What is now the United States was crisscrossed by an extensive network of trails long before the advent of railroads or highways. Even though long-distance travel frequently included a combination of canoe and foot travel, trails connected nearly every person on the continent. The paths of the American Indians, used for war and trade, were usually along relatively high ground or ridges where the soil dried quickly after rains and where there were few streams to be crossed; soft footgear made stony ground less favorable. Major trails followed important mountain passes to connect river drainages, and trails traveling across rather than along rivers usually followed the fall line. Major trails crossed tribal boundaries, although long-term warfare would cause paths between some tribes to become overgrown. Numerous minor trails branched off from principal trails in much the same way as today's highways feed local roads. Indians sometimes blazed trees along a trail so that seasonal changes might not confuse them should they or others see fit to make a return journey.

One of the great trails of the North American Indians was the Iroquois trail from Albany, up the Mohawk River, through the site of Rochester, and on to the site of Buffalo on Lake Erie. Also, there was the Great Warrior Path that connected the mouth of the Scioto to Cumberland Gap and Tennessee Country. Both of these trails followed important routes through the Appalachian Mountains. The trail through CUMBERLAND GAP led early colonial migrations into Kentucky and middle Tennessee. The route eventually became known as Boone's Trail, or the WILDERNESS ROAD. The Chickasaw-Choctaw Trail became the noted Natchez Trace between Nashville and Natchez. The Occaneechi Trail, from the site of Petersburg, Virginia, southwest into the Carolinas, followed the Atlantic coast fall line.

Trails following the Missouri and Yellowstone River crossed the Rocky Mountains and followed the Columbia River, connecting the Mississippi Valley with the Pacific Northwest. Along the Columbia River was an important crossroads known as the Dalles. From this junction other trails headed south. Trails following the Pacific Coast or the valleys on either side of the Cascades and Sierra Nevadas provided communication between tribes in Puget Sound and Baja California. Heading west from California, trails passed through the towns of the Pueblos and eastward down the Canadian and Red Rivers to return to the Mississippi, Santa Fe, and Taos. They became important junctions in the trading paths of the Southwest. Only in sparsely settled regions like the Great Basin were there few major trails.

Few individuals followed these trails for their entire transcontinental extent, but exchange along the routes transported valuable materials great distances. Copper from the Upper Great Lakes reached Georgia and the Rocky Mountains; conch shells from the Gulf of Mexico have been found in Oklahoma. Later explorers, traders, and colonists followed these major routes. When future generations laid rails and asphalt for their own transportation networks, they frequently followed paths that had been trodden for centuries.

BIBLIOGRAPHY

Salisbury, Neal. "The Indians' Old World." *William and Mary Quarterly* 53 (1996): 435–458.

Swagerty, William R. "Indian Trade in the Trans-Mississippi West to 1870." In *Handbook of North American Indians.* Edited by William C. Sturtevant et al. Vol. 4: *History of Indian-White Relations*, edited by W. E. Washburn. Washington, D.C.: Smithsonian Institution, 1988.

Tanner, Helen H. "The Land and Water Communications Systems of the Southeastern Indians." In *Powhatan's Mantle: Indians in the Colonial Southeast.* Edited by Peter Wood, et al. Lincoln: University of Nebraska Press, 1989.

Samuel C. Williams / J. H.

See also **Portages and Water Routes; Roads; Transportation and Travel.**

INDIAN TREATIES were the means that Europeans and Americans used to secure alliances with, and most often acquire land from, Native Americans. Historians disagree about the number of treaties negotiated between European powers and the United States between 1492 and the end of the formal treaty-making period in 1871. Because municipalities, companies, and state and national governments all made treaties, the number may well be in the thousands.

Origins

After Christopher Columbus discovered the New World for Spain in 1492, Spanish explorers and conquistadors used the Caribbean as a base from which to explore North and South America. At first, conquistadors ruthlessly took land from Native Americans, whom they considered heathen or subhuman. By the 1540s, however, Spanish cleric Francisco de Vitoria was already trying to convince the Spanish Crown and its explorers that Indians were indeed human, and thus Spain should treat them with respect rather than take land by conquest. Vitoria succeeded. As friars began to supersede conquistadors on the frontier of New Spain in an attempt to Christianize Native Americans, they introduced a treaty system.

Other nations followed suit. France, less interested in planting permanent colonies but eager to establish a footing in North America, negotiated agreements with native groups that enabled them to fish and trade in peace. Over time, French colonial officials and priests used treaties to secure an extensive web of relationships that guarded the western borders of their North American domain and ensured access to the rich fur trade of the Great Lakes region.

The Dutch used treaties. Like the French, Dutch traders forged agreements with local tribes to gain access to the western fur trade. Settlers in the lower Hudson valley also purchased land and the rights to certain hunting areas with trade goods.

English settlers tried warfare and brutality to cow Native Americans. The English at Jamestown, Virginia, tried to negotiate treaties with local tribes, even attempting at one point to "crown" Powhatan, the leader of a Chesapeake Confederacy, "king" of the Indians (see POWHATAN CONFEDERACY). Powhatan's own ambitions and the

Englishmen's ongoing desire for new farmlands undermined these efforts, however. The parties maintained a fragile peace during Powhatan's lifetime (a peace sealed with the marriage of his daughter Pocahontas to an English planter), but after his death the chief's brother, Opechancanugh, reignited warfare with the English.

In New England, Pilgrim settlers on Cape Cod negotiated informal agreements with local WAMPANOAGS that allowed them to settle at Plymouth, Massachusetts. Their Puritan brethren followed a similar path when they settled in Boston in 1630. Eventually, however, the English crowded members of the Nipmuck, Narragansett, and Wampanoag tribes onto reservations in Massachusetts. In 1675 the Wampanoag leader Metacomet, known to the English as King Philip, launched a war against the Puritans. Metacomet led warriors from all three groups against the English in the two-year struggle. Puritans won, but only after losing one-sixth of their male population. Ironically, while the English victory meant the end of an era of peaceful treaty making, it was made possible by the assistance of Hudson valley groups who refused to come to Philip's assistance because of their treaty commitments to the British.

Historical Development

During the eighteenth century, the strength of Indian confederacies, imperial threats from other nations, and a renewed interest in empire and mercantilism by the Crown (joint-stock companies had arranged early English settlements with little or no interest from the Crown) convinced England to rely more on diplomacy and treaties in relations with Indians. KING GEORGE'S WAR (1744–1748), which saw England and France vying for control of the Ohio River valley (and subsequently North America), was an example.

The Treaty of Aix-la-Chapelle ended King George's War, but in truth it decided nothing. Both France and England jockeyed for position in preparation for renewed warfare. Native Americans, however, did not understand military truces, for once they proclaimed themselves enemies of another they intended to stay that way. French colonists capitalized on that confusion in an attempt to draw some of the IROQUOIS Confederacy (the Senecas, Cayugas, Onondagas, Oneidas, and Mohawks who had earlier laid claim to the Ohio valley) away from their ally, England. To the south, at the mouth of the Mississippi River in New Orleans, French agents scored treaties with Creeks, Chickasaws, and some CHEROKEES.

Pennsylvania traders, led by George Croghan, realized that the British Navy had so devastated French trade routes that French Indian allies could not get the trade goods they wanted. In August 1748, Croghan and fellow traders signed the Treaty of Logstown with leaders of the DELAWARES, SHAWNEES, Iroquois, and Wyandotte Indians. It established a perpetual trade and defensive alliance between England and the Indians.

In the FRENCH AND INDIAN WAR (1754–1763), the last of the great wars for the British Empire, the Iroquois Confederacy remained allied with England but did little in the way of fighting against France. The confederacy did not want to be enemies with France if France won the war. British victory in 1763 saw a deterioration in relations with the confederacy, which itself became plagued with infighting.

Upon taking control of all of North America to the Mississippi River, England encountered more trouble with former French-allied Indians. In 1763 on the upper Ohio, an Ottawa chief named Pontiac and an alliance of Indians attacked Americans (still British subjects) headed west. British soldiers put down Pontiac's rebellion, but England realized it had to conduct aggressive diplomacy with western Indians to make the region safe for settlement.

Parliament passed the PROCLAMATION OF 1763, which prohibited Americans from settling west of the Appalachian Mountains. The proclamation would enable Parliament to both control land dispersal and establish treaties with Indians before Americans took the land.

The spread of Americans to the West scared Indians. In an attempt to create a permanent boundary between whites and Indians, William Johnson, the English Indian commissioner for the North, and John Stuart, an agent in the South, treated with the Iroquois Nations in 1768. The Treaty of Fort Stanwix negotiated such a line, but failed to halt the westward white movement.

After American victory in the Revolutionary War, the United States inherited diplomatic trouble with Indians on the frontier. Indians formed new confederacies to oppose American expansion. One of them, including MIAMI, Shawnee, and Delaware Indians, tried to prevent white expansion north of the Ohio River. President George Washington chose force to move the Indians off the land. In 1790 he sent a small army under General Arthur St. Clair, but Miamis under Little Turtle defeated him. They did likewise to General Josiah Harmer the next year, killing 630 American troops and scoring the biggest victory over whites that Native Americans would ever win.

In 1794, with 4,000 troops, General "Mad" Anthony Wayne marched into the Miamis' region, and defeated them at the Battle of Fallen Timbers. In the subsequent Treaty of Greenville (1795), Miamis ceded to the United States most of Ohio, part of Indiana, and areas for trading posts along strategic waterways.

Indian Displacement and Nineteenth-Century Treaties

The presidency of Thomas Jefferson saw many Indian tribes east of the Mississippi River cede territory to the United States. In 1804 SAUK and FOX (see MESQUAKIE) Indians ceded much of what would become northwestern Illinois. In 1805 Cherokees gave up land in Georgia, Mississippi Territory, and Tennessee. That same year, CHOCTAWS, who had ceded land in southwest Mississippi Territory in 1801, gave up more nearby. Chickasaws gave up land in middle Tennessee in 1805, and in 1806 Cherokees gave up more in southern Tennessee.

When Jefferson made the windfall purchase of Louisiana from France in 1803, he had in mind using part of it for the removal of eastern Indians. Jefferson could rightly see that white expansion would not cease, and the United States would have to deal with uprooted Indians. He suggested a large "INDIAN TERRITORY," sections of which the government could reserve for Indians. Jefferson was also interested in Indians of the West, dispatching Meriwether Lewis and William Clark on their journey of exploration across the northern Louisiana Purchase (1804–1806), in part to open friendly relations with Indians. By the end of their journey, the LEWIS AND CLARK EXPEDITION had executed no treaties, but had established friendly relations with such groups as the SHOSHONES, MANDANS, Flatheads, and Clatsops.

The white land grab continued east of the Mississippi. In Indiana, the territorial governor and military commander William Henry Harrison wanted to pad Indiana's boundaries. In September 1809 Harrison called a conference of local Indians, including Delawares, POTAWATOMIES, and Shawnees, at Fort Wayne, Indiana. So concerned were the Native Americans about the future of their remaining lands that more than 1,100 of them attended. Harrison, no lover of Indians, dictated terms and greased the slide with money and trade baubles. With the signing of the Treaty of Fort Wayne, Native Americans ceded to the United States another 3 million acres of land in return for $7,000 up front and $1,750 yearly.

The Shawnee warrior chieftain Tecumseh protested the treaty on the grounds that the land belonged to no one tribe; hence, no one tribe or representative could sign it away. But Harrison defended its legality. Tecumseh and his half-brother, the tribal prophet named Tenskwatawa, would soon found a confederacy of Indians with the intent of stopping further white incursions.

While previous Indian treaties had moved tribes to reservation land near their traditional homes, Native Americans in the Lake Plains regions south of the Great Lakes (in an area Americans then called the Northwest—Michigan, Wisconsin, Illinois, Indiana, and Ohio) would be some of the first subjected to removal west of the Mississippi River. At the behest of military and political authorities, 1,000 representatives of northwestern tribes gathered at Prairie du Chien, Wisconsin, in 1825, and began signing the Treaties of Prairie du Chien in which they sold millions of acres of land in return for reservations in the West. Small groups of northwestern Indians signed treaties with Indian agents for the next four years.

In the Southeast, Cherokees, Choctaws, Chickasaws, Creeks, and SEMINOLES (the so-called "FIVE CIVILIZED TRIBES" because whites thought they had somewhat assimilated into white culture) faced continuing pressure to get off their traditional lands. In the presidential election of 1828, the Tennessee politician and general Andrew Jackson had promised southerners he would oust Indians from their land to clear the way for American agriculture. At Jackson's urging, Congress passed the Indian Removal Bill of 1830, which gave the federal government authority to negotiate with tribes for their removal to the West. Cherokees tried to fight the bill in court with two landmark cases, *The Cherokee Nation v. Georgia* (1831) and *Worcester v. Georgia* (1832) (see CHEROKEE NATION CASES).

While ultimately unsuccessful, these U.S. Supreme Court decisions established two principles that would guide treaty making in the future. First, the Court noted that the sovereignty of the United States could not be compromised. The justices declared that treaties with tribes were not the same as treaties with foreign governments. Second, Justice John Marshall insisted that treaties were instruments of federal power and that the states could not interfere with their implementation. Federal bullying and local hostility finally persuaded a small minority of the Cherokees to sign an agreement, the Treaty of New Echota, that provided for their removal to the West, but most tribesmen refused to leave Georgia until they were forced out by the U.S. Army.

Other southeastern tribes signed similar treaties. The rapid expansion of the United States to the Pacific in the 1840s—the result of annexing Texas, settling the Oregon boundary dispute with Great Britain, and acquiring the Southwest from Mexico after the Mexican-American War—inevitably brought Americans into more conflict with Indians. U.S. officials negotiated treaties with tribes in the Northwest that exchanged land for small reservations and guaranteed access to fish and other subsistence foods, while at Fort Laramie, Wyoming, in 1851 they signed an agreement that tried to define tribal hunting grounds on the Plains and to ensure safe passage of American settlers to the West (see LARAMIE, FORT, TREATY OF [1851]). Government negotiators also agreed to treaties that established tribal reservations in California, but the chaos of the gold rush and the virulent anti-Indian racism of the day blocked the ratification of those agreements in Congress. The result was further bloodshed and the establishment of far smaller refuges. In the Southwest and along the "middle border" of Kansas and Nebraska, similar agreements attempted to define tribal reservations and set Indian communities apart from white settlers. Unfortunately, the sanctity of these areas "reserved" for tribal use and occupancy was frequently short-lived.

The discovery of gold in Colorado in 1859 drew more than 100,000 whites across the Plains and into the Rocky Mountain region. Those miners simply took Indian lands as they went. The U.S. government attempted to alleviate the situation in 1861 by calling leaders of the primarily affected tribes—the CHEYENNES and ARAPAHOS—to Fort Lyon, in Colorado Territory. Officials abandoned the Fort Laramie Treaty, instead giving the tribes smaller parcels of land in southeastern Colorado. Angered, many tribal warriors launched a war against eastern

Coloradoans. In 1864 the Colorado militia under Colonel John Chivington attacked and killed most of a band of Cheyennes under Chief Black Kettle at SAND CREEK, Colorado, site of one of the 1861 reservations.

The Civil War diverted Americans' attention from westward expansion and Indian troubles for four years. But in 1866 Red Cloud's War between SIOUX warriors and U.S. soldiers in Wyoming Territory spawned a new search for answers. Convinced that peace on white terms was possible, the U.S. government created a Peace Commission to handle Native American location problems. The commission decided to establish two reservations—one in the Black Hills of South Dakota, the other in western Indian Territory—to handle the estimated 140,000 Plains Indians.

Peace commissioners brought representatives of the KIOWAS, COMANCHES, southern Cheyennes, and Arapahos to Medicine Lodge Creek, Kansas, for treaty talks in October 1867. After bribery and some coercion, the tribal leaders at the Medicine Lodge Treaty talks accepted some 3 million acres in western Indian Territory. American negotiators again failed to realize that tribal leaders did not speak for all members of their tribes. Thus when warriors of different tribes refused the treaty, warfare was again imminent. In November 1868 Lieutenant Colonel George Armstrong Custer's Seventh Cavalry attacked Black Kettle's Cheyennes on the Washita River in retaliation for depredations that another band of warriors had committed. Black Kettle died in that attack.

In 1868 peace commissioners met with Sioux leaders at Fort Laramie. In a new Fort Laramie Treaty (see LARAMIE, FORT, TREATY OF [1868]), they promised the United States would stop protecting the Powder River Road, which threatened Sioux hunting lands, if the Sioux would accept permanent reservation land in the Black Hills. The Sioux agreed, but in vain. The discovery of gold in the Black Hills in 1874 lured more whites to the area, who shoved the Sioux out of the way.

The U.S. government abandoned treaty making with Indians in 1871. In 1870 the Supreme Court had ruled in the *Cherokee Tobacco* case that all Indian treaties were subject to unilateral congressional action. The next year, angered that the executive branch and the Senate had never placed many Indian cessions into the public domain, but rather shunted them directly to land-grant railroads, the House of Representative attached a rider to an Indian Office appropriations bill abolishing treaties. The bill became law. It did not nullify existing treaties, however, and it did not end the practice of negotiating agreements with tribes. In fact several such agreements were negotiated in the late nineteenth century (most prominently with the Blackfeet, Gros Ventres, and Assiniboines in Montana in 1884 and with the Sioux in Dakota Territory in 1889).

The Twentieth Century and Future Developments

In the twentieth century treaties had a complicated history. In 1903 the Supreme Court in *LONE WOLF V. HITCHCOCK* seemed to seal its fate. In a case involving the dissolution of the Kiowa reservation in Oklahoma, the Court declared that Congress had the power to abrogate treaties, even ones that promised that its terms could not be altered without the consent of the tribe. But at century's end, the courts upheld the sovereign power of treaty-guaranteed tribal courts and councils and struck down state attempts to regulate hunting and fishing rights established in treaties. The existence of treaties has also been an important argument in favor of modern tribal "sovereignty" within the context of the United States. The exact fate of treaty guarantees in the twenty-first century remains to be determined.

BIBLIOGRAPHY

Billington, Ray Allen, and Martin Ridge, eds. *Westward Expansion: A History of the American Frontier.* 5th ed. New York: Macmillan, 1982.

Brinkley, Alan, Richard N. Current, Frank Freidel, and T. Harry Williams, eds. *American History: A Survey.* 8th ed. New York: McGraw-Hill, 1991.

Bonds, Ray, ed. *The Illustrated Directory of Native Americans: Their History, Dress, and Lifestyles.* London: Salamander, 2001.

Holm, Tom. "Indian Treaties and Congresses" and "Native Americans, U.S. Military Relations With." in *The Oxford Companion to American Military History.* Edited by John Whiteclay Chambers, II. New York: Oxford University Press, 1999.

R. Steven Jones

See also **Indian Policy; Indian Reservations; Indian Removal; Wars with Indian Nations;** *and vol. 9:* **Fort Laramie Treaty of 1851; Treaty with the Six Nations, 1784.**

INDIAN TREATIES, COLONIAL. One of the most striking features of the American colonial period was the treaty system created by Indians and Europeans. The system was the outcome of efforts by all parties to achieve separate goals and at the same time to manage relations with each other. These relations were not characterized by constant hostility, as is sometimes supposed. Instead, they were adjustments to each other's presence, and they often involved cooperation in the pursuit of mutual goals such as trade or an alliance against a common enemy. The result was a complex set of relationships outstanding for its flexibility and for its blending of elements from different cultural and diplomatic traditions.

The several European powers, while at odds with each other, were at one in their views of diplomacy. Whether British, French, Spanish, Swedish, or Dutch, they assumed centralized authority and a top-down, closeted approach to negotiations. In colonial America, they encountered Indians whose assumptions of equality and openness did not fit this pattern. Since the Indians who held these views showed no sign of changing them, new approaches to diplomatic negotiations had to be worked out.

It was a case of necessity being the mother of adjustment. For the Europeans, it was the necessity of Indian help for survival in a strange land and for Indian allies in their ongoing struggles with each other. For the Indians, it was the necessity of a reliable supply of weapons and trade goods and for European allies in their ongoing struggles with each other.

Thus, each party adjusted to the other, and a rich multilateral, multicultural treaty system took shape. The system continued as a potent force for control and cooperation until the American Revolution ended the competition of European powers that had given the Indians room to maneuver and freedom to seek the best diplomatic bargains they could. In that competitive environment even the Spanish felt compelled to make treaties with the southeastern Indians, unlike their practice in areas where they had no such competition.

The most prominent component of the colonial treaty system was the covenant chain of northeastern America. The six nations of the Iroquois and various groups of British colonists had created this set of relationships, but the imagery and style were strictly Iroquois. The ritual smoothing of the road to peace, the symbolic casting away of weapons, and the exchange of wampum belts to validate each item of an agreement reflected the Iroquois, not the European, worldview. Nor was this a case of style without substance. Agreements were made the Iroquois way or they were not made at all, a state of affairs that no one wanted. Both the British and the Indians hoped to use the covenant chain to extend their influence—the Iroquois over the Shawnees and Delawares to the south and west, the British over the French and the Hurons to the north. Meanwhile, through conferences and formal and informal agreements, the partners managed their relations with each other.

The covenant chain is only one example of the different sets of treaty relationships that developed in colonial America. There the Indian inhabitants and the European newcomers created a new kind of diplomacy that provided a means for exchanges of mutual benefit in a multicultural setting.

BIBLIOGRAPHY

Jennings, Francis. *The Ambiguous Iroquois Empire: The Covenant Chain Confederation of Indian Tribes with English Colonies.* New York: Norton, 1984. The pioneering work.

Jones, Dorothy V. *License for Empire: Colonialism by Treaty in Early America.* Chicago: University of Chicago Press, 1982. Changes in the treaty system from accommodation to U.S. domination.

———. "British Colonial Indian Treaties." In *Handbook of North American Indians.* Edited by William C. Sturtevant et al. Volume 4: *History of Indian–White Relations,* edited by Wilcomb E. Washburn. Washington, D.C.: Smithsonian Institution, 1988. Comprehensive coverage.

Williams, Robert A., Jr. *Linking Arms Together: American Indian Treaty Visions of Law and Peace, 1600–1800.* New York: Oxford University Press, 1997. A fresh approach.

Dorothy V. Jones

See also **Indian Policy, Colonial; Indian Treaties; Iroquois.**

INDIAN TRIBAL COURTS constitute the frontline American Indian tribal institutions that most often confront issues of self-determination and sovereignty, while at the same time providing reliable and equitable adjudication in the many and diverse matters that come before them. In addition, they constitute a key tribal entity for advancing and protecting the rights of self-government. The work of the courts has also become a way to assess the current status of tribal self-determination and reservation well-being.

Tribal courts are established either by tribal constitutions or by tribal legislation. They usually consist of a trial court and an appellate branch. In criminal matters they have jurisdiction over American Indians for offenses where the penalty does not exceed one year in jail or a $5,000 fine or both. In civil cases they have wide-ranging authority over both Indians and non-Indians for matters that take place on the reservation, such as commercial activities, actions involving negligence, and actions involving important matters such as elections and civil rights. Many tribal courts use respected elders and peacemakers to resolve disputes in a traditional way.

Some smaller reservations have courts that operate under the authority of the Bureau of Indian Affairs. Established in the nineteenth century as instruments of federal authority, these courts are referred to as Courts of Indian Offenses.

During the late twentieth century the jurisdiction and procedures of tribal courts began to undergo change. They heard more cases of greater complexity and impact than ever before. As part of this process of significant change, tribal courts crafted a unique jurisprudence of vision and cultural integrity. In other words, tribal courts responded competently and creatively to federal oversight pressures and cultural values, synthesizing the best of both traditions—as in *National Farmers Union Insurance Companies v. Crow Tribe of Indians* and the work of the Navajo Peacemaker Courts, for example.

Despite the weight of history and the attendant legal complexity that often surround tribal courts, they also address a more basic and profoundly human concern. The key to a more benign and morally coherent era is based on the core values of respect and dignity. The basic unity of important purpose and commitment dominates the daily workings of tribal courts, demonstrating both the tenacity and the hope that underpin the struggle to flourish. The struggle takes place in small tribal courthouses throughout Indian country as reservation inhabitants interact with the law in an ongoing effort to construct an enduring future. The central elements of this interaction continue to focus on establishing a meaningful relationship with federal courts and improving the quality of justice rendered within tribal courts.

BIBLIOGRAPHY

Deloria, Vine, Jr., and Clifford M. Lytle. *The Nations Within: The Past and Future of American Indian Sovereignty.* New York: Pantheon Books, 1984.

Pommersheim, Frank. *Braid of Feathers.* Berkeley: University of California Press, 1995.

Frank Pommersheim

See also **Bureau of Indian Affairs.**

INDIAN TRIBES. *See* **Tribes.**

INDIANA, often called "the crossroads of America," was a center of commerce even before the arrival of European explorers in the 1670s. Bounded on the north by Lake Michigan and on the south by the Ohio River, the state's several important rivers and portages made it a strategic military location as well. The dominant Indian tribe in the region, the Miamis, lived throughout the state from the early 1600s. They were joined by bands of Shawnee and Delaware Indians in the southern part of the state and by groups of Delaware, Potawatomi, Piankashaw, and Wea in the north. By 1700, the Miamis had settled in several villages throughout the region, including large villages at Kekionga (present-day Fort Wayne), Ouiatanon (near present-day Lafayette), Vincennes, and Vermillion. In 1679, led by the French explorer Robert Cavelier, Sieur de La Salle, the first Europeans reached the region. Eager to establish outposts for the fur trade, the French laid claim to the area and erected military forts at Kekionga (known as Fort Miami, possibly as early as the late 1680s and permanently after 1704), Ouiatanon (1719), and Vincennes (1732). Although they had survived primarily as an agricultural people, the tribes eagerly entered into the fur trade, especially after epidemics from smallpox, measles, and other diseases decimated their numbers and made farming more difficult. By the 1750s, only about 2,000 Indians of various tribes survived in the region.

During the French and Indian War, French claims over the territory were ceded to the British, a concession ratified by the Treaty of Paris on 10 February 1763. British rule over the region was brief, however. In 1778 and 1779, during the American Revolution, forces led by George Rogers Clark controlled the area after capturing Vincennes. After the Revolution, the United States took possession of the land between the Appalachians and the Mississippi River in another Treaty of Paris, signed in 1783. The United States reorganized the region under the Ordinance of 1787, recognizing it as the Northwest Territory the following year. In July 1800, the region was divided into an eastern section that later became the state of Ohio and a western section that extended to the Mississippi River on the west and up to Canada in the north. Known as the Indiana Territory, a name that reflected it as "the land of the Indians," the territory later was divided even further to create the Michigan Territory (January 1805) and the Illinois Territory (February 1809). Thus, by 1809, the boundaries of present-day Indiana were secure.

Beginning with the Treaty of Greenville in 1795, which ceded a portion of eastern Indiana to the United States, federal authorities gradually purchased land from various Indian tribes through the 1830s. The governor of the territory, William Henry Harrison, signed the Treaty of Fort Wayne in 1809 with the Delawares, Potawatomis, and Miamis, adding the southern third of the territory to federal reserves; other agreements, including the Treaty of St. Mary's (1818) and the Treaty of Wabash (1826), completed the transfer of land from Indian hands. In the meantime, however, major conflicts occurred, most notably with Harrison's victory over Indian forces led by Tenskwatawa (also known as the Prophet) at Tippecanoe in 1811. During the War of 1812, British and Indian forces combined to fight American troops throughout the territory. The last major battle was between Miami and American forces and took place on the Mississinewa River on 17 and 18 December 1812; the battle concluded with the Miamis' defeat.

Early Statehood

With the opening of U.S. land offices at Vincennes (1804), Jeffersonville (1807), Terre Haute (1817), and Brookville (1819), almost 2.5 million acres of Indiana land were sold to speculators and settlers through 1820. Later, additional offices opened at Fort Wayne (1822), Crawfordsville (1823), and La Porte (1833). With the territory's population reaching 24,520 in 1810, agitation for statehood gained momentum, and on 11 December 1816, Indiana was admitted to the Union as the nineteenth state. The location of its first capital, Corydon, in south-central Indiana reflected the fact that the overwhelming majority of the state's population resided close to its border with the Ohio River. On 7 June 1820, the capital was relocated to Indianapolis, a site chosen for its location in the geographical center of the state.

In its first decade as a state, Indiana's population surged as migrants from the Carolinas, Kentucky, Tennessee, and Virginia bought newly opened federal lands; later, arrivals from Ohio, Pennsylvania, and New York joined them. Although slavery was prohibited by the 1816 state constitution, other legal restrictions kept some African Americans from settling in Indiana. By 1830, just over 1 percent of the state's 343,031 inhabitants was African American, a figure that remained steady until well after the Civil War. A surge in the number of foreign-born immigrants, particularly German-speaking arrivals

to central and southern Indiana, contributed to well over 5 percent of the state's population after 1850.

With land well suited to farming and raising livestock throughout the state, most of the newcomers settled into agricultural pursuits. Early attempts at industrial concerns included furniture making, farm implement production, and food processing. However, small-town life characterized Indiana throughout the nineteenth century; even up to 1850, the state's largest city, the Ohio River town of New Albany, held no more than 8,181 residents. While the towns of Indiana remained important trading centers for commercial farmers, the state's cultural fabric was constructed by thousands of small family farms. At the end of the antebellum era, more than 91 percent of Indiana residents lived in rural areas. From the predominance of its small-town character, the appellation "Hoosier" was affectionately bestowed upon Indiana's residents from the 1820s onward. Although many folkloric explanations have been given for the term, one of the most likely is that it came from the employment of Indiana canal workers by the Kentucky contractor Samuel Hoosier. The workers became known as "Hoosiers," and the name soon became generalized to describe all Indianians.

Although only a few minor engagements of the Civil War touched Indiana soil, the state's unity was tested by its commitment to the Union's cause. With so many recent migrants from southern states, support for the Confederacy ran high during the conflict's early days. However, a majority of residents—especially antislavery Quaker migrants from the Carolinas who came to the state in the 1810s and 1820s—eventually made the state a stalwart supporter of the Union. After the war, political allegiance shifted back once again, and the state remained roughly divided between the Democratic and Republican parties, a trait it retained through succeeding generations.

While Indiana engaged in the internal improvement craze of the 1840s with heavy state investment in canal building, the state's geographic importance between the agricultural centers of the Midwest and the markets of the East became more apparent after the Civil War. While the Ohio River trade favored the growth of Evansville and New Albany in the first half of the nineteenth century, railroads covered central and northern Indiana by the 1880s. Indianapolis and Terre Haute ranked as major rail centers. The latter city witnessed the formation of the American Railway Union by Eugene V. Debs in 1893, one of the first labor unions of industrial workers in the United States. Rail traffic also spurred commercial and manufacturing growth throughout the state. In 1852, the Studebaker brothers founded a blacksmith shop that made South Bend the site of the largest wagon works after the Civil War; the company would produce automobiles under the Studebaker name in the northern Indiana city until 1963. Another city, Muncie, gained fame as the site of the Ball Brothers Company; relocated to Indiana from New York in 1886, the factory immediately became the leading producer of glass jars and canning instruments in the United States. The most dramatic urban development, however, occurred in the northwestern corner of the state. Founded and built largely to serve the U.S. Steel Corporation's mills, the city of Gary grew from its inception in 1907 to have over 100,000 residents by 1940. The refineries of the Standard Oil Company in Whiting, opened in 1889, along with numerous other major steel and metal works throughout the area made northwest Indiana's Calumet region the most heavily industrialized in the state.

Like many state capitals, Indianapolis owed most of its early growth to its status as a center of government. Located on the White River, with insufficient depth to allow commercial navigation, the city had to wait until the railroad era to take advantage of its strategic location in the center of the state. Although hampered by a lack of natural resources in the immediate area, Indianapolis eventually developed a diverse manufacturing base to supplement its role as a center of government and commerce.

Hoosier Values

Even as the state edged into urbanism, it retained much of the small-town values from its early days. As explored by Robert S. Lynd and Helen Merrell Lynd in their classic sociological study of Muncie, *Middletown: A Study in Mod-*

ern American Culture (1929), typical Hoosiers valued consensus and conformity, even as they embraced modern conveniences at home and at work. Although Middletown's residents respected differences in religion and politics, they were suspicious of beliefs deemed foreign or strange. The source of both the state's strength and weakness, these dichotomous characteristics were the basis for some of the best literary works produced by Indiana writers, including native sons such as Booth Tarkington, James Whitcomb Riley, and Theodore Dreiser.

Increasingly, the white, Anglo-Saxon character of small-town Hoosier life became more heterogeneous in the twentieth century. In 1920, a bare majority of the state's almost three million residents lived in urban areas. Foreign-born residents represented over 5 percent of the population; the Great Migration of African Americans northward after World War I increased their presence to almost 3 percent. These demographic changes, along with a conservative reaction to the spread of Jazz Age culture in the 1920s, fueled a rebirth of the Ku Klux Klan in Indiana. The state became the midwestern center of the organization in the 1920s. Under the banner of patriotism, combined with directives against Roman Catholics, the foreign-born, and African Americans, the Klan attracted upwards of 300,000 Hoosier members by 1923 in urban and rural areas alike. By the following year, Klan-endorsed candidates controlled the Indiana legislature and the governor's office as well. Only in 1925, after the conviction of Klan leader D. C. Stephenson for murder and rape, did the organization relinquish its hold on Indiana politics. A 1928 Pulitzer Prize–winning campaign by the *Indianapolis Times* against the Klan finally purged it from legitimate political circles.

Industrial Strength

Aside from the conservative politics of the decade, the driving force in Hoosier life was the state's continuing industrialization that linked it firmly with the national economy, especially the automobile industry. By the end of the 1920s, steel production was the state's largest industry, with automobile and auto parts manufacturing and electrical component production ranked just behind it. Most northern and central Indiana cities were tied to the auto industry with at least one automobile or parts production factory employing their citizens, while the Calumet cities continued to expand their steel output. To the south, Evansville became a major center of refrigeration unit production. The state's natural resources also continued to make Indiana a center of limestone, sand, and coal output, particularly throughout the southern part of the state.

Given the economy's growing dependence on durable goods manufacturing by 1930, the onset of the Great Depression hit the state hard. Industrial employment plunged to almost half its pre-Depression level by 1932, as employers such as U.S. Steel, which had doubled its production capacity in the 1920s, shut down. In the midst of New Deal attempts to revive the economy, Hoosier workers responded with a number of organizational efforts to form labor unions. A sit-down strike at Anderson's Guide Lamp factory in 1936 and 1937 led by the United Auto Workers (UAW) was a pivotal action in forcing General Motors to recognize the right of workers to collectively bargain through their unions. Anderson became a bastion of UAW support in politics and society, while Evansville witnessed the rise of the United Electrical Workers and the Calumet region, the United Steel Workers. As it had been since the 1890s, the United Mine Workers remained a strong force in the lives of thousands of Hoosiers in the coal mining towns of southern Indiana.

Spurred on by lucrative federal contracts to industrial employers during World War II, the state's emphasis on manufacturing investment continued into the postwar era. By 1958, over 40 percent of the state's total earnings came from the manufacturing sector, a rate that far outpaced the national average. Even as the national economy moved away from durable goods manufacturing, Indiana remained a bastion of manufacturing strength: in 1981, the national economy derived less than 17 percent of its earnings from durable goods production, while in Indiana, the rate was over 31 percent. Although the manufacturing sector provided many Hoosiers with high-wage jobs and advantageous benefits, the state's dependence on the industrial sector came under criticism during the recession from 1979 to 1982. With prohibitively high interest rates and energy prices, many industrial corporations failed to reinvest in new technology and equipment; as a result, many of the so-called "smokestack industries" lost their competitive advantage during the recession. About one-quarter of the employees in the durable goods sector lost their jobs in Indiana, and unemployment rates in Muncie and Anderson topped 18 percent in 1982.

While those without a college degree had previously obtained high-paying jobs in the manufacturing sector, public leaders were concerned that the state's economy might not provide such opportunities in the future. Calls for greater access to Indiana's system of higher education prevailed in the 1980s and 1990s. Although the Purdue University and Indiana University systems had expanded greatly with branch campuses around the state after World War II, in 1990 the college attendance rate of 37 percent continued to trail the national average of 45 percent. Indiana also ranked low on the number of college graduates who completed their degrees and remained in the state's workforce.

As it emerged from the recession of the early 1980s, Indiana's manufacturing base contributed to the recovery and the state remained one of the top five producers of aircraft engines and parts, truck and bus bodies, steel, surgical supplies, and pharmaceuticals. In 1999, manufacturing jobs made up 23.4 percent of nonfarm employment. While the overall number of manufacturing jobs in Indiana increased throughout the 1990s, the service sector became the single largest provider of nonagricultural jobs, with a 24.3 percent share. Agricultural production, once a mainstay of the state's development, represented just 1.8 percent of Indiana's economic output in 1997. In Indianapolis, the Eli Lilly Company, making products from insulin to Prozac, ranked as the state's largest corporation, with global sales approaching $11 billion in 2000. Overall, the Hoosier economy was the nation's eighteenth largest in 1997; with 27 percent of its manufacturing workforce making products for export, Indiana ranked fifteenth in the nation as an exporting state.

At the millennium, Indiana had 6,080,485 inhabitants, making it the nation's fourteenth most populous state. African Americans comprised the state's largest minority group, with 8.4 percent of the total population; 87.5 percent of Hoosiers identified themselves as white. Indianapolis had a population of more than 750,000 people, but no other city other than Fort Wayne had more than 200,000 residents. Indeed, Indiana's reputation remained rooted in a small-town, Hoosier identity. Steve Tesich's portrait of town-and-gown relations in Bloomington, the subject of the coming-of-age movie *Breaking Away* (1979), won an Academy Award for best screenplay. Hammond resident Jean Shepherd's wry reminiscences of the 1940s served as the basis for the movie *A Christmas Story* (1983). The movie *Hoosiers* (1986), based on the basketball team from the town of Milan that won the state championship in the 1950s, also thrilled audiences who rooted for the underdog team. Few other states follow high school and college sports teams so avidly. Basketball remains the top Hoosier pasttime, and Indianapolis waged a successful campaign to become the home of the National Collegiate Athletic Association in 1999. The NCAA Hall of Champions museum, along with the annual five-hundred-mile race at the Indianapolis Motor Speedway, has added to the city's popularity as a tourist destination.

While the ascendancy of Dan Quayle to vice president in 1988 led some observers to herald a period of Republican dominance in the state, Indiana voters remained steadfastly centrist in their habits. The Indiana legislature typically was evenly split between Republicans and Democrats. After a twenty-year run of Republican governors, the Democrat Evan Bayh in 1989 began the first of two terms as governor. In 1998, Bayh went on to the U.S. Senate in a landslide victory with 63 percent of the vote. He was replaced by another Democrat, Frank O'Bannon, who in 2000 won another term in office with 57 percent of the vote. Like Bayh, the state's senior senator, Republican Richard Lugar, was regarded as a political centrist, holding conservative views on fiscal matters while avoiding stridency on foreign relations or public policy issues. Avoiding the political extremes, both senators embodied the central values of their Hoosier constituents.

BIBLIOGRAPHY

Cayton, Andrew R. L. *Frontier Indiana.* Bloomington: Indiana University Press, 1996.

Critchlow, Donald T. *Studebaker: The Life and Death of an American Corporation.* Bloomington: Indiana University Press, 1996.

Lynd, Robert S., and Helen Merrell Lynd. *Middletown: A Study in Modern American Culture.* New York: Harcourt, Brace, 1929.

Madison, James H. *The Indiana Way: A State History.* Bloomington: Indiana University Press, 1986.

———, ed. *Heart Land: Comparative Histories of the Midwestern States.* Bloomington: Indiana University Press, 1988.

Nelson, Daniel. *Farm and Factory: Workers in the Midwest, 1880–1990.* Bloomington: Indiana University Press, 1995.

Timothy G. Borden

See also **Indianapolis; Iron and Steel Industry; Miami (Indians); Midwest; Northwest Territory.**

INDIANA COMPANY originated with a group of Indian traders and their merchant backers who lost goods during Pontiac's War (1763). The Iroquois, to compensate for these losses, presented the traders with a large tract of land (now part of West Virginia) in a treaty agreement. Company executives attempted to secure royal confirmation of the title, but the claim was swallowed up in the project for the Grand Ohio Company. When the Revolution broke out, the Indiana Company reorganized and proceeded to sell land, but Virginia blocked its operations and contested its land claims. The company eventually brought suit against Virginia in the U.S. Supreme Court *(Grayson v. Virginia)*, but the case was ultimately dismissed on the ground that the Court had no jurisdiction under the Eleventh Amendment.

BIBLIOGRAPHY

Bayard, Charles Judah. *The Development of Public Land Policy, 1783–1820.* New York: Arno Press, 1979.

Cayton, Andrew R. L. *Frontier Indiana.* Bloomington: Indiana University Press, 1996.

Max Savelle / s. b.

See also **Baynton, Wharton, and Morgan; Colonial Commerce; Frontier; Indian Land Cessions; Trading Companies.**

INDIANAPOLIS ranked as the twelfth largest city in the United States in 2000. The Indiana legislature selected the area as the state's capital in 1821 due to its central location, but the city remained a small and commercially insignificant town until the 1840s because of its inaccessibility. In 1847, railroads linked the city to national markets, attracting businesses and residents. From that time through the 1970s, Indianapolis served as a manufacturing and agribusiness hub for the Midwest. The "Rust Belt" phenomenon, and particularly the recession of 1979–1982, effected changes in the national economy that forced many of the city's largest employers to eventually close or move elsewhere, resulting in a blighted and

Indianapolis. A panoramic photograph of Monument Place, 1914. LIBRARY OF CONGRESS

depressed inner city. Revitalization efforts focusing on sports and attracting high technology and science-related industry slowly reversed the blight and transformed the city into a model for urban renewal. Circle Centre Mall, the Canal Walk, and the placement of several museums and other venues in an education corridor continued the beautification of downtown after 1990.

Since the early 1970s, the city's leaders have endeavored to link the Circle City with sports, creating the Indiana Sports Corporation to coordinate efforts to bring competitive events to the city, spending more than $400 million between 1979 and 2001 for sporting venues and related structures with the help of private organizations, and eagerly seeking to host professional sports teams. Indianapolis remains best known for AUTOMOBILE RACING and the Indianapolis Motor Speedway, with the Indianapolis 500, the Brickyard 400, and the U.S. Grand Prix—the highest attended events for each racing series. Approximately 2 million visitors per year travel to Indianapolis for the various sporting events and conventions, making tourism a major factor in the city's economy.

The revitalization efforts of the 1970s and 1980s may not have been possible without a consolidated city-county government with a strong mayor and city-county council at its center. Most city and county offices were consolidated and placed under the authority of a mayoral appointee in 1969, in what is popularly known as Unigov. The borders of the city of Indianapolis became contiguous with those of Marion County, expanding the size of the city to 361 square miles.

Major employers in Indianapolis in the early twenty-first century include government, hospitals, pharmaceutical companies, grocery outlets, universities, and manufacturing. As of 2002, the three largest employers were Clarion Health, Eli Lilly and Company, and Marsh Supermarkets. The 2000 U.S. Census revealed that Indianapolis's population stood at 860,454 (70.2 percent non-Hispanic, white; 24.8 percent African American; 3.9 percent Hispanic; 1.3 percent Asian; and 0.6 percent Native American).

BIBLIOGRAPHY

Bodenhamer, David J., and Robert G. Barrows, eds. *The Encyclopedia of Indianapolis.* Bloomington and Indianapolis: Indiana University Press, 1994.

Bodenhamer, David J., Lamont Hulse, and Elizabeth B. Monroe. *The Main Stem: The History and Architecture of North Meridian Street.* Indianapolis: Historic Landmarks Foundation of Indiana, 1992.

Taylor, Rich. *Indy: Seventy-Five Years of Racing's Greatest Spectacle.* New York: St. Martin's Press, 1991.

Bradford W. Sample

See also **Capitals.**

INDIANS AND ALCOHOL. Most of the indigenous peoples of North America possessed no alcohol before Europeans arrived in the Western Hemisphere. Only the Native peoples of the modern-day southwestern United States and Mexico consumed alcohol in any form. Thus, the majority of Native Americans were exposed to alcohol at the same time that they had to cope with the far-reaching changes in their lives brought about by European colonization. The enduring stereotype of the "drunken Indian" suggests a common belief that Indians have suffered more than others from liquor.

Before European Contact

The peoples who possessed alcohol before 1492 used fermented beverages only in specific rituals. The Tepehuanes and Tarahumaras, who inhabited territory in modern-day northern Mexico, fermented corn to produce *tesvino*, which they consumed at ceremonies to mark important stages in an individual's life, such as the passage to adulthood. The belief in the sacred potential of alcohol survived for centuries. In modern times, these indigenous peoples began to offer some of their alcohol to Jesus before they drank. The Pimas and Papagos, who continue to inhabit traditional lands in the southwestern United States, extracted an intoxicating juice from saguaro cactus. They drank in a ritual designed to appease the divine forces that brought rain to their often-arid world. Believing the amount of rain in a year depended on the amount of the cactus liquor they consumed during a specific ritual, they often drank to the point of drunkenness. The Aztecs of Mexico drank pulque, which they fermented from the maguey. Like other indigenous peoples, they believed alcohol had sacred force, that whoever drank it gained access to divine powers. As a result, the Aztecs created elaborate rules for when alcohol could be consumed and who could drink it. If someone drank at an illegal time or if someone who did not have the right to drink it consumed alcohol, the punishment was death. By contrast, the Mayas, who fermented *balche* from bark and honey, allowed more widespread consumption of alcohol though still within set limits. In Maya society drinking *balche* on certain days allowed *macehuales* (commoners) to express their emotions freely and thus relieve potential tension that might otherwise exist between them and the *principales*, who controlled the resources of the society. For the Mayas, consumption of *balche* remained a fixture of holidays long after the Spanish arrived.

European Influences

Although these peoples possessed alcohol and established rules for its consumption before Europeans arrived, colonization altered drinking patterns. The Spanish created facilities to produce *aguardiente* (burning water), thereby expanding the amount of alcohol available. Soon, drinking became more widespread and was no longer confined to set holidays. The increase in the amount of drinking contributed to an increase in social pathologies, such as violence within communities, though scholars believe Native peoples' prior experience with alcohol enabled them to exert some control over the potentially most devastating threats posed by liquor.

In other parts of North America, most of modern-day United States and Canada, liquor first arrived when Europeans landed, but the trade did not start at the dawn of the colonial period. Although some Europeans no doubt offered Native Americans alcohol when they met, possibly in gestures meant to solidify nascent alliances, the real trade in alcohol did not begin until the mid-seventeenth century, when British and French colonists recognized that sugar produced in the West Indies could be distilled in the Western Hemisphere and sold as liquor in North America. From 1650 onward, alcohol became a common item in the fur trade. Native Americans who had developed a taste for alcohol purchased rum from the English and brandy from the French. The trade had particular importance for the English, because North American colonists and American Indians had a greater fondness for rum than Europeans. In fact, colonists consumed far more alcohol than Native Americans—perhaps seven shots of distilled beverages each day by 1770 according to one estimate. But whatever social pathologies they suffered did not undermine their society, and thus no widespread movement for temperance took hold during the colonial period.

As soon as the liquor trade began, colonists came to believe that it created havoc in Native communities. They were right. Indigenous and colonial observers reported that Native Americans who consumed alcohol did so only to become intoxicated. Those who became drunk fought with each other and with members of their families; they eroded the civility that normally characterized relations in indigenous communities; they fell into fires or off cliffs or drowned; and they at times murdered others, thereby opening raw wounds that communities struggled to heal. Not all Indians drank, and surviving records suggest that those most likely to drink to drunkenness and then engage in some form of social pathology were young men, though ample examples of women and the elderly drinking exist as well. Since young men were the community members who often had control of the furs or skins taken during the hunting season, their desire for alcohol had devastating consequences when some of them chose to exchange the rewards of their annual hunt for liquor, which they drank quickly. As a result, poverty became more widespread, thereby diminishing indigenous peoples' efforts to cope with the threats to their cultural, spiritual, and economic existence brought by colonists.

Over time, Natives and newcomers alike tried to find ways to limit the horrific consequences of the alcohol trade. Each colony passed laws to prohibit the commerce in liquor. More important, Native peoples organized opposition to the trade. They protested to colonial officials about nefarious traders who lured young men with alcohol, and they organized temperance campaigns to halt consumption. Although some of these efforts reflected the teachings of Catholic and Protestant missionaries, the most successful antidrinking programs might have emanated from within Indian communities. Eventually, such programs also helped solidify Native Americans' critique of colonial mores. As the Catawba headman Hagler put it when he met with North Carolina emissaries in 1754, "You Rot Your grain in Tubs, out of which you take and make Strong Spirits." Colonists should desist from such practices, he and others argued, since the liquor trade only caused violence and despair in Indian country.

Despite their efforts, the liquor trade thrived in the colonial period, because traders recognized that alcohol was an ideal commodity. The demand for most trade items, such as manufactured clothing, was limited, but the demand for alcohol was theoretically infinite. Colonial officials in New France and British America who realized the horrors caused by alcohol also recognized the value of the trade. As Sir William Johnson, superintendent of Indian affairs for the northern colonies, informed the Lords of Trade in 1764, the commerce might cause problems, but "the Trade will never be so extensive" without rum.

After the American Revolution, the liquor trade spread farther west. Wherever traders went, alcohol followed. Federal officials became alarmed at the continuing prospect of Indian drinking, so they enacted the Trade and Intercourse Act of 1802, which granted the president the authority to halt the sale of alcohol to Indians. Although various federal and state officials, including Thomas Jefferson, wanted to stop the flow of alcohol into Indian country, they were unable to end the business. As in the colonial period, the economics of the trade proved overwhelming to government officials. Since the profits to be made on alcohol were often greater than those that could be made on other commodities, especially since traders watered down their alcohol so they had more to sell, traders were willing to face any legal risks to sustain the commerce. Missionaries, too, often failed in their efforts to stop drinking in indigenous communities.

Temperance Efforts

The most notable temperance efforts in the nineteenth-century West were those led by Native Americans. The Pawnees, for example, limited alcohol consumption in their communities in the early nineteenth century, and so did various Native peoples who followed the teachings of indigenous revival movements. Thus, the Iroquois Handsome Lake, the Shawnee prophet Tenkswatawa, and a Delaware woman named Beate convinced their followers to abandon alcohol. Later leaders of cultural revival movements also embraced temperance. The Paiute Wovoka, for example, made temperance part of the Ghost Dance, a movement that swept the Plains in the late nineteenth century.

Still, neither federal laws nor temperance efforts ended the scourge of drinking in Indian country. By the mid-nineteenth century, alcohol abuse had taken a toll on the Sioux and Chippewas, among others, according to one government report. In the following decades, which brought untold horror to Native Americans across the Plains and in the West, liquor continued to arrive in indigenous communities. During the twentieth century, the range of social pathologies associated with liquor was simply astonishing. According to estimates, the alcoholism mortality rate was six times higher for Indians than for the general U.S. population, and alcohol-related trauma or disease accounted for seven out of ten admissions to Indian Health Service clinics. Fetal alcohol syndrome had a devastating impact in indigenous communities. Despite the fact that many Native Americans avoided liquor, alcohol also played an enormous role in homicides, suicides, and accidental deaths caused by motor vehicles and exposure. Although alcohol-related problems in indigenous communities were widespread, no single pattern of drinking existed.

Ever since the seventeenth century, observers of Indian alcohol use have suggested that something about the indigenous peoples of the Americas made them particularly susceptible to alcohol abuse. Some have claimed that their problems stem from a genetic trait that makes them more likely to become alcoholics. At the beginning of the twenty-first century, there was no evidence that Native Americans possess any greater genetic predisposition to alcoholism than the general population. Alcohol, however, continued to take a devastating toll in Indian country, a tragic legacy of the European colonization of the Western Hemisphere.

BIBLIOGRAPHY

Dorris, Michael. *The Broken Cord.* New York: Harper and Row, 1989.

Kunitz, Stephen J., and Jerrold E. Levy. *Drinking Careers: A Twenty-Five-Year Study of Three Navajo Populations.* New Haven, Conn.: Yale University Press, 1994.

Mancall, Peter C. *Deadly Medicine: Indians and Alcohol in Early America.* Ithaca, N.Y.: Cornell University Press, 1995.

———. "Men, Women, and Alcohol in Indian Villages in the Great Lakes Region in the Early Republic." *Journal of the Early Republic* 15 (1995): 425–449.

Taylor, William B. *Drinking, Homicide, and Rebellion in Colonial Mexican Villages.* Stanford, Calif.: Stanford University Press, 1979.

Unrau, William E. *White Man's Wicked Water: The Alcohol Trade and Prohibition in Indian Country, 1802–1892.* Lawrence: University Press of Kansas, 1996.

Waddell, Jack O., and Michael W. Everett, eds. *Drinking Behavior among Southwestern Indians: An Anthropological Perspective.* Tucson: University of Arizona Press, 1980.

Peter Mancall

See also **Alcohol, Regulation of; Indian Religious Life; Indian Social Life;** *and vol. 9:* **Life of Ma-ka-tai-me-she-kai-kiak, or Black Hawk.**

INDIANS AND SLAVERY. Prior to contact with Europeans, American Indian groups throughout North America enslaved each other. From the Pacific Northwest to the Southeast, large confederacies and alliances often targeted smaller societies and took captives for laborers, warriors, or kinspeople. Many groups incorporated captives into their societies, and they generally did not keep captives in a state of perpetual or chattel slavery.

The nature and magnitude of Indian slavery forever changed following European contact. Desperate to secure immediate wealth, Europeans organized large slave-raiding campaigns against Indian populations and greatly encouraged intertribal slaving, particularly in the hinterlands of colonial societies. From California to Florida the Spanish enslaved captives directly, bought slaves from Indian groups, and institutionalized slave hierarchies within colonial society. Wealth, the Spanish believed, came from Indian labor and tribute. Despite the protests of the church, Indian slavery flourished. In New Mexico, detribalized Indian captives became known as *genizaros* and formed a distinct ethnic and racial group within colonial society. Similar hybrid racial and ethnic social relations characterized portions of French colonial societies along the Mississippi River, particularly at New Orleans and St. Louis. Most captives in these colonial societies were young children, especially girls, whose domestic and sexual labor became integral to colonial economies and demographic stability.

As the Indian slave trade remade colonial hinterlands throughout the North American continent, Indian groups often responded in kind to European and intertribal slaving. Groups migrated away from slaving societies, joined with neighboring groups for protection, and increasingly became fierce slavers themselves. In the Northeast and on the southern Plains the Iroquois and Comanches built large empires in which captive taking and slavery became important institutions. Along with the escalation of violence and disease, Indian slavery became a clear indicator of the disruptive and traumatic influences engendered by European contact and colonization. Although often grafted onto existing intertribal divisions and antagonisms, postcontact Indian slavery held little resemblance in scope or scale to pre-Columbian practices.

In English colonies, Indian slaves often labored for whites, but bonded laborers from England and later from Africa formed the majority of the servile labor force along the Atlantic Coast. In the Southeast, Indian captives were forced to labor on Carolina plantations, but increasingly Indian slaves were sent away from the continent to other colonies in the Caribbean. Creeks, Choctaws, and Cherokees enslaved each other and sold captives to the British in exchange for guns, ammunition, and supplies. As African American slavery grew and swept throughout the South, Indians incorporated runaways into their societies, returned slaves to white owners, and bought black slaves for their own slaveholding purposes. Desperate to maintain access to their homelands, Indians such as the Cherokees constructed plantation economies in an attempt to maintain viable livelihoods within southern society. Upon their eventual removal from the South to Indian Territory, slaveholding Indians took many black slaves with them. Other groups, particularly the Seminole and Creek Nations, offered former slaves community rights and privileges within their new societies.

Following emancipation, many African Americans moved west into Indian Territory and settled among Indian nations, where they developed extended kinship and community networks. The mixture of Indians and Africans became a defining characteristic of many Oklahoma and southeastern Indian nations.

BIBLIOGRAPHY

Lauber, Almon Wheeler. *Indian Slavery in Colonial Times within the Present Limits of the United States.* Williamston, Mass.: Corner House Publishers, 1979. Reprint of the 1913 original edition.

Perdue, Theda. *Slavery and the Evolution of Cherokee Society, 1540–1866.* Knoxville: University of Tennessee Press, 1979.

Ned Blackhawk

See also **Slavery.**

INDIANS AND THE HORSE. Spaniards brought horses to the Americas, but traditional Indian stories about the acquisition of the HORSE do not begin with a bow toward the Iberian Peninsula. Rather, the stories speak of the holy people or brave individuals within the community who bestowed or obtained these remarkable animals. In the Great Plains, the Southwest, and the Plateau regions, the horse made possible new horizons and new dreams for Native communities.

During the 1600s, Indian peoples began acquiring horses and realizing their potential for the hunt, for transportation, and for war. Given the Spanish presence in the South, horses moved through Indian Country from south to north, and Santa Fe was a vital center for the trade. Through trade and purchase, by "borrowing" and raiding, Indians began to gain sufficient horses for their purposes. The results could be dramatic, and in no location were they more dramatic than in the Plains. In this area successful farming communities like the Mandans, Hidatsas, and Arikaras had held the advantage. With the arrival of horses (and new diseases like smallpox), such sedentary communities suddenly were vulnerable, and other peoples like the Lakotas and the Cheyennes became dominant. In the Southwest, Pueblo communities now had to confront newly powerful groups like the Apaches, the Navajos, and the Comanches. Although horses transformed daily life, they did not necessarily change central values. An individual among the Cheyennes still sought to be generous and to be courageous; the horse allowed new means of achieving those objectives.

Horses therefore are associated with an era of Native ascendancy, and Indians on horseback became indelibly stamped in the American public memory as a central representation of who Indians were. In film, in art, and in imagination, Indians on horses chased buffalo, rode over ridges to ambush the army, and accompanied the wind. In the twenty-first century, filmmakers, artists, and storytellers continued to seize upon this element in their renditions of Native life. Their depictions suggested that "real" Indians are on horseback rather than in pickup trucks.

Indian on Horseback. Chief Looking Glass, a Nez Perce military strategist, photographed in the 1870s. NATIONAL ARCHIVES AND RECORDS ADMINISTRATION

When Indian peoples were confined to reservations in the second half of the nineteenth century, horses remained important. Indian family names like Riding In (Pawnee), Her Many Horses (Lakota), and Buckinghorse (Navajo) exemplified the significance of horses. Many Native groups turned to cattle ranching as a central economic and cultural activity and of course employed horses. Horse racing proved a popular pastime at newly organized gatherings like Crow Fair. Indians started to compete in rodeos, and legendary cowboys like Jackson Sundown (Nez Perce), George Defender (Lakota), Sam Bird-in-Ground (Crow), and Tom Three Persons (Blood) achieved great success. The Native fondness for horses encouraged the proliferation of tribal herds with consequent complications in regard to soil erosion. During the New Deal era, the commissioner of Indian affairs, John Collier, attempted to eradicate horses, but he met stiff resistance from the Navajos and other tribes. The Navajos in fact applied a new term to the worst-looking horses, the ones with little economic value but whose owners liked having them around. They called them "john colliers."

Indian communities became more urban by the twenty-first century, but demographic and technological change did not diminish the appeal of horses. Cattle ranching remained important on some Indian reservations, and rodeos continued to involve thousands of Native men, women, and children. A good horse is the key to success in roping events, steer wrestling, and barrel racing and thus to bringing honor to self, family, and community. Indian artists portray horses in all the colors of the rainbow, not only black, white, and brown but also blue and red. Children learn that horses are a sacred gift that represents a cultural obligation. The Crow Fair features an endless parade of horses, and john colliers live in pastures a few miles north of Nazlini. Horses thus have endured as symbols of Indian identity and significant parts of Indian life.

BIBLIOGRAPHY

Holder, Preston. *The Hoe and the Horse on the Plains: A Study of Cultural Development among North American Indians.* Lincoln: University of Nebraska Press, 1970.

Iverson, Peter. *When Indians Became Cowboys: Native Peoples and Cattle Ranching in the American West.* Norman: University of Oklahoma Press, 1994.

———. *Riders of the West: Portraits from Indian Rodeo.* Seattle: University of Washington Press, 1999.

Peter Iverson

See also **Indian Economic Life; Indian Social Life; Warfare, Indian.**

INDIANS AND TOBACCO. There are more than a dozen species of tobacco, all of them native to the New World. Although *Nicotiana tabacum* is the most prevalent form in present-day commercial use and was the species encountered by Columbus, *N. rustica* was more widely distributed in Native America. Its range was largely coincident with the distribution of maize agriculture, spreading from Chiloe Island in Chile, to New Brunswick, Canada, but many nonfarmers among American Indians raised or traded tobacco. Another species, *N. attenuata*, grew in the Great Basin and southern Plains, and was spread into western Canada. The fact that the Inuit lacked tobacco before Russian contact and that the northwestern tribes of the continent made only limited use of the plant suggests that tobacco in its various forms was still in the process of diffusion at the time of first contact with Europeans. The various tobacco types were the most widely raised plants among natives in the New World.

Given so bewildering an array both of species and of uses, it is virtually impossible to point to origins. Tobacco appears wild both in the tropics and in desert areas. Its spread and hybridization by man, the fact that it was smoked in many forms, eaten, chewed, sniffed, and drunk, and employed ceremonially, socially, and individually are all features suggestive of considerable antiquity. The tropical forests of South America offer the greatest aboriginal variation in uses of tobacco and are probably where tobacco domestication began. The narcotic properties of the various species of tobacco may have been discovered not once but several times in the course of American Indian cultural development.

Generally, even among farmers, tobacco was planted separately, always by men, and was frequently associated with ritual. The sacred element in tobacco, reflected in ceremonies and offerings, often diffused with the plant itself. Full inhalation of smoked tobacco was common in native America, as was holding the breath to produce intoxication. Some tobaccos had so pronounced a narcotic effect that they were adulterated with bark and grasses. In California, the Great Basin, and southeastern Alaska, tobacco was commonly eaten with lime. In southern California some Indian tribes drank a mixture of tobacco and datura (the jimsonweed, or toloache). Tropical South America and the Antilles had the cigar, Mexico and the Pueblo region knew corn-husk cigarettes, and pipes appeared all over in great variety.

Pipes of stone, wood, clay, and bone were used among various tribes of the differing culture areas of the present United States. Tubular pipes, not unlike a modern cigar holder, had a scattered distribution. The elbow pipe, with stem and bowl, appeared mostly in the Plains and Woodlands. In the Great Lakes region, where smoking took on a ritual aspect, the association of the pipe with peace deliberations gave rise to the American "peace pipe" concept. Folklore, not all of it accurate, surrounds the American Indians' use of the pipe. The common idea of the peace pipe, for example, is somewhat overdrawn, at least in respect to the sharing of a pipe to symbolize cessation of hostilities. Pipe-smoking rituals, it is true, were stressed by the Plains and Woodlands peoples, but tobacco and the items associated with it were sacred almost everywhere they appeared. A Plains Indian bundle, the wrapped tribal or group fetish, frequently contained a carved pipe bowl of catlinite, along with the reed or wooden stem, the calumet; the latter, carved, incised, and otherwise decorated, was often the more important element. In the Woodlands, the eastern Plains, and some of the Gulf area, the calumet, like wampum, might be carried by ambassadors between federated tribes and might symbolize states of war and peace, but it might also be employed in an appeal to spiritual beings. The passing of the pipe, solemnly ritualized as it was, became a social adjunct to its intertribal symbolic use.

Pipes with stem and bowl were introduced in the mid-sixteenth century to Europe, which by then was familiar with smoking tobacco. In 1559 Portugal and Spain were already importing leaves for their alleged medical properties. Tobacco pipes became current in England after 1586, when Sir Walter Raleigh is said to have made it current among the members of the court. Tobacco spread across the world remarkably rapidly. By 1600 tobacco was raised widely in Europe despite initial adverse reactions from both church and state. In the seventeenth century the Russians fined, imprisoned, and even tortured tobacco users, while the Ottoman Turks made the use of tobacco a capital offense. But despite such opposition, tobacco spread from Russia across Siberia, and into Japan, China, and Southeast Asia; by the beginning of the nineteenth century it had reached the Alaskan Inuit, bringing the American plant to a people who still did not use it.

BIBLIOGRAPHY

Gill, Sam D. *Native American Traditions.* Belmont, Calif.: Wadsworth, 1983.

Goodman, Jordan. *Tobacco in History: The Cultures of Dependence.* New York: Routledge, 1993.

King, Jonathan C. H. *Smoking Pipes of the North American Indian.* London: British Museum Publications, 1977.

Robert F. Spencer / J. H.

See also **Agriculture; Indian Religious Life; Indian Technology; Medicine, Indian; Tobacco Industry.**

INDIANS IN THE CIVIL WAR. American Indians who fought in the Civil War did so only reluctantly and almost all of them with the hope that federal officials would reward them by protecting them in their homelands. This was certainly true of the Ojibwes and Ottawas from Michigan and the Senecas from New York, who, at the outbreak of the war, saw their small land bases continually reduced. Others, like the Pequots and Mohegans from Connecticut, may have joined the war effort for purely economic reasons, hoping that service in the war would lead them out of poverty.

In the West, the war had unintended tragic consequences. Because regular army troops were called east to fight, some western posts were manned by poorly trained and undisciplined local militia. One of these militia units was led by John Chivington against a peaceful band of Cheyennes at Sand Creek in Colorado in November 1864. Chivington's forces slaughtered hundreds of people (mostly women and children) and mutilated their bodies in one of the most brutal massacres of Native people that this country has ever seen.

American Indians in the South, remembering that it was the U.S. government that had signed treaties with them, initially wished to maintain neutrality in this "fight between brothers." According to the Cherokee "declaration," "no other course was consistent with the dictates of prudence or could secure the safety of their people and immunity from the horrors of a war waged by an invading enemy than a strict neutrality." But neutrality could not be sustained; feeling pressure from all sides, some tribes in Indian Territory took up arms for the South. Never happy with the removal process that had moved them from their traditional lands, they feared that if the North won, they might be displaced from their lands once again. In addition, some southern tribal leaders had cultural affiliations with the South; indeed, some Native people were also slave owners. Again in the words of the Cherokee "declaration," "Whatever causes the Cherokee peo-

Ely Samuel Parker. A Seneca, the secretary to General Ulysses S. Grant during the Civil War, and President Grant's appointee as the first Native American commissioner of Indian affairs, 1869–1871; he sought to reform U.S. government policies toward Indians, though he also supported church-run programs to "civilize" them. DEPARTMENT OF ANTHROPOLOGY, SMITHSONIAN INSTITUTION

ple may have had in the past, to complain of some of the Southern States, they cannot but feel that their interests and their destiny are inseparably connected with those of the South."

The Five Civilized Tribes declared their allegiance to the South, but many towns in their territory in the Southeast stayed out of the war. The Indian units from both sides distinguished themselves. In fact, the last Confederate general to surrender was Stand Watie, the Cherokee leader of the Indian brigades of the Army of the Trans-Mississippi, who gave up the fight on 23 June 1865, two months after General Robert E. Lee's surrender on 9 April.

After the war, it became evident that the fears of the Native people were well-founded. The western tribes were subjected to intense pressure to give up their free lives on the Plains and move to reservations. Despite their loyal service in the war, Oneida, Seneca, and Ojibwe communities continued to face hostile neighbors with little federal protection. Virtually all the tribal communities that fought in the war were also deeply affected by the death and destruction the conflict wrought. With large numbers of orphans and widows living on reservations, it became very difficult to rebuild these communities, and many fell even deeper into poverty and despair. Finally, after the war, the Five Civilized Tribes were forced to sign new treaties with the United States that undermined their land base and permitted new intrusions into their territories.

BIBLIOGRAPHY

Hauptman, Laurence M. *Between Two Fires: American Indians in the Civil War.* New York: Free Press, 1995.

Starr, Emmet. *History of the Cherokee Indians and Their Legends and Folk Lore.* Oklahoma City: Warden, 1921.

Phil Bellfy

See also **Cherokee; Civilized Tribes, Five; Indian Brigade; Indian Policy, U.S., 1830–1900; Indian Removal; Indians in the Military; Sand Creek Massacre;** *and vol. 9:* **Head of Choctaw Nation Reaffirms His Tribe's Position.**

INDIANS IN THE MILITARY. Before the advent of whites in North America, Native American peoples engaged in various forms of organized violence, almost none of which the European colonists would have regarded as "true" war. Native Americans fought pitched battles that tested the agility, skills, and courage of their young men, and Native nations raided each other for goods, foodstuffs, religious objects, and captives. Wars made for territorial gain or to destroy entire societies were rare if not absent in precontact Native North America.

War in North America changed considerably after the European invasion. While the Europeans held an advantage in weapons technology in the form of muskets and cannon, Indian knowledge of the terrain gave the tribes great tactical advantages. Native Americans were also motivated: they were defending their homelands. European colonists soon recognized that they needed Native American allies, auxiliaries, and scouts to maintain their territorial claims and defend their trade routes.

In the colonial era, trade rivalry, new diseases, and warfare all contributed to the widespread disruption and displacement of numerous tribal societies. New alliances were forged, totally new Native groups appeared, new tribal nation-states emerged, and many Native American peoples became more thoroughly militarized than ever before. For a great many tribes, military participation became highly valued, even if it was in the service of the whites.

The United States followed in the tradition of the colonial powers. United States officials recruited Native American allies for war and sought to divide tribal alliances formed to oppose them. During the revolutionary war, the Continental Congress authorized George Washington to recruit 2,000 Native American warriors. The first ratified U.S.-Indian treaty was in effect a military alliance with the Delawares. After this pact, Native Americans began to serve with the U.S. armed forces in ever-increasing numbers. When in the early 1790s the federal government had two armies destroyed in a war against a tribal confederacy on the northwest frontier, it sent General "Mad" Anthony Wayne, accompanied by Choctaw scouts, to crush the tribes. Thereafter, Native American contingents fought in American campaigns in the War of 1812 and aided the United States against "rebellious" Native Americans throughout the nineteenth century.

When the Civil War erupted in 1861, the Confederacy actively sought alliances with several Native nations, including the Five Civilized Tribes of Indian Territory as well as the Comanches, Osages, and Quapaws. On the Union side, "loyal" Cherokees, Creeks, and others formed independent battalions that eventually assisted in retaking Indian Territory, a strategic area on the border of Arkansas and Texas. The Union also recruited a company of Chippewa sharpshooters who served in the siege of Petersburg and helped chase the Army of Northern Virginia to its final surrender. The Seneca general Ely S. Parker, later promoted to brigadier general, is remembered as the staff officer who drafted the terms of surrender at Appomattox. A Cherokee, Stand Watie, became the last Confederate general to surrender to the United States.

Following the Civil War, the primary military foe of the United States was the various Native nations located in the West. Once again American military leaders recognized that fighting Indians required the aid of other Indians. In 1866, Congress authorized the army to establish a special Indian scouting corps. Indian scouts served throughout the Indian wars of the latter half of the nineteenth century and gained an unparalleled reputation for bravery in action. The Indian scouting corps was not disbanded until the 1940s.

Eventually, Native Americans were fully integrated into the regular army divisions. In 1891, the War Department formed a few infantry and cavalry companies made up entirely of Native American personnel. The Indian companies were strictly segregated and commanded by white officers. This experiment did not last, however, and the all-Indian companies were disbanded in 1895. A few Native Americans served in some of the units in the Spanish-American War, most notably in Theodore Roosevelt's Rough Rider regiment. The Indian scouting corps was kept active, and General John J. Pershing took a contingent of Apache scouts with him during the American incursion into Mexico in 1916.

The U.S. entrance into World War I essentially changed the military outlook toward Native Americans. While the scouting corps remained, white political leaders insisted that Natives be fully integrated into the divisions that made up the American Expeditionary Forces. At the same time, Native Americans who had been made

Mitchell Red Cloud. The Winnebago Indian who received a Medal of Honor as a U.S. Army corporal during the Korean War; during World War II he had served in the U.S. Marine Corps, and he is shown here in his marine uniform. LIBRARY OF CONGRESS

U.S. citizens under the General Allotment Act were subject to the draft. About 12,000 Native Americans served in World War I, and a large number distinguished themselves in the trenches. Notably and perhaps prophetically, the army began using Choctaw and Cherokee speakers to send messages over telephone lines from the edge of no-man's-land to command posts in the rear. The Germans who tapped into these telephone lines could not understand what was being said, thus ensuring the security of secret transmissions.

In the course of World War II, about 44,000 Native Americans, now all citizens, joined or were drafted into the military services—a number far out of proportion to their relative population in the United States. Three Native Americans, Van Barfoot, Jack Montgomery, and Ernest Childers, won Medals of Honor for their valor and leadership against the Germans. Native Americans fought in every branch of the armed forces and in every theater of war. The Marine Corps recalled the use of Native American speakers to secure lines of communications during World War I and recruited a body of Navajos, who in turn created a code from their language that was never broken. The NAVAJO CODE TALKERS served in every marine campaign in the Pacific. The U.S. Army likewise recruited a group of Comanche speakers to create another code that was utilized in the European theater.

Native Americans in World War II contributed more than their linguistic knowledge. Because many whites believed Native American warriors possessed extraordinary abilities, Native American soldiers were often given dangerous military assignments. In Korea, where two more Native Americans earned Medals of Honor, and Vietnam, where 42,000 Native Americans served, Native Americans took part in patrols and ambushes and "walked point" to give the rest of their units advanced warning of enemy hiding places. In Vietnam, Indian soldiers and marines joined long-range reconnaissance teams and force reconnaissance battalions. Native Americans also participated in the U.S. incursions into Grenada and the Panama Canal Zone. Among the first soldiers killed during the Gulf War of 1991, where 3,000 Native Americans served, was an Apache soldier from the San Carlos Reservation in Arizona.

BIBLIOGRAPHY

Bernstein, Alison R. *American Indians and World War II: Toward a New Era in Indian Affairs.* Norman: University of Oklahoma Press, 1991.

Britten, Thomas A. *American Indians in World War I: At Home and at War.* Albuquerque: University of New Mexico Press, 1997.

Dunlay, Thomas W. *Wolves for the Blue Soldiers: Indian Scouts and Auxiliaries with the United States Army, 1860–1890.* Lincoln: University of Nebraska Press, 1982.

Ferguson, R. Brian, and Neil L. Whitehead, eds. *War in the Tribal Zone: Expanding States and Indigenous Warfare.* Santa Fe, N.Mex.: School of American Research Press, 1992.

Franco, Jere Bishop. *Crossing the Pond: The Native American Effort in World War II.* Denton: University of North Texas Press, 1999.

Holm, Tom. *Strong Hearts, Wounded Souls: Native American Veterans of the Vietnam War.* Austin: University of Texas Press, 1996.

Townsend, Kenneth William. *World War II and the American Indian.* Albuquerque: University of New Mexico Press, 2000.

Tom Holm

See also **Indians in the Civil War; Indians in the Revolution; Warfare, Indian.**

INDIANS IN THE REVOLUTION. Many Indian tribes, out of traditional loyalty, the need for British trade goods, or a fear of land-hungry colonists, sided with Britain during the American Revolution. It is important to note, however, that almost all tribes were divided between neutral, pro-British, and pro-American factions. For the Ohio Valley tribes, especially the Shawnees and Mingos, war with the Americans began when they fought against the expansionist policies of Virginia in 1774. Virginia's victory led to the Shawnees' forced cession of their claims to Kentucky. As a consequence, this tribe, along with most other Ohio Valley-Great Lakes area tribes, quickly joined the British when fighting began.

The Shawnees clamored for American blood after the murder of their unarmed Chief Cornstalk by Virginia militia in 1777, while during the same period the Mingos tried to wipe out American settlements in Kentucky. Britain's superior supplies won over many Great Lakes tribes in 1778; the powerful Delawares waited until 1781. In 1782 American militia massacred one hundred peaceful, Christian Delawares (men, women, and children who had been converted by Moravian missionaries) at their Gnadenhutten, Ohio, town. This atrocity enraged other Delawares who had moved to the Ohio Valley. Later in 1782 the Delawares turned back Colonel William Crawford's invasion of their Ohio homelands and tortured Crawford to death. That same year the Shawnees and Wyandots successfully ambushed American militia at Blue Licks, Kentucky, killing dozens of rebels (including one of Daniel Boone's sons).

The Northeast proved a more contested area. In March 1775 Massachusetts formed an alliance with the Christian Stockbridge Indians, and made overtures for similar arrangements to the Iroquois, Penobscots, and St. Francis Abenakis. Sir Guy Johnson, British superintendent of Indian affairs in the northern colonies, also tried to secure Indian allies. Johnson's great council at Oswego in July 1775 failed when the American invasion of Canada, otherwise a disaster, cut off British supplies, undercutting the British agent's ability to offer "presents" to his potential allies. Continental commissioners gained the neutrality of some of the Iroquois at Albany that September and of some of the Ohio Valley tribes at Fort Pitt in October. Nevertheless, after it became clear that the American invasion of Canada had failed, many northern tribes rejoined the British. The Continental Congress's inability to support the subsidy policy of Indian agent George Morgan at Fort Pitt, combined with long-standing settler-Indian animosity, also influenced Indians' decisions. Chief Joseph Brant led his Mohawks and other Iroquois (minus the Oneidas and Tuscaroras, who remained officially neutral) in the British Burgoyne–St. Leger campaign of 1777. After Burgoyne's failure, Brant's men operated independently, terrorizing the New York frontier until an American army under General John Sullivan utterly devastated the Iroquois heartland in 1779.

In 1776 the Cherokees, hoping for British aid in dislodging settlers from North Carolina's Watauga and Nolichuckey Valleys, launched a war on frontier settlements in North Carolina and Virginia. The ferocity of these attacks led Thomas Jefferson to write of King George's "merciless Indian savages" in the Declaration of Independence. The raids backfired horrifically, however, and the Cherokees were forced to cede the disputed territory in the Treaty of Holston on 20 July 1777. The Cherokees later renewed their attacks on Americans, hoping to capitalize on recent British successes in the South, but militias from Virginia and Carolina crushed them again at the

Battle of Boyd's Creek and won additional land cessions. The Creeks had generally avoided the war until 1781. Then, as General "Mad" Anthony Wayne sought to complete the restoration of American control in Georgia, Creeks under Emistesigo made a heroic but futile attempt to relieve the British besieged at Savannah.

While the Cherokees were much chastened by the war, and Iroquois military capabilities were all but obliterated, many tribes remained uncowed by the rebels' victory. In the Ohio Valley, the Treaty of Paris in 1783 meant nothing, and the violent struggle to keep the Americans out of that strategic region continued for more than a decade. West of the Mississippi, the Revolution had almost no effect on Native American communities and their British and Spanish allies.

BIBLIOGRAPHY

Calloway, Colin G. *The American Revolution in Indian Country: Crisis and Diversity in Native American Communities.* New York: Cambridge University Press, 1995.

Hatley, Thomas M. *The Dividing Paths: Cherokees and South Carolinians through the Era of Revolution.* New York: Oxford University Press, 1995.

Ward, Harry M. *The American Revolution: Nationhood Achieved, 1763–1788.* New York: St. Martin's Press, 1995.

Robert M. Owens

See also **Wars with Indian Nations: Colonial Era to 1783.**

INDIGO CULTURE came to South Carolina at the inception of that colony, but it was not until 1744 that Eliza Lucas, married in that same year to Charles Pinckney, demonstrated on her father's plantation near Charleston that indigo production was practical with slave labor. Neighboring planters promptly adopted her idea as a supplement to the cultivation of rice. The industry stabilized first in 1748, when the British government granted a bounty of sixpence a pound on indigo shipped to Great Britain, and then in 1756, when Moses Lindo, an experienced indigo sorter, came to South Carolina. For some thirty years indigo was second only to rice in the colony's agricultural economy. On the eve of the American Revolution, growers annually exported more than a million pounds. In the closing decades of the eighteenth century, however, the production declined rapidly. The causes were the withdrawal of the bounty, the tedium and health dangers of indigo curing, and the development of cotton production. Nonetheless, agriculturalists, mostly in the Orangeburg area, continued to cultivate the dyestuff for local consumption until the end of the Civil War.

BIBLIOGRAPHY

Olwell, Robert. *Masters, Slaves, and Subjects: The Culture of Power in the South Carolina Low Country, 1740–1790.* Ithaca, N.Y.: Cornell University Press, 1998.

Young, Jeffrey Robert. *Domesticating Slavery: The Master Class in Georgia and South Carolina, 1670–1837.* Chapel Hill: University of North Carolina Press, 1999.

Francis B. Simkins/A. E.

See also **Agriculture; Bounties, Commercial; Colonial Commerce; Enumerated Commodities; Navigation Acts; Plantation System of the South; Slavery; South, the: Antebellum; South Carolina.**

INDIVIDUAL RETIREMENT ACCOUNT, or IRA, was created in 1974 for those individuals not covered by company pensions. Initially individuals could make tax-deductible contributions of up to $1,500 per annum to an IRA account, but in 1981, a new tax law allowed individuals to make tax-deductible contributions up to $2,000 per annum; the sum was raised to $3,000 for tax year 2002. The Taxpayer Relief Act of 1997 gave employees already in corporate pension programs the ability to contribute monies to their own IRA accounts. IRA contributions can be placed in high-yield investments, with taxation deferred until the money is withdrawn. In most cases, IRA contributions cannot be withdrawn without penalty until after age fifty-nine and a half. Congress did make some exceptions to the rule, however, for qualified education expenses through the creation of an Education IRA and for first-time home purchases. The Taxpayer Relief Act also created the Roth IRA, in which the earnings are tax-free, but there are no tax-deduction benefits for the contributions made each year. Contributions to a Roth IRA are made with after-tax rather than pre-tax dollars, but earnings are tax-free. If certain conditions are met, the earnings are free of Internal Revenue Service penalties. Unlike a traditional IRA, Roth contributions are allowed beyond age seventy and a half.

BIBLIOGRAPHY

Bamford, Janet, et al. *The Consumer Reports Money Book: How to Get It, Save It, and Spend It Wisely.* Yonkers, N.Y.: Consumer Reports, 2000.

Downing, Neil. *The New IRAs and How to Make Them Work for You.* Chicago: Dearborn Trade, 2002.

Meg Greene Malvasi

See also **Retirement Plans.**

INDIVIDUALISM. One of our most familiar terms of analysis, individualism is also one of the most elusive. It is employed in so many different ways—approving and disapproving, descriptive and normative, social and psychological, economic and political—that one never knows quite what is meant when the word is trotted out. It is rarely clear, for example, whether "individualism" is describing a consciously held set of formal philosophical or ideological doctrines or merely an ingrained ethos, or *mentalité*, a set of assumed internalized social norms that is not being articulated. Even more bewildering, the student of American culture is likely to find that "individualism" is first highly praised and then roundly condemned in nearly the same breath. Everyone, it seems, finds something to dislike about individualism, but rarely the same thing. Conservatives may be severe critics of individualism in the moral and expressive spheres, but tend to be staunch supporters of individualism in the economic sphere. By the same token, liberal critics of individualism are likely to restrict their criticism to economics and distributive justice, preferring instead to celebrate the very moral and expressive individualism that conservatives deplore.

Such confusion should not blind us to the irreducible core of validity in this often nebulous concept. A widely shared belief in the dignity and worth of the individual person has long been a distinctive feature of what we imprecisely call Western civilization. As the medievalist Colin Morris well expressed the matter, "We [Westerners] think of ourselves as people with frontiers, our personalities divided from each other as our bodies visibly are. . . . It is to us a matter of common sense that we stand apart from the natural order in which we are set, subjects over against its objectivity, and that we have our own distinct personality, beliefs, and attitude to life." But in fact, he continues, Western individualism is so far from "expressing the common experience of humanity" that it might more aptly be regarded as "an eccentricity among cultures." And yet this "eccentricity" forms the indispensable basis for the ideas of liberty and equality, which are among the West's chief gifts to humanity. Belief in the independent standing of the individual human being loses none of its central importance as a legitimizing principle of Western moral and political life because it emerged only in fits and starts over the course of Western history; has nearly always been applied selectively and inconsistently; and is often more honored in the breach than the observance.

The first stirrings of this emphasis on the individual person can be detected as far back as the world of classical antiquity, in the emergence of philosophical inquiry and democratic institutions in Greece, and especially in the intensely self-directed moral discipline of Hellenistic-era Epicureanism and Stoicism. The ideas and institutions arising out of biblical monotheism also played a vital part in the formation of an individualistic ideal, placing heavy emphasis upon the infinite value, personal agency, and moral accountability of the individual person. That emphasis reached a pinnacle of sorts in the synthetic vision of Western Christianity, which incorporated the divergent legacies of Athens and Jerusalem into a single universalized faith.

Yet none of these expressions of belief should be equated with what we mean by modern individualism. Such freedom as the premodern individual enjoyed, particularly after the advent of Christianity, was always constrained by belief in the metaphysical existence of an objective moral order, which could not be violated with impunity by antinomian rebels or advocates of romantic subjectivity. It was equally constrained by belief in the inherent frailty of human nature, which insisted that moral virtue could not be produced in social isolation. Although nearly all influential Western thinkers had conceded the signal importance of the individual, none employed the term "individualism" to express that belief. Only with the dawning of modernity did essential components of modern individualism such as the belief in natural rights—that is, rights that precede the creation of political society—began to fall into place and prepare the way for what was to come.

As for "individualism" itself, like many of our most useful words, it began life as a term of abuse, appearing first in the discourse of opponents of the French Revolution. The nineteenth-century French archconservative Joseph de Maistre used the word "individualism" to describe the Revolution's overturning of established social hierarchies and the dissolution of traditional social bonds in favor of an atomizing and leveling doctrine of natural individual rights, which freed each individual to be his or her own moral arbiter. Maistre's idea of "individualism" was not an affirmation of personal human dignity. Instead, for him it represented a disordered nightmare of egotism and moral anarchy.

Alexis de Tocqueville also employed the term critically, albeit much more moderately so, in his classic study *Democracy in America* (1835–1840), a locus classicus for the consideration of the term's American career. Individualism is, he argued, a characteristic pitfall for all societies that are "democratic," by which he meant societies lacking any legally sanctioned distinctions of rank or status among their members. Indeed, he concluded that the American propensity for individualism was characteristic of all modernity, because America, as the first "great republic," represented the avant-garde of human history, and therefore served as a pioneering exemplar of what the future would likely bring to Europe.

Tocqueville's complaint was very different from Maistre's, however. Egotism, he thought, was a mere emotional disorder, the passionate and exaggerated self-love one could find manifested throughout human history. But individualism was also something else. It was a more or less self-conscious social philosophy, "a mature and calm feeling, which disposes each member of the community to sever himself from the mass of his fellow-creatures: and to draw apart with his family and friends: so that . . . he willingly leaves society at large to itself." In other words, individualism was a conscious and calculated withdrawal, not from all human contact, but more specifically from the responsibilities of citizenship and public life. For Tocqueville—who was, unlike Maistre, a qualified friend of democracy, which he believed to be the God-ordained direction of human history—there was no greater threat to the health and stability of this new order than such a tendency toward privatism.

So "individualism" began its life as a critical term, and a reasonably precise one. But it did not remain so. Indeed, the critical view of individualism taken by these two French writers seems strikingly at odds with the self-conception that would come to be characteristic of most Americans, who had little or no comparable experience of feudal, aristocratic, monarchical, and other premodern political institutions, and who saw individualism in a largely favorable light. In the American context, especially with the social opening that came with the rise of Jacksonian democracy, the word has only rarely taken on pejorative connotations. It was more likely to refer to the sturdy values of the self-reliant frontiersman or the self-made entrepreneur—or to a broadly libertarian understanding of the relationship between the individual and society or the state, wherein the liberty and dignity of the former are shielded from the grasping hands of the latter. As such, it pointed toward a view of all political and social groups as mere aggregations of otherwise naturally self-sufficient individuals, whose social bonds are largely governed by choice and consent. Even more radically, it might point toward a view, increasingly pervasive in our own day, that to the maximum degree possible, the individual should be regarded as an entirely morally autonomous creature—accountable to no person and no "higher law," armed with a quiver of inviolable rights, protected by a zone of inviolable privacy, and left free to "grow" and "develop" as the promptings of the self dictate.

In any event, there seems little reason to doubt that the dominant view in our own day tends to endorse the highest possible degree of individual liberty and self-development in political, religious, social, and economic affairs. American history is a record of the defeat or weakening of nearly all competing ideas. The language of individual rights—the tendency to regard individual men and women as self-contained, choosing, contract-making, utility-maximizing, and values-creating actors, who accept only those duties and obligations they choose to accept—grew steadily more powerful and pervasive in the latter part of the twentieth century, and now stands triumphant. The recourse to individual rights, whether expressed as legal rights, voting rights, expressive rights, reproductive rights, sexual rights, membership rights, or consumer rights, has become the near-invincible trump card in most debates regarding public policy. Although there are serious challenges to the hegemony of such "rights talk," particularly as evidenced in the critical works of such communitarian thinkers as Mary Ann Glendon, Philip Selznick, and Amitai Etzioni, such challenges have yet to find a broad audience.

The Unique Development of American Individualism

This has not always been the state of affairs in America, and we are reminded of just this fact by much of the best scholarship in colonial and early national history in recent years. The crucial role of Protestant Christianity in making the early American social and political ethos has been repeatedly emphasized. For example, the political scientist Barry Alan Shain has made the case that it was not Enlightenment liberalism but a very constrained form of communitarian Reformed Protestantism that best represented the dominant social and political outlook of early America. The political theorist Michael Sandel has argued that, until the twentieth century, America's public philosophy was based largely on the "republican" assumption that the polity had a formative, prescriptive, "soulcraft" function to perform in matters of the economy, the family, church-state relations, personal morality, free speech, constitutional law, privacy, productive labor, and consumption. Like so much else about the early American milieu, that assumption has been so completely erased by the individualistic liberalism of our own day that we have forgotten it was ever there.

In retrospect, however, it is hard not to see those earlier perspectives as fatally fragile. Certainly by the middle of the nineteenth century, figures such as Ralph Waldo Emerson and Walt Whitman—romantic American nationalists and prophets of the unconstrained self—were already trumpeting the note that would have the most lasting resonance in the American imagination. It was Emerson who declared famously that a society is a "conspiracy against the manhood of every one of its members," and that "nothing is at last sacred but the integrity of your own mind." And it was Whitman who declared that "the Great Idea" is "the idea of perfect and free individuals," and that "nothing, not God, is greater to one than one's-self is." One could hardly deny that such driving, self-interested ambition was itself a logical corollary to the spirit of unrestrained self-development, although both men would live long enough to be disappointed in the crass materialism that seemed to take hold of American society in the post–Civil War years. So, too, there is the irresistible story of Mark Twain's Huckleberry Finn, the semi-noble, semi-savage boy who lit out for the territory rather than enduring the phony rigors of civilization. Indeed, one sure index of the hold that individualism has had on American thought and expression is the culture's richness in figures of heroic individuality—and its relative poverty in providing convincing representations of community or social obligation.

There have always been a few important countercurrents, however, to this pervasive celebration of individuality. One such current emerged from women writers, both inside and outside the nascent feminist movement. Individualism being a game still reserved largely for males, the fiction and "domestic economy" literature produced by such nineteenth-century writers as the sisters Catharine Beecher and Harriet Beecher Stowe often had a very different tone, emphasizing the satisfactions of settlement, family life, nurture, and human connectedness—all the things that Henry David Thoreau and Huck Finn sought to escape. Such arguments were carried to a high pitch by the southern anti-suffragist Louisa McCord, who urged women to stand at a critical distance from the coarse individualism of the male public world. To be sure, the works of northern feminists such as Margaret Fuller and Elizabeth Cady Stanton were nothing if not individualistic in tone, testifying to the fact that some women were eager to get in on the game. Various forms of that same tension between equality and difference have persisted into the twenty-first century and continue to color our discussions of individualism and gender.

The immense human suffering and social dislocation wrought by industrialization was another stimulus to anti-individualistic thinking. One can see some elements of this critique emerging idiosyncratically in the antebellum years—for example, in the fascinating career of the anti-capitalist Catholic convert Orestes Brownson, who railed against individualism for destroying the grounds of human solidarity; or in the works of pro-slavery apologist George Fitzhugh, who presented slavery as an organic and patriarchal institution, far preferable to the inhumane and predatory institution of "wage slavery." But the best example could be found in one of the most widely read books of the nineteenth century, Edward Bellamy's 1888 fantasy *Looking Backward*, an effort to imagine a perfected postindustrial Boston, reconstituted as a socialist cooperative commonwealth in the year 2000. Bellamy openly reviled individualism, proposing in its place a post-Christian "religion of solidarity," which would radically de-emphasize the self, and instead emphasize social bonds over individual liberty (and traditional Christian doctrine).

The popularity of Bellamy's book showed that there was a market hungry for such ideas, and many of the most "progressive" forces of the day—ranging from the cooperation-minded Knights of Labor, the theological advocates of a modernist "social gospel," to Progressive reformers such as Herbert Croly, Jane Addams, and John Dewey—unreservedly admired and emulated its spirit. Indeed, the Progressive movement itself, at least in some of its manifestations, advanced a new corporate ideal that sought to downplay individualism and instead to defend and preserve "the public interest" in the face of industrial capital's power. In the hands of a sophisticated thinker like Dewey, a case was made that the values of community and individuality, far from being in opposition, are mutually supporting and mutually sustaining, particularly in an age dominated by large industrial combinations, immense asymmetries of wealth and power, and vast impersonal networks of communication. It was pointless, in their view, to restore the small-scale community of days past. Economic and social forces had rendered such community, with its personal bonds and face-to-face business transactions, impossible. The task ahead was the creation of something new, which Dewey called "The Great Community," a systematically reconstituted social order that, it was hoped, would adapt the best features of the old community forms to the inexorable realities of the new economy and society, and thereby preserve the possibility of a healthy form of individuality as well.

Individualism in a Postindustrial World

In retrospect, though, a social and political ideal based on solidarity seems never to have had much of a chance. Even the crisis of the Great Depression did little to dislodge Americans' individualistic assumptions, and a decisive blow to communitarian alternatives was administered by the rise of the totalitarian regimes of Europe, whose terrifying success in suppressing the individual for the sake of the nation threw all communitarian and corporate ideals into a disrepute from which they have yet to recover. The concerns generated thereby decisively shaped both the liberalism and the conservatism of the postwar years. Libertarians like Ludwig von Mises and Friedrich Hayek and liberals like David Riesman, Lionel Trilling, and Reinhold Niebuhr—even conservatives like Robert Nisbet and Russell Kirk—all paid their disrespects to the Leviathan nation-state and thereby called into question the efficacy of any modern corporate or communitarian ideal. Instead, the social and political thought of postwar America seemed to be devoted to an entirely different ideal: the guardianship of the self.

The 1950s were awash in works devoted to that cause. Riesman's *The Lonely Crowd* (1950) warned against the conformism of "other-direction" in the American personality, and William Whyte's *The Organization Man* (1956) deplored the predominance of a "social ethic" in America's white-collar classes. Ayn Rand's fierce pop-Nietzschean novels celebrated the autonomy of the individual creative genius, sneered at altruism as a form of self-betrayal, and gave rise to the still lively intellectual movement called Objectivism. Neo-Freudian psychology concerned itself with the problems of the ego, and such leading psychological theorists as C. G. Jung and Erik Erikson focused obsessively on the problem of "individuation." Even the emergence of a New Left movement in the early 1960s, which purported to challenge the bourgeois assumptions of its liberal forebears, did little to alter this trend, since the movement's communitarian tendencies were no match for its commitment to a radical, near-anarchic standard of behavioral and expressive liberty.

In the age of postmodernity, then, the self has become the chief source of moral value. But one need only state such a proposition to realize how deeply problematic it is. Notwithstanding the naive certitude of Descartes's cogito, there is nothing more elusive than the self, which is both something that we "are" and something that we "have" in our less-than-full custody. Not only is it the ultimate seat of our subjectivity, it is equally the object of our therapeutic ministrations. Moreover, it is an entity whose highest refinement is its reflexive ability to stand outside of itself, enacting a selfhood that is beyond self. Indeed, the tortuous complexity of this description lends plausibility to one of the most powerful themes of postmodernism: its assertion that the modern idea of the unitary self cannot bear the weight placed upon it by fragmented modern life, and that in fact what we call the "self" is finally deconstructible into an ensemble of social roles. If so, though, then in what can individualism, let alone morality, be grounded?

It may be, too, that what appears to be unrestricted individualism turns out, on closer examination, to be something rather different. It may be that our broadened individual liberty is constrained in ways we hardly notice, so that we have been granted greater and greater freedom to live lives of less and less heft and consequence. A choosing consumer is not the same thing as a deliberating citizen, because the freedom to choose is not the same thing as freedom to shape. The philosopher Alasdair MacIntyre, among others, has argued that the expanding moral freedom of the modern world has been purchased at a very considerable price in public disempowerment. In our "bifurcated" modern world, moral evaluation has been relegated to "the realm of the personal," he says, while vast public bureaucracies and private corporations rule unchallenged over "the realm of the organizational" by means of impersonal procedural dicta. Hence individuals are remarkably free to order their personal lives as they see fit, but at the cost of having ceded any substantial voice in the shaping of public life. There is, MacIntyre has asserted, a "deep cultural agreement" between the ideal of the unencumbered private self and the corporatist ideal of rule by bureaucracy. Both accept a diminished understanding of humanity. In this view, we may already resemble the soma-numbed denizens of Aldous Huxley's *Brave New World* (1932) more than we would like to think.

Such a state of affairs bears an uncanny resemblance to the condition Tocqueville most feared, in which individualism enervates Americans' will to act in public ways. Accordingly, it would seem that the most useful response to the disintegration and diminution of the self might be a movement away from the characteristic preoccupations of modern sociology and psychology, and toward a fresh reconsideration of our political natures, in all their complexity, contingency, and promise. Just such a view was put forward memorably by the late American historian Christopher Lasch, who argued that it is in the school of public life, and in the embrace and exercise of the title of "citizen," that the selves of men and women become most meaningfully equal, individuated, mature, and free—not in those fleeting, and often illusory, moments when they evade the constraints of society and retreat into a weightless zone of privacy, subjectivity, and endlessly reconstructed narratives of the "self." This insight will be well worth our pondering in the years to come.

BIBLIOGRAPHY

Arieli, Yehoshua. *Individualism and Nationalism in American Ideology.* Cambridge, Mass.: Harvard University Press, 1964.

Brown, Gillian. *Domestic Individualism: Imagining Self in Nineteenth-Century America.* Berkeley: University of California Press, 1990.

Curry, Richard O., and Lawrence B. Goodheart, eds. *American Chameleon: Individualism in Trans-National Context.* Kent, Ohio: Kent State University Press, 1991.

Hewitt, John P. *Dilemmas of the American Self.* Philadelphia: Temple University Press, 1989.

Lasch, Christopher. *The Culture of Narcissism: American Life in an Age of Diminishing Expectations.* Revised, New York: Norton, 1991.

———. *The True and Only Heaven: Progress and Its Critics.* Reprint, New York: Norton, 1991.

Lukes, Steven. *Individualism.* Reprint, Oxford, U.K.: Blackwell, 1985.

McClay, Wilfred. *The Masterless: Self and Society in Modern America.* Chapel Hill: University of North Carolina Press, 1994.

Morris, Colin. *The Discovery of the Individual, 1050–1200.* Reprint, Toronto: University of Toronto Press, 1995.

Sandel, Michael. *Democracy's Discontent: America in Search of a Public Philosophy.* Cambridge, Mass.: Belknap Press, 1996.

Taylor, Charles. *Sources of the Self: The Making of the Modern Identity.* Cambridge, Mass.: Harvard University Press, 1989.

Wilfred McClay

INDUSTRIAL MANAGEMENT. Industrial management, in its most comprehensive meaning, refers to the systematic management of all aspects of the factory, and more specifically, to early studies of production efficiency known as scientific management. The term came into use in the United States around the turn of the twentieth century, when the Industrial Revolution dramatically shifted methods of generating output from craftsmanship to mass production and automation. Massive centralized production facilities, like those of the Ford Motor Company, Bethlehem Steel, and Western Electric, brought with them the unprecedented need to understand work that had become increasingly complex. To bring some measure of control and discipline to the industrial behemoths, such luminaries as Frederick Taylor, Henry Ford, and Frank and Lillian Gilbreth developed "scientific" methods of observation in factories. The term "scientific" brought a patina of respectability to a field of study, which by its very nature contained some measure of dehumanization with regards to work methods. Frederick Taylor sought the "one best way to manage" by systematically recording the time to perform work elements that comprised a laborer's repetitive movements, while the Gilbreths developed "time and motion" studies. Henry Ford is credited with institutionalizing division of labor in factories with his development of the assembly line, an innovation that dramatically reduced the time it took to produce an automobile.

Little attention was paid to the motivational content of work until the accidental discovery of the importance of human relations by the Hawthorne studies from 1927 to 1932, research supervised by Elton Mayo. While conducting productivity studies at Western Electric, Mayo demonstrated that workers' efficiency depended on a wide range of relations within groups as well as on compensation. This finding led to an eventual split in the study of industrial management, with one branch emphasizing an understanding of organization theory and behavior and the other emphasizing the mechanics of production, also known as operations. While science continued to provide the basis for academic studies of both branches, the practice of management was increasingly recognized as a complex set of knowledge and skills. Later, increased specialization of management talents led to the dissipation of comprehensive studies in industrial management, with more attention paid to specialties like financial management, human resources management, and operations management.

Following World War II, many of the dehumanizing aspects of factory life were a leading concern of both union movements and studies to improve quality of work life. Work design and sociotechnical approaches to work became the focus of industrial management. By the 1960s, however, the U.S. economy had shifted to a service economy, with more than half of the labor in the country employed in services. This shift was to be followed by the information revolution and extraordinarily high rates of global competitiveness, changes that had dramatic impacts on work content. The term "industrial management" became increasingly irrelevant as the nature and content of work shifted to computerization and other spheres of the economy.

In the early twenty-first century, the segment of management that seeks improvements in efficiency and productivity is known as service and operations management. Its most recent developments include integrated methods of management that contain elements of programmable technology, quality improvement, just-in-time delivery, lean production, and supply chain management.

BIBLIOGRAPHY

Boone, Louis E., and Donald D. Bowen, eds. *The Great Writings in Management and Organizational Behavior.* Tulsa, Okla.: PPC, 1980.

Dertouzos, Michael L., et al. *Made in America: Regaining the Productive Edge.* New York: HarperPerennial, 1990.

Lacey, Robert. *Ford: The Men and the Machine.* Boston: Little, Brown, 1986.

Russell, Roberta S., and Bernard W. Taylor III. *Operations Management.* 3rd ed. Upper Saddle River, N.J.: Prentice-Hall, 2000.

Zuboff, Shoshana. *In the Age of the Smart Machine: The Future of Work and Power.* New York: Basic Books, 1988.

Patricia Nemetz

See also **Industrial Revolution; Scientific Management;** *and vol. 9:* **Deming's Fourteen Points for Management.**

INDUSTRIAL RELATIONS. The term "industrial relations" has developed both a broad and a narrow meaning. Originally, industrial relations was broadly defined to include the totality of relationships and interactions between employers and employees. From this perspective, industrial relations covers all aspects of the employment relationship, including human resource (or personnel) management, employee relations, and union-management (or labor) relations. Since the mid-twentieth century, however, the term has increasingly taken on a narrower, more restricted interpretation that largely equates it with unionized employment relationships. In this view, industrial relations pertains to the study and practice of collective bargaining, trade unionism, and labor-management relations, while human resource management is a separate, largely distinct field that deals with nonunion employment relationships and the personnel practices and policies of employers. Both meanings of the term coexist in the twenty-first century, although the latter is the more common.

Origins

The term "industrial relations" came into common usage in the 1910s, particularly in 1912 upon the appointment by President William Taft of an investigative committee titled the Commission on Industrial Relations. The commission's charge was to investigate the causes of widespread, often violent labor conflict and make recommendations regarding methods to promote greater cooperation and harmony among employers and employees. Shortly thereafter, the term gained even greater saliency in the public mind due to the wave of strikes, labor unrest, and agitation for "industrial democracy" that accompanied the economic and political disturbances associated with World War I. As a result, by the beginning of the 1920s universities began to establish industrial relations centers and programs to conduct research and train students in employer-employee relations, while progressive business firms established the first "industrial relations" or "personnel" departments to formalize and professionalize the management of labor.

Although the term "industrial relations" came into prominent usage in the 1910s, its roots extend back at least three decades into the nineteenth century. It was during this period, beginning in the 1870s, that the process of industrialization began in earnest in the United States, leading to the emergence of a growing urban-based wage-earning labor force working in large-scale factories, mills, and mines. Conditions growing out of the industrialization process—twelve-hour work days, tens of thousands of work-related fatalities, low wages, extremely high rates of labor turnover, and poor employee work effort and attitudes—led to growing numbers of strikes, revolutionary economic and political movements, and demands for social and economic reform. These maladjustments and frictions between employers and employees, and the conflict they precipitated, came to be known as "the Labor Problem."

The emergence of industrial relations in the 1910s as an academic field of study and area of business practice was thus intimately associated with the rise and growing seriousness of the Labor Problem, and industrial relations came to be widely defined during this period as the study of labor problems and alternative methods to resolve such problems. Social scientists identified three major types of solutions: the "employer's solution" of personnel management, the "workers' solution" of trade unionism and collective bargaining, and the "community's solution" of government-enacted protective labor legislation and social insurance programs (for example, minimum wages and unemployment insurance). In its early years, therefore, industrial relations was broadly conceived because it subsumed all three types of solutions to labor problems, while in terms of ideology and approach to social policy industrial relations tended to be reformist, progressive, and critical of laissez-faire.

Historical Development

During the prosperous and politically conservative 1920s, the American labor movement suffered a significant loss in membership, influence, and public approval, while restrictive court rulings and conservative political opposition hobbled the extension of labor legislation. In this period the major line of advance in industrial relations was the employer's solution of personnel management. Numerous firms established personnel departments and in various ways tried to reduce the most serious causes of labor unrest and turnover. The apogee of this effort was among several hundred liberal/progressive employers who adopted the new model of welfare capitalism. Intended to promote greater employee morale, cooperation, and productivity—as well as to undercut the threat of unions and government intervention—this employment strategy entailed many new employee welfare benefits (paid vacations and company doctors, for example), promises of employment security, curbs on the right of foremen to hire and fire, payment of fair wages, and the introduction of employee representation plans to promote resolution of grievances and employee participation and voice in the enterprise.

The decade of the 1930s saw a near-revolution in American industrial relations practices and policies. The GREAT DEPRESSION, beginning in late 1929 and extending to 1939, caused widespread suffering and hardship among the industrial workforce, leading to the re-emergence of numerous labor problems, such as low wages, long hours, and mass unemployment. Many workers became disillusioned with employers when firms succumbed to economic pressures and cut wages and other labor conditions, while some became embittered when they perceived that companies took advantage of labor in a harsh and opportunistic way. As the employer's solution lost credibility and effectiveness, focus turned toward other solutions. This shift gained speed when the new administration of Franklin D. Roosevelt was elected in late 1932 and soon thereafter Roosevelt instituted his New Deal economic recovery measures. Under Roosevelt's leadership, public policy turned favorable to labor unions and government labor legislation as a way to promote economic recovery, protect the underdog in the employment relationship, and establish greater industrial democracy. The three major initiatives were the NATIONAL LABOR RELATIONS ACT (encouraging and protecting the right to join a union and bargain collectively), the Social Security Act (establishing old age and unemployment insurance), and the FAIR LABOR STANDARDS ACT (setting minimum wages and maximum hours).

The labor movement also transformed itself in the 1930s. More dynamic, aggressive union leaders came to the fore, such as John L. Lewis, Sidney Hillman, and Philip Murray. A more effective method of organizing and representing workers was emphasized ("industrial" unions that organize all workers in an industry, rather than the traditional "craft" union model that includes only workers of a particular occupation or skill). And a new federation of industrial unions, called the Congress of Industrial Organizations (CIO), was established to rival the traditional federation of craft unions, the American Federation of Labor (AFL).

As a result of these events and developments in the economic, legislative, and trade union worlds, a great shift in industrial relations practices and policies occurred in the 1930s. Union membership mushroomed from only 10 percent of the workforce in the early 1930s to 27 percent a decade later. The American laissez-faire approach to employer-employee relations was reversed and the beginnings of both greater government regulation of employment and the development of a social welfare state were initiated. Finally, employers emerged from the 1930s with much-reduced power in industrial relations, while personnel management came to be regarded in many quarters as largely ineffective and often an overt or covert union-avoidance device.

The decade of the 1940s saw a consolidation of the trends unleashed a decade earlier. As a result of World War II, industrial employment boomed and the federal government instituted a system of wage-price controls on the economy. The net effect of these developments was to further spread collective bargaining and government regulation of the labor market, in the case of the former due in part to government pressure on employers to accede to union organizing efforts and bargaining demands in order to prevent strikes and interruptions to war production. With the end of the war, wage-price controls were lifted and a strike wave erupted in 1946 as employers sought to recoup some of their lost prerogatives while unions fought to maintain their gains. The result was largely to leave intact the industrial relations system that had evolved out of the war, but with a discernible spread of opinion among the public that union power needed to be reined in and made more responsible. The result was the passage in 1947 of the Taft-Hartley amendments to the National Labor Relations Act. The law prohibited certain practices of unions, such as the closed shop, and gave the government the ability to temporarily end strikes that cause national emergencies.

Adverse changes in federal law notwithstanding, for roughly another decade organized labor continued to expand its membership and influence. Unity was also restored in the labor movement through the creation of a single labor federation in 1955, the AFL-CIO, under the leadership of George Meany. Although not discernible at the time, the high water mark for the labor movement came in the mid-1950s when the union share of the nonagricultural workforce peaked at slightly above one-third. Hidden in this number is the remarkable fact that over a twenty-year period unions had succeeded in organizing most of the medium-large firms in the manufacturing, mining, and transportation sectors of the economy. Also of significance, unions were seen as the primary innovators in employment practices, using collective bargaining to win formal grievance systems, wage classification systems, cost-of-living wage adjustment clauses, and a plethora of new employee benefits.

Starting in the early 1960s, the New Deal industrial relations system, with its emphasis on collective bargaining as the major institution for determining wages and labor conditions in the economy, began to erode and be replaced by a new system. The new system that emerged, and then became consolidated in the 1980s and 1990s, featured a much smaller role for collective bargaining with a much-expanded role for personnel management—now called human resource management—and direct government regulation of employment conditions.

Several trends and developments were responsible for this shift. One was a slow but cumulatively significant shrinkage in the size and influence of the union sector of the economy. In the private (non-government) sector, the unionized share of the workforce began to contract in the 1960s and continued to do so until the end of the century. While 32 percent of private sector workers were covered by collective bargaining contracts in 1960, in the year 2000 this proportion had shrunk to 9 percent—a level roughly equal to that in the early 1930s. A number of factors were responsible for the union decline. Unions gradually increased wage and benefits for their members up through the mid-1980s, but in so doing the production costs at organized firms also became increasingly higher than at nonunion firms. The result was a slow loss of competitiveness and jobs in the union sector in the 1960s and 1970s, followed in the 1980s by a hemorrhaging of jobs due to widespread plant closings and layoffs. Another complementary factor was the intensification of competition in product and financial markets. Due to globalization and domestic deregulation of industries, American firms experienced a gradual increase in competitive pressure, leading them to more aggressively resist union organizing drives and downsize and eliminate existing unionized plants. This trend was also complemented by greater pressure from financial markets (Wall Street) for higher earnings and short-run profit performance. Finally, during the presidency of Ronald Reagan in the 1980s government policy toward organized labor turned more hostile, as reflected in the firing of the striking air traffic controllers and the pro-management rulings of the National Labor Relations Board.

The situation for unions from the 1960s to the 1990s was not entirely negative, however. The most positive development was the spread of collective bargaining to the public sector. Due to a liberalization of state and federal laws in the 1960s and 1970s, union coverage in the public (government) sector greatly expanded, from 11 percent in 1960 to 37 percent in 2000. As a result of the shrinkage of private sector unionism and the expansion of unionism in the public sector, the latter accounts for nearly 40 percent of total union members in the United States. (However, even in the private sector unions continue to represent over 9 million workers [and 7 million in the public sector] and, encouragingly for organized labor, surveys indicate that one-third of American workers would vote to have a union if given the opportunity.)

A second development that undermined the New Deal system of industrial relations was the re-emergence and revitalization of the employer's solution of labor problems in the form of human resource management. The decline of the unionized sector of the economy opened the door for personnel/human resource management to reassert itself as a leading force in industrial relations, and new ideas and practices in human resource management allowed companies, in turn, to effectively take advantage of this opportunity. Through the 1960s, personnel management had a reputation as a largely low-level, heavily administrative, and nonstrategic business function. Starting in the 1960s, however, academic research in the behavioral and organizational sciences led to a flowering of new ideas and theories about how to better motivate people at work, structure jobs for increased productivity and job satisfaction, and organize and operate business firms for competitive advantage. These new insights were gradually incorporated into personnel management, leading to a shift in both its name—to human resource management—and its approach to managing employees (from viewing employees as a short-run expense to a long-term asset). As a result, human resource management gradually replaced labor-management relations (increasingly thought of as synonymous with industrial relations) in the eyes of academics and practitioners as the locus of new and exciting workplace developments.

In the 1970s American companies started to introduce these new employment practices into selected plants and facilities, culminating in the development of what is often called a "high-performance" work system. Since the 1970s this system, and individual parts of it, have spread widely. A high-performance work system is a package of employment practices that include self-managed work teams, gainsharing forms of compensation, promises of employment security, formal dispute resolution systems, and an egalitarian organizational culture. These work systems not only boost productivity but also typically increase employee job satisfaction, leading to reduced interest in union representation. Companies have also become much more adept at keeping out unions, not only through progressive human resource management methods but also through more aggressive and sophisticated union-avoidance practices.

The third major force undermining the New Deal industrial relations system has been the spread of greater government regulation of employment conditions. After the passage of the Social Security and Fair Labor Standards Acts in the 1930s, the federal and state governments enacted little new employment legislation until the mid-1960s. Starting with the Civil Rights Act of 1964, however, government has become increasingly active in the employment sphere. In addition to a host of laws and regulations pertaining to discrimination (racial, gender, age, physical disability, sexual orientation), federal and/or state governments have passed numerous laws relating to other employment areas, such as pension plans, family and medical leave, and the portability of health insurance. It is widely considered that these laws and attendant agencies, courts, and attorneys have to some degree served as a substitute for unions, thus also explaining a portion of the union decline in the late twentieth century.

Conclusion

The field and practice of industrial relations began in the early years of the twentieth century and evolved in numerous ways in reaction to a host of far-reaching changes in the economic, political, and social realm. It began with a broad emphasis on the employment relationship and the labor problems that grow out of this relationship. As a result of the rise of mass unionism between 1935 and 1955, the field became identified in the academic and practitioner worlds with, first and foremost, the study and practice of collective bargaining and labor-management relations. Since then the unionized sector of the economy has shrunk considerably, while a rival field of human resource management has grown and spread—a product of both new ideas and practices and the opening up of a much-expanded unorganized sector in the labor market. Thus the term "industrial relations" is increasingly associated with the unionized sector of the labor market. But a minority of participants continue to view industrial relations as pertaining to the entire world of work and, in particular, the three solutions to labor problems: personnel/human resource management, trade unionism and collective bargaining, and government legislation.

BIBLIOGRAPHY

Bennett, James, and Bruce Kaufman. *The Future of Private Sector Unionism in the United States.* Armonk, N.Y.: M. E. Sharpe, 2001.

Derber, Milton. *The American Idea of Industrial Democracy, 1865–1965.* Champaign: University of Illinois Press, 1970.

Dunlop, John. *Industrial Relations Systems.* New York: Holt, 1958.

Freeman, Richard, and Joel Rodgers. *What Workers Want.* Ithaca, N.Y.: Cornell University Press, 1999.

Jacoby, Sanford. *Employing Bureaucracy: Managers, Unions, and the Transformation of Work in American Industry, 1900–1945.* New York: Columbia University Press, 1985.

Kaufman, Bruce. *The Origins and Evolution of the Field of Industrial Relations in the United States.* Ithaca, N.Y.: ILR Press, 1993.

———. "Human Resources and Industrial Relations: Commonalities and Differences." *Human Resource Management Review* 11, no. 4 (2001): 339–374.

Kochan, Thomas, Harry Katz, and Robert McKersie. *The Transformation of American Industrial Relations.* New York: Basic Books, 1986.

Nelson, Daniel. *Shifting Fortunes: The Rise and Decline of American Labor from the 1820s to the Present.* Chicago: Ivan Doe, 1997.

Bruce Kaufman

See also **Labor; Trade Unions.**

INDUSTRIAL RESEARCH. The emergence and growth of industrial research and development during the twentieth century must rank as one of the most important economic developments in modern American history. There is no doubt that technological innovation is the primary driver of economic growth, and that it is the business firm that is at the core of the American system of technological innovation. Industrial research conducted by and substantially funded by business firms has thus played a key role in American prosperity. It was also key to the outcomes in both world wars, and arguably to the ending of the Cold War. What then, is the genius behind this system? How did it emerge, how does it work, and how did it change in the twentieth century?

Industrial research and development (R&D) is the activity in which scientific and engineering knowledge is used to create and bring to market new products, processes, and services. R&D encompasses several different activities that can occur in any order. There is basic research, which is aimed purely at the creation of new knowledge. Its purpose is to create new understandings of phenomena. Its core foundations are usually quite abstract. There is applied research, which is work expected to have a practical, but not a commercial, payoff. While basic research is aimed at new knowledge for its own sake, applied research has practicality and utility as its goal. There is also development, in which the product is honed for commercial application. Boundaries among these activities are quite fuzzy, and the manner in which they have been organized and linked has changed over time.

The roots of American industrial research can be found in the late nineteenth century when a discernible amount of science and technology began being applied to industry. This is the period when the science-based industries in dyestuffs, chemicals, electricity, and telecommunications began to emerge.

The first organized research laboratory in the United States was established by the inventor Thomas Edison in 1876. In 1886, an applied scientist by the name of Arthur D. Little started his firm which became a major technical services/consulting firm to other enterprises. Eastman Kodak (1893), B. F. Goodrich (1895), General Electric (1900), Dow (1900), DuPont (1902), Goodyear (1909), and American Telephone and Telegraph (AT&T; 1907) followed soon thereafter.

Growth of the Organized R&D Laboratory (1890–1945)

The industrial laboratory constituted a significant departure from an earlier period when innovation was largely the work of independent inventors like Eli Whitney (the cotton gin), Samuel Morse (telegraph), Charles Goodyear (vulcanization of rubber), and Cyrus McCormick (the reaper).

The founding of formal R&D programs and laboratories stemmed in part from competitive threats. For instance, AT&T at first followed the telegraph industry's practice of relying on the market for technological innovation. However, the expiration of the major Bell patents and the growth of large numbers of independent telephone companies helped stimulate AT&T to organize Bell Labs. Competition likewise drove George Eastman to establish laboratories at Kodak Park in Rochester, New York, to counteract efforts by German dyestuff and chemical firms to enter into the manufacture of fine chemicals, including photographic chemicals and film.

During the early years of the twentieth century, the number of research labs grew dramatically. By World War I there were perhaps as many as one hundred industrial research laboratories in the United States. The number tripled during the war, and industrial R&D even maintained its momentum during the Great Depression. The number of scientists and research engineers employed by these laboratories grew from 2,775 in 1921 to almost 30,000 by 1940. The interwar period also saw the industrial research labs produce significant science. In 1927 Clinton Davisson began his work at Bell Labs on electron defraction. His work led to a Nobel Prize in physics in 1937. At DuPont, Wallace Carothers developed and published the general theory of polymers, and went on in 1930 to create synthetic rubber; and then, a strong, tough, water-resistant fiber called nylon. These technological breakthroughs were in and of themselves of great importance, but it took time and money to leverage them into marketable products. For instance, over a decade elapsed to get from the beginning of research in super polymers to the production of nylon on commercial terms.

The Golden Era of "Big Science" (1945–1980)

Building on wartime success, including the Manhattan Project, the era of big science began, fueled by the optimism that well-funded scientists and engineers could produce technological breakthroughs that would benefit the economy and society. University scientists, working together with the engineers from corporate America, had indeed produced a string of breakthrough technologies including radar, antibiotics, the digital electronic computer, and atomic energy. The dominant intellectual belief of the immediate postwar period was that science-driven research programs would ensure the development of an endless frontier of new products and processes. The development of the transistor at Bell Labs gave strength to this view. Many firms augmented their commitments to industrial R&D. For instance, in 1956 IBM established a research division devoted to world class basic research.

As tensions increased during the Cold War, government funding increased considerably. In 1957, government funding of R&D performed by industry eclipsed the funding provided by the firms themselves. By 1967, it went back the other way, with private funding taking the lead. By 1975, industry funding of industry conducted R&D was twice the federal level, and the ratio was expanding. Government procurement was perhaps even more important to the technological development of certain industries, as it facilitated early investment in production facilities, thus easing the cost of commercialization. The newly emergent electronics industry in particular was able to benefit from the Defense Department's demand for advanced components and advanced products. By 1960, the electronics industry had come to rely on the federal government for 70 percent of its R&D dollars. Perhaps as an unfortunate consequence, the United States ceased to be the leader in consumer electronics as it became preoccupied with the requirements of the U.S. military, which was more performance-oriented in its requirements than the consumer markets.

By the early 1970s, however, management was beginning to lose faith in the science-driven view of industrial research and technological innovation, primarily because few blockbuster products had emerged from the research funded during the 1950s through the 1970s.

From the mid-1970s on, there has been a marked change in organization and strategy, as both industry and government have come to recognize that the classical form of R&D organization—with centralized research and a science driven culture—was simply not working, in part because new technology was not getting into new products and processes soon enough. Foreign competitors began undermining the traditional markets of many U.S. firms.

Many companies were confronted by the paradox of being leaders in R&D and laggards in the market. The fruit of much R&D was being appropriated by domestic and foreign competitors, and much technology was wasting away in many research laboratories. In telecommunications, Bell Lab's contribution to the economy at large far outstripped its contribution to AT&T. In the semiconductor industry, Fairchild's large research organization contributed more to the economy through the spin-off

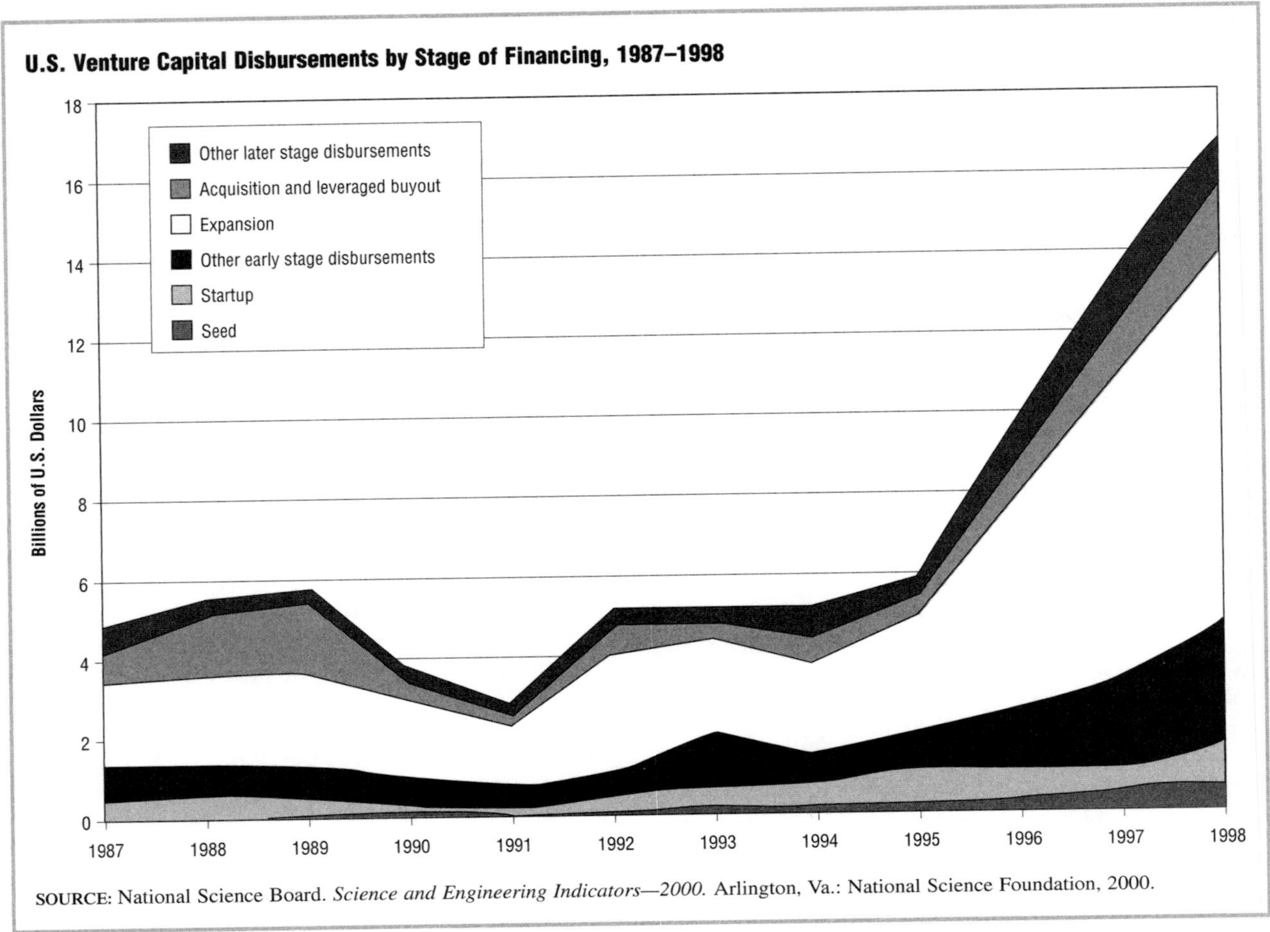

SOURCE: National Science Board. *Science and Engineering Indicators—2000.* Arlington, Va.: National Science Foundation, 2000.

companies it spawned than to its parent. Xerox Corporation's Palo Alto Research Center made stunning contributions to the economy in the area of the personal computer, local area networks, and the graphical user interface that became the basis of Apple's Macintosh computer. Xerox shareholders were well served too, but most of the benefits ended up in the hands of Xerox's competitors.

Emergence of the "Distributed" Approach to Industrial R&D

Different modes of organization and different funding priorities were needed. The distinctive competence of firms was understood to depend upon knowledge diffused throughout the firm and embedded in new products promptly placed into the marketplace, rather than being confined to the R&D laboratory. A new way of conducting R&D and developing new products was needed.

By the 1980s and 1990s, a new model for organizing research became apparent. First, R&D activity came to be decentralized inside large corporations themselves, with the aim to bring it closer to the users. Intel, the world leader in microprocessors, was spending over $1 billion per year on R&D, but did not have a separate R&D laboratory. Rather, development was conducted in the manufacturing facilities. It didn't invest in fundamental research at all, except through its funding of Sematech and university research.

Second, many companies were looking to the universities for much of their basic or fundamental research, maintaining close associations with the science and engineering departments at the major research universities. Indeed, over the century the percentage of academic research funded by industry grew from 2.7 percent in 1960 to 6.8 percent in 1995. However, strong links between university research and industrial research is limited primarily to electronics (especially semiconductors), chemical products, medicine, and agriculture. For the most part, university researchers are insufficiently versed in the particulars of specific product markets and customer needs to configure products to the needs of the market. Moreover, in many sectors the costs of research equipment are so high that universities simply cannot participate.

Third, corporations have embraced alliances involving R&D, manufacturing, and marketing in order to get products to market quicker and leverage off complementary assets already in place elsewhere. (It is important to note, however, that outsourcing R&D is a complement,

TABLE 1

Industrial R&D Expenditures by Funding Source: 1953–1997 (millions of 1998 U.S. dollars)

Calendar year*	Total	Federal Government[a]	Industry[b]
1953	3,630	1,430	2,200
1954	4,070	1,750	2,320
1955	4,517	2,057	2,460
1956	6,272	2,995	3,277
1957	7,324	3,928	3,396
1958	8,066	4,436	3,630
1959	9,200	5,217	3,983
1960	10,032	5,604	4,428
1961	10,353	5,685	4,668
1962	11,037	6,008	5,029
1963	12,216	6,856	5,360
1964	13,049	7,257	5,792
1965	13,812	7,367	6,445
1966	15,193	7,977	7,216
1967	15,966	7,946	8,020
1968	17,014	8,145	8,869
1969	17,844	7,987	9,857
1970	17,594	7,306	10,288
1971	17,829	7,175	10,654
1972	19,004	7,469	11,535
1973	20,704	7,600	13,104
1974	22,239	7,572	14,667
1975	23,460	7,878	15,582
1976	26,107	8,671	17,436
1977	28,863	9,523	19,340
1978	32,222	10,107	22,115
1979	37,062	11,354	25,708
1980	43,228	12,752	30,476
1981	50,425	14,997	35,428
1982	57,166	17,061	40,105
1983	63,683	19,095	44,588
1984	73,061	21,657	51,404
1985	82,376	25,333	57,043
1986	85,932	26,000	59,932
1987	90,160	28,757	61,403
1988	94,893	28,221	66,672
1989	99,860	26,359	73,501
1990	107,404	25,802	81,602
1991	114,675	24,095	90,580
1992	116,757	22,369	94,388
1993	115,435	20,844	94,591
1994	117,392	20,261	97,131
1995	129,830	21,178	108,652
1996	142,371	21,356	121,015
1997	155,409	21,798	133,611

Note: Data are based on annual reports by performers except for the nonprofit sector; R&D expenditures by nonprofit sector performers have been estimated since 1973 on the basis of a survey conducted in that year.
*These calendar-year expenditure levels are approximations based on fiscal year data.
(a) For 1953–1954, expenditures of industry Federally Funded Research and Development Centers (FFRDC) were not separated out from total federal support to the industrial sector. Thus, the figure for federal support to industry includes support to FFRDCs for those two years. The same is true for expenditures of nonprofit FFRDCs, which are included in federal support for nonprofit institutions in 1953–1954.
(b) Industry sources of industry R&D expenditures include all non-federal sources of industry R&D expenditures.

SOURCE: National Science Foundation, Division of Science Resources Studies (NSF/SRS). *National Patterns of R&D Resources: 1998.* Arlington, Va.: NSF/SRS, 1998.

not a substitute, to in-house R&D.) Outsourcing and co-development arrangements had become common by the 1980s and 1990s (for example Pratt & Whitney's codevelopment programs for jet engines) as the costs of product development increased, and as the antitrust laws were modified to recognize the benefits of cooperation on R&D and related activities. The National Cooperative Research Act of 1984 and its amendment in 1993 provided greater clarity with respect to the likely positive treatment of cooperative efforts relating to technological innovation and its commercialization. Cooperation was also facilitated by the emergence of capable potential partners in Europe and Japan.

These developments meant that at the end of the twentieth century, R&D was being conducted in quite a different manner from how it was organized at the beginning of the century. Many corporations had closed their central research laboratories, or dramatically scaled back, including Westinghouse, RCA, AT&T, and Unocal to name just a few. Alliances and cooperative efforts of all kinds were of much greater importance.

Importantly, a transformation in industry structure brought about through venture capital funded "start-ups" was well under way. New business enterprises or "start-ups" were in part the cause for the decline of research laboratories; but in many ways the start-ups still depended on the organized R&D labs for their birthright.

The Role of Start-ups and Venture Capital

Beginning in the late 1970s, the organized venture capital industry, providing funding for new enterprise development, rose to significance. This was particularly true in industries such as biotech and information services. While venture capital in one form or another has been around for much of the twentieth century—the Rockefellers, Morgans, Mellons, Vanderbilts, Hillmans, and other significant families had been funding entrepreneurs for quite some time—institutional sources of money, including pension funds and university endowments, had become significant sources by the 1980s. This dramatically increased the funds that were available, as well as the professionalism by which "the money" provided guidance to a new breed of entrepreneurs, eager to develop and market new products.

As a result, venture funded start-ups have proliferated in many sectors. Thus while in the 1970s Apple Computer "bootstrapped" itself into the personal computer industry, in the 1980s Compaq and others received large infusions of venture capital to get started in the computer industry. In biotechnology, venture funding has also grown to great significance. However, it is extremely unusual for venture funds to support the efforts of companies making investments in early stage research. Rather, venture funding tends to be focused on exploiting research, not doing it. Successful start-ups frequently begin with an idea, and often personnel, that has been incubated to some level in a research program of an already established firm. Absent incumbent firms and their research programs, there would be far fewer start-ups. Figure 1 shows that significant venture funding was present in the early 1990s, and that it grew drastically from 1995 on, in part driven by the Internet boom. In 1995, however, it had risen to a level equal to 5.5 percent of the funds allocated by industry to R&D ($6 billion, compared to $108 billion). The comparison, however, should be used with care, because only a fraction of venture capital disbursements are likely to qualify as R&D. Nevertheless, the phenomena of venture funding is significant, as it is now a very important channel by which new products and processes come to the market.

Conundrum at the New Millennium

At least compared to half a century earlier, privately funded research had become more short run in its focus, and more commercial in its orientation at the millennium. International competition and the competition from spin-outs forced that outcome. The leakage of technology was such that the earlier stage the research was, the greater the chance one's competitors would also benefit from it. For example, half a century earlier, AT&T could rely on the Bell operating companies (BOCs) to each more or less pay their pro-rata share of the cost of Bell Labs; but the BOCs were divested in 1984. Their contracts to pay a fixed percent of revenues to supporting research and development were set aside in the breakup of AT&T. There no longer was an easy appropriability mechanism in place.

By 2000, it was easy in many cases to get a free ride on the efforts of others, scooping up from the public domain the product of R&D funded by others. Domestic and foreign rivals were so quick and capable that it was extremely difficult to justify the support for long-range research.

Industry and society was thus left with a deep concern—the concern that insufficient resources were being invested in the scientific "seed corn." Perhaps the solution would lie in more collective funding of research? Perhaps industrially relevant basic and applied research in universities could be expanded? The issues related more to the allocation of resources than to the amount. Clearly, as shown in Table 1, the federal government had continued throughout the postwar period to provide considerable resources to support industrial R&D. But whereas it was more than half of the total in 1960, it was only about 16 percent by 1995. A reallocation of resources from government labs to private and university labs would be one possible avenue to improve programs and augment prosperity.

BIBLIOGRAPHY

Chandler, Alfred D. *Scale and Scope: The Dynamics of Industrial Capitalism.* Cambridge, Mass.: Belknap Press, 1990.

Houndshell, David A. "The Evolution of Industrial Research in the United States." In *Engines of Innovation: U.S. Industrial Research at the End of an Era.* Edited by R. S. Rosenbloom and W. J. Spencer. Boston: Harvard Business School Press, 1996.

Mansfield, Edwin. *The Economics of Technological Change.* New York: Norton, 1968.

Moore, Gordon E. "Some Personal Reflections on Research in the Semiconductor Industry." In *Engines of Innovation: U.S. Industrial Research at the End of an Era.* Edited by R. S. Rosenbloom and W. J. Spencer. Boston: Harvard Business School Press, 1996.

Mowery, David C. "The Emergence of Growth of Industrial Research in American Manufacturing, 1899–1945." Ph.D. diss., Stanford University, 1981.

Teece, David J. "Profiting from Technological Innovation." *Research Policy* 15, no. 6 (1986): 285–305.

———. "The Dynamics of Industrial Capitalism: Perspectives on Alfred Chandler's Scale and Scope (1990)." *Journal of Economic Literature* 31 (March 1993).

David J. Teece

See also **AT&T; Bell Telephone Laboratories; Capitalism; Laboratories.**

INDUSTRIAL REVOLUTION. The industrial revolution can be defined as a drastic transformation both of the processes by which American (and European) society produced goods for human consumption, and of the social attitudes surrounding these processes. The first non-ambiguous use of the term is attributed to the French economist Adolphe Blanqui in 1837, but the idea of a "revolution" in the industrial sphere showed up in various forms in the writings of many French and British intellectuals as early as the 1820s. The expression underlines the depth and speed of the changes observed, and the fact that they seemed to derive from the introduction of machine-based factories. Although in Great Britain the slow process of industrial transformation has led historians there to question the very notion of an "industrial revolution," the speed and radical character of the change that took place in the United States in the nineteenth century largely precludes any such discussion.

An Economic and Social Revolution

The spread of new, powerful machines using new sources of power (water, then coal-generated steam) constituted the most obvious aspect of this process of change. Alexander Hamilton's *Report on Manufactures* (1791) made explicit reference to "the extension of the use of machinery," especially in the British cotton industry, and in 1812, Tench Coxe, a political economist and career official in the Treasury Department, peppered his *Report on the State of Manufactures in the United States* with paeans to "labor-saving machinery." Factories built around new machines became a significant element in the urban landscapes of several eastern cities in the 1830s, while railroads brought steam-powered engines into the daily life of rural areas. The new industrial order included productivity increases that made available a wealth of new, nonagricultural goods and activities. Three out of four American male workers accounted for in the census of 1800 worked full time in

Textile Mill. Workers in 1869 leave a mill in Lawrence, Mass., one of the world's leading manufacturing centers for woolen textiles. ARCHIVE PHOTOS, INC.

agriculture; by 1900 more than two-thirds of the workforce was employed in the manufacturing and service sectors. Another, less visible evolution was even more momentous: in 1800 virtually all Americans were working in family-sized units of production, based on long-term or permanent (slaves, spouses) relationships and included such nonquantitative characteristics as room and board and "moral" rules of behavior. When wages were paid, their amount was a function of these "moral" customs (some historians even speak of a "moral" economy) and the prosperity of the business as much as of the supply and demand of labor. A century later, wages determined by the labor market were becoming the norm, with little attention paid to "custom" or the moral imperative of "fair wages." Moreover, employers and employees lived increasingly disconnected lives, both socially and spatially. Among many other consequences, this shift eventually led to a reevaluation of "women's work," hitherto left unpaid within the household, and made untenable first slavery, then the segregation with which southern white supremacists hoped to create their own racist version of the labor market. It is thus impossible to overstate the social and political impact of the industrial revolution.

From New Machines to Modern Businesses

While the existence of an industrial revolution is hard to dispute, its chronology and causes are more open to discussion. Technologically, the United States took its first steps toward mass production almost immediately after independence, and had caught up with Great Britain by the 1830s. Following the British lead, American innovation was concentrated in cotton and transportation. In 1793, after fifteen years of experimentation in the Philadelphia and Boston areas, Samuel Slater set up the country's first profitable cotton-spinning factory in Pawtucket, Rhode Island. Thomas Jefferson's decision in 1807 to stop trade with Europe, and the subsequent War of 1812 with Great Britain, created a protected environment for American manufacturers, and freed commercial capital. This led to such ventures as the Boston Manufacturing Company, founded under the impulse of Boston merchant Francis Cabot Lowell in 1813 in Waltham, Massachusetts. The company's investors went on to create a whole series of new factories in Lowell, Massachusetts, in 1822. Thanks to a combination of immigrant British technicians, patent infringements, industrial espionage, and local innovations, American power looms were on a par

Child Labor. In this photograph by Lewis W. Hine, c. 1910, two young boys climb up on the spinning frame to do work in a textile mill in Macon, Ga. LIBRARY OF CONGRESS

with the English machines by the end of the 1810s. Moreover, Waltham, which combined under one roof all the processes of textile production, particularly spinning and weaving, was the first wholly integrated textile factory in the world. Still, despite the development of a high-pressure steam engine by inventor Oliver Evans in Philadelphia in 1804, American cotton manufacturers, and American industry in general, lagged in the use of steam. In 1833, Secretary of the Treasury Louis McLane's federal survey of American industry reported few steam engines outside of the Pittsburgh area, whereas James Watt's steam engine, perfected between 1769 and 1784, was used throughout Great Britain by 1800.

However, in 1807, the maiden run of Robert Fulton's first steamboat, the *Clermont*, on the Hudson River marked the first commercial application of steam to transportation, a field in which Americans were most active. The first commercial railroad in the United States, the Baltimore and Ohio, was launched in 1828, three years after its first British counterpart. In 1829, the British inventor George Stephenson introduced his Rocket engine; the New Jersey transportation magnate John Stevens bought one two years later and had built three improved (and patent-infringing) copies by 1833. His son, Robert L. Stevens, added his own contribution by creating the modern T-rail. John Stevens also gave technical information to young Matthias Baldwin of Philadelphia, who launched what would become the Baldwin Locomotive Works with his first engine, the Ironsides, built in 1832. With the opening of the ERIE CANAL in 1825, and the ensuing "canal craze," a spate of canal construction extending into the 1840s, all the ingredients of the so-called transportation revolution were in place.

Between the 1820s and the Civil War, American machinery surpassed that of their British competitors, a superiority made public at the CRYSTAL PALACE EXHIBITION in London in 1851. For instance, under the impulse of John Hall, a machinist who began working at the Harpers Ferry federal gun factory in 1820, American gun makers developed a production process precise and mechanized enough to produce standardized, interchangeable gun parts; such an approach would make the fortune of gun maker Samuel Colt in the 1850s. Standardized production was eventually applied to other goods, starting with

Isaac Merritt Singer's sewing machines, sold commercially from 1851 on. The biggest advance in communications technology since the railroad greatly improved mail delivery, was the telegraph, an American innovation introduced by Samuel F. B. Morse between Washington, D.C., and Baltimore in 1844. The 1830–1860 period is most important, however, for its organizational innovations. Up to then, cotton manufacturers, steamboat promoters, and railroad administrators alike were less concerned with productivity than with turning a quick profit through monopolies, cartels, and niche markets. Accounting was sloppy at best, making precise cost control impossible. Subcontracting was the rule, as well as piecework rather than wages. In this environment, technical innovations that sped production could lessen costs for the manufacturer only if piece rates were cut accordingly. This began to occur in American cotton factories from 1828 on (leading to the first modern industrial conflicts in Manayunk and other factories around Philadelphia, six years before the better-known strikes in Lowell and other New England centers in 1834). It was not until the 1840s and 1850s that modern business procedures were introduced. These included the accounting innovations of Louis McLane, at this time president of the Baltimore and Ohio Railroad, and his chief engineer, Benjamin Latrobe, and the organizational overhaul of the Pennsylvania Railroad launched by its president, J. Edgar Thompson, in 1853.

By the Civil War, competent technicians and productivity-minded administrators were revolutionizing one industry after another, a process that became generalized after 1870. Organizers and inventors systematically allied with each other; in Pittsburgh, Alexander L. Holley built for Andrew Carnegie the most modern steel mill in the world, the Edgar Thomson works, which opened in 1875. Sometimes organizer and inventor were one and the same, as in the case of Thomas Edison, who set up an experimental laboratory in Menlo Park, New Jersey, in 1876, developed the first electric lightbulb in 1879, and went on to build what became General Electric. In other fields, the pioneers were superseded by outsiders. Colonel Edwin Drake was the first person to successfully use drilling to extract oil from the earth, which he did in Titusville, Pennsylvania, in 1859, but John D. Rockefeller was the man who succeeded in gaining control over 90 percent of American refineries between 1865 and 1879, creating with Standard Oil the first modern monopoly in America. The systematized search for productivity led to systematized research and development through the combined use of applied research and funding from large corporations, university-based science, and federal subsidies. From oil and electricity to chemistry, the pace of innovation became such that the period has been called a "second industrial revolution" (actually a misnomer, since rates of growth were not significantly higher than in the previous period). Similarly, the search for economies of scale led to giant factories, great concentrations of workers, and widespread urbanization. The search for new outlets for constantly increasing output led to mass consumption and advertisement. And the search for lower costs prompted bloody battles with workers. Compromise in this area was slowly reached; in 1914, Henry Ford introduced the idea that high wages meant efficient workers and useful consumers, and Roosevelt and the New Deal, from 1933 on, set up a social security system giving those same workers a safety net in hard times. Thus, much of the history of the late-nineteenth and the twentieth centuries is the history of the struggle to come to terms with the economic, political, and social consequences of the new forms of organization of human production developed before the Civil War and systematized in the Gilded Age. More generally, the industrial revolution inaugurated trends that perpetuated themselves into the twenty-first century and can properly be described as the matrix of the contemporary world.

BIBLIOGRAPHY

Chandler, Alfred D., Jr. *The Visible Hand: The Managerial Revolution in American Business.* Cambridge, Mass.: Belknap Press, 1977.

Cochran, Thomas C. *Frontiers of Change: Early Industrialism in America.* New York: Oxford University Press, 1981.

Cohen, Isaac. *American Management and British Labor: A Comparative Study of the Cotton Spinning Industry.* New York: Greenwood Press, 1990.

Hounshell, David A. *From the American System to Mass Production, 1800–1932: The Development of Manufacturing Technology in the United States.* Baltimore: Johns Hopkins University Press, 1984.

Jeremy, David J. *Transatlantic Industrial Revolution: The Diffusion of Textile Technologies between Britain and America, 1790–1830s.* Cambridge, Mass.: MIT Press, 1981.

Licht, Walter. *Industrializing America: The Nineteenth Century.* Baltimore: Johns Hopkins University Press, 1995.

Scranton, Philip. *Endless Novelty: Specialty Production and American Industrialization, 1865–1925.* Princeton, N.J.: Princeton University Press, 1997.

Zunz, Olivier. *Why the American Century?* Chicago: University of Chicago Press, 1998.

Pierre Gervais

See also **Embargo Act; Railroads; Standard Oil Company; Steam Power and Engines; Steamboats;** *and vol. 9:* **Mill Worker's Letter on the Hardships in the Textile Mills.**

INDUSTRIAL WORKERS OF THE WORLD

(IWW) had a major impact on the American labor movement, despite its rotating membership and controversial methods. The activities of its members, called "Wobblies" for the "W" in its acronym, entered the folklore of an underclass of hoboes and migratory labor.

The unprecedented American economic development in the late nineteenth century expanded the factory system and mechanization. The new kinds of industries subsumed the labor previously performed by skilled craftspeople and required an increase in the hired workforce.

To meet the need for workers, industries relied heavily on migration from rural America and massive immigration from overseas. Proponents of American labor organizations faced a complex and layered workforce in an industrial environment that had outgrown the existing form of unionism. By the early 1880s, the Knights of Labor had organized hundreds of thousands of workers of all sorts into a fraternal, cooperative order that lacked a clear focus on the workplace. By 1886, skilled workers who had such a focus formed the American Federation of Labor (AFL), which was preoccupied with the defensive protection of "craft unionism" and its privileges.

As the panic of 1893 created conditions conducive to unionization, three notable currents adamantly urged what was called "industrial unionism." First, ideologically motivated working-class radicals launched the Socialist Trade and Labor Alliance (STLA), hoping to follow the success of the German social democracy in organizing new unions. Second, working conditions on the railroads, arguably the most important industry of the age, convinced growing numbers of engineers, firemen, brakemen, switchmen, conductors, porters, and others that they needed to replace or supplement their craft organizations with the common American Railway Union (ARU). In the harsh and often violent circumstances of the Far West, local unions combined into the Western Federation of Miners (WFM). While the STLA largely degenerated into a propaganda vehicle for the Socialist Labor Party, the local, state, and federal authorities intervened with troops to break the ARU in the 1894 Pullman Strike and over the next few years clashed with armed WFM members in bitter disputes at Cripple Creek and Leadville, Colorado, and Coeur d'Alene, Idaho. Blaming the fraternal and defensive AFL for protecting membership concerns rather than expressing class interests, the tough-minded miners attempted to form the nucleus of a rival general association of workers in conjunction with the Western Labor Union (1898) and the American Labor Union (1902), but those efforts came to naught. Based on the prestige of having led a series of tough campaigns against Colorado employers in 1903 and 1904, the WFM sponsored a January 1905 conference in Chicago that called for a new national union.

On 27 June 1905, the convention gathered in Chicago's Brand Hall. The more than two hundred delegates included Daniel De Leon, the reorganizer of the Socialist Labor Party and the inspiration for the STLA; Eugene Debs, the once-imprisoned president of the old ARU and at the time of the convention the most prominent national spokesperson for the new Socialist Party; the white-haired and aged "Mother" Mary Jones, long an organizer of coal miners in the East; and Lucy Parsons, the mulatto anarchist widow of Albert Parsons, who was judicially murdered only blocks away from Brand Hall almost twenty years earlier over the Haymarket affair. This gathering, which William D. "Big Bill" Haywood of the WFM called "the Continental Congress of the working-class," launched the IWW.

Big Bill Haywood. Miner and militant cofounder of the IWW, he was acquitted in 1907 in the assassination two years earlier of the former governor of Idaho but convicted a decade later of sedition during World War I, after which Haywood fled to Russia, where he died in 1928. UPI/CORBIS-BETTMANN

The AFL, the Knights of Labor, and numerous other unions had started with resolutions discussing a class struggle between capital and labor, but the new movement discussed the subject as a matter of course. "We are here," said Haywood, "to confederate the workers of this country into a working-class movement that shall have for its purpose the emancipation of the working-class from the slave bondage of capitalism." The preamble to the constitution of the IWW stated bluntly: "The working class and the employing class have nothing in common. There can be no peace so long as hunger and want are found among millions of working people and the few, who make up the employing class, have all the good things of life."

The founders of the IWW were vague about how they might achieve their goals and made no commitment regarding politics. The seriousness of those omissions became evident at the second convention in 1906. There, in the absence of Haywood, Debs, and other prominent founders, De Leon led a successful movement in opposition to what the socialists called the conservative WFM leadership, though, in fact, Vincent St. John and other WFM leaders backed the opposition as well. The movement not only ousted President Charles Sherman but abolished the office itself, assigning William Trautmann as their "general organizer."

Meanwhile, the WFM faced a major crisis. In the closing hours of 1905, someone assassinated the Idaho governor Frank Steunenberg, who had confronted the WFM at Coeur d'Alene. During early 1906, Idaho authorities illegally crossed state lines to kidnap the WFM officials Haywood and Charles Moyer and the prounionist Denver shopkeeper George A. Pettibone. As the WFM debated the factional battle that transformed the IWW, its leaders prepared for a trial (9 May–27 July 1907) that made them an international cause célèbre defended by the famed criminal attorney Clarence Darrow. Their acquittal publicized the new union without resolving its studied ambiguities about politics and power.

In its first years, the IWW organized workers and led strikes from Portland, Oregon, to Skowhegan, Maine. Determined to organize unskilled workers regardless of sex, ethnicity, or race, the IWW rarely won a strong, permanent membership capable of withstanding reversals in many of these communities. Many workers joined to strike and left with its completion. Where other unions had sought to lead, the IWW was led by its own sense of principle and duty to take up workers' grievances. That same mistrust of would-be leaders that had turned out the Sherman regime in 1906 seemed to mandate a repudiation of De Leon's doctrinaire "socialist industrial unionism" at the 1908 convention. The IWW had defined itself by deciding what it was not, embracing a broad spectrum of currents initially and then removing selected ones. By 1908, this process had reduced the membership in the organization to 3,700.

Nevertheless, the IWW was a distinctive labor movement. Under St. John (1908–1915) and later Haywood (1915–1918), the union became what the latter called socialism "with its working clothes on." This new kind of unionism advocated the overthrow of capitalism not at the ballot box, which it mistrusted, but through "direct action" on the job. Rooted in the North American experience, the IWW developed a distinctive version of what was coming to be called "syndicalism" in Europe. It sought to organize all workers into "one big union," a new, democratized, and self-governing power, through the ongoing quest for a consensus in practice. Its version of a labor movement was "the frame of the new in the shell of the old." Using progressively stronger methods of "direct action," workers broke through the shell of capitalist ownership in production and distribution. The process precluded the kinds of legal recognition and contract agreements essential to the "pure and simple" unionism of the AFL.

The IWW approach became a touchstone for the radicals who later gained prominence in socialist circles. Adhering to the IWW vision, William Z. Foster nevertheless insisted on "boring from within" the established AFL unions to win them to socialism. Many young radicals, like James P. Cannon, alternated between functioning as a Wobbly and as a member of the Socialist Party. In the flush of success after the Russian Revolution of 1917, Foster, Cannon, John Reed, Elizabeth Gurley Flynn, and a number of others associated with the revolutionary goals of the IWW founded the Communist Party, USA, although the party expelled Cannon for criticisms of the Soviet regime rooted in his IWW preoccupations with the democratic standards essential to a future working-class self-government.

Small but militant, the IWW determined to organize some of the most disadvantaged of the unorganized, particularly the unemployed or the marginally and often-migratory employed workers. Farm laborers and other migrant workers regularly traveled by freight train and gathered in the large markets near the rail yards. IWW organizers sought to carry their message of unionism to these workers in the yards and in the railroad cars themselves.

At the time, municipal governments struggled to regulate public life, imposing requirements for special permits to hold meetings and establishing armed police departments to enforce such ordinances. Accusing authorities of placing an admission price on the use of the Bill of Rights, IWW speakers had no alternative but to defy these restrictions, and they faced arrest when they did so. The otherwise powerful IWW base found its real strength in numbers here. As the authorities seized one after another IWW speaker, they found hundreds of unemployed people filling their jails to capacity. The IWW pursued this approach deliberately, waging impressive "free speech fights" at Missoula, Montana (1909); Spokane, Washington (1909–1910); Fresno, California (1910–1911); Aberdeen, South Dakota (1911–1912); San Diego, California (1912); and Kansas City, Missouri (1914).

Wobblies brought the same kind of militancy into its strikes. Perhaps the most successful strike waged by the IWW came in the textile industry in Lawrence, Massachusetts, from 12 January to 14 March 1912. The estimated twenty-three thousand strikers not only represented, with their dependents, about three-fifths of the city's population, they also represented over two dozen nationalities and nearly four dozen languages. Their success despite the odds brought the IWW to national attention.

The IWW doubtlessly began the process that enabled the Congress of Industrial Organizations to successfully establish industrial unions in the 1930s. The IWW organized drives and strikes in steel at McKees Rocks, New Castle, and Butler in Pennsylvania (1909); in silk textiles at Paterson, New Jersey (1913); in rubber at Akron, Ohio (1913); and in automobiles at Detroit, Michigan (1913). Significantly, in 1911–1912, southern veterans of the IWW efforts in the Northwest returned to the Louisiana-Texas border, sparking a series of labor struggles characterized by a distinctive interracial solidarity.

Joe Hill. The IWW organizer and singer-songwriter shortly before his arrest in 1914 on murder charges and his execution in 1915; at least two songs were inspired by this posthumous folk hero of the labor movement—whose last message, sent to Bill Haywood, was, "Don't waste any time in mourning. Organize." © SEATTLE POST-INTELLIGENCER COLLECTION; MUSEUM OF HISTORY & INDUSTRY/CORBIS

After 1912–1913, IWW activity tended to refocus on the West. The union inspired the "riot" of farm labor at Wheatland, California, in 1913, and miners elbowed the IWW into prominence within the intensely unionist town of Butte, Montana, in 1914 and on the Mesabi Range north of Duluth, Minnesota, in 1916. Activities among the lumberjacks of the Northwest created a large following in western Canada and Washington. These endeavors saw local surges of interest in the IWW that receded after the struggle's close. Membership officially reached around thirty thousand in 1912, but fell to nearly half that in each of the next three years. Wildly fluctuating membership and a base largely among the most transitory workers inspired speculation that as many as 60,000 to 100,000 workers passed through the organization.

Violent repression characterized the history of the IWW. In company towns or work camps, employers ruled under their own law and ruthlessly met any move toward unionization, particularly by an organization that denied their claim to profit. Some city governments sometimes grudgingly conceded unionism a platform due to the moral suasion of the free speech fights. San Diego and other municipalities frankly sought to defeat the free speech fights by sanctioning beatings and torture of jailed unionists who would exercise free speech. Authorities at Salt Lake City arrested and convicted the Swedish-born IWW songwriter Joe Hill of a murder based on so little substantive evidence that it disappeared after his trial. Despite an international defense campaign, Hill was executed in 1915. In Washington State, when Seattle supporters took the public passenger boat *Verona* to Everett in 1917 for a rally in support of local strikers, armed deputies opened fire on the boat, resulting in over sixty casualties, including a dozen fatalities. Subsequently, Seattle authorities arrested and tried seventy-four of the passengers. So many Wobblies were behind bars together at different points that their hunger strikes and other means won concessions in often unheated and overcrowded jails. Vigilantes assailed not only strikers but their families. In Bisbee, Arizona, twelve hundred men, women, and children were illegally detained, loaded onto cattle cars, and dumped in the desert on 12 July 1917.

Governments at every level turned a blind eye toward extralegal assaults on the IWW, though in the proper progressive fashion, they soon assumed that function themselves. Beginning in 1917, states passed unconstitutional "criminal syndicalist" legislation that made it a crime to advocate self-government through a labor organization. By then the federal authorities had determined to preclude any discussion of the merits of its decision to bring the United States into World War I. On the day after President Woodrow Wilson asked for a declaration of war but before that declaration had been passed, on 3 April 1917, local police escorted "off duty" military to close the IWW headquarters in Kansas City. The action inspired similar attacks in Detroit, Duluth, and other IWW centers. A "mob" in Butte lynched the part-Indian organizer Frank Little from a railroad trestle on 31 July 1917. As in other industrial nations, officials in the United States, frustrated by the constitutional, legal, and cultural checks on their authority, found extralegal means to remove from public discourse those who had broken no law but who disagreed with government policy.

Modern war among similar industrial nations required government involvement in the economy, including the labor movement. The IWW's refusal to participate in contractual wage agreements in this context made it appear treasonable. Aided by what became the Federal Bureau of Investigation, the government arrested, imprisoned, and eventually tried a considerable number of the IWW's leadership. Those behind bars in Chicago; Sacramento, California; Wichita, Kansas; and Omaha, Nebraska, totaled nearly three hundred. Alongside the mechanisms of government, state-sponsored vigilantism continued, as when the American Legion assaulted the IWW hall in Centralia, Washington, on 11 November 1919, murdering Wesley Everest, a distinguished war veteran as well as an IWW member.

The IWW survived the repression, though clearly it did not and could not have done so as the sort of organization that had existed before. The radical unionism of the IWW reemerged briefly in the massive postwar strike wave in 1919, but other organizations had displaced the IWW. Out of jail on bail, Haywood fled to Russia. In some localized industries, notably the docks of Philadelphia, the IWW survived through the 1920s and 1930s by negotiating contracts and functioning as a trade union. As a small group urging more militant unionism and the necessity of "one big union," the IWW survived. The Wobblies' faith in social transformation through class solidarity and their demonstrations of that power provided a legacy that outlasted the later illusions in Soviet Russia.

BIBLIOGRAPHY

Bird, Stewart, Dan Georgakas, and Deborah Shaffer, comps. *Solidarity Forever: An Oral History of the IWW.* Chicago: Lake View Press, 1985.

Conlin, Joseph Robert. *Bread and Roses Too: Studies of the Wobblies.* Westport, Conn.: Greenwood, 1974.

———, ed. *At the Point of Production: The Local History of the IWW.* Westport, Conn.: Greenwood, 1981.

Dubofsky, Melvyn. *We Shall Be All: A History of the Industrial Workers of the World.* Urbana: University of Illinois Press, 1988.

Foner, Philip S. ed. *Fellow Workers and Friends: IWW Free Speech Fights as Told by Participants.* Westport, Conn.: Greenwood, 1981.

Hall, Greg. *Harvest Wobblies: The Industrial Workers of the World and Agricultural Laborers in the American West, 1905–1930.* Corvalis: Oregon State University Press, 2001.

Werstein, Irving. *Pie in the Sky: An American Struggle: The Wobblies and Their Times.* New York: Delacorte, 1969.

Mark A. Lause

See also **American Federation of Labor–Congress of Industrial Organizations; American Railway Union; Knights of Labor; Labor; Lawrence Strike; Socialist Labor Party; Steel Strikes; Strikes; Trade Unions; Western Federation of Miners.**

INDUSTRIES, COLONIAL. During the colonial period most people engaged in agriculture. A greatly diversified agriculture in the North contrasted with the extreme importance of tobacco in the South. However, from the earliest days of settlement many other industries developed. The vast natural resources of the coast and continent facilitated many of these early enterprises. Shipbuilding, fishing, fur trapping, iron making, and the production of textiles and naval stores helped provide the basis of the colonial economy.

Shipbuilding was an industry of primary importance. Colonists built wooden vessels varying in weight from a few to several hundred tons for the fisheries, the coastal trade, and trade with the West Indies, Great Britain, and foreign countries. Boston, Salem, New Haven, Portsmouth, and Philadelphia became shipbuilding centers. Shipbuilding created or stimulated many other industries. Among these were the making of sails, rope, nails, spikes, anchors, and chain plates, as well as caulking and painting.

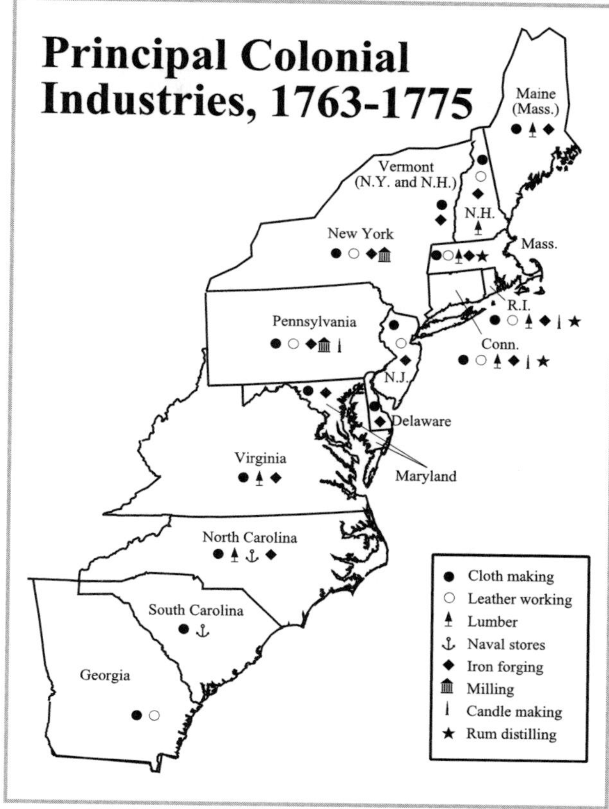

Coastal fishing and whaling were carried on in most colonies, but in New England fishing the banks for cod, mackerel, bass, herring, halibut, hake, sturgeon, and other ocean fish developed into a leading industry. Allied to the fishing industry, and often considered a part of it, was whaling. By the close of the seventeenth century, Plymouth, Salem, and Nantucket, Massachusetts, and villages on the eastern end of Long Island were doing a profitable business in supplying the demand for spermaceti, sperm oil, whalebone, and ambergris. After the opening of the eighteenth century, whaling expanded to a remarkable extent, as whalers often pursued their prey to Arctic waters. Before the colonial period ended, several hundred vessels were engaged in this perilous industry.

The fur trade was also important from the time the first settlements were founded. The abundance of fur-bearing animals provided opportunities for trapping, frequently as an occupation supplemental to farming. The trade in furs, large quantities of which were secured from the Indians, provided a valuable source of income. Significant in its industrial and commercial aspects, the fur trade was also of great importance in pointing the way to the West, as trappers and traders pressed after the retreating fur-bearing animals. Like the fisheries, the fur trade was an important factor in colonial rivalries, especially between England and France, and was partly responsible for many of the intercolonial struggles.

Iron making was an industry that reached relatively large proportions. The basic mining and smelting processes generally occurred on plantations or large estates where fuel for the ironworks and food for the workers could be obtained. From the bar iron produced, blacksmiths and other artisans, scattered in villages, towns, and cities, fashioned tools, implements, and other hardware.

Textile production was largely a household industry. Imported textiles were expensive and therefore almost every home had a spinning wheel and handloom to produce rough serges and linsey-woolseys. Textiles were made chiefly from wool and flax; cotton was used to a much lesser extent. Before the Revolution a few shops were established in New England and in other places where several looms were brought together under one roof, thus prefiguring the coming factory system. Among the long list of home manufactures in addition to textiles were furniture, tools and other implements, wagons, harnesses, and nails. Meal, hominy, maple sugar, dried fruits, candles, lye, and soap were also produced on the farms.

Pine forest products—TAR, pitch, rosin, and turpentine—as well as masts and spars were exported to the mother country from all sections of the seaboard, especially from the southern colonies. In addition to naval stores, quantities of planks, boards, shingles, barrel staves, and even house frames were produced at sawmills and exported to the West Indies and elsewhere. Among forest industries, the production of potash and pearl ash—which are made from wood ashes—must be included. Mainly incidental to the clearing of land, these two products were in demand, especially in England, for bleaching and soap making.

Other important colonial industries included tanning and leatherworking establishments, fulling mills, GRISTMILLS, powder mills, saltworks, paper mills, printing shops, glassworks, brick kilns, firearms shops, copper shops, breweries, and distilleries. In connection with the last-mentioned industry, the distillation of rum in New England was important and lucrative.

BIBLIOGRAPHY

McCusker, John J., and Russell R. Menard. *The Economy of British America, 1607–1789.* Chapel Hill: University of North Carolina Press, 1985.

Perkins, Edwin J. *The Economy of Colonial America.* New York: Columbia University Press, 1988.

Shepherd, James F., and Gary M. Walton. *Shipping, Maritime Trade, and the Economic Development of Colonial North America.* Cambridge, U.K.: Cambridge University Press, 1972.

Tunis, Edwin. *Colonial Craftsmen and the Beginnings of American Industry.* Cleveland, Ohio: World Publishing, 1965.

Vickers, Daniel. *Farmers and Fishermen: Two Centuries of Work in Essex County, Massachusetts, 1630–1850.* Chapel Hill: University of North Carolina Press, 1994.

Arthur C. Bining/H. S.

See also **Colonial Commerce; Colonial Ships; Fur Trade and Trapping; Iron and Steel Industry; Naval Stores; Salt; Textiles.**

INFLATION. The definition of "inflation" cannot be separated from that of the "price level." Economists measure the price level by computing a weighted average of consumer prices or so-called "producer" prices. The value of the average is arbitrarily set equal to one (or one hundred) in a base year, and the index in any other year is expressed relative to the base year. The value of the consumer price index in 1999 was 167, relative to a value of 100 in 1982 (the base year). That is, prices in 1999 were 67 percent higher on average than in 1982.

Inflation occurs when the price level rises from one period to the next. The rate of inflation expresses the increase in percentage terms. Thus, a 3 percent annual inflation rate means that, on average, prices rose 3 percent over the previous year. Theoretically, the rate of inflation could be by the hour or the minute. For an economy suffering from "hyperinflation"—Germany in the 1920s is an example—this might be an appropriate thing to do (assuming the data could be collected and processed quickly enough). For the contemporary United States, which has never experienced hyperinflation, the rate of inflation is reported on a monthly basis.

Deflation is the opposite of inflation: a fall in the price level. Prior to World War II deflation was quite common in the United States, but since World War II, inflation has been the norm. Prewar deflation took two forms. First, the price level might decline very sharply during an economic downturn. This happened, for example, in the early 1840s, when the country was hit by a severe depression, as well as during the Great Depression of the 1930s. Second, deflation might occur over long periods of time, including periods of economic expansion. For example, the price level in the United States in 1860 was lower than in 1820, yet during these four decades the economy grew rapidly and experienced much structural change.

Measuring Inflation

The measurement of the price level is a difficult task and, therefore, so is the measurement of the inflation rate. For example, many economists believe that the consumer price index has overstated the rate of inflation in recent decades because improvements in the quality of goods and services are not adequately reflected in the index. An index that held quality constant, according to this view, would show a smaller rate of price increase from year to year, and thus a smaller average rate of inflation.

It is important to recognize that a positive rate of inflation, as measured by a price index, does not mean that all prices have increased by the same proportion. Some prices may rise relative to others. Some might even fall in absolute terms, and yet, on average, inflation is still positive.

The distinction between absolute and relative price change is important in understanding the theory behind the effects of inflation on economic activity. In the simplest "static" (one-period) economic model of consumer behavior, a fully "anticipated" (understood and expected by consumers and producers) doubling of all prices—the prices of the various consumer goods and the prices of the various productive "inputs" (factors of production, like labor)—does not change the structure of relative prices and therefore should have no effect on the quantities of goods demanded. Similarly, the conventional model of producer behavior predicts that a doubling of all prices would not affect output price relative to the cost of production and therefore would not affect the quantity of goods supplied. The nominal value of GNP (gross national product) would double, but the real value would remain constant. In such a model, money is said to be "neutral," and consumers and producers are free of "money illusion." In more complex, dynamic models, it is possible that a sustained, higher rate of inflation would alter consumers' desired holds of money versus other assets (for example, real estate) and this might change real economic activity.

When inflation is unexpected, however, it is entirely possible—indeed, almost inevitable—that real economic activity will be affected. Throughout American history there is evidence that money wages are "sticky" relative to prices; that is, changes in money wages lag behind (unexpected) changes in the price level. During the early years of the Great Depression of the 1930s, nominal hourly wages fell but not nearly as much as prices. With the real price of labor "too high," unemployment was the inevitable result. When inflation is unexpected, consumers or producers may react as if relative prices are changing, rather than the absolute price level. This can occur especially if the economy experiences a price "shock" in a key sector—for example, an unexpected rise in the price of oil—that sets off a chain of price increases of related products, and a downturn in economic activity.

Causes of Inflation

All of which begs the underlying question: What ultimately causes inflation (or deflation)? Although this is still a matter of dispute among economists in the details, most believe that inflation typically occurs when the supply of money increases more rapidly than the demand for money; or equivalent, when the supply of money per unit of output is increasing. This might occur within a single country; in a global economy, it can also spill over from one country to another. The supply of money per unit of output can increase either because the "velocity" at which it circulates in the economy has increased or, holding velocity constant, because the stock of money per unit of output has increased.

This leads to another question: What factors determine the rate of growth of the money supply relative to money demand? The demand for money depends on the overall scale of economic activity, along with interest rates, which measure the opportunity cost of holding money balances. The supply of money depends on the so-called "monetary regime"—the institutional framework by which money is created.

During the nineteenth century and part of the twentieth, the United States adhered to the gold standard and, at times, a bimetallic (silver) standard. Under the gold standard, the money supply was "backed" (guaranteed) by holdings of gold, so the supply of money could grow only as rapidly as the government's holdings of specie. If these holdings increased more slowly than the demand for money, the price level would fall. Conversely, if holdings of specie increased more rapidly than the demand for money, the price level could rise. Generally, the latter would occur with the discovery of new deposits of gold (or silver) in the United States—or elsewhere, because gold flowed across international borders—as occurred in California in the late 1840s, or in South Africa in the late 1890s.

During periods of war the money supply was augmented with paper money. For example, during the Civil War, both the Union and Confederate governments issued greenbacks as legal tender. The price level rose sharply during the war years. Real wages fell, producing an inflation "tax" that both sides used to help pay for the war effort.

In the contemporary United States, the main institutional determinant of the money supply is the Federal Reserve. The Fed can affect the growth of the money supply in several ways. First, it can engage in open market operations, the buying and selling of government securities. When the Fed buys securities, it injects money into the system; conversely, when it sells securities, it pulls money out. Second, the Fed can alter certain features of the banking system that affect the ability of banks to "create" money. Banks take in deposits, from which they make loans. The supply of loanable funds, however, is larger than the stock of deposits because banks are required only to keep a fraction of deposits as reserves. The Fed can alter the reserve ratio, or it can alter the rate of interest that it charges itself to lend money to banks.

Most economists believe that the Federal Reserve, when deciding upon monetary policy, faces a short-run trade-off between inflation and unemployment. In the long run, unemployment tends toward a "natural" rate that reflects basic frictions in the labor market and that is independent of the rate of inflation. If the goal in the short run is to reduce unemployment, the Fed may need to tolerate a moderate inflation rate. Conversely, if the goal is to lower the inflation rate, this may require a slowdown in economic activity and a higher unemployment rate. Since World War II, the Federal Reserve has sought to keep inflation at a low to moderate level. This is because a high or accelerating rate of inflation is typically followed by a recession. Some economists believe that, rather than trying to "fine-tune" the economy, the Fed should "grow" the money supply at a steady, predictable pace.

It is sometimes argued that inflation is good for debtors and bad for creditors, and bad for persons on fixed incomes. A debtor, so goes the argument, benefits from inflation because loans are taken out in today's dollars, but repaid in the future when, because of inflation, a dollar will be worth less than today. However, to the extent that inflation is correctly anticipated—or "rationally expected"—the rate of interest charged for the loan—the "nominal" rate—will be the "real" rate of interest plus the expected rate of inflation. More generally, any fixed income contract expressed in nominal terms can be negotiated in advance to take proper account of expected inflation. However, if inflation or deflation is unanticipated, it can have severe distributional effects. During the Great Depression millions of Americans lost their homes because their incomes fell drastically relative to their mortgage payments.

Inflation in American History

In the eighteenth and nineteenth centuries and, indeed, in the first half of the twentieth century, inflation was uncommon. Major bouts of inflation were associated with wars, minor bouts with short-term economic expansions ("booms"). The booms usually ended in financial "panics," with prices falling sharply. During the nineteenth century this pattern played itself out several times, against a backdrop of long-term deflation.

The first wartime experience with inflation in U.S. history occurred during the American Revolution. Prior to the Revolution inflation did occur periodically when colonial governments issued bills of credit and permitted them to circulate as money, but these were banned by Parliament between 1751 and 1764. When war broke out, bills of credit were again circulated in large numbers. Because the increase in the money supply far exceeded the growth of output during this period, the price level rose sharply.

Wartime inflations in American history have typically been followed by severe deflations, and the Revolution was no exception. After dropping by two-thirds between 1781 and 1789, prices rebounded and eventually stabilized. The next big inflation occurred with the War of 1812. Briefer and less intense than its revolutionary counterpart, prices fell sharply after peaking in 1814. The price level continued to trend downward in the 1820s but reversed course in the mid-1830s during a brief boom. A financial panic ensued, and the country plunged into a severe downturn accompanied by an equally severe deflation. The economy began to recover after 1843, and the price level remained stable until the mid-1850s, when, fueled by the recent gold discoveries in California, inflation returned. Again, however, a financial panic occurred and prices fell. In 1860, the eve of the Civil War, the price level in the United States was 28 percent below the level in 1800; that is, the preceding six decades were characterized by long-term deflation.

To help finance the war effort, Congress and the Confederacy both issued paper money. Inflation followed, peaking in 1864. The price level dropped sharply after the war and, except for a brief period in the early 1880s, continued on a downward course for the remainder of the nineteenth century.

The discovery of gold in South Africa in the mid-1890s signaled another expansion of the money supply. Prices rose moderately after 1896, stabilizing in the years just prior to World War I. Inflation returned with a vengeance during the war, with prices rising by nearly 228 percent between 1914 and 1920. Once again, a sharp postwar recession was accompanied by deflation, but recovery ensured the price level remained stable for the remainder of the 1920s.

Following the stock market crash in October 1929, a deep and prolonged deflation accompanied the dramatic bust that became the Great Depression. Prices fell by one-third between 1929 and 1932. Nominal hourly wages did not fall as much as prices, however, and unemployment rose sharply, to nearly a quarter of the labor force. Convinced that higher wages and higher prices were the key to renewed prosperity, the "New Deal" administration of President Franklin D. Roosevelt adopted a multipronged attack: raising prices directly via the National Recovery Act, reforming the banking system, and expanding the money supply. The price level did turn around beginning in 1933 but fell once again in 1938 during a brief recession.

It took the Nazis and the Japanese invasion of Pearl Harbor to reinvigorate the inflationary process in the United States. Unemployment dropped sharply, putting considerable upward pressure on wages and prices. To some extent this pressure was abated through the use of wage and price controls that lasted from 1942 to 1946, although it is widely believed that official price indexes for the period understate the true inflation because many transactions took place at high "black market" prices, and these are not incorporated into the official indexes.

In the years since World War II the United States has experienced almost continuous inflation, the only exception being very slight deflation in the early 1950s. The inflation rate was nonetheless quite moderate until the expansion of the Vietnam War in the late 1960s. A reluctant President Richard Nixon mandated a series of price controls from 1971 to 1974, but these did little to stem the tide of rising prices, particularly after an international oil embargo in 1973–1974 caused energy prices to skyrocket. Overall in the 1970s the consumer price index rose at an average annual rate of nearly 7.5 percent, compared with 2.7 percent per year in the 1960s. A sharp recession in the early 1980s coupled with activist monetary policy cut the inflation rate to an average of 4.6 percent between 1980 and 1990. Inflation fell further in the 1990s, to an average of 2.7 percent (1990–1999).

As noted, the federal government reports the inflation rate on a monthly basis. Recent data may be found in the U.S. Census Bureau's publication, *Statistical Abstract of the United States*, and on-line at the Bureau's Web site (www.census.gov) or the Web site of the Bureau of Labor Statistics (www.bls.gov). For long-term historical data on the price level, readers should consult the various editions of *Historical Statistics of the United States* or the volume by McCusker (2001).

BIBLIOGRAPHY

Friedman, Milton, and Anna Jacobson Schwartz. *A Monetary History of the United States.* Princeton, N.J.: Princeton University Press, 1963.

Hanes, Chris. "Prices and Price Indices." In *Historical Statistics of the United States, Millennial Edition.* Edited by Susan B. Carter, Scott S. Gartner, Michael Haines, Alan L. Olmstead, Richard Sutch, and Gavin Wright. New York: Cambridge University Press, 2002.

McCusker, John J. *How Much Is that in Real Money? A Historical Price Index for Use as a Deflator of Money Values in the Economy of the United States.* Worcester, Mass.: American Antiquarian Society, 2001.

Parkin, Michael. "Inflation." In *The New Palgrave: A Dictionary of Economics.* Edited by John Eatwell, Murray Milgate, and Peter Newman. Vol 2. New York: Stockton Press, 1987.

Rolnick, Arthur J., and Warren E. Weber. "Money, Inflation, and Output Under Fiat and Commodity Standards." *Journal of Political Economy* 105 (December 1997): 1308–1321.

U.S. Department of Commerce. *Historical Statistics of the United States from Colonial Times to 1970.* Washington, D.C.: Government Printing Office, 1975.

———. *Statistical Abstract of the United States: The National Data Book.* 120th ed. Washington, D.C.: Government Printing Office, 2000.

Robert Margo

See also **Business Cycles; Consumer Purchasing Power; Cost of Living; Economic Indicators; Price and Wage Controls; Prices; Stagflation.**

INFLATION IN THE CONFEDERACY began in May 1861 with an issue of $20 million of non-interest-bearing treasury notes. The Confederate congress continued to issue treasury notes throughout the remainder of the year so that it had $105 million in such notes outstanding at the end of 1861. These paper dollars depreciated almost immediately, setting off a spiral of rising prices that, over the next four years, threatened to undermine the Confederate cause.

The principal methods available to finance the war were taxation, borrowing, and printing money. The Confederacy was able to raise little of its wartime revenue from taxes, and usually Confederate bonds found but a meager market. Consequently, the government met most of its expenses by issuing ever-increasing amounts of treasury notes. By the end of 1862, treasury notes outstanding plus issues by the various southern states totaled $500 million and were worth only one-third that amount in gold. A year later this amount had increased to more than $700 million, and gold was quoted in paper notes at 20 for 1. By the end of 1864, the amount of currency had risen to $1 billion, and the gold quotation was 40 for 1 before that year-end.

The Confederate government was not the only one issuing notes in the South. States, counties, cities, and private businesses also issued their own money. Banks, which had been freed from the compulsion to redeem notes in specie early in the war, issued large quantities. And counterfeit notes swelled this sea of paper. As a consequence, the South experienced runaway inflation. During the war, prices in the Confederacy rose more than 9,000 percent. The inflation rate in the North was only about 80 percent.

Although the collapse of the currency came with the loss of the war, it would have occurred shortly in any event. The inflation in the Confederacy ended in a complete loss of value of Confederate issues and exacerbated the burdens of the war upon southerners.

BIBLIOGRAPHY

Ball, Douglas B. *Financial Failure and Confederate Defeat.* Urbana: University of Illinois Press, 1991.

Donald, David Herbert, ed. *Why the North Won the Civil War.* New York: Touchstone Books, 1996 (orig. pub. 1960).

McPherson, James M. *Battle Cry of Freedom: The Civil War Era.* New York: Oxford University Press, 1988.

Frederick A. Bradford / C. P.

See also **Civil War; Confederate States of America; Inflation; Prices; Taxation.**

INFLUENZA, commonly called "the flu," reached America early in colonial history, and its periodic visitations have continued since then. John Eliot described the first epidemic, which struck in 1647, as "a very depe cold, with some tincture of a feaver and full of malignity. . . ." In the succeeding years a series of outbreaks, described in such terms as "a general catarrh," "winter feavers," "epidemical colds," and "putrid pleurisies," swept through the colonies, bringing death on a large scale. The cause of these epidemics remains unknown, but from accounts of the symptoms and the pandemic nature of the outbreaks, some strain of influenza is a logical suspect. Colonial records show many local outbreaks, with some form of respiratory disease reaching major epidemic proportions in

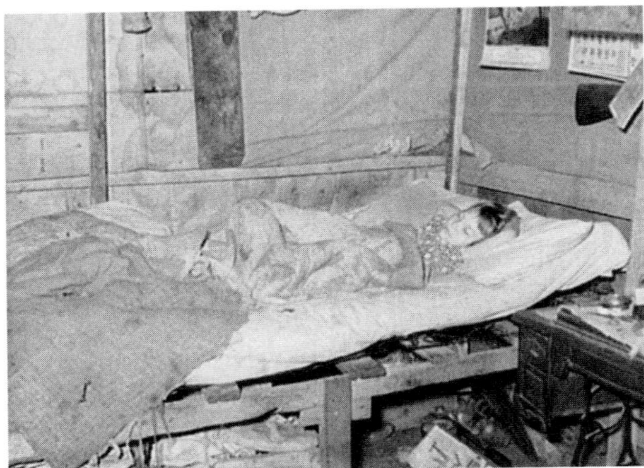

Influenza Case. Russell Lee's 1939 photograph, taken near Jefferson, Texas, shows a migrant worker's child ill with the flu. LIBRARY OF CONGRESS

1675, 1688, 1732–1733, 1737, 1747–1750, 1761, and 1789–1791.

The nineteenth century saw a similar pattern of influenza epidemics—major pandemics interspersed with local or regional outbreaks. The disease spread through Europe and America in 1830, 1837, and 1847, eased up for a long period, and then broke out on a worldwide scale from 1889 to 1893. There were two minor outbreaks involving an unusual number of pneumonic complications in 1916 and 1917. In the summer of 1918, a deceptively mild wave of influenza swept through army camps in Europe and America, immediately followed by the second and third waves of the greatest recorded pandemic of influenza in history. In America the heaviest toll was exacted by a major wave lasting from September to November of 1918; the pandemic killed an estimated 15 million individuals worldwide. In the United States, the disease infected approximately 28 percent of the population, killing 450,000, with half of the deaths occurring among young adults between the ages of twenty and forty.

Several outbreaks struck in the 1920s, but the morbidity and mortality from influenza gradually declined in the succeeding years, although a Metropolitan Life Insurance Company study showed that influenza combined with pneumonia consistently remained the third-ranking cause of death among its policyholders as late as 1935.

Various forms of influenza have persisted; rarely do as many as three years go by without a fairly serious outbreak. Most occurrences are minor, but once or twice every decade the disease flares up. The introduction of new therapeutics in the 1940s led to a steady drop in the overall influenza mortality rate until the outbreaks of Asiatic influenza in 1957, 1958, and 1960. The influenza death rate per 100,000 reached 4.4 in the latter year, the last time this figure exceeded 4 per 100,000.

In 1933 the influenza virus now known as influenza virus A was identified, and other strains were later discovered. Although the impact of influenza vaccines has been limited, the introduction of sulfonamides, penicillin, and antibiotics in the World War II era greatly improved the treatment for pneumonia associated with influenza and thus helped reduce the fatality rate from influenza. Improved sanitary standards have also most likely helped reduce the number and virulence of influenza outbreaks.

BIBLIOGRAPHY

Bett, Walter R. *The History and Conquest of Common Diseases.* Norman: University of Oklahoma Press, 1954.

Crosby, Alfred W. *America's Forgotten Pandemic: The Influenza of 1918.* New York: Cambridge University Press, 1989.

Duffy, John. *Epidemics in Colonial America.* Baton Rouge: Louisiana State University Press, 1953.

Frost, W. H. "The Epidemiology of Influenza." *Journal of the American Medical Association,* 73 (1919): 313–318.

Kolata, Gina Bari. *Flu: The Story of the Great Influenza Pandemic of 1918 and the Search for the Virus that Caused It.* New York: Farrar, Straus and Giroux, 1999.

John Duffy / C. W.

See also **Centers for Disease Control and Prevention; Epidemics and Public Health; Microbiology.**

INFOMERCIALS are program-length (usually thirty or sixty minutes) television productions designed exclusively to feature and sell a product. They often employ formats borrowed from other genres in an effort to disguise partially the fact that they are commercials. Many infomercials are designed as talk shows, for example, and Bell Atlantic introduced a "sitcommercial" in 1992. Although some high-end products have been featured in high-budget infomercials, like those for General Motors' Saturn automobiles, the form is generally associated with more gimmicky merchandise. Hair extensions, miracle cleaning products, food preparation gadgets, and psychic reading services are among the things frequently sold on infomercials. Production values are usually comparatively low, and the style of the sales pitch is often reminiscent of the snake oil salesman.

Program-length commercials on television were forbidden by Federal Communication Commission (FCC) regulations until 1984. Once the ban was lifted, however, infomercials became a significant part of the TV programming mix, especially in the late-night hours. By filling unprofitable time slots with infomercials, cable and broadcast stations avoided the need to pay for programming for that time slot while at the same time generating income by selling that time to the provider of the infomercial. Infomercials aimed at children are still illegal. Perhaps the most unfortunate result of the rise of the infomercial is that many stations now air infomercials in time periods that were once used for public affairs and local programs.

BIBLIOGRAPHY

Head, Sydney W., Thomas Spann, and Michael A. McGregor. *Broadcasting in America: A Survey of Electronic Media.* 9th ed. Boston: Houghton Mifflin, 2001.

Robert Thompson

See also **Advertising; Television: Programming and Influence.**

INFRASTRUCTURE. Human settlements started as simple places, where people could live with some level of convenience and enjoy some measure of security against outside threats. Although hunting, gathering, and fishing were the first preoccupations of primitive man, it was soon discovered that some kinds of tools had to be made for even these elementary activities. In addition, they soon found out that provisions should be made to help them face the adversities of the local weather and the hostilities of other tribes and wild animals. These support facilities were the first elemental components of an urban infrastructure that made living, gathering, hunting, and producing possible.

All these old truths remain relevant to more recent human habitation experiences. The first "towns" of the Far West in the United States almost instinctively were formed where transport was available and where the provision of water was secure. Settlements that neglected to pay proper attention to these two primary components of the needed support systems, or failed to have an elemental concern and provision for drainage, usually experienced an early demise.

Concerns for additional support structures continued in most settlements soon after their establishment. A marketplace, some form of a city hall, a police station, and a courthouse tended to pop up soon in the life of a city. A school was added before long, as well as a clinic or doctor's office. In this way the first infrastructure services and facilities were included very early in the life of most urban developments.

Throughout history, infrastructure systems and services have continuously evolved in both technology and organization. Indeed, in many instances, social scientists measure the level of civilization or advancements of a society on the basis of the richness and articulation of the infrastructure systems that society has in place. Another way to gauge the importance of infrastructure is to note that all the progressive movements of the nineteenth and twentieth centuries have, in essence, focused on the need to improve one or another infrastructure system in meeting one or another social, humanitarian, or economic need. In the case of the American metropolis of the early twenty-first century, one can easily distinguish at least fifty systems and subsystems that constitute the city's infrastructure, ranging from large-scale transportation and water projects to neighborhood medical clinics and libraries.

Birth of Modern Infrastructure: The Great Depression

The "new era" of American infrastructure started in the Great Depression. In 1932 Americans elected a president and Congress that believed in an active role for the federal government in creating jobs for the multitude of unemployed Americans. Within the framework of a newly coined economic theory in macroeconomics by John Maynard Keynes, the new president started with a modest list of infrastructure projects, such as federal administrative buildings. He soon extended the enterprise to railroad stations, post office buildings, irrigation projects, road repairing and expansion, hydroelectric dams, and even a regional multipurpose district of major proportions under the name of the TENNESSEE VALLEY AUTHORITY. Even in outlying areas, the Rural Electrification Administration extended another infrastructure system.

Following the example of the federal government, many states initiated plans for infrastructure systems in their territories. Notable among these are the projects carried out by Robert Moses in New York, city and state, who extended and improved the transportation and parks systems of the greater New York region by leaps and bounds, adding many miles of parkways, bridges, and tunnels. The new age of great urban public works was on.

The intervention of World War II interrupted this stream of initiatives throughout the country. But at the same time, additional infrastructure components were added as new airports, new towns, and new harbors appeared on the map as a result of the war effort.

Immediately after the war, government leaders worried about a potential new economic recession and, desiring to do something good for the returning millions of victorious war veterans, initiated a major housing assistance program. This action was followed by the 1947 Urban Renewal Act and then with the Housing Act of 1954, both of which placed all three levels of government in the midst of a new nationwide effort to plan and improve the service systems of all cities with more than 50,000 people.

In particular the 1954 act included section 701, which invited each of these cities to produce a community plan in which six of the seven central components were focused on transportation and the other infrastructure systems needed for the growth of the community. Once the plan was approved by local, state, and federal agencies, each community could apply for a major share of the cost of construction paid by the federal (and state) government. Since then, section 701 and its extensions have produced a multitude of local infrastructure improvements and expansions for most of the cities of the country.

Interstate Highway System

In 1956, Congress approved the Interstate Highway Act, proposed by President Eisenhower as both a national defense program in the midst of the Cold War (permitting large-scale military units' rapid movement from one part of the country to the other) and as an economic measure that would increase the efficiency of the American economy. The program initially proposed 41,000 miles of expressways crisscrossing the continental United States, with an initial overall budget not to exceed $41 billion. By 1962 the program was extended to about 42,500 miles and included not only the interstate expressways but also components for all major metropolitan areas of the country. The actual plans in each case included segments connecting the suburban areas with the central business districts of each region, crosstown expressways, and one or two beltways. By the time the whole program was completed in the late 1980s, the expenditures had reached about $111 billion, making it the largest single public works project in history, far exceeding the pyramids of Egypt, the Tennessee Valley Authority multipurpose program, and the federal hydroelectric and irrigation dams program of the western states.

The interstate expressway system has been a major force for change in urban America, influencing national location patterns of American industry and substantially increasing the productivity and efficiency of both the primary and secondary sectors of the economy. With regard to the residential patterns of American metropolitan areas, the expressway program of the 1960s, 1970s, and 1980s contributed to the changes and upheavals of that period. Many significant mistakes have been noted on specific, localized parts of the system, due frequently to administrative directives that were very constrictive and necessitated the elimination of whole neighborhoods and/or historical communities.

Environmental Regulations: Land, Water, and Air

Another federal program that had a major impact on urban infrastructure systems is the one based on section 208 of the CLEAN WATER ACT of 1970. This program required that the sewage of all urban areas be cleaned before its emission into streams, rivers, and lakes. Federal assistance was in most cases up to 90 percent of the cost of each project. As a result of this program, the level of impurities in streams, rivers, and lakes in the United States improved dramatically. Primary sewage treatment became universal, removing about 65 percent of all impurities. Secondary and tertiary treatments were expanded on a scale that removed 90 to 95 percent of the impurities (and in some cases, up to 98 percent). By the end of the century, U.S. urban areas were disposing of effluent in streams, rivers, and lakes that was typically cleaner than the natural flow of their waters would produce.

The Clean Water Act also has assisted many cities in building whole new water and sewerage systems, as well as expanding and improving existing ones. In some cases improvements were essential, as in the case of Manhattan Island, where, for the first time, purification plants made it possible to discontinue the practice of releasing raw sewage into the Hudson River. The Clean Water Act and its amendments also mandated improvement of the effluents emitted by industries, commercial enterprises, and even major private residential construction sites. The National Environmental Protection Act of 1969 (NEPA) introduced sweeping measures for cleaning up the American natural environment, making the thirty years between 1970 and 2000 a historic period in the environmental and infrastructure history of the country and of the world.

The solid waste collection and disposal system was also radically improved between 1970 and 2000. Gone are the casual solid waste dumps at the outskirts of the cities, replaced by sanitary landfills. Almost gone, thanks to air pollution regulations, are the solid waste incinerators in some central parts of cities, built there to minimize the transport costs of collected waste. In their place are either electrolytic burners or sophisticated trash-to-energy installations where high-temperature burners generate electricity for local electric utilities. Solid waste collection and disposal has been improved with new trucks designed to carry compacted waste. Such trucks bring the waste to special stations where further compacting produces uniform, high-density cubes that are transported to far-away sanitary disposal sites and used as landfill in natural cavities, excavation sites, or abandoned surface-mining sites. On the other side of the spectrum, extensive recycling of paper, glass, plastics, and aluminum had in some cities reached the level of 30 percent of the total volume of municipal solid waste by the beginning of the twenty-first century, creating new markets for such materials and extending the useful life of the basic product.

Libraries and Medical Facilities

Infrastructural improvements also include the extensive urban and rural library systems in operation today throughout the country, a far cry from the typical unitary central library of the past. Branch libraries in almost every neighborhood or community are a common practice, with computerized data systems that permit almost instant service and control of the operations. Similarly, most major U.S. cities have networks of community clinics, with readily available first-aid service backed up by additional ambulatory transport service and connections with major hospitals.

Public Transportation

Improvements in urban transportation in the last half of the twentieth century took the form of new and expanded heavy and light rail systems, an improved bus service system, and a paratransit system serving special population groups and communities.

Six heavy rail systems were introduced (Washington, D.C., Atlanta, Baltimore, Miami, Los Angeles, and San Francisco) in addition to the four systems already in place since before World War II (New York, Chicago, Philadelphia, and Boston). Ten light rail systems were introduced (Miami, Detroit, San Diego, Buffalo, Pittsburgh,

Portland, Sacramento, Denver, Hoboken, and Camden-Trenton). Several systems also have undergone continuous expansion (San Francisco and Los Angeles, for example). In all cases the budget and the effort has been enormous. For example, the Washington Metropolitan Area Transit Authority took more than thirty-four years to complete its 103-mile system, which began in 1967 with a projected cost of $2.5 billion and concluded in 2001 with an actual cost of about $10 billion.

At the beginning of the twenty-first century almost all major urban regions were planning major new transit systems and extensions of older ones. In Boston, the "Big Dig" of Central Avenue was expected to require more than $15 billion to accommodate all the transit and highway facilities. In the New York metropolitan region, the Regional Plan Association advanced plans that would require an expenditure of at least $20 billion in mass transit systems alone. In Philadelphia three major proposals for heavy rail would require a budget exceeding $7 billion. During this period there were vastly expanded budget revisions of the 1991 Interstate Surface Transportation Efficiency Act ($156 billion) and the 1998 Transportation Equity Act ($216 billion), but these federal funds were clearly not enough to accommodate the need for new mass transit systems projected throughout the country.

Planning for the Future

Infrastructure needs in the early twenty-first century were based on three major considerations. The first was the nationwide anti-sprawl campaign calling for substantive improvements in mass transit and limitation of other infrastructure systems in suburban areas so that development could be significantly curbed. The second was the aging of many infrastructure systems of most older cities (such as sewerage systems), which were built in the late nineteenth and early twentieth centuries with minimal dimensions and impermanent design and materials. The third factor was the rapid growth of American urban areas and the constantly evolving technology of almost all urban infrastructure systems, including telecommunications (fiber optics), steam distribution systems (heat-resistant pipes), sewerage systems (chemical-resistant reinforced concrete), and transportation systems (automated people movers).

Specialists in the field considered the need of improvements and renovations in the infrastructure system of the country as the greatest challenge for the United States in the early 2000s. Many systems were simply too old to continue without major renovations (water systems, sewage networks) while others were functionally obsolete in terms of size or operations (schools, hospitals, solid waste disposal projects). The complex juxtaposition of old city centers, decaying early suburbs, expanding new suburbs, and a narrowing envelope of environmental constraints in and around the metro areas of the United States (as of many other countries of the world) produced major policy dilemmas.

How It Gets Done: Public or Private?

Primary to the construction of modern public works are the issues of who makes the decision to build it (known as provision of services) and who should actually build and/or run it (production of services). Specialists in urban infrastructure draw a sharp distinction between provision and production of services. Although there is almost unanimous agreement that in most cases it is the government that should decide whether an infrastructure system should be provided in a city, agreement is far from certain in deciding exactly how much an infrastructure service or system should be produced through, for example, a publicly owned enterprise or a privately owned business under proper licensing as a utility or as a totally free market provision.

The production of any service or commodity is an industrial process with additional requirements of continuous technological improvements and undiminished managerial attention and skills. Additional requirements of quality, modernity, and minimization of production and distribution costs enter the discussion and impose solutions, which sometimes suggest public-sector production and distribution and sometimes private-sector involvement.

The aversion of taxpayers toward financing speculative ventures decided by civil servants at little personal risk and with dubious competence in what they decide usually holds government agencies back from improved technologies, untested managerial scenarios, and newly established social needs. This is where the private sector's entry usually is welcomed and where it is usually proven to be very useful in expanding the frontier of urban infrastructure networks. Examples of such infrastructure abound in telecommunications, health, energy, and education. In all these cases the government role stays very vigorous in regulation, in standardization, in nondiscriminatory provision, and in safety matters, but stays back from actual production.

Legislation introduced in the 1990s included extensive provisions for private sector participation in many aspects of infrastructure systems development. Under the principal of "private money for public purposes" the various programs attempt to explore the possibility of attracting private entrepreneurs to invest in projects of clear public benefit. The underlying reason in all cases is the desire to conserve public capital investment funds and to achieve additional efficiency and innovation in both the construction and operation of the new infrastructure systems components.

Another debated issue in the provision of services is the role of the three levels of government and their institutions. In theory the notion of federalism finds its perfect application in the process of building infrastructure networks in urban areas. In this scenario, the federal government establishes a national policy for the improvement and enrichment of the specific infrastructure systems and services. As part of these policies, it sponsors a national investment program in which the federal government establishes the goals, the process, the standards, and the states' and localities' roles and financial participation. The funds for many types of infrastructure projects are distributed by a formula for each state or region or on a project-by-project basis. In addition, both the 1993 Interstate Surface Transportation Efficiency Act and the Transportation Equity Act included provisions for the states and regions to exercise discretion and choice on some proportion of the funds on the basis of their local priorities and preferences. In all cases the proportion of local contribution (by state, by region, or by specific locality) is determined by the federal legislation, and it is a precondition for any further action.

Environmental Impacts

The matter of protecting the physical environment during construction and operation of infrastructure systems is an increasingly challenging issue. Most of the major environmental battles of the past have revolved around highway projects, major sewage systems, solid waste disposal sites, and water containment projects, with the conflict extending to include school sites, hospital expansion, and even mass transit lines and stations.

Environmental concerns focus on all three parts of the environment—air, land, and water—and involve concerns for human health and species retention as well as aspects of aesthetics, culture, and history. Conflicts arise over the use of nonrenewable energy resources for infrastructure operations and the sustainability of a given metropolitan region. In many cases, the arguments reach a pitch that prevents reasonable discussion and an unbiased search for solutions.

Even after all available solutions for minimizing the environmental impact of a given project have been explored, however, circumstances may require that either a major intervention on the environment will have to take place or the project must be canceled. Such has been the case on a number of solid waste disposal projects, water conservation projects, and highway projects, such as the West Side Expressway project on Manhattan Island. Nevertheless, in many other locations pressure from community and environmental groups has produced admirable solutions and very agreeable completion of infrastructure projects. Such an example is the Vine Street Expressway in Philadelphia, which was constructed as a depressed expressway with green parapets on both sides, with reasonable construction costs and very important neighborhood-friendly impacts. Still, environmental issues will continue to loom large in the future, underscoring the need for development of new and appropriate public policy guidelines and design options.

BIBLIOGRAPHY

Abbott, Carl. *Portland: Planning, Politics and Growth in a Twentieth Century City.* Lincoln: University of Nebraska Press, 1983.

Goddard, Stephen B. *Getting There: The Epic Struggle Between Road and Rail in the American Century.* New York: Basic Books, 1994.

Goodrich, Carter. *Government Promotion of American Canals and Railroads, 1800–1890.* New York: Columbia University Press, 1965.

Kaszynski, William. *The American Highway: The History and Culture of Roads in the United States.* Jefferson, N.C.: McFarland, 2000.

Larson, John Lauritz. *Internal Improvement: National Public Works and the Promise of Popular Government in the Early United States.* Chapel Hill: University of North Carolina Press, 2001.

Melosi, Martin V. *The Sanitary City: Urban Infrastructure in America from Colonial Times to the Present.* Baltimore: Johns Hopkins University Press, 2000.

Schuyler, David. *The New Urban Landscape: The Redefinition of City Form in Nineteenth-Century America.* Baltimore: Johns Hopkins University Press, 1986.

Silver, Christopher, and Mary Corbin Sies, eds. *Planning the Twentieth Century American City.* Baltimore: Johns Hopkins University Press. 1996.

Tomazinis, Anthony R. *New Concepts in Urban Transportation.* Philadelphia: Institute for Environmental Studies, 1972.

United States Advisory Commission on Intergovernmental Relations. *Toward a Federal Infrastructure Strategy: Issues and Options.* Washington, DC: Advisory Commission on Intergovernmental Relations, 1992.

Anthony R. Tomazinis

See also **American System; City Planning; Environmental Protection Agency; Interstate Highway System; Railways, Interurban; Railways, Urban, and Rapid Transit; Urbanization; Waste Disposal; Water Pollution; Water Supply and Conservation.**

INHERENT POWERS. Inherent powers are those that the Constitution has not expressly given but which "necessarily derive from an office, position, or status" of the national government (*Black's Law Dictionary*, 7th ed., 1999). The U.S. Supreme Court has discovered federal inherent powers to take land through eminent domain proceedings, to acquire land by discovery and occupation, to exclude or admit aliens, and to sell munitions to belligerent nations. After the Court had, during most of the twentieth century, broadly construed the commerce clause to allow expanded federal regulation, the doctrine was rarely invoked.

BIBLIOGRAPHY

Robinson, Donald L. "Inherent Powers." In *The Oxford Companion to the Supreme Court.* Edited by Kermit L. Hall. New York: Oxford University Press, 1992.

Stephen B. Presser

See also **Constitution of the United States.**

INHERITANCE TAX LAWS. Two types of death duties are popularly called inheritance taxes. They are levied, essentially, as excise taxes on the right to transfer property at time of death. The primary death tax has been the federal estate tax, which is based on the net value of the deceased's estate. In addition, most states have imposed inheritance taxes, based on the value of the shares received by individual heirs.

The federal government adopted an estate tax in 1916. Prior to that, it had imposed an inheritance tax on three occasions: 1797–1802, 1862–1870, and 1898–1902. These acts were all initially adopted as emergency revenue measures. In addition, the income tax statute of 1894 taxed, as income, money and personal property received by inheritance, but this law was held unconstitutional. A federal gift tax was first enacted in 1924, repealed in 1926, and revived in 1932. This tax was designed to complement the estate tax by taxing transfers that would reduce the donor's taxable estate. In 1976, the estate and gift tax structures were combined into a single unified gift and estate tax system, which might be more accurately described as a wealth transfer tax.

Estate and gift tax rates have been designed to be progressive, with exemptions for the vast majority. The exemption was initially $50,000, and this fluctuated within a narrow band through 1976, when it was $60,000. At this point, estate taxes returns were filed following about 8 percent of adult deaths. By 1986, the exemption rose to $500,000 and only about 1 percent of adult deaths yielded estate taxes. From 1941 until 1976, the marginal tax rate started at 3 percent and climbed to 77 percent on estates exceeding $10,000,000. The top marginal rate was cut to 50 percent in 1981. The share of federal revenue from estate and gift taxes has generally fallen over time, averaging over 4 percent in 1941, 1.5 to 2 percent between 1945 and 1980, and a bit over 1 percent during the 1990s. Simultaneously, estate tax law has grown progressively more complicated, with provisions for marital deductions, generation-skipping transfers, the valuation of business assets, deductions for charitable contributions, conservation easements, credits for state death taxes, and tax deferral, among others.

Inheritance, estate, and gift taxes were originally seen as a method of breaking up large accumulations of wealth without harming the economy. Beginning in the late 1970s, however, empirical studies by economists across the political spectrum began to question the efficacy of these taxes, showing that they had little impact on the wealth distribution and suggesting that they created incentives for owners of capital to transfer resources away from their most productive uses. Analysis suggested that the estate tax increased the effective tax burden on capital income, thus discouraging saving, encouraging consumption, and reducing long-run economic growth. Economists estimated that the costs of complying with or avoiding these taxes were as large as the revenues raised by the tax and that they may actually result in net losses for the federal government. Others complained that these taxes unfairly hit those not adept at estate planning and required the breakup of family farms and businesses. Opponents caught the public's attention by labeling them "death taxes." In a 1982 referendum, Californians voted two to one to eliminate that state's inheritance taxes. Other states followed suit, as did Canada, Australia, and Israel. In 2001, President George W. Bush signed a bill that gradually increased exemptions (from $1 million to $3.5 million) and slightly reduced the top tax rate between 2002 and 2009, before completely eliminating the federal estate tax in 2010. However, the law reverts back to the initial levels in 2011, unless otherwise changed.

BIBLIOGRAPHY

Gale, William G., and Joel B. Slemrod. "Policy Watch: Death Watch for the Estate Tax?" *Journal of Economic Perspectives* 15, no. 1 (2001): 205–218.

Joint Economic Committee Study, U.S. Congress. "The Economics of the Estate Tax." December 1998. http://www.house.gov/jec/fiscal/tx-grwth/estattax/estattax.pdf

Joulfaian, David. "A Quarter Century of Estate Tax Reforms." *National Tax Journal* 53, no. 3 (September 2000): 343–360.

Pechman, Joseph. *Federal Tax Policy.* 5th ed. Washington, D.C.: Brookings Institution, 1987.

Robert Whaples

See also **Income Tax Cases; Taxation.**

INITIATIVE, the process by which citizens, rather than legislators, propose statutes or constitutional amendments and place them before voters for approval. The initiative is not applicable at the federal level because the U.S. Constitution vests all national legislative powers in Congress, but by 2001 twenty-four states and the District of Columbia allowed the process in some form. All jurisdictions require the proponent to gather signatures from state residents, usually 5 to 10 percent of the electorate, supporting a vote on the issue, and some regulate the nature or wording of the issue. Where the direct initiative is employed, the proposition goes directly on the ballot. In states with an indirect initiative, the proposal must be submitted first to the legislature, which may adopt it or send it to the voters, possibly with modifications.

The initiative grew out of the popular disenchantment with state legislatures that gave rise to the Populist and Progressive movements in the late nineteenth and early twentieth centuries. Reformers, angered by the influence of big business on government and what they saw as unresponsiveness and corruption among elected representatives, sought to restore "direct democracy" and allow the people to participate in policymaking and hold politicians accountable. From 1898 to 1918, nineteen states, beginning with South Dakota, provided for the initiative, and the process was one element of the Progressive Party platform of presidential candidate Theodore Roosevelt in 1912.

From its first actual use in Oregon in 1904 until 2001, approximately 2,000 initiatives have appeared on state ballots, and voters approved about 40 percent of them. Initiative use is something of a regional phenomenon, as six states alone account for nearly two-thirds of its use—Oregon, California, Colorado, North Dakota, Arizona, and Washington, in that order. New or relatively young western states facing problems of economic development and political discontent were more likely to adopt the process, while strong political parties often blocked it in the East and South. There have been three periods of greatest use of the device: the 1910s, during the Progressive era; the 1930s, during the Great Depression and New Deal; and in the last two decades of the twentieth century. In all three periods, strong social movements arose questioning the ability of government to provide for public needs and calling for more democratic or populist reforms. Among recent initiative propositions there have been questions on taxation, term limits for elected officials, and public morality issues such as gambling, abortion, and gun control.

Advocates of the initiative argue that it represents a genuine forum for democratic participation in policymaking, operates as a safety valve for political discontent, and helps shape the agenda of public officials. Skeptics charge that it circumvents the more deliberative legislative process and allows well-organized and well-funded special interests to take advantage of impassioned, even irresponsible, public opinion, possibly to the detriment of minority groups. There is no clear correlation between the influence of money or the media and the outcome of a proposition, though initiative campaigns increasingly rely on professional polling and marketing services rather than on grassroots volunteers.

BIBLIOGRAPHY

Bowler, Shaun, Todd Donovan, and Caroline J. Tolbert, eds. *Citizens as Legislators: Direct Democracy in the United States.* Columbus: Ohio State University Press, 1998.

Cronin, Thomas E. *Direct Democracy: The Politics of Initiative, Referendum, and Recall.* Cambridge, Mass.: Harvard University Press, 1989.

Ellis, Richard J. *Democratic Delusions: The Initiative Process in America.* Lawrence: University Press of Kansas, 2002.

Jeffrey T. Coster

See also **Proposition 13; Proposition 187; Proposition 209.**

INJUNCTIONS, LABOR. In the late nineteenth century, America saw a dramatic increase in state intervention against labor protest. Beginning with the railway strikes of the 1870s and spreading to every major industry by century's end, the nation's courts vastly enlarged their role in regulating and policing industrial conflict through labor injunctions.

The substantive law governing the bounds of workers' collective action changed little from the beginning of the nineteenth century until the first and second decades of the twentieth century. Strikes to improve wages and working conditions at individual workplaces were legal, but boycotting or striking to gain union recognition or to support fellow workers in "unfair" shops was outlawed. What changed, then, was not the substantive law but its application.

Until the late nineteenth century, conspiracy trials were the chief way that courts enforced this body of law; and they were rare. By 1895, conspiracy prosecutions for strike activities had dwindled to a handful each year, while labor injunctions were multiplying. By a conservative reckoning, at least 4,300 injunctions were issued between 1880 and 1930—by the 1920s 25 percent of strikes were limited by injunctions. While capital consolidated and individual plants and firms merged into large-scale, nationwide corporations, workers' ability to join together to enlarge their economic might was sharply curtailed.

The switch in form from conspiracy trial to injunction also signified an enormous increase in the pervasiveness of judicial regulation. Every injunction represented a new, particularized set of legal commands—a kind of custom-made criminal statute—addressed to strikers and often to whole working-class communities, or to all the members of a national union. A single injunction's language often ranged from the broadest proscriptions against interfering with a plaintiff-employer's business to prohibiting the aiding or abetting of a strike or boycott down to the most minute tactics and customs. The appeal of the labor injunction from an employer's perspective lay not only in this breadth, but also in the ease and swiftness of obtaining and enforcing it. The criminal process was slow; but one could appear before an equity judge with a handful of affidavits and obtain a temporary decree against a strike in a matter of hours; one did not even have to notify the defendants until after the order was issued. Local juries, moreover, often stymied criminal prosecutions against strikers, but strikers accused of violating an injunction were tried by the judge who issued the decree. Juries often acquitted, lending popular legitimacy to the underlying labor action, whereas judges almost always meted out jail sentences. Injunction proceedings circumvented more than just local juries. An injunction suit could be used to override the judgments of local mayors, sheriffs, and police chiefs, whom courts as well as employers constantly accused of siding with strikers.

Thus, in the late nineteenth and early twentieth century, the labor injunction enabled hostile employers and public officials to depict peaceful protest and mutual aid as the acts of outlaws. From the 1890s until the New Deal, the chief political goal of the American Federation of Labor (AFL) was repealing this judge-made law. Repeatedly, trade unionists brought to state and federal lawmakers their stories of broken strikes and their claims of constitutional wrongs by the nation's courts—of judicial violations of the freedom of speech and association, and the freedom to quit, individually and in concert. From the 1890s through the 1920s, labor prevailed on both state legislatures and Congress to pass roughly forty "anti-injunction statutes," loosening the judge-made restraints on collective action. However, at least twenty-five of these statutes were voided on constitutional grounds, and most of those not struck down were vitiated by narrow construction. Until the Great Depression and the New Deal, courts had both the power and the will to trump these measures. In 1932, Congress enacted the NORRIS-LAGUARDIA ACT, which stripped federal courts of authority to issue injunctions in labor disputes. The new anti-injunction law did not undergo Supreme Court scrutiny until 1938. By then, however, New Deal judges and jurisprudence had begun to vanquish the old legal order, of which "government by injunction" had been a central pillar.

BIBLIOGRAPHY

Forbath, William E. *Law and the Shaping of the American Labor Movement.* Cambridge, Mass.: Harvard University Press, 1991.

Frankfurter, Felix, and Nathan Greene. *The Labor Injunction.* New York: Macmillan, 1930.

William E. Forbath

See also **American Federation of Labor–Congress of Industrial Organizations; Collective Bargaining; Labor Legislation and Administration; Picketing; Right-to-Work Laws; Strikes; Taft-Hartley Act; Yellow-Dog Contract.**

INLAND LOCK NAVIGATION.

In 1792 the New York legislature granted charters to the Western Inland Lock Navigation Company to open water communication along the Mohawk River between the Hudson River and Lakes Ontario and Seneca. The legislature also granted charters to the Northern Inland Lock Navigation Company to connect the Hudson with Lakes George and Champlain, which, for lack of money, it never succeeded in accomplishing. The Western Company, by locks and short canals, opened a crude navigation between the Hudson and the lakes, but it never earned a profit and was eliminated after the completion of the Erie Canal in 1825.

BIBLIOGRAPHY

Bourne, Russell. *Floating West: The Erie and Other American Canals.* New York: Norton, 1992.

Shaw, Ronald E. *Canals for a Nation: The Canal Era in the United States, 1790–1860.* Lexington: University Press of Kentucky, 1990.

Alvin F. Harlow / A. E.

See also **Canals; Erie Canal.**

INLAND WATERWAYS COMMISSION.

By the beginning of the twentieth century, conservationists regarded development of the nation's waterways as an integral component of CONSERVATION policy. In 1907 President Theodore Roosevelt appointed the Inland Waterways Commission to prepare "a comprehensive plan for the improvement and control" of U.S. river systems. In 1908 the commission submitted a bulky preliminary report on rivers, lakes, canals, and railroad competition, urging that future plans for navigation improvement take account of water purification, power development, flood control, and land reclamation. Congress created the NATIONAL WATERWAYS COMMISSION in 1909 to carry on the work of the Inland Waterways Commission.

BIBLIOGRAPHY

Hull, William J., and Robert W. Hull. *The Origin and Development of the Waterways Policy of the United States.* Washington, D.C.: National Waterways Conference, 1967.

Hunchey, James R., et al. *United States Inland Waterways and Ports.* Fort Belvoir, Va.: U.S. Army Engineers Institute for Water Resources, 1985.

William J. Petersen / C. P.

See also **River and Harbor Improvements; Waterways, Inland.**

INSECTICIDES AND HERBICIDES.

Farmers first discovered cultural and physical pest controls such as crop rotations, nutrient management, intercropping, and residue destruction. They also learned to use dust prepared from plants containing naturally occurring insecticides, such as nicotine and pyrethrum. Applied entomologists studied the life history of insects, seeking the keys to control strategies. U.S. Department of Agriculture entomologists imported a predaceous ladybug, known as the Vedalia beetle, from Australia in 1888 to control cottony-cushion scale on California citrus trees. The spectacular success touched off a quest for biological control agents.

The use of chemical arsenical compounds as insecticides dates from at least 1681. Paris green and London purple, both arsenical insecticides, became the main stomach poisons of chewing insects in the late nineteenth and early twentieth centuries. Other uses of insecticides in the late nineteenth century included carbon bisulfide to disinfect stored grain and control root lice and hydrocyanic acid gas to fumigate California citrus trees. In 1880, lime sulfite was employed against the San Jose scale, and in 1882 the grape phylloxera was controlled with naphthalene. Lead arsenate, first used against the gypsy moth in New England forests in 1892, was used against the cotton boll weevil until the development of calcium arsenate was recommended in 1916. In 1906, the U.S. Department of Agriculture began using arsenical dips against the Texas fever-carrying cattle tick.

During World War II, many new chlorinated hydrocarbon insecticides were produced, DDT being the most effective and widely used. These organic, contact insecticides (usually attacking the nervous system) proved more effective than the internal arsenicals, which often scorched plants during application and built up toxic residues in the soil. But with the publication of Rachel Carson's *Silent Spring* in 1962, people became increasingly aware of the danger such insecticides posed to other animal life. The Environmental Protection Agency banned most uses of DDT in December 1972. Scientists concentrated more on developing the organophosphorous and carbamate insecticides, which generally circumvented the problem of transmittable residues but were more toxic to man and animals during application. The Department of Agriculture also developed systemic insecticides to protect plants and animals. In 1958, ronnel became the first systemic insecticide ingested by cattle to kill the cattle grub.

The so-called second generation of insecticides encountered two other problems: development of insect resistance and killing of nontargeted insects. In some cases, pests quickly developed resistance to organophosphates, increasing the impact of both major and previously minor pests. Furthermore, when these broad-spectrum pesticides killed parasites and predators, minor pests were released from natural controls and exploded into major pest status.

In the 1960s, entomologists started preaching integrated pest management (IPM), which utilized mutually supporting systems of cultural, biological, chemical, and other controls. Pheromones, sexual attractants, and sterile-males techniques were added to the strategies. Genes from strains of the naturally occurring bacterium *Bacillus thuringiensis* were introduced into several crops to ward off insect damage. Insecticides continued to be a part of IPM, but more recently developed insecticides (pyrethroids, insect growth regulators, neonicotinoids) were generally targeted to a narrower range of insects and were applied in lower doses.

American and European scientists discovered several chemicals that acted as herbicides in certain situations, including copper salts, carbolic acid, caustic soda, arsenical compounds, and kerosene. But expense, the toxicity of arsenical compounds to plants, the flammability of oils, and the lack of selectivity retarded the use of chemical weed killers. Farmers generally relied on mowing, cultivation, hoeing, fire, and crop rotation to combat weeds.

Some agriculturists recognized that it would be desirable to eliminate frequent plowing and cultivation, which bared the soil to wind and water erosion and caused the loss of organic matter and soil compaction. Just before World War II, researchers in the United States and Canada experimented with "trashy fallow." The idea was to pull blades under the soil surface to cut off the moisture-sapping roots, leaving wheat stubble and other crop residues on the surface. Plant growth regulators presented the possibility of planting through the crop residues. The herbicide 2,4D, released for use in 1946, selected broadleaf plants and was used to control weeds in grasses, including wheat, oats, and corn. By the late 1950s, herbicides such as paraquat and diquat, which killed all herbaceous plants, had been introduced. These herbicides had the added advantage of being deactivated when they touched the ground, leaving the soil ready to accept the next crop. During the 1950s and 1970s, researchers tested combinations of equipment, chemicals, and growing methods. The Farm Bill of 1985 gave no-till and other forms of reduced tillage, known collectively as conservation tillage, a boost. The law required that farmers who received assistance from the Department of Agriculture, including price support payments, had to reduce erosion on highly erodible land to an acceptable level. Conservation tillage utilizing herbicides was the most cost-effective way for many farmers to meet the requirements. Farmers utilized conservation tillage methods on 73 million acres in 1990, 98 million acres in 1995, and 108 million acres in 2000.

BIBLIOGRAPHY

Berenbaum, May R. *Bugs in the System: Insects and Their Impact on Human Affairs.* Reading, Mass.: Addison-Wesley, 1995.

Insects: The Yearbook of Agriculture. Washington, D.C.: U.S. Department of Agriculture, 1952.

Little, Charles E. *Green Fields Forever: The Conservation Tillage Revolution in America.* Washington, D.C.: Island Press, 1987.

Sprague, Milton A., and Glover B. Triplett, eds. *No-Tillage and Surface Tillage Agriculture.* New York: Wiley, 1986.

Douglas Helms

See also **Agricultural Price Support; Agriculture.**

INSIDER TRADING. Gaining an unfair advantage in buying or selling securities based on nonpublic information, or insider trading, has plagued Wall Street from its earliest days. Prior to the formation of the Securities and Exchange Commission (SEC) in 1934 in response to the stock market crash of 1929, insider trading occurred more frequently. Since the mid-1930s, the SEC has regulated trading and attempted to make it a trustworthy system. Spotting and prosecuting illegal insider trades has been a major priority.

Although insider trading is usually associated with illegal activity, it also happens when corporate officers, directors, and employees buy and sell stock within their own companies, for example, exercising stock options. Legal insider trading occurs every day and is permitted within the rules and regulations of the individual company and federal regulations governing this kind of trade, which the SEC requires be reported. Because legal insider trading is reported to the SEC, it is considered part of normal business activity. Illegal insider trading, however, is corrupt, since all parties involved do not have all the information necessary to make informed decisions. Most often, the average investor is duped in insider trading scandals.

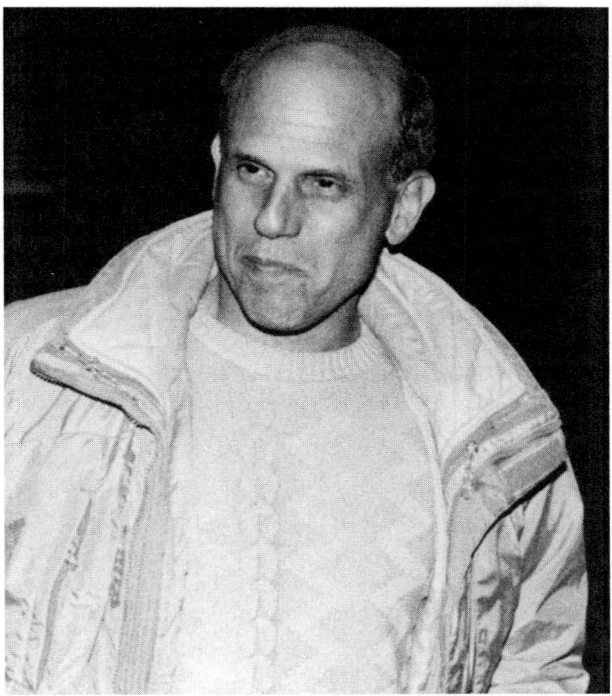

Michael Milken. A 1993 photograph of the 1980s junk bond king, who was brought down by charges of insider trading that resulted in guilty pleas, a short prison term, and an unprecedented $600 million in fines for securities fraud. GETTY IMAGES

Illegal insider trading gained great notoriety in the 1980s, epitomized by the criminal charges brought against junk bond king Michael Milken and financial speculator Ivan Boesky. The hit motion picture *Wall Street* (1987) centered on insider trading and brought the catchphrase "greed is good" into the popular lexicon. Tom Wolfe's best-selling novel *Bonfire of the Vanities* (1987) employs a Milken-like figure as its main character.

Given that in the late twentieth century people placed a larger percentage of their money in the stock market and that they tied retirement funds to stock-based 401K programs, any hint of an unfair advantage undermines the spirit of fairness that the general public associates with democracy and capitalism. Breaches in insider trading laws and enforcement efforts routinely become headline news, which helps perpetuate the idea that the stock market is a dependable institution.

Insider trading is punishable by hefty fines and imprisonment, and is prosecuted as a civil offense. Milken pleaded guilty to six counts filed against him and paid fines of $600 million, the most ever levied against an individual. The SEC has broad authority to investigate violations of securities laws, including subpoena power and the ability to freeze profits from illegal activities. In the early years of the twenty-first century, insider trading returned to the forefront of the national conscience as a result of the downfall of Houston-based energy company Enron and many other corporations that used illegal accounting procedures to artificially bolster stock prices.

BIBLIOGRAPHY

Chernow, Ron. *The House of Morgan: An American Banking Dynasty and the Rise of Modern Finance.* New York: Atlantic Monthly Press, 1990.

Gordon, John Steele. *The Great Game: The Emergence of Wall Street As a World Power, 1653–2000.* New York: Scribner, 1999.

Holbrook, Stewart H. *The Age of Moguls: The Story of the Robber Barons and the Great Tycoons.* New York: Doubleday, 1954.

Stewart, James B. *Den of Thieves.* New York: Simon and Schuster, 1991.

Bob Batchelor

See also **Stock Market.**

INSPECTION, GOVERNMENTAL. One way that federal, state, and local governments enforce their regulations. Most inspections pertain to safety (e.g., elevators), health (e.g., eggs), or environmental protection (e.g., clean air). Inspection can be controversial. Some critics argue that it violates the constitutional protection against unreasonable searches, and courts have occasionally ruled that regulatory agencies must obtain warrants before conducting inspections. Others contend that the protection of public health and safety supersedes the right to privacy.

Though businesses have typically considered inspections to be unnecessary government interference, some of the first American inspection laws were passed on behalf of commercial interests. In the mid-eighteenth century, for example, the tobacco colonies of Virginia and Maryland initiated tobacco inspection to raise prices, which were low because too many growers tried to sell "junk tobacco."

A few inspection programs geared toward consumer protection appeared in the early nineteenth century. For instance, many cities created health agencies empowered to conduct inspections when epidemics struck. Nevertheless, government regulation and inspection did not really take off until after the Civil War, when a hectic new society characterized by rapid immigration, industrialization, and urbanization seemed to require elaborate forms of control.

Facing another cholera outbreak, New York City in 1866 created an extremely powerful Metropolitan Board of Health to deal with the problem. Dozens of inspectors were assigned to specific neighborhoods to clean streets and dispose of garbage and thereby prevent the spread of the disease. The epidemic was less severe in New York than in most other American cities, many of which soon adopted rigorous programs of health and sanitary inspection of their own. Gradually over the next several decades, cities hired inspectors to enforce a number of new building, fire, and health codes. States were also involved in early regulation and inspection efforts, such as mine inspection in Illinois and agricultural inspection in Wisconsin. All these efforts belonged to the emerging Progressive movement, whose members believed that only an active government could curb abuses of private power.

The federal government was slower to enact Progressive legislation, but after the Interstate Commerce Commission was created to regulate railroads in 1887, Congress started using its power under the commerce clause to regulate and inspect a variety of industries. The most important regulatory legislation of the Progressive Era provided for the inspection of food products. A weak law covering ham and bacon for export passed in 1890, followed the next year by legislation covering most kinds of meat for domestic and foreign markets. Early in 1906, Upton Sinclair published his muckraking novel, *The Jungle*, which documented the awful squalor of meatpacking plants. President Theodore Roosevelt ordered an investigation, and Congress passed the Meat Inspection Act and the Pure Food and Drug Act on the same day (the Pure Food and Drug Act did not mandate inspection until it was amended in 1938). These 1906 laws were pillars of Progressive regulation, and similar legislation in a number of other areas quickly followed. In 1911 Congress created the Bureau of Mines to monitor mine safety, and federal grain inspection began in 1916.

The biggest post–Progressive Era wave of regulation and inspection came in the late 1960s and early 1970s, another period in which grassroots consumer and environmental movements were agitating for a more active government. After the consumer advocate Ralph Nader published his auto safety expose *Unsafe at Any Speed* (1965), more than ten states passed new auto inspection laws. In 1970, Congress established two large and important regulatory agencies: the Occupational Health and Safety Administration (OSHA), which inspects workplaces, and the Environmental Protection Agencies, which inspects air and water quality.

By the late 1970s and early 1980s, however, regulation had fallen out of favor. President Ronald Reagan promised to limit the role of government, and he started by slashing the budgets of regulatory agencies. Though George H. W. Bush and Bill Clinton slowed the trend, regulation and inspection has not enjoyed the full support of government since Reagan took office.

Although a wealth of regulatory agencies continue to do their work, inspection is often spotty due to budget and staff limitations. OSHA inspectors, for example, cannot cover all 6.2 million workplaces in the country. Spurts of regulation and inspection have tended to follow disastrous events and popular movements. In normal times, communities' inspection needs often slip under the radar.

BIBLIOGRAPHY

Eisner, Marc Allen. *Regulatory Politics in Transition.* 2d ed. Baltimore: Johns Hopkins University Press, 2000.

Goodwin, Lorine Swainston. *The Pure Food, Drink, and Drug Crusaders, 1879–1914.* Jefferson, N.C.: McFarland, 1999.

Mintz, Joel A. *Enforcement at the EPA: High Stakes and Hard Choices.* Austin: University of Texas Press, 1995.

Rosenberg, Charles E. *The Cholera Years: The United States in 1832, 1849, and 1866.* Chicago: University of Chicago Press, 1987.

Jeremy Derfner

See also **Food and Drug Administration; Muckrakers; Pure Food and Drug Movement.**

INSTALLMENT BUYING, SELLING, AND FINANCING

INSTALLMENT BUYING, SELLING, AND FINANCING refers to the use of short- and intermediate-term CREDIT to finance the purchase of goods and services for personal consumption, scheduled to be repaid in two or more installments. Statistics supplied by the board of governors of the Federal Reserve System show the amounts of credit extended and outstanding to finance automobiles, mobile homes, and other consumer goods. Data on home repair and modernization loans and personal loans reflect the use of cash installment loans to acquire consumer goods and services.

The origin of installment sales credit lies in the open-book credit provided consumers by retailers in colonial times. Although there were no formally scheduled payments, business proprietors expected consumers to pay when funds were available. In agricultural areas, this arrangement meant that retailers extended credit from crop to crop. In 1807 the furniture firm of Cowperthwaite and Sons first introduced consumer installment selling. In about 1850, the Singer Sewing Machine Company began to sell its products on the installment plan. After the CIVIL WAR, manufacturers of pianos, organs, encyclopedias, and stoves were quick to broaden their markets by providing for installment payments.

The single largest component of consumer installment credit is AUTOMOBILE credit. Installment financing of consumers' automobile purchases began in 1910. Sales finance companies formed to purchase the installment notes of consumers from automobile dealers. In 1915 the Guarantee Securities Company began buying consumers' installment notes from Willys-Overland dealers. Other firms that entered the field were the Commercial Credit Company of Baltimore, the Commercial Investment Trust of New York, and the National Bond and Investment Company of Chicago. By the end of 1917 as many as twenty-five companies were financing automobiles. By 1925 this number swelled to a peak of about 1,700. After 1930, commercial banks became active in financing automobiles and gradually came to dominate the market. In the mid-1970s the major automobile sales finance companies were factory-owned subsidiaries: General Motors

Acceptance Corporation, Ford Motor Credit Company, and Chrysler Financial Corporation. Commercial banks held about 60 percent of outstanding automobile installment credit; finance companies, 25 percent; and other financial lenders, principally credit unions, 15 percent.

The development of installment selling was an accompaniment to, and prerequisite of, the growth of the mass production of a variety of consumer durable goods, of which the automobile was the most significant. As they gained experience, firms providing installment credit gradually lowered required down payments and lengthened the maturities of contracts, thus making credit available to more and more consumers. In 1924 the National Association of Finance Companies adopted standards of a minimum down payment of one-third of the cash price for a new car and two-fifths for a used car, with a maximum maturity of twelve months for both classes. By 1937 maturities had generally lengthened to eighteen months and by 1952 to twenty-four months on new cars. During 1955, a further lengthening to thirty-six months fostered a rapid growth in new-car sales, and in the early 1970s, some contracts allowed for repayment over forty-two and even forty-eight months. By 2002, sixty-month loan periods were common in the auto industry, as higher car prices made it necessary to extend repayment periods.

In addition to longer payment terms, a new finance option became available that made cars more affordable. Called "leasing," consumers essentially "rented" a car from a dealer, as they paid only for the portion of the car that they used over a set period of time, usually twenty-four or thirty-six months. At the end of the lease, the car was returned to the automobile dealer instead of becoming the property of the lease-holder, as there was still a large amount of the car's purchase price that remained unpaid. The consumer then had an option to purchase the leased vehicle (for a price that represented the unpaid amount of the car's value after the lease had been paid), which meant that a new sales repayment contract was negotiated, or they could simply walk away from the deal and choose to lease or purchase a new vehicle from that or another dealer. First popular in the early 1990s, the Better Business Bureau estimated that leasing would account for 33 percent of new car sales in the year 2002.

By the end of the 1920s, retailers other than automobile dealers offered two primary types of credit plan: the thirty-day charge account and the installment account that a specific purchase generated and secured. Buyers seldom paid the thirty-day account in thirty days. In 1938, to provide customers more extended terms on a formal basis, Wanamaker's of Philadelphia introduced the first revolving credit plan for soft goods. Although the permitted payment period was four months, no charge accrued for the use of the credit service. After World War II, as restrictions on all forms of installment credit disappeared, the modern revolving charge account emerged as a credit arrangement that enabled a consumer to buy from time to time, charging purchases against an open line of credit, and to repay at least from one-tenth to one-sixth of the unpaid balance outstanding at the end of a billing cycle. Credit users pay some portion of the cost of providing this service through a monthly charge ranging from 1 to 1.5 percent of a specified unpaid balance.

A later innovation in credit selling was the development of bank charge credit plans, first inaugurated in 1951 by the Franklin National Bank of New York. A plastic credit card issued by a bank provided participating retailers with evidence that the bank has granted the consumer a line of credit. After making a sale, the retailer deposited the sales slip with the bank and receives a credit to his or her account, less a discount from the face of the sales slip. The bank then billed the consumer monthly for his or her accumulated purchases on the credit card. As in the case of retail revolving credit, if the consumer pays within a specified grace period, there is no finance charge. After that point the finance charge levied monthly parallels that assessed by retailers. In the early 2000s, the use of CREDIT CARDS had reached almost epidemic proportions in the United States. Nearly every person in the country had at least one card, and credit companies had started targeting younger and younger consumers, usually those of college age. Interest rates also became much higher—as high as the mid-20 percent range—as more and more people overextended and defaulted on their credit card debt.

An increasing amount of state and federal legislation has governed consumer installment credit. At the state level, in 1968 the National Conference of Commissioners of Uniform State Laws introduced the Uniform Consumer Credit Code to replace existing segmented state laws affecting consumer credit. At the federal level the Consumer Credit Protection (or Truth-in-Lending) Act (1969) required disclosure of finance charges as annual percentage rates. In 1974 other federal legislation significantly affecting consumer credit came into effect. The Fair Credit Billing Act protects consumers against inaccurate and unfair credit billing and credit card practices. The purpose of the Equal Credit Opportunity Act is to require credit grantors to make credit equally available to all creditworthy customers, regardless of sex or marital status.

BIBLIOGRAPHY

"BBB Warns Consumers That Auto Leasing Isn't for Everyone." Better Business Bureau Serving Metropolitan New York. Available from http://www.newyork.bbb.org/alerts/buying.html.

Guttmann, Robert. *How Credit-Money Shapes the Economy: The United States in a Global System*. Armonk, NY: M.E. Sharpe, 1994.

Mandell, Lewis. *The Credit Card Industry: A History*. Boston: Twayne, 1990.

Ommer, Rosemary E., ed. *Merchant Credit and Labour Strategies in Historical Perspective*. Fredericton, New Brunswick, Canada: Acadiensis Press, 1990.

Schor, Juliet B. *The Overspent American: Upscaling, Downshifting, and the New Consumer.* New York: Basic Books, 1998.

Robert W. Johnson / A. E.

See also **Automobile Industry; Consumer Protection; Economic Indicators; Financial Services Industry; Sewing Machine.**

INSTITUTE FOR ADVANCED STUDY. The Institute for Advanced Study at Princeton, New Jersey, was founded in 1930 by a gift from Louis Bamberger and his sister, Caroline Bamberger Fuld. During the preceding year, they had decided to sell their business, R. H. Macy and Company, and devote their time and fortune to philanthropic endeavors. Although they remained involved in structuring and formulating the Institute, they created a board of trustees and a directorship to supervise academic programs and oversee administration. Abraham Flexner, a classicist as well as an innovator of American medical education, was chosen as the first director and, in many ways, determined the Institute's future course.

In an early letter to the board of trustees, the founders envisioned the Institute as a place for "the pursuit of advanced learning and exploration in fields of pure science and high scholarship to the utmost degree that the facilities of the institution and the ability of the faculty and students will permit." The Institute has retained the spirit of the founders' vision, while also revising its particular mission. The Bambergers had initially imagined establishing an entirely new university, but as they discussed their ideas with Flexner, they devised a new model of scholarship, unburdened by the administrative demands of a university. Primarily under the leadership of Flexner, the Institute carved out an identity somewhere between the traditional roles of university and research institute. The Institute still does not award any higher degrees and does not provide any formal graduate training. Its small size and highly specialized academic agenda remain points of pride.

In the fall of 1932, Albert Einstein and Oswald Veblen were approved as the first academic appointments to the Institute's newly established School of Mathematics. Two years later, the Schools of Humanistic Studies and Politics were added to the Institute's academic scope. In the following six decades, the Institute formally designated five areas of study, including the Schools of Mathematics (1933), Historical Studies (1948), Natural Sciences (1966), Social Sciences (1973), and, most recently, Theoretical Biology (1998). Each school has a small permanent faculty but relies quite heavily on the academic strength and contributions of the approximately 180 fellows invited to the Institute each year.

Although the Institute enjoys a close, symbiotic relationship with nearby Princeton University, it is administratively and financially independent. Funding comes from a number of different private and public sources, including gifts from corporations and individuals and grants from government agencies. Fellows and faculty of the Institute are given the opportunity to explore Princeton's resources and attend lectures and seminars sponsored by the university, but they are not expected to teach any courses. Likewise, members of the Princeton community can attend events at Institute facilities.

The historical moment of the Institute's founding, when Nazism and fascism were on the rise in Europe, set a precedent for close ties to the international scholarly community. In its early years, the Institute provided academic asylum for many refugee scholars from the Continent. To this day, the Institute invites scholars from around the world to engage in serious learning and research. It also is committed to providing opportunities for new scholars to focus on their independent work in the company of other scholars, without the demands of teaching. The Institute houses its faculty and fellows and offers a number of cultural activities, lectures, and seminars to foster a sense of academic exchange.

Over the last decades of the twentieth century the faculty of the Institute has included scholars such as Clifford Geertz, George Kennan, Joan Wallach Scott, and Michael Walzer. From 1991, Phillip A. Griffiths served as director.

BIBLIOGRAPHY

The Institute for Advanced Study: Some Introductory Information. Princeton, N.J., 1975.

Institute for Advanced Study home page at http://www.ias.edu.

Lila Corwin Berman

See also **Princeton University.**

INSTRUCTIONS, issued to every royal governor on his departure for the colonies, delineated the specific powers established in the governor's commission. They were most often prepared in the king's name by special committees of the Privy Council or, subsequent to its organization in 1696, the Board of Trade, in consultation with English merchants, other royal officials, and colonial agents. Royal governors received instructions on every facet of colonial administration, including colonial councils and assemblies, finances, the courts, military matters, trade, navigation, commerce, and religious establishment.

A newly appointed governor sometimes had the opportunity to make suggestions about his own instructions. The Board of Trade also consulted royal commissioners, including those of the Admiralty, the Treasury, and the Customs. English merchants wielded considerable influence in the drafting of instructions. Merchants who objected to colonial legislation had only to petition the Board of Trade, which, in keeping with mercantilist interests, disallowed laws "prejudicial to the trading interests of Great Britain." Colonists objected to those trade-based instructions that seemed frequently to represent

British interests at the expense of the colonists. Such instructions, however, were issued to nearly all of the royal governors until the American Revolution.

BIBLIOGRAPHY

Labaree, Leonard Woods. *Royal Government in America.* 2d ed. New York: Frederick Ungar, 1964.

———, ed. *Royal Instructions to British Colonial Governors, 1670–1776.* New York: D. Appleton-Century, 1935. Reprint, New York: Octagon Books, 1967.

Leslie J. Lindenauer

See also **Board of Trade and Plantations; Colonial Policy, British; Privy Council; Royal Disallowance.**

INSULAR CASES. Following its victory in the Spanish-American War (1898), the United States acquired Hawaii, Puerto Rico, Guam, and the Philippines. In the Insular Cases (1901–1922), the U.S. Supreme Court determined the constitutional and political status of the new territories. In *De Lima v. Bidwell* (1901), a customs dispute, a 5-to-4 majority ruled that Puerto Rico was not a "foreign country" for tariff purposes. In subsequent cases, the Court addressed the territories' relationship to the United States and whether "the Constitution follows the flag"; that is, whether and how constitutional provisions applied to these acquisitions. Many of the later cases were also decided by divided Courts, reflecting disagreement about the constitutional issues underlying American expansionism.

The "incorporation" approach emerged as a central doctrine in the Court's decisions. This principle held that incorporated territories—those that Congress intended to become part of the United States and, eventually, states—were directly protected by the Constitution as written. However, it also held that only a limited set of rights applied to unincorporated possessions that Congress had not yet determined to make permanent parts of the Union. Thus, in *Rassmussen v. United States* (1905), the Court ruled that the Sixth Amendment required jury trials in Alaskan criminal cases because Alaska had been incorporated into the United States, while in *Dorr v. United States* (1904), it determined that jury trials were not required in the Philippine Islands, because they had not been incorporated. Puerto Rico, for which the doctrine of the Insular Cases would have the most enduring consequences, was unincorporated, according to *Downes v. Bidwell* (1901). Thus, it was treated as subject to the political authority of Congress, unrestrained by the full protections of the Constitution.

BIBLIOGRAPHY

Kerr, James. *The Insular Cases: The Role of the Judiciary in American Expansionism.* Port Washington, N.Y.: Kennikat Press, 1982.

Ramos, Efren Rivera. "The Legal Construction of American Colonialism: The Insular Cases (1901–1922)." *Revista Jurídica Universidad de Puerto Rico* 65 (1996): 225–328.

Torruella, Juan R. *The Supreme Court and Puerto Rico: The Doctrine of Separate and Unequal.* Río Piedras: University of Puerto Rico, 1985.

Gabriel J. Chin
Diana Yoon

See also **Guam; Hawaii; Puerto Rico; Territories of the United States.**

INSURANCE. The insurance business, one of the oldest in America, has its roots in the early years of the Republic, when the nation's business was carried on primarily in seaport coffeehouses, the gathering point for sea captains, merchants, and bankers. Marine and fire insurance were the earliest forms of the property and liability branch of the insurance business; later additions include inland marine, aviation, workers' compensation, automobile, multiple-line, and suretyship insurance. Marine insurance has been a necessary adjunct to commerce, and insurance against losses from frequent fires in colonial seaports also had a colorful history.

The other major branches of insurance, life and health, did not assume importance until the 1840s, when the Industrial Revolution created a need for security that land had traditionally given to a nation of farmers. The Mutual Life Insurance Company of New York, which began writing policies in 1843, was the first commercial life insurance company making policies available to the general public. Health insurance began as accident insurance about 1850. The first auto insurance was issued in 1898.

Marine Insurance

The first marine insurance policies sold in America were contracted through the local agents of English underwriters in the coffeehouses of American seaports. Always a necessary adjunct to commerce, forms of marine insurance were known in the times of the ancient Babylonians, Phoenicians, Greeks, and Romans, as well as the Europeans of the fifteenth and sixteenth centuries. Modern marine insurance had its origins in England in the seventeenth century, and American marine insurance owes its beginnings to the English marine underwriters of that era.

By 1741 Philadelphia was the most important city in the colonies, outranking Boston in volume of shipping and commerce and serving as the country's political center; it also emerged as the center of the early development of American insurance. By 1760 the insurance center of Philadelphia was the London Coffee House of Philadelphia, in which the Old Insurance Office was maintained by the Philadelphia underwriters during regular hours. The English underwriters also met there. The rival of the Philadelphia underwriters—the New York Insurance Office—maintained an office next door.

During the Revolution City Tavern in Philadelphia became the gathering place of soldiers, statesmen, and important merchants, superseding the London Coffee House as the headquarters for marine underwriting. As the headquarters of the marine underwriters, it was also the place where plans were later made for the formation of the Insurance Company of North America, founded in 1792—the first stock insurance company in the nation and the first American company capable of writing satisfactory marine contracts. Since fire insurance was already being written by two companies in Philadelphia, and since the subscribers already had considerable experience in marine underwriting, a decision was made to concentrate on that form of insurance. American marine underwriting contributed directly to the growth and prosperity of the shipping trade in the new nation. Managed well, it was successful as a stock company and paid regular dividends; it has thrived for nearly two hundred years.

In the 1840s and 1850s the revolutionary design of the American clipper ship inaugurated one of the most prosperous eras in American shipping and American marine insurance, for marine insurance kept pace with the increased prosperity of ocean commerce. Between 1840 and 1861, the combined value of American exports and imports more than doubled, while marine premium receipts tripled. This prosperity lasted until the 1890s, when the British steamship made the clipper ship obsolete. Then, in the early twentieth century, the Panama Canal undercut the clipper ship's role in the growing trade between the Atlantic coast and California.

After the depression of 1893, Congress limited U.S. coastal trade to U.S. ships, a boon to domestic shipowners. New ships were built, and American marine underwriters found their business increasing again. But the greatest growth came with World War I. Although the outbreak of war created unstable conditions in the quoting of marine insurance rates, the Bureau of War Risk Insurance—created by Congress in 1914—made it possible to quote stable rates. The great increase in the volume of shipping boosted demand for marine insurance, the value of vessels and cargoes soared, and freight charges increased, leading to millions of dollars worth of insurance orders and the revitalization of American marine underwriting. The gross tonnage of ships built jumped from 316,250 in 1914 to 3,880,639 in 1920, the value of cargo carried reached $12 billion, and the demand for insurance coverage created the first major expansion in the marine insurance market since the clipper-ship era. Between the end of World War I and the beginning of World War II, the large number of new companies entering the field caused an excess capacity in marine underwriting that resulted in intense competition and lower underwriting profits.

Congressional encouragement of risk-spreading through syndicates in World War II made underwriting insurance on merchant vessels possible in the period between the Neutrality Act of 4 November 1939 and April 1942, when the government requisitioned all American vessels. At the request of the Maritime Commission, the American Hull Syndicate wrote war risk insurance on hulls, and the American Cargo War Risk Exchange made vital shipping possible by creating a market large enough to spread insurance coverage among many marine underwriters.

After World War II Congress again promoted the U.S. marine insurance market with the McCarran-Ferguson Act of 1945, which exempted marine insurance from antitrust laws and made American marine insurance competitive in world markets. The Ship Sales Act of 1946 required mortgagees of merchant ships to place not less than 75 percent of the required hull insurance in the U.S. market.

From 1965 to 1974, the American marine insurance market grew substantially in relationship to the English market (primarily Lloyd's of London). Ships grew in size and cost, and construction during this decade of huge oceangoing rigs designed for oil drilling and costing tens of millions of dollars created another expansion of the marine market. In the 1980s and 1990s, the introduction of automated handling procedures, satellite tracking, and the use of standardized containers transformed the shipping industry, leading to larger and larger ships and payloads. By the end of the twentieth century, some 60 percent of the world's merchant fleet had moved to countries under open registries such as Panama, Liberia, the Bahamas, and Greece, which have fewer taxes, lower wages, and less regulation.

Inland Marine Insurance

Initially designed to insure cargo on inland waterways, inland marine insurance expanded to include movement on land as the interior of the country developed. Some of the first policies insured the possessions of traveling salesmen. In the twentieth century, bridges and tunnels used for transportation, as well as tourist baggage and postal shipments, were included.

Aviation Insurance

Aviation insurance covers the hull and liability hazards of both commercial airlines and private aircraft; it does not include accidental injury or death coverage, which companies issue separately. During the 1960s and 1970s, many new companies entered this field, primarily as reinsurers. These companies compete among themselves and with foreign insurance carriers (mainly Lloyd's of London) for both U.S. and foreign aviation business.

One problem associated with aviation insurance is the constant exposure to catastrophic loss. As speed, size of equipment, fuel load, and passenger capacity continue to increase, the catastrophe hazard grows in direct proportion. There are too few commercial aircraft at risk to allow successful operation of the "law of large numbers," upon which underwriters rely to predict losses. Therefore, aviation underwriters must rely on their own judgments in determining rates.

Fire Insurance

Fire insurance is a direct descendant of marine insurance. It developed in the American colonies from ideas brought by English settlers. American merchants realized the need for protection from loss from fire after the Great Fire of London in 1666 destroyed three-fourths of the city's buildings. Like the first marine insurance company, the first fire insurance company in America began in Philadelphia, and, like the earliest marine companies, that company provided policies based on mutual agreement rather than stock subscription. Largely through the efforts of Benjamin Franklin, America's first fire insurance company and its oldest mutual insurance company formed in 1752—the Philadelphia Contributionship for Insurance of Houses From Loss by Fire. Experiencing difficulty in fighting fires at houses surrounded by trees, the Philadelphia Contributionship decided, in 1781, not to insure houses that had trees in front of them. Out of opposition to this policy grew the Mutual Assurance Company in 1784, popularly known as the Green Tree because of the circumstances of its founding and because of its fire mark. Then, in 1794, the Insurance Company of North America—primarily a marine underwriter—became the first company to market insurance coverage on a building and its contents and to underwrite fire risk beyond the city limits.

The success of Philadelphia's mutual fire insurance companies inspired the formation of mutual companies in other cities. The history of large fires in the growth of American cities and seaports gave rise to improvements in fire underwriting. The 1835 fire in New York, in which almost the entire business district burned to the ground, ruined most New York companies. Because of state discriminatory taxes, much of the risk had been underwritten by small local companies that had too little surplus to meet the $18 million loss. Subsequently, the underwriting business grew throughout the nation to spread the risk.

The Factory Mutual Fire Insurance Company made its appearance in New England in 1835. The firm was pioneered by Zachariah Allen, who, along with other mill owners—who had been refused fire insurance for their factories by the mutual companies and found the high premiums of stock companies excessive—formed their own company. Skillful underwriting kept the costs low and, as the system grew, it had an effect far beyond that field, forcing stock companies to reduce their rates. At the same time, the factory mutuals expanded with the growth of American industry until they underwrote the risks of the wide industrial field created by the expansion of American business and extended coverage to include loss from other damage such as lightning. In 1866 the fire companies formed the National Board of Fire Underwriters, which disseminated information on the compensation of agents, fire prevention, and the discovery and prevention of arson.

In 1909 Kansas responded to the widespread belief that fire insurance companies were making excessive profits by enacting a law that gave the state insurance commissioner power over rates charged by fire insurance companies. In 1910 the New York legislature responded to the same belief by appointing a joint committee, under state senator Edwin A. Merritt, Jr., to investigate the insurance companies. The Merritt committee's recommendations for sweeping changes in the industry produced a number of key reforms that served as models for other states.

Fire insurance continued to grow steadily during the twentieth century. In 1948 almost $1.3 billion in premiums were written ($9.7 billion in 2002 dollars); $8.4 billion ($8.7 billion in 2002 dollars) in premiums were written in 2000. Since its beginning in the early 1950s, the trend toward multiple-line coverage and packaging of property and casualty lines in either indivisible or divisible premium contracts has been gathering momentum, both in the growth of homeowners policies and in commercial packages.

Workers' Compensation Insurance

Federal and state laws requiring workers' compensation insurance have created the market for this form of liability insurance, which is sold by property and liability insurance companies. Prior to the development of workers' compensation, an injured worker's legal rights were based upon common law. As the cost and inequity of the common law created public dissatisfaction, changes gradually took place.

Between 1909 and 1913, thirty-one investigatory commissions were established; nine more were set up during the next six years. The consensus from this research was that employers' liability legislation should be replaced with what would become state workers' compensation laws. These laws derived from an entirely new legal concept—liability without regard to fault. Industrial accidents and disease have traditionally fell under the theory of occupational risk. Workers' compensation legislation provided for prompt payment of medical and disability benefits and thus eliminated the cost of litigation and encouraged the employer to promote safe working conditions.

Before 1908 a few states had passed narrow compensation acts with low benefits. The first major law, the federal Employee's Compensation Act of 1908, provided benefits for civil employees of the federal government and public employees of the District of Columbia. Ten states passed workers' compensation laws in 1911; all but six states had followed suit by 1920. The trend has been toward more comprehensive coverage for a larger group of workers. In 1934 only 33 percent of the total workforce was covered by workers' compensation; by 1957 the figure had grown to 62 percent. By the mid-1970s about 75 percent was covered. Workers' compensation, the third largest individual line of insurance, had premiums of $23.2 billion in 2000.

Automobile Insurance

The first automobile insurance policy was issued by the Travelers Insurance Companies in 1898, and since then more and more of America's 120 million motorists have recognized its value. In 1973 automobile insurance premiums reached $17.15 billion ($69.46 billion in 2002 dollars) and accounted for 42.3 percent of total property-liability premium volume. Because of inflation, increasing claims frequency, and larger claim settlements, automobile premiums have increased rapidly, and, in 1973, were more than double those of 1965. By the end of the 1970s, most states had made the purchase of automobile insurance by car owners compulsory.

Following consumer unhappiness over automobile insurance rates in the late 1980s and 1990s, some states instituted no-fault automobile insurance to reduce litigation. Typical state no-fault insurance laws permit accident victims to recover such financial losses as medical and hospital expenses and lost income from their own insurance companies and usually place some restrictions on the right to sue.

Life Insurance

Early colonists were skeptical of life insurance. Benjamin Franklin said that men were willing to insure their homes, their goods, and their ships, yet neglected to insure their lives—the most important asset to their families and the most subject to risk. Many considered life insurance a form of gambling and therefore against their religion. As late as 1807, the Massachusetts legislature argued against the morality of life insurance.

The earliest life insurance policies in America were written as a sideline by marine underwriters on the lives of sea captains for the duration of a voyage. The tontine, a life insurance lottery, formed by a group who insured themselves together, first appeared in 1790. When one died, the others divided his assets. Subscribers to the Universal Tontine used their funds to form an insurance company in 1792; the tontine policy was not used again until 1867.

The great expansion of the American economy from 1830 to 1837 made Americans more dependent on financial institutions. The prosperity engendered the founding of large stock insurance companies, but the recession after 1837 gave impetus to the mutuals because the shortage of capital during the depression years made it difficult to sell stock in life insurance companies. Four great mutual companies were founded during that period. The first, the Mutual Life Insurance Company of New York founded in 1843, is the oldest commercial life insurance company in continuous existence.

In 1855 Massachusetts became the first state to establish an insurance department. Elizur Wright, insurance commissioner of Massachusetts from 1858 to 1867 and often called the father of legal reserve life insurance, developed the first American table for establishing policy reserves. By 1890, most states had established insurance departments; by 1940, insurance departments were regulating the business in all states. State regulation of life insurance was firmly established by the SUPREME COURT in *Paul v. Virginia* (1868), which declared that life insurance was not interstate commerce and not subject to federal jurisdiction.

As the industry grew after the CIVIL WAR, it became more and more important to ensure the mortality experience on which rates were based. Sheppard Homans published the first mortality table, based on the experience of insured lives in America, in 1868. Other developments included the requirement of nonforfeiture provisions under state statues and the growing employment of full-time agents. The fervor for expansion during the period following the Civil War was characterized by extreme competition between companies—particularly proprietary stock companies and mutual companies—and influenced all aspects of the business. Quality was frequently sacrificed for quantity, and the dividend policies of the companies eventually led to abuse.

Competition also encouraged strong leaders and the control of large life insurance companies by powerful executives rather than by owners or investors. For example, although Henry B. Hyde of the Equitable Life Assurance Society had appointed a capable president to succeed him, the controlling stock passed at Hyde's death to his son. His son so misused his control as to bring about much unfavorable publicity and the ultimate transformation of the company into a mutual. In the case of the mutuals, interlocking directorates led to investments in syndicates and in entrepreneurial activities that did not always serve the best interests of the policyholders. Life insurance companies ultimately invested in every phase of the economic expansion of the United States and became competitors of investment bankers.

The climate in which the life insurance business operated between 1890 and 1905—the peak of the trust-busting period—was one of severe public criticism of business and finance. New York legislators could not ignore the dubious practices any longer. In July 1905 the Assembly and Senate concurred in a resolution directing a committee to investigate and examine the business and affairs of life insurance companies operating in the state. With Sen. William W. Armstrong as chairman and Charles Evans Hughes as counsel, the committee issued its report in 1906. Although it declared the life insurance business to be fundamentally sound, it brought to light numerous practices detrimental both to policyholders and to the national economy. The committee's recommendations led to state legislation prohibiting these practices and strengthened the industry.

The professional approach to life insurance was important to its growth. Between 1890 and 1906, several professional associations were formed, including the Actuarial Society of America, the National Association of Life Underwriters, the American Life Convention, and the Association of Life Insurance Presidents. Ownership of U.S. government life insurance by young men entering the military service in World War I caused their families to reappraise their own need for life insurance and stimulated sales—a situation that repeated itself during World War II. The Great Depression of the 1930s also favored the growth of life insurance, and American insurance companies outperformed most businesses during that time.

In the late 1930s the Temporary National Economic Committee's investigations into the sources of economic power in the country endorsed the soundness of the life insurance industry and disclaimed any disposition toward governmental regulation of the industry. However, in *United States v. South-eastern Underwriters Association et al.* (1944), the Supreme Court held that no commercial enterprise that conducts its business across state lines is wholly beyond the regulatory power of Congress. Subsequently Congress passed the McCarran-Ferguson bill in 1945, which stated that continued regulation and taxation of the insurance industry by the states was in the public interest and that silence on the part of Congress did not stand as any impediment to state regulation. The bill thereby strengthened state regulation and helped to guarantee more qualified insurance management.

Entry into mutual funds and variable annuities by life insurance companies made them subject to the federal securities laws, since these products are considered securities. Agents for the variable annuity and mutual funds must meet the requirements of both state and federal regulation. Simultaneously, changes in financial enterprises began affecting the marketing of life insurance products. Members of the Midwest stock exchange began selling life insurance in 1970, and other exchanges permitted their members to follow this lead. Thus, large life insurance companies began to enter the property and liability insurance field.

Liability insurance became a political issue in the 1980s, when businesses, manufacturers, and physicians fought to reform liability laws to reduce what they considered extensive jury awards. Life insurance also underwent a major change. Once sold only to wage-earning males to provide comfort to would-be widows, new-style life insurance policies became opportunities to accumulate tax-free savings, causing life and annuity insurance sales to boom from $63.2 billion ($137.78 billion in 2002 dollars) in 1980 to $216.5 billion ($277.12 billion in 2002 dollars) in 1992. Brokerage houses began selling life insurance with good returns and long-term growth, attracting money from banks and savings and loans. In 1995 the Supreme Court agreed with the position of the U.S. comptroller of the currency that annuities were investments rather than insurance, opening the door to bank participation in the $72-billion-a-year annuity market.

Group Insurance

Group insurance is a phenomenon of the twentieth century. The Equitable Life Insurance Company issued the first group life insurance policy, covering employees of the Pantasote Leather Company, in June 1911. Since then group insurance has expanded rapidly. By the end of the twentieth century, low-cost group life, health, and disability coverages were available through companies with twenty-five or more employees and through many professional associations. More than two-thirds of all employed persons in the United States are covered by some form of group insurance.

Health Insurance

Health insurance had its start in the mid-nineteenth century. Accident insurance came first, and then the policyholder began to be protected against loss of income from a limited number of diseases. Although stemming from accident insurance, life insurance companies are the primary marketers of modern health insurance. These companies are committed to group life insurance, which pairs naturally with health insurance.

Rail and steamboat accidents in the mid-nineteenth century precipitated the first demand for an insurance policy to protect against loss of income because of accident. The Franklin Health Assurance Company of Massachusetts is credited with being the first insurer to write accident insurance in America in 1850. However, the Travelers Insurance Company, founded in 1863, was the first company in America to write health insurance, providing a schedule of stated benefits payable to the insured for each illness or injury. The Fidelity and Casualty Company of New York issued the first contract to protect against loss of income from accident and from certain diseases (1891).

Workers' compensation laws, first effectively enacted by the federal government in 1908, stimulated an interest in group health insurance contracts for illness and non-work-related injuries not covered by the law; in 1914 the Metropolitan Life Insurance Company issued the first group health contract, covering its home office employees. The economic depression of the 1930s engendered a wide concern for individual and family security, stimulating group health insurance sales. What became Blue Cross in 1948 began when a group of schoolteachers entered an agreement with Baylor Hospital in Dallas, Texas, to provide hospital care on a prepayment basis. In response, traditional insurance companies also developed reimbursement policies for hospital and surgical care.

During World War II the fringe benefit became a significant element in collective bargaining, and group health insurance became an important part of fringe-benefit packages. Sharply escalating costs for health care after the war prompted continued improvement of health insurance. Perhaps most significant was the development of major medical insurance in response to the family's need for protection against serious and prolonged illness.

During the 1970s, health insurance companies developed dental insurance plans that provided scheduled benefits for various types of dental surgery. Some companies added payments during the 1980s and 1990s for routine dental checkups or teeth cleaning.

Health insurers found themselves embroiled in a major debate after the 1992 election, when the administration of President Bill Clinton argued that the insurance industry's practices harmed the medical community. President Clinton and First Lady Hillary Rodham Clinton favored a competitive model generally known as managed competition, but the insurance industry mobilized a successful television campaign against it. Large insurers, meanwhile, responded by developing health maintenance organizations to manage care and costs and halt the year-to-year double-digit rise in medical costs.

A string of catastrophic claims in the 1980s and 1990s resulting from major natural disasters threatened the industry far more than any possible federal regulation. Hurricane Hugo caused $4.2 billion in insured losses in 1989—the first hurricane to cause more than $1 billion in losses—and three years later Hurricane Andrew produced $16.5 billion ($21.12 billion in 2002 dollars) in insured losses. Altogether, the insurance industry counted thirty-six catastrophes in 1992, resulting in $22.9 billion ($29.3 billion in 2002 dollars) in losses. An earthquake in California in 1989 and riots in Los Angeles in 1992 incurred insured losses of $1.1 billion ($1.41 billion in 2002 dollars). Flooding of the Missouri and Mississippi rivers and tributaries caused another $1 billion in privately insured losses.

Despite these challenges, during the late 1980s and early 1990s the industry proved itself durable and adaptive, and greatly expanded the risks that individuals or businesses can insure against: automobile, home, life, health, annuities, disability, workers' compensation, nursing home, flood, earthquake, and numerous specific liabilities. As the industry has grown, insurance has become a major expense for most Americans. U.S. households in 1992 spent 6.3 percent of their income on automobile, home, health, and other forms of insurance coverage. The United States is the largest insurance market in the world, accounting for almost one-third of all insurance expenditures. In 1994, premiums totaled $561.7 billion ($678.93 in 2002 dollars)— $316.8 billion for life and health and $244.9 billion for property and casualty, a total equal to Spain's annual economic output.

Insurance companies invest billions of dollars in credit and equity markets and employ nearly 2.2 million people in 4,000 companies. The collapse of several major national companies, including the $18 billion Executive Life, prompted calls for federal regulation that the politically powerful insurance industry successfully opposed.

BIBLIOGRAPHY

Bainbridge, John. *Biography of an Idea: The Story of Mutual Fire and Casualty Insurance.* Garden City, N.Y.: Doubleday, 1952.

Black, Samuel P., Jr. *Entrepreneurship and Innovation in Automobile Insurance: Samuel P. Black, Jr. and the Rise of Erie Insurance.* New York: Routledge, 2001.

Clough, Shepard B. *A Century of American Life Insurance: A History of the Mutual Life Insurance Company of New York, 1843–1943.* New York: Columbia University Press, 1946.

Cunningham, Robert, III. *The Blues: A History of the Blue Cross and Blue Shield System.* DeKalb: Northern Illinois University Press, 1997.

James, Marquis. *The Metropolitan Life: A Study in Business Growth.* New York: Viking Press, 1947.

Huber, Peter W. *Liability: The Legal Revolution and its Consequences.* New York: Basic Books, 1988.

Schulte, Gary. *The Fall of First Executive: The House that Fred Carr Built.* New York: HarperBusiness, 1991.

Brent Schondelmeyer
Edmund Zalinski / C. W.

See also **Banking; Disasters; Earthquakes; Fires; Floods and Flood Control; Health Care; Health Insurance; Health Maintenance Organizations; Hurricanes; Medicare and Medicaid; Social Security.**

INSURRECTIONS, DOMESTIC. An insurrection is an uprising against government or civil authority. Inasmuch as local officials are always charged with intervening to curb behavior understood to be outside the law, the broadest conception of the term would include race and ethnic revolts, such as slave revolts, lynchings, and the New York Draft Riot of 1863 (which had a combination of causes); violent labor unrest; and popular assaults directly targeting the political process (that is, political violence encompassing a range of uprisings from Bacon's Rebellion in Virginia in 1675 to anti-abortion violence in the 1980s and 1990s). Looked at this way, insurrections have always been a part of the American experience.

Rioting revealing racial and ethnic tensions goes back to colonial America. Lynchings and other brutality against slaves and freemen were matched by slave revolts, including the Negro Plot of 1741 in New York; the Charleston, South Carolina, slave revolt of 1822; Nat Turner's Rebellion of 1831; and the Harpers Ferry Raid in Virginia in 1859. There were urban race and anti-abortion riots (more than a dozen) in many major cities in 1834 and 1835; race riots in East St. Louis in 1917 and in Chicago in 1919; the Watts Riot in Los Angeles in 1965 and similar upheavals in Newark, Detroit, and New York City in 1967; and another major race riot in Los Angeles in 1992.

Industrial working-class rioting and its violent repression were commonplace, starting with widespread labor riots around Pittsburgh and in Ohio in 1877. The Homestead Strike in Pittsburgh in 1892 and the Pullman Strike in Illinois two years later were both repressed brutally, with loss of life. Succeeding generations saw more of the same: the Ludlow Massacre of 1914 in Colorado and the Detroit Sitdown Strike of 1936 are two examples.

Political insurrection against a broad array of governmental authorities was always in season. In colonial America, for example, Leisler's Rebellion in New York in 1689 and rent riots in New Jersey in the 1740s were but two examples of many, precursors of the widespread upheavals that accompanied the coming of the American Revolution. The opening shots of that revolution were heard in the Stamp Act Riots of 1765 and 1766 in Boston, New York, and elsewhere. These were followed by, among many possible examples, the Regulator Wars in North Carolina from 1769 to 1771 and the Boston Tea Party of 1773. In the immediate postwar era, more violence marred the American landscape; the most serious upheaval was Shays's Rebellion in western Massachusetts in 1786. No generation escaped: widespread political upheavals deriving from a variety of causes in 1834 and 1835, the Astor Place Riot of 1849 in New York City, and the Native-American Party–led Know-Nothing Riots in the 1850s in Baltimore, New York, and Louisville, among many other places, attest to this fact.

In the twentieth century, insurrectionary political causation was inherent in all of the many race riots, but purely political rioting was evident as well: the suppression following the "Red Scare" of the 1920s, and the repression of World War I veterans in Washington, D.C., following their Bonus March at the height of the Great Depression offer up well-known examples. The "days of rage" of the radical group the Weathermen was but one of many insurrections in the tumultuous 1960s. The same era gave rise to antiwar demonstrations, some violent, everywhere in America, directed at the nation's military involvement in Vietnam. No section of the country was spared the largely urban anti-abortion rioting that began in the mid-1980s and continued at the start of the twenty-first century.

The above is but a partial catalog of ubiquitous American insurrectional activity. To some American historians of the subject, rioting is as American as apple pie; to others, it is violence against civil society and the broadly protective laws of the land guaranteed by the First Amendment. Historians on both sides of the question count and catalog domestic insurrections endlessly. As they have done so, they have developed a body of theory about the role of rioting and violence in the shaping of the American Republic. While these historians and other social scientists differ on the constructiveness and validity of insurrection, they nevertheless all accept certain ideological touchstones.

First, of course, the very presence of First Amendment rights (the freedoms of speech, the press, and assembly) has underpinned claims that crowd actions in general have a quasi-legal standing (or at least debatable legal standing) in the American political process. Americans have always voted with their feet, some historians say; taking to the streets is an extension of constitutional civil rights. Those opposed will argue that it is a matter of degree; that is, when demonstrations turn violent, they become lawless. Second, while rural and small-town violence has always been with us, the rise of large cities from the early nineteenth century on conferred an anonymity on its inhabitants that made crowd actions a tempting way to redress grievances. And third, most scholars would agree, throughout its history America's very diversity and openness—though perceived to be two of its greatest strengths—have made episodic racial, religious, cultural, industrial, generational, and class hostility almost inevitable.

The very birth of the Republic was accompanied by the repeated crowd actions that characterized the American Revolution. To a degree, these mobs drew legitimacy in turn from crowds going back to the Magna Carta. Thus born of insurrection, Americans, the historian Paul Gilje has concluded, "have persisted in rioting throughout American history." Crowd actions have intermittently played important roles in moving the nation forward, with independence in 1776 being the prime example. Other instances of constructive results arising from domestic insurrection include democratic reforms growing out of the crowd actions of the Age of Jackson; working-class gains and the right to collective bargaining emerging from the industrial labor riots that extended from 1877 to 1937; and impressive racial progress and gains in race relations forged first through assaults on slavery by whites and African Americans before the Civil War, and then by the civil rights upheavals of the 1960s.

Violence always introduces danger, and many good people have died over more than three centuries of domestic insurrection, but—to paraphrase Thomas Jefferson—the tree of liberty must be watered each generation by the blood of patriots.

BIBLIOGRAPHY

Gilje, Paul. *Rioting in America.* Bloomington: Indiana University Press, 1996.

Graham, Hugh Davis, and Ted Robert Gurr, eds. *Violence in America: Historical and Comparative Perspectives.* Rev. ed. Beverly Hills, Calif.: Sage, 1979.

Carl E. Prince

See also **Bonus Army; Chicago Riots of 1919; Detroit Riots; Los Angeles Riots; Radicals and Radicalism; Riots; Riots, Urban; Riots, Urban, of 1967.**

INTEGRATION. During the colonial and antebellum periods, the southern slave codes were draconian and the slave regimen was harsh, yet chattel slavery was basically incompatible with racial segregation. Although the civil and social status of blacks was rigidly subordinate, blacks and whites often worked side by side, and racial mingling and miscegenation in the South were widespread. Racial segregation, known as JIM CROW in the South, first emerged in the antebellum North, where rights gained by free blacks through the thrust of the Revolution, especially the franchise and rights in court, were subsequently whittled away.

The RECONSTRUCTION period (1865–1877) witnessed the passage of the Fourteenth Amendment (1868), which recognized African Americans as citizens, accorded them equal protection under the laws, and secured their civic privileges and immunities from state violation. Also at this time, the Fifteenth Amendment (1870), which barred disfranchisement on grounds of race, color, or previous condition of servitude, was passed. But by 1877 white America had wearied of the strains of Reconstruction, abandoning the freedmen and freedwomen to conservative Democratic home rule in the southern states. In the absence of slavery and the strict enforcement of Reconstruction legislation intended to guarantee blacks' civil rights, southern whites reasserted racial dominance through segregation, disfranchisement, and lynching. The federal government sanctioned segregation in the states and practiced it in its agencies; indeed, Jim Crow prevailed in Washington, D.C. The conservative Supreme Court so narrowly interpreted the Fourteenth Amendment (the 1883 Civil Rights Cases) and the Fifteenth Amendment (*UNITED STATES v. REESE,* 1876) that African Americans were for the most part denied the intended benefits of emancipation. In 1894, Congress repealed all but seven of the forty-nine sections of the Reconstruction's enforcement provisions in civil rights. In 1896, the Supreme Court endorsed the segregationist principle in *PLESSY v. FERGUSON,* proclaiming the constitutionality of a Louisiana law compelling "equal but separate" railroad facilities "for the white and colored races."

Into the 1960s, rigid Jim Crow laws separated blacks and whites virtually everywhere in the South. Despite the Supreme Court's "separate but equal" provision, facilities for blacks were far inferior to those for whites. Whites contended that the Bible justified racial discrimination, and that blacks preferred segregation. Whites in the Northeast, Midwest, and West practiced segregation through social pressure, antimiscegenation ordinances, and racial covenants preventing blacks (and in some areas, other people of color and Jews) from purchasing homes in certain neighborhoods. In 1941 and 1942, white immigrants in Buffalo and Detroit agitated against blacks moving into federally funded housing projects. Asian Americans and Mexican Americans in some western and southwestern communities were subjected to segregated educational facilities, confined to slum housing, and refused service in white-only businesses.

Civil rights activists endeavored to eliminate segregation through the courts and appeals to presidents. In the 1930s and 1940s, the Supreme Court dealt blows to segregation by ruling against the segregation of blacks at universities in Missouri, Texas, and Oklahoma, all-white primaries (*Smith v. Allwright*, 1944), and segregation on interstate transportation (*Morgan v. Virginia*, 1946). In 1941, civil rights leader A. Philip Randolph demanded that President Franklin D. Roosevelt desegregate the federal government and defense industries. In response, Roosevelt issued Executive Order 8802, although the Fair Employment Practices Committee, charged with investigating allegations of racial discrimination, proved ineffectual in carrying out its mission.

In 1946, President Harry Truman created a committee to report on violations of civil rights and propose solutions. World War II (1939–1945) had furnished occasions for racial integration in employment, public venues, and housing, but segregationists tried to restore racial hierarchy, viciously attacking black veterans upon their return to the United States. In 1947, the President's Committee on Civil Rights released a report recommending federal legislation and action to outlaw racial assaults, overcome obstacles to enfranchisement, desegregate housing, and address other breaches of civil rights. In 1948, President Truman signed executive orders prohibiting racial discrimination in the civil service (EO 9980) and the armed forces (EO 9981). Although the Korean War (1950–1953) is hailed as the first war fought by an integrated armed forces since the American Revolution, white supremacists attempted to sustain segregation at military bases in the United States and abroad.

The momentum gained by civil rights activists during the 1940s carried into the next decade. The Supreme Court's unanimous 1954 ruling in *BROWN v. BOARD OF EDUCATION OF TOPEKA* found the "equal but separate" provision of *Plessy v. Ferguson* unconstitutional, thus hastening the decline of segregation. Although the Court determined in 1955 that local school boards were to oversee desegregation in their districts, it set no deadline and thus gave whites little incentive to carry out the order. Although many schools in the Midwest, southern border states, and Washington, D.C., desegregated peaceably, southern states allowed schools to circumvent the Supreme Court's *Brown* rulings by closing down, and repealed compulsory attendance laws so that parents could withdraw children from desegregating schools. During the 1957–1958 school year, nine African American teenagers, backed by the National Association for the Advancement of Colored People (est. 1909), integrated into Central High School in Little Rock, Arkansas. White hostility, and Governor Orval Faubus's refusal to ensure state protection of the "Little Rock Nine," compelled President Dwight Eisenhower to deploy federal troops to keep order and safeguard the students.

As civil rights activists grew bolder, they developed strategies of "direct action" to bring about integration, and to that end organized mass sit-ins, boycotts, and marches. Members of the interracial CONGRESS OF RACIAL EQUALITY engaged in sit-ins at segregated eating establishments and "FREEDOM RIDES" on interstate buses in the 1940s, and joined forces with other integrationist groups in the 1960s. In Montgomery, Alabama, the NAACP launched a yearlong boycott (1955–1956) that accomplished the desegregation of the city's bus system. College students who mobilized sit-ins at southern lunch counters and recreational facilities formed the STUDENT NONVIOLENT COORDINATING COMMITTEE (SNCC) in 1960, which subsequently organized projects to register black voters in the rural Deep South.

Cold War politics also entered into the issue of segregation. Foreign foes as well as allies of the United States called attention to the contradiction between Americans' claims to advocate freedom, democracy, and equality while subjecting citizens and foreign visitors to racial discrimination. "White-only" hotels, apartments, and restaurants that denied entry to foreign officials of color insulted the visitors and, some critics argued, threatened to harm U.S. foreign relations.

The wide-ranging CIVIL RIGHTS ACT OF 1964, which created the EQUAL EMPLOYMENT OPPORTUNITY COMMISSION, and the VOTING RIGHTS ACT OF 1965 represented the fruits of decades of activism. Yet by the time Congress passed this legislation, some activists doubted that integration was the ultimate solution for achieving racial equality. Black separatists advocated building communities apart from whites, whom they believed would never accept African Americans as equals. In this view, black-only communities would most effectively foster the social and economic progress of their members, and also would allow African Americans to define themselves according to their own values, rather than futilely striving to conform to white society. Critics also contended that integration was a goal of members of the black middle class, who would benefit the most from incorporation into white-dominated capitalist society, and that integration would not solve the economic problems of poorer African Americans. Such ideas influenced SNCC members, whose 1966 election of Stokely Carmichael as chairman over the more moderate John Lewis marked SNCC's shift away from integration as a primary goal and toward radicalism and separatism.

Since the 1960s, integration in the South proved most successful in public schools. The proportion of African American children in the South attending all-black schools dropped from two out of three in 1960 to one out of ten in 1972. In contrast, de facto segregation characterized schools and housing in the North and West during the 1970s and beyond as whites moved out of neighborhoods increasingly populated by people of color. In 1971, the Supreme Court's controversial decision (*Swann v. Charlotte Mecklenburg Board of Education*) on busing to integrate public schools riled parents who considered it an extreme means to achieve racial equality. Into the twenty-first century, colleges and universities, the government, public transportation, professional sports, and other venues experienced varying degrees of integration, although concerns persisted about social and economic inequalities that perpetuated racial separation.

BIBLIOGRAPHY

Banner-Haley, Charles T. *The Fruits of Integration: Black Middle-Class Ideology and Culture, 1960–1990.* Jackson: University Press of Mississippi, 1994.

Beals, Melba Pattillo. *Warriors Don't Cry: A Searing Memoir of the Battle to Integrate Little Rock's Central High.* New York: Pocket Books, 1994.

Brooks, Roy L. *Integration or Separation? A Strategy for Racial Equality.* Cambridge, Mass.: Harvard University Press, 1996.

Fairclough, Adam. *Better Day Coming: Blacks and Equality, 1890–2000.* New York: Viking, 2001.

King, Desmond. *Separate and Unequal: Black Americans and the U.S. Federal Government.* New York: Oxford University Press, 1995.

Romano, Renee. "No Diplomatic Immunity: African Diplomats, the State Department, and Civil Rights, 1961–1964." *Journal of American History* 87, no. 2 (Sept. 2000): 546–579.

Sitkoff, Harvard. *The Struggle for Black Equality, 1954–1992.* Rev. ed. New York: Hill and Wang, 1993.

Donna Alvah

See also **Civil Rights and Liberties; Civil Rights Movement; Desegregation; Discrimination: Race; Race Relations; Segregation.**

INTELLECTUAL PROPERTY describes the interests protected by the laws of patents, copyrights, trademarks, and trade secrets. It is a phrase of convenience rather than a term of art; its precise boundaries are not agreed upon, or crucial. Patents, copyrights, and trademarks all predate the term "intellectual property," which, though known in the nineteenth century, was not widely used until the 1960s. Historically, property was divided into two classes, real and personal. Real property consisted of interests in land; personal property consisted of everything else. Personal property included not only tangibles, such as goods, but intangibles such as shares of stock, rights to receive payment, and copyrights and patents. It was understood by the eighteenth century that patents and copyrights were socially desirable because potential inventors and authors, unless rewarded, would underinvest in inventing and writing. Patents and copyrights provide rewards proportional to the value of the work. By exploiting monopolies over patentable and copyrightable subject matter, creators can charge amounts sufficient to recapture their capital investment plus make a profit; this is comparable to granting farmers the exclusive rights to harvest crops that have required labor to plant and tend.

Patents are granted after examination by the Patent Office and confer twenty (previously seventeen) years of monopoly rights in works that have the characteristics of utility, novelty, and nonobviousness. Copyrights arise upon embodiment of works of authorship in a tangible medium and now last for much longer than previously; today, in most cases, they endure for the life of the author plus seventy years. Registration, though desirable, is not essential.

Trademarks are usually counted as intellectual property but have quite a different rationale and arise differently from either patents or copyrights. The reason for protecting trademarks is not to promote investment in their creation but to protect consumers from being deceived as to the origin of goods bearing them. Trademark rights develop as consumers associate the marks on the goods with a single source. Courts have often said trademark rights are not property rights but are part of tort law (though recent developments arguably render trademarks more propertylike). Whatever the theory, the practice persists of calling trademarks a species of intellectual property, if only because the same lawyers who do patent and copyright work also advise on trademark questions.

Trade secret law confers on those who manage to keep valuable information to themselves the competitive advantage of exclusive access to that information. It is arguably tort law, rather than property law, but since the subject matter of the secret is often identical to the subject matter of the patent or copyright, its designation as intellectual property is not surprising.

BIBLIOGRAPHY

Chisum, Donald S., and Michael A. Jacobs. *Understanding Intellectual Property Law.* New York: Matthew Bender, 1992.

Halpern, Sheldon W., Craig Allen Nard, and Kenneth L. Port. *Fundamentals of United States Intellectual Property Law: Copyright, Patent, and Trademark.* The Hague, Netherlands: Kluwer Law International, 1999.

John A. Kidwell

See also **Copyright; Patents and U.S. Patent Office; Trademarks.**

INTELLIGENCE, MILITARY AND STRATEGIC. Military and strategic intelligence includes the collecting, processing, analyzing, evaluating, integrating, and interpreting openly or covertly acquired information about foreign countries and areas, regions of actual or potential military operations, and hostile or potentially hostile forces. Military intelligence has to be related to and significant to military operations and planning; strategic intelligence is used in formulating policy on national and international levels. The intelligence community in the United States consists of the Central Intelligence Agency (CIA); the National Security Agency (NSA); the Defense Intelligence Agency; the State Department's Bureau of Intelligence and Research; the National Reconnaissance Office; the intelligence agencies of the army, navy, and air force; and the Federal Bureau of Investigation (FBI). The Department of the Treasury and the Department of Energy have limited intelligence capabilities and missions as well. Almost exclusive reliance on data collected by human sources (HUMINT) was superseded in importance in the last decades of the twentieth century by signals intelligence (SIGINT), communications intelligence (COMINT), electronics intelligence (ELINT), telemetry intelligence (TELINT), and photography (PHOTINT).

Although intelligence was used in all military conflicts in which the United States was engaged as early as the Revolutionary War, the first sustained intelligence organizations were the Office of Naval Intelligence, created in 1882, and the Military Information Division (MID), established by the U.S. Army in 1885. In 1888, service attachés were appointed to U.S. missions abroad to collect information on foreign armed forces. Nevertheless, during World War I, American forces had to rely mostly on military intelligence supplied by the British and the French.

The advent of communications technology such as the telegraph in the late 1830s, the telephone in the 1870s, and the radio in the 1920s shifted intelligence collection to COMINT and to code-breaking. A Cipher Bureau was created within MID in 1917 that became the nucleus of the American Black Chamber, or MI-8, which was created in 1918 and headed by Herbert O. Yardley. It worked for the army and state departments to break the diplomatic codes of several nations. During World War II, the Office of Strategic Services (OSS) coordinated most of the intelligence work; integration with data compiled by other services through the Joint Intelligence Committee, however, was not satisfactory. The National Security Act of 1947 created a centralized structure with the establishment of the National Security Council (NSC) and the CIA. The NSA is responsible mostly for COMINT, cryptology, and decoding. The work of the FBI, responsible for internal security, bears on military and strategic intelligence particularly in its dealings with foreign intelligence services, and dissident or terrorist movements operating within the United States.

Since World War I, and increasingly after World War II, technology has played a significant role in collecting data. SIGINT helped establish troop movements and naval operations during World War II. Relying on wireless communications, it did not, however, detect Japanese forces (who kept strict radio silence) advancing on Pearl Harbor in 1941.

In the 1960s, PHOTINT collected by overflights of U-2 spy planes, led to the detection of military activities and missile deployment in and by the Soviet Union and other nations, and confirmed the construction of missile launching sites on Cuba. Satellites later become a major source of PHOTINT, fulfilling the same functions better without endangering pilots or invading other nations' air space. With the advent of the Internet and mobile telephony, COMINT has become an increasingly important source for intelligence.

The volume of data to be handled by intelligence services increased enormously since the 1960s, threatening to overwhelm analysis. Raw intelligence, however acquired, must be collated, scrutinized, and processed; technically procured data may require translation, decryption, interpretation, and computer analysis. The National Intelligence Estimate is the highest form of finished national intelligence. It usually reflects the consensus of the intelligence community and often attempts to predict a potential adversary's course.

During most of the COLD WAR, intelligence focused on the Soviet Union. Since the 1990s it has shifted to international arms and drug trafficking, to transnational crime and concentrated on so-called "rogue state" (Iran, Iraq, and North Korea among them). After the terrorist attacks on the United States in September 2001, international terrorism has received increased attention by the intelligence community.

Failures and Oversight

Intelligence estimates, however, have hardly been foolproof. In 1962, the American intelligence community failed to predict the movement of Soviet missiles into Cuba. The CIA's large-scale involvement in Vietnam resulted in a major dispute in 1967 between the army command in Vietnam and CIA analysts about the number of enemy troops. Coupled with the CIA's pessimism about long-term prospects for military success, it undermined the army's claim to be winning the war. CIA appraisals did not alert government officials to the fall of the shah of Iran in 1979 or to the collapse of the Soviet Union in 1991. In the 1980s, CIA Director William Casey was suspected of slanting CIA estimates for political reasons, especially with regard to the Soviet Union and Nicaragua. Given Casey's belief and that of President Ronald Reagan that the Soviet Union was bent on subjugating the world, it is not surprising that the CIA or the intelligence community rarely argued that Soviet capabilities were much lower than projected.

Oversight of U.S. intelligence began with the establishment of a permanent Senate Select Committee on Intelligence in 1976 and the creation the following year of the House Permanent Select Committee on Intelligence. These committees were established following the investigations of previous congressional committees into intelligence community abuses including domestic spying and illegal and unethical programs, such as kidnappings and assassinations of foreign leaders. Both committees reviewed budgets, programs, and covert activities. The Iran-Contra investigations of 1986 and 1987, which revealed an elaborate Reagan administration plan to sell arms to Iran in exchange for the release of U.S. hostages in Lebanon and the diversion of funds from these transactions to support the Contras in Nicaragua, shattered whatever progress the intelligence community had made toward regaining the trust of Congress. The Reagan administration promised a new era of cooperation with Congress, and the administrations of George H. W. Bush and Bill Clinton attempted to maintain cooperative relations. The end of the Cold War in the early 1990s also led to questions in Congress about the enormous cost of the U.S. intelligence effort. (Criticism that increased after revelations that optimal cooperation between the CIA and FBI might have prevented the attacks of 11 September 2001.)

Persian Gulf War

The administration of George H. W. Bush enjoyed overwhelming congressional support for the Persian Gulf War of 1991 and U.S. intelligence activities during that conflict. The Gulf War was the first major military conflict following the end of the Cold War, and U.S. intelligence, both strategic and tactical, played an important role. The primary focus of intelligence operations, particularly during Operations Desert Shield and Desert Storm, was to provide the theater and component commanders with an accurate picture of Iraqi capabilities and intentions. Extensive use was made of both strategic and tactical intelligence, with U.S. commanders having access to a vast array of impressive intelligence capabilities. These officers, nevertheless, were often frustrated and dissatisfied with the intelligence support they received. Operation Desert Storm tended to blur the distinction between tactical and strategic intelligence, and commanders often found the intelligence furnished to them too broad. Frequently, tactical units were sent finished estimates rather than detailed, tailored intelligence needed to plan operations. The overwhelming military victory against Iraq during Operation Desert Storm was attributable, nevertheless, in no small part to accurate intelligence provided both to national policymakers and command theater-level decision makers. The same can be said about the Kosovo Conflict in 1999, where American intelligence provided the vast majority of military information for the operations of NATO forces.

Because of the failure of the intelligence services to predict and prevent the attacks of 11 September 2001 on the World Trade Center and the Pentagon, President George W. Bush, on 6 June 2002, proposed a permanent cabinet-level Department of Homeland Security.

BIBLIOGRAPHY

Andrew, Christopher M. *For the President's Eyes Only: Secret Intelligence and the American Presidency from Washington to Bush.* New York: HarperCollins, 1995.

Jeffreys-Jones, Rhodri. *Cloak and Dollar: A History of American Secret Intelligence.* New Haven, Conn.: Yale University Press, 2002.

May, Ernest R., ed. *Knowing One's Enemies: Intelligence Assessment before the Two World Wars.* Princeton, N.J.: Princeton University Press, 1984.

Watson, Bruce W., Susan M. Watson, and Gerald W. Hopple, eds. *United States Intelligence: An Encyclopedia.* New York: Garland, 1990.

Gerald Haines
Michael Wala

INTELLIGENCE TESTS. Although the tests created specifically to gauge intelligence were introduced to the United States in the early twentieth century, their roots go back much farther, even to exams in ancient China. The American tests, however, emerged directly from the work of nineteenth-century English scientists who were laying the foundation for the field of psychometrics: the scientific approach to measurement of psychological characteristics.

Early European Testing and the Stanford-Binet Test

Sir Francis Galton produced the first systematic investigations of the concept of intelligence. Galton seemed uniquely qualified for this task, as he was known for collecting and quantifying massive amounts of data. Galton's statistical analyses included seemingly random and subjective assessments. Nonetheless, his groundbreaking pronouncement endures: that intelligence is a trait normally distributed among populations. A normal distribution means that most people were of average intelligence, while a minority fell above or below this middle range. Plotting this distribution resulted in the formation of the now familiar bell curve.

Reflecting popular nineteenth-century theories of evolution, including those of his cousin, Charles Darwin, Galton viewed intelligence as a single, inherited trait. His landmark 1869 publication, *Hereditary Genius*, established the parameters of the scientific investigation of mental processes for years to come; his understanding of intelligence as a fixed and predetermined entity would remain largely unchallenged for nearly a century.

Eager to further explore Galton's ideas, psychologist James McKeen Cattell returned from his studies in Europe to the University of Pennsylvania in the late 1880s and began his own work. Cattell's "mental tests," a term he introduced, reflected his skills at statistical analysis. Similar to Galton's, however, his tests ultimately failed to show any real correlation between scores and demonstrated achievement. Still, Cattell's work earned growing recognition and respect for the emerging field of psychology.

The earliest intelligence tests to move beyond the theoretical and into the practical realm were the work of the French researcher Alfred Binet. The passage of a 1904 law requiring that all children attend school prompted the French government to decide what to do with children who could not keep up with classroom work. Binet and his colleague, Théodore Simon, set out to devise a test as a means of identifying these students, who would then receive tutoring or be placed in alternative classes.

Binet's first test was published in 1905. Like its subsequent revisions, this early version asked students to demonstrate proficiency at a variety of skills. Starting with the most basic and increasing in difficulty, they were designed to measure childrens' vocabulary and their ability to understand simple concepts and identify relationships between words. An age level or "norm" was assigned to each task, based on the age at which approximately 70 percent of children could successfully complete that task. Totaling the individual scores would yield a child's "mental age." This would be subtracted from his or her chronological age; a difference of two or more indicated that a child was mentally retarded.

Binet's research differed from that of previous investigators in several important ways: test scores were meant to measure classroom performance, not innate intelligence, and they were intended to target students who could benefit by receiving extra help. Binet was one of the few who challenged popular perceptions of intelligence as an inherent and unchangeable entity.

American professor of psychology Lewis Terman set out to refine what became widely known as the Binet-Simon Scale. Named after his long and distinguished career at Stanford University, the Stanford-Binet Intelligence Test emerged as the one to which all future tests would be compared. First published in 1916, the Stanford-Binet asked students to demonstrate competency in a variety of areas, including language comprehension, eye-hand coordination, mathematical reasoning, and memory. Terman advanced the idea proposed in 1912 by German psychologist Wilhelm Stern that intelligence could more accurately be expressed as a ratio, dividing mental age by chronological age. This would be multiplied by one hundred (to avoid the use of decimals) to arrive at what Stern labeled the "mental quotient." This quickly became known as an intelligence quotient, or IQ.

This formula ultimately yielded to new methods of calculation. Still predicated on Galton's assumption that intelligence is normally distributed, tables of raw data are statistically adjusted so that the mean scores are set at 100, with the middle two-thirds of the distribution set between 85 and 115 to form the "normal" range. This scale defines those who score below 70 as mentally retarded; those with 130 or above are often labeled gifted.

Testing the Masses

The United States entry into World War I in 1917 prompted an immediate and unprecedented demand for standardized tests. The federal government sought a way to quickly and efficiently determine the abilities of large numbers of military recruits to determine appropriate assignment of duties. Robert Yerkes of Harvard and other prominent psychiatrists created a committee in response to this need. Adopting the work of Arthur Otis, whose research in this field already was underway, they quickly produced two versions of a workable test. The Army Alpha was a written exam and the Army Beta was a verbal assessment for the considerable number of men who were unable to read. The tests resulted in grades ranging from A to E. Within weeks a group of four thousand recruits completed the first trial run.

By the end of the war over 1.7 million men had taken either the Army Alpha or Beta. Based on their scores, tens of thousands of men were promoted or assigned a lower-level duty. An additional 8,000 men received discharges as a result of their poor performance. The impact of the Army testing program reached far beyond the military service. Its success convinced the nation of the usefulness of wide-scale standardized testing. The popularity of the Alpha, in particular, launched a rapidly expanding intelligence test industry. In the years immediately following the war, schoolchildren across the country began taking its numerous revisions; by 1930 over seven million American students had taken the test.

As the popularity of mass testing continued to grow, the need for individual tests as diagnostic tools remained. The Wechsler-Bellevue Intelligence Scale supplemented the Stanford-Binet in 1939. Devised by David Wechsler of Bellevue Hospital in New York City, results included both verbal and nonverbal scores. The test was named the Wechsler Scale in 1955 (WAIS), later revised to WAIS-R. The expanded group of tests, including the Wechsler Intelligence Scale for Children, Revised (WISC-R), and the Wechsler Preschool and Primary Scale of Intelligence (WPPSI), form a battery of tests that continue to be widely used. While schools no longer routinely offer individual tests specifically designed to measure intelligence, their use continues, usually as a follow-up to demonstrated academic difficulty or to determine eligibility for special programs, such as those for gifted children. Educators continue to rely on the relative ease and efficiency of administering group tests.

Although they date back to the 1917 prototype designed for military use, standardized tests at the start of the twenty-first century offer the promise of a more reliable and sophisticated means to predict future success. There are additional advantages as well: no special training is required to administer them, they can be given to large groups at once, and computers quickly and accurately generate results. The Cognitive Abilities Test (CAT) and the School and College Ability Test (SCAT) are among the more popular. Developers of these tests compare them favorably to both the Stanford-Binet and Wechsler series. Many high school students take the Scholastic Assessment Test (SAT) as part of the college application process. Its earliest version going back to 1926, the SAT is calculated to measure both verbal and mathematical ability. Proponents point to its usefulness as one indicator of future success, and claim that it counters inevitable disparities in grading practices nationwide.

Defining Intelligence: The Debate Continues

Alfred Binet rejected the idea of tests as providing a fixed label; he believed that children could indeed grow smarter. Binet's optimism notwithstanding, the history of intelligence testing in the United States reveals that early tests reflected the prejudices of the society in which they were produced. Not surprisingly, few questioned the idea that intelligence is innate and inherited. Tests made no accommodations for the disparate social and cultural backgrounds of test takers, and indeed, helped to fuel popularly held assumptions of the need to rank entire groups based on their racial or ethnic origins. They were hailed by some as a "measuring stick to organize society." Early-twentieth-century concerns about "feeblemindedness" validated the need for testing. Amidst growing concerns over an influx of immigration, tests were proposed to reduce the flow of "mental defectives" into the country. Congress, aided by the findings of prominent psychologists, passed the 1924 Immigration Act, which restricted admission for those believed to be of inferior intellect; especially targeted were Russians, Italians, Jews, and others primarily from southern and eastern Europe. Entry examinations given at Ellis Island seemingly ignored the numerous language and cultural barriers that would be readily apparent today.

While standardized tests continue to play a dominant role in American society, many critics argue that subtle inequities remain, producing results that more accurately represent the social and economic background of the test taker rather than providing a true measure of one's capabilities. The SAT and other tests, meanwhile, retain their foothold in the academic arena. The ability to "coach" students to produce greater scores has launched a multi-million-dollar mass tutoring industry. This has prompted many to further renounce their use as an "objective" means of assessment, arguing that they are more accurate indicators of students' social and economic backgrounds.

Meanwhile, biological interpretations of intelligence endure. Interrogating the degree to which race or ethnicity are determining factors, the 1994 publication of *The Bell Curve: Intelligence and Class Structure in American Life*, pushed the debate to new heights. While authors Richard Herrnstein and Charles Murray suggested the merits of acknowledging genetic differences, some critics immediately decried a racist agenda and uncovered studies they believed to be scientifically unsound.

Experts continue to voice disagreement over methods of measuring intelligence. At the core of the debate lie questions regarding the very concept of intelligence itself. Some embrace interpretations that echo the theories of turn-of-the-twentieth-century psychologist Charles Spearman of England, who pointed to a single, overarching general intelligence, or "g" factor. At the other extreme is the more recent twentieth-century model created by J. P. Guilford of the University of Southern California, who has identified no less than 150 components of intelligence. Arguably the most detailed model, it has had limited impact on the field of testing; many have adopted his claim, however, that intelligence is comprised of multiple parts.

The psychologist Robert Sternberg believes that the logical or analytical reasoning that most intelligence tests measure is only one of several factors. He had added to this two other areas of assessment—practical intelligence, or the ability to cope amidst one's environment, and experiential intelligence, or propensity for insight and creativity—to form his triarchic theory of intelligence. Sternberg's theory has advanced the notion that psychological assessments move beyond the written test toward those that seek measures of practical knowledge that guide our day-to-day experiences. Also believing that traditional IQ tests ignore critical components of intelligence, Howard Garner has introduced what he calls "multiple intelligences," which range from musical ability to self-awareness. Not surprisingly, Gardner is among those who advocate more expansive interpretations of intelligence, suggesting decreased reliance on the standardized tests of the past and more emphasis on real-life performance.

Experts continue to explore the concept of intelligence. New lines of inquiry widen the scope of investigation and questions abound. Should traits of character and morality be examined? Should the ability to form emotional bonds and display musical talent be considered? Will more comprehensive approaches replace short-answer tests? And does the ability to determine one's IQ necessarily define how this score should be used? Studies are moving beyond the realm of psychological inquiry. Increasingly sophisticated ways of measuring brain activity suggest new modes of interpretation while technological advances have produced an "artificial intelligence" that previous generations of researchers could barely imagine. While we may be no closer to finding a universally accepted definition of intelligence, clearly the quest to do so remains.

BIBLIOGRAPHY

Chapman, Paul Davis. *Schools as Sorters: Lewis Terman, Applied Psychology, and the Intelligence Testing Movement, 1890–1930.* New York: New York University Press, 1988.

Eysench, H. J., and Leon Kamin. *The Intelligence Controversy.* New York: Wiley, 1981.

Fancher, Raymond E., ed. *The Intelligence Men: Makers of the IQ Controversy.* New York: Norton, 1985.

Gardner, Howard. *Frames of Mind: The Theory of Multiple Intelligences.* New York: Basic Books, 1983.

———. "Who Owns Intelligence?" *Atlantic Monthly* (February 1999).

Gould, Stephen Jay. *The Mismeasure of Man.* New York: Norton, 1983.

Herrnstein, Richard J., and Charles Murray. *The Bell Curve: Intelligence and Class Structure in American Life.* New York: Free Press, 1994.

Sokal, Michael M., ed. *Psychological Testing and American Society, 1890–1930.* New Brunswick, N.J.: Rutgers University Press, 1987.

Sternberg, Robert J. *Beyond IQ: A Triarchic Theory of Human Intelligence.* Cambridge, U.K.: Cambridge University Press, 1985.

Yam, Philip, ed. "Exploring Intelligence." Spec. issue of *Scientific American* (Winter 1998).

Zenderland, Leila. *Measuring Minds: Henry Herbert Goddard and the Origins of American Intelligence Testing.* Cambridge, U.K.: Cambridge University Press, 1998.

Christine Clark Zemla

See also **Education; Racial Science.**

INTEREST GROUPS are organizations that seek to influence public policy. When defined in this manner, an enormous variety of organizations can be thought of as interest groups. Interest groups range from large, mass-membership organizations, such as the AMERICAN ASSOCIATION OF RETIRED PERSONS (AARP), to labor unions, such as the UNITED AUTO WORKERS (UAW), to large corporations, such as Exxon Mobil. Because of the enormous variety of interest groups, it is useful to divide them into several categories. One obvious distinction is between interest groups that are membership organizations; their future depends to an important degree on persuading individuals to become and remain members. At the other extreme are organizations such as corporations that are often very active in influencing public policy but that have no "members" as such; interest group activity is something in which they engage in order to protect their primary activities, such as making and selling a product or service. Another distinction that can be made is between interest groups that exist to promote a particular cause (such as the NATIONAL RIFLE ASSOCIATION, which exists primarily to oppose gun control) and interest groups such as corporations that may become involved in a wide range of public policies such as taxation, environmental protection, and trade policy that affects their interests.

Interest groups have long been thought to be central to American politics. The writers of the *Federalist Papers* (especially in Numbers 10 and 51) cast their arguments in favor of the Constitution in large part on how it would both facilitate and restrain interest-group activity. Alexis de Tocqueville's famous description of the United States in the Jacksonian era, *Democracy in America*, began the tradition of describing Americans as more likely to form and join interest groups than people in other countries. Whether or not this is the case depends on how the question is framed. It is true that Americans claim to be members of more interest groups than are the citizens of other advanced democracies such as Britain. However, certain types of interest groups, particularly those that are defined in terms of economic role, are often weaker than those in other democracies. For example, labor unions in the United States are much less successful in recruiting potential members than are unions in Germany, Britain, or above all, the Scandinavian democracies. American interest groups also tend to be fragmented. In many advanced democracies, a single interest group speaks for a broad sector of society, such as labor, farmers, or business. In the United States, however, there are generally numerous competing interest groups that claim to represent a sector of society. The NATIONAL ASSOCIATION OF MAN-

UFACTURERS, the Business Roundtable, the National Federation of Independent Business, and the Chamber of Commerce have all claimed to be the voice of business; a similar competitive situation could be described among farmers' organizations (the National Farmers Union, the American Farm Bureau, the National Farmers' Organization, plus numerous organizations representing producers of a single commodity) and environmental groups (the SIERRA CLUB, Friends of the Earth, Greenpeace, World Wildlife Fund, and many others).

Throughout American history, different types of interest groups have been brought to prominence as the products of socioeconomic changes, social movements, and government policies. The recurring economic crises of American agriculture from the late nineteenth century onward prompted the creation of a succession of agricultural interest groups—the Grange, the American Farm Bureau Federation, and the National Farmers' Union. Craft unions representing skilled workers became established in the late nineteenth century; not until the 1930s did industrial unions representing less skilled workers reach a secure footing, largely through the help of the federal government. The major social movements of the late twentieth century also left an impact. Civil rights groups came to prominence in the 1960s, followed by groups representing women (especially the NATIONAL ORGANIZATION FOR WOMEN [NOW]), consumers, and environmentalists. Business interest groups, seeking to counter the influence of unions and public-interest groups, set the pace in terms of fund-raising and organization in the 1980s and 1990s. While some of these interest groups have since seen their influence decline, all retain an important presence in American politics today. The interest-group landscape thus reflects a complex geology in which, like different rocks, different interest groups are created by a variety of forces.

Interest groups have used a wide array of tactics over the years, ranging from campaigning in elections to bribery. The most obvious tactics used today are lobbying and making campaign contributions. All major interest groups—such as the AMERICAN FEDERATION OF LABOR-CONGRESS OF INDUSTRIAL ORGANIZATIONS (AFL-CIO), the Business Roundtable, and individual companies such as Exxon Mobil or DuPont—employ professionals whose job is to persuade legislators and executive-branch officials of the wisdom and justice of the group's case. Most studies of lobbyists have concluded that the most effective lobbyists are those who have established a long-term relationship of trust and confidence between themselves and the legislators with whom they deal. Most lobbyists feel that they are more likely to gain a hearing for their arguments if their interest group makes campaign contributions to the politicians with whom they deal. Since 1974, campaign contributions made directly to candidates (known as hard money) must be made through POLITICAL ACTION COMMITTEES (PACS) that are linked to the interest group but legally separated from its general funds. Contributions are limited to a maximum of $5,000 for each election (primary and general) and must be reported to the Federal Election Commission (FEC.) It was hoped that the combination of limiting contributions considerably and publicizing them would prevent abuses. In the late twentieth century, however, interest groups were allowed to make unlimited contributions through parties to candidates. This "soft money" could come directly from the interest group's general funds and need not have been raised explicitly for political purposes. In 2002, federal legislation was passed to block soft money contributions to candidates in federal elections. Whether the legislation would survive the inevitable constitutional challenge in the courts remained to be seen. It also was likely that the legislation contained enough large loopholes by which its purpose could be circumvented, for example, by funneling soft money through state parties.

Interest groups also use other tactics. It has been very common for interest groups to go to court to challenge the constitutionality of legislation. The cases brought by the NATIONAL ASSOCIATION FOR THE ADVANCEMENT OF COLORED PEOPLE (NAACP) to undermine segregation, most notably *Brown v. Board of Education of Topeka*, are among the most influential. Almost equally famous is the 1973 Supreme Court decision *Roe v. Wade*, establishing the right of women to choose to have an abortion in the first two trimesters of pregnancy. The case was supported and the precedent defended in subsequent cases by feminist organizations such as NOW. Business interest groups, environmental groups, and unions also go to court frequently to challenge regulations that they dislike.

Interest groups have also become more active in campaigns to change public opinion. Individual companies such as Exxon Mobil have run many advertisements to both enhance their general image and to project their opinions of issues such as environmental regulation. The AFL-CIO and individual unions have also tried to mobilize their members and their families in support of both labor and more general policy issues. Interest groups were very zealous in both supporting and opposing the nomination of controversial figures to the Supreme Court, such as Justice Clarence Thomas.

In spite of their ubiquity, a debate has raged throughout American history about whether interest groups are an aid or a barrier to the practice of democracy. Defenders of interest groups argue that they are both a central aspect of democratic politics and an aid to good government. The Bill of Rights protects the right of the people to petition their government, and interest groups exist to do just that. The clash of interests between interest groups aids policymakers by providing more and better information for making policy decisions. However, interest groups have also generated considerable concern. First, it is often feared that instead of policymakers being aided by a clash of opinions and interests, in practice there will be a single interest group that dominates a policy area to the disadvantage of the public as a whole. Second, it is feared that the interest group system distorts democracy because the resources required to be effective are distributed unequally. Environmental or consumer protection groups must struggle hard to attract members and money; the large corporations that they confront can easily command the resources they need to staff a Washington office for their lobbyists, to create a PAC, or to make soft money contributions.

These defects in the interest group system are real and important. The dilemma set out by Madison in the *Federalist Papers* remains. Attempts to restrain the power of interest groups by restricting their activities may cure some of the "mischiefs" of the interest group system but at the cost of liberty. Madison's solution was to set interest against interest in what was later called a pluralist interest group system. Interest groups have experienced considerable growth in number and range during the beginning of the twenty-first century. For example, corporations are now opposed by public interest groups, and the National Rifle Association by Handgun Control. While the inequality of resources between these groups is still disturbing, this proliferation of interest groups creates a system that is more varied, inclusive, and representative of American society than in the past.

BIBLIOGRAPHY

Goldstein, Kenneth M. *Interest Groups, Lobbying, and Participation in America.* Cambridge, U.K.: Cambridge University Press, 1999.

Hamilton, Alexander, James Madison, and John Jay. *The Federalist Papers.* Edited by Isaac Kramnick. Harmondsworth: Penguin, 1987.

Tocqueville, Alexis de. *Democracy in America.* Edited by J.P. Mayer. New York: Harper and Row, 1988.

Wilson, Graham K. *Interest Groups.* Oxford: Blackwell, 1990.

Graham K. Wilson

See also **Lobbies.**

INTEREST LAWS. In the modern world, interest is ordinarily charged on all loans, with only exorbitant rates considered usurious. During the Middle Ages, however, any repayment in excess of the amount lent constituted usury, which was both a violation of civil law and a sin against God. Medieval Christians had inherited inconsistent precedents to govern the lending of money. The ancient Hebrews proscribed charging interest to their own people, but permitted it to be exacted from foreigners. At the same time, the Talmud declared money "sterile," implying that no one should expect to profit from lending it. The Greeks and Romans regulated interest rates, although the requirements of commerce and finance in the ancient world precluded an absolute prohibition. Despite this confused legacy, medieval churchmen concurred that usury, which they believed occasioned covetousness and greed, was evil.

Lawyers disagreed with theologians on the issue of usury, however. Medieval law allowed entrepreneurs to profit from lending money if they could demonstrate that they would have earned more from investing in another enterprise. The attempt to make up the difference between the amount of a loan and the profits that a lender might otherwise have attained gave rise to the modern distinction between usury—the illicit charges enjoined upon a debtor—and interest—the legitimate costs paid for borrowing.

The Massachusetts general assembly enacted the first usury law in American history in 1661. By 1791, all of the original thirteen states had adopted similar legislation. The charters of the First and Second Banks of the United States prohibited charging more than 6 percent on loans. In the twentieth century, state laws fixed maximum interest rates between 6 and 12 percent.

The federal government did not begin to monitor interest rates until 1969, when the Consumer Credit Protection Act, or the Truth-in-Lending Act as it is more commonly known, went into effect. Among other regulatory provisions, this law requires commercial lenders to disclose the total cost of borrowing as an annual average percentage rate. In addition, the Credit Control Act of 1969 authorizes the Federal Reserve Board to set national maximum and minimum interest rates on all credit transactions.

There are also laws designating the amount of interest institutional lenders may pay to attract public investment. To remedy the banking crisis of the 1930s, the Banking Act of 1933 discontinued interest payments on demand deposits (checking accounts) by all Federal Reserve Banks and by nonmember banks with deposits insured by the Federal Deposit Insurance Corporation (FDIC). The law further limited interest payments on time deposits (savings accounts) to the maximum rates that the Federal Reserve Board had established according to Regulation Q of the Federal Reserve Act.

To create financial markets more receptive to changing economic conditions, bankers have lobbied Congress to relax or repeal restrictions on interest rates since the 1960s. In response, the Senate and House banking committees fashioned the Depository Institutions Deregulation and Monetary Control Act of 1980 (DIDMCA). The DIDMCA phased out Regulation Q over a period of six years, annulled state usury laws for all federally insured lenders, and sanctioned interest-bearing checking accounts. Deregulation increased competition, lowered profit margins, and led to bank failures and consolidations, but it did not consistently raise the interest rates paid on deposits or reduce the interest rates charged for loans.

BIBLIOGRAPHY

De Roover, Raymond. *San Bernardino of Siena and Sant'Antonino of Florence: The Two Great Economic Thinkers of the Middle*

Ages. Boston: Harvard Graduate School of Business Administration, 1967.

Fry, Maxwell J. *Money, Interest, and Banking in Economic Development*. 2d ed. Baltimore: Johns Hopkins University Press, 1995.

Homer, Sidney, and Richard Sylla. *A History of Interest Rates*. 3d rev. ed. New Brunswick, N.J.: Rutgers University Press, 1996.

Nelson, Benjamin N. *The Idea of Usury: From Tribal Brotherhood to Universal Otherhood*. Princeton, N.J.: Princeton University Press, 1949.

Meg Greene Malvasi

INTERESTS, or "vested interests," was an expression popularly used around the opening of the twentieth century to designate the colossal business corporations that dominated the American scene. Among these interests were the so-called money trust, sugar trust, tobacco trust, oil trust, beef trust, and steel trust, all of which became subjects for strong attacks by muckraking reformers, especially during the presidency of Theodore Roosevelt. These attacks, published in books, magazines, and newspapers and delivered from the political platform, inaugurated an era of reform at the local, state, and national levels that lasted until the United States entered World War I.

BIBLIOGRAPHY

Hofstadter, Richard. *The Age of Reform, from Bryan to F. D. R.* New York: Vintage Books, 1955.

Erik McKinley Eriksson / C. W.

See also **Muckrakers; Progressive Movement, Early Twentieth Century; Trusts.**

INTERIOR, DEPARTMENT OF THE. The sixth department of cabinet rank, the U.S. Department of the Interior (DOI) was created 3 March 1849 to be the nation's principal conservation agency. Originally placed with the General Land Office, the Office of Indian Affairs, the Pension Office, and the Patent Office, it was reorganized by Reorganization Plan III of 1940, as amended. Since its creation, the department has been charged with a conflicting mission. One set of statutes stipulates it must develop the nation's lands and get natural resources such as trees, water, oil, and minerals out into the marketplace; another demands the conservation of these same resources. Since the president appoints the secretary of the interior, the compromise between these conflicting regulations is determined in part by whoever is in the Oval Office.

DOI serves as steward for approximately 436 million acres of public lands, which represent almost 19 percent of the nation's land surface and 66 percent of federally owned land. The department manages mineral development on 1.48 billion acres of the U.S. outer continental shelf. DOI also assists 556 tribes in managing 56 million acres of Indian trust land, and provides elementary and secondary education to over 50,000 Indian students. The department generates scientific information and assessments in a variety of areas: it monitors water quantity and quality, and helps local planners identify and deal with natural hazards, by earthquake monitoring and assessing environmental health and trends, for example. Millions of cultural and historic resources benefit from DOI protection. The department works to protect and recover imperiled plant and animal species, and helps to provide green space and recreation opportunities for urban America. Each year, the DOI hosts almost 290 million visitors to 379 national parks, 36 million visitors to 530 wildlife refuges, and 75 million visitors to public lands. The department manages dams and reservoirs, providing water to over 30 million people a year for municipal, agricultural, and industrial use, and generates enough power to make it the fifth largest energy utility in the seventeen western states.

The secretary of the interior heads the DOI, reporting directly to the president, and is responsible for the direction and supervision of all operations and activities of the department. The DOI is a large organization with multiple programs, which are administered by eight separate and distinct bureaus, including the Bureau of Land Management (BLM), the Minerals Management Service (MMS), the Office of Surface Mining Reclamation and Enforcement (OSM), the Bureau of Reclamation (BOR), the U.S. Geological Survey (USGS), the Fish and Wildlife Service (FWS), the National Park Service (NPS), and the BUREAU OF INDIAN AFFAIRS (BIA). Four assistant secretaries assist the secretary and deputy secretary in overseeing the eight bureaus.

The mission of the Bureau of Land Management is to sustain the health, diversity, and productivity of the public lands. The BLM operates on the principles of multiple use and sustained yield to manage public lands and resources, including energy and mineral resources, outdoor recreation, rangelands, timber, and fish and wildlife habitats. The bureau manages 264 million acres of public lands, about one-eighth of the U.S. land mass, and about 370 million acres of subsurface mineral estate. It was established 16 July 1946 by the consolidation of the General Land Office (1812) and the Grazing Service (1934).

The Minerals Management Service manages the mineral resources (including oil and natural gas) on the outer continental shelf in an environmentally sound and safe manner and collects, verifies, and distributes mineral revenues from federal and Indian lands in a timely fashion. It collects revenues from offshore federal mineral leases and from onshore mineral leases on federal and Indian lands and disburses them to states, tribes, and the U.S. Treasury. The service collects more than 4 billion dollars each year from oil and gas leasing programs. The

MMS was established on 19 January 1982 by secretarial order.

The Office of Surface Mining Reclamation and Enforcement fulfills the requirements of the Surface Mining Control and Reclamation Act in cooperation with the states and tribes. The OSM ensures that surface coal mines are operated safely and in an environmentally sound manner; it also works to restore lands after they have been mined and mitigates the effects of past coal mining through the reclamation of abandoned mines. Each year the OSM reclaims over 10,000 acres of mined lands in its efforts to protect the environment. The office was established by the Surface Mining Control and Reclamation Act of 1977.

The Bureau of Reclamation manages, develops, and protects water and related resources in an environmentally and economically sound manner. The BOR manages dams, reservoirs, and irrigation facilities, supplying water for agriculture and communities in the West. The bureau is the second largest producer of hydroelectric power and the fifth largest electric utility in the nation. It is also the largest water wholesaler, supplying household, agricultural, and industrial water to one-third of the population in the seventeen western states. The BOR was established pursuant to the Reclamation Act of 1902.

The U.S. Geological Survey produces the scientific information necessary to make sound natural resource management decisions and provides information on the effects and risks of natural hazards such as earthquakes and volcanoes. The USGS also provides data on the status of the nation's natural resources, such as the quality and quantity of water resources. It is also the federal government's largest natural science and mapping agency, and as such, produces information that contributes to public and environmental health and safety. The USGS was established by the Organic Act of 3 March 1879.

The Fish and Wildlife Service manages the lands of the National Wildlife Refuge System with the primary goal of conserving and protecting fish, wildlife, plants, and their habitats. It administers the Endangered Species Act for all but certain marine species, and consults with other agencies to help recover protected species. In total, the service manages 530 national wildlife refuges and sixty-seven national fish hatcheries. The FWS was created in 1940 by Reorganization Plan III by the consolidation of the Bureau of Fisheries (1871) and the Bureau of Biological Survey (1885).

The National Park Service preserves the natural and cultural resources of the national parks. The NPS cooperates with other agencies to extend the benefits of natural and cultural resource conservation and outdoor recreation in the United States and throughout the world. The NPS manages 379 national parks, conserving, preserving, and protecting the nation's resources. It was established on 25 August 1916.

The Bureau of Indian Affairs fulfills its responsibilities to, and promotes self-determination on behalf of, American Indians and their tribal governments. The BIA provides an array of services comparable to most of those provided by county and local governments. The BIA was created in 1824 as part of the War Department and transferred to the DOI in 1849.

BIBLIOGRAPHY

Babbitt, Bruce. "Science: Opening the Next Chapter of Conservation History." *Science* 267, no. 5206 (1995): 1954.

Office of the Federal Register, National Archives and Records Administration. *United States Government Manual.* Washington, D.C.: Government Printing Office, 2001–2002.

Mary Anne Hansen

See also **Geological Survey, U.S.; Mines, U.S. Bureau of; National Park System; Reclamation.**

INTERMEDIATE CREDIT BANKS. A system of unified Federal Intermediate Credit Banks (FICBs) was created with the passage of the Agricultural Credits Act on 4 March 1923. The twelve regionally dispersed intermediate credit banks received an initial infusion of $60 million in capital from the U.S. Treasury and were established as separate divisions of the Federal Land Banks, with the intention of providing a permanent source of seasonal production credit for agriculture and livestock production.

In the early 1920s Federal Reserve policy had shifted toward tighter credit, and country banks were reluctant to lend to farmers due to the precipitous decline in farm commodity and land prices (which had peaked in 1920) and the large proportion of agricultural loans already on their books. In response to these credit conditions, declining demand for their products, and the liquidation of the War Finance Board (which had discounted agricultural paper on an emergency basis from 1921 to 1923), agricultural interest groups, such as the American Farm Bureau Federation, began to clamor for more dependable and improved sources of credit. The authorizing legislation that created the FICBs in 1923 was passed in response to the intensive lobbying efforts of the "Farm Bloc," a bipartisan coalition of congressmen.

The FICBs were authorized to provide credit for the production of crops and livestock, for cooperative marketing of staple agricultural products, and for the cooperative purchase of farm supplies. To carry out these functions, the banks could sell collateral trust debentures to increase their capital stock, discount agricultural paper, and make loans to cooperative associations. Loans typically had short maturities and could not exceed three years by law.

The initial impact of the banks was limited. Loans and discounts outstanding at the end of 1929 totaled approximately $76 million, but the loans amounted to less than 2 percent of all non–real estate agricultural loans outstanding in that year. In part, this was due to their design. The credit banks were not authorized to make loans directly to individual farmers. Instead, local cooperative marketing associations, finance corporations, and livestock loan companies provided FICB funds indirectly to farmers. However, throughout the 1920s, these agencies complained about the cumbersome loan procedures of the credit banks and did not utilize them extensively. The rediscounting function of the banks also proved to be unprofitable for country banks relative to Federal Reserve banks since caps on their profit margins were imposed.

The Farm Credit Act of 1933 significantly altered the federal farm credit system; it created twelve production credit associations to assist the FICBs in reaching out to individual farmers. By executive order in that same year, supervision of the banks was also transferred from the Federal Farm Loan Board to the Farm Credit Administration (FCA). Despite these changes, through 1970, FICBs never provided more than 2 percent of the non–real estate agricultural loans outstanding.

In 1988 Federal Credit Banks were created by merging the FICBs with Federal Land Banks. The Federal Credit Banks were authorized to extend loans to Production Credit Associations, Agricultural Credit Associations, and Federal Land Credit Associations, and to make long-term real estate mortgage loans in areas not serviced by direct lenders. These banks are owned and operated by their member-borrowers and have elected boards that guide the institutions' policies and ensure compliance with the FCA's regulations.

BIBLIOGRAPHY

American Institute of Banking. *Farm Credit Administration.* New York: American Institute of Banking, 1934.

Benedict, Murray R. *Farm Policies of the U.S., 1790–1850: A Study of their Origin and Development.* New York: Twentieth Century Fund, 1953.

Sparks, Earl Sylvester. *History and Theory of Agricultural Credit in the United States.* New York: Thomas Y. Crowell, 1932.

Kris Mitchener

See also **Credit.**

INTERNATIONAL BROTHERHOOD OF TEAMSTERS began on 27 January 1899, when the American Federation of Labor (AFL) issued a charter to the 1,700 members of the Team Drivers International Union (TDIU). While today "teamsters" are associated with trucks, the term originally referred to those who drove "teams" of horses. Organizations other than TDIU still represented teamsters, including the Teamsters National Union, which included team owners as well as drivers, and Chicago's International Team Drivers Union, which formed in 1903 to exclude owners. Competing unions met in 1903 at Niagara Falls, New York, and formed the International Brotherhood of Teamsters (IBT). A bloody defeat, suffered while supporting a tailor's strike at Chicago's Montgomery Ward Company in 1905, weakened the new union. The 1907 IBT convention elected the president of Boston's Local Union 25, Daniel J. Tobin, as general president, a position he retained for forty-five years.

Early Growth and Transformation of the Teamsters

The Teamsters grew slowly, adding new job categories, and in 1909 changed its name to the International Brotherhood of Teamsters, Chauffeurs, Stablemen, and Helpers. The IBT prospered because it represented both the disappearing horse-and-wagon workers, as well as the truck drivers who were replacing them. This led to some internal conflict, but the conversion was very gradual. In 1920 there were scarcely 1,000 to 2,000 trucks in the United States, and the Teamsters continued to focus on local businesses that delivered such goods as coal, ice, meat, and laundry. In 1920, Tobin affiliated the IBT with the Canadian Trades and Labour Congress. The Great Depression that followed the 1929 stock market crash initially hurt the IBT, and membership reached a low of 75,000 in 1933. However, during the latter half of the 1930s, both the trucking industry and the Teamsters experienced major growth spurts, due in large part to labor and commerce regulations passed by the federal government. Labor laws controlled wages, hours, and working conditions, and ensured the right to bargain collectively. The most significant of these laws was the 1935 National Labor Relations Act (also called the Wagner Act). Equally significant for the Teamsters was the passage of the Motor Carrier Act of 1935, which gave the Interstate Commerce Commission authority to regulate the trucking industry. In 1937 the IBT again altered its name, becoming the International Brotherhood of Teamsters, Chauffeurs, Warehousemen, and Helpers of America. The Teamsters' 277,000 members made it the largest union in the AFL, and there were more than 70,000 trucks on U.S. roads in 1938. In that supportive political climate the Teamsters were very powerful, and a sympathetic strike by the IBT lent Teamster power and strength to weaker unions.

Teamsters' Boom Years in the 1940s and 1950s

The post–World War II economic boom created further IBT growth, and membership exceeded one million in 1950. The political climate became less friendly, as Congress restricted labor's power with the Labor-Management Relations Act of 1947 (usually called the Taft-Hartley Act). At the 1952 convention, Dan Tobin announced his retirement as president. The number of Teamsters continued to climb under new president Dave Beck, who settled a twenty-five-state contract in 1955 covering all over-the-road and local freight companies. The number of trucks increased greatly in 1956, when the federal government created the Interstate Highway System. The IBT continued to support workers through sympathetic

Labor Troubles. Violence during the 1934 Teamsters strike in Minneapolis, Minn. About 200 were injured in clashes with the police and National Guard.

strikes, refusing to pick up or deliver goods anywhere there was a work stoppage. This power brought intense scrutiny and backlash from businesses and increasing government hostility. A Senate investigation into racketeering and corruption led to the IBT's expulsion from the American Federation of Labor and Congress of Industrial Organizations (AFL-CIO) in 1957. Teamster membership reached 1.5 million at the 1957 convention, when James P. (Jimmy) Hoffa was elected president. In 1959, Congress passed the antiunion Labor-Management Reporting and Disclosure Act (also known as the Landrum-Griffin Act). The law prohibited sympathetic strikes, significantly reducing the Teamsters' ability to assist less powerful unions. The Senate in the late 1950s also convened the McClellan Committee, which investigated corruption in the IBT. Dave Beck went to prison in 1962 for larceny and income tax violations.

Union Decline and Evolution of the New Teamsters

Hoffa negotiated the first National Master Freight Agreement in 1964, covering 400,000 Teamsters employed at more than 16,000 trucking companies. Hoffa was convicted of jury tampering in 1963, began a prison term in 1967, and resigned as IBT president on 22 June 1971. He was released from prison later in 1971 and was attempting to reenter union politics when he mysteriously disappeared in 1975. Teamster membership passed the two million mark in 1976. Deregulation of the trucking industry began in 1980, which created a steady decline in Teamster membership. Throughout the 1980s and 1990s attacks by business and government, along with economic globalization, severely impacted the labor movement, and the Teamsters. IBT President Roy Williams was convicted of bribing a U.S. senator in 1982, and President Jackie Presser was indicted for embezzling union funds. The IBT sought shelter under the AFL-CIO umbrella, and rejoined the organization in 1988. IBT President William McCarthy signed a 1989 consent decree settling a federal government racketeering suit, and a court-appointed trustee supervised the first direct election of union officers in 1991. Won by Ronald R. Carey, a former United Parcel Service (UPS) worker and New York City local union president, the union again changed its name, reverting to the original International Brotherhood of Teamsters. Carey won reelection in 1996 and led a successful national strike at UPS in 1997, providing a boost to the sagging labor movement. One significant national issue Carey addressed was the use of part-time workers. The victory was short lived, as the government overseer controlling the union ruled that Carey participated in a plan to funnel dues money into his 1996 reelection campaign. Carey was barred from running in a special election, and James P. Hoffa Jr., son of the former IBT leader, became president. By 1998 membership stabilized at 1.4

James P. (Jimmy) Hoffa. The powerful president of the Teamsters union from 1957 to 1971 disappeared in 1975. ARCHIVE PHOTOS/FILMS

million members. By that date only 16 percent of the "new" Teamsters were truck drivers, and the union represented a diverse assortment of workers such as policemen, teachers, school principals, nurses, airline pilots, and zookeepers. Even the character dressed in the Mickey Mouse costume in Disney World is a Teamster.

BIBLIOGRAPHY

Brill, Steven. *The Teamsters.* New York: Simon and Schuster, 1978.

La Botz, Dan. *Rank and File Rebellion: Teamsters for a Democratic Union.* New York: Verso, 1990.

Romer, Sam. *The International Brotherhood of Teamsters: Its Government and Structure.* New York: Wiley, 1962.

Sloane, Arthur A. *Hoffa.* Cambridge, Mass.: MIT Press, 1991.

John Cashman

See also **Labor; Trade Unions.**

INTERNATIONAL BROTHERHOOD OF TEAMSTERS V. UNITED STATES,

431 U.S. 329 (1977), a Supreme Court decision that involved the employer T.I.M.E.-D.C., Inc., a national common carrier of motor freight, and the International Brotherhood of Teamsters, a labor union representing a large group of employees. The federal district and circuit courts held that T.I.M.E.-D.C. had violated Title VII of the Civil Rights Act of 1964 by engaging in a pattern or practice of employment discrimination against African Americans and Spanish-surnamed Americans. The lower courts also held that the union had violated the act by cooperating with the employer to create and maintain a seniority system that perpetuated past discrimination.

On appeal, the Supreme Court agreed with the government that the company had engaged in a systemwide practice of minority discrimination in violation of Title VII. The Court denied, however, the government's claim that the union's seniority system, which was exempt from Title VII, also violated the provision because it perpetuated discrimination. The Court also rejected the notion that victims suffering discriminatory acts prior to Title VII qualified for judicial relief under it.

In dissenting opinions, Justices Thurgood Marshall and William J. Brennan argued that the law granting exemption to seniority plans was not "plainly and unmistakenly clear" regarding perpetuation of discrimination, and thus the union's seniority system should not be protected. The Court's decision provided broad immunity to seniority plans that are on their face neutral, even if they perpetuate the effects of past discrimination.

BIBLIOGRAPHY

Kleinman, Kenneth. "Seniority Systems and the Duty of Fair Representation: Union Liability in the *Teamsters* Context." *Harvard Civil Rights-Civil Liberties Law Review* 14, no. 3 (Fall 1979): 711–782.

Schlei, Barbara Lindemann, and Paul Grossman. *Employment Discrimination.* 2d ed. Washington, D.C.: American Bar Association, BNA Books, 1983.

Tony Freyer / A. R.

See also **American Federation of Labor–Congress of Industrial Organizations.**

INTERNATIONAL COURT OF JUSTICE

(ICJ), sometimes known as the "World Court." The principal judicial organ of the United Nations (UN) since 1946, its statute is a multilateral agreement annexed to the charter of the United Nations.

The court serves as a principal vehicle for furthering the UN's mandate to facilitate the peaceful resolution of international disputes, acting as a permanent, neutral, third-party dispute settlement mechanism rendering binding judgments in "contentious" cases initiated by one state against another. Parties to dispute before the court must consent to the exercise of the court's jurisdiction. This may be demonstrated in one of three ways: (1) by special agreement or *compris,* in the context of a particular case; (2) by treaty, such as a multilateral agreement that specifies reference of disputes arising under it to the court; or

(3) by advance consent to the so-called "compulsory" jurisdiction court on terms specified by the state concerned. The court also has the power to render advisory opinions at the request of international institutions such as the UN General Assembly.

Located in The Hague, the ICJ is the successor to the Permanent Court of International Justice, an organ of the League of Nations, which itself was the culmination of earlier international movements to promote international arbitration as an alternative to armed conflict. After World War II, the United States became party to the statute and accepted the compulsory jurisdiction of the court on terms specified by the Senate, including the famous Connally amendment, in which the United States declined to give its consent to "disputes with regard to matters which are essentially within the domestic jurisdiction of the United States of America, as determined by the United States of America." Over the subsequent decade and a half the United States unsuccessfully initiated a series of cases against the USSR, Hungary, Czechoslovakia, and Bulgaria concerning aerial incidents in Europe. The court as a whole had relatively few cases on its docket during the 1960s, but the United States successfully appealed to the ICJ to vindicate its position as a matter of legal right during the Iranian hostage crisis.

A case initiated by Nicaragua in 1984 challenging U.S. support of the Contra militias and the mining of Nicaraguan ports proved to be a watershed in U.S. dealings with the court. After vigorously and unsuccessfully contesting the court's jurisdiction in a preliminary phase, the United States declined to appear on the merits and subsequently withdrew its consent to the compulsory jurisdiction of the court in 1985. However, the United States continues to be party to cases relying on other jurisdictional grounds.

BIBLIOGRAPHY

Rosenne, Shabtai. *The Law and Practice of the International Court, 1920–1996.* The Hague and Boston: Nijhoff, 1997.

Eyffinger, Arthur. *The International Court of Justice 1946–1996.* The Hague and Boston: Kluwer Law International, 1996.

Pomerance, Michla. *The United States and the World Court as a "Supreme Court of the Nations": Dreams, Illusions, and Disillusion.* Dordrecht, Netherlands: Nijhoff, 1996.

David A. Wirth

See also **League of Nations; United Nations.**

INTERNATIONAL GEOPHYSICAL YEAR,

eighteen months (1 July 1957–31 December 1958) of geophysical observations by about 30,000 scientists and technicians representing more than seventy countries. The extension of this program for an additional year (until 31 December 1959) was officially called International Geophysical Cooperation (IGC), but that period is generally included in the term "International Geophysical Year" (IGY). The IGY and IGC attempted simultaneous observations in eleven fields of earth, near-earth, and solar physics: aurora and airglow, cosmic rays, geomagnetism, glaciology, gravity, ionospheric physics, latitude and longitude determination, meteorology, oceanography, seismology, and solar activity. The IGY oversaw the launching of the first artificial earth satellites, inaugurating the age of space exploration.

International cooperation in science began in the 1830s with the networks of scientific observers organized by Karl Friedrich Gauss in Germany to observe and record geomagnetic changes, and by W. Whewell and Sir John W. Lubbock in England to make tidal observations. Because observations in high northern latitudes could not be made routinely, Lt. Karl Weyprecht of the Austrian Navy organized the First International Polar Year in 1882–1883, during which scientists and military men from ten European countries and the United States operated twelve stations in the Arctic and two in the Antarctic. The American stations were at Point Barrow, Alaska, and at Grinnell Land in the Canadian Arctic. The rescue of the latter's observers (under army Lt. A. W. Greely) is famous in the annals of polar exploration. Fifty years later the Second International Polar Year (1932–1933) saw fourteen countries (twelve from Europe, plus the United States and Canada) occupy twenty-seven stations, again mostly in the Arctic. Of the scientific publications that resulted, more came from the United States than from any other country.

By 1950, the rapid advances in geophysics and the need to restore the international network of scientists that had been ruptured by World War II led Lloyd V. Berkner of the United States to propose another international polar year to be held only twenty-five years after the previous one, in 1957–1958. The international scientific bodies to whom he referred his proposal, organized under the umbrella International Council of Scientific Unions, broadened it to include the entire earth; thus the IGY replaced its predecessors' limited programs with a comprehensive program of observations in fields where data recorded simultaneously at many places could yield a picture of the whole planet. Scientists occupied more than 2,500 stations worldwide at a cost of about $500 million.

Two of the most prominent achievements of the IGY were the discovery of the Van Allen radiation belts and the calculation of a new, pear-shaped model of the shape of the earth. Both these results came from rocket-launched satellites, the IGY's most spectacular new feature. So successful was the IGY that it has been followed by a number of other cooperative research programs, including the International Year of the Quiet Sun (1964–1965), the International Hydrological Decade (1965–1975), and the International Decade of Ocean Exploration (1970–1980).

BIBLIOGRAPHY

International Council of Scientific Unions. *Annals of the International Geophysical Year.* London, New York: Pergamon Press, 1957–1970.

Sullivan, Walter. *Assault on the Unknown: The International Geophysical Year.* New York: McGraw-Hill, 1961.

Wilson, J. Tuzo. *I.G.Y.: The Year of the New Moons.* New York: Knopf, 1961.

Harold L. Burstyn/A. R.; C. W.

See also **Geophysical Explorations; Greely's Arctic Expedition; Observatories, Astronomical.**

INTERNATIONAL HARVESTER COMPANY.

To solve bitter competition among farm machinery manufacturers, Cyrus McCormick Jr., son of the inventor of the reaper, spearheaded the 1902 consolidation of the industry's leading companies, including the McCormick Harvesting Machine Company; Deering Harvester Company; Plano Manufacturing Company; Warder, Bushnell and Glessner Company; and Milwaukee Harvester Company. Capitalized at $120 million, the merger acquired other concerns as its lines diversified. The federal government brought action against the company, and in 1914 the Supreme Court found the company an illegal combination under the SHERMAN ANTITRUST ACT and ordered division of the company's property among independent corporations (*United States v. International Harvester Company*, 214 U.S. 987).

BIBLIOGRAPHY

McCormick, Cyrus H. *The Century of the Reaper: An Account of Cyrus Hall McCormick, the Inventor of the Reaper.* Boston: Houghton Mifflin, 1931.

Sullivan, E. Thomas, ed. *The Political Economy of the Sherman Act: The First One Hundred Years.* New York: Oxford University Press, 1991.

Roger Burlingame/C. W.

See also **Agricultural Machinery; Antitrust Laws; McCormick Reaper.**

INTERNATIONAL LABOR DEFENSE.

The International Labor Defense (ILD) was formed in 1925 by the Central Committee of the Communist Party of the United States as the party's legal arm. The group's goal was to provide legal and moral aid to people it considered victims of an ongoing class war. Under the leadership of William L. Patterson and Vito Marcantonio, the ILD came to the defense of strikers and workers confronting labor injustices, foreign-born individuals faced with discrimination and deportation, and African Americans in the Deep South challenged by oppression and racism.

In 1927, lifelong labor activist and eventual African American rights advocate Lucy Parsons became a member of the National Committee of ILD. Parsons believed that militant strikes and direct action would lead to equality and enable a working-class movement that could seize the methods of production. Similarly, the ILD believed that direct action would lead to equality in a legal arena that was politically motivated. With that in mind, the group launched political protests and campaigns that included legal defense, as well as massive levels of publicity-garnering action. The scope and aggressiveness of ILD protests, however, often contrasted sharply with the less-combative methods of other civil rights groups.

Included in the ILD's list of controversial protest actions was a campaign to keep Italian immigrants Nicola Sacco and Bartolomeo Vanzetti from receiving the death penalty. Sacco and Vanzetti, who were anarchists, were convicted for robbing and killing two men who were delivering the payroll of a shoe factory. The ILD argued that the men were convicted, and eventually executed, because of their poor grasp of the English language and status as immigrants. Other efforts taken on by the ILD included a campaign to force the release of convicted trade unionists Tom Mooney and Warren K. Billings and the criminal defense of the Scottsboro Boys.

During the depression and early wartime years, the ILD introduced many African Americans to Communist rhetoric and teachings. But its involvement in the Scottsboro case, more than any other protest, garnered a great deal of African American support for the ILD and its Communist Party leanings. The Scottsboro case began in 1931 after two white women on a freight train near Paint Rock, Alabama, accused nine African American men of rape. The ILD protested that the men were arrested and tried without adequate access to counsel—eight of the nine were sentenced to death. The ILD initiated a campaign to gain the men's freedom and engaged the National Association for the Advancement of Colored People (NAACP) in an intense battle for control of the case. After a prolonged battle between the two organizations and an attempted witness bribe by attorneys associated with the ILD, an alliance between the ILD, the NAACP, the American Civil Liberties Union (ACLU), and the American Scottsboro Committee (ASC) was able to obtain releases for four of the nine defendants.

Until the end of World War II, the ILD also published a monthly magazine called the *Labor Defender* in an effort to extend its challenge of racial, class, and political oppression. In 1946, the group merged with two other organizations to form the Civil Rights Congress.

BIBLIOGRAPHY

Martin, Charles H. "The International Labor Defense and Black America." *Labor History* 26 (Spring 1985).

James T. Scott

See also **Communist Party, United States of America; Industrial Workers of the World; Sacco-Vanzetti Case; Scottsboro Case.**

INTERNATIONAL LABOR ORGANIZATION.

Founded in 1919 as part of the League of Nations, the

International Labor Organization (ILO) is the only surviving creation of the Treaty of Versailles. In 1946 the ILO became the first agency of the United Nations.

The ILO formulates international labor standards, aiming to establish basic labor rights such as a prohibition on forced labor; the right to organize; the right to bargain collectively; and the right to equal opportunity across ethnic, racial, and gender differences. Western powers founded the ILO with the goal of diffusing the appeal of Bolshevism and harnessing the wartime loyalties of labor movements to a reformist internationalism; they also emphasized the practical importance of multilateral cooperation in the arena of labor reform—sweated labor in one country endangered decent labor standards among its competitors.

The United States, which never joined the League of Nations, did not join the ILO until 1934. However, Samuel Gompers, head of the American Federation of Labor, chaired the Labor Commission created by the 1919 Peace Conference to draft the ILO Constitution, which established the "tripartite" principle of organization that remains the ILO's cornerstone. Under tripartism—which makes the ILO unique among the UN and other international agencies—not only governments, but also workers and employers are represented (in a 2:1:1 ratio) in the ILO.

Tripartism proved the heart of U.S.-ILO tensions from the early 1950s through 1977, when the United States withdrew from the ILO. Interpreting tripartism to mean independent workers' and employers' representatives, the United States complained that Soviet, Eastern European, and some Third World union and employers' representatives were voting on government instructions. The issue was a thorny one: the ILO Credentials Committee pointed out in 1954 that "refusing to admit . . . persons duly nominated by their government . . . on the ground that the state concerned had a socialized economy would be an unwarranted interpretation of the [ILO] Constitution." Moreover, observers noted that U.S. representatives had not objected to the seating of government-controlled trade unions from Franco's Spain.

Another source of controversy lay in the ILO's expanding agenda from traditional labor standards to broader questions of political economy, full employment, development policies, and human rights concerns—which flowed from the increasing proportion of Third World nations among ILO members. The United States objected, partly on ideological grounds, partly because its representatives believed that the changes distracted the organization from its traditional focus upon verifiable commitments to specific rights and freedoms. Injured by the loss of U.S. dues, which accounted for one-quarter of the organization's budget, the ILO trimmed its sails, and the United States rejoined in 1980.

At the end of the twentieth century, the ILO enjoyed membership from over 160 nations, and had concluded 183 conventions. The ILO's main enforcement mechanism was publicity—the organization's stately hearings and reports continued to expose member nations' labor laws and practices to scrutiny. The need for international labor standards was never greater than in the era of "globalization," and the ILO's strongest supporters continue to lament the absence of stronger means of enforcement.

BIBLIOGRAPHY

Alcock, Antony E. *History of the International Labor Organization.* New York: Octagon Books, 1971.

Ghebali, Victor Yves. *The International Labour Organization: A Case Study on the Evolution of U.N. Specialized Agencies.* Boston: M. Nijhoff, 1989.

William E. Forbath

See also **American Federation of Labor–Congress of Industrial Organizations; Child Labor; Labor; Labor Legislation and Administration; League of Nations; Wages and Hours of Labor, Regulation of.**

INTERNATIONAL LADIES GARMENT WORKERS UNION (ILGWU), founded in 1900, a major factor in American labor, radical, socialist, and Jewish history. The first leaders of the ILGWU, moderate Jewish socialists and labor veterans, were the victorious survivors of many years of labor struggles and internecine political warfare in the New York garment industry, which had been inundated by immigrant Jewish "greenhorns." These "Columbus tailors" found their advocate in Abraham Cahan's *Jewish Daily Forward*, which was struggling to assimilate them into socialist-flavored Americanism.

As a small, moribund, craft-minded organization, the early ILGWU narrowly beat off an Industrial Workers of the World (IWW) challenge in 1905–1907. But an immigrant flood revitalized the Jewish labor movement in the aftermath of the 1905 Russian Revolution. Radicalized by the revolution and trained in trade unionism by the Jewish Labor Bund, this huge wave of immigrants waged a series of mass garment strikes. The 1909–1910 "rising of the twenty thousand" in the New York shirtwaist industry was the first mass strike of women workers in American history. The weak ILGWU left much of the day-to-day administration of the strike in the hands of rank-and-file workers, laborite-feminist activists from the Women's Trade Union League, and woman volunteers from the Socialist Party (SP). The success of the strike paved the way for the unionizing "great revolt" of fifty thousand New York cloak makers, mostly males, in 1910, which established the ILGWU as the third-largest member of the AMERICAN FEDERATION OF LABOR (AFL) by 1914.

The "great revolt" was resolved through a "protocol of peace," brokered by Louis Brandeis, that was widely hailed as the Progressive Era model for permanent cooperation between capital and labor. This Progressive pipe dream broke down rapidly. The ILGWU was shaken

Enduring Symbol. Fifty years after the Triangle Shirtwaist fire of 1911, New York City garment workers sit in front of a poster of some of the victims, whose deaths galvanized the labor movement—the International Ladies Garment Workers Union in particular. Associated Press/World Wide Photos

by a massive cloak makers' rebellion against the protocol that prefigured later internal conflicts. The combatants reached a settlement through SP mediation, solidifying the union's Socialist ties, and the ILGWU became a powerful American institution. The union initially opposed World War I, and hailed the Russian Revolution, but its officers continued to face rank-and-file leftist dissent. They hinted that youthful female dissidents radicalized by the Triangle Shirtwaist Fire and revolution abroad were victims of sexual frustration.

During the great labor upsurge of 1919, dissidents formed workers councils, inspired by workers' councils in Seattle and Petrograd. The ILGWU formed the strongest trade union base of the early American Communist Party (CP). The political, generational, ethnic, and gender contradictions within the ILGWU led to a decade of internecine warfare between pro-CP insurgents and pro-SP union leaders. The hardnosed anticommunist Morris Sigman, a former Wobbly (IWW member), kept a tenuous grasp on the ILGWU's national machinery but had to concede control of the New York ILGWU to the rebels. The peak of the insurgency was the left-led 1926 New York cloak makers' strike. The strike achieved ambiguous results, which Sigman seized on as his golden opportunity to purge the left New York officers, touching off a bloody civil war in the whole garment industry. Several lives were lost, and scores of workers were hospitalized. ILGWU leaders managed to regain control with assistance from business, government, and organized crime. The ILGWU's street general was SP spokesperson Abe Beckerman, who was involved in the Jewish gangster "Lepke" Buchalter's infamous "Murder Incorporated." When the dust cleared, little was left of the ILGWU. Wages plunged, hours lengthened, and sweatshop conditions were restored.

The left attempted to replace the ILGWU with a "red union," but the effort was stillborn due to bureaucratic dithering by the "Lovestonites," a CP faction led by Jay Lovestone, and ultraleftist policies imposed by the increasingly Stalinized CP. The ensuing purge of the Lovestonites from the party enabled the ILGWU to regain control of the trade.

The ILGWU experienced a resurgence during the New Deal. The Jewish needle trades unions had a friend in the White House in Franklin D. Roosevelt. The massive ILGWU strikes in 1933 and 1934 benefited from a rare combination of government sympathy, weak resistance from manufacturers, and a tremendous release of pent-up militancy. Soon the ILGWU totally dominated

Memorial Procession. Horses draped in mourning capes lead workers and other sympathizers marching on 5 April 1911 in memory of the 146 garment workers who died eleven days earlier in the Triangle Shirtwaist Company fire in New York City. LIBRARY OF CONGRESS

the industry. The ILGWU leader David Dubinsky, a veteran of the Jewish Labor Bund, became one of America's most important union leaders. A Tammany politician quipped that "the Jews have drei veltn—di velt, yene velt, un Roosevelt" (three worlds—this world, the other world, and Roosevelt). Consequently, during the Holocaust the ILGWU did not militantly challenge Roosevelt's refusal to admit Jewish refugees. As late as 1947 hourly wages for ILGWU members were higher than wages for autoworkers. The New Deal alliance between the Roosevelt administration and the Congress of Industrial Organizations (CIO), which shaped later American trade unionism, was molded on the template of the special relationship between Roosevelt and Jewish Socialist needle trades officials like Dubinsky.

During the Roosevelt and Truman administrations the ILGWU pioneered many hallmarks of American unionism. But while most American workers experienced dramatically increased prosperity in the Eisenhower era, ILGWU leaders, fearful of nonunion competition, orchestrated a decline in garment wage levels that made the ILGWU notorious for "fighting for lower wages." The ILGWU experienced a major demographic transformation. Jews exited the shop floor, replaced by blacks, Puerto Ricans, and eventually Asians. By 2002, Jews in the garment industry were predominantly union officers or employers.

After World War II the ILGWU, in close collaboration with the U.S. government, threw its considerable resources into the struggle against communism. Lovestone became the ILGWU director of international affairs and the key personal link between the AFL-CIO, led by George Meany, a Dubinsky protégé, and the Central Intelligence Agency. After Dubinsky retired in 1966, the ILGWU became one of the foremost labor opponents of foreign imports.

In the late twentieth century the rapidly declining ILGWU attempted to organize new immigrant sweatshop labor and defended the rights of undocumented workers. But the old pattern of collaboration with employers to protect the industry persisted. Indeed, some Hong Kong sweatshops moved to New York in the 1980s and set up as union shops. Former ILGWU officials dominated The Union of Needletrades, Industrial, and Textile Employees, which was formed in 1995 through a merger of the ILGWU with the Amalgamated Clothing and Textile Workers Union, an old rival based in the men's clothing industry.

BIBLIOGRAPHY

Dubinsky, David, and A. H. Raskin. *David Dubinsky: A Life with Labor.* New York: Simon and Schuster, 1977.

Epstein, Melech. *Jewish Labor in U.S.A: An Industrial, Political, and Cultural History of the Jewish Labor Movement.* 2 vols. New York: 1950–1953. Reprint, New York: Ktav Publishing House, 1969.

Foner, Philip S. "Revolt of the Garment Workers (I and II)." In *History of the Labor Movement in the United States.* Vol. 5. New York: International Publishers, 1988.

Gurowsky, David. "Factional Disputes within the ILGWU, 1919–1928." Ph.D. diss., State University of New York at Binghamton, 1978.

Kwong, Peter, and JoAnn Lum. "Hard Labor in Chinatown: How the Other Half Lives Now." *Nation*, 18 June 1988.

Liebman, Arthur. *Jews and the Left.* New York: Wiley, 1979.

Myerson, Michael. "ILGWU: Fighting for Lower Wages." *Ramparts*, October 1969.

Tyler, Gus. *Look for the Union Label: A History of the International Ladies' Garment Workers' Union.* Armonk, N.Y.: M. E. Sharpe, 1995.

John Dewey Holmes

See also **Clothing Industry; Labor; Trade Unions.**

INTERNATIONAL LAW is traditionally understood to be the law governing the relations among sovereign states, the primary "subjects" of international law. Strictly speaking, this definition refers to public international law, to be contrasted with private international law, which concerns non-state actors such as individuals and corporations. Public international law originates from a number of sources, which are both created by and govern the behavior of states. Treaties or international agreements are a familiar source of international law, and are the counterpart of domestic contracts, which create rules for the states that accept them. Customary international law, which has fewer analogues in domestic law but which is binding as a matter of international law, originates from a pattern of state practice motivated by a sense of legal right or obligation. Particularly since World War II, international institutions and intergovernmental organizations whose members are states, most notably the United Nations (UN), have become a principal vehicle for making, applying, implementing and enforcing public international law.

The United States is a modified "dualist" legal system, which means that international law does not necessarily operate as domestic law. In fact, both the Congress and the president may violate international law under certain circumstances. Similarly, the Constitution is held superior to international law in the event of an outright conflict, and in such cases the courts will recognize the primacy of domestic legal authorities over international law. Article I, section 8 of the Constitution apportions certain exclusive powers related to foreign relations and international law to the Congress. These include the authority to declare war, to regulate international trade, to establish and maintain an army and navy and to establish rules governing them, and to "define and punish Piracies and Felonies committed on the high Seas, and Offences against the Law of Nations." Otherwise, the president, as commander in chief and chief executive, exercises considerable unenumerated powers in such areas as the recognition of foreign states and governments, and is "the sole organ of the nation in its external relations, and its sole representative with foreign nations" (*United States v. Curtiss-Wright Export Corp.*, 1936).

The Constitution likewise gives the president the power to negotiate treaties, subject to Senate advice and consent by a two-thirds majority. In the early 2000s, many of the nation's international agreements were nonetheless concluded as executive agreements, without congressional participation. While treaties, according to Article VI of the Constitution, are the supreme law of the land, U.S. courts make a distinction between "self-executing" treaties that will be applied as rules of decision in domestic litigation and those that will not. Article I, section 10 of the Constitution prohibits the states of the Union from entering into treaties or alliances, or from engaging in most other functions related to the conduct of foreign affairs.

Modern international law is generally taken to originate with the Treaties of Westphalia of 1648, which ended the Thirty Years' War. The system of co-equal sovereign states that resulted, with no authority such as an international legislature or court of general jurisdiction superior to that of the state, required the application of legal approaches different from those found in most municipal legal systems. Early treatments of international law by such writers as Hugo Grotius (1583–1645) were strongly influenced by concepts of natural law and the religious tradition on which it drew. In the nineteenth through the early twenty-first centuries, positivism became the dominant perspective in international law. In contrast to abstract principles of ethics or morality, legal positivism relies on affirmative acts of states to establish the law.

As demonstrated by the references in its Constitution, the United States has both acknowledged the importance of and contributed to the development of international law from the earliest days of the Republic. American contributions have been particularly important in the development of the law of neutrality, the body of law defining the rights and obligations of a third state adopting an attitude of impartiality toward belligerents in armed conflict with each other. During the first century of its existence, the law governing neutrality was among the most important international legal concerns of the new nation, whose commerce was dependent on the freedom to trade with belligerents on both sides of the French Revolution and the Napoleonic Wars.

Washington's Neutrality Proclamation of 1793, followed by the Neutrality Act of 1794, were innovations in the law of neutrality. Before asserting expanded rights as a neutral, the U.S. implicitly acknowledged the need to clarify the obligations associated with that legal status. These authorities stressed the then-new concept of neutral states' duties to regulate certain activities of their citizens. They further contributed to a distinction between acts which neutral governments and their citizens by international law are forbidden to commit, and acts which neutral governments are obliged to suppress. The United States alleged that its rights as a neutral state had been violated in disputes with Britain over its practice of seizing cargoes of U.S. merchant vessels trading with France and impressing U.S. sailors into the British navy, both precipitating factors leading to the War of 1812. During the Civil War, the United States was similarly assertive in pressing the duties of neutral states, most famously in the Treaty of Washington (1871) and the subsequent Alabama arbitration (1872), which established the liability of Great Britain for violating its legal status as a neutral state by allowing private parties under its jurisdiction to build and outfit vessels of war for the Confederacy. Since the late eighteenth century, the U.S. Supreme Court has advanced the development of international law in such areas as the immunity of foreign governments from suit.

The United States also substantially contributed to the use of international arbitration as a mechanism for the peaceful settlement of disputes between states. The Treaty of Amity Commerce and Navigation with Britain, popularly know as Jay's Treaty (1794), designed to address certain unsettled issues remaining after the American War of Independence, contained a number of arbitration clauses that were important developments in international law and practice. In the latter part of the nineteenth century, the United States and Great Britain conducted arbitration over fur seals in the Bering Sea (1893), and the American-Mexican Mixed Claims Commission, established by international convention in 1868, adjudicated more than 200 claims between 1871 and 1876.

In the late 1800s, the United States' approach to international law was influenced by peace movements advocating international arbitration as a mechanism for settling disputes and as an alternative to armed force. These trends bore fruit in the form of the Hague Peace Conferences of 1899 and 1907, of which the former established the Permanent Court of Arbitration. The United States, however, failed to participate in the next major step in the development of international arbitration: the establishment of the Permanent Court of International Justice (PCIJ) under the auspices of the League of Nations in 1920. Although the Senate failed to approve U.S. membership in the League of Nations, the United States signed the agreement establishing the PCIJ. A protocol was adopted in 1929 amending the PCIJ's Statute, the institution's governing instrument, in a manner intended be responsive to the concerns of the U.S. Senate so as to permit U.S. accession. That agreement, however, failed to receive the necessary two-thirds majority in a Senate vote in 1935. Nonetheless, a judge of U.S. nationality served on the court throughout its existence, which terminated at the end of World War II. In the interwar period, the United States also articulated and asserted an international standard of "prompt, adequate and effective compensation" as a remedy for governmental expropriation of foreign nations' property, a matter that continues to be both highly relevant and controversial in the law of foreign investment.

In the latter part of the twentieth century, dominated by the Cold War and the emergence of the United States as a global superpower, the United States continued in its rhetorical commitment to international law as a vehicle for ensuring a stable and peaceful world order. Among other things, it consented to the compulsory jurisdiction of the International Court of Justice the successor to the PCIJ, albeit with significant reservations. However, instances in which the International Court of Justice adjudicated that the United States had violated international law, most notably in mining Nicaraguan ports and supporting the Contra militias, tended to undermine some of the United States' credibility as an adherent to the rule of law. Criticisms have also been directed at the United States' apparent hostility to some major multilateral agreements including the United Nations Convention on the Law of the Sea, the Comprehensive Nuclear Test Ban Treaty, the Convention on the Rights of the Child, the Rome Statute of the International Criminal Court, the Kyoto Protocol on global climate change, and conventions adopted by the International Labor Organization.

With the end of the Cold War in the last decade of the twentieth century, international institutions and international law have become increasingly important. The creation of new intergovernmental national organizations such as the World Trade Organization and the European Bank for Reconstruction and Development, and the reinvigoration of international institutions like the UN Security Council, are evidence of the importance of the rule of law in the new millennium. The United States' reliance on the UN Security Council's prior authorization before initiating hostilities to expel Iraq from Kuwait (1991) was interpreted by many international lawyers as an indicator of a newly enhanced stature for international law and institutions. At the same time, the United States as the sole remaining superpower seems to be searching for an appropriate role for law in its foreign policy for situations such as Kosovo, in which U.S. and NATO intervention was not authorized by the Security Council and rested on an uncertain legal foundation. Two challenges to the application of capital punishment to foreign nationals, initiated by Paraguay and Germany in the International Court of Justice, suggest as well that in the United States international law may play a small role in the face of competing domestic political considerations.

BIBLIOGRAPHY

Akehurst, Michael B. *A Modern Introduction to International Law.* 6th ed. Boston: Allen and Unwin, 1987.

Brierly, James Leslie. *The Law of Nations.* 6th ed. Edited by Humphrey Waldock. New York: Oxford University Press, 1963.

Brownlie, Ian. *Principles of Public International Law.* 5th ed. New York: Clarendon Press, 1998.

Butler, William E., ed. *International Law and the International System.* Boston: M. Nijhoff, 1987.

Corbett, Percy E. *The Growth of World Law.* Princeton, N.J.: Princeton University Press, 1971.

Fawcett, James E. S. *Law and Power in International Relations.* London: Faber and Faber, 1982.

Heere, Wybo P., ed. *International Law and Its Sources.* Boston: Kluwer Law and Taxation Publishers, 1989.

Henkin, Louis. *How Nations Behave: Law and Foreign Policy.* New York: Praeger, 1968.

Higgins, Rosalyn. *Problems and Process: International Law and How We Use It.* New York: Oxford University Press, 1994.

Janis, Mark W. *An Introduction to International Law.* 3d ed. Gaithersburg, Md.: Aspen Law and Business, 1999.

Jessup, Philip C. *Transnational Law.* New Haven, Conn.: Yale University Press, 1956.

Kaplan, Morton A., and Nicholas deB. Katzenbach. *The Political Foundations of International Law.* New York: Wiley, 1961.

Lauterpacht, Hersch. *The Function of Law in the International Community.* Hamden, Conn.: Archon Books, 1966.

Maris, Gary L. *International Law: An Introduction.* Lanham, Md.: University Press of America, 1984.

McDougal, Myres S., and W. Michael Reisman. *International Law in Contemporary Perspective: The Public Order of the World Community.* Mineola, N.Y.: Foundation Press, 1981.

Nussbaum, Arthur. *A Concise History of the Law of Nations.* New York: Macmillan, 1954.

Oppenheim, Lassa. *Oppenheim's International Law.* 9th ed. Edited by Robert Jennings and Arthur Watts. Essex, England: Longman, 1992.

Restatement (Third) of the Foreign Relations Law of the United States. St. Paul, Minn.: American Law Institute Publishers, 1987.

David A. Wirth

See also **International Court of Justice; United Nations.**

INTERNATIONAL LONGSHOREMEN'S AND WAREHOUSEMEN'S UNION. Although founded in 1937, the International Longshoremen's and Warehousemen's Union (ILWU) has origins rooted in the early years of the twentieth century. In 1912, a group of West Coast locals bolted the International Longshoremen's Association (ILA) in opposition to the undemocratic practices of East Coast ILA presidents Dan Keefe and T. V. O'Connor. Like his predecessor Keefe, who resigned in 1908, O'Connor continued the practice of buying votes through his grip on the abusive hiring system. Lacking job security, longshoremen often sold their votes in exchange for being selected to join daily work crews. On the West Coast, the ILA emerged within a more militant and democratic context, as the radical Industrial Workers of the World exercised influence among longshoremen. In 1915, the clash between militant and corrupt union practices caused a split in ILA West Coast leadership. Company unions emerged, which longshoremen unsuccessfully challenged in a 1919 strike. For a decade, company unions and the Waterfront Employers Association undermined genuine longshoremen organization.

In 1933, longshoremen revived ILA locals on the Pacific Coast. The next year, company unions collapsed when ILA members struck all Pacific ports. ILA locals demanded unified bargaining by all West Coast maritime unions over wages, union hiring halls, and hours. The conflict resulted in the death of six workers, and hundreds of strikers were injured. After a four-day general strike in San Francisco led by militant workers and supported by the Communist Party, employers finally agreed to arbitration, which granted the union most of its demands. Moreover, the strike entrenched militant leaders like Harry Bridges, who became president of the San Francisco ILA local in 1936.

In 1936, Bridges entered into dispute with East Coast–based ILA president Joseph Ryan over strategy pursued by West Coast locals to unite all maritime unions into one federation. Ideological differences and ILA refusal to ally itself with unskilled workers sharpened the conflict. As an American Federation of Labor (AFL) affiliate, the anticommunist ILA adhered to craft unionism and declined entering into bargaining agreements with the unskilled. In February 1937, Bridges defied Ryan and led workers in a ninety-eight-day strike that failed to make significant gains for West Coast locals. While Bridges blamed Ryan and his lack of support for the strike's failure, the East Coast ILA leader called Bridges and his lieutenant, Louis Goldblatt, "puppets of the international communist conspiracy." In 1937, growing ideological hostility, coupled with opposing trade union philosophies, prompted the Bridges-led Pacific Coast ILA to break with Ryan and affiliate with the recently formed and more inclusive Congress of Industrial Organizations (CIO). This event resulted in the West Coast locals receiving a CIO charter to form the ILWU. The separation was finalized when ILWU members elected Harry Bridges as their president.

Because the ILWU constitution prohibited political discrimination, Communist Party influence remained, and some of its members held several key union posts. The Soviet-American alliance during World War II ensured ILWU enforcement of no-strike pledges and maximum productivity. The ILWU then expanded its activities into Hawaii, organizing not only longshoremen, but also workers in agriculture, hotels, and tourism. The ILWU became one of the first multiracial and multiethnic unions as Asians, Latinos, and African Americans filled its ranks.

Cold War politics threatened the union's stability and survival. The 1947 Taft-Hartley Act required the signing by union leaders of affidavits disavowing communist affiliation. The initial refusal by ILWU officials to sign affidavits left the union vulnerable to raids by rival unions. The ILWU responded by seeking National Labor Relations Board (NLRB) intervention. In exchange for NLRB protection, ILWU officials ultimately signed the affidavits. This did not end the union's political problems, and in 1950 the CIO expelled the ILWU for alleged communist domination.

Despite political isolation, the ILWU had successfully maintained control over the hiring hall and entered into a new era of cooperation with employers. Contributing to this was the Communist Party's diminishing influence resulting from growing Cold War political consensus. A "new look" approach to collective bargaining marked an era of harmonious labor-employer relations, which was highlighted by the 1960 Mechanization and Modernization Agreement. Virtually suspending existing work rules, it reduced the size of the labor force, provided no-layoff guarantees, and started a longshoremen retirement plan. Although company-ILWU cooperation generally prevailed throughout this period, ILWU politics remained leftist. The union strongly supported the civil rights actions of the 1950s, and in 1967 the ILWU passed a resolution calling for the withdrawal of U.S. troops from Vietnam.

While the ILWU battled in the political trenches, the increasing rationalization of the maritime industry, which included the introduction of containerized shipping, led to a breakdown of the mechanization and modernization agreement. In 1971, the ILWU struck for 135 days, ending the period of company-union cooperation. The final agreement resulted in a substantial workforce reduction, and, as a result, in 1988 ILWU rank-and-file—seeking strength in numbers—voted to affiliate with the AFL-CIO. The union's radical legacy and its continued democratic practices, such as electing its president by the full membership, placed the ILWU to the left of most AFL-CIO unions.

BIBLIOGRAPHY

Cherny, Robert W. "The Making of a Labor Radical: Harry Bridges, 1901–1934." *Pacific Historical Review* 64 (1995): 363–388.

Fairley, Lincoln. *Facing Mechanization: The West Coast Longshore Plan.* Los Angeles: Institute of Industrial Relations, University of California, 1979.

Larrowe, Charles P. *Harry Bridges: The Rise and Fall of Radical Labor in the United States.* 2d rev. ed. New York: Lawrence Hill, 1977.

Nelson, Bruce. *Workers on the Waterfront: Seamen, Longshoremen, and Unionism in the 1930s.* Urbana: University of Illinois Press, 1988.

Norman Caulfield

See also **American Federation of Labor–Congress of Industrial Organizations; Industrial Workers of the World; Strikes; Trade Unions.**

INTERNATIONAL MONETARY FUND (IMF), created at the Bretton Woods Conference in 1944, began operations on 1 March 1947. It had its inception on 1 July 1944, when delegates of forty-four nations met at Bretton Woods, New Hampshire, and proposed two associated financial institutions—the IMF, with $8 billion capital, and the International Bank for Reconstruction and Development. A recurrence of the restrictive trade policies, exchange instability, and international lending abuses that had characterized the interwar era was feared. After World War I, nations had sought monetary stability by returning to the gold standard, but in many instances the gold standard took the form of a weak version of the gold exchange standard. Its breakdown contributed to the 1929–1936 economic debacle.

The IMF's original purpose was to support world trade by reestablishing a stable international system. To this end, it was given the mandate to monitor the exchange rate policies of member countries and provide short-term loans in case of balance of payments problems.

Since the IMF and member nations accepted the dollar as equal to gold, the growing number of dollars in their central bank reserves, especially after 1958 and in turn the consequence of chronic U.S. government deficits, stimulated worldwide inflation. The gold exchange standard broke down in 1968–1971, notably after the United States ceased redeeming dollars in gold on 15 August 1971, thereby severely damaging the prestige of the IMF.

With the collapse of fixed exchange rates in 1973, the dominant role of the IMF was to provide financial support for member countries. As of 1993, it had 178 members and had become a major financial intermediary. Its involvement is virtually required before international bankers will agree to refinance or defer loans for Third World countries. The IMF was also instrumental in providing funds for the emerging market economies in eastern Europe following the breakup of the Soviet Union in 1991. The fund also provides information to the public, and technical assistance to governments of developing countries.

The IMF can make loans to member countries through standby arrangements. Depending on the size of the loan, the fund imposes certain conditions. Known as IMF conditionality, these measures often interfere with the sovereignty of member countries with regard to economic policy. IMF conditions can require devaluation of currencies, removal of government subsidies, cuts in social services, control over wages, trade liberalization, and pressure to pursue free-market policies. IMF conditionality has been criticized as being too severe, imposing hardship on debtor countries. Because IMF policies are imposed by an international agency consisting of industrialized countries, they give the appearance of maintaining the dependency of the Third World.

Critics point out that balance-of-payment problems in the Third World are often structural and long term, with the result that short-term stabilization by the IMF may lead to long-run development problems. Access of member countries to the fund's assets is determined by quota. Each member receives a quota based on the size of its economy. The quotas are defined in terms of Special Drawing Rights (SDRs), reserve assets created by the IMF to supplement world reserves. The value of SDRs for member nations requesting loans is determined by an IMF accounting system based on a weighted average of major economic powers' currencies.

BIBLIOGRAPHY

Aufricht, Hans. *The International Monetary Fund: Legal Bases, Structure, Functions.* New York: F. A. Praeger, 1964.

Horsefield, J. Keith, ed. *The International Monetary Fund, 1945–65: Twenty Years of International Monetary Cooperation.* Washington, D.C.: International Monetary Fund, 1969.

International Monetary Fund. "Supplement on the IMF." *IMF Survey* 22 (October 1993): 1–28.

Salda, Anne C. M. *The International Monetary Fund.* New Brunswick, N.J.: Transaction, 1992.

Marie D. Connolly
Donald L. Kemmerer / A. G.

See also **Banking; Banks, Export-Import; Bretton Woods Conference; Corporations; Dumbarton Oaks Conference; Foreign Aid.**

INTERNATIONAL UNION OF MINE, MILL, AND SMELTER WORKERS. In its first incarnation as the Western Federation of Miners (WFM), established at a convention in Butte, Montana, on 15 May 1893, the International Union of Mine, Mill, and Smelter Workers (IUMMSW) organized workers who mined copper, bauxite, nickel, uranium, lead, zinc, gold, and silver as well as those who smelted and refined copper. Earning a reputation as one of the leading radical institutions in the American West, the union won some important organizing drives in its early years, including a key victory at Cripple Creek, Colorado, in 1894. With ownership of mining companies increasingly consolidated among a few corporations, however, the WFM dissolved a number of its locals and was nearly defunct by World War I. Hoping to put aside its radical reputation, the union reemerged as the IUMMSW in 1916.

In the anti-union atmosphere of the Roaring Twenties, the IUMMSW remained a shell of its former self. As with many other industrial unions, however, its leadership seized upon the promise of the New Deal to reassert its presence in the western mines. After a five-month strike in Butte and Anaconda, Montana, in 1934, the IUMMSW was not only revitalized as a labor organization, but also firmly established as a partner in the New Deal coalition of labor leaders, social reformers, and other activists. Yet internal divisions continued to plague the union under the presidency of Reid Robinson, elected to office in 1936 under a pledge to renew the union's aggressive organizing and bargaining stance. Robinson roused controversy when he appointed Communist Party member Maurice Travis to an international IUMMSW office. Anticommunist IUMMSW members forced Robinson's resignation from office in 1947 over the move, but were further incensed when Travis succeeded Robinson as IUMMSW president. Although Travis formally severed his ties to the Communist Party in order to meet the TAFT-HARTLEY ACT's prohibition against labor leaders holding membership in the party, the publicity over the flap drew national attention to the union at the height of the McCarthy-era red scares.

Further sapping the union's energy was its expulsion from the Congress of Industrial Organizations (CIO) in 1950. Although it was a founding member of the CIO in 1935, the IUMMSW was one of eleven unions expelled in a move to eliminate communist elements from the organization. The IUMMSW also faced renewed charges of communist influence with the 1954 movie *Salt of the Earth*, based on a strike against Empire Zinc by IUMMSW Local 890 in Hanover, New Mexico. With its producer, director, screenwriter, and lead actor already on a movie industry blacklist for their leftist activities, the film appeared to justify suspicions of communist dominance in the IUMMSW at the time of its release.

During the 1950s, the IUMMSW faced numerous challenges from the UNITED STEEL WORKERS OF AMERICA (USWA), which used anticommunist and racist rhetoric to raid the union's locals. Although it retained about 37,000 members in 300 local unions, IUMMSW officials voted to merge with the USWA on 30 June 1967. An additional 13,000 workers in Canadian IUMMSW locals joined the merger the next day. IUMMSW Local 598 in Sudbury, Ontario, however, refused to agree to the merger, and after 1985 retained an affiliation with the Canadian Auto Workers union.

BIBLIOGRAPHY

Jameson, Elizabeth. *All That Glitters: Class, Conflict, and Community in Cripple Creek.* Urbana: University of Illinois Press, 1998.

Mercier, Laurie. "'Instead of Fighting the Common Enemy': Mine Mill versus the Steelworkers in Montana, 1950–1967." *Labor History* 40, no. 4 (1999): 459–480.

Zieger, Robert H. *The CIO, 1935–1955.* Chapel Hill: University of North Carolina Press, 1995.

Timothy G. Borden

INTERNET. Arguably the most important communications tool ever created, the Internet connects millions of people to online resources each day. Grown from seeds planted during the Cold War, the roots of the Internet were formed to develop a reliable, national system for communications. Although early pioneers disagree over whether the computer-based communications network was built to withstand nuclear attack, the uneasy tension between the United States and the Soviet Union during the Cold War certainly increased the resolve of the United States to fund and develop relevant scientific and defense-related projects aimed at national security.

Home to many of the preeminent scientists of the time, the Massachusetts Institute of Technology (MIT) served as the birthplace of the Internet. It was there, in Cambridge, Massachusetts, that President Harry Truman's administration formed MIT's Lincoln Laboratories to begin work on the Semi-Automatic Ground Environment.

SAGE's primary goal was to develop an air defense system that involved a network of interconnected computers across the United States. The push for advanced technology received an even larger boost in August 1957, when the Soviet Union test fired its first intercontinental ballistic missile and subsequently launched its *Sputnik* orbiter in October of that same year. Shortly thereafter, President Dwight D. Eisenhower convened a meeting of his Presidential Science Advisory Committee. From that meeting and subsequent congressional testimony on the progress of U.S. defense and missile programs, it became clear that the "science gap" between the two superpowers had widened. Eisenhower sought funding for the Advanced Research Projects Agency (ARPA) late in 1957 and obtained it the following year.

In the early 1960s, the Lincoln Laboratory researchers Lawrence Roberts and Leonard Kleinrock worked on developing a method of digitizing and transmitting information between two computers using a communications method called packet switching. Similar work on systems that used store-and-forward switching was also underway in the late 1950s under the direction of Paul Baran and Donald Davies at the National Physical Laboratory in England. At the heart of both research projects was the development of a communications system in which information would be distributed among all nodes on a network, so that if one or more nodes failed, the entire network would not be disabled. This type of network, in which messages were passed from node to node, with no single node responsible for the end-to-end traffic, was called hot-potato routing.

ARPA's first director, J. C. R. Licklider, moved from Lincoln Laboratory to a small Cambridge, Massachusetts–based consulting firm, Bolt, Beranek, and Newman (BBN), where researchers continued to explore the use of computers as tools of communication. While there, Licklider and his colleagues developed the necessary hardware to connect computers to telephone lines and also researched the collection of data from a wide array of other sources including antennae, submarines, and other real-time sensors. Most of BBN's projects were ARPA supported and sought to achieve ARPA's ultimate goal of helping close the science gap by creating a nationwide network of interconnected computers.

In the summer of 1968, ARPA issued a request for proposals to more than 130 different research centers with the goal of creating a digital network of computers conforming to ARPA's technical specifications. Roberts developed the criteria and served as the chief architect of the network's overall design, which included the deployment of "packet switching technology, using half-second response time, with measurement capability, and continuous operation"—that is, an Internet. Frank Heart and the team of scientists at BBN were awarded the contract in December 1968. Outfitted with specialized minicomputers and interface hardware, BBN set out to connect their "packet switches" or Interface Message Processors (IMPs), at each ARPA-determined remote location (node), which would then communicate with the host computer at that location. Robert Kahn and Vincent Cerf, with Jon Postel and Charles Kline, developed the software to connect host computers to the IMPs, a host-to-host protocol on how packets would be routed. While America was absorbed in NASA's race to land on the moon in the summer of 1969, BBN air shipped its first IMP computer across the country—no small feat for the time. It arrived safely and was working at the first node, the University of California at Los Angeles, in August 1969.

Internet Pioneer. Gene Kan shows off the Gnutella Web site and some of the innovative file-swapping software that he developed and promoted; Kan committed suicide on 29 June 2002, at the age of twenty-five. AP/Wide World Photos

This phase of the ARPA-BBN project was completed in nine months. Meanwhile, work continued on equipping the second node, the Stanford Research Institute (SRI) in Palo Alto—some four hundred miles away—to the interface message processor. On 1 October 1969 the Stanford node came online and the first message, "LO," was passed that day. BBN continued to progress, installing nodes three and four at the University of California at Santa Barbara (1 November 1969) and the University of Utah (1 December 1969). Only in March of the following year did BBN connect its Cambridge offices to the newly created ARPAnet.

The ARPAnet continued to evolve through the early 1970s with the addition of more diverse data networks such as the University of Hawaii's ALOHAnet packet radio network and the European-based packet satellite network. During this period, the first terminal interface processor (TIP) was introduced to the network, thereby allowing computer terminals to call directly into the ARPAnet using standard telephone lines. In 1972, the first electronic messaging program (e-mail) that supported incoming and outgoing messages was developed. In that same year, a file transfer protocol specification (FTP) to allow for the transmission of data files across the network was designed and tested. With these additions, ARPAnet truly began to fulfill its mission as an open-architecture network, accommodating a variety of different environments and allowing the free sharing of resources.

As the uses of the network grew, more efficient methods for carrying data were needed, forcing an evolution of transmission protocols—the underlying control layer in which the messages flowed—and addressing schemes. After many refinements, TCP/IP (transmission control protocol/Internet protocol) became the de facto standard for communicating on the network. A naming scheme also became necessary and the Domain Name System (DNS) was developed by Paul Mockapetris of the University of Southern California. DNS allowed for the assignment of names to networks and nodes, supplanting the use of numeric addresses. In 1973, Ethernet technology was developed, allowing for the rapid addition of nodes and workstations to the network. With the birth of the personal computer and local area networks (LANs) in the early 1980s, the network grew at a staggering pace.

The federal government funded the network and its infrastructure through 1995. The work of the National Science Foundation (NSF) was instrumental for understanding the future evolution of the Internet as a true "information superhighway." However, federal funding of the Internet was terminated as a result of the NSF's privatization initiative to encourage commercial network traffic. Control of the large backbones of the network—the set of paths with which local or regional networks connected for long-haul connectivity—was redistributed to private regional network service providers.

The Internet serves as a vital network of communication in the form of e-mail, news groups, and chat. It also provides unparalleled resource sharing and resource discovery through the World Wide Web. At the end of 2001, the Internet continued its phenomenal annual rate of growth of 100 percent. At its start in 1981, the Internet connected just over two hundred researchers and scientists. By the end of 2002, it is estimated that the Internet had the capacity to reach more than six billion people worldwide.

BIBLIOGRAPHY

Abbate, Janet. *Inventing the Internet.* Cambridge, Mass.: MIT Press, 1999.

Hauben, Michael, and Ronda Hauben. *Netizens: On the History and Impact of Usenet and the Internet.* Los Alamitos, Calif.: IEEE Computer Society Press, 1997.

Quarterman, John S., and Smoot Carl-Mitchell. *The Internet Connection: System Connectivity and Configuration.* Reading, Mass.: Addison-Wesley, 1994.

Segaller, Stephen. *Nerds 2.0.1: A Brief History of the Internet.* New York: TV Books, 1998.

Michael Regoli

See also **Communications Industry; Computers and Computer Industry; Electronic Mail; National Science Foundation.**

INTERNMENT, WARTIME. Internment has long been recognized in American and international law. By World War II, it was regulated by a system of rules—the Geneva Convention—that governed the treatment of prisoners of war and civilian enemy nationals, including diplomats, resident in or captured by a belligerent nation. The United States first used internment during the War of 1812, when some resident British, mostly merchants, were ordered to remove themselves fifty miles inland. British merchants in New York City were exiled up the Hudson at Newburgh, but left at liberty.

The United States next resorted to internment during World War I. At that time about 500,000 unnaturalized resident aliens of German birth were in the United States; they were proclaimed "alien enemies" after war was declared in April 1917. Some 8,000 enemy aliens—the vast majority of them Germans, and almost all the rest subjects of Austria-Hungary—were arrested under presidential warrants, but nearly three-quarters of them were released within a short time. Only about 2,300 enemy nationals resident in the United States were actually interned, 90 percent of them German and all but a few of them male.

During World War II, internment of Germans and Italians began more than two years before the United States formally entered the war. Seamen from German vessels stranded in U.S. ports were interned shortly after the outbreak of war in September 1939. In June 1940, when Italy entered the conflict, perhaps a thousand Italians, consisting of seamen and a group of food workers from the Italian exhibition at the New York World's Fair of 1939–1940 were also seized. All were persons without permanent resident status.

Shortly after the fall of France, Congress passed the Alien Registration Act of 1940. Among the several million registrants were 695,363 Italians, 314,715 Germans, and 91,858 Japanese, so that after the United States went to war, there were about a million unnaturalized natives of the Axis nations resident in the United States, all potential internees.

When war came, President Franklin D. Roosevelt signed three similar public proclamations declaring that "all natives, citizens, denizens, or subjects of [Japan, Germany, and Italy] being of the age of fourteen years and upward, who shall be in the United States and not actually naturalized, shall be liable to be apprehended, restrained, secured, and removed as alien enemies." Austrian and Korean resident aliens, who had German and Japanese nationality, were not declared alien enemies.

The administration of President Franklin D. Roosevelt never intended to intern any sizable percentage of the one million alien enemies. Attorney General Francis

Manzanar Relocation Camp. Well over 100,000 Japanese Americans were interned during World War II in camps such as this one in eastern California—now the Manzanar National Historic Site. National Archives and Records Administration

Biddle and his staff in the Department of Justice wanted a minimal program and were aware of the gross injustices suffered by German and Italian resident aliens in Winston Churchill's Britain. In preparation for war, various federal security agencies had prepared custodial detention lists, better known as the "ABC lists," of persons who were deemed potentially dangerous. Persons on the A list were identified as "known dangerous" aliens; those on the B list were labeled "potentially dangerous"; and those appearing on the C list were persons who were believed to warrant surveillance because of pro-Axis sympathies or propaganda activities. As is common with internal security lists, they were largely based on guilt by association rather than on individual investigations, as most of the names came from membership and subscription lists of organizations and publications deemed subversive.

It is not yet possible—and may never be—to give precise figures for either the total number of persons interned or the numbers of each nationality. Several civilian agencies, chiefly the Federal Bureau of Investigation, the Immigration and Naturalization Service (INS), and the military authorities made arrests. Furthermore, the surviving records are incomplete. Until the spring of 1943, civilian internees were largely under military custody; most were then transferred to the INS, which had held some civilians since early in the war. At various times the INS reported, with what seems like studied vagueness, on the number of persons it held, but its reports did not always make clear what categories of persons were being counted. In late 1944, J. Edgar Hoover reported that 14,807 enemy aliens had been taken into custody by the FBI, of whom nearly two-fifths had "been ordered interned by the Attorney General and the military authorities." Hoover's seemingly precise figures leave room for doubt. Early in the war many individuals were arrested by various local authorities and held under military auspices in places like Camp Forrest, Tennessee, and they probably were not included in his totals. The 40,000 Japanese nationals who were incarcerated by the War Relocation Authority along with 80,000 American citizens of Japanese ancestry were alien enemies who were not on the government's lists. The best estimate of the total number of interned persons is something under 11,000, broken down as follows: Japanese, perhaps 8,000; Germans, possibly 2,300; and only a few hundred Italians. Many more were arrested and held in custody for days and even weeks without being officially interned. Of the total, at least 2,254 Japanese, chiefly from Peru, and 4,058 Germans and 288 Italians were brought from fifteen Latin American countries and interned in INS camps.

BIBLIOGRAPHY

Corbett, P. Scott. *Quiet Passage: The Exchange of Civilians between the United States and Japan during the Second World War.* Kent, Ohio: Kent State University Press, 1987. An account based largely on U.S. Department of State documents.

Culley, John J. "The Santa Fe Internment Camp and the Justice Department Program for Enemy Aliens." In *Japanese Americans: From Relocation to Redress.* Edited by Roger Daniels et al. Salt Lake City: University of Utah Press, 1986.

Fiset, Louis. *Imprisoned Apart: The World War II Correspondence of an Issei Couple.* Seattle: University of Washington Press, 1997. The best treatment of the internment of Japanese nationals.

Friedman, Max Paul. *Nazis and Good Neighbors: The United States Campaign against the Germans of Latin America in World War II.* New York: Cambridge University Press, forthcoming. The first multinational approach to this topic.

Gardiner, C. Harvey. *Pawns in a Triangle of Hate: The Peruvian Japanese and the United States.* Seattle: University of Washington Press, 1981. A pathbreaking work.

Saunders, Kay, and Roger Daniels, eds. *Alien Justice: Wartime Internment in Australia and North America.* St. Lucia, Australia: Queensland University Press, 2000. An anthology covering experiences in both world wars.

Roger Daniels

See also **Geneva Conventions; Japanese American Incarceration;** *and vol. 9:* **The Japanese Internment Camps, 1942.**

INTERSTATE COMMERCE COMMISSION.

On 31 December 1995, after 108 years of operation, the Interstate Commerce Commission (ICC) closed its doors in compliance with the ICC Termination Act of 1995 (P.L. 104-88). This archetypal American independent regulatory commission, once feared by the transportation industry, saw the functions it still performed diminish until, at the end, they were assumed by offices in the Federal Highway Administration and the newly-created Surface

Transportation Board, both elements of the U.S. Department of Transportation.

Those with the greatest stake in the ICC, which was created in 1887, were midwestern farmers and the owners and operators of the newly emergent railroad transportation systems. The railroads opened midwestern markets to those in the East, but charged what the market would bear, which was significantly less between two cities connected by more than one carrier than between towns that did not have the benefit of such competition. "Long haul" rates were more beneficial than "short haul" rates, leading farmers and merchants (members of the Grange) to redress their grievances through politics.

This post–Civil War reform movement helped initiate state regulation of railroads and grain elevators. In 1877 the Supreme Court, in *Munn v. Illinois*, ruled that the states could indeed regulate those properties vested with a public interest. However, in 1886 the Court reversed itself in *Wabash, St. Louis and Pacific Railway v. Illinois*, saying that only Congress could regulate interstate commerce. In 1887 Congress passed an Act to Regulate Commerce, known thereafter as the Interstate Commerce Act, which President Grover Cleveland signed into law on 4 February 1887. The law established a five-person commission to be appointed by the president and confirmed by the Senate.

From its inception until the end of the century, the ICC, seeking to negotiate "reasonable and just" rates, was hobbled by the vagueness of its enabling act, the failure of Congress to give it enforcement power, and the Supreme Court's strict interpretation of the COMMERCE CLAUSE of the Constitution, which emasculated the commission's power. During its first eighteen years, the ICC brought sixteen cases before the Court, fifteen of which were decided in favor of the railroads.

Nevertheless, the ICC would become the model for effective regulation later on. Responding to President Theodore Roosevelt and the Progressive movement, Congress passed the HEPBURN ACT (1906) and the Mann-Elkins Act (1910), which gave the commission wider authority to set aside rates charged by railroads, set profit levels, and organize mergers. The Hepburn Act extended the ICC's jurisdiction to include sleeping car companies, oil pipelines, ferries, terminals, and bridges. Through a broader interpretation of the Commerce Clause, the Court accepted a more muscular role for the ICC. This allowed for passage of the Esch-Cummins Transportation Act of 1920 and the commission's gradual assumption of regulatory jurisdiction over all other common carriers by 1940 (the MOTOR CARRIER ACT of 1935 regulated trucks; the Transportation Act of 1940, water carriers), except the airlines. In addition, the ICC had regulated telephone, telegraph, wireless, and cable services from 1910 until the FEDERAL COMMUNICATIONS COMMISSION was established in 1934.

Congress, in the 1940 Transportation Act—and again in the Transportation Act of 1958—attempted to persuade the ICC to prepare a national transportation policy that would impartially regulate all modes of transportation and preserve the advantages of each. In 1966, this mission was shifted to the newly established Department of Transportation, as were the ICC's safety functions, which traced back to the Railroad Safety Appliance Act of 1893.

If the transfer of functions set a new tone for the ICC, the move to deregulate the transportation industry rendered it increasingly irrelevant. Passage of the Motor Carrier Regulatory Reform and Modernization Act of 1980 and the STAGGERS RAIL ACT of 1980 deregulated the trucking and rail industries, respectively. In 1982, Congress pared the membership of the ICC—which had grown to eleven—back to five. Staff dwindled from 2,000 to around 200. And on 29 December 1995, President William Clinton signed the ICC Termination Act into law.

BIBLIOGRAPHY

Hoogenboom, Ari. "Interstate Commerce Commission." In *A Historical Guide to the U.S. Government*. Edited by George Thomas Kurian. New York: Oxford University Press, 1998.

———, and Olive Hoogenboom. *A History of the ICC: From Panacea to Palliative*. New York: Norton, 1976.

R. Dale Grinder

See also **Federal Agencies; Granger Cases; Granger Movement; Interstate Commerce Laws; Interstate Trade Barriers; Restraint of Trade; Transportation Act of 1920.**

INTERSTATE COMMERCE LAWS. The scope of interstate commerce laws in the United States is much broader than the jurisdiction of the Interstate Commerce Commission, which covers only some forms of transportation. However, at its formation in 1887, constitutional doctrine largely confined federal powers in the regulation of interstate commerce to transportation and communications. Much of the history of interstate commerce in the United States has to do with this expansion of federal powers over interstate commerce during the twentieth century. The Constitution specifically grants the federal government power "to regulate Commerce . . . among the several States." Chief Justice John Marshall stated in *Gibbons v. Ogden* (1824) that federal legislation was supreme over a state law that might affect interstate or foreign commerce. But for a century, there was little federal regulation of interstate commerce other than transportation and communications, for, with regard to the reserved powers of the states in the absence of federal legislation, the Supreme Court has tended to be generous to the states. The states have regulated grade crossings and public utilities, controlled practices in food production and sanitation, and limited the loads of trucks on their highways. Indeed, the main body of commercial law in the United States is state law.

It was not until the post–Civil War period, when the growth and power of the modern corporation became clearly evident through corrupt, arbitrary, and discriminatory practices, that the national political environment began to change. The Interstate Commerce Act of 1887 was only the first major example of a long series of important and complex federal statutes regulating business under the authority of the commerce clause, only a few of which can be noted here.

The Sherman Antitrust Act of 1890, aimed at curbing monopolies, was supported in 1914 by the Clayton Act, Labor Provisions (which, in addition, exempted labor organizations from antitrust laws) and by the creation of the Federal Trade Commission in 1914 to regulate "unfair methods in restraint of trade." The food and drug acts of 1906 and 1938 as amended—plus a series of related laws, such as the Meat Inspection Act of 1906—have been aimed at preventing adulteration and mislabeling. Additional powers given to the Federal Trade Commission in 1938 forbid false advertising. The Truth-in-Packaging Act of 1966 and the Consumer Credit Protection (Truth-in-Lending) Act of 1969 brought further protection to consumers. The publicity acts of 1903 and 1909 were forerunners of the Securities and Exchange Act of 1934, all of which were aimed at the sale of fraudulent securities.

Controls over additional modes of transport came with the Shipping Act of 1916, which established the U.S. Shipping Board, whose authority was reestablished in 1936 under the Maritime Commission. Federal regulation of utilities came with the creation in 1920 of the Federal Power Commission. The Federal Radio Commission of 1927 was broadened into the Federal Communications Commission in 1934. Government regulation of the labor relations of industries engaged in interstate commerce culminated in the formation of the National Labor Relations Board in 1935, whose powers and duties were revised by the Taft-Hartley Act of 1947 and several amendments to it. The Civil Aeronautics Act of 1938, setting up the Civil Aeronautics Authority (later Civil Aeronautics Board), concluded formation of the series of agencies known as the independent regulatory commissions. Moreover, some regulatory authority derived from the interstate commerce clause lies in the hands of the traditional departments and other agencies, such as the Atomic Energy Commission.

Interstate commerce laws are not limited to regulative and punitive measures. Subsidies are available, for example, to maritime shipping and to large segments of agriculture. Many federal agencies engage in, and disseminate the results of, research of interest to business and commercial organizations of all kinds. The Tennessee Valley Authority was created in 1933 to help in the total development of an entire economic area. Moreover, the federal government has from its beginning stimulated commerce through statutes implementing its additional powers over coinage and money, the mails, weights and measures, and copyrights and patents.

As the political environment changed and a network of federal laws evolved, the views of the Supreme Court on federal powers under the interstate commerce clause gradually broadened. Thus, for some decades, the implementation of certain statutes was modified or negated by the Court's opinions on what constituted interstate commerce. Not until the late 1930s did the Court include manufacturing plants and processes, for example, within the scope of regulation under the commerce clause: child-labor laws were struck down in 1918 (*Hammer v. Dagenhart*) and 1922 (*Bailey v. Drexel Furniture Company*), and it was frequently difficult to apply the Sherman Antitrust Act to some corporate combinations. By 1946, in the case of the *American Power and Light Company v. Securities and Exchange Commission*, the Court concluded that "the Federal commerce power is as broad as the economic needs of the nation." The determination of what interstate commerce is, and what shall be done in support or regulation of that commerce, now lies essentially in the political arena.

In the 1980s, the Reagan Administration pushed through Congress a sweeping package of deregulatory legislation that rolled back government regulation of business. Moreover, President Reagan and his successor, George H. W. Bush, appointed justices to the Supreme Court who were skeptical of the federal government's role in private economic affairs. Events took a different turn in the mid-1990s when the federal government began prosecution of the Microsoft Corporation for monopolistic business practices. The Microsoft case divided Congress, pitting liberal supporters of business regulation against conservative critics of regulation. In the early 2000s, the federal government's role in business regulation remained highly controversial.

BIBLIOGRAPHY

Breyer, Stephen G. *Regulation and Its Reform.* Cambridge, Mass.: Harvard University Press, 1982.

McCloskey, Robert Green. *American Conservatism in the Age of Enterprise, 1865–1910.* Cambridge, Mass.: Harvard University Press, 1951.

Miller, Arthur S. *The Supreme Court and American Capitalism.* New York: Free Press, 1968.

Shapiro, Martin M. *The Supreme Court and Administrative Agencies.* New York: Free Press, 1968.

Taft, William Howard. *The Anti-Trust Act and the Supreme Court.* Littleton, Colo.: F. B. Rothman, 1993.

Paul P. Van Riper/A. G.

See also **Bland-Allison Act; Civil Service; Commerce, Department of; Consumer Protection; Deregulation; Federal Aid; Government Regulation of Business; Railroad Mediation Acts.**

INTERSTATE COMPACTS. Article I, Section 10, of the U.S. Constitution authorizes the states, with the consent of Congress, to make compacts among themselves. The Compact Clause says, "No state shall, without the Consent of Congress, . . . enter into any Agreement or Compact with another State, or with a foreign Power. . . ." The U.S. Supreme Court has interpreted this provision to mean that Congress must approve only those interstate agreements that affect the balance of power within the federal system. Furthermore, such approval can be implicit, found in subsequent Congressional acts recognizing the results of the interstate compact (*Virginia v. Tennessee*, 1893). Administrative agreements or administrative amendments to other agreements do not require congressional approval.

States began making agreements among themselves early in the nation's history. In the colonial period, nine agreements on boundaries existed, and four more were made under the ARTICLES OF CONFEDERATION. In the first century of the Republic, interstate compacts were limited chiefly to a few boundary agreements; only twenty-four were ratified from 1783 to 1900. A large increase in compacts began in the 1930s, when the Council of State Governments and other organizations began wholehearted encouragement of interstate cooperation as an alternative to federal administration of all interstate issues. By the mid-1970s, the number of compacts approved was over 200, and they affected important governmental responsibilities.

Perhaps the most significant agreements are the river development compacts, which deal with irrigation, pollution control, fishing, and navigation. Federal sponsorship of the Colorado River Compact (1928) did not succeed in precluding a long litigation between two of the six states involved, Arizona and California, but the Upper Basin agreement seems to have worked well. The Delaware River Basin Compact (1936) was novel in that it included the federal government as a participating member, as well as the four states directly affected—New York, New Jersey, Pennsylvania, and Delaware. The New England Interstate Water Pollution Control Commission, which was formed in 1947, expanded its powers to include regulatory activities in the early 1970s. The Susquehanna River Basin Compact of 1969 (which deals with planning land use), like the Delaware compact, also includes federal participation.

States have made agreements among themselves covering a wide range of other issues and activities, including child custody and placement, educational policy, administration of criminal law, use of natural resources, protection of the environment, transportation, and utility regulation. There are a number of regional development and planning compacts. And one important compact, the Port Authority of New York (1921)—also the first joint administrative agency of a continuing nature—does a multibillion dollar business involving airports, bridges, and tunnels.

The federal government, especially Congress, has had no consistent policy on compacts. Sometimes it has encouraged them; sometimes it has discouraged them. Because interstate compacts are a means by which states retain some control over some of their activities, this vacillation reflects the national government's uncertainty about the appropriate scope of its own power and the role of the states in an ever changing federal system.

BIBLIOGRAPHY

Council on State Governments. *Interstate Compacts and Agencies.* Lexington, Ky.: The Council of State Governments, 1983.

Council on State Governments. *Interstate Compacts, 1783–1977: A Revised Compilation.* Lexington, Ky.: The Council of State Governments, 1977.

Florestano, Patricia S. "Past and Present Utilization of Interstate Compacts in the United States." *Publius* 24, no. 4 (1994): 13–25.

Ridgeway, Marian E. *Interstate Compacts: A Question of Federalism.* Carbondale: Southern Illinois University Press, 1971.

George C. S. Benson / C. P.

See also **Port Authority of New York and New Jersey; State Sovereignty.**

INTERSTATE HIGHWAY SYSTEM. The Dwight D. Eisenhower System of Interstate and Defense Highways includes more than 46,000 miles of intercity highways. With just 1 percent of U.S. highway mileage, the interstate system carries 21 percent of highway travel, including half of all heavy truck travel. The interstate is a major economic asset, and high design requirements have helped to make it the world's safest highway system. The states own and operate most highways; the interstate is a national system of state highways. The program made federal funds available for specific activities to encourage states to pursue federal interests in national defense and interstate commerce, though commerce always has been more central to the program.

The Federal-Aid Highway Act of 1944 first authorized a 40,000-mile interstate as part of the Federal-Aid Primary System, established in 1921. In 1947, the Bureau of Public Roads designated 37,681 miles, with 2,900 miles in urban areas. Another 2,319 miles were reserved for urban distribution routes and circumferentials (beltways). However, the 1944 act dedicated no funds for the interstate system and applied the Primary System's principle of covering 50 percent of costs with federal money. Without dedicated funds or a higher federal share of costs, no projects emerged. In 1952, Congress authorized $25 million annually for fiscal years 1953 through 1955, then $175 million annually for 1956 and 1957, with a 60 percent federal share. A few projects got under way, with $5.6 million spent in 1953, increasing to $90 million in 1956.

The Federal-Aid Highway Act of 1956, under President Eisenhower, established the "real" interstate pro-

Interstate Highway. This 1972 photograph by Charles O'Rear shows Interstate 8 cutting through farmland in the Imperial Valley, in the southeastern corner of California. NATIONAL ARCHIVES AND RECORDS ADMINISTRATION

gram. Congress added 1,000 miles to the system, established a trust fund, and raised the federal share of project costs to 90 percent. Funding increased to $1 billion in 1957, with accelerating authorizations through 1969. Congress also added 1,500 miles in 1968, bringing the total to 42,500 miles. Another several hundred miles were added as "continuation" mileage, but these links were not eligible for interstate funds. With new funding and high federal shares, construction began in earnest. Expenditures reached $1.25 billion in 1958 and nearly $2 billion in 1959. At $2.6 billion in 1963, the interstate accounted for 73 percent of all Federal Highway Administration (FHWA) expenditures. Outlays increased steadily, peaking at $4.1 billion in 1986 and 1988, though the program had slipped to less than 50 percent of all FHWA outlays.

The interstate program enjoyed strong public support, but some groups soon characterized it and the urban renewal program as "urban removal" of low-income neighborhoods. Early criticism was perceived as "obstructing progress," but opposition increased among the displaced, environmentalists, academics, and others, especially over new urban projects, some of which were never built. In response, beginning in 1962, Congress steadily increased the role of local governments in the program, particularly in urbanized areas, and increased planning requirements to ensure consideration of environmental effects and transit alternatives. After 1973, states needed local governments' approval for urban interstate projects. Later, with local agreement, states could transfer funds from one highway program to another and could finance transit construction with interstate funds. The interstate program financed much of the subsequent expansion in urban rail systems. Congress also raised the federal share on noninterstate highways to 70 percent in 1973, then to 80 percent, equaling the federal share for transit construction.

Simultaneously, most of the interstate system approached completion. By 1980, the goal of a new system of "superhighways" had essentially been achieved. Controversial urban links accounted for most remaining mileage. In 1981, Congress began redirecting funds from new construction to preservation through resurfacing, restoration, rehabilitation, and reconstruction of existing mileage ("4R"). Bridge replacement needs also began to reduce the role of new interstate construction.

Finally, the Intermodal Surface Transportation Efficiency Act (ISTEA) of 1991 fundamentally restructured the entire federal-aid highway program. Those changes have been reinforced in subsequent acts. The ISTEA established a 155,000-mile (260,000-kilometer) National Highway System of arterial highways, including the interstate as a distinct subset. The ISTEA also authorized forty-two "high-priority corridors," some of which have been added to the interstate system. However, new construction was no longer a core objective. The federal share on interstate projects changed to 90.66 percent for

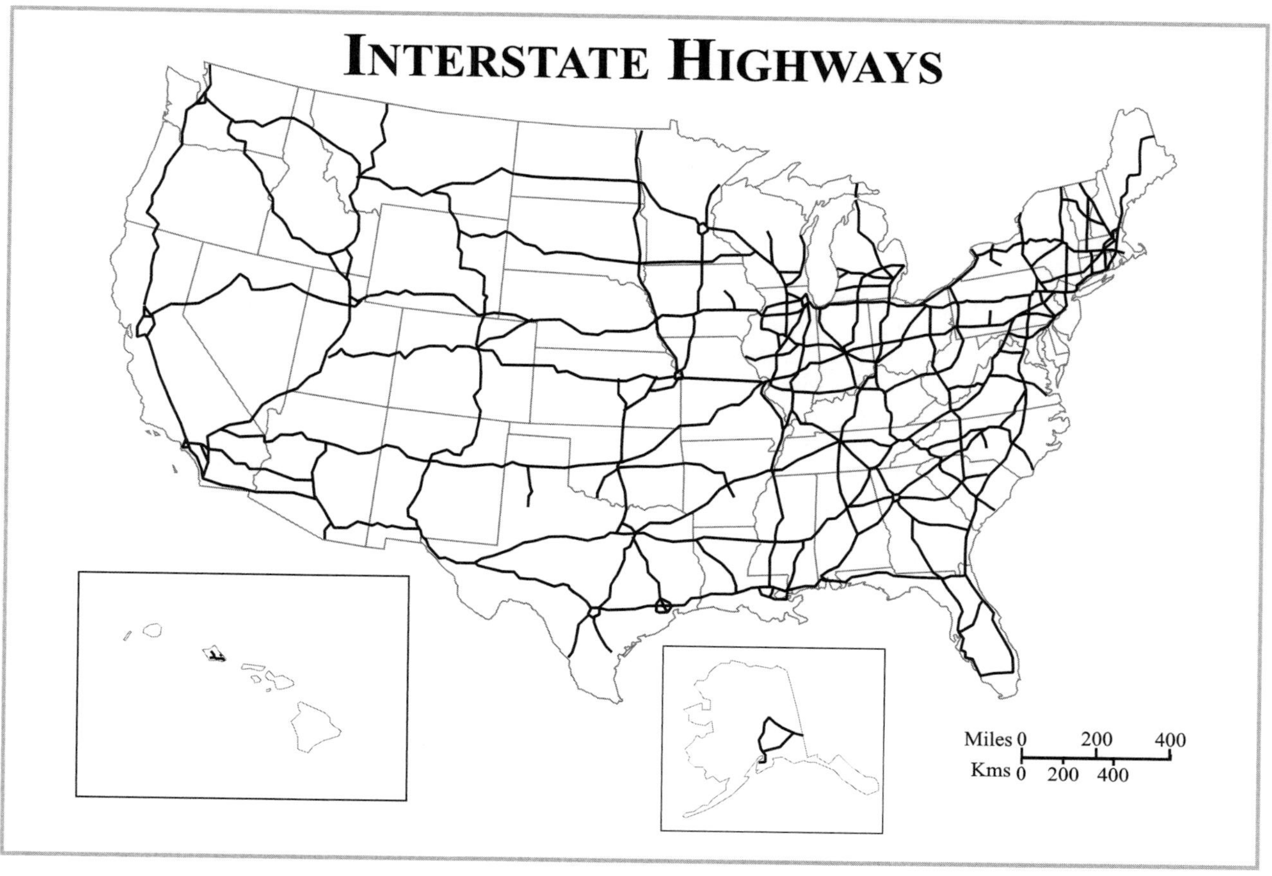

4R, and 86.5 percent if projects added capacity other than high-occupancy vehicle lanes. Construction for new capacity fell to just $363 million in 1999, while total interstate spending ($3.2 billion) fell to 15.7 percent of total FHWA spending. Nevertheless, the interstate remains a monumental public works program that met its goal of providing a national system of safe, high-performance highways.

BIBLIOGRAPHY

Cox, Wendell, and Jean Love. *The Best Investment a Nation Ever Made.* Washington, D.C.: Highway Users Federation, 1996. A history of the interstate system and an assessment of its economic and social benefits.

Gomez-Ibáñez, José, William B. Tye, and Clifford Winston. *Essays in Transportation Economics and Policy.* Washington, D.C.: Brookings Institution, 1999. A discussion of contemporary issues confronting transportation in general in the United States.

Highway Statistics. Washington, D.C.: Federal Highway Administration, 1947–. Annual publication providing data on highway mileage, travel, and finance.

Robert Matthews

See also **Federal-Aid Highway Program; Infrastructure; Roads; Transportation and Travel.**

INTERSTATE TRADE BARRIERS. During the early years of the Confederation, states broadened and intensified the commercial blockages that had grown up among the colonies in the era before independence. A principal reason for calling the Constitutional Convention of 1787 was to eliminate this cause of friction. The Constitution granted authority over interstate commerce to Congress, except for "absolutely necessary . . . inspection" provisions, which it reserved for the individual states. As a result, for nearly a century and a half the United States had the most extensive free trade area in the world. The size and unimpeded nature of the domestic market in the nineteenth century invited the emphasis on economies of large-scale production so characteristic of American capitalism.

During the Great Depression, beginning in 1929, states sought more and more to impose limitations on the national free flow of commerce to raise revenue for hard-pressed state treasuries and to protect intrastate business against the competition of neighboring states. Devices were varied and often disingenuous: taxes on incoming goods and out-of-state corporations; requirements for inspection of commodities and, in some cases, lengthy quarantine; demands that incoming trucks pay fees and have certain equipment; and the creation of state "ports of entry" reminiscent of frontier customs stations in Europe. California went so far as to restrict "immigration" to individuals possessing a certain amount of cash.

The threat that the United States would be "Balkanized" (fragmented) led to a conference of state governments in 1939. President Franklin D. Roosevelt begged the states to "take effective steps toward the removal of all barriers to the free flow of trade within our union." Instead, over the following twenty-five years, restraints increased in number and incidence. The Supreme Court struck down the most undisguised discriminations but tolerated exactions that furnished states with revenues that the federal government would otherwise have had to supply. The court justified this leniency by noting that it was the province of Congress, not the judiciary, to disallow repugnant practices. A committee of the House of Representatives, after hearings in 1965, concluded that "the present system of State TAXATION as it affects interstate commerce works badly for both business and the States." Complex rules bred disregard of law; for all but large enterprises, the costs of compliance exceeded the taxes. Many prefered standardization of state restrictions to rigid enforcement of constitutional prohibition. States, in the face of increasing dependence on federal aid and discipline, pled states' rights.

The rapid growth of electronic commerce in the 1990s intensified the debate over interstate trade barriers. INTERNET companies asked Congress for tax exempt status under the Commerce clause of the Constitution. The companies argued that, although headquartered in particular localities, they did business across the nation on the electronic "superhighway," and thus fell outside the tax jurisdiction of any one particular state. They also argued that granting tax exempt status to Internet companies would benefit the national economy by promoting high-tech expansion. As the nation entered the twenty-first century, the issue of state taxation and Internet commerce remained unresolved.

BIBLIOGRAPHY

Frankfurter, Felix. *The Commerce Clause Under Marshall, Taney, and Waite.* Chapel Hill: University of North Carolina Press, 1937; Chicago: Quadrangle Books, 1964.

Swisher, Carl Brent. *The Growth of Constitutional Power in the United States.* Chicago: University of Chicago Press, 1963.

Tribe, Laurence H. *God Save This Honorable Court: How the Choice of Supreme Court Justices Shapes Our History.* New York: Random House, 1985.

Broadus Mitchell/C. W; A. G.

See also **Commerce, Court of; Commerce Clause; Laissez-Faire; Supreme Court.**

INTERURBAN ELECTRIC RAILWAYS. *See* **Railways, Interurban.**

INTERVENTION involves the unsolicited interference of one nation in the affairs of another. It may be directed against a single state, factions within that state, or interactions among a group of states. It does not necessarily take the form of military action but may involve economic or social pressure. When applied to international law, the concept can be elusive. Because many relations between states involve elements of coercion, it is difficult to determine at which point pressure becomes sufficiently coercive as to be deemed intervention. Although states always claim the right to intervene on the basis of "vital interests," they never agree as to what this term involves.

During most of the nineteenth century, the United States intervened to consolidate control of the American mainland, and major instances included successful efforts to acquire Florida, Texas, and California from Spain and Mexico. The United States also engaged in efforts to expose China, Japan, and Korea to American trade. For instance, Commodore Matthew C. Perry "opened" Japan in 1854 with an armed squadron. Prior to 1899, at least fifty minor incidents took place, usually in the Pacific or the Caribbean, in which U.S. forces raided pirate villages, landed marines to protect resident Americans, and bombarded foreign towns in reprisal for offensives directed toward American traders and missionaries. In 1900, U.S. troops took part in an international expedition to relieve Beijing from Chinese revolutionaries called the Boxers. Because of the Spanish-American War (1898), itself the result of U.S. pressure upon Spain to liberate Cuba, the United States gained the Philippines, Puerto Rico, and Guam. The United States also annexed Hawaii in 1898 and in 1899 took part in the partition of the Samoan Islands, gaining the harbor of Pago Pago. In both cases, the United States sought to protect trade routes and, in the case of Hawaii, the economic and political prerogatives of the powerful American colony there.

By the late nineteenth century, the nation's leaders proclaimed their right to intervene in the Western Hemisphere. During the Venezuela boundary dispute, Secretary of State Richard Olney claimed on 20 July 1895, "The United States is practically sovereign on this continent, and its fiat is law upon the subjects to which it confines its interposition." In his corollary to the Monroe Doctrine, first set forth in 1904, President Theodore Roosevelt issued a unilateral declaration asserting the U.S. prerogative to exercise "international police power" in the Western Hemisphere.

The Caribbean was a particular focal point, as the United States continually sought to protect its isthmian canal and to create political and financial stability favorable to its interests. In 1903, Roosevelt sent warships to the Isthmus of Panama to ensure Panama's successful secession from Colombia and thereby to ensure the building of the Panama Canal. President Woodrow Wilson intervened twice in Mexico, first in occupying Veracruz in 1914 after an alleged insult to American seamen and

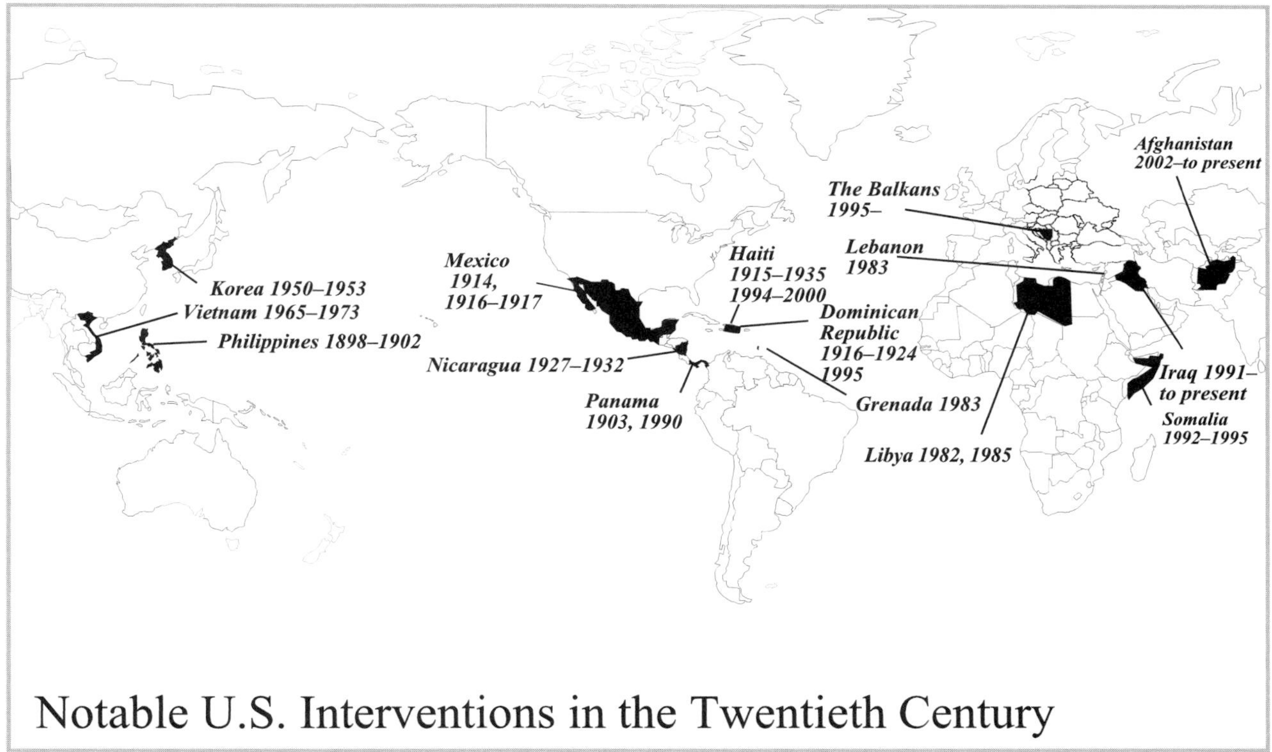

Notable U.S. Interventions in the Twentieth Century

second in a "punitive expedition" in 1914 in search of the revolutionary Pancho Villa.

U.S. troops directly occupied several Caribbean nations. American forces entered Cuba in 1898, 1906, 1912, and 1917, at times remaining several years. Americans occupied Haiti from 1915 to 1924, the Dominican Republic from 1916 to 1924, and Nicaragua in 1909, from 1912 to 1924, and from 1927 to 1933.

In 1917 and 1941 the United States became a full-scale belligerent in World War I and World War II, respectively. In efforts to contain communist expansion, the United States led in the formation of the North Atlantic Treaty Organization (1949), entered the Korean War (1950–1953), and fought a full-scale conflict in Vietnam (1965–1975). Other examples of Cold War intervention include the Greek civil war (1947), the Berlin Airlift (1948), Guatemala (1954), and Lebanon (1958). Cuba was subject to an American-sponsored invasion in 1961 and an American blockade during the missile crisis of 1962.

Several Cold War presidents issued interventionist doctrines. On 12 March 1947, President Harry S. Truman pledged support for "free peoples who are resisting attempted subjugation by armed minorities or by outside pressures." On 5 January 1957, the Eisenhower Doctrine authorized the dispatching of military forces to any Middle Eastern state requesting assistance against "overt armed aggression controlled by international communism." In the Carter Doctrine, promulgated on 23 January 1980 in the wake of the Soviet invasion of Afghanistan, Jimmy Carter threatened military action against any "attempt by any outside force to gain control of the Persian Gulf region."

On 6 February 1985, when Ronald Reagan spoke of backing "freedom fighters," his statement was dubbed by journalists the Reagan Doctrine. During his presidency, the United States opposed left-wing insurgencies in Angola, Mozambique, Grenada, Cambodia, Afghanistan, Nicaragua, and El Salvador. Under Presidents George H. W. Bush and William J. Clinton, the United States maintained sanctions against South Africa, sent troops to Somalia and Lebanon, invaded Panama, entered into Operation Desert Storm against Iraq, and ordered eight thousand ground forces to Kosovo. The 2001 terrorist attack on the United States inspired prompt retaliatory intervention in Afghanistan and elsewhere.

BIBLIOGRAPHY

Graber, Doris A. *Crisis Diplomacy: A History of U.S. Intervention Policies and Practices.* Washington, D.C.: Public Affairs Press, 1959.

———. "Intervention and Nonintervention." In *Encyclopedia of American Foreign Policy: Studies of the Principal Movements and Ideas.* Rev. ed. Edited by Alexander DeConde et al. New York: Scribners, 2002.

Haass, Richard N. *Intervention: The Use of American Military Force in the Post–Cold War World.* Washington, D.C.: Carnegie Endowment, 1994.

Justus D. Doenecke

See also **Carter Doctrine; Cuba, Relations with; Eisenhower Doctrine; Guatemala, Relations with; Haiti, Relations with; Lebanon, U.S. Landing in; Mexico, Relations with; Panama Invasion; Truman Doctrine.**

INTOLERABLE ACTS. The four Intolerable Acts, also known as the Coercive Acts, formed Britain's punishment of both the town of Boston and the province of Massachusetts for the destruction of the East India Company's tea on 16 December 1773. They were rushed through Parliament in the spring of 1774. Their purpose was to show rebellious colonials that, unlike 1766, when the Stamp Act was repealed, and 1770, when four of the five Townshend taxes were withdrawn, Britain would not retreat this time.

The Boston Port Act closed Boston to seaborne commerce until the town paid for the tea. Since trade was the town's life, the act and its enforcement by the Royal Navy amounted to a blockade, which was an act of war. The Massachusetts Government Act abolished the province's royal charter of 1692. The new structure would replace a provincial council elected by the assembly with one appointed by the governor in the name of the king. Towns would meet once per year, solely to elect local officers. County courts would enforce the act's provisions. The Administration of Justice Act let the Crown remove the trials of public officials under accusation to another province or to Britain on the ground that they could not get fair trials in local courts. The Quartering Act allowed British commanders to billet soldiers in colonials' homes if no barracks or public buildings could be found. The commander in chief in America, General Thomas Gage, became governor of Massachusetts.

The Quebec Act, passed at the same time, granted legal privileges to the Catholic Church in the former French province, established nonrepresentative government there, and gave Quebec control of much of the interior north of the Ohio River. It was not part of the package of punishments. But the Intolerable Acts, the Quebec Act, and the naming of Gage all figured among the "abuses and usurpations" listed in the Declaration of Independence.

BIBLIOGRAPHY

Ammerman, David. *In the Common Cause: American Response to the Coercive Acts of 1774.* New York: Norton, 1975.

Bushman, Richard L. *King and People in Provincial Massachusetts.* Chapel Hill: University of North Carolina Press, 1985.

Edward Countryman

See also **Boston Tea Party; Revolution, American.**

INTREPID, formerly the Tripolitan ketch *Mastico,* was captured by Stephen Decatur during the war with Tripoli and used by him on 16 February 1804 in burning the *Philadelphia,* which had been captured by the Tripolitans. On the night of 4 September 1804, the vessel, carrying 15,000 pounds of powder and 150 large shells, solid shot, and combustibles, was sailed into the harbor of Tripoli by Lt. Richard Somers, accompanied by two other officers and ten men, where it exploded before getting sufficiently near the enemy gunboats to destroy them. The thirteen Americans were all killed. Also bearing the name was the World War II era aircraft carrier U.S.S. *Intrepid,* currently decommissioned and site of the Intrepid Sea Air Space Museum in New York City.

BIBLIOGRAPHY

Lewis, Charles Lee. *The Romantic Decatur.* Philadelphia: University of Pennsylvania Press, 1937.

Charles Lee Lewis/A. R.

See also **Barbary Wars; Gunboats; Navy, United States.**

INUIT. Inuit (people) is the collective name of a widely distributed group of people inhabiting the northernmost areas of North America and Greenland. "Eskimo," a term formerly used by outsiders, has lost favor because of its offensive origins in an Algonquian word roughly meaning "eaters of raw flesh."

Early European Exploration

Inuit were the first inhabitants of the Americas to encounter Europeans. Archaeological evidence suggests that groups of Inuit moved eastward from Alaska, inhabiting the entire Arctic coast of North America and portions of Greenland about a century before the explorations of the Greenland coast by the Viking Gunnbjörn Ulfsson around A.D. 875. Eric the Red established settlements in southern

Inuit Home. A woman emerges from a tent in the Arctic as a man stands nearby, c. 1901; a photograph from the collection of the polar explorer Frederick A. Cook. Library of Congress

Inuit Education. Early-twentieth-century students stand outside a public school in Kivalina, a small Inuit village on the northwestern coast of Alaska. LIBRARY OF CONGRESS

Greenland in 982 or 983. Contact between the Norse colonies in Greenland and the Inuit was uneasy and major conflict seems to have ended the Viking colonization of Greenland in the fifteenth century. Danish colonization began with the arrival in 1721 of missionaries, who pressured the Inuit to adopt European customs and language.

The first appearance of Russians took the form of an expedition of explorers to Alaska in 1741 led by Vitus Bering. The Russians subsequently claimed all of Alaska by virtue of their colonies on the southern coast. Russian contact with Inuit was limited to the area of these settlements; Inuit in northern Alaska had only indirect contact with Russians and their trade goods through trade by northern Inuit with their neighbors in southwest Alaska. British and American whaling ships began hunting the Arctic and wintering in northern Alaska in the late 1840s and Russia sold its Alaskan claims to the United States in 1867. Inuit east from the Mackenzie Delta to Hudson Bay did not meet Europeans until the late nineteenth century.

Pre-Colonial Inuit Society

The primary mode of Inuit settlement has been the village, although until recently relations between villages were not socially fundamental. Rather, power manifested itself mostly within the village. Men hunted and fished, women cooked and skinned animals; family cooperation was essential to survival. Social networking within the extended family and between extended families within the village served as the mediator of power. More recently, Inuit people began to organize themselves at the village level, the regional level, and the international level in order to interact with their colonial governments, but the importance of the family persists.

The Inuit economy before European development was one of subsistence. Sea and land mammals, including whales, walrus, seals, and in some areas, caribou, were the staple targets of hunts. Most Inuit technology, including harpoons, stone oil lamps, dogsleds, skin boats, water resistant boots, and tailored clothing, served either the tasks of the hunt or the tasks of the home. Individual contribution to the hunt, proper sharing of the yield with the elderly and infirm, honesty, and other forms of cooperation for the common good were enforced by general approval or disapproval through social networks rather than by a government or corporate apparatus. Economic life, like political life, centered on the family's internal networks and its connections to other families.

The Impact of Colonial Status

Ongoing colonial status has brought changes to Inuit communities. Missionaries have proselytized among them, anthropologists have studied them, governments have imposed laws and regulations on them, and corporations have pressed them to enter the capitalist cash economies of the modern nation-states in which they have found themselves. The colonial relationship between the modern nation-states and Inuit communities across the Arctic has been and is the overarching problem with which the Inuit and their southern neighbors must cope.

The social problems of colonization manifest themselves most strongly among the Inuit in politics and economy. Caught up in the drive to advance the frontiers of "civilization," Inuit people have sometimes willingly appropriated economic, political, and social structures from their colonizers, and sometimes those structures have been imposed. One important event in this process has been the discovery and exploitation of the petroleum resources in northern Alaska. Through legal intricacies, Alaskan Inuit and other Native Alaskans were deprived of enforceable legal claim to their lands and resources. Most petroleum-bearing lands in northern Alaska were acquired by the state in the early 1960s, and then leased to a group of oil companies in 1969. Afterward, in the Alaska Land Claims Settlement Act of 1971, the U.S. Congress acted to settle Native Alaskan groups' land and resource claims, awarding a relatively large cash and land settlement and creating regional- and village-based corporations to administer it. The imposition of corporate structures was supposed to help draw Native Alaskans into the American economy, but instead most of the corporations have been unable to turn profits.

Inuit people often are eager to take advantage of snowmobiles, motorboats, rifles, and other technological advances that can make their ways of life less difficult and dangerous, but such items are only available from within the American cash economy. From the perspective of the colonizers, the question was how to compel Inuit to labor and create surplus value, thereby establishing wage relations, and it was answered with a host of vocational training programs. However, the contradiction between the American corporate expectation that Inuit work regular schedules and the Inuit social expectation that able-bodied men hunt to provide subsistence for their families creates obstacles to Inuit employment in non-Inuit-run corporations in the Arctic. Thus, the petroleum industry has not employed many Inuit.

In Canada and Greenland, governmental attempts to deal fairly with Inuit have differed from the approach taken by the United States. Greenland acquired home rule from Denmark by popular referendum in 1979, and governs itself by parliamentary democracy. Canada has passed claims settlement acts like that of the United States, but in 1993 the Canadian Parliament voted to partition the Northwest Territories and create a new territory called Nunavut (our land). The population of Nunavut is around 85 percent Inuit; thus, the Inuit of Nunavut enjoy a measure of home rule within the Canadian nation. These developments in Alaska, Canada, and Greenland have succeeded in large part because of organizing and pressure by Inuit themselves. On the international level, Inuit in all three countries joined in 1977 in a statement of common interest to form the Inuit Circumpolar Conference, a United Nations NGO (nongovernment organization).

Political and economic interactions illustrate the fundamental problem of colonialism, the answer to which will continue to be worked out in the future. To what extent will Inuit culture be characterized as "traditional" in distinction to "modern," such that Inuit must inevitably adopt modern customs, like working regular schedules for wages, and to what extent will Inuit culture be characterized as an identity to be formed by Inuit themselves, regardless of what customs they choose to adopt?

BIBLIOGRAPHY

Burch, Ernest S. *The Iñupiaq Eskimo Nations of Northwest Alaska.* Fairbanks: University of Alaska Press, 1998.

Chance, Norman A. *The Iñupiat and Arctic Alaska: An Ethnography of Development.* Fort Worth, Tex.: Holt, Rinehart, and Winston, 1990.

Dorais, Louis-J. *Quaqtaq: Modernity and Identity in an Inuit Community.* Toronto: University of Toronto Press, 1997.

Jorgensen, Joseph G. *Oil Age Eskimos.* Berkeley: University of California Press, 1990.

Frank C. Shockey

See also **Alaska; Alaska Native Claims Settlement Act.**

INVESTIGATING COMMITTEES have developed over two centuries into one of Congress's principal modes of governance. Since the mid-twentieth century, congressional investigations have grown increasingly spectacular even as they have become commonplace, invading business, culture, politics, and every other sphere of American life with increasingly powerful tools to compel testimony and production of documents.

Things started episodically. While the U.S. Constitution does not explicitly authorize Congress to conduct investigations, both the British Parliament and several colonial assemblies had done so repeatedly. In 1792, the first congressional investigation under the Constitution had authority to "call for such persons, papers, and records, as may be necessary to assist their inquiries" into the defeat of General Arthur St. Clair's army by Indians in the northwest. In 1827, Congress enacted a statutory penalty of up to a $1,000 fine and a year in prison for refusal to appear, answer questions, or produce documents. But when the Jacksonian era's so-called Bank War began five years later, the House of Representatives declined to launch an open-ended inquiry into the operations of the Bank of the United States. On at least one occasion, moreover, President Andrew Jackson declined to provide information requested by a House committee. In 1859, the Senate initiated contempt proceedings against a witness who refused to testify during an investigation of John Brown's raid on the federal armory at Harpers Ferry. By the time the nineteenth century closed, the idea had been established that congressional power to investigate reached both private persons and executive agencies. Congress had also learned that it was easier to force private persons to cooperate than the chief executive.

In the first half of the twentieth century, congressional investigations were aimed more frequently toward crafting federal legislation. In 1912, for example, the House Banking and Currency Committee, chaired by Arsene Paulin Pujo, investigated J. P. Morgan and the "money trust." Pujo Committee findings were instrumental in passage of the Federal Reserve Act of 1913 and the Clayton Antitrust Act of 1914. Senator Gerald Nye led another major investigation in 1934–1936 that again focused on Wall Street—along with munitions manufacturers and British propagandists. Nye's specific subject was U.S. entry into World War I, and his conclusions led to the Neutrality Acts of the mid- and late 1930s. During World War II, Senator Harry S. Truman led a third major investigation as chair of the Special Committee to Investigate the National Defense Program; and from 1939–1945 Martin Dies led a fourth—the Special House Committee to Investigate Un-American Activities. The latter's principal concern was communist infiltration of the Franklin D. Roosevelt administration, especially the New Deal's alphabet agencies.

In World War II's last year, the House institutionalized Dies's mission by creating a standing House Committee on Un-American Activities (HUAC). The Senate followed in 1951 by creating an Internal Security Subcommittee (SISS) and allowing Joseph R. McCarthy's Permanent Subcommittee on Investigations (PERM) free reign. Making use of a new medium, television (as would Senator Estes Kefauver's investigation of organized crime in 1950–1951), all three committees tried to make the general argument that President Truman and the Democratic Party were "soft on communism." HUAC broke the Alger Hiss case in 1948 and held hearings on communist infiltration of the motion-picture industry. Subpoenaed witnesses were always required to "name names" (that is, inform on others). Refusal to do so on First Amendment grounds meant jail for contempt of Congress. Refusal on Fifth Amendment grounds meant that the witness would stay out of jail but be thrown out of work and onto the Hollywood blacklist or one of the other dozen blacklists operating at the time. McCarthy initially focused in 1950 on communist infiltration of the Department of State. In 1953, he moved on to look for communists in the United States Army. The televised Army-McCarthy hearings led to McCarthy's demise largely because President Dwight D. Eisenhower made his own general argument: the army's work was too important to the nation's security to allow irresponsible congressional investigators to interfere. A few years later, Attorney General William Rogers coined the term "executive privilege" to signal White House refusal to cooperate with any congressional request for information.

Executive privilege was more the rule than the exception until the Richard M. Nixon administration (1969–1974) collapsed under the weight of the Watergate scandals. Both the House of Representatives, with Peter Rodino serving as chair, and the Senate, with Sam Ervin serving as chair, established Watergate investigating committees. Both Houses also established special committees to explore the intelligence community, best known by the names of their chairs (Senator Frank Church and Congressman Otis Pike). Other scandals inspired more committees, including the joint committee that investigated the Ronald Reagan administration's Iran-Contra affair, and the various committees that endlessly probed the Bill Clinton administration under the general umbrella investigation called Whitewater.

Two basic questions remain in dispute. First, what are the parameters of investigating committee authority? The Supreme Court has been less than a consistent voice here, generally coming down in favor of executive privilege on most occasions while opposing the claim when criminal violation is alleged. The controlling case, *United States v. Nixon* (1974), basically held that executive privilege challenges should be heard on a case-by-case basis. Second, are investigating committees useful tools for Congress when pursuing its principal legislative mission? Or are such committees more often than not blunt partisan instruments wielded by majorities against minorities?

BIBLIOGRAPHY

Berger, Raoul. *Executive Privilege: A Constitutional Myth.* Cambridge, Mass.: Harvard University Press, 1974.

Schlesinger, Arthur M., Jr., and Roger Bruns, eds. *Congress Investigates: A Documented History, 1792–1974.* 5 vols. New York: Chelsea House, 1975.

Kenneth O'Reilly

See also **Clinton Scandals; McCarthyism.**

INVESTMENT COMPANIES. As defined by the 1940 Investment Company Act, investment companies are publicly held corporations or trusts "in the business of investing, reinvesting, owning, holding, or trading in securities." In the form of mutual (or open-end) funds, they constituted the most spectacular growth industry on Wall Street in the late twentieth century, which is all the more remarkable in light of the role that (closed-end) investment companies played in the speculative mania leading up to the October 1929 stock market crash.

Early Developments and Abuses

The first investment companies in the United States developed out of public utility holding companies and were organized to gain control of corporations. Public utility holding companies issued bonds and used the proceeds to purchase controlling shares of utility companies. In 1905, the Electric Bond and Share Company (EB&S) became the most prominent investment company of the pre–

World War I period by taking the next step and issuing preferred stock in order to use the proceeds to purchase controlling shares of utilities. EB&S was organized by General Electric (GE). It purchased controlling shares of utilities because they were, or would become, major purchasers of GE equipment.

Although public utility holding companies remained a major factor in the investment company movement of the 1920s, a structural change in the source of new savings available for investment purposes ensured an increasingly prominent role for the investment companies organized by investment banks. Prior to World War I, firms like J. P. Morgan and Company and Kuhn, Loeb and Company dominated investment banking because of their access to British and German savings, respectively. But after the war, which destroyed Britain and Germany as sources of new savings, dominance shifted to investment banks like Dillon, Read and Company and Goldman, Sachs and Company because of their success in organizing investment companies that served as magnets for the savings of salaried workers and small business owners in the United States. The keys to their success were large sales forces dependent on commissions for their incomes, installment payment plans for customers, and mass advertising campaigns designed to persuade millions of Americans that, by purchasing shares of investment companies, they could gain the same diversification, liquidity, and continuous supervision of their investments enjoyed by the wealthy.

This message proved illusory insofar as the closed-end investment companies of the 1920s were concerned. Closed-end investment companies assumed no responsibility for issuing new shares or redeeming outstanding shares at their net asset value. As the speculative mania of the 1920s gathered momentum, this lack of responsibility, combined with the absence of government regulation and supervision, created an irresistible temptation for the investment banks that sponsored investment companies to make profits at the expense of the investors in them.

Such profits came from the fact that the investment companies placed deposits with and loaned money to the investment banks that sponsored them, served as depositories for the stocks they underwrote, issued shares to the investment banks' partners for a fraction of their market price, and paid underwriting fees and in some cases salaries to the investment banks' partners for sitting on the boards of directors of the investment companies.

For example, the most prominent investment company in the 1920s was the United States and Foreign Securities Company (US&FS). It was organized in 1924 by Dillon, Read and Company, which raised $25 million from the public by issuing 250,000 shares of US&FS common stock as attachments to 250,000 shares of 6 percent first preferred stock, for $100 a bundle. Dillon, Read and Company maintained control by putting $5 million into US&FS in exchange for 750,000 shares of common stock attached to 50,000 shares of 6 percent second preferred stock, for $100 a bundle. Dillon, Read partners also paid themselves a $339,000 underwriting fee and gave themselves common stock in US&FS, which traded as high as $73 per share, for about 13 cents per share.

As remarkable as these profits were, they were nothing compared with the profits Dillon, Read and Company made in 1928 by pyramiding a second investment company, the United States and International Securities Corporation (US&IS), onto US&FS. Dillon, Read raised another $50 million from the public by issuing 500,000 shares of US&IS common stock as attachments to 500,000 shares of 5 percent first preferred stock, for $100 a bundle. It maintained control—and created the pyramid—by having US&FS spend $10 million on 2 million shares of US&IS common stock that were attached to 100,000 shares of 5 percent second preferred stock, for $100 a bundle. For the time and trouble of thus leveraging its initial investment of $5 million in US&FS into control of $75 million of the public's savings, Dillon, Read partners gave themselves a $1 million underwriting fee and US&IS stock for pennies per share.

This kind of pyramiding of investment companies by investment banks accounts for the spectacular growth in the number of investment companies in the 1920s, from about 40 in 1921 to about 700 in 1929. Most of the investment companies were organized in the 1926–1929 period, with over 250 organized in 1929 alone. Indeed, nearly one-third of all new corporate financings in the months leading up to the crash were stock in investment companies.

The largest pyramid, which included four of the fourteen investment companies with total assets of more than $100 million in 1929, was started in December 1928 by Goldman, Sachs and Company, when it issued stock in the Goldman Sachs Trading Corporation (GST). GST merged with the Financial and Industrial Securities Corporation, which became a major depository for GST stock. GST then joined with the Central States Electric Corporation (CSE) to organize the Shenandoah Corporation, which organized the Blue Ridge Company as a major depository for CSE stock. CSE held controlling shares of American Cities Power and Light Company, which held controlling shares of Chain Stores, Inc., which held controlling shares of a company that was actually in business, Metropolitan Chain Stores. However, the profits of Metropolitan Chain Stores were insufficient to pay dividends on all the stock issued by the six investment companies and one public utility holding company pyramided onto it, and by 1932, GST stock, issued to about 40,000 investors for $104 a share, was trading for $1.75 a share.

The collapse of the pyramid of investment companies built by Goldman, Sachs and Company illustrates the larger trend of the investment company movement in the early 1930s, whereby the total market value of investment companies dropped from a peak of about $8 billion immediately prior to the October 1929 crash to less than $2 billion in 1932.

Reforms and New Trends

The passage of the 1933 Securities Act, the 1934 Securities Exchange Act, the 1935 Public Utility Holding Company Act, and the 1940 Investment Company Act (amended in 1970) created rules and enforcement mechanisms to prevent the practices of the investment banks in organizing investment companies in the 1920s. Most importantly, new laws required that directors of the investment companies be independent of the sponsoring investment banks, and thus free of the conflict of interests that allowed investment banks to profit at the expense of the shareholders in the investment companies they sponsor.

Nonetheless, closed-end investment companies never recovered from the October 1929 stock market crash. What has taken their place, and become the principal means by which salaried workers and small business owners save, are open-end investment companies, or mutual funds. Mutual funds continuously issue new shares and stand ready to redeem outstanding shares at their net asset value. Even in 1929 mutual funds constituted over 500 of the 700 investment companies; they were just dwarfed by the publicity, size, and seemingly easy money to be made by purchasing the shares of closed-end investment companies. At the time of the passage of the 1940 Investment Company Act, there were only sixty-eight mutual funds left, with about $400 million in assets. But after World War II, they began to grow. Gross sales of new shares in them was more than $10 billion between 1946 and 1958, by which time there were 453 investment companies (238 mutual funds) with total assets of about $17 billion. By 1960, mutual funds alone had $17 billion in total assets, and by 1970 there were 361 mutual funds with assets of $47.6 billion. Meanwhile, closed-end investment companies were marginalized, with only $4 billion in assets.

In the 1970s, money market funds became a significant new trend in the investment company movement. It was during the 1970s that the government removed the interest rate ceilings on bank deposits that had been in effect since the 1930s, starting with the ceilings on large-denomination time deposits. Money market funds were attractive to small investors because, by pooling their savings, the money market funds could obtain the higher returns on the large-denomination time deposits. By also allowing shareholders to write checks, money market funds became an attractive alternative to placing savings with commercial banks, savings and loans, credit unions, and mutual savings banks.

The first data available on money market funds is for 1974. They constituted $1.7 billion of the $35.8 billion of total assets in mutual funds. (There was a severe downturn in the market in 1974–1975.) By 1979, money market funds were up to $45.5 billion, practically catching up with all other mutual funds at $49 billion, for total mutual fund assets of $94.5 billion. In 1983 they surpassed all other mutual funds in total assets ($179.3 billion versus $113.6 billion, for a total of $292.9 billion).

In the mid-1980s another trend began in the investment company movement. Salaried workers and small business owners stopped making new investments in the stock market except through mutual funds. Whereas net purchases of equities by households outside mutual funds has been negative since the mid-1980s, their purchases of equities through mutual funds grew from $5 billion in 1984 to a peak of $218 billion in 1996, but was still a hefty $159 billion in 1999.

On account of the growth of equity funds, in 1985 mutual funds other than money market funds were once again larger than the money market funds, at $251.7 billion and $243.8 billion, respectively, for a total of $495.5 billion. In 1993, equity funds became larger in value than money market funds, at $740.7 billion and $565.3 billion, respectively. In 1999, the total assets of 7,791 mutual funds reached about $6.8 trillion. Equity and money market funds accounted for a bit more than $4 trillion and $1.6 trillion of the total, respectively.

BIBLIOGRAPHY

Bullock, Hugh. *The Story of Investment Companies.* New York: Columbia University Press, 1959.

Carossa, Vincent P. *Investment Banking in America: A History.* Cambridge, Mass.: Harvard University Press, 1970.

Investment Company Institute. *Mutual Fund Fact Book.* Washington, D.C.: Investment Company Institute, 2000.

Edwin Dickens

See also **Banking: Investment Banks; Financial Services Industry; Stock Market.**

INVISIBLE MAN (1952) is widely considered one of the finest examples of American literature. Written by Ralph Ellison (1914–1994) at the outset of the civil rights movement, the popular best-seller won the National Book Award in 1953.

Invisible Man is a complex and richly layered tale in which the pointedly unnamed African American narrator tells both his own story and the story of millions of others like him. The novel traces the narrator's experiences from his humiliating teenage participation in a battle royal for the amusement of white southern businessmen through his engagement in—and, significantly, his withdrawal from—the black culture of Harlem. His constant battle is one of and for identity, and it is a battle the narrator shares with millions of Americans in every time and circumstance.

Ellison's characters offer rich variations of doubling and dichotomy. Bledsoe, president of the college the narrator briefly attends, should enlighten his young black students; instead, he is just as oppressive as the surrounding white southern culture. Jack, the leader of the Brotherhood, professes the desire to express the voice of the masses, yet he cannot allow his prized orator to speak his own mind. Ras, who derides the Brotherhood's moderate tactics as a white-sponsored fraud, ends up isolated, the victim of his own radical push for the unity of all African brothers. The narrator illustrates many dichotomies within and around himself, although they are in fact universal influences: South and North, black and white, coercion and freedom, underground and exposure, darkness and light, silence and voice. The appeal of Ellison's narration lies in the fact that the hopes, disappointments, fears, frustrations, and viewpoints that he expresses resonate as strongly with the experience of any alienated group in the United States today—and those who would alienate them—as they did when Ellison published his only novel.

BIBLIOGRAPHY

Sundquist, Eric J., ed. *Cultural Contexts for Ralph Ellison's* Invisible Man. Boston: Bedford/St. Martin's, 1995.

Barbara Schwarz Wachal

IOWA, located in the center of the Midwest in the north-central region of the continental United States, is characterized by its gently rolling terrain and bountiful agriculture. The earliest European explorers to visit Iowa observed a lush landscape covered primarily by tall prairie grass with trees mostly along rivers and streams. A century and a half later, the first white settlers quickly sensed the immense agricultural potential of that lush landscape. The newcomers' initial impressions held true. By 1870, with most of Iowa settled, the state was recognized nationally as a premier agricultural area.

Exploration and Changes

Iowa's recorded history began with the journey of Louis Joliet and Father Jacques Marquette when they explored the Mississippi River. On 25 June 1673, the exploring party stepped ashore on Iowa soil, the first Europeans to do so. During the next 100 years, numerous explorers traveled up and down the Mississippi and visited Iowa. In 1682, French explorer René-Robert Cavelier, Sieur de La Salle traveled the Mississippi River, claiming the river and its valley for France. He named the area Louisiana, in honor of Louis XIV. The French sold Louisiana to Spain in 1762, but some forty years later regained control of the territory, and in 1803, sold it to the United States. The area containing the future state of Iowa then belonged to the United States. Little remained of the Spanish presence in the Upper Mississippi area, but French legacy continued in the names of Mississippi River towns such as Dubuque and Prairie Du Chien.

Iowa's early history also includes the presence of seventeen Native American tribes. All tribes were a part of the Prairie-Plains Indian culture where members lived both a sedentary and a migratory lifestyle. The Ioway were the first prominent tribe in Iowa, but in 1830, sold their land and relocated in Kansas. The two largest tribes, the Sauk and Meskwaki, dominated the eastern part of Iowa for almost 100 years. By 1845, the two tribes had sold their lands to the federal government, and were relocated in Kansas. The Sauk remained there but some Meskwaki returned to Iowa and later purchased land, creating the Meskwaki settlement in east-central Iowa.

From 1803 until Iowa became an independent territory in 1838, the area underwent continual political change. It was first a part of the District of Louisiana that extended from the 33-degree parallel northward to the Canadian border. From 1805 to 1838, the area was a part of four different territories. In reality, federal officials had simply assigned Iowa to the nearest political entity for most of that period. For a time, between 1821 and 1834, Iowa had no governmental jurisdiction. Finally in 1838, Congress created the Territory of Iowa.

Almost immediately Iowans began to agitate for statehood. They made the first attempt in 1844 but Congress rejected the proposed constitution. In 1846, Iowans tried again and were successful. The state benefited from the delay, as the area included in 1846 was larger than two years earlier. The state's final boundaries were the Mississippi River on the east; the Missouri–Big Sioux Rivers on the west; 43 degrees, 30 minutes on the north; and the Missouri border on the south. On 18 December 1846, Iowa became the twenty-ninth state to enter the Union.

Even before Iowa became an independent territory, white settlers had crossed the Mississippi River and staked out land in eastern Iowa. Federal officials started land surveys in 1836, and land sales began two years later. Settlement moved across Iowa in a fairly steady manner, moving from the southeast to the northwest. By 1870, small towns and farms covered most of the state and settlement in northwest Iowa signaled the end of the frontier era. Towns also appeared quickly, especially along the Mississippi River, and included Dubuque, Davenport, and Keokuk. Early settlements along the Missouri River included Council Bluffs and Sioux City. Iowa's population grew rapidly, reaching 1,194,020 by 1870.

The Late Nineteenth Century

Iowa's agricultural production varied in the nineteenth century. Farmers raised large quantities of wheat before the Civil War (1861–1865). They also raised oats, barley, hay, and sorghum. Unlike farmers in the Great Plains or the South who relied on staple crops, Iowa farmers diversified their production, providing greater economic stability in the event of drought or low farm prices. With ever-increasing agricultural production, farmers were soon looking for ways to market their surplus crops and livestock. Before the Civil War, farmers relied heavily on the Mississippi River for transportation, but in the 1850s, railroad construction got under way in Iowa. In 1867, the Chicago and North Western Railroad was the first route to reach Iowa's western border. By 1870, three more railroads—the Illinois Central, the Burlington Northern, and the Rock Island—had completed east-west routes across the state. Later, the Chicago, Milwaukee, St. Paul, and Pacific Railroad also spanned the state. From 1870 until the early twentieth century, railroads would not only dominate transportation in the state, but they would also be a powerful political entity in the state legislature.

The Civil War brought disruption to economic development, including railroad building, in a state still in the process of initial settlement. Even so, Iowa still contributed some 70,000 men to fight for the Union. No battles of any consequence took place on Iowa soil. On the home front, Iowa women contributed to the war effort, working tirelessly to provide clothing and food for Iowa soldiers. Women also took over family businesses and operated family farms while their husbands were away at war.

Following the Civil War, great expansion and change took place in both agriculture and the industrial sector. By 1870, Iowa farmers had switched from raising wheat to specializing in the production of corn and hogs. Iowa farmers had discovered by the 1870s that the state's climate and soil were especially well suited to raising corn. They also discovered they could realize greater profit from feeding corn to hogs, which they then marketed, rather than selling their corn commercially. The development of these economic practices produced the so-called corn-hog complex and resulted in the state being ranked first or second in the production of corn and hogs. Women also played major roles in Iowa farm life. Women typically raised poultry, which by 1900 made Iowa first in the nation in egg production, helped process dairy products, and raised huge vegetable gardens. With these practices, farm families were nearly self-sufficient in food needs. Women also routinely bartered eggs, cream, and butter for staple groceries. During difficult economic times, women's food production sustained many Iowa farm operations.

Iowans also began to create businesses and manufacturing firms in the nineteenth century, most of which were agriculture-related. Before the Civil War, the first ones appeared in towns along the Mississippi River. Most river towns had pork-slaughtering operations and breweries, and many also developed specialties. Davenport became a flour-milling center in the 1850s, while Burlington workers manufactured shoes and carriages. All river cities benefited from the daily steamboat travel on the Mississippi. Following the construction of railroads, larger agriculture-related industries appeared. Quaker Oats constructed an oat processing plant in Cedar Rapids, and John Morrell and company set up a meatpacking operation in Ottumwa. By century's end, meatpacking had become the most visible industrial operation in the state with plants in Cedar Rapids, Waterloo, Des Moines, Mason City, and Sioux City. Eventually, Sioux City became Iowa's largest meat processing center. After 1900, more industries appeared, many not related to agricultural production. Frederick Maytag began to manufacture washing machines, and a tractor works developed in Waterloo. In southeastern Iowa, Sheaffer Pen Company began operations.

Iowa's second largest industry in the late nineteenth and early twentieth centuries was coal mining. Beginning in the 1840s in southeastern Iowa, the industry gradually moved into south central Iowa. By 1880, the state had 450 underground mines with a total of 6,028 miners, and Iowa's operation was ranked fifteenth nationally. The industry was tied to railroad development and as railroad mileage increased, so did the number of coal mines.

Population

Throughout the nineteenth century, as more land opened for settlement and as new industries developed, the need for additional labor was often filled by immigrants. The majority of foreign-born workers arrived from Western Europe and the British Isles. Germans composed the largest group. German Americans settled everywhere within the state, with most of the newcomers going into farming. German Americans were also numerous in the Mississippi River cities where they established small businesses and worked in industry. Even in the early twenty-first century, cities like Dubuque, Davenport, and Burlington are known for their high numbers of German descendants.

Other major immigrant groups in Iowa included the Irish, the state's second largest foreign-born group. Many Irish helped build railroads across the Midwest, and some workers settled permanently in Iowa. A large number of Irish settled in Dubuque, where they worked in factories. Some Irish families also became farmers. Today, several communities, including Emmetsburg, annually celebrate their Irish ancestry.

People of many other nationalities from Western Europe and the British Isles also immigrated to Iowa. Scandinavians constituted Iowa's third largest group, including Swedes, Norwegians, and Danes, with the largest group being the Swedes. Swedes settled in southwest and west-central Iowa, where most became farmers. Many Swedish men also worked as coal miners. Norwegians settled in northeastern and central Iowa, where most families took up farming, and the Danes created a large farming community in southwestern Iowa. Other groups settling in Iowa included the English, especially in southern Iowa, and also Dutch, Welsh, Scots, and Czechs. Most of these ethnic groups still celebrate their heritage by operating ethnic museums and holding ethnic festivals.

Around 1900, immigration patterns changed. The foreign-born continued to emigrate from Western Europe and the British Isles, but people also began arriving from Eastern and Southern Europe, although in smaller numbers than the earlier groups. Newcomers arriving after 1900 included emigrants from Russia, Italy, Poland, Croatia, Serbia, and Slovenia. Frequently lacking resources to begin farming, many of these newcomers went to work in the coal mines and in meatpacking plants. Italians also set up small businesses in Des Moines, and others went to work for the Chicago Great Western Railroad in Oelwein. Like their fellow immigrants elsewhere, Iowa's Southern and Eastern Europeans often suffered discrimination because of their national origins and their Roman Catholic religion.

The Twentieth Century and After

Like all states, Iowa was strongly influenced by the two world wars. During World War I (1914–1918), federal government subsidies encouraged farmers to expand their landholdings and to increase their production. Following the war, many farmers were unable to meet mortgage payments and lost their farms through foreclosure. World War II (1939–1945) brought greatly increased production and a strong push for greater mechanization in farming. Corn yields increased as more and more farmers adopted hybrid seed corn.

After World War II, farmers moved quickly to mechanize farming, using combines, corn pickers, and larger tractors. They also began using chemicals to control weeds and increase yields. Farm acreages increased and farmers began to specialize in corn and soybean production, but they continued to raise large numbers of hogs. These many developments had changed the face of agriculture and the way farm families lived. By 1960, Iowa farms had a new look. Gone were the flocks of chickens, the small dairy herds, and often the large gardens. Farm families had begun to buy their food rather than produce it. With rural electrification, which started in 1935, farm homes could be as modern as town and city homes.

For most of its history, Iowa has been a Republican state even though Iowans initially voted for Democrats. During the 1850s Iowans shifted to the Republican Party and remained almost solidly Republican until the 1930s. Between 1854 and 1932, only one Democrat, Horace Boies, was elected governor. Between 1932 and 1974, four Democrats and eight Republicans served as governor. In the more recent past, Iowans have distinguished themselves by keeping Republicans in the governorship for long periods of time. In 1968, Robert D. Ray was elected governor and remained in that office for fourteen years. Republican Terry Branstad was elected in 1982 and served sixteen years as governor. Iowans have elected both Democrats and Republicans to the U.S. Congress but tend to elect Democrats to the state legislature. Since the 1950s, Iowa has been regarded as a two-party state.

Iowa experienced major economic and social change in the second half of the twentieth century. Most evident has been the trend toward urbanization. Shifts from rural to urban populations had been moderate but steady since the latter nineteenth century. In 1880, 84.4 percent of Iowans lived in rural areas, including towns of fewer than 2,500 people. But in 1956, for the first time, more Iowans lived in urban areas than in rural areas. As more Iowans moved to the cities and as farming became more mechanized and specialized, rural institutions began to disappear. Rural churches closed their doors, public schools consolidated at a rate faster than before, and small-town businesses began to close. Reapportionment of the state legislature in 1972 led to a lessening of rural influence in the state government. Given these changes along with the founding of new industries such as Winnebago Industries, Iowa has developed a political balance between rural and urban interests and a steadily growing industrial sector.

The decade of the 1980s brought major change to the agricultural sector as the farm economy suffered a major depression and farmland values plummeted. By mid-decade, news of the farm crisis dominated all statewide media. By the end of the decade, conditions had improved but more than 140,000 people had moved off Iowa farms. Although by the end of the twentieth century, Iowa remained either first or second in production of corn, hogs, and soybeans, approximately 50 percent of farm families augmented their income through off-farm employment. By 2000, the number of Iowa farms had shrunk to 94,000. While many Iowa farmers still raise hogs, a major shift in the countryside has been the development of large-scale hog confinement operations. Large poultry confinement facilities have also been constructed. These changes have produced strong protest, especially from rural residents, because such facilities produce environmental pollution and sometimes reduce their quality of life.

Iowans have also faced numerous key political issues with long-term social and economic implications. In 1962, Iowans adopted liquor-by-the-drink, allowing the establishment of bars and abolishing the State Liquor Commission. At the same time, a struggle to reapportion the state legislature, where both legislative chambers were weighed heavily in favor of rural residents, pitted the state's liberal and conservative forces against each other for more than a decade. After various efforts by the legislature, the state supreme court stepped in, declaring reapportionment legislation unconstitutional. The court then drew up its own reapportionment plan, effective in 1972, which gave Iowa the most equitably apportioned legislature in the nation.

Two political issues of the 1980s and 1990s proved contentious. In 1985, in strongly contested legislation, Iowa established a state lottery. Opponents, many of them church officials, predicted that the lottery was only the first step in opening the state to all types of gambling. The creation of the lottery was quickly followed by an increase in pari-mutuel betting facilities and the building of steamboat casinos and three Native American gambling casinos. A second issue dealt with gender. In 1980 and 1992, Iowans considered adding an equal rights amendment to the state constitution. The amendment was defeated both times, in 1992 by a vote of 595,837 to 551,566. In analyzing the defeat, supporters pointed to a long ballot, which confused some voters, and to the amendment's unclear wording.

Iowa demographics have changed slowly since the 1960s. In 2000, Iowa had 2,926,324 residents and its population had grown just 5.4 percent since 1990. Since its admission to the Union in 1846, Iowa gradually increased in population until 1980 (with the exception of the 1910 census) and then lost population for each of seven years. In 1987, that trend was reversed, and the state experienced the beginning of slow but steady population increases. Iowa has long had a high percentage of elderly residents; by 2000, Iowa's percentage of people age sixty-five and older had risen to 14.9 percent, one of the highest in the nation. The percentage of urban and rural residents also changed: in 2000, fewer than one in ten Iowans lived on a farm.

For most of its history, Iowa has remained a state characterized by cultural variations but with little racial diversity. African Americans have historically been the largest racial group although their total numbers have been small. In 2000, they constituted approximately 2 percent of the state's total population. African Americans have traditionally lived in Iowa's larger cities, although early in 1900 many men worked as coal miners. Since the 1970s, however, the state has become more racially diverse. In 1975, 13,000 Southeast Asian refugees were resettled in Iowa, mainly due to the efforts of then-Governor Robert D. Ray. By the 1990s, their numbers had increased to 25,037. Beginning in the 1960s, a small but increasing number of Hispanics arrived in Iowa. Hispanics had earlier worked as migrant farmworkers, but in the 1990s, they were employed in a wider range of industries, especially in meatpacking. They had settled in both large cities and small towns. In the 1990s, the number of Hispanics rose sharply, an increase of almost 40 percent in ten years. The newly arrived Hispanics came from Mexico as well as from California and Texas. Spanish is the second major language used in the state on an everyday basis. In 2002, the number of Hispanics in Iowa was 82,473. In the 1990s, Iowa also became home to small numbers of Bosnian and Sudanese refugees who settled in Iowa's larger communities.

Despite severe economic dislocations in most segments of Iowa's economy during the latter twentieth and early twenty-first centuries, Iowans remain unchanged in major ways. They continue to express strong support for public education and to produce well-educated young people who often score highest in the nation on college entrance exams. Iowa communities remain stable, with community institutions—family, church, and school—intact and still held in high esteem. Although the state now experiences a balance between rural and urban interests and between agriculture and other industries, its character is still defined largely by the culture of its small towns and its agricultural preeminence. As Iowans experience the twenty-first century, they remain somewhat conservative in their politics, usually liberal in their social thinking, and almost always optimistic about their economic future.

BIBLIOGRAPHY

Bergman, Marvin, ed. *Iowa History Reader.* Ames: State Historical Society of Iowa in association with Iowa State University Press, 1996.

Sage, Leland L. *A History of Iowa.* Ames: Iowa State University Press, 1974.

Schwieder, Dorothy. *Iowa: The Middle Land.* Ames: Iowa State University Press, 1996.

———. "Iowa: The Middle Land." In *Heartland: Comparative Histories of the Midwestern States.* Edited by James H. Madison. Bloomington: Indiana University Press, 1988.

Wall, Joseph Frazier. *Iowa: A Bicentennial History.* New York: Norton, 1978.

Dorothy Schwieder

IOWA BAND, a group of eleven young ministers from Andover Theological Seminary who came to Iowa in 1843 as missionaries of the American Home Missionary Society, supported largely by the Congregational and New School Presbyterian churches. Their hope was that each one should found a church and that together they might found a college. In this they succeeded. Each man founded one or more Congregational churches, and the group was instrumental in founding Iowa College, which opened its doors at Davenport in November 1848. In 1859 it was moved to Grinnell.

BIBLIOGRAPHY

Adams, Ephraim. *The Iowa Band.* Boston: The Pilgrim Press, 1902.

Ruth A. Gallaher / A. R.

See also **Congregationalism; Iowa; Missionary Societies, Home; Presbyterianism.**

IPSWICH PROTEST. In March 1687, Edmund Andros, governor of the newly formed Dominion of New England, moved to increase colonial revenue. Although Andros's tax was small in comparison to those levied both prior and subsequent to the Dominion, it placed a special burden on the colony's poorer farmers: tax laws abolished the discount for cash payment, and set at an artificially low level the price for produce acceptable for payment. Resistance to the direct tax imposed by Andros—a single "country rate" of twenty pence per poll and one penny on the pound on estates—was, according to John Wise, leader of a group of protestors from Ipswich, Massachusetts, a matter of principle. The government, however, quickly prevailed. Wise and other protestors were arrested, imprisoned, tried, and fined.

BIBLIOGRAPHY

Craven, Wesley Frank. *The Colonies in Transition, 1660–1713.* New York: Harper and Row, 1968.

Johnson, Richard R. *Adjustment to Empire: The New England Colonies, 1675–1715.* New Brunswick, N.J: Rutgers University Press, 1981.

Kammen, Michael. *Empire and Interest: The American Colonies and the Politics of Mercantilism.* Philadelphia: Lippincott, 1970.

Leslie J. Lindenauer
James Duane Squires

See also **Taxation.**

IRA. *See* **Individual Retirement Account.**

Relations with Iran. President Jimmy Carter *(right)* shares a happy moment with the shah of Iran—but the shah was overthrown in 1979, and the subsequent 444-day hostage crisis wrecked Carter's chances for reelection in 1980. Getty Images

IRAN, RELATIONS WITH. Americans had relatively little contact with Iran until the 1940s. The United States largely deferred to British policy, whose commercial and diplomatic approach focused on extracting oil for a nominal fee and confronting Russian influence in Iran. In August 1941, fearing German influence, the British and the Soviets invaded Iran and deposed the pro-Axis ruler Reza Shah Pahlavi. They installed his son, Mohammad Reza Pahlavi, depriving the new shah of popular legitimacy. Franklin D. Roosevelt attended the November 1943 Teheran Conference of the Allied leaders, the first visit of an incumbent U.S. president to the country.

As the Cold War began, the USSR tried to overwhelm Iran, Turkey, and Greece, while the mantle of protecting Western interests moved from the British to the Americans. The continued Soviet occupation in Iran triggered the first threat of direct U.S. intervention in the Near East. President Harry S. Truman's threat to send marines to aid Iran coupled with Iranian diplomatic maneuvering in the United Nations convinced the Red Army to retreat in May 1946. In March 1947, the Truman Doctrine promised support to those resisting Soviet subversion. Iran became part of the American sphere of influence thanks to its abundant supply of oil and its strategic location at the juncture of the Persian Gulf, the Middle East, and the Caucasus.

In August 1953, the United States orchestrated a military coup to overthrow the popular Iranian prime minister Mohammad Mosaddeq, who opposed the shah, briefly forcing him into exile, and the predominance of the West in his country, especially the exploitation of oil companies. The restoration of the pro-American regime, while damaging its credibility, secured an alliance between the two countries. The growing revenues generated by more local control over oil transformed Iran into a consumer of American products, such as advanced technology and defense equipment. A stronger, more industrialized Iran became an anti-Soviet pillar.

The October 1973 oil crisis, in which Iran remained loyal to the United States and to Israel, in stark contrast to its Arab neighbors, further increased Iran's importance to the United States. The shah's aspirations to regional hegemony and accelerated modernization in Iran heightened commercial, military, cultural, and educational ties with the United States. While U.S. training of Iranian pilots was a mutual source of pride, the presence of American military personnel and their alleged help to the notorious secret police, the SAVAK, were controversial.

The shah's downfall was due in part to corruption and to the widening disparity in wealth caused by his aggressive White Revolution. These failures were compounded by his weak legitimacy and by opposition of the leading members of the Muslim clergy, who portrayed him as an agent of incursion for American interests and a promoter of Western decadence, which they claimed jeopardized the values and structure of a traditional society.

The most memorable year in U.S. relations with Iran was 1979, which reversed decades of collaboration. The year began with mass demonstrations against the shah and his overthrow. He left for exile on 16 January. President James Earl Carter refused to intervene for the fledgling regime, and even had he chosen to act, success would have been unlikely. The Muslim fundamentalists prevailed on 11 February. Previous U.S. support for Ayatollah Ruhollah Khomeini's foe, an internal struggle between factions vying for control, and U.S. permission for the cancer-stricken shah to receive medical care in New York City triggered a hostage crisis that lasted 444 days. On 4 November, members of the Revolutionary Guards attacked the American Embassy and seized dozens of staff members. Among their explicit demands were the extradition of the shah for a public trial and an American apology for aiding his regime. Some leaders of the new government also feared a covert action to reverse their political gains.

The Iranian government sided with this violation of diplomatic immunity partly because of its domestic election campaign in early 1980. As negotiations to redeem the remaining fifty-two American hostages proved futile, President Carter turned to coercion. After freezing Iranian assets, he ordered a rescue attempt in April 1980. Eight U.S. soldiers died in an accident during the aborted mission. This debacle, coupled with alleged Republican manipulations to delay any release of the hostages prior to the presidential elections, sealed Carter's loss to Ronald Reagan in November 1980. The shah had died in August 1980, and the hostages were released in exchange for unfreezing Iranian assets on 20 January 1981, the day of the presidential transition from Carter to Reagan.

In the mid-1980s, during the Iran-Iraq War, the Iran-Contra scandal unfolded in the United States. National Security Council officials, notably Colonel Oliver North, secretly sold arms to Iran, and some of the proceeds were diverted to help the anticommunist Contras in Nicaragua in contravention of the U.S. Constitution. The hope was to gain influence among moderates in Iran and to secure the release of American hostages in Lebanon. The contacts had only limited success. During the 1990–1991 Persian Gulf War, Iran remained neutral as the United States and its allies defeated Iraq.

Only in 1997, when the reformer Mohammad Khatami won the presidential elections in Iran, did relations visibly improve, although rhetorical animosity remained the norm, especially among Iranian clergy. The June 1998 World Cup soccer game, in which Iranian and American players exchanged mementos, embodied the hopes for more friendly relations.

BIBLIOGRAPHY

Bill, James A. *The Eagle and the Lion.* New Haven, Conn.: Yale University Press, 1988.

Kuniholm, Bruce Robellet. *The Origins of the Cold War in the Near East.* Princeton, N.J.: Princeton University Press, 1980.

Sick, Gary. *October Surprise: America's Hostages in Iran and the Election of Ronald Reagan.* New York: Times Books, 1991.

Itai Sneh

See also **Iran-Contra Affair; Iran Hostage Crisis; Persian Gulf War.**

IRAN-CONTRA AFFAIR. On 8 July 1985, President Ronald Reagan addressed the American Bar Association and described Iran as part of a "confederation of terrorist states . . . a new, international version of Murder, Inc." Ironically, that same month, members of the Reagan administration were initiating a clandestine policy through which the federal government helped supply arms to Iran in its war with Iraq, the nation supported by the United States. Millions of dollars in profits from the secret arms sales were laundered through Israel and then routed to Central America in support of rebel forces known as the contras, whose professed aim was to overthrow the duly elected government in Nicaragua. Both Secretary of State George P. Shultz and Secretary of Defense Caspar Weinberger opposed the policy but lost the debate to members of the NATIONAL SECURITY COUNCIL. The Iran-Contra Affair, arguably the crisis that did most to erode public confidence in the Reagan presidency, occupied the nation's attention through much of the next two years.

Reagan's staunch opposition to communism and his commitment to the safety of U.S. citizens throughout the world fostered the crisis. In 1979, a communist Sandinista government assumed power in Nicaragua. Soon after Reagan assumed office in 1981, his administration began to back the contra rebel forces with overt assistance. Congress terminated funding for the contras when evidence of illegal covert actions surfaced and public opinion turned against administration policy. At the same time, the public shared the president's disillusion with events in the Middle East because of the October 1983 bombing of a U.S. marines barracks in Beirut, Lebanon, that killed 241 Americans, and the contemporaneous abduction in Lebanon of several U.S. citizens as hostages. Events in both hemispheres came together in the late summer of 1985. From then until 1986, the United States provided Iran with TOW antitank missiles and parts for ground-launched Hawk antiaircraft missiles. The actions violated both the government's embargo on weapons sales to Iran and its avowed policy of not arming terrorists, because the Iranian government apparently was sponsoring Lebanese TERRORISM. The administration's rationale for its actions was the benefits promised for the contras. Private arms dealers, acting with the knowledge and approval of Reagan's National Security Council staff, overcharged Iran for the weapons and channeled the money to the rebels.

Reagan on Iran-Contra. The president *(center)* talks with members of the President's Special Review Board, the first and briefest of the investigations. © REUTERS/CORBIS-BETTMANN

During a White House ceremony early in November 1986, reporters asked the president to comment on rumors that the United States had exchanged arms for hostages. He repudiated the stories, then appeared on national television one week later to explain the administration's case, a case grounded in denial of any wrongdoing. "We did not," he declared in his conclusion, "repeat—did not trade weapons or anything else for hostages, nor will we." Just six days later, however, on 19 November, Reagan opened a press conference by announcing that he had based his earlier claims on a false chronology constructed by the National Security Council and the White House staff. He announced formation of the President's Special Review Board, known as the TOWER COMMISSION. Headed by former Senator John Tower, the board included former Secretary of State Edmund Muskie and former national

Oliver North. The U.S. Marine and former National Security Council staff member testifies at joint congressional hearings in 1987 about his key role in Iran-Contra. AP/Wide World Photos

security adviser Brent Scowcroft. In late February 1987, the board concluded that the president was guilty of no crime but found that Reagan's lax management allowed subordinates the freedom to shape policy.

Concurrent executive branch and congressional investigations of Iran-Contra proceeded into 1987. As independent counsel, a position created by the Ethics in Government Act of 1978, former federal Judge Lawrence E. Walsh explored allegations of wrongdoing. In May 1987, a joint Senate and House committee hastily convened for what became four months of televised hearings that included 250 hours of open testimony by thirty-two public officials. In its report on 17 November, the committee held President Reagan accountable for his administration's actions because his inattention to detail created an environment in which his subordinates exceeded their authority. In the spring of 1988, former national security adviser Robert C. McFarlane pleaded guilty to withholding information from Congress and later attempted suicide. Criminal indictments were returned against Rear Adm. John M. Poindexter, the president's national security adviser; arms dealers Richard V. Secord and Albert A. Hakim; and Lt. Col. Oliver L. North of the National Security Council staff. The convictions of North and Poindexter were ultimately dismissed because evidence against them was compromised by their congressional testimony. In December 1992, just before leaving office, President George H. W. Bush pardoned six others indicted or convicted in the Iran-Contra Affair, including Weinberger, whose diaries allegedly would have shown that both Reagan and Bush knew of the arms-for-hostages deal. "Ollie" North, viewed by some as an unfairly censured patriot, went on to win the Republican Party's nomination in the 1994 Virginia senatorial election. Although he lost to the Democratic incumbent Chuck Robb, he remained in the public eye as a conservative pundit, columnist, and radio personality.

BIBLIOGRAPHY

Busby, Robert. *Reagan and the Iran-Contra Affair: The Politics of Presidential Recovery.* New York: St. Martin's Press, 1999.

Cannon, Lou. *President Reagan: The Role of a Lifetime.* New York: Public Affairs, 2000.

Cohen, William S., and George M. Mitchell. *Men of Zeal: A Candid Inside Story of the Iran-Contra Hearings.* New York: Viking, 1988.

Fried, Amy. *Muffled Echoes: Oliver North and the Politics of Public Opinion.* New York: Columbia University Press, 1997.

Lynch, Michael. *The Spectacle of History: Speech, Text, and Memory at the Iran-Contra Hearings.* Durham, N.C.: Duke University Press, 1996.

President's Special Review Board. *The Tower Commission Report: The Full Text of the President's Special Review Board.* New York: Bantam Books, 1987.

Thelen, David P. *Becoming Citizens in the Age of Television: How Americans Challenged the Media and Seized Political Initiative during the Iran-Contra Debate.* Chicago: University of Chicago Press, 1996.

Walsh, Lawrence E. *Iran-Contra: The Final Report.* New York: Times Books, 1994.

———. *Firewall: The Iran-Contra Conspiracy and Cover-Up.* New York: Norton, 1997.

*David Henry/*a. r.

See also **Corruption, Political; Hostage Crises; Iran, Relations with; Nicaragua, Relations with; Scandals; Special Prosecutors;** *and vol. 9:* **Report on the Iran-Contra Affair.**

IRAN HOSTAGE CRISIS. On 4 November 1979, Islamic militants overran the American embassy in Teheran, Iran, initiating a crisis that lasted through the end of President Jimmy Carter's term. The militants held fifty-two of the embassy's personnel hostage for 444 days. Relations between the United States and Iran began to disintegrate in early 1979, during the Iranian revolution. Following the overthrow of the U.S. ally Muhammad Reza Shah Pahlevi, the new government, led by the Muslim fundamentalist Ayatollah Ruhollah Khomeini, focused much of its fervor against the United States, culminating with the embassy takeover following Carter's decision to allow the shah to enter the United States for cancer treatment. The United States attempted to pursue political, diplomatic, and economic measures to broker the release of the hostages. Carter also organized a military contingency plan in the event that nonmilitary solutions failed.

The White House attempted several failed diplomatic initiatives and mounted a campaign of international pressure on Iran, which brought condemnations from governments around the world. The sole successful diplomatic measure was an initiative from Palestinian Liberation Organization (PLO) representatives that gained the release of thirteen female and African American hostages. Carter also signed an order to freeze all of Iran's assets in American banks.

Despite continued pressure on Iran, the hostages remained in captivity five months after the crisis began, and pressure mounted on the Carter administration to find a more effective solution. After much deliberation, Carter authorized an ill-fated military mission to rescue the hostages. The 24 April 1979 rescue mission suffered from military miscalculations and untimely mechanical failures, forcing the mission to be aborted. The final mishap came during a refueling stop, when two of the helicopters collided, killing eight servicemen. When President Carter informed the nation of the mission and its failure, he suffered politically.

The failure of the rescue mission did not end negotiations, but the administration appeared to be paralyzed by the crisis. The Iranians released the hostages on 20 January 1981, minutes after Ronald Reagan took the oath of office as president. U.S. relations with Iran did not return to their earlier cordial nature during the twentieth century. Presidents Reagan, George H. W. Bush, and Bill Clinton faced a hostile Islamic state on the borders of the Persian Gulf.

BIBLIOGRAPHY

Carter, Jimmy. *Keeping Faith: Memoirs of a President.* New York: Bantam, 1982.

Jordan, Hamilton. *Crisis: The Last Year of the Carter Presidency.* New York: Putnam, 1982.

Sick, Gary. *All Fall Down: America's Tragic Encounter with Iran.* New York: Random House, 1985.

Stephanie Wilson McConnell

See also **Iran, Relations with;** *and vol. 9:* **Interrogation of an Iran Hostage.**

IRANIAN AMERICANS. Iranian immigration to the United States was insignificant until the 1950s and 1960s, when many young Iranians began to study at American universities. After the 1979 revolution in Iran, many Iranian students stayed in the United States and were joined by their families, taking up residence mostly in metropolitan areas. According to statistics from the U.S. Census Bureau, in 1990 the median age of all Iranian immigrants in the United States was just over thirty years old. Since the early 1980s, notable Iranian American communities, made up almost entirely of immigrants, developed in New York, Texas, Maryland, and Virginia, with the largest population centers found in southern California. It is estimated that more than half the Iranian American population resides in the San Fernando Valley, Orange County, and the west side of Los Angeles.

According to the 1980 census, there were 121,000 Iranian Americans living in the United States at that time. In the 1990 census, 236,000 Americans identified themselves as having Iranian ancestry, with 211,000 reporting Iran as their place of birth. Of the total Iranian American population, just over 27 percent were listed as naturalized citizens. Between 1981 and 1990, 154,800 Iranians were admitted to the United States as immigrants; of those, nearly 47,000 were granted permanent resident status as refugees. Continued turmoil in the Persian Gulf in the 1990s meant continued refugee migration from Iran. Between 1991 and 1998 another 96,900 Iranian immigrants were admitted into the United States, of which 22,327 were listed as refugees. Estimates from the 2000 census for the total population of Iranian Americans range from 500,000 to as high as 800,000 or 1,100,000—numbers that members of the Iranian American community say underrepresent the population, due to the uncertain reporting methods on ancestry and race.

Iranian Americans are among the more educated immigrants in the United States, and most are members of the technical, professional, and entrepreneurial classes. More than 80 percent of Iranian Americans are fluent in English, and nearly half have earned college degrees. The majority are engineers, teachers, doctors, and business owners, and the median income of Iranian Americans is higher than the national average. In spite of their success as immigrants, Iranian Americans have suffered discrimination at times because they are mistakenly associated with the actions of the government of Iran (a regime they fled) and because they are sometimes mistakenly identified as being from various countries in the Middle East. After the terrorist attacks on New York and Washington, D.C., in September 2001, more restrictions were placed on temporary visas from Iran and on Iranian immigration as the relationship between Iran and the United States continued to be strained.

BIBLIOGRAPHY

Bahrampour, Tara. *To See and See Again: A Life in Iran and America.* New York: Farrar, Straus and Giroux, 1999.

Bill, James A. *The Eagle and the Lion: The Tragedy of American-Iranian Relations.* New Haven, Conn.: Yale University Press, 1988.

Farhang, Mansour. *U.S. Imperialism: The Spanish-American War to the Iranian Revolution.* Boston: South End Press, 1981.

Sullivan, Zohreh T. *Exiled Memories: Stories of Iranian Diaspora.* Philadelphia: Temple University Press, 2001.

Paul Hehn

IRAQ-GATE is the name given to a scandal centered on loans guaranteed by the United States government to Iraq. The allegations of the scandal arose after the Persian Gulf War in 1991, in which the United States fought against Iraq, led by Saddam Hussein. Subsequent investigations uncovered evidence that between 1985 and 1989, the Atlanta branch of Banca Nazionale del Lavoro (BNL), the Italian national bank, issued more than $5 billion in secret and illegal loans to Iraq. The loans were backed by the Export-Import Bank and the Commodities Credit Corporation, two executive branch agencies. While the purpose of these loans was for food and agricultural products, the grant of the money allowed Hussein to use money for arms that he could have spent on feeding the nation. The loans operated by lending money to companies that were supplying Hussein with weapons-manufacturing products.

After being indicted for fraud and other related charges, the BNL Atlanta branch manager, Christopher Drougal, testified before the House Banking Committee as to the details of the loans. He claimed that the BNL loans were part of a covert operation designed to finance the secret rearming of Iraq. He claimed that he was merely the instrument of a secret U.S. policy to aid Hussein. The operation was coordinated with Italian officials by the administration of President Ronald Reagan and continued by President George H. W. Bush. The United States was involved in the arming of Iraq to gain bargaining leverage for U.S. hostages in Iraq. Despite these accusations, the Bush administration denied any involvement in the illegal loans. However, in October 1992, Attorney General William Barr instructed the Federal Bureau of Investigation to begin an investigation into allegations of obstruction of justice by the government. During the 1992 presidential election, Bill Clinton promised that if elected he would investigate the scandal. On 17 January 1995, Attorney General Janet Reno issued the final report resulting from the Clinton administration's investigation into the matter. The report concluded that there had been no violation of the law.

BIBLIOGRAPHY

Krosney, Herbert. *Deadly Business: Legal Deals and Outlaw Weapons: The Arming of Iran and Iraq, 1975 to the Present.* New York: Four Walls Eight Windows, 1993.

Timmerman, Kenneth. *The Death Lobby: How the West Armed Iraq.* Boston: Houghton Mifflin 1991.

Shira M. Diner

IRAQI AMERICANS are the fourth largest group of immigrants from the Arab world in the United States. According to the 1990 U.S. census, there were approximately 45,000 people of Iraqi descent living in the United States. Since then, the number has grown to 250,000, constituting 2 percent of the Arab Americans living in the United States. Like many other Arab groups, Iraqi Americans have concentrated in the Midwest. More than 70,000 live in Michigan, primarily in Detroit, with another 15,000 in and around Chicago. More than 30,000 Iraqis live in California, most residing in the southern part of the state.

Some of the first Iraqi immigrants to come to the United States were Iraqi nationals and Iraqi Jews. In the years between 1900 and 1905, approximately twenty Jewish families arrived from Iraq to settle in New York City. With the breakup of the Ottoman empire after World War I, more Jewish Iraqi immigrants came to America. Other Iraqis flocked to Detroit, and like thousands of other Arab immigrants who preceded them, found work in the automobile factories. Many had soon saved enough money to bring over other members of their families. The following decades brought a steady stream of Jewish Iraqi immigrants, many of whom were drawn by the better educational and business opportunities in the United States. The exodus from Iraq continued until 1953, when more than 124,000 Iraqi Jews left their homeland.

The number of Iraqis coming to America remained relatively low until 1974. It peaked in 1976 and then began to decline, but never fell to pre-1974 levels. Between 1983 and 1993, immigration from Iraq again increased, with approximately 23,600 Iraqis arriving in the United States. The jump in Iraqi immigration to the United States began in 1992 and reflected the large number of Iraqis admitted to the country after the 1991 Persian Gulf War, when more Iraqis came as refugees fleeing political persecution.

Many large cities are home to Iraqi American communities that are filled with Iraqi-run bakeries, grocery stores, and barbershops. In Detroit alone, there are an estimated 70,000 Iraqis. About 30,000 live in California, and another 15,000 live in and around Chicago. Compared to other Arab groups, Iraqi Americans rarely voice their political concerns in public, and maintained an especially low profile during the Gulf War. Although the majority of Iraqi Americans dislike Iraqi leader Saddam Hussein, they are also growing increasingly distrustful of American policy in the Arab world. As a result, more Iraqi American civic and religious leaders are beginning to address the concerns of their people.

After the terrorist attacks of 11 September 2001, the government of the United States tightened its restrictions on immigrants from the Middle East, including those from Iraq. As of 2002, the only Middle Eastern immigrants permitted to enter the United States were those who had been recognized as refugees, and the government reserved the right to deport them. According to statistics compiled by the Immigration and Naturalization Service, 46 Iraqi refugees were deported on criminal charges between 1997 and 2002.

BIBLIOGRAPHY

Abraham, Sameer Y., and Nabeel Abraham, eds. *Arabs in the New World: Studies on Arab-American Communities.* Detroit, Mich.: Center for Urban Studies, Wayne State University, 1983.

Gammage, Jeff. "Iraqi Immigrants in Detroit Want U.S. to Target Saddam, not Iraq." *The Philadelphia Inquirer,* February 20, 1998.

Meg Greene Malvasi

See also **Arab Americans; Arab Nations, Relations with.**

IRELAND, RELATIONS WITH. James Joyce's *Ulysses* (1922) wistfully refers to America as "our greater Ireland beyond the sea." These words capture the bond between the two nations, forged through immigration and negotiated in light of British colonialism. The Irish first landed in the colonies following the conquest of William III (William of Orange, son of William, Prince of Orange) in 1689–1691. The enactment of the first penal laws (1695), a series of codes that initially secured and enlarged Protestant landholdings and ultimately led to the severe restriction of Catholic liberties, coupled with economic uncertainty in the textile industry, led to another significant exodus of Irish to the colonies in the 1720s. But not all those leaving were oppressed or poor. Some were Anglo-Irish Protestants who, like their Anglo-American counterparts, opposed the taxations of British imperialism.

The nineteenth century saw significant changes in relations between Ireland and America. By the 1830s the laboring class of Ireland had grown into a formidable force giving rise to calls for Irish nationalism. Outspokenly backing Daniel O'Connell and his Repeal Association, a group calling for the repeal of the Act of Union (1801) and laws against Catholic practice, many Irish Americans sent money back home to support a nationalist agenda. The great Irish potato famine (1845–1847) led to a four-year period of mass exodus and institutionalized immigration as a permanent feature of Irish-American relations. Fleeing a dire situation yet near the bottom of the socioeconomic ladder in America, Irish demands for a resolution to the problems at home took a radical turn. Following the American Civil War, groups such as the Fenians and the Irish Revolutionary Brotherhood plotted publicly to overthrow English rule. Despite diplomatic efforts by England to obtain American help in restraining these groups, such requests were largely ignored by the U.S. government.

America's emergence on the international political stage made relations between Ireland and America considerably more complex. Earlier animosities with Britain faded and the two nations became wartime allies. Under the leadership of Cardinal James Gibbons and others, Irish Americans continued to support nationalism. Bloody Sunday, on 21 November 1920, ushered in a series of battles between the Irish Republican Army and British auxiliaries. The American Commission on Conditions in Ireland condemned both parties. Calls for peace and independence continued across the Atlantic. On 6 December 1921 Irish representatives signed a treaty with Britain granting dominion status to Ireland as the Irish Free State.

Disputes over a united Ireland, terrorist activities in Ulster, and a fragmentation of political interests framed relations during the remainder of the century, with varying levels of engagement being pursued by different U.S. administrations. On 10 April 1998 the Good Friday Accord, which established Protestant and Catholic political representation in Northern Ireland, was negotiated under the direction of former U.S. senator George Mitchell and the administration of President Bill Clinton.

BIBLIOGRAPHY

Dumbrell, John. *A Special Relationship: Anglo-American Relations in the Cold War and After.* New York: St. Martin's Press, 2001.

McCaffrey, Lawrence J. *The Irish Diaspora in America.* Washington, D.C.: Catholic University of America Press, 1984.

O'Grady, Joseph P. *How The Irish Became Americans.* Boston: Twayne, 1973.

Kent A. McConnell

See also **Irish Americans.**

IRISH AMERICANS. More than 7 million Irish immigrants have come to America since the 1600s. This mass movement transformed Irish society and played a significant role in shaping American politics, religion, culture, and economics during the country's most formative years. More than 40 million people in the United States claim some degree of Irish ancestry.

Colonial and Pre-Famine Immigration

Approximately 50,000 to 100,000 Irishmen, over 75 percent of them Catholic, came to America in the 1600s, while 100,000 more Irish Catholics arrived in the 1700s. A small number of prosperous merchants formed communities in Philadelphia and other cities, but most immigrants were indentured servants who eventually blended into the mainstream society. A few were prominent citizens, like wealthy Charles Carroll who migrated to Maryland in 1681, establishing a family that produced the only Catholic signer of the Declaration of Independence and the first American archbishop.

Between 250,000 and 500,000 Protestant Irish arrived in the eighteenth and early nineteenth centuries. While some were southern Irish Anglicans and Quakers, over three-fourths were Scotch-Irish Presbyterians from Ulster. In search of land and religious freedom, these "Wild Irish" settled in New England, New York, and Pennsylvania, later migrating to the wilderness backcountries of Virginia, Georgia, and the Carolinas. Known for their hatred of the British and their rugged individualism, many fought bravely in the American Revolution. More came in the early 1800s to settle Kentucky and Tennessee, becoming the nation's first "Indian fighters" and producing such American heroes as President Andrew Jackson (1767–1845) and frontiersman Davy Crockett (1786–1836).

The end of the Napoleonic Wars in 1815 caused widespread changes in Irish society and opened the floodgates of poor Catholic immigration. Landlords began to turn from grain production to cattle, raising rents and evicting tenants by the thousands. During this time, the population in Ireland rose from 6.8 million in 1821 to 8 million in 1841, with the largest increase among poor cottiers—landless laborers who received access to land for working the landlord's crops. Partible inheritance (dividing land among all sons), early marriage, and high fertility doubled their numbers from 665,000 to 1.3 million between 1831 and 1841. Fathers could no longer provide for every child, creating scores of young men and women with no alternatives but delayed marriage, permanent celibacy, or emigration. As a result, 1.3 million people left Ireland for America between 1815 and 1845.

Famine Immigration and Settlement

Conditions for those who remained behind in Ireland continued to worsen. As plots of land shrunk and the population grew, cottiers came to rely increasingly on the potato, a nutritious root that grew quickly and easily in Irish soil, as their main source of food. In August 1845, a fungus destroyed the potato crop, returning for the next four years and causing widespread destruction. Despite assistance from public and private sources, approximately 1.5 million people starved or died of famine-related diseases between 1846 and 1855, the most during "Black '47." Another 2.1 million emigrated, mainly to the United States, accounting for almost half of all immigration to the States during the 1840s and over a third during the 1850s.

In America, initial sympathy for the starving peasants gave way to anti-Catholic hostility as they began to arrive in droves, forming enclaves in Northern cities. In Boston, for example, immigration rates rose from 4,000 in 1820 to 117,000 in 1850. By the 1850s–1860s, 28 percent of all people living in New York, 26 percent in Boston, and 16 percent in Philadelphia had been born in Ireland. Irish Catholics also dominated immigration to Southern cities before the Civil War (1861–1865); New Orleans was the second-largest port of arrival after New York by 1850.

Throughout the nation, work advertisements stated, "No Irish Need Apply," while nativist political parties like the Know-Nothings gained power. Hostility often turned violent, as in 1834 when mobs burned an Ursuline convent in Charlestown, Massachusetts. Such episodes were etched in Irish American memory, contributing to a separatist mentality long after they achieved success.

Unskilled Irish men became manual laborers, competing with free African Americans for jobs, which sometimes caused bitter race riots. Over 3,000 Irish helped build New York's Erie Canal, while thousands of others worked on the railroad, in Pennsylvania's coal mines, or as farm laborers. The more enterprising traveled out west to San Francisco, finding greater opportunity and less discrimination. In the South, Irish workers were deemed less valuable than slaves and less dangerous than free blacks, perfect for urban areas. Irish women nationwide overwhelmingly worked as domestic servants, becoming known as "Bridgets," or in the growing needle trades.

Various charitable and social organizations helped the Irish settle into American life, while such financial societies as New York's Irish Emigrant Savings Bank (established 1851) assisted immigrants with sending remittances back home. The most important institution was the Catholic Church, which created a national network of churches, hospitals, schools, and orphanages. Irish priests, such as New York's Archbishop John Hughes (1797–1864) and Charleston's Bishop John England (1786–1842) dominated the hierarchy and shaped the course of American Catholicism. On the local level, the parish church served as the center of Irish American life, becoming the means of both preserving ethnic culture and Americanizing immigrants.

Their service during the Civil War also helped the Irish gain respect and acceptance. While criticized for their role in the 1863 New York draft riots, as many as 170,000 Irish-born men served in the Northern army. In the South, the Irish contributed the largest number of troops of any foreign-born group.

Post-Famine Immigration and Life

The Great Famine accelerated changes already at work in Irish society. With no land to inherit, younger children had few options in Ireland. As a result, approximately 3 million Irish men and women came to America between the end of the Famine and Irish independence (1856–1921). Departures were often marked by an "American wake," illustrating the finality of the journey. While most would never see Ireland again, many emigrants sent money back home, providing for their families and paying for siblings or parents to follow.

While the vast majority of Irish immigrants remained in the Northeast and Midwest, a significant minority of mainly skilled, single men migrated west. In 1890, the cities with the largest Irish-born populations were New York-Brooklyn (275,156, or 12 percent of the combined population), Philadelphia (110,935, 11 percent), Boston (71,441, 16 percent), Chicago (70,028, 6 percent), and San Francisco (30,718, 10 percent). The Irish-born population peaked that year at 1,871,509; the second generation totaled 2,924,172, growing to its highest level of 3,375,546 in 1900.

The late nineteenth century showed few improvements in Irish occupational mobility. While Irish-born men made up 11 percent of America's policemen and 6 percent owned their own businesses, they were concentrated in unskilled, dangerous, and low-paying jobs. While the violent methods of the Molly Maguires, a secret society of Pennsylvania coal miners, sometimes made their activities suspect, labor unions more often helped improve working conditions, and also served as a means of mobility. By 1900, Irish Americans of birth or descent held the leadership of almost half of the 110 unions in the American Federation of Labor. Some prominent labor leaders included Terence Powderly (1849–1924), head of the Knights of Labor, and Leonora O'Reilly (1870–1927), a founder of the Women's Trade Union League.

Westward migration greatly affected occupational mobility for men; 20 percent of the Irish in San Francisco in 1880 held white-collar positions as opposed to 13 percent of those in New York. For women, there was less of a disparity, as domestic service remained one of the few options for Irish-born women across the country until the 1920s. The second generation showed slightly more mobility, with many becoming clerks, teachers, priests, nuns, and nurses. By 1900, almost 5 percent of Irish American men held white-collar jobs, as opposed to 2 percent of the Irish-born. Second-generation women had greater opportunities as well, composing 10 percent of all female teachers of foreign parentage in 1900.

For most second-generation men, the church and politics were the best means for upward mobility. The cornerstone of the Irish community was the parish, with the parochial school at its center. Priests served not only as spiritual guides, but also as cultural brokers, social workers, and peacemakers in their parishes—good training for rising in the hierarchy. By 1900, 50 percent of American bishops and 13 out of 17 cardinals were of Irish birth or descent.

Unable to penetrate rigid social hierarchies, politics was one of the few ways the Irish could advance in Eastern cities. Irish ward bosses dominated Democratic city machines beginning with "Honest John" Kelly (1822–1886), who took over New York's Tammany Hall in 1873. Bosses created patronage networks, exchanging services for immigrant votes. Such notable politicians as New York's Charles F. Murphy (1858–1924) and Boston's James Michael Curley (1874–1958) used these methods with great success.

By the end of the century, more Irish Americans began to enter the middle class and work for acceptance. Saint Patrick's Day parades became a way to exhibit not only a love of Ireland, but also pride in America. Likewise, support for Irish nationalist causes was often motivated by a desire not only for Irish freedom, but also to prove to nativists that they did not come from a conquered race. This desire for respect was aided by such entertainers as vaudevillians Harrigan and Hart, the composer Victor Herbert, Broadway mogul George M. Cohan, and singer John McCormick, who all helped to change the stage Irishman image and popularize Irish music and song in mainstream entertainment. John Boyle O'Reilly, Louise Imogen Guiney, and Eugene O'Neill revealed demonstrated Irish literary talents. In addition, the Catholic Church established such universities as Notre Dame, Boston College, and Fordham to provide higher education for Irish Americans.

New York Police Officer. An Irish American stereotype with a basis in fact, there and in other cities. Library of Congress

Post-1920s Irish America

Irish America became more American than Irish in the twentieth century. Changes in immigration laws in 1924 and 1965, along with the Great Depression and the world wars, slowed immigration to a trickle. In addition, the arrival of other immigrant groups, war service, and intermarriage ensured Irish Americans' gradual assimilation into mainstream American society. By 1924, Irish American politicians began to attract national recognition with the nomination of Al Smith (1873–1944) as the first Catholic presidential candidate. In 1960, complete Irish acceptance was finally achieved with the election of President John F. Kennedy.

During this time, the Irish also started to achieve success in theater, film, sports, business, and the professions. In the 1950s, the Irish began leaving their urban enclaves for the suburbs, although certain neighborhoods in Boston, New York, Chicago, and Philadelphia retained many Irish residents, resulting in clashes with blacks and other new arrivals. While a significant number remained in the working class throughout the century, by the 1970s the Irish were the best educated and highest-paid white Catholic ethnic group in America.

The 1970s and 1980s brought a revival of Irish identity and a new connection to modern-day Ireland. This interest was stimulated by a new national preoccupation with ethnic roots, the escalation of the Troubles in Northern Ireland, and the arrival of the "New Irish"—mostly illegal, highly educated Irish immigrants whose numbers ranged from 40,000 to 150,000. Settling mainly in Irish American cities like New York and Boston, these immigrants helped to revive interest in Irish culture. Through lobbying organizations like the Irish Immigration Reform Movement, they sought the support of Irish American politicians, businessmen, and clergy in changing immigration laws.

With the help of Irish American businessmen and its membership in the European Union, Ireland emerged in the 1990s as an economic powerhouse, dubbed the "Celtic Tiger." President Bill Clinton, George Mitchell (D-ME), Representative Peter King (R-NY), Senator Daniel Patrick Moynihan (D-NY), and Senator Edward Kennedy (D-MA) played important roles as negotiators between nationalist and loyalist forces in Northern Ireland, leading to the 1998 "Good Friday" Agreement and a lasting cease-fire. The cultural renaissance inspired by Frank McCourt's *Angela's Ashes* (1996), Bill Whelan's music and dance phenomenon *Riverdance*, Irish rock bands like U2 and Black 47, and various Irish studies programs at American universities continues to renew interest in all things Irish for both Irish and non-Irish Americans.

BIBLIOGRAPHY

Almeida, Linda Dowling. *Irish Immigrants in New York City, 1945–1995*. Bloomington: Indiana University Press, 2001.

Blessing, Patrick J. "Irish." In Stephan Thernstrom, ed. *Harvard Encyclopedia of American Ethnic Groups*. Cambridge, Mass.: Belknap Press of Harvard University Press, 1980.

Diner, Hasia. *Erin's Daughters in America: Irish Immigrant Women in the Nineteenth Century*. Baltimore: Johns Hopkins University Press, 1983.

Gleeson, David T. *The Irish in the South, 1815–1877*. Chapel Hill: University of North Carolina Press, 2001.

Kenny, Kevin. *The American Irish: A History*. New York: Longman, 2000.

Miller, Kerby A. *Emigrants and Exiles: Ireland and the Irish Exodus to North America*. New York: Oxford University Press, 1985.

O'Hanlon, Ray. *The New Irish Americans*. Niwot, Colo.: Roberts Rinehart Publishers, 1998.

Williams, William H. A. *'Twas Only an Irishman's Dream: The Image of Ireland and the Irish in American Popular Song Lyrics, 1800–1920*. Urbana: University of Illinois Press, 1996.

Meaghan M. Dwyer

IRON ACT OF 1750 was passed by Parliament to encourage iron production in the colonies. It provided for duty-free importation of colonial pig iron and (by a later extension of the law) bar iron into any English port. English manufacturers supported restrictive clauses in the law, which stipulated that colonists could not erect slitting mills, steel furnaces, and plating mills, although those already in operation could continue. The law was not very successful. Colonists sent increasing amounts of iron to England but not in such quantities as manufacturers had expected. Colonial suppliers also ignored the more restrictive aspects of the law, and they built many forbidden ironworks in the colonies.

BIBLIOGRAPHY

Church, R. A., ed. *The Coal and Iron Industries*. Oxford: Blackwell Publishers, 1994.

McCusker, John J., and Kenneth Morgan, eds. *The Early Modern Atlantic Economy*. Cambridge, Mass.: Cambridge University Press, 2000.

Arthur C. Bining / S. B.

See also **Colonial Commerce; Colonial Policy, British; Iron and Steel Industry; Mercantilism.**

IRON AND STEEL INDUSTRY. Iron and steel, although closely related, are not the same thing. Iron begins as iron ore, which is melted in a blast furnace and blown through with air. Then it is manipulated so as to limit its content of carbon and other impurities. Steel is a particular kind of iron that is approximately one percent carbon, with the carbon content spread throughout the metal evenly. Steel is harder than iron and does not rust as easily. However, for most of history steel was harder to make than iron. That is why ironmaking was by far the bigger industry in America until the late nineteenth century.

The first iron works in America, called Hammersmith, began operation in 1647 in Saugus, Massachusetts, but lasted only five years. Subsequent ironmaking firms would be small operations that tended to be located close to local ore supplies, water power, and major transportation routes. Some of the most important ironmaking regions of the country in colonial America were in eastern Pennsylvania near the Delaware River, western Pennsylvania around the Allegheny and Monongahela Rivers, and the Hudson River valley in New York and New Jersey. Most of these firms remained small because of the high cost and low efficiency of available fuel to run their furnaces. When Americans switched fuels from charcoal or wood to coal in the early nineteenth century, larger operations became possible. The discovery of huge iron ore deposits in the northern Great Lakes region during the 1840s gave a further boost to production.

The Expansion of Iron Production in the Nineteenth Century

The widespread adoption of puddling as a technique to make iron also contributed to growth in production. In the early days of American ironmaking, craftsmen used a method called fining to produce iron. This meant that the mixture of iron and slag expelled from a blast furnace was separated out by hammering it. Puddling involved adding iron oxide to the blast furnace charge because the chemical reaction made it easier to separate impurities from the iron. Puddlers did the separating by stirring the melted product with a long iron rod. The slag that rose was poured off the top and the iron at the bottom was shaped into balls. The balls were squeezed into iron bars that were worked into the mill's final product (such as rails or rods) by other workers. Puddling required many judgment calls based on experience. Therefore, it could take up to two years of training to become a skilled puddler. Many puddlers in the mid-nineteenth century were successful enough to later move into the ranks of owners.

Both fining and puddling were pioneered in Great Britain and adopted by American producers in subsequent decades. As they gained more experience, American ironmasters developed their own variations of these English techniques, depending on local resources like the quality of their iron and the efficiency of their fuel. A means of automating iron production was not developed until the 1930s.

In the nineteenth century, the American iron market produced a wide variety of products. Stoves, gun parts, cannons, and machinery were among key early uses for iron. Iron also played a crucial role in the development of railroads. Once again, the English pioneered techniques for making high-quality iron rails. In fact, American railroads imported all their rails from British mills until 1844. In 1857, John Fritz's Cambria Iron Works in Johnstown, Pennsylvania, created a technique to automate partially the production of iron rails. The resulting increase in productivity made the railroad boom of the next two decades possible.

Iron and Steel Industry. At iron and steel plants like this one in Pittsburgh, photographed in 1905, blast furnaces convert iron ore into iron; a variety of processes purify iron and convert it into steel. Library of Congress

Steel Manufacturing: Henry Bessemer and Andrew Carnegie

Before the Civil War, American manufacturers made only small quantities of steel. Because they were unable to master the demanding requirements to create steel through puddling, imports from England's Sheffield mills dominated the American market. That all changed with the application of the Bessemer process. Henry Bessemer was a British inventor who created a way to refine iron into steel using air alone in 1855. His machine, the Bessemer converter, blew air over molten iron from a blast furnace so as to remove impurities and create a substance of a uniform consistency. The American engineer Alexander Holley brought Bessemer technology to America in 1864, but did not perfect the Bessemer design until he created his first plant from the ground up as opposed to adapting an existing facility. This was the Edgar Thomson Works in Braddock, Pennsylvania. The mill, which opened in 1875, was the model for all subsequent Bessemer facilities.

Holley built the Edgar Thomson Works for Andrew Carnegie, who used it mostly to produce steel rails for the Pennsylvania Railroad. Carnegie's first experience in industry came when he invested in the iron business during the 1860s. His genius was to champion technological innovations like the Bessemer converter and the Jones mixer, which sped the delivery of iron from the blast furnace to the converter, in order to cut production costs and undersell his competitors. Carnegie also had a genius for picking good associates. For example, William R. Jones, the inventor of the Jones mixer, served as superintendent of the Edgar Thomson Works and was just one of many men who shared in Carnegie's business success. Another Carnegie protégé, Charles Schwab, would go on to form Bethlehem Steel in 1904.

Carnegie's devotion to vertical integration also contributed to his success. His firm eventually controlled supplies of everything needed to make steel: iron ore and coal deposits; railroads to transport everything; and marketing networks for the finished product. By the 1890s, Carnegie Steel made more steel than the entire country of Great Britain. In 1900, its annual profit was $40 million.

Between the mid-1870s and the early 1890s steel replaced iron in more and more markets that iron had once dominated, such as rails and nails. The key reason for this was increased steel production. Accelerated by the innovations in Carnegie's mills, Bessemer steelmaking allowed firms to make thousands of more tons of metal per year than when iron had dominated the market. And because the Bessemer method required less skill than ironmaking, labor costs dropped too. As steel prices dropped dramatically, consumers increasingly chose the cheaper, harder, more durable metal.

As this trend accelerated, puddlers began to find that their skills were no longer needed. Steelmakers came to depend on immigrant labor, particularly workers from southern and eastern Europe. In the Homestead lockout of 1892, the only major union in the iron and steel industry, the Amalgamated Association of Iron and Steel Workers, made one last violent stand to prevent managers from driving the union out of the industry at Carnegie Steel's Homestead Works. Its effort failed. From 1892 to 1937, American steelmakers operated in an almost entirely union-free environment.

The U.S. Steel Corporation

As in other industries, many steel producers joined forces at the beginning of the twentieth century. However, the effect of the great merger movement in the American steel industry is particularly noteworthy. The United States Steel Corporation formed in 1901 when a group of firms dominated by J. P. Morgan decided to buy out Andrew Carnegie so that the latter would no longer undercut their selling price. Carnegie's take from the deal made him the richest man in the world.

U.S. Steel was the first business in history to be valued by the stock market at over one billion dollars ($1.4 billion, to be exact). This figure represented one sixty-seventh of the total wealth of the United States at that time. U.S. Steel controlled 72 percent of Bessemer steel production in the United States and 60 percent of the market in open hearth steel, a new steelmaking process that made steel in a furnace which achieved high heat by recycling exhaust gases. U.S. Steel's ten divisions reflected the diversity of steel products made at that time, including steel wire, steel pipe, structural steel (for bridges, buildings, and ships), sheet steel (which would go largely for automobile bodies in subsequent decades), and tin plate (once used for roofing shingles, it would increasingly go to make tin cans). Like Carnegie Steel, the U.S. Steel Corporation was also vertically integrated, with substantial interests in iron ore, coal, shipping, and railroads.

Although it held one of the largest monopolies in an age of monopolies, U.S. Steel deliberately let its market share decline over the first few decades of its existence to avoid dissolution through antitrust prosecution by the federal government. Even though the Justice Department filed suit against U.S. Steel in 1911, this policy helped it survive when the Supreme Court resolved the case in 1920. U.S. Steel's largest competitors took advantage of the policy and the opportunities afforded them by World War I to grow at U.S. Steel's expense. Bethlehem Steel, for example, grew big during the war by selling armaments to Europe and ships to the U.S. Navy. Nevertheless, other firms took their cues from U.S. Steel for everything from product prices to wages and labor policy. The American Iron and Steel Institute, the industry trade organization formed in 1911 and led by U.S. Steel chairman Elbert Gary, helped spread many of U.S. Steel's policies and practices.

An important effect of the corporation's dominance was its imposition of the Pittsburgh Plus pricing system upon the entire industry. This system dictated that all steel prices be based upon the costs of production and transportation from Pittsburgh, no matter where the steel was originally produced. This allowed producers based in Pittsburgh to compete with local producers all around the country, since these producers were unable to undersell steel made in markets that U.S. Steel dominated. Although its origins are obscure, Pittsburgh Plus was firmly in place by 1901 and U.S. Steel championed its continued existence. Despite losing a suit by the Federal Trade Commission in 1924, U.S. Steel fought to keep the Pittsburgh Plus system in place in a modified form until it lost a U.S. Supreme Court decision on the matter in 1948.

The Steel Industry and Organized Labor

Throughout the early twentieth century, steel executives were determined to prevent the return of organized labor to their industry. Managers fought off national organizing campaigns in 1901, 1919, and 1933 through a combination of the carrot and the stick. They used hard-nosed tactics like spies, blacklists, and the fomenting of racial strife along with softer policies like safety improvements and employee stock ownership plans. However, when the Committee on Industrial Organization (later the Congress of Industrial Organizations, or CIO) started the Steelworkers Organizing Committee (SWOC) in 1936, it used the impetus of the National Labor Relations Act (1935) to gain a foothold in U.S. Steel. Rather than risk a costly strike at a time when production was just beginning to recover from the Depression, U.S. Steel recognized the SWOC without a strike in March 1937.

Although many other steel producers followed the steel corporation's lead, its largest competitors did not. Firms like Bethlehem Steel, Youngstown Sheet and Tube, and Republic Steel were part of a group known as Little Steel, not because they were small, but because they were smaller than U.S. Steel. Rather than recognize the union on terms similar to those agreed to by their larger competitor, these firms started the Little Steel Strike of 1937. Despite violence, particularly the so-called Memorial Day Massacre in Chicago, the Little Steel firms won the strike relatively easily. However, government pressure during World War II to keep production moving forced each of these firms to recognize the SWOC's successor organization, the United Steel Workers of America (USWA), over the course of that conflict.

World War II and Postwar Decline

During World War II, industry production increased sharply because of steel's importance to war mobilization. Some of this increase was a result of production returning to full capacity after the depression, but new plants also came on line. For example, the government loaned the shipbuilder Henry J. Kaiser enough money to build the first steel mill on the West Coast so as to ensure his yards would have enough product to meet his many navy contracts. U.S. Steel used both its money and money from the federal government to expand its production capacity during the war, particularly around Pittsburgh. By 1947, the United States controlled 60 percent of the world's steelmaking potential.

When the war ended, steelmakers wanted to roll back union gains that the administration of Franklin D. Roosevelt had forced the industry to accept, but the USWA had grown too big to destroy. Between 1946 and 1959, the USWA struck five times in an effort to win higher wages and more control over workplace conditions for its members. Each of these strikes shut down the industry. The 1952 strike led to President Harry Truman's historic decision to seize the entire steel industry. The Supreme Court ruled this action unconstitutional in *Youngstown Sheet and Tube Company v. Sawyer* (1952). The 1959 dispute lasted 116 days and was the largest single strike in American history. As a result of these disputes, America's steelworkers were among the highest paid manufacturing employees in the country. The cost of these wage gains contributed to the collapse of the industry in subsequent decades.

Foreign competition also contributed to the industry's decline. Countries like Japan and Germany first became major players in the international steel market during the 1960s. Later on, countries like Brazil and South Korea would break into the American market to the detriment of domestic producers. Although friends of the American steel industry would often complain of unfair competition from abroad, foreign producers' use of new technology and the failure of American steelmakers to innovate also explain these developments. For example, two Austrian firms developed the Basic Oxygen Furnace (BOF) in 1952. This process, which used pure oxygen as the only fuel in the furnace, was much more efficient than the then-traditional open hearth method. No major American steelmaker adopted this technology until 1957. U.S. Steel, still the largest firm in the industry, did not commission its first BOF unit until 1964. Close proximity to cheaper raw materials was another advantage that foreign steel producers had over their American counterparts.

The collapse of the steel industry began in the late 1960s and has only grown worse since then. Old-line firms like Wisconsin Steel and Republic Steel went bankrupt and ceased operations. Even survivors like U.S. Steel closed old plants in order to cut back capacity. U.S. Steel's decision to buy two oil companies in the 1980s and then change its name to USX symbolized the company's break with its roots. The elimination of much of America's steel capacity devastated the communities that had depended on these mills, including Pittsburgh, Pennsylvania, and Youngstown, Ohio. The Monongahela River valley around Pittsburgh lost approximately thirty thousand jobs during the 1980s. Many of these workers experienced significant psychological distress as they went from having high-paying jobs to joining the ranks of the long-term unemployed. Alcohol and drug abuse, depression, and suicide all increased dramatically as deindustrialization progressed.

The only sector of the American steel industry to expand since the 1960s has been the mini-mills. These facilities use large electric furnaces to melt scrap steel and reshape it rather than making new steel from scratch. Among the advantages that mini-mills have over traditional facilities are lower start-up costs, greater freedom of location, and more flexible job organization. Because these facilities tend to be built in rural areas and because workers need fewer skills than those at larger mills, mini-mills tend to be nonunion. The Nucor Corporation of North Carolina, which operates in ten states (mostly in the South), has had great success filling this niche in the international steel market. As this technology has improved in recent years, mini-mills have been able to break into more and more markets that large producers once dominated. Because of global and domestic competition, it has become increasingly unlikely that the American steel industry will ever return to the way it was in its heyday.

BIBLIOGRAPHY

Gordon, Robert B. *American Iron, 1607–1900.* Baltimore: Johns Hopkins University Press, 1996.

Hogan, William T. *Economic History of the Iron and Steel Industry in the United States.* 5 vols. Lexington, Mass.: D C. Heath, 1971.

Misa, Thomas J. *A Nation of Steel: The Making of Modern America, 1865–1925.* Baltimore: Johns Hopkins University Press, 1995.

Tiffany, Paul A.. *The Decline of American Steel: How Management, Labor, and Government Went Wrong.* New York: Oxford University Press, 1988.

Warren, Kenneth. *Big Steel: The First Century of the United States Steel Corporation, 1901–2001.* Pittsburgh, Pa.: University of Pittsburgh Press, 2001.

Jonathan Rees

See also **Homestead Strike; Monopoly; Steel Strikes; U.S. Steel; United Steelworkers of America.**

IRON CURTAIN, a phrase made popular by the former British prime minister Winston S. Churchill in a speech in Fulton, Missouri, on 5 March 1946. He referred to the influence of the Soviet Union in Eastern Europe: "From Stettin in the Baltic to Trieste in the Adriatic an iron curtain has descended across the Continent." As the Cold War emerged, President Harry S. Truman and other politicians used Churchill's metaphor to describe a dividing line in Europe between "West" and "East." The expression "behind the iron curtain" conjured an image of "captive peoples" suffering in a Soviet "bloc." Although Soviet influence over its neighbors varied country by country and the "curtain" did not move westward, the dark symbol served as anticommunist propaganda and helped spur the Marshall Plan, the North Atlantic Treaty Organization, and Radio Free Europe. The Berlin Wall, erected by the Soviets in 1961, gave the symbol credence. In 1989 the communist governments in Eastern Europe collapsed and the Berlin Wall came down, and in 1991 the Soviet Union disintegrated. Consequently, the term lost its relevance and its value as a Cold War epithet.

Naval Revolution. The inconclusive but historic first battle between ironclad warships: the Union's *Monitor (foreground)* and the Confederates' *Merrimack* (or *Virginia*) at Hampton Roads, Va., a narrow channel at the mouth of Chesapeake Bay, 9 March 1862. © CORBIS

BIBLIOGRAPHY

Harbutt, Fraser J. *The Iron Curtain: Churchill, America, and the Origins of the Cold War.* New York: Oxford University Press, 1986.

Paterson, Thomas G. *On Every Front: The Making and Unmaking of the Cold War.* Rev. ed. New York: Norton, 1992.

Thomas G. Paterson

See also **Anticommunism; Cold War.**

IRONCLAD OATH. In 1862, Congress mandated that civil servants and military personnel take an Ironclad Test Oath that they had never voluntarily aided the Confederacy. As Reconstruction evolved, the Ironclad Oath emerged as the strictest of several possible standards for the readmission of Southerners into the political life of the Union. The Radical WADE-DAVIS BILL (1864) would have required Southerners to take the oath before regaining the right to vote, but President Lincoln pocket-vetoed it. The Second Reconstruction Act (1867) made the oath a condition for holding federal office, but it was not consistently enforced.

BIBLIOGRAPHY

Dorris, Jonathan Truman. *Pardon and Amnesty Under Lincoln and Johnson: The Restoration of the Confederates to Their Rights and Privileges, 1861–1898.* Chapel Hill: University of North Carolina Press, 1953.

Foner, Eric. *Reconstruction: America's Unfinished Revolution, 1863–1877.* New York: Harper and Row, 1988.

Jeremy Derfner

See also **Loyalty Oaths; Reconstruction.**

IRONCLAD WARSHIPS. Thickening a ship's sides against enemy fire was common practice in the sailing-ship era. The perfection of the rifled cannon by 1850, however, spurred the development of new armored warships. During the Civil War inadequate shipbuilding facilities forced the Confederates to fit armor onto existing hulls; the captured Union steam frigate *Merrimack* (renamed *Virginia*) was the first so converted, with a waterline belt and an armored central casemate. The Union generally relied on newly constructed iron or wooden vessels designed to carry metal armor. The *Monitor* was the first completed, and its success against the *Virginia* on 9 March 1862 led to the construction of many others of the same type—characterized by a very low freeboard, vertically armored sides, and armored revolving gun turrets—based on the designs of engineer James B. Eads.

On 12 October 1861 the Confederate privateer ram *Manassas* became the world's first ironclad steamer in action. Although Confederate ironclads achieved startling victories in the early years of the Civil War, such as the *Arkansas*' single-handed passage of the combined fleets of Adm. David G. Farragut and Adm. Charles H. Davis above Vicksburg, Miss., 15 July 1862, the United States quickly gained ironclad superiority, which contributed largely to the splitting of the Confederacy in 1863. The ironclad war on inland waters ended with the surrender of the Confederate ship *Missouri* in the Red River, 3 June 1865.

BIBLIOGRAPHY

Baxter, James P. *The Introduction of the Ironclad Warship*. Hamden, Conn.: Archon Books, 1968 (orig. pub. 1933).

Still, William N., Jr. *Iron Afloat: The Story of the Confederate Armorclads*. Nashville, Tenn.: Vanderbilt University Press, 1971.

Dudley W. Knox/A. R.

See also **Armored Ships; Mobile Bay, Battle of; *Monitor* and *Merrimack*, Battle of; Navy, Confederate; Navy, United States; Rams, Confederate; Warships.**

Through European Eyes. A 1701 engraving, reproduced in 1930, of a tattooed Iroquois with a snake and pipe. Library of Congress

IROQUOIS. The Iroquois of the seventeenth century were a confederation of five closely related but separate nations: the Mohawks, Oneidas, Onondagas, Cayugas, and Senecas. Around the year 1500, these were independent nations speaking related languages that were arrayed in the order given from east to west across what became upstate New York. They were related to other Iroquoian-speaking nations and confederacies of the interior Northeast, namely the Neutrals, Petuns, Hurons, Wenros, Eries, and Susquehannocks. Even closer linguistic relatives, the Tuscaroras and Meherrins, lived in interior North Carolina. Iroquoians began expanding northward into what are now New York and Ontario beginning around A.D. 600. They were horticulturalists attracted by improved climatic conditions and fertile glacial soils, and they absorbed or displaced the thinner hunter-gatherer populations they encountered. The expansion also cut off the Eastern Algonquian-speaking peoples of the Northeast from the Central Algonquians of the Great Lakes basin.

Iroquois Communities

The ancestral Iroquois depended upon maize, beans, and squash as staples. Wild plant and animal foods supplemented this diet and deer hides provided most of their clothing prior to the introduction of trade cloth. Communities appear to have been organized along matrilineal lines from an early date. Communal households were led by senior women whose sisters and daughters comprised its social framework. Men moved to their wives' houses when they married. This household form eventually led to the emergence of the classic Iroquois longhouse, a segmented structure that accommodated pairs of nuclear families that shared common hearths in individual compartments. A single long aisle connected compartments, which were added to the ends of the longhouses as new marriages required.

Iroquois longhouse villages of the seventeenth century were compact and densely populated communities that could hold up to two thousand people before becoming politically unstable. They were lived in year round, but were designed to last only a decade or two. Without large domesticated animals and the fertilizer they might have provided, fields became unproductive after a few years. In addition, local firewood supplies became exhausted and longhouses were strained by changes in family age and composition. These pressures led to relocations, often to places just a few miles away. If displaced by warfare, Iroquois villagers moved much greater distances, a practice that accounts for their colonization of new regions and the clustering of village sites around those destinations as the result of subsequent shorter moves.

Warfare and the League of Iroquois

Both archaeology and oral tradition point to a period of internecine warfare in the fifteenth and sixteenth centu-

Iroquois Gathering. A panoramic photograph by William A. Drennan, 1914. LIBRARY OF CONGRESS

ries. By the latter part of the sixteenth century, the League of the Iroquois (Hodenosaunee) developed as a mutual nonaggression pact between the five Iroquois nations. This did not stop regional warfare, but it allowed the Iroquois nations to redirect their aggression toward other nations and emerging confederacies in the region. The Iroquois numbered around 22,000 by this time. By the middle of the seventeenth century, they had destroyed or dispersed the Huron, Neutral, and Erie confederacies as well as the independent Petun and Wenro nations. The Susquehannocks held out only a few years longer.

The Iroquois League, and the political confederacy that it eventually became, was founded on existing clan structure and funerary ritual. Leading clan segments from each of the five constituent nations provided league chiefs (sachems) who met frequently to maintain internal peace and discuss external affairs. Much of the earlier violence had been predicated on the shared assumption that most deaths were deliberately caused by enemies. Even what might otherwise have been considered natural deaths were usually attributed to witchcraft, which prompted cycles of revenge violence. Thus, a principal activity of the league chiefs was mutual condolence designed to stop cycles of revenge-motivated warfare. The vehicle for this was elaborate funerary ritual and the prompt raising up of new leaders to replace deceased ones. Replacements assumed the names of the deceased, providing both continuity and comfort to the bereaved.

Relations with Europeans

Smallpox and other diseases devastated the Iroquois beginning about 1634. The nations survived by taking in large numbers of refugees. Some of these were displaced from New England and other parts of the eastern seaboard that were experiencing European colonization. Many others were the remnants of nations that the Iroquois had defeated in war. The immigrants replaced lost relatives, often taking on their identities.

The Iroquois became the principal native power brokers in the colonial Northeast, treating first, in 1615, with the Dutch on the Hudson River and the French on the St. Lawrence River. After the English seized New Netherland in 1664 they forged a "covenant chain" with the Iroquois, principally through the Mohawks, who lived closest to Albany. French Jesuit missionaries established missions in several Iroquois villages. When the Jesuits retreated back to New France in the face of English expansion they took many Mohawks, Onondagas, and some other Iroquois with them.

The Iroquois also made peace with the French at the beginning of the eighteenth century, and successfully played the two colonial powers off each other until the English expelled the French from North America in 1763, after the French and Indian War. The Iroquois survived the war politically intact despite the fact that while many were allied with the English, Catholic Mohawks and other pro-French Iroquois fought with the other side. By that time, the Iroquois had absorbed many native refugees, both individually and as whole nations. The Tuscaroras moved north in the early part of the eighteenth century to become a sixth member of the confederacy. A large fraction of the Delawares were absorbed as a dependent nation in the mid-eighteenth century. The Tutelo refugees took shelter in New York under Iroquois protection at about the same time, with other refugee communities doing the same soon after. By this time, the traditional longhouses had been replaced by dispersed communities of individual cabins.

The American Revolution shattered the Iroquois confederacy. Most Oneidas sided with the colonists while most other Iroquois aligned with the British. The Mohawks soon fled to Canada and large fractions of western Iroquois communities were eventually also displaced by the fighting. The League of the Iroquois was dissolved.

After the League's Dissolution

Many Iroquois took up residence on Canadian reserves awarded to them after the war by a grateful English government. Others remained on new reservations in central and western New York, under the protection of the Canandaigua Treaty of 1794 and other agreements. While the Tuscaroras and four of the five original Iroquois nations achieved reservation status, the Mohawks did not return. Their only presence in New York was on the small St. Regis (Akwesasne) reservation-reserve, which straddles the New York, Ontario, and Quebec boundaries.

The League of the Iroquois was recreated both at Onondaga in New York and on the Six Nations Reserve in Ontario, but neither revival could hope to wield much power in the face of the U.S. and Canadian governments. Poverty and alcoholism on the reservations prompted a native religious revival in 1799. The prophet of the updated revival of Iroquois traditional belief was Handsome Lake, a Seneca. The Handsome Lake religion eventually spread to most other Iroquois communities and continues to provide both a rallying point and a source of controversy in many of them.

Iroquois reservation lands were reduced through the course of relocations and land deals in the nineteenth century. The legality of some these cessions were still being argued in courts in the early twenty-first century. A few gains were also realized by the Iroquois, and by the end of the twentieth century, there were even two new Mohawk communities in eastern New York. The Senecas remained on three reservations in western New York, while the Tuscaroras, Onondagas, and Oneidas had one each. The Cayugas had a small presence and claims on a larger one. The Oneidas, who had close relatives on a reservation in Wisconsin and a reserve in Ontario, pursued a land claim and had business success in casino operations. Many other Iroquois lived on reserves in Canada.

BIBLIOGRAPHY

Fenton, William N. *The Great Law and the Longhouse: A Political History of the Iroquois Confederacy.* Norman: University of Oklahoma Press, 1998. For the serious reader, a masterpiece by the dean of Iroquoian scholars.

Morgan, Lewis Henry. *League of the Iroquois.* New York: Corinth Books, 1962. Originally published in 1851 as *League of the Ho-dé-no-sau-nee or Iroquois.*

Snow, Dean R. *The Iroquois.* Cambridge, U.K.: Blackwell, 1994. The best place to start for the general reader.

Sturtevant, William C., gen. ed. *The Handbook of North American Indians.* Vol. 15, *Northeast.* Edited by Bruce G. Trigger. Washington, D.C.: Smithsonian Institution, 1978. This volume is the best single source for the Algonquian and Iroquoian speaking tribes of the Northeast.

Dean Snow

See also **Architecture, American Indian; French and Indian War; Indian Economic Life; Indian Land Cessions; Indian Languages; Indian Policy, Colonial; Indian Policy, U.S.: 1775–1830, 1830–1900, 1900–2000; Indian Political Life; Indians in the Revolution; Tribes: Northeastern; Warfare, Indian; Wars with Indian Nations: Colonial Era to 1783;** *and vol. 9:* **The Origin of the League of Five Nations; Treaty with the Six Nations, 1784.**

IRREPRESSIBLE CONFLICT, a term originating with William H. Seward in an 1858 speech in which he predicted the collision of the socioeconomic institutions of the North and the South. This confrontation, Seward maintained, would determine whether the nation would be dominated by a system of free labor or slave labor. Abraham Lincoln posited the same idea in his 1858 "House Divided" speech. At the time, the use of the phrase did not include the assumption that the "irrepressible conflict" would necessarily find expression in violence or armed conflict.

BIBLIOGRAPHY

Cole, Arthur C. *The Irrepressible Conflict: 1850–1865.* New York: Macmillan, 1934.

Freehling, William W. *The Road to Disunion: Secessionists at Bay, 1776–1854.* New York: Oxford University Press, 1991.

Arthur C. Cole
Gordon E. Harvey

See also **Civil War; House Divided.**

IRRIGATION, the delivery of water to grow crops, has been a factor in North American society and agriculture since long before the existence of the United States. Mostly practiced in the arid western regions of the country, its expansion in the twentieth century dramatically altered the national landscape and food production.

Possibly as early as A.D. 300, the HOHOKAM erected the first large-scale irrigation systems in the area that later became the southwestern United States. Although their rawhide and basket tools were simple and their dams small by modern standards, these indigenous societies maintained thousands of acres under irrigation for centuries. The Papago and PUEBLO nations later practiced similar techniques, though they generally irrigated only smaller fields near arroyo mouths and seasonal streambeds. The coordinated efforts to construct and maintain this sophisticated infrastructure required these early irri-

Irrigation Ditch. Help stretches into the distance for thirsty fields on both sides of this ditch, c. 1940. © HORACE BRISTOL/CORBIS

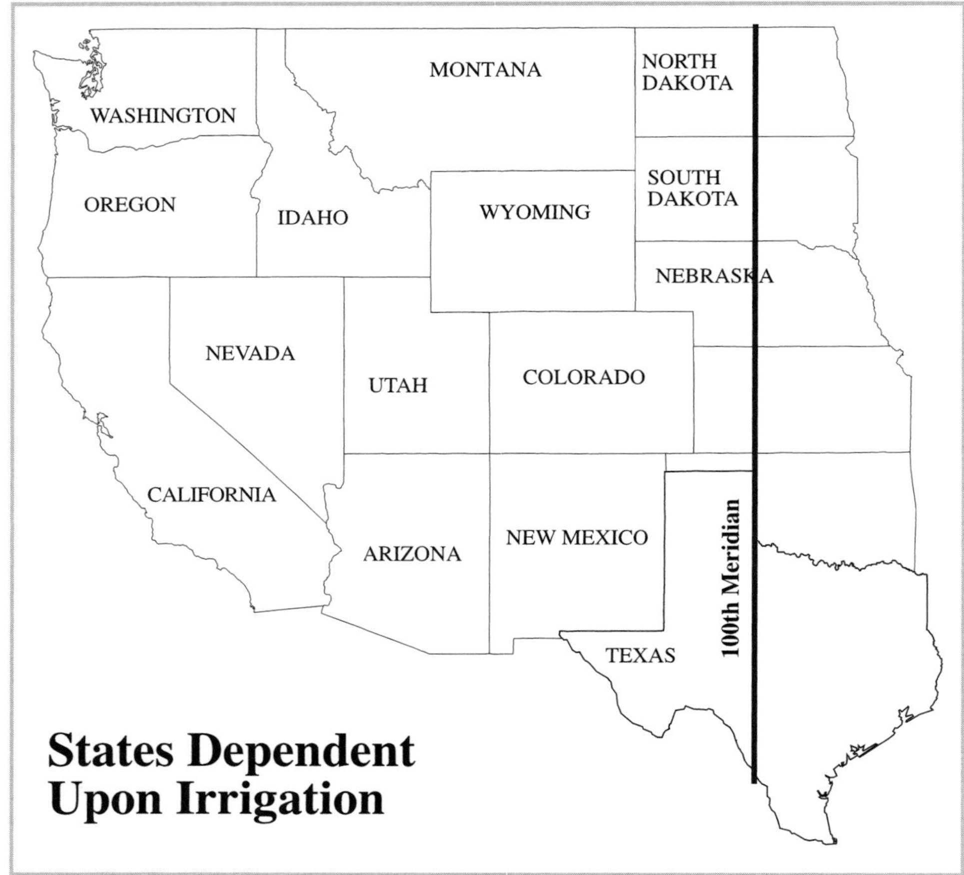

States Dependent Upon Irrigation

gators to develop political institutions and tribal affiliations larger than those of their hunter-gatherer neighbors.

Spanish and Mexican settlers in New Mexico created similar irrigation systems to support their own agriculture. Many of their villages and fields were actually built around an *acequia madre* or "mother ditch," and they boasted well-articulated lines of command and labor expectations to maintain the ditch. This social and physical system still existed in some of these villages at the end of the twentieth century.

The Mormon settlers arriving in the Salt Lake area in the 1840s drew on these precedents in the erection of their own irrigation networks. Using the cooperative religious institutions that characterized their society, by 1850 they grew such diverse crops as potatoes, wheat, hay, and oats on more than sixteen thousand irrigated acres.

The westward expansion of the United States in the nineteenth century brought the regions where irrigation was needed to practice extensive agriculture under American control. At first, however, migrating Americans were slow to recognize the challenge that aridity posed to their traditional agricultural practices. At less than twenty inches a year, the average rainfall west of the one-hundredth meridian—roughly the line that runs north and south through the middle of the states of Texas, Oklahoma, Kansas, Nebraska, and the Dakotas—is just below the amount needed to grow wheat, and ten inches less than that needed by corn.

The enormous challenge of the arid West was initially difficult to recognize. During the 1880s, when thousands of farmers settled on the Great Plains, rainfall was significantly above average, in some cases twice as heavy as the long-term pattern. Farmers and policymakers were thus lulled into a false sense of security. One theory even held that the plowing of so much virgin territory had in fact fundamentally changed the natural patterns of rainfall, increasing precipitation to facilitate the conquest of the continent.

Private efforts to irrigate the arid regions of the West met with very limited success. Irrigation was generally outside the reach of individual farmers for the simple reason that it required the control of large stretches of rivers and streams and the erection of sizable dams for storage. In the 1870s and 1880s, private land companies entered the irrigation business, constructing dams, building extensive canal systems, and then selling nearby lands to farmers who would remain dependent on the companies for their water. High capital costs, however, constrained these efforts. Only the most opportune sites were irrigated, the total acres under irrigation soon stagnated, and by 1900 nearly nine out of ten of these irrigation companies were in financial jeopardy.

The Federal Role

The failure of private efforts created an opening for those who thought that the federal government should build massive irrigation works. John Wesley Powell, a pioneering scientist and ethnographer who headed the United States Geological Survey, had made the most radical proposals in this regard. Surveying the lands of the arid West in the 1870s, Powell came to the conclusion that the country's model for the settlement of newly acquired territory was deeply flawed. Extinguishing the public domain by giving settlers 160-acre tracts (under the provisions of the Homestead Act) might work where enough rain fell to grow crops, but the development of the West hinged on water rather than land. Since very little of the West could be farmed in the traditional way, the government, Powell believed, should divide the region by watershed. Much like the Mormons—whose communal irrigation made quite an impression on Powell—settlers should govern themselves by watershed, forming a cooperative to raise the capital for the necessary irrigation network. Irrigated farms, more productive and labor intensive, would be smaller than farms back east, probably about 80 acres. Unirrigated lands, which he thought would always comprise the vast majority of the West, would be reserved for ranching in large tracts of 2,500 or more acres.

Powell's vision was at once too radical and too modest to gain the political support it needed to be implemented. Western boosters were enraged by his assumption that little of the region's land was fit for agriculture, and even fewer were willing to accept the drastic revision in territorial laws for which his watershed proposal called. After the failure of private irrigation in the West, the form that federal intervention took was much more modest. The 1902 Newlands Reclamation Act created the Bureau of Reclamation, a federal agency charged with building dams, reservoirs, and irrigation canals for the benefit of private farmers. The West, in other words, was meant to resemble the East, with a little more help from the federal government.

The Newlands Act married conservation's technical expertise with its emphasis on antimonopoly. Farmers were to repay the construction costs through annual charges for their water. Individuals could buy water for a maximum of only 160 acres. The Newlands Act thus extended the provisions of the Homestead Act, seeking to create egalitarian farming communities with dispersed land ownership.

The Bureau of Reclamation was remarkably successful in its goal of irrigating the West. Whereas in 1906, fewer than thirty thousand acres west of the one-hundredth meridian were under irrigation, by 1992 that number had skyrocketed to more than 45 million. The Bureau of Reclamation, the Army Corps of Engineers, and other federal agencies erected more than one thousand dams in the West. These massive structures not only provided water for crops, but also generated much of the electricity that lit the region's cities and towns. For decades, the politics of irrigation proved irresistible. The construction of dams, aqueducts, and canals created numerous jobs, and the lands that they opened up for agriculture benefited real estate speculators and the local tax rolls alike. While the New Deal saw a significant expansion in the scope of these projects, the fact that their ultimate goal was to support private agriculture kept them attractive to more antistate politicians.

Aiming the Water. J. G. Milne directs water to where his farm in Colorado needs it most, c. 1993. © MICHAEL L. LEWIS/CORBIS

In the 1930s, affordable pumps and low-cost electricity opened up a new dimension in irrigation: groundwater pumping. By 1970, such pumping watered more than 40 percent of the nation's irrigated acreage, most of it on the Great Plains. This irrigation differed from federal projects in that it drew upon generally unrenewable aquifers and was easily affordable by individual farmers.

Social and Environmental Issues

Such intensive irrigation, however, generated its own social and environmental effects. From its inception, the Bureau of Reclamation operated much differently than its founders had envisioned. Very few irrigation projects were actually paid for by their beneficiaries, and so these public works quickly became subsidies. The proliferation of modest homesteads that had been so important to justify giving the federal government primary responsibility for irrigation never came to be. Land speculators bought much of the land where they anticipated dams might be built, and the bureau showed little interest in enforcing its 160-acre limit on what came to be some of the most powerful political interests in the West. In most areas served by the bureau's projects, it was actually impossible to purchase small tracts of land. The high productivity and costs of irrigated lands meant that such agriculture tended to be more market-oriented, more mechanized, and to employ more migrant labor than elsewhere. In practice, then, irrigation helped to solidify the dominance of large-scale agribusiness in the West.

Environmental problems have increasingly limited the effectiveness of irrigation and reduced its public support. The damming of most of the West's major rivers has decimated their salmon runs. Natural river flows have been dramatically altered. The Colorado River, for example, once mighty enough to carve the Grand Canyon, was so heavily drawn on for irrigation that it did not reach the Pacific from 1964 to 1983. Proposals to build further dams on the Colorado sparked an environmental backlash as early as the 1950s. The buildup of silt behind reservoir walls quickly became a problem; by 2000, most reservoirs built before 1945 had lost from 7 to 15 percent of their capacity. Salinization, the accretion of salt in perpetually water-logged soil, puts thousands of acres out of production each year. Groundwater pumping on the Great Plains seemed headed for extinction, with the aquifer predicted to dry up within a few decades.

No large federal irrigation projects were approved from the late 1970s to the turn of the century. In part this was because so many of the most feasible dam sites had been taken, but the loss of support for federal irrigation also reflected the growing political power of more environmental-minded urbanites. Nevertheless, irrigation continues to be a decisive force in American agriculture and the landscape of the West.

BIBLIOGRAPHY

Hundley, Norris, Jr. *The Great Thirst: Californians and Water—A History*. Rev. ed. Berkeley: University of California Press, 2001.

Pisani, Donald J. *To Reclaim a Divided West: Water, Law, and Public Policy, 1848–1902*. Albuquerque: University of New Mexico Press, 1992.

Reisner, Marc. *Cadillac Desert: The American West and Its Disappearing Water*. Rev. ed. New York: Penguin, 1993.

Walton, John. *Western Times and Water Wars: State, Culture, and Rebellion in California*. Berkeley: University of California Press, 1992.

Worster, Donald. *Rivers of Empire: Water, Aridity, and the Growth of the American West*. New York: Pantheon, 1985.

Benjamin H. Johnson

See also **Agriculture; Agriculture, American Indian; Reclamation; Water Supply and Conservation.**

ISLAM. There are roughly six million Muslims scattered throughout the United States. By 1992 there were over twenty-three hundred Islamic institutions in North America, including schools, community centers, mosques, publishing houses, and media units. To coordinate activities of this dispersed, growing American Muslim community, Muslims organized conferences, the first of which was held in Cedar Rapids, Iowa, in 1952. Succeeding conferences were coordinated by the Muslim Students of America (MSA), which held its first conference at the University of Illinois in 1963. The Islamic Society of North America (ISNA), the principal national organization for mainstream (Sunni) American Muslims, started in 1982 as an outgrowth of MSA. In 1993 the first Muslim chaplain began working with Muslims in the U.S. armed forces, who now number in the thousands. Although there are no reliable population figures for the Muslim community in the United States, the consensus is that by 2015 the American Muslim community will be the nation's largest non-Christian religion.

Muslims have been in North America since the sixteenth century. Isfan the Arab was a guide for the Franciscan explorer Marcos de Niza in Arizona in 1539. Nosereddine, an Egyptian, settled in the Catskill Mountains of New York State in the 1500s and was burned at the stake for murdering an Indian princess. As many as 20 percent of the West African slaves brought to the United States during the eighteenth and nineteenth centuries were Muslims. At the beginning of the nineteenth century, the first Arab Muslims began to form communities in the United States. One of these Arab Muslims, Haj Ali, assisted the U.S. Army with camel-breeding experiments in the Arizona desert in the 1850s. He is remembered in folk legend as Hi Jolly. By the end of the nineteenth century, large numbers of male Muslim immigrants, mostly from the eastern Mediterranean, had come to the Midwest as migrant workers. Three thousand Polish Muslims and a small community of Circassian (Russian) Muslims settled in New York. The latest wave of Muslim immigrants, one that is continuing, began after the repeal of the Asian Exclusion Act in 1965. These immigrants, arriving from a variety of countries, generally are highly educated and have western educations.

Muhammad Alexander Webb, an American consul in Manila, converted to Islam in 1868 and opened a mosque in New York City in 1893. The next mosque was opened in Ross, North Dakota, followed by one in the Detroit suburb of Highland Park in 1919. By 1952 there were twenty mosques joined together by the Federation of Islamic Associations of North America. In 1957 the Islamic Center was dedicated in Washington, D.C., sponsored by fifteen Islamic countries. During the 1970s considerable mosque construction began and continues to the present day.

African Americans, who have been converting to Islam since the 1920s, make up 40 percent of the American Muslim community (with Indo-Pakistanis and Arabs each comprising about 25 percent of the community). In 1913 Noble Drew Ali founded the Moorish Science Temple of America, headquartered in Baltimore. His successor, Wallace D. Fard, probably of Turkish or Iranian descent, began the Lost-Found Nation of Islam in the Wilderness of North America in Detroit in 1930 (in 1995 the Lost-Found Nation had nineteen temples in the United States). He claimed that African Americans were really Muslims who had been denied their heritage. Designated by Fard as the "messenger of God," Elijah Muhammad became the leader of the Nation of Islam (NOI) in 1934. Members stressed education and black-owned businesses, with the goal of a separate black nation. When Elijah died in 1975, there were about seventy NOI temples and 100,000 members in the United States. Since whites were excluded from membership and since Elijah Muhammad was considered a prophet (the last prophet is the seventh-century Muhammad, according to Muslim orthodoxy), in addition to other beliefs unique to NOI, the larger worldwide Muslim community does not consider members of the NOI to be Muslims. The Ansaar Allah and Five Percenters are offshoots of NOI.

Mosque. A house of worship of the Islamic Foundation in St. Louis. © G. John Renard

Malcolm X, the best-known disciple of Elijah Muhammad, left NOI in 1964 after experiencing the lack of racial and color distinctions during his pilgrimage to Mecca. The issue of joining mainstream Islam or of maintaining a separate African American community created leadership struggles after 1975 when Warith Deen Muhammad, Elijah Muhammad's son, succeeded his father. In 1985 he led most of the NOI members to merge with the larger mainstream Muslim community. Louis Farrakhan became the new leader of the NOI and continued the agenda of Elijah Muhammad, including organizational structure, racist ideology, and the goal of a separate nation. The merger of Warith Deen's community into mainstream Islam did not affect the sixty Clara Muhammad schools, which provide high-quality secular and religious education to elementary and secondary school students.

Ahmadiyya Muslims, believing in the prophethood of the northern Indian Mirza Ghulam Ahmad (1835–1908), began to proselytize in the United States in 1921 and achieved success in the African American community. As of 1992, headquartered in Washington, D.C., they had ten thousand members and active centers in thirty-seven cities. The Tablighi Jama'at, headquartered in Pakistan, has sent Muslim missionaries to the United States since 1952 to preach the creation of separate communities of observant Muslims. Since the 1970s the growth of Islam among New York City's Latin American population has been fostered by PIEDAD (Propagación Islámica para la Educación y Devoción de Ala' el Divino) and in California by ALMA (Asociación Latina de Musalmanes en las Américas). Among Native Americans, Islam is slowly gaining ground, as a mosque on a Navajo reservation demonstrates. Seminoles in Florida claim that escaped Muslim slaves converted Seminoles to Islam during the nineteenth century. Cherokees state that their chief in 1866 was a Muslim named Ramadhan ibn Wati. Shia Muslims, who look for a descendant of the Prophet for leadership and form 10 percent of the Muslim community worldwide, have formed their own national organizations, the Shia Association of North America and the Ismaili Council for the U.S.A. In 1987 there were thirty thousand Nizari Ismailis in seventy-five centers around the United States. Shias usually worship in mosques separate from the mainstream Sunni Muslim community.

Caucasian Muslim converts in the United States often come to Islam through small groups of mystics, or Sufis. Hazrat Inayat Khan (1882–1927) of the Indian Chishti lineage came to the United States in 1910 and set up the Sufi Order. Its leadership was continued by his son, Pir Vilayat Khan, who has turned over the leadership of the order in the United States to his son, Zia Khan. One of the largest Sufi communities in the United States is that of Bawa Muhaiyaddeen (d. 1986), who came to Philadelphia from Sri Lanka in 1971 and whose tomb is becoming a place of pilgrimage. There are over three thousand people affiliated with this group.

There are clear ethnic, cultural, and theological differences between Muslims living in the United States. Due to the Wahhabi influence (a theological perspective named after an eighteenth-century Arab ideologue, Muhammad ibn Abd al-Wahhab, whose followers teamed up with the first king of the Saudi dynasty to create Saudi Arabia), an extreme Arab form of Islam is increasingly becoming normative in the United States. In reaction to the self-declared authoritative Wahhabi stance that does not permit any other way of being a Muslim, ethnic mosques are continually being established. There appears to be minimal social contact between immigrant and African American Muslims—including separate mosques and celebration of holidays. Often African Americans are attracted to Islam by its ideal of genuine racial equality, only to find that the actual practice is far from the stated ideal.

American Islam—specifically MSA, ISNA, and ICNA (Islamic Circle of North America), its mainstream organizations—has received considerable funding from foreign donors who seek to further an Arab Wahhabi theological perspective in the United States. Some African Americans perceive these organizations as catering primarily to the needs of the immigrant community. The ideological, conservative, anti-Sufi stance promoted by these mainstream organizations has been influenced by political ideologues of the Jamaat Islami and Ikhwan al-Musilmin and often has been funded by Saudi Arabia. These groups have managed to control the Islamic symbols and belief systems (i.e., to define Islam) in American Muslim communities, because they have a long-term strategy (political control in majority Islamic countries) and an organization with ample funding. They strongly influence mainstream American Islam—the majority of the mosques in the United States are funded by Saudi Arabia and/or their imams are trained in Saudi Arabia. This Arab version of Islam, already the norm for most American Muslims, contrasts sharply with the actual pluralism of the American Muslim community. To what extent foreign political interests will influence funding of American Muslim activities is unclear, since Persian Gulf nations cut off aid to various American Muslim organizations when many immigrant Muslims did not support Saudi policies during the Gulf War. Clearly, as in other religions, common identity as a Muslim does not guarantee community. In view of the tragic events of 11 September 2001, it remains to be seen whether more moderate American Muslims will prevail over their more vocal and well-funded co-religionists in an ever-evolving mosaic of Islamic diversity in the United States.

BIBLIOGRAPHY

Haddad, Yvonne, and John Esposito, eds. *Muslims on the Americanization Path?* Atlanta: Scholars Press, 1998.

———, and Jane Smith, eds. *Muslim Communities in North America.* Albany: State University of New York Press, 1994.

Melton, J. Gordon. *Encyclopedia of American Religions.* 6th ed. Detroit, Mich.: Gale, 1999.

Smith, Jane I. *Islam in America.* New York: Columbia University Press, 1999.

Arthur F. Buehler

See also **Nation of Islam.**

ISLAND NUMBER TEN, OPERATIONS AT. From 15 March to 7 April 1862, six ironclads and ten mortar boats commanded by Union flag officer Andrew H. Foote cooperated with twenty-five thousand men led by Major General John Pope in capturing Island Number Ten, located in the upper part of a triple bend of the Mississippi, fifty-five miles below Cairo, Illinois. It was protected by forty-nine guns on the island and—on the opposite Tennessee shore—by a floating battery of nine guns and twelve thousand men. The decisive factor was the running of the batteries at night by the *Carondelet* and *Pittsburg*, which enabled Pope's forces to cross the river south of the island and capture about half of the Confederate defenders. This operation was the first achievement in the campaign to divide the Confederacy by gaining control of the Mississippi.

BIBLIOGRAPHY

Daniel, Larry J. *Island No. 10: Struggle for the Mississippi Valley.* Tuscaloosa: University of Alabama Press, 1996.

Charles Lee Lewis / A. R.

See also **Mississippi River; Vicksburg in the Civil War.**

ISOLATIONISM was the dominant ideology guiding American foreign policy from the era of the founders until the end of World War II. Its central tenet was that the United States should take advantage of its geographic distance from Europe and refrain from intervention in Old World affairs. Supporters of isolationism also thought America was better off pursuing its interests in other parts of the world without participating in alliances or foreign wars. Isolationists thought the best way to secure democracy and prosperity was to build it at home.

Although isolationist assumptions were widely accepted for over 150 years, the terms "isolationism" and "isolationist" were actually seldom used until after World War I. When the war ended in 1917, President Woodrow Wilson wanted the United States to enter the League of Nations. Those who opposed American participation, fearing the United States would lose its autonomy over foreign affairs, were pejoratively labeled "isolationists." In the 1930s, the term was used even more frequently to refer to the politicians and lobbyists who actively opposed U.S. intervention in World War II.

Origins

Isolationism has its roots in the experiences of America's colonists. Those settlers crossed the Atlantic Ocean to escape constant war, religious persecution, and other adversities in Europe. They considered the vast body of water separating them from continental strife a blessing from the Divine. They believed the New World was morally superior to the Old World. The colonists' hunger for land and trade brought them into conflict with the Native Americans, the French, and the Spanish. Some of the wars waged over territory were driven by the colonists' desire for security; others arose from rivalries between the European powers. Nevertheless, the colonists came to feel unfairly burdened by these conflicts and resented having their fate in the hands of the British Crown. After the English victory over the French in Canada in 1763, colonial leaders argued that they ought to avoid further involvement in European wars. Although the colonies' alliance with France was crucial in winning the revolutionary war, they viewed the break with England as the definitive step in severing ties to Europe.

During the early years of the republic, French efforts to draw the United States into supporting its postrevolutionary wars against England, Holland, and Austria put isolationism to the test. French diplomats unsuccessfully attempted to influence the 1796 presidential election; they led Americans to believe that if Federalist John Adams became president over the pro-French Thomas Jefferson, a war with France would be imminent. President George Washington, in his Farewell Address of 1796, issued the most significant statement of isolationist principles in American history. He called for vigilance against "the insidious wiles of foreign influence" and argued that it would be unwise to "implicate ourselves, by artificial ties, in the ordinary vicissitudes of [European] politics, or the ordinary combinations and collisions of her friendships or enmities." Washington, however, did not advocate the United States completely cut its ties to other nations. He called on Americans to engage in trade abroad with "as little political connection as possible." And, he noted that circumstances might require further engagement. "Tis our true policy to steer clear of permanent alliances with any portion of the foreign world . . . [but] we may safely trust to temporary alliances for extraordinary emergencies."

Expansion Without Intervention

Isolationism was strongest in the nineteenth century, when the growing nation needed to concentrate on domestic development. Moreover, the United States did not yet have the means to support the naval forces necessary to sustain a more active foreign policy. After the War of 1812, the United States was able to continue western expansion without incursions from foreign powers. However, in the 1820s, American leaders grew concerned about the possibility of renewed European intervention in the Pacific Northwest and in Latin America. In response, President James Monroe announced his 1823 doctrine, which reiterated and expanded Washington's neutrality policy. He proclaimed that the "American continents . . . are henceforth not to be considered as subjects for future colonization by any European powers." He also warned that the United States would consider any European move "to extend their system to any portion of this hemisphere as dangerous to our peace and safety." Lastly, Monroe pledged that the United States would not take part in "wars of the European powers in matters relating to themselves."

International circumstances in the nineteenth century reinforced Americans' confidence in isolationism. The United States did not become involved in dangerous foreign engagements largely because a balance of power was maintained on the Continent. The British navy provided a security blanket for American commerce. Thus, the United States was able to act unilaterally in expanding in Latin America and even the Far East. Americans considered the nation's growth and prosperity a consequence of its adherence to a foreign policy of nonintervention and neutrality.

By the 1880s, domestic and international developments were making isolationism less relevant. For example, the expansion of American industrial and agricultural production dictated a search for new markets abroad. Busier foreign trade led the United States to establish a large navy. The days of relative peace in Europe were also fading. Germany and Japan were building up their military forces, prompting a European arms race. Meanwhile, all the powers scrambled for empire in Asia and Africa. In 1898, the United States demonstrated its newfound status as a world power by winning its war against Spain. The spoils included the Philippines, Puerto Rico, and Cuba.

World War I and the League of Nations

When Europe went to war in 1914, President Woodrow Wilson vowed not to break the tradition of American isolation. However, Wilson's neutrality policies worked to favor England and France. German attacks on American ships and Germany's attempt to ally with Mexico eventually led Wilson to seek congressional approval for a declaration of war in 1917. In keeping with the American preference to see itself as morally superior to the Europeans, Wilson said the United States needed to go to war to "vindicate the principles of peace and justice in the life of the world against selfish and autocratic power" and because "the world must be made safe for democracy." Only the most ardent isolationists failed to vote for war.

Wilson believed that if, after a peace settlement was reached, the United States joined a collective security organization, the world would be spared another devastating conflict. But his mostly Republican opposition was not convinced. Some feared the United States would become the world's policeman if it joined the league. Other isolationists argued Congress would lose its power over warmaking. The Senate rejected the treaty that would have ratified American participation in the organization.

World War II and the Rise of Internationalism

In the 1930s, Japan's invasion of China and Nazi Germany's militarism in Europe failed to sway the United States from its policy of noninvolvement. The Great Depression had reinforced Americans' conventional isolationist sentiments. Americans were already concerned about the expansion of federal powers to revive the economy; they feared involvement in another war could bring a dictatorship to American soil. Although isolationism was a nationwide and bipartisan phenomenon, its strongholds were in landlocked midwestern, Great Plains, and Rocky Mountain states. Important ethnic groups also favored isolationism: the Germans, Irish, Italians, and Scandinavians. Isolationist leaders in Congress, such as senators William E. Borah of Idaho, Gerald P. Nye of North Dakota, and Arthur Vandenberg of Michigan led investigations that concluded greedy arms makers and Wall Street bankers had unduly influenced President Wilson's decision to become involved in World War I. If it was a mistake to have fought the last war, as another war loomed, most Americans concluded that the United States should remain aloof from Old World conflicts.

When the first signs of overt aggression were evident in 1935 with Italy's Ethiopian conquest and Germany's 1936 reoccupation of the Rhineland, isolationists fashioned neutrality legislation. Congress passed laws forbidding arms sales and loans to warring nations, and restricting American travel on belligerent ships. Only in the wake of Germany's 1939 invasion of Poland did the tide of public opinion begin to turn against isolationism. President Franklin Roosevelt, an internationalist, who, needing support for his domestic policies, acceded to isolationists' demands and convinced Congress to repeal the arms embargo. This move away from isolationism sparked zealous lobbying by groups such as the America First Committee, whose most famous member was the aviator Charles A. Lindbergh. Roosevelt's efforts to assist England, which was attacked in 1940, were championed by both the Committee to Defend America by Aiding the Allies and the Fight for Freedom Committee.

The Japanese attack on Pearl Harbor on 7 December 1941 and U.S. entry into World War II ended isolationism. The United States emerged as a superpower after the Allied victory and internationalism became the dominant ideology guiding foreign policy in the latter half of the twentieth century. Even former isolationists rallied behind the creation of the United Nations. The onset of the Cold War with the Soviet Union led the United States to become intimately involved in European affairs through the Marshall Plan and the North Atlantic Treaty Organization. Subsequent efforts to contain the spread of communism led the United States to expand its reach globally. During debates over various interventions, such as Korea in 1950, Vietnam in the 1960s, or Bosnia in the 1990s, isolationist arguments resurfaced in a phenomenon labeled "neo-isolationism." But by the start of the twenty-first century, America's vast global responsibilities had rendered the tradition of noninvolvement and unilateralism obsolete.

BIBLIOGRAPHY

Adler, Selig. *The Isolationist Impulse: Its Twentieth-Century Reaction.* New York: Abelard-Schuman, Ltd., 1957.

Cole, Wayne S. *America, Roosevelt, and the Isolationists, 1932–1945.* Lincoln: University of Nebraska Press, 1983.

Dallek, Robert A. *The Illusion of Neutrality.* Chicago: University of Chicago Press, 1962.

———. *The American Style of Foreign Policy: Cultural Politics and Foreign Affairs.* N.Y.: Knopf, 1983.

Jonas, Manfred. *Isolationism in America, 1935–1941.* Ithaca, N.Y.: Cornell University Press, 1966.

Ellen G. Rafshoon

See also **Anti-Imperialists; Imperialism; Intervention; Neutrality;** *and vol. 9:* **America First; The Monroe Doctrine and the Roosevelt Corollary.**

ISRAEL, RELATIONS WITH. The phrase "special relationship" describes U.S.-Israeli ties, suggesting an association uncommon in international affairs. The closeness of the bond between the two countries is extraordinary, and the U.S. commitment to Israel encompasses moral, religious, diplomatic, economic, and strategic dimensions. Israeli leaders have pursued such relations since the establishment of the Jewish state in May 1948, but no special relationship existed before the mid-1970s. By the early 1980s, a confluence of interests based mainly on Cold War considerations brought about an unwritten alliance that has allowed Israel to achieve a high degree of accord with the United States. However, the United States has dictated the extent of the commitment and the pace of its development. Israel is highly dependent upon the United States, and in the post–Cold War era, a continued convergence of major interests will determine the durability of the special nature of the relationship.

1948: Israel's Orientation and an American Moral Commitment

Upon attainment of statehood, Israel adopted a policy of nonalignment between East and West, pursuing close ties with both the United States and the Soviet Union in order to avoid choosing sides in the Cold War. In terms of both the nature of its regime and its view of the international system, Israel leaned clearly toward the United States. American public opinion recognized this affinity and assumed a moral responsibility toward the Jewish state, a responsibility attributable in great part to the Holocaust. Moreover, the religious orientation of many American Christians brought them to support modern Zionism. President Harry S. Truman supported the United Nations plan in 1947 for the partition of Palestine, thus overriding the objections of the State Department and the Department of Defense and creating the basis for early recognition of the state of Israel. Yet, a general moral commitment brought the United States to provide neither a formal guarantee of its security nor arms to Israel. In fact, the United States imposed an arms embargo on the parties to the Arab-Israeli conflict that it maintained in near-complete fashion until the early 1960s.

1949–1960: Economic Aid on a Background of Bilateral Tension

Between 1949 and 1959, about 10 percent of the capital that Israel imported came directly from the United States. In January 1949, the United States averted a collapse of the Israeli economy by extending $100 million in credits. By 1960, total U.S. economic aid (grants and loans) had reached $1.5 billion. This support was modest compared to later periods, but it heightened both Israel's perception and the fact of dependence upon the United States.

At the same time, the administration of President Dwight D. Eisenhower considered Israel the more aggressive of the sides in the Arab-Israeli conflict. His administration gave Israel vague assurances that the United States would not allow its destruction. But the United

States saw in Israel an impediment to a Middle East policy, the main objective of which was to achieve closer relations with the Arab states in order to bring them into a pro-Western alliance and ensure a steady supply of oil. This administration opposed Israel's practice of severe retaliation in response to raids from Arab states, withheld diplomatic support when it viewed Israel's use of force as excessive (as in 1953, during a dispute over the waters of the Jordan River), and planned, with Britain, to require Israeli territorial concessions in order to resolve the Arab-Israeli conflict. In early 1957, President Eisenhower threatened Israel with sanctions to force it to withdraw from Egyptian territory it had conquered during the 1956 Sinai campaign, and U.S.-Israeli relations during the second Eisenhower administration (1957 to 1961) remained cool.

1961–1973: The Strategic Background to a Growing Accord

President John F. Kennedy adopted a more accommodating approach toward Israel, and in 1962 authorized the sale of U.S. Hawk anti-aircraft missiles. Yet, at the same time, he attempted to elicit Israeli agreement to a significant unilateral concession on the Palestinian refugee problem and took a tough stance toward Israel's nuclear development, warning Prime Minister David Ben Gurion in May 1963 that an Israeli nuclear option would disturb both global and regional stability.

President Lyndon Johnson's rapport with Prime Minister Levi Eshkol seemed to usher in a new period in U.S.-Israeli relations. In reality, Johnson was determined that the United States not become a purveyor of arms to Israel, a policy aimed at avoiding a far-reaching political commitment. Nevertheless, during the early-to-mid 1960s, the Soviet Union transferred arms on a large scale to Egypt, Iraq, and Syria, and offered to supply advanced arms to Jordan. In early 1966, the United States decided to sell Jordan jet fighters, and the Johnson administration, seeking to avoid a political battle with Israel's supporters in Washington, reluctantly agreed to sell Israel jet bombers (the A-4 Skyhawk) in what it stipulated would be a "one-time deal."

A close patron-client relationship that included a steady supply of modern arms emerged gradually after the Six Day War of 1967. By 1969, President Richard M. Nixon and his national security adviser, Henry Kissinger, had come to view Israel as a Cold War asset, and during the 1969–1970 Israeli-Egyptian War of Attrition, supplied it with more advanced arms. In September 1970, during the large-scale clash between the Jordanian army and Palestinian guerrillas, Israel deterred Syria from employing its air force to support the armor with which the Syrians had invaded Jordan, thus earning Washington's appreciation for aiding the pro-Western monarchy. Yet, from 1971 to 1973, U.S. acquiescence to the lack of receptivity of the government of Golda Meir to negotiate with Egypt contributed to the stalemate that led to war in 1973. U.S.-Israeli relations had become much closer, but during the 1973 Yom Kippur War, the United States again demonstrated that strategic interests, and not a nascent special relationship, determined its policies.

1973–1979: Toward Israeli-Egyptian Peace

The U.S. role during the 1973 war and the diplomatic process that eventually led to an Israeli-Egyptian peace treaty demonstrate that even after the establishment of a patron-client relationship, in the framework of which Israel acquired nearly all of its military hardware from the United States, ties were much closer when Washington could reconcile support of Israel with its other policies in the Middle East. The United States flew arms to Israel during the 1973 war but prevented a defeat of Egypt on a scale that would have obviated a later U.S.-Egyptian rapprochement. From 1974 to 1976, the United States granted Israel $5.8 billion in combined civilian and military assistance, a level at which aid has since approximately remained. Yet, in 1975, President Gerald Ford and Secretary of State Kissinger warned that they would "reassess" relations, forcing Israel to sign an agreement that included partial withdrawal from the Sinai Peninsula. In 1978, at Camp David, President Jimmy Carter threatened to cut Israeli aid should they fail to evince more flexibility in the negotiations.

President Carter used the term "special" to describe the U.S.-Israeli relationship, and he maintained the high levels of support his predecessor had established. But he also called for the creation of a Palestinian "homeland" and reminded Israel that close relations did not mean U.S. acquiescence to the policies of Prime Minister Menachem Begin of the right wing Likud party, policies intended to perpetuate Israel's presence in the West Bank, the Gaza Strip, and the Golan Heights.

1981–1992: Harmony and Discord

During the 1980s and early 1990s, the interests of Israel and the United States converged over a common view of the threat from the Soviet Union but diverged over problems of the Middle East. In June 1981, the Reagan administration condemned Israel for bombing Iraq's nuclear facility. Israel's (unsuccessful) opposition to the sale of sophisticated U.S. arms to Saudi Arabia in a manner that the administration considered interference further strained relations. The United States intended a strategic memorandum of understanding it signed with Israel in November 1981 to compensate for the U.S.-Saudi deal, and the memorandum noted agreement to "deter all threats from the Soviet Union in the region." But in December 1981, Washington suspended the memorandum in response to Israel's annexation of Jerusalem and the extension of Israeli law to the Golan Heights.

In the view of the Reagan administration, Israel's invasion of Lebanon in June 1982 exceeded the strategic exigency of ending the Palestinian Liberation Organization (PLO) threat to Israel's northern region. The Septem-

A Moment of Hope. President Bill Clinton brings together Prime Minister Yitzhak Rabin *(left)* and Palestinian leader Yasir Arafat after the signing of the historic—but not lasting—framework for peace, commonly called the Oslo Accords, in Washington, D.C., 13 September 1993. REUTERS/GARY HERSHORN/GETTY IMAGES

ber 1982 Reagan Plan called for a halt to Israeli settlement of the occupied territories and opposed the extension of Israeli sovereignty. The administration referred to Palestinian self-determination in federation with Jordan, but its concern for the Palestinian people pointed out Washington's consistent disagreement with Israeli policies oriented toward any solution other than that of land-for-peace.

Such discord notwithstanding, by the mid-1980s the United States and Israel had achieved a high level of cooperation on strategic issues that included the reinstatement of the November 1981 memorandum. Israel became the only non-NATO country to contribute to the U.S. Strategic Defense Initiative, and cooperation increased despite the Pollard affair (espionage by a U.S. citizen who passed documents to Israeli handlers) and the U.S.-PLO dialogue. The U.S.-Israeli strategic consensus encompassed both governments' views of most major global and regional matters.

Following the U.S.-led war against Saddam Hussein's Iraq in 1991, the Bush administration considered the time propitious for a Middle East peace initiative and viewed the policies of Israel's Likud-led government under Yitzhak Shamir the major obstacle to an accord. Israeli leaders took exception to U.S. relegation of their country to a passive role during the Gulf War. They also resented the Bush administration's suspension of a $10 billion guarantee of loans for Israel's absorption of immigrants as a means to pressure the Shamir government to participate in the peace conference at Madrid. In truth, despite tension between that administration and the Shamir government, the bilateral relationship was by then based on a long-term U.S. commitment and twenty years of close strategic ties, and during this period, the United States signed (in 1989 and 1992) additional strategic memoranda with Israel.

1993–2002: From Success at Oslo to Renewed Arab-Israeli Strife

U.S.-Israeli relations reached their highest point during the presidency of Bill Clinton and the prime ministership of the Labor Party's Yitzhak Rabin. The 1993 Israeli-Palestinian Declaration of Principles and an Israeli-Jordanian peace treaty the following year heightened both the perception and substance of an Israeli regional role that accorded well with the interests of the United States during the post–Cold War period. The Clinton administration placed the greater onus for lack of further progress toward peace during the years 1996–1999 upon Prime Minister Binyamin Netanyahu of the Likud. In 1999, Ehud Barak led Israel's Labor Party back into a two-year period of leadership. Although Barak allowed the expansion of settlements in the territories, his willingness to consider a complete withdrawal from the Golan Heights for peace with Syria, the removal in 2000 of Israeli forces from southern Lebanon, and the far-reaching concessions he offered the Palestinians at a Camp David summit that year earned him the Clinton administration's enthusiastic support.

The administration of George W. Bush inherited a regional configuration that included ongoing U.S. hostility to Iraq's Saddam Hussein, concern for the stability of conservative Arab regimes, the view that Syria had rejected Israeli overtures, and the conviction that Palestinian Authority leader Yasir Arafat bore responsibility for the failure of the 2000 Camp David summit. The United States wished to restart negotiations based on a land-for-peace formula that would include a dismantling of Israeli settlements beyond the 1967 border. Yet, no sharp deterioration in U.S.-Israeli relations attended the 2002 invasion of West Bank towns by an Israeli government under hardliner Ariel Sharon. The Palestinians' extensive use of terror in 2001 and 2002, including frequent suicide bombings, both deepened U.S.-Israeli cooperation and heightened the perception among the American public that, in the wake of the 11 September 2001 attacks in the United States, the two countries have a very great deal in common.

BIBLIOGRAPHY

Bar-Siman-Tov, Yaacov. "The United States and Israel since 1948: A 'Special Relationship?'" *Diplomatic History* 22, no. 2 (1998): 231–262.

Ben-Zvi, Abraham. *Decade of Transition: Eisenhower, Kennedy, and the Origins of the American-Israeli Alliance.* New York: Columbia University Press, 1998.

Bialer, Uri. *Between East and West: Israel's Foreign Policy Orientation, 1948–1956.* Cambridge, U.K.: Cambridge University Press, 1990.

Levey, Zach. *Israel and the Western Powers, 1952–1960.* Chapel Hill: University of North Carolina Press, 1997.

Organski, A. F. K. *The $36 Billion Bargain: Strategy and Politics in U.S. Assistance to Israel.* New York: Columbia University Press, 1990.

Safran, Nadav. *Israel: The Embattled Ally.* Cambridge, Mass.: Belknap Press, 1981.

Schoenbaum, David. *The United States and the State of Israel.* New York: Oxford University Press, 1993.

Spiegel, Steven. *The Other Arab-Israeli Conflict: Making America's Middle East Policy, from Truman to Reagan.* Chicago: University of Chicago Press, 1985.

Zach Levey

See also **Arab Nations, Relations with; Camp David Peace Accords; Cold War; Foreign Aid; Foreign Policy; Israel-Palestine Peace Accord; Treaties with Foreign Nations.**

ISRAELI-PALESTINIAN PEACE ACCORD. In 1993, the government of the state of Israel and the Palestine Liberation Organization (PLO) began a series of secret discussions on relations between the two groups called the Oslo Accords in hopes of resolving the deep-seated tensions between them. The conflict between the Palestinian residents of the Israeli-occupied West Bank and Gaza Strip began with the Intifada, a Palestinian uprising in 1987, and revolve around the Palestinian desire for independence from Israeli control and Israel's constant threat of violence from her Arab neighbors. However, conflict between Israel and its Arab neighbors existed before the declaration of the state of Israel in 1948 and manifested itself in five wars between Israel and her Arab neighbors between 1948 and 1987, when the Palestinian uprising began. Many of the Palestinians living in the West Bank and Gaza Strip are persons displaced during the 1948 and 1967 wars when Israel gained control of these areas.

The January 1993 conversations, which focused on water rights, refugees, security matters, and other topics, were held in Oslo, Norway, under the cover of a conference hosted by Fafo, a Norwegian social research institute. The meetings were secret, and Johan Jorgen Holst, the Norwegian Foreign Minister, aided the two groups in the negotiations and acted as an intermediary. After eleven rounds of talks in the summer of 1993, the Israelis and Palestinians reached a provisional agreement on partial autonomy in the occupied territories. This so-called "Declaration of Principles on Interim Self-Government Arrangements" (DOP) was not a regular peace treaty. It was an agreement that set out specific steps to reach a permanent solution to the conflict and established a five-year timetable over which to complete them.

The accords reached at Oslo set forth a process by which Israel would transfer portions of the West Bank and Gaza Strip to the control of a new body, the Palestinian Authority, which would be elected by the Palestinian people. The authority would guarantee Israel's security by fighting terrorism. This would enable the parties to build enough trust and confidence to proceed with negotiations on the "final status" that was to occur in 1999. Many of the most controversial issues between the two sides, including the future of Jerusalem, were left for the final status talks. The accord set up a joint Israeli-Palestinian economic cooperation committee to carry out economic development programs in the West Bank and Gaza, critical to the success of Palestinian autonomy.

On 13 September 1993, the DOP was formally signed. United States President Bill Clinton hosted the official signing ceremony. Israeli Foreign Minister Shimon Peres and PLO official Abou Abbas signed the accords, granting self-government to Palestinians in the Israeli-occupied Gaza Strip and West Bank, while Prime Minister Yitzhak Rabin and PLO Chairman Yasir Arafat shook hands, a historic gesture. Clinton's statement that "Today marks a shining moment of hope for the people of the Middle East; indeed, of the entire world" captured the monumental nature of the event.

In September 1995, the Oslo Accords were followed up with an interim agreement (Oslo II), which expanded Palestinian self-rule by the withdrawal of the Israeli military from six large West Bank cities. The Israeli Army was replaced by Palestinian police forces, and elections for a Palestinian Counsel were held in 1996, during which Yasir Arafat was elected.

While the Oslo Accord was a great step toward peace in the region, many groups on both sides were opposed to its implementation. In February 1994, an Israeli settler, Baruch Goldstein, killed twenty-nine Palestinians at a mosque in the West Bank town of Hebron. In November 1995, a right-wing Israeli named Yigal Amir assassinated Prime Minister Rabin. In February and March 1996, the Islamic fundamentalist movement Hamas, which had gained support after the signing of the Oslo Accords, conducted a series of suicide bombings in Israel that killed fifty-seven Israelis. This prompted Shimon Peres, the acting prime minister, to break off the peace talks.

As a result of the violent backlash against the peace accords, Peres was defeated by Benjamin Netanyahu, a hard-line right-winger. In his bid to be prime minister, Netanyahu put up many obstacles to the peace process, including lifting a four-year ban on building new Jewish settlements in the West Bank. He did, however, in January 1997, turn over 80 percent of the town of Hebron to Palestinian control as called for in the accord. This was the last transfer of land by the Israelis until October 1998, when the United States pushed Israel to turn over additional land, as part of the Wye River Accord. The 1999 deadline for final status talks passed without any sort of discussions, and the conflict in the area has worsened.

BIBLIOGRAPHY

Ellis, Marc H. *Israel and Palestine: Out of the Ashes.* Sterling, Va.: Pluto Press, 2002.

Finkelstein, Norman G. *Image and Reality of the Israel-Palestine Conflict.* New York: Verso, 1995.

Freedman, Robert Owen, ed. *The Middle East and the Peace Process: The Impact of the Oslo Accords.* Gainesville: University Press of Florida, 1998.

Gerner, Deborah J. *One Land, Two Peoples: The Conflict over Palestine.* Boulder, Colo.: Westview Press, 1994.

Pappé, Ilan, ed. *The Israel/Palestine Question.* New York: Routledge, 1999.

Shira M. Diner

See also **Arab Nations, Relations with; Israel, Relations with.**

ITALIAN AMERICANS. Italian influence on American history can be traced back to the navigators Christopher Columbus and Amerigo Vespucci. America's founding fathers, especially Thomas Jefferson and Benjamin Franklin, were familiar with the Italian language and culture and with Roman history. Jefferson was a supporter of the Italian physician and merchant Filippo Mazzei and encouraged him in the early 1770s to bring Italian vintners to Virginia. Though not successful in that venture, Mazzei became actively involved in the colonists' struggle with England. Writing in the Virginia newspapers as "Furioso" he was one of the first people to urge Americans to declare independence and form a unified constitution to govern all thirteen colonies. Some of his phraseology later found its way into Jefferson's Declaration of Independence. William Paca, an early governor of Maryland, was one of the signers of the Declaration of Independence.

Italian Americans in the Eighteenth and Nineteenth Centuries

During the eighteenth and nineteenth centuries a number of Italian-named missionaries such as Friar Eusebio Kino and Friar Samuel Mazzuchelli operated in present-day Arizona and in the Wisconsin-Michigan area, respectively. Though the presence of Italian individuals in the United States was sparse before 1850, Lorenzo Da Ponte, who wrote librettos for Mozart, taught Italian language and literature at Columbia University. In 1825 he produced his *Don Giovanni* in New York.

Italian style and Italian artisans heavily influenced the design of buildings in Washington, D.C. Constantino Brumidi painted numerous frescoes in the Capitol between 1855 and 1880. There was a modest migration of Italians to California during and after the gold rush. Many in this group became prosperous farmers, vintners, and business leaders, including Domenico Ghirardelli (the chocolate maker), the Gallo and Mondavi families (wine producers), and Amadeo Giannini (the founder of Bank of America).

Though New York City had an Italian colony in the 1850s, Italians did not have serious impact until the mass migration of the 1880s. Italian unification in the 1860s failed to bring economic prosperity and in many places in the South the new government policies intensified *la miseria* (poverty). Moreover, basic advances in medicine in this period lowered the death rate and swelled the population. This led to massive migration of *contadini* (peasants), first to Latin America and then, in the 1880s, to the United States.

Most early Italian migrants were young men who originally intended to work for a season or two on the railroads or in the mines. Living frugally, they could save most of their meager wages and send remittances back to their mothers and wives. In the period from 1880 to 1920 about $750 million was sent to Italy. The impact of these remittances, the monetary investments of returning Italian Americans (*rimpatriati*), or the practical knowledge Italian Americans transferred back to Italy is impossible to calculate precisely. Yet it is clear that Italian migration to the United States was a two-way street. Migrations were not unique, one-time events, but rather represented a continuous relationship sometimes lasting over a century.

Estimates of the number of Italian immigrants are made murky by repeated crossings by the same individual, the undocumented entry of untold thousands, and inconsistencies in the spelling of names. About 4.5 million Italians made the trip to the United States and readily found work as unskilled laborers in the burgeoning industrial American economy. America needed the immigrants as much as the immigrants needed America. Between 1900 and 1910, 2 million Italians emigrated. The numbers peaked in 1907 at 285,000, in 1914 at 284,000, and in 1921 at 222,000. After 1900 Italian immigrants began in earnest to bring their families from Italy and Italian neighborhoods in large cities began to have more stability. In this "chain migration," *paesani* (townspeople) from a particular town in Italy transferred (over varying time periods) to specific neighborhoods and suburbs in the United States. In this manner, they created a near-replica of their hometown, adhering more or less to the social customs, dialect, and family patterns of Italy, even while beginning their journey to Americanization.

Italians brought with them an agrarian, Catholic, and family-based culture. Hard work and self-sufficiency were facts of life. Of all the social institutions in Italian society, the family was the only one that could be relied on consistently. In this sense, it was ironic that the early immigrants had to leave their families in order to save their families. The immigrants founded *Società di Mutuo Soccorso* (Mutual Benefit Societies) that often hired a physician on retainer and that provided modest benefits to survivors in case of death.

Italian immigrants were ambivalent toward the Catholic Church. On the one hand, they were all baptized Catholics, they believed in the saints, and were devoted to the Blessed Virgin Mary; on the other hand, the Church was a large landholder, deeply involved in Italian politics in coalition with the upper classes, and opposed to unification. In contrast to Irish and Polish immigrants whose national identity was championed by the Church, Italian nationalists saw the Church as an enemy. The immigrants brought with them a certain anticlericalism, a casual attitude toward strict rules, and a devotion to folk practices including a belief in *mal occhio* (the evil eye). The establishment by Bishop Giovanni Battista Scalabrini of the Missionaries of St. Charles Borromeo in the 1890s was the first concentrated effort by the Catholic Church to minister to the needs of migrants. Over the century that followed, the order built and staffed hundreds of churches, schools, and hospitals in the United States, Canada, Latin America, and Australia. Among the disciples of Scalabrini was St. Frances (Mother) Cabrini.

The first Italian newspaper in the United States was New York's *L'Eco D'Italia* in 1849. Dozens of Italian American socialist, anarchist, religious, fascist, antifascist, unionist, and literary magazines have been published since then. *Il Progresso Italo-Americano* (New York, 1880–1989) was the most continuous mirror of Italian American history. Since its daily circulation was above 100,000, Generoso Pope, its editor during the 1930s and 1940s, was perhaps the most influential Italian leader of his time.

There was virtually no migration during World War I. General racism, the red scare, the anarchist bombings of 1919–1920, and pressure from organized labor led to the harsh immigration quotas of the Johnson-Reed Act of 1924. This law reduced the allowable number of Italian immigrants from over 200,000 to 6,000. Several events—America's harsh immigration policy, the policies of the Italian dictator Benito Mussolini that sought to keep Italians in Italy, the Great Depression of the 1930s, and World War II—kept Italian migration numbers very low between 1924 and the end of World War II.

By the end of the 1930s the number of American born surpassed the number of emigrants in the Italian American population. Although Mussolini's regime had been popular among both the elite and the general American public, the socialists and other Italian American elements waged a spirited but unsuccessful campaign to undermine immigrant support for Mussolini. When Italy joined the Axis, and when the war began, public opinion shifted drastically. In 1942, especially on the West Coast, suspected Italian Fascist sympathizers and fishermen were arrested and harassed. Though the scale of this maltreatment in no way compares to the incarceration of Japanese Americans, it became a sore point for modern-day Italian American activists.

The age cohort for the second generation of Italian Americans coincided closely with the age group most suitable for military service. More than 1 million Italian American males in their late teens and twenties served in the U.S. armed services in World War II. For many, it was their first experience beyond their own neighborhood. All of them were "Americanized" to one degree or another by the military and most of them subsequently benefited from military training and the educational/home-loan benefits of the GI Bill. All of these forces worked to draw young people away from the old neighborhood, its culture, and the Italian language.

In World War II Italy experienced defeat abroad, the fall of the Fascist government, occupation by Germans, invasion by American forces, and what amounted to a civil war in many parts of the Italian peninsula. The devastation and poverty of the postwar period triggered another wave of migration out of Italy to Canada, Latin America, Australia, and the United States. Various provisions for refugees and for the relatives of Italian immigrants who had acquired claims to U.S. citizenship allowed for considerable migration that reunited families and continued the chain migration into the 1970s. The Marshall Plan helped create the Italian "economic miracle" of the 1960s and by the early 1990s the Italian Gross National Product surpassed that of England. These developments, the attainment in Italy of zero population growth, and the progress of the European Union, virtually ended outmigration of Italians.

Italian American Grocery. Many Italian immigrants settled in New York City, where dozens of small Italian neighborhoods sprung up. New immigrants tried to settle in the same areas as their fellow townspeople, creating virtual replicas of Italian villages in the middle of the city. Italian American culture stressed hard work and family life, and it is likely that the Italian American grocery pictured here was a family-owned operation. Library of Congress

Twentieth-Century Trends

The social mobility of Italian Americans was steady throughout the twentieth century. In the early years group members were likely to be the object of social work in settlement houses like Jane Addams's Hull-House. They were likely to be victimized by sharp politicians and labor agents. The 1920s were prosperous times for most Americans and many Italian American colonies received infusions of capital derived from the near-universal practice of breaking Prohibition laws. Hard hit by the Great Depression, Italian Americans reacted by becoming part of Franklin D. Roosevelt's Democratic coalition. The full employment of the war years and general prosperity of the 1950s and 1960s brought the vast majority of Italian Americans safely into the middle class. More precisely, a strategy of underconsumption, the pooling of extended family resources, hard work in small family businesses, and entry into unionized skilled and unskilled jobs earned middle-class status for the vast majority of Italian Americans. By the mid-1970s Italian American young people were attending college at the national average.

The public image of Italian immigrants has been a continuing source of conflict. Salvatore LaGumina's *Wop: A Documentary History of Anti-Italian Discrimination in the United States* (1973) enumerates and quotes a vicious race prejudice against Italian workers in the articles and editorial cartoons of the nation's finest magazines. Into the 1920s, social science professionals fabricated an elaborate pecking order that established the superiority and inferiority of the races and nationalities of the world. Italians turned up near the bottom. The fact that the earliest Italian neighborhoods were overcrowded, crime-ridden, and dominated by *padroni* (often unscrupulous labor agents) intensified the negative image. Sensational newspaper stories of cases of blackmail and vendettas among Italian immigrants gave rise to the mafia myth that has dogged Italian ethnics in the United States since the late nineteenth century.

This climate of public opinion played a role in the 1891 lynching in New Orleans of eleven Italians. There were more victims in this incident than in any other single lynching in U.S. history. The controversial execution in 1927 of anarchists Nicolo Sacco and Bartolomeo Vanzetti for a murder-robbery in Braintree, Massachusetts, in 1920 haunted the headlines for over seven years. The flamboyance and style of Italian American bootleggers during Prohibition overshadowed the image of all other gangsters in that period and has since become the baseline stereotype of Italian Americans. The thousands of books and media productions on the subject of Italian gangsters include some of the best and some of the worst artistic expression in American culture. But whatever the quality of the art, in the eyes of the Italian American leadership the result was the same: the intensification in the public's mind of a negative image of Italians Americans.

In the world of pop culture, some of America's universally admired entertainers and sports figures were Italian: Frank Sinatra, Dean Martin, Liberace, Jimmy Durante, Joe DiMaggio, and Vince Lombardi. Sports celebrities Tommy Lasorda and Lawrence "Yogi" Berra were Italian. Moreover, the image of Italians as leaders in entertainment (consider Madonna), fashion (Donatella Versace), and cuisine was strong in the twenty-first century.

Statistics vary widely when discussing ethnicity in the third, fourth, and fifth generations. Many Americans can claim four or five ethnicities. Surnames can be confusing when there are married couples that change or hyphenate their last names. Ethnic organizations often exaggerate their numbers to further a specific agenda. And the statistical formatting of the U.S. Census makes it hard to discern exactly how many Italian Americans there are in the United States. The 2000 census estimated about 16 million Americans (or 6 percent of the total U.S. population) are of Italian ancestry.

The most heavily Italian American states are New Jersey (1.5 million, 18.5 percent), Connecticut (653,000, 19.8 percent), and Rhode Island (202,735, about 20 percent). The Italian American population of New York is about 2.7 million, or 14.8 percent; Pennsylvania, 1.4 million or 13 percent; Nevada, 142,658 or 7.3 percent; California, 1.4 million or 4.3 percent; and Massachusetts, 890,000 or 14.5 percent. Other states with significant Italian American populations are Illinois (706,000, 5.8 percent), Florida (1 million, 6.5 percent), Ohio (713,015, 6.7 percent), and Louisiana (360,333, 5.2 percent).

This ethnic concentration during the twentieth century resulted in the election of Italian American political leaders, including Fiorello LaGuardia, the mayor of New York City in the 1930s and 1940s; John O. Pastore of Rhode Island, the nation's first Italian American in the U.S. Senate; Mario Cuomo, governor of New York in the 1980s; Geraldine Ferraro, a New York congresswoman and Democratic nominee for vice president in 1984; Alphonse D'Amato, a U.S. senator from New York; Ella Grasso, the first woman to serve as governor of Connecticut; and Rudolph Giuliani, the mayor of New York City in the 1990s.

Contemporary Italian Americans rarely vote as a bloc. Their politics seem to be based on social class and income rather than ethnicity. There appear to be few overriding ethnic-based issues as there might be for African American or Jewish voters. Moreover, in many places on the East Coast, Italian-named candidates from diverse parties and philosophical camps often run against each other.

BIBLIOGRAPHY

Alba, Richard D. *Italian Americans: Into the Twilight of Ethnicity.* Englewood Cliffs, N.J.: Prentice-Hall, 1985.

Alfonsi, Ferdinando, ed. *Poeti Italo-Americani: Italo-American Poets, a Bilingual Anthology.* Catanzaro, Italy: A. Carello, 1985.

American Italian Historical Association. *Proceedings of Annual Conferences.* New York: Author, 1970. 33 vols. Contains some 500 articles on all aspects of Italian American life. Available from http://www.moblito.com/aiha.

Barolini, Helen, ed. *The Dream Book: An Anthology of Writings by Italian-American Women.* 2d ed. Syracuse, N.Y.: Syracuse University Press, 2000.

Italian American Review: A Social Science Journal of the Italian American Experience. New York: John Calandra Institute, Queens College.

Italian Americana: A Cultural and Historical Review. Kingston: University of Rhode Island.

LaGumina, Salvatore. *Wop: A Documentary History of Anti-Italian Discrimination in the United States.* 2d ed. Toronto and Buffalo, N.Y.: Guernica, 1999. The original edition was published in 1973.

LaGumina, Salvatore, et al. *The Italian American Experience: An Encyclopedia.* New York: Garland, 2000.

Mangione, Jerre, and Ben Morreale. *La Storia: Five Centuries of the Italian American Experience.* New York: HarperCollins, 1992.

Tamburri, Anthony J., Paolo A. Giordano, and Fred L. Gardaphé, eds. *From the Margin: Writings in Italian Americana.* 2d ed. West Lafayette, Ind.: Purdue University Press, 2000. Anthology of contemporary Italian American poets, writers, and critics.

Tusiani, Joseph. *Ethnicity: Selected Poems.* Edited with two essays by Paolo Giordano. Lafayette, Ind.: Bordighera, 2000. Accessible poems that focus on the full spectrum of Italian American history and culture. Includes commentary by the editor.

VIA: Voices in Italian Americana, A Literary and Cultural Review. Lafayette, Ind.: Bordighera. Since 1990 has published cutting-edge poetry, short stories, nonfiction, interviews, and literary criticism.

Dominic Candeloro

See also **Italy, Relations with.**

ITALY, RELATIONS WITH. United States relations with Italy began when Italy became a nation-state in 1861.

Soon after independence Italian immigrants, especially from the poor southern region of the country, began coming to the United States, Canada, Australia, South America, and other countries. These immigrants, in addition to seeking relief from poverty, sought freedom from political oppression. From 1876 to 1976, the United States received more Italian nationals than any other country; Census figures show 484,027 Italians in residence in 1900. That number continued to increase until Congress passed laws restricting immigration from Italy.

U.S. relations with Italy's parliamentary monarchy were cordial; problems arose in 1922, however, when Benito Mussolini came to power and ended parliamentary government. Mussolini, a fascist, found the poor economic conditions that followed World War I (Italy was

Relations with Italy. President Richard M. Nixon *(right)* meets with Premier Giulio Andreotti, head of a center-right coalition elected in 1972. That government fell in 1973, a year before Nixon himself resigned, and Andreotti's return to power twice more was followed by charges of corruption and other crimes (ending in his acquittal). LIBRARY OF CONGRESS

allied with the United States) fertile soil for establishing a dictatorship. He opposed the communists who had become influential in the unions and claimed to favor a type of National Socialism that would benefit all Italians.

Mussolini had many defenders in the United States, including a number of Italian Americans. Praised for getting the railroads to run to schedule and for his early opposition to Adolf Hitler, Mussolini began to lose favor in the United States when he attacked Ethiopia in 1935 and began to draw closer to Hitler. In 1936, Italy and Germany formed the Rome-Berlin Axis to oppose France. In 1939, Italy invaded Albania and solidified its links with Germany, links that had first been forged with their cooperation during the Spanish Civil War (1936–1939).

Remaining neutral until it seemed German victory was inevitable, Italy declared war on France in 1940. As World War II raged on, many Italians became American sympathizers and fought for the Allies as guerillas. In 1943, Italy declared war on Germany and armed conflict broke out within Italy between Italians loyal to the Allies and those loyal to the German Nazis.

After World War II, the United States helped establish a republic in Italy. When Italy seemed likely to elect a communist government, the United States increased MARSHALL PLAN aid and encouraged Italian Americans to engage in a letter writing campaign urging their friends and relatives in Italy to vote for a non-Communist government.

Italy joined a number of U.S.-sponsored initiatives and was a charter member of the NORTH ATLANTIC TREATY ORGANIZATION (NATO), founded in 1949; it was also a charter member of the European Economic Community (EEC), formed in 1957. Italy has strongly supported other European initiatives for cooperation and unification, including the European Monetary Union in 1999. The United States was the only country to promise military support of Italy immediately after World War II. Ties between Italy and the United States have remained close and political cooperation has been a constant.

BIBLIOGRAPHY

Albrecht-Carrié, René. *Italy from Napoleon to Mussolini.* New York: Columbia University Press, 1950.

Barzini, Luigi. *The Italians.* New York: Athenaeum, 1964.

Berner, Wolfgang. "The Italian Left, 1944–1978: Patterns of Cooperation, Conflict, and Compromise." In *The European Left: Italy, France, and Spain,* edited by William E. Griffith. Lexington, Mass.: Lexington Books, 1979.

Keefe, Eugene K., et al. *Area Handbook for Italy.* Washington, D.C.: Government Printing Office, 1977.

Kogan, Norma. *A Political History of Italy: The Postwar Years.* New York: Praeger, 1983.

Frank A. Salamone

ITT AFFAIR, (1971–1972) involved allegations that the Justice Department settled an antitrust suit against International Telephone and Telegraph Corporation (ITT) in return for a $400,000 donation to help pay for holding the Republican National Convention in San Diego in 1972. Newspaper columnist Jack Anderson broke the story on 29 February 1972, by publishing ITT lobbyist Dita Beard's 25 June 1971, memo admitting a quid pro quo. Beard claimed forgery, and the Richard M. Nixon administration pressured the Federal Bureau of Investigation to agree. But the FBI refused. In June 1973, the Watergate special prosecutor created an ITT task force to determine whether Attorney General Richard Kleindienst had committed perjury at his 1972 Senate Judiciary Committee confirmation hearings when he denied there had been White House pressure to drop the antitrust action. He pled guilty to a misdemeanor count, receiving a one-month prison sentence (later suspended) and a $100 fine. California Lieutenant Governor Ed Reinecke was also convicted for testifying falsely before the Senate regarding discussions with Kleindienst's predecessor as attorney general, John Mitchell. That conviction was overturned because the Senate lacked a quorum during his testimony. San Diego lost the convention to Miami.

BIBLIOGRAPHY

ITT Task Force. Record Group 460.9. *Records of the Watergate Special Prosecution Force, 1971–1977.* Washington, D.C.: National Archives and Records Service.

Sampson, Anthony. *The Foreign State of ITT.* New York: Stein and Day, 1973.

Kenneth O'Reilly

IVY LEAGUE was coined in 1937 by a newspaper columnist to describe football competition at ivy-covered northeastern universities. The term came to identify eight prestigious private American universities that admit less than 20 percent of their applicants and require an academically rigorous curriculum. Their alumni often enter highly influential and lucrative careers. Once overwhelmingly male, white, and Protestant, they now enroll a diverse student body by recruiting cultural, ethnic, racial, and religious minorities. Seven of the eight were established as colonial colleges: Harvard, Congregational, was established at Cambridge, Massachusetts in 1636; Yale, Congregational, was established in 1701 and relocated to New Haven in 1715; the College of New Jersey, Presbyterian, was established in 1746 and renamed Princeton University in 1896; Franklin's Academy in Philadelphia, nonsectarian, was established in 1749, chartered in 1754, and renamed the University of Pennsylvania in 1791; King's College, nonsectarian but Anglican-controlled, was established in New York City in 1754 and renamed Columbia College in 1784; Rhode Island College, Baptist, was established at Providence in 1764 and renamed Brown University in 1804; and Dartmouth College, Congregational, was established in 1769 and relocated to Hanover, New Hampshire, in 1770. The eighth, Cornell University, chartered in 1865 at Ithaca by the New York legislature, was endowed with federal land grants and by Ezra Cornell. Strong presidents and outstanding faculty transformed the institutions into national universities. Charles William Eliot (Harvard); James Rowland Angell (Yale); Nicholas Murray Butler (Columbia); Woodrow Wilson (Princeton); and Andrew Dickson White (Cornell).

The first Ivy Group Agreement on football in 1945 committed the eight universities to similar academic standards, eligibility rules, and need-based financial aid practices with no athletic scholarships. The Ivy League was officially founded in February 1954 by extending that agreement to all sports. Between 1956, the year of the first round-robin schedule in football, and 1995, Dartmouth won the most Ivy League championships, eight, and tied for another eight. In May 1974, five years after Princeton and Yale admitted women undergraduates, the Ivy Group inaugurated league championship competitions in women's sports.

BIBLIOGRAPHY

Bernstein, Mark F. *Football: The Ivy League Origins of an American Obsession.* Philadelphia: University of Pennsylvania Press, 2001.

Birmingham, Frederic Alexander. *The Ivy League Today.* New York: Thomas Y. Crowell, 1961.

Goldstein, Richard. *Ivy League Autumns: An Illustrated History of College Football's Grand Old Rivalries.* New York: St Martin's Press, 1996.

Lillard, Dean, and Jennifer Gerner. "Getting to the Ivy League: How Family Composition Affects College Choice." *Journal of Higher Education* 70, no. 6 (November–December 1999): 706–730.

McCallum, John. *Ivy League Football Since 1872.* New York: Stein and Day, 1977.

Iwo Jima. Under heavy fire, the Fifth Marine Division slowly advances from Red Beach One toward Mount Suribachi at the southern end of the small island. NATIONAL ARCHIVES AND RECORDS ADMINISTRATION

www.IvyLeagueSports.com, official Web site for Ivy League athletics.

Marcia G. Synnott

See also **Brown University; Columbia University; Cornell University; Dartmouth College; Harvard University; Princeton University; University of Pennsylvania; Yale University.**

IWO JIMA (16 February–17 March 1945). The capture of the Japanese island of Iwo Jima in World War II by three U.S. Marine divisions supported by more than 800 warships and landing craft has been described as the classic amphibious assault of World War II. One of the Volcano Islands 750 miles south of Tokyo, Iwo Jima could give Japan two hours' warning of U.S. B-29 raids from the Mariana Islands and provided a fighter base for the harassment of U.S. bombers. To reverse this situation and afford a haven for crippled American aircraft, the Joint Chiefs of Staff directed that Iwo Jima be seized.

The eight-square-mile island is dominated at one end by Mount Suribachi (556 feet). The island's defenses—the most elaborate, dense, and best integrated in the Pacific—included three airfields; more than 730 major installations with 120 guns larger than 75 mm; 220 large mortars, howitzers, and rocket launchers; and 10 miles of underground tunnels linking hundreds of bunkers and blockhouses. One of Japan's most able generals, Lieutenant General Tadamichi Kuribayashi, with 21,000 troops, defended Iwo Jima. The overall commander of the marines was Lieutenant General H. M. Smith, supported by Admiral R. K. Turner. The 82,000-man landing force (Third, Fourth, and Fifth Marine Divisions) was under the command of Lieutenant General H. Schmidt.

Following three days of bombardment from six battleships and five cruisers, the marines landed on 19 February under cover of the heaviest prelanding bombardment of the war—more than 6,000 tons of shells and bombs pounded the island before noon. Because of the massive preparation, beach casualties were moderate. However, capture of the remainder of the island required the most bitter battle of the Pacific, in which—amid black volcanic sands, grotesque crags, and steaming sulfur pits—gains were counted in yards. Heavy casualties were inflicted by both sides. Seizure of Mount Suribachi (23 February) by the Twenty-eighth Marine Division gave attackers the dominant terrain, from which a ten-day struggle ensued to overrun the fire-swept airfields and capture ridges, buttes, and deep caves in which Kuribayashi made his last desperate stand. Although Iwo Jima was officially declared secured on 17 March, resistance was not extinguished until nine days later.

The battle cost the United States 4,590 lives and wounded 24,096; more than 20,000 Japanese were killed and 1,083 captured. By the end of the war, 2,251 B-29 aircraft carrying 24,761 airmen had made safe emergency landings on Iwo Jima.

BIBLIOGRAPHY
Bartley, W. S. *Iwo Jima: Amphibious Epic.* Washington, D.C.: U.S. Marine Corps, 1954.

Isely, Jeter A., and Philip A. Crowl. *The U.S. Marines and Amphibious War, Its Theory, and Its Practice in the Pacific.* Princeton, N.J.: Princeton University Press, 1951.

Marling, Karal A. *Iwo Jima: Monuments, Memories, and the American Hero.* Cambridge, Mass.: Harvard University Press, 1991.

Newcomb, Richard F. *Iwo Jima.* New York: Holt, Rinehart and Winston, 1965.

Robert Debs Heinl Jr. / A. R.

See also **Task Force 58; Underwater Demolition Teams; World War II, Air War against Japan; World War II, Navy in.**

JACKSONIAN DEMOCRACY. The phrase "Jacksonian Democracy" has a dual and ambiguous meaning. In its narrower sense, it denotes both the political party organized under Andrew Jackson, which called itself the American Democracy, and the program espoused by that party. The broader connotation, taking its cue from Alexis de Tocqueville's classic *Democracy in America* (1835), suggests an ethos and an era: the flowering of the democratic spirit in American life around the time of Jackson's presidency. Tocqueville toured the United States in 1831–1832, and found there "the image of democracy itself, with its inclinations, its character, its prejudices, and its passions." To Tocqueville and other commentators, both favorable and critical, the United States represented the democratic, egalitarian future, Europe the aristocratic past. Andrew Jackson's partisans (and some sympathetic historians) appropriated this broader meaning to themselves, counterposing the Democratic Party's democracy to the opposing Whig Party's "aristocracy." But this identification should not be accepted uncritically.

The Jacksonian Democratic Party

The Democratic Party and its program emerged in stages out of the largely personal following that elected Andrew Jackson president in 1828. The core issues through which the party defined its membership and philosophy concerned economic policy. As fully developed by the end of the 1830s, the Democratic outlook was essentially laissez-faire. Deeming themselves preservers of the Jeffersonian legacy, Democrats demanded simple, frugal, and unintrusive government. They opposed protective tariffs along with federal (and often state) bank charters and internal improvement projects. As president, Jackson articulated this policy through a series of vetoes, most notably the Maysville Road in 1830 and the Bank of the United States in 1832. In official messages, he cast himself as protector of "the humbler members of society—the farmers, mechanics, and laborers" against moneyed, privileged interests seeking to turn the public powers of government to unfair private advantage. In Jackson's reading, tariffs, public works, and corporate charters (especially of banks, whose right of note issue gave them tremendous leverage over credit and the currency) were all devices to siphon wealth from the poor to the rich and to steal power from the many to benefit the few.

Again following Jeffersonian tradition, the Democratic Party embraced anticlericalism and rigorous separation of church and state. Democrats resisted the hegemonizing impulses of the nation's powerful interdenominational (but primarily Presbyterian-Congregational) benevolent and philanthropic associations, and they denounced the intrusion into politics of religious crusades such as Sabbatarianism, temperance, and abolitionism. Democrats thus garnered adherents among religious dissenters and minorities, from Catholics to freethinkers.

Under Jackson and his adviser and successor Martin Van Buren, Democrats pioneered in techniques of party organization and discipline, which they justified as a means of securing the people's ascendancy over the aristocrats. To nominate candidates and adopt platforms, Democrats perfected a pyramidal structure of local, state, and national party conventions, caucuses, and committees. These ensured coordinated action and supposedly reflected opinion at the grass roots, though their movements in fact were often directed from Washington. Jackson practiced "rotation in office"—the periodic replacement of government officials, often on partisan criteria—and defended it as offering the chance for employment to all citizens alike and thus forestalling the creation of an officeholding elite. His followers frankly employed the spoils of office as rewards for party workers.

Jackson and the Democrats cast their party as the embodiment of the popular will, the defender of the common man against the Whig "aristocracy." The substance behind this claim is still hotly disputed. After the War of 1812, constitutional changes in the states had broadened the participatory base of politics by easing property requirements for suffrage and making state offices and presidential electors popularly elective. By 1828, when Jackson was first elected president, nearly all white men could vote, and the vote had gained in power. Jackson and his partisans benefited from and capitalized upon these changes, but they in no sense initiated them.

The presence of a class component in Jacksonian parties, setting Democratic plain farmers and workers against the Whig bourgeoisie or business elite, has been often asserted and as often denied. Some historians read Democratic paeans to the plain people as a literal description of their constituency. Others dismiss them as artful pro-

General Jackson Slaying the Many Headed Monster. This 1836 lithograph by Henry R. Robinson depicts President Andrew Jackson's long struggle against a new charter for the Bank of the United States, with its many branches; after his reelection in 1832, Jackson shifted federal deposits from the central bank to state banks. LIBRARY OF CONGRESS

paganda. Sophisticated efforts to quantify class divisions in politics through electoral data have yielded uncertain results. While Democrats usually marshaled a slightly larger (and better organized) following than the Whigs, clearly the latter too had a mass popular appeal. Whether Democratic laissez-faire policies actually worked to the benefit of their claimed plebeian constituency has also been questioned.

Looking beyond the white male electorate, many of the Democrats' postures seem profoundly antiegalitarian and antidemocratic, judged not only by a modern standard but against the goals of the burgeoning humanitarian and reform movements of their own day. On the whole, Democrats were more aggressively anti-abolitionist and racist than Whigs, acting to suppress antislavery's intrusion into politics and to curtail the liberties of free blacks. Jackson's original core constituency was southern. At their competitive height in the 1840s, the two parties were nearly evenly matched throughout the country, but in the 1850s, Jacksonian Democracy would return to its sectional roots as the party of slaveholders and their northern sympathizers.

Democrats outdid Whigs in justifying and promoting ethnic, racial, and sexual exclusion and subordination. Democrats championed territorial acquisition and conquest, portraying it in Jeffersonian terms as securing to all (white) citizens the chance for a landed independence. In 1845, a leading Democratic editor coined the phrase "manifest destiny." Andrew Jackson's drive to compel the remaining eastern Indian tribes beyond the Mississippi produced the Indian Removal Act of 1830, a slew of coerced treaties, and the infamous Cherokee Trail of Tears in 1838. The annexation of Texas in 1845 and war against Mexico in 1846–1848 were Democratic initiatives, denounced by many Whigs. Lastly, though no major party advocated female suffrage, Democrats more than Whigs identified politics as a distinctly masculine activity and relegated women to a subordinate, confined sphere.

The Democratic Spirit of the Age

Given this complex picture, no glib generalizations about Jacksonian Democracy's democracy are sustainable. An alternative, suggested by Tocqueville and other contemporary commentators, is to view democracy as the reigning spirit of the age and to trace its workings in all areas of American life, both within and outside party politics. As Tocqueville famously observed, "the people reign in the American political world as the Deity does in the universe. They are the cause and the aim of all things; everything comes from them, and everything is absorbed in them." To Tocqueville, Americans' energetic voluntarism, their enthusiasm for societies, associations, reforms, and crusades, their vibrant institutions of local government, the popular style and leveling spirit of their manners, customs, pastimes, art, literature, science, religion, and intellect, all marked democracy's pervasive reign. From this perspective, the fact that Andrew Jackson—a rough-hewn, poorly educated, self-made frontiersman—could ascend to the presidency spoke more than his policies in office. His rhetorical championship of the plain people against the aristocrats, whatever its substance or sincerity, was itself the sign and harbinger of a social sea change toward democracy, equality, and the primacy of the common man. Jackson stands in this view not as the leader of a party, but as the symbol for an age.

Seen thus, many of the particular phenomena that Andrew Jackson and his party treated with indifference or hostility seem themselves emanations of a broader Jacksonian democratic spirit. Within politics, Whigs as well as Democrats championed the common man and marshaled the masses at barbecues and rallies. Both parties appealed to ordinary voters with riveting stump speeches and by crafting candidates into folk heroes. Whigs answered the popularity of "Old Hickory" Andrew Jackson, hero of the Battle of New Orleans, with figures like "Old Tippecanoe" William Henry Harrison, victor of the rousing "log cabin" presidential campaign of 1840. Close party competition enlivened voter interest, sending turnout rates spiraling upward toward 80 percent of the eligible electorate.

In the religious sphere, evangelical preachers, especially Baptist and Methodist, carried a message of individual empowerment and responsibility, sparking massive revivals and winning thousands of converts. Older, more staid denominations either modified their methods and message to compete in the contest for souls or saw their influence dwindle. Reform crusades from temperance to abolitionism likewise pitched their appeals toward everyman and everywoman, building networks of local affiliates and mounting massive membership and petition drives. Self-help and mutual-aid societies flourished; experiments in popular education proliferated. Poets and philosophers celebrated the egalitarian ethic and the worth of the individual.

All these may be read as evidence of social democratization. Yet some historians emphasize opposing signs of growing stratification, inequality, and repression in these same years. Jackson's own symbolism can be turned many ways: spokesman for the plain people, he was also a wealthy slaveholder and Indian fighter. Scholars will continue to dispute the extent (and definition) of democracy in the era of Jacksonian Democratic ascendancy, along with the social reality underlying politicians' celebration of the common man. What does seem certain is that, rightly or not, during these years the United States became in both American and foreign eyes "the image of democracy itself" for generations to come.

BIBLIOGRAPHY

Benson, Lee. *The Concept of Jacksonian Democracy: New York as a Test Case.* Princeton, N.J.: Princeton University Press, 1961. Repudiation of class analysis; egalitarianism as a pervasive, not partisan, impulse.

Feller, Daniel. *The Jacksonian Promise: America, 1815–1840.* Baltimore: Johns Hopkins University Press, 1995. Brief synthetic treatment.

Pessen, Edward. *Jacksonian America: Society, Personality, Politics.* Rev. ed. Urbana: University of Illinois Press, 1978. Iconoclastic assault on Jackson's character, party, era, and scholarly admirers.

Schlesinger, Arthur M., Jr. *The Age of Jackson.* Boston: Little, Brown, 1945. Riveting account, strongly pro-Jackson; starting point for modern debate.

Sellers, Charles. *The Market Revolution: Jacksonian America, 1815–1846.* New York: Oxford University Press, 1991. Class analysis: Democrats as anticapitalist.

Tocqueville, Alexis de. *Democracy in America.* Translated by Henry Reeve, corrected by Phillips Bradley. New York: Knopf, 1945. Preeminent interpreter of American national character.

Ward, John William. *Andrew Jackson: Symbol for an Age.* New York: Oxford University Press, 1955. Jackson as embodiment of national self-image.

Daniel Feller

See also **Democratic Party; Jeffersonian Democracy; Maysville Veto; Removal Act of 1830; Rotation in Office; Spoils System.**

JACKSONVILLE, city located on the Saint Johns River twenty miles from the Atlantic Ocean in northeast FLORIDA. French Huguenots settled in the area in 1564 and built Fort Caroline. The Spanish took control of the area the following year, and the English followed in the late eighteenth century. In 1822, settlers laid out a town named for Andrew Jackson. The city was incorporated in 1832 and served as a base for blockade-runners during the Civil War. A fire destroyed much of the city in 1901 but it was quickly rebuilt. In 2000, Jacksonville was Florida's largest incorporated city, with a land area of 765 square miles and a population of 735,617. The population of the metropolitan area was 1,121,580. African Americans were the largest racial minority in Jacksonville—25 percent of the population. Jacksonville's consolidation with Duval County in 1968 ended much duplication of urban services and provided political access for minorities. It also kept middle-income residents as taxpayers and voters, while attracting national corporations to relocate, providing jobs and tax revenues. Crime, drugs, teenage pregnancies, school dropouts, and homelessness were serious problems for the city in the 1990s. The U.S. Navy is Jacksonville's largest employer. Banking, insurance, finance, medicine, transportation, wholesale and retail trade, construction, and tourism are other major industries. The Jacksonville Jaguars expansion team in the National Football League began play in 1995 in an entirely new Gator Bowl. Downtown, the Jacksonville Landing and Riverwalk helped revitalize the waterfront. In 1995, a renaissance plan to include a new city hall and civic auditorium was under way, which by 2002 had resulted in a rebuilt Performing Arts Center, the Florida Theatre, and the Ritz Theatre, and had moved city hall to the St. James Building on Hemming Plaza. Historically, Jacksonville has been mainly a blue-collar city. In the 1980s, that image began to change with the establishment of new upscale communities in Amelia Island and Ponte Verde, and the Professional Golf Association (PGA) Hall of Fame in adjacent Saint Johns County.

BIBLIOGRAPHY

Martin, Richard A. *A Quiet Revolution: Jacksonville-Duval County Consolidation and the Dynamics of Urban Political Reform.* Jacksonville, Fla.: White Publishing, 1993.

Ward, James Robertson. *Old Hickory's Town: An Illustrated History of Jacksonville.* Jacksonville, Fla.: Florida Publishing, 1982.

James B. Crooks/A. G.

See also **Frontier; South, the: The New South; Trading Posts.**

JACOBIN CLUBS, activist political clubs that appeared in the cities of the United States in the years from 1793 to 1795. The first club began in Paris under the name Club Breton, in October 1789: it met in a Dominican, or Jacobin, convent in the Rue St. Honoré. The Jacobin clubs gained increasing influence in the French Revolution after France declared itself a republic in 1792. Led by Maximilien Robespierre in 1793, the clubs helped support the most radical phase of the French Revolution. The French Jacobins believed in universal equality among citizens, the freedom of the individual, and universal brotherhood. By July 1794 the Paris Jacobin club was closed after the Jacobin leaders associated with Robespierre lost power. In November 1794 the clubs were suppressed.

The first American club began in Philadelphia in 1793. Some of the members were skilled craftsmen, others were merchants and professionals, and many were prominent intellectuals. Their membership overlapped with the Democratic Society of Philadelphia. Similarly, the Jacobin Club of Charleston, South Carolina, overlapped with the Republican Society there. The Charleston Club had connections through the prominent Huguenots in that city to other sympathizers with the French Revolution in the West Indies and in France. The Jacobin clubs in the United States sought to promote the broad aims of the French Revolution, including democracy and support for the French government against the European monarchies warring against it. Initially, their aims were popular in the cities, but after American disillusionment with the French minister Edmond Charles Genêt, the influence of the Jacobin clubs waned.

By 1795 the clubs had largely disbanded. "Jacobinism," however, had become a loaded epithet in American political rhetoric, used by FEDERALISTS to target not only radical democrats but also any follower of Thomas Jefferson, or any member of the Democratic Republican Party. The word "Jacobin" as an epithet still appeared occasionally in American conservative journals in the 1820s, a generation after the Jacobins in France had become politically moribund.

BIBLIOGRAPHY

Kennedy, Michael L. "A French Jacobin Club in Charleston, South Carolina, 1792–1795." *South Carolina Historical Magazine* 91 (1990): 4–22.

———. *The Jacobin Clubs in the French Revolution.* Princeton, N.J.: Princeton University Press, 1988.

Link, Eugene Perry. *Democratic-Republican Societies, 1790–1800.* New York: Columbia University Press, 1942.

Andrew W. Robertson

JAMES RIVER AND KANAWHA COMPANY. The vision of connecting tidewater Virginia with the Ohio River arose in colonial Virginia, with George Washington as a leading proponent. In 1785, the James River Company was founded to make improvements on the James River, and Washington was its first president. In 1820, the company's mandate was extended to connecting the James River to the Kanawha River and thus the Ohio, but it failed to accomplish its mission.

A new venture, the James River and Kanawha Company, was incorporated in 1832 and organized in 1835 to accomplish its predecessor's task. In 1851 the canal reached Buckhannon in western Virginia (later West Virginia), but with the company unable to refinance the venture, the canal ended there. Facing fierce railway competition, the canal company attempted to reach Clifton Forge and make a connection with the Chesapeake and Ohio Railroad by establishing the Buchanan and Clifton Forge Railway Company, organized in 1876. Work began in 1877 but languished because of financial exigency, and the company was sold to the Richmond and Alleghany Railway Company, which began construction of a 230-mile line from Richmond to Clifton Forge. The work was expedited by laying track on the canal towpath. In 1888 the Richmond and Alleghany Company was sold to the C&O Railroad Company.

BIBLIOGRAPHY

Dunaway, Wayland F. "History of the James River and Kanawha Company." Ph.D. diss. *Columbia University Studies in History, Economics, and Public Law.* Vol. 104. New York: Columbia University Press, 1922.

Kemp, Emory L. *The Great Kanawha Navigation.* Pittsburgh, Pa.: University of Pittsburgh Press, 2000.

Emory L. Kemp

See also **Canals; Ohio River.**

JAPAN, RELATIONS WITH. Relations between Japan and the United States have been a complex mix of cooperation, competition, and conflict from the moment that Commodore Matthew C. Perry arrived at Edo Bay in 1853 and demanded an end to more than two centuries of Japanese isolation. Just a decade earlier, Britain had imposed the unequal Treaty of Nanjing on China after the First Opium War. Perry's display of naval power persuaded Japan's leaders to sign the Treaty of Kanagawa in 1854, providing for the opening of two ports to U.S. ships, better treatment of American shipwrecked sailors, acceptance of a U.S. consul at Shimoda, and most-favored-nation privileges. Townsend Harris, the first U.S. minister to Japan, negotiated additional agreements to expand U.S. rights in Japan. The United States thus had demonstrated to Japan how economic weakness had left it vulnerable. Hostility to foreign dictation ignited a rebellion that restored the Meiji emperor and initiated a process of rapid modernization and industrialization in which Japanese leaders learned and borrowed from Western nations, especially the United States.

Japanese Power in East Asia

In 1871, Iwakura Tomomi led a mission to the United States and Europe that sought revision of the unequal treaties and access to foreign knowledge. This firsthand contact with the West confirmed the necessity for wholesale economic, political, and social changes to attain equality. After two decades of Japanese westernization, the United States acknowledged Japan's rising power and importance in the U.S.-Japan Treaty of Commerce and Navigation, signed in 1894, which abolished extraterritoriality (exemption of foreign residents from the laws of the host country) and provided for reciprocal rights of residence and travel. That same year, Japan went to war against China, registering an easy victory and obtaining control over Korea, Taiwan, and southern Manchuria. Russia then challenged Japan's dominance over Korea, resulting in the Russo-Japanese War in 1904. Japan's decisive triumph on land and at sea over a Western nation marked its arrival as a major power.

At first, President Theodore Roosevelt welcomed Japan's success in checking Russia's challenge to the Open Door policy in Asia, but he soon feared Japanese domination. In 1905, he acted to create a balance of power in the area when he mediated a treaty ending the war. Aware that Japan held the strategic advantage, Roosevelt acknowledged its control over Korea in the 1905 TAFT-KATSURA MEMORANDUM in return for Japanese recognition of U.S. rule in the Philippines in the 1908 ROOT-TAKAHIRA AGREEMENT. Meanwhile, rising tension between the two nations had reached a climax after California placed limits on the rights of Japanese Americans, which Roosevelt condemned and ameliorated with the Gentlemen's Agreement in 1908, stipulating that the Japanese government would restrict Japanese emigration to the United States, while Roosevelt would work to repeal discriminatory laws. President William Howard Taft's "dollar diplomacy" in Manchuria then angered Japan, but this did not prevent the signing of a bilateral treaty in 1911 granting full tariff autonomy to Japan.

During World War I, Japan once again challenged the U.S. Open Door policy when it declared war on Germany and seized its Pacific colonies and leaseholds in China. When President Woodrow Wilson did not protest, Japan concluded that Washington would not interfere in its expansion as long as it threatened no vital U.S. interests in the Pacific. In 1915, Secretary of State William Jennings Bryan reinforced this assumption after Japan imposed the Twenty-one Demands on China, when he informed Tokyo and Beijing that the United States only would refuse to recognize limits on the Open Door policy. But after the United States declared war on Germany in April 1917, Washington, to display unity with its Japanese ally, signed the Lansing-Ishii Agreement, affirming the open door in China, as well as China's independence, but also conceding contradictorily that Japan had special interests in China. Tokyo would confirm its wartime territorial gains in the Versailles Treaty ending World War I, but resented Wilson's refusal to include a racial equality clause in the League of Nations Covenant. Angry and bitter, Japan resorted thereafter to militarism and war to achieve the status and respect that it thought it had earned.

American leaders targeted Japan as the main threat to peace and stability in east Asia during the 1920s, although Tokyo at first endorsed international cooperation. At Washington in 1922, Japan signed treaties that provided for U.S. and British superiority in naval armaments and ensured an open door in China. Nevertheless, the U.S. military prepared plans in 1924 for war with Japan. China's unification in 1928 then accelerated the triumph of Japanese militarism because of Chinese determination to regain Manchuria, Japan's primary target for imperial trade and investment. Acceptance of new limits on Japanese naval power in the London Naval Treaty of 1930 so infuriated the Japanese military that extremists assassinated the prime minister. In September 1931, young officers in the Japanese army stationed in Manchuria staged an explosion on the South Manchuria Railway and blamed it on Chinese forces, exploiting the incident to justify total military occupation of the region. In response, Secretary of State Henry L. Stimson sent letters of protest to both Japan and China, declaring that Washington would not recognize changes in the status quo achieved through a resort to force.

Neither Stimson's words nor the threat of sanctions from the League of Nations deterred Japan, as Tokyo created the puppet state of Manchukuo in 1932. Thereafter, the Soviet Union's support for communist parties in Asia reinforced increasing sympathy for Nazi Germany, leading Japan to join the Anti-Comintern Pact in 1936. Militants determined to create a "New Order in Asia" under Japanese direction then gained control over the government. Exploiting an exchange of gunfire between Chinese and Japanese soldiers near Beijing in July 1937, Japan initiated what would become a protracted war that led to the occupation of China's most populated and productive areas. Washington continued to issue only verbal protests against Japan's aggressive behavior because the refusal of the American people to risk a new war precluded stronger action. President Franklin D. Roosevelt's speech in October 1937 calling for a "quarantine" of aggressors ignited a firestorm of criticism. In December, a Japanese pilot attacked and sunk the U.S.S. *Panay* on the Yangtze River, but this incident merely reinforced American isolationism.

World War II and Aftermath

After World War II began in Europe in September 1939, Japan invited war with the United States the next year when it signed the Tripartite Pact with Germany and Italy and invaded French Indochina. To deter Japan, the United States imposed sweeping economic sanctions, while also providing increasing aid and advice to China. During negotiations in Washington with Japan's ambassador in April 1941, Secretary of State Cordell Hull insisted that Japan not only respect the Open Door policy but evacuate all captured territories. In July, after Japan occupied southern Indochina, Roosevelt cut off oil and froze Japanese assets in the United States. In October, Japan's leaders decided that compromise was unlikely and opted for war, hoping to deliver a knockout blow to U.S. naval power in the Pacific before the United States could mobilize, thereby compelling Washington to accept Japanese dominance over east Asia. The strategy failed because Japan's 7 December attack on the U.S. naval base at Pearl Harbor in Hawaii scored only a tactical victory, while galvanizing Americans for an all-out war against Japan.

Japan quickly conquered the Philippines, Malaya, and Burma, expecting realization of its dream of creating a Greater East Asia Co-Prosperity Sphere. The Japanese mistakenly believed the United States would accept their new order in Asia or be unable to penetrate an impregnable defensive perimeter of fortified bases. Americans mobilized far superior military potential and economic resources to overwhelm Japan. By the summer of 1942, U.S. naval forces had won key victories at Coral Sea and Midway, imposing thereafter a suffocating blockade that created severe shortages of food and raw materials. After island-hopping isolated Japanese outposts, the United States bombed Japan's industry and housing from the air. The Japanese fought on ferociously, suffering massive losses on Iwo Jima and Okinawa. In August 1945, Japan was in ruins when U.S. atomic bombs destroyed Hiroshima and Nagasaki, forcing Japan to surrender.

Japan expected a harsh and vindictive occupation, but American rule was benevolent and constructive. As Supreme Commander for the Allied Powers (SCAP), General Douglas MacArthur and his staff enacted a series of reforms that helped create an open society based on capitalism and representative government. Article 9 of Japan's new constitution renounced war forever. But in 1947, the adverse impact of SCAP's economic reforms designed to eliminate the foundations of authoritarianism and militarism became obvious, as the atmosphere of physical and psychological devastation had not disappeared. Consistent with its new containment policy, the United States abandoned further reforms in favor of promoting rapid economic recovery, pursuing a "reverse course" aimed at transforming Japan into a bulwark against Soviet expansion in Asia. Prime Minister Yoshida Shigeru believed, however, that the occupation had to end if Japan was to emerge as a genuine U.S. partner in the Cold War. In September 1951, the Japanese Peace Treaty provided for a restoration of Japan's sovereignty the following April, but at the price of dependence, as Japan signed a security treaty with the United States that guaranteed its military protection in return for American use of air bases.

During the 1950s, Japan's relationship with the United States remained a source of heated controversy, not least because pacifism remained strong in Japan as a consequence of the devastation of war and public horror after the atomic attacks. Opposition to nuclear weapons intensified in 1954 after radioactivity from an American hydrogen bomb test on Bikini Atoll showered a Japanese fishing boat. Public protests persuaded the Socialists to reunite, which brought gains in the 1955 elections and motivated conservatives to form the Liberal Democratic Party (LDP). That same year, in negotiations for revision of the security treaty, the United States resumed pressure on Japan to expand the overseas role of its Self-Defense Force. This enraged many Japanese because it seemed to suggest that Japan might undertake military commitments in the Pacific. Prime Minister Kishi Nobosuke defied critics and in 1960 signed a revised treaty that, despite providing for a more equal partnership, was the target of fierce opposition in the Diet, Japan's national legislature. Ratification of the treaty in May in the absence of the boycotting dissenters set off massive street demonstrations during June that resulted in President Dwight D. Eisenhower canceling his scheduled visit to Tokyo.

Japanese Economic Power

During the 1960s, Japan adopted a "low posture" in foreign policy that placed a priority on transforming itself into an economic power. The U.S. government cooperated by encouraging high levels of Japanese exports to the United States, while allowing Japan's protection of its domestic market. Despite disputes over trade, the relationship remained stable because Japan achieved double-digit annual economic growth, while the United States ran a favorable balance of trade. U.S. military involvement in Southeast Asia soon strained relations, as many Japanese criticized Washington for suppressing nationalism rather than communism. There also were protests against the periodic visits of U.S. nuclear submarines to Japan. Led by the conservative LDP, the Japanese government endorsed the military effort in Vietnam, but rebuffed U.S. pressure to do more. More important, Japanese industry used the profits from the sale of many nonmilitary supplies for use in Vietnam to modernize and shift its exports to the United States from textiles, cameras, and transistor radios to sophisticated consumer electronics, automobiles, and machinery. After 1965, in a dramatic reversal, Japan sold more to the United States than it bought, its annual surplus increasing from a few billion dollars early in the 1970s to the $60 billion range by the 1990s.

A more immediate and serious source of friction was the U.S. refusal to end its occupation of the Ryukyu and Bonin Islands. Washington considered the military base on Okinawa as vital to containing the People's Republic of China (PRC) and sustaining the war in Southeast Asia. In November 1969, President Richard Nixon, having begun withdrawal from Vietnam, agreed to restore Japanese control of Okinawa, while retaining U.S. base rights. But the "Nixon shocks" rocked U.S.-Japan relations, the first coming in July 1971, when Nixon announced that he would visit the PRC. Since the Korean War, Japan had supported the U.S. policy of isolating the PRC and placed limits on Sino-Japanese trade. Prime Minister Sato Eisaku was stung after learning about the opening of relations with Beijing just hours before the announcement. Japan's rising trade surplus with the United States was responsible for the other shocks. Nixon imposed taxes on imports, ended the convertibility between dollars and gold, and threatened quotas on textile imports. Japan acquiesced to U.S. demands, but exports continued unabated.

A receding communist threat in Asia after 1975 made it more difficult for the United States to dictate relations with Japan. Only after persistent pressure from Washington did Japan agree to pay more of the costs incurred by U.S. military forces there and elevate levels of internal defense spending. Frustrated U.S. officials and business leaders attributed Japan's continuing economic growth to an alliance between bureaucrats, corporations, and the LDP ("Japan, Inc."), who conspired to control foreign markets, while using various ruses to limit U.S. access to Japanese consumers. U.S. workers and politicians blamed the decline of the U.S. automobile industry on Japan's car exports. During the 1980s, huge budget deficits resulted in Japanese banks lending hundreds of billions of dollars to the U.S. government, and Japanese corporations bought U.S. real estate and companies. A 1989 poll revealed that more Americans feared Japanese economic competition than the Soviet military threat. That same year, a Japanese politician and business leader coauthored a popular book that called on Japan to resist U.S. bullying.

Despite the troubled state of U.S.-Japanese relations during the 1980s, President Ronald Reagan established an effective working relationship with Prime Minister Nakasone Yasuhiro, who supported his anti-Soviet policies. Then, in 1991, the fall of the Soviet Union eliminated the main reason for the postwar U.S.-Japan security alliance. But Tokyo already was resisting U.S. pressure to assume greater responsibility for preserving world peace and security. Japan contributed $13 billion to finance the Gulf War of 1991, but this was ridiculed as "checkbook diplomacy," especially after the Diet delayed passage of a bill to allow Japan's military forces to join in United Nations peacekeeping activities. By then, Japan's "bubble economy" had collapsed, and Tokyo was reluctant, as the recession continued, to abandon protectionist economic policies. In 1995, President Bill Clinton threatened tariff retaliation, while Japanese officials warned of an impending trade war. Two years later, the financial collapse in Asia created an economic crisis in Japan that provided Washington with leverage to achieve some success in persuading Tokyo to increase domestic demand and lower tariffs, thereby reducing the U.S. trade deficit. As the new century began, U.S.-Japan relations were unstable and unpredictable, as the two nations struggled to redefine their roles.

BIBLIOGRAPHY

Buckley, Roger. *U.S.-Japan Alliance Diplomacy, 1945–1990.* New York: Cambridge University Press, 1992.

LaFeber, Walter. *The Clash: A History of U.S.-Japan Relations.* New York: Norton, 1997.

Matray, James I. *Japan's Emergence as a Global Power.* Westport, Conn.: Greenwood Press, 2000.

Neu, Charles E. *The Troubled Encounter: The United States and Japan.* New York: Wiley, 1975.

Schaller, Michael. *Altered States: The United States and Japan Since the Occupation.* New York: Oxford University Press, 1997.

James I. Matray

See also **Dollar Diplomacy; Open Door Policy; *Panay* Incident; World War II;** *and vol. 9:* **War against Japan.**

JAPANESE AMERICAN INCARCERATION.

In the spring and summer of 1942, the United States, as an ostensible matter of military necessity, incarcerated virtually the entire Japanese American population of the West Coast states. All told, more than 120,000 persons, over two-thirds of them native-born citizens, were confined for as long as forty-seven months in what the government called assembly centers and relocation centers, but which many later termed concentration camps. While fear of possible attacks by imperial Japanese forces and of sabotage by Japanese Americans was the proximate cause, a long history of anti-Japanese measures and attitudes made it possible for the public, shocked by the growing dimensions of the U.S. military debacle in the Pacific war,

Relocation Center. The scenery was bleak and the weather was often extreme at internment camps, such as this one at Minidoka, Idaho. NATIONAL ARCHIVES AND RECORDS ADMINISTRATION

to accept and even approve measures that clearly contradicted American values.

The triggering mechanism for incarceration was Executive Order 9066, drafted in the War Department and signed by Franklin Delano Roosevelt on 19 February 1942, seventy-four days after the attack on Pearl Harbor. The executive order specified no particular group of persons, and some in the War Department would have applied it to enemy aliens and perhaps others anywhere in the United States. It empowered Secretary of War Henry L. Stimson and subordinates designated by him to exclude "any or all persons" from areas he might designate and to "provide . . . transportation, food, shelter, and other accommodations . . . to accomplish the purpose of this order." Read without context, it seems to be a relief measure, but government spokesmen, chief of whom was the future attorney general and U.S. Supreme Court justice Tom Clark, explained to the press that it was aimed chiefly at Japanese, who would be moved away from the West Coast.

Moving toward Incarceration

Even before the promulgation of the executive order, the lives of the West Coast Japanese, alien and citizen, had been disrupted by a series of wartime government decrees. Apart from an 8 December 1941 proclamation empowering a selective internment of Japanese "alien enemies" conforming to existing statute law, a Justice Department order forbade "alien enemies" and persons of Japanese ancestry from leaving the country. In addition, Treasury Department orders froze the bank accounts of alien enemies and all accounts in American branches of Japanese banks, which immobilized most of the liquid assets of the entire Japanese American community. In addition, a joint Justice and War Department directive in late December effectively nullified the Fourth Amendment as far as Japanese Americans were concerned, as it authorized warrantless searches of any premises housing "alien enemies," which meant, in practice, any Japanese American home.

Sometime after the issuance of Executive Order 9066, government lawyers realized that no federal law required civilians to obey military orders without a declaration of martial law. Therefore, the War Department drafted and Congress—without significant debate or recorded vote—enacted Public Law 503 on 21 March 1942. This measure made it a misdemeanor to violate an order by the secretary of war or any officer designated by him to leave a "military area." On 18 March, Roosevelt had issued Executive Order 9102, establishing the civilian War Relocation Authority (WRA) to take charge of "persons designated" under Executive Order 9066.

Carrying Out Relocation and Incarceration

With these legal underpinnings in place, the army, with the clandestine and illegal help of the Bureau of the Census, divided the West Coast states into 108 separate districts, most of which contained about one thousand Japanese persons. General John L. DeWitt, who was in charge of West Coast defense, issued a series of civilian exclusion orders, one for each district, ordering "all persons of Japanese ancestry, both alien and non-alien" to "report to a specified place in the vicinity," bringing whatever belongings they could carry, for transportation to an assembly center. Although the government did not confiscate property, except for fishing boats, firearms, explosives, and some radios, most Japanese American families lost, or disposed of at fire-sale prices, the bulk of their personal and real property.

Once in military custody, Japanese Americans were moved first to one of sixteen assembly centers and, from there, to one of ten relocation centers under the authority of the civilian WRA. The whole mass movement began on 31 March 1942, with 257 persons taken from Bainbridge Island in Puget Sound and sent to Manzanar in the desert country northeast of Los Angeles. It was not completed until the end of October, with shipments of 655 persons from the Santa Anita Racetrack camp to WRA camps in Wyoming, Colorado, and Arkansas.

The assembly centers utilized existing facilities; some families were housed in horse stalls at racetracks and cattle pens at fairgrounds. The inmates were, however, not far from home and could be visited by non-Japanese friends and neighbors. The relocation centers, however—built in slapdash fashion for their current purpose—were located, by design, in desolate places.

Forced Evacuation. Soldiers watch baggage being loaded onto trucks as Japanese Americans await removal from their homes in San Francisco. NATIONAL ARCHIVES AND RECORDS ADMINISTRATION

Resistance

The overwhelming majority of Japanese Americans simply complied with the successive government orders as their community leaders recommended. Several thousand were able to avoid being seized by moving to territory east of the forbidden zone that comprised California, western Washington and Oregon, and a small part of Arizona before the government closed that escape route in March 1942. A dozen or so of those who remained either challenged the government orders through the courts or tried to avoid its clutches by attempting to assume non-Japanese identities. The legal protesters greatly concerned government leaders, but they need not have worried: the federal judiciary, with a few nonbinding exceptions, simply accepted the government's rationale about military necessity and the inherent untrustworthiness of Japanese Americans.

Three of the legal challenges eventually made their way to the U.S. Supreme Court. In June 1943, the Court decided unanimously in *Hirabayashi v. United States* that an American citizen of Japanese ancestry had to obey a curfew order; the Court avoided ruling on incarceration. The two other cases were not decided until December 1944. In *Korematsu v. United States*, the Court, now divided in a 6–3 vote, ruled that a citizen had to obey the military evacuation orders. Paradoxically, however, in the *Ex parte Endo* decision handed down the same day, the Court decided unanimously that a citizen of undoubted loyalty might not be held in camp or prevented from returning to California.

Life in the Camps

Life in the concentration camps was severe but generally not brutal, although on three occasions at three separate camps, troops guarding them shot and killed unarmed inmates, most of whom were protesting conditions. The civilian War Relocation Authority, in many ways a typical New Deal agency, tried to treat the prisoners humanely as long as they obeyed the rules. In many ways the administration resembled that of Indian reservations, and, in fact, the WRA head, Dillon S. Myer, later ran the Bureau of Indian Affairs. The WRA rules allowed thousands of Japanese Americans to leave the camps for work, for education, and, eventually, for military service. Some 3,600 young men entered the U.S. Army directly from camps, first as volunteers and then as draftees. Several hundred young men, however, resisted the draft, claiming that since they had been deprived of their liberty, they should not have to serve. The courts disagreed and sentenced 263 to terms in federal penitentiaries.

Redress

After the war the government slowly receded from its actions. In a 1945 ceremony, President Harry S. Truman honored Japanese American soldiers, telling them that "you have fought prejudice and won." In 1948, the Japanese American Claims Act provided limited compensation for certain property losses. Decades later, in 1976, President Gerald R. Ford issued a proclamation revoking Executive Order 9066, declaring that "Japanese Americans were and are loyal Americans." Finally, responding to a 1983 recommendation of the Commission on the Wartime Relocation and Internment of Civilians, the government in 1988 awarded each of some eighty thousand survivors a $20,000 tax-free redress payment and eventually sent each a check and a letter of apology signed by President George H. W. Bush.

BIBLIOGRAPHY

Daniels, Roger. *Prisoners without Trial: Japanese Americans in World War II.* New York: Hill and Wang, 1993.

Daniels, Roger, ed. *American Concentration Camps: A Documentary History of the Relocation and Incarceration of Japanese Americans, 1941–1945.* 9 vols. New York: Garland, 1989. A collection of archival documents.

Houston, Jeanne Wakatsuki, and James D. Houston. *Farewell to Manzanar: A True Story of Japanese American Experience during and after the World War II Internment.* Boston: Houghton Mifflin, 1973. The best-known memoir of incarceration.

Maki, Mitchell T., Harry H. L. Kitano, and S. Megan Berthold. *Achieving the Impossible Dream: How Japanese Americans Obtained Redress.* Urbana: University of Illinois Press, 1999.

Myer, Dillon S. *Uprooted Americans: The Japanese Americans and the War Relocation Authority during World War II.* Tucson: University of Arizona Press, 1971. An apologia by the head of the War Relocation Authority.

Taylor, Sandra. *Jewel of the Desert: Japanese American Internment at Topaz.* Berkeley: University of California, 1993. The best account of a single incarceration camp.

Roger Daniels

See also **Internment, Wartime;** *and vol. 9:* **The Japanese Internment Camps, 1942.**

JAPANESE AMERICANS have contributed significantly to the political strength, economic development, and social diversity of the United States. Like all Asian Americans, they are a heterogeneous group, the most obvious distinction being between those from the Japanese home islands and those from Okinawa, which was an independent kingdom until 1879, when Japan incorporated it as a prefecture. In 1970, Japanese Americans were the largest group among Asian Americans in the total U.S. population, but Chinese and Filipinos had passed them by 1990, In 2000, the Census Bureau asked respondents to identify themselves as one or more races in combination. Japanese Americans were most likely to report one or more other ethnic groups, but with a total population of 1,148,932, they still ranked sixth among Asian Americans, having also fallen behind Asian Indians, Vietnamese, and Koreans. Japanese Americans increased least among Asian Americans by immigration after 1980 because Japan's economy provided its citizens with a high living standard. Also, Japanese Americans did not manifest a huge gender imbalance like other Asian American groups, and in fact was the only group prior to 1965 in which women outnumbered men. By far most Japanese Americans live in California and Hawaii, with the states of Washington, New York, and New Jersey a distant third, fourth, and fifth.

Early Settlement in Hawaii and California

U.S. commercial expansion in the Pacific during the early nineteenth century initiated the history of Japanese movement to America. After American traders established a presence in Hawaii, the United States secured a commercial treaty with China in 1844. It then gained access to Japan in 1854, signing an agreement that ended Japan's policy of national isolation. Thereafter, Hawaiian sugar planters, mostly U.S. citizens, began to recruit Japanese as contract laborers. In 1869, the first Japanese arrived on the mainland and settled near Sacramento, where they established the Wakamatsu Tea and Silk Farm Colony on 600 acres. This settlement soon disappeared because the mulberry shoots and tea seeds that the immigrants brought from Japan could not survive in the dry California soil. In 1871, Japan sent the Iwakura Mission to the United States in search of Western scientific knowledge as a way to preserve its political and cultural independence. Significant numbers of individual Japanese resettled in the United States thereafter for the same reason and generally were

Formal Portrait. Japanese immigrants pose dressed as samurai. NATIONAL ARCHIVES AND RECORDS ADMINISTRATION

well received until Congress passed the Chinese Exclusion Act of 1882. U.S. labor recruiters from the mainland then went to Hawaii to lure Japanese workers with promises of higher wages and better working conditions. Seeking escape from the rigors of sugar plantation life, 34,000 Japanese left Hawaii from 1902 to 1906 for the West Coast.

Anti-Japanese agitation in the United States began almost with the arrival of the first Issei (first-generation Japanese Americans). Not only did reactionary politicians favor action to block Japanese immigration, but reformers also called for restrictions. Progressives talked of the "Yellow Peril" and prevailed on legislatures in western states to pass anti-Japanese laws that barred Japanese Americans from interracial marriage and excluded them from clubs, restaurants, and recreational facilities. Racial segregation greatly reduced opportunities in education, housing, and employment, and alien land laws thwarted advancement in agriculture.

Japan protested these measures to defend its national honor and to protect itself against the same imperialist exploitation China endured. In response, President Theodore Roosevelt arranged the 1908 Gentlemen's Agreement with Japan, whereby Tokyo agreed not to issue passports to Japanese workers seeking to migrate to the United States in return for Roosevelt's promise to press for repeal of discriminatory laws. At that time, California had roughly 50,000 Japanese residents in a population of 2,250,000, working mostly as tenant farmers, fishermen, or small businessmen. But many owned farms, and there was a small professional class of lawyers, teachers, and doctors. From 1908 to 1920, the migration of Japanese women, mainly as "picture brides" and wives, helped even the mainland gender ratio. In 1924, the National Origins Act effectively ended Japanese immigration.

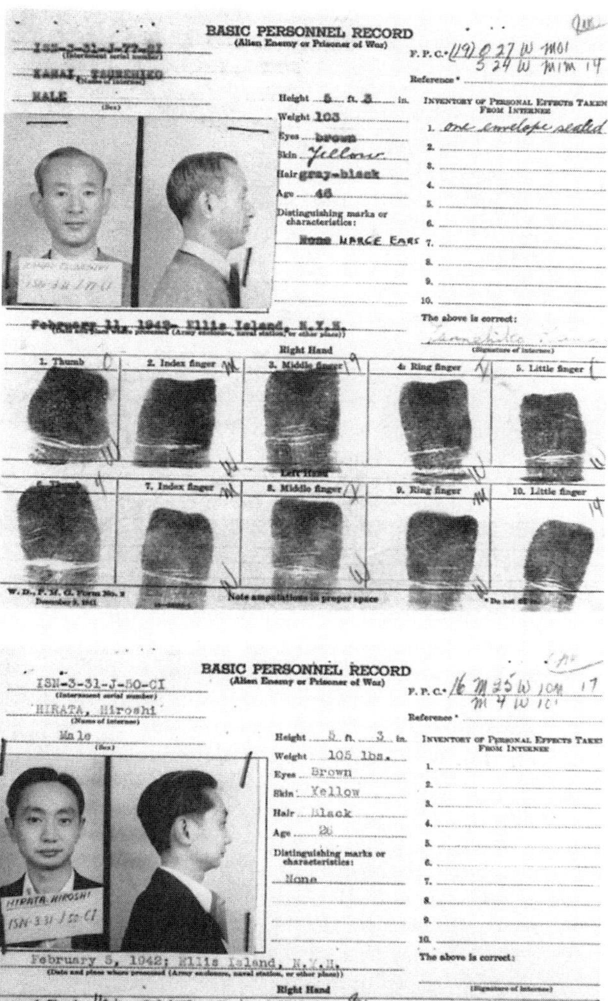

Japanese American ID. An identification record, featured in an exhibit at Ellis Island on the treatment of Japanese Americans during World War II; photographed in 1998 by Bebeto Matthews. AP/WIDE WORLD PHOTOS

World War II and Incarceration

By 1941, about 120,000 Japanese lived in the United States, 94,000 in California. Earlier, most Japanese immigrants had settled in towns, but by then, 40 percent lived outside urban centers and worked in agriculture, forestry, and fishing. In Hawaii, racism against the Japanese was strong, but not as strong as in California. Many bowed to pressure to give up their language and embrace Christianity, yet they were still excluded from white schools. After Japan's attack on Pearl Harbor forced U.S. entry into World War II, Japanese Americans were targeted for special persecution because of an exaggerated fear that they would conspire to aid the enemy. *Time* magazine explained to its readers in late December 1941 how they could distinguish the "kindly placid, open" faces of the Chinese, who were allies of the United States, from the "positive, dogmatic, arrogant" expressions of "the Japs." Barred from U.S. citizenship were 47,000 Issei, but their 70,000 American-born offspring (Nisei) were citizens. Congressman Leland Ford of California insisted that any "patriotic native born Japanese, if he wants to make his contribution, will submit himself to a concentration camp." Despite their having committed no crimes, General John DeWitt, head of the Western Defense Command, declared Japanese of any citizenship enemies.

In Hawaii the U.S. government declared martial law but imposed no further limitations on the Japanese living there. On the mainland, however, President Franklin D. Roosevelt's Executive Order 9066 of 19 February 1942 declared parts of the country "military areas" from which any or all persons could be barred. The U.S. Army gained authorization to remove all Japanese Americans from the West Coast. In May, the War Relocation Authority gave forty-eight hours or less to Japanese Americans to pack their belongings and sell or otherwise dispose of their property. More than 112,000 people were moved to ten detention facilities, mostly located in remote and desolate areas of the West. Thirty thousand children were taught in schools about democratic values, while being denied their civil liberties.

No one ever was charged with treason or sedition, as the pretext was disloyalty, which was not against the law. Yet since only 1,466 Japanese in Hawaii were placed in detention facilities over the course of the war, it is clear that racism, not fears of disloyalty, motivated the massive mainland incarceration. Facilities in the camps were primitive, services poor, and privacy virtually nonexistent. But nearly all Japanese Americans complied without objection, performing menial labor under armed guard. In 1943, the U.S. Supreme Court upheld as legal the racial curfew for reasons of military security. With three judges dissenting, the Court ruled in 1944 that the relocation was justified by the exigencies of war.

Dozens of Japanese Americans refused to be drafted from the camps into the military to protest their incarceration, with some claiming conscientious objector status. At the same time, many young Japanese American men and women made important contributions to the U.S. war effort. The 442d Infantry Combat Team, comprised entirely of Nisei volunteers and serving in Europe, became the most decorated unit for bravery in action in the entire American military service. Others worked in the Pacific theater as translators, interpreters, or intelligence officers. Meanwhile, the numbers of Japanese Americans in the camps steadily declined as students were allowed to attend college, workers received temporary permits, and some internees gained permission to leave after agreeing to settle in eastern states. In 1944, the Supreme Court ruled in *Ex Parte Endo* that a loyal U.S. citizen could not be deprived of his or her freedom. That October, martial law ended in Hawaii. By January 1945, the camps still held 80,000 people, but finally that summer all could leave. A fortunate few found that friends had protected their homes and businesses, but most lost the work of a lifetime.

Postwar Acculturation

After World War II, Americans who had fought against Nazism started to question older notions of white superiority and racism. During the war, California had vigorously enforced an alien land law that led to the seizure of property declared illegally held by Japanese. In November 1946, a proposition endorsing the measure appeared on the state ballot, but voters overwhelmingly rejected it in part because the Japanese American Citizens League (JACL) organized a campaign to remind Californians of the wartime contributions of Nisei soldiers. Two years later, the Supreme Court declared the alien land law unconstitutional, labeling it as "nothing more than outright racial discrimination." In Hawaii, Japanese American veterans entered politics, organized the Japanese American vote, and reshaped the Democratic Party in the islands, ending nearly fifty years of Republican Party rule in the "revolution of 1954." The 1952 McCarran-Walter Act removed the ban on Japanese immigration and made Issei eligible for naturalized citizenship. Japanese Americans lobbied aggressively for the new law and rejoiced in its passage. By 1965, some 46,000 immigrant Japanese had taken their citizenship oaths.

Like other World War II veterans, Japanese Americans used the GI Bill to gain college educations. This brought a steady increase in postwar years in the percentage of professionals and city dwellers in this Asian American group. Because the rise in education levels and family incomes appeared so spectacular, especially after the impoverishment caused by World War II detention, commentators heaped praise on Japanese Americans as a "model minority." These writers attributed their economic advancement not only to determined effort but also cultural values that resembled dominant American ideals, including the centrality of the family, regard for schooling, a premium placed on the future, and belief in the virtues of hard work. As early as 1960, Japanese Americans had a greater percentage of high school and college graduates than other groups, and in later years median family incomes were higher by nearly $3,000 than those of other Americans. Observers noted, however, that Japanese Americans had greater numbers of workers per household, accounting in part for higher median incomes. According to a study of Asian Americans in California's San Francisco Bay area, based on the 1980 census, Japanese American individuals worked more hours.

Passage of the Immigration Act of 1965 abolished the national origins quotas of 1924 and opened the gates widely for many Third World peoples. Adopting the principle of "first come, first served," it also gave preference to professionals and the highly skilled. By 1986, immigrants from Asia rose from 1 to 5 million, comprising 40 percent of new immigrants as opposed to 7 percent twenty years earlier. But the portion of Japanese immigrants plummeted from 52 percent of all Asian Americans in 1960 to 15 percent in 1985. This decline accelerated the integration and assimilation of Japanese Americans into the mainstream of American society.

Japanese American Community Since the 1980s

During the 1980s, the Japanese American community experienced a transition from a relatively exclusive and excluded group to a fragmented and diverse collectivity. Among Sansei (third generation) and Vonsei (fourth generation), there was declining participation in Japanese American institutions and a lack of cultural connection to things Japanese. Rejecting assimilation, some younger Japanese Americans criticized the JACL for supporting cooperation with internment and opposing wartime draft resistance to strengthen its power position.

Japanese American political agitation grew during an era of greater social, economic, and political opportunities, focusing especially on gaining compensation for relocation and internment. Congress had offered a token payment in 1948, but it was not until the 1980s that several Japanese Americans convicted of wartime offenses successfully reopened their cases. The Justice Department and the Federal Bureau of Investigation were forced to release files showing how prosecutors withheld evidence proving that no danger existed to justify wartime civil rights violations. Civil organizations, political activists, and congressmen then lobbied successfully for passage of the Civil Rights Restoration Act of 1987, resulting in the U.S. government apologizing for wrongs done to Japanese Americans during World War II and authorizing monetary redress in the amount of about $20,000 per surviving internee. After determining terms of payment and definition of eligibility in 1988, over 82,000 received payments.

Japanese American assertiveness in this matter and against other forms of discrimination caused many observers to reexamine the accuracy of describing the group as the "model minority." Some writers saw a basic flaw in comparative analysis, stressing that Japanese Americans had to overcome "structural restraints" that white European immigrants did not have to face. Their success was largely attributable to a Japanese culture that emphasized the primacy of group survival over and above the retention of specific beliefs and practices. Others pointed to a sharp contrast between traditional American values that stressed individualism, independent goals, achieving status, and a sense of optimism, and Japanese values emphasizing group reliance, duty and hierarchy, submissiveness to authority, compulsive obedience to rules and controls set by those with status, a sense of fatalism, and success through self-discipline. Yet Japanese Americans arguably have been able to achieve assimilation into the American mainstream more fully than any other Asian American group. Despite the increasing complexity of the Japanese American community, new stereotypes have surfaced to limit options for Sansei and Vonsei that are less visible and more subtle. Meeting this challenge has caused younger Japanese Americans to rely on voluntary social groups to deal with collective needs. Persistent ethnic cohesiveness, as well as a commitment to build orderly and meaningful lives, thus remain key sources of strength in the Japanese American community.

BIBLIOGRAPHY

Daniels, Roger. *Asian America: Chinese and Japanese in the United States Since 1850.* Seattle: University of Washington Press, 1988.

Hazama, Dorothy Ochiai, and Okamoto Komeiji. *Okage Sama De: The Japanese in Hawai'i, 1885–1895.* Honolulu: University of Hawaii Press, 1986.

O'Brien, David J., and Stephen S. Fugita. *The Japanese American Experience.* Bloomington: Indiana University Press, 1991.

Spickard, Paul R. *Japanese Americans: The Formation and Transformations of an Ethnic Group.* New York: Twayne, 1996.

Takahashi, Jere. *Nisei/Sansei: Shifting Japanese American Identities and Politics.* Philadelphia: Temple University Press, 1997.

James I. Matray

Japanese Cherry Trees. Eleanor Roosevelt enjoys the first of thirteen years of blossoms while she is first lady, 3 April 1933.

See also **Asian Americans; Japan, Relations with; Japanese-American Incarceration;** *and vol. 9:* **Gentlemen's Agreement.**

JAPANESE CHERRY TREES, in Potomac Park, Washington, D.C., attract thousands of visitors during blossom time each April. They were presented by the city of Tokyo as a token of goodwill from the people of Japan to the people of the United States. The first shipment in 1909 had to be destroyed because of insect pests. The city of Tokyo then, in a special nursery, grafted flowering cherry trees onto wild cherry stock, and the trees reached Washington in perfect condition. The first two were planted by then first lady Helen Taft and the wife of Japanese ambassador Count Sutemi Chinda on 27 March 1912.

BIBLIOGRAPHY

Jefferson, Roland M. "Cherry Blossoms—Restoring a National Treasure." *Agricultural Research* 47, no. 4 (April 1999): 4–8.

Fred A. Emery/H. S.

See also **Japan, Relations with.**

JAVA SEA, BATTLE OF, an early World War II naval engagement off the northern coast of Java. A fleet comprising American, British, Dutch, and Australian units, under Rear Admiral Karel W. F. M. Doorman of the Netherlands, attempted to halt a Japanese invasion of Java. Trying to locate the Japanese troop transports, Doorman's force, late on 27 February 1942, encountered a Japanese covering force under Rear Admiral T. Takagi. Although the Japanese force was of approximately equal numbers, they alone had air support. The two Allied heavy cruisers, USS *Houston* and HMS *Exeter*, were outgunned by two Japanese cruisers. In the first clash, the *Exeter* was severely damaged, and two Allied destroyers were sunk. Retiring in hope of shaking off Takagi and finding the transports, Doorman lost another destroyer to a mine and, after dark, again ran into Takagi's fleet and lost two light cruisers, including his own flagship. The surviving ships retired. Neither the *Houston* nor any of the five U.S. destroyers was damaged. However, the following day, as the *Houston* and the light cruiser HMS *Perth* tried to escape southward, they encountered the main Japanese armada. Four Japanese transports were sunk, but both the *Houston* and the *Perth* were lost, and the Japanese invasion proceeded.

BIBLIOGRAPHY

Schultz, Duane P. *The Last Battle Station: The Story of the USS Houston.* New York: St. Martin's Press, 1985.

Thomas, David A. *The Battle of the Java Sea.* London: Deutsch, 1968; New York: Stein and Day, 1969.

Charles B. MacDonald / A. R.

See also **Aircraft Carriers and Naval Aircraft; Coral Sea, Battle of the; Midway, Battle of.**

JAY-GARDOQUI NEGOTIATIONS. John Jay's negotiations with Don Diego de Gardoqui of Spain began in New York City on 20 July 1785 in an effort to solve problems regarding the southwest boundary between the new nation and Spanish America, and American rights to navigate the Mississippi River to New Orleans. In 1779, Jay had gone to Spain to seek its endorsement of the war against England. Spain rejected Jay's appeal, but agreed to secret loans to help Americans purchase armaments. After the peace treaty ending the Revolutionary War was signed in 1785, Spain rejected America's right to navigate the Mississippi between Natchez and New Orleans.

One year after the Jay-Gardoqui negotiations began, Spain granted American commercial privileges for Spain's European ports, but still refused American rights on the Mississippi River to New Orleans. In August 1786, the Continental Congress voted seven to five for Spain's proposal, but lacked the necessary nine votes for ratification. In 1788, Spain granted Americans the right to navigate to New Orleans, provided they paid 15 percent duties to Madrid. The issue of Mississippi trade restrictions was finally resolved through the Pinckney Treaty of 1795.

BIBLIOGRAPHY

Bemis, Samuel Flagg. *Pinckney's Treaty: America's Advantage from Europe's Distress, 1783–1800.* Rev. ed. New Haven, Conn.: Yale University Press, 1962.

Weeks, William Earl. *Building the Continental Empire: American Expansion from the Revolution to the Civil War.* Chicago: Dee, 1997.

Whitaker, Arthur Preston. *The Spanish-American Frontier, 1783–1795: The Westward Movement and the Spanish Retreat in the Mississippi Valley.* Boston: Houghton Mifflin, 1927.

Lester H. Brune

See also **Pinckney's Treaty.**

JAYHAWKERS, a name applied to the Free State bands active in the Kansas-Missouri border war between 1856 and 1859, particularly the band captained by Charles R. Jennison. It was also applied to Union guerrilla bands during the Civil War and to the Seventh Kansas Cavalry, commanded by Jennison. Because of real and alleged depredations attributed to the Jayhawkers, the term became one of opprobrium. The term's origin is uncertain, but a party of gold seekers from Galesburg, Illinois, may have coined it in 1849 and used it in California. (Traditional stories of the term's origin in Kansas are apocryphal.) After the Civil War, "Jayhawker" became the popular nickname for a Kansan.

BIBLIOGRAPHY

Napier, Rita, ed. *History of the Peoples of Kansas.* Lawrence: University of Kansas, 1985.

Samuel A. Johnson / C. W.

See also **Border Ruffians; Border War; Kansas-Nebraska Act; Lecompton Constitution; Pottawatomie Massacre.**

JAY'S TREATY (1794). Both the United States and Great Britain failed to live up to the terms of the 1783 peace treaty that ended the Revolutionary War. American violations reflected the weakness of its central government; state governments passed laws blocking the repayment of prewar debts to British creditors and Americans continued to discriminate against American loyalists. British violations resulted from a more deliberate policy—failing to evacuate Northwest forts and posts, especially to please its Indian allies and to assuage its fur traders.

Mounting American dissatisfaction came up against the Federalist-Republican split in government. To such Federalists as Secretary of the Treasury Alexander Hamilton, friendship with Britain was too important to risk over these issues; Hamilton needed trade with Britain, America's key trading partner, to finance his plans. To Republicans, such as Secretary of State Thomas Jefferson, who were committed to France, the only recourse was a firm insistence on Britain's honoring of its treaty obligations.

Britain had issues as well. By this point a war had begun between France and Britain, and it would not end for nearly two decades. As the world's premier naval power, Britain rejected America's view that it should, as a neutral state, be able to trade freely with all interested parties. Britain seized hundreds of American neutral ships, and Sir Guy Carleton, Baron Dorchester, the governor-general of Canada, made a bellicose speech to western Indians implying that they would soon be able to recover their lands in the Great Lakes region from the United States.

In this environment, President George Washington sent Chief Justice John Jay, a staunch Federalist and a strong Anglophile, to London as minister plenipotentiary and envoy extraordinaire on a special mission. As the historian Samuel Flagg Bemis has noted, Jay could have made more of the American cause. He acquiesced in British maritime measures for the duration of the war with France in return for the creation of a mixed commission to adjudicate American spoliation claims for damages made "under color" of British Orders in Council. On 19 November 1794, Jay and the British foreign minister Lord Grenville signed a Treaty of Amity, Commerce, and Navigation. Britain agreed to evacuate frontier posts by 1 June 1796 (which it mostly did); the United States guaranteed payment of British private prewar debts. Another term of the treaty stated that mixed boundary commissions were to establish the boundaries in the northwest and northeast. The boundary commission for the northwest never met, and the commission for the northeast set the boundary at the Saint Croix River. Jay did not obtain any satisfaction on issues of impressment, neutral (shipping) rights, ending so-called paper or unenforced blockades, and no indemnification for slaves that departing British soldiers took from the United States in 1783.

Washington got the treaty through the Senate and the House only with great difficulty and at some cost. The temporary acquiescence in British maritime measures was the price the Federalists paid for redemption of American territorial integrity in the Northwest, and peace with Britain. Britain wanted a treaty to keep its best foreign customer and to keep the United States neutral during the continuing conflict with France. There certainly were protests in the United States, and Jay was burned in effigy while Secretary of the Treasury Alexander Hamilton was stoned while publicly defending the treaty. France regarded the treaty as a violation of its commercial treaty with the United States and, as Alexander DeConde has written, engaged in a kind of undeclared naval war with America between 1798 and 1800.

BIBLIOGRAPHY

Bemis, Samuel Flagg. *Jay's Treaty: A Study in Commerce and Diplomacy.* New Haven, Conn.: Yale University Press, 1962.

Combs, Jerald A. *The Jay Treaty: Political Background of the Founding Fathers.* Berkeley: University of California Press, 1970.

DeConde, Alexander. *Entangling Alliance: Politics and Diplomacy under George Washington.* Westport, Conn.: Greenwood Press, 1974.

Reuter, Frank T. *Trials and Triumphs: George Washington's Foreien Policy.* Fort Worth, Tex.: Texas Christian University Press, 1983.

Charles M. Dobbs

JAZZ as a term can act as an adjective, noun, or verb, and refers to a performance method or the music itself that is called jazz. The term was only applied to music around 1915 and was even then disliked by some musicians because it was a vulgar term for sexual intercourse. Jazz music encompasses many substyles that can be characterized by comparative time periods, geography, style, ensemble, function, venue, and audience. The importance of individuality and improvisatory interaction in jazz, requiring mastery of expression and technical skill, should not be underestimated.

Origins

Like the BLUES, jazz was at first an oral tradition founded by African Americans as a passionate expression of social condition, combining both African American and European American influences. New Orleans, the birthplace of jazz, was a slave trade port, and its Congo Square was a gathering place on Sundays for the African Americans who danced, sang of their history and ritual with expressive African inflections, and played drums. In the late

Duke Ellington. Pianist, leader of a legendary and long-lasting big band, and preeminent composer of jazz and other African American music. AP/WIDE WORLD PHOTOS

Fletcher Henderson's Orchestra. The bandleader (*sitting at the piano*) hired extraordinary talent such as Louis Armstrong (*center, rear*)—with the group from late 1924 to late 1925, just before his revolutionary Hot Fives and Hot Sevens recordings—and Coleman Hawkins (*with tenor saxophone at left*). ARCHIVE PHOTOS, INC.

1800s, European American music, spirituals, Creole music, and the same African American field hollers and work songs that influenced blues influenced this oral tradition.

Another early influence on New Orleans jazz was RAGTIME, which began to be published around 1890 and became the first African American tradition to gain widespread popularity. Ragtime's primary musical model was the marching band, and most of its repertoire was for piano, such as the rags of St. Louis's Scott Joplin and Harlem's James P. Johnson. Larger ragtime ensembles called syncopated orchestras (syncopation was a prominent ragtime feature) were also popular in America and Europe; one of the most famous was James Reese Europe's Clef Club Orchestra. In addition, Europe founded what could possibly be the first modern association of African American musicians, also called Clef Club.

New Orleans was a melting pot of African, Caribbean, Creole, European, and local traditions. Its small bands played in parades, funerals, and other social gatherings and were typified by a celebratory spirit and rhythmic intensity. Buddy Bolden, Louis Armstrong, and Jelly Roll Morton began their careers in New Orleans and became some of the greatest soloists of the time. Most jazz in New Orleans was performed as dance music in the venues of Storyville (the red-light district between 1896 and 1917). When Storyville closed, many musicians migrated to Chicago, Kansas City, and New York to find employment.

The Jazz Age and Modernity (1920s)

The displaced Dixieland sounds characterized the JAZZ AGE. Some believe the Original Dixieland Jazz Band (founded 1916), set a standard that started the Jazz Age, while others point to King Oliver's Creole Jazz Band (founded 1922) in Chicago. Louis Armstrong and his Hot Five (1925) are often credited with exemplifying the spirit of the era. New York became the center for jazz performance and recording after 1925. By 1930, successful artists included Coleman Hawkins, Fletcher Henderson, Duke Ellington, Fats Waller, and Benny Carter.

The Jazz Age characterized the sound of modernity because it emphasized the individual voice and had a great impact on genres and styles in the visual arts, including film, and modernist literature, in works by such authors as Langston Hughes and T. S. Eliot. Socially, musicians were successful in presenting jazz to the general public as well as making strides in overcoming racial boundaries.

The Big-Band Swing Era (1930–1940s)

As early as 1924, Louis Armstrong was in New York playing with Fletcher Henderson's orchestra, and by the mid-1930s, swing style was already widely popular. The term "swing" was first used to describe the lively rhythmic style of Armstrong's playing and also refers to swing dance music.

Duke Ellington, best known for his colorful orchestration, led a group that played at Harlem's Cotton Club;

Glenn Miller, Benny Goodman, and Count Basie led other successful orchestras. While these big bands came to characterize the New York jazz scene during the Great Depression, they were contrasted with the small, impoverished jazz groups that played at rent parties and the like. During this time the performer was thoroughly identified by popular culture as an entertainer, the only regular venue was the nightclub, and African American music became synonymous with American dance music. The big-band era was also allied with another popular genre, the mainly female jazz vocalists who soloed with the orchestras. Singers such as Billie Holiday modernized popular-song lyrics, although some believe the idiom was more akin to white Tin Pan Alley than to jazz.

Some believe that the big band at its peak represented the golden era of jazz because it became part of the cultural mainstream. Others, however, consider it furthest from the ideal of jazz's artistic individuality.

Bebop, Post-Bop, Hard Bop, and Free Jazz (1940s–1960s)

Post–World War II jazz contrasted with the big bands and had parallels with abstract expressionist painters and Beat writers. It was not dance music and was primarily played by smaller ensembles and often called combo jazz. The new style was more harmonically challenging, maintained a high level of virtuosity, and pushed the established language to its extremes. Dizzy Gillespie, Charlie "Bird" Parker, and Stan Getz played in this new style. In the late 1940s and 1950s this style, described onomatopoeically as bebop, became even more complex.

A smoother, more relaxed "cool" sound, a reaction to the intensity of bebop, was developed by Miles Davis in his 1949 album *Birth of the Cool;* it is often called mainstream jazz and was successful into the 1970s. Cool performers in the 1950s, including Davis, the Modern Jazz Quartet, and Dave Brubeck, gained popularity for jazz as an art. There were many other post-bop styles, such as modal jazz (based on musical modes), funk (which reprised early jazz), and fusion, which blended jazz and rock and included electronic instruments. Miles Davis in his later career and Chick Corea were two influential fusion artists.

Dizzy Gillespie. The pioneer of bebop (along with Charlie Parker) expands his famous cheeks as he plays his trademark bent trumpet. AP/Wide World Photos

Hard bop was a continuation of bebop but in a more accessible style played by artists such as John Coltrane. Ornette Coleman (1960) developed avant-garde free jazz, a style based on the ideas of Thelonius Monk, in which free improvisation was central to the style.

Postmodern Jazz Since 1980

Hybridity, a greater degree of fusion, and traditional jazz revivals merely touch the surface of the variety of styles that make up contemporary jazz. Inclusive of many types of world music, it is accessible, socially conscious, and draws almost equally from its vast musical past. Performers such as David Grisman, B. B. King, Wynton Marsalis, Harry Connick Jr., Toshiko Akiyoshi, and Tito Puente attest to this variety. Since the 1980s, mainstream jazz education has developed, along with more serious concern for the study of jazz documentation and scholarship.

BIBLIOGRAPHY

Clark, Andrew, ed. *Riffs and Choruses: A New Jazz Anthology.* London and New York: Continuum, 2001.

Erlewine, Michael, et al., eds. *All Music Guide to Jazz: The Experts' Guide to the Best Jazz Recordings.* 3d ed. San Francisco: Miller Freeman Books, 1998.

Gridley, Mark C. *Jazz Styles: History and Analysis.* 7th ed. Upper Saddle River, N.J.: Prentice Hall, 2000.

Kirchner, Bill, ed. *The Oxford Companion to Jazz.* Oxford, U.K., and New York: Oxford University Press, 2000.

Monson, Ingrid. *Saying Something: Jazz Improvisation and Interaction.* Chicago: University of Chicago Press, 1996.

Townsend, Peter. *Jazz in American Culture.* Edinburgh: Edinburgh University Press, 2000; Jackson: University of Mississippi Press, 2000.

Christina Linsenmeyer-van Schalkwyk

See also **Music: African American.**

JAZZ AGE. The novelist F. Scott Fitzgerald coined the term "Jazz Age" retrospectively to refer to the decade after World War I and before the stock market crash in 1929, during which Americans embarked upon what he called "the gaudiest spree in history." The Jazz Age is inextricably associated with the wealthy white "flappers" and socialites immortalized in Fitzgerald's fiction. However, the era's soundtrack was largely African American, facilitating what Ann Douglas has described as a "racially mixed social scene" without precedent in the United States. Postwar U.S. supremacy and a general disillusion with politics provided the economic base and social context of the Jazz Age. In his 1931 essay, "Echoes of the Jazz Age," Fitzgerald referred to "a whole race going hedonistic, deciding on pleasure," a rather glib exaggeration, as 71 percent of American families lived below the poverty line during the Roaring Twenties. Nevertheless, a young white elite put this pleasure principle into practice by embracing jazz. As the historian Lawrence Levine observed, many whites identified this black music as libidinal and "primitive," the liberating antithesis of mainstream, middle-class conventions. White New Yorkers went "slumming" at jazz clubs in Harlem. Boosted by the emergence of radio and the gramophone, black singers like Bessie Smith and Clara Smith became stars. The motion picture *The Jazz Singer* (1927) brought the music to the big screen in the first-ever "talkie," although the eponymous hero was the white performer Al Jolson in blackface.

BIBLIOGRAPHY

Cowley, Malcolm, and Robert Cowley, eds. *Fitzgerald and the Jazz Age.* New York: Scribners, 1966.

Douglas, Ann. *Terrible Honesty: Mongrel Manhattan in the 1920s.* London: Picador, 1996.

Fitzgerald, F Scott. "Echoes of the Jazz Age." In *The Crack-Up with Other Pieces and Stories.* Harmondsworth, U.K.: Penguin, 1965.

Levine, Lawrence. *Black Culture and Black Consciousness: Afro-American Thought from Slavery to Freedom.* New York: Oxford University Press, 1977.

Martyn Bone

See also **Flapper.**

The Jazz Singer. Al Jolson stars in this 1927 feature film, the first with synchronized dialogue as well as singing (though much of it was still a silent movie using subtitles); there were some earlier shorts and features with sound effects, but this motion picture revolutionized the industry. AP/WIDE WORLD PHOTOS

JAZZ SINGER, THE, a motion picture released by Warner Brothers in October 1927, was the first successful feature-length production to include sound, ushering in the end of the silent film era. Audiences thrilled when Al Jolson, in the title role, broke into song and proclaimed, "You ain't heard nothing yet!" Directed by Alan Crosland (filming Alfred A. Cohn's screen adaptation of Samson Raphaelson's play *Day of Atonement*), *The Jazz Singer* tells the tale of Jakie Rabinowitz, the young Jewish son of a New York City cantor who would rather "sing jazzy" than follow five generations of cantors. Jakie runs away from home to pursue his dreams of stardom; years later, under the name Jack Robin, Jakie returns to New York City. Conflict arises when Jakie must decide between singing "Kol Nidre" in place of his sick father on Yom Kippur and opening his Broadway show. Jakie decides to chant "Kol Nidre" for his father in the synagogue, postponing his debut. This decision does not hamper Jakie. The film ends with Jolson crooning "My Mammy" in blackface to his mother in the audience of his Broadway show. The film suggests that in America one can be both hugely successful and remain true to one's roots while also suggesting interesting connections between African American traditions and Jewish American identity.

BIBLIOGRAPHY

Carringer, Robert L. ed. *The Jazz Singer.* Madison: University of Wisconsin Press, 1979.

Crafton, Donald. "*The Jazz Singer*'s Reception in the Media and at the Box Office." In *Post Theory: Reconstructing Film Studies.* Edited by David Bordwell and Noël Carroll. Madison: University of Wisconsin Press, 1996.

Saposnik, Irv. "Jolson, the Jazz Singer, and the Jewish Mother: Or, How My Yiddishe Momme Became My Mammy." *Judaism: A Quarterly Journal of Jewish Life and Thought* 43 (1994): 432–442.

Matthew R. Davis

See also **Film.**

JEFFERSON TERRITORY was established under a spontaneously formed provisional government that had a precarious existence in COLORADO from 1859 to 1861. Legally, the new settlements that grew up in Pikes Peak country following the discovery of gold nearby in 1858 were under Kansas' jurisdiction. They were so far from the seat of the KANSAS government, however, that the territory was unable to exercise effective authority. Denver residents took the first step toward organizing a new government in November 1858 when they elected a delegate to Congress and asked that a new territory be created. Torn with dissension over slavery, Congress did not act until January 1861. Meanwhile, through several successive conventions and elections, inhabitants formed Jefferson Territory without Congressional authorization. They adopted a constitution, elected officials, determined territorial boundaries, and established a legislature, which created counties and courts and passed laws pertaining to personal and civil rights. The nascent government's attempt to collect taxes generally failed, however, mainly because the nearby Arapahoe County, the Kansas government, and the local miners' courts remained the chief means of maintaining law and order. Jefferson Territory came to an end after Congress created the Territory of Colorado in 1861. Jefferson Territory stands as an example of many similarly short-lived attempts to establish provisional governments in unorganized territories. As was the case in Jefferson Territory, these territories—including Deseret (Utah) and the State of Franklin (Tennessee)—lasted only until settlers used legal channels to establish territorial governments recognized by Congress.

BIBLIOGRAPHY

Abbott, Carl, et al. *Colorado: A History of the Centennial State.* 3rd ed. Niwot: University Press of Colorado, 1994.

Smith, Duane A. *Rocky Mountain West: Colorado, Wyoming, and Montana, 1859–1915.* Albuquerque: University of New Mexico Press, 1992.

Colin B. Goodykoontz / S. B.

See also **Deseret, State of; Franklin, State of; Mining Towns; Pikes Peak Gold Rush; Territorial Governments; West, American; Westward Migration.**

JEFFERSONIAN DEMOCRACY has never been described more economically or elegantly than in Thomas Jefferson's inaugural address in 1801. For twelve years after George Washington's inauguration, the infant federal government had been directed by a Hamiltonian design for national greatness. The election of 1800, Jefferson informed one correspondent, was "as real a revolution in the principles of our government as that of 1776 was in its form"; it rescued the United States from policies that had endangered its experiment in popular self-governance and had undermined the constitutional and social groundwork of a sound republican regime, from leaders whose commitment to democracy itself had seemed uncertain. The Jeffersonian Republicans would set the Revolution back on its republican and popular foundations. They would certainly, as most historians would see it, loose a spirit of equality and a commitment to limited government that would characterize the nation for a century or more to come.

Thomas Jefferson. Painting by Rembrandt Peale, 1800.

As Washington's secretary of the Treasury, Alexander Hamilton had faced toward the Atlantic and supported rapid economic growth, envisioning the quick emergence of an integrated state in which the rise of native manufactures would provide materials for export and a large domestic market for the farmers. Supported by a broad interpretation of the Constitution, his economic and financial policies were intended to equip the young nation with institutional foundations comparable to those that had permitted tiny Britain to compete effectively with larger nation-states, and he carefully avoided confrontation with that power. The Republicans, by contrast, were more concerned about the preservation of the relatively democratic distribution of the nation's wealth. While they had always advocated freeing oceanic commerce and providing foreign markets for the farmers, they believed that Federalists had rendered the United States subservient to Britain and had actually preferred a gradual reintroduction of hereditary rule.

Jeffersonian ambitions for the nation focused much more on the West, where a republic resting on the sturdy stock of independent farmer-owners could be constantly revitalized as it expanded over space. Under Jefferson's (and then James Madison's) direction, the central government would conscientiously withdraw within the boundaries that they believed had been established when the Constitution was adopted, assuming that the states, "in all their rights," were "the most competent administrations for our domestic concerns and the surest bulwarks against antirepublican tendencies." The national debt would be retired as rapidly as preexisting contracts would permit, not clung to for its broader economic uses while the interest payments steadily enriched a nonproductive few and forged a dangerous, corrupting link between the federal executive and wealthy moneyed interests. State militias, not professional armed forces, would protect the nation during peacetime. Internal taxes, during peacetime, would be left to the states. The federal government would cultivate "peace, commerce, and honest friendship with all nations, entangling alliances with none." Committed to "equal and exact justice to all men, of whatever state or persuasion, religious or political," to religious freedom, freedom of the press, and other constitutional protections (many of which, as Jefferson conceived it, had been gravely threatened during the final years of Federalist rule), the Jeffersonians would conscientiously pursue "a wise and frugal government which shall restrain men from injuring one another, shall leave them otherwise free to regulate their own pursuits of industry and improvement, and shall not take from the mouth of labor the bread it has earned." The Jeffersonian Republicans, as Jefferson or Madison conceived it, were quintessentially the party of the people and the champions of the republican Revolution. Their principles democratized the nation, profoundly shaping its religious landscape as well as its political institutions and ideas. They may also have protected slavery, produced a war with Britain, and contributed essentially to both sides of the argument that led to civil war.

BIBLIOGRAPHY

Banning, Lance. *The Jeffersonian Persuasion: Evolution of a Party Ideology.* Ithaca, N.Y.: Cornell University Press, 1978.

Hatch, Nathan. *The Democratization of American Christianity.* New Haven, Conn.: Yale University Press, 1989.

McCoy, Drew R. *The Elusive Republic: Political Economy in Jeffersonian America.* Chapel Hill: University of North Carolina Press, 1980.

Lance Banning

See also **Federalist Party; Republicans, Jeffersonian.**

JEHOVAH'S WITNESSES, one of the most prominent Adventist and apocalyptic sects to have emerged in America. Charles Taze Russell—raised a Presbyterian and heavily influenced by Adventist teachings—founded the denomination in the early 1870s, when his loosely structured Bible study groups evolved into a discernible movement. In 1879, Russell published *Zion's Watchtower and the Herald of Christ's Presence* (later known as *The Watchtower*), which served as the principal means of spreading the Witnesses's prophetic interpretations and doctrines. In 1884, Russell incorporated the movement as the Watchtower Bible and Tract Society, which would become known as the Dawn Bible Students, the Russellites, and the International Bible Students before adopting its current name in 1931.

Although the church has no ordained ministry, it has been led by a succession of powerful directors. After Russell died in 1916, leadership passed to the charismatic and volatile Joseph Franklin Rutherford, who expanded the fledgling sect into an organized international movement. Upon Rutherford's death in 1942, the more bureaucratic Nathan Homer Knorr took over. He further developed the Witnesses's publishing enterprise and instituted a series of international and regional assemblies. Frederick Franz succeeded Knorr in 1977, and Milton Henschel replaced Franz in 1994.

Like other Adventist groups, Jehovah's Witnesses emphasize the apocalyptic sections of the Bible, particularly the books of Daniel and Revelations. They worship Jehovah (the term comes from the name for God in the Jewish Bible) and believe in universal atonement through the crucifiction; in an Arian Christology—the nontrinitarian belief that Christ was an archangel who chose to become a human; and in the imminence of the millennium. In that golden age, they believe, 144,000 elected will share in Christ's rule as citizens of a messianic kingdom based in Jerusalem. According to Russell, the movement had reached 144,000 converts by 1881 (although, because of apostasy [abandoning one's faith], no one could know the absolute number of spiritually baptized saints). The numerical limit of saved converts has necessitated a unique doctrine in which there are two "classes" of Witnesses: the 144,000 elected, and others who may escape destruction and achieve limited rewards provided they join the Witnesses during their lifetimes.

Today, this tightly organized movement engages in widespread evangelism. Their principal activities include Bible study, door-to-door witnessing, and the publication and sale of religious literature. In the United States, Jehovah's Witnesses have attracted legal controversy due to their claim of exemption from military service, which is based on their commitment to fight in no battle except Armageddon; their proselytizing activities; their rejection of blood transfusions; and their refusal to pledge allegiance to the American flag (Witnesses pledge obedience to Jehovah alone). Popular animosity notwithstanding, the courts have consistently affirmed their right to dissent. Despite increasing defections, the Jehovah's Witnesses estimate their membership to be nearly one million in the United States and approximately six million worldwide, with international membership concentrated in Latin America and Africa. U.S. headquarters, including the Watchtower publishing center, are located in Brooklyn, New York.

BIBLIOGRAPHY

Conkin, Paul K. *American Originals: Homemade Varieties of Christianity.* Chapel Hill: University of North Carolina Press, 1997.

Harrison, Barbara Grizzuti. *Visions of Glory: A History and a Memory of the Jehovah's Witnesses.* New York: Simon and Schuster, 1978.

Newton, Merlin Owen. *Armed with the Constitution: Jehovah's Witnesses in Alabama and the U. S. Supreme Court, 1939–1946.* Tuscaloosa: University of Alabama Press, 1995.

Peters, Shawn Calvin. *Judging Jehovah's Witnesses.* Lawrence: University Press of Kansas, 2000.

Glenn T. Miller/Shelby Balik

See also **Adventist Churches; Conscientious Objectors; Conscription and Recruitment; Evangelicalism and Revivalism; Protestantism; Religion and Religious Affiliation; Religious Liberty.**

JENKINS' EAR, WAR OF (1739–1743), was a struggle between England and Spain. It preceded the War of the Austrian Succession (known in North America as King George's War), which lasted until 1748. The war was named for Robert Jenkins, a British seaman who lost an ear in a brush with the Spaniards off the coast of Florida. Commercial rivalry on the seas and disputes over proprietary rights to Georgia contributed to the conflict. England and Spain fought at sea and on land, in two major theaters: the Caribbean and the Georgia-Florida borderlands.

The war resulted in no significant gains for either side. The British admiral Edward Vernon captured Portobelo on the Isthmus of Panama in 1739 but met with disastrous failure in 1741 at Cartagena, Colombia's principal port. James Oglethorpe, having clinched an alliance with the Creek Indians at a meeting on the Chattahoochee River, invaded Florida early in 1740 and seized two forts on the St. Johns River. He attacked St. Augustine the following summer but failed to take it. In 1742 a force of five thousand Spaniards sought to end the Georgia colony but was turned back at the Battle of Bloody Marsh, on St. Simons Island. The next year, Oglethorpe again invaded Florida without success.

BIBLIOGRAPHY

Dowd, Gregory Evans. *A Spirited Resistance: The North American Indian Struggle for Unity, 1745–1815.* Baltimore, Md.: Johns Hopkins University Press, 1992.

Merrell, James H. *The Indians' New World: Catawbas and Their Neighbors from European Contact through the Era of Removal.* New York: Norton, 1989.

Usner, Daniel H., Jr. *Indians, Settlers, and Slaves in a Frontier Exchange Economy: The Lower Mississippi Valley before 1783.* Chapel Hill: University of North Carolina Press, 1992.

Shelby Balik
E. Merton Coulter

See also **Colonial Wars; Indian Treaties; King George's War.**

JERSEY PRISON SHIP, a dismantled sixty-four-gun British man-of-war moored in Wallabout Bay, in the New York harbor, during the American Revolution. It confined American naval prisoners taken by the British. Although it was only one of several prison ships in the harbor, it became notorious for the ill treatment of prisoners. They received inadequate, often spoiled, and poorly cooked rations. Although the ship housed as many as twelve hundred captives at one time, all prisoners, whether able-bodied or sick and dying, spent each night below deck, where the heat, vermin, and stench were intolerable. Dysentery, smallpox, and yellow fever were prevalent, and the death rate was appalling.

BIBLIOGRAPHY

Bowman, Larry G. *Captive Americans: Prisoners during the American Revolution.* Athens: Ohio University Press, 1976.

Louis H. Bolander
Angela Ellis

See also **Atrocities in War; Prison Ships.**

JESUIT *RELATIONS*. Each Jesuit missionary in colonial and frontier America was required to report every year to his superior the events of his mission and the prospects for further exploration. Beginning in 1632 these reports were published annually in a volume entitled *Relations* and forwarded to the chief of the order in France or

Jesuits in the New World. A missionary preaches to Indians in New France (Canada) in this line drawing by C. W. Jefferys. Granger Collection, Ltd.

Rome. The Jesuit missionaries wrote reports of the regions of Canada, the Great Lakes, and the Mississippi Valley that could not be surpassed. In 1673 the publication was suspended; however, the missionaries continued to send in reports, which remained in manuscript for almost two centuries.

In all, forty-one separate *Relations* were published, and several American libraries have the full series. In 1896 Reuben G. Thwaites edited an expanded version entitled *Jesuit Relations and Allied Documents*, covering the period 1610 to 1791. This edition included not only the published *Relations* but also other documents secured from many sources in America and Europe. It forms a source of unusual quality for the conditions of the North American continent at the time: accounts of the fauna and flora; descriptions of the lakes, rivers, and country; and mention of indications of minerals and other resources. It is especially useful to scholars for the information it provides about the customs and migrations of the native Americans, their relationship to the environment, the impact of European conquest and settlement on them, and European responses to indigeneous cultures.

BIBLIOGRAPHY

Chapple, Christopher, ed. *The Jesuit Tradition in Education and Missions: A 450-Year Perspective.* Scranton, Pa.: University of Scranton Press, 1993.

Thwaites, Reuben G., ed. *The Jesuit Relations and Allied Documents: Travels and Explorations of the Jesuit Missionaries in New France, 1610–1791.* New York: Pageant Book Co., 1959.

Louise Phelps Kellogg/A. R.

See also **Catholicism; French Frontier Forts; Indian Missions; Jesuits; Religious Thought and Writings.**

JESUITS. The history of the Jesuits in America can be divided into three periods. The first, a period of Jesuit missionary enterprise, begins in 1566 with Pedro Martínez landing in Florida, and ends in 1773, when Pope Clement XIV suppresses the order. The second period stretches from the restoration of the Jesuits in 1814 to the early 1960s, and traces the broad shift toward educational and academic ministries and parish work. The third period begins in 1962 with the Second Vatican Council.

Pedro Martínez died in a clash with the indigenous people of Florida. Neither he nor any of the other Spanish Jesuits established enduring Catholic settlements in the region north of modern-day Mexico. However, in the seventeenth and eighteenth centuries Jesuits had more success, especially in southern Arizona, where Eusebio Kino worked among the people of Pimería Alta, and in Maryland, where a handful of British Jesuits settled in the one colony enthusiastic about Catholic immigrants. By the late eighteenth century, 144 Jesuits had served in missions in British territories in North America. French Jesuits moved south from Canada into the colonies of New York and modern-day Maine; they also inhabited the southern portion of the Great Lakes region. Jesuit willingness to blend Christian and Native traditions facilitated conversions. Eventually the Jesuits established cadres of Catholic Indians throughout the region.

The primary difficulty faced by Jesuits in the seventeenth and eighteenth centuries was anti-Catholicism and anti-Jesuitism brought to the New World by British colonists weaned on the fundamental texts of the Reformation. In 1620, William Brewster brought on board the *Mayflower* a just-published translation of the Venetian historian Paulo Sarpi's attack on the Council of Trent and the papacy. Fears of popery and Jesuits shaped the rhetoric of settlers in colonial New England just as in Britain. New England Protestant missionaries asked Abenaki Indians in 1699 to abandon "those foolish superstitions and plain idolatries with which the Roman Catholics and especially the Jesuits and missionaries have corrupted [religion]." In 1724, Sébastian Råle, a French Jesuit working among Maine Indians, was murdered and his scalp carried back to Boston.

The papal suppression of the Jesuits occurred in 1773, and though the new nation was growing rapidly, Catholic priests were few. Still, in 1789 John Carroll (1735–1815) became the first American bishop. In the same year Carroll founded the first Jesuit college, Georgetown College (now Georgetown University) in Washington, D.C. By the first decade of the nineteenth century, Pope Pius VI allowed ex-Jesuits to begin to affiliate with each other.

The restoration of the Jesuits by Pope Pius VII in 1814 allowed the order to begin again. The initial efforts in the United States were halting, as only a small number of Jesuits spread throughout the East, Midwest, and Louisiana. Their focus was often on setting up missions for Native Americans. Pierre-Jean De Smet (1801–1873) became the most famous Jesuit missionary; he traveled back and forth across the continent and consulted with Indian chiefs and governmental officials. During the nineteenth century, the primary task of the Jesuits switched from missionary work to education. Their students were the Catholic immigrants pouring into the United States in the latter half of the nineteenth century; the first were immigrants from Ireland and Germany, with slowly increasing numbers from Italy and Poland. Here the distinctive mentality of the nineteenth-century Jesuits—suspicion of modern philosophical trends, wariness toward any deviation from Roman orthodoxy—helped create a Catholic educational system that saw itself as countercultural, protecting the faith in a hostile environment. By 1916, the Jesuits, then numbering 2,626, had founded twenty-four Catholic colleges and a larger number of Catholic high schools. Virtually all of the students in these institutions were male, and the Jesuits understood themselves to be training a lay Catholic elite of teachers, doctors, lawyers, and businessmen to defend the church in the world.

Since they were busy establishing schools, few American Jesuits became intellectual leaders until the middle of the twentieth century. Pushed by coeducation and even more by the effect of the G.I. bill after World War II, Jesuits found themselves struggling to keep pace with the 130,000 students enrolled in their colleges by 1963. Still, from the middle of the nineteenth century forward, Jesuits provided much of the energy behind Catholic publishing, founding such magazines as *America* in 1909. By the 1930s, there were roughly twenty Jesuit labor schools, attesting to the growing interest in social reform and mobilization of the Catholic working classes.

Not until the 1940s did individual Jesuits begin to exert intellectual leadership. They primarily used a natural law template to argue that moral values were universal and that reason could lead to faith. The most important figure was John Courtney Murray (1904–1967). A brilliant stylist and deeply learned, Murray became a leading figure in the church-state debates of the 1940s and 1950s, arguing that America's founders did not intend as rigid a separation of church and state as contemporary American liberals assumed. Within the church, he became the foremost spokesman for the position that Catholics should embrace religious freedom along the American model, not grudgingly accept it while formally proclaiming "error has no rights." These heterodox views led Roman authorities to suppress Murray's writings on the topic during the latter 1950s. Yet, Murray's views triumphed at the Second Vatican Council, with the adoption by the assembled bishops in 1965 of a document he helped draft, *Dignitatis Humanae*, also called the "Declaration on Religious Freedom."

At the time of the Council almost one quarter of the 36,038 Jesuits in the world were American. Within thirty years, the number of American Jesuits had fallen almost by half, even as the worldwide Jesuit population fell by one-third. The dwindling order focused more on interior spiritual development than on fighting secularists. Yet, the primary Jesuit ministry remained education. Many Jesuits pushed their colleges and high schools toward what one worldwide gathering of the Jesuits called the "struggle for justice," meaning greater engagement with social evils such as poverty and the suppression of human rights. At the same time, fears that the declining number of Jesuits signaled an evisceration of Catholic institutional identity were widespread. Jesuit high schools (now primarily coeducational) seemed more stable in this regard than universities, which were overwhelmingly staffed by laypeople, many, if not most, of whom were non-Catholic.

At the beginning of the twenty-first century, Jesuits remain as leaders in every aspect—editorial, liturgical, pastoral, and intellectual—of Catholic life. In addition a small number of Jesuits have achieved prominence in the wider world of the American academy. One American Jesuit theologian, Avery Dulles (b. 1918), noted for his defense of the theological views of Pope John Paul II, was even named a cardinal in 2001, the first American theologian so honored.

BIBLIOGRAPHY

Axtell, James. *The Invasion Within: The Contest of Cultures in Colonial North America.* New York: Oxford University Press, 1985.

Garraghan, Gilbert J., S.J. *The Jesuits of the Middle United States.* 3 vols. Chicago: Loyola University Press, 1983. The original edition was published in 1938.

McDonough, Peter. *Men Astutely Trained: A History of the Jesuits in the American Century.* New York: Free Press, 1992.

O'Malley, John. *The First Jesuits.* Cambridge, Mass.: Harvard University Press, 1993.

John T. McGreevy

See also **Anti-Catholicism; Education, Higher: Denominational Colleges; Explorations and Expeditions: French; Indian Missions.**

JEWISH DEFENSE LEAGUE. Created in 1968, the Jewish Defense League (JDL) emerged as a militant and sometimes violent organization of working-class Jews disaffected with the growing urban crisis, the rise of black ANTI-SEMITISM, and the bureaucratic lethargy of mainstream national Jewish organizations. The Orthodox rabbi Meir Kahane founded the group, which counted over 15,000 members at the height of its popularity in the early 1970s. The JDL combined strident Zionism with American identity politics to create a right-wing alternative to the left-leaning ethnic revival of the 1960s. Its mottos, "Never Again" and "Every Jew a .22," recalled the Shoah and played on the larger Holocaust consciousness emerging among American Jews during the late 1960s and 1970s.

The Jewish Defense League entered the 1968 New York City Teachers' Strike, siding with the teachers, most of whom were Jewish, in a dispute with black parents over community control of the schools. It reached the apex of its influence with participation in the Soviet Jewry movement. While the Jewish Defense League is credited for raising the national profile of the Soviet Jewry cause, it often resorted to violence to achieve its goals. In 1972, two JDL members pleaded guilty to bomb possession and conspiracy to blow up the residence of the Soviet Union's mission to the United Nations. Seven years later, another member of the JDL interrupted a Soviet orchestra performance at Carnegie Hall by setting off a smoke bomb.

With Meir Kahane's 1971 emigration to Israel and 1990 assassination while on a speaking tour in New York City, the JDL ceased to be a meaningful force in American Jewish life. Few in the American Jewish community empathized with the organization's fears of an impending Holocaust. In December 2001, Meir Kahane's successor as JDL head, Irv Rubin, was arrested on charges of conspiring to blow up a California mosque and the offices of an Arab American member of the U.S. Congress.

BIBLIOGRAPHY

Dolgin, Janet L. *Jewish Identity and the JDL.* Princeton, N.J.: Princeton University Press, 1977.

Kahane, Meir. *Never Again! A Program for Survival.* Los Angeles: Nash, 1971.

Rosenthal, Richard. *Rookie Cop: Deep Undercover in the Jewish Defense League.* St. Paul, Minn.: Leapfrog Press, 2000.

Marc Dollinger

See also **Zionism.**

JEWS. In September 1654, twenty-three Sephardic Jews sailed into New Amsterdam's harbor aboard the *St. Catherine.* Fleeing the collapse of Dutch colonial rule in Brazil, the Jews sought refuge in New Amsterdam. They received a cold welcome from New Amsterdam's governor, Peter Stuyvesant, a Calvinist who viewed Jews as "blasphemers of the name of Christ" as well as a potential burden on his colonial coffers. Undeterred, the Jews appealed to brethren in Amsterdam to intervene on their behalf to the directors of the Dutch West India Company.

They succeeded. In 1655, the directors granted Jews permission to settle in New Amsterdam as long as they did not worship publicly, a right Jews had enjoyed in both Brazil and Amsterdam, and they assumed total responsibility for their indigent. In the colonies, economic potential often outweighed religious affiliation, and most white people enjoyed an equality of opportunity. The colonies consistently complained of labor shortages and the directors knew that Jews made good colonists: they quickly established roots in their new home, they remained loyal citizens, they developed international trade networks through contacts in Europe and the Caribbean, and wealth tended to flow along these networks. By forcing the poor Jews who arrived in 1654 to become a viable colonial population, perhaps the directors hoped that the new arrivals would stimulate needed economic growth. Beginning with New Amsterdam, Jews established communities in numerous colonial port cities, including New Port (1677), Savannah (1733), Philadelphia (1745), and Charleston (1750).

Establishing Communities

The Jews who settled in Dutch and, after 1664, British North America participated in a broad international migration that continued well into the twentieth century. They were Sephardim, part of the Iberian-Jewish diaspora created by the expulsion of all Jews from Spain and Portugal during the fifteenth and sixteenth centuries. Soon, Ashkenazi Jews, who traced their roots to northern and central Europe, began to join the Sephardim. Generally poorer, and differing in religious ritual and Hebrew pronunciation, the Ashkenazim constituted the majority of American Jews by 1720.

Immediately upon arrival in North America, Jews established the necessities of full political and religious freedom. In 1655, the Jewish community received permission to construct a cemetery so they could bury the dead according to Jewish religious ritual. In 1656, one year after Lutherans lost their right to worship in their homes, Jews gained that exact privilege. After two years of legal wrestling, Asser Levy, one of New Amsterdam's, and later New York's, most prominent Jews, won Jews burgher rights—citizenship—in 1657. Although Jews did not receive the official right to worship publicly until the end of the seventeenth century, the nascent community worshiped in a building on Mill Street commonly known as the "Jew's Synagogue." The building, which included a mikveh, or ritual bath used primarily by women for rituals associated with family purity laws, served as colonial Jews' house of worship until 1728, when they established Shearith Israel, North America's first permanent synagogue.

Outwardly, the Jews who settled in America during the seventeenth and eighteenth centuries could not be distinguished from their neighbors. This, as well as the low number of marriageable Jews, led to the emergence of intermarriage as a common feature of American Jewish life. Jews differed from their peers, however, in their professional activities. Whereas non-Jewish immigrants tended to work in agriculture or artisanry, Jews concentrated in commerce. Relying primarily upon family and community ties, Jews established trade networks among the colonies, with the Caribbean, and with Europe. These business arrangements provided Jews with the bonds necessary to sustain religious, cultural, economic, and familial interests. By 1730, when about 300 Jews lived in New York, only two Jews listed occupations other than commerce.

While most Jewish merchants traded in rum, hardware, spices, candles, lumber, and fur, some found the most lucrative commodity to be African slaves. Lured by the promise of substantial profit, Jewish notables from the shipping center of Newport, Rhode Island, participated in the traffic of humans. Moreover, like many of their white neighbors, Jews in both the North and the South owned slaves. In fact, the 1703 census revealed that 75 percent of Jewish households owned slaves. Because slavery functioned as the central determinant of American political, economic, and social systems, owning—or seeking to liberate—slaves existed as a central feature of American life for both Jews and non-Jews alike until the Civil War (1861–1865).

The American Revolution and subsequent ratification of the Constitution legitimized the rights and ad hoc privileges that had organized American Jewish life during the past century. The Constitution instituted the legal separation of church and state—a condition of existence quite different from Europe, where religion could determine an individual's political and legal rights.

Nineteenth Century Arrivals

Beginning in the 1820s, a new migration of Jews from Europe began, one that would continue unabated until its climax during the first decades of the twentieth century.

Jews migrated westward between 1820 and 1920 in response to upheavals in European society caused by political emancipation, industrialization, and urbanization. Unlike other immigrant groups, that often returned to Europe after earning enough money to sustain a family, Jews tended to immigrate permanently.

Between 1820 and 1880, the Jewish population in America rose from 4,000 to almost 250,000. Historians usually refer to members of this first wave as "German" immigrants, but the name is incorrect. Jewish immigrants who arrived in America between 1820 and 1880 generally left from areas eventually included in unified Germany (1871) or countries deeply influenced by German culture, such as Austria, Hungary, Bohemia, and Moravia. Yet the pre-1880 contingent also included many Jews whose culture was decidedly Polish, from Silesia and Posen, provinces annexed by Prussia and later assumed into unified Germany, as well as Lithuania, western Russia, and Galicia. These Polish and Eastern European Jews, characterized by poverty, religious traditionalism, and the Yiddish language, more closely resembled the Jews who would begin their exodus to America in the final decades of the nineteenth century.

By the Civil War, Jews lived in over 160 communities in America. Many earned their keep by peddling, a profession that required no initial investment and functioned entirely on credit. Moreover, if successful, an itinerant peddler could earn enough to become a store owner. At a time when few retail stores existed outside the large cities, peddlers provided rural Americans and ethnic neighborhoods with their everyday necessities. Peddlers bought their supplies in large cities like New York, Chicago, or St. Louis and set out either for the hinterlands or the city streets. With their wares slung over their backs, on horsecarts, or on pushcarts, they roved from town to town or neighborhood to neighborhood selling small items like buttons, stoves, glass, needles, old clothes, and plates. Peddling resulted in the creation of extensive peddler-supplier-creditor networks in which Jews across the United States became linked in a collective endeavor to earn a living from the constant pulse of supply and demand. Indeed, this network of peddlers, general stores, and wholesalers served as the foundation for the evolution of the American department store.

Early Judaism in America

After the establishment of Shearith Israel in 1728, synagogues began to spring up wherever Jews settled, including the Touro Synagogue in Newport (1762) and Mikveh Israel in Philadelphia (1782). These first synagogues followed the traditional Sephardic rite. In 1801, resenting Sephardic control over synagogue administration and ritual, a group of Ashkenazim in Philadelphia formed the first "second" synagogue in an American Jewish community.

Because no ordained rabbi arrived in the United States until the 1840s, American Judaism developed almost entirely by improvisation. Moreover, due to their white skin color and their position outside the scope of nativist concerns with Irish Catholics, American Jewish modes of worship and religious institutions developed relatively free from outside interference. Laypeople generally led congregations and a synagogue's board determined religious ritual. Negotiating Jewish tradition, congregational demands, and desires for social acceptance, Jewish leaders oversaw a burgeoning American Judaism as chaotic and diverse as its new homeland. By the close of the 1800s, three major institutions—the Union of Orthodox Jewish Congregations of America, the Jewish Theological Seminary of America, and the Union of American Hebrew Congregations—all claimed to speak for American Jewry.

Starting in 1870, the same processes that had led earlier arrivals to immigrate to America—market capitalism, industrialization, urbanization, and growing anti-Jewish violence—set in motion a new migration from eastern Europe to America. Between 1870 and 1924, when Congress officially legislated the end of free and open immigration, the 2.5 million Jews who immigrated to the United States radically altered American Jewry's demography, social structure, cultural life, and communal order.

Adjusting to America

After crossing the Atlantic, Jewish immigrants landed at Ellis Island. There, they encountered employees of the U.S. government, who checked papers and performed rigorous medical exams, and representatives of settlement houses or the Hebrew Immigrant Aid Society, organizations founded in the late nineteenth century to guide immigrants through landing procedures and provide financial aid, shelter, professional training, and acculturation skills. Whether meeting a family member already established in America or arriving alone, most immigrants headed directly from Ellis Island to one of the major ethnic neighborhoods that saturated America's cities, such as Chicago's West Side, Boston's North End, downtown Philadelphia, or New York's Lower East Side.

The immigrant neighborhood bustled. A cacophony of life, work, and leisure, one square block could hold among its tenements workshops of the garment trades, synagogues, saloons, cafes, wives, children, intellectuals, political functionaries, religious students, gamblers, con artists, and prostitutes. By 1910, 540,000 Jews lived within the 1.5 square miles considered the Lower East Side, cramped into five- or six-story tenement houses. Entire families, as many as seven or eight people, lived in three- or four-room apartments. Often, they took in boarders to help pay the rent. Usually a single male, the boarder would occupy one full room in the tiny apartment, cramping the rest of the family into even smaller quarters.

In order to meet their monthly expenses, every family member earned wages. Generally poorer and more religious than their predecessors, the new arrivals made work a top priority. Unlike their predecessors, the Eastern European Jews who arrived in the decades surrounding the

Rabbi Ralph Stone, Jewish Theological Seminary, New York. A photograph by Alfred T. Palmer, c. 1942, associated with wartime government promotion of the freedom of worship as one of President Franklin D. Roosevelt's "Four Freedoms." LIBRARY OF CONGRESS

turn of the century tended to be skilled laborers, primarily in the garment industry. In fact, in 1900, one out of every three Jewish immigrants labored in the garment trades, although cigar making, peddling, and butchering were also popular professions. Due to the pressure to earn money, women, working in the needle trades, and children, who labored on assembly lines or in the streets selling whatever possible, joined men in the factories, backroom sweatshops, and small street stalls.

To compensate for these tough conditions, Jews developed an array of cultural and political responses to their new environment. The Yiddish theater offered low-cost, high-quality performances of original plays, translations, comedies, and variety shows. Likewise, socialism and Zionism became the dominant secular ideologies of the immigrant neighborhood. The language of these political ideologies, Yiddish, served as a source of literary and theatrical productions. Between 1885 and 1914, over 150 Yiddish dailies, weeklies, monthlies, quarterlies, and yearbooks appeared in print.

Jewish immigrants also produced institutional responses to immigration. Modeled after American fraternal orders, Jews organized *landsmanschaften*, societies for individuals who originated from the same town. The *landsmanschaften* provided various forms of financial aid such as sick and bereavement benefits, and organized small synagogues, lectures, and social opportunities. Trade unionism also provided Jews with opportunities for mutual aid and political expression. The International Ladies' Garment Workers' Union, the most famous of the Jewish trade unions, organized in 1900 to provide support to the thousands of women working in the needle trades. The union opened a health center, experimented in cooperative housing, provided unemployment and health insurance and retirement benefits, and offered recreational and vocational programs. In 1909, the union participated in one of the largest strikes to date, known as the "Uprising of the 20,000," where women shirtwaist workers protested their poor salaries, poor working conditions, and culture of sexual abuse.

The ethnic neighborhood served primarily as a way station for new immigrants. Although it served as the first place of residence for a tremendously high percentage of immigrant Jews, its piteous living conditions encouraged immigrants to move to better neighborhoods as quickly as possible. In these areas of second settlement, public schools, interethnic contacts, and American popular culture all served as a cauldron of integration, tutoring immigrants and their children how to look, sound, and act like Americans. Indeed, by the 1930s, American Jewry became, for the first time, a largely native-born population. Thus, when the depression hit, Jews, like all Americans, suffered financial hardship, bankruptcies, and barriers to financial and educational advancement, as well as the disappointment of the expectations that accompanied general upward mobility.

Following World War II (1939–1945), in which over half a million American Jews served in the armed forces, American Jewry experienced a profound period of social and economic mobility. The Holocaust caused many American Jews to approach life with a new sense of responsibility. Now the world's largest Jewish community, American Jewry aimed for success, both as Americans and as Jews. Most important, they aimed to eradicate the distinctions that had marked earlier generations. Because of the opportunities offered by the GI Bill, Jewish men and women entered higher education in record numbers. As a result, by the end of the twentieth century most of America's 6 million Jews claimed college degrees, worked in white-collar jobs, and enjoyed comfortable lifestyles. Moreover, Judaism experienced a second period of transformation.

As America's Jews became increasingly assimilated, they diversified from the orthodoxy that had characterized the eastern European immigrants to more Americanized forms of Jewish expression. The birth of the State of Israel catalyzed the American Zionist movement. Numerous Jews participated in a wellspring of Jewish cultural expression in literature, academia, dance, and film. Others chose new religious opportunities. Some found "modern" Orthodoxy, a movement to combine traditional Judaism's strict lifestyle constraints with the realities of modern American society. Others chose the Havurah movement, which sprang up in the 1960s. Influenced by 1960s counterculture, members of havurot rejected traditional Judaism's formalism and sought to invest Jewish ritual with greater spirituality and attention to social justice. Most American Jews, however, identified as Reform or Conservative, American Jewry's mainline religious movements.

BIBLIOGRAPHY

Ashton, Dianne. *Rebecca Gratz: Women and Judaism in Antebellum America.* Detroit, Mich.: Wayne State University Press, 1997.

Diner, Hasia R. *A Time for Gathering: The Second Migration, 1820–1880.* Baltimore: Johns Hopkins University Press, 1992.

Ewen, Elizabeth. *Immigrant Women in the Land of Dollars: Life and Culture on the Lower East Side, 1890–1925.* New York: Monthly Review Press, 1985.

Faber, Eli. *A Time for Planting: The First Migration, 1654–1820.* Baltimore: Johns Hopkins University Press, 1992.

Glenn, Susan A. *Daughters of the Shtetl: Life and Labor in the Immigrant Generation.* Ithaca, N.Y.: Cornell University Press, 1990.

Goldman, Karla. *Beyond the Synagogue Gallery: Finding Places for Women in American Judaism.* Cambridge, Mass.: Harvard University Press, 2000.

Goren, Arthur A. *New York Jews and the Quest for Community: The Kehillah Experiment, 1908–1922.* New York: Columbia University Press, 1970.

Grinstein, Hyman. *The Rise of the Jewish Community of New York, 1654–1860.* Philadelphia: The Jewish Publication Society of America, 1945.

Gurock, Jeffrey S., and Schacter, Jacob J., *A Modern Heretic and a Traditional Community: Mordecai M. Kaplan, Orthodoxy, and American Judaism.* New York: Columbia University Press, 1997.

Heinze, Andrew R. *Adapting to Abundance: Jewish Immigrants, Mass Consumption, and the Search for American Identity.* New York: Columbia University Press, 1990.

Jacobson, Matthew Frye. *Whiteness of a Different Color: European Immigrants and the Alchemy of Race.* Cambridge, Mass.: Harvard University Press, 1998.

Jick, Leon A. *The Americanization of the Synagogue, 1820–1870.* Hanover, N.H.: University Press of New England: Brandeis University Press, 1976 [1992].

Markowitz, Ruth Jacknow. *My Daughter, The Teacher: Jewish Teachers in the New York City Schools.* New Brunswick, N.J.: Rutgers University Press, 1993.

Moore, Deborah Dash. *At Home in America: Second-Generation New York Jews.* New York: Columbia University Press, 1981.

Morawska, Ewa T. *Insecure Prosperity: Small-Town Jews in Industrial America, 1890–1940.* Princeton, N.J.: Princeton University Press, 1996.

Rischin, Moses. *The Promised City: New York's Jews, 1870–1914.* Cambridge, Mass.: Harvard University Press, 1962.

Soyer, Daniel. *Jewish Immigrant Associations and American Identity in New York, 1880–1939.* Cambridge, Mass.: Harvard University Press, 1997.

Svonkin, Stuart. *Jews Against Prejudice: American Jews and the Fight for Civil Liberties.* New York: Columbia University Press, 1997.

Wenger, Beth S. *New York Jews and the Great Depression: Uncertain Promise.* New Haven, Conn.: Yale University Press, 1996.

Wertheimer, Jack, ed. *The American Synagogue: A Sanctuary Transformed.* Hanover, N.H.: University Press of New England: Brandeis University Press, 1987.

Josh Perelman

JIM CROW LAWS, which regulated social, economic, and political relationships between whites and African Americans, were passed principally to subordinate blacks as a group to whites and to enforce rules favored by dominant whites on nonconformists of both races. The name "Jim Crow" came from a character in an early nineteenth-century minstrel show song.

Beginning with a ban on interracial marriages in Maryland in 1664, the laws spread north as well as south, but they were neither uniform nor invariably enforced. The campaign against them, initiated in the 1840s by both black and white Massachusetts antislavery activists, reached a symbolic end in the 1967 U.S. Supreme Court case, *Loving v. Virginia,* that finally ruled anti-intermarriage laws unconstitutional.

The most widespread laws mandated racial segregation in schools and public places such as railroads, restaurants, and streetcars. Since segregation laws often replaced customary or legal exclusion of African Americans from any services at all, they were initially, in a sense, progressive reforms. They tended to be adopted earliest and were more strictly enforced in cities where diverse crowds intermingled, than in the countryside where other means of racial subordination were readily available.

During Reconstruction in the 1860s and 1870s, seven southern states passed laws requiring equal access to places open to the public; Louisiana and South Carolina, as well as seven northern states, promised integrated schools. After a long struggle over whether to include a school integration provision, Congress in 1875 passed the Civil Rights Act, which prohibited racial discrimination in public accommodations. But in 1883, the U.S. Supreme Court ruled in *The Civil Rights Cases* that Congress had no power under the Fourteenth Amendment to regulate an individual's discriminatory behavior.

While virtually all northern states that had not already banned Jim Crow practices rushed to enact state versions of the invalidated national Civil Rights Act, most southern states during the 1880s and 1890s passed laws requiring segregation. The Supreme Court held up the southern laws in *Plessy v. Ferguson* (1896), accepting assurances that separate accommodations would be equal. Freed of legal restraints, some southern cities and states went on to prescribe separate drinking fountains, restrooms, entrances to public buildings, and even Bibles for use in court. More significantly, they disfranchised the vast majority of African Americans through literacy and property tests and discrimination against blacks who could pass such tests.

The National Association for the Advancement of Colored People (NAACP) led the long effort to overturn Jim Crow through lawsuits such as those that led to *Brown v. Board of Education of Topeka* (1954), as well as by lobbying for new state and federal laws. Beginning in the 1890s and greatly intensifying in the 1950s, African Americans boycotted segregated transit, held sit-ins at segregated restaurants, picketed discriminatory businesses, registered black voters, and braved frequent violence in an ultimately successful effort to force Americans to abolish the most blatant legal inequities. The 1964 Civil Rights Act, the 1965 Voting Rights Act, and a host of state and federal court decisions institutionalized the crusaders' victories. The demise of explicitly discriminatory laws, however, was only one giant step on the unfinished journey toward racial equality.

BIBLIOGRAPHY

Kousser, J. Morgan. *Dead End: The Development of Nineteenth-Century Litigation on Racial Discrimination in Schools.* Oxford: Clarendon Press, 1985.

Rabinowitz, Howard N. *Race Relations in the Urban South, 1865–1890.* New York: Oxford University Press, 1978.

Woodward, C. Vann. *The Strange Career of Jim Crow.* 3rd rev. ed. New York: Oxford University Press, 1974.

J. Morgan Kousser

See also **Black Codes; *Brown v. Board of Education of Topeka*; Civil Rights Movement; Literacy Test; National Association for the Advancement of Colored People; Poll Tax; Segregation.**

JINGOISM, in American usage, a term for the blatant demand for an aggressive foreign policy. The word is probably derived from a music-hall song popularized in England during a crisis with Russia in 1877–1878:

> We don't want to fight, but, by jingo, if we do,
> We've got the ships, we've got the men and got the money too.

By March 1878 "jingo" was a term of political reproach. In the United States it has been directed toward those who have advocated the annexation of Canada, the seizure of Mexico, expansion in the Caribbean or the Pacific, or a bellicose interpretation of the Monroe Doctrine.

BIBLIOGRAPHY

Beisner, Robert L. *From the Old Diplomacy to the New, 1865–1900.* New York: Crowell, 1975; Arlington Heights, Ill.: Harlan Davidson, 1986.

Stanley R. Pillsbury / D. B.

See also **Foreign Policy; Monroe Doctrine.**

JOB CORPS is a federal program that provides food, shelter, work clothes, health care, and job training to teenagers and young adults at 115 campuses across the United States. Begun during the War on Poverty in the 1960s, and meant to offer alternatives to young disadvantaged Americans who might otherwise turn to crime, its fortunes have risen and fallen in the decades since its founding. At the end of the twentieth century, the program cost approximately $1.2 billion annually, had enrollment of about 70,000 (70 percent of them minorities), and had served more than 1.9 million.

The Job Corps was created as a major arm of the antipoverty program through the Economic Opportunity Act, which President Lyndon B. Johnson signed into law on 20 August 1964. The new agency was built on lessons learned from the Civilian Conservation Corps and the Farm Security Administration of the 1930s, Ford Foundation experiments in community development, urban renewal programs, and welfare reforms of the U.S. Department of Health, Education, and Welfare. It was also influenced by scholarly studies suggesting the complex interrelationships of such variables as economic growth, mental health, racial and ethnic biases, illiteracy, local power structures, and family lifestyles. Under the leadership of Sargent Shriver, director of the Office of Economic Opportunity, the Job Corps was dedicated not to creating and finding jobs for the unemployed, but rather to the more ambitious goals of human reclamation and social mobility.

The Job Corps provides general and vocational education, technical training, and useful work experience at residential centers for young people from poverty backgrounds ages sixteen through twenty-one years to prepare them for responsible citizenship and productive employment. The program was founded on the assumption that such young people must be removed from their home environments before effective reclamation might be accomplished.

The administration of the Job Corps during the Johnson years was continuously challenged by such problems as a high dropout rate, misbehavior at the centers, managerial disputes, community hostility toward nearby centers, difficulty in finding suitable locations for centers, high administrative financial costs, and sharp congressional and other political opposition. The administration of President Richard M. Nixon closed many Job Corps centers and curtailed the program's budgets; what remained of the agency was transferred to the Manpower

Administration in the Department of Labor. Emphasis was shifted from residential centers to centers within commuting distance of the enrollees' homes. Also, technical training largely replaced general remedial education.

Although the Job Corps was more thoroughly studied and evaluated than any other antipoverty agency, its long-range impact remains an open question. In the 1990s, Job Corps faced a number of challenges, threats, and criticism: Critics charged that the program was wasteful because it was spending $26,000 per student, and fewer than 15 percent of participants were completing the program. A 1995 bill sought to turn control over to the states and to close numerous programs, but Congress voted that the federal government should retain control and that fewer centers should be closed. Attempts to boost the program's reputation backfired, however, when a study to demonstrate the Job Corps' effectiveness as an anticrime measure turned out to have used a highly controversial methodology. The study, which Labor Secretary Robert Reich commissioned from Mathematica Policy Research, intentionally denied admission to one in every twelve eligible applicants in order to use them as a control group. It then paid them $10 each for follow-up interviews to study their subsequent fate; the study's architects worked from the assumption that they would find a higher rate of criminal behavior in the control group because participants had been denied the opportunities Job Corps offered. The study cost $17.9 million and took nine years. In September 1998, the 6,000 control subjects filed a class-action lawsuit against the Labor Department. A U.S. District Court judge ruled that the Labor Department should have subjected the study's methodology to public review, and halted the study. The Labor Department reached a preliminary settlement with the plaintiffs, under which it pledged to locate those in the control group and invite those who are still eligible to enroll in Job Corps. Fifteen of the plaintiffs received $1,000 for providing information to the court, but none received any money in damages.

President Bill Clinton gave something of a boost to Job Corps during his administration, but his successor, President George W. Bush, showed little intention of continuing such support. The future of Job Corps is likely to continue to rise and fall, depending on the presidential administration and the composition of Congress.

BIBLIOGRAPHY

Levitan, Sar A., and Garth L. Mangum. *Federal Training and Work Programs in the Sixties.* Ann Arbor: Institute of Labor and Industrial Relations, University of Michigan, 1969.

McCarron, Kevin M. "Job Corps, AmeriCorps, and Peace Corps: An Overview." *Occupational Outlook Quarterly* 44, 3 (Fall 2000): 18–25.

Price, John. "Job Corps Lottery." *Mother Jones* 24, 1 (January 1999): 21.

Sidney Baldwin / D. B.

See also **Crime; Labor; Labor Legislation and Administration; Poverty; Unemployment; War on Poverty; Work.**

JOHN BIRCH SOCIETY was founded in December 1958 by Robert Welch, a retired Boston candy manufacturer who considered President Dwight D. Eisenhower "a dedicated conscious agent of the Communist conspiracy." According to Welch and other society members, coconspirators ranged from Franklin D. Roosevelt to the various chairs of the Federal Reserve Board. John M. Birch was a Baptist missionary and Air Force officer who was killed by Chinese communists in 1945, ten days after V-J Day. Welch never met Birch, but he named his society in honor of the man he called the Cold War's first hero. The society quickly emerged as perhaps the most well-known far-right anticommunist group in the United States. By the early 1960s, the group peaked after enlisting some ten thousand members, including hundreds who sat on school and library boards or held other civic offices. Headquartered in Belmont, Massachusetts, society activists ran campaigns calling for the impeachment of Supreme Court Chief Justice Earl Warren and the United States' withdrawal from the United Nations. On a more regular basis, the Birch Society publishes a journal, *American Opinion*, and runs youth camps, book distribution services, and intellectual cadres of "Americanists" scattered throughout the nation. Its members have never advocated violence.

BIBLIOGRAPHY

Broyles, J. Allen. *John Birch Society: Anatomy of a Protest.* Boston: Beacon Press, 1964.

Hardisty, Jean. *Mobilizing Resentment: Conservative Resurgence from the John Birch Society to the Promise Keepers.* Boston: Beacon Press, 1999.

Kenneth O'Reilly

See also **Anticommunism; Radical Right;** *and vol. 9:* **The Blue Book of the John Birch Society.**

JOHNNY APPLESEED. As the American frontier moved into Ohio, Indiana, and Illinois, the settlers lacked fruit until orchards could be planted and could grow. Since the settlers did not have money, they could not have bought young trees even if nurseries had existed. Not surprisingly, horticulture languished. Therefore, between 1801 and 1847, John Chapman dedicated himself to bringing seed from Pennsylvania to the frontier forests and planting flowers and fruit trees, especially apple trees. He intended them to be ready for the free use of the settlers when they arrived. Meager documentary evidence and rich tradition have preserved Chapman's fame under the sobriquet "Johnny Appleseed."

BIBLIOGRAPHY

Price, Robert. *Johnny Appleseed: Man and Myth.* Bloomington: Indiana University Press, 1954.

Bliss Isely / A. E.

See also **Folklore; Frontier; Fruit Growing.**

JOHNS HOPKINS UNIVERSITY, a private, nonsectarian institution of higher learning, opened on 22 February 1876 in Baltimore, Maryland, as the country's first research-based, graduate-level university. Funded by the Baltimore Quaker merchant Johns Hopkins with a bequest of $7 million—the largest philanthropic gift given to that date in the United States—the university was modeled after the great European universities. It was the first to combine the liberal arts, the classics, and scientific research. Known since its inception for innovative programs, many consider Johns Hopkins to be the first modern American research university. It revolutionized higher education, medical training and practice, and, not least, provided an unlikely arena in the battle for women's equality.

The university, which has eight academic divisions, first opened in modest classrooms in downtown Baltimore, but soon moved north to Baltimore's more spacious Homewood section, where the main campus is still located. The university's first president, Daniel Coit Gilman, launched what many at the time considered to be an audacious and unprecedented academic experiment to merge teaching and research. He dismissed the idea that the two were mutually exclusive: "The best teachers are usually those who are free, competent, and willing to make original researches in the library and the laboratory," he stated. To implement his educational plan, Gilman recruited internationally known luminaries such as the biologist Henry Newell Martin; the Greek scholar Basil Gildersleeve; the classicist Charles D. Morris; the economist Richard T. Ely; and the chemist Ira Remsen, who became the second president of the university in 1901.

The Johns Hopkins Hospital in East Baltimore opened to much fanfare in 1889. The university's research-based pedagogy soon attracted world-renowned faculty members who became giants in the emerging field of academic medicine, including William Osler, William Halsted, Howard Kelly, and William Welch.

In the age of scientific discovery and bacteriology, the opening of the country's first research-based hospital was propitious. John Shaw Billings, a surgeon and the country's leading expert on hospital construction, designed the pioneering hospital, the first in the country to offer, among a host of innovations, central heating. With its well-equipped laboratories and rooms, patients benefited from the new "bench-to-bedside" transfer of research from laboratory to patient. Faculty became clinician-physicians. The hospital's charter, reflecting the Quaker philosophy of its founder, mandated hospital care for the "sick and indigent" of Baltimore.

The founder of the university had always hoped to establish a modern medical school, sorely needed in the late nineteenth century, when medical education was in its infancy. At the time, there were few academic standards and even fewer known medical cures. A student could study for a few months at a proprietary medical school or apprentice with a physician. But the university faced a major hurdle. Soon after the completion of the hospital, the remaining endowment earmarked to start the medical school sank with the misfortunes of the 1880s stock market. In 1889, President Gilman put forth a national plea for a "man of large means" to endow the proposed medical school. The search for a benefactor took four years. The person who stepped up to the plate was Mary Elizabeth Garrett, the thirty-eight-year-old daughter of John Work Garrett, a Hopkins trustee and president of the powerful Baltimore and Ohio Railroad from 1858 until his death in 1884.

Despite Gilman's stated intention to make the university a place to "to develop character and to make men," it soon became a battleground for women's rights. Mary Garrett headed the national Women's Medical School Fund, founded in 1890 to raise money to make the proposed Hopkins medical school coeducational. The fund's roster included the country's wealthiest and most prominent grande dames and activists. They organized into fifteen chapters across the country and eventually raised $100,000. Garrett contributed $354,000, one of the largest amounts given by a woman in the nineteenth century, for the balance needed to open the medical school. She insisted on several unprecedented conditions, notably that women were to be admitted "on the same terms as men," and that the new medical students have a baccalaureate degree with a background in science and language.

One commentator at the time called the Hopkins victory the "crowning achievement for American feminism in the nineteenth century." In the fall of 1893, three women medical students took their place with fifteen male students. Hopkins became the nation's first coeducational, graduate-level medical school and the prototype for academic medicine. The Hopkins medical school ushered in a heightened era of medical standards, which emphasized bedside learning, research projects, and laboratory training. The new medical school produced some of the most outstanding scientists and physicians in the United States during the twentieth century.

Hopkins is known for a range of other groundbreaking programs. The Johns Hopkins University Press, founded in 1878, is the oldest American university press in continuous operation. In 1909, the university was among the first in the country to start adult continuing education programs and by the end of the century offered classes in numerous sites around Maryland and the District of Columbia. In the mid-twentieth century, the university began to focus on international programs. Since 1950, the

Johnstown Flood. A photograph dated 31 May 1889 shows a riverside shack whose enterprising owner, the legend underneath states, "made a fortune from selling souvenirs" of that date's natural disaster. © BETTMANN/CORBIS

Paul H. Nitze School of Advanced International Studies in Washington, D.C., has been a division of Hopkins. In addition to the nation's capital, the school has campuses at Nanjing, China, and Bologna, Italy. In 1977, the university acquired the famed Peabody Institute in Baltimore, a leading professional school of music, founded in 1857.

In 2001, Hopkins enrolled 18,000 students and employed more than 25,000 full-time, part-time, and temporary employees, making it one of the top five employers in Maryland. In 1999, it ranked first in federal research and development funds, receiving $770.5 million, given primarily to the Applied Physics Laboratory. The School of Medicine is the largest recipient of National Institutes of Health grants and Hopkins consistently is named among the top universities and medical centers in the world. Its endowment tops $1.8 billion, making it the twenty-third wealthiest university in the United States.

BIBLIOGRAPHY

Chronicle of Higher Education, Almanac Issue, 2001–2002.

Harvey, A. McGehee, et al. *A Model of Its Kind.* Vol. 1, *A Centennial History of Medicine at Johns Hopkins.* Vol. 2, *A Pictorial History of Medicine at Johns Hopkins.* Baltimore: Johns Hopkins University Press, 1989.

Schmidt, John C. *Johns Hopkins: Portrait of a University.* Baltimore: Johns Hopkins University Press, 1986.

Warren, Mame. *Johns Hopkins: Knowledge for the World, 1876–2001.* Baltimore: Johns Hopkins University Press, 2000.

Kathleen Waters Sander

See also **Coeducational Movement; Education, Higher: Colleges and Universities; Medical Education; Medical Research.**

JOHNSON IMPEACHMENT. *See* **Impeachment Trial of Andrew Johnson.**

JOHNSTOWN FLOOD of 1889 was the worst natural disaster in the United States. The city of Johnstown is located in southwestern Pennsylvania, in a narrow valley where the Little Conemaugh and Stony Creek rivers merge to create the Conemaugh River. In 1880, Johnstown was a leading industrial center with 10,000 inhabitants and 20,000 more in its surrounding communities.

In 1852, construction was completed on the South Fork Dam upstream on the Little Conemaugh River, creating a man-made reservoir. The dam gave way in 1862 and the damaged dam and surrounding property was sold. It was acquired in 1879 by the South Fork Fishing and Hunting Club, whose members were the wealthy elite from Pittsburgh and other eastern cities. From 1879 to 1881 the earth and rock dam was rebuilt, stretching 918 feet across and 72 feet high. The reservoir expanded to nearly three miles in length, one mile in width, and about sixty feet in depth at the dam face.

In late May 1889, torrential rains caused flooding in more than twenty western Pennsylvania counties. By 31 May, the water level climbed to within two feet of the top of the South Fork Dam, and it breached. The center collapsed, sending a wall of water one-half mile wide and seventy-five feet deep through the valley. Within another hour, the then forty-foot wall of water descended on Johnstown. The estimated 20 million tons of water was partially blocked at the Pennsylvania Railroad viaduct, creating a thirty-acre field of debris, drowned livestock, and human bodies, which eventually caught fire. In ten minutes, at least 2,209 people were killed (although contemporary records claim as many as 5,000), 1,600 homes damaged or destroyed, and the iron and steel factories ruined.

The *New York Times* of 1889 characterized the flood as "a symbol of the havoc created by the elements gone wild," while the *London Chronicle* condemned the shoddiness of American engineering. The dam lacked a core of masonry or puddle, and did not represent accepted construction practices even for the time. Survivors held the South Fork club members responsible, but the courts affirmed the disaster to be an "act of God" and no legal compensation was made to the survivors. The responsibility for the flood remains undetermined and has attracted the attention of numerous scholars.

Another major flood on 17 March 1936 caused $50 million in damage and resulted in a U.S. Army Corps of Engineers flood-control project in 1942. However, the city was again flooded in July 1977.

BIBLIOGRAPHY

Ferris, George T. *The Complete History of the Johnstown and Conemaugh Valley Flood.* New York: H. S. Goodspeed, 1889.

Frank, Walter S. "The Cause of the Johnstown Flood." *Civil Engineering* 58, no. 5 (May 1988): 63–66.

Johnson, Willis Fletcher. *History of the Johnstown Flood.* Bowie, Md.: Heritage Books, 2001. The original edition was published in 1889.

McCullough, David G. *The Johnstown Flood.* New York: Simon and Schuster, 1968.

Charles C. Kolb

See also **Disasters; Floods and Flood Control; Hydroelectric Power; Pennsylvania.**

JOINT CHIEFS OF STAFF (JCS) came into existence in 1942. The JCS consisted of the chief of staff, U.S. Army; the chief of naval operations; and the chief of staff, U.S. Air Force. Their functions were to advise the president on the military, give strategic direction to the army and navy, and facilitate U.S.-British military cooperation. In 1949, an amendment to the National Security Act of 1947 established the position of chairman of the Joint Chiefs of Staff; the chairman was to preside over the meetings of the JCS, but had no vote. Moreover, he was not to exercise military command over the JCS or any of the military services. In 1952, Public Law 82-416 authorized the commandant of the Marine Corps to meet with the JCS as a co-equal whenever any matter concerning the Marine Corps was under consideration. On 28 October 1978, Public Law 95-485 made the commandant of the corps a permanent and fully participating member of the JCS.

The Goldwater-Nichols Act of 1986 prescribed the most important changes in the Joint Chiefs of Staff organization since 1949. It increased the responsibilities of the chairman, naming him the principal adviser to the president, the National Security Council, and the secretary of defense. The chairman was to attend and participate in meetings of the National Security Council, and his responsibilities were expanded to include assisting the president with strategic direction of the armed forces; preparing strategic plans and joint logistic and mobility plans; and advising the secretary of defense on requirements, programs, and budgets, particularly on budget proposals for activities of each unified and specified combatant command. In addition, the act created the position of vice chairman of the Joint Chiefs of Staff to rank after the chairman and ahead of all other officers of the armed forces.

BIBLIOGRAPHY

Millett, Allan R. *The Reorganization of the Joint Chiefs of Staff: A Critical Analysis.* Washington, D.C.: Pergamon-Brassey's, 1986.

Robert S. Driscoll

See also **Defense, Department of; National Security Council.**

JOINT COMMISSIONS. The arbitration of international disputes by joint commissions is usually distinguished from the negotiation of formal treaties by more than one diplomatic agent—such as the Definitive Treaty of Peace of 1783, the termination of Franco-American hostilities by the Convention of 1800, the Louisiana Purchase of 1803, the Treaty of Ghent of 1814, the WEBSTER-ASHBURTON TREATY of 1842, and the Peace of Paris of 1898. Most arbitrations are the work of joint commissions, as indicated in the monumental six-volume work on international arbitration by John Bassett Moore. Since its publication in 1898, further cases have arisen for settlement, notably the Alaskan boundary dispute of 1903.

Of the numerous arbitrations to which the United States has been a party, some of the more important ones were conducted for the following purposes: settling pre-Revolution American debts to the British, British spoliation claims, and the Maine-Canada boundary, under the Jay Treaty of 1794; for settling French spoliation claims in 1803, 1831, and 1880; for determining various articles under the Treaty of Ghent; for claims of American citizens against Mexico, in 1839, 1849, and 1868; for U.S. claims against Colombia in 1861 and against Peru in 1863; and for Spanish claims in 1871. Most significant of all was the Alabama Claims dispute with Britain, which led to the Geneva award of 1872. To these may be added fact-finding commissions as an indispensable adjunct of modern diplomacy.

Since the mid-twentieth century, reservations have increased toward the use of joint commissions to settle international disputes. In 1946, the United States accepted the compulsory jurisdiction of the International Court (except in domestic matters), but continued its reluctance to accept any other binding arbitration.

BIBLIOGRAPHY

Bailey, Thomas A. *A Diplomatic History of the American People.* New York: F. S. Crofts, 1940; 1942; 1946; New York: Appleton-Century-Crofts, 1950; 1955; 1958; 1964; 1969; Englewood Cliffs, N.J.: Prentice Hall, 1974; 1980.

Moore, John Bassett. *History and Digest of the International Arbitrations to Which the United States Has Been a Party, Together with Appendices Containing the Treaties Relating to Such Arbitrations, and Historical and Legal Notes.* Washington, D.C.: Government Printing Office, 1898; Buffalo, N.Y.: William S. Hein, 1995.

Paterson, Thomas, J. Garry Clifford, and Kenneth J. Hagan. *American Foreign Relations: A History.* Lexington, Mass.: D.C. Heath, 1995; Boston: Houghton Mifflin, 2000.

Louis Martin Sears / T. G.

See also **Diplomatic Missions; Ghent, Treaty of; Paris, Treaty of (1898); Prize Cases, Civil War; Treaties with Foreign Nations.**

JOINT COMMITTEE ON RECONSTRUCTION was established by the Thirty-Ninth Congress on 13 December 1865 to investigate and report on conditions in the former Confederate states after the Civil War and to propose necessary legislation. Congress referred to this committee the credentials of senators and representatives from former Confederate states that had been reconstructed according to President Andrew Johnson's mild Reconstruction program. The Senate initially rejected a provision barring the seating of any congressman from the former Confederacy until the committee reported, but both houses passed a concurrent resolution to this effect after Johnson vetoed the Freedmen's Bureau Bill in February 1866. Chaired by the senior senator William Pitt Fessenden from Maine, a moderate Republican informally recognized as the Senate majority leader, the committee consisted of six senators and nine representatives, all but three of whom were Republicans. Although the senior representative was the Pennsylvania Radical Republican Thaddeus Stevens, Fessenden's counterpart in the House, Radical Republicans were a minority on the committee. Also important was Representative John A. Bingham, the leading moderate House Republican, who developed the committee's proposal to amend the Constitution to protect civil rights.

From January to May, but mostly in February, four subcommittees took testimony in Washington from U.S. military and Freedmen's Bureau officers; former Confederate political and social leaders, including General Robert E. Lee and the Confederate vice president Alexander H. Stephens; northern immigrants and visitors to the South; southern Unionists, and a few black southerners. The testimony was designed both to gather information and to make a public record justifying congressional legislation. While former Confederates generally insisted that the southern states were peaceful and ready for restoration, the other witnesses indicated that the former slaves and those who had remained loyal to the Union were subject to violence and intimidation and that restored southern governments would deny African Americans' basic civil rights. In light of the testimony, the committee fashioned amendments to the Constitution to modify the apportionment of congressional representation in light of the emancipation of the slaves and to secure the rights of American citizens.

However, in February and March, Congress refused to agree to initial committee proposals, instead passing civil rights legislation emanating from the Senate Judiciary Committee. Congress finally agreed to the Reconstruction Committee's proposal of a multipart Fourteenth Amendment in June 1866, sending it to the states for ratification. The committee's report explaining why the amendment was necessary and its compilation of testimony, published in 1866, were two of the most effective documents justifying Republicans' Reconstruction policy. But Congress tabled the committee's Reconstruction Act, which would have recognized the restoration of former Confederate states to normal relations in the Union upon their ratification of the proposed amendment and its incorporation into the Constitution.

In February 1867, after every former Confederate state but Tennessee rejected the proposed Fourteenth Amendment, the Joint Committee proposed a bill to put all the other southern states under military authority. As amended by the House and Senate, this measure became the Reconstruction Act of 1867, under the terms of which the southern states were placed under military authority, reconstructed, and restored. The Joint Committee was not renewed by the Fortieth Congress and ceased to exist upon the expiration of the Thirty-Ninth Congress on 2 March 1867.

BIBLIOGRAPHY

Kendrick, Benjamin B. *The Journal of the Joint Committee of Fifteen on Reconstruction, 39th Congress, 1865–1867.* New York: Columbia University Press, 1914. Reprint New York: Negro Universities Press, 1969.

Lowe, Richard. "The Joint Committee on Reconstruction: Some Clarifications." *Southern Studies* 3 (Spring 1992): 55–65.

Wilbur, W. Allan. "Joint Committee on Reconstruction, 1865." In *Congress Investigates: A Documented History, 1792–1974.* Edited by Arthur M. Schlesinger Jr. and Roger Bruns. New York: Chelsea House, 1975.

Michael Les Benedict

See also **Reconstruction.**

JOINT OCCUPATION, a term designating the 1818 U.S.-British agreement regarding the joint occupation of the Oregon territory as being "free and open" to subjects of both states for trade and commerce during the next ten years. The joint occupation was one part of the CONVENTION OF 1818 WITH ENGLAND that Richard Rush and Albert Gallatin negotiated with British delegates Henry Goulburn and Frederick J. Robinson. The delegates signed the treaty on 20 October 1818, and it was unanimously ratified by the U.S. Senate on 30 January 1819. Subsequently, on 6 August 1826, the United States and Great Britain renewed the joint occupation until either party gave one-year notice to terminate it. The agreement remained in effect until December 1845, when President James K. Polk asked Congress to annex all the Oregon territory if Britain refused to divide it at the forty-ninth parallel (see OREGON TREATY OF 1846).

The 1818 convention was a first step in moving the two states away from their 1812 controversy toward rapprochement. The convention also dealt with fishing rights near Labrador, agreed to use arbitration to determine indemnity for slaves the British carried away in 1812, and renewed an 1815 trade agreement.

BIBLIOGRAPHY

Merk, Frederick. *The Oregon Question: Essays in Anglo-American Diplomacy and Politics.* Cambridge, Mass.: Harvard University Press, 1967.

Rakestraw, Donald A. *For Honor or Destiny: The Anglo-American Crisis over the Oregon Territory.* London: Peter Lang, 1995.

Weeks, William Earl. *Building the Continental Empire: American Expansion from the Revolution to the Civil War.* Chicago: Ivan R. Dee, 1997.

Lester Brune

JOINT-STOCK LAND BANKS were chartered under the authority of the Federal Farm Loan Act, approved 17 July 1916. These banks were financed with private capital and were permitted to make loans in the states in which they were chartered and in one contiguous state. About eighty-seven charters were granted, but not all of the banks opened for business. The joint-stock banks were most numerous in the more prosperous agricultural areas—Iowa, Illinois, Minnesota, Missouri, Texas, and California. The original law did not limit the size of loans, but an amendment to the act in 1923 limited the loans to agricultural purposes only and reduced the size of loans to $50,000 per borrower. The federal government appraised the borrower's land, and the amount of a loan was limited to a percentage of the value of the appraised land and buildings.

These banks thrived during the World War I land booms but declined rapidly when the agriculture industry slumped in the late 1920s. Many of the banks failed. Accusations of mismanagement followed, and many banks reorganized or liquidated. The Emergency Farm Mortgage Act of 1933 ordered the joint-stock land banks liquidated. To help with the liquidation, the Farm Credit Act of 1933 provided the Land Bank Commission with $100 million for two years and renewed the provision for two more years in 1935.

BIBLIOGRAPHY

Farm Credit Administration. *Annual Reports.* Since 1933.

Federal Farm Loan Board. *Annual Reports.* 1916–1933.

Wright, Ivan. *Farm Mortgage Financing.* New York: McGraw-Hill, 1923.

Ivan Wright / A. R.

See also **Agriculture; Banking; Financial Panics.**

JOLLIET-MARQUETTE EXPLORATIONS. Louis Jolliet was a native of New France who, after being educated at the Jesuit schools of Quebec, embarked on a career of exploration in the far western country during the seventeenth century. On one of his voyages to Lake Superior in 1669, he met the Jesuit missionary Jacques Marquette, then at the mission of Sault Ste. Marie. Three years later, the authorities of New France commissioned Jolliet to undertake the discovery of the great central river of the continent, which American Indians called the Mississippi. Jolliet requested that Marquette be appointed chaplain of the expedition. Late in the autumn of 1672 he set out for the Northwest to join Marquette at the mission of St. Ignace on the north shore of Mackinac Straits; there the two explorers prepared the voyage.

On 17 May 1673 Jolliet and Marquette left St. Ignace in two canoes with five voyageurs. They went by way of Lake Michigan, Green Bay, and the Fox River, a route that was well known as far as the upper villages on the Fox. At the Mascouten, village guides were obtained to lead them to the portage. A month after departure their canoes shot out from the Wisconsin into a great river, which they instantly recognized as the one they sought. Marquette wished to name the river the Conception for the Immaculate Conception of the Virgin Mary. Jolliet called it first the Buade, after Louis de Buade, Comte de Frontenac, governor of New France. Ultimately, he christened it the Colbert, for the prime minister of France. However, the Indian name persisted.

The two explorers in their canoes drifted downriver as far as the Arkansas; they met few Indians, and these for the most part were friendly. They saw paintings on the

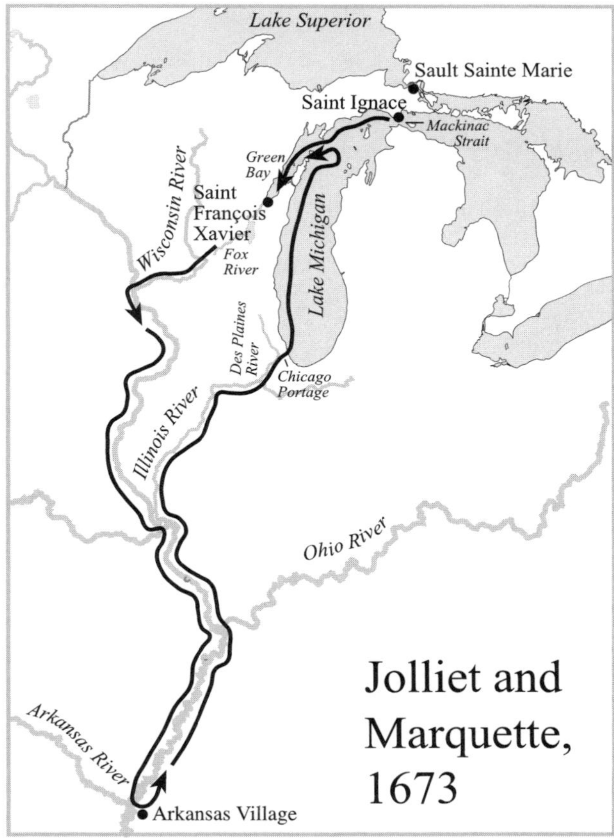

cliffs high above the stream, which are now known as the Alton Petroglyphs. From the Arkansas they turned back upstream, fearing to encounter Spaniards on the lower river. Acting on Indian advice, they did not return to the Fox-Wisconsin waterway but ascended the Illinois and the Des Plaines, portaging at Chicago to Lake Michigan. They were thus the first Europeans to stand on the site of Chicago.

Via Lake Michigan and Green Bay, they journeyed to the mission at De Pere, where Marquette remained to regain his health when Jolliet embarked for Canada in 1674 to report their discoveries. Just before Jolliet reached Montreal, his canoe overturned in the rapids. He lost all his journals, notes, and maps and saved his life only with difficulty. Thus, Marquette's journal has become the official account of the voyage, and Jolliet's voice has been somewhat muted. Jolliet was an expert mapmaker, later the official hydrographer of New France. His maps of the expedition, however, were drawn from memory, and Marquette's maps superseded them.

The Jolliet-Marquette discovery was widely heralded in France and formed the basis for the exploration and exploitation of the Mississippi Valley by Robert Cavelier de La Salle and other French explorers later in the seventeenth century.

BIBLIOGRAPHY

Kellogg, Louise Phelps. *The French Régime in Wisconsin and the Northwest.* Wisconsin History Series, vol. 1. Madison: State Historical Society of Wisconsin, 1925.

Louise Phelps Kellogg/A. R.

See also **Explorations and Expeditions: French; French Frontier Forts; Jesuit "Relations"; Mississippi River.**

JONES ACT, or Organic Act of the Philippine Islands, passed by Congress on 29 August 1916, provided for the government of the Philippines and committed the United States to the future independence of the archipelago. The act gave the right to vote to all male citizens over twenty-one years of age who could read and write. The two houses of the Philippine Congress were made wholly elective; the president of the United States was to appoint, subject to confirmation by the Senate, justices of the Philippine Supreme Court and a governor-general. Full independence of the Philippines was realized in 1946.

BIBLIOGRAPHY

Carlson, Keith Thor. *The Twisted Road to Freedom: America's Granting of Independence to the Philippines.* Diliman, Quezon City: University of the Philippines Press, 1995.

Paredes, Ruby R., ed. *Philippine Colonial Democracy.* Southeast Asia Studies Monograph Series, no. 32. New Haven, Conn.: Yale University Southeast Asia Studies, Yale Center for International and Area Studies, 1988.

John Colbert Cochrane/T. M.

See also **Insular Cases; Paris, Treaty of (1898); Philippines; Tydings-McDuffie Act.**

JONES V. VAN ZANDT, 46 U.S. 215 (1847), provided abolitionists with an opportunity to challenge the constitutionality of the 1793 federal Fugitive Slave Act and attack slavery itself as contrary to "natural right." American jurist Salmon P. Chase contended that the law violated the Fourth, Fifth, Seventh, and Tenth Amendments. But Justice Levi Woodbury of the U.S. Supreme Court rejected these arguments, insisting that the fugitive slave clause of Article IV was one of the "sacred compromises" of the U.S. Constitution and Congress had power to enforce it. According to the ruling, the constitutionality or injustice of slavery itself was a "political question" left to the states and which federal judges could not resolve.

BIBLIOGRAPHY

Wiecek, William M. "Slavery and Abolition Before the United States Supreme Court, 1820–1860." *Journal of American History* 65, no. 1 (1978): 34–59.

William M. Wiecek

See also **Fugitive Slave Acts.**

JONESTOWN MASSACRE, 18 November 1978, was the mass suicide of 913 members, including 276 children, of the Peoples Temple cult led by the Reverend Jim Jones. After moving his Peoples Temple to California in 1965, Jones persuaded his followers to relocate to an agricultural commune in Jonestown, Guyana, in 1977, following allegations of financial misconduct. In Guyana, Jones confiscated passports, manipulated his followers with threats of blackmail and beating, and staged bizarre rehearsals for mass suicide. Friends and relatives of cult members warned U.S. officials that Jones was using physical and psychological torture to prevent defections from Jonestown. On 14 November 1978, U.S. Congressman Leo Ryan of California flew to Guyana with a group of journalists and relatives of cult members to investigate the charges. As Ryan's party, along with fourteen cult defectors, prepared to leave, Jones ordered them assassinated. Upon learning that only four of them had been killed, Jones organized a mass suicide ritual. On 18 November, Jones presided over the enforced suicide ceremony during which his followers drank cyanide-laced punch. Jones died later that day from a gunshot wound, possibly self-inflicted.

BIBLIOGRAPHY

Kilduff, Marshall. *The Suicide Cult: The Inside Story of the Peoples Temple Sect and the Massacre in Guyana.* New York: Bantam Books, 1978.

Klineman, George. *The Cult that Died: The Tragedy of Jim Jones and the Peoples Temple.* New York: Putnam, 1980.

Weightman, Judith Mary. *Making Sense of the Jonestown Suicides: A Sociological History of Peoples Temple.* New York: E. Mellen Press, 1984.

Carolyn Bronstein / H. S.

See also **Cults.**

Jonestown. Bodies everywhere: 913 members of the Peoples Temple cult lie dead at their agricultural commune in Guyana after a mass suicide ritual on 18 November 1978. © CORBIS

JOURNAL OF CONGRESS, the official record of the proceedings of the legislative branch of the U.S. government. When the Continental Congress in 1774 appointed Charles Thomson as secretary, he kept a manuscript journal recording its resolves and other decisions and also the attendance of the members. This journal was published contemporaneously in thirteen volumes. Thomson also kept a secret journal that was not published until 1821. These journals, together with information from auxiliary records and papers, formed the core of the thirty-four-volume Library of Congress edition of the *Journals of the Continental Congress*, published 1904–1937, to reconstruct the fuller story of the activities of the Congress from 1774 to 1789.

The Constitution provides that "each House shall keep a Journal of its Proceedings." In the earliest congresses, the journals were printed in parts and distributed during the session. At the end of each session since 1789, verbatim reports have been published with indexes, one or more volumes for each house. After the burning of the Capitol in 1814, which destroyed all printed copies belonging to both houses, the journals of the first thirteen congresses were reprinted (1820–1826). Until 1861 the journals were printed by contract and thereafter by the Government Printing Office under the authority of each house. They are also substantially incorporated in the *Annals of Congress* (covering 1789–1824), in the *Register of Debates* (1824–1837), in the *Congressional Globe* (1833–1873), and in the *Congressional Record* since 1873. The Senate also keeps an executive journal, which has been published from time to time.

BIBLIOGRAPHY

Schmeckebier, L. F., and Roy B. Eastin. *Government Publications and Their Use.* Washington, D.C.: Brookings Institute, 1969.

Roscoe R. Hill / C. W.

See also **Congressional Record; Continental Congress; Washington Burned.**

JUDAISM. The first Jews in North America arrived from Holland in 1654, their ancestors having been expelled from Spain and Portugal at the end of the fifteenth century. The religion of these Sephardic (Spanish) Jews was different from that of the Ashkenazic Jews who arrived in the United States two centuries later from Central and Eastern Europe. Sephardic Jews followed a ritual different from their Ashkenazic counterparts and came from a region where, until the 1490s, they had enjoyed relative peace, security, and wealth under both Muslim and Christian rulers. They were eager to assimilate into American society and did so successfully. During the American Revolution, a Hessian mercenary serving in Newport, Rhode Island, commented that the Jews were "not distinguishable by their beards and attire . . . while their women wear the same French finery as the other faiths." The arrival of Ashkenazic Jews during the nineteenth century altered the character of Judaism in the United States. Although many gravitated toward the Reform tradition, the majority remained Orthodox, especially those coming from Lithuania, Poland, Romania, and Russia between 1880 and 1924. As a consequence, Orthodox Judaism in the United States became synonymous with Central and Eastern European Jewry.

Orthodox Judaism

By the 1820s three Orthodox Ashkenazic rite synagogues had been established in North America: the first in Easton, Pennsylvania in 1761, followed by Rodeph Shalom in Philadelphia in 1802 and, in 1825, by B'nai Jeshurun in New York City. The first Orthodox rabbi, however, did not arrive in the United States until 1840 when Abraham Rice came from Germany to serve the Orthodox congregation in Baltimore.

Orthodox Jews strictly observe the *Halachah* (Jewish laws). Derived from the Torah, the *Mishna* (commentaries on the Torah), and the *Gemara* (commentaries on the commentaries), the laws make up the Talmud, the authoritative text of Judaism. Orthodox Judaism is preeminently a religion of laws and practices that direct and regulate every aspect of life for the faithful. Among Orthodox Jews, however, community is also essential. To worship, Orthodox Jews require only the presence of ten adult Jewish males, the *minyan*; they need no synagogue or rabbi. Such a community could theoretically be small and self-contained, having no formal connection with other Jews; in practice, however, such isolation has proven impossible to sustain. Complex issues involving ritual and law frequently compel adjudication from an outside authority. As a result, questions of, and disputes about, faith, law, and practice have linked one Jewish community to another.

Isaac Mayer Wise. One of the rabbis who led the movement to create an institutional structure for Reform Judaism in the nineteenth century; he founded several organizations, edited two periodicals, and wrote prolifically. © CORBIS-BETTMANN

The Retreat from Orthodoxy

The years between 1840 and 1880 were turbulent for the American Jewish community. Jews increasingly rejected the Halachi prescriptions as old-fashioned and inapplicable to their circumstances in the United States. Everywhere Orthodoxy was in retreat.

Reform Jews attempted to accommodate Judaism more completely to the modern world. From the 1840s until the turn of the twentieth century, Reform Judaism was the primary form of Judaism in the United States, losing its dominance to Conservative Judaism only in the 1920s. With roots in the eighteenth-century Enlightenment, Reform Judaism emphasized the ethical and moral aspects of religion at the expense of ritual and theology. Only in the United States, however, did Reform Judaism attract substantial numbers of adherents.

The first Reform organization in the United States began among members of the Congregation Beth Elohim of Charleston, South Carolina. They wanted briefer services, greater use of English, and the mixed seating of men and women. (Orthodox Jews separate men and women at worship.) When the majority of the congregation refused to yield, the dissidents withdrew and, in 1824, founded the Reformed Society of Israelites.

The principal impetus behind the growth of Reform Judaism in the United States came from German immigrants who created Reform *Vereine* (Reform Societies) that eventually developed into temples, as they called synagogues. In 1842 Temple Har Siani in Baltimore became the first first Reform temple in the United States, followed in quick succession by Temple Emanu-El in New York City (1845), and later by Sinai in Chicago (1858). During the second half of the nineteenth century, the efforts of Rabbis Isaac Mayer Wise, David Einhorn, and Kaufman Kohler gave institutional order and theological substance to Reform Judaism.

Reform Judaism

Reform Judaism radically altered Jewish belief, ritual, practice, and law. Meeting in Philadelphia in 1869, Reform Jews, guided by the liberal David Einhorn, rabbi at Adath Jeshurun (later Beth-El) in New York City, rejected the hope for a restoration of Israel and a rebuilding of the temple in Jerusalem. Einhorn declared, alternately, that the "messianic aim" of Judaism was a union of all the children of God, not merely the Jews. He also downplayed the customary dietary restrictions and the ritual of male circumcision.

The Pittsburgh Platform of 1885, drafted by Kaufman Kohler, rabbi at Temple Beth-El in New York City and Einhorn's son-in-law, superseded the Reform statement of 1869 and repudiated all Jewish laws and practices not in keeping with "the views and habits of modern civilization." In the Pittsburgh Platform, which Isaac Mayer Wise called the "Jewish Declaration of Independence," Kohler asserted that the Jews were not a nation or people in exile, but a religious community. As such, Jews could anticipate "neither a return to Palestine, nor a sacrificial worship under the sons of Aaron, nor the restoration of any laws concerning the Jewish state." Kohler and the signatories of the Pittsburgh Platform characterized Judaism as a "progressive religion, ever striving to be in accord with the postulates of reason."

Controversy and Antagonism

Relations between Reform and Orthodox Judaism could not have been more antagonistic. Reform Jews looked upon the Orthodox as ignorant rabble who had given themselves over entirely to vulgar superstitions. The Orthodox considered Reform Jews heretics and pagans. Yet the majority of the 2.5 million Jewish immigrants who came to the United States between 1880 and 1924, or at least their children, gradually abandoned Orthodoxy and embraced Reform Judaism. Although they accepted the tenets of Reform Judaism, Jewish immigrants from Central and Eastern Europe were unwilling to renounce their Jewish cultural heritage and ethnic identity. Many were ardent Zionists, and by the 1930s had compelled the Reform movement to change its position on Zionism. Originally rejecting Zionism, by 1937 the Central Conference of American Rabbis, which Isaac Wise had founded in 1889 as one of the institutional centers of Reform Judaism, adopted a statement of principles that called for the creation of a Jewish state in Palestine.

Conservative Judaism

The effort to accommodate to American circumstances and concurrently to preserve Jewish tradition led to the emergence of Conservative Judaism. By the end of the twentieth century Conservative Judaism was the largest branch of American Judaism, consisting of 850 congregations that represented 1.5 million members.

Conservative Judaism originated from a breach that developed in the Reform movement. At a banquet held in 1883 to honor the first graduating class of Hebrew Union College in Cincinnati, Ohio, the caterer, who was himself Jewish, served shrimp, one of the foods forbidden to Jews who follow *kashrut,* the Jewish dietary laws. Several members of the board of trustees along with a number of rabbis left the banquet in a rage, convinced that they could not make common cause with Reform Jews who apparently sought to ridicule them and to denigrate the customs and precepts they cherished. From this relatively minor incident Conservative Judaism was born.

Although the infamous "*trefa* (forbidden food) banquet" was the immediate cause of the Jewish division into Reform and Conservative factions, Conservative Judaism had more significant antecedents. Not all Jews in the United States endorsed the radical break with tradition that the reformers espoused in the Pittsburgh Platform. Under the direction of Isaac Lesser, Sabato Morais, Henry Pereira Mendes, Marcus Jastrow, and Benjamin Szold, Conservative Jews sought to perpetuate the Jewish dietary laws, which Isaac Wise had disparaged as "Kitchen Judaism," the identity of Jews as a people in exile, and the unity of American Jews with their brethren scattered throughout the world. The Conservatives did not oppose change—surely God had not sanctioned all elements of the tradition; some were the work of men and thus men could and, when necessary, should alter them.

Conservatives maintained, however, that Reform Jews encouraged purely utilitarian modifications. They opposed the attitude that the law needed to be replaced not because it had been tried and found wanting but because it had been tried and found impractical and difficult. Conservative Jews did not wish to impugn the tradition but to infuse it with new life. Rabbi Alexander Kohut of Ahavath Chesed in New York City expressed the ideals of Conservative Judaism in a sermon delivered in 1885: "I desire a Judaism full of life . . . a Judaism true to itself and its past, yet receptive of the ideas of the present."

Reconstructionist Judaism

Conservative Jews saw their movement as a compromise between the iconoclasm of Reform Judaism and the rigidity of Orthodox Judaism. They emphasized *klal Yisrael* (universal Israel), and aspired to unite Jews everywhere into a single community as the chosen people of God. In that larger purpose Conservative Jews failed; their commitment, moreover, alienated liberals, some of whom created a fourth American denomination, Reconstructionist Judaism.

A continuation of the ideas of Mordecai M. Kaplan, who urged American Jews to "reconstruct the Jewish civilization," Reconstructionist Judaism dispensed with belief in the supernatural while retaining some commitment to the Jewish tradition in an effort, as Kaplan wrote, "to maintain the historic continuity of the Jewish people and to express, or symbolize, spiritual values or ideals which can enhance the inner life of Jews." Most Reconstructionist Jews, however, emphatically reject the idea of Jews as the chosen people of God. Although not an independent movement until the 1960s, Reconstructionist Judaism, by the1990s, boasted a membership of fifty thousand, with sixty congregations and one hundred and fifty rabbis.

American Judaism in the Twenty-First Century: Problems and Prospects

In the two decades between 1945 and 1967 Jews in the United States, though internally divided, enjoyed a peace and security that enabled them to pursue their version of the American dream. That tranquil period ended with the Arab-Israeli War of 1967. Although the Israelis prevailed, the threat to the existence of Israel brought Jewish history, including the Holocaust, to the forefront of Jewish concerns. Since the late 1960s, the preservation of Jewish traditions, the maintenance of Jewish identity, and the survival of the Jewish people have come to be of paramount importance to American Jews, including many in the Reform and Reconstructionist movements.

Common concerns notwithstanding, relations have not been cordial among Jews in the United States. No issue inspired greater conflict than the debate over the role of women. The introduction of integrated seating at worship, a practice that both Reform and some Conservative Jewish congregations adopted, ignited a terrible quarrel. From the Orthodox perspective, though, the worst violation of Jewish tradition and law were changes authorizing greater participation of women in religious services. The first alteration came in 1973, when the law committee of the Conservative Rabbinical Assembly issued a *takhana* (legislative enactment) that permitted women to be counted in the minyan. A ten-year conflict also ensued over whether to admit women to the rabbinate. The dispute ended in 1983 when the faculty of the Conservative Jewish Theological Seminary in New York City voted thirty-four to eight to accept female students. Reform Jews had voted even earlier, in 1972, to ordain women; the Reform decision to consider ordaining homosexuals increased tensions with Orthodox and Conservative Jews.

Predictably, Orthodox Jews have been the most resistant to making concessions. Their defiance strengthened Orthodoxy, which since the 1970s has been the most dynamic and vibrant Jewish denomination. By 2000 the United States had 1,075,000 Orthodox Jews. As young Jews feel increasingly alienated from the secular world and as many seek to rediscover their cultural and religious heritage, Orthodox Judaism has become more attractive. The dramatic and often salutary alternative that Orthodox Judaism presents to those who have grown weary of the degeneracy of modern American society explains, at least in part, its continued appeal. At the dawn of the twenty-first century, however, Orthodox Jews have had to consider whether, and to what extent, their community can maintain it insularity and protect itself from the contamination of the modern world and how much its survival depends upon adaptation to American life.

BIBLIOGRAPHY

Davis, Moshe. *The Emergence of Conservative Judaism: The Historical School in Nineteenth Century America.* Philadelphia: Jewish Publication Society of America, 1963.

Eisen, Arnold. *The Chosen People in America: A Study of Jewish Religious Ideology.* Bloomington: Indiana University Press, 1983.

Glazer, Nathan, ed. *American Judaism.* 2d ed. Chicago: University of Chicago Press, 1972.

Goldsmith, Emanuel S., Mel Scult, and Robert M. Seltzer, eds. *The American Judaism of Mordecai M. Kaplan.* New York: New York University Press, 1990.

Herberg, Will. *Protestant, Catholic, Jew: An Essay in American Religious Sociology.* New York: Doubleday, 1955.

Libowitz, Richard. *Mordecai M. Kaplan and the Development of Reconstructionism.* Lewiston, N.Y.: E. Mellen Press, 1983.

Neusner, Jacob, ed. *Sectors of American Judaism: Reform, Orthodoxy, Conservatism, and Reconstructionism.* New York: Katv, 1975.

Olitzky, Kerry M., Lance J. Sussman, and Malcolm A. Stern, eds. *Reform Judaism in America: A Biographical Dictionary and Sourcebook.* Westport, Conn.: Greenwood Press, 1993.

Plaut, W. Gunther. *The Rise of Reform Judaism.* 2 vols. New York: World Union for Progressive Judaism, 1963–1965.

Rosenblum, Herbert. *Conservative Judaism: A Contemporary History.* New York: United Synagogue of America, 1983.

Sachar, Howard M. *A History of Jews in America.* New York: Knopf, 1992.

Mark G. Malvasi

See also **Religion and Religious Affiliation; Religious Thought and Writings.**

JUDICIAL REVIEW. When a court measures a statute or an executive action against a constitution, treaty, or other fundamental law, judicial review has occurred. The antecedents of modern judicial review were three: first, Edward Coke's opinion in Bonham's Case (1610), in which he declared an act of Parliament to be against "common right and reason" and therefore void; second, the opinions of the British Privy Council finding certain measures of colonial legislatures to have exceeded authorization under their royal charters; and third, early U.S. state government decisions that state statutes exceeded the permissible bounds set forth in the state constitutions. There were also some early state and federal decisions suggesting that even where the state or federal constitutions were silent, certain basic principles of "republican governments" could not be disregarded by legislators, principles that would be grounds for striking down statutes. In *Calder v. Bull* (1798), Supreme Court Justice Samuel Chase gave examples of the violation of these principles, such as taking one person's property to give to another, deeming an action criminal that was not illegal when committed, and making persons judge and party in their own cases.

Judicial review in America is often dated from John Marshall's opinion in *Marbury v. Madison* (1803). According to Marshall, a provision of the Judiciary Act of 1789 improperly extended the jurisdiction of the U.S. Supreme Court, and was therefore unconstitutional. This was the first opinion in which the Court exercised judicial review *en banc* (with full judicial authority). The idea of judicial review had been employed previously by several of the justices, riding circuit, to question both federal and state legislation. In *Federalist* No. 78, published at the time of the ratification of the U.S. Constitution, Alexander Hamilton asserted the power of judicial review in terms almost identical to those employed by Marshall in *Marbury*. Opponents of the Constitution believed judicial review gave the justices too much discretion, but Hamilton defended the doctrine by arguing that when the judges struck down a statute on the grounds that it was barred by the Constitution, they were merely fulfilling their task as agents of the American people—the sovereign that dictated the Constitution.

Dred Scott Case and the Fourteenth Amendment

Judicial review was infrequent during the Republic's early years, although in several notable cases, including *Fletcher v. Peck* (1810), *Dartmouth College v. Woodward* (1819), and *Gibbons v. Ogden* (1824), the Marshall Court ruled that state legislatures had exceeded the bounds permitted them under the federal Constitution. Not until the Taney Court decided the *DRED SCOTT CASE* (1857), however, was a second federal statute ruled unconstitutional. In a 7 to 2 decision, Chief Justice Taney ruled that Congress had no power to forbid slavery in the territories, because the Fifth Amendment to the Constitution barred Congress from taking property without "due process." According to Taney, forbidding slavery amounted to the obliteration of a property interest that could not be "dignified with the name of due process."

At the beginning of the twenty-first century the *Dred Scott* case is regarded with universal disapprobation. Still, Taney's statement of the proper philosophy of judicial review—that the Court should interpret the Constitution's provisions as they were understood at the time of the Constitution's ratification—has merit and is itself in accordance with the understanding of the framers. Taney's elevation of property rights to the central constitutional concern is also in keeping with the framers' views.

Nevertheless, in *Dred Scott*, Taney belied his own judicial philosophy when he failed to recognize that at the time of the framing of the Constitution there was a presumption in favor of human freedom and a widespread belief that slavery was contrary to natural law. As such, there was less protection for slavery than for other forms of property, and congressional prohibition of slavery where it had not been established by positive law should have been permissible. Another principal holding of *Dred Scott*—that even free blacks were not regarded as "citizens" at the time of the ratification of the Constitution—is similarly debatable. Through 2002, *Dred Scott* continued to be invoked as a symbol of judicial review's excesses.

After the Civil War a series of constitutional amendments were passed, some provisions of which reversed *Dred Scott*. The Thirteenth Amendment forbade slavery and the Fourteenth Amendment made clear that citizenship could not be denied because of race. The Fourteenth Amendment also further circumscribed the powers of state governments by providing that no state could deprive any person of the "equal protection of the laws," take a person's "life, liberty or property without due process of law," or "abridge the privileges and immunities of citizens of the United States." The meaning of these provisions is obscure, but thereafter the Fourteenth Amendment was invoked in the most dramatic instances of judicial review.

The Fourteenth Amendment was intended to improve the lot of the newly freed slaves, but it soon came to be employed in a different context. As states began to impose new forms of economic regulation, many businesses and corporations argued that they possessed Fourteenth Amendment rights that had been infringed. They asserted a "right to contract" that they claimed inhered in the due process provision of the Fourteenth Amendment. Just as Taney believed that a congressional statute that took away a right to property in slaves could not be regarded as due process, so some began to argue that to infringe on the right to contract with one's employees did not meet the requirements of due process. Because this argument did not deal with "process" in its usual sense, it came to be known as substantive due process. This doctrine assumes that there are some subjects on which legislation simply should not be permitted.

A number of Supreme Court decisions found state regulatory legislation unconstitutional. The most famous was *LOCHNER V. NEW YORK* (1905), in which the Court invalidated, on substantive due process grounds, New York legislation that set maximum hours for bakers. *Lochner's* majority was chastised by Oliver Wendell Holmes Jr. in a fiery dissent. He claimed that the majority was imposing its own policy preferences on New York, and was reading into the Constitution a particular economic theory which the framers had not intended.

The New Deal

Until 1937 the U.S. Supreme Court continued to employ judicial review in service of a conservative, business-oriented view of the Constitution. When the Great Depression led to federal regulatory efforts of an unprecedented scope, it was inevitable that the Court would be asked to review the constitutionality of these measures. There were a number of decisions, some upholding New Deal legislation. But in the most notable cases, the Court held that Congress's power to regulate interstate commerce was limited and could not be stretched to include manufacturing or processing which took place within a single state. *SCHECHTER POULTRY CORPORATION V. UNITED STATES* (1935), for example, invalidated the National Industrial Recovery Act (1933).

Schechter Poultry infuriated President Franklin Roosevelt, who bemoaned the Court's use of a "horse-and-buggy" definition of interstate commerce. Roosevelt challenged the Court's interpretive strategy of defining terms the way they had been understood by the framers, and argued for a dynamic interpretation to fit the Constitution to the needs of the times. Roosevelt, in his fulmination, threatened to pack the court by appointing additional justices sympathetic to his views. But before he could, the Court dramatically changed interpretive course.

The case that demonstrated the Court's interpretive shift most clearly was *National Labor Relations Board v. Jones and Laughlin Steel Corporation* (1937), in which the Court allowed Congress to use its powers to regulate interstate commerce to create the National Labor Relations Board, with jurisdiction to mandate collective bargaining and union organizing within manufacturing plants. The Court's logic was that a strike at the Pennsylvania steel plant in question might have consequences for interstate commerce and that this possibility permitted federal regulation. This logic could support federal regulation of nearly anything, and was employed until late in the twentieth century. *Jones* and a number of other cases also rejected the predominance earlier given to freedom of contract, and substantive economic due process died.

The Warren Court

Several striking instances of modern judicial review occurred during the chief justiceship of Earl Warren, who adopted the notion advanced by Franklin Roosevelt that the Constitution ought to be perceived as a "living document." In the landmark case of *Brown v. Board of Education of Topeka* (1954), the Warren Court announced that constitutional jurisprudence could not "turn back the clock." Warren, writing for a unanimous Court, held that racially segregated schools violated the Fourteenth Amendment's guarantee of equal protection of the laws, and that the practice had to end. There was strong evidence that this had not been the intention of the amendment, but the Court brushed this objection aside. The events *Brown* set in motion altered racial relations in America forever, and initiated a pattern of judicial activism unlike any other.

The Warren Court embraced earlier decisions which had held, in spite of a paucity of evidence, that the Fourteenth Amendment was intended to extend the Bill of Rights' prohibitions against the federal government to forbid actions by the states. The Court proceeded, wholesale, to refashion state and local government and law enforcement. The Court ruled that state laws requiring compulsory Bible reading or school prayer violated the First Amendment. It decided that the Fourth Amendment's prohibition on unreasonable searches and seizures meant that local law enforcement officials had to follow particular procedures dictated by the federal courts or have the evidence they obtained thrown out of court. The Court read the Fourteenth Amendment's equal protection language to mean that both houses of the state legislatures had to be apportioned on the basis of population, refusing to allow the states to emulate the federal Constitution's model of one chamber determined by population, and another by political subdivision.

Roe v. Wade

For most of the period of the Burger and Rehnquist Courts, much of the reformist zeal of the Warren Court prevailed. In an exercise of constitutional interpretation second in boldness only to *Brown*, the Court in *Roe v. Wade* (1973) ruled 7 to 2 that state prohibitions on abortion during the first trimester of pregnancy violated the Fourteenth Amendment's requirement of due process. Thus did substantive due process return, though in neither the property rights guise of *Dred Scott* or the economic aspect of *Lochner.*

The audacity of *Roe* led to an unsuccessful struggle in the legal academy to articulate a theory of judicial review that might reconcile the Court's conduct with Hamilton's idea that judicial review merely carried out the will of the people. Although the Court had been unwilling to overturn *Roe*, by 2002 it survived by the slimmest of margins. The Warren Court's decisions regarding state-sponsored prayer were generally upheld as late as 2002, with the Rehnquist Court barring officially selected prayers at school graduations and even at football games. Lower federal courts nibbled away at the school prayer decisions at the beginning of the twenty-first century, however, by permitting schools to impose "moments of silence" with prayer among the permitted meditative activities.

The Rehnquist Court

With the landmark case of *United States v. Lopez* (1995), the Supreme Court, under Chief Justice William Rehnquist, announced for the first time since the New Deal that a federal regulatory measure was not permitted under the commerce clause. Congress had sought to impose federal criminal penalties on those who carried unauthorized firearms in or near any school in the nation. Proponents of the act argued that firearms disrupted education and that the disruption of education would eventually have an adverse affect on interstate commerce. This rationale was no more strained that that which had permitted the Court to allow many New Deal measures, but in a 5 to 4 ruling, the Court decided that to permit this commerce clause argument to prevail in *Lopez* would be to allow unlimited federal regulation.

A later Rehnquist Court case, *United States v. Morrison* (2000), applied similar logic to reject some provisions of the federal Violence Against Women Act, holding that basic criminal law enforcement was a matter for the state and local governments rather than the federal government. *Lopez* and *Morrison*, and a variety of other cases concerned with the assertion of state sovereign immunity and the prohibition on conscripting state and local officials into federal law enforcement, were perceived in the 1990s as the Rehnquist Court's assertion of a "new federalism." Critics charged that the Court's newly activist conservative majority was bent on construing the Constitution in a manner that sharply restricted what the federal government could do, and threatened its role as the protector of civil rights. The Rehnquist Court's defenders argued that it was returning to a jurisprudence of original understanding, and receding from the wanton readings of the Constitution during the Warren Court years.

But if the Rehnquist Court's new federalism decisions could be defended as an exercise in returning the Constitution to its original scheme, it was difficult to make that argument in support of the Rehnquist Court's most ambitious act of judicial review, in *Bush v. Gore* (2000). For the first time, the Supreme Court, at the instance of a presidential candidate, held that a state court's interpretation of state election law violated the equal protection clause of the Fourteenth Amendment. Seven justices agreed there was an equal protection violation, but only five concurred in the Court's remedy of barring further ballot recounts in Florida, in effect awarding the presidency to George W. Bush.

In 2001 and 2002, justifications were advanced for what the Court did (most centering around the country's need to put an end to election proceedings that threatened to drag out for months or years). But the Court's equal protection reasoning was dubious and the Court itself took pains to limit its holding to the case at hand. Many sympathetic to the Gore candidacy believed that the Court stole the election for Bush. Not surprisingly, no sooner did the Democrats take control of the Senate in early 2001 than a series of hearings was scheduled on "judicial ideology." Democratic senators were concerned about preserving the legacy of the Warren Court, and worried that the Rehnquist Court was embarked upon "judicial activism." During the first months of 2001, no Bush nominees were confirmed to the federal courts and Democrats asserted that there was a need for a balance of interpretive approaches on the bench. Republicans countered this argument by asserting that ideology had no place in judging, which, they claimed, ought to be conceived of as an objective search for the original understanding of the legislature or the sovereign people. The nature of judicial review had once again become one of the most important issues in national politics.

BIBLIOGRAPHY

Dionne, E. J., Jr., and William Kristol, eds. *Bush v. Gore: The Court Cases and the Commentary.* Washington, D.C.: Brookings Institution, 2001.

Ely, John Hart. *Democracy and Distrust: A Theory of Judicial Review.* Cambridge, Mass.: Harvard University Press, 1980.

Perry, Michael J. *The Constitution, the Courts, and Human Rights: An Inquiry into the Legitimacy of Constitutional Policymaking by the Judiciary.* New Haven, Conn.: Yale University Press, 1982.

Presser, Stephen B. *Recapturing the Constitution: Race, Religion, and Abortion Reconsidered.* Lanham, Md.: National Book Network, 1994.

Wolfe, Christopher. *The Rise of Modern Judicial Review: From Constitutional Interpretation to Judge-Made Law.* New York: Basic Books, 1986.

Wood, Gordon S. *The Creation of the American Republic, 1776–1787.* Chapel Hill: University of North Carolina Press, 1969.

Stephen B. Presser

See also **Supreme Court.**

JUDICIARY. In the early 1830s Alexis de Tocqueville observed that sooner or later, every important American political issue ends up in the courts. The judiciary of the United States thus occupies a unique institutional role. Americans are a litigious people, and lawyers are a higher percentage of the population in the United States than in any other nation. It is the judiciary that must resolve these disputes. Judges occupy a venerated position in the United States, unlike those of most other nations, where they are regarded more as bureaucrats than as important formulators of policy. Because the rule of law occupies a place in the United States something like the monarchy or the established church once did in European nations, those who administer the law are particularly venerated. They are also the subject of great controversy, and have been since the earliest days of the Republic.

English and Colonial Antecedents

The American judicial system is based on that of Great Britain, but the manner in which justice was administered in England and the colonies is not what it came to be in the United States. Until the twentieth century, English judges were regarded as executive officials, "lions under the throne," as a sixteenth-century term had it. The king was regarded as the law speaking, and although the king's place as the font of law was challenged by the common law judges and this role of the monarch was later displaced by Parliament, throughout much of English history judges were removable at the discretion of the Crown or Parliament. Colonial judges were subject to dismissal by the royally appointed colonial governors or by officials in London. Colonial courts applied English common law, but the decisions of those courts could be overruled by English administrators. Thus, prior to the American Revolution it could not be said that judges had much prestige or that Americans had an independent judiciary.

From Independence to the Civil War

The new state constitutions in 1776, like the federal Constitution in 1789, generally established independent judiciaries as branches of government coequal to the legislatures and executives. The notions expressed in constitutions that liberty requires separating judging from legislating and that it was the job of the judges independently to implement the sovereign will of the people began to take hold. Judges were no longer removable at executive or legislative whim but were, at the federal level and increasingly at the state level, guaranteed tenure during good behavior. An early tension between the state and federal courts was resolved after the political struggles over the Judiciary Act of 1789 and the Judiciary Act of 1801, which generally favored the state courts as the principal forums for the resolution of legal disputes and the development of private law doctrines, such as property, torts, contracts, and corporations.

At a time when the "United States" was a plural rather than a singular noun, it is not surprising that state courts and state governments in general exercised the greatest influence over the lives of American citizens. Nevertheless, even in the early years of the Republic the federal courts and in particular the U.S. Supreme Court, in the exercise of judicial review, enforced some constitutional restrictions against the states. In one of the most important decisions of this kind, Chief Justice John Marshall held in *McCulloch v. Maryland* (1819) that the state of Maryland could not tax the federally incorporated Bank of the United States. That same year in the *Dartmouth College Case,* Marshall overturned the decision of the New Hampshire Supreme Court that the state legislature could alter the charter of Dartmouth College, in effect transforming it from a public to a private university. Somewhat later, in *Swift v. Tyson* (1842), Justice Joseph Story, in spite of a provision of the 1789 Judiciary Act that required him to follow the laws of the states in which the federal courts were situated, ruled that in commercial law matters, the federal courts could impose a rule based on general understandings of the common law rather than the case law of the state in which the federal court sat.

These were exceptional cases, however. In general, unless a clear conflict existed between state and federal statutes or between state law and the federal Constitution, the federal courts gave the state courts and legislatures broad discretion. The best example of this attitude is the *Charles River Bridge Case* (1836), decided shortly after Chief Justice Roger Taney replaced Chief Justice Marshall. The state of Massachusetts had chartered a bridge to compete with the Charles River Bridge, the beneficiary of an earlier state charter. The Charles River Bridge attorneys argued that its charter implied that the state would not authorize at some future date a new bridge that would drive the Charles River Bridge out of business. *Dartmouth College* could have been read to support this argument, but Taney, writing for the Court, rejected it, arguing that the country's developmental needs required competition and progress in the means of transportation and that Massachusetts should be permitted to charter competing bridges in the public interest.

The goals of commercial progress and social mobility reflected in Taney's *Charles River Bridge* decision seem also to have motivated scores of state common law judges, who altered private law doctrines taken from the hierarchical, status-based and agricultural English society to fit an increasingly democratic, growth-orientated, and entrepreneurial American culture. In the early days of the Republic, Americans feared that judges, and in particular federal judges, might turn into an inconvenient aristocracy, oppressing the people with the great discretion the power of judicial review conferred on them. Instead, as Tocqueville predicted, judges and lawyers seem to have moved the law in a more democratic direction. Indeed, in the state judiciaries, to keep judges responsive to the people, election of judges became more common than executive appointments.

The controversy over slavery in the territories in the fifth decade of the nineteenth century, however, resulted in a Supreme Court decision that seriously damaged the prestige of the Court. That decision may have contributed to a climate in which the judiciary ceased for a time to play a significant role in refashioning the law in keeping with social needs. In the *Dred Scott Case* (1857), Chief Justice Taney, writing for the Court in a 7 to 2 decision, ruled that the Constitution prevented Congress from prohibiting slavery in the territories, and also ruled that even freed slaves could not, in the contemplation of the Constitution, be treated as citizens. The decision may have been conceived as way of quelling sectional discontent, but it had the opposite effect. Many historians believe it was instrumental in causing the Civil War.

From the Civil War to the New Deal

From the end of the Civil War until the third decade of the twentieth century, the Supreme Court for the most part played what might be described as a conservative role in national political life, defending the freedom of businesses to make contracts and generally reining in legislatures that sought to impose regulations. For example, in *Lochner v. New York* (1905), over a strong dissent from Justice Oliver Wendell Holmes Jr., the Court held that to allow New York to regulate the hours of bakers would violate the freedom of contract guaranteed by the Fourteenth Amendment.

The Court did, however, permit some federal regulations to pass constitutional muster, for example, with regard to the Interstate Commerce Act (1887) and the Sherman Antitrust Act (1890). Moreover, while the Court was, in *Lochner* and other cases, hostile to the general idea of regulating freedom of contract, it did permit states to regulate wages and hours in particularly dangerous industries or to protect groups that might not possess sufficient bargaining power. Among other significant decisions, the Court held in *Plessy v. Ferguson* (1896) that it was permissible to impose racial separation in public transportation so long as the facilities provided were "separate but equal." And in *Bradwell v. Illinois* (1872) the Court held that, in spite of the Fourteenth Amendment's guarantee of "equal protection of the law" to all persons, women did not have to be admitted to the practice of law.

The reforms at the end of the nineteenth century and the beginning of the twentieth century were characterized more by constitutional amendments and legislative initiatives than by progressive decisions of the courts. Similarly, the common law administered by the state courts was changed relatively little. Democratic and egalitarian advances, such as the progressive income tax, securing the franchise and professional equality for women, giving adopted children rights of inheritance, or creating property rights for spouses, were accomplished by amendments or laws, not by court decisions. Indeed, many commentators have suggested that judges at both the state and federal levels were generally hostile to such changes and narrowly construed both constitutional amendments and legislation where it differed from the common law or previously prevailing constitutional jurisprudence.

From the New Deal to the Twenty-First Century

All of that changed in the last six decades of the twentieth century. During the Great Depression, the federal government under Franklin D. Roosevelt instituted an ambitious program of social legislation unlike anything ever seen before. At first the Supreme Court tended to rule that the federal government did not possess the constitutional power to dictate rules for the general management of the nation's economy, for example, in *SCHECHTER POULTRY CORPORATION v. UNITED STATES* (1935). That decision held that congressional power to regulate interstate commerce did not permit the setting of wages, hours, and reporting requirements for a New York chicken slaughterhouse, even if the chickens had been transported from other states. But by 1937 the Court seemed to change course in a move some called "the switch in time that saved nine." In *NATIONAL LABOR RELATIONS BOARD v. JONES AND LAUGHLIN STEEL CORPORATION,* the Court held that the federal government could set up a scheme to foster collective bargaining on wages and hours and other matters that could reach even manufacturing plants within particular states. From 1937 until 1995 no federal regulatory scheme was held insufficient on interstate commerce grounds. At the same time that the Supreme Court embraced doctrines permitting greater federal regulation, it also rejected the expansive notion of freedom of contract that previously had hindered both state and federal measures.

The reasons for the Supreme Court's abrupt about-face on these matters have been the subject of debate ever since, but it seems safe to say that two factors were of importance. One was the continued popularity of President Roosevelt, whose landslide victory in 1936 and whose attacks on the "nine old men" who were frustrating his plans for national economic recovery may have struck home. Indeed, Roosevelt's threat to "pack the Court" by increasing the number of justices with appointments of persons more friendly to regulation may have been taken seriously.

Just as important as politics was a change in jurisprudential understanding that occurred roughly contemporaneous with the "switch in time." After Oliver Wendell Holmes Jr. published his classic *The Common Law* in 1881, lawyers and law professors more commonly understood that the judicial role, over the course of American history, included a strong legislative component. At the beginning of the twentieth century even establishment figures, like Harvard's dean Roscoe Pound, railed against "mechanical jurisprudence" and urged its replacement with "sociological jurisprudence," in which the judges as well as legislators understood more clearly their obligation to alter the law in a progressive manner. In the early 1930s, some critics, calling themselves legal realists, began to challenge the whole idea of following precedent and the claim that legal and doctrinal questions had objective answers. Whether or not legal realism had a strong influence on what some called the judicial revolution of 1937, the doctrine was profoundly influential in fomenting the explosion of legal doctrinal change that was ushered in with Chief Justice Earl Warren.

The Warren Court (1953–1969). The Warren Court's most famous decision, rendered soon after the new chief justice ascended the bench, was *BROWN v. BOARD OF EDUCATION OF TOPEKA* (1954), in which the court ruled that state-sponsored school segregation violated the Fourteenth Amendment. This decision departed from the original understanding of the amendment, but Warren justified it on the grounds that the country could not "turn back the clock" to the time of the amendment or the time of the framing of the Constitution. This signaled that the Court had expressly embraced the notion of a "living Constitution," made equally clear in the jurisprudence of other liberal members of the Court, including in particular William O. Douglas and William Brennan. Other justices, most prominently Hugo L. Black, urged interpretation according to the original understanding of constitutional provisions. Still others, such as Felix Frankfurter and John Marshall Harlan II, counseled what came to be referred to as judicial restraint, the notion that legal change should be left to other branches of government.

To a great extent, however, the views of Warren, Douglas, and Brennan prevailed, and the Supreme Court proceeded expansively to cite the Fourteenth Amendment, in particular to end the practice of state-sponsored school prayer, to rewrite the rules of criminal prosecution in the states, and to order legislative reapportionment of both houses of state governments according to the principle of "one person one vote." The Court also considerably broadened the freedoms of speech and press guaranteed under the First Amendment far beyond that contemplated by the framers, believing that such expansion was necessary to achieve the country's professed democratic and egalitarian goals.

The tendency in American legal history is for changes in the interpretation of common law doctrines to accompany or to follow changes in constitutional law jurisprudence. Just as an explosion of common law changes followed the establishment of an independent United States and a federal Constitution, so a major alteration of the common law followed in the wake of the Warren Court's activities. State court judges, who then comprised (and continued to comprise into the twenty-first century) roughly 95 percent of the nation's judiciary, began to alter the rules regarding contracts, torts, and property.

Contract law, which had tended to defer to the expressed intentions of the parties, increasingly was interpreted to allow the courts to set aside agreements in which one party had taken unconscionable advantage of another or to allow them, when unanticipated events occurred, more or less to rewrite the parties' arrangements. The law of torts, which had generally not imposed liability where actors had performed in a manner that was not negligent, changed in the case of the manufacturers of consumer goods to impose liability where products left the factory in an "unreasonably dangerous" condition, even in the absence of negligence. In addition, the rules of property, which had tended to favor landlords and had been strictly interpreted in favor of established ownership interests, were relaxed to favor tenants, and lease agreements were interpreted more liberally to promote equity rather than to increase certainty. Just as the general culture seemed to undergo radical change in the 1960s, both constitutional and private law were dramatically altered at the hands of the judiciary.

The Burger Court (1969–1986). Not everyone in the legal profession or the nation was comfortable with the activist legal realist approach of the Warren Court. In 1969, when Richard Nixon had the opportunity to name a new chief justice upon Warren's retirement, he nominated Warren Earl Burger, a conservative from Minnesota. Some Burger Court decisions restricted the ambit of the Warren Court era by, for example, limiting access to the federal courts, particularly for those seeking to overturn decisions of the executive branch. Still, in one of its most notable decisions, *United States v. Nixon* (1974), the Court, while recognizing the doctrine of executive privilege, ruled that under the circumstances the president could not conceal evidence of wrongdoing when sought by a prosecutor in a criminal case. The implication was clear as well that executive privilege could not be used to conceal evidence of presidential wrongdoing in the course of impeachment proceedings, as the federal courts were to rule a quarter of a century later in the case of President William Jefferson Clinton.

From the vantage point of history, it is striking how little the Burger Court altered the "living Constitution" philosophy of the Warren Court or the jurisprudence of the "switch in time." The Burger Court did not significantly diminish the regulatory power of the federal government, which dramatically expanded during those years, and the Warren Court's emphasis on the rights of the individual was if anything dramatically increased by the most famous decision of the Burger Court, *ROE v. WADE* (1973). An earlier decision of the Warren Court, *GRISWOLD v. CONNECTICUT* (1965), had announced an implicit "right to privacy" in the Constitution, said to inhere in "emanations and penumbras" of various amendments. In *Roe* this "right of privacy" became solidly anchored in the Fourteenth Amendment's due process clause, and the Court announced in a remarkable 7 to 2 decision that for any state to prohibit abortion in the first three months of a woman's pregnancy would be a violation of due process. Thus, substantive due process, the doctrine invoked in *Dred Scott*, endorsed in *Lochner*, and rejected during the course of the "switch in time," reappeared in a new guise and established constitutional "freedom of choice."

Many constitutional scholars sought a coherent doctrinal defense for *Roe* based on precedent, but virtually all conceded that the decision represented a policy choice made by the justices against prohibiting abortion. Their choice was consistent with emerging legislative trends in the states, but the availability of abortion by judicial choice was difficult for many Americans to accept. Subsequently, this sort of judicial activism became a hot topic of political debate. Each year on the anniversary of *Roe*, antiabortion and pro-choice demonstrators stage noisy rallies in front of the Supreme Court's august edifice, and political campaigns and judicial nominations often turn on the issues of reproductive freedom and judicial legislation.

The Rehnquist Court. Ronald Reagan, elected president in 1980, followed the Republicans' practice of campaigning on a platform of ending judicial activism. Consequently, his nominations to the Court were expected to be persons committed to rolling back the expansionist decisions of the Warren and Burger Courts. Accordingly, some of his nominees encountered resistance in the Senate from those who favored the decisions, primarily Democrats. One nominee, Robert Bork, was defeated on the explicit charge that he would "turn back the clock" to a time when unfair racial treatment and "back-alley" abortions prevailed. This charge was undoubtedly unfounded, but it demonstrated the vitriol often employed regarding the courts and the strong influence they had come to wield in American society. Indeed, it often seemed as if not only did every political dispute sooner or later become a judicial matter, as Tocqueville had said, but that virtually all judicial matters eventually became political fodder.

When President Reagan nominated a conservative sitting justice, William S. Rehnquist, to become chief justice, Rehnquist too encountered strong resistance and the suggestion by critics that he would move the Court in a reactionary direction. Nevertheless, the Senate confirmed Rehnquist, and though he personally dissented, his Court in 1992 affirmed two of the most controversial Warren and Burger Court decisions. The Court ruled in *Lee v. Weisman* (1992) that the school prayer decisions should be extended to prohibit state-sponsored prayer at graduation ceremonies. In *PLANNED PARENTHOOD OF SOUTHEASTERN PENNSYLVANIA v. CASEY* (1992), the Court reaffirmed the declaration in *Roe v. Wade* of a constitutional right of privacy and interpreted it to bar all prohibitions on abortion that imposed an "undue burden" on a woman's right to choose. Unlike *Roe*, *Casey* did not dictate a solution based on a trimester model of pregnancy. But *Casey* did continue to recognize the right of the states to protect the potential life of the fetus and to prohibit abortion when the fetus was viable, except in cases where the life or health of the mother was at stake.

In other areas, however, and increasingly at the end of the twentieth century, the Rehnquist Court showed signs of changing constitutional jurisprudence. Most important in this regard was a series of decisions called the Court's "new federalism," of which *United States v. Lopez* (1995) was the most important. In *Lopez* the Court sought to impose limits on the federal government's exercise of regulatory powers and to move closer toward the original constitutional scheme in which the states were the primary lawmakers. For the first time since the "switch in time," the Court seemed prepared to strike down federal regulations on a regular basis. At the beginning of the twenty-first century, judicial activism was again at the center of national politics, as the presidential candidates Al Gore and George W. Bush stated their preferences or dislikes for the jurisprudence practiced by individual members of the U.S. Supreme Court. In an ironic development, the Rehnquist Court decided the outcome of that election for Bush by a 5 to 4 vote in *Bush v. Gore* (2000).

At the beginning of the twenty-first century, the Court faced difficult choices between the jurisprudences of the "living Constitution" and the "original understanding" in cases involving state aid to religious schools, affirmative action, and the balance between the powers of the state and federal governments. In 2001 the Senate held hearings on "judicial ideology," and because the Rehnquist Court decided many controversial cases by 5 to 4 majorities, any vacancies on the Supreme Court were expected to result in confirmation struggles. Indeed, so delicate was the matter of judicial selection that nine months into George W. Bush's term, with more than one hundred vacancies on the lower federal court benches, the Senate had confirmed only a handful of the new president's judicial nominees.

In the state courts, the rules of the common law did not seem to undergo reformulation in the same activist manner as previously. Indeed, a movement began for legislative "civil justice reform" to reverse the tendency of state juries to render multimillion-dollar and in some cases multibillion-dollar verdicts against corporate defendants. State legislatures began to pass such civil justice reforms, including limiting the amount of recoverable damages and putting other procedural roadblocks in the way of plaintiffs and their lawyers. Many of these "reforms" were ruled unconstitutional by state courts, based on provisions in state constitutions that guaranteed plaintiffs rights to trial by jury and that mandated the separation of the judicial power from the legislative.

State and federal courts and legislatures also seemed engaged in the promulgation of rules designed to protect property owners and investors in order to strengthen an American economy that faced stiffer competition from European and Asian concerns. Some American industries, such as asbestos, tobacco, and commercial aviation, were bankrupted or severely damaged by litigation, and antitrust regulators at the state and federal levels sought to move against titans, such as Microsoft, accused of predatory practices against consumers and competitors. The outcome of these struggles was unclear, but the trend at the beginning of the twenty-first century, at least, was toward the resolution of these important economic disputes by legislatures and executives rather than by the courts.

BIBLIOGRAPHY

Berger, Raoul. *Government by Judiciary.* Cambridge, Mass.: Harvard University Press, 1977.

Bickel, Alexander M. *The Supreme Court and the Idea of Progress.* New York: Harper and Row, 1970.

Hall, Kermit L. *The Magic Mirror: Law in American History.* New York: Oxford University Press, 1989.

Horwitz, Morton J. *The Transformation of American Law, 1780–1860.* Cambridge, Mass.: Harvard University Press, 1977.

———. *The Warren Court and the Pursuit of Justice.* New York: Hill and Wang, 1998.

Kelly, Alfred H., Winfred A. Harbison, and Herman Belz. *The American Constitution: Its Origins and Development.* 7th ed. New York: Norton, 1991.

Kutler, Stanley I. *Privilege and Creative Destruction: The "Charles River Bridge" Case.* Philadelphia: Lippincott, 1971.

McCloskey, Robert G. *The American Supreme Court.* 3d ed. Chicago: University of Chicago Press, 2000.

Nelson, William E. *The Americanization of the Common Law: The Impact of Legal Change on Massachusetts Society, 1760–1830.* Cambridge, Mass.: Harvard University Press, 1975.

Olson, Walter K. *The Litigation Explosion: What Happened When America Unleashed the Lawsuit.* New York: Truman Talley Books–Dutton, 1991.

Pound, Roscoe. *The Formative Era of American Law.* Boston: Little, Brown, 1938.

Presser, Stephen B., and Jamil S. Zainaldin, eds. *Law and Jurisprudence in American History.* 4th ed. St. Paul, Minn.: West Group, 2000.

Yarbrough, Tinsley E. *The Burger Court: Justices, Rulings, and Legacy.* Santa Barbara, Calif.: ABC–CLIO, 2000.

———. *The Rehnquist Court and the Constitution.* New York: Oxford University Press, 2000.

Stephen B. Presser

See also **Common Law; Supreme Court.**

JUDICIARY ACT OF 1789. While the framers of the U.S. Constitution agreed upon the division of the federal government into three branches, the delegates disagreed over whether the Constitution should create inferior federal courts. In the end, the Constitution left the issue open, and the construction of Article III, establishing the national courts, was left to Congress. At the initial session of the First Congress in 1789, the initial Judiciary Act was passed; it would serve as the model for all subsequent judicial legislation.

The path of the legislation involved the appointment of the Senate Committee for Organizing the Judiciary, consisting of members from each state. The committee had to overcome residual hostility to the idea of national courts, the relative youth of the government, and the fierce partisanship that threatened to erupt at any time. In addition to these problems, very few of the senators on the committee were lawyers. The Judiciary Act, or Senate Bill No. 1, was adopted in September 1789—following an entire congressional session of debate—as a compromise and, presumably, as a temporary measure.

The most important set of provisions in the Judiciary Act of 1789 created a three-tiered federal court structure. At the top was the United States Supreme Court (the only one expressly named in the Constitution), to consist of one chief justice and five associate justices. At the bottom were the district courts, one judge to each court and one court for each of the thirteen states, except for the states of Virginia and Massachusetts, each of which had two. The middle tier was the circuit courts, which would sit twice a year in each of the districts. There were three circuits to be ridden by the justices, one each for southern, eastern, and middle states. The original plan was for the circuit courts to consist of two Supreme Court justices joining the district court judge, but the difficulty of riding circuits very quickly resulted in only one Supreme Court justice on a circuit court.

The Constitution gave a limited amount of original jurisdiction to the Supreme Court, but the 1789 Judiciary Act made the district courts and the circuit courts the preeminent trial courts. Under the terms of the act, many civil matters, particularly admiralty cases, came before the district courts, and the circuit courts, among other assignments, had a general federal criminal jurisdiction. The lower federal courts were directed to follow the laws and procedures of the states in which they sat. Because of the politically controversial nature of the creation of the federal courts, these provisions of the first judiciary act were designed to calm fears about the possibly unbridled discretion of a national judiciary. The Supreme Court was prohibited from overturning factual determinations made by lower courts, and while the federal courts were permitted to hear cases that involved citizens from different states (diversity jurisdiction), they were not yet granted the jurisdiction to hear every matter that might arise under federal law, and indeed, under certain circumstances, the federal courts could not rule on federal questions until the highest state court had passed upon the issue. These provisions were designed to counter critics who feared that the national courts would intervene in all areas, rendering the state judiciaries impotent and obsolete.

The three-tiered structure first established by the 1789 legislation remains in effect, although the judges in the middle tier now sit in their own courts and exercise only appellate jurisdiction. The matters that can be heard by the federal courts have expanded far beyond the contemplation of the 1789 law, although its structural and jurisdictional provisions lingered until almost the end of the nineteenth century, and its procedural provisions still govern the basic operations of the federal courts.

BIBLIOGRAPHY

Goebel, Julius. *History of the Supreme Court of the United States.* Vol. 1. *Antecedents and Beginnings to 1801.* New York: Macmillan, 1971.

Marcus, Maeva, ed. *Origins of the Federal Judiciary: Essays on the Judiciary Act of 1789.* New York: Oxford University Press, 1992.

Ritz, Wilfred J. *Rewriting the History of the Judiciary Act of 1789: Exposing Myths, Challenging Premises, and Using New Evidence.* Edited by Wythe Holt and L. H. LaRue. Norman: University of Oklahoma Press, 1990.

Stephen B. Presser

See also **Circuits.**

JUDICIARY ACT OF 1801. In the waning years of the John Adams administration, the operation of the federal judiciary became a divisive political issue when the federal courts were used to prosecute Jeffersonian editors for seditious libel, when Federalist judges applied the doctrine of the common law of crimes, and after several prosecutions were conducted for treason arising out the Whiskey Rebellion in western Pennsylvania and the Fries Rebellion in eastern Pennsylvania. Criticism of the courts helped ensure Thomas Jefferson's party victories in the presidential and congressional elections of 1800, but the Adams Federalists, before they were swept from power, sought to reform the judiciary in order to retain it as a bastion against the Jeffersonian Republicans.

Thus, as lame ducks, the Federalists secured passage of the Judiciary Act of 1801. Some of the provisions of this act were sensible reforms, but the statute has generally been scorned. The act reduced the number of U.S. Supreme Court justices from six to five and ended the justices' duty—imposed by the Judiciary Act of 1789—of sitting with a federal district court judge to handle criminal and some civil matters, known as "riding circuit." Instead, a system of six new circuit courts was to be set up and staffed by sixteen new circuit judges, to be appointed by the outgoing President Adams. The sixteen appointments were all given to Federalists, and these became known as the "midnight judges," because their positions were filled as time was running out for Adams.

The 1801 law also enlarged the scope of operation of the circuit courts to give them jurisdiction over all federal questions and, in particular, exclusive jurisdiction over litigation concerning the recent Bankruptcy Act of 1800. The 1801 legislation also expanded the opportunities for the federal courts to hear disputes between citizens of different states, made it easier to transfer cases from state to federal courts, and provided jurisdiction over disputes involving the granting of titles to land by the states.

Until the 1800 election, issues regarding the judiciary had not been particularly important in American life, but Jefferson and the Republicans saw the 1801 law as a tremendous danger to liberty. Believing that the U.S. Constitution granted Congress power to abolish the lower federal courts, they proceeded to eliminate the new circuit courts in the Judiciary Act of 1802 and revert to the provisions of the Judiciary Act of 1789. Supreme Court justice Samuel Chase sought to rally his fellows to declare the 1802 act unconstitutional in that it removed the sixteen new judges without benefit of impeachment, but the Republicans countered that they were legitimately disbanding courts, and not illegitimately extracting judges. In *Stuart v. Laird* (1803), the Supreme Court declined to rule the 1802 law unconstitutional. The expanded jurisdiction granted to the lower federal courts in 1801 was not reinstated until after the Civil War, and for the most part, the important judicial decisions during the formative period of American law were made by the state courts.

BIBLIOGRAPHY

Ellis, Richard E. *The Jeffersonian Crisis: Courts and Politics in the Young Republic.* New York: Oxford University Press, 1971.

Presser, Stephen B. *Original Misunderstanding: The English, The Americans, and the Dialectic of Federalist Jurisprudence.* Durham, N.C.: Carolina Academic Press, 1991.

Turner, Kathryn. "Federalist Policy and the Judiciary Act of 1801." *William and Mary Quarterly* 22 (1965): 3–32.

Stephen B. Presser

See also **Midnight Judges.**

JUILLIARD V. GREENMAN, 110 U.S. 421 (1884), was a case in which the SUPREME COURT upheld the implied power of Congress to make U.S. government notes legal tender—and therefore money—in peacetime as well as in wartime. In *Hepburn v. Griswold* (1870), the Court had held the legal-tender acts of 1862 and 1863 unconstitutional, but, in 1871, the Court upheld the legal-tender acts as a war measure. *Juilliard v. Greenman* upheld the acts without reference to the war power. In this case, the Court inferred the power from the express power to borrow money and the implied power to issue bills of credit.

BIBLIOGRAPHY

Dunne, Gerald T. *Monetary Decisions of the Supreme Court.* New Brunswick, N.J.: Rutgers University Press, 1960.

Kutler, Stanley I. *Judicial Power and Reconstruction Politics.* Chicago: University of Chicago Press, 1968.

Schwartz, Bernard. *A History of the Supreme Court.* New York: Oxford University Press, 1993.

Hugh E. Willis/A. E.

See also **Legal Tender; Legal Tender Act; Legal Tender Cases; Repudiation of Public Debt.**

JUMPING-OFF PLACES, the towns along the border of American frontier settlement where emigrants completed their outfitting for the journey across the Plains during the 1840s and 1850s. Independence, Mo., was the best known of these places. Among the others were Council Bluffs, Iowa; Saint Joseph, Mo.; and Fort Smith, Ark.

BIBLIOGRAPHY

Faragher, John Mack. *Women and Men on the Overland Trail.* New Haven, Conn.: Yale University Press, 1979.

Dan E. Clark/F. B.

See also **Migration, Internal; Oregon Trail; Westward Migration.**

JUNGLE, THE, Upton Beall Sinclair's novel of labor exploitation in Chicago's meatpacking industry, advanced groundbreaking food and drug legislation rather than the anticapitalist outcry the author anticipated. A member of the Socialist Party of America, in 1904 Sinclair accepted a $500 commission from the socialist newspaper *Appeal to Reason* to write a fiction series comparing northern "wage slavery" to the South's antebellum slave system. Published in book form in 1906, *The Jungle* interpreted the hardships of ethnic workers as an odyssey toward socialist rebirth. Protagonist Jurgis Rudkus, a Lithuanian immigrant to Packingtown, at first gladly accepts meatpacking employment. He endures long workdays in miserable conditions; loses his job in defense of his wife, whom a foreman has seduced; is bereaved of his home, wife, and family; and, finally, after months of aimless wandering, discovers new dignity and purpose in the socialist movement. Sinclair's novel was the product of nearly two months' research in Packingtown, the laboring community adjacent to Chicago's stockyards.

However, popular reaction to the best-seller fell short of his hopes: as Sinclair famously observed, "I aimed at the public's heart, and by accident hit it in the stomach." Shocked at the unhygienic processing methods and product misrepresentation portrayed in the novel, consumers shunned dressed meat, while President Theodore Roosevelt launched an inquiry into packinghouse sanitation. The findings, which confirmed Sinclair's account, prompted Congress to pass both the Meat Inspection Act and the Pure Food and Drug Act in 1906.

Since the Progressive Era, scholars have valued *The Jungle* as a document of America's industrial and immigrant experience. Sinclair's apt descriptions of the stockyards and workday retain their emotional impact, and his celebrated portrayal of an ethnic wedding in Packingtown offers a rare glimpse of community ritual and interactions.

BIBLIOGRAPHY

Bloodworth, William A., Jr. *Upton Sinclair.* Boston: Twayne, 1977.

Harris, Leon. *Upton Sinclair, American Rebel.* New York: Crowell, 1975.

Yoder, Jon A. *Upton Sinclair.* New York: Ungar, 1975.

Rae Sikula Bielakowski

See also **Meatpacking;** *and vol. 9:* **Conditions in Meatpacking Plants.**

JUNIOR LEAGUES INTERNATIONAL, ASSOCIATION OF. Nineteen-year-old Mary Harriman, daughter of the railroad financier Edward Henry Harriman, founded the Junior League for the Promotion of Settlement Movements in 1901. She conceived a plan whereby the debutante class of 1901 would organize and put on a benefit for the New York College Settlement on Rivington Street on the Lower East Side of Manhattan. Eighty debutantes joined the Junior League.

In 1902, members volunteered in settlement houses themselves. They worked in the Rivington Street settlement as well as Greenwich House and Hartley House. Eleanor Roosevelt became a volunteer at Rivington Street in 1903. She later brought her future husband, Franklin Delano Roosevelt, to see the poverty and desperation of the immigrants living on the Lower East Side.

The Junior League of New York had 700 members by 1911, when it built a residential hotel for workingwomen, Junior League House, that housed 338 women. Dorothy Payne Whitney raised $250,000 for this ambitious project.

As the debutantes married and moved from New York City, they established Junior Leagues in Boston, Chicago, Portland, Oregon, and Montreal. In 1921, thirty Junior Leagues formed the Association of Junior Leagues International. During the 1920s, Barnard College provided the New York Junior League with the first training course for volunteers. From that time forward, the Junior Leagues were noted for their emphasis on training and leadership. By 1930, there were over one hundred Leagues.

During the Great Depression, Junior Leagues addressed problems of widespread hunger by providing nutrition centers and milk stations. Franklin Roosevelt appointed founder Mary Harriman Rumsey to posts within the New Deal. During World War II, many Junior Leaguers were active in the Red Cross. Member Oveta Culp Hobby was appointed head of the Women's Army Corps.

The baby boom of the 1950s turned the attentions of the Junior Leagues to projects such as improving the public schools and creating quality television programming for children. In the decades that followed, many Leagues worked on urban issues and social problems. The organization also sought to diversify its membership. By the 1980s, the empowerment of women had become a major goal. Sandra Day O'Connor, the first woman justice on the Supreme Court, had been a member.

The diversity that had been nourished in the 1970s bore fruit in the 1990s, when the first Hispanic president of the Junior Leagues, Clotilde Pérez-Bode Dedecker, took office. In 2000, Deborah Brittain, the first African American president, saw the Leagues into a new century. In 2001, the Leagues celebrated their first one hundred years of service.

The organization was 96 percent white in 2000. But although it had once been strictly Protestant, 22 percent of its members at the end of the century were Roman Catholic—very different from the group that had denied Rose Kennedy entrance because of her religion. One percent was Jewish. While the Junior Leagues were more diverse than ever before, it was still an elite organization comprised of middle- and upper-class women. At the start of the twenty-first century, a majority of members worked outside the home and the program has been modified to meet their needs. As the new century began, the Junior Leagues addressed problems such as child abuse, domestic violence, substance abuse, and HIV/AIDS.

BIBLIOGRAPHY

Jackson, Nancy Beth. *The Junior League: 100 Years of Volunteer Service.* Nashville, Tenn.: Favorite Recipe Press, 2001.

Yeomans, Jeannine. "Junior League Remakes Itself for the 21st Century." *Women's News,* 28 November 2000.

Bonnie L. Ford

See also **Girl Scouts of the United States of America.**

JUNK BONDS. Michael Milken, the notorious investment banker of the 1980s, allegedly coined the term "junk bonds" to describe the portfolio of low-grade bonds owned by one of his early clients, Meshulam Riklis. Companies issue low-grade, also called "high-yield," bonds at high interest rates because of the associated high risk of nonpayment. Unlike investment-grade bonds, the low-grade variety is not backed by assets or cash-flow statements. Companies frequently issue these bonds as a way of borrowing money. An outside, third-party credit rating agency, such as Moody's Investors Service or Standard and Poor's Corporation, judges the creditworthiness of such companies and then ranks them from least to most likely to default. The more financially secure the company, the less risky the debt, or bond. A bond's rating can be downgraded to "junk" status if the company gets into financial trouble. Historically, the use of junk bonds has been a minor part of Wall Street's activity because of the high risks. In the 1920s, however, high-yield bonds flourished. Tempted by the skyrocketing stock market in the

1920s, companies issued bonds with high interest rates in order to raise money by cashing in on booming stock profits and the robust economy. When the market collapsed in 1929, many companies defaulted on the low-grade bonds, and many investment-grade bonds were downgraded to junk status.

For forty years, Wall Street shunned high-yield bonds. In the late 1970s, Milken, as an investment banker with Drexel Burnham, rediscovered their potential. He encouraged his clients, largely fringe players on Wall Street, to issue junk bonds, and within a few years he, his company, and his clients became very successful. Milken's success bred imitators, and junk bonds became a popular way to raise money. In 1984 companies issued close to $16 billion in high-yield bonds—ten times the amount in 1981. In 1986 more than $33 billion worth of high-yield bonds were issued. Profits from the sale of junk bonds frequently financed mergers and acquisitions through leveraged buyouts and hostile takeovers. The transactions involved high fees, which induced investment bankers to underwrite increasingly risky bonds and to engage in fraud. Companies lured by the successes of earlier junk-bond deals took increasingly greater risks in issuing bonds. Enticed by the high interest rates, buyers continued to purchase the risky bonds.

The frenzy lasted until 1989, when the junk-bond market collapsed as the economy went into a recession and companies could no longer generate profits to pay their debts. In 1990 companies issued a mere $1.4 billion in high-yield bonds. Defaults totaled $20 billion. Milken and his imitators, such as Ivan Boesky, were disgraced, and many went to jail for fraud. Milken himself served time and paid fines for six counts of securities fraud.

Junk bonds left a dual legacy. They provided financing for the cable television and computer industries and encouraged companies to emphasize efficiency to realize profits to pay off the high interest on the bonds. On the flip side, the unchecked and frantic pace of the junk-bond market led to fraud, overspeculation, layoffs, and lost fortunes.

In the 1990s, the junk-bond market partially recovered despite the scandals of the previous decade. The high returns possible on such risky deals continue to make them attractive to daring investors. Some less adventurous investors, however, have attempted to temper the risks of purchasing junk bonds by placing their money in special mutual funds that deal solely in high-yield bonds rather than buying junk bonds directly themselves. This approach allows them to depend on the investment savvy of specialists in the field of low-grade bond trading.

BIBLIOGRAPHY

Auerbach, Alan J., ed. *Mergers and Acquisitions.* Chicago: University of Chicago Press, 1988.

Platt, Harlan D. *The First Junk Bond: A Story of Corporate Boom and Bust.* Armonk, N.Y.: M.E. Sharpe, 1994.

Stein, Benjamin. *A License to Steal: The Untold Story of Michael Milken and the Conspiracy to Bilk the Nation.* New York: Simon & Schuster, 1992.

Yago, Glenn. *Junk Bonds: How High Yield Securities Restructured Corporate America.* New York: Oxford University Press, 1991.

Erik Bruun / A. E.

See also **Crime; Financial Services Industry; Leveraged Buyouts; Scandals; Wall Street.**

JURY TRIAL is the traditional mode of determining issues of fact at COMMON LAW. Its development dates back far into the Middle Ages. Early jurors were drawn from the local community and thus brought to trials their own knowledge of the parties and events at issue. Property qualifications for jury duty existed in England, where officials selected juries from those qualified to serve. The jury trial was transplanted from England to the American colonies and became an integral part of their legal system in both civil and criminal law cases, with the exception that a more summary procedure was permitted in petty cases. In the early years of the Republic, Americans embraced the jury trial and attempted to utilize it as a limitation on despotic government. The U.S. Constitution, in Article III, section 2, contains the provision that "The Trial of all Crimes, except in Cases of Impeachment, shall be by Jury." No mention is made of juries in civil cases. The omission was much criticized, but in the seventh of the ten articles of amendment adopted soon afterward to quell the fears of those concerned about the omission of a bill of rights, a provision was included to the effect that in common law suits involving more than twenty dollars, the right to trial by jury should be preserved. The Sixth Amendment elaborated upon the use of juries in criminal cases by providing that "the accused shall enjoy the right to a speedy and public trial, by an impartial jury of the State and district wherein the crime shall have been committed."

The jury system came under serious criticism in the late nineteenth and twentieth centuries, partly because of clogged court calendars and the perceived inadequacy of juries to deal with complex questions outside the limits of jurors' experiences. While civil juries were subjected to the heaviest criticism, criminal juries came under similar attack. Jury selection had become slow and cumbersome, and many citizens attempted to avoid jury duty. Furthermore, opponents of juries began to focus not on the jurors' role in defending individual liberty, but rather on the claim that the jury was an expression of oppressive public opinion. These trends resulted in substantial changes in American jury practices, most of which attempted to control the jury and increase predictability. Some states did not adhere rigidly to the old common law requirement that the jury be composed of not more or less than twelve persons and that the verdict be unanimous. Increasingly, jury trials were not required in cases involving petty offenses, and in all cases, including cases involving serious crimes, the right to trial by jury could often be waived by the parties.

Traditionally, only men acted as jurors, and in practice only white men served. After the Civil War, several southern states enacted legislation preventing blacks from acting as jurors. In *Strauder v. West Virginia* (1879), the U.S. Supreme Court struck down a West Virginia statute that stipulated that only white men could act as jurors. Despite this decision, southern states often found less explicit methods of excluding black jurors.

BIBLIOGRAPHY

Alschuler, Albert W., and Andrew G. Deiss. "A Brief History of the Criminal Jury in the United States." *University of Chicago Law Review* 61 (1994): 867.

Friedman, Lawrence M. *Crime and Punishment in American History.* New York: Basic Books, 1993.

R. Blake Brown
Carl Brent Swisher

See also **Bill of Rights in U.S. Constitution; Constitution of the United States; *Milligan, Ex Parte*; *Strauder v. West Virginia.***

JUSTICE, DEPARTMENT OF. Congress created the Department of Justice (DOJ) on 22 June 1870, naming the attorney general as its head. The department's mandate includes, among other obligations, representing citizens of the United States, protecting them against criminal activity through proper law enforcement, ensuring healthy business competition, and enforcing drug, immigration, and naturalization laws. In addition, the department represents the United States in any case argued before the Supreme Court that involves U.S. interests, assists the government in various legal matters by offering legal advice, and provides legal opinions to the president and heads of executive departments.

Prior to the 1870, the U.S. attorney general, whose post was created in the Judiciary Act of 1789, served as a member of the president's cabinet but did not head a specific department. The attorney general is responsible for ensuring that the federal government does not exercise power unfairly, inconsistently, or arbitrarily. For many years, attorneys general served almost solely as legal counsel to the president. Other cabinet departments used their own attorneys for legal affairs; the U.S. district attorneys trying federal cases operated independently. (The attorney general led a staff so small that special counsel and investigators had to be retained whenever an important case arose.)

As the number of federal offenses rose and civil litigation increased, Congress expanded the scope of the Department of Justice, putting the attorney general in charge of substantially all federal prosecution and litigation and creating an organization that could grow in response to future legislation and government needs. During the Progressive Era around the turn of the twentieth century, many Americans came to believe that the government needed to intervene in daily life to create justice. Accordingly, a need to expand the Department of Justice was perceived.

On 26 July 1908, Attorney General Charles Bonaparte named a group of former Secret Service employees and Department of Justice investigators to posts as special agents of the Department of Justice. This investigative arm, led by Chief Examiner Stanley W. Finch, was dubbed the Bureau of Investigation, which later expanded its name to the Federal Bureau of Investigation (FBI). In 1909, the DOJ established a criminal division charged with enforcing and supervising application of federal criminal law.

The federal government's increased interest in developing public lands resulted in the development of a lands division in 1910; this division later became the land and natural resources division. Eventually, other legislation, such as antitrust laws, created a need for more special offices. In the extensive departmental reorganization of 1933, several of these offices were expanded into divisions, including the tax division and antitrust division, which is charged with keeping markets competitive by policing acts that restrain trade or commerce. The claims division, which later became the civil division, also emerged from this reorganization. The largest legal assembly in the Department of Justice, the civil division legally represents the United States, its departments and agencies, members of Congress, cabinet officers, and other federal employees when the need arises.

Other specialized divisions continued to be created. In 1940, the government officially moved control of the Immigration and Naturalization Service (INS) office from the Department of Labor to the Department of Justice. In 1957, a time when the civil rights movement was at its height, the DOJ created a civil rights division and gave it the task of enforcing federal statutes that prohibited discrimination. In 1964, the DOJ created the Office of Criminal Justice. The following year, the DOJ extended its criminal justice efforts when it created the Office of Law Enforcement Assistance, which had the task of helping states and local jurisdictions upgrade their criminal justice systems. The department's mandate to ensure civil rights was reinforced in 1966 when the Community Relations Service was transferred from the Department of Commerce to the DOJ. Created by the Civil Rights Act of 1964, the Community Relations Service has a mission of preventing and resolving incidents that occur because of differences in race, color, or national origin.

As the drug trade burgeoned in the 1960s, Congress authorized the creation of the Bureau of Narcotics and Dangerous Drugs in 1968. In 1972, President Richard Nixon created the Office for Drug Abuse Law Enforcement, which was charged with coordinating all federal and state efforts, and the Office of National Narcotics Intelligence, which was developed to be a clearinghouse for information on drug trafficking. The next year, President Nixon streamlined the war on drugs by combining five federal drug enforcement agencies to create the Drug Enforcement Administration (DEA) within the Department of Justice. The DEA is the main domestic enforcer of federal drug laws and bears sole responsibility for coordinating and pursuing U.S. drug investigations abroad. In 2002, the DOJ again stepped up efforts to stop the growing, importation, and sale of illegal drugs when it established the National Drug Intelligence Center, which was as the nation's principal center for strategic domestic counterdrug intelligence.

Following major terrorist acts on American soil in 2001, the DOJ shifted its focus from battling drugs to combating terrorism. On 5 March 2002, the department created the National Security Coordination Council of the Department of Justice; its principal mission is to facilitate seamless coordination of department functions relating to national security and terrorism. The council included the attorney general, the director of the FBI, the commissioner of the INS, the chief of staff of the attorney general, the assistant attorney general of the criminal division, and the assistant attorney general for the Office of Justice programs.

The Department of Justice, which is the largest law office in the world, has grown from its meager beginnings to an organization comprising nearly forty components and more than 30,000 employees.

BIBLIOGRAPHY

Huston, Luther A. *The Department of Justice.* New York: Praeger, 1967.

Langeluttig, Albert George. *The Department of Justice of the United States.* Baltimore: Johns Hopkins University Press, 1927.

James T. Scott

See also **Federal Agencies.**

JUSTICE OF THE PEACE. Justices of the peace were originally medieval English officials authorized to keep the peace and to try felonies and trespasses at the king's suit. In more recent times, they dealt with numerous other affairs of local government. The office flourished in the colonies from the beginning. The justices exercised both criminal and civil jurisdiction—the former through the courts of Quarter or General Sessions, the latter by statutory authority that authorized them to try all manner of debts, trespasses, and other matters involving not more than forty shillings, or, in Virginia, "one hogshead of tobacco not exceeding 350 pounds." In Maryland the justices of a county made up the county court, and later the governor designated some of their number, known as "justices of the quorum," for court service. In New York the justices gradually supplanted the old Dutch commissaries. In North Carolina they possessed exclusive jurisdiction over the crimes of slaves.

In most of the colonies, the justices in court sessions exercised sweeping local executive and administrative powers; drew up the levy; collected the tax; appointed road commissioners and supervised highways; made disbursements; granted licenses to keep taverns and retail liquors; and appointed and controlled administrators, executors, and guardians. They generally took acknowledgments of deeds and depositions and performed marriage ceremonies, but they seldom exercised the sweeping authority of the English and Welsh justices of levying wage assessments of laborers.

While the institution still exists in some states, the criminal jurisdiction of justices has narrowed, and they are now mainly committing magistrates. Appointive officers in colonial times, they are now generally elected, with compensation from fees paid by parties losing in litigation. As in colonial days, they are usually members of the laity. By World War I, justices of the peace no longer existed in most urban areas.

BIBLIOGRAPHY

Botein, Stephen. *Early American Law and Society.* New York: Knopf, 1983.

Friedman, Lawrence Meir. *A History of American Law.* New York: Simon and Schuster, 1985.

Richard B. Morris / A. E.

See also **Hundred; *Marbury v. Madison*; Midnight Judges.**

JUVENILE COURTS. The first specialized juvenile court in the United States was created on 1 July 1899 under an Illinois legislative act establishing the juvenile court division of the circuit court for Cook County. The civic leaders who propelled this reform sought to separate children and youth from the ugly conditions in prisons and to improve their opportunities for constructive citizenship. Conceptual forerunners of the juvenile court were the equity jurisdiction of the English Court of Chancery, common-law traditions limiting or prohibiting the criminal liability of juveniles below certain ages, and the doctrine of the inherent power of a state to protect the welfare of children. Influenced by these precedents, various American institutions in the nineteenth century developed privately operated houses of refuge, where juveniles toiled long hours in manufacturing tasks within an overall repressive environment, first in New York and then in other eastern cities in the 1820s and 1830s; developed probation, first in Massachusetts in 1868; and began holding separate hearings for juveniles accused of criminal violations, first in Massachusetts in 1879.

The 1899 Illinois legislation not only established separate courts for juveniles but also incorporated other reforms in juvenile justice. Since the intent was to help rather than to hurt, the state law kept legal proceedings simple and summary and eschewed lawyers. Social workers and behavioral scientists appeared in court to assist the judge in making and carrying out the most appropriate disposition of the cases. Court wards who were to be confined were segregated from adult offenders and placed in training and industrial schools—and some were placed in private foster homes and institutions. The state employed probation officers to facilitate adjustment.

Colorado passed a similar statute in 1903, formalizing and extending a Denver juvenile court that, under Judge Ben Lindsey, had been hearing juvenile cases separately prior to 1899, under a preexisting juvenile disorderly persons act. Specialized juvenile courts were quickly created in the larger cities of the East and Midwest, and by 1925 a juvenile court in some form existed in all but two states.

Constitutional challenges to juvenile court practices and procedures were consistently overruled until the 1960s. State appellate court rulings swept aside concerns that children were denied a right to bail, to counsel, public trials, jury trials, immunity against self-incrimination, and that children could be convicted on hearsay testimony or by only a preponderance of the evidence. Rulings found that juvenile proceedings were civil in nature and that their purpose was to obtain rehabilitation rather than to order punishment. Legislative reform in California and New York in 1961 and 1962, respectively, began to place a more regularized procedure on the historically informal juvenile court practices. Research on the juvenile justice system had shown that juvenile court judges not infrequently lacked legal training; that probation officers were undertrained and that their heavy caseloads often prohibited meaningful social intervention; that children were still regularly housed in jails; that juvenile correctional institutions were often, in reality, little more than breeding grounds for further criminal activity; and that juvenile recidivist rates were high.

In 1967, in the case *In Re Gault*, the U.S. SUPREME COURT ruled that constitutional due process protected any juvenile whose liberty was threatened by juvenile court action and mandated formal rather than informal fact-finding hearings, together with the juvenile's right to be represented by an attorney and to avoid self-incrimination. The Court ruled in 1970 that the criminal justice system's principle of proof beyond a reasonable doubt must be utilized in juvenile court trials, but in 1971 it confirmed that juveniles were not entitled to a jury trial under the Constitution.

These Supreme Court rulings stimulated an ongoing legal challenge of juvenile court practices and procedures and signaled the beginning of a conspicuous role for lawyers in juvenile courts. Lawyers began to replace judges and probation officers as children's advocates. Benevolent intentions and broad juvenile court jurisdiction still applied, however. Noncriminal juvenile offenses—running away, habitual truancy, and incorrigibility—remained subject to sanction in all the states.

Although the customary maximum age limit for juvenile court jurisdiction is eighteen, public concerns regarding the extent and seriousness of juvenile law violations stimulated efforts in the 1970s to lower the age, to make more serious offenses subject exclusively to criminal rather than juvenile court sanctions, and to encourage the application of the juvenile code provision of many states for the discretionary transfer of juveniles from juvenile to criminal court jurisdiction. An opposition movement sought to narrow juvenile court jurisdiction by transferring primary responsibility for minor offenses to social service agencies and by extending the array of available community service alternatives for juvenile rehabilitation to avoid the necessity for state institutional commitment.

In the 1970s juvenile courts in all states had jurisdiction over dependent and neglected children as well as juvenile law violators (delinquents) and youths who commit noncriminal offenses (status offenders). Nearly a quarter of those courts also had jurisdiction over the voluntary relinquishment of children and their adoption and over the determination of paternity and support proceedings. The 1970s saw increased popularity of community-based programs and deinstitutionalization for juveniles in the justice system, and the passage of the 1974 Juvenile Justice and Delinquency Prevention Act required states to keep juvenile offenders separate from adult offenders and to follow several other custody requirements in order to qualify for grants.

However, the 1980s brought a dramatic shift toward "law and order" policies, in response to misperceptions that a juvenile crime wave was occurring. A number of states passed more punitive laws. Some of these new laws moved certain classes of offenders from juvenile court to adult court, and others required juvenile courts to function more like adult courts by treating certain classes of juvenile offenders as adults. People charged with certain offenses would be excluded from juvenile court jurisdiction and thus face mandatory or automatic waiver to criminal court. In some states, prosecutors have discretion to file certain cases directly in criminal court, and in other states, mandatory sentencing laws apply to some juvenile offenders. In response to concern that the weight of this crackdown was falling disproportionately on minority youths, the Juvenile Justice and Delinquency Prevention Act was reauthorized in 1992 to require states to examine the issue and demonstrate the efforts made, if necessary, to reduce such injustices.

The Supreme Court also had a significant effect on juvenile justice in the 1980s. *Eddings v. Oklahoma* (1982) called for considering a defendant's age in deciding whether to apply the death penalty and *Thompson v. Oklahoma* (1988) and *Stanford v. Kentucky* (1989) set the minimum age for the death penalty at sixteen.

The 1990s brought further changes. Forty-five states made it easier to transfer juvenile offenders from the juvenile to the criminal justice system. Thirty-one states expanded the sentencing options in both juvenile and criminal court. Forty-seven states removed or modified the juvenile courts' confidentiality provisions, making proceedings and records less private. In twenty-two states laws increased the role for victims of juvenile crime in the juvenile justice system, and, finally, correctional administrators in both juvenile and adult facilities developed new correctional programs. Recently, states have also added language to their juvenile codes. The language addresses holding juveniles accountable for their criminal behavior, providing effective deterrents, protecting the public from criminal activity, balancing attention to offenders, victims, and the community, and imposing punishment suitable to the crime. Seventeen states increased the age to which juvenile courts had jurisdiction over juvenile offenders, but no states mandate a minimum age limit for transfering juveniles to criminal court. Twenty states incorporate "blended sentencing," which allows courts to combine juvenile and adult correctional sanctions on juvenile offenders. During the last few decades, states have shifted the purpose of juvenile courts from rehabilitation toward "punishment, accountability and public safety" and from considering an offender's individual situation toward basing the punishment on the offense.

BIBLIOGRAPHY

American Bar Association. *Facts about the American Judicial System.* 1999.

Clapp, Elizabeth J. *Mothers of All Children: Women Reformers and the Rise of Juvenile Courts in Progressive Era America.* University Park: Pennsylvania State University Press, 1998.

Getis, Victoria. *The Juvenile Court and the Progressives.* Urbana: University of Illinois Press, 2000.

Knupfer, Anne Meis. *Reform and Resistance: Gender, Delinquency, and America's First Juvenile Court.* New York: Routledge, 2001.

Polier, Justine Wise. *Juvenile Justice in Double Jeopardy: The Distanced Community and Vengeful Retribution.* Hillsdale, N.J.: L. Erlbaum, 1989.

Ted Rubin / D. B.

See also **Chicago; Childhood; Crime; *In Re Gault;* Prisons and Prison Reform.**

KANSAS. The geographic center of the 48 contiguous states of the United States is in Kansas, one mile north of the city of Lebanon. The geodetic center (which takes into account the curvature of the earth) of North America is in Osborne County in north-central Kansas. The state is rectangular, approximately 408 miles east to west, and 206 miles north to south. Kansas is bordered to the east by Missouri, to the south by Oklahoma, to the west by Colorado, and to the north by Nebraska. Because of its geographic center and because of its agricultural prominence, Kansas is often referred to as "the heartland of America."

The state is customarily divided into four different geologic regions. The northeastern part of Kansas is the Dissected Till Plains, so-called because the retreating glaciers of the last ice age left the land looking as though it had been divided and plowed. It has forests and an abundance of water. The southeastern part of Kansas, known as the Southeastern Plains, is marked by limestone hills, the Osage Plains, and grass. To the west of these two regions is the Plains Border, so called because its western edge borders the eastern edge of the foothills of the Rocky Mountains. This region is plagued by severe droughts and tornadoes. Also prone to drought are the High Plains, which occupy the western part of Kansas and rise westward up into the Rockies. It is a dry area whose people rely on an underground aquifer for irrigation of their crops.

The most historically important of Kansas's rivers are the Missouri, Kansas, Arkansas, and Cimarron. The Missouri River forms part of the northeastern border and has been important for shipping. The Kansas River begins in north central Kansas at the confluence of the Republican and Smoky Hill Rivers and flows eastward to the Missouri. It formed a natural boundary between the Native American tribes, in the northeast, and the rest of the state. The Arkansas River enters Kansas a third of the way north on Kansas's western border, meanders east, then northeast, then crosses the border into Oklahoma. The Santa Fe Trail, used by hundreds of thousands of migrants and traders, followed the Kansas River, then turned southwest to the Arkansas River and followed it to the west. Some people chose a quicker but more hazardous route by crossing south over the Arkansas River and heading southwest to cross the Cimarron River, which originates in the High Plains and flows southeastward to Oklahoma.

Prehistory

It is not known when humans first arrived in what is now Kansas. Archaeologists and paleoanthropologists have continued to push backward in time the era when the first people arrived in North America, probably more than 100,000 years ago. During the last ice age, a glacier extended southward into northeastern Kansas and would have obliterated evidence of habitation earlier than 11,000 B.C.

There is much evidence of humans south of the glacier in 11,000 B.C., including long sharpened stone points for spears. These Paleo-Indians, a term meaning people who predate the Native American cultures that existed after 7000 B.C., were nomads who hunted mammoths and giant bison, as well as other big game. By 7000 B.C., the glacier had retreated far to the north, leaving the gouged landscape of the Dissected Till Plains; as the climate of Kansas warmed, new cultures were introduced. The archaic Indians of 7000 B.C. were not the wanderers their predecessors had been. With the extermination of large game, they became focused on small animals and on plants as sources for food. During the period between 5000 B.C. and 3500 B.C., people formed small settlements, and they often hunted with atlatls, slotted spear throwers that added greater power than was possible when throwing a spear by hand alone. These people also developed techniques for making ceramics.

By A.D. 1, the people in Kansas lived off of the wildlife of Kansas's forest. They still used stone tools, but they were making great strides in their pottery making. During this era, bows and arrows began to supplant spears and atlatls, with spear points becoming smaller and sharper. Maize, first grown in Mexico and Central America, appeared in Kansas, perhaps between A.D. 800 and 1000, probably coming from an ancient trade route that extended southwestward into what is now Mexico. Settlements became larger, and in eastern Kansas large burial mounds were built, suggesting evolution of complex societies.

After A.D. 1000, Native Americans in Kansas grew not only maize, but squash and beans as well. They used the bow and arrow to hunt bison and small game. The

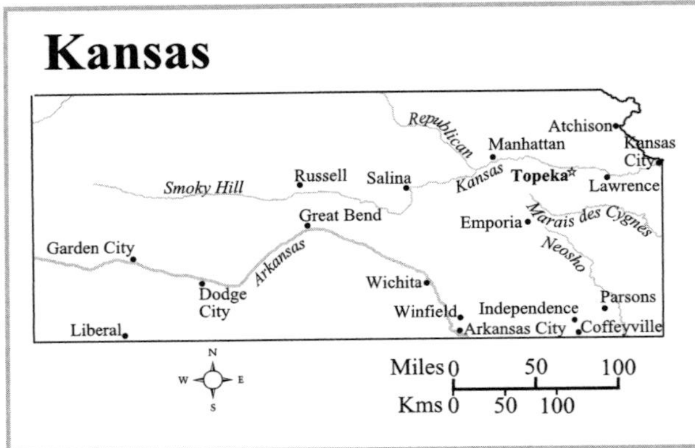

Native Americans of northern Kansas and southern Nebraska lived in large communal lodges built of sod. Those to the south made thatched-roofed, plaster-covered houses. These people likely traded with the Pueblo Indians to the southwest, and at least one habitation within what is now Kansas was built by the Pueblo.

By the time of the arrival of the first European explorers in 1541, the settled cultures probably had already been driven out by numerous invasions of warlike nomadic cultures such as the APACHE. The PAWNEES inhabited northwestern Kansas, the KIOWAS the high western plains, the COMANCHES the central part of Kansas, and the Wichita the southern plains. The Kansas, "the people of the south wind," for whom the state is named, and the OSAGES had yet to migrate into eastern Kansas; they would arrive in the 1650s. There were frequent wars among these tribes, and they often fought the nomadic Apaches, who tended to follow the herds of bison.

Exploration

The first recorded European explorer of the Kansas region was Francisco Vásquez de Coronado and his followers, who were looking for riches. In Kansas, he found a land rich in farms and diverse Native American cultures. Some of the tribes he encountered resented Roman Catholic priests for trying to convert them, and one priest was killed. Pieces of Spanish chain mail have been uncovered in central Kansas, indicating that a few Spanish soldiers also may have died there.

France claimed the region of Kansas in 1682, but it was not until 1724 that explorers from Europe and European American colonies began coming to Kansas on a regular basis. The first was Étienne Veniard de Bourgmont, who traveled through Kansas as a trader, while exploring the land for the French government. In 1739, Paul and Pierre Mallet led several traders through Kansas to the southwest, blazing a trail for other traders. The French built Fort Cavagnial, near what would become Leavenworth, to aid French travelers and to provide a meeting place for Native Americans and French traders; the fort was closed in 1764. In 1803, the United States purchased the Louisiana territory, which included Kansas, from France.

Kansas was still a frontier when the LEWIS AND CLARK EXPEDITION passed through it in 1804. In 1806, Zebulon M. Pike led an expedition through Kansas, helping to blaze trails from east to west that Americans would follow. In 1819, Major Stephen H. Long explored part of Kansas and the Great Plains, calling the region the Great American Desert, probably because of a drought and the seemingly endless dry, brown grass. Perhaps he missed or dismissed the large forest that still covered much of Kansas.

Early Settlements

IRRIGATION had been introduced to Kansas along Beaver Creek in western Kansas in 1650 by the Taos Indians, setting the stage for year-round settlements in the dry High Plains. The explorer William Becknell established the Santa Fe Trail in 1821, beginning the busy travel of traders through Kansas to the American southwest. In 1827, Fort Leavenworth was established by Colonel Henry Leavenworth to provide a place for settling disputes among the Native American tribal factions. That same year, Daniel Morgan Boone, son of Daniel Boone, became the first American farmer in Kansas. In 1839, Native Americans imported wheat from the east and became the first wheat farmers in Kansas, clearing and farming plots of land along rivers. Treaties with the American government supposedly protected the Native American farmers in what was called "Indian Country." In 1852, the Native American Mathias Splitlog established Kansas's first flour mill just west of the Missouri River in what is now Wyandotte County.

Bleeding Kansas

In 1854, in the KANSAS-NEBRASKA ACT, the U.S. Congress established Kansas as an official territory, but in so doing, Congress violated a compromise between slave states and free states that was supposed to make both Kansas and Nebraska free states. Instead, Congress said that the people of Kansas and Nebraska would vote on whether to make the territories free or slave states when they applied for statehood.

In 1855, Kansas tried to elect a legislature that would write a state constitution to present to Congress as part of its application for statehood. Most of the settlers in Kansas, such as Mennonites and Quakers, were antislavery (known as "free staters"), but proslavery men from outside Kansas were imported to vote in the election, and through intimidation of antislavery voters and ballot-box stuffing, they "won" the election. The new legislature quickly wrote a proslavery constitution, which Congress rejected because the state legislature was not recognized as legitimate. In 1855, the Topeka Movement favoring a free state was begun, and its followers wrote their own state constitution; this, too, was rejected by Congress because the authors had not been properly elected.

By 1856, proslavery terrorists were killing free-state farmers. On 21 August 1856, an out-of-state proslavery gang invaded Lawrence, Kansas, an overwhelmingly free-state community, and murdered over 150 people and burned down most of the town. The antislavery fanatic John Brown gathered some of his followers and invaded farms along Pottawatomie Creek, south of Kansas City, Kansas, murdering five proslavery men; this became known as the POTTAWATOMIE MASSACRE. A proslavery militia later attacked John Brown and some of his followers, only to be captured by those they tried to kill. This made John Brown a hero among many antislavery people. These events inspired the nickname "Bleeding Kansas," and the violence and murders continued even after the conclusion of the Civil War (1861–1865).

Statehood

Beginning in 1860 and lasting until telegraph lines were established between America's West and East, the Pony Express passed through Kansas. By 1861, Kansas had managed to have an election that Congress recognized as valid, and the resulting territorial legislature wrote a state constitution forbidding slavery that Congress also recognized as valid. On 29 January 1861, Kansas was admitted as the thirty-fourth state in the Union, although a large chunk of its western territory was ceded to what eventually would become the state of Colorado. Topeka was declared the state capital. On 12 April 1861, the Civil War began, pitting proslavery Southern states, the Confederacy, against the rest of the country, the Union.

Over 20,000 Kansans, out of only 30,000 eligible men, enlisted in the Union army; at the war's end, 8,500 (28.33 percent) of the Kansas soldiers had been killed, the highest mortality rate of any Union state. The first skirmishes against Confederate regulars occurred in 1861 along the Missouri River, with the first significant combat for Kansan troops occurring near Springfield, Missouri, in the Battle of Wilson's Creek, with the First Kansas Volunteer Infantry suffering heavy losses. Kansan historians claim that the first African Americans to see significant combat in the Civil War were the First Kansas Colored Infantry, who were formed into a regiment in August 1862, and who fought Confederate troops at Butler, Missouri, on 29 October 1862 in the Battle of Toothman's Mound. Under Colonel James M. Williams, white and black Union troops fought together as a unit for the first time in a battle at Cabin Creek on 2 July 1863 in the Indian Territory (now Oklahoma), against Confederate troops who had raided a train.

The most significant battle in Kansas during the Civil War occurred when Union forces under the command of Major General James G. Blunt and Confederate forces under General Douglas Cooper met in a series of clashes involving more than 25,000 troops, concluding in the Battle of Mine Creek, in which 10,000 troops fought. The First Kansas Colored Infantry underwent a forced march northeastward through Kansas to the battle and was stationed in the Union line's center. The regiment advanced to within thirty yards of the Confederate center, enduring heavy losses until the Confederate line broke and fled, ending the major Confederate threat to Kansas.

During the war, Confederate guerrilla units raided Kansan settlements. Under the command of Captain William Clarke Quantrill, "Quantrill's Raiders" executed farm families and burned villages and towns. On 21 August 1863, Quantrill led 450 of his troops into Lawrence, Kansas; with most of the men of Lawrence off to war, Quantrill's Raiders killed nearly 200, few of them men. Quantrill remains despised in Kansas.

Building a State

From 1867 to 1869, a fierce war between the United States and Native Americans was fought in western Kansas. The Pawnees and others had objected to violations of treaties that guaranteed them the right of ownership of some of the land in Kansas. In 1868, General Phil Sheridan led an offensive against the warring tribes, and in 1869 the tribes were forced to settle in the Indian Territory, southwest of Kansas.

The 1870s and 1880s saw an influx of over 300,000 people into Kansas. Many were guided there by the New England Emigrant Aid Society (NEEAS) of Massachusetts. Among the people the NEEAS guided to Kansas were Mennonites from Russia, who in 1874 brought with them a hardy, drought-resistant, cold-resistant strain of dwarf wheat called "Turkey red wheat." This soon became the favorite winter wheat of Kansas, and it helped advance the growing of wheat throughout the United States.

One of the first actions of the new state legislature in 1861 was to grant women the right to vote in school board elections. It was a small advance for voting rights, but it was considered progressive at the time. Even so, some women activists scorned it, making enemies where they once had friends. During the 1870s and 1880s (known as the sodbuster decades for the sod houses that were built), many women activists were sidetracked by the prohibitionist movement, which was seen as a woman's issue because of the severe social problem of drunken husbands beating their wives. In 1880, Kansas voters approved the prohibition of sale or consumption of alcoholic beverages in the state. The law was ignored throughout Kansas; saloons operated openly in many towns.

In 1874, locusts invaded Kansas and much of the Midwest, denuding farmlands. It was an era of drought, and an adequate irrigation system did not yet exist. Over 30,000 people fled the drought. Once the rains returned in the late 1870s, the influx of settlers renewed. During 1879–1880, 30,000 "Exodusters" (a play on "sodbuster" and "exodus"), African Americans fleeing Southern states, migrated into Kansas.

Kansas was proud of its progressive image, and in 1887, women at last received the right to vote in municipal elections. Within a few weeks, the first female mayor elected in America, Susanna Madora Salter, became mayor of the town of Argonia. The next year, five towns had female mayors and city councils consisting entirely of women. The Populist Party (a.k.a. the People's Party) was founded in Topeka in 1890, and Populist Kansas governors, beginning with Lorenzo Lewelling in 1892, were supported by women. By 1911, over 2,000 women held public office in Kansas. In 1912, Kansas voted to give women full suffrage, the same voting rights as men had. In 1932, Kansas elected its first female member of the U.S. House of Representatives, Kathryn O'Loughlin McCarthy.

In 1900, Kansas had an official population of 1,470,495 people. Before 1907, maize was the state's principal crop, but it was replaced in 1907 by wheat, much of it descended from the Turkey red wheat brought by Russian immigrants. The land still suffered from drought, about once every twenty years, but it was not until 1920 that farmers began to extensively irrigate their farmland. The irrigation system created a boom that made Kansas the world's leader in wheat production. In 1923, a motorized combine was introduced to Kansas, allowing a couple of men to do what had been the work of several horses and a score of men in 1900. In 1930, portable irrigation sprinkler systems were introduced, and the state became an example of prosperity.

Dust Bowl

Drought hit Kansas again during the 1930s. Most of the state's forest had been converted to farmland; its native grasses and other plants had been supplanted by sweeping farms, rich in wheat, maize, sorghum, and other cultivated grains. When streams dried up, and when the irrigation system could not find enough water for the central and western parts of the state, the soil dried. The topsoil had become powder. Kansas had always had high winds, and in the 1930s, the winds blew the powdery soil high into the air, often making day as dark as night. During 1934, the region became known as the "dust bowl."

Many farmers abandoned their farms. Some found work in Kansas's factories. Oil and natural gas strikes in southern Kansas and zinc mining in the western hills helped provide Kansas with income. By 1937, the prohibition law was seen as oppressive. Kansas changed the law to allow 3.2 percent beer to be produced and taxed; it also instituted a sales tax.

World War II and the 1950s

During World War II, Fort Riley, established in 1853 to protect travelers on the Santa Fe Trail, became a major military training base. In 1942, a prisoner of war camp was built near Concordia. The factories of Kansas became important parts of the production for war, and the oil and natural gas suppliers gained in importance. In 1943, Dwight David Eisenhower, who had been raised in Abilene, became Supreme Commander of Allied Forces in Europe, and he helped the growth of the military industry in Kansas.

The "progressive" state of Kansas had long had a dirty secret: racial segregation. On 28 February 1951, the father of eleven-year-old Linda Brown, an African American, filed suit in the United States District Court against Topeka's Board of Education, asking that she be allowed to attend a whites-only school and alleging that segregation violated Amendment XIV of the U.S. Constitution. On 17 May 1954, a team of attorneys led by Thurgood Marshall won a ruling from the U.S. Supreme Court that racial segregation was inherently unequal and therefore a violation of the Constitution. *Brown v. Board of Education* became the landmark court decision that would change the course of American society during the next fifty years.

The Modern Era

By 1960, the population of Kansas had increased to over 2,000,000 people. In 1969, part of the Kansas National Guard was called to duty and sent to serve in Vietnam. In 1970, the student union at Kansas University was set afire, probably as part of protests against the war.

In 1972, the state's constitution was amended, reducing the number of elected officials in the executive branch and extending to four years from two the terms of the elected officials of the executive branch. During that year, the Kansas legislature ratified the ill-fated Equal Rights Amendment that would have added a statement to the United States Constitution that women and men were to have the same civil rights. In 1973, the Wolf Creek nuclear power plant was begun; it would not come on line until 1985. In 1978, Nancy Landon Kassebaum, daughter of Alf Landon, Republican nominee for president in 1936, was elected to the United States Senate. She was the first woman who was not a widow of a senator to be elected to the Senate.

In 1980, Kansas established and funded programs to prevent child abuse. In 1986, Kansas changed its alcoholic beverage laws to allow serving liquor "by the drink." It also approved a state lottery. Its population was just under 2,500,000 in 1990. In 1991, Joan Finney became Kansas's first woman governor. Former Governor Mike Hayden was placed in charge of the United States Fish and Wildlife Service and the National Park Service. During the 1990s, the elaborate irrigation system for the High Plains and Plains Border regions became severely strained because the underground aquifer, consisting of sand mixed with water, was being seriously diminished, creating sinkholes and threatening an end to the underground water supply. In 2000, nearly 3,000,000 people lived in Kansas, mostly in cities.

BIBLIOGRAPHY

Anderson, George L., Terry H. Harmon, and Virgil W. Dean, eds. *History of Kansas: Selected Readings.* Lawrence: University Press of Kansas, 1987.

Bader, Robert Smith. *Hayseeds, Moralizers, and Methodists: The Twentieth-Century Image of Kansas.* Lawrence: University Press of Kansas, 1988.

Davis, Kenneth S. *Kansas: A Bicentennial History.* New York: Norton, 1976.

Masters, Nancy Robinson. *Kansas.* New York: Grolier, 1998.

Napier, Rita, ed. *A History of the Peoples of Kansas.* Lawrence: Independent Study, Division of Continuing Education, University of Kansas, 1985.

Shortridge, James R. *Peopling the Plains: Who Settled Where in Frontier Kansas.* Lawrence: University Press of Kansas, 1995.

Wedel, Waldo R. *Central Plains Prehistory: Holocene Environments and Culture Change in the Republican River Basin.* Lincoln: University of Nebraska Press, 1986.

Kirk H. Beetz

See also **Midwest; Tribes: Great Plains.**

Kansas City. An aerial view of the city's downtown, with the Missouri River in the background, c. 1929. LIBRARY OF CONGRESS

KANSAS CITY. Located in northwest MISSOURI at the junction of the Kansas (or Kaw) and Missouri Rivers, Kansas City sits very close to the geographic center of the United States. From its beginning the area has served as a transportation hub, first for the Kansa (or Kansas) tribe of Native Americans and later for European and American traders and settlers who established permanent settlements. French trader François Chouteau established a trading post along the river near the present downtown in 1821, while American John C. McCoy built Westport to service the Santa Fe Trail a short distance away in 1835. The river settlement was platted and renamed the City of Kansas in 1853 and incorporated with Westport in 1889 to form Kansas City. With fifteen railroads and the river system at its heart, the city quickly became a major shipment point for agricultural products from the Great Plains to the West and a processing center for livestock from the Southwest.

As the twentieth century progressed, Kansas City's industrial base expanded to include steel making and machine tools, automobile assembly plants, oil refining, and a large garment industry. The Pendergast machine of brothers James and Thomas controlled much of the city's Democratic politics from the 1890s until 1939, when Thomas was jailed on income tax evasion charges. Despite this, the city managed to develop an innovative city council with six members elected on a district basis and six elected at large, along with the mayor. During the twentieth century the civic leaders embarked on major city beautification and cultural projects to change the city's image from that of a dingy "cow town." The late nineteenth and early twentieth centuries saw the development of ragtime by Scott Joplin and the Kansas City style of JAZZ with more saxophones and constant background riffs as performed by musicians such as Charlie Parker and Count Basie. Through the twentieth century the city remained a major transportation center, particularly with the coming of three interstate highways during the 1950s and 1960s. It continues to expand, growing to an area of 313.6 square miles by 2001 and a population of 441,545 according to the 2000 Census—up from 434,829 in 1990, but still down from 448,159 in 1980. Kansas City also serves as the regional center for an eleven-county metropolitan region of nearly five thousand square miles in both Missouri and Kansas. Drawing on the rural areas around it, the metropolitan population has continued to grow; from 1.5 million in 1990, it increased to nearly 1.8 million in 2000.

BIBLIOGRAPHY

Glaab, Charles Nelson. *Kansas City and the Railroads: Community Policy in the Growth of a Regional Metropolis.* Madison: State Historical Society of Wisconsin, 1962.

Hartmann, Rudolph H. *The Kansas City Investigation: Pendergast's Downfall, 1938–1939.* Columbia: University of Missouri Press, 1999.

Matthew L. Daley

See also **Transportation and Travel.**

KANSAS COMMITTEE, NATIONAL. After the sack of Lawrence on 21 May 1856, during civil war in Kansas Territory over the slavery issue, emigrant aid societies and Kansas relief committees sprang up throughout the free states. On 9 July 1856, representatives of these groups, and of older organizations like the New England Emigrant Aid Company and the New York State Kansas Committee, met at Buffalo, New York, and formed the National Kansas Committee with headquarters in Chicago. It raised and spent some $200,000, sending arms, supplies, and recruits to the Free-State (antislavery) Party in Kansas. In 1861 Congress incorporated Kansas into the Union as a free state.

BIBLIOGRAPHY

Potter, David M. *The Impending Crisis, 1848–1861.* New York: Harper and Row, 1976.

Rawley, James A. *Race and Politics: "Bleeding Kansas" and the Coming of the Civil War.* Philadelphia: Lippincott, 1969.

Samuel A. Johnson / A. G.

See also **Emigrant Aid Movement; Kansas-Nebraska Act; Lawrence, Sack of.**

KANSAS FREE-STATE PARTY. Organized by aggrieved settlers in 1855, the Kansas Free-State Party rejected the territorial legislature elected by the controversial means spawned by the flawed Kansas-Nebraska Act of 1854. Emigrants primarily from free states resented that residents of the slave state of Missouri nonetheless voted in the Kansas territorial election of 30 March 1855. The territorial government elected by such methods rebuffed several "free-state" delegates while endorsing a slave code seeking to organize Kansas as a slave state.

Protest meetings culminating at Big Springs on 5 September 1855 launched the Free-State political organization that supported a shadow "free-state" territorial government formed at Topeka. Competition emerged between Dr. Charles Robinson, a representative of antislavery New England emigrants, and James H. Lane, a former Democrat from Indiana. Lane led Midwestern settlers in resisting slavery's establishment in Kansas but also in promoting the exclusion of free blacks from the territory. On 15 December 1855 free-state voters approved a discriminatory referendum, 1,287 to 453. The eventual free-state constitution did not formally exclude blacks; it did deny blacks the suffrage while allowing segregated schools.

The Free-State Party encouraged Republicans in Congress to block pro-slavery efforts to control Kansas. A referendum authorized by the English bill of 1858 prevented such pro-slavery hopes while delaying the admission of Kansas as a free state until January 1861. Identified with national Republicans, the Free-State Party formally merged with that party in 1859 at an Osawatomie meeting attended by Horace Greeley. Turmoil in territorial Kansas contributed to the onset of the Civil War in 1861.

BIBLIOGRAPHY

Rawley, James A. *Race and Politics: "Bleeding Kansas" and the Coming of the Civil War.* Philadelphia: Lippincott, 1969.

SenGupta, Gunja. *For God and Mammon: Evangelicals and Entrepreneurs, Masters and Slaves in Territorial Kansas, 1854–1860.* Athens: University of Georgia Press, 1996.

Vernon L. Volpe

See also **Republican Party.**

KANSAS-NEBRASKA ACT of 1854 organized the northern Great Plains into the territories of Kansas and Nebraska. It also repealed the Missouri Compromise of 1820, which had prohibited slavery's expansion into the territories northwest of the border between the states of Arkansas and Missouri. Under the terms of the act, the residents of the Kansas and Nebraska territories would decide for themselves whether they would enter the Union as free or slave soil states. By repealing the Missouri Compromise, the Kansas-Nebraska Act reopened the divisive issue of slavery's expansion and brought the United States closer to civil war.

After the passing of the Compromise of 1850, which settled the slavery issue in New Mexico and Utah, many Americans hoped that further controversy over slavery would be avoided. But it soon arose again, largely because of plans for building a transcontinental railroad to the Pacific coast. Because the settlement of the western territories depended upon the construction of a transcontinental railroad, the railroad's location took on tremendous importance. Naturally, northern congressmen advocated a northern route, while southern congressmen supported a southern route. The sectional debate over the railroad's path threatened to block its construction, until Senator Stephen A. Douglas of Illinois entered the fray. An ardent supporter of western expansion and a tireless promoter of the Midwest's development, Douglas understood that a transcontinental railroad was indispensable for that region's political and economic future. Douglas also realized that if the transcontinental railroad took a northern route, Chicago would most likely serve as its eastern terminus. The resulting political and economic benefits that would accrue to Douglas's home state of Illinois were obvious. But Douglas also had national interests in mind. He genuinely believed that a populous and prosperous Midwest would be able to mediate sectional conflicts between North and South, and thus would promote sectional harmony and national unity.

Douglas recognized, however, that a transcontinental railroad running from Chicago to San Francisco would be possible only after the settlement of the vast midwestern lands between the Rocky Mountains and the Missouri River. Douglas thus introduced a bill to organize the land into the territories of Kansas and Nebraska, a move he believed would encourage settlers to migrate into the northern Great Plains.

In his effort to secure support for the Kansas-Nebraska bill, Douglas found an important ally in Missouri's influential senator, David R. Atchison, who was seeking reelection in 1854. Atchison's reelection campaign pitted him against Senator Thomas Hart Benton, a prominent opponent of slavery's westward expansion. Unlike Benton, Atchison was a staunch supporter of slavery's expansion, and he saw in the Kansas-Nebraska bill an opportunity to expand slavery's domain. Atchison promised Douglas that he would support the creation and settlement of the Kansas and Nebraska territories, but with one critical condition. He insisted that the Missouri Compromise be repealed so that his slaveholding constituents would be allowed to move into the new Kansas and Nebraska territories with their human property.

In an effort to mollify Atchison's concerns, Douglas introduced a bill for the territorial organization of Kansas and Nebraska, a bill that included a provision that effectively repealed the Missouri Compromise. The bill asserted that the Compromise of 1850 had superseded the 1820 principle that slavery would not be extended north and west of the Arkansas-Missouri state border. The bill also stated that the question of slavery in the territories should be settled by the people living in them, an idea known as POPULAR SOVEREIGNTY.

This language conveniently favored Atchison in his senatorial campaign, for it confronted his opponent, Thomas Hart Benton, with a difficult dilemma. If Benton voted for the bill, he would betray his antislavery sympathies; but if he voted against it, he would be defaulting on his promise to work for expansion into Kansas and Nebraska. He voted against the bill and suffered defeat in the race with Atchison. The final bill explicitly repealed the Missouri Compromise, and the possibility of slavery in the new territories was made real.

The political ramifications of the enactment of the Kansas-Nebraska bill reached deeply into the general political climate in which it was passed. Support for it from southern members of Congress was nearly unanimous. Northern Democrats were seriously split, half of their votes in the House going for the measure and half against it. Nearly all northern Whigs opposed the bill.

This severe political division fractured the structure of the political party system. The Whig Party was essentially destroyed in the South. The Democrats were so seriously divided that their tenuous congressional majority became highly vulnerable. A coalition of anti-Nebraska Democrats, northern Whigs, Know-Nothings, and nativist groups joined the newly organized Republican Party, making it a viable political force. By 1856 the Whigs had all but disappeared, and the Republican Party was able to confront the weakened Democrats with strong opposition.

In addition to these basic political changes, the Kansas-Nebraska Act had direct ramifications. Kansas and Nebraska were promptly opened for settlement in 1854. Although Nebraska remained relatively quiet, Kansas, the destination of most of the new settlers, became a political hotbed. Settlers came to Kansas not only to develop the frontier but also—and perhaps more importantly—to lend their weight in the determination of whether Kansas would be free or slave.

Almost from the outset, political stability was lacking in Kansas. From the South, proslavery Missourians traveled into Kansas to vote in favor of slavery, often arriving in armed bands. Groups in the North and East, such as the Emigrant Aid Company, helped so large a number of antislavery settlers move into the territory that it was generally thought that an honest referendum of actual settlers would not permit slavery in Kansas. But Missouri raiders entering the territory in great numbers made an honest count impossible. In 1855 a proslavery territorial legislature was established in the town of Lecompton, Kansas, while at the same time an antislavery legislature was established in Topeka. Almost inevitably, civil war erupted in Kansas as proslavery and antislavery forces clashed for control of the territory. Although bloody, the conflict remained inconclusive until the 1860s, when Kansas was finally admitted to the Union as a free soil state.

The violence and political chaos in Kansas not only presaged the CIVIL WAR but also helped to trigger it. In 1857 the proslavery territorial government in Lecompton presented to Congress a constitution that would have incorporated Kansas into the Union as a slave state. Chastened by the disastrous failure of his Kansas-Nebraska Act, Stephen Douglas led congressional opposition to the Lecompton constitution. Douglas and a diverse coalition of northern political factions in Congress narrowly managed to defeat Kansas's proposed admission to the Union as a slave state. The divisive battle over Lecompton, however, shattered the unity of the national Democratic Party, which in 1860 would divide into northern and southern wings. The collapse of the Democratic Party, the one remaining national party, set the stage for southern secession in 1860.

BIBLIOGRAPHY

Gienapp, William E. *The Origins of the Republican Party, 1852–1856.* New York: Oxford University Press, 1987.

Holt, Michael F. *The Political Crisis of the 1850s.* New York: Wiley, 1978.

———. *The Rise and Fall of the Whig Party: Jacksonian Politics and the Onset of the Civil War.* New York: Oxford University Press, 1999.

Malin, James C. *The Nebraska Question, 1852–1854.* Lawrence, Kans.: The author, 1953.

Potter, David M. *The Impending Crisis, 1848–1861.* New York: Harper and Row, 1976.

Rawley, James A. *Race and Politics: "Bleeding Kansas" and the Coming of the Civil War.* Philadelphia: Lippincott, 1969.

Jeannette P. Nichols/S. K.

See also **Democratic Party; Emigrant Aid Movement; Free Soil Party; Lecompton Constitution; Know-Nothing Party; Republican Party; Slavery; States' Rights; Transcontinental Railroad, Building of; Whig Party;** *and vol. 9:* **The Crime Against Kansas.**

KASSERINE PASS, BATTLE OF. In a series of engagements in Tunisia during World War II that reached a climax near the Algerian border at the Kasserine Pass, combined Italian and German forces in February 1943 drove American and French troops back about fifty miles from the Eastern to the Western Dorsale mountains. These events grew out of two actions: the British victory at El Alamein on 23 October 1942, which precipitated the retreat of German General Erwin Rommel's army across Libya and into southern Tunisia; and the Anglo-American invasion of French North Africa on 8 November 1942, which prompted the Axis nations to dispatch troops from Italy to northern Tunisia. By January 1943, Rommel's troops, pursued by Lieutenant General Bernard L. Montgomery's Eighth Army, were settling into the Mareth positions. At the same time, General D. Juergen von Arnim held Bizerte and Tunis against Lieutenant General Kenneth Anderson's First Army, composed of British, French, and American units.

The Americans were inexperienced and overconfident, and the French lacked modern and mechanized weapons and equipment. There were too few men for the large area they defended, yet the roads and railways from Algeria made support for larger forces impossible.

The battle opened 30 January 1943, when Arnim overwhelmed the French at Faïd Pass, and the Americans failed to restore the situation. Arnim attacked again on 14 February and marooned American forces on the Lessouda and Ksaira hills. At Sidi bou Zid he soundly defeated the U.S. First Armored Division, which lost ninety-eight tanks and about half of its combat effectiveness in two days. Allied troops abandoned Gafsa, Fériana, and Thélepte after destroying equipment and supplies, including facilities at two airfields, and the Americans were forced out of Sbeïtla.

Hoping to gain a great strategic victory by a wide envelopment through Tebéssa to Annaba (Bone), which would compel the Allies to withdraw from Tunisia, Rommel continued the offensive on 19 February. He thrust north from Sbeïtla toward Sbiba and sent two columns through the Kasserine Pass, one probing toward Tebéssa and the main effort toward Thala. After fierce fighting, all were stopped by determined defensive work. On 22 February a discouraged Rommel sent his units back to the Mareth positions to prepare for Montgomery's inevitable attack. Unaware of Rommel's withdrawal, the Allies moved cautiously forward, retook the Kasserine Pass on 25 February, and found the Italians and Germans gone.

The Americans learned their lessons and restructured their training programs. Major General George S. Patton Jr. replaced Major General Lloyd R. Fredendall at the head of the II Corps and restored the fighting spirit of the troops. General Harold Alexander instituted a better command system for the ground forces, and the French were rearmed and reequipped. Less than three months later, the Allies defeated the Italians and Germans and won control over all of North Africa.

BIBLIOGRAPHY

Blumenson, Martin. *Kasserine Pass.* Boston: Houghton Mifflin, 1967.

Greenfield, Kent R. *American Strategy in World War II: A Reconsideration.* Baltimore: Johns Hopkins University Press, 1963.

Macksey, Kenneth. *Crucible of Power: The Fight for Tunisia, 1942–1943.* London: Hutchinson, 1969.

Martin Blumenson / A. R.

See also **North African Campaign; World War II.**

KEARNEYITES were followers of Denis Kearney, who formed the Workingmen's party of California in 1877 to protest a variety of issues that troubled the state's workers, including rampant unemployment, dishonest banking, inequitable taxation, land monopoly, the growing power of railroads, and the immigration of Chinese laborers. In 1879, the Kearneyites became a significant political force in California and sent fifty-one delegates to the state's constitutional convention. Although California's new constitution met many of their demands, the Kearneyites apparently had little direct influence on the proceedings. By the presidential campaign of 1880, Kearney's party had lost most of its momentum and had practically disappeared from the stage of California politics.

BIBLIOGRAPHY

Gyory, Andrew. *Closing the Gate: Race, Politics, and the Chinese Exclusion Act.* Chapel Hill: University of North Carolina Press, 1998.

Saxton, Alexander. *The Indispensable Enemy; Labor and the Anti-Chinese Movement in California.* Berkeley: University of California Press, 1971.

P. Orman Ray / E. M.

See also **California; Chinese Exclusion Act; Labor.**

KEARNY'S MARCH TO CALIFORNIA. Just after the start of the MEXICAN-AMERICAN WAR in June 1846, General Stephen Watts Kearny led the Army of the West out of Fort Leavenworth, Kansas, with orders to march down the Santa Fe Trail into Upper CALIFORNIA and take possession of the territory for the United States. His swift, forceful invasion of Mexico's thinly populated northern frontier met no resistance. On 15 August, the Army of the West marched into Las Vegas, New Mexico, and three days later entered Santa Fe. On 25 September, Kearny moved west again, his numbers considerably reduced as his volunteers had turned south into Mexico to join the war there.

On 6 October at Socorro, New Mexico, Kearny met the renowned scout Kit Carson coming east with the news that California was already in American hands. Knowing the worst of the trail lay before him and believing the fighting to be over, Kearny reduced his force to one hundred dragoons and a few hunters, now all mounted on mules, and commandeered the services of a protesting Carson.

The army pushed west along the Gila River, through the harsh Sonoran desert. Halfway there Kearny learned that the Californios had revolted, throwing the Americans out of Los Angeles and Santa Barbara. The army pushed on under conditions that reduced men and beasts to starvation. Almost dead, they stumbled into eastern California on 2 December. Coming upon a party of Californio horsemen four days later in the Indian village of San Pascual, Kearny attacked—perhaps to get the fresh horses. Recent rains made the Americans' guns useless; the Californios counterattacked with lances and *reatas* (lassos). In the furious skirmishing, twenty-two Americans died. Kearny himself was wounded. Harassed by the Californios, his army staggered into San Diego on 12 December, where it joined forces with Commodore Robert F. Stockton. On 10 January 1847 Kearny and Stockton marched into Los Angeles and ended the revolt. Kearny never fully recovered from his wounds and died in 1848.

BIBLIOGRAPHY

Clarke, Dwight L. *Stephen Watts Kearney: Soldier of the West.* Norman: University of Oklahoma Press, 1961.

Cecelia Holland

KEARNY'S MISSION TO CHINA. Dispatched to the Far East in 1842 to protect American trading interests in China, Commodore Lawrence Kearny arrived in Canton at the close of the Anglo-Chinese War, generally known as the Opium War. Kearny sent a note to the Chinese high commissioner requesting that American citizens be granted trading rights equal to those of the "most favored" merchants operating in China. The two nations subsequently agreed to Cushing's Treaty, the first U.S. treaty with China, which established the most-favored-nation doctrine as the standard for American trade relations with China. The treaty constituted the genesis of the open-door doctrine proclaimed by Secretary of State John Hay some fifty-seven years later.

BIBLIOGRAPHY

Clymer, Kenton J. *John Hay: The Gentlemen as Diplomat.* Ann Arbor: University of Michigan Press, 1975.

Holt, Edgar. *The Opium Wars in China.* Chester Springs, Pa.: Dufour Editions, 1964.

McCormick, Thomas J. *China Market: America's Quest for Informal Empire, 1893–1901.* Chicago: Quadrangle Books, 1967.

Foster Rhea Dulles / A. G.

See also **Boxer Rebellion; Cushing's Treaty; Dutch West India Company; Root Arbitration Treaties; Trade Agreements; Trading Companies.**

KEELBOAT, a type of craft that was used on American rivers, chiefly in the West. The earliest keelboat seems to have been a skiff with a plank nailed the length of the bottom to make the boat easier to steer, but by about 1790 the keelboat had become a long narrow craft built on a keel and ribs, with a long cargo box amidships. It was steered by a special oar and propelled by oars or poles, pulled by a cordelle, or occasionally fitted with sails. Keelboats were 40 to 80 feet long, 7 to 10 feet in beam, 2 feet or more in draft, with sharp ends. A cleated footway on each side was used by the pole men. The success of Henry M. Shreve's shallow draft steamboats drove the keelboats from the main rivers by about 1820, except in low water, but they were used quite generally on the tributaries until after the Civil War. The chief utility of the keelboat was for upstream transportation and for swift downstream travel. It was used extensively for passenger travel.

BIBLIOGRAPHY

Baldwin, L. D. *The Keelboat Age on Western Waters.* Pittsburgh, Pa.: University of Pittsburgh Press, 1941.

Haites, Erik F. *Western River Transportation: The Era of Early Internal Development, 1810–1860.* Baltimore: The Johns Hopkins University Press, 1975.

Leland D. Baldwin / A. R.

See also **Flatboatmen; Galley Boats; Lewis and Clark Expedition; Missouri River; River Navigation; Waterways, Inland.**

KELLOGG-BRIAND PACT (also called the Pact of Paris), signed 27 August 1928 by 15 nations, reflected the movement to outlaw war to prevent a recurrence of the carnage of World War I. French foreign minister Aristide Briand initially proposed a bilateral treaty renouncing war as a method of settling disputes between France and the United States and drawing the United States into its defensive system against Germany. U.S. support for the pact came from both ends of the political spectrum. Interventionists thought it would lead to U.S. acceptance of the League of Nations; isolationists and peace groups hoped it would end war. Charles Lindbergh's successful solo crossing of the Atlantic and subsequent landing in Paris in May 1927 also helped boost Briand's efforts. Secretary of State Frank Kellogg, fearful that signing the treaty could drag the United States into a European war on the side of France, expanded the proposed agreement to a multilateral treaty renouncing war. Briand had no choice but to accept the pact, which was moral in tone but lacked force and did not bind America to any European treaty system. Subsequently, when Japan seized Manchuria in 1931, when Italy took over Ethiopia in 1935, and later when Germany began its expansion in the late 1930s, the Pact was exposed as the toothless treaty it had been all along.

BIBLIOGRAPHY

Ferrell, Robert H. *Peace in Their Time: The Origins of the Kellogg-Briand Pact.* New Haven, Conn.: Yale University Press, 1952.

Charles M. Dobbs

KELLY'S INDUSTRIAL ARMY was one of a number of "industrial armies," born of the panic of 1893, that pressed the federal government to help the unemployed. During the 1890s, Californian Charles T. Kelly rallied fifteen hundred men, many out of work, to this cause. In the spring of 1894, Kelly's followers boarded railroad boxcars bound for Washington, D.C. They planned to join Jacob S. Coxey's army, which had recently captured national headlines by marching from Ohio to the nation's capital. At Council Bluffs, Iowa, the railroad ejected Kelly's army. Many of Kelly's supporters, however, continued their journey on foot and eventually joined Coxey's army in Washington.

BIBLIOGRAPHY

McMurry, Donald Le Crone. *Coxey's Army: A Study of the Industrial Army Movement of 1894.* 1929. Reprint, Seattle: University of Washington Press, 1968.

Schwantes, Carlos A. *Coxey's Army: An American Odyssey.* Lincoln: University of Nebraska Press, 1985.

Carl L. Cannon/E. M.

See also **Coxey's Army; Financial Panics.**

KENESAW MOUNTAIN, BATTLE OF (27 June 1864). As Union general William Tecumseh Sherman advanced southward from Chattanooga, Tennessee, in his campaign to Atlanta, he used flanking movements to avoid a protracted confrontation with his opponent, General J. E. Johnston. As he neared Atlanta, Sherman came upon the Confederate army, drawn up with its center occupying the crest of Kenesaw Mountain. His frontal attack was repulsed with heavy losses. Several days later, he resumed his flanking movements, forcing Johnston southward to the line of the Chattahoochee River. The unnecessary assault on Kenesaw Mountain was one of Sherman's few serious errors in the campaign.

BIBLIOGRAPHY

Fellman, Michael. *Citizen Sherman: A Life of William Tecumseh Sherman.* New York: Random House, 1995.

McDonough, James L. *"War So Terrible": Sherman and Atlanta.* New York: Norton, 1987.

Royster, Charles. *The Destructive War: William Tecumseh Sherman, Stonewall Jackson, and the Americans.* New York: Knopf, 1991.

Thomas Robson Hay/A. R.

See also **Atlanta Campaign; Sherman's March to the Sea.**

KENNEBEC RIVER SETTLEMENTS of Maine were the focus of colonial competition among English investors, the Crown, Puritans, and French Acadians during the seventeenth century. Sir John Popham, the lord chief justice of England, was one of the first British sponsors to attempt settlement in North America, establishing a colony called Sagadahoc in 1607. Sagadahoc was abandoned in 1608 upon the death of its president, George Popham. In 1622 King James I granted land for the "Province of Maine" to Sir Fernando Gorges. By 1639 the province had pressed claims against Acadia, the French colony to the north, as far as the St. Croix River, the modern U.S.-Canadian boundary. In 1643 the proprietary governor of Maine, Thomas Gorges, returned to England to fight in the Civil War. Soon the Puritans of Massachusetts annexed Maine and its Kennebec River settlements, transforming them from the domain of an ineffectual proprietor into the frontier of Puritan society for the next century.

BIBLIOGRAPHY

Reid, John G. *Acadia, Maine, and New Scotland: Marginal Colonies in the Seventeenth Century.* Toronto: University of Toronto Press, 1981.

Timothy M. Roberts

KENNEDY ASSASSINATION. *See* **Assassinations, Presidential.**

KENSINGTON STONE is either an important fourteenth-century relic or an impressive hoax. It purports to be the inscribed account of a pre-Columbian Scandinavian exploration into the Great Lakes territory of North America. The stone was supposedly discovered in Kensington, Minnesota, in 1898 by a Swedish immigrant and farmer, Olof Ohman, who claimed to have unearthed the stone on his property. The stone is an irregularly shaped rectangular slab of graywacke, a sedimentary rock, and is about two and a half feet high, three to six inches thick, and fifteen inches wide. After the stone was discovered, it was kept in a bank in Kensington until early 1899, when its existence was publicized in newspapers. The stone's symbols were then discovered to be runic and were translated into several languages. When translated into English, the inscription reads:

> Eight Swedes and Twenty-two Norwegians on an exploration journey from Vinland westward. We had our camp by 2 rocky islets one day's journey north of this stone. We were out fishing one day. When we came home we found ten men red with blood and dead. AVM save us from evil. We have ten men by the sea to look after our ships, fourteen days' journey from this island. Year 1362.

When news of the inscription was released, it was quickly dismissed by academics at American and Scandinavian universities as a hoax or a forgery. The stone was then returned to Ohman, who claimed to use it as a doorstop until 1907, when the writer Hjalmar Rued Holand acquired the stone with the intent to prove its authenticity. Holand spent the rest of his life arguing for the legitimacy of the stone. He believed that Vikings had reached Minnesota territory in the fourteenth century and that an expedition led by Paul Knutson through Hudson Bay, Lake Winnipeg, and the Red River was the expedition that the stone chronicled. If Holand was correct, then the Norse explored wider areas of the North American continent and had enjoyed a longer era of exploration than previously supposed. Holand's theory became popular among the Scandinavian communities of Minnesota who helped perpetuate the idea of the stone's authenticity despite academic dismissal.

There has been a good deal of scholarly examination and debate surrounding the stone, and the overwhelming conclusion is that it is a forgery. This is based on the runic characters and style of inscription, which are dated by philologists and runologists as nineteenth century in style. Those who argue for the stone's authenticity find the use of "AVM," a medieval abbreviation for "Ave Maria," to be particular to the fourteenth century and most likely unknown to nineteenth-century forgers.

Although still considered by many to be a hoax and by some to be genuine artifact, the Kensington Stone is a curiosity and remains displayed at the Runestone Museum of Alexandria, Minnesota.

BIBLIOGRAPHY

Blegen, Theodore Christian. *The Kensington Rune Stone: New Light on an Old Riddle.* St. Paul: Minnesota Historical Society, 1968.

Hall, Robert Anderson. *The Kensington Rune-Stone Is Genuine: Linguistic, Practical, Methodological Considerations.* Columbia, S.C.: Hornbeam Press, 1982.

Williams, Stephen. *Fantastic Archaeology: The Wild Side of North American Prehistory.* Philadelphia: University of Pennsylvania Press, 1991.

Deirdre Sheets

See also **Norsemen in America.**

KENT STATE PROTEST. On 4 May 1970 Ohio national guardsmen opened fire on Kent State University students protesting the VIETNAM WAR. In a mere thirteen seconds four students were killed, and nine others wounded. What had begun as a small campus demonstration turned Kent State into a symbol of the Vietnam era worldwide.

Kent State students protested President Richard M. Nixon's 30 April announcement that troops would invade Cambodia to strike against suspected guerrillas. Nixon's declaration set off a chain reaction, and 1.5 million students protested around the country. The president fueled the confrontation by calling them "bums" who were "blowing up the campuses." Tensions in Kent, Ohio, escalated in the days leading up to 4 May. Mayor Leroy Satrom declared the city under a state of emergency after a disturbance downtown got out of hand. On 2 May Satrom requested that the Ohio National Guard deploy.

Despite the presence of armed soldiers, Kent State students continued to hold rallies. The situation spiraled out of control when a fire burned down the university Reserve Officers' Training Corps (ROTC) building. Governor James Rhodes arrived on 3 May and condemned student radicals, comparing them to nazis and communists. In response protesters gathered on campus but were teargassed.

On 4 May a rally drew approximately two thousand students, many merely curious onlookers. National Guard officers ordered the protesters to disburse, shooting tear gas into the crowd. Next more than one hundred armed guardsmen advanced on the students. The troops moved toward the protesters, up a hill, and then down to a practice football field. Reaching a fence at the far end, some knelt and aimed their weapons. Students retreated into a parking lot between several buildings, but some lobbed rocks and tear gas canisters back at the guardsmen.

After ten minutes the troops moved back up the hill. When they reached the crest, a group of twenty-eight guardsmen turned quickly and shot in the direction of the parking lot and the main group of protesters. They fired sixty-one rounds of ammunition. Of the thirteen people killed or injured, only two were actively participating in the confrontation. One student was killed while walking to class, and another ironically was an ROTC student. Others were more than one hundred yards away.

As news spread Kent State and nearly five hundred other colleges were closed. Ten days later another shooting occurred, this time at Jackson State University in Mississippi. Police and state patrolmen fired into a dormitory at the all-black school, killing two students and wounding nine others. The lack of attention given to the deaths at Jackson State embittered many in the African American community.

Kent State immediately transformed from a sleepy midwestern college into the symbolic epicenter of student protest in the Vietnam era. Lingering romantic notions of the 1960s ended with the Kent State shootings. The incident has been immortalized in countless books and even a television movie, but nothing was more stinging than the song by the group Crosby, Stills, Nash, and Young, "Ohio," with its haunting lyrics, "Tin soldiers and Nixon's coming. . . . Four dead in Ohio!"

BIBLIOGRAPHY

Bills, Scott L., ed. *Kent State, May 4: Echoes through a Decade.* Kent, Ohio: Kent State University Press, 1982.

Davies, Peter. *The Truth about Kent State: A Challenge to the American Conscience.* New York: Farrar, Straus, and Giroux, 1973.

Eszterhas, Joe, and Michael D. Roberts. *Thirteen Seconds: Confrontation at Kent State.* New York: Dodd, Mead, 1970.

Gordon, William A. *The Fourth of May: Killings and Coverups at Kent State.* Buffalo, N.Y.: Prometheus Books, 1990.

Heineman, Kenneth J. *Campus Wars: The Peace Movement at American State Universities in the Vietnam Era.* New York: New York University Press, 1993.

Michener, James A. *Kent State: What Happened and Why.* New York: Random House, 1971.

Bob Batchelor

KENTUCKY. The date the first human walked on the land that now comprises Kentucky remains unknown to history. Archaeologists indicate it took place over twelve thousand years ago. But leaving no written record, no history, those lives can only be re-created by archaeological investigations, which describe the Native American presence in four stages. Paleoindians, living from 12,000 years before the present (B.P.) to around 10,000, saw the end of the Ice Age. They were hunter-gathers who moved often, and their lives centered on simple survival. During the Archaic Period (1000 B.P.–3000 B.P.) the people in Kentucky continued to hunt and developed some limited trade routes. In the third culture, that of the Woodland Indians, which included the Hopewell and Adena subcultures, a more settled lifestyle resulted from agricultural cultivation. The final period, dating from the years A.D. 1000 to around A.D. 1700, has been called the Late Prehistoric or in the east the Fort Ancient and in the west the Mississippian. The latter featured sizable fortified villages with mounds organized around the water courses that supported farms.

Having been the lone occupiers of the land for century after century, Native Americans finally found that the place called Kentucky no longer would be theirs without conflict. The region quickly became a middle ground, a place of contact. Unfortunately one of the critical contacts came in the form of microbes. Disease probably had a greater impact than any other forms of contact with the European colonies. Death swept the land, tribal patterns changed, Indian numbers fell, and Native life never returned to past ways. When the first explorers from the colonies arrived, they found a different place than what had existed only a few years before. Once heavily peopled, Kentucky seemed vacant of inhabitants. The last recorded interior Indian village, Eskippakithiki, was abandoned by the 1750s. The region seemed to be more of a fought-over buffer between tribes to the north and south, and while various groups hunted the land, early English hunters and explorers left no record of seeing semipermanent villages. To their land-hungry eyes the area seemed to be a prize waiting to be taken.

Word soon spread across the colonial backcountry that beyond the mountains lay a land of much promise with fine forests, abundant game, and rich soil. Driven by this image of plenty and promise, imbued with "Kentucky fever," more and more ventured across the mountains to this First West. A series of long hunters, of whom Daniel Boone, James Harrod, and Simon Kenton are the best known, started the process, and land companies soon sent their own surveyors to map out the unexplored territory. Conflict with the Native peoples intensified. Mostly occurring while the Revolutionary War raged, the settlement of Kentucky represented simply another front in that conflict and a bloody one.

Coming down the Ohio River, Harrod established the first permanent settlement at Harrodsburg in 1774. Boone, working for the Transylvania Land Company, followed buffalo trails in part and blazed the Wilderness Road from Cumberland Gap to the central Bluegrass. These two paths were followed by thousands of men and women over the next two decades, and by the first census in 1790 some seventy-three thousand people (16 percent of them slaves) had moved to what was then part of Virginia. Others, about one in seventy who migrated, had been killed in the attempt. In those decades from settlement in the 1770s until the peace that followed the War of 1812, Kentucky started as the first step in the new nation's move westward, represented a testing ground for new ideas and plans, and matured into a new state, the first state west of the mountain barriers. Yet none of that came easily.

The land of milk and honey was also, as one Indian called it, "a dark and bloody ground." Yet the hopes and dreams of those in less-promising situations to the east brought many to risk all to try to find a better future. Some in fact did just that, and their descendants lived better lives as a result. However, for some the myth of plenty proved elusive. By 1800 half of Kentuckians owned land, but as many did not. That contradictory nature of early Kentucky has been a theme throughout the state's history.

Statehood and Slavery

As the region filled with people, questions arose on what future course should be followed, separation from Virginia and statehood, or something else? The so-called Spanish conspiracy, which left many Kentucky leaders under the pay of Spain, failed in its efforts to encourage Kentucky to become a separate nation. In 1792 Kentucky entered the Union as the fifteenth state with Isaac Shelby as its governor, and within a few months Frankfort became its capital. But issues of separation and of a state's role in the Union continued. Distrust of federal support for Kentucky's needs caused several prominent leaders, including the war hero George Rogers Clark, to aid the so-called French conspiracy in 1794 and later the Burr conspiracy. Reaction to Federalist actions in 1798 and 1799 brought forth the Kentucky Resolutions defending states' rights and even nullification. Yet these sentiments were partly muted over succeeding decades as Kentuckians fought in the nation's wars and as the rise of Henry Clay and his American System stressed the idea of a powerful, united country. Still Kentucky remained that middle ground of frontier times, only now a meeting place for South, North, and West.

The contrasting aspects present in early Kentucky emerged in the first constitution in 1792. While containing many elements that restricted the role of the people, indirect selection of state senators and the governor, for instance, it also included universal manhood suffrage except for slaves, the first to do so in the United States. In more debatable terms it opened the floodgates toward what became 120 counties, the third highest number in the nation. For a considerable time these almost self-perpetuating, feudal-like entities, those "little kingdoms," dominated the political face of Kentucky.

That contrast between an almost aristocratic heritage and a democratic one, as shown early in the settling of the land and in the formation of the first constitution, represented only one of the divisions that brought the historian Thomas D. Clark to call Kentucky a "land of contrast." Those divisions were clearly demonstrated when citizens turned to the subject of slavery. From the earliest English explorations, such as that of Christopher Gist in 1750–1751, black slaves had been a part of discovering the "new Eden." Harrodsburg's 1777 census showed that one in ten in that frontier post were enslaved peoples, and blacks fought side by side with whites against the common Indian foe, sometimes at the cost of their lives. But when the Indian wars ended and decision time came, ruling whites placed more emphasis on establishing slavery as a way to regulate race relations and as an economic system than on the idea of equality. By 1830 slaves made up 24 percent of the commonwealth's population, and on the eve of the Civil War, Kentucky had the third highest number of slaveholders among the slave states.

At the same time Kentucky had the third lowest average number of slaves held, 5.5 per family, and many places, such as the eastern mountains, held few slaves at all. Moreover a vocal antislavery movement existed throughout the antebellum period, ranging from the conservative colonization-oriented plans of Henry Clay and Robert J. Breckinridge to the vocal opposition of Cassius M. Clay to the true egalitarianism of John G. Fee. Yet as the eloquent voices of escaped Kentucky slaves, such as Henry Bibb, Josiah Henson, and the novelist William Wells Brown, showed, freedom came to most bondspeople through their own actions.

Slavery represented another paradox in a state that before the Civil War had become one of the most important and prosperous in the nation. In 1840 it stood first in the United States in the production of hemp and wheat, second in tobacco and corn, third in flax, and fourth in rye. Its reputation for producing fine thoroughbreds had already been established and later was enhanced with the Kentucky Derby, which began in 1875. Moreover for a time Kentucky's Transylvania University, with its medical and law schools, was the place of choice for the education of southern gentlemen as it was one of the best schools in the nation. In religion the Great Revival of 1801 spread from Kentucky across the nation as well, and a more diversified worship emerged. By 1850 Kentucky stood eighth in the United States in population and had a reputation as a modern, forward-looking commonwealth, a place for the ambitious and eager.

The state's antebellum importance came through clearly in the area of politics. Between 1824 and 1860 a Kentuckian ran for either president or vice president in seven of the ten presidential races. Three times the Whig leader Henry Clay won electoral votes. Twice Kentuckians served as vice president, the Democrats Richard M. Johnson and John C. Breckinridge, the latter also a presidential candidate who lost in 1860 to the native Kentuckian Abraham Lincoln. Ten Kentuckians filled presidents' cabinets, and three served as Speaker of the House.

When the threat of civil war emerged in the late 1850s, Henry Clay and his Whig Party had both died, the Know-Nothings had won a governorship in 1855 after a bloody riot in the state's economic center Louisville, and a divided commonwealth faced an uncertain future. With the failure of the Kentuckian John J. Crittenden's attempt at a compromise to keep the Union together, the state officially chose a pattern of neutrality from May to September 1861, and the nation divided into the United States, the Confederate States, and Kentucky. But, indicative of the state's past, Kentucky wanted both the Union and slavery and did not see the war as one against the "peculiar institution" at the conflict's beginning. Elections and enlistments showed a pro-union emphasis, and the commonwealth abandoned neutrality and remained officially a loyal state. Those friendly to the southern cause called a rump convention and declared the state a part of the Confederacy, and Kentucky became a star in both flags. Before it all ended perhaps as many as 100,000 fought for the North (23,000 of them former slaves, the second largest number of all the states), while some 40,000 entered the ranks of the Confederacy. It truly was a brothers' war for Kentucky.

The initial southern defense line from Cumberland Gap to the Mississippi splintered after defeats at Mill Springs and Fort Donelson in early 1862. That fall a major Confederate invasion tasted early success at the Battle of Richmond in Kentucky but then ended in retreat after the bloody Battle of Perryville on 8 October 1862. Thereafter raids by General John Hunt Morgan and brutal guerrilla warfare marked the rest of the conflict.

Perhaps the greatest effect of the war came from developments away from the battlefield. As the issue of slavery became a war aim, that, together with the unpopular Union military rule, turned Kentuckians more and more against the cause they had initially supported. By the war's end the commonwealth had become as sympathetic to the South as any of the seceding states. As a loyal state it never went through Reconstruction officially, but the "lost cause" attitudes displayed toward former slaves and toward the federal government brought martial law and the Freedmen's Bureau to Kentucky. The state became almost a spokesperson for the South, especially through the columns of the powerful *Louisville Courier-Journal*, edited by

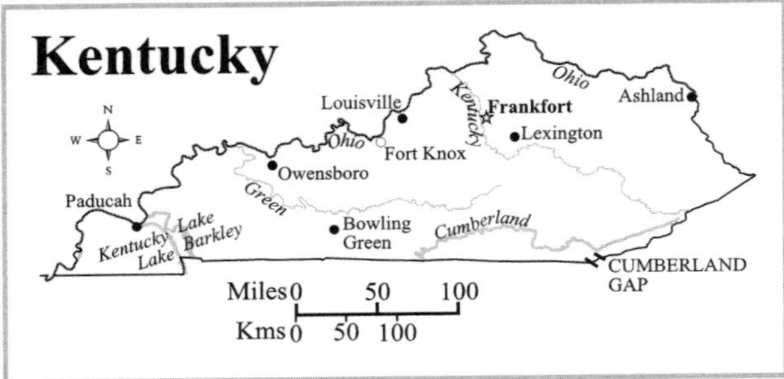

Henry Watterson. For the next three decades the once-minority Democrats ruled with few challenges, and ex-Confederates, not the once-dominant Unionists, guided it.

Postwar Kentucky

Few reform elements emerged in those years. A fledgling women's rights group did organize in 1881, the first in the South. Advocates such as Laura Clay and Madeline McDowell Breckinridge eventually earned national leadership roles and made the state a strong force for suffrage, ratifying the federal amendment in 1920. During the same time the commonwealth once more showed its varied faces in its ability to reconcile racing, red-eye WHISKEY, and religion all at the same time. Kentucky voted in statewide prohibition despite its role as the nation's leading producer of bourbon, and in the 1920s it even seriously debated ending pari-mutuel betting despite its dependence on the horse industry.

But more reflective of the half century following the Civil War was the role violence played in Kentucky. In lynchings and in personal, honor-based actions, the commonwealth varied little from southern patterns. However, in the Appalachian Mountains feud violence broke out in a dozen or more major conflicts, the best-known (but not the bloodiest) of which was the Hatfield-McCoy dispute. Kentucky's increasing image as a place of violence intensified in January 1900 with the assassination of Governor William Goebel, the only governor to die in office as a result of assassination, and with the Black Patch War in the first decade of the twentieth century. That war united farmers against tobacco companies in what has been called the largest mass agricultural protest movement in the nation. Night riders used violence to enforce the growers' will and to intimidate the buyers, and the state's reputation suffered. With the boom and bust cycles in the eastern coal fields, labor and management divisions in the 1930s gave "Bloody Harlan" its name. But by the end of the twentieth century Kentucky ranked low on the crime scale in a drastic reversal.

The violent acts one after the other, the effect of prohibition on the economy, the lack of leadership, and a decline in education from its once-strong place in the South hurt Kentucky in the twentieth century. Despite the presence of military bases, such as Fort Knox with its gold depository, World War II also affected that growth, for of all the southern states Kentucky grew tenth slowest. Outmigrations to jobs in the North intensified in wartime and continued in the 1950s as the coal mines mechanized and Appalachians left for urban areas beyond the Ohio. But almost quietly Kentucky's economy changed. The 1960s War on Poverty did help those of lower income levels. Jobs also resulted when businesses expanded or new ones started, chiefly in Louisville and Lexington, including GE, Ford, Corvette, Brown-Foreman, Humana, Toyota, UPS, IBM (later Lexmark), Ashland Oil, and Kentucky Fried Chicken (Yum!Brands). While tardy in constructing highways, the state built interstates and toll roads that soon provided an excellent system that, coupled with river routes and rails as well as the state's central location, made it increasingly attractive to businesses. By the start of the twenty-first century the state's working profile largely resembled the nation's regarding manufacturing jobs. Kentucky was the third leading producer of motor vehicles and carried on extensive world trade, for example. Yet the one-time mainstays of the state, thoroughbreds, coal, and tobacco, still heavily influenced an economy that had moved beyond them in some ways.

Education remained a key to the so-called "new economy," and Kentucky for many decades of the 1900s stood near the bottom of the states in that regard. State-funded institutions of higher education began with the present-day University of Kentucky in 1865, Kentucky State University (as a segregated school) in 1886, various teacher colleges in 1908 and again in 1922, and the University of Louisville and Northern Kentucky University at the end of the 1960s. Combining those with an extensive community college system and strong private colleges, such as Transylvania, Centre, and Georgetown, the state offered the instruction needed, but too few attended. By 1980 the commonwealth stood near the bottom in high school and college graduates. In a 1989 decision the state supreme court ruled the existing elementary and secondary system unconstitutional, and the Kentucky Education Reform Act (KERA) crafted an entirely new approach in 1990. Other states began to look on the commonwealth as a model for reform, and statistical improvements did follow. However, long decades of neglect and a poorly educated population meant that the issue remained.

Ironically, given the state's poverty and low educational attainments, Kentucky has had an exceptionally strong literary tradition and rich folklife element. Robert Penn Warren provided the most visible example of that, winning Pulitzer Prizes in both fiction and poetry, the only American so honored. But many others have made significant impacts as well, including James Lane Allen, John Fox Jr., Annie Fellows Johnston (*The Little Colonel*), Alice Hegan Rice (*Mrs. Wiggs of the Cabbage Patch*), Irvin S. Cobb, Elizabeth Maddox Roberts, Allen Tate, Caroline Gordon, Cleanth Brooks, Jesse Stuart, James Still, Harriette Arnow (*The Dollmaker*), A. B. Guthrie, Janice Holt Giles, Thomas Merton, Bobbie Ann Mason, and Wendell Berry. Some strengths appeared in art over the years, such as Matthew Jouett, Paul Sawyier, and Frank Duveneck, and a few in film, such as the director D. W. Griffith, but another real area of contribution has been music. The bluegrass style of Bill Monroe represented part of a rich tradition in folk and country, with Kentuckians standing second in the number of representatives in the Country Music Hall of Fame. A strong arts community in Louisville, with its festival of new plays the centerpiece, showed the range of interests in the commonwealth.

But in some ways politics, even more than basketball, where the commonwealth's university and college teams have won many national titles, long dominated conversation. From 1895, when the first Republican governor was elected, until 1931 a fairly strong two-party system operated. The New Deal, with its actions that helped bring blacks and labor into the Democratic fold, gave that party almost unbroken control of the legislature and governor's office over the next decades. In the last three-quarters of the twentieth century Republicans held the executive office only eight years. At the same time the state's conservative voting nature emerged in elections for national office, with citizens selecting Republicans more often than Democrats in the late twentieth century. A 1992 amendment to the outdated 1891 state constitution finally allowed governors to serve two terms, which countered somewhat a growing legislative independence. Serious political corruption in the BOPTROT scandal that erupted in the early 1990s ended in the convictions of over a dozen legislators and one of the strongest ethics laws in the nation. Throughout all that the state produced several strong leaders at both the national and state levels, including Senator Alben Barkley, majority leader under Franklin Roosevelt; A. B. "Happy" Chandler, senator, two-term governor, and baseball commissioner; Chief Justice Fred Vinson; Senators John Sherman Cooper and Wendell Ford, the latter a majority whip; and Governors Earle Clements and Bert Combs.

Only slowly have two groups shared in that success. African Americans, for example, found their life after the Civil War segregated and restricted, varying little from southern patterns. The last integrated college in the South, Berea, was forced by state action to segregate in 1904. Yet unlike in the South, Kentucky blacks continued to vote, giving them an important power that translated into some support. Still, what the historian George C. Wright called a facade of polite racism dominated efforts at real equality. Work by Kentucky leaders, such as Charles W. Anderson Jr., the first black state legislator in the South after decades of exclusion; Whitney M. Young Jr., the head of the Urban League; and state senator Georgia Powers, helped break down the legal barriers. Nevertheless racism and lack of economic opportunity convinced many to migrate, and the state's African American population fell to some 7 percent. The commonwealth's Civil Rights Act of 1966 and Fair Housing Act two years later were the first in the South, and studies placed state schools as the most integrated in the nation by the 1990s.

After getting the vote, women reflected the state's dual character as well. The commonwealth elected one of the first eight women to Congress, Katherine Langley, and one of the first half-dozen women governors, Martha Layne Collins. It supported women's rights in the early struggle and ratified the failed Equal Rights Amendment decades later. Yet in the early twenty-first century Kentucky ranked near the bottom in the percentage of women legislators in its 138-member body and low in females in managerial positions and as business owners.

By the first decade of the twenty-first century the commonwealth stood exactly in the middle of the states in population, and its 4,041,769 residents ranked high in the nation in the percentage of people who still lived in the state of their birth. More urban than rural for the first time in 1970, a half century after the nation as a whole, Kentucky remained tied to the ideals of the family farm, small town life, and a sense of place. But another side of Kentucky reflected all the elements of modern America. In short, the contrasts that marked the state over the years continued.

BIBLIOGRAPHY

Aron, Stephen. *How the West Was Lost: The Transformation of Kentucky from Daniel Boone to Henry Clay.* Baltimore: Johns Hopkins University Press, 1996.

Clark, Thomas D. *Kentucky: Land of Contrast.* New York: Harper and Row, 1968.

Harrison, Lowell H. *The Civil War in Kentucky.* Lexington: University Press of Kentucky, 1975.

Harrison, Lowell H., ed. *Kentucky's Governors, 1792–1985.* Lexington: University Press of Kentucky, 1985.

Harrison, Lowell H., and James C. Klotter. *A New History of Kentucky.* Lexington: University Press of Kentucky, 1997.

Kleber, John E., ed. *The Kentucky Encyclopedia.* Lexington: University Press of Kentucky, 1992.

Klotter, James C. *Kentucky: Portrait in Paradox, 1900–1950.* Frankfort: Kentucky Historical Society, 1996.

Klotter, James C., ed. *Our Kentucky: A Study of the Bluegrass State.* Rev. ed. Lexington: University Press of Kentucky, 2000.

Lewis, R. Barry, ed. *Kentucky Archaeology.* Lexington: University Press of Kentucky, 1996.

Lucas, Marion B., and George C. Wright. *A History of Blacks in Kentucky.* 2 vols. Frankfort: Kentucky Historical Society, 1992.

Tapp, Hambleton, and James C. Klotter. *Kentucky: Decades of Discord, 1865–1900.* Frankfort: Kentucky Historical Society, 1977.

Ulack, Richard, ed. *Atlas of Kentucky.* Lexington: University Press of Kentucky, 1998.

Ward, William S. *A Literary History of Kentucky.* Knoxville: University of Tennessee Press, 1988.

James C. Klotter

See also **Bluegrass Country; Coal Mining and Organized Labor; Feuds, Appalachian Mountain; Horse Racing and Showing; Music: Bluegrass; Westward Migration.**

KENTUCKY CONVENTIONS. In the 1780s the Kentucky frontier, then part of Virginia, became the scene of violent confrontations between white settlers and local Indians. As the white population increased, the ferocity of such conflicts escalated correspondingly. In 1784 a convention of representative delegates met in Danville to petition Virginia for assistance. Between 1784 and 1790 nine conventions were held. A tenth convention met in April 1792 to frame the state constitution.

The conventions reshaped Kentucky's relationship to Virginia and cleared the way for Kentucky's incorporation into the Union as a state in its own right. In particular, they broadened Virginia's laws for frontier defense and passed four enabling acts. These latter acts gave the Kentuckians three privileges: first, they provided specific rules for registry of land; second, they established definite terms of separation; and, third, they secured Kentucky representation in the Congress of the Confederation. In the numerous debates, pioneer statesmen clarified many issues that faced the western people. Navigation and trade rights down the Mississippi River were partially guaranteed, the Spanish conspiracy was defeated, and a reasonably democratic constitution was drafted. Perhaps the most important accomplishment of all was the excellent political training early Kentucky leaders secured as delegates to the conventions.

BIBLIOGRAPHY

Channing, Steven A. *Kentucky: A Bicentennial History.* New York: Norton, 1977.

Horsman, Reginald. *The New Republic: The United States of America, 1789–1815.* Harlow, U.K.; New York: Longman, 2000.

T. D. Clark / A. G.

See also **Backcountry and Backwoods; Frontier Defense; Tobacco and American Indians; Trading Companies; Virginia Indian Company; Wars with Indian Nations: Early Nineteenth Century (1783–1840).**

KEOGH PLANS. *See* **Retirement Plans.**

KERNER COMMISSION. In the summer of 1967, serious rioting broke out in many American cities, causing property damage estimated at between $75 and $100 million and resulting in eighty-four deaths. In Detroit, federal troops were deployed to quell unrest. That city suffered the most serious rioting, with forty-three deaths, seven thousand arrests, and 1,383 burned buildings. In July 1967, President Lyndon Johnson created the National Advisory Commission on Civil Disorders to investigate the causes of the civil unrest and to recommend remedies. Johnson suspected that the commission would find evidence of a political conspiracy among urban black militants. The commission was more popularly known by the name of its chair, Otto Kerner, whom Johnson appointed because of his long legal career as a judge and prosecuting attorney and his political experience as a former Democratic governor of Illinois. Other important members of the commission included Oklahoma senator Fred Harris, NAACP executive director Roy Wilkins, and New York City mayor John Lindsay. Lindsay's efforts were of particular importance as he played an important role in the drafting of the commission's final report, which was issued on 1 March 1968.

The commission found no evidence of a political conspiracy at work in the rioting. Rather, the panel concluded that economic deprivation and racial discrimination created great anger in the ghettos and thus created the conditions for rioting. In its most famous phrase, the report found that "Our nation is moving toward two societies, one black, one white—separate and unequal" and that a program of racial integration and economic uplift was the only preventative step that could be taken to avoid rioting in the hot summers of the future. The commission called for steep increases in federal aid to the cities, a federal jobs program to employ one million workers, and an increase in the minimum wage, among other redistributive policy proposals. The report attracted a vast amount of public attention as a commercial press reprint of the report sold two million copies and made the best-seller lists. The policy impact of the report was minimal. Urban riots peaked out after the difficult summer that prompted the formation of the commission and a conservative Republican administration came to power in January 1969. With its linkage of white racism with black poverty, the report entered into the lexicon of social science and policy analysis debate.

BIBLIOGRAPHY

Lipsky, Michael, and David J. Olsen. *Commission Politics: The Processing of Racial Crisis in America.* New Brunswick, NJ: Transaction Books, 1977.

United States. National Advisory Commission on Civil Disorders. *Report of the Commission on Civil Disorders.* New York: Dutton, 1969.

Richard M. Flanagan

See also **Civil Rights Movement; Great Society; Riots, Urban, of 1967.**

KEROSINE OIL. Americans knew something of petroleum deposits as early as 1700, but oil rarely entered commerce until 1849 when Samuel M. Kier of Pittsburgh began selling "Kier's Petroleum or Rock Oil, Celebrated for its Wonderful Curative Powers" on a large scale. Meanwhile, other men were taking steps destined to reveal the true value of the oil. James Young of Glasgow, Scotland, began distilling lubricating and illuminating oils from a petroleum spring in Derbyshire, England, in 1847. In Prince Edward Island, Canada, Abram Gessner distilled kerosine from local coal as early as 1846. He patented his process in the United States and sold his rights to the North American Kerosene Gas Light Company of

New York, which began commercial manufacture in March 1854. By 1859, the country had between fifty and sixty companies making kerosine from coal, shale, and other carbons. The business grew rapidly, replacing older illuminants such as whale oil and camphine.

Although Kier had begun distilling kerosine from petroleum in 1850, he had made little headway, and the effective pioneer was Col. A. C. Ferris of New York, who obtained most of the output of the Tarentum, Pennsylvania, wells. In 1858 the crude petroleum business of the United States amounted to 1,183 barrels. Then in 1859 E. L. Drake made his momentous oil strike in western Pennsylvania, and the supply of crude oil rapidly grew enormous. By 1860 more than 200 patents had been granted on kerosine lamps, and within years kerosine became the world's principal illuminant. About 1880 the Standard Oil Company perfected a safe kerosine stove. Meanwhile, by-products of kerosine manufacture, such as paraffin, Vaseline, and lubricating oils, had taken an important place in American life.

During the twentieth century, additional uses were found for kerosine—as an ingredient in jet engine fuel, for domestic heating, as a cleaning solvent and insecticide, and, although largely replaced by electricity, for illumination. In 1972 the United States produced approximately 2.3 billion barrels (42 gallons each) of kerosine.

BIBLIOGRAPHY

Black, Brian. *Petrolia: The Landscape of America's First Oil Boom.* Baltimore: Johns Hopkins University Press, 2000.

Yergin, Daniel. *The Prize: The Epic Quest for Oil, Money, and Power.* New York: Simon and Schuster, 1991.

Allan Nevins / c. w.

See also **Coal; Oil Fields; Petroleum Industry; Standard Oil Company.**

KEYNESIANISM is a term that identifies both a school of economic theory and a distinctive approach to public policy. Regarding theory, it can be said that the English economist John Maynard Keynes (1883–1946) invented modern macroeconomics with the publication in 1936 of his masterwork *The General Theory of Employment, Interest, and Money.* That book shifted the focus of attention from the microeconomic actions of individuals and firms to the overall behavior of a capitalist economy.

Keynes argued that, contrary to the conventional wisdom embodied in Say's Law, the capitalist economy did not contain a self-correcting or homeostatic mechanism that would necessarily return it to a healthy equilibrium over the course of the business cycle. Rather, as the contemporaneous Great Depression seemed to demonstrate, a deficiency in effective demand could result in equilibrium at an intolerably high level of unemployment. In the Keynesian model, government policy to bolster aggregate demand, especially fiscal action (spending and taxing) to increase either consumption or the particularly volatile element of investment, could be used to drive an underperforming economy to full employment. Because of the so-called "multiplier effect" that Keynes invoked as a central element in his model, such action could have an ultimate economic impact several times larger than the magnitude of the government's initial corrective intervention.

In the period from World War II through the early 1970s, Keynesianism rose to ever greater influence as both a theory and a guide for public policy. The Keynesian analysis gained a prominent place in textbooks, and its terminology increasingly became the common language of both economists and policymakers. The experience of World War II, with its massive deficit spending, seemed to validate Keynes's approach, and the subsequent Cold War and the later expansion of social spending left the federal government with a sufficiently large presence in the U.S. economy to serve as a Keynesian lever. The size of postwar budgets meant that changes in federal spending and taxing had a powerful impact on the overall economy. Embraced most fervently by Democrats but influential also in Republican circles, the Keynesian policy approach gained its fullest expression in the liberal presidencies of the 1960s, most prominently in the Kennedy-Johnson tax cut of 1964. In 1965, *Time* magazine put Keynes's picture on its cover in a tribute to the influence of his economic vision.

With the onset of stagflation in the 1970s, Keynesianism began to lose influence both as a theory and as a policy. Unable to explain adequately the economic malaise of simultaneous stagnation and inflation, it came under theoretical assault by the monetarist and the rational expectations schools of economic thought. Suspected of being itself a primary contributor to inflation, Keynesianism was increasingly supplanted by policy approaches aimed more at the supply side of the economy.

At the end of the twentieth century, Keynesianism still provided much of the lingua franca of macroeconomics. However, both as a theory and as a policy, it lived on only in a much chastened and attenuated form, more a limited analysis and a special prescription for particular circumstances than the general theory Keynes had originally proclaimed it to be.

BIBLIOGRAPHY

Collins, Robert M. *More: The Politics of Economic Growth in Postwar America.* New York: Oxford University Press, 2000.

Keynes, John Maynard. *The General Theory of Employment, Interest, and Money.* London: Macmillan, 1936.

Skidelsky, Robert. *Keynes.* Oxford: Oxford University Press, 1996.

Stein, Herbert. *The Fiscal Revolution in America.* Chicago: University of Chicago Press, 1969.

Robert M. Collins

See also **Economics; Great Depression; Reaganomics; Supply-Side Economics.**

Baby Lone. A Kickapoo medicine man, 1917. Library of Congress

KICKAPOO. The exact origins of the Kickapoo remain uncertain, though tribal tradition tells of their separating from the Shawnee after a dispute over a bear's foot. Equally unknown is the meaning of "kiikaapoa," the name Kickapoo call themselves. The Kickapoo have maintained a marked independence from outside influences. To this day, they remain an exceptionally conservative people, as evidenced by their reluctance to marry outside the tribe. In addition to the Shawnee, the Kickapoo are strongly related to the Miami, Sauk, Fox, and especially the Mascouten.

The Kickapoo reckoned kinship patrilineally, and were organized into clans bearing the names of animals. They also had a Berry clan and a Tree clan, though clans named after plants were unusual in most tribes. Leaders from the clans formed a council, which governed along with a hereditary chief, usually from the Eagle clan. Women sometimes acted as chiefs, although in a religious, not political, role. By the 1950s, traditional organization became largely ceremonial, and matrilineal chiefs were acceptable. Kickapoo religion centers on relations with several important deities, including Creator, the four winds, the sky, moon, sun, stars, and earth.

Kickapoo women provided much of the tribe's food through agriculture and gathering. Men hunted and fished. Hunting and gathering are still important to a band of Kickapoo who settled in Mexico. Women also constructed the rectangular, bark-over-pole lodges in Kickapoo villages, and made clothing.

The Kickapoo migrated frequently both before and after encountering Europeans. They first met the French in the mid-seventeenth century when they lived in southern Wisconsin, and initially resisted any attempted control by France. Kickapoo hostility against the French increased in the 1680s, as they blamed French influence for Iroquois and Siouan invasions. The Kickapoo also fought France's Illinois allies, though their longest standing enemies were the Chickasaw and the Osage.

Kickapoo-French relations improved considerably in 1729, and they joined France for a time in the war against the Fox. The Kickapoo remained allied to France, and also the Spanish, even after France's surrender to England in 1763. They joined Pontiac's war against the English in 1763–1764. In the late 1760s they, along with the Potawatomi, Ottawa, and Chippewa, drove the Illinois tribes from the Illinois River, and the Kickapoo moved into central Illinois. During the American Revolution (1775–1783) the Kickapoo were largely neutral or even pro-American, until American land hunger led them to side with Britain. They joined the Miami's confederacy against the Americans in the 1790s, and for years after the Treaty of Greenville (1795) refused to even pick up their annuities from the United States.

Never a huge tribe, the Kickapoo combined with the Mascouten (whom they gradually absorbed) to number only about 2,250 people in 1700, and 1,500 by 1750. In the latter half of the eighteenth century, the Kickapoo divided into two principal bands, about equal in size. The Prairie Kickapoo lived in central Illinois, while the Vermilion Kickapoo inhabited the western fringes of the Wabash River Basin, between modern Danville, Illinois, and Lafayette, Indiana. After 1800, small groups also migrated west of the Mississippi River. The Vermilion Kickapoo became fierce adherents to Tenskwatawa (the Shawnee Prophet) and Tecumseh. The Prairie Kickapoo joined the Vermilion Band against the United States during the War of 1812 (1812–1815). Even after 1815, some Kickapoo resisted further American settlement. By 1819, however, both bands ceded their lands in Illinois and Indiana, and were ordered west in 1832. The last holdouts went west in 1834. By the twentieth century, the Kickapoo had three main bands in Kansas, Oklahoma, and Mexico, numbering 185, 247, and approximately 400, respectively.

BIBLIOGRAPHY

Gibson, A. M. *The Kickapoo: Lords of the Middle Border.* Norman: University of Oklahoma Press, 1963.

Trigger, Bruce G., ed. *Handbook of North American Indians, vol. 15 Northeast.* Washington, D.C.: Smithsonian Institution, 1978.

Robert M. Owens

KIDNAPPING. Powerful stories about abduction predate the history of the United States. Biblical, mythological, and historical tales recount the fates of prominent people—Joseph, the Sabine women, Helen of Troy, and various members of royalty—taken from their homelands. During the Middle Ages, peripatetic Jewish merchants talked of abduction as just another business risk, and contributing to a ransom fund for a landsman qualified as a substantial mitzvah.

The conquest and colonizing of the Americas generated new abduction tales. The slave trade, the business of abducting and enslaving millions of Africans (and lesser numbers of Indians), took shape during the early seventeenth century. As European diseases exacted a heavy toll on indigenous people, Indian warfare increasingly aimed at abducting members of other tribes to replenish populations. At the same time, stories of Indians carrying off European women, "captivity narratives," such as that of Mary Rowlandson, formed one of the earliest Euro-American literary genres. The term "kidnapping," which joined two English slang terms, emerged toward the end of the seventeenth century. It first denoted abducting young people from Britain and transporting them to North America as indentured laborers. Consequently, Sir William Blackstone, the eighteenth-century common-law jurist, characterized kidnapping, then a misdemeanor rather than a felony, as the crime of carrying someone away from their homeland and depriving them of their "personal liberty."

Stories about other kinds of kidnapping, many with an ethnic dimension, proliferated during the nineteenth and early twentieth centuries. The antislavery movement characterized the capture of runaway slaves, authorized by the Constitution and the FUGITIVE SLAVE ACTS of 1793 and 1850, as a pernicious form of kidnapping. Drawing on Blackstonian legal terminology, many Northern legislatures passed "personal liberty laws" that unsuccessfully interposed state power against slave hunters. Other ethnically charged situations, such as the 1904 "rescue"—by Anglo-Protestant vigilantes—of forty Catholic orphans who had been placed with Mexican American families in Arizona could legally excuse abductions that might otherwise have been seen as cases of kidnapping.

Meanwhile, a much-publicized 1874 abduction in Philadelphia, in which several career criminals abducted for ransom (and later killed) four-year-old Charley Ross, inaugurated a growing emphasis on urban kidnapping stories. In response to the Ross case, Pennsylvania enacted a stiff antikidnapping law that made kidnapping a serious felony offense and became an early model for other states. As kidnapping for ransom became a highly publicized underworld enterprise, some perpetrators avoided the stigma attached to child abduction by making wealthy adults their target of opportunity. George "Machine Gun" Kelly became J. Edgar Hoover's "Public Enemy Number One" after kidnapping an Oklahoma City business leader in 1933. Around the same time, a brazen, daylight kidnapping of a wealthy businessman by gangsters in an upscale neighborhood of St. Paul ended a police-gangster arrangement that had long made Minnesota's capital city a haven for interstate fugitives such as John Dillinger.

Two other widely publicized incidents, though, reinforced the connection between kidnapping and young children. The 1924 case of Nathan Leopold and Richard Loeb, who abducted and killed a young boy in Chicago, focused attention on cases involving sexual motives, while the 1932 kidnapping of Charles Lindbergh Jr., son of the fabled aviator, dramatized abduction for ransom. These cases produced lengthy, controversial "trials of the century" and sparked debate over broader issues including the insanity defense and the death penalty in the Leopold-Loeb case. In the aftermath of the Lindbergh case, Congress passed the "Lindbergh Act" of 1932, which expanded federal authority over kidnapping with its presumption that any abduction of more than twenty-four hours involved transportation across state lines. Many states adopted their own tougher, new antikidnapping measures called "Little Lindbergh laws."

During the last half of the twentieth century, kidnapping stories encompassed an ever wider array of fictive and real-life scenarios. The 1974 abduction of Patricia Hearst, the daughter of a prominent media mogul, by the Symbionese Liberation Army, recalled politically motivated kidnappings in other countries. Several years later, when an anti-American faction in Iran seized nearly one hundred people at the American Embassy in Tehran, the media proclaimed "America Held Hostage," and the incident played a key role in the 1980 presidential election of Ronald Reagan and the defeat of incumbent Jimmy Carter. The kidnapping of U.S. businesspeople and diplomats remained a prominent concern overseas, while abductions that accompanied carjackings and other crimes attracted considerable attention in the United States.

Still, cases involving young children attracted the most intense interest. Bitter controversy over child custody laws, for example, publicized a form of abduction in which one parent resorted to kidnapping in order to circumvent a court order granting custody to the other. In 1980, Congress responded with the Parental Kidnapping Prevention Act, which mandated greater state-to-state cooperation in custody-related abductions. Advocates for children, though, insisted on a clear distinction between parental kidnappings and "stranger abductions," which became firmly associated with the specter of sexual exploitation. Several tragic cases of stranger abductions prompted new legislation, such as "MEGAN'S LAW," which aimed for the registration and monitoring of "sexual predators." Other prominent kidnappings produced new nationwide organizations, including the Adam Walsh Children's Fund and the Polly Klaas Foundation for Missing Children.

BIBLIOGRAPHY

Fass, Paula S. *Kidnapped: Child Abduction in America.* New York: Oxford University Press, 1997.

Gordon, Linda. *The Great Arizona Orphan Abduction.* Cambridge, Mass.: Harvard University Press, 1999.

Morris, Thomas D. *Free Men All: Personal Liberty Laws of the North, 1780–1861.* Baltimore: Johns Hopkins University Press, 1974.

Norman Rosenberg

See also **Captivity Narratives; Iran Hostage Crisis; Leopold-Loeb Case; Lindbergh Kidnapping Case; Slave Trade.**

"KILROY WAS HERE," possibly the most popular graffiti in military history, has uncertain origins. Folklore traces the saying to a World War II shipyard worker, James J. Kilroy, who inspected the bottoms of warships under construction, indicating his inspection with a chalk mark. However, this mark was susceptible to erasure, so Kilroy began the practice of scrawling "Kilroy was here" in crayon. Servicemen around the world saw the slogan on the ships, and word spread that "Kilroy" had been there first. They began placing the graffiti wherever U.S. forces landed. Kilroy thus became a symbol of reassurance for soldiers in threatening situations—a "Super G.I." who had always already been wherever the real soldier went.

BIBLIOGRAPHY

Dickson, Paul. *War Slang: Fighting Words and Phrases of Americans from the Civil War through the Persian Gulf War.* New York: Pocket Books, 1994.

Fussell, Paul. *Wartime: Understanding and Behavior in the Second World War.* New York: Oxford University Press, 1989.

Timothy M. Roberts

See also **World War II.**

"KING COTTON" was an expression much used by southern authors and orators before the Civil War. The idea appeared first as the title of a book, *Cotton Is King*, by David Christy in 1855. In a speech in the U.S. Senate on 4 March 1858, James H. Hammond declared, "You dare not make war upon cotton! No power on earth dares make war upon it. Cotton is king." The phrase expressed the southern belief that COTTON was so essential that those who controlled it might dictate the economic and political policies of the United States and of the world. Southern confidence in cotton's economic power contributed to the decision to establish the Confederacy in 1861. During the Civil War, however, northern industry proved far more decisive than southern agriculture in the war's outcome.

BIBLIOGRAPHY

Faust, Drew Gilpin. *James Henry Hammond and the Old South: A Design for Mastery.* Baton Rouge: Louisiana State University Press, 1982.

Wright, Gavin. *The Political Economy of the Cotton South: Households, Markets, and Wealth in the Nineteenth Century.* New York: W.W. Norton, 1978.

Hallie Farmer/T. G.

See also **Commodity Exchanges; Cotton Gin; Inflation in the Confederacy; Lower South; Mason-Dixon Line.**

KING GEORGE'S WAR (1744–1748). Nominally at peace from 1713 to 1744, France and England conflicted over boundaries of Acadia in Canada and northern New England and over claims in the Ohio Valley. When the War of Jenkins's Ear (England's commercial war with Spain, 1739–1743) merged into the continental War of Austrian Succession (1740–1748), England and France declared war on each other. The French at Louisburg (Cape Breton Island) failed in an early attack in which they attempted to take Annapolis (Port Royal). In retaliation, New Englanders captured Louisburg and planned, with English aid, to attack Quebec and Montreal simultaneously. Seven colonies cooperated to raise forces in 1746, but the promised English aid did not arrive, and the colonials finally disbanded the next year.

Meanwhile, France sent a great fleet in June 1746 to recapture Louisburg and devastate English colonial seaports. However, assorted fiascoes—including storms, disease, and the death of the fleet's commander—frustrated the attempt. British squadrons defeated a second French fleet on the open sea in 1747. Gruesome raids along the New England–New York borders by both conflicting parties and their Indian allies characterized the remainder of the war, with no result except a temporary check on frontier settlement. Weary of futile and costly conflict, the warring parties signed the Peace of Aix-la-Chapelle in October 1748, granting mutual restoration of conquests but leaving colonial territorial disputes unresolved.

BIBLIOGRAPHY

Merrell, James H. *Into the American Woods: Negotiators on the Pennsylvania Frontier.* New York: Norton, 1999.

White, Richard. *The Middle Ground: Indians, Empires, and Republics in the Great Lakes Region, 1615–1815.* New York: Cambridge University Press, 1991.

Shelby Balik
Raymond P. Stearns

See also **Colonial Wars; Jenkins's Ear, War of; Ohio Valley.**

KING PHILIP'S WAR (1675–1676). White New Englanders who coveted farmland but needed help surviving in harsh conditions built uneasy partnerships with neighboring American Indians during the seventeenth century. By 1660, however, most Anglo-American communities had achieved economic and demographic stability, and white New Englanders who valued agriculture and fishing over the fur trade increasingly downplayed their economic partnership with Indians and justified seizures of Indian land. Conversely, many Indians suspected English motives, resisted English laws, and resented Puritan missionary efforts. When Massasoit died (1662), new Indian leaders rejected alliances with Anglo-Americans, who in turn accused the Indians of conspiring against them.

According to white settlers, the chief conspirator was Massasoit's son, Metacomet, or Philip, sachem (chief) of the Wampanoags. Philip renewed the peace covenant with Plymouth Colony, but repeated reports of plots with the Narragansets and the French heightened tensions with Plymouth leaders. Philip avowed peaceful intentions and agreed to surrender firearms. A tentative peace followed, but when whites executed three Wampanoags for murdering a Christian Indian informer, warriors attacked and plundered nearby farms. On 18 June 1675, Wampanoag marauders provoked Swansea settlers to begin hostilities. The war that ensued actually was a series of Indian raids with retaliatory expeditions by the English.

The English counterattack was ill planned and indecisive and antagonized other tribes. Jealous colonial commanders and troops cooperated badly, soldiers were poorly equipped and ignorant of Indian warfare, and troops lacked scouts to track the enemy and refused at first to employ friendly Indians. When Plymouth and Massachusetts forces drove Philip from Mount Hope into Pocasset swamps, he easily slipped into central Massachusetts. Then, colonial forces raided Narraganset territory and compelled a few lingerers to sign a treaty of neutrality, but Narraganset warriors had already joined in Philip's War. When the English sold captives into West Indian slavery and slaughtered Christian Indians, they drove many former allies into opposition—although these Indians never united under one leader.

Before the end of 1675, disaster overtook New England on all sides. Mendon, Brookfield, Deerfield, Northfield, and other Massachsuetts towns were devastated, abandoned, or both. Indians had ambushed and destroyed two colonial forces, and similar raids devastated New Hampshire and Maine settlements. During the winter of 1675–1676, the Indians planned to attack the eastern settlements to concentrate English forces there while they planted crops in the Connecticut Valley. In February they attacked Lancaster—where Mary Rowlandson was captured—and threatened Plymouth, Providence, and towns near Boston.

Meanwhile, the colonies reorganized their forces, destroyed Narraganset food supplies, and captured and executed Narraganset warrior Canonchet in April. The Mohawks threatened to attack the Connecticut Valley Indians from the west, thereby helping the English. In May an English force of 180 men surprised and massacred the Indians at Deerfield and broke their resistance in the valley. Soon, the tide turned in the west. English scouts harried Philip and his followers in swamps near Taunton and Bridgewater. In August they captured Philip's wife and son, surrounded his camp, and shot and killed Philip as he tried to escape. Philip's death marked the end of the war, although hostilities continued in New Hampshire and Maine, where the Abenakis and others, with French support, attacked English settlements.

The war was disastrous for both the English and the Indians. It wreaked havoc on the New England economy. Sixteen English towns in Massachusetts and four in Rhode Island were destroyed. No English colonist was left in Kennebec County (Maine), and the Indian population of southern New England was decimated. Although Indians no longer posed a threat to colonists in southern New England, tension between Indians and white settlers persisted to the northeast and northwest, where these conflicts merged with political and territorial clashes between England and France.

BIBLIOGRAPHY

Carroll, Peter N. *Puritanism and the Wilderness: The Intellectual Significance of the New England Frontier, 1629–1700.* New York: Columbia University Press, 1969.

Kupperman, Karen Ordahl. *Indians and English: Facing Off in Early America.* Ithaca, N.Y.: Cornell University Press, 2000.

Lepore, Jill. *The Name of War: King Philip's War and the Origins of American Identity.* New York: Knopf, 1998.

Slotkin, Richard. *Regeneration through Violence: The Mythology of the American Frontier, 1600–1800.* Middletown, Conn.: Wesleyan University Press, 1973; New York: HarperPerennial, 1996.

Shelby Balik
Raymond P. Stearns

See also **Frontier Defense; Indian Policy, Colonial; Warfare, Indian.**

KING WILLIAM'S WAR (1689–1697). This first of the French and Indian wars was already smoldering on the New England frontier when England declared war on France in May 1689. English traders had recently established the Hudson's Bay Trading Company, which competed with French traders in Canada. Angry at British interference in the fur trade, the French incited the Abenaki tribes of Maine to destroy the rival English post of Pemaquid and attack frontier settlements. By this time, political divisions had fragmented the northern British colonies, each jealous of its own frontiers. These divisions interfered with relations between white settlers and American Indians and rendered British colonists susceptible to military assault. When the European conflict known as the War of the League of Augsburg erupted on the North American frontier, it became a struggle for colonial supremacy.

Conditions were unstable in Canada, as well. When Louis de Buade, Comte de Frontenac, arrived in 1689 to begin his second term as governor, he found the colony plagued by Iroquoian raids. To calm the French settlers and regain the allegiance of his Indian allies, he sent out three war parties in 1690: the first destroyed Schenectady, the second attacked and burned the little settlement of Salmon Falls on the New Hampshire border, and the third forced the surrender of Fort Loyal, an outpost at the site of the present city of Portland, Maine.

Terror spread throughout the English colonies, and Massachusetts raised a fleet of seven ships, one of which captured and plundered Port Royal, Nova Scotia. In May 1690, representatives of Massachusetts, Plymouth, Connecticut, and New York met in New York City. They planned a united attack by land on Montreal with the promised cooperation of the Iroquois. At the same time, Massachusetts and the other New England colonies undertook to attack Quebec by sea. Both expeditions were failures. New York and Connecticut troops, traveling from Albany, could not advance farther than the foot of Lake Champlain. The New England fleet fared no better.

Realizing that they lacked sufficient financial resources and military organization, the leaders of the northern English colonies appealed repeatedly to the English government for help. Britain sent a fleet to North America, but it arrived with a fever-stricken crew, so the contribution amounted to little. Frontenac made similar appeals to France for help, with no better luck. The French squadron sent to capture Boston was delayed by head winds, ran short of provisions, and could do nothing.

Although the French won this war, the Treaty of Ryswick, which settled the conflict, was inconclusive and did not result in significant transfers of North American land between European powers. The consequences for the American Indians in the region, however, were severe. The war ignited a much longer struggle between the Algonquins and the Iroquois, which proved disastrous for both as they tried to negotiate with French and British colonists and officials. Because so many of the tensions that initially provoked the conflict remained unresolved, the North American frontier would again erupt in violence five years later, in Queen Anne's War.

BIBLIOGRAPHY

Gallay, Alan, ed. *Colonial Wars of North America: 1512–1763: An Encyclopedia*. New York: Garland, 1996.

Leach, Douglas Edward. *Arms for Empire: A Military History of the British Colonies in North America, 1607–1763*. New York: Macmillan, 1973.

A. C. Flick/Shelby Balik

See also **Colonial Settlements; Colonial Wars; French Frontier Forts; French and Indian War; Fur Trade and Trapping; Hudson's Bay Company; Iroquois.**

KING'S PROVINCE was a portion of the mainland of Rhode Island between the Pawcatuck River and Narragansett Bay. Known as the Narragansett Country, it was claimed by Rhode Island, Connecticut, and Massachusetts. Attempting to settle the controversy in 1665, a royal commission named this territory King's Province and placed it under the jurisdiction of Rhode Island, although Connecticut still claimed authority over it. The matter was settled when Sir Edmund Andros took possession of both colonies. In 1729 King's Province became Kings County, and in 1781 its name was changed to Washington County, Rhode Island.

BIBLIOGRAPHY

Daniels, Bruce C. *Dissent and Conformity on Narragansett Bay: The Colonial Rhode Island Town*. Middletown, Conn.: Wesleyan University Press, 1983.

James, Sydney V. *Colonial Rhode Island: A History*. New York: Scribner, 1975.

R. W. G. Vail/H. S.

See also **Narragansett Bay; Narragansett Planters; Rhode Island.**

KING, MARTIN LUTHER, ASSASSINATION. At 6:01 P.M. on Thursday, 4 April 1968 a fatal rifle shot hit Martin Luther King Jr. as he stood on a balcony outside his second-floor room at the Lorraine Motel in Memphis, Tennessee. The civil rights leader had arrived in Memphis the previous day to prepare for a march planned for the following Monday on behalf of the city's striking sanitation workers. Late in the afternoon of the fourth, SOUTHERN CHRISTIAN LEADERSHIP CONFERENCE (SCLC) Executive Director Andrew Young and attorney Chauncey Eskridge returned to the Lorraine to report on their successful effort to convince District Judge Bailey Brown to lift his antiprotest restraining order that was prompted by violence which disrupted a march a week earlier. Pleased that he would be able to proceed with the planned march, King was preparing to leave for a dinner at the home of Memphis minister Billy Kyles when he stepped out on the balcony of room 306. As King talked with SCLC colleagues standing in the parking area below, an assassin fired a single shot severely wounding the lower right side of King's face. As Ralph Abernathy cradled King's head, other SCLC aides rushed toward him. Some of those on the balcony pointed across the street toward the rear of a boarding house on South Main Street. An ambulance rushed King to St. Joseph's Hospital where doctors pronounced him dead at 7:05 P.M.

News of King's assassination prompted outbreaks of racial violence, resulting in forty-six deaths and extensive property damage in dozens of American cities, including Washington, D.C. President Lyndon Johnson attended a memorial for King on the fifth and called for a national day of mourning to be observed two days later. A march was held in Memphis on the eighth to honor King and to support the sanitation workers. The march attracted thousands of participants, including King's widow and other family members. King's funeral, attended by many of the nation's political and civil rights leaders, occurred the following day in Atlanta at Ebenezer Baptist Church, where King served as co-pastor along with his father, Martin Luther King Sr., and his brother, A. D. King. Morehouse College President Benjamin Mays delivered the eulogy. After another ceremony on the Morehouse campus, King's body was interred at Southview Ceme-

Martin Luther King Jr. The civil rights leader *(second from right)* arrives at the Lorraine Motel on 3 April 1968 with *(left to right)* Hosea Williams, Jesse Jackson, and Ralph Abernathy; the next day he would be assassinated there. AP/WIDE WORLD PHOTOS

tery; it was later moved to a crypt at the site of the King Center, an institution founded by King's widow, Coretta Scott King, located next to Ebenezer Church.

Search for the Assassin

Within minutes of the assassination, a policeman who had rushed to the area discovered a bundle containing a 30.06 Remington rifle in the doorway of the Canipe Amusement Company, located on South Main next door to the boarding house. Based on its serial number, investigators from the Federal Bureau of Investigations determined that the weapon had been purchased at Aeromarine Supply Company in Birmingham, Alabama, by a person using the name Harvey Lowmeyer. FBI agents learned that the Ford Mustang found on 10 April abandoned in Atlanta was registered to Eric Starvo Galt and subsequent handwriting analysis indicated that Galt and Lowmeyer were the same person. These discoveries led FBI agents to an apartment in Atlanta, where they found a thumbprint matching that of James Earl Ray, a fugitive who had escaped from a Missouri prison in April 1967. FBI agents and police in Memphis produced further evidence that Ray had registered on 4 April at the South Main rooming house under the alias John Willard and had taken a second-floor room near a common bathroom with a view of the Lorraine Motel.

The identification of Ray as a suspect led to an international search. After examining passport application photographs, Canadian officials found that a passport had been issued on 24 April to a person using the name Ramon George Sneyd, who resembled Ray and whose handwriting matched samples of Ray's. They also determined that the person using the passport had left Canada for London. On 8 June British immigration officials on the alert for Ray detained him while he prepared to board a flight to Brussels (Ray later explained that his ultimate destination was the white-ruled nation of Rhodesia [later Zimbabwe]). On 18 July Ray arrived in the United States after being extradited to stand trial.

Prosecution of James Earl Ray

In a plea bargain, Tennessee prosecutors agreed in March 1969 to forgo seeking the death penalty if Ray pled guilty to murder charges. The circumstances leading to this decision later became a source of controversy, because Ray recanted his confession soon after being sentenced to a ninety-nine-year term in prison and claimed that his attorney, Percy Foreman, had provided inadequate representation due to his fear that lucrative arrangements to publish Ray's story would be compromised if the defendant testified in open court. Ray fired Foreman, but he was unsuccessful in his subsequent attempts to reverse his conviction and gain a new trial.

Unresolved Questions

During the years following King's assassination, doubts about the adequacy of the case against Ray were fueled by revelations of extensive surveillance of King by the Federal Bureau of Investigation and other government agencies. In the aftermath of the Watergate scandal that ended Richard Nixon's presidency, congressional investigations of illegal FBI activities during the 1960s prompted calls for a reopening of the assassination investigation. *Frame-Up* (1971) by Harold Weisberg and *Code Name "Zorro"* (1977) by Mark Lane (Ray's lawyer during the late 1970s) and Dick Gregory raised questions about the evidence against Ray. In 1976 the House Select Committee on Assassinations launched a re-examination of the evidence concerning King's assassination as well as that of President John F. Kennedy. The committee's final report, released by Chairman Louis Stokes (Democrat, Ohio) in January 1979, suggested that Ray may have been motivated by a reward offered by two St. Louis businessmen and may have had coconspirators, possibly his brothers, John and Jerry Ray. Despite detailing the FBI's activities targeting King, the report nonetheless concluded that there was no convincing evidence of government complicity in the assassination. Rather than ending conspiracy speculation, the report and twelve volumes of evidence assembled during the House investigation provided a wealth of information that would continue to fuel speculation.

After recanting his guilty plea, Ray consistently maintained his innocence. In his 1992 memoir, he claimed to have been framed by a gun smuggler he knew as Raoul (sometimes spelled Raul). In 1993 William F. Pepper, who had become Ray's lawyer, sought to build popular support for a reopening of the case by staging a televised mock trial of Ray (the "jury" found Ray not guilty). Pepper later published *Orders to Kill: The Truth Behind the Murder of Martin Luther King* (1995), which cast suspicion on the FBI, local police, a local businessman allegedly linked to the Mafia, and military intelligence personnel assigned to Memphis at the time of the assassination. In 1997 members of King's family publicly supported Ray's appeal for a new trial, and King's son, Dexter Scott King, proclaimed Ray's innocence during a televised prison encounter. Despite this support, Tennessee authorities refused to reopen the case, and Ray died in prison on 23 April 1998.

Even after Ray's death, conspiracy allegations continued to surface. Despite several attempts, test bullets fired from the rifle linked to Ray were never conclusively matched to the slug removed from King's body. In March 1998, retired FBI investigator Donald Wilson claimed he had found pieces of paper in Ray's car with the name "Raul" on them. In 1999 Pepper won a token civil verdict on behalf of King's widow and children against Lloyd Jowers, owner of the Jim's Grill on the rooming house's ground floor, "and other unknown co-conspirators." Jowers had stated during a 1993 during an appearance on ABC-TV's *Prime Time Live* that he was given $100,000 to arrange King's murder. Although the trial produced considerable testimony that contradicted the original case against Ray, the Justice Department announced in 2000 that its own internal investigation, launched in 1998 at the King family's request, had failed to find sufficient evidence to warrant a full investigation. In April 2002, at a news conference in Gainesville, Florida, the Reverend Ronald Denton Wilson announced that his deceased fervently anticommunist father, Henry Clay Wilson, had spoken of killing King with the aid of two other conspirators after Ray supplied the weapon, but this claim was also met with widespread skepticism.

BIBLIOGRAPHY

Pepper, William F. *Orders to Kill: The Truth behind the Murder of Martin Luther King.* New York: Carroll & Graf Publishers, Inc., 1995.

Posner, Gerald L. *Killing the Dream: James Earl Ray and the Assassination of Martin Luther King, Jr.* New York: Random House, 1998.

Ray, James Earl. *Who Killed Martin Luther King, Jr.? The True Story by the Alleged Assassin.* 2d ed., New York: Marlowe and Company, 1997.

United States Department of Justice. *Investigation of Recent Allegations Regarding the Assassination of Dr. Martin Luther King, Jr.* Washington, D.C.: Government Printing Office, June 2000.

Clayborne Carson

See also **Assassinations and Political Violence, Other; Civil Rights Movement; Conspiracy.**

KING, RODNEY, RIOTS. *See* **Los Angeles Riots.**

KINSEY REPORT is comprised of two studies by Alfred Kinsey exploring male and female sexuality. Detailed scientific studies based on eleven thousand interviews, *Sexual Behavior in the Human Male* (1948) and *Sexual Behavior in the Human Female* (1953), challenged widely held beliefs about human sexuality, including prevalent medical literature that posited that women were not sexual beings. Kinsey's work effectively separated sexuality from morality and emphasized the importance of sexual adjustment to a stable union. More than any previous book, Kinsey's studies placed sex on the national stage and inspired public discourse on American sexuality.

Kinsey, a biologist by training, became involved in sex research in 1938, when he was placed in charge of an interdisciplinary course on marriage and family at Indiana University. Although physicians had engaged in research on sexual behavior in the 1920s and 1930s, such research remained controversial. By Kinsey's own accounts, he sought to reconfigure sexual research, to free it from moral judgment, and to treat it as a scientist would from data collection to its presentation, replete with charts, graphs, and a comprehensive review of the literature in the field. He assembled and trained a team of researchers and interviewers who collected over eighteen thousand interviews with men and women. Kinsey conducted eight thousand of the interviews himself.

Until the publication of the Kinsey Report, public exposure to topics in human sexuality had been primarily through hygiene courses, where teachers warned of the dangers of sexually transmitted diseases, masturbation, and any sex act deemed outside a narrowly defined norm. No one could have predicted the magnitude of the response to Kinsey's studies. The demand for his *Sexual Behavior in the Human Male* far outpaced its print run. The book sold 250,000 copies and spent twenty-seven weeks on the *New York Times* best-seller list. His *Sexual Behavior in the Human Female* was also a runaway best-seller.

Members of the scientific community condemned Kinsey's studies for what they claimed were specious scientific methods and conclusions tainted by Kinsey's own cultural attitudes toward sex. In addition, his findings shocked traditional moralists. The general public, however, seemed ready to consume what the report had to offer. Because Kinsey's data was so extensive, his report offered readers documentation of a wide range of sexual variations and revealed a vast undercurrent of sexual practices that countered what the public had assumed was the sexual "norm." At a time when television especially glorified a picture of family life altogether devoid of sex, Kinsey revealed that masturbation and premarital petting were almost universal and that women, like men, were sexual beings. Moreover, over a third of adult males had homosexual experiences.

Although widely renounced for the pretense that sexual data could be or even should be presented as an objective science devoid of discussion of moral or social implications, Kinsey's work altered the American sexual landscape forever. Of particular concern both in the 1950s and in the early twenty-first century were the sections of the report that discuss incidents of pedophilia. The scientific context of the report legitimized open discussion of sexual subjects in the media, at universities, and in the home. The Kinsey Report encouraged more open discussion of homosexuality, which Kinsey presented as but another form of sexual activity, and female sexuality.

BIBLIOGRAPHY

D'Emilio, John, and Estelle B. Freedman. *Intimate Matters: A History of Sexuality in America.* New York: Harper and Row, 1988.

Jones, J. H. *Kinsey: A Public/Private Life.* New York: Norton, 1997.

Leslie J. Lindenauer

See also **Sex Education; Sexual Orientation; Sexuality.**

KINSHIP. All human beings are connected to some others by blood or marriage. While cultural variations shape the nature and meaning of those relationships, sociologists and anthropologists have identified general categories that appear to apply widely to human societies. Connections between people based on genetic ties (such as between parents and children and among siblings) are known as consanguineal or blood relationships. Relationships based on marriage are known as affinal relationships. Individuals also may recognize as kin others who are related neither by blood nor marriage, such as adopted children who are legally defined as kin, fictive kin (godparents, blood brothers), a special family friend who is called "aunt" or "uncle," or a homosexual partner, even though same-sex marriage is not presently recognized as such by the state. The basic components of the kinship system in every society are marriage, family, postmarital residence (where a couple resides after marriage), the incest taboo (rules that prohibit sexual relations and therefore marriage between certain categories of kin), descent (the rules of reckoning one's relatives), and kinship terminology (the terms used to label kin).

In the contemporary United States the idealized kinship customs—promulgated through popular culture, religious custom, and the law—are heterosexual monogamous marriage, neolocal residence (residence apart from both families after marriage), nuclear families (one husband/father, one wife/mother and their children), incest prohibitions within the nuclear family, bilateral descent (kin are traced through both the mother's and the father's lines), and kin terms that reflect an emphasis on biological versus affinal ties. In some cultures kinship relations are highly structured and rigid with different categories of kin, such as brothers and sisters or in-laws who are expected to behave toward one another in highly stylized ways. Kinship in America is loosely structured, with considerable individual freedom to pick and choose among kin for different purposes. Thus many kin might be invited to a wedding but only a few are invited to a more intimate family gathering such as a holiday dinner.

Nonetheless, in the late twentieth century there was much variation in some features of kinship within American society. While monogamous marriage was the ideal, millions of people remained unmarried and millions married and divorced. Given the high divorce rate (about one in two marriages formed each year ended in divorce) and high remarriage rate, some social scientists argued that the marriage norm was better described as serial monogamy. In addition, homosexual marriages and families were on the rise, and some employers responded by providing spousal benefits, such as health care insurance, to homosexual partners of employees. While nuclear family households were still common, other family arrangements, such as mother-children families, families composed of parents and their adult children, families with stepparents and children, and blended families formed from portions of two former nuclear families, became common. Beyond these broad variations across U.S. society, there were variations in the structure and nature of kin relations across religions, ethnic groups, and social classes.

BIBLIOGRAPHY

Fox, Robin. *Kinship and Marriage: An Anthropological Perspective.* Harmondsworth, Eng.: Penguin, 1967.

Levinson, David, ed. *Encyclopedia of Marriage and the Family.* New York: Macmillan, 1995.

Schneider, David M. *American Kinship: A Cultural Account.* Chicago: University of Chicago Press, 1980.

David Levinson / A. R.

See also **Demography and Demographic Trends; Family; Genealogy; Marriage.**

KIOWA. Classified in the Uto-Aztecan language family, Kiowa is remotely linked to the Tanoan languages of the Eastern Pueblos. This suggests divergence and prehistoric northward migrations to the mountainous Yellowstone River region of western Montana, the ancestral lands of the pre-contact hunting-and-gathering Kiowa.

Migrations and Alliances to the Mid-Nineteenth Century

Leaving their homelands in the late seventeenth century in search of horses, the Kiowa and an affiliated group of Plains Apache migrated southeastward, befriending the Crow, reaching the Black Hills (in present-day South Dakota) around 1775, and then establishing trading relations with the Mandan and Arikara before the Lakota and Cheyenne drove them south to the Arkansas River. At the time of the first direct contact with whites in the late eighteenth century, the Kiowa had relocated to the Southwestern Plains. They numbered barely two thousand individuals and were compelled to form an alliance with the more numerous Comanche between 1790 and 1806. Like the Comanche, the Kiowa fashioned a lucrative equestrian raiding economy in the lands of mild winters and ample grazing that were within striking distance of Spanish settlements in Colorado, New Mexico, Texas, and northern Mexico. The Kiowa, Comanche, and Plains Apache (KCA Indians) coalition fought common northern enemies, particularly the Lakota, Cheyenne, and Pawnee. By 1840, additional intertribal alliances had been forged with the Osage, Lakota, and Cheyenne.

By the mid-nineteenth century, the KCA Indians dominated the Southwestern Plains: the Kiowa and Plains Apache inhabited the northern region adjacent to the Arkansas River in present-day west-central Kansas, and the Comanche controlled the Staked Plains region of the Texas Panhandle. Intertribal raiding parties skirmished with Ute, Navajo, and Pawnee enemies, and plundered Mexican and Texan settlements for livestock and captives.

Decline and Dependency

KCA hegemony, however, waned after the Civil War. Squeezed between rapidly expanding Euro-American settlements in Texas, Colorado, and Kansas, the Kiowa and Comanche signed the Little Arkansas Treaty of 1865, forfeiting lands in Kansas and New Mexico. In 1867, provisions of the Medicine Lodge Treaty reserved almost three million acres for the group; the lands encompassed the Wichita Mountains in southwestern Oklahoma. Residing exclusively within the confines of the KCA Reservation proved difficult, however, and raiding sorties into Texas inevitably provoked military responses from the U.S. Army. These conflicts culminated in the Red River War of 1874 and 1875, after which the Kiowa and their allies were forced to reside permanently on their reserve.

KCA subsistence changed after 1879 with the extinction of the Southern Plains bison herds, rendering the Indians totally dependent on rations and beef issues provided by the Kiowa Agency. Subsequent efforts to transform the Kiowa into farmers and ranchers failed, and hunger often resulted from inadequate government assistance. Leasing reservation grasslands to Texas cattlemen starting in 1886 brought temporary solace until the September 1892 arrival of the Jerome Commissioners (David H. Jerome, former governor of Michigan; Warren G. Sayre of Indiana; and Alfred M. Wilson of Arkansas), who forced the KCA Indians into agreeing to take individual 160-acre allotments and sell surplus reservation lands to white settlers. The Kiowa protested this fraudulent agreement because it violated the terms of the Medicine Lodge Treaty. Their protest reached all the way to the U.S. Supreme Court, but lost in *Lone Wolf v. Hitchcock* (1903). Ironically, the decision came seventeen months after the "opening" by lottery of the 2.8 million–acre KCA Reservation to settlement on 6 August 1901. Inhabiting clusters of allotments north of the Wichita Mountains, early twentieth-century Kiowa meagerly survived on subsistence hunting and fishing and per capita interest payments for former reservation lands; some even worked as manual laborers on their own allotments, leased to non-Indian farmers.

Kinship System

Nineteenth-century Kiowa kinship typified what anthropologists call Hawaiian systems that distinguish relatives by sex and generation; with exceptions, the Kiowa grouped kin into generation sets of grandparents, parents, siblings, and children. Cousins are still reckoned as "brothers" and "sisters." Indicative of Hawaiian kinship systems, the Kiowa acknowledged bilateral descent and formed kindreds, extended family groups usually led by the oldest brother. Pre-reservation Kiowa society consisted of from approximately ten to twenty kindreds representing the prominent, or *ondedw* (rich) Kiowa families, along with *ondegup'a* (second best), *kwwn* (poor), and *dapom* (worthless) families. Marriage alliances were based on wealth in horses, materials, and the reputation and war accomplishments of family leaders. Postnupital residence patterns

Kiowa. This mural by Kiowa artist Steven Mopope depicts a bison hunt. NATIONAL ARCHIVES AND RECORDS ADMINISTRATION

preferred the wealthier of the two families. Leaders of each prominent kindred, or band, were called *topadok'i* (main chief), derived from the Kiowa word *topadoga* (band).

Notable among band leaders, Dohasan "Little Bluff" was the undisputed principal Kiowa chief from 1833 until his death in early 1866, after which leadership presumably passed to Guipago, "Lone Wolf," although Tene-angopte, "Kicking Bird," and Set-t'ainte, "White Bear," led rival factions until the Kiowa surrendered in May 1875. Afterward, the *topadok'i* were relegated to serving as "beef chiefs" responsible for the distribution of meat to their families. The allotment period further eroded traditional leadership as former bands settled into various enclaves largely in later Kiowa and Caddo counties in Oklahoma, where approximately one-half of the nearly ten thousand Kiowa live.

Belief Systems

Traditional Kiowa belief systems centered around *dw_dw_* (power), a spirit force that permeated the universe, and was present in all natural entities inhabited by spirits or souls. Young men fasted in the Wichita Mountains and other elevated areas seeking *dw_dw_* from the spirit world. Those fortunate enough to receive power visions became either great warriors or curers who painted their power symbols on war shields, and often formed shield societies. Besides personal medicine bundles associated with individual *dw_dw_*, tribal bundles included the *talyi-da-i* (boy medicine) or Ten Medicines, whose keepers were civil servants who settled domestic disputes and prayed for the well-being of the people, and the Taime, or Sun Dance icon central to the renewal ceremony that united the people socially and spiritually. The Sun Dance had collapsed by 1890 because of the extinction of the Southern Plains bison herds and government pressures. The GHOST DANCE movement of 1890–1891 and 1894–1916 and the advent of the peyote religion after 1870 filled the spiritual void following the collapse of the horse and buffalo culture. At the end of the twentieth century, most Kiowa attended Baptist and Methodist churches and Native American Church peyote ceremonies.

The Kiowa still venerate warfare, as indicated by the many twentieth-century Kiowa combat veterans, and by the number who continue to serve in the U.S. armed forces. Notable Kiowa include N. Scott Momaday, awarded the Pulitzer Prize in fiction for 1969, and Everette Rhoads, former U.S. assistant surgeon general.

BIBLIOGRAPHY

Mishkin, Bernard. *Rank and Warfare among the Plains Indians.* 1940. Reprint. Lincoln: University of Nebraska Press, 1992.

Mooney, James. *Calendar History of the Kiowa Indians.* 1895–1896. Reprint. Washington, D.C.: Smithsonian Institution Press, 1979.

Richardson, Jane. *Law and Status among the Kiowa Indians.* Seattle: University of Washington Press, 1940.

Benjamin R. Kracht

See also **Dawes General Allotment Act; Indian Land Cessions; Indian Reservations; Indian Treaties; Indians and the Horse; Indians in the Military; Native American Church; Nativist Movement (American Indian Revival Movements); Red River Indian War; Sun Dance; Tribes: Great Plains; Wars with Indian Nations: Later Nineteenth Century (1840–1900).**

"KITCHEN CABINET," a title derisively applied by President Andrew Jackson's political enemies to an informal group of advisers who were credited with exercising more influence on the president than his regular cabinet. From 1829 until 1831, when the cabinet was reorganized, the Kitchen Cabinet, or "lower cabinet," as it was often called, was especially influential. Thereafter, Jackson relied less on his informal advisers and more on regular members of the cabinet. The most important members of the Kitchen Cabinet were Amos Kendall, Francis Preston Blair, Sr., William B. Lewis, A. J. Donelson, Martin Van Buren, and John H. Eaton.

BIBLIOGRAPHY

Latner, Richard B. "The Kitchen Cabinet and Andrew Jackson's Advisory System." *Journal of American History* 65 (September 1978): 367–388.

Erik McKinley Eriksson / L. T.

See also **Jacksonian Democracy; President, U.S.**

KITCHENS. Long before the European colonists arrived, Native Americans had cooked on open fires or hot stones. The colonists brought the idea of a more permanent hearth within a specific room—the kitchen. In New England, early colonists lived in small, landscape-hugging farmhouses. The kitchen was the hub of the house, with an eight- to ten-foot-wide medieval-style fireplace. While the husband and field hands worked democratically side by side taming the land, the housewife, usually with a servant who was treated as extended family, worked from dawn to dark. She lit fires using a tinder box; tended an orchard and kitchen garden; grew flax; carded wool; spun yarn; wove fabric; knitted stockings; dipped tallow candles; made soap for laundering; preserved food; baked bread from home-grown grain ground at a mill; and produced a large family to aid with chores.

Kitchens in the Eighteenth Century

Kitchen improvements were invented throughout the eighteenth century. Fireplaces were reduced in size and chimneys given more efficient flues. Forged iron swinging cranes held heavy iron pots conveniently over the fire. Brick beehive-shaped baking ovens were equipped with iron doors. Adjuncts to the kitchen included a smokehouse (sometimes in the attic), a root cellar, an icehouse—which might double as a springhouse to chill milk—a dairy for cheese and butter-making, and a poultry yard. Pewter plates and mugs, and wood trenchers (bowls and spoons used by the earliest colonists) were gradually augmented by glass and earthenware vessels and by 1750, imported china. Prospering villages and towns attracted shopkeepers who began to offer ready-made cloth, foodstuffs, and other staple items, lessening the housewife's workload.

Martha Washington's Kitchen. The restored late-eighteenth-century room at Mount Vernon, Va. LIBRARY OF CONGRESS

In the southern states, large plantations prospered from cash crops—rice, tobacco, and cotton—ideally suited to the warm, humid climate. Slaves from Africa worked the fields, and some were trained as house servants and cooks. To keep cooking smells, heat, and the threat of fire from the main house, kitchens became separate buildings with food carried into the main house through a covered breezeway. By the beginning of the nineteenth century, housewives on southern plantations were able to live a genteel life while servants took care of kitchen drudgery—although they kept a strict eye on everything and carried keys to all the storerooms.

As European settlers spread westward, they built houses from logs in Scandinavian style. Pioneer women bore much of the brunt of the hard labor, coaxing meals in primitive kitchens from alien meats such as bear, beaver tail, buffalo tongue, and snake.

The Nineteenth Century Brings Changes

The nineteenth-century kitchen had a large work table; a dresser or step-back cupboard with shelves for plates and cups and drawers for cutlery and kitchen linens; a pie safe with perforated tin doors that kept mice and insects away from freshly baked goods; a sink of iron, soapstone, or granite set in a wooden dry sink; and a kitchen clock, needed to time cookery now gleaned from published recipe books instead of handwritten family recipes. Water was carried in from exterior wells. As the century progressed, water was conveyed to interior sink pumps by pipes. By 1850, windmill power pumped water to roof cisterns and interior plumbing delivered water to faucets.

Two inventions, the range and the stove, revolutionized cooking methods; the former was a large iron structure with an oven and several top burners all set in brickwork engineered with flues, and the latter was a freestanding iron cookstove with built-in flues. Both included hot water reservoirs and could be fueled with wood or coal. By 1850, even in country areas, one or the other of these cooking devices was in use, and many of the old walk-in fireplaces were bricked up.

From the 1830s until the Civil War (1861–1865), immigrants became the "help," but were referred to as "domestic servants." Town house kitchens were relegated to the rear with back stairs to ensure that servants were unseen, or to a half basement with a separate entrance. The hands-on housewife's role changed to that of supervisor with the parlor her realm, although she still prided herself on doing fancy cooking for company.

The Civil War and encroaching industrialization depleted the supply of domestic servants, but it created a need for portable food for troops and boosted canning companies who mechanized their industries, making canned goods widely accepted by housewives. Household tools patented in the mid-nineteenth century included the Boston Carpet Sweeper (1850) and several early washing machines (late 1850s), although mechanical washers were not in general use until after 1920. Advice on efficiency came from an increasing number of women's magazines. Help also came from influential books extolling economy, system, and scientific methods in cooking, organizing a kitchen, and house maintenance. By 1896, *The Boston Cooking-School Cook Book*, by Fanny Farmer, was published.

With fewer servants, kitchens became smaller toward the end of the nineteenth century, but more attention was paid to their appearance. Efforts at "natural" colors, such as beige and soft green, replaced whitewashed walls. Tiles or washable oilcloth covered the floor—to be superseded by linoleum (invented in 1863 by Frederick Walton, founder of The American Linoleum Company). Many kitchens had "sanitary" tin ceilings, which could be wiped clean. With the growing awareness of hygiene, carbolic acid was used for cleaning, and "white vitriol" for disinfecting, both home-mixed. By the 1920s, cleaning supplies and soaps could be bought ready-made.

The first gas stove was made by Wm. W. Goodwin & Company in 1879 and became commonplace in many American towns by the 1890s. In the 1870s, enameled kitchenware (granite ware or agate ware) became available in speckled blue, black, brown, and gray designs. By the 1900s, aluminum ware was adopted. Pyrex cookware was in use by the 1920s.

Mail-order catalogs advertised furnishings and household appliances. Wooden iceboxes lined in metal—later porcelain—were filled by the iceman. The first hermetically sealed electric refrigerator was the GE Monitor-Top in 1927. By then, electric appliances—toasters, percolators, mixers, and vacuums—were used in towns, but many rural areas were without electricity until the mid-twentieth century.

The "work station" developed from a wooden baker's table with drawers and bins for flour in the 1830s to an all-purpose baker's cupboard in the 1890s, and to the klearfronts or hoosier cabinets of the 1920s and 1930s. Named after the Hoosier Mfg. Co., which was founded in 1899, these had enameled extensions for worktables and sliding or glass-fronted cupboards above, and came with many options in various sizes.

A Century of Convenience

The servant population shrank drastically after World War I (1914–1918). Housewives searched for laborsaving devices. Sinks were porcelain-lined with cupboards below to hold cleaning supplies and to hide pipes. Nearby were racks to dry plates. The Fuller Brush man sold cleaning products door-to-door. With no maid to carry and serve food, meals were often eaten in the kitchen on an enameled-top table, and dining rooms got less use. By the mid-twentieth century, many houses were built without them altogether. Household linens were no longer starched white damask but casual and colored. By the 1930s, smart new kitchens were "streamlined." Counters and shelves had curved edges, and white enameled refrigerators—now used as food cupboards—were given rounded corners. With continually changing technology, the average American kitchen was the most frequently renovated room in the house.

After World War II (1939–1945), women who had been working in munitions factories were encouraged to give up their jobs to returning GIs. They became full-time, dedicated mothers and housekeepers. Although much of the world was devastated, America was on a boom and the housewife became an important consumer. Manufacturers responded to their desire for perfect, modern kitchens. Appliances were made in standardized sizes, so counters, stovetop, and sink ran at an even 36-inch continual height around walls. Electric outlets at working level became essential for plug-in countertop appliances—mixers, blenders, and toaster ovens with rotisserie attachments. Inventive marketing trends included Tupperware parties run by local salespeople and held in private homes to sell plastic food containers. Essentials now included paper towels, clear plastic wrap (Saran wrap), and aluminum foil in appropriate containers.

Family habits by the 1960s were changing. Spurred by the women's liberation movement, college-educated women seized the chance to "have it all"—a career and a family. Meals were no longer as formal as in the first half of the twentieth century, with the whole family gathered around the table at set times, but casual and often help-yourself from the now head-height well-stocked fridge with its companion freezer. Husbands shared duties, often cooking meat—especially outdoors on a charcoal grill. The sink, sometimes double, had a nozzle spray in addition to a mixing valve that could regulate water from a hot and a cold tap to blend in one faucet. Some states permitted a sink garbage disposal unit. Next to the sink was a dishwasher—many baby boomers have never hand washed dishes! Appliances were offered in a variety of colors—gold, avocado, and brown.

By the last quarter of the twentieth century, kitchens were designed on an open plan, where not only cooking but also family activities—doing homework or crafts, watching television—took place. Glass-fronted wall ovens in addition to stoves became familiar. Broilers that had been confined to a bottom section of the oven in the 1950s were relocated to the top to lessen stooping. Electric stoves had timed, self-cleaning ovens; the tops of many were designed with completely flat surfaces for wipe-off cleaning. In the 1980s, high-tech kitchens filled with brushed steel appliances were fashionable. Convection ovens circulated heat evenly for greater efficiency. Workstations became islands centered in the room or bar/counters dividing the kitchen from the living room. Both husband and wife cooked "gourmet" meals while entertaining guests. The versatile food processor took the place of gadgets for chopping, slicing, mixing, and grating. Microwave ovens, used for heating food more than for cooking, became universal. Kitchens had recycling bins for metal, glass, plastic, and paper. By 2000, a more traditional style of kitchen took hold, with expensive milled woodwork and granite counters.

BIBLIOGRAPHY

Beecher, Catharine E., and Harriet Beecher Stowe. *The American Woman's Home: or, Principles of Domestic Science; being a Guide to the Formation and Maintenance of Economical, Healthful, Beautiful, and Christian Homes.* New York: J.B. Ford & Company, 1869.

Franklin, Linda Campbell. *300 Years of Kitchen Collectibles.* Florence, Ala.: Books Americana, 1991.

Grey, Johnny. *Kitchen Design Workbook.* New York: DK Publishers, 1996.

Grow, Lawrence. *The Old House Book of Kitchens and Dining Rooms.* New York: Warner Books, 1981.

Harrison, Molly. *The Kitchen in History.* Reading, Pa.: Osprey Publishing, 1972.

Holt, Emily. *The Complete Housekeeper.* New York: McClure, Phillips & Co., 1904.

Krasner, Deborah. *Kitchens for Cooks—Planning Your Perfect Kitchen.* New York: Viking Studio Books, 1994.

Lifshey, Earl. *The Housewares Story; A History of the American Housewares Industry.* Chicago: National Housewares Manufacturers Association, 1973.

Miller, Judith. *Period Kitchens: A Practical Guide to Period-Style Decorating.* London; Mitchell Beazley, 1995.

Plante, Ellen M. *The American Kitchen, 1700 to the Present: From Hearth to Highrise.* New York: Facts On File, 1995.

Thompson, Frances. *Antiques from the Country Kitchen.* Lombard, Ill.: Wallace-Homestead Book Company, 1985.

Chippy Irvine

KLAMATH-MODOC. The ancestral lands of the Klamaths and Modocs span southern Oregon, northeastern California, and parts of northern Nevada. Prior to 1820, approximately 2,000 Klamaths and 1,000 Modocs lived in this area. Their numbers decreased dramatically after contact with non-Indians. Scholars claim that these tribes were once the same and that the Modocs split from the Klamaths and moved south after 1780. The tribes' origin stories give a different account, suggesting divergent points of origins, social structures, and environment. The two tribes belong to the same language group, Lutuami, but speak different dialects. The designation "Maklak" or "Moadoc" translates as "southern people."

The political differences that caused the Modocs to split from the Klamaths do not mean that the Klamaths and the Modocs cut ties with each other. Their relationship developed along both friendly and hostile lines through trade, intermarriage, and warfare.

The Klamaths' traditional environment was humid, whereas the Modocs' homeland was arid and experienced harsh winters. Subsistence for both depended on the marshes that produced camas, wocus, waterfowl, fish, and small game animals. Housing depended on the season. During the winter months the Modocs and Klamaths lived in earth lodges or pit houses. In summer they set up temporary housing near fishing, hunting, and gathering areas. Both tribes maintained a sexual division of labor. Women wove intricate baskets, tended children, and gathered, prepared, and cooked food; men hunted, protected villages, raided neighboring tribes, and fought enemies. Male leadership depended on a person's ability to orate, fight, and provide for the community. Although men held public positions, women's roles in selecting and advising leaders were equally important. Because of their smaller numbers and environment, Modoc leadership was more flexible than that of the Klamaths.

Both the Klamaths and the Modocs were important in the trade networks linking California to the Pacific Northwest. The Klamaths had direct access to major trade centers, especially the Dalles, while the Modocs played an important role in securing captives for the slave trade to the north. Contact with non-Indians further distinguished the Klamaths and the Modocs. The Klamaths came into contact with non-Indians first through material

Modocs. The tribe maintained various ties to the Klamaths in the Northwest but was far less conciliatory toward white settlers and policies of the U.S. government. © CORBIS

goods and then, beginning in 1826, with fur traders. The Modocs also came in contact with trade goods, but the volume of exchange in Modoc territory was minimal. The discovery of gold in the late 1840s changed this. The Klamaths and Modocs contended with thousands of miners and settlers moving through and settling in their territories. The Modocs took exception to the wagon trains moving through their lands and polluting the area. They sought to stop these incursions by frightening newcomers away. The Klamaths, reluctant to take action against newcomers, tried to develop friendly relations with them.

In line with federal Indian policy, the Klamath treaty of 1864 created a reservation on Klamath lands where the Klamaths and Modocs would settle in exchange for protection against settlers and miners. During the reservation era, the Klamaths took center stage in relations with agency officials. Allen David emerged as a leader on the reservation through the end of the nineteenth century. When the Modocs moved to the reservation they experienced agency neglect and came into conflict with the Klamaths. Eventually, half the Modocs returned to California under the leadership of Kintpuash (Captain Jack). This migration set off conflicts with white settlers, leading to the Modoc War of 1872–1873. At its end, four Modoc men, including Kintpuash, were executed, and 153 Modocs were exiled to Indian Territory in Oklahoma.

The Klamaths and Modocs who remained on the Klamath reservation secured a living by creating irriga-

Klondike Rush. In 1900 a horse-drawn wagon makes a delivery to a meat market in Dawson, then the capital of Yukon Territory and a major distribution center for the Klondike mining region in both Canada and Alaska. © CORBIS

tion projects and a lumber business. They established a council under the supervision of agency officials and have successfully managed affairs to the present. The exiled Modocs suffered a dramatic population decline, but through hard work and determination they became successful farmers. The Dawes Severalty Act of 1887 allotted land to individuals on reservations throughout the United States. Although this act adversely affected many Native Americans, it enabled fifty-one Modocs to return to Oregon in 1909.

Twentieth-century Indian policy disrupted the course of economic development on the Klamath reservation. Most important, in 1954 the federal authorities "terminated" the Klamaths and Modocs in an effort to make them self-sufficient and less dependent on government services. Federal protections were withdrawn and individuals were allowed to sell property previously held in trust. As a consequence, many Klamaths lost their lumber enterprises. In 1978 the Modocs were recognized and in 1985 the Klamaths were reinstated as a federally recognized tribe. At the beginning of the twenty-first century, the Klamaths and Modocs still resided in Oregon, and descendants of those Modocs exiled to Indian Territory still resided in Oklahoma under the Modoc Tribe of Oklahoma. In 2002 approximately 3,100 people claimed Klamath ancestry and 600 claimed Modoc ancestry.

BIBLIOGRAPHY

Curtin, Jeremiah. *Myths of the Modocs: Indian Legends of the Northwest.* Boston: Little, Brown, 1912.

Howe, Carrol B. *Ancient Tribes of the Klamath Country.* Portland, Ore.: Binford and Mort, 1968.

———. *Ancient Modocs of California and Oregon.* Portland, Ore.: Binford and Mort, 1979.

Ray, Verne F. *Primitive Pragmatists: The Modoc Indians of Northern California.* Seattle: University of Washington Press, 1963.

Stern, Theodore. *The Klamath Tribe: A People and Their Reservation.* Seattle: University of Washington Press, 1966.

Rebecca Bales

See also **Modoc War; Tribes: California; Tribes: Northwestern.**

KLONDIKE RUSH. On 16 August 1896 gold was discovered by George Carmack and his two Indian brothers-in-law on Bonanza Creek of the Klondike River, a tributary of the Yukon River in Canada's Yukon Territory. News of the discovery reached the United States in January 1897, and in the spring of that year a number of people made preparations to depart by boat up the Yukon, or up the Inside Passage and the Chilcoot and White passes and then down the upper tributaries of the Yukon. On 14 July 1897 the steamer *Excelsior* arrived at San Francisco with $750,000 in gold; on 17 July the *Portland* arrived at Seattle with $800,000. The press made the Klondike Rush a national sensation, partly because there was little other important news at the time. Chambers of commerce, railroads, steamship lines, and outfitting houses received thousands of inquiries, and, seeing the commer-

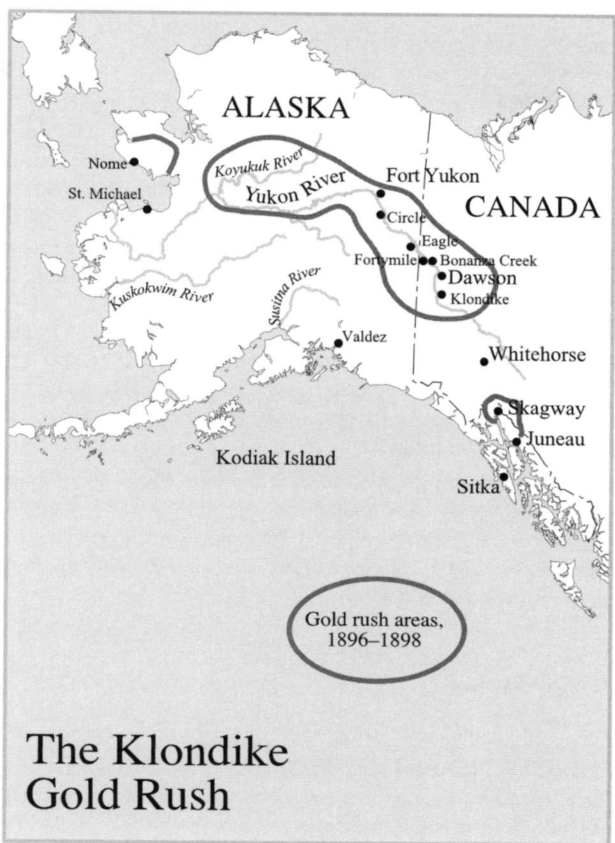

The Klondike Gold Rush

cial possibilities, began a well-financed propaganda campaign that precipitated the rush. The peak of the rush occurred from 1897 to 1899, when 100,000 people left for Alaska, although only about half reached the mines, because of the harsh weather and terrain.

The Klondike Rush had far-reaching economic results, particularly for Alaska. Those unable to secure claims on the Klondike spread over Alaska, finding gold at Nome, Fairbanks, and numerous less famous places. Many turned to other pursuits. Taken together, participants in the rush were the principal factor in the diffuse settlement of Alaska and the economic development of the territory.

BIBLIOGRAPHY

Hunt, William R. *North of the 53 Degree: The Wild Days of the Alaska-Yukon Mining Frontier, 1870–1914.* New York: Macmillan, 1974.

Shape, William. *Faith of Fools: A Journal of the Klondike Gold Rush.* Pullman: Washington State University Press, 1998.

Wharton, David. *The Alaska Gold Rush.* Bloomington: Indiana University Press, 1972.

V. J. Farrar / H. S.

See also **Alaska; Gold Mines and Mining; Yukon Region.**

KNIGHTS OF LABOR. The Noble Order of the Knights of Labor reached a peak membership of around 700,000 in the mid-1880s, making it the largest and most important labor organization in nineteenth-century America. The complexities of its organization, ideology, and activities reflected the problems that afflicted the American labor movement. Antebellum working-class involvement with fraternal orders, such as the Freemasons and the Odd Fellows, inspired associations like the Mechanics' Mutual Protection Association and the Brotherhood of the Union. From the Civil War and the panic of 1873 emerged new clandestine labor organizations, including the shoemakers' Knights of St. Crispin and the miners' "Molly Maguires," along with the broader Sovereigns of Industry, Industrial Brotherhood, and Junior Sons of '76. The Knights of Labor eventually subsumed all of these.

Long a hotbed of such activities, the Philadelphia needle trades built the Garment Cutters' Union during the Civil War. On 28 December 1869, Uriah Stephens gathered a handful of workers in that craft to launch the Knights of Labor. Members paid a 50-cent initiation fee. Ten members could form an assembly, though at all times at least three-quarters of the assembly had to be wage earners. Initially, membership in the Knights expanded among Philadelphia textile workers, but in the mid-1870s it spread into western Pennsylvania and began recruiting large numbers of miners. Expansion into other trades required not only the "trade assembly" but the industrially nonspecific "local assembly." The presence of the order in different communities with growing numbers of organizations inspired the formation of a "district assembly" to coordinate the work.

After an insurrectionary railroad strike in 1877, the order assumed a more public presence, and membership expanded at an unprecedented pace. The Knights numbered nearly 9,300 in 1878; over 20,000 in 1879; over 28,000 in 1880; and almost 52,000 in 1883. With the radically expanding membership, new leaders like Terence V. Powderly displaced the old fraternalists like Stephens. This turnover in leadership represented a deeper ideological shift.

The Knights of Labor proclaimed the underlying unity of the condition of all who work and urged solidarity. They asserted the equal rights of women and included them in the order despite the often Victorian values of the leadership. Calling for the unity of brain and brawn—the solidarity of all who labor—the Knights essentially shaped the popular notion of class in American life. Notwithstanding national chauvinism and ethnic rivalries, the order organized assemblies of immigrants from across Europe and Jewish associations. By some estimates, as many as ninety-five thousand African Americans became Knights. Glaringly, however, the Knights established a terrible record regarding treatment of Chinese Americans, even defending the massacre of Chinese workers by white miners at Rock Springs, Wyoming.

The order pursued legislative and political means to undermine the "money power," banks and monopolies, and favored the legislation of an eight-hour day, equal pay for equal work, abolition of child labor and convict labor, and public ownership of utilities. On the other hand, in the midst of major third-party movements, the Knights struggled, usually without success, to remain aloof. Largely to placate the active hostility of the hierarchy of the Catholic Church, the leadership of the Knights explicitly denied an interest within the order in more radical politics.

These contradictions gave the Knights great power, yet largely predisposed the order to use its power in an uncoordinated and chaotic fashion. Railroad workers in the Knights in 1883 launched a series of strikes against the widely hated railroads that came to fruition in the southwestern strike of 1885 against the Jay Gould interests. Powderly and the Knights successfully organized national boycotts in support of the strike movements. As a result of the consequent publicity and the temporary demise of third-party politics, the Knights expanded to massive proportions, attaining 110,000 members by July 1885 and over 700,000 members by October 1886. By then, the movement embraced virtually every current in the American labor movement. Some thought the strike, wage agreements, boycott, and cooperatives were sufficient. The order avoided support of the 1886 eight-hour-day strike movement and remained ambiguous about nonpolitical means of attaining its goals.

Members of the trades assemblies, including printers, molders, cigar makers, carpenters, glassworkers, ironworkers, and steelworkers, combined into the Federation of Organized Trades and Labor Unions (FOTLU) in 1881. Although initially cooperative with the concerns of these trade unionists, the leadership of the Knights became increasingly cautious even as their successes inspired intense opposition, and the FOTLU reorganized as the American Federation of Labor (AFL) in 1886. Membership in the Knights quickly fell to 100,000 by 1890, and neither its dalliance with populism nor interventions by the Socialist Labor Party kept it from plummeting during the twentieth century.

BIBLIOGRAPHY

Voss, Kim. *The Making of American Exceptionalism: The Knights of Labor and Class Formation in the Nineteenth Century.* Ithaca, N.Y.: Cornell University Press, 1993.

Weir, Robert E. *Beyond Labor's Veil: The Culture of the Knights of Labor.* University Park: Pennsylvania State University Press, 1996.

Mark A. Lause

See also **American Federation of Labor–Congress of Industrial Organizations; Industrial Workers of the World; Labor; Strikes.**

KNIGHTS OF THE GOLDEN CIRCLE. The Knights of the Golden Circle (KGC) was a pre–Civil War, pro-Southern secret society founded in Ohio in 1854 by George W. L. Bickley, a Virginian, who soon moved the KGC to the South. Members were known as Copperheads. Wishing to extend slavery into Mexico and to form a country that surrounded the Gulf of Mexico, a "golden circle," they opposed abolition and fought for secession. KGC was reorganized in 1863 as the Order of American Knights, and again in 1864 as the Order of the Sons of Liberty. Republicans tried to discredit Democrats by associating them with the KGC; their efforts failed, making themselves look bad instead.

BIBLIOGRAPHY

Crenshaw, Ollinger. "The Knights of the Golden Circle: The Career of George Bickley." *American Historical Review* 47, no. 1 (1941): 23–50.

Klement, Frank L. "Ohio and the Knights of the Golden Circle: The Evolution of a Civil War Myth." *Cincinnati Historical Society Bulletin* 32, nos. 1–2 (1974): 7–27.

Milton, George F. *Abraham Lincoln and the Fifth Column.* New York: Vanguard, 1942.

Mary Anne Hansen

See also **Slavery.**

KNOW-NOTHING PARTY, or American Party, organized as the political expression of nativism, hostility directed against German and Irish Roman Catholics, who immigrated heavily in the 1840s and 1850s. Nativism first impacted politics in the form of election-day riots provoked by secret fraternal organizations such as the Order of the Star Spangled Banner, organized in New York in 1849. When questioned about this order, members replied, "I know nothing." By 1854 the "Know-Nothings" achieved national prominence and had an estimated membership of a million. From 1854 to 1856 Know-Nothing candidates won local, state, and congressional offices across the nation. The Know-Nothing platform reflected the party's political and moral conservatism. It included calls for extension of the immigrant naturalization period from five to twenty-one years; restriction of the right to vote to citizens; restriction of office-holding to native-born citizens; prohibition of the manufacture and sale of alcohol; and requirement of the reading of the King James Bible in schools.

Know-Nothings drew from both the Democratic and Whig Parties, but most heavily from the latter, whose traditional makeup of middle-class and skilled working-class Protestants was susceptible to nativist appeals. The Whigs, already damaged by division over the slavery issue, were dealt a mortal blow by Know-Nothing defections in 1854–1855. Know-Nothings occasionally found support among antislavery groups, although most abolitionists and Free Soilers denounced nativism as a form of bigotry and as a distraction from the main goal of restricting slavery. Moreover, the Know-Nothings themselves became divided over the slavery issue. Still, the effects of

Know-Nothing Party. An 1844 campaign ribbon of the secretive anti-immigrant, anti-Catholic organization. © CORBIS

the Know-Nothing Party were to pave a transition from Whiggery to Republicanism. In 1856 Know-Nothings in the Northeast supported the Republican candidate John C. Frémont. The Republican Party was primarily an antislavery party but it absorbed and reflected the nativism of the Know-Nothings well into the twentieth century.

BIBLIOGRAPHY

Anbinder, Tyler G. *Nativism and Slavery: The Northern Know Nothings and the Politics of the 1850s.* New York: Oxford University Press, 1992.

Gienapp, William E. *The Origins of the Republican Party, 1852–1856.* New York: Oxford University Press, 1987. Argues the rise of the Republican Party was a response to nativism.

Osofsky, Gilbert. "Abolitionists, Irish Immigrants, and the Dilemmas of Romantic Nationalism." *American Historical Review* 80 (1975): 889–912. Evaluates immigrants' ambivalence over antislavery as a result of nativist hostility.

Timothy M. Roberts

See also **Nativism;** *and vol. 9:* **American Party Platform.**

KNOX, FORT. In 1918 an army camp named Camp Knox, for General Henry T. Knox, was established in Kentucky, thirty-one miles southwest of Louisville. Made permanent in 1932 as Fort Knox, the post became the main repository of U.S. gold in 1937. More than 140 million ounces of gold, worth billions of dollars, are kept in the U.S. Bullion Depository, a two-story granite, steel, and concrete vault managed by the Treasury Department. The 109,000-acre army installation at Fort Knox also includes an artillery training school, the Godman Army Air Field, and the Patton Museum.

BIBLIOGRAPHY

Truscott, Lucian K., Jr. *The Twilight of the U. S. Cavalry: Life in the Old Army, 1917–1942.* Lawrence: University Press of Kansas, 1989.

Andrew C. Rieser

See also **Army, United States; Currency and Coinage; Fortifications; Mint, Federal; Treasury, Department of the.**

KOREA, RELATIONS WITH. In August 1866, the American merchant W. B. Preston dispatched the *General Sherman*, a merchant ship, to a port in northern Korea demanding trade unilaterally, a private endeavor that did not officially involve the U.S. government. The entire crew died when the Hermit Kingdom had the ship set on fire. In two retaliatory campaigns during 1871, U.S. naval ships bombarded Korean forts, killing some 250 Koreans. The undeclared hostilities were settled by a treaty of commerce and amity in 1882. Yet military and diplomatic encounters failed to develop further as Korea soon became a target of Chinese, Japanese, and Russian imperialism. In 1910, it fell prey to Japanese military rule. Full-scale and enduring U.S.-Korean relations developed as a result of Japan's surrender at the close of World War II; the ensuing American military occupation of South Korea by 40,000 American personnel and servicemen (1945–1948); and the Korean War (1950–1953), which engaged about 1.6 million American servicemen. These events started a wave of Korean immigration consisting largely of some 20,000 Korean wives of U.S. servicemen and their children, who arrived in the United States from 1945 to 1965. Beginning in the 1950s, many American families adopted Korean war orphans. Also, the Immigration Act of 1965, with its family reunification provision, gave a tremendous boost to the presence of Korean Americans, who would surge from some 100,000 in 1965 to about 1.3 million at century's end.

Still, the major pillars of U.S.–South Korean relations after the Korean War were the U.S. security umbrella against external communist threats and the opening of U.S. markets to Korean exports. The Korea-gate scandal of 1976–1978, in which dozens of U.S. congressmen reputedly received bribes from lobbyists for the South Korean government, and diplomatic friction during the Jimmy Carter presidency over human rights abuses in South Korea, were just minor glitches. In fact, making the most of U.S. military, diplomatic, and economic commitments, South Koreans achieved annual economic growth of more than 9 percent for the three decades following the mid-1960s. From 1980, Korean exports to the United States underwent a structural changeover from nondurable consumer goods to consumer electronics and computers, high technology and durable goods, steel, and automobiles. Meanwhile, U.S. exports to Korea in the area of service industries and popular culture steadily grew relative to heavy industry and chemical products. Owing to South Korea's prosperity, the United States often scored trade surpluses in the 1990s; in the mid-1990s, they averaged $10 billion annually.

As of 2001, the United States had not established any formal diplomatic relationship with North Korea, a nation cut off from the noncommunist world for a half century. George W. Bush's administration practically brushed aside the Bill Clinton administration's efforts to bring North Korea to the diplomatic table to resolve any alleged threat of North Korea's development and sale of missiles and nuclear weapons.

BIBLIOGRAPHY

Baldwin, Frank, ed. *Without Parallel: The American-Korean Relationship since 1945.* New York: Pantheon, 1974.

Lee, Yur-Bok, and Wayne Patterson, eds. *One Hundred Years of Korean-American Relations, 1882–1982.* University: University of Alabama Press, 1986.

Sutter, Robert, and Han Sungjoo. *Korea-U.S. Relations in a Changing World.* Berkeley: University of California Press, 1990.

David Park

See also **Cold War; Korea War of 1871; Korea-gate; Korean Americans; Korean War;** *and vol. 9:* **War Story.**

KOREA WAR OF 1871. In 1871 the United States engaged in undeclared hostilities with Korea as a result of the murder of Americans who illegally entered closed ports and the subsequent refusal of the Koreans to open their kingdom to foreign trade. By ancient custom, violation of Korean seclusion was a capital offense. Nonetheless, in 1866 an American merchant dispatched the *General Sherman* to open trade. When the schooner grounded on a sandbar, the Koreans—acting by royal command—burned the ship and murdered the crew.

The U.S.S. *Shenandoah,* sent to investigate, was denied all communication with the Korean capital. George F. Seward, consul general at Shanghai, suggested a punitive expedition, and on 26 May 1871 an American squadron arrived to survey the coast and meet with the king. When no favorable response came from the Koreans, the squadron began to move upriver. On 1 June masked batteries opened fire, and the Americans returned that fire.

The guardian-general of Fu-ping prefecture formally complained of the American presence but declared himself too humble to communicate the American message to his king. The Americans sent a second expedition and took five Korean batteries, but the Koreans still would not give the Americans an audience. On 2 July Edward B. Drew, acting secretary of legation at Peking, announced the squadron would withdraw to consult with Washington. Korea and the United States secured no treaty until 1882.

BIBLIOGRAPHY

LaFeber, Walter. *The American Age: United States Foreign Policy at Home and Abroad since 1750.* New York: Norton, 1989.

———. *The New Empire: An Interpretation of American Expansion, 1860–1898.* Ithaca, N.Y.: Cornell University Press, 1963, 1998.

Angela Ellis
Harry Emerson Wildes

See also **Imperialism; Korea, Relations with.**

KOREA-GATE surfaced in the immediate aftermath of the Watergate scandal of the mid-1970s when journalists began attaching "gate" to any event that suggested scandal in government. "Korea-gate" developed following reports in 1976–1978 of South Korean efforts to influence U.S. policy and of U.S. congressmen who profited from the efforts. Most attention focused on the behavior of Tongsun Park, a wealthy South Korean businessman who from 1970 to 1975 reportedly spent huge sums of money on gifts to numerous U.S. congressmen. The activities occurred when U.S. relations had soured with South Korea, largely because of the dictatorial practices of President Park Chung Hee. President Jimmy Carter's announcement in July 1977 that virtually all U.S. troops would be withdrawn from South Korea brought the issue to a crisis. Meanwhile, the Korea-gate affair ran its course. Richard T. Hanna of California, who reportedly received $246,000 from Park, served a prison sentence of approximately one year. Three congressmen were reprimanded for misconduct; one was found innocent. Relations between South Korea and the United States improved, and Carter canceled his order to withdraw troops. Park, the object of U.S. dissatisfaction, was assassinated that same year.

BIBLIOGRAPHY

Buss, Claude A. *The United States and the Republic of Korea.* Stanford, Calif.: Hoover Institution Press, Stanford University, 1982.

Kwak, Tae-Hwan, et al., eds. *U.S.–Korean Relations, 1882–1982.* Seoul: Kyungnam University Press, 1982.

Ross Gregory / A. G.

See also **Corruption, Political; Political Scandals; Watergate.**

KOREAN AIRLINES FLIGHT 007. Originating in New York, Korean Airlines flight 007 left Anchorage, Alaska, for Seoul just before 3:30 A.M. on 31 August 1983. A few minutes after takeoff, it deviated from its assigned course, taking the 747 into Soviet airspace and over a major Soviet military installation. Five hours into the flight, two missiles fired from a Soviet interceptor struck the plane, sending it into the sea west of Sakhalin Island. All 269 people on board, including 61 Americans, died. Soviet authorities took nearly a week to admit their fighter had downed the civilian aircraft. The Soviet claim that KAL 007 was a spy plane caused a chorus of condemnations in the United Nations. Arms limitation talks in Geneva stalled. The West subsequently boycotted flights into and out of the Soviet Union. For years, the Soviet Union refused to accept any blame and kept U.S. investigators from the crash site. Later explanations pointed either to mistaken identity or pilot incompetence. Korean Air Lines, which paid pilots a bonus to arrive on time and "any way they can," was also deemed guilty. A final theory alleged that the jet wandered into a Soviet-American air battle and was destroyed. Still a mystery, the destruction of KAL 007 worsened escalating tensions in the COLD WAR.

BIBLIOGRAPHY

Brun, Michael. *Incident at Sakhalin: The True Mission of KAL Flight 007.* New York: Four Walls Eight Windows, 1995.

Dallin, Alexander. *Black Box: KAL 007 and the Superpowers.* Berkeley: University of California Press, 1985.

Hersh, Seymour M. *"The Target Is Destroyed": What Really Happened to Flight 007 and What America Knew about It.* New York: Random House 1986.

Johnson, Richard W. *Shootdown: Flight 007 and the American Connection.* New York: Viking, 1986.

Bruce J. Evensen
James I. Matray

KOREAN AMERICANS. The first Korean immigrants came to the United States in the last years of the nineteenth century as Hawaiian sugar plantation workers or students of higher education. However, their numbers were very small, estimated at fewer than 100. Between 1903 and 1905, some 7,200 Koreans arrived in Hawaii to work on sugar plantations for the Hawaiian Sugar Planters' Association. The vast majority of them were single men, and their arrival was soon followed by about 1,000 Korean women called "picture brides," because their marriages had resulted from exchanging photographs. That first wave of Korean immigration was heavily promoted not only by labor recruiters but also by American missionaries in Korea, who billed Hawaii as a Christian paradise. In fact, about 40 percent of those Korean immigrants were Protestants, while few people in Korea were Protestants at the time.

The first wave came to a sudden halt. In 1905, upon making Korea a protectorate, Japan shut down the Korean Emigration Office. The Gentlemen's Agreement of 1907 between the United States and Japan restricting Japanese immigration applied to Koreans as well by default, and the U.S. Congress enacted highly restrictive immigration acts in 1920 and 1924. As a consequence, few Koreans immigrated until the late 1940s. The 1910 U.S. census reported 4,994 Korean immigrants, and the 1940 census reported 8,562, most in Hawaii and California.

The majority of those early immigrants engaged in agriculture as tenant farmers, growing rice, fruits, and vegetables, and many women worked in domestic service. A small number took up mining and railroading. By the early 1910s, a few "rice kings" and fairly large farm entrepreneurs had emerged, and by the 1930s, some successful restaurants, groceries, and other small businesses had appeared around Los Angeles. By the 1940s, a small group had become professionals, entering medicine, science, and architecture. Nevertheless, throughout the first half of the twentieth century, most Korean Americans had to eke out a harsh living owing to linguistic and cultural barriers, the prevalent perception of the "yellow peril" during the Progressive Era, and the rampant racial bigotry of the 1920s. Until 1952, the U.S. government denied first-generation Korean immigrants the right to become naturalized U.S. citizens, and California enforced discriminatory educational, tax, licensing, and leasing policies. Over time the third- to fifth-generation Korean Americans scattered all over the country, where most intermarried and led middle-class lives in the larger society.

A second wave of Korean immigrants consisted of some 20,000 Korean women, who married U.S. servicemen and immigrated to the United States between 1945 and 1965, the children of U.S. servicemen, and war orphans. The second wave was largely a by-product of the U.S. military rule over Korea (1945–1948) and the Korean War (1950–1953). A small but growing number of Korean professionals who had originally arrived as students became permanent residents and U.S. citizens. As

Koreatown. Signs indicate urban neighborhoods, such as this one in New York City, where large numbers of Korean Americans have congregated, especially since a liberalized immigration law took effect in 1968. AP/Wide World Photos

of 1965, an estimated 100,000 Korean Americans lived in the United States. Yet a major and sustained influx of Korean immigrants did not occur until 1968, when the Immigration Act of 1965 took effect with an epoch-making provision for family reunification. Subsequently, the Korean American population grew by leaps and bounds to about 1.3 million at the beginning of the twenty-first century. After reaching its peak in 1987, Korean immigration slowed down, largely due to a dramatic rise in living standards in Korea between the 1970s and the 1990s but partly on account of the Los Angeles riots of 1992.

Most of the newcomers after 1975 came to the United States in pursuit of better economic opportunities, political or social freedom, or professional aspirations. A vast majority of the adults were college-educated with an urban middle-class background. Although about 20 percent became professionals in academia, medicine, science, engineering, finance, and so on, a great majority entered various lines of small business. Most notably, Korean Americans owned about 25 percent of the laundry and dry cleaning businesses across the country and a large number of groceries and delicatessens in New York City. Working long hours on hard jobs, six or even seven days a week, often in inner cities and minority neighborhoods, almost 70 to 75 percent of these newcomers turned to their ethnic Christian churches for practical needs of all kinds as well as spiritual rejuvenation and fraternal association, much as their predecessors had in Hawaii and California in the early decades of the century.

On the other hand, while they often mixed with fellow Korean immigrants, joined local Korean immigrant meetings or alumni clubs, ate Korean food, watched Korean television and videotapes, read Korean newspapers and magazines, listened to Korean music, and checked out Korean Web sites, first-generation Korean immigrants put much emphasis on the acculturation and education of their children. As a result, most of their American-born children earned college degrees, and many attended graduate or professional schools. They landed financially secure jobs, but frequently at the expense of their Korean language and cultural heritage.

With the growing number of old-timers and the increasing financial security of most Korean immigrants, the Korean American population after the 1980s began moving gradually but visibly away from urban centers and traditional ethnic enclaves to middle-class suburbs around the country. In the 1990s, the average household income of Korean American families was substantially higher than that of white American families. Politically, the majority of first-generation and a large proportion of second-generation Korean Americans, owing to their overriding concerns for financial security, evangelical Christian faith, and law and order, leaned toward the Republican Party. This preference is despite the fact that they have long benefited from the immigration, civil rights, Korean policies, and broader political and social climate more often supported by Democrats.

BIBLIOGRAPHY

Kim, Hyung-chan, and Wayne Patterson, eds. *The Koreans in America, 1882–1974.* Dobbs Ferry, N.Y.: Oceana, 1974.

Patterson, Wayne. *The Korean Frontier in America.* Honolulu: University of Hawaii Press, 1988.

Takaki, Ronald. *Strangers from a Different Shore.* Boston: Little, Brown 1989.

David Park

See also **Immigration Act of 1965; Immigration Restriction; Korea, Relations with; Korean War;** *and vol. 9:* **Gentlemen's Agreement; War Story.**

KOREAN WAR. The Korean War began on 25 June 1950, when forces of the Democratic People's Republic of Korea (DPRK) attacked southward across the thirty-eighth parallel against the army of the Republic of Korea (ROK). Trained and armed by the Soviet Union and the People's Republic of China (PRC) and substantially out-

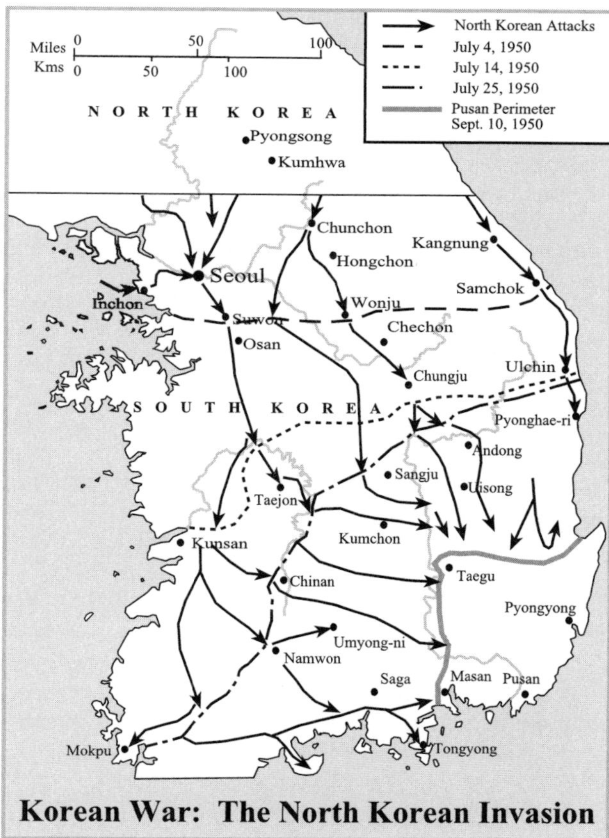

Korean War: The North Korean Invasion

numbering the South Koreans along the front, the North Koreans advanced rapidly, capturing Seoul, the ROK capital, on 28 June.

The U.S. administration of Harry S. Truman reacted sharply. With Secretary of State Dean G. Acheson taking the lead in advising the commander-in-chief, the United States rushed the Korean issue to the United Nations Security Council in New York. The Soviet Union was boycotting that body over its refusal to grant China's seat to the recently founded PRC under Mao Zedong, thus making possible the quick passage of U.S.-drafted resolutions on 25 and 27 June. The first called for a cessation of hostilities and the withdrawal of DPRK forces north of the thirty-eighth parallel, the second for assistance from member states to the ROK "necessary to repel the armed attack and to restore international peace and security in the area." Already the United States was aiding the ROK with arms, ammunition, and air and naval forces. On 30 June, as the North Koreans advanced south of Seoul, Truman committed to the battle U.S. combat troops stationed in Japan. On 7 July the UN Security Council passed another U.S.-drafted resolution creating a United Nations Command (UNC) in Korea under American leadership. Truman appointed General Douglas MacArthur, the commander-in-chief of U.S. Forces, Far East, to head the UNC.

The Korean War lasted for over three years. Although the United States and ROK provided over 90 percent of the manpower on the UN side, fourteen other governments sent forces of some kind and unofficially Japan provided hundreds of laborers in critical Korean industries and in its former colony's harbors operating American vessels. On the North Korean side, the PRC eventually committed over a million troops, and the Soviet Union contributed large-scale matériel assistance and hundreds of pilots and artillery personnel. United States forces suffered in battle alone over 142,000 casualties, including 33,000 deaths; the Chinese nearly 900,000 casualties, including 150,000 deaths. Koreans on both sides endured far greater losses. Total casualties in the war, military and civilian combined, numbered over 3 million.

Origins of the War

The war originated in the division of the peninsula in August 1945 by the United States and the Soviet Union. Korea had been under Japanese rule since early in the century. American leaders believed that, with its defeat in World War II, Japan should lose its empire but that Koreans would need years of tutelage before being prepared to govern themselves. The United States surmised that a multipower trusteeship over the peninsula, to involve itself, the Soviet Union, China, and perhaps Great Britain, would provide Koreans with the necessary preparation while averting the great-power competition that had disrupted northeast Asia a half century before. Yet as the Pacific war approached its end, the Allied powers had not reached precise agreements on Korea. On the eve of Japan's surrender, President Truman proposed to Soviet premier Joseph Stalin that their governments' forces occupy Korea, with the thirty-eighth parallel as the dividing line between them. Stalin agreed.

At the Moscow Conference of Foreign Ministers in December 1945, the United States did advance a trusteeship proposal, but the Soviets watered it down to include merely negotiations toward trusteeship in a joint commission made up of representatives of the two occupation commands in Korea. The new body soon became stalemated, adjourning in May 1946. The Americans aligned with the Korean right in the south, while the Soviets sided with the extreme left in the north. Despite a second attempt to resolve differences in the joint commission in the spring and summer of 1947, the Soviet-American stalemate continued, as the escalating Cold War in Europe and the Middle East dampened prospects for accommodation in other areas. In September the United States referred the Korean issue to the UN General Assembly.

By this time South Korea was in considerable turmoil. Since the beginning of the occupation, the Americans had favored conservative Korean groups who had either collaborated with the Japanese or spent most of the period of Japan's rule in exile. The economic division of

On the Offensive. An American tank crests a hill, followed by U.S. Army troops. NATIONAL ARCHIVES AND RECORDS ADMINISTRATION

the country, the influx of over a million Koreans into the territory south of the thirty-eighth parallel from Japan, Manchuria, and North Korea, and poorly conceived occupation policies combined to produce widespread discontent. Meanwhile, the extreme right, led by Syngman Rhee, agitated aggressively for establishment of an independent government in the south. With support in Congress waning for the U.S. occupation, the Truman administration decided to refer the Korean issue to the United Nations.

The Soviets refused to cooperate in creating a unified government in Korea, so the United States persuaded the international organization to supervise elections below the thirty-eighth parallel. These occurred on 10 May 1948, and the boycott of them by leftist and some rightist leaders ensured a victory for Rhee and his allies. When the ROK came into being on 15 August, Rhee stood as its president and the conservative Democratic party dominated the National Assembly. Less than a month later, the Soviet Union brought into existence the DPRK in the north, led by the Communist Kim Il Sung as premier. Confident of the relative strength of their creation, the Soviets withdrew their occupation forces at the end of the year. Given the widespread turmoil in the south, which included guerrilla warfare in mountain areas, the Americans did not withdraw their last occupation forces until June 1949. Even then, they left substantial quantities of light arms for the ROK army and a 500-man military advisory group to assist in its development.

Beginning in March 1949 Kim Il Sung lobbied Stalin for approval of and matériel support for a military attack on the ROK. Stalin initially demurred. At the end of January 1950, with the Communists having won the civil war on mainland China, with Mao in Moscow negotiating a military alliance with the Soviet Union, and with support for the ROK in the United States appearing less than firm, he changed his mind. Over the next several months, Stalin approved the shipment to North Korea of heavy arms, including tanks, thus giving the DPRK a clear military advantage over the ROK. North Korea was also strengthened by the return of tens of thousands of Korean nationals who had fought on the Communist side in China. In meetings with Kim in Moscow in early April, Stalin explicitly approved a North Korean attack on South Korea, provided Mao also gave his blessing. Although he believed that the United States would not intervene, especially if the North Koreans won a speedy victory, he made it clear that, if Kim ran into difficulty with the Americans, he would have to depend as a counter on direct Chinese, not Soviet, intervention. When in mid-May Mao endorsed Kim's proposal for an early attack on the ROK, the plans proceeded to their final stage.

The Course of the War

Even with the intervention of U.S. troops in July, the DPRK nearly drove the enemy out of Korea. By early August forces fighting under the UN banner were squeezed into the Pusan perimeter, on the southeastern corner of the peninsula. At the end of the month DPRK forces launched an offensive that over the next two weeks inflicted more enemy casualties than in any other comparable period during the war.

Yet UN troops now outnumbered their opponents and, on 15 September, General MacArthur launched a counteroffensive at Inchon, the port for Seoul. By month's

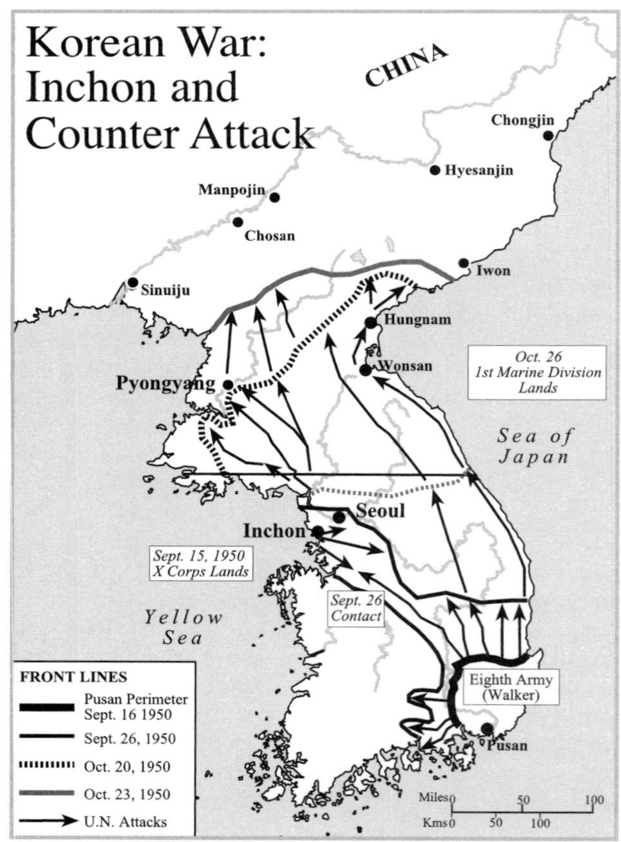

On the Defensive. Members of the U.S. Army's Second Infantry Division man a machine gun in a foxhole, 1950.

end UN forces had broken out of the Pusan perimeter and retaken Seoul. DPRK forces were in headlong retreat northward and the United States had altered its objective from reestablishing the thirty-eighth parallel to destroying the enemy and reuniting the peninsula under a friendly government. ROK units began crossing the old boundary on 1 October and other UN units followed a week later, by which time the UN General Assembly had given its endorsement.

Long anticipating such developments, the PRC now moved decisively toward intervention. The DPRK appealed to Beijing for aid on 1 October and Stalin urged Mao to comply. The "Chinese People's Volunteers" (CPV) under General Peng Dehuai commenced large-scale movements into Korea on 19 October.

Despite contact with CPV soldiers from 25 October on, UN ground forces did not stop their movement northward. General MacArthur was determined to win a quick and total victory and, despite reservations in the Pentagon and the State Department, Washington proved unwilling to order him to halt. On 24 November UN forces began what they hoped would be an "end-the-war offensive." Four days later, with CPV forces over 200,000 strong engaged in a strong counterattack against severely overextended UN units, MacArthur declared that he faced "an entirely new war."

Over the next month UN troops retreated to the thirty-eighth parallel. On New Year's Eve CPV units crossed the old boundary in an attempt to push enemy forces off the peninsula. MacArthur told Washington that the U.S. choice was between expanding the war to air and naval attacks against mainland China and accepting total defeat.

Adhering to a Europe-first strategy and faced with allied pressure to both persevere in Korea and contain the war there, the Truman administration refused to follow MacArthur's lead. During the second week of January the CPV offensive petered out below Seoul in the face of severe weather, supply problems, and the regrouping of UN forces under the leadership of General Matthew B. Ridgway, who had taken over the U.S. Eighth Army in Korea in late December. Over the next three months, UN forces, outnumbered on the ground but controlling the air and enjoying a sizable advantage in artillery, gradually pushed the enemy northward, retaking Seoul in mid-March. A month later UN units held a line slightly north of the thirty-eighth parallel in all sectors except the extreme west.

This evolving situation produced a final showdown between Truman and MacArthur. The president was content, if possible, to settle the war roughly where it had begun the previous June, and he was under steady pres-

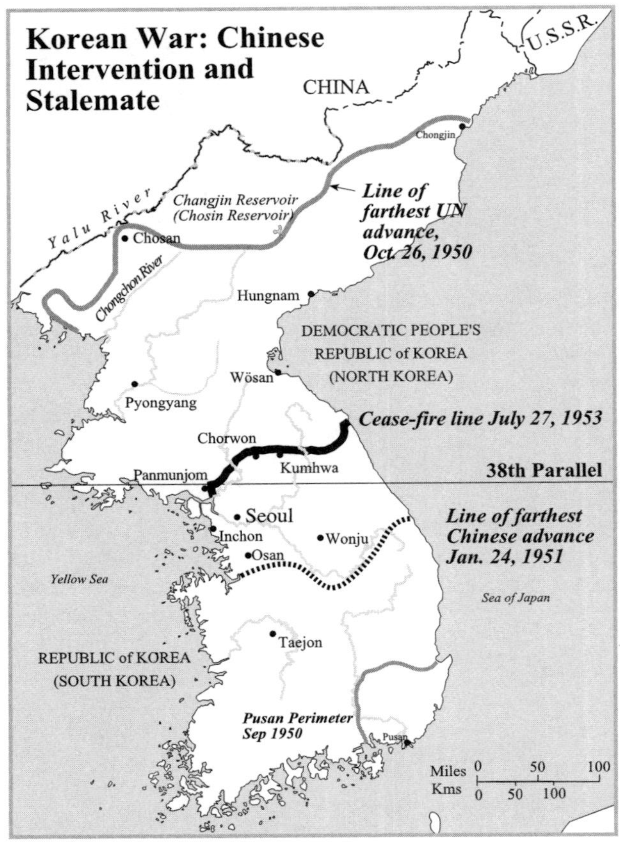

sure to do so from allies and neutrals in the United Nations. Dissatisfied with less than total victory, the UN commander continued to scheme for an expanded war. Anticipating a Chinese spring offensive at any moment and facing continued public dissent from MacArthur, Truman on 11 April removed his field commander from all his positions, appointing Ridgway in his place. The action set off a storm of protest in the United States, but Truman held firm, aided by UN forces in Korea, which repulsed massive Chinese offensives in April and May. Following consultations in Moscow in early June, the Communist allies decided to seek negotiations for an armistice.

Peace Negotiations

On 10 July negotiations began between the field commands at Kaesong, just south of the thirty-eighth parallel. Despite restraint on both sides from seeking major gains on the battlefield, an armistice was not signed for over two years.

The first issue negotiated was an armistice line, and this took until 27 November to resolve. The Communists initially insisted on the thirty-eighth parallel; the UN command, which was dominated by the United States, pressed for a line north of the prevailing battle line, arguing that this would be reasonable compensation for its agreement in an armistice to desist its pounding of North Korea from the air and sea. After much acrimony, the suspension of the talks for two months, and small battlefield gains by the UN side, the parties agreed to the existing "line of contact"—provided, that is, that agreement on all other issues was reached within thirty days.

Two main issues remained on the agenda: "arrangements for the realization of cease fire and armistice . . . including the composition, authority, and functions of a supervising organization for carrying out the terms;" and "arrangements relating to prisoners of war." With the UN command relaxing its military pressure on the ground and the Communists securing their defensive lines as never before, neither side had a compelling reason to give way. Nonetheless, by April 1952 essential agreement had been reached on the postarmistice rotation of troops in Korea, the replacement and introduction of matériel, and the makeup and authority of a Neutral Nations Supervisory Commission. The one remaining item was the fate of prisoners of war (POWs).

The POW issue was bound to be difficult, as it involved captured personnel on both sides who had participated in the ongoing civil conflicts in Korea and/or

POWs in North Korea. One of the American and South Korean prisoners of war being paraded through the streets of Pyongyang on 3 October 1950 is forced to dress as Adolf Hitler and to drag an American flag on the ground. Archive Photos, Inc.

China. Many of the prisoners held by the United Nations had begun the war in South Korea, been captured by the DPRK army, and eventually been impressed into it. Others had fought in Nationalist armies during the Chinese civil war and later been integrated into the CPV. Not all of these prisoners wanted to return to the DPRK or PRC at war's end. Negotiations eventually became stalemated over the fate of Chinese prisoners. In October 1952, after months without progress, the UNC suspended talks.

Negotiations did not resume until April of the following year. By this time Dwight D. Eisenhower had replaced Truman as president of the United States (20 January) and Stalin had died (5 March). When negotiations failed to achieve quick success, the American president ordered the bombing of dikes in North Korea, which threatened the DPRK's food supply; he also threatened to terminate the talks and expand the war. In early June the Communists finally accepted the U.S. position on POWs. The centrality of Eisenhower's actions in this outcome remains uncertain.

The fighting would have ended in mid-June had it not been for the action of Syngman Rhee, who opposed an armistice without Korea's unification. His wishes ignored, he ordered ROK guards to release over 25,000 anti-Communist Korean POWs held in the south. This action on 18 June led to strong protests from the Communists and a crisis in U.S.-ROK relations. After the Communists launched successful limited offensives against ROK forces along the battlefront and the Americans promised to negotiate a defense treaty with the ROK immediately following the conclusion of fighting, Rhee finally agreed not to disrupt—but not to sign—an armistice. The Communists joined the UNC in signing the agreement on July 27.

Ending the Fighting. Lieutenant General William K. Harrison (*seated at left*) and General Nam Il, spokesman for the Communist delegation (*seated at right*), sign multiple copies of the armistice at Panmunjom, just below the thirty-eighth parallel, on 27 July 1953. ARCHIVE PHOTOS, INC.

Impact of the War

The war left Korea at once devastated and less likely than at any time since 1945 to become the focal point of international military conflict. Unlike the thirty-eighth parallel, the armistice line based on established battlefield positions was defensible on both sides. More important, while leaders of the divided country refused to rule out forceful unification—indeed, Rhee positively craved it—the great powers were now sufficiently committed to preventing its success by the other side to discourage their clients from initiating the effort.

Although the war was limited almost entirely to Korea, its impact was global. Fearful that the North Korean attack of June 1950 represented the beginning of the Soviet Union's use of force to achieve its purposes, the United States instituted a fourfold increase in defense spending; signed military pacts with Japan, the Philippines, Australia, New Zealand, and the ROK; added Greece and Turkey to the North Atlantic Treaty Organization (NATO); created a NATO command led by an American general; increased the U.S. troop presence in Europe from two to six divisions; and pushed for the rearming of West Germany. The United States also intervened to save Taiwan from the Communists, eventually signing a defense pact with the Nationalist government there, and initiated formation of the Southeast Asia Treaty Organization, which in the following decade played a pivotal role in the direct U.S. military intervention in Indochina.

If the prudence of some of these actions may be questioned, there can be little doubt that the long-term impact of the war was contrary to Soviet interests. The Soviet Union was in a poor position economically to compete with a U.S.-led alliance system partially mobilized for war on a permanent basis. Furthermore, although the Korean War brought the Soviet Union and the PRC closer together for the short term, it helped tear them apart within less than a decade of its end. China's intervention in Korea to prevent a total U.S. victory greatly enhanced the PRC's self-confidence and prestige. The limited scope and initial delay of Soviet aid to the Chinese effort produced resentment in Beijing and reinforced its determination to develop an independent capacity to defend itself and project power beyond its borders.

Yet the war also produced both short- and long-term problems in Sino-American relations. In addition to augmenting feelings of bitterness and fear between the PRC and the United States, the conflict led to American intervention to save Taiwan from conquest by the Communists. U.S. involvement in the island's fate represents the single most acrimonious issue in Sino-American relations to the present day.

BIBLIOGRAPHY

Blair, Clay. *The Forgotten War: America in Korea, 1950–1953.* New York: Times Books, 1987.

Chen, Jian. *China's Road to the Korean War: The Making of the Sino-American Confrontation.* New York: Columbia University Press, 1994.

Cumings, Bruce. *The Origins of the Korean War.* Vol. 1, *Liberation and the Emergence of Separate Regimes, 1945–1947.* Vol. 2, *The Roaring of the Cataract, 1947–1950.* Princeton, N.J.: Princeton University Press, 1981–1990.

Goncharov, Sergei N., John W. Lewis, and Xue Litai. *Uncertain Partners: Stalin, Mao, and the Korean War.* Stanford, Calif.: Stanford University Press, 1993.

Kaufman, Burton I. *The Korean War: Challenges in Crisis, Credibility, and Command.* New York: Knopf, 1986.

Pierpaoli, Paul G., Jr. *Truman and Korea: The Political Culture of the Early Cold War.* Columbia: University of Missouri Press, 1999.

Stueck, William. *The Korean War: An International History.* Princeton, N.J.: Princeton University Press, 1995.

Thornton, Richard C. *Odd Man Out: Truman, Stalin, Mao, and the Origins of the Korean War.* Washington, D.C.: Brassey's, 2000.

West, Philip, and Suh Ji-moon, eds. *Remembering the "Forgotten War."* Armonk, N.Y.: M. E. Sharpe, 2001.

Zhang, Shu Guang. *Mao's Military Romanticism: China and the Korean War, 1950–1953.* Lawrence: University Press of Kansas, 1995.

William W. Stueck Jr.

See also **China, Relations with; Cold War; Korea, Relations with; Southeast Asia Treaty Organization; United Nations;** *and vol. 9:* **General Douglas MacArthur's Speech to Congress; A Personal Narrative of the Korean War; War Story.**

KOREAN WAR, AIR COMBAT IN. When the Democratic People's Republic of Korea (North Korea) invaded the Republic of Korea (South Korea) on 25 June 1950 the North Korean army was supported by a small but effective force of Russian-built aircraft. In the emergency, President Harry S. Truman directed the U.S. Far East Command to act as the United Nations Command and assist in repelling the communist aggression. The U.S. Air Force's Far East Air Forces and the U.S. Navy's Seventh Fleet and First Marine Air Wing were the major elements of UN airpower, which also included Royal Australian and South African air force fighter squadrons, Royal Thai and Royal Hellenic air force troop carrier detachments, and a growing Republic of Korea air force.

The Korean conflict has been called the first jet air war. In the initial weeks American jet pilots quickly destroyed the North Korean air force, so establishing an air superiority that was critical during the summer months of 1950, as UN ground forces were driven into a perimeter around Pusan in southeastern Korea. By 15 September 1950 when U.S. forces launched a bold amphibious invasion at Inchon, the combination of UN ground defenses, strategic air attacks against North Korea, air interdiction operations against extended enemy supply lines, and very strong close air support decimated the initially victorious North Korean army. This permitted a march into North Korea, which turned into retreat in November 1950 when Chinese MIG-15 jet fighters appeared at the Yalu River and overwhelming Chinese armies poured into Korea.

After November 1950 the MIG-15s sought to establish air superiority, but their efforts were thwarted by U.S. Air Force F-86 Sabre fighter screens, which destroyed 792 MIGs in air-to-air combat at a cost of seventy-eight F-86s shot down. UN airpower also provided extensive close air support to outnumbered ground forces and, equally important, proved effective in interdicting the movement of communist troops and supplies to the battle area. By June 1951 UN forces defeated communist ground offensives, thus setting the stage for truce talks the following month.

The air war in Korea called into question the United States' deeply held tenets of air doctrine that emphasized the efficacy of strategic attack against enemy vital industrial centers. The North Koreans had few industries against which to concentrate strategic bomber attacks. Moreover, when air strikes destroyed existing industrial areas, the North Koreans obtained supplies from their Soviet and Chinese allies. When the strategic campaigns had destroyed North Korean industries, air leaders turned to aerial interdiction to produce decisive effects on the battlefield. Operation Strangle, the interdiction effort against the North Korean road and railway system that lasted from 18 August 1951 until the summer of 1952, represented an attempt to isolate front-line troops from their sources of supply. U.S. analysts eventually realized that as long as the United Nations and communist armies remained locked in a stalemate on the front, supply requirements remained so low that airpower alone could have little effect on communist fighting capabilities.

After the talks stalemated in mid-1952, UN air forces were authorized to wage air pressure attacks inside North Korea, culminating in the destruction of several irrigation dams and resultant flooding. Early in 1953 President Dwight D. Eisenhower indicated that the United States might act even more forcefully. This warning may have led the communists to accept the military armistice agreement ending hostilities on 27 July 1953.

During the three-year Korean War, UN air forces flew a total of some 1,040,708 air sorties of all kinds and expended approximately 698,000 tons of ordnance in combat. The United States Air Force missed opportunities to learn from the Korean experience. Slightly more than a decade later, in the Vietnam War, airmen attempted to apply strategic airpower against a foe that was not susceptible to its effect.

BIBLIOGRAPHY

Bruning, John R. *Crimson Sky: The Air Battle for Korea.* Dulles, Va.: Brassey's, 1999.

Crane, Conrad C. *American Airpower Strategy in Korea, 1950–1953.* Modern War Studies. Lawrence: University Press of Kansas, 2000.

Futrell, Robert Frank. *The United States Air Force in Korea, 1950–1953.* Rev. ed. Washington, D.C.: Office of Air Force History, United States Air Force, 1983.

Thompson, Wayne, and Bernard C. Nalty. *Within Limits: The U.S. Air Force and the Korean War.* Washington, D.C.: Air Force History and Museums Program, 1996.

Warnock, A. Timothy, ed. *The USAF in Korea: A Chronology, 1950–1953.* The Korean War fiftieth anniversary commemorative ed. Washington, D.C.: Air Force History and Museums Program in association with Air University Press, 2000.

Y'Blood, William T. *Mig Alley: The Fight for Air Superiority.* Korean War fiftieth anniversary commemorative ed. Washington, D.C.: Air Force History and Museums Program, 2000.

Anthony Christopher Cain
Robert Frank Futrell

See also **Air Force, United States; Air Power, Strategic; Aircraft Armament; Aircraft, Bomber; Aircraft, Fighter.**

KOSOVO BOMBING. In the aftermath of the Bosnian peace agreement, which the United States brokered in the fall of 1995 in Dayton Ohio, conflict in the Balkans soon spilled over into Kosovo, a province of Serbia. There, increasing Serbian repression directed against the Albanian Kosovar majority triggered violent encounters between members of the newly formed Kosovo Liberation Army (KLA) and Serbian military forces.

After news of a particularly gruesome atrocity committed by Serbian forces at Racak became known, an outraged Secretary of State Madeleine Albright pushed hard for a form of diplomatic and military intervention to end the violence in Kosovo. Consequently, she persuaded President Bill Clinton to adopt a policy designed to prevent further ethnic cleansing by the Serbians in Kosovo.

Following the failure of a diplomatic effort directed at the Serbians to end their violence, Clinton, on March 24, 1999, ordered an air assault on Serbian positions in Kosovo and Serbia proper. Backed by NATO, this undertaking provided an alternative to a land invasion, which the Defense Department, Congress, and a majority of the American people flatly opposed. Thus, NATO aircraft flew over 34,000 sorties, firing 23,000 bombs and missiles in its air mission in Kosovo. Among the targets hit by American missiles, however, was the Chinese embassy in Belgrade, which caused several deaths inside the embassy and produced a furious uproar in Beijing. As a result of this incident, an American apology and indemnity soon followed.

The bombing produced mixed results. It did not fully degrade the Serbian Army, as NATO had hoped, and it produced many civilian deaths in both Kosovo and Serbia while accelerating the forced flight of refugees from Kosovo itself. Yet as the war ended, Bill Clinton was relieved, knowing that the mission had avoided American casualties and had reinforced America's senior and dominant role within NATO's command structure.

BIBLIOGRAPHY

Ash, Timothy Garton. "Kosovo: Was It Worth It?" *New York Review of Books.* Vol. XLVII, Number 14 (September 21, 2000): 50–64.

Berman, William C. *From the Center to the Edge: The Politics and Policies of the Clinton Presidency.* Lanham, Md.: Rowman & Littlefield, 2001.

Clark, Wesley. *Waging Modern War: Bosnia, Kosovo, and the Future of Combat.* New York: Public Affairs, 2001.

William C. Berman

See also **Bombing; Human Rights; North Atlantic Treaty Organization; Yugoslavia, Relations with.**

KU KLUX KLAN. A Reconstruction-era terrorist group founded in Pulaski, Tennessee, in 1866, the Ku Klux Klan has been resurrected in a variety of forms from that time to the present; it is one of the powerful, enduring symbols of violent white supremacy and bigotry in American history.

Initially a fraternal organization for a small group of Confederate veterans, the Reconstruction-era Klan quickly turned in a violent, overtly political direction. Like similar groups that appeared across the South in 1866 and 1867 (the Knights of the White Camellia, for example), the Klan used violence and the threat of violence to thwart perceived challenges to white supremacy and Democratic rule. Its mayhem was intended, among other purposes, as a means of controlling black labor, reinforcing social deference to whites, disciplining perceived instances of interracial sexual relationships, and punishing any whites sympathetic to or working on behalf of the Republican Party. Most often, the Klan's victims were African American community leaders—ministers, teachers, politicians, former or current soldiers, or anyone else who clearly held a place of special importance among the former slaves. Murders, floggings, beatings, and sexual assaults carried out against these leaders often achieved the intended goal not only of undermining Reconstruction government, but also of demoralizing the wider black community. Klan terror erupted on a vast scale during the election year of 1868, leading to more than two thousand political assassinations and murders in the former Confederate states, often carried out with the approval or even direct support of local Democratic leaders. "Run nigger, run, or the Kuklux will catch you," warned one Democratic newspaper in Alabama (Trelease, *White Terror,* p. 63). The violence completely eliminated Republican opposition in some areas of the South. Similar waves of Klan activity in 1870 and 1872 led to a series of congressional acts that gave the federal government historic new authority to enforce civil rights under the Fourteenth and Fifteenth Amendments. The most significant of these

Racial Hatred. Famous for their white robes and hoods and the burning crosses (like this one in Edinburg, Miss., in 1967) that were the centerpieces of their rallies, the Ku Klux Klan is one of the most enduring American symbols of racism, bigotry, and violence. © AP/Wide World Photos

were the Enforcement Act of 1870 and the Ku Klux Klan Act of 1871. The Klan faded from the scene after Reconstruction came to an end in 1877, but remained a vivid symbol of barbarous racial violence in the minds of African Americans—and an equally powerful emblem for many whites of what they saw as a just struggle against the tyranny of Reconstruction and "black rule."

By the early twentieth century, idealized images of the Klan as savior of white civilization had become a mainstay of scholarly and popular representations of the Reconstruction era. Thomas Dixon's best selling, turn-of-the-century novels *The Leopard's Spots* and *The Clansman* told the story of heroic Klansmen with melodramatic flair. In 1915, the motion picture visionary D. W. Griffith used *The Clansman* as the basis for his sweeping epic, *Birth of a Nation*.

In that same year, previously unsuccessful fraternal organizer William J. Simmons capitalized on the enormous popularity of Griffith's film by launching a new Klan movement. For five years the "second" Klan barely survived, maintaining a small membership in Georgia and Alabama. In 1920, however, in the wake of extensive postwar labor and racial strife and the onset of national Prohibition, it began a five-year period of enormous, nationwide popularity. The revived Klan was based on romantic images of the original, but ultimately was a very different organization. While the first Klan had little formal structure or leadership outside of individual communities, the second had a highly developed organization, with a hierarchy of local, state, and national leaders, public relations advisers, a string of newspapers, and a marketing operation that sold official uniforms and other paraphernalia. Using recruiting agents—who earned a 25 percent commission on each ten-dollar initiation fee—and holding mass public ceremonies, parades, and social events to attract widespread attention, the second Klan enrolled perhaps as many as five million male and female members (women joined a separate organization, Women of the Ku Klux Klan). Its largest state memberships and greatest local influence came outside the South, in the Midwest and the West. The Indiana Klan enrolled approximately 25 percent of all native-born white men in the state; at least one half million men and women became Klan members in Ohio.

The goals and tactics of the second Klan also differed markedly from those of the first. While the original movement used terror to confront the significant challenge to white supremacy that came with Reconstruction, the Klan of the 1920s faced no such threat and was focused instead on upholding a more general sense of white, Protestant hegemony within American society. The perceived threat came from Catholics, Jews, immigrants, African Americans, Prohibition-related lawlessness, gambling, prostitution, immoral popular culture and personal behavior, and a sense of decline in religion, "pure womanhood," and the family. Vigilante violence did occur in association with the new Klan, most often in the South, targeted in some instances, of course, against African Americans. But more often, when violence did occur, it was directed against fellow white Protestants as punishment for drinking, gambling, adulterous behavior, or other perceived moral lapse. Mob violence was also directed against the Klan, particularly in northern and midwestern cities where ethnic minorities vastly outnumbered native, white Protestants and Klan parades and demonstrations were not well received. The main thrust of the second Klan movement, however, was to elect its members and supporters to public office. Promising to uphold traditional values and enforce the law—Prohibition in particular—the Klan won control of mayor's offices, city councils, school boards, sheriff and district attorney offices, and judgeships in many communities across the nation. It gained complete control of state politics for a time in Indiana, Colorado, Oregon, Oklahoma, and Alabama, and was an important political force in almost every state outside the Northeast. The second Klan began to lose its momentum by 1925 when Klan politicians proved as incapable as other elected officials of halting Prohibition-related vice and other unwanted conditions. Membership dropped precipitously after a series of scandals, the most famous involving Indiana Klan leader D. C. Stephenson, who was convicted of second-degree murder after committing a brutal sexual assault against an Indianapolis woman who eventually died from her injuries.

By the end of the 1920s only small pockets of Klan members remained, most of them in the South and devoted primarily to perpetuating the tradition of racial vigilantism. After World War II, support for Klan groups began to increase again as war-related social changes and the rising expectations of African Americans threatened the Jim Crow system. Once the civil rights movement took hold, the spirit of massive white resistance and the leadership of the White Citizens' Council gave birth to a number of independent, regional Klan organizations. Like the Reconstruction-era Klan cells, these new groups operated mainly through terror, committing hundreds of murders, and countless other acts of violence and intimidation, with the goal of stopping the second Reconstruction. In the face of intense media coverage and the persistent courage of civil rights workers, however, Klan violence actually backfired by broadening public sympathy for the cause of racial justice. Klan groups have continued to exist since that time as part of a diverse, sometimes violent right-wing element in American life, although consistently and effectively assailed by the Southern Poverty Law Center and other groups. In one notable instance, one-time Louisiana Klan leader David Duke gained widespread national attention during the late 1980s and early 1990s by proclaiming himself a mainstream conservative Republican, winning election to the state legislature, and falling just short of the governors' office. National party leaders, however, rejected Duke, underscoring the fact that the Klan itself had lost any place of legitimacy or influence in American life.

BIBLIOGRAPHY

Blee, Kathleen M. *Women of the Klan: Racism and Gender in the 1920s.* Berkeley: University of California Press, 1991.

Chalmers, David M. *Hooded Americanism: The History of the Ku Klux Klan.* 3d ed. Durham, N.C.: Duke University Press, 1987. The original edition was published in 1965.

Jenkins, William D. *Steel Valley Klan: The Ku Klux Klan in Ohio's Mahoning Valley.* Kent, Ohio: Kent State University Press, 1990.

Moore, Leonard J. *Citizen Klansmen: The Ku Klux Klan in Indiana, 1921–1928.* Chapel Hill: University of North Carolina Press, 1991.

Trelease, Allan W. *White Terror: The Ku Klux Klan Conspiracy and Southern Reconstruction.* New York: Harper and Row, 1971.

Leonard J. Moore

See also **Discrimination: Race; Force Acts; Jim Crow Laws; Race Relations.**

KWANZAA. Maulana Karenga, a professor and chairman of the Department of Black Studies at California State University, Long Beach, created the African American cultural festival of Kwanzaa in 1966. The celebration takes place annually from 26 December through 1 January. Although the American origins of this holiday are found in the struggles for black nationalism that transpired in the 1960s, its African origins are rooted in the historic "first fruits" celebrations that have been associated with successful harvests from time immemorial.

Essential to the celebration are the *Nzugo Saba* (seven principles), which outline the pan-African origins of African American peoples. The principles are: *umoja* (unity), *kujichagulia* (self-determination), *ujima* (collective work and responsibility), *ujamaa* (cooperative economics), *nia* (purpose), *kuumba* (creativity), and *imani* (faith). One of the seven principles is featured on each day of the week-long celebration.

Millions of African Americans commemorate Kwanzaa annually in either family-centered or community-centered celebrations. These events highlight the reaffirmation of community, a special reverence for the Creator and Creation, a respectful commemoration of the past, a recommitment to lofty ideals, and a celebration of all that is inherently good. During these cultural celebrations Kwanzaa candles are lit, children receive heritage gifts, and a commemorative meal takes place.

BIBLIOGRAPHY

Karenga, Maulana. *Kwanzaa: A Celebration of Family, Community, and Culture.* Los Angeles: University of Sankore Press, 1998.

Junius P. Rodriguez

See also **African Americans; Holidays and Festivals.**

ISBN 0-684-80526-X